Monographs in
Mediterranean Archaeology
3

Executive Editor
A. Bernard Knapp

Editorial Board
Piotr Bienkowski, Robert Chapman, John F. Cherry,
Richard Hodges, Andrew G. Sherratt,
Simon Stoddart, Norman Yoffee

Sheffield Academic Press

MIRIAM S. BALMUTH
MUSEO ARCHAEOLOGICO NAZIONALE, CAGLIARI

> Where then? Spain or Sardinia. Spain or Sardinia. Sardinia, which is like nowhere. Sardinia, which has no history, no date, no race, no offering. Let it be Sardinia. They say neither Romans nor Phoenicians, Greeks nor Arabs ever subdued Sardinia. It lies outside; outside the circuit of civilisation. Like the Basque lands. Sure enough, it is Italian now, with its railways and its motor omnibuses. But there is an uncaptured Sardinia still. It lies within the net of this European civilisation, but it isn't landed yet. And the net is getting old and tattered. A good many fish are slipping through the net of the old European civilisation. Like that great whale of Russia. And probably even Sardinia. Sardinia then. Let it be Sardinia.
>
> D.H. Lawrence (*Sea and Sardinia*, 1923)

At the time that D.H. Lawrence wrote his novel, Sardinia was certainly considered peripheral to European civilization, both ancient and modern. Little was known of the island's history beyond the successive waves of (civilized) conquering peoples. Lawrence did recognize, however, that there was something unique, something special about Sardinia, something as yet uncaptured.

In the last few decades, more of Sardinia's history has been found, and the island has gone from 'nowhere' to a place of central importance in the ancient Mediterranean world. We owe much of this recognition to the efforts of Miriam S. Balmuth, who did not let Sardinia slip through the net. This volume is offered as a token of our appreciation for her inspirational role in our lives as teacher, mentor and friend, and as evidence of the broad influence she has had on the study of Sardinian archaeology.

Sardinia in the Mediterranean: A Footprint in the Sea

Studies in Sardinian Archaeology
Presented to Miriam S. Balmuth

edited by Robert H. Tykot
and Tamsey K. Andrews

Copyright © 1992 Sheffield Academic Press

Published by
Sheffield Academic Press Ltd
343 Fulwood Road
Sheffield S10 3BP
England

Typeset by Sheffield Academic Press
and
Printed on acid-free paper in Great Britain
by Alden Press
Oxford

British Library Cataloguing in Publication Data

A catalogue record for this book is available
from the British Library.

ISBN 1-85075-386-5
ISSN 0960-6432

Contents

Editors' Preface	9
Foreword Giovanni Lilliu	11
A Biography of Miriam S. Balmuth Tamsey K. Andrews and David Gordon Mitten	13
A Bibliography of Miriam S. Balmuth	15
Introduction/Introduzione Robert H. Tykot and Tamsey K. Andrews	17

Part I: Palaeolithic, Neolithic and Chalcolithic

Palaeolithic Sardinians? Some Questions of Evidence and Method John F. Cherry	28
Early Human Settlement in Sardinia: The Palaeolithic Industries Fabio Martini	40
Pleistocene Humans in the Island Environment of Sardinia Gerard Klein Hofmeijer and Paul Y. Sondaar	49
The Sources and Distribution of Sardinian Obsidian Robert H. Tykot	57
Western Mediterranean Obsidian Distribution and the European Neolithic Patricia Phillips	71
New Contributions to the Study of the Function of Sardinian Obsidian Artifacts Linda Hurcombe	83
Elementi Architettonici e del Culto Funerario nella Domus de Janas di Su Littu (Ossi-Sassari) Maria Luisa Ferrarese Ceruti	98
New Contributions to the Study of the Megalithic in Corsica Joseph Cesari	105
The Megalithic Monuments of Corsica and Sardinia: A Comparative Study François de Lanfranchi	118
The Megalithic in Sardinia, Southern France and Catalonia Jean Guilaine	128

6 *Sardinia in the Mediterranean*

Paleosardi e Protosardi dal Paleolitico all'Età del Bronzo Recente
Franco Germanà   137

Cuccuru S'Arriu (Cabras). L'Orizzonte Eneolitico Sub-Ozieri
Vincenzo Santoni   157

Part II: Nuragic Architecture and Settlement

Tipologie Nuragiche: I Protonuraghi con Corridoio Passante
Lucia Manca Demurtas e Sebastiano Demurtas   176

Sui Protonuraghi del Marghine e della Planargia
Alberto Moravetti   185

Militarism in Nuragic Sardinia
David H. Trump   198

**Cultural Uniformity during the Italian Iron Age:
Sardinian Nuraghi as Regional Markers**
Marshall Joseph Becker   204

**Territorial Boundaries, Buffer Zones and Sociopolitical Complexity:
A Case Study of the Nuraghi on Sardinia**
Renée M. Bonzani   210

Considerazioni sullo Sviluppo dell'Architettura e della Società Nuragica
Giovanni Ugas   221

**Aegean Architectural Links with the Central Mediterranean:
Sardinian Sacred Wells and Lipari's Thermal Tholos**
Paolo Belli   235

**Le Tecniche Edilizie del Periodo Nuragico nell'Architettura delle Acque,
Presenti nel Territorio della Barbagia**
Maria Ausilia Fadda, Caterinella Tuveri e Giuseppe Murru   250

Phoenician Echoes in a Nuragic Building
Barbro Santillo Frizell   262

**A Temporal Analysis of the Ceramic Industry at Duos Nuraghes:
A Step toward Chronology**
Aviva Weiss Grele   271

**Vertebrate Faunal Remains at the Nuragic Village of Santa
Barbara, Bauladu (OR)**
Lenore J. Gallin and Ornella Fonzo   287

Part III: Sardinia and the Mediterranean World

Un'Altra Fibula 'Cipriota' dalla Sardegna
Fulvia Lo Schiavo   296

Nuragic Sardinia and the Mediterranean: Metallurgy and Maritime Traffic
Claudio Giardino   304

New Light on the Provenience of the Copper Oxhide Ingots Found on Sardinia
Zofia A. Stos-Gale and Noël H. Gale   317

Some Metallurgical Remarks on the Sardinian Bronzetti
C. Atzeni, L. Massidda, U. Sanna and P. Virdis   347

Sardinia and History
David Ridgway and Francesca R. Serra Ridgway   355

Osservazioni sulla Ceramica Attica in Sardegna
Carlo Tronchetti   364

Miti e Rituali nella Sardegna Preistorica
Giovanni Lilliu   378

Greeks in Sardinia: Myth and Reality
Jean M. Davison   384

Part IV: Interaction and Acculturation:
Phoenician, Punic and Roman Settlement in Sardinia

La Facies Orientalizzante in Sardegna: Problemi di Individuazione e Metodologia
Paolo Bernardini   396

The Phoenician Foundation of Cities and Towns in Sardinia
Brian Peckham   410

Lucerne Arcaiche da Sulcis
Piero Bartoloni   419

I Gioielli Punici di Tharros
Enrico Acquaro   424

Testimonianze Fenicio-Puniche nella Sardegna Centro-Settentrionale
Giovanni Tore   429

Divertimento 1991. Ancora sulla Cartagine di Sardegna
Maria Giulia Amadasi Guzzo   439

Toward the Study of Colonial–Native Relations in Sardinia from c. 1000 BC–AD 456
Gary S. Webster and Maud Teglund   448

Carthaginians in the Countryside?
Robert J. Rowland, Jr   474

Roman Sardinia and Roman Britain
Stephen L. Dyson   484

Sardinian Amphora Studies: Past and Future
Elizabeth Lyding Will   493

List of Contributors   497

Tabula Gratulatoria   500

Indexes   503

Editors' Preface

'A Festschrift should be fun, at least for the authors', said one of the contributors to this volume. That this has been true for the editors as well is due in large part to the enthusiastic support we have received throughout this project: from the overwhelming response to our call for papers, to the generosity of both institutions and individuals in underwriting the inevitable costs, to invaluable editorial assistance in the actual preparation of the manuscript.

The publication of this volume would not have been possible without the generosity of the following:

Chancellor Jean Mayer, Provost Sol Gittleman, and the Office of the Dean of the College of Liberal Arts, all of Tufts University; Edward H. Merrin; the Dr M. Aylwin Cotton Foundation, and the Royall House Association; Elie and Batya Borowski, Count Cinelli, Lia Glovsky, Anne Rossi, Mr and Mrs Edward Shapiro, Elizabeth Lyding Will, and Marianne Witherby. Also, Monni Adams, Ralph Appelbaum, Jane A. Barlow, Marilyn M. Beaven, Philip P. Betancourt, Larissa Bonfante, Estelle Brettman, John Brownson, Victoria Bunker, Jose Bustamente, Madeline H. Caviness, Marie Cleary, Patricia Crawford, Frank Moore Cross, Jeanne C. Dillon, Julia Dubnoff, Ernestine S. Elster, Thomas R. Fenn, David N. Fixler, Carolyn Frazer, Eleanor M. Garvey, Esther Stoddard Graves, Judith P. Hallett, Alice Ryerson Hayes, Amy K. Hirschfeld, R. Ross Holloway, Sarah Hood, Gertrude Howland, Debra A. Hudak, Mr and Mrs James D. Hume, the Joukowsky Family Foundation, Ann O. Koloski-Ostrow and Steven E. Ostrow, Christine Kondoleon, Neal A. Konstantin, Guenter Kopcke, Gilbert Lawall, Heather Lechtman, Albert Leonard, Jr, Mary Louise Lord, Susan S. Lukesh, Gioconda Cinelli McMillan, Regina F. Merzlak, Leo Mildenberg, Andrew M.T. Moore, Susan Tufts Moore, Peter L.D. Reid, Brunilde S. Ridgway, Eleanor Robbins, William and Elizabeth Ruf, Sondra and Milton Schlesinger, Jane Ayer Scott, Philippa D. Shaplin, S. Amber Somes, Dennis Trout, Jane C. Waldbaum, Howard Weintraub, Shelby White and Leon Levy, Malcolm H. Wiener and Susan Wood.

Equally invaluable were the following for assistance in the production of the manuscript: Gloria Bates and Amélie Beyhum, who translated articles from French into English; Marisa Ciani, who translated summaries into Italian and proofread Italian-language articles; and Lia Glovsky, Debra Hudak, Paula Kay Lazrus, Laura Maniscalco McConnell, Amber Somes and Ruth Thomas, who proofread and corrected both articles and summaries. Both Kay Teahan, of the Classics Department at Tufts, and Gretchen Traister, of the Graduate Dean's Office, helped track down former Tufts University students for the *tabula gratulatoria*.

Finally, we would like to thank Marshall Joseph Becker, David Gordon Mitten, Elizabeth Lyding Will, Ladislaus Bolchazy, A. Bernard Knapp and last but not least, Norman Balmuth, for their advice and direction.

On behalf of everyone involved, we offer this Festschrift in appreciation of Miriam Balmuth's own enthusiasm for the archaeology of Sardinia, and the inspiration she has given several generations of students—one of whom wrote, 'Whenever I think of Tufts, Miriam is the first person who comes to mind: she was a mentor, role model and friend for me'. The production of this volume has been most satisfying for the editors, and it is our hope that it will also be fun for Miriam.

Robert H. Tykot
Tamsey K. Andrews
December 1991

Foreword

La Sardegna è una terra di forte suggestione, dove il passato segna ancora un'orma profonda. Ad evocarlo stanno gli splendidi monumenti megalitici, i nuraghi soprattutto che coprono l'isola in migliaia, immersi in un paesaggio mitico. Queste originali e remotissime evidenze archeologiche hanno richiamato da lungo tempo la curiosità o la considerazione di visitatori e studiosi. Un interesse romantico nell'800, un'attenzione scientifica nel nostro secolo.

Da qui memorie di viaggio di stranieri, soprattutto ricerche, studi e pubblicazioni, via via cresciuti in valore e nella diffusione, per cui l'isola, grazie principalmente alle memorie di radice, è entrata, dove più e dove meno, nella conoscenza del mondo. Ad esternarla hanno lavorato con diligenza gli archeologi italiani, tra di essi i sardi più di tutti con l'intento anche di scoprire e valorizzare la loro identità di popolo. Ma vi hanno contribuito pure, con importanti studi, i ricercatori stranieri: francesi, inglesi e tedeschi, per primi.

In anni più vicini, si è aggiunta la cooperazione degli esperti Americani, con metodi di indagine più sofisticati, i cui utili risultati riscattano il recente sopraggiungere. A titolo di merito vanno menzionati ricerche e scavi, condotti in diversi luoghi dell'isola da archeologi universitari o professionali, accompagnati da loro allievi. L'*équipe* Penn State di G.S. Webster e J.W. Michels ha operato nella regione del Marghine, avendone materiali litici e ceramici computerizzati onde meglio evidenziarne le valenze. Note su talune 'hydration dates' di ossidiane raccolte presso nuraghi del Marghine e del Montiferru, si devono a S.L. Dyson, L. Gallin, M. Klimkiewicz, R.J. Rowland, Jr, e C.M. Stevenson. S.L. Dyson e R.J. Rowland, Jr (progetto di 'Maryland-Wesleyan survey') hanno attivato ricerche di superficie per l'individuazione di monumenti nuragici e connessi materiali di varia epoca nel territorio di Bauladu e in Val di Tirso, e R. Tykot ha percorso la zona del Monte Arci con lo scopo di localizzare le fonti e le reti di scambio di ossidiana. È da menzionare anche il fatto che lo scavo di L. Gallin nel nuraghe Santa Barbara di Bauladu ha fornito risultati interessanti.

Questa notevole attività di ricercatori Americani è stata certamente stimolata dalla 'pioniera' in tale opera: la professoressa Miriam S. Balmuth in cui giusto onore esce il presente lavoro *Sardinia in the Mediterranean: A Footprint in the Sea*. La Signora Balmuth è stata la prima americana a indirizzare l'attenzione scientifica alla preistoria sarda, con gli scavi di Tufts University al nuraghe Ortu Còmidu (Sardara) che sono stati utilmente pubblicati nelle *Notizie degli Scavi di Antichità* editi dall'Accademia dei Lincei (1986). Le precedenti ricerche qui effettuate da Antonio Taramelli, risultano arricchite e chiarificate nel senso vero funzionale del monumento, ed i nuovi materiali esaminati da P. Phillips, P. Nicholson, e H. Patterson (in *La Sardegna nel Mediterraneo tra il Secondo e il Primo Millennio a.C.* 1987), rivelano una sequenza culturale e cronologica dalla fine del II millennio all'VIII-VII secolo a.C., prima non conosciuta. La Professoressa Balmuth si è anche interessata alla metallurgia sarda della tarda età del Bronzo, con lo studio dei lingotti di rame del tipo 'oxhide,' analizzati in collaborazione con R.F. Tylecote (in *Journal of Field Archaeology* 1976). È da ricordare anche il contributivo articolo sulle figurine di bronzo nuragiche conservate in Musei americani, nel quale L.P. Stodulski del Fogg Art Museum offre, per la prima volta, sicure analisi chimiche dei famosi 'bronzetti' (in *Studi Sardi* 1978).

I risultati delle esperienze archeologiche in Sardegna sono stati ripetutamente illustrati e divulgati dalla Professoressa Balmuth in conferenze internazionali (Tufts 1983, Roma 1986, Tufts 1991). Ma se tutto ciò non bastasse a dimostrare il grande interesse e il valore riconosciuto dalla Professoressa Balmuth alla più remota civiltà dei Sardi, specialmente nei tempi di quella che ne fu la più fulgida e libera manifestazione—la civiltà nuragica—la Balmuth ha chiamato illustri esperti di vari paesi americani ed europei, ad indagarla e proporla nei vari aspetti e nel suo lungo svolgimento. Ne rendono significativa e preziosa testimonianza i tre volumi *Studies in Sardinian Archaeology*, editi dalla Balmuth a cura dell'Università di Michigan (1984, 1986) e del British Archaeological Reports (1987). Non posso non ricordare, a titolo personale, il piacere e l'onore avuti nel ricevere in dono dalla Professoressa Balmuth il primo volume, con la dedica 'Al Professor Lilliu—alla fonte della ñostra ispirazione'.

In riconoscenza di questo amichevole attestato, ma soprattutto nella considerazione dell'importante apporto venuto all'archeologia preistorica e protostorica della Sardegna dall'opera dell'insigne studiosa, sento il dovere di ringraziare la Professoressa Balmuth anche a nome degli archeologi sardi, per i suoi alti meriti. L'opera della Professoressa ha fatto sì che la conoscenza dell'archeologia sarda acquisita in America tramite l'opera nell'isola di ricercatori statunitensi e specialmente della Balmuth stessa, torna anche utile all'immagine nel grande paese americano della Sardegna che, in tal modo, non sarà più una terra dimenticata.

Giovanni Lilliu
Cagliari, 23 ottobre 1991

A Biography of Miriam S. Balmuth

Tamsey K. Andrews and David Gordon Mitten

Those of us who believe that intellectual depth, courage and wit can only be the products of an unhappy childhood stand swiftly corrected by the example of Miriam S. Balmuth. *La Professoressa* was born in New Brunswick, New Jersey to a gregarious household headed by Sigmund Scharf, a self-made success in clothing manufacturing and a pillar of the community. Her mother, Rose Scharf, was influential in the development of that strong-minded determination that we have come to recognize as one of her daughter's own most characteristic qualities.

In 1946, Miriam graduated from Cornell University with a degree in Classics, and later that year married Norman Balmuth. The couple moved to Columbus, Ohio, where Norman entered graduate school at Ohio State University and Miriam went to work. Within two weeks those roles were reversed: while Norman took employment at a nearby private laboratory, Miriam enrolled in the Department of Classical Languages. In the next two years the Balmuths celebrated the birth of their first son, Paul, and Miriam completed her Master's Degree in Classics. In 1951, after moving to Waltham, Massachusetts, their second son, Jeremy, was born. For the next few years Miriam devoted herelf to her growing family, but in 1955 she became a volunteer assistant to Professor George M.A. Hanfmann, and in 1961 formally entered Harvard University's Department of Classics in pursuit of a doctorate in classical archaeology.

At Harvard, Miriam was one of the first Keepers of Coins in the Fogg Art Museum. In this capacity she worked closely with Professor Hanfmann in overseeing the Museum's share by bequest of the famed David M. Robinson collection of Classical art and antiquities. From Hanfmann's example she learned the energetic, multi-pronged approach to complex historical problems that would mark her later, mature scholarship. In 1961, the Robinson Collection Exhibition Catalogue was published under the co-authorship of Miriam and her mentor. Then, in 1964, Miriam successfully completed her doctoral dissertation, 'Forerunners of Coinage in the Aegean and the Mediterranean'.

In the halcyon days of the 1960s when the humanities were in increasing demand, Miriam was immediately employed by the Tufts University Department of Classics where she had served as a teaching assistant while still in graduate school. Then followed her Directorship of the New England Latin Workshop, and her rise to Associate Professor. However, Miriam has always abhorred narrow professional specialization and soon the ever-vigorous expansion of her professional interests—another characteristic Balmuth quality—would express itself in quite unforeseen ways.

During the 1970s, the Boston archaeological community was host to a series of discussions about one of the most engrossing problems in the ancient Mediterranean: the sources of copper, tin and lead, and the maritime trade routes by which these metals were transported to various centers of industry and craftsmanship. This search for the origins of ancient bronze focused on the eastern Mediterranean, spurred by George Bass's publications of the spectacular finds from the Cape Gelidonya shipwreck. In 1970, while Miriam was on holiday in the Mediterranean, these issues and the general problems of east–west Mediterranean interchange were fresh in her mind. Her love of the Italian language drew her to the western Mediterranean, and by chance she sailed to Sardinia. Several things became clear to her immediately: Sardinia was a primary source for copper; its rich archaeological history was plain to see in the thousands of unexcavated *nuraghi* strewn across the landscape; and the island was strategically located in the path of western Mediterranean trade routes. Furthermore, Sardinia, with its great natural beauty and archaeological treasures, was being completely ignored by scholars outside the island itself who dismissed it as a place of ancient pestilence and exile.

The result of these insights has been the opening of the world's eyes to the fundamental importance of Sardinia in western Mediterranean archaeology by means of excavations, publications and international colloquia, all spearheaded by Miriam Balmuth. In 1975, she led the excavation of the Nuraghe Ortu Còmidu, assisted by Dr Patricia Phillips of Sheffield University, and concluded this work in 1978. At once she began a series of publications on the Ortu Còmidu results, as well as the wider problems of the Sardinian *bronzetti*, the interpretation of the *nuraghi* and, in collaboration with the late Ronald F. Tylecote, analyses of Sardinia's place in the copper and bronze trade of the ancient Mediterranean. In 1979, she began the first of her annual colloquia on problems in Sardinian history and archaeology, held at Tufts University. These colloquia have represented an important opportunity for international groups of scholars to gather and discuss pivotal problems in Sardinia's relations with the western Mediterranean. In addition to directing these colloquia, Miriam herself has contributed a paper at each meeting. In 1984, her first edited volume of *Studies in Sardinian Archaeology* was published in collaboration with Robert J. Rowland, Jr. Two more edited volumes appeared in 1986 and 1987, and a fourth volume is planned. In the course of these publications and colloquia, Miriam has expanded her subject area further to include ancient Iberia and its contacts with Sardinia and the western Mediterranean. Her most recent colloquium, 'New Perspectives in Western Mediterranean Archaeology', held at Tufts University in 1991, has opened new areas of research and discussion in Tyrrhenian archaeology.

Miriam Balmuth's record as a scholar speaks for itself. But we who speak for Miriam as a person—her biographers, her students, friends and professional colleagues—bear witness to a teacher of great warmth, dedication and personal loyalty. We have seen how some of Miriam's greatest satisfactions have come from following and encouraging the careers of her students, present and former, official and unofficial. Most notable is how she supports and encourages her students to become active participants in all aspects of collegial scholarly enterprise. Her favorite motto is 'persistence over brilliance'. Her enthusiasm for her work and her students is legendary and contagious, and her never-failing sense of humor has saved many a precarious situation in the field and in the lecture hall. We would like to conclude this biographical tribute to Miriam Balmuth with the personal recollection of a former student, Ms Esther Stoddart Graves, who speaks for us all:

'I recall warm waters quietly rolling up to the edges of the peninsula just outside Cagliari... Miriam Balmuth, Sardinian archaeologist extraordinaire, small and mighty, shins down an unsteady ladder, lowering herself through the hole which is the entry into the ancient stone *nuraghe*. I, her pupil, follow her down the ladder. I am a neophyte, an admiring student, endeavoring to grasp exactly what it is I am standing inside of. Miriam explains precisely what we are exploring in quick, easily understood language. We walk through one empty, cell-like room to another until, through her ritual words, the entire structure takes on in my mind a distinct role in a society three thousand years old.'

'One pupil, one teacher—the ideal learning experience. Miriam taught me more than Sardinian archaeology: that night she taught me how the best teaching is done.'

'To Miriam, with gratitude.'

A Bibliography of Miriam S. Balmuth

Compiled by the Editors with the assistance of David Smart

1956   *Ancient Coins* (with G.M.A. Hanfmann).

1957–58   Greek coins of the fifth and fourth centuries BC. *Fogg Art Museum Annual Report*: 19-21.

1959   Portraits and coins. *The Connoisseur* 143(575): 58-61.

1961   *The David Moore Robinson Collection of Classical Art and Antiquities.*

1963a   The birth of Athena on a fragment in the Fogg Art Museum. *American Journal of Archaeology* 67: 69.

1963b   Epigraphical intimations of early coinage in the Near East (abstract). *American Journal of Archaeology* 67: 208.

1965   The image of an Anatolian goddess at Sardis. *Jahrbuch für Kleinasiatische Forschung* 1.1-2: 261-69 (with G.M.A. Hanfmann).

1966a   Athens or Phlius? *Schweizer Münzblatter* 16(16): 1-3.

1966b   From Wappenmünzen to owls (abstract). *American Journal of Archaeology* 70: 183.

1967   Monetary forerunners of coinage in Palestine and Phoenicia. In *International Numismatic Convention, Jerusalem 1963: The Patterns of Monetary Development in Palestine and Phoenicia in Antiquity*, 25-32. Jerusalem: Schocken Books.

1970   Lucanian three-color Geometric pottery. In R. Ross Holloway (ed.), *Satrianum. The Archaeological Investigations Conducted by Brown University in 1966 and 1967*, 88-91. Providence: Brown University.

1971a   Remarks on the appearance of the earliest coins. In *Studies Presented to George M. A. Hanfmann*, 1-8. Cambridge, MA: Fogg Art Museum.

1971b   Reconsideration of the earliest coinage (abstract). *American Journal of Archaeology* 75: 195.

1973   The origins of coinage. In *A Survey of Numismatic Research 1965-1970*, 27-35. New York: International Numismatic Commission.

1974   An unpublished bronze figurine from Sardinia in the Fogg Art Museum (abstract). *American Journal of Archaeology* 78: 160-161.

1975   The critical moment: the transition from currency to coinage in the Eastern Mediterranean. *World Archaeology* 6(3): 293-98.

1976a   The filial complaint. In S. Bertman (ed.), *The Conflict of Generations in Ancient Greece and Rome*, 129-33. Amsterdam: Gruner.

1976b   Ancient copper and bronze in Sardinia: excavation and analysis. *Journal of Field Archaeology* 3: 195-201 (with R.F. Tylecote).

1976c   Jewellers' hoards and the development of early coinage. In *Proceedings of the 8th International Congress of Numismatics, New York and Washington, September 1973*, 27-30. Paris.

1977   Bronzes from Cyprus and Sardinia: geographical and chronological problems. In R. Crossland (ed.), *Proceedings of the Third International Colloquium on Aegean Prehistory: The Sea Peoples, Sheffield 1973*. Announced as Duckworth, apparently never published.

1978   Sardinian bronzetti in American museums. *Studi Sardi* 24(1975–77): 145-56.

1980a   Money before coinage. In M. Jessup Price (ed.), *COINS: An Illustrated Survey 650 BC to the Present Day*, 20-25. London: Methuen.

1980b   The relationship of Nuragic Sardinia with the Bronze Age civilizations of the eastern Mediterranean (abstract). *American Journal of Archaeology* 84: 193.

1981a   Una risposta. *Dialoghi di Archeologia* 16(1):109-11.

1981b   The nuraghi towers of Sardinia. *Archaeology* 34(2): 35-43.

1981c   Scale weights, weight names and early coin denominations (abstract). *American Journal of Archaeology* 85: 185.

1982a   Material for the study of the origins of coinage. In *Proceedings of the 9th International Congress of Numismatics, Berne, September 1979*, 31-35. Louvain-la-Neuve.

1982b   Ortu Còmidu: A contribution to Sardinian archaeology (abstract). *American Journal of Archaeology* 86: 253.

1984a   *Studies in Sardinian Archaeology*. Ann Arbor: University of Michigan Press (ed. with R.J. Rowland, Jr).

1984b   The nuraghi of Sardinia: An introduction. In M.S. Balmuth and R.J. Rowland, Jr (eds.), *Studies in Sardinian Archaeology*, 23-52. Ann Arbor: University of Michigan Press.

1984c   Copper and bronze metallurgy in Sardinia. In M.S. Balmuth and R.J. Rowland, Jr (eds.), *Studies in Sardinian Archaeology*, 115-51. Ann Arbor: University of Michigan Press (with R.F. Tylecote and R. Massoli-Novelli).

1984d   Advances in Sardinian archaeology. In R. Ross Holloway (ed.), *Crossroads of the Mediterranean*, 247-54. Archaeologia Transatlantica 2. Louvain-la-Neuve: Art and Archaeology Publications, Collège Erasme.

1985   Landscape and architecture: origins of Neolithic and Bronze Age architectural styles in Sardinia (abstract). *American Journal of Archaeology* 89: 324.

1986a   Nuraghe Ortu Còmidu (Sardara-CA): Preliminary report of excavations 1975–1978. *Notizie degli Scavi di Antichità* 37(1983): 353-410.

1986b   *Studies in Sardinian Archaeology, Volume II: Sardinia in the Mediterranean*. Ann Arbor: University of Michigan Press (ed.).

1986c   Epilogue. In M.S. Balmuth (ed.), *Studies in Sardinian Archaeology, Volume II: Sardinia in the Mediterranean*, 273-79. Ann Arbor: University of Michigan Press.

1986d   Mycenaean Greece and Nuragic Sardinia: Late Bronze Age interaction? (abstract). *American Journal of Archaeology* 90: 203.

1987a   Studio architettonico del Nuraghe Ortu Còmidu. In G. Lilliu G. Ugas and G. Lai (a cura di), *La Sardegna nel Mediterraneo tra il Secondo e il Primo Millennio a.C. Atti del II Convegno di studi 'Un millennio di relazioni fra la Sardegna e i Paesi del Mediterraneo', Selargius-Cagliari, 29-30 novembre 1986*, 219-23. Cagliari: Amministrazione Provinciale di Cagliari.

1987b   *Studies in Sardinian Archaeology III: Sardinia and the Mycenaean World*. BAR International Series 387. Oxford: British Archaeological Reports (ed.).

1987c   Introduction. In M.S. Balmuth (ed.), *Studies in Sardinian Archaeology III: Sardinia and the Mycenaean World*, 1-5. BAR International Series 387. Oxford: British Archaeological Reports.

1987d   A Punic kitchen in Nuraghe Ortu Còmidu (Sardara-CA) in Sardinia (abstract). *American Journal of Archaeology* 91: 325.

1989   Review of *Archaeology and Language: The Puzzle of Indo-European Origins*, by C. Renfrew. *The Journal of Interdisciplinary History* 20(2):257.

1990   Bronze, sea and Sardinia (abstract). *American Journal of Archaeology* 94: 340.

1991a   The contribution of R.F. Tylecote to the archaeometallurgy of Sardinia. *Journal of the Historical Metallurgy Society*. 25(1): 7-8.

1991b   Nuragic camouflage. In B. Santillo Frizell (ed.), *Arte Militare e Architettura Nuragica. Nuragic Architecture in its Military, Territorital and Socio-economic Context. Proceedings of the Frst International Colloquium on Nuragic Architecture at the Swedish Institute in Rome, 7-9 December, 1989*. Acta Instituti Romani Regni Sueciae, Series In 4°, 48: 19-22. Stockholm: Svenska Institutet i Rom.

1992   Archaeology in Sardinia. *American Journal of Archaeology* 96(4).

in press   Phoenician chronology in Sardinia: prospecting, trade, and settlement before 900 BC. In *Premonetary and Monetary Economy in the Phoenician and Punic World. Symposium at Louvain-la-Neuve (Belgium), May 13, 1987*, 144-57.

Introduction

Robert H. Tykot and Tamsey K. Andrews

This Festschrift in honor of Miriam S. Balmuth continues in spirit the series of edited works collected under the title *Studies in Sardinian Archaeology*, based on the proceedings of her colloquia begun in 1979 at Tufts University. When *Studies in Sardinian Archaeology* appeared in 1984, it was the first such volume in English since Margaret Guido's *Sardinia* (1963). Since that time, Early Neolithic settlements dating back to c. 6000 BC have been discovered, Sardinian obsidian has been found in Corsica, mainland Italy, and southern France, and Late Bronze Age Aegean-type ceramics and metal artifacts have been identified at a number of sites on the island; the number of *nuraghi* (towers), *tombe di giganti* (giants' tombs), *domus de janas* (witches' houses), *pozzi sacri* (sacred wells), and other characteristic manifestations of Sardinian culture that were under investigation had increased significantly, as had also the number of professional archaeologists in the *Soprintendenze di Archeologia* for the provinces of Cagliari/Oristano and Sassari/Nuoro, and at the Universities of Cagliari and Sassari. The cumulative result of this expanded picture of Sardinia's past has been the realization of both the depth of the island's own cultural history, and its intimate relationship with other areas of the Mediterranean.

Also in that period, excavations began to be directed by foreign scholars for the first time: David Trump in the Bonu Ighinu Valley (1971–72, 1979–80), Miriam Balmuth at Nuraghe Ortu Còmidu (1975–78), Joseph Michels and Gary Webster at Nuraghi Toscono and Urpes in the Marghine (1982), and Paul Sondaar and colleagues at Corbeddu Cave beginning in 1982. This growing involvement of American and British scholars in Sardinian studies, the escalation of research results, and the increased awareness in the larger archaeological community—due in part to the major exhibition at Karlsruhe, Germany in 1980—of the importance of Sardinia in the Mediterranean, all mandated the publication of a volume to bring English readers up to date on Sardinian archaeology.

This initiative was continued and expanded upon in *Studies in Sardinian Archaeology, Volume II: Sardinia in the Mediterranean* (1986), the revised proceedings of the First International Colloquium on Sardinian Archaeology, held at Tufts University in September 1983. Thematic sections on early settlement, Nuragic art, east and west, Sardinia and the Greeks, trade and contact, and metallurgy emphasized both the island's singular developments and its relationship to other areas of the Mediterranean. The volume, a mixture of period studies and topical investigations, covered a wide range of disciplines reflecting the increasing complexity of Sardinian archaeology and the still accelerating pace of research.

Studies in Sardinian Archaeology III (1987), the proceedings of the colloquium held at the American Academy in Rome in 1986, was dedicated to a single topic: Nuragic Sardinia and the Mycenaean World. A broadly international group of scholars participated in this colloquium, and for the first time their edited papers were published in both English and Italian.

In addition to this foreign-sponsored research and publication, Sardinian scholars have increased even further the number of their own field surveys, excavations, and scientific, art-historical, and epigraphical research over the last several years. Major conferences have been held in Cuglieri (1984), Selargius (1985, 1986, 1987), Ozieri (1986–87), Olièna (1988), and Sassari-Monte d'Accoddi (1990), with research articles also appearing in the new journal *Nuovo Bullettino Archeologico Sardo* (vols. 1–3, 1986, 1989, 1990), in the *Quaderni* published by the Soprintendenze, as well as in the well-established *Studi Sardi*, *Notizie degli Scavi*, and other Italian periodicals. Among the most important recent books are Giovanni Lilliu's revised and expanded *La Civiltà dei Sardi* (1988), the full excavation report *Il Nuraghe S. Antine nel Meilogu-Logudoro* (1988), and the corrected version of *La Civiltà Nuragica* (1990).

This history of international, scholarly dialogue, cooperation, and collaboration in recovering Sardinia's past is carried on in this Festschrift, with articles by 53 authors from seven countries, in both English and Italian. The Editors wanted this volume to reflect the entire range of current Sardinian studies, and invited contributions on the Palaeolithic through Roman periods, from specialists in anthropology, classics, art history, epigraphy and laboratory sciences. The articles were organized into thematic groupings and sequences on the basis of both chronology and disciplinary approach.

The Prenuragic section starts off with a survey by John Cherry of the evidence for Pleistocene settlement in Sardinia. This subject, barely 10 years old, represents an area of Sardinian studies that opens up a new line of inquiry into early island settlement and ecology. The most fundamental issue, whether the island was settled in the Pleistocene, profoundly affects our interpretation of subsequent Neolithic and Bronze Age developments. His call for more complete information on the lithic finds is answered by Fabio Martini, who describes and illustrates several of the stone tool assemblages. Gerard Klein Hofmeijer and Paul Sondaar argue that the discovery in Corbeddu Cave of cusp fragments which can be refitted to molars in deer mandibles proves that the mandibles were used in the cave *post mortem*, probably as cutting or scraping instruments, between 11,000 and 17,000 BP. The evidence of the cusp fragments may satisfy Cherry and others who feel that the excavators should bear the burden of disproving the possibility that the assemblage is the result of non-human activity, before we generally recognize a Palaeolithic settlement of Sardinia.

The Holocene levels of Corbeddu Cave, on the other hand, are of unquestionable human origin, and rival those of Grotta Filiestru (Mara-SS) in their importance for understanding the chronology and ecology of Prenuragic Sardinia. Particularly significant will be the palynological and faunal data since so few of these studies have been done in Sardinia.

Whether Sardinia was initially settled in the Palaeolithic, or in the Mesolithic/Early Neolithic, it was certainly not isolated from other regions of the western Mediterranean at any time during the Prenuragic period. Robert Tykot, who presents new data on the sources and distribution of Sardinian obsidian, and Patricia Phillips, who examines its distribution as a larger European Neolithic phenomenon, conclude that the exploitation of individual sources varied both geographically and chronologically. Use-wear analyses by Linda Hurcombe supplement this data by showing how function could affect the form and circumstances under which obsidian was distributed. Obsidian studies remain most promising in their potential for revealing economic and subsistence activities, and future investigation will enhance the foundation begun here.

The Late Neolithic of Sardinia is represented by the relatively uniform Ozieri cultural horizon, characterized by significant developments in artistic and religious expression. Maria Luisa Ferrarese Ceruti presents as an example the *domus de janas* of su Littu (Ossi), and offers an interpretation of the bull's horn and anthropomorphic figure reliefs carved on its walls. Along with dolmens and menhirs, the construction of these cultural monuments did not take place in isolation from concurrent developments in Corsica, and can be considered manifestations of an even more widespread megalithic phenomenon. Joseph Cesari reviews the Corsican monuments, which are noteworthy because of their frequent occurrence in large groups, and François de Lanfranchi offers a simplified classification of these monuments into two types. The architectural evidence of stone circles and burials *a tafone* in both southern Corsica and northern Sardinia are supplemented by the presence in Corsica of imported obsidian and Sardinian-type ceramics. Jean Guilaine shows us that striking similarities also exist between the Sardinian monuments and examples in southern France and eastern Spain. The distances involved, however, make it difficult to tell whether these similarities are due to reciprocal influence or simply convergent architectural development.

The period between the Neolithic and Bronze Age in Sardinia comprises a complex Chalcolithic period lasting nearly a millennium. Vincenzo Santoni provides a detailed examination of the ceramic and other material remains from the sub-Ozieri levels of Cuccuru s'Arriu-Cabras, and relates them to other Sardinian sites. He also suggests that the subsequent Filigosa and Abealzu-Monte d'Accoddi facies may be pushed chronologically closer to the more widespread Monte Claro (evolved Chalcolithic) horizon.

The Neolithic, Chalcolithic and Bronze Age populations themselves are examined by Franco Germanà in his important study of the corpus of human skeletal material found on Sardinia. The appearance of individuals with brachymorphic cranial features starting in the Monte Claro period, accounting for up to 35% of samples from Early Bronze Age northwestern Sardinia, may be attributed to some population shifts in the Chalcolithic, but many of the typical features of native Sardinians today may be traced to a hybridization process that was mostly complete by the Late Neolithic Ozieri period.

It is in the Middle Bronze Age that nuraghi, the most characteristic architectural feature of ancient Sardinia, first appear. This nuraghi-based way of life endured for approximately two millennia, encompassing the Phoenician, Punic and Roman periods, during which these structures were continuously elaborated and reoccupied. The Editors have divided the articles concerning this long period into three sections: Part II deals strictly with architecture and Nuragic settlement; Part III examines Sardinia's relations with the outside world; and Part IV covers the period of foreign settlement on the island.

Beginning in the Middle Bronze Age, the megalithic phenomenon of Sardinia, limited in earlier periods to sacred-religious architecture, is extended to the domestic sphere in the form of nuraghi. The major questions surrounding these stone towers—in the ancient Mediterranean second in size only to the Egyptian pyramids—concern their use and their relation to other (Aegean) architectural traditions.

The function of the nuraghi is addressed by Lucia Manca Demurtas and Sebastiano Demurtas in their examination of 55 protonuraghi *a corridoio passante*. They emphasize that these structures were in their own right successful attempts at constructing an enclosed space with a dual function of habitation and defense. Alberto Moravetti, in his survey of the Marghine and Planargia regions, integrates geological, soil, and topographic data in modelling the functions and interrelationships of both corridor and tholos nuraghi in the same territory.

David Trump cautions us against projecting the latent military function of the complex nuraghi-fortresses back in time to the protonuraghi, and notes that the transition from classic to complex nuraghe requires a more profound social explanation than that from corridor to tholos. By means of an analogy from mainland Italy, Marshall Becker also points out that we should be careful about ascribing a single function to all nuraghi, since it is unlikely that a static form of social organization applied simultaneously throughout Sardinia. Renée Bonzani uses ethnographic data to relate the use of territorial space to particular types of social organization, and proposes a testable model which focuses on the occupation of buffer zones between clusters of nuraghi.

Giovanni Ugas notes that funerary practices such as those evidenced by the Tomb of the Warriors in Decimoputzu indicate dramatic changes in social organization in the Nuragic period. He also maintains that the transition to the classic, tholos nuraghe may yet have some relationship with Aegean architectural developments. While the early nuraghi predate Aegean tholos architecture, the Sardinian *pozzi sacri* do not. Paolo Belli's survey of Mediterranean architecture related to water sources and storage, including the thermal bath of S. Calogero on Lipari, shows that similar types of structures—both in form and in function—were used contemporaneously with the Sardinian wells. He suggests, therefore, that architectural concepts and influences could have accompanied the well-documented ceramic and metal products known to have flowed between East and West in the Late Bronze Age. The religious function of these buildings, documented by the study by Maria Ausilia Fadda *et al.* of the materials used in constructing Nuragic wells, springs and sanctuaries, could then be seen as a Sardinian elaboration of an architectural type more widespread in the Mediterranean. Barbro Santillo Frizell also argues for foreign architectural influence, specifically in the sacred well at Santa Cristina (Paulilatino) where the Tanit-shaped entry and the geometry of the dromos could be explained by the intervention of Phoenician craftsmen familiar with ship-building.

The development and elaboration of domestic and religious architecture in Sardinia is in stark contrast to Nuragic ceramic production, which Aviva Weiss Grele demonstrates to have been remarkably conservative. Her preliminary study of data from the Pennsylvania State University excavations in the Borore region, however, does show an increase in the number of vessel types in the Late Bronze Age, and implies a rising demand for material goods beginning in that period. Faunal data from the Late Bronze Age village of Nuraghe Santa Barbara (Bauladu), presented by Lenore Gallin and Ornella Fonzo, illuminate the pastoral aspect of Nuragic subsistence: the raising of cattle, pigs, sheep and goats for meat, wool, and possibly milk products.

In Part III, Fulvia Lo Schiavo adds to the growing inventory of imported and imitated Aegean-type artifacts found in Sardinia with her presentation of a Cypriot-type fibula found at Nuraghe Nurdole; the possibility of its manufacture in Iberia only supports the likelihood of Sardinian maritime contacts with both the East and the West in the Late Bronze/Early Iron Age. That the island became a focal point in the Mediterranean metals' trade in these periods is demonstrated by Claudio Giardino's synthesis of Sardinian metallurgy. His investigation of marine currents and navigational capabilities is a systematic assessment of the actual routes and times of year favorable to long-distance trade.

Zofia Stos-Gale and Noël Gale give us the latest

results of their ongoing provenience study of the copper oxhide ingots found on Sardinia. Thirty ore deposits in Sardinia have now been tested, and none match the 31 oxhide ingots analyzed in their lead isotope composition, although some additional ores remain to be checked. All 31 do, however, match the Cypriot fields for both lead isotope composition and gold/silver ratios, and a scenario is offered to explain how foreign copper can be found on an island with its own rich copper sources. Furthermore, there is no evidence that any foreign copper was melted down to make Nuragic artifacts.

David and Francesca Ridgway suggest that between 1200 and 900 BC, the Cypriots may have been exchanging copper for iron, as described in the *Odyssey*; this could explain both the late appearance of oxhide ingots in Sardinia, and the similarities between Sardinian and Cypriot metalsmithing tools. They also suggest that the lost-wax bronze-casting process used to make the *bronzetti* could have been introduced to Sardinia by Cypriots. C. Atzeni *et al.* report here the results of metallographic analysis of some *bronzetti* in the National Archaeological Museum in Cagliari, the first time that a Sardinian collection has been analyzed; the discovery of a figurine made of a copper-silver alloy rather than tin bronze points out the need for further investigation of the use of silver in Sardinia.

After the Phoenician colonization of the island in the 8th century BC, imported materials, especially ceramics, increased markedly. The Phoenicians and their Carthaginian successors served as a medium for the importation not only of Levantine products, but also Greek and Etruscan material. Carlo Tronchetti describes the Attic Greek ceramics found in Sardinia, mostly of the 6th–4th centuries BC, and notes the importance of both drinking vessels and perfume containers. He suggests that an exponential increase in Greek imports in the 5th century BC is the result of Hellenization of the Punic civilization, rather than of direct Greek contact. According to the ancient authors, however, the Greeks did settle in Sardinia; among them was Sardus who gave his name to the island. Giovanni Lilliu summarizes these legendary accounts, and concludes that while they contain some threads of truth, they are not confirmed by archaeological evidence. Jean Davison suggests that the Hellenization of Sardinian culture, through Phoenician–Punic commercial contacts, resulted in Sardinians adapting a view of their own mythic history that was essentially Hellenocentric. Since this adoption probably occurred in the 6th and 5th centuries BC, the later historians Diodorus Siculus and Pausanias would then have observed Sardinian cultic practices based on, and therefore apparently validating, these originally Greek legends.

The effects on the indigenous Nuragic population of Phoenician, Carthaginian and Roman colonization are examined in Part IV. Paolo Bernardini points out the difficulties in defining an Orientalizing 'culture' after the establishment of Phoenician colonies in Sardinia in the 8th and 7th centuries BC, despite the quantity of Orientalizing artifacts found on the island. His argument, that the Nuragic society encountered by the Phoenicians was neither static nor homogenous, is borne out in his discussion of the influence of Orientalizing art and culture on indigenous craft production and social relations. Brian Peckham, conversely, highlights the diversity of the Phoenician colonists themselves who, from several independent city-states, headed west for different reasons, by different routes, and at different times: first the Sidonians, and later the Tyrians, ultimately landing at Bosa, Nora, Sulcis and Tharros. The presence of votive Nuragic lamps in the earliest phase of the tophet at Sulcis, illustrated here by Piero Bartoloni, shows not only that native Sardinians had access to Phoenician sacred rites, but that there may have been an indigenous component to the settlement and urbanization of this site from its foundation in the 8th century BC. Through these coastal interactions, Orientalizing art, exemplified here by Enrico Acquaro in his presentation of some jewelry from Tharros, was introduced to Sardinia.

Giovanni Tore also cautions against generalizing the archaeological and historical data concerning the interaction between Phoenicians, Carthaginians and indigenous Sardinians. The northern coast of the island, for example, also had particularly close relations with Etruria during the 8th–6th centuries BC; during the Carthaginian domination, Tore argues, an antagonistic relationship did not necessarily exist in all parts of the island, and certainly not at all times. Further light is shed on the Phoenician–Punic colonization of Sardinia by epigraphic evidence, comprehensively catalogued by Maria Giulia Amadasi Guzzo; here she presents two Punic inscriptions from Olbia and Tharros which refer to settlements called 'new city'.

Gary Webster and Maud Teglund, integrating archaeological, historical and epigraphic evidence, suggest a three-zone model of Phoenician, Punic and Roman interaction with native Sardinians. The intermediate, middle altitude zone is where they see the most significant chronological change. This zone was occupied by socially stratified, organizationally complex Nuragic peoples during the Phoenician period, was later abandoned and/or controlled in the Punic period, and was then reoccupied by a newly emerging elite in the Roman period. Their study underscores the central theme of Part IV, that colonial–native interaction was a melding of dynamic, heterogeneous cultures, and requires careful, region-specific interpretation rather than broad island-wide generalization. Robert Rowland focuses on the extent of Punic settlement in the interior of the island; he concludes that although some Carthaginians actually settled in the countryside, the archaeological evidence from both funerary and habitation sites is best explained by the effects of Punicization on native Sardinians.

The Romanization of Sardinia, like that of other Roman colonies, is thought to have involved the military domination of highland Nuragic settlements, with rural villas marking *latifundia* worked by slave labor. Stephen Dyson uses new survey data to show that far fewer villas existed in Sardinia than in Roman Britain which, along with the continuity shown at native sites within Roman *territoria*, indicate dialogue rather than domination in this period of the island's history. Finally, Elizabeth Lyding Will's study of Sardinian amphora collections provides yet another line of inquiry into the economy of Roman Sardinia; her observation that olive oil was imported from mainland Italy in the 1st century BC, and then from Spain in the 1st century AD, once again reflects both the long-standing, yet ever-changing relations of Sardinia in the Mediterrean.

Editorial Notes

The opposite-language summaries following each paper were written by the Editors, who take full responsibility for their contents. Summaries, rather than abstracts, were provided to serve as useful tools for research. Some homogenization of spelling and format was done; although all article titles are capitalized, Italian conventions for numbers were retained. The bibliographic format is that of the *Journal of Mediterranean Archaeology*. The chronological conventions used are BP for raw radiocarbon dates, uncal BC for uncalibrated dates, and cal BC for calibrated dates. Whenever possible, the raw date with reference is given so that recalibration can be done by the reader as necessary.

Introduzione

Robert H. Tykot e Tamsey K. Andrews

Il *Festschrift* in onore di Miriam S. Balmuth continua in spirito la serie di opere pubblicate e raccolte sotto il titolo *Studies in Sardinian Archaeology*, basate sui colloqui organizzati da Miriam Balmuth a Tufts University a partire dal 1979. Il primo volume di *SSA* pubblicato nel 1984 è stato il primo volume redatto in lingua inglese (riguardante l'archeologia in Sardegna) dopo *Sardinia* di Margaret Guido (1963). Sucessivamente, sono stati scoperti insediamenti appartenenti al Neolitico antico che risalgono al 6000 a.C., è stata ritrovata ossidiana sarda in Corsica, in Italia e nella Francia meridionale, e presso numerosi siti dell'isola sono stati identificati ceramiche e metalli di tipo egeo appartenenti al Bronzo tardo. Il numero di nuraghi, di tombe di giganti, di pozzi sacri, di domus de janas, e di altre strutture architettoniche sarde prese in esame è aumentato considerevolmente così come è aumentato il numero di archeologi nelle Soprintendenze delle Provincie di Cagliari e Oristano, di Sassari e Nuoro, e nelle Università di Cagliari e Sassari. I risultati cumulativi dell'espansione del quadro storico sardo, sono consistuti in un approfondimento della storia culturale dell'isola e delle sue relazioni con altre aree del Mediterraneo.

Durante quel periodo, per la prima volta, scavi archeologici sono stati diretti da studiosi stranieri: David Trump nelle Valle di Bonu Ighinu (1971–1972, 1979–1980), Miriam Balmuth presso il nuraghe Ortu Còmidu (1975–1978), Joseph Michels e Gary Webster presso i nuraghi Toscono e Urpes nella Marghine (1982), e Paul Sondaar e i suoi colleghi presso la Grotta di Corbeddu (dal 1982). La crescente partecipazione di studiosi inglesi e americani nelle ricerche in Sardegna e l'aumentata consapevolezza nella comunità archeologica dell'importanza della Sardegna all'interno del Mediterraneo—dovuta in parte all'esibizione presso Karlsruhe in Germania nel 1980—hanno contribuito alla pubblicazione di un volume (*SSA*) che aggiornava i lettori di lingua inglese sull'archeologia in Sardegna.

Questa iniziativa è continuata ed è stata ampliata con la pubblicazione del secondo volume, intitolato *Studies in Sardinian Archaeology*,

Volume II: Sardinia in the Mediterranean (1986). Il volume è basato sulla Prima Conferenza Internazionale sull'Archeologia in Sardegna tenutasi presso Tufts University nel settembre del 1983. Le sezioni dedicate ad insediamenti antichi, al commercio, alla metallurgia, enfatizzano lo sviluppo dell'isola e le sue relazioni con altre aree del Mediterraneo. All'interno del volume, che è caratterizzato da studi di determinati periodi e da studi delle caratteristiche dei periodi in questione, è presente una vasta gamma di discipline e ciò riflette la crescita della complessità dell'archeologia sarda e allo stesso tempo l'incremento delle ricerche in atto.

Studies in Sardinian Archaeology III (1987) è basato sulla conferenza tenutasi all'American Academy a Roma nel 1986, e è concentrato principalmente sulla *Sardegna Nuragica e il Mondo Miceneo*. Un gruppo di studiosi internazionali ha partecipato alla conferenza e per la prima volta i loro articoli furono pubblicati in lingua inglese ed in lingua italiana.

Durante gli scorsi anni, studiosi sardi hanno aumentato il numero di scavi, di ricerche scientifiche, artistiche, storiche ed epigrafiche da loro condotte, aggiungendosi alle ricerche sponsorizzate da stranieri e ai volumi sopra menzionati. Si sono tenute conferenze a Cuglieri (1984), a Selargius (1985, 1986, 1987), ad Ozieri (1986–87), ad Olièna (1988), e a Sassari-Monte d'Accoddi (1990). Articoli sono apparsi nel *Nuovo Bullettino Archeologico Sardo* (volumi 1-3: 1986, 1989, 1990), nei *Quaderni* pubblicati dalle Soprintendenze, nei rinomati *Studi Sardi*, nelle *Notizie degli Scavi*, ed in altri periodici italiani. Tra i più importanti libri pubblicati recentemente sono da menzionare la edizione riveduta ed ampliata de *La Civiltà dei Sardi* di Giovanni Lilliu (1988), il rapporto completo degli scavi presso *Il Nuraghe S. Antine nel Meilogu-Logudoro* (1988), e la versione redatta de *La Civiltà Nuragica* (1990).

La cooperazione internazionale nel recuperare il passato della Sardegna continua con questo *Festschrift*, cui 53 autori provenienti da 7 nazioni hanno contribuito con la stesura di articoli redatti in lingua inglese ed italiana. Gli Editori hanno voluto che questo volume riflettesse l'intera gamma degli attuali studi sardi, e hanno invitato specialisti in antropologia, in studi classici, in arte storica, e in scienze di laboratorio a contribuire con lavori che partono dal Paleolitico e vanno fino al periodo romano. Gli articoli sono stati organizzati in gruppi tendendo conto dei temi e del periodo a cui si riferiscono.

La sezione prenuragica si apre con un'indagine di John Cherry sulle testimonianze degli insediamenti pleistocenici in Sardegna. Questa recente area di studio (iniziata dieci anni fa) crea nuovi quesiti a proposito dei primi insediamenti sull'isola e della sua ecologia. La risposta alla domanda secondo la quale ci si chiede se sono esistiti insediamenti umani nel periodo pleistocenico ha una profonda influenza sull'interpretazione degli sviluppi avvenuti durante il Neolitico e durante l'Età del Bronzo. Martini fornisce a Cherry maggiori informazioni sui ritrovamenti litici: egli descrive e illustra parecchi complessi di utensili di pietra. Klein Hofmeijer e Sondaar sostengono che il fatto che i frammenti di cuspidi ritrovati nella Grotta di Corbeddu corrispondono ai molari delle mandibole di cervo ritrovate nello strato 3 del vano 2, prova che le mandibole furono usate *post mortem*, probabilmente come strumenti di taglio o di raschiamento, tra 11.000 e 17.000 BP. Le testimonianze sopra menzionate potrebbero soddisfare Cherry ed altri studiosi i quali sostengono che il solo modo per dimostrare che durante il Paleolitico esistettero degli insediamenti umani è di provare che il complesso di ritrovamenti non è frutto di attività non-umana.

I livelli olocenici della grotta di Corbeddu sono senza dubbio di origine umana e sono importanti, come lo è la grotta di Filiesteru (Mara-SS), per comprendere la cronologia e l'ecologia della Sardegna prenuragica. Sono anche da menzionare i dati sul polline e sulla fauna raccolti, dal momento che in Sardegna il numero di ricerche condotte a proposito è limitato.

Anche se non è certo che insediamenti umani esistessero nel Paleolitico o nel Mesolitico/Neolitico antico, è sicuro il fatto che durante il periodo prenuragico la Sardegna non era isolata dal resto delle regioni del Mediterraneo occidentale. Robert Tykot, il quale presenta nuovi dati riguardanti i giacimenti e la distribuzione di ossidiana sarda, e Patricia Phillips, la quale esamina la distribuzione di ossidiana come un esteso fenomeno neolitico europeo, affermano che lo sfruttamento dei singoli giacimenti varia a seconda dei luoghi e dei tempi. Analisi di tracce d'uso compiute da Linda Hurcombe, confermano questa ipotesi e dimostrano come la funzione dell'ossidiana abbia influenzato il modo e le circostanze secondo le quali essa sarebbe stata distribuita. Le ricerche sull'ossidiana sono le più promettenti nel rivelare le attività economiche di quel periodo, e studi futuri approfondiranno ciò che è stato scoperto fino ad ora.

Il tardo Neolitico sardo è rappresentato dalla relativamente uniforme cultura di Ozieri, la quale è caratterizzata da importanti sviluppi artistici e religiosi. Maria Luisa Ferrarese Ceruti presenta come esempio architettonico della cultura Ozieri la domus de janas del su Littu (Ossi), e offre un'interpretazione delle corna di bue e delle figure antropomorfiche scolpite nelle mure. La costruzione di questi monumenti, e di menhirs e dolmens, non fu immune dagli sviluppi contemporanei della Corsica, e può essere considerata come la manifestazione di un vasto fenomeno megalitico. Joseph Cesari riesamina i monumenti corsi che spesso sono presenti in grandi gruppi, e François de Lanfranchi classifica questi monumenti in due categorie. La testimonianza architettonica di circoli funerari e di tombe a tafone sia nella Corsica meridionale che nella Sardegna settentrionale è accompagnata dalla presenza in Corsica di ossidiana importata e di ceramiche di tipo sardo. Jean Guilaine ci mostra che esistono similitudini impressionanti tra i monumenti sardi ed alcuni monumenti nella Francia meridionale e nella Spagna orientale, ma la distanza esistente tra queste due aree rende difficile definire se queste similitudini sono dovute ad influenze reciproche o semplicemente a sviluppi architettonici convergenti.

In Sardegna l'arco di tempo esistente tra il Neolitico e l'Età del Bronzo è caratterizzato da un complesso periodo calcolitico che dura quasi un millennio. Vincenzo Santoni fornisce un dettagliato esame delle ceramiche e di altri materiali provenienti dai livelli sub-Ozieri del Cuccuru s'Arriu-Cabras, e li mette in relazione con i ritrovamenti di altri siti sardi. Egli suggerisce anche che le facies successive di Filigosa e di Abealzu-Monte d'Accoddi potrebbero essere cronologicamente più vicine al più esteso periodo culturale di Monte Claro (tardo Calcolitico).

Franco Germanà esamina le popolazioni del Neolitico, del Calcolitico, e dell'Età del Bronzo, mediante il suo importante studio del materiale scheletrico ritrovato in Sardegna. L'apparizione di individui con caratteristiche craniche brachiformi (35% dei campioni raccolti nella Sardegna nord-occidentale del Bronzo antico) a partire dal periodo di Monte Claro, potrebbe essere attribuita a dei cambiamenti di popolazioni nel Calcolitico, ma molte caratteristiche tipiche dei sardi nativi d'oggi potrebbero risalire al processo di ibridazione che fu quasi completato nel periodo Ozieri.

É durante la Media Età del Bronzo che i nuraghi, strutture architettoniche tipiche dell'antica Sardegna, fanno la loro apparizione. Lo stile di vita basato sui nuraghi durò circa due millenni: durante il periodo fenicio, il periodo punico e il periodo romano, i nuraghi infatto furono continuamente elaborati e rioccupati. Gli Editori hanno raggruppato gli articoli riguardanti questo lungo periodo in tre sezioni: la seconda parte si concentra principalmente sull'architettura degli insediamenti nuragici; la terza parte esamina le relazioni della Sardegna con il mondo esterno; la quarta parte discute gli insediamenti stranieri sull'isola.

A partire dalla Media Età del Bronzo, il fenomeno megalitico sardo, che si era precedentemente limitato all'architettura sacro-religiosa, si estende alla sfera domestica con l'erezione dei nuraghi. Le principali questioni su queste torri di pietra—nell'antico Mediterraneo esse erano seconde per dimensioni solo alle piramidi egiziane—riguardano il loro uso e la loro relazione con altre tradizioni architettoniche (egee).

La funzione dei nuraghi è esaminata da Lucia Manca Demurtas e da Sebastiano Demurtas nella loro analisi di 55 protonuraghi a corridoio passante. Essi sottolineano che queste strutture rappresentano dei tentativi riusciti di costruire edifici che servissero come abitazioni e come luoghi di difesa. Alberto Moravetti, mediante le ricerche effettuate nelle regioni di Marghine e di Planargia, fornisce dati geologici e topografici che contribuiscono a definire le funzioni e le relazioni fra i corridoi ed i nuraghi a tholos situati nello stesso territorio.

David Trump sostiene che bisogna essere cauti quando si afferma che la funzione militare dei nuraghi a fortezza deriva dai protonuraghi, e aggiunge che la trasformazione da nuraghe classico a nuraghe complesso richiede una spiegazione sociale più approfondita di quella data alla trasformazione da corridoio a tholos. Utilizzando l'Italia come paragone, Marshall Becker sostiene che si dovrebbe essere cauti nell'attribuire una sola funzione a tutti i nuraghi, dal momento che è improbabile che una forma statica di organizzazione sociale possa aver dominato simultaneamente l'intera Sardegna. Renée Bonzani utilizza dati etnografici per mettere in relazione l'uso del territorio con particolari tipi di organizzazioni sociali, e propone un modello che si concentra sull'occupazione delle zone cuscinetto esistenti tra un agglomerato di nuraghi ed un altro.

Giovanni Ugas nota che le pratiche funerarie, come quella testimoniata dalla Tomba dei Guerrieri di Decimoputzu, indicano che durante il periodo nuragico dei cambiamenti drammatici sono avvenuti nell'organizzazione sociale. Egli sostiene anche che il passaggio al classico nuraghe a tholos possa aver avuto a che fare con gli sviluppi architettonici egei. Mentre i primi nuraghi precedono l'architettura egea delle tholos, i pozzi sacri sardi sono successivi. L'indagine di Paolo Belli sulla architettura mediterranea connesse con sorgenti d'acqua, come le terme di S. Calogero a Lipari, mostra che strutture di tipo simile—sia nella forma che nella funzione—furono usate contemporaneamente ai pozzi sardi. Egli suggerisce che durante la tarda Età del Bronzo idee architettoniche potrebbero aver accompagnato prodotti di ceramiche e di metalli che circolavano tra Est e Ovest. La funzione religiosa di queste strutture, documentate dagli studi di Maria Ausilia Fadda *et al.* dei materiali usati per costruire pozzi, sorgenti, e santuari nuragici, può quindi essere vista come un'elaborazione sarda di un fenomeno architettonico esteso in tutto il Mediterraneo. Barbro Santillo Frizell afferma che è esistita un'influenza architettonica straniera, specialmente nel pozzo sacro di Santa Cristina (Paulilatino), dove l'entrata a forma di Tanit e la geometria del dromos possano essere spiegati dall'intervento di artigiani fenici esperti nel costruire navi.

Lo sviluppo e l'elaborazione delle forme architettoniche religiose e domestiche sarde è in forte contrasto con la produzione di ceramiche nuragiche, che al contrario sembra essere veramente tradizionale, come è dimostrato da Aviva Weiss Grele. I suoi studi preliminari dei dati provenienti dagli scavi compiuti dalla Pennsylvania State University nel comune di Borore, comunque mostrano un aumento dei tipi di vasellame prodotto durante il Bronzo tardo, e ciò implica un aumento della domanda di beni materiali a partire da quel periodo. Dati presentati da Lenore Gallin e Ornella Fonzo sulla fauna del villaggio del Nuraghe Santa Barbara (Bauladu) durante il Bronzo antico, sottolineano l'aspetto pastorale dell'economia nuragica e mostrano l'esistenza di allevamento di bestiame, suini, ovini e caprini, e la loro utilizzazione per la carne, la lana, e il latte.

Nella terza parte Fulvia Lo Schiavo presenta una fibula di tipo cipriota ritrovata nel nuraghe di Nurdole. Così facendo allunga la lista dei materiali di tipo egeo, importati o imitati, ritrovati in Sardegna. La possibilità che la fibula sia stata costruita in Iberia, conferma la probabilità che durante il tardo Bronzo/antica Età del Ferro la Sardegna abbia avuto contatti marittimi sia con l'Est che con l'Ovest. Gli studi compiuti da Claudio Giardino sulla metallurgia sarda dimostrano che durante questo periodo, la Sardegna diventò un punto focale nel commercio dei metalli. I suoi studi sulle correnti marine e sulla capacità di navigazione, indicano le rotte e i periodi dell'anno favorevoli al commercio di lunga distanza.

Zofia Stos-Gale e Noël Gale hanno fornito gli ultimi risultati del loro recente studio sui lingotti *oxhide* ritrovati in Sardegna. Sono stati esaminati trenta giacimenti sardi ma nessuno di questi corrisponde nella loro composizione isotopica di piombo ai 31 lingotti *oxhide* analizzati, ma altri giacimenti devono ancora essere analizzati. Tutti e 31 campioni corrispondono invece a giacimenti ciprioti sia per quanto riguarda la loro composizione isotopica di piombo, sia per quanto riguarda il loro rapporto oro/argento. Un'ipotesi è formulata per spiegare il motivo per cui del rame straniero è presente su un'isola che ha ricchi giacimenti di rame. Inoltre non esistono testimonianze che provano che rame straniero sia stato fuso per costruire oggetti in metallo nuragici.

David e Francesca Ridgway suggeriscono che tra il 1200 e 900 a.C. è possibile che i Ciprioti scambiassero rame per il ferro come è descritto nell'Odissea. Questo spiegherebbe la tarda apparizione di lingotti *oxhide* in Sardegna e le similitudini esistente tra gli utensili per lavorare i metalli usati dai Sardi e quelli usati dai Ciprioti. Essi sospettano anche che il processo a cera perduta usato per gettare i bronzetti potrebbe essere stato introdotto dai Ciprioti. C. Atzeni *et al.* presentano i risultati delle analisi metallografiche di alcuni bronzetti del Museo Archeologico Nazionale di Cagliari: è la prima volta che una collezione sarda viene analizzata. La scoperta che una delle figurine è realizzata in una lega di rame e argento invece che di rame e stagno, mostra che sono necessarie ulteriori ricerche sull'uso dell'argento in Sardegna.

In seguito alla colonizzazione fenicia dell'isola durante l'ottavo secolo a.C., c'è stato un aumento di materiali importati, specialmente di ceramiche. I Fenici ed i Cartaginesi sono serviti da mediatori non solo per l'importazione di prodotti Levantini, ma anche per l'importazione di materiale etrusco e greco. Carlo Tronchetti descrive ceramiche attiche appartenenti dal VI al IV secolo a.C. ritrovate in Sardegna, e sottolinea l'importanza sia del vasellame da mensa che dei contenitori di profumi. Egli sostiene che durante il V secolo a.C. l'aumento di prodotti greci importati è il risultato di un'ellenizzazione della civiltà punica invece che di un contatto diretto con i Greci. Secondo gli autori antichi invece, i Greci si sarebbero stabiliti in Sardegna; tra di loro ci fu Sardus, il quale diede il nome all'isola. Giovanni Lilliu riassume queste storie leggendarie, che se anche contengono una parte di verità, non sono confermate da testimonianze archeologiche. Jean Davison sostiene che l'ellenizzazione della cultura sarda, attraverso contatti commerciali fenicio-punici, risulta dal fatto che i Sardi ebbero una visione ellenocentrica della loro storia mitica. Dal momento che questa visione si sarebbe sviluppata nel VI e nel V secolo a.C., gli storici successivi, Diodoro Siculo e Pausania, avrebbero osservato culti sardi basati su leggende greche convalidando ciò che loro credevano.

Gli effetti della colonizzazione fenicia, cartaginese, e romana sono analizzati nella quarta parte. Anche se in Sardegna sono stati ritrovati materiali orientalizzanti, Paolo Bernardini sottolinea la difficoltà di definire una 'cultura' orientalizzante in seguito alla fondazione di colonie fenicie in Sardegna nell'VIII e IX secolo a.C. Egli sostiene che la società nuragica che i Fenici incontravano non era né omogenea né statica, e discute l'influenza orientalizzante sull'arte e sulle relazioni sociali indigene. J. Brian Peckham invece sottolinea la disparità dei colonizzatori fenici, i quali originavano da città-stato indipendenti, e si diressero verso ovest per diverse ragioni, seguendo rotte diverse, e in tempi diversi: prima i Sidoniani e più tardi i Tiriani, arrivando in fine a Bosa, Nora, Sulcis, e Tharros. La presenza di alcune lampade votive nuragiche nella prima fase del Tofet a Sulcis, illustrata da Piero Bartoloni, mostra che le popolazioni sarde avevano accesso a riti sacri fenici, e che è possibile che sia esistita una componente indigena nell'insediamento e nell'urbanizzazione di questo sito, a partire dalla sua fondazione nell'VIII secolo a.C. Attraverso queste relazioni costiere, fu introdotta in Sardegna l'arte orientalizzante rappresentata da alcuni gioielli da Tharros, presentati da Enrico Acquaro.

Giovanni Tore, comunque, sostiene che bisogna stare attenti quando si generalizzano i dati archeologici e storici riguardanti le relazioni esistenti tra i Fenici, Cartaginesi e le popolazioni sarde. Per esempio, dell'VIII al VI secolo a.C., la costa settentrionale dell'isola ebbe delle strette relazioni con l'Etruria; Tore afferma che durante la dominazione cartaginese non esistevano necessariamente rapporti negativi in tutta la parte dell'isola e certamente non durante tutto il periodo. Ulteriori testimonianze epigrafiche sulla colonizzazione fenicio-punica sono offerte da Maria Giulia Amadasi Guzzo, che presenta due iscrizioni puniche da Olbia e Tharros riferentesi ad insediamenti chiamati 'città nuova'.

Gary Webster e Maud Teglund completano le testimonianze storiche, archeologiche ed epigrafiche, e propongono un modello a tre zone, delle relazioni dei Fenici, dei Punici e dei Romani, con le popolazione sarde. I maggiori cambiamenti cronologico sembrano avvenire nella zona intermedia, la zona della media altitudine. Durante l'occupazione fenicia questa zona fu occupata da popolazioni nuragiche socialmente stratificate e con una complessa organizzazione sociale, più tardi fu abbandonata e/o fu controllata nel periodo punico, e fu rioccupata da un'elite emergente durante il periodo Romano. Le loro ricerche sottolineano il tema principale della quarta parte, ossia che le relazioni tra colonizzatori e popolazioni native fu un fondersi di culture dinamiche ed eterogenee, e richiede un'attenta interpretazione, e l'analisi di ciascuna regione invece che una vasta generalizzazione di tutta l'isola. Robert Rowland si concentra sulla dimensione dell'insediamento punico all'interno dell'isola; egli conclude affermando che anche se alcuni Cartaginesi si stabilirono nella campagna, le testimonianze archeologiche sia dei siti funerari che di quelli abitativi è spiegabile tramite gli effetti della punicizzazione su Sardi.

Durante la romanizzazione della Sardegna, come nel caso di altre colonie, sembra che i Romani abbiano dominato militarmente gli insediamenti nuragici degli altipiani, e che siano esistite ville rurali e latifondi lavorati da schiavi. Stephen Dyson, usando nuovi dati, mostra che in Sardegna esistevano meno ville che nella Britannia romana, e che ci fu una continuità di siti indigeni all'interno del territorio romano. Tutto ciò indica che nell'isola in questo periodo esisteva un dialogo anziché una dominazione. Infine, lo studio di Elizabeth Lyding Will sulle collezioni di anfore sarde fornisce altre testimonianze sull'economia della Sardegna romana; ella osserva che durante il I sec. a.C. l'olio d'oliva veniva importato dall'Italia e successivamente dalla Spagna nel I sec. d.C. Ancora una volta questo riflette le lunghe e allo stesso tempo mutevoli relazioni della Sardegna nel Mediterraneo.

Note Editoriali

I riassunti bilingui che seguono ciascun articolo sono stati redatti dagli Editori, i quali si assumono la piena responsabilità per i loro contenuti. I riassunti sono stati scritti per funzionare da utili strumenti di ricerca. É stata compiuta un'omogenizzazione della grafia e del formato; anche se i titoli degli articoli sono in maiuscolo, sono state mantenute le convenzioni italiane per i numeri. La forma della bibliografia è quella del *Journal of Mediterranean Archaeology*. Le convenzioni cronologiche utilizzate sono 'BP' e 'uncal BC' per date radiocarboniche non calibrate e 'cal BC' per date calibrate. Quando è possibile viene fornita la data non calibrata cosicché la ricalibrazione può essere fatta dal lettore a seconda dalla necessità.

PART I

Palaeolithic, Neolithic and Chalcolithic

Palaeolithic Sardinians?
Some Questions of Evidence and Method

John F. Cherry

A Festschrift should be fun, at least for the authors: among other things, it offers a legitimate and guilt-free chance to try out risky and unpopular ideas, or to dawdle in fascinating lay-bys off the main highways of research. So by offering a paper whose prevailing tone is negative and cautionary to a collection celebrating the decisively positive contributions to Sardinian archaeology which Miriam Balmuth has achieved over many years, I may make myself as unwelcome as an undertaker at a party. Besides, as Dena Dincauze (1984: 285) remarked in a similar context (one to which I shall return), 'Nay-saying is always less gratifying than announcing exciting discoveries, and as an activity it does little to forward careers'. Nonetheless, as I hope to show, to the extent that archaeology is a scientific discipline, drawing attention to weaknesses in the nature and use of evidence may actually promote the growth of knowledge by encouraging tests of existing data or fresh observations against current models and assumptions. Problems in the earliest archaeology of Sardinia, in any case, turn out not to be unique to that island.

My argument, in a nutshell, is the following. Research on Sardinia during the past decade or more has produced material which, in some quarters, has been claimed as evidence of a human presence on the island during the Palaeolithic, perhaps reaching as far back as two or three hundred thousand years ago. The evidence in question, however, is weak or circumstantial (though it may, of course, improve with time). So, as Vigne (1989) put the matter in a recent article title, 'le peuplement paléolithique des îles: le débat s'ouvre en Sardaigne'. Everything we currently know about the beginnings of human impact on Sardinia, about the antiquity of human presence on other Mediterranean islands, and indeed about island colonization on a worldwide basis, in fact counsels caution in accepting these claims without the closest scrutiny of the evidence. Yet to my mind the most surprising aspect has been neither the data themselves nor the assertions made about them, but rather the fact that they have thus far generated little debate—presumably because the idea of Palaeolithic humans on Sardinia has widely been considered *un*surprising. Something else is involved here: the prominence and *cachet* attached to the earliest sites in any given region, which predisposes their proponents to argument by assertion, and their opponents to dissection of the ambiguities of incomplete or incongruent data. Such head-on confrontations about alleged early sites are a feature of the archaeology of many other parts of the world, and they have a distinct tendency to dissolve into stalemate over the nature and use of evidence. Perhaps, then, in Sardinia we can learn from experience elsewhere?

In what follows, I begin by discussing and evaluating the Sardinian material, and I do so very concisely for at least three reasons. First, papers by several of the fieldworkers most closely involved may be found elsewhere in this volume, and they no doubt incorporate their most recent thoughts and the most up-to-date evidence. Secondly, although a prehistorian, I am not a specialist Palaeolithic archaeologist, and there are many aspects of cave taphonomy, lithic technology, zoo-archaeology, or evolutionary ecology which are best left to experts. Thirdly, what I regard as the most salient points of the Sardinian evidence have already been summarized, with full references, in a recent review of evidence for the first human colonization of the Mediterranean islands (Cherry 1990: 173-78). It is to the wider Mediterranean setting that I turn in my second section, and the pattern that emerges from that discussion inevitably calls into play our current theoretical understanding of the human colonization of insular environments as a more general phenomenon. Lastly, I touch on disputes about an early or Pleistocene human presence in several regions beyond the Mediterranean, and the lessons we might draw from them. Let it be clearly understood at the outset, however, that my failure to be convinced by the currently proffered evidence for early sites in Sardinia has no bearing on my estimation of the ultimate likelihood that unambiguous evidence may yet emerge: on that issue I am merely agnostic, yet also hopeful that sound scientific method will carry the day.

The Sardinian Evidence

When was Sardinia first colonized by humans? The question is not trivial, because establishing the first settlers' probable time of arrival has obvious relevance for the proper understanding of the ecological and demographic background to the florescence of the Neolithic and Bronze Age cultures on the island, about which so much has been learned in recent decades. A firm starting point is provided by the growing number of later 8th and 7th millennium BP Early Neolithic Tyrrhenian Impressed Ware sites: Grotta dell'Inferno (Muros), Filiestru (Mara), Grotta Verde (Alghero), Grotta Sa Korona, Monte Maiore (Thiesi), and Su Carroppu de Sirri (Carbonia) are the best known (for refs., see Atzeni *et al.* 1981; Lewthwaite 1981; 1982; Foschi 1982; Tanda 1982; Trump 1983). Of particular interest is the clear evidence at some of these sites, and even in somewhat later contexts too, that certain elements of the larger Pleistocene endemic fauna survived alongside domesticates introduced to the island by human occupants (Vigne 1987: 170, and fig. 1, with refs.; Cherry 1990: fig. 9). Sardinian obsidian found in Corsica already in the 8th millennium BP (Hallam *et al.* 1976; cf. Lanfranchi 1980) tells of inter-island contacts which are hardly surprising: the straits of Bonifacio (joined, but not much enlarged, at the glacial maximum) lie at -65 m, and at about 9000 BP the seaway between them would only have been about 10 km wide, as compared with the c. 50-55 km gap between Corsica and Italy (Shackleton *et al.* 1984: 311 fig. 4).

So far, so good: this earliest Neolithic horizon, attested in several parts of the island, finds good support in artifactual, stratigraphic and chronometric evidence, and, moreover, is paralleled by broadly comparable developments at much the same time in Corsica, Sicily, Crete, and Cyprus (Cherry 1990). But are there yet older phases of occupation? What demonstrates a human presence on Sardinia—or, perhaps more accurately, on the Corsican-Sardinian massif—at substantially earlier periods? Unless fresh data, unknown to me or not yet published, have come to light, I am aware of three distinct strands of evidence or lines of argument.

Lithic Assemblages

The first concerns lithic finds at half a dozen localities near Perfugas in the Anglona region, first briefly reported by Martini and Pitzalis (1981; 1982), and then published in detail by Arca *et al.* (1982a; 1982b); additional detailed typological studies were presented by Martini and Pitzalis and by Martini and Palma di Cesnola at the 1988 Olièna conference, and a further account by Martini appears in the present volume. The material in question comprises chipped stone solely from secondary or surface contexts (although there has been a small excavation of a 'chipping floor' at Pantallinu: Arca *et al.* 1982b), and there seem to exist no clearly associated palaeontological finds, no radiometric dates, nor any geostratigraphic context. Two of the localities, Riu Altana and Interiscias, represent heavily abraded and water-rolled finds in recent alluvium along stream channels, while others (Codrovulos, Laerru, Preideru and Giuanne Malteddu) are isolated relict alluvial terraces whose Rissian date seems to be derived mainly from comparison with Conchon's relative chronology of fluvial terraces in Corsica (Arca *et al.* 1982a: 10).

In techno-typological terms, two distinct lithic facies have been recognized (Klein Hofmeijer *et al.* 1989: 989; Sondaar *et al.* 1991: 194-98). The oldest (Riu Altana industry), described as evolved Clactonian with Protolevallois elements, has been attributed to an early period of the Middle Pleistocene (prior to the Mindel-Riss interglacial?); a flake industry without bifaces (Sa Pedrosa-Pantallinu), characterized as Clacto-tayacian, is thought to be younger (Rissian, or last interglacial), and to correspond with Tayacian and Evenosian assemblages of southern France, and similar complexes in peninsular Italy.

To those involved in its discovery, this evidence appears wholly convincing and it has been repeatedly presented, without additional documentation, as established fact. Others, myself included (Cherry 1984: 10-11; 1990: 175), have emphasized the need for caution and better data. Peretto and Piperno (1985) drew attention to the peculiarities of these assemblages (especially the lack of bifaces), the absence of palaeontological context, and continuing uncertainties about the connections between Sardinia and the continent at the periods in question—criticisms which Sondaar *et al.* (1991: 195) have brushed off as irrelevant or explicable through lack of research. Vigne (1989: 41) even wondered out loud whether the 'Sardinian Clactonian' could have some connection with the still poorly-known 'pre-Neolithic' finds from the basal levels of Corsican sites such as Curacchiaghiu, Araguina-Sennola and Strette.

But what seems odd, from the methodological point of view, is the seeming lack of a sense of controversy on the part of those proposing sites which, if their dates were accepted, would fall earlier by a margin of at least 100,000 years than any other yet known in the Mediterranean islands, and solely on typological grounds. In such circumstances, it seems reasonable to expect relatively stringent standards of demonstration, yet I cannot envisage how this might be achieved with the data advanced thus far. The root problem is that the archaeological materials are not enclosed in sediments that could allow the agency, environment and time of their deposition to be investigated, but were found either in secondary stream-bed contexts or as surface sites whose geological setting can allow only the loosest *post quem* chronology. Where sites have no matrix, depositional history and site integrity become serious research problems that often end inconclusively because associations cannot be shown to be original. In fact Dincauze (1984: 299-300) quite rightly asserts that 'the chronological problems inherent in matrix-free sites are so complex that it is unlikely that such sites will ever support demonstration of great age independently of more favored locations elsewhere.' On Sardinia, no such other locations are yet known, so the case rests entirely on comparative lithic typology—which, as we all know, can sometimes prove to be very subjective.

Corbeddu Cave

We are on firmer ground in the case of the excavations at Corbeddu Cave (Oliéna) in east-central Sardinia, even if some of the claims emanating from them are just as problematic. The international and multi-disciplinary research group led by Paul Sondaar and Mario Sanges includes palaeontologists, palynologists, physical anthropologists, cave taphonomists and archaeologists, whose preliminary results since work began in 1982 have poured forth in a series of papers (e.g. Sondaar *et al.* 1984; Sondaar *et al.* 1986; Spoor and Sondaar 1986; Spoor and Sondaar 1987; Sondaar and Spoor 1989; Klein Hofmeijer, Martini *et al.* 1987; Klein Hofmeijer, Sondaar *et al.* 1987; Klein Hofmeijer and Sondaar, and Kalis *et al.*, this volume). Latest reports (Klein Hofmeijer *et al.* 1989; Sondaar *et al.* 1991) present AMS radiocarbon dates which allow the effective correlation of the rather different sequence and taphonomy of the deposits in Halls 1 and 2 within the cave.

The uppermost units (levels A-B) in Hall 1 are evidently somewhat disturbed and, since they reach into the Bronze Age, are of longer duration than their stratigraphic and radiocarbon counterparts in Hall 2 (levels 1-2), whose sequence and distinction is clearer (Sondaar *et al.* 1991: figs. 1-2, table 1). Level 1 is unambiguously of Early–Middle Neolithic date, with Cardial pottery, flint and obsidian, domesticated animals (sheep, dogs), and other mainland species. An upper level (1a), with a ^{14}C date on charcoal (6260 ± 180 BP; GR N-11433), is separated by a stalagmitic floor from a lower one (1b), whose ^{14}C date of 8040 ± 100 (UT-C22-3568) makes this the earliest Cardial assemblage anywhere in the Mediterranean (Lewthwaite 1989: 546).

The chronology of level 2 is now firmly tied down by half a dozen ^{14}C assays on charcoal and bone, ranging between 7860 ± 130 BP (UtC-301) and 11040 ± 130 BP (UtC-250). While no ceramic and scarcely any lithic artifacts have been recovered from it, level 2 contained huge quantities of bones of the extinct endemic 'rabbit-rat' (pika), *Prolagus sardus*, some of them butchered and burned, as well as other members of the endemic Upper Pleistocene *Tyrrhenicola* fauna, including the endemic deer *Megaceros cazioti*. There are other reported traces of human activity—such as earth spoil apparently from a well dug to reach groundwater (Sondaar *et al.* 1986: 20)—and traces of humans themselves, in the form of a few skeletal fragments, including a left maxilla, a right temporal bone, and part of an ulna (Sondaar *et al.* 1986: 21-23; Spoor and Sondaar 1986; 1987; Sondaar 1987: 163; Sondaar *et al.* 1991: 185). These latter, associated with a ^{14}C date of 8750 BP (UtC-300), are certainly the oldest from the Corsican–Sardinian massif, slightly pre-dating those from Araguina-Sennola XVIII (Lanfranchi and Weiss 1977; Lanfranchi *et al.* 1973). Certain morphological characteristics are said to lie outside the range of variation of modern *Homo sapiens*, which the excavators have taken as evidence of endemism (implying a long history of isolation in a pre-existing Sardinian population of which we have, as yet, no fossil evidence); Vigne (in press), on the other hand, believes that such suggestions should not be pressed too far. Despite such uncertainties, the general character of Corbeddu level 2—few, if any, artifacts and heavy dependence on individual endemic Pleistocene species—suggests similarities with the earliest levels at Mallorcan sites such as So'n Muleta and So'n Matge, and the earliest, 'pre-Neolithic' occupation levels at the Corsican sites of Curacchiaghiu, Araguina-Sennola and Strette, with which it overlaps chronologically (cf. Cherry 1990: 178-89 for a summary).

Real problems of interpretation, however, are presented by the lowest levels of the sequence (levels C-F in Hall 1, level 3 in Hall 2), for which the earliest AMS ^{14}C date now stands at 14370 ± 190 (UtC-242). The red calcareous breccia includes concentrations of bone, notably those of *Megaceros cazioti* which (it is claimed) have been grouped into patterns not explicable by processes of natural transport, showing preferential selection (e.g. over-representation of jaws from young deer), and exhibiting various types of deliberate cut, scratch, groove and polish marks (Sondaar *et al.* 1984; 1986: 19-20; 1991: 186-93). Unfortunately, the anthropogenic origin of all this material is hotly disputed, and even its examination at first hand by delegates to the 1988 Oliéna conference did not suffice to convince the skeptics (summary in Vigne 1988: 43; 1989: 41). It is true that some features in the data (e.g. the atypical mortality profile of the *Megaceros* sample) remain difficult to explain. But there is no consensus that any of the bone 'tools' provide unequivocal proof of human intervention (as distinct from, for instance, gnawing by the canid *Cynotherium sardous*), and many taphonomic aspects of the cave deposits remain hazy in all the reports so far (e.g. the sorting and scouring effects of the stream that deposited much of the lower part of the profile in layer 3 of Hall 2). The lithic finds—one in layer 3, and a small, but unspecified, quantity from layers C-F—do not clinch the question. Only a handful have so far been illustrated in print and we await quantitative or statistical presentation. Mostly of the same limestone as the cave itself, the lithic industry is said to comprise 'de traces peu abondantes de l'intervention de l'homme...', and to have 'un aspect indifférencié, dénué d'éléments typologiques caractéristiques...une technique de façonnage très rudimentaire faisant appel à l'emploi très sommaire et répétif des techniques de retouche ainsi qu'un débitage et un choix des supports qui sont peu élaborés' (Sondaar *et al.* 1991: 194). Even if we can be convinced that these finds are indeed mainly artifacts rather than geofacts, they clearly have nothing in common with the contemporaneous evolved and late Epigravettian industries of the Italian peninsula, and it is sensible to characterize them not as Upper Palaeolithic but simply as 'pre-Neolithic' (Sondaar *et al.* 1991: 198). Certainly, the dubious status of the lithics, and the absence of hearths or charcoal, of clear traces of butchery, and of incontrovertible bone tools, leave lingering uncertainties about the role of Corbeddu Cave in substantiating a Pleistocene human presence in Sardinia (Vigne 1987: 168-70; in press).

The Middle Pleistocene

Sondaar's published suggestions about the antiquity of human presence in Sardinia are, in fact, even more far-reaching, since he has proposed that the ancestors of the population at Corbeddu can only have immigrated during the earlier part of the Middle Pleistocene, some 200,000 or 300,000 years earlier. The argument rests on the alleged role of humans in the extinctions of several taxa of the Lower Pleistocene *Nesogoral* fauna (which included a monkey, a pig and an antelope) and their replacement by the *Tyrrhenicola* fauna, with *Megaceros cazioti*, *Prolagus sardus*, and the small canid *Cynotherium sardous* (Sondaar 1986: fig. 3; 1987: fig. 2; Sondaar and Spoor 1989). Sondaar notes that, unlike the general pattern of Pleistocene island faunas in which lack of predation by large carnivores leads to dwarfing and low-gear locomotion, the unbalanced endemic Sardinian fauna includes a deer of 'normal mainland proportions' (in contrast, for instance, to that of Crete: Dermitzakis and de Vos 1987), implying the presence of a large predator—perhaps humans? Moreover, he has proposed a more general model (Sondaar 1987) to suggest that islands are susceptible to permanent Pleistocene human colonization only if they provide suitable natural resources. On most of the Mediterranean islands, the endemic dwarf mammals, being easily-taken prey with slow reproduction and recovery rates, would have been too susceptible to overkill, while other types of fauna, such as the murids, were too small to constitute a significant food resource; only Sardinia offers a substantially-sized mammal with high reproduction rates (i.e. *Prolagus sardus*), as well as a swift, large-bodied deer, and it was this unique circumstance, together with the island's proximity to the mainland, that facilitated its alleged Palaeolithic occupation.

This theoretically plausible account, however, has been vigorously opposed by Vigne (in press), who points to the strong size increase throughout the Pleistocene of potential human prey species such as *Prolagus*—which would imply weak predation pressure (Thaler 1973)—and the reverse tendency during the post-glacial period, when humans were certainly not only present, but also hunting *Prolagus* (Vigne 1983; 1987; Vigne *et al.* 1981). In any case, it is difficult to conceive of a human presence for several hundred thousand years on the Corsico-Sardinian massif which has not yet produced any visible traces, despite the sustained research efforts of palaeontologists, geologists, and archaeologists. The case must, for now, be regarded as *sub judice*.

The Wider Mediterranean Context

How surprising would it be if the antiquity of the human presence on Sardinia really did reach back as far as some of these claims maintain? Would such a finding square with our current knowledge of the first colonization of the other islands in the Mediterranean, or, indeed, of insular environments in general? It is worth admitting immediately that the reluctance of an earlier generation of scholarship to allow Pleistocene humans any competence in seafaring now seems misplaced. The occurrence of Melian obsidian at the Franchthi Cave in the Greek Peloponnese by c. 13,000 BP—the movement of a raw material which can only have been accomplished by over-water travel (Perlès 1979)—is now very well known. Far earlier and more impressive are the voyages involved in the colonization of southeast Asia and Australasia at least 40,000 years ago. The realization that water gaps need not have been an overwhelming impediment to human movement, especially when taken in conjunction with our improved knowledge of Pleistocene shorelines (e.g. Shackleton *et al.* 1984), puts previously labored discussions of land-bridges in a new light. How much does it really matter, for example, whether Sardinia (joined to Corsica) was, or was not, linked via Capraia and Elba to the Tuscan coast of Italy (Conchon 1976; Sondaar *et al.* 1991: 182-83), if the crossing of the narrow seaway that probably existed until a few thousand years ago posed such a trivial problem? Nonetheless, to say that humans in the Pleistocene *could* undertake significant maritime crossings is a quite different matter from demonstrating empirically that they *did* do so.

Several generations of archaeologists, palaeontologists and geologists working in the Mediterranean islands have been attempting to find tangible evidence of such ventures. Of the many claims that have been advanced, few are well founded; yet speculative or undocumented propositions have a tendency to enjoy an afterlife in the literature, even after they have been shown to be fatally flawed. It may be helpful, therefore, to take a whistle-stop tour of some other islands of the Mediterranean, in order to remind ourselves of the current position regarding evidence of pre-Neolithic or Pleistocene occupation. Much more thorough discussions, with full references to all the following material, may be found elsewhere (Cherry 1981; 1990).

Cyprus

Until 1987, the only evidence proposed in support of suggestions that humans were present on the island already in the Palaeolithic was based on the morphological characteristics of lithic artifacts which were found either as isolated items on the surface, or in contexts whose date and geological settings have not been rigorously explored. Held (1989: 7) is surely correct in pointing out that both the absence of culturally antecedent basal layers at excavated aceramic Neolithic sites, and the lack of diagnostically pre-Neolithic artifacts among the finds from the systematic field surveys of recent years, contribute to a persuasive argument from silence. Excavations at Aetokremnos on the Akrotiri peninsula in 1987–90 (Simmons 1988; 1989), however, have brought to light the clear conjunction of cultural material and huge quantities of bone from pygmy hippopotami and other extinct endemic fauna. A consistent group of a dozen ^{14}C dates spanning a period of c. 1300 years, with a weighted average of 10,030 ± 35 BP, sets the site at least two millennia before the *floruit* of the aceramic Neolithic period; nothing earlier is known, despite systematic exploration of fossiliferous palaeontological sites throughout the island.

Crete

Aceramic Stratum X at Knossos, the basal layer in the deep soundings beneath the central and west courts of the Palace of Minos associated with an earliest ^{14}C date of 8050 ± 180 (BM-124), remains the oldest unambiguous cultural context on the island. Substantial palaeontological research in Crete in recent years (for refs., see Cherry 1990: 161-62) has provided ample opportunity for the discovery of instances of the co-existence of humans with extinct Pleistocene fauna: none have yet come to light. Various types of evidence alleged to indicate a Palaeolithic human presence, all demonstrably flawed, include 'osteokeratic' bone artifacts (subsequently shown to be the likely outcome of bone-gnawing by deer or other ungulates), the possible use of bones of the now-extinct megacerine deer, so-called 'Aurignacian' lithics and parietal art. Recent announcements of a possible Epipalaeolithic or Mesolithic site in the Samaria Gorge have likewise turned out to be premature, since the material in question is actually of natural rather than artifactual origin. F. Facchini and G. Giusberti reported to the Olièna conference in 1988 on a human skeleton of supposed Middle Würm age from Crete, but the date seems to depend solely on palynological evidence and further details are awaited.

The Aegean Islands

Lithic assemblages of Palaeolithic date have come to light during the 1980s on Euboea and on

Thasos in the north Aegean, but in both cases the island was continental at times of depressed sea level. On the Cycladic island of Kythnos, doubt has been cast on a claimed Mesolithic site at Maroula (Cherry 1979), while no further details have emerged about any possible cultural associations of a ^{14}C-dated Pleistocene fossil elephant site on the same island; the same is true of the Charkadio Cave on Tilos in the Dodecanese. This leaves the Palaeolithic finds—fossilized large mammal bones and white flint tools of Mousterian types, associated with *terra rossa* deposits—from Mikro Kokkinokastro, Glipha, Steni Vala, Spartines (Halonnisos), Agios Petros (Kyra Panagia) and Akhili (Skyros), all in the Northern Sporades. Despite poor reporting, there is no good reason to doubt these discoveries, and indeed Efstratiou (1985: 6) claims them as 'the first time that the Aegean basin has yielded Palaeolithic finds... [providing] evidence that *Homo sapiens* did occupy islands that were separated from the mainland by shallow stretches of water'. The crucial question, however, is whether or not these islands were joined to each other and to the adjacent mainland to the east at the time in question; but there remain too many uncertainties about the precise timing and rates of global sea-level rise, and too few bathymetric details for the areas immediately around and between the islands, for immediate resolution of the issue.

The Ionian Islands

Middle Palaeolithic material at Nea Skala in the north of Kephallinia, said to be of around 50,000 years BP, has now been published (cf. Cherry 1990). The island was insular throughout the Pleistocene, and at the last glacial maximum would have been linked with Zakynthos and Ithaka to form the only significant island off the west coast of Greece. Even during the higher sea levels at some stages of the Middle Pleistocene the use of Lefkas as a stepping-stone would have necessitated only quite short crossings, although the island has never been closer than 20 km to the mainland. This seems to be an important exception to the generalization (e.g. Shackleton *et al.* 1984) that *archaic* hunter-gatherers did not reach islands in the Mediterranean.

Corsica

Despite biogeographic considerations which offer no real obstacles in principle to the notion of colonization episodes during the Pleistocene, when lowered sea levels afforded 'windows of opportunity', current evidence continues to suggest otherwise (perhaps for the ecological reasons proposed by Lewthwaite 1985: 48-50). The earliest sites, certainly, are 'pre-Neolithic' rock-shelters, with consistent ^{14}C dates in the 9th or late 10th millennium BP, indicating a period of foraging that preceded the introduction of food production by at least a millennium.

Balearic and Pitiussae Islands

Major advances in the archaeology of this island group have pushed back human ancestry here to at least the 7th millennium BP, but not into the Pleistocene. The cave sites of So'n Muleta (Sùller) and So'n Matge (Valldemossa) on Mallorca both offer evidence of human predation of the extinct antelope-like ruminant *Myotragus balearicus*, perhaps as early as 8570 ± 350 BP (UCLA-1704c) in the former case; *Myotragus* does not disappear from the record until after the introduction of the earliest pre-Talayotic pottery and domesticated animals, at about 4650 ± 120 BP (QL-988). At Ca'n Canet (Esporles), anthropogenic deposits containing *Myotragus* bones may even reach back to the 9th millennium BP. At all these sites, the 'pre-Neolithic' cultural material is both rare and exceedingly impoverished. The first human evidence from the other islands of the group is in each case some millennia younger.

Other West Mediterranean Islands

The Maltese group was settled no earlier than the late 7th millennium BP, at a relatively late stage of the development of Impressed Ware cultures in the West Mediterranean, and the Aeolian group likewise as yet has no material pre-dating the Middle Neolithic Stentinello pottery horizon. On the other hand, Liparian obsidian reached sites in Sicily and Calabria from at least the 8th millennium BP, and found its way to Mesolithic Arma dello Stefanin in Liguria during the 9th millennium; the pre-Neolithic exploitation of insular obsidian sources is thus a feature of the west Mediterranean, as well as the Aegean. Sicily is a different matter, of course. It has a clear sequence of lithic industries, ^{14}C-dated and associated with Pleistocene hippo–elephant–deer fauna, reaching back in some cases to the Acheulian. But it is a false island, having been joined to the continent for much of the Pleistocene by a narrow land-bridge at a depth of -90 m, and even after separation divided only by the narrowest of straits. In a way, this is a positive advantage, because Sicily provides a useful test case of the Pleistocene faunal and vegetational composition of an island on which humans were indisputably present for much of the Palaeolithic.

Discussion

This breathless survey of the current state of affairs provides, I hope, a useful background for evaluating the Sardinian material discussed above. It shows fairly clearly that, notwithstanding decades of palaeontological and archaeological exploration (the pace of which has accelerated notably in the past 20 years), traces of Pleistocene humans in insular environments remain vanishingly elusive. As in politics, so in archaeology one should never say never (as the evidence from Kephallinia evidently reminds us); but the cumulative argument from silence is growing more powerful as the years pass. What *has* recently become much clearer, however, is the evidence of a significant phase of island exploitation before the arrival of the fully-fledged Neolithic 'package'. On Cyprus, Corsica, Sardinia and the Balearics, this 'pre-Neolithic' seems to be characterized by two features: (1) heavy reliance on endemic, Pleistocene mammalian fauna which, not being adapted to the pressures of predation, may have been 'naive', easily taken, and therefore readily driven to extinction by overkill; and (2) a very rudimentary and impoverished material culture, which bears little resemblance either to contemporary assemblages on adjacent mainland areas or to those of succeeding Neolithic cultures. Expressed in millennia BP, the dates are locally variable, but form a coherent horizon: Cyprus (10th–11th), Corsica (9th–late 10th), Balearics (7th, or perhaps 9th), and Sardinia (at Corbeddu Level 2; early 8th–early 11th). These dates are of roughly the same order as the earliest signs of the exploitation of raw materials from islands in the Aegean (13th millennium BP) and western Mediterranean (8th–9th millennium BP).

This chronological picture raises some intriguing questions. For instance, is it not striking—even paradoxical—that what seems to be the period of 'take-off' in the radiation of humans into Mediterranean island environments should have been the very time when rising sea-levels had made most islands substantially smaller, had severed land-bridges with other islands or with the mainland, and had rendered water crossings to the islands more problematic than they had been for many millennia? Similarly, does the date and character of a site such as Aetokremnos on Cyprus suggest that it should be considered as the product of fully pre-Neolithic hunter-gatherers, or as a specialized adaptation to unusual ecological conditions (i.e. an island without human or other ground predators) by people with an affiliation of some sort to early food-producing cultures on the adjacent mainland? The currently available data from Aetokremnos do not allow either possibility to be wholly excluded, and its dates, while roughly in line with the Levantine Pre-Pottery Neolithic A, also overlap with the later stages of the Natufian. So what term should be used in describing this and similar sites further west? 'Epipalaeolithic', 'proto-Neolithic', and 'pre-Neolithic' have all been suggested. Even if some of them are equivalent in date to the terminal stage of the Upper Palaeolithic on the continent, these sites are not 'Palaeoithic' in the usual sense of that word, and neutral terminology is preferable until we know more about their chronology, function and cultural affinities.

This discussion leads me back to the Sardinian evidence, and two observations about it. First, I have noted above some unresolved questions about the cultural status of the lowest levels of the Corbeddu sequence (levels C-F in Hall 1, level 3 in Hall 2). But if it were established with certainty that they were all anthropogenic, they would nonetheless be very similar in character to the overlying 'pre-Neolithic' phase and to the equivalent instances on other islands just discussed, nor remarkably earlier in date. It may therefore be more helpful to consider this evidence not (as stressed in the initial reports) as a *unique* instance of 'Palaeolithic culture' or 'Pleistocene deer hunters', but rather as one member of a small group of pre-Neolithic Mediterranean island sites which reflect interesting human-animal interactions at the Pleistocene/Holocene transition. Secondly, it would clarify debate about 'the Palaeolithic of Sardinia' if a clear distinction were drawn between (1) the evidence for terminal Pleistocene culture at Corbeddu, and (2) hypotheses which propose an enormously greater time-depth for the human occupation of Sardinia. My preceding summary makes it plain that the attempt to infer human presence there even 100,000 years ago, let alone 300,000, would place Sardinia in a position that is wildly anomalous not only by comparison with every other Mediterranean island, but also with the known pattern of human colonization of insular environments on a global scale (Keegan and Diamond 1987). Were Sondaar and his colleagues aware of quite how controversial their claims actually are? We have to hope that their strongly scientific orientation will lead to comprehensive presentation of evidence, high standards of documentation, and sober evaluation of data which have a bearing on their hypotheses.

Establishing Early-Site Status: Some Broader Issues

In considering the claims and counter-claims that have been advanced over the years for a Pleistocene human presence on Mediterranean islands, I have been forcibly struck by similarities with the problems encountered in evaluating the status of alleged early sites in other parts of the world. Of particular interest is the ease with which controversy about such sites slide into inconclusiveness and factional debate between enthusiastic proponents and skeptics, even though in most cases the central questions at issue are amenable to resolution through the application of appropriate research strategies and accepted geological and archaeological methods. There is, of course, a great temptation to rush into print with early-site claims, because both the discipline of archaeology and the popular media display an interest in them which is disproportionate to their significance in terms of available evidential support. The quest for the Very First Site clearly represents a sort of Holy Grail in the competition for which unsupported claims are just as useful as solid and indisputable archaeological evidence. Dincauze (1984: 292) calls this the *prodigious fallacy*, best expressed in archaeology 'when overriding importance is claimed on the basis of great age, historical precedence, size, or some other subjective measure of value unsupported by a theoretical context'.

A good example is provided by the debate, now rising to fever pitch, about the Boqueirão de Pedra Furada rock-shelter in an area of northeastern Brazil already known for its prehistoric rock-art. The excavators, Nièdé Guidon and Fabio Parenti, first claimed to have found painted rock spalls from the cave walls going back to at least 17,000 years ago, and ash-filled hearths and stone implements from the early levels ^{14}C-dated to 32,000 years BP (Guidon and Delibrias 1986). This itself was very surprising. Now—significantly, in a newspaper report (*The New York Times*, 17 April 1990)—the claim has been extended in an unbroken sequence to 47,000 years ago, with charcoal and burned rocks in hearth arrangements associated with the earliest dates from radiocarbon and thermoluminescence measurements. That, of course, is more than 30,000 years older than the first well-documented and universally accepted dates for humans in the New World. Brian Fagan (1990), in an article in *Archaeology* magazine, was entirely correct, therefore, in insisting that such a grand claim is not necessarily *wrong*, but that the basis for it needs very careful demonstration, and certainly something more than the assertion 'I observed this; trust my observations'. A heated exchange of letters has ensued.

A better model, perhaps, is provided by the unfolding debate about the Monte Verde site in northern Chile (Dillehay and Collins 1988), whose lower levels have yielded wood fragments and some modified stones associated with dates in the 33,000 BP range. The excavator's research strategy has involved, *inter alia*, publication in monograph form of the upper, less contentious units of the site; the comparative investigation of nearby deposits that seemed devoid of human activities; and elaborate studies of the site's taphonomy and palaeoenvironmental setting, in order to rule out as many agencies as possible other than the human which might have created the site's structure and contents. Monte Verde will likely remain controversial, but evaluation procedures are in place to an extent that is unusual among all the many other claims of glacial-age sites in South America (Lynch 1990).

Yet another debate that has recently erupted in a quite different part of the world concerns the first human colonization of Australia. Not so many years ago, the issue at stake was the validation of claims pushing the settlement of Sahul back to the 35–40,000 BP range. This age estimate is now universally accepted, not only because of the multiplication of good cases from various parts of the continent providing conclusive demonstration of the proposition (Jones 1989; Allen 1989), but also because of supporting evidence from adjacent regions such as New Guinea (Groube *et al.* 1986) and New Britain (Allen *et al.* 1989) which fit within a coherent theoretical framework for how and why the process might have occurred. But this consensus has been disrupted by the claim of thermoluminescence dates between 50,000 and 60,000 years ago from the Malakunanja II rock-shelter in Arnhem Land (Roberts *et al.* 1990a). The debate is up and running, centering at present on questions of dating resolution, deposit stability and models of the colonizing process (Hiscock 1990; Roberts *et al.* 1990b); its quality is impressive.

Examples from elsewhere could be multiplied: but it is certainly in regard to the case for pre-Clovis (i.e. pre-12,000 BP) occupation of North America that the fiercest debate and the sloppiest arguments can be found (for recent summaries see, e.g., Fagan 1987; Carlisle 1988; Meltzer 1989). Everyone interested in this discourse, or in the problems associated with establishing early-site status, should read the brilliant analysis of the difficulties involved in the paper by Dincauze (1984): many of her telling criticisms apply with little change to the Mediterranean also. She is not the only person in recent years, of course, to have noted the unquestioning presumption of artifact status for roughly broken bones and stones in archaeological context, and the ease with which this leads to 'myths' about past human behavior (Binford 1981). But she extends the idea as a *typological fallacy* which mistakes simple for old (and vice versa), so that people 'accept as cultural remains various combinations of "geofacts", concentrations of broken bones, and burned areas, without asking what such unstructured phenomena might imply for human behavior' (Dincauze 1984: 292). Another set of problems concerns the difficulty of falsifying statements which are expressed only as possibilities, and of refuting the widespread belief that 'many possibles make a probable' (whereas the probability of a series of assertions being true is the product, not the sum, of their individual probabilities).

There is an underlying methodological issue of some importance here. In the pre-Clovis debate, skeptics tend to insist that properly substantiated data *must* include sound stratigraphy coupled with a series of chronometric determinations of artifacts indisputably of human manufacture in direct association—i.e. *artifacts*, *stratigraphy* and *dates*. Proponents tend to complain that this imposes standards of demonstration which are quite unreasonably stringent, and which are not demanded of later, less controversial sites; and, in any case, would it not be the case that the groups responsible for early sites were small, very mobile, highly conservative, and equipped with 'material cultures so rudimentary that those can be distinguished from naturally broken stones and bones only with difficulty, if at all' (Dincauze 1984: 298)? The skeptics reply that these are questionable assumptions about the nature of early human societies, and that in any case the criteria for establishing artifact status for broken bones and stones have become much clearer and more demanding as a result of experimental, ethnoarchaeological and taphonomic studies. This debate seems likely to run and run. Yet when there is 'a carefully reasoned analysis of the controversy and a line-by-line response to critics' concerns' (Fagan 1990: 19)—as has occurred recently in respect of the 19,000 BP levels at the Meadowcroft rock-shelter near Pittsburgh (Adovasio *et al.* 1990)—one feels that knowledge is making progress. (Ironically, Adovasio was one of those who, some years ago, proposed a wholly unsubstantiated Upper Palaeolithic date for a series of chipped stone assemblages from surface sites in northwest Cyprus!)

So back again to the earliest prehistory of Sardinia, the lessons for which I hope are self-evident from the preceding discussion. With respect to the data from the lowest levels at Corbeddu Cave, I take the side of those who think it not unreasonable (especially in the light of widespread skepticism by those who have themselves examined the data) to expect the excavators next to disprove the hypothesis that the assemblage could be the result of *non*-human agents, using techniques that are now becoming better established; the broken bones and stones, and their spatial and stratigraphic relationships, will otherwise float in a limbo of uncertainty. As for the possibility of a staggeringly long ancestry of man on Sardinia, it is helpful that Sondaar (1987) has cast some of his thinking in the form of a *model*, and one that is generalizable outside the specific island context that gave rise to it; but it has also proved vulnerable to immediate criticism. Is it testable on a comparative sample of islands? Do we have the methodological tools to factor out unambiguously human impact on the long-term evolutionary ecology of endemic mammalian fauna on islands? A 300,000-year history for *Homo sardus* is too large a claim to swallow without documentation beyond a reasonable doubt; and the earliest phases of the fascinating prehistory of the island of Sardinia deserve no less.

References

Adovasio, J., J. Donahue & R. Stuckenrath
 1990 The Meadowcroft Rockshelter radiocarbon chronology 1975–1990. *American Antiquity* 55(2): 348-54.

Allen, J.
 1989 When did humans first colonize Australia? *Search* 20: 149-54.

Allen, J., C. Gosden & J.P. White
 1989 Human Pleistocene adaptations in the tropical island Pacific: Recent evidence from New Ireland, a Greater Australian outlier. *Antiquity* 63: 548-61.

Arca, M., F. Martini, C. Tuveri, G. Pitzalis & A. Ulzega
 1982a Il paleolitico dell'Anglona (Sardegna settentrionale). Ricerche 1979–80. *Quaderni della Soprintendenza Archeologica per le Provincie di Sassari e Nuoro* 12.
 1982b Il deposito quaternario con industrie del Paleolitico inferiore di Sa Pedrosa-Pantallinu (Sassari). *Rivista di Scienze Preistoriche* 37(1-2): 31-53.

Atzeni, E., F. Barreca, M. L. Ferrarese-Ceruti, E. Contu, G. Lilliu, F. Lo Schiavo, F. Nicosia & E. Equini Schneider (eds.)
 1981 *Ichnussa: La Sardegna dalle origini all'età classica*. Milano: Libri Scheiwiller.

Binford, L.R.
 1981 *Bones: Ancient Men and Modern Myths*. New York: Academic Press.

Carlisle, R. (ed.)
 1988 *Americans Before Columbus: Ice Age Origins*.

Cherry, J.F.
1979 Four problems in Cycladic prehistory. In J.L. Davis and J.F. Cherry (eds.), *Papers in Cycladic Prehistory*, 22-47. UCLA Institute of Archaeology Monograph 14. Los Angeles: UCLA Institute of Archaeology.
1981 Pattern and process in the earliest colonization of the Mediterranean Islands. *Proceedings of the Prehistoric Society* 47: 41-68.
1984 The initial colonization of the West Mediterranean islands in the light of island biogeography and paleogeography. In W.H. Waldren, R. Chapman, J. Lewthwaite and R.-C. Kennard (eds.), *The Deya Conference of Prehistory: Early Settlement in the Western Mediterranean Islands and the Peripheral Areas*, 7-23. BAR International Series 229. Oxford: British Archaeological Reports.
1990 The first colonization of the Mediterranean islands: A review of recent research. *Journal of Mediterranean Archaeology* 3: 145-221.

Conchon, O.
1976 The human settlement of Corsica: Palaeogeographic and tectonic considerations. *Journal of Human Evolution* 5: 241-48.

Dermitzakis, M.D., & J. de Vos
1987 Faunal succession and the evolution of mammals in Crete during the Pleistocene. *Neues Jahrbuch für Geologie und Paläontologie, Abhandlungen* 173(3): 377-408.

Dillehay, T.D., & M. Collins
1988 Early cultural evidence from Monte Verde in Chile. *Nature* 332: 150-52.

Dincauze, D.F.
1984 An archaeo-logical evaluation of the case for pre-Clovis occupations. In F. Wendorf and A. Close (eds.), *Advances in World Archaeology*, III, 275-323. Orlando: Academic Press.

Efstratiou, N.
1985 *Ayios Petros: A Neolithic Site in the Northern Sporades*. BAR International Series 241. Oxford: British Archaeological Reports.

Fagan, B.M.
1987 *The Great Journey: The Peopling of Ancient America*. New York: Thames & Hudson.
1990 Tracking the first Americans. *Archaeology* 43(6): 14-20.

Foschi, A.
1982 Il neolitico antico della Grotta Sa Korona di Monte Majore (Thiesi, Sassari): Nota preliminare. In R. Montjardin (ed.), *Le Néolithique Ancien Méditerranéen: Actes du Colloque International de Préhistoire, Montpellier 1981*, 339-47. Sète: Fédération Archéologique de l'Hérault.

Groube, L., J. Chappell, J. Muke & D. Price
1986 A 40,000 year-old occupation site at Huon Peninsula, Papua New Guinea. *Nature* 324: 453-55.

Guidon, N., & G. Delibrias
1986 Carbon-14 dates point to man in the Americas 32,000 years ago. *Nature* 321: 769-71.

Hallam, B., S. Warren & C. Renfrew
1976 Obsidian in the western Mediterranean: Characterisation by neutron activation analysis and optical emission spectroscopy. *Proceedings of the Prehistoric Society* 42: 85-110.

Held, S.O.
1989 Colonization cycles on Cyprus, 1: The biogeographic and paleontological foundations of early prehistoric settlement. *Reports of the Department of Antiquities, Cyprus*: 7-28.

Hiscock, P.
1990 How old are the artefacts in Malakunanja II? *Archaeology in Oceania* 25: 122-25.

Jones, R.
1989 East of Wallace's Line: Issues and problems in the colonisation of the Australian continent. In P. Mellars and C. Stringer (eds.), *The Human Revolution: Behavioural and Biological Perspectives on the Origins of Modern Humans*, 743-82. Edinburgh: Edinburgh University Press.

Keegan, W., & J. Diamond
1987 Colonization of islands by humans: A biogeographic perspective. *Advances in Archaeological Method and Theory* 10: 49-92.

Klein Hofmeijer, G., C. Alderliesten, K. van der Borg, C.M. Houston, A.F.M. de Jong, F. Martini, M. Sanges & P.Y. Sondaar
1989 Dating of the Upper Pleistocene lithic industry of Sardinia. *Radiocarbon* 31: 986-91.

Klein Hofmeijer, G., F. Martini, M. Sanges, P.Y. Sondaar & A. Ulzega
1987 La fine del Pleistocene nella Grotta Corbeddu in Sardegna. Fossili umani, aspetti paleontologici e cultura materiale. *Rivista di Scienze Preistoriche* 41(1-2): 1-36.

Klein Hofmeijer, G., P.Y. Sondaar, C. Alderliesten, K. van der Borg & A.F.M. de Jong
1987 Indications of Pleistocene Man on Sardinia. *Nuclear Instruments and Methods in Physics Research* B29: 166-68.

Lanfranchi, F. de
1980 L'obsidienne prehistorique corse: Les échanges et les axes de circulation. *Bulletin de la Société Préhistorique Française* 77(4): 115-22.

Lanfranchi, F. de, & M.-C. Weiss
1977 *Araguina-Sennola: Dix Années de Fouilles Préhistoriques à Bonifacio*. Archeologia Corsa 2. Ajaccio: Maison de la Culture de la Corse.

Lanfranchi, F. de, M.-C. Weiss & H. Duday
1973 La sépulture prénéolithique de la couche XVIII de l'abri d'Araguina-Sennola. *Bulletin de la Société des Sciences Historiques et Naturelles de la Corse* 606: 7-26.

Lewthwaite, J.
1981 Ambiguous first impressions: A survey of recent work on the Early Neolithic of the West Mediterranean. *Journal of Mediterranean Anthropology and Archaeology* 1(2): 292-307.
1982 Cardial disorder: Ethnographic and archaeological comparisons for problems in the early prehistory of the West Mediterranean. In R. Montjardin (ed.), *Le Néolithique Ancien Méditerranéen: Actes du Colloque International de Préhistoire, Montpellier 1981*, 311-18. Sète: Fédération Archéologique de l'Hérault.
1985 From precocity to involution: The Neolithic of Corsica in its west Mediterranean and French contexts. *Oxford Journal of Archaeology* 4(2): 47-68.
1989 Isolating the residuals: The Mesolithic basis of man–animal relationships on the Mediterranean islands. In C. Bonsall (ed.), *The Mesolithic in Europe: Papers Presented at the Third International Symposium, Edinburgh 1985*, 541-55. Edinburgh: John Donald Publishers.

Lynch, T.F.
  1990   Glacial-age man in South America? A critical review. *American Antiquity* 55(1):12-36.
Martini, F., & G. Pitzalis
  1981   Il paleolitico in Sardegna. In E. Atzeni *et al.* (eds.), *Ichnussa: La Sardegna dalle origini all'età classica*, 603-604. Milano: Libri Scheiwiller.
  1982   Il paleolitico inferiore in Sardegna. In *Atti del XXIII Riunione Scientifica 'Il Paleolitico inferiore in Italia,' Firenze, 7-9 maggio 1980*, 249-55. Firenze: Istituto Italiano di Preistoria e Protostoria.
Meltzer, D.J.
  1989   Why don't we know when the first people came to North America? *American Antiquity* 54(3): 471-90.
Peretto, C., & M. Piperno
  1985   The earliest phases of human settlement in Italy. *Homo: Journey to the Origins of Man's History*, 249-58. Marseilles: E.D.
Perlès, C.
  1979   Des navigateurs méditerranéens il y a 10,000 ans. *La Recherche* 10(96): 82-85.
Roberts, R.G., R. Jones & M.A. Smith
  1990a   Thermoluminescence dating of a 50,000 year-old human occupation site in northern Australia. *Nature* 345: 153-56.
  1990b   Stratigraphy and statistics at Malakunanja II: Reply to Hiscock. *Archaeology in Oceania* 23: 125-29.
Shackleton, J.C., T.H. van Andel & C.N. Runnels
  1984   Coastal palaeogeography of the Central and Western Mediterranean during the last 125,000 years and its archaeological implications. *Journal of Field Archaeology* 11: 307-14.
Simmons, A.H.
  1988   Extinct pygmy hippopotamus and early man in Cyprus. *Nature* 333(6173): 554-57.
  1989   Preliminary report on the 1988 test excavations at Akrotiri-Aetokremnos, Cyprus. *Reports of the Department of Antiquities, Cyprus*: 1-5.
Sondaar, P.Y.
  1986   The island sweepstakes: Why did pygmy elephants, dwarf deer, and large mice once populate the Mediterranean? *Natural History* 95(9): 50-57.
  1987   Pleistocene man and extinctions of island endemics. *Mémoires de la Société Géologique de France* 150: 159-65.
Sondaar, P.Y., P.L. de Boer, M. Sanges, T. Kotsakis & D. Esu
  1984   First report on a paleolithic culture in Sardinia. In W.H. Waldren, R. Chapman, J. Lewthwaite and R.-C. Kennard (eds.), *The Deya Conference of Prehistory: Early Settlement in the Western Mediterranean Islands and the Peripheral Areas*, 29-47. BAR International Series 229. Oxford: British Archaeological Reports.
Sondaar, P.Y., F. Martini, A. Ulzega & G. Klein Hofmeijer
  1991   L'homme pléistocène en Sardaigne. *L'Anthropologie* (Paris) 95: 181-200.
Sondaar, P.Y., M. Sanges, T. Kotsakis & P.L. de Boer
  1986   The pleistocene deer hunter of Sardinia. *Geobios* 19(1): 17-25.
Sondaar, P.Y., & C.F. Spoor
  1989   Man and the pleistocene endemic fauna of Sardinia. In G. Giacobini (ed.), *Hominidae: Proceedings of the Second International Congress of Human Paleontology (Turin, 28 September-3 October 1987)*. Turin.
Spoor, C.F., & P.Y. Sondaar
  1986   Human fossils from the endemic island fauna of Sardinia. *Journal of Human Evolution* 15: 399-408.
  1987   The first palaeolithic human fossils from Sardinia. *Bones: Treasuries of Human Experience in Time and Space* 1: 69-71.
Tanda, G.
  1982   Il neolitico antico della Sardegna. In R. Montjardin (ed.), *Le Néolithique Ancien Méditerranéen: Actes du Colloque International de Préhistoire, Montpellier 1981*, 327-31. Sète: Fédération Archéologique de l'Hérault.
Thaler, L.
  1973   Nanisme et gigantisme insulaire. *La Recherche* 37: 741-50.
Trump, D.
  1983   *La Grotta Filiestru a Bonu Ighinu, Mara (SS)*. Quaderni 13. Sassari: Dessì.
Vigne, J.-D.
  1983   *Les mammifères terrestres non-volants du post-glaciaire de Corse et leurs rapports avec l'homme: étude paléo-ethno-zoologique fondée sur les ossements*. Thèse 3e cycle, P. et M. Curie Université, Paris.
  1987   L'extinction holocène du fonds de peuplement mammalien indigène des îles de Méditerranée occidentale. *Mémoires de la Société Géologique de France* 150: 167-77.
  1988   Colloques: Early Man in Island Environments, Olièna (Sardaigne), 25 settembre-2 ottobre 1988. *Les Nouvelles de l'Archéologie* 34: 42-43.
  1989   Le peuplement paléolithique des îles: Le débat s'ouvre en Sardaigne. *Les Nouvelles de l'Archéologie* 35: 39-42.
  in press Biogeographical history of the mammals on Corsica (and Sardinia) since the final Pleistocene. In *Proceedings of the International Symposium on Biogeographical Aspects of Insularity (Rome 1987)*. Rome: Accademia Nazionale Lincei.
Vigne, J.-D., M.-C. Marinval-Vigne, F. de Lanfranchi & M.-C. Weiss
  1981   Consommation du 'Lapin-Rat' (*Prolagus sardus* Wagner) au Néolithique ancien méditerranéen: Abri d'Araguina-Sennola (Bonifacio, Corse). *Bulletin de la Société Préhistorique Française* 78: 222-24.

Riassunto

Quando è avvenuta la prima colonizzazione umana in Sardegna? La risposta a questa domanda è importante per comprendere le caratteristiche geologiche e demografiche della Sardegna durante il periodo neolitico e l'inizio dell'età del Bronzo. Sono state ritrovate ceramiche impresse di tipo tirrenico che risalgono al settimo e all'ottavo millennio BP, sono stati anche ritrovati elementi di fauna pleistocenica ed alcuni animali domestici introdotti in quel periodo: tutto ciò indica una presenza umana nell'isola durante questo periodo. C'è da aggiungere che il ritrovamento di ossidiana dell'ottavo millennio BP in Corsica, indica l'esistenza di contatti tra le due isole in questo periodo.

Ricerche e studi effettuati nell'ultimo decennio hanno mostrato l'esistenza di una presenza umana nell'isola durante il Paleolitico, ed è stato suggerito che la prima presenza umana sull'isola risale a 200.000 e 300.000 anni fa, ciò vuol dire al Pleistocene Medio. L'Autore rivede quest'affermazione basandosi su ciò che è noto riguardo alla colonizzazione dell'isola in altre aree del Mediterraneo.

I ritrovamenti litici presso sei località vicino a Perfugas nella regione di Anglona (cf. Martini, in questo volume) hanno provocato il sorgere di parecchie controversie. Si tratta di sassi scheggiati da contesti di superficie e secondari, purtroppo non accompagnati da altri ritrovamenti paleontologici, non hanno date radiometriche e non provengono da un contesto geostratigrafico. Questi ritrovamenti sono stati ripetutamente presentati come dati di fatto senza essere accompagnati da un'ulteriore documentazione. L'Autore, seguendo Peretto e Piperno, e Vigne, sostiene che questi litici sono insoliti, specialmente per il fatto che nessuno di loro è bifacciale. Ma il fatto più inquietante è che i siti in cui sono stati trovati risalerebbero a 100.000 anni prima di ogni altro sito conosciuto nelle isole Mediterranee e questa interpretazione è stata fatta basandosi unicamente su dati tipologici. La datazione di questi ritrovamenti fatta attraverso la tipologia ignora la complessità della storia di deposizione, l'integrità del sito ed i problemi di interpretazione soggettiva. Per questo motivo i ritrovamenti devono essere interpretati con cautela e messi da parte fino a quando non si avranno ulteriori dati.

Una seconda fonte che afferma che una presenza umana è esistita nella Sardegna Pleistocenica proviene dalla Grotta Corbeddu nella Sardegna centro-orientale (cf. Klein Hofmeijer e Sondaar, in questo volume). Nella parte superiore dei vani 1 e 2 della suddetta grotta, sono stati ritrovati ossa e carboni i cui dati radiocarbonici indicano che risalgono a 11,000 BP. I ritrovamenti della Grotta Corbeddu sono simili a quelli fatti a So'n Muleta e So'n Matge a Mallorca, e ai ritrovamenti pre-neolitici di Curacchiaghiu, Araguina-Sennola, e Strette in Corsica.

Ci sono però seri problemi di interpretazione per quanto riguarda i ritrovamenti fatti nella parte inferiore della grotta. Infatti sono state ritrovate mascelle di cervo che sembrano essere state incavate e levigate da mano umana. Non è ancora sicuro il fatto che le ossa sopra menzionate siano state degli utensili, ed è possibile che i ritrovamenti litici del livello 3 siano dei 'geofatti' anziché dei manufatti. L'assenza di focolari, di carboni, di tracce di processi di macellazione, e la dubbia interpretazione che le ossa ritrovate siano stati utensili, ci lascia poco convinti del fatto che durante l'età Pleistocenica ci sia state una presenza umana a Corbeddu. Infine Vigne non ha accettato su una base teorica il fatto che tra 200.000 e 300.000 anni fa l'uomo sia stato il responsabile della sostituzione faunistica Nesogoral-Tyrrhenicola, e questa ipotesi non può essere accettata a meno che siano ritrovate ulteriori indubbie testimonianze di attività umana.

L'Autore esamina la scarsa evidenza di insediamenti pleistocenici in altre isole mediterranee e afferma che il materiale ritrovato in Sardegna, che mostra l'evidenza di una presenza umana durante il Pleistocene, non corrisponde al quadro generale della regione. Nonostante i ritrovamenti di ossidiana di Melos presso la grotta di Franchthi datata al 13.000 BP, le date più antiche per le isole di Cipro (10.000 BP) e Creta (8000 BP) risalgono al periodo pre-Neolitico e Neolitico. In Corsica i più antichi siti pre-neolitici risalgono al nono e al decimo millennio BP. Le ossidiane lipariche non hanno raggiunto la Sicilia e la Calabria prima dell'ottavo millennio BP, ma hanno raggiunto la Liguria nove mila anni fa. Tranne i ritrovamenti risalenti al Paleolitico medio presso Nea Skala (Kephallinia, Grecia), le isole mediteranee non sono state testimoni di una presenza umana durante il periodo Pleistocenico.

L'Autore osserva che esiste un fase significativa di sfruttamento delle isole mediterranee prima del vero e proprio Neolitico, ma le date riguardanti la prima colonizzazione umana delle isole del Mediterraneo risalgono tutte intorno al decimo e undicesimo millennio BP. L'Autore nota con interesse il fatto insolito che la colonizzazione delle isole coincide con un periodo in cui il livello del mare si è innalzato ed ha fatto in modo che le isole divenissero più piccole e che ponti naturali tra le isole e il continente fossero tagliati.

L'Autore conclude l'articolo con una discussione riguardante la psicologia che si cela dietro le scoperte di alcuni archeologi. L'Autore teorizza che il prestigio e lo status associati con il ritrovamento di testimonianze che indicano l'esistenza di una prima colonizzazione umana, spesso conducono a tirare conclusioni affrettate. Inoltre i mass-media tendono a giudicare tali ritrovamenti senza tener conto delle conoscenze teoriche esistenti. Ciò nonostante, bisogna essere sempre certi che manufatti, date e stratigrafie siano direttamente associati tra di loro. Per sostenere una tale affermazione sarebbe necessario che le circostanze dei primi insediamenti siano formulate in modo da potere essere applicate in altri luoghi. Per quanto riguarda la Sardegna, il fatto che un *Homo sardus* sia esistito 300.000 anni fa, non può essere stabilito basandosi unicamente sui correnti dati comparativi ed archeologici.

Early Human Settlement in Sardinia: The Palaeolithic Industries

Fabio Martini

The first discoveries of lithic industries that led scholars to believe in the existence of Palaeolithic settlements in Sardinia date from 1979 (Cornaggia Castiglioni and Calegari 1979). Since then, a research program developed by the University of Siena and the Archaeological Superintendency for the Provinces of Sassari and Nuoro has focused on the Lower Palaeolithic period (Martini and Pitzalis 1982). In 1982, the Rijksuniversiteit Utrecht joined the program with studies on the Late Pleistocene. This program has not only confirmed the early findings, but has also made it possible to outline a relatively complex picture of Palaeolithic settlement in Sardinia.

Currently there are about 10 Palaeolithic sites known on the island; some have been the object of stratigraphic excavations and others of only surface research. With the exception of Corbeddu Cave (see Klein Hofmeijer and Sondaar, this volume), which has a Late Pleistocene–Early Holocene occupation, all the other archaeological sites date to the Lower Palaeolithic.

These sites have yielded materials from different facies of the Clactonian phylum. Clactonian lithic assemblages are usually characterized by tools with massive striking platforms, unsophisticated retouch, and an overall lack of bifacially flaked tools. Unfortunately, in Sardinia these lithic assemblages have never been found associated with palaeontological remains; in addition, the deposits themselves have always proven to be palynologically sterile. Therefore, the age of these sites has been based on the geomorphological and pedological context of the finds, as well as the technological and typological features of the lithic artifacts themselves. I use the term Clactonian, therefore, as a conventional nomenclature to highlight the class of flaking technique used; early and late are used only to indicate relative chronological sequence.

The Early Clactonian

The oldest Clactonian period in Sardinia is represented by two industrial complexes near Perfugas (SS): a surface collection of artifacts showing the most physical alterations, gathered along the Riu Altana river bed, and some assemblages in primary deposits found during stratigraphic excavations at Sa Coa de Sa Multa.

The Riu Altana assemblage is composed of various industrial complexes, both Pleistocene and Holocene, that were identified on the basis of their physical attributes (Martini and Palma di Cesnola 1988). The older series 1 has very abraded edges (Fig. 1), while artifacts classified as series 3 have relatively fresh edges. Series 2 artifacts are considered intermediate in form.

Series 1, the most altered, is attributed to the Early Clactonian and would seem to represent a facies comparable to the peninsular Protolevallois. In typometric terms[1] the size of the items ranges from medium (c. 72%) to large (c. 24%), with a prevalence of flakes (c. 37%) and laminar flakes (c. 24%), and a reasonable number of blades (c. 22%), including some very narrow elements. Flat (c. 41%) and subcarinated (c. 31%) forms dominate, while carinated (c. 13%) and very flat pieces (c. 15%) are less significant. Flakes and medium-size flat laminar flakes are the most common lithic reduction products.

The recognizable striking platforms are mostly smooth with uneven edges, and are either triangular or rhomboid. Both the size and the elongation of the platform are ample, with little inclination relative to the vertical face (about 110-115°); at times the angles barely exceed 90°.

Morphological studies of the reduction process have revealed little utilization of the core. In fact, there is a prevalence of artifacts with one or two dorsal ribs and with some cortex still present.

---

[1] For the typometric nomenclature used, see Laplace (1968) for length, Bagolini (1968) for elongation indices, and Martini (1975) for carination indices.

Only the more elongated pieces have great numbers of ribs, which are a sign of more prolonged use of the core. The direction of the dorsal attachments is mostly random (about 58%). There is a significant amount of centripetal (about 5%) or parallel (about 35%) detachments which are indicative of a relatively systematic flaking technique. The few cores that were found were not sufficient to permit in-depth study of the reduction process.

The typology of the Riu Altana assemblage is not very significant since only a few dozen instruments were found. These include short, lateral and transverse scrapers that are either carinated or denticulated, while retouched blades are rare. There is one unifacial pointed chopper with an uneven, rounded contour. The retouch is either overlapping or, more often, marked by wide scars. Rarely do we see small, single flake scars. The origins of this industry have been traced to the peninsular Protolevallois facies of the Early Clactonian, found along the Adriatic coast (Puglia, Abruzzo, Marche and Emilia) and even perhaps in Tuscany.

When compared to the Protolevallois, the Riu Altana industry seems to have utilized a more systematic and predetermined flaking technique; however, it is still acceptable to classify both of these industries within the same stylistic and technological group. On the continent as well there is a lack of chronostratigraphic and naturalistic data that could provide chronological markers, but through typological comparisons with some Emilian materials found out of context in pedogenized Mindelian gravels, the Riu Altana facies could also be as early as the Mindel glaciation.

The second Early Clactonian complex was recently discovered in a primary deposit at Sa Coa de Sa Multa. The assemblage (Fig. 2) lies in a severely altered terrain with soils formed during a temperate climatic moment in the Middle Pleistocene. The artifacts are part of an inhabited palaeosurface of which only 15 sq m have been studied to date, although excavations are currently in progress. Many flaked tools have been found along with a number of cores, blocks and large flakes of primary siliceous material. The industry can be described as medium to large in size, and is characterized mainly by instruments with significantly raised retouch which is often unique. A preliminary analysis indicates that these artifacts resemble the Riu Altana finds in their general technological features, although they seem to be lacking in Protolevallois characteristics.

The Late Clactonian

This subsequent industrial stage is represented in the Province of Sassari by a series of assemblages: Giuanne Malteddu, Interiscias, Preideru, Codrovulos-Pantallinu, Laerru and Riu Altana series 3 (Arca *et al.* 1982a; 1982b). The assemblage from Sa Pedrosa-Pantallinu (Fig. 3) is typical of this complex. It was found *in situ* in an orographic terrace which has been dated to the Riss glaciation on the basis of the sequence of terraces in the entire local basin, and by correspondence with similar terraces in nearby Corsica. The Sa Pedrosa terrace is attributed to the Pantallinu order in the cold climatic conditions of this penultimate glacial period, with soil formation and alteration occuring during the last interglacial era, and with significant erosion during the Würm glaciation. Pedological analyses attribute the soil containing the assemblage to the pre-Würmian.

The lithic assemblage comes from a single level of dwellings associated with breakage due to frost. It is stratigraphically related to a great quantity of siliceous material found in blocks at the base of the soil, and above the underlying Miocene layer which supports the archaeological finds. A small number of tools are accompanied by a great quantity of unretouched items and residual cores, especially in the form of debris. The abundance of raw materials at the site, the high ratio between unretouched items and tools, and the great number of residual cores have led me to propose the existence of a lithic workshop at Sa Pedrosa.

A tentative synthesis of the Sardinian Late Clactonian takes into consideration the following preliminary results from the analysis of the above assemblages. In typometric terms, medium-sized items are the most common, but with good representation of large and even small sizes. Laminarity is low and laminar waste is exceptionally narrow and elongated; flakes prevail, with many wide elements. Flat and very flat pieces of debitage are the most common.

Comparing these features with the Early Clactonian, we can see a decrease in size in the later stage along with a decrease of laminarity in favor of wide striking platforms, and a decrease in the number of carinated pieces. The striking platforms are mostly elongated and narrow, and less broad than those of the Riu Altana series 1. Their inclination with respect to the ventral face (mainly 116-120°) is accentuated more than in the older stage. In addition, striking platforms with almost right angles are extremely rare.

42 *Sardinia in the Mediterranean*

Fig. 2 Sa Coa de Sa Multa: lithic industry.

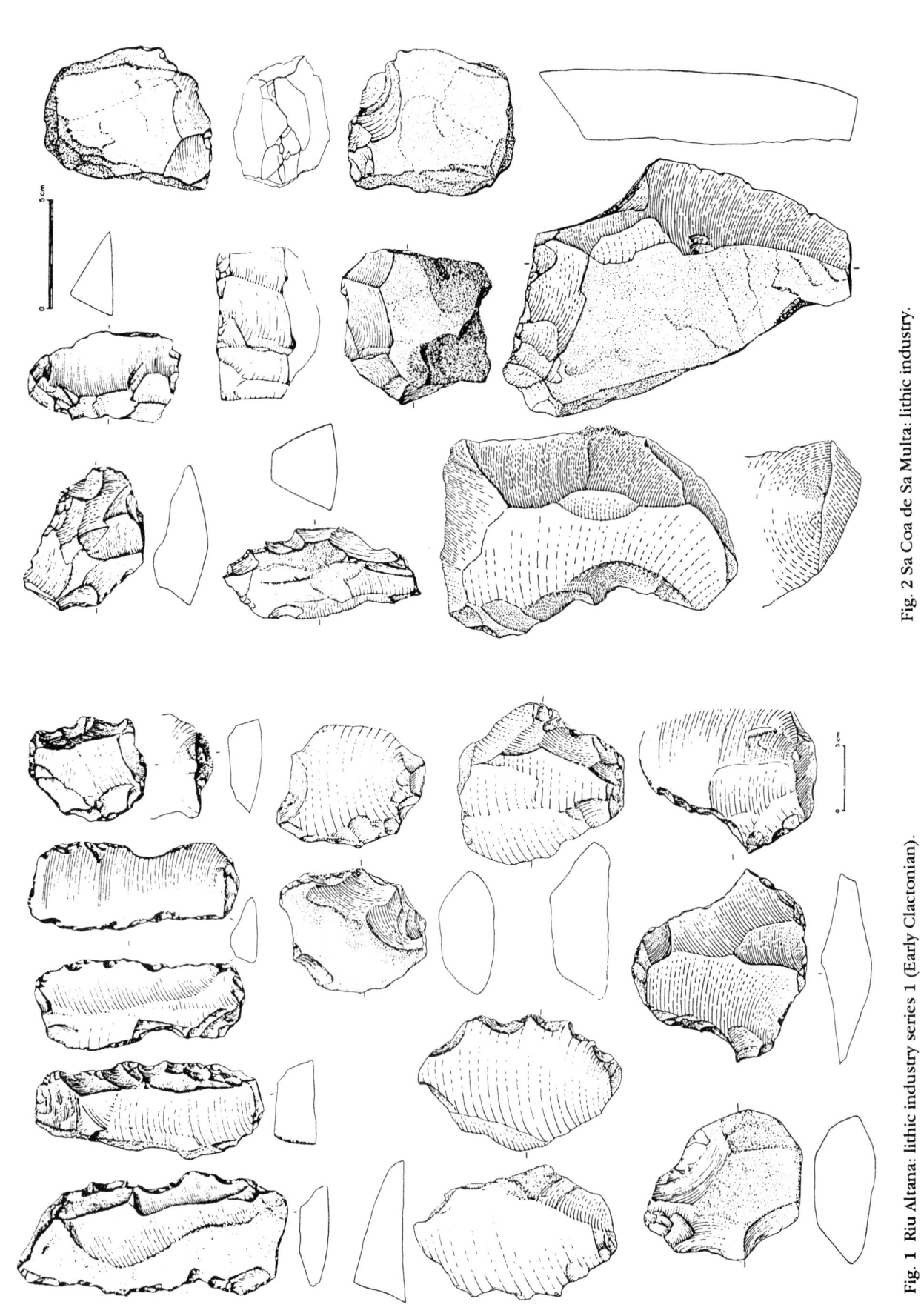

Fig. 1 Riu Altana: lithic industry series 1 (Early Clactonian).

Fig. 4 Corbeddu Cave (hall 1): lithic industry.

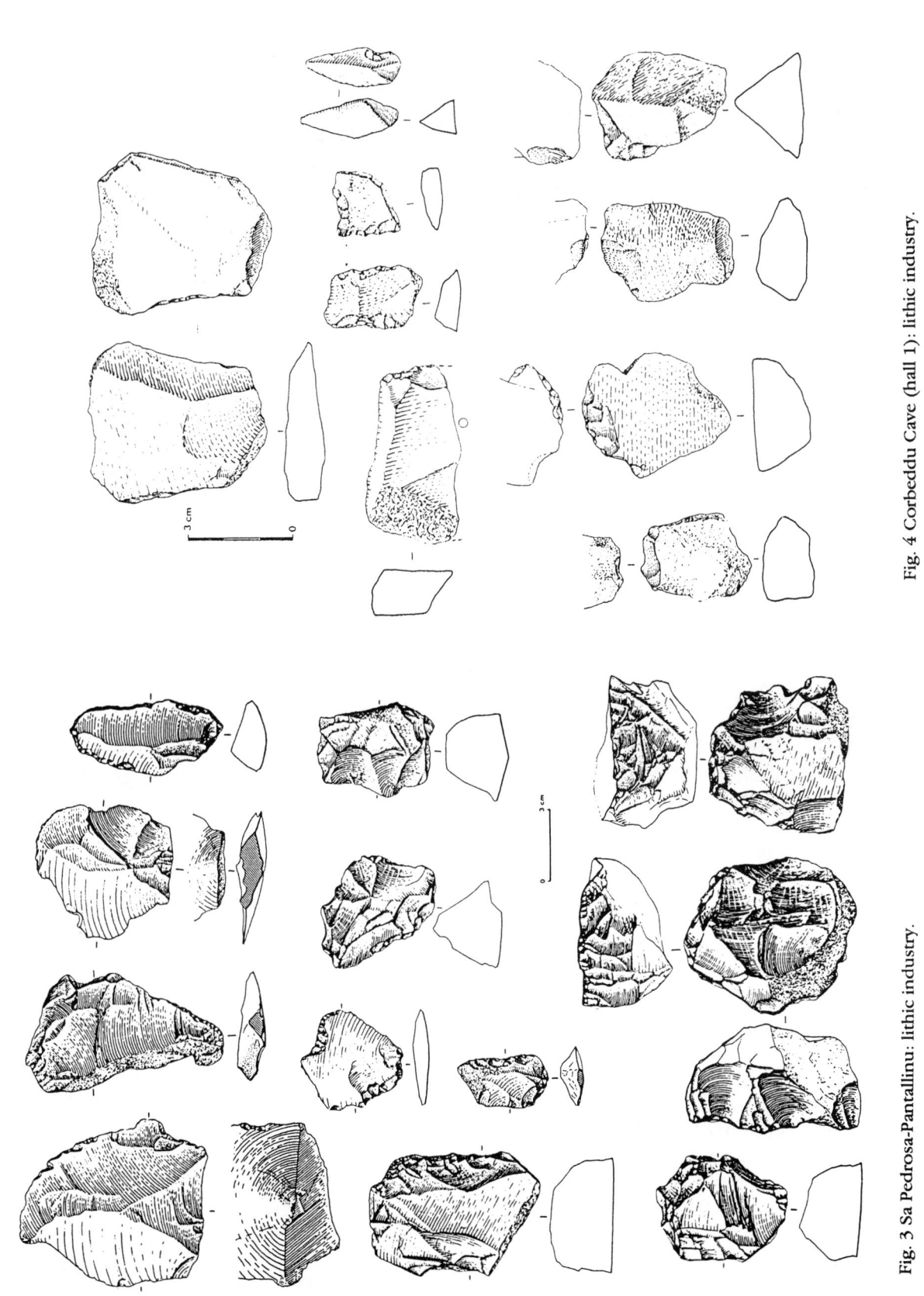

Fig. 3 Sa Pedrosa-Pantallinu: lithic industry.

In all Late Clactonian industries there is a certain frequency of elements with two or three dorsal ribs; but there is no lack of pieces with more ribs and these occur more frequently than in the Early Clactonian. This is further evidence of more elaborate utilization of the cores. The flaking sequence is very elementary and hardly predetermined at all, with few parallel and centripetal detachments, in marked contrast to the apparently greater organization and planning of Early Clactonian flaking. In typological terms, scrapers and denticulated items are equally dominant. There is more lateral retouch and some transverse retouch among the scrapers, while a few 'rabots' can be seen in the former. The retouch technique is that of simple flake scars, not always invasive and rarely overlapping. All of these features lead me to place the Sa Pedrosa industry, and all those associated with it, within an aspect of the Clactonian which differs from Riu Altana and the peninsular Clactonian, the latter presumably dating to the Mindelian era. Various aspects of the Sardinian Late Clactonian seem comparable to some more evolved, but not terminal, continental complexes of the Clactonian phylum found in Abruzzo (Madonna del Freddo, Terrazzi Zannini) and in Campania. It is not always possible to date these complexes accurately, but they seem to center around the Riss glaciation. The Sa Pedrosa industries can certainly be dated to the pre-Würmian on geomorphological grounds. Nor are the Sardinian Late Clactonian industries wholly comparable to other continental complexes, probably dating from the end of the Clactonian and attributed to Riss and Riss-Würm, which are characterized by Levallois techniques and the widescale use of laquinoid-type overlapping retouch (e.g. Latial Protopontinian, Late Clactonian in the Valle Giumentina, and pre-Mousterian from Grotta dell'Alto and Grotta del Colombo).

The Late Pleistocene Industry of Corbeddu Cave

If our knowledge of the earliest human settlements on the island begins with a probably articulated sequence of different industries in the Middle Pleistocene, we know nothing further about Sardinian prehistory until the Late Pleistocene, the period from which the archaeological finds at Corbeddu Cave (Olièna-NU) are dated. In this cave settlement, still under excavation, a Late Pleistocene through Early Holocene sequence has been discovered, along with signs of Neolithic and Bronze Age occupation (cf. Klein Hofmeijer and Sondaar, this volume). The preliminary results, regarding lithic industries, have revealed the presence in Hall 1 of a flint complex and considerable siliceous limestone dated c. 14,000–12,000 BP. The tools are characterized by a very elementary and undifferentiated technology with little organized flaking, complementing the more widescale use of naturally flaked material (Fig. 4). The assemblage is typologically very generic and lacks the tools which characterize Upper Palaeolithic complexes on the continent. At Corbeddu Cave we find almost solely scrapers and splintered pieces which were only rarely produced by careful and continuous workmanship.

The layer 2 complex (Hall 2) belongs to a slightly more recent period, c. 9000 BP, but there is not sufficient material for an exhaustive definition. In an associated layer, some human fossils have been found which we feel have a peculiar morphology and should be interpreted as a probable sign of endemism (the result of specialization due to isolation). The archaeological and anthropological data, along with the endemic character of the fauna, have led to a hypothesis of human presence in Sardinia c. 14,000 BP, and probably lasting up to Neolithic colonization. These humans had an economy based on hunting, and created tools with such a low level of specialization that they cannot even be compared with their contemporary counterparts on the continent. Today we have no way to determine when this isolation began, and why it led to such an unspecialized lithic complex. This hypothesis, based only on the evidence from Corbeddu Cave, requires further confirmation that only similar discoveries at other sites can provide. The fact remains, however, that if we deny the possibility of Sardinian endemism in the Late Pleistocene, we must admit—even without any supporting evidence to date—that around 14,000 to 13,000 BP humans were already capable of sailing long distances with no land in sight; during that period, both Sardinia and Corsica were islands with sea-level conditions comparable to their current status. Furthermore, we must find an explanation for the existence of an endemic faunal equilibrium which would not be upset until Neolithic colonization.

Pre-Neolithic Industries in Corsica

Sardinia's prehistory cannot be separated from contemporary events taking place on nearby Corsica; both islands were part of a single land mass during the maximum regression of the sea at various times in the Pleistocene. Currently we have no information about Pleistocene lithic industries in Corsica. The only pre-Neolithic archaeological evidence belongs to an industrial complex identified at a few sites on the island, dated between the 10th and 9th millennium BP and provisionally called 'pre-Neolithic'. The Araguina-Sennola and Curacchiaghiu assemblages are characterized by medium-sized and frequently quite thick tools, rich in denticulates but not in backed forms, and overall very undifferentiated. They seem comparable to the slightly older complex of Corbeddu Cave because of their typologically complex structure which is dominated by scrapers and denticulates. But if Corbeddu predates the Corsican pre-Neolithic by about 4000 years, and a hypothesis of endemism is used to justify the nature of the lithic assemblage there, we cannot advance the same hypothesis for these Corsican industries. In fact, in the burials associated with these tools, the human fossil remains are typical of *Homo sapiens sapiens*, and without any endemic features. This fact would seem to substantiate the hypothesis of intentional maritime contacts between the islands and the mainland prior to the Neolithic.

The origin of the Corsican pre-Neolithic remains to be identified. However, we cannot exclude the theory that it could be related to some Preboreal complexes characterized by a regressive phenomenon that produced undifferentiated industries with scrapers, denticulates and perhaps splintered pieces, with a near absence of microliths. There are similar industries, however, with a very basic, simplified flake and retouch technology. Such industries were widespread throughout the Mediterranean basin and have been identified in the Iberian and Italian peninsulas, the Balkans, Greece and Cyprus (Martini, unpublished data; Martini and Ulzega in press). This would seem to be a particular Epipalaeolithic aspect which should be studied in depth to identify the origin of these industries (which currently—at least for certain areas—seem to be final Epigravettian) and their evolutionary development. At present, it is sufficient to remember that the makers of this Corsican pre-Neolithic complex must have reached the island by sea. Therefore, notwithstanding their territorial unity during certain phases of the Pleistocene, current research indicates that Sardinia and Corsica present quite distinctive archaeological evidence, each inspiring strikingly different historical hypotheses. Only new discoveries on both islands can integrate and unite our current knowledge of their most ancient settlements, which must have originated in the same way.

Routes of Arrival in the Human Settlement of Corsica and Sardinia

The question of settlement in Sardinia during the Palaeolithic is linked to the possibility of moving from the mainland to the Corsica–Sardinia island block. The issue must be faced by keeping in mind the archaeological finds and the results of palaeographic and palaeontological studies. I will present only a brief outline of my hypotheses about Pleistocene human arrival in Sardinia, since more complete details can be found elsewhere (Klein Hofmeijer *et al.* 1987–88; Martini 1988; Martini and Ulzega in press; Sondaar *et al.* 1991).

At the end of the Middle Pleistocene (170,000–160,000 BP), at the greatest lowering of sea-levels, Corsica and Sardinia formed a single land mass, a territorial continuity that was maintained for several thousand years. The Tuscan Archipelago was joined in an extension of the Tuscan coast (Fig. 5). Between Capo Corso and Capraia there was a channel, five nautical miles wide, forming a narrow strait that was practically a calm, closed sea. This palaeogeographic situation, with the sea about 130 m lower than its modern level, reoccurred during two other glacial maximums in the Upper Pleistocene (70,000–50,000 BP and c. 20,000 BP). For the earlier periods, which concern our interest here, there is evidence of even greater sea-level lowering, but these events are difficult to date. We can suppose, however, that even in the pre-Rissian era the area's palaeogeography did not differ from the situation as documented for the end of the Middle Pleistocene, and even then there was a strait between the islands at a greater depth. In fact, there is no neotectonic, vulcanological, or sedimentological evidence that would suggest major upheavals of the sea bottom which could have resulted in the emergence of the strait.

These geomorphological data lead us to suppose that Lower Palaeolithic humans were indeed capable of crossing narrow sea channels in sight of land. The palaeontological evidence also supports this theory. In fact, at an early period of the Middle Pleistocene, a new animal population comprised of only two species—*Megaceros cazioti* and *Cynotherium sardus*—reached the Corsican–Sardinian block. This *Tyrrhenicola* population replaced the existing *Nesogoral* which became extinct. Only *Prolagus sardus* was to survive and populate the island until the Holocene period. Human arrival is assumed to be contemporaneous with that of these animals due to the fact that in the Middle Pleistocene an ecological balance was created on the island that was not modified until Neolithic colonization. If humans had reached the island

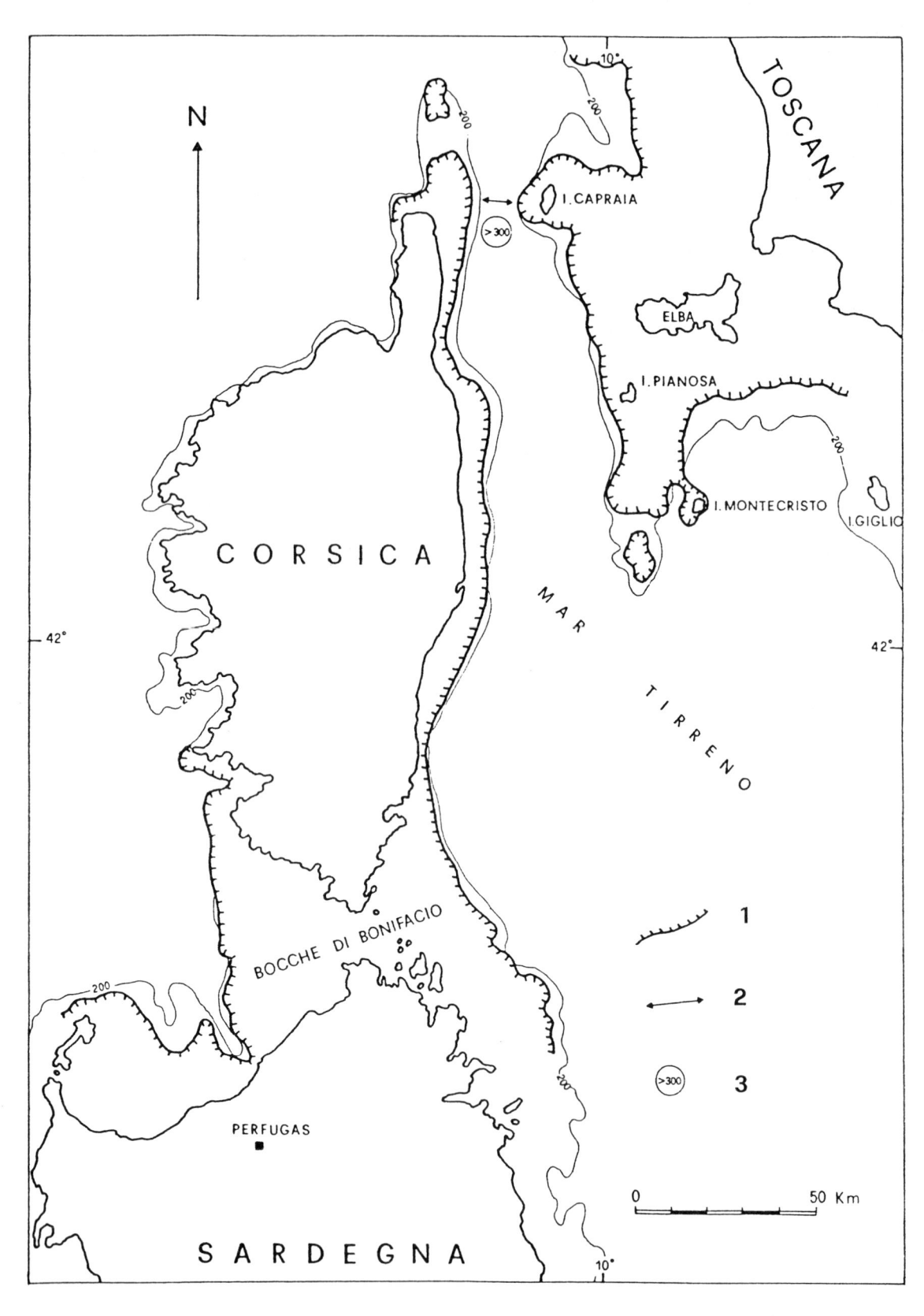

Fig. 5 Palaeogeography of Corsica and Sardinia. 1. Coastline in Glacial periods (c. 170,000–160,000, 70–50,000 and 20,000 BP); 2. Narrowest sea-crossing between mainland (near Capraia) and Corsica; 3. Sea depths greater than 300 m.

after the deer and the canid, that balance would not have been maintained.

When islands are not connected to the mainland by a continuous land bridge, their animal populations tend to lack some species that are frequent among continental fauna, and are comprised only of those few capable of crossing narrow straits. This is precisely the case with Sardinia. According to the Simpsonian model of 'dispersion through obstacles', the strait between Corsica and Capraia served as a selective filter for the possibility of moving from the peninsula to the Corsica–Sardinia block which was only reached by the most capable species. Assuming that Pleistocene humans arrived on Sardinia along with the deer and the canid, the chronology of the faunal replacement, documented by palaeontologists at the beginning of the Middle Pleistocene, concurs with the dating of the Early Clactonian on Sardinia, which we will recall, in the case of Sa Coa de Sa Multa, is based on pedological interpretation.

The matter of the relationships between Early and Late Clactonian still remains open. My current position is that there are two possibilities.

1. The Early Clactonian, imported to Sardinia during an early period of the Middle Pleistocene, gave rise phyletically to the Late Rissian Clactonian. The technical and typological similarities between this last period and some continental Rissian complexes would lead us to assume a phenomenon of convergence between the Sardinian and the continental Late Clactonian.
2. The Late Sardinian Clactonian, with substantial similarities to the continental Late Clactonian, was imported to Sardinia through a new human migration that can be dated to the maximum Rissian sea-level regression.

A great time span separates the Late Clactonian from the Late Pleistocene complex at Corbeddu Cave. Currently we do not have any archaeological data about this interval. Theoretically speaking, the survival of stable human groups could have been assured not so much by the deer and the canid as by *Prolagus*, which was present on the island in considerable numbers. In fact, this animal reproduces rapidly and is an excellent source of protein. At this point, however, we must await the discovery of new and different lithic assemblages that can fill these gaps before we can speak of any continuity between these periods.

References

Arca, M., F. Martini, C. Tuveri, G. Pitzalis & A. Ulzega
  1982a Il Paleolitico dell'Anglona (Sardegna settentrionale). Ricerche 1979–80. *Quaderni della Soprintendenza Archaeologica per le Provincie di Sassari e Nuoro* 12.
  1982b Il deposito quaternario con industrie del Paleolitico inferiore di Sa Pedrosa-Pantallinu (Sassari). *Rivista di Scienze Preistoriche* 37(1-2): 31-53.

Bagolini, B.
  1968 Ricerche sulle dimensioni dei manufatti litici preistorici non ritoccati. *Annali dell'Università di Ferrara* 15(1)10: 195-219.

Cornaggia Castiglioni, O. & G. Calegari
  1979 Prima segnalazione del Paleolitico in Sardegna. *Natura* 70: 1-2.

Klein Hofmeijer, G., F. Martini, M. Sanges, P.Y. Sondaar & A. Ulzega
  1987–88 La fine del Pleistocene nella Grotta Corbeddu in Sardegna. *Rivista di Scienze Preistoriche* 41(1-2): 1-36.

Laplace, G.
  1968 Recherches de typologie analitique. *Origini* 2: 7-64.

Martini, F.
  1975 Il Gravettiano della Grotta Paglicci nel Gargano. II: Tipometria dell'industria litica. *Rivista di Scienze Preistoriche* 30(1-2): 179-223.
  1988 Il popolamento umano delle isole del Mediterraneo nel Pleistocene e nel primo Olocene: Corsica e Sardegna. In *Early Man in Island Environments: Proceedings of the Olièna (Sardinia) Colloquium, 25 September-2 October 1988*. Sassari: Industria Grafica Stampacolor.

Martini, F. & A. Palma di Cesnola
  1988 L'industria paleolitica di Riu Altana (Sassari): Il complesso clactoniano arcaico. In *Early Man in Island Environments: Proceedings of the Olièna (Sardinia) Colloquium, 25 September-2 October 1988*. Sassari: Industria Grafica Stampacolor.

Martini, F., & G. Pitzalis
  1982 Il Paleolitico inferiore in Sardegna. In *Atti del XXIII Riunione Scientifica 'Il Paleolitico inferiore in Italia', Firenze 7-9 maggio 1980*, 249-55. Firenze: Istituto Italiano di Preistoria e Protostoria.

Martini, F., & A. Ulzega
  in press L'insularità e i suoi effetti sul popolamento umano delle isole del Mediterraneo nel Pleistocene e nel primo Olocene. *Rivista di Scienze Preistoriche* 42.

Sondaar, P.Y., F. Martini, A. Ulzega & G. Klein Hofmeijer
  1991 L'homme pléistocène en Sardaigne. *L'Anthropologie* 95(1): 181-200.

Riassunto

Anche se le prime tracce di insediamenti paleolitici in Sardegna sono state scoperte nel 1979, oggi nell'isola si conoscono 10 siti paleolitici. Tutti i siti tranne uno (Grotta Corbeddu) risalgono al Pleistocene Medio. Le date a cui risalgono i siti sono state identificate grazie alla scoperta di manufatti di pietra, attribuili alle diverse *facies* del Clactoniano.

La *facies* arcaica del Clactoniano di Sardegna, identificata a Riu Altana presso Perfugas (SS), è confrontabile con il Clactoniano arcaico peninsulare di *facies* protolevalloisiana. I ritrovamenti di Sa Coa de sa Multa provengono da un deposito in giacitura primaria che risale al Pleistocene Medio iniziale; il materiale di Riu Altana proviene dalle raccolte di superficie lungo il torrente omonimo.

La *facies* evoluta del Clactoniano è rappresentato in Sardegna da ritrovamenti provenienti da numerosi siti nella provincia di Sassari. Una possibile officina litica è stata ritrovata a Sa Pedrosa-Pantallinu *in situ* su una terrazza alluvionale che risale al Riss. Questo complesso è caratterizzato da strumenti litici più piccoli e da una minore organizzazione nella scheggiatura rispetto alla *facies* Clactoniana arcaica.

L'Autore suggerisce due ipotesi: 1) il Clactoniano arcaico è stato introdotto in Sardegna durante il Pleistocene Medio iniziale e si è sviluppato parallelamente al Clactoniano continentale; 2) il Clactoniano evoluto è giunto in Sardegna tramite una seconda migrazione umana avvenuta nel Riss.

Durante il Pleistocene Medio, c. 170,000–160,000 BP (ed ancora nel Pleistocene Superiore c. 70,000–50,000 BP e c. 20,000 BP) durante i massimi regressivi e il conseguente abbassamento del livello marino, individuato a circa -130 metri dall'attuale, solo uno stretto canale divideva la Corsica dall'estensione della costa toscana. È possibile che l'uomo, anche con una navigazione non organizzata, abbia attraversato questo stretto nel Pleistocene medio iniziale. Infatti è in questo periodo che la fauna *Tyrrhenicola* ha sostituito la fauna *Nesogoral*. L'assenza di squilibri ecologici fino al Neolitico fa pensare ad un arrivo in contemporanea dell'uomo paleolitico, del cervo e del canide.

C'è un ampio vuoto cronologico tra i ritrovamenti risalenti al Pleistocene Medio e quelli della Grotta di Corbeddu, datati c. 14,000–12,000 BP. I complessi litici in selce e calcare siliceo provenienti dalla sala 1 non sono molto elaborati e sono stati adottati anche supporti naturali. L'industria di Corbeddu è diverso dai complessi appartenenti al Paleolitico Superiore continentale. Solo alcuni strumenti sono stati ritrovati nella sala 2, che è datato c. 9000 BP.

I più antichi ritrovamenti archeologici in Corsica risalgono al pre-Neolitico e sono datati tra il nono e il decimo millennio BP. I complessi di Araguina-Sennola e Currachiaghiu sono genericamente paragonabili a Corbeddu ma sono più antichi di 4000 anni. Al contrario di Corbeddu, dove la particolarità della litotecnica può essere spiegata con un isolamento dalle popolazioni continentali (i fossili umani a Corbeddu mostrano caratteri endemici), il materiale Corso è associato a fossili di tipo continentale. Ciò suggerisce che ci sono stati contatti marittimi post-Pleistocenici tra le isole e il continente, prima della colonizzazione neolitica di queste isole.

Pleistocene Humans in the Island Environment of Sardinia

Gerard Klein Hofmeijer and Paul Y. Sondaar

Introduction

Islands often differ from mainlands by their impoverished endemic flora and fauna. The ability of land animals to swim or to keep afloat for a long time determines their chances of reaching an island. Once they have arrived, they will colonize and, in relatively little time, adapt to the island's characteristic biotope. An established, adapted island fauna will remain remarkably stable if their equilibrium is not disturbed by new faunal or human arrivals or the subsequent formation of a land bridge back to the mainland.

For Pleistocene Mediterranean islands, the fauna include larger mammals represented mainly by the fossils of elephants, hippopotami and deer. The absence of large predators (except birds of prey) and limited space were important factors in this process of adaptation. Elephants, hippopotami and deer became extremely small and the deer developed especially short legs with some leg bones becoming fused (Sondaar 1977). Early Pleistocene Sardinia is consistent with this picture. But during the Middle Pleistocene Sardinia's fauna changed drastically. The older *Nesogoral* fauna was suddenly replaced by the *Tyrrhenicola* fauna, which remained unchanged until the Neolithic. Both these fauna are typical island fauna in that they consist of only a few endemic species (Sondaar et al. 1986). However, the younger *Tyrrhenicola* fauna is remarkable because of the presence of the endemic deer *Megaloceros cazioti*, which is not dwarfed and has not developed short legs, and the presence of the small canid *Cynotherium sardous*.

In search of an explanation for this exception, an excavation was begun in 1982 in Corbeddu Cave in central Sardinia. It soon became apparent that the distribution of the fossils of *Megaloceros cazioti* was unusual when compared with other deer fossils excavated in previous years on the island of Crete. Also, the Sardinian fossils showed *post mortem* damage that is hard to explain by merely natural processes (Sondaar et al. 1984; 1986; Klein Hofmeijer et al. 1986). Human fossils and artifacts of flint and limestone, found later, confirmed the idea of a human component in the taphonomy. They also proved that humans and Pleistocene island fauna occupied the island together. Long-term human settlement in such an isolated environment in the Mediterranean had not been known previously.

Corbeddu Cave

Corbeddu Cave is situated in the valley of Lanaittu, southeast of the village of Olièna (Nuoro). The steep slopes of this tectonic valley are made of Jurassic and Cretaceous limestone. At present, the Sa Oche-Su Bentu subterranean karst system, which includes Corbeddu Cave, constitutes the main drainage of the karstic water. The sedimentological infill history of Corbeddu Cave, however, shows that the latter played only a minor role in this drainage system at least for the last 40,000 years. The cave is divided into four halls (Fig. 1). The single entrance in Hall 1 is a very small opening at the top of collapsed limestone blocks just below the roof. The earlier opening must have been considerably larger and probably extended from the northeast to the east. Palynological data from Hall 2 suggest that this hall too was connected with the open air until about 10,000 BP. The only possible location for this entrance is now covered with stalagtitic deposits of unknown age.

Stratigraphy

In Hall 2 the completeness of the stratigraphic succession is remarkable. With only minor intervals of non-deposition, there is an almost complete sedimentological representation of the period from at least 42,000 BP up to and including the Bronze Age. The pre-Neolithic deposits are now exposed to a depth of 2 m below the surface, reaching an estimated age of c. 17,000 BP. The lower part, Layer 3, consists of red silty clay with abundant fossils of the endemic deer *Megaloceros cazioti*. The upper part, Layer 2, consists of a limestone breccia. The formation of this layer started around 11,000 BP. It is very rich in fossils of the ochotonid *Prolagus sardus*. Two human fossils (Spoor and Sondaar 1986), limestone and flint artifacts (Sondaar *et al.* 1991; Martini, this volume), and charcoal show human presence in this hall during the last 4000 years before the arrival of the first Neolithic people. This pre-Neolithic succession is overlain by deposits bearing Neolithic and Bronze Age material.

In Hall 1, the pre-Neolithic deposits (Layers C-G) mainly consist of limestone breccia and red clay alternations. Up to now four fossil units have been recognized. The lower three all appear as floors due to the association of deer fossils with stones which are often polished at the top, suggesting intensive trampling. The youngest fossil unit contains mainly small elements of the deer—especially phalanges—together with phalanges of birds of prey like *Aquila* and *Athene*. The overlying Neolithic deposits seem to be more disturbed by soil formation processes and Bronze Age human activity than is observed in Hall 2. Layer B bears a mixture of pre-Neolithic, Neolithic and Bronze Age material. Therefore the age of the human fossils found in this layer is hard to establish, especially since no collagen was left in the bones for radiocarbon dating. The uppermost Layer A represents the Bronze Age and is extremely rich in ash. Neither the Neolithic nor the Bronze Age material has been studied in detail.

Radiocarbon Dates
Milligram samples of both bone collagen and charcoal have been dated by AMS at the Robert J. Van de Graaff Laboratory of the Rijksuniversiteit Utrecht. Samples from sections in Hall 1 (Klein Hofmeijer *et al.* 1989) and Hall 2 (Klein Hofmeijer *et al.* 1987) have been dated (Fig. 2). A new date for the base of Layer 1, Hall 2 (an Early Neolithic fireplace) of 6690 ± 80 BP (UtC-1251) indicates that the earlier obtained date of 8040 ± 180 BP is incorrect. Bioturbation by worms might be the cause of upward transport of charcoal from the top of Layer 2 into the lower part of Layer 1.

The Human Fossils
Two human fossils, a right temporal bone and a left maxilla, were found in Hall 2 in Layer 2, 25 cm below the boundary with Layer 1 (^{14}C date: 8750 ± 140 BP). They are the oldest human fossils from the Mediterranean islands and are the first human fossils found in association with a pre-Neolithic endemic island fauna.

The articular eminence of the temporal bone is wide and flat in its medio-lateral direction, and lacks the 'normal' concave shape. The maxilla (Fig. 3) bears a robust zygomatic process and the palate is narrow. The latter is due to the characteristic combination of relatively small alveoles of the incisors and the extremely large alveoles of the molars. In these aspects, which have no pathological origin, the morphology of the cranial fossils is outside the variation found in modern *Homo sapiens sapiens*, and possibly that of *Homo sapiens* in general. The aberrant morphology might be an indication of endemism in the isolated pre-Neolithic population on Sardinia (Spoor and Sondaar 1986). In the Neolithic period the morphology of these bones in the Sardinian population is not significantly different from those of the European mainland, and the aberrant morphology of the Palaeolithic Sardinian fossils is not found in Neolithic Sardinian skulls (Spoor and Germanà 1987; Germanà, this volume). This may be the consequence of an absence of interbreeding between a pre-Neolithic population and the early Neolithic colonizers, or of rapid morphological changes after the colonization.

The Lithic Industry
For a description of the lithic industry found in both Hall 1 and Hall 2 the reader is referred to the contribution by Martini in this volume. Of significance in this paper is the fact that, based on the radiocarbon dates, it can be concluded that the levels C to E in Hall 1 are the time equivalent of Layer 3 in Hall 2 (see Fig. 2). This means that the large amount of deer fossils in the second hall, associated with only one possible stone artifact, is related to fossil unit 1 in Hall 1 which is associated with several limestone artifacts. This at least shows us that humans were present in the cave in the period when the Hall 2 accumulation was formed.

Megaloceros cazioti
The accumulation of deer fossils in Layer 3 of Hall 2 is remarkable. Up to now 14 field levels have been distinguished within 1 m of clay. Even if detailed analysis of this stratification were to reduce the recognizably distinct fossil levels, the fact remains that this layer, representing a timespan of c. 7000 years, was formed by a periodically repeated process that time and time again accumulated substantial quantities of deer fossils. From a sedimentological point of view, a geologically controlled process of fossil accumulation is extremely unlikely. The homogeneous clay points to a very low energy environment and there are

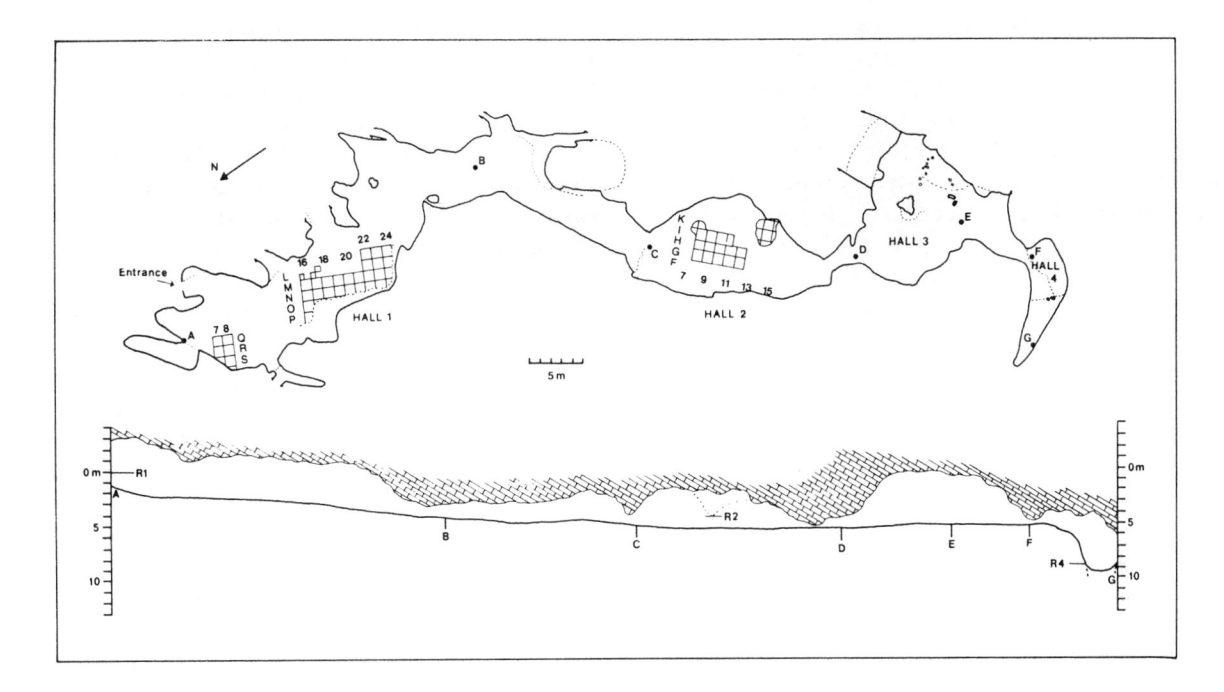

Fig. 1 Plan and longitudinal section of Corbeddu Cave (Olièna-NU) showing the location of the main excavation pits.

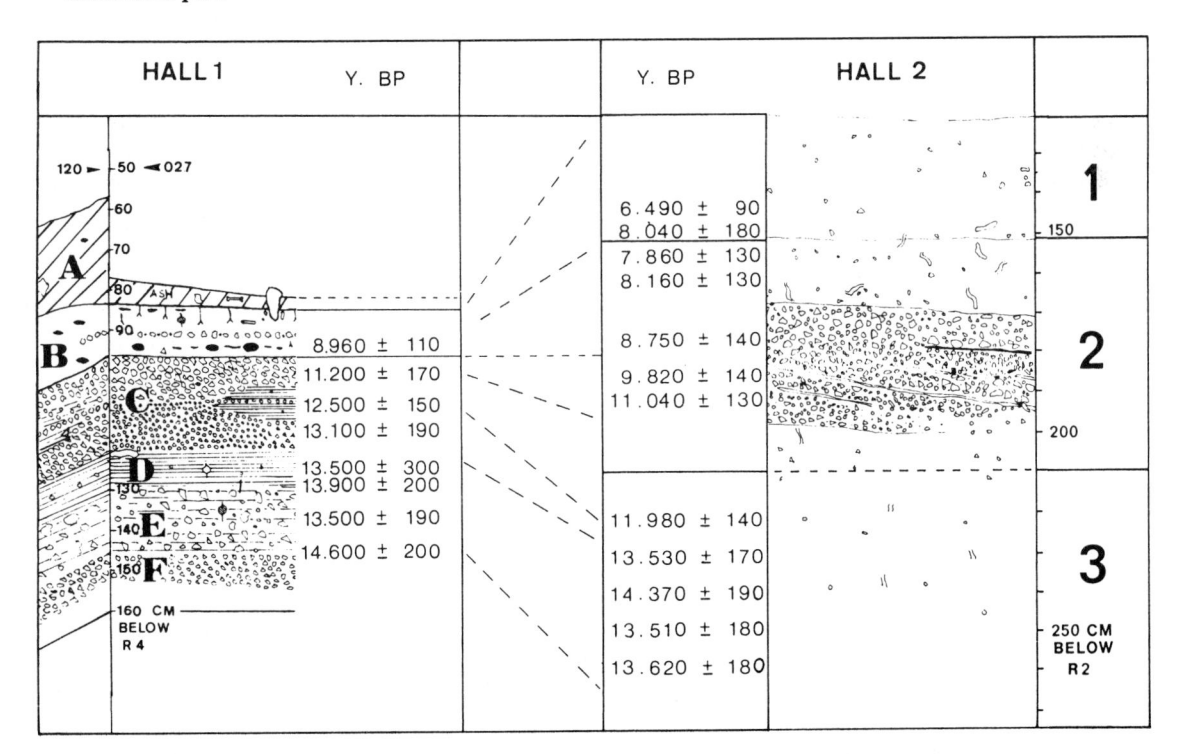

Fig. 2 Correlation between the stratigraphic sections of Halls 1 and 2 of Corbeddu Cave, based on radiocarbon dating.

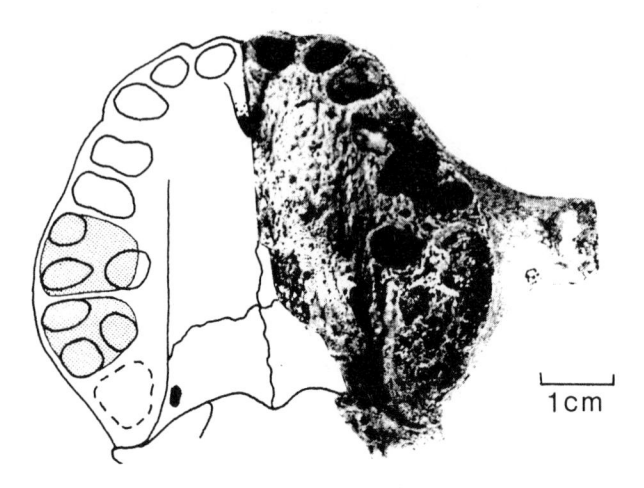

Fig. 3 The inferior aspect of the left human maxilla CB85-3031) from layer 2 (Hall 2) of Corbeddu Cave, with the right half reconstructed. Dotted areas indicate the estimated size of the first two molars.

no examples of accumulation due to mass transport. Probably the clay precipitated out of suspension in a standing shallow pool; preserved shrinking cracks show that there were alternating wet and dry periods. Furthermore, taphonomic analysis shows that even extremely fragile parts of the skeleton, such as skulls with complete antlers, scapulae, ribs, etc., are often found unfractured. This unfractured state of the skeletal elements is one of the characteristics of the Hall 2 deer assemblage, and also contradicts an accumulation due to canine activity, which would have resulted in a much more damaged state of the bones. Although traces of gnawing are present in some exceptional cases (Sondaar *et al.* 1991), the assemblage as a whole is the antithesis of a typical carnivore den. It is believed that the small *Cynotherium sardous* only occasionally took advantage of the presence of deer remains.

Human Activity

Some features of the fossil assemblage suggest human influence on the taphonomy. Notwithstanding the unfractured state of the fossils, many specimens exhibit numerous striations and a high degree of polish. The fact that this type of surface modification is most frequent and most clear on the diaphyses of the long bones, including the mandibles, contradicts the hypothesis that it was caused by flowing water, a process that would have also—or even especially—affected the skeletal extremities. Many of the non-long bone elements do not show any

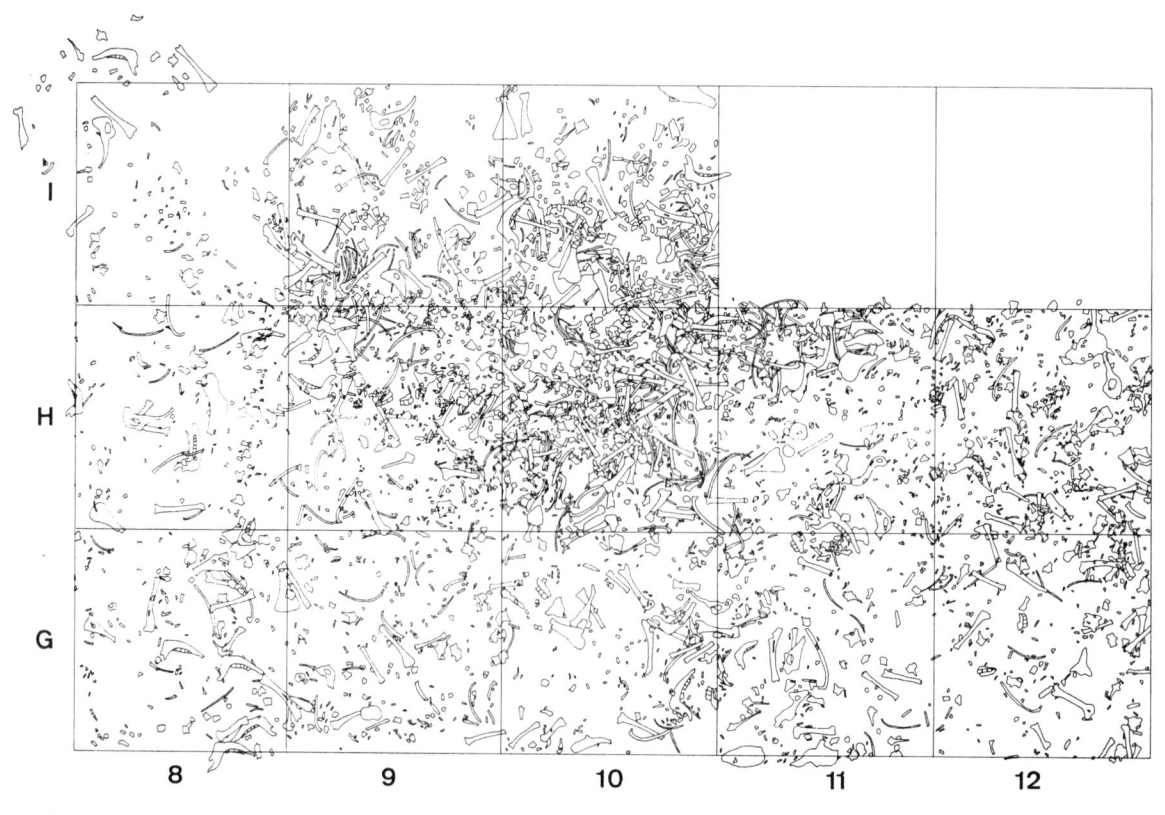

Fig. 4 Plan of Level 7, Layer 3, Hall 2 of Corbeddu Cave, showing the accumulation of fossils of the endemic deer of *Megaloceros cazioti* (^{14}C date: 13,620 ± 180).

kind of polish or striation, as is also the case with the elements of a complete skeleton of *Cynotherium sardous* that was found spread over the entire excavation floor in the uppermost part of Layer 3. It could be argued that these striations and polish might be the result of trampling. Although there are indeed some cases of damage due to trampling, the overall unfractured state of the assemblage does not permit the assumption that most of the fine striations and the very frequent polish is merely the result of trampling. If so, this process should have been so frequent and intensive that much more damage to the fossils would have been observed. Figure 4 shows a plan of Level 7 of Layer 3 in Hall 2. The abundance of undamaged but fragile bones, the large number of complete ribs for example, clearly indicates that if trampling occurred it must have been occasional. The fact that surface modifications are observed particularly on the long bones suggests a selective agent for this feature, which cannot be trampling.

Damage to the molars and other teeth is of particular interest. The incisors, most of them found isolated from the jaws, are often damaged at the occlusal surface. One specimen shows a clear cut 3 mm long and 1 mm wide from the occlusal surface down into the crown. In many other cases pieces of enamel are broken off (Sondaar *et al.* 1986). The molars also show a particular type of wear on the occlusal surface (Sondaar *et al.* 1991). Unlike the incisors, only a few lower molars were found isolated from the mandibles, showing the unfractured state of the mandibles. Furthermore, it was often observed that molar cusps had been broken off. Here again a type of damage is present that cannot be explained by trampling because of the extremely selective nature of the agent: mandibles remained unfractured while the much more resistant crowns of the molars are damaged. In several cases where a cusp fragment was large enough, the pulp cavity became fully exposed. Pre-*mortem* occurrence due to aberrant chewing on hard material seems unlikely because of the lack of traces of infections or any kind of healing. Only in those cases in which the damage is limited to only the uppermost top of the cusp, resulting in a broken-off fragment that is smaller than 2 mm, may the remaining surface be found repolished. This kind of molar damage is considered to be of possible pre-*mortem* origin. The question of pre-*mortem* versus *post mortem* origin of the molar damage in the Corbeddu Cave assemblage is obviously of crucial importance for the hypothesis of human use of the mandibles. New evidence has been found that seems to confirm the *post mortem*

theory. Analysis of the sieved sediments revealed a large number of broken molar cusps, ranging in height from 2 mm to more than 10 mm (Fig. 5). An attempt to find the corresponding mandibles resulted in eight fragments that could be fitted with seven mandibles (Fig. 6). The fact that at least some of the little cusp fragments appear to be present next to their corresponding mandibles seems to be hard evidence for the *post mortem* origin of this damage. Another significant aspect is the fact that juvenile specimens are more frequently damaged than adult specimens. The difference in fragility between the higher cusps in juveniles and the more worn ones in adults is obvious but this is true for both pre-*mortem* and *post mortem* agents. However, a pre-*mortem* theory demands that this kind of damage inflicted in youth should still be recognizable in adulthood. If the damage were due to human use of the mandibles as cutting or scraping instruments, then the broken-off molar fragments are expected to be found at the place where this activity took place. The discovery of the fragments in Hall 2 indicates that these mandibles were used there. A better understanding of the Hall 2 taphonomy is required before we can speculate about the precise relationship between this human activity and the accumulation of deer bones.

Hall 1

In contradistinction to the situation in Hall 2, most bones from Hall 1 are fragmentary. The low energy environment, reconstructed from the characteristics of the sediments, confirms the assumption of no or minor geological transport. Fossil unit 1 (Layers C-D) is of particular interest because it is the time equivalent of Layer 3 in Hall 2. Nevertheless its taphonomy is rather different. It is characterized by the presence of many deer bone fragments, lots of isolated teeth, and an extreme over-representation of phalanges. Besides those belonging to deer, phalanges of large birds of prey, such as *Aquila* and *Athene*, are common. Units 2 and 3 differ from Unit 1 in containing more large bones of *Megaloceros cazioti* and being poor in bird fossils. Remarkable are the damaged lower jaws. The representation of the original element ranges from an almost complete mandible, missing only a small anterior part, through a reduction process that finally leads to a small part of the horizontal ramus with only two molars. All stages in between seem to be present. Also some specimens with broken-off molar cusps have been found. It was very surprising to discover that several left and right pairs were present, each showing a remarkable symmetry in reduction pattern of the two mandibles.

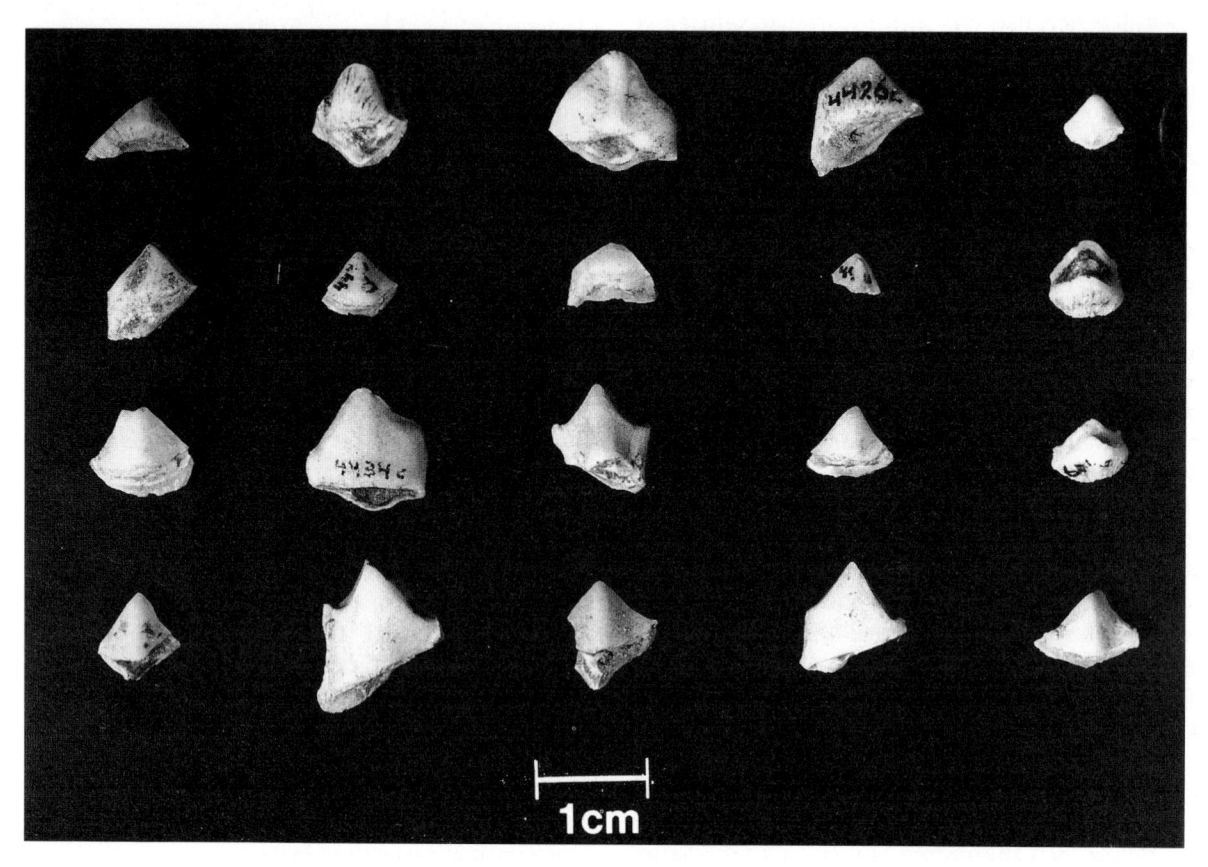

Fig. 5 Fragments of the molar cusps of *Megaloceros cazioti* found in Layer 3, Hall 2 of Corbeddu Cave.

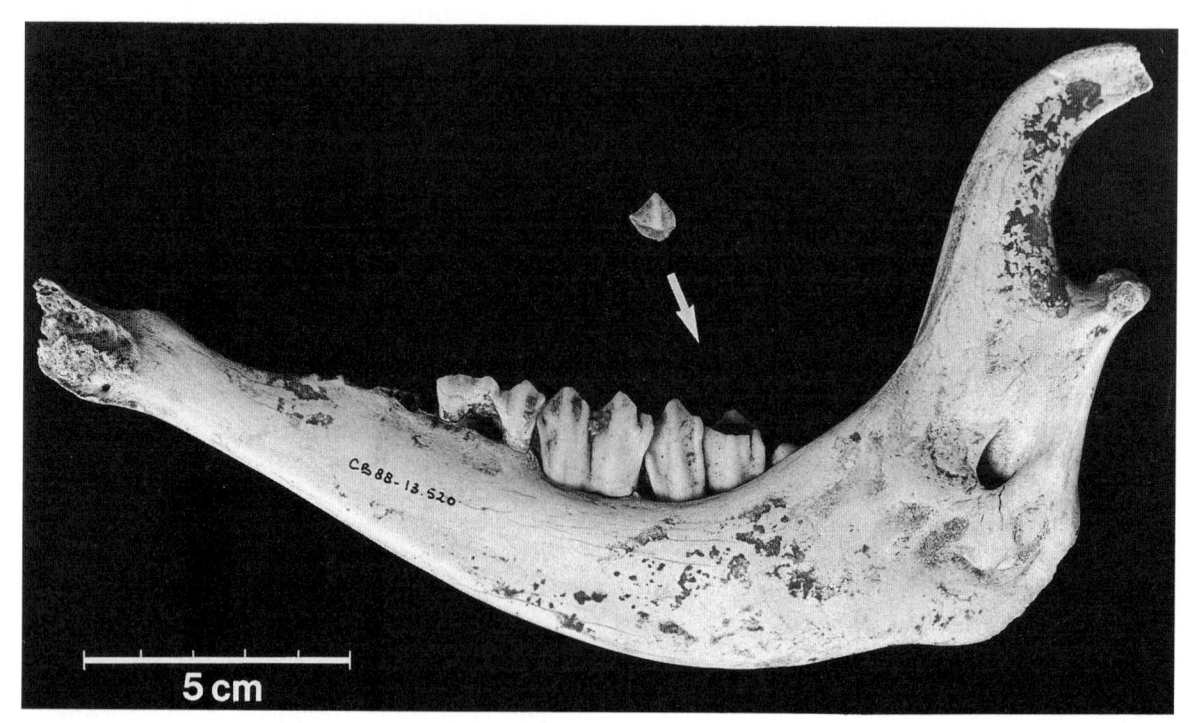

Fig. 6 Right mandible of *Megaloceros cazioti* (CB88-13520) from Level 8, Layer 3, Hall 2 of Corbeddu Cave, with a corresponding cusp fragment (CB87-10595b) found in the washed sediment sample from the same quadrant G09.

The presence of pairs in the mandible specimens is peculiar because the entire fossil assemblage is characterized by a high degree of damage, fracturing and reduction of most elements.

Discussion

The taphonomy of the deer fossils in Corbeddu Cave is not easy to explain. Further detailed analysis is necessary for a better understanding of the different agents involved and to establish the human role in the complex. During the 1988 Olièna conference the origin of the damage of the teeth was hotly debated and two opinions were put forward: (1) The damage is caused during life by chewing on stones. This opinion was defended mainly by the archaeologists; (2) The origin of the damage is *post mortem* and caused by human activity. This opinion was held mainly by the palaeontologists. The new evidence of the fitting of cusp fragments excludes the first explanation and proves that the damage has a *post mortem* origin. Cherry (1990) doubts the human involvement in the taphonomy of Layer 3, Hall 2, despite the lithic industry of the time-equivalent layers in Hall 1. This datum alone points out the Palaeolithic occupation of Sardinia in contradiction to the supposition of Vigne (1990). The fitting of the broken molars cusps is another argument for the palaeolithic human occupation of Corbeddu Cave.

Acknowledgments

The authors are grateful to a number of persons and institutions that supported the excavation in Corbeddu Cave over the last 10 years. We especially thank Dr Fulvia Lo Schiavo and Mario Sanges of the Soprintendenza Archeologica di Sassari e Nuoro, the town of Olièna, and the Gruppo Grotto Nuorese; and Will den Hartog for taking the photographs. IBM-Nederland supported the project with hardware and software. Last but not least we are grateful to the many students and volunteers who worked at the excavation and on other stages of the research.

References

Cherry, J.F.
1990   The first colonization of the Mediterranean islands: A review of recent research. *Journal of Mediterranean Archaeology* 3: 145-221.

Klein Hofmeijer, G., C. Alderliesten, K. van der Borg, C. Houston, A. de Jong, F. Martini, M. Sanges, P.Y. Sondaar & J.A. de Visser
1989   Dating of the Upper Pleistocene lithic industry of Sardinia. *Radiocarbon* 31(3): 986-91.

Klein Hofmeijer, G., F. Martini, M. Sanges, P.Y. Sondaar & A. Ulzega
1986   La fine del Pleistocene nella Grotta Corbeddu in Sardegna. *Rivista di Scienze Preistoriche* 41(1-2): 1-36.

Klein Hofmeijer, G., P.Y. Sondaar, C. Alderliesten, K. van der Borg & A. de Jong
1987   Indications of Pleistocene Man on Sardinia. *Nuclear Instruments and Methods in Physics Research* B29: 166-68.

Sondaar, P.Y.
1977   Insularity and its effects on mammal evolution. In Hecht et al. (eds.), *Major Patterns in Vertebrate Evolution*, 671-707. New York.

Sondaar, P.Y., P.L. de Boer, M. Sanges, T. Kotsakis & D. Esu
1984   First report on a paleolithic culture in Sardinia. In W.H. Waldren, R. Chapman, J. Lewthwaite and R.-C. Kennard (eds.), *The Deya Conference of Prehistory: Early Settlement in the Western Mediterranean Islands and the Peripheral Areas*, 29-47. BAR International Series 229. Oxford: British Archaeological Reports.

Sondaar, P.Y., F. Martini, A. Ulzega & G. Klein Hofmeijer
1991   L'homme pleistocene en Sardaigne. *L'Anthropologie* 95(1): 181-200.

Sondaar, P.Y., M. Sanges, T. Kotsakis & P.L. de Boer
1986   The pleistocene deer hunter of Sardinia. *Geobios* 19(1): 17-25.

Spoor, C., & F. Germanà
1987   Proportions of the neolithic human maxillae from Sardinia. *Bulletin et Memoire de la Société d'Anthropologie de Paris* 14(2): 143-50.

Spoor, C.F., & P.Y. Sondaar
1986   Human fossils from the endemic island fauna of Sardinia. *Journal of Human Evolution* 15: 399-408.

Vigne, J.-D.
1990   Biogeographical history of the mammals on Corsica (and Sardinia) since the final Pleistocene. In *Proceedings of the International Symposium on Biogeographical Aspects of Insularity (Rome 1987)*. Rome: Accademia Nazionale Lincei.

Riassunto

Spesso ciò che differenzia un'isola dalla terraferma è il fatto che l'isola possiede una fauna limitata, che ha un equilibrio stabile a meno che non sia disturbata dall'arrivo di nuova fauna, da esseri umani, o dall'emergere di nuovi ponti naturali che connettono l'isola con la terraferma. In Sardegna durante il Pleistocene Medio la vecchia fauna *Nesogoral* è stata sostituita dalla fauna *Tyrrhenicola*, che include il cervo endemico non rimpicciolito *Megaloceros cazioti* e il piccolo canide *Cynotherium sardous*. Le caratteristiche del cervo sardo sono alquanto insolite se comparate a quelle del resto della fauna mediterranea insulare se teniamo conto che generalmente gli animali tendono a diventare più piccoli in assenza di predatori.

Nel 1982 sono iniziati degli scavi presso la Grotta di Corbeddu per far luce su questa eccezione. Nei vani 1 e 2 della grotta è stato trovato del materiale pre-neolitico. Nel vano 2, lo strato 3 contiene fossili di *Megaloceros cazioti*, e i dati radiocarbonici di questi ritrovamenti risalgono a 17,000 BP. Lo strato 2, risalente a 11,000 BP, è ricco di fossili di *Prolagus sardus*, e contiene due fossili umani, e alcuni manufatti litici. I fossili umani, datati 8750 ± 140 BP, sono i fossili umani più antichi fino ad ora ritrovati nelle isole mediterranee e sono anche i primi ad essere ritrovati insieme a fauna insulare endemica pre-neolitica. I fossili umani mostrano una variazione morfologica, il che può indicare una presenza di endemismo nella popolazione umana del periodo pre-neolitico, facendo pensare quindi ad insediamenti sardi ancora più antichi.

Gli strati C-G del vano 1 corrispondono allo strato 3 nel vano 2. Gli strati C-G contengono anch'essi depositi pre-neolitici che includono fossili di cervo e parecchi manufatti di calcare. L'esistenza di questi oggetti mostra che esseri umani erano presenti nel vano 1 nello stesso momento in cui numerose ossa di cervo sono state depositate nel vano 2. È da notare l'accumulo di ossa di cervo in quanto molte di esse non sono fratturate e secondo gli Autori ciò significa che non c'è stata attività canina. Secondo gli Autori la presenza di striature e levigature nelle ossa insieme al fatto che i molari sono stati rotti non è senz'altro dovuto al calpestio di altri animali.

Otto frammenti di cuspidi di molari sono stati reinseriti in sette mandibole e mostrano che le ossa di mandibole ritrovate nei vani 1 e 2 sono state utilizzate *post mortem* come strumenti di taglio o di raschiamento. È necessario che siano effettuati ulteriori scavi e ricerche presso questo sito, per capire la relazione esistente tra l'attività umana e l'accumulo di ossa di cervo. È chiaro però il fatto che il danno subito dai molari dei cervi non può essere stato causato dal fatto che i cervi abbiano masticato sassi, come è stato sostenuto da numerosi archeologi presenti alla conferenza di Olièna nel 1988. Il fatto che cuspidi di molari siano state reinserite nelle mandibole ritrovate nel vano 2, e che siano stati fatti ritrovamenti litici nel vano 1 risalenti allo stesso periodo, mostra che presso la Grotta di Corbeddu è esistita una occupazione umana durante il periodo Paleolitico.

The Sources and Distribution of Sardinian Obsidian

Robert H. Tykot

Introduction

The following paper summarizes the history of obsidian studies pertaining to Sardinia, and assesses our current knowledge of the geological sources in Sardinia, and of the 'trade' of archaeological obsidian around the island, to Corsica, Elba and mainland Italy and France. The pattern and chronology of obsidian distribution have the potential to increase our understanding of the extent of interaction between insular and extra-insular populations, and of Neolithic and Bronze Age social and economic organization. With sufficient data, it should be possible to infer the parallel movement of more perishable goods (e.g. plants, animals and animal products), cultural ideas, and technological information, and their significance in the cultural development of prehistoric Sardinia (Tykot forthcoming). The long history of obsidian studies in Sardinia reflects the realization of this potential, and current efforts continue to build upon the foundation established by previous research.

History of Research

The presence in Sardinia of geological sources of obsidian, a volcanic glass frequently used to make stone tools because of its superior conchoidal fracture, is not a new discovery. Count Alberto de la Marmora (1839–40) made the first substantial contribution to our geological knowledge of the island in general, and in particular of the Monte Arci region where obsidian is found, more than a century ago (Fig. 1). De la Marmora (1839–40: 499-501) describes rhyolites of various types, including black obsidian, in the narrow valleys (*concas*) on the southwestern side of Monte Arci; he found obsidian *in situ*, as dikes or beds between rhyolite flows, in only a few places, however, although he does mention scatters so abundant that they could have come from a glass bottle factory. De la Marmora (1839–40: 153, 479, 489, 532, 583, 631) also mentions several minor sources of obsidian, at Tacco Ticci (Seulo), in the

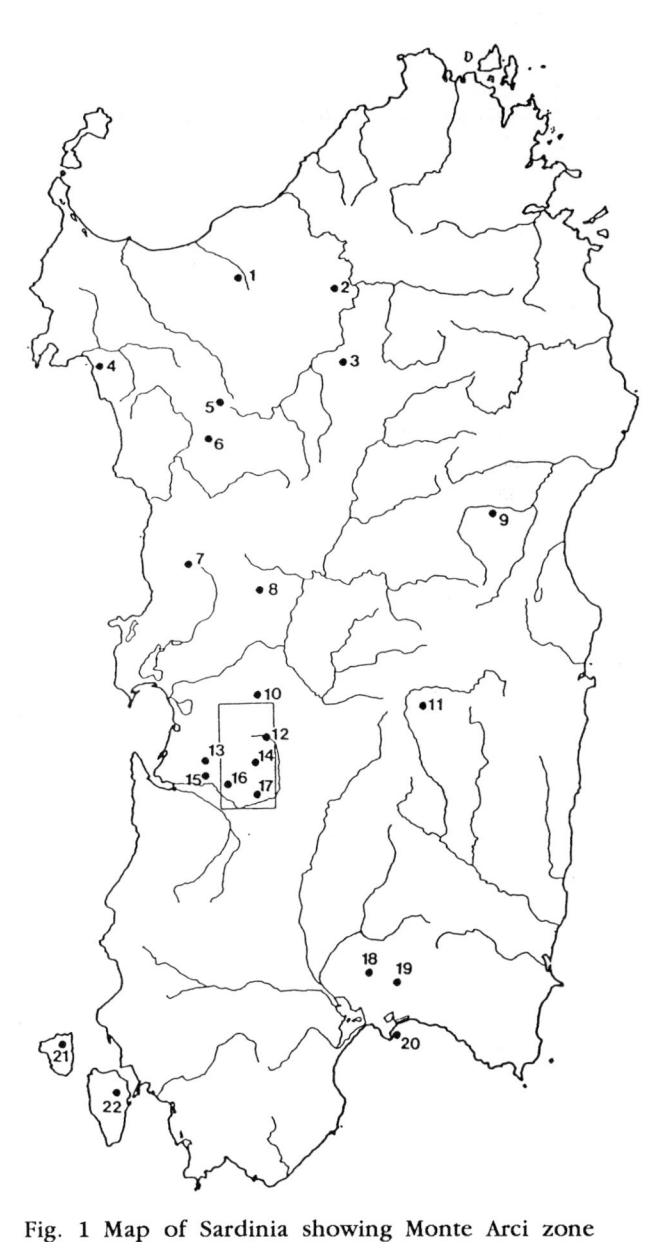

Fig. 1 Map of Sardinia showing Monte Arci zone (rectangle) and sites mentioned in text.
1. Osilo; 2. Tula; 3. Ozieri; 4. Alghero; 5. Monte Traessu; 6. Filiestru-Mara; 7. Cuglieri; 8. Losa-Abbasanta; 9. Corbeddu-Olièna; 10. Villaurbana; 11. Seulo; 12. Pau; 13. Marrubiu; 14. Morgongiori; 15. Terralba; 16. Uras; 17. Mogoro; 18. Sestu S. Gemiliano; 19. Settimo S. Pietro; 20. S. Bartolomeo-Cagliari; 21. S. Pietro; 22. S. Antioco.

Sarcidano, on the islands of S. Pietro and S. Antioco, in the altopiano of Sassu between Ozieri and Tula, at Muros (Villaurbana) and at Monti Urtigu (Cuglieri).

The first archaeological mention of Sardinian obsidian was by Giovanni Spano (1870: 19) in his notice about the prehistoric site of Monte Urpinu (CA). This site would come to the attention of mainland officialdom a decade later (Pigorini 1879: 45), was fully excavated by Edoardo Mannai in 1901, and was published on his behalf by Romualdo Loddo (1903). Significantly, two distinct types of obsidian, translucent and opaque, were recognized at Monte Urpinu, and attributed to sources on Monte Arci and Monte Trebina (Loddo 1903: 47). Meanwhile, the discovery by Melosi of a rock-shelter near Alghero with arrowheads of obsidian, quartz, agate and jasper had been reported (Spano 1873: 20-22); and Pio Mantovani (1875: 84) had discovered near Osilo (SS) an obsidian and flint workshop about 200 m wide, which was explored further by D. Lovisato (1875: 82; 1879: 18) and Filippo Nissardi (1886: 467). By 1903 a number of other prehistoric sites with obsidian had been discovered, including S. Gemiliano (Sestu) (Pigorini 1903), Settimo S. Pietro, and the Grotta di S. Bartolomeo (Cagliari), and it became clear that obsidian was an extremely important raw material for the prehistoric inhabitants of Sardinia.

Henry Washington (1913), a geologist with the Carnegie Institution, visited Sardinia in 1905 and spent two days studying the western flanks of Monte Arci. He confirmed de la Marmora's observation that Monte Arci consists of a domal core of feldspathic rhyolites, covered by a later mantle of trachyte, dacite, andesite and basalt flows. Washington (1913: 590-82) cites highly vitreous ash-gray perlites and black obsidians, usually intercalated with lithoidal rhyolites, near Uras in the Canale Perdera, above Conca s'Ollastu and at Conca Cannas; some small pieces of reddish-brown obsidian with black streaks are reported from the Rione Prassueda east of Conca s'Ollastu.

It thus became apparent by the early 1900s that obsidian from Monte Arci was to be found at nearly all prehistoric and protohistoric sites in Sardinia. Zanardelli (1899: 109-77), for example, lists 25 sites in the Campidano around Oristano from which he collected some 6661 pieces of obsidian; Taramelli (1926) summarizes his own extensive finds, and those of Lovisato, Ardu-Onnis, Zanardelli, Pischedda, Orsoni, Cara, Nissardi, Loddo and Mannai. Puxeddu (1958: 10-20), in a publication resulting from his thesis work at the University of Cagliari, was the last to compile this obsidian-site information, adding sites reported by Luigi Congiu (1947), Carlo Porru (1947), and Giovanni Lilliu, who has described obsidian as 'oro nero'. Puxeddu's major contribution was in the location and description of the Monte Arci obsidian sources, and the incorporation of that geological/geographical information into an archaeological framework for the interpretation of prehistoric sites with obsidian artifacts.

In a zone of about 200 km^2 which today includes 19 centers of habitation, Puxeddu reports 35 Roman sites, 93 nuraghi, and 246 locations with obsidian. The latter are classified as: sources (4); collection centers (11); workshops (74); and stations (157). Puxeddu (1958: 24, 33-37, 46, 48) found abundant *in situ* material at Roia Cannas near Uras, cites de la Marmora's finds of obsidian veins at Sonnixeddu, and notes probable sources at Tzipanéas in the territory of Marrubiu, and at Perdas Urias near Pau.

Puxeddu (1958) also reported some green, red and hazel-brown obsidians from the Monte Arci zone, but these are actually jasper (Francaviglia 1984: 314). Monte Arci obsidian can have red streaks, however, and a few samples of blue obsidian have been reported (Francaviglia 1984: 314).

By the time of Puxeddu's research, numerous sites with obsidian artifacts were known not only in Sardinia, but also in Corsica, on Elba and other islands in the Tuscan archipelago, in Liguria and southern France, and elsewhere on the Italian peninsula (cf. Buchner 1949). It was also recognized that the Mediterranean sources were limited to Pantelleria (Pa), Lipari (Li), Palmarola (Pl), Monte Arci in Sardinia, Melos, and the mountains of Hungary and Transylvania. It is therefore not surprising that the obsidian in central and northern Italy was attributed to Sardinian and Liparian sources (Bernabò Brea 1947; Bernabò Brea and Cavalier 1956).

It was in the early 1960s that chemical methods of analysis were first applied to the question of obsidian provenience. Cornaggia Castiglioni *et al.* (1962–63) tried using ordinary wet chemical analysis of major elements to distinguish between the Palmarolan, Liparian, Melian and Pantellerian sources, with the surprising (and erroneous) result that obsidian artifacts in Malta were thought to be mainly of Melian origin.

The first successful application of chemical analysis relied instead on trace elements, measured by optical emission spectroscopy, to characterize the Mediterranean obsidians (Cann and Renfrew 1964). Using the trace elements barium, zirconium, niobium and yttrium, they were able to differentiate many of the sources in the Mediterranean region. Among those sources which could not be differentiated were Lipari and Palmarola (their group 4a), and only two of the Sardinian sources (2a and 6a) were represented among the four Sardinian specimens analyzed.

Hallam, Warren and Renfrew (1976) followed up on this initial study with a more detailed examination of the western Mediterranean obsidians. Of the 148 samples analyzed, 63 were Sardinian: these fell into three chemical groups, suggesting that there were three Sardinian sources, all presumably in the Monte Arci region of the island. Only 7 were geological specimens, however, all from a source near Uras, which was now labelled as the SA source, and was equivalent to the 2a group from Cann and Renfrew's earlier study (Hallam et al. 1976: 88). Type SB archaeological material was tentatively identified as coming from the northern part of Monte Arci, while the source of type SC artifacts was considered to be possibly near the SA source in the Roja Cannas area east of Uras (Hallam et al. 1976: 95). This study also revealed an extensive distribution of Sardinian obsidian to Corsica, southern France, and northern Italy (Fig. 2a), with different patterns of individual source utilization. In order to explain this variation, it became urgently necessary to locate and characterize the SB and SC sources.

It was also considered unusual for such chemically disparate obsidians (SC is calcalkalic to tholeiitic; SA is more alkaline) to occur together in the same volcanic center (Hallam et al. 1976: 95), but tectonic plate movement over a few million years can substantially change lava composition (Tykot 1982). Although calcalkalic obsidian of Oligocene-Miocene age (K-Ar date of 16.8 mya) has been reported in the rhyolitic massif of Monte Traessu west of Giave in northwestern Sardinia (Coulon 1971; Coulon et al. 1974), this material was never considered a possible source of the SC archaeological material found near Monte Arci (Dixon 1976: 291), although the obsidian of Monte Arci was attributed to an early phase of the Oligocene-Miocene by earlier scholars (cf. Lauro and Deriu 1957; Dixon 1976: 290-91). In any case the Monte Traessu obsidian is highly localized and unsuitable for tool use (personal observation), perhaps because of its great age.

The potassium-argon dating of Italian obsidians by Belluomini et al. (1970) included a vertical series of 8 samples in the Uras quarry which showed that flow to be about 3.0 ± 0.2 million years in age; the obsidians from Palmarola (1.6 ± 0.2) were significantly younger, and those from Lipari and Pantelleria were so young as to be unmeasurable by this technique. Fission-track dating by Bigazzi and his colleagues (Bigazzi et al. 1976; Bigazzi et al. 1971; Bigazzi and Bonadonna 1973) initially confirmed the age of the Uras and Palmarolan obsidians, and provided ages of about 11,000 BP for Liparian and 135,000 BP for Pantellerian obsidian; thus the individual island obsidian sources could be differentiated by their geological age as well as their chemistry. It was later realized that a correction factor had to be applied to these dates to account for argon loss in the rhyolitic flows, so that the Uras obsidian should be dated to about 5 million years (Bigazzi et al. 1976). Dating by potassium argon of obsidian samples from Conca s'Ollastu and Riu Murus (near Monte Sparau North) (di Paola et al. 1975); and by fission-track of two specimens each from a quarry at Perdas Urias and at Pira Inferta (to the northwest of Monte Arci) (Bigazzi et al. 1976: 1568), showed these obsidian deposits to be of the same age as the Uras material. Thus, Bigazzi and Radi (1981) were unable to individuate the Sardinian sources in their analysis of archaeological material, which included 7 (of 13) artifacts from Tuscany found to be of Sardinian origin.

It was only in 1976 that a complete geological and petrographic study of Monte Arci was published, including a detailed 1: 50,000 map of the region (Assorgia et al. 1976; cf. also Beccaluva et al. 1974). This research illustrates the wide distribution of acidic lavas in the Pliocene levels of Monte Arci, where they frequently appear as massive, strongly vesiculated flows, often grading into a perlitic facies where obsidians are likely to occur (Assorgia et al. 1976: 383). Areas of prevailing perlites and obsidians include a small zone around Conca Cannas; a large area around Su Paris de Monte Bingias, reaching northwest to Santa Suina and northeast to Punta Perda de Pani; an equally large but more diffuse zone on the western side of Monte Arci, encompassing Bruncu Perda Crobina and s'Allostiraxiu, Conca s'Ollastu, Seddai, Cucru Is Abis, the western flanks of Monte Sparau North, Cuccuru Porcufurau, and Punta Su Zippiri; the isolated pockets of Tu Passetti at the center of Monte Arci, and several to the northwest including Pira Inferta; and a zone stretching northwest from Punta Pizzighinu to Su Varongu, west of Pau (Fig. 3).

Pyroclastic deposits, for example at Pala Sa Murta (southwest of Morgongiori) and Fustiolau (north of Perdas Urias), also tend to have obsidian and perlite mixed with pumice (Assorgia et al. 1976: 380-81), and obsidian-perlite volcanics have been reported in the Riu Acqua Bella valley, at Punta Feuraxi and at Laccu Sa Vitella to the northwest of Fustiolau (Bigazzi et al. 1976: 1557). Rarely do the geological studies specifically mention the size or extent of the obsidian outcrops, and whether the obsidian is of workable quality.

It should also be noted that glassy, peralkaline comendites are found on the islands of S. Antioco and S. Pietro off the southwest coast of Sardinia (Araña *et al.* 1974), and an artifact made of this material has been found on the surface at Nuraghe Losa (Abbasanta) by Francaviglia (1984: 316). These comendites are, however, chemically distinguishable from the obsidians (Hallam *et al.* 1976: 95).

Meanwhile, additional archaeometric studies of western Mediterranean obsidian were being done in the late 1970s/early 1980s by Noël Gale at Oxford, by Stanley Warren at Bradford (with several colleagues), by Vincenzo Francaviglia at CNR-Rome, by a group at CNR-Cagliari, and by Joseph Michels at Penn State. These studies included attempts at using strontium isotopes, Mössbauer spectroscopy, magnetic parameters, and X-ray fluorescence to characterize source material, and the neutron activation and atomic absorption analysis of archaeological material from northern Italy, southern France, and Sardinia.

Gale (1981) demonstrated that it was possible using a combination of strontium isotopes and elemental measurements of strontium and rubidium to separate all of the Mediterranean sources; all five geological samples from Sardinia, however, were from a single source. The two Sardinian artifacts analyzed did not match this group, and suggested the existence of additional sources.

Only the SA type of Sardinian obsidian has been tested by Mössbauer spectroscopy (Longworth and Warren 1979; Aramu *et al.* 1983), and it is differentiable from Liparian obsidian; this method cannot, however, differentiate the Liparian and Palmarolan sources. The use of magnetic parameters was also not entirely successful, as it separated Pantellerian, Liparian and Palmarolan obsidian, but the Sardinian groups overlapped with all of these sources (McDougall, Tarling and Warren 1983). This technique can, however, differentiate the SA, SB and SC sources, and two archaeological samples and one geological specimen from the Perdas Urias zone fell into a fourth group, called SD (McDougall *et al.* 1983: 448).

The analysis of 57 artifacts from northern Italy (Williams Thorpe *et al.* 1979) and 10 pieces from southern France (Williams Thorpe *et al.* 1984) supplemented Hallam *et al.*'s (1976) original study. In northern Italy, the primary use of both Liparian (22 of 68 overall) and Sardinian SA (32) sources was confirmed, while in southern France type SA was by far the most common source material (15 of 21 analyses overall). While the quantity of obsidian found at mainland sites is small, it is significant that this imported material is found at so many sites (40 in northern Italy, 50 in southern France).

The actual location of the Monte Arci obsidian sources and their relationship to archaeological artifacts was addressed at this time by Maria Mackey for her doctoral dissertation in geology at the University of Nottingham. Unfortunately, her work was temporarily abandoned, and when she finally submitted her thesis, it was turned down. The only available information comes from a brief conference paper (Mackey and Warren 1983), which is summarized here. Mackey was able to locate, in addition to the Conca Cannas source, *in situ* outcrops with medium-sized obsidian nodules towards the summit of Monte Sparau North, with small 1 cm nodules at higher levels of Cucru Is Abis, and with sub-millimeter specks of obsidian in a hard perlitic matrix at Le Trebine and Monte Sparau South (Mackey and Warren 1983: 421). Neutron activation analyses of 'relatively small' numbers of geological samples were able to differentiate the Conca Cannas (SA), Perdas Urias (SC), Monte Sparau North, and Cucru Is Abis sources; all 51 archaeological artifacts (from 12 Ozieri sites and 1 Nuragic site) analyzed could be attributed to one of these four groups. The original SB group matched most closely, but not exactly, the Cucru Is Abis source.

Another geochemical study of the Monte Arci sources was done independently by Vincenzo Francaviglia (1984), as part of a Mediterranean-wide survey using classical methods. Using X-ray fluorescence, a total of 172 geological specimens from Sardinia were analyzed for both major/minor and trace elements. Unfortunately, little information about the deposits themselves is given for the five localities tested: the quarry at Conca Cannas (77 samples), Funtana Figu (next to Cucru Is Abis) (30), Mitza Sa Tassa (near Perdas Urias) (27), S. Pinta (18), and Cave della Ceca (Morgongiori) (20) (Francaviglia 1984: 314). The most significant results were that the Cave della Ceca material actually consisted of a mixture of Conca Cannas and Funtana Figu-type obsidian in a detrital deposit; the western Mediterranean sources (Li, Pl, Pa, SA, SB, SC) could be differentiated using just major/minor element composition; and that the Mitza Sa Tassa and S. Pinta collections, both near Perdas Urias, were perhaps partially distinguishable using trace elements.

Finally, Michels *et al.* (1984) analyzed 104 artifacts from 10 sites in southern Sardinia using

Fig. 2a Map of western Mediterranean sites with obsidian tested by means of chemical analysis (after Crummett and Warren 1985; with additions). Circles = Sardinian (Monte Arci) obsidian; triangles = Liparian obsidian; squares = Palmarolan obsidian; and diamonds = Pantellerian obsidian.

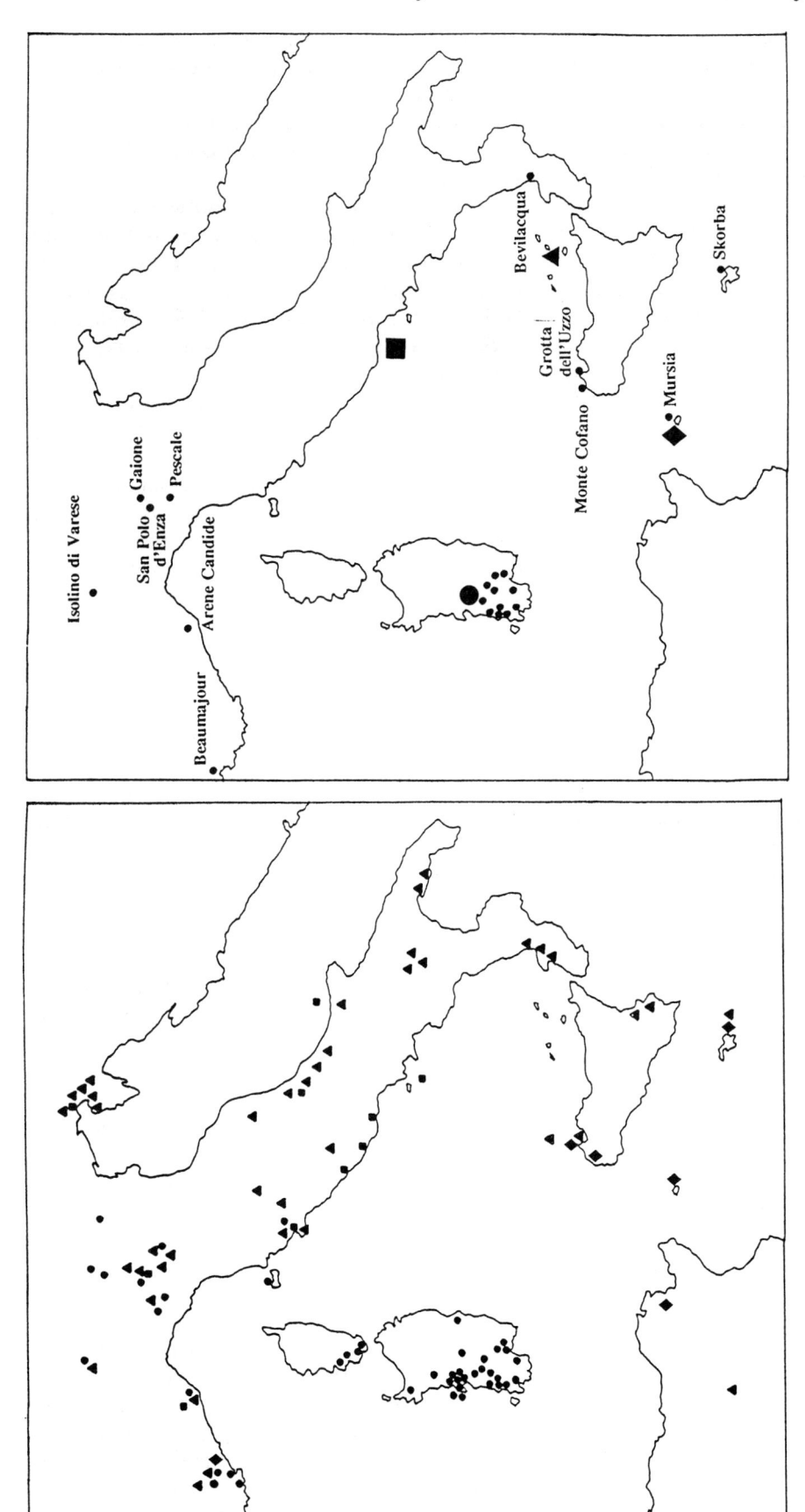

Fig. 2b Map of western Mediterranean sites with more than 5 pieces of obsidian tested. Sources: Monte Arci (circle); Palmarola (square); Lipari (triangle); and Pantelleria (diamond).

atomic absorption, in conjunction with an obsidian hydration dating program. The number of artifacts analyzed, in addition to those previously reported, greatly enhanced our knowledge of *Sardinian* use of Monte Arci obsidian, and alerted us to the potential chronological changes in source exploitation.

Current Research

Despite the numerous research efforts outlined above, there still remained a number of problems regarding the sources and usage of Sardinian obsidian. While the SA source seems well characterized, the SC source had not been located *in situ*, and the type SB archaeological artifacts analyzed did not match exactly with either of the Santa Maria Zuarbara localities tested by Mackey and Warren. The research by McDougall *et al.* (1983) and Francaviglia (1984) suggested that additional source groups may also have existed. Furthermore, while obsidian from about 100 western Mediterranean sites had been analyzed (Fig. 2a), most sites were represented by only a few samples, many from unscientific excavations. Only a fraction of these sites had more than five analyses (Fig. 2b), and only four had more than ten; one of these is Gaione in northern Italy, where Ammerman *et al.* (1990) recently found 3 of the 17 pieces tested to be of Sardinian type SC obsidian. Skorba in Malta is the only site where we can look at chronological change in source utilization.

My own research into the problems of Sardinian obsidian comprises three parts: (1) the location and characterization of the geological sources; (2) the provenience analysis of archaeological material; and (3) the interpretation of the resulting distribution patterns at various levels of inference. The results of the chemical analysis, by electron microprobe and ICP mass spectrometry, will be reported elsewhere (Tykot forthcoming); a description of the geological survey (cf. also Tykot 1991) and some preliminary interpretations of the archaeological data follow.

My fieldwork at Monte Arci began in 1987 with a survey of the zones previously identified as containing acidic lavas, and hence possibly obsidian (Fig. 3). Obsidian is usually formed under rapid cooling conditions from lavas that would otherwise form granitic rocks such as rhyolite and trachyte. If too much water is present, pumice or tuff can also be produced. After formation, obsidian can hydrate, turning into perlite, so that few obsidian sources are older than 10 million years.

Some quantity of obsidian was in fact found in most of these zones, although often as millimeter-sized pieces in a rock matrix. For each locality, the presence of obsidian was noted as *in situ* (found in geologically-formed strata), float (large, naturally produced blocks found on the surface or in secondary deposits), scatter (unworked obsidian found in loose soil, presumably naturally transported), or archaeological (worked artifacts and/or flaking debris). The exact position, including altitude, and extent of each locality was recorded, along with the range and average size of the obsidian finds. Physical properties such as color, glassiness, translucency, and the presence of phenocrysts were also described. Approximately 600 specimens were selected from more than 30 localities and, with the permission of the Soprintendenza Archeologica per le Provincie di Cagliari ed Oristano, taken to the United States for analysis.

The most well-known source is located below the peak of Conca Cannas, northeast of Uras, where obsidian occurs in an abandoned perlite quarry along with rhyolite and trachyte. Obsidian is frequently found as small specks within a perlitic matrix along the Riu Cannas, and rising up to Conca Cannas itself (elevation 382 m a.s.l.). No trace of obsidian was found near Perda Arrubia. One can find rather small, unworkable nodules of obsidian in a broad area to the south and east of the quarry, while fist-sized obsidian nodules are abundant in a more restricted area. These nodules average 10-15 cm in diameter, and can reach nearly 40 cm in length (cf. also Lanfranchi and Weiss 1973: 124). Conca Cannas obsidian is generally quite glassy, black but often so translucent that individual particles of colorant can be seen by eye. The particles are sometimes oriented so as to represent the original flow structure. Very occasionally the obsidian will contain red streaks.

The zone where type SB obsidian occurs is located near the church of Santa Maria Zuarbara but often at much higher elevations. A few kilometers northeast of the church, obsidian may be found *in situ* on the slope of Cuccuru Porcufurau, in bombs up to 30 cm in length; 3-5 cm nodules of obsidian occur at Punta Su Zippiri, at an elevation of 500 m. And it occurs along the Riu Murus near Monte Sparau North, in workable-sized blocks.

The Cucru Is Abis source appears to begin at an elevation of 230 m and flows down to the west near Funtana Figu, where large blocks may be found in a modern gravel quarry below the Seddai cliff-face (cf. also de Michele 1975: 172-73; Exel 1986: 78). Material still in the quarry measures up to 1 m in length; interestingly enough, hardly

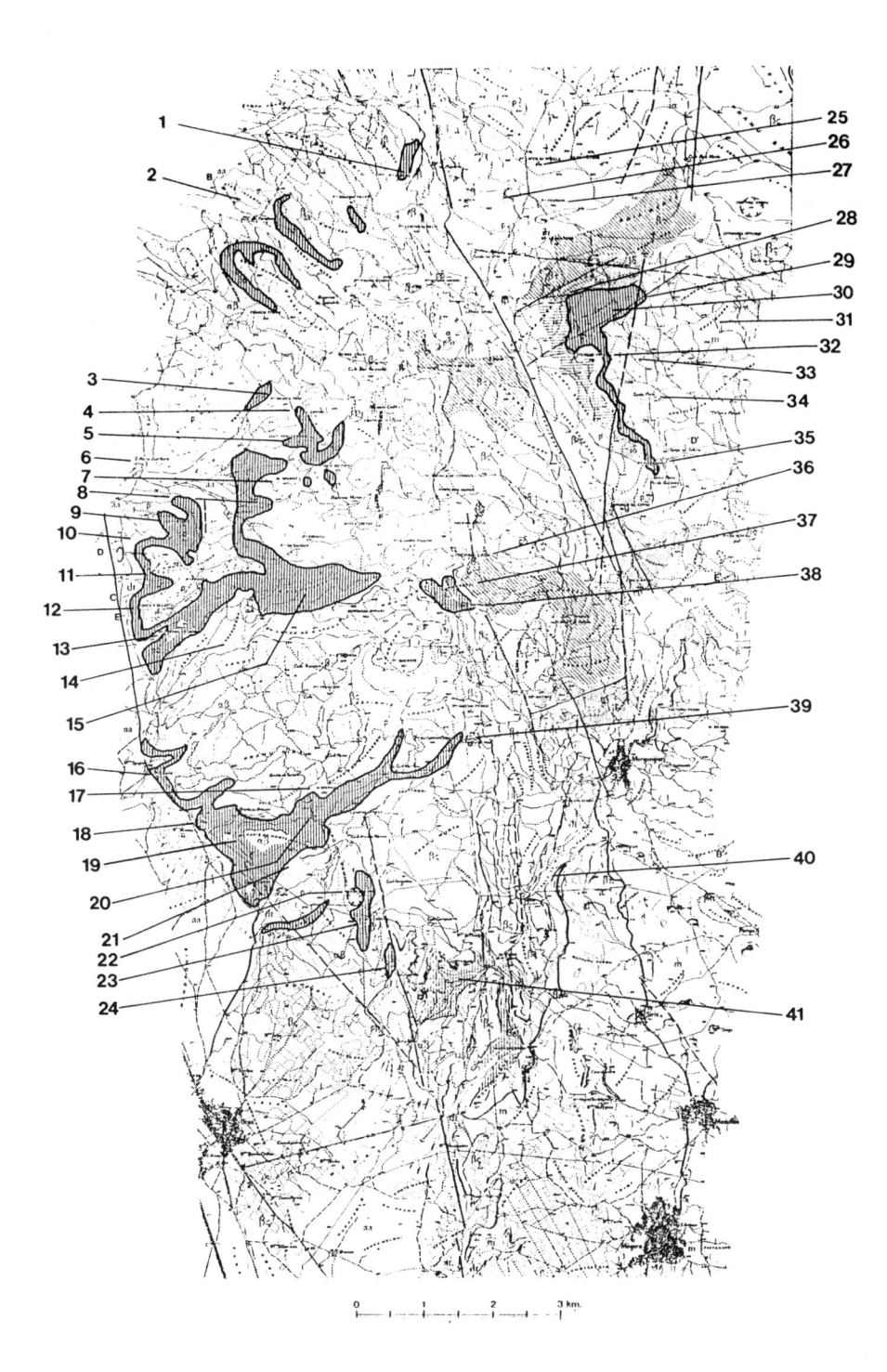

Fig. 3 Monte Arci: location of geological obsidian samples (probable obsidian-bearing lavas in outline, after Assorgia *et al.* 1976).
1. Punta Muroni; 2. Pira Inferta/Campo dei Forestieri; 3. Punta Nigola Pani; 4. Punta Su Zippiri; 5. Cuccuru Porcufurau; 6. Santa Maria Zuarbara; 7. Monte Sparau (North); 8. Riu Murus; 9. Cucru Is Abis; 10. Funtana Figu; 11. Seddai; 12. Conca s'Ollastu; 13. Bruncu Perda Crobina; 14. Rione Prasuedda; 15. S'Allostiraxiu; 16. S. Suina; 17. Monte Sparau (South); 18. C. Pies; 19. Su Paris de Monte Bingias; 20. Riu Solacera; 21. Canale Perdera; 22. Perda Arrubia; 23. Conca Cannas; 24. Uras Quarry; 25. Punta Laccu Sa Vitella; 26. Riu Acqua Bella; 27. Punta Feuraxi;; 28. Fustiolau; 29. Mitza Troncheddu; 30. Su Varongu; 31. Cazzighera; 32. Perdas Urias; 33. Mitza Sa Tassa; 34. Santa Pinta; 35. Punta Pizzighinu; 36. Trebina Lada; 37. Tu Pasetti; 38. Scala Antruxioni; 39. Perda de Pani; 40. Pala Sa Murta/Cave della Ceca; 41. Sonnixeddu.

any obsidian occurs in another quarry less than 1 km to the north.

Obsidian-bearing deposits continue to the south, along the western flanks of Monte Arci. *In situ* obsidian bombs 15-17 cm in length can be found on the slope of Bruncu Perda Crobina, beginning at an elevation under 100 m in the west, and up to an elevation of perhaps 400 m to the northeast. Scatters of unworked obsidian are common in the low plain to the west of Cucru Is Abis and Conca s'Ollastu.

No obsidian was observed between Santa Suina and C. Pies, but small pieces of *in situ* obsidian can be found even further south, near the peak of Su Paris de Monte Bingias, and near Monte Sparau South as specks within a perlitic matrix. Quarries have been operating in both locations for about 30 years, and according to the manager only small pieces have been found. Francaviglia (1984: 314), however, reports pieces several tens of centimeters in size along the Canale Perdera and the Riu Solacera.

Obsidian from the western flanks localities is frequently as glassy as the Conca Cannas material, but may be less translucent and grayer in color. This obsidian also is often broken up by white spots of crystalline material which can make the fracture sub-conchoidal. Not all pieces have white spots however, and visual techniques of source identification are not entirely accurate.

On the northeastern side of Monte Arci lies the Perdas Urias source zone, which is actually a large ridge running north-northwest from Punta Pizzighinu to the plateau of Su Varongu. *In situ* material has been located for the first time, in a perlitic matrix at about 600 m altitude, near Punta Pizzighinu, and includes specimens up to 17 cm in length. Abundant material also occurs in secondary contexts at lower altitudes. Natural blocks up to 30 cm may be found redeposited near Santa Pinta, just below the actual peak of Perdas Urias, near Mitza Troncheddu to the north, and in the low hills of Cazzighera to the east. The nearby site of Sa Tassa has been called a lithic production center, but this needs to be investigated. It appears that if a concentration of large obsidian nodules like that found near Conca Cannas exists, it is mostly overlain by later geological deposits. Thus, although there clearly exists considerable geological material—and the archaeological evidence proves that this source was exploited to a great extent—it must have required greater effort to collect raw material than at the SA and SB sources. Certainly, the landscape in the Perdas Urias zone is much more mountainous than the western side of Monte Arci; with parts reaching altitudes over 800 m a.s.l., no roads cross Monte Arci from east to west.

Obsidian from the Perdas Urias zone exhibits a great range in physical appearance. Some material is highly devitrified and weathered on its surface, while other pieces are glassy and have no evidence of flow banding. The type SC obsidian tends to be more opaque than both types SA and SB, but again it is difficult to visually distinguish archaeological artifacts.

Lastly, near Pala Sa Murta south of Morgongiori, some obsidian is found in the Ceca quarry, which Francaviglia (1984) had reported as being of two types. Elemental analyses are currently in progress, but in any case the only *in situ* obsidian I found was never greater than 1 cm in diameter, and there were no surface scatters of natural or flaked obsidian to suggest human activity there. Regarding other zones with the geological potential for obsidian formation, only the most meager surface scatter was found in the localities adjacent to the Campo dei Forestieri, near where Bigazzi *et al.* (1976) took a sample for fission-track dating; and no material was found near Punta Muroni, also to the northwest of Monte Arci. The locality of Tu Passetti/Scala Antruxioni was not visited.

To summarize the geological source data, we can say that: (1) large quantities of type SA obsidian occur near Conca Cannas; (2) equally large quantities of workable-size material occur in diffuse localities along the western flanks of Monte Arci, and the source at Cucru Is Abis has been shown chemically to be close, but not identical with the archaeologically-determined SB group; (3) large quantities of type SC obsidian are available at several localities in the Perdas Urias zone; and (4) small pieces of unworkable-sized obsidian may be found *in situ* at several additional localities, in either a perlitic or pyroclastic matrix. The extent to which all these sources were exploited at various period in prehistory can be easily estimated by testing archaeological material, but the dynamic behavior resulting in individual sources being favored, and some even ignored, will be more difficult to reconstruct.

Interpretation

Obsidian exploitation must be considered in chronological perspective, from the Neolithic to the end of the Bronze Age; we must also differentiate between local, regional and inter-regional levels of exchange, and the different economic and social mechanisms governing each. Settlement patterns, land routes and water crossings will also affect how raw source material ended up at various archaeological sites.

Although only part of the analytical data is now available, a few things can be said about regional interaction. A simple calculation of the relative usage of the different west Mediterranean obsidian sources shows that within Sardinia, type SA accounts for 37% of the artifacts analyzed, type SC 58%, and type SB, only 6% (Table 1). In Corsica, however, type SB (42%) is nearly as common as type SC (53%), with very little SA (5%); yet on the mainland, type SA (76% in northern Italy, 94% in southern France) is by far the most common type of Sardinian obsidian used. These frequencies are statistically different (at a 95% confidence level) than those for the Sardinian sources within Sardinia, and require a cultural explanation (among the possibilities, simply chronological variation in the sites tested so far). Whether these patterns will hold up after more material has been analyzed remains to be seen, but the current data imply that in the Neolithic—which most of the analyzed artifacts represent—different exchange mechanisms existed between Sardinia, Corsica and the mainland.

The routes taken by Mesolithic and Early Neolithic colonists of Corsica and Sardinia may be reflected in the directional distribution of obsidian finds. For example, obsidian from a Cardial site on Pianosa Island, between Elba and Corsica, is of Sardinian type C (unpublished data), and shows that there was bi-directional interaction in the Early Neolithic between the mainland and Sardinia.

Examination of the relative quantities of obsidian at sites in Tuscany and Liguria suggests that early navigators hugged the coasts and traveled from island to island. Specifically, it is proposed that long-distance traders may have transported the readily-accessible type SA obsidian directly to the Gulf of Oristano, where ships sailed north past Corsica to the Tuscan coast (cf. also Cocchi Genick and Sammartino 1983). Type SC obsidian, occurring on the eastern side of Monte Arci, may also have been carried to the Gulf, but was mainly distributed through an extensive land-based network. Type SB, used only locally in Sardinia, was nevertheless readily accessible to sea-borne carriers, and this may account for its increased representation in Corsica. Mechanical and visual properties of the obsidian sources cannot be discounted as influential in the selective exploitation of individual sources. The large quantities of obsidian at mainland sites like Pescale and Faenza, and the sheer number of sites where obsidian is present, show that this exchange was at least socially, if not economically, significant.

The fact that Sardinian obsidian was widely distributed in the Early Neolithic, yet is not found in the pre-Neolithic levels of Corbeddu Cave (cf. Hofmeijer and Sondaar and Martini this volume), certainly does not help the case for Pleistocene settlement of Sardinia.

Continuity or change in the distribution pattern established in the Early Neolithic may parallel other economic or technological developments (e.g. the introduction of animal domesticates and cereal agriculture in the Neolithic, or improvements in maritime technology); once again the direction of importation may also be reflected in the obsidian distribution pattern. Of particular interest is the possibility that the Near Eastern neolithic 'package' was introduced to Sardinia and Corsica from Sicily and North Africa, rather than from the European continent; this hypothesis would be supported if Sardinian obsidian were present in Tunisian assemblages, e.g., that of Zembra Island (J.-D. Vigne, pers. comm.).

Finally, I will test Michels's hypothesis that by the Middle Bronze Age access to obsidian sources had come under the control of local communities, which had specific trading relationships with their neighbors. For most Sardinian sites, it appears that variety in obsidian sources is the rule in the Neolithic and Early Bronze Age (and Gaione in northern Italy also has 3 types present), but that in the Middle and Late Bronze Age obsidian from only one source at a time was used at a particular site (Table 2). For example, the assemblage from Nuraghe Antigori on the Bay of Cagliari is entirely of type SC obsidian, a composition which is statistically different from the island-wide figure of 58%; in fact, the only sites which are statistically different are Nuragic in date. When territorial control emerged is important for our understanding of the function of the nuraghi. If access to obsidian sources were restricted prior to the earliest nuraghi, the latter could then be interpreted as having military significance from their inception; if territorial control came later, alternative explanations for the protonuraghi must be found (cf. Trump; Bonzani; and Ugas, this volume). Again, this suggestion is based on minimal data, and we will see if this pattern holds up after more sites have been examined.

In conclusion, we must be cautious in our extraction of information from lithic distribution patterns, but it is certainly a worthwhile endeavor. This is especially true for Sardinia, the only Mediterranean island source where distribution patterns on that island itself can be studied. The collection of appropriate data in the course of geological and archaeological survey and excavation, and the determination of the sources of the raw materials, are only the first steps in this direction.

Table 1

Regional use of Sardinian obsidian in the western Mediterranean

Region	Source	Number analyzed	Percent	p̄	Var	z value
W. Mediterranean	SA	122	43.9			
	SB	28	10.1			
	SC	128	46.0			
Sardinia total:		178				
	Li	80	–			
	Pa	11	–			
	PI	16	–			
Sardinia	SA	67	37.0			
	SB	10	5.5			
	SC	104	57.5			
total:		181				
France	SA	15	93.75	0.42	0.017	-4.36*
	SB	0	0	0.05	0.003	1.00
	SC	1	6.25	0.53	0.017	3.93*
Sardinia total:		16				
	Li	3	–			
	Pa	2	–			
N. Italy	SA	32	76.2	0.44	0.007	-4.68*
	SB	3	7.1	0.06	0.017	-0.12
	SC	7	16.7	0.50	0.007	4.88*
Sardinia total		42				
	Li	34	–			
	PI	6	–			
Corsica	SA	1	5.3	0.34	0.013	2.78*
	SB	8	42.1	0.09	0.005	-5.28*
	SC	10	52.6	0.57	0.014	0.41
total:		19				

p̄, Var, and z are statistical values which are used to test for the difference between two sample proportions; here the Sardinian use of each source is compared with regional percentages of each type. Regional z-values with asterisks (*) are significantly different from the Sardinian pattern:

the probability of /z/ < 1.96 is 95%
the probability of /z/ < 1.65 is 90%

p̄ = total successes/($n_1 + n_2$)   n = # analyzed for each region

Var $(p_1 - p_2) = p̄(1-p̄)(1/n_1 + 1/n_2)$

z = $(p_1 - p_2)/\sqrt{Var}$

Calculation comparing type SA in France and in Sardinia:

p̄ = (67 + 15)/(181 + 16) = 0.42
Var = (0.42)(.58)(1/181 + 1/16) = 0.017
z = (0.37-0.938)/$\sqrt{0.017}$ = -4.36*

Table 2

Chronological use of obsidian within Sardinia
(sites with more than 5 analyses)

Site	Source	Number analyzed	Percent	Date	p	Var	z value
Su Carroppu	SA	6	46.0	E Neo	0.38	0.019	-0.65
	SB	1	8.0		0.06	0.004	-0.40
	SC	6	46.0		0.57	0.020	0.81
Buon Cammino	SA	5	42.0	M Neo	0.37	0.021	-0.35
	SB	0	0.0		0.05	0.004	0.87
	SC	7	58.0		0.58	0.022	-0.03
Tracasi	SA	5	50.0	L Neo	0.38	0.025	-0.82
	SB	2	20.0		0.06	0.006	-1.87
	SC	3	30.0		0.57	0.026	1.71
Barbusi	SA	2	18.0	L Neo	0.36	0.022	1.28
	SB	0	0.0		0.05	0.005	0.78
	SC	9	82.0		0.59	0.023	-1.62
San Benedetto	SA	3	60.0	L Neo	0.38	0.048	-1.05
	SB	0	0.0		0.05	0.010	0.55
	SC	2	40.0		0.57	0.050	0.78
C. Craboni	SA	5	38.0	EBA	0.37	0.019	-0.07
	SB	0	0.0		0.05	0.004	0.87
	SC	8	62.0		0.58	0.020	-0.32
Serra Cannigas	SA	3	25.0	EBA	0.37	0.021	0.85
	SB	0	0.0		0.05	0.005	0.78
	SC	9	75.0		0.59	0.022	-1.18
Antigori	SA	0	0.0	Nuragic	0.35	0.019	2.68*
	SB	0	0.0		0.05	0.005	0.78
	SC	13	100.0		0.60	0.020	-3.01*
Domu Beccia	SA	10	100.0	Nuragic	0.40	0.025	-3.98*
	SB	0	0.0		0.05	0.005	0.78
	SC	0	0.0		0.54	0.026	3.57*
Ortu Comidu	SA	16	41.0	Nuragic	0.38	0.007	-0.48
	SB	0	0.0		0.05	0.001	1.74
	SC	23	59.0		0.58	0.010	-0.15

References

Ammerman, A., A. Cesana, C. Polglase & M. Terrani
    1990   Neutron activation analysis of obsidian from two neolithic sites in Italy. *Journal of Archaeological Science* 17(2): 209-20.

Aramu, F., V. Maxia, S. Serci & I. Uras
    1983   Mössbauer study of Mount Arci (Sardinia) obsidian. *Lettere al Nuovo Cimento* 36(5): 102-104.

Araña, V., F. Barberi & R. Santacroce
    1974   Some data on the comendite type of S. Pietro and S. Antioco islands, Sardinia. *Bulletin Volcanologique* 38(3): 725-36.

Assorgia, A., L. Beccaluva, G. di Paola, L. Maccioni, G. Macciotta, M. Puxeddu, R. Santacroce & G. Venturelli
    1976   Il complesso vulcanico di Monte Arci (Sardegna Centro-Occidentale). Nota illustrativa alla carta geopetrografica 1: 50.000. *Bollettino della Società Geologica Italiana* 95: 371-401.

Beccaluva, L., L. Maccioni, G. Macciotta & G. Venturelli
    1974   Dati geologici e petrochimici sul massiccio vulcanico di Monte Arci (Sardegna). *Memorie di Società Geologica Italiana* Supplemento 2(13): 387-405.

Belluomini, G., A. Discendenti, L. Malpieri & M. Nicoletti
    1970   Studi sulle ossidiane italiane II. Contenuto in 40Ar radiogenico e possibilità di datazione. *Periodico di Mineralogia* 39: 469-79.

Bernabò Brea, L.
    1947   Commerci e industrie della Liguria neolitica. *Rivista di Studi Liguria Italiana* 13: 3-16.

Bernabò Brea, L., & M. Cavalier
    1956   Isole Eolie e Milazzo. *Bullettino di Paletnologia Italiana* 1956.

Bigazzi, G., & F. Bonadonna
    1973   Fission track dating of the obsidian of Lipari Island (Italy). *Nature* 242(5396): 322-23.

Bigazzi, G., & G. Radi
    1981   Datazione con le tracce di fissione per l'identificazione della provenienza dei manufatti di ossidiana. *Rivista di Scienze Preistoriche* 36(1-2): 223-50.

Bigazzi, G., G. Belluomini & L. Malpieri
    1971   Studi sulle ossidiane Italiane IV. Datazione con il metodo delle tracce di fissione. *Bollettino della Società Geologica Italiana* 90: 469-80.

Bigazzi, G., F. Bonadonna, L. Maccioni & G. Pecorini
    1976   Research on Monte Arci (Sardinia) subaerial volcanic complex using the fission-track method. *Bollettino della Società Geologica Italiana* 95: 1555-70.

Buchner, G.
    1949   Ricerche sui giacimenti e sulle industrie ossidianiche in Italia. *Rivista di Scienze Preistoriche* 4(3-4): 162-86.

Cann, J.R., & A.C. Renfrew
    1964   The characterization of obsidian and its application to the Mediterranean region. *Proceedings of the Prehistoric Society* 30: 111-33.
Cocchi Genick, D., & F. Sammartino
    1983   L'ossidiana utilizzata nelle industrie preistoriche del livornese. *Quaderni del Museo di Storia Naturale di Livorno* 4: 151-61.
Congiu, L.
    1947   Saggio di Catalogo Archeologico della Carta d'Italia, Foglio 225, Quadrante IV, Tavolette SE-NE. Tesi di Laurea, Anno Accademico 1946-47, Università di Cagliari.
Cornaggia Castiglioni, O., F. Fussi & M. D'Agnolo
    1963   Indagini sulla provenienza dell'ossidiana in uso nelle industrie italiane. *Atti della Società Italiana di Scienze Naturali e del Museo Curcio di Storia Naturale in Milano* 102: 310.
Coulon, C.
    1971   La genèse du massif rhyolitique du Mont Traessu (Sardaigne septentrionale): Evolution de son dynamisme volcanique. *Bollettino della Società Geologica Italiana* 90: 73-90.
Coulon, C., A. Demant & H. Bellon
    1974   Premières datations par la methode K/Ar de quelques laves cenozoiques et quaternaires de Sardaigne nord-occidentale. *Tectonophysics* 22: 41-57.
Crummett, J.G., & S.E. Warren
    1985   Appendix I. Chemical analysis of Calabrian obsidian. In A. Ammerman (ed.), *The Acconia Survey: Neolithic Settlement and the Obsidian Trade*, 107-14. Institute of Archaeology Occasional Publication 10. London: Institute of Archaeology.
de la Marmora, A.
    1839-40 *Voyage en Sardaigne*. Turin: J. Bocca.
de Michele, V.
    1975   *Guida Mineralogica d'Italia*. Novara: Istituto Geografico De Agostini.
di Paola, G., M. Puxeddu & R. Santacroce
    1975   K-Ar ages of Monte Arci volcanic complex (central-western Sardinia). *Rendiconti della Società Italiana di Mineralogia e Petrografia* 31: 181-90.
Dixon, J.E.
    1976   Obsidian characterization studies in the Mediterranean and Near East. In R.E. Taylor (ed.), *Advances in Obsidian Glass Studies. Archaeological and Geochemical Perspectives*, 288-333. Park Ridge, NJ: Noyes Press.
Exel, R.
    1986   *Sardinien: Geologie, Mineralogie, Lagerstatten, Bergbau*. Sammlung geologischer Fuhrer, Bd. 80. Berlin: Borntraeger.
Francaviglia, V.
    1984   Characterization of Mediterranean obsidian sources by classical petrochemical methods. *Preistoria Alpina* 20: 311-32.
Gale, N.H.
    1981   Mediterranean obsidian source characterisation by strontium isotope analysis. *Archaeometry* 23(1): 41-51.
Hallam, B.R., S.E. Warren & A.C. Renfrew
    1976   Obsidian in the western Mediterranean: Characterisation by neutron activation analysis and optical emission spectroscopy. *Proceedings of the Prehistoric Society* 42: 85-110.

Lanfranchi, F. de, & M.-C. Weiss
    1973   *La Civilisation des Corses. Les origines*. Ajaccio: Cyrnos et Méditerr.
Lauro, C., & M. Deriu
    1957   Il vulcanismo cenozoico in Sardegna; le manifestazioni 'oligoceniche'. *Congresso Geologico Internazionale XXe session, Mexico 1956* (2): 469-86.
Loddu, R.
    1903   Stazione neolitica del Monte Urpino (Cagliari). *Bullettino di Paletnologia Italiana* 29: 45-52.
Longworth, G., & S.E. Warren
    1979   Mössbauer spectroscopy and the characterisation of obsidian. *Journal of Archaeological Science* 6(2): 179-93.
Lovisato, D.
    1875   Una pagina di Preistoria Sarda. *Atti della R. Accademia dei Lincei* 4: 82.
    1879   Gita inaugurale della sezione di Sassari al Club Alpino Italiano. *Bullettino di Paletnologia Italiana* 6: 18.
Mackey, M., & S.E. Warren
    1983   The identification of obsidian sources in the Monte Arci region of Sardinia. In A. Aspinall & S.E. Warren (eds.), *Proceedings of the 22nd Symposium on Archaeometry, University of Bradford, Bradford, U.K. March 30th—April 3rd 1982*, 420-31.
Mantovani, P.
    1875   Una stazione dell'età della pietra in Sardegna. *Bullettino di Paletnologia Italiana* 1: 81-90.
McDougall, J., D. Tarling & S.E. Warren
    1983   Magnetic sourcing of obsidian samples from the Mediterranean. *Journal of Archaeological Science* 10(5): 441-52.
Michels, J., E. Atzeni, I.S.T. Tsong & G.A. Smith
    1984   Obsidian hydration dating in Sardinia. In M.S. Balmuth and R.J. Rowland, Jr (eds.), *Studies in Sardinian Archaeology*, 83-114. Ann Arbor: University of Michigan.
Nissardi, F.
    1886   Sardinia-XXI. Sassari. *Notizie degli Scavi* 1886: 467.
Pigorini, L.
    1879   *Bullettino di Paletnologia Italiana* 5: 45.
    1903   Stazione neolitica di S. Gemiliano di Sestu (Cagliari). *Bullettino di Paletnologia Italiana* 29: 42-43.
Porru, C.
    1947   Saggio di Catalogo Archeologico della Carta d'Italia, Foglio 225, Quadrante I, Tavolette NE-SE. Tesi di Laurea, Anno Accademico 1946-47, Università di Cagliari.
Puxeddu, C.
    1958   Giacimenti di ossidiana del Monte Arci in Sardegna e sua irradiazione. *Studi Sardi* 14-15 (1955-1957) Parte I: 10-66.
Spano, G.
    1870   *Scoperte Archeologiche in Sardegna 1870*. Cagliari.
    1873   *Scoperte Archeologiche in Sardegna 1873*. Cagliari.
Taramelli, A.
    1926   La ricerca archeologica in Sardegna. In *Il Convegno Archeologico in Sardegna, Reggio Emilia, giugno 1926*, 9-80.
Tykot, R.
    1982   Problems in obsidian: Nuragic manufacture and use. Paper read at the Fourth Annual Colloquium on Sardinian Archaeology, Tufts University, November 12th, 1982.

| 1991 | Survey and analysis of the Monte Arci (Sardinia) obsidian sources. *Old World Archaeology Newsletter* 14(2-3): 23-27. |
| forthcoming | Prehistoric trade in the western Mediterranean: The sources and distribution of Sardinian obsidian. PhD dissertation, Department of Anthropology, Harvard University. |

Washington, H.
1913 Some lavas of Monte Arci, Sardinia. *American Journal of Science* 36: 577-90.

Williams Thorpe, O., S.E. Warren & L.H. Barfield
1979 The distribution and sources of archaeological obsidian from Northern Italy. *Preistoria Alpina* 15: 73-92.

Williams Thorpe, O., S.E. Warren & J. Courtin
1984 Sources of archaeological obsidian from Southern France. *Journal of Archaeological Science* 11(2): 135-46.

Zanardelli, T.
1899 Stazioni litiche del Campidano d'Oristano. *Bullettino di Paletnologia Italiana* 25: 109-77.

Riassunto

L'ossidiana, un vetro vulcanico frequentemente utilizzato per fabbricare utensili di pietra, è un importante indicatore del commercio nell'area mediterranea antica. Nel Mediterraneo occidentale, l'ossidiana è stata spesso ritrovata a centinaia di chilometri dai giacimenti insulari di Lipari, di Palmarola, di Pantelleria, e della Sardegna.

I giacimenti e la distribuzione di ossidiana sono stati esaminati dettagliatamente. Importanti contributi a questo proposito sono stati fatti da numerosi studiosi sardi tra cui de la Marmora nell'Ottocento e da Puxeddu alla metà del Novecento. Puxeddu ha compiuto un'indagine dettagliata nella zona di Monte Arci in Sardegna, dove già si sapere che l'ossidiana era presente *in situ*. Puxeddu ha identificato quattro giacimenti, undici centri di raccolta, settantaquattro officine, e centocinquantasette stazioni.

All'inizio del 1960 sono state sviluppate tecniche analitiche capaci di trovare il giacimento geologico corrispondente ad un materiale archeologico. Ricerche compiute da Renfrew e dai suoi colleghi, mostrano che è possibile trovare ossidiana sarda presso siti archeologici in Corsica, nell'Elba, nella Penisola Italiana, e nella Francia meridionale, e che esistono almeno tre giacimenti sardi. Ci sono state numerose speculazioni riguardo l'esatta posizione di questi giacimenti, ma soltanto all'inizio del 1980 sono stati raccolti campioni provenienti dai giacimenti geologici per farli corrispondere con quelli provenienti dai siti archeologici.

I geologi Mackey e Francaviglia, lavorando indipendentamente, hanno raccolto ed analizzato campioni di ossidiana provenienti dalla Sardegna, ma i risultati di queste ricerche sono stati pubblicati solo brevemente. Più recentemente l'Autore ha condotto una ricerca più estensiva nella regione del Monte Arci, e per la prima volta egli ha trovato ossidiana di tipo SC in situ. Sono in corso le analisi chimiche sia del materiale geologico che dei campioni archeologici provenienti da più di 50 siti in Sardegna e in Corsica.

Le informazioni sui giacimenti e sulla distribuzione di ossidiana possono essere riassunte così:

1. Il tipo di ossidiana SA si presenta *in situ* presso Conca Cannas, a nord-est di Uras ed è associato con perlite. L'ossidiana è nera e vetrosa e appare in forma di noduli (con il diametro medio di cm 10-15). In Sardegna questo tipo di ossidiana è quello del 40% dei materiali fino ad ora analizzati. In Francia e nell'Italia settentrionale, il tipo di ossidiana SA è decisamente il tipo di ossidiana sarda più comune (85%), ma in Corsica esso rappresenta meno del 5% dell'ossidiana analizzata.

2. Il tipo di ossidiana SC si trova *in situ* a Punta Pizzighinu, a sud di Perdas Urias, a circa 600 m s.l.m. Questo tipo appare più comunemente in depositi secondari ad altitudini più basse vicino a Santa Pinta, sotto Perdas Urias, e probabilmente anche a nord e ad ovest di Su Varongu. L'ossidiana di tipo SC è nera, spesso non è così vetrosa come quella di tipo SA, ma appare in blocchi di cm 30. È il materiale più comune in Sardegna ed in Corsica, e anche se è stato ritrovato nel continente, è presente in quantità minori dell'ossidiana di tipo SA.

3. Il tipo di ossidiana SB, originariamente identificato solo da campioni archeologici, può essere trovato sui pendii occidentali del Monte Arci, vicino a Santa Maria Zuarbara. Materiale lavorabile è stato ritrovato *in situ* presso numerose località che includono le zone del Monte Sparau Nord, Cucru Is Abis, Cuccuru Porcufurau, Punta Su Zippiri, Bruncu Perda Crobina e Su Paris de Monte Bingias. Sono stati osservati blocchi di m 1, ed entrambi i giacimenti di Cucru Is Abis e Bruncu Perda Crobina contengono noduli di cm 15-20. L'ossidiana di queste zone è nera e tende ad essere vetrosa come quella di tipo SA, ma forse meno traslucida e spesso con accenni di grigio. Alcuni pezzi hanno delle caratteristiche macchie bianche, ma generalmente non è possibile dif-

ferenziare ad occhio nudo l'ossidiana proveniente dai giacimenti sardi.

Nonostante i numerosi giacimenti locali di ossidiana, sembra che il tipo di ossidiana SB sia stato usato raramente in Sardegna, visto che rappresenta solo il 5% degli oggetti analizzati. Analisi preliminari suggeriscono che il giacimento di Cucru Is Abis corrisponde ai pochi campioni archeologici analizzati.

4. L'uso diverso dei diversi tipi di ossidiana in Sardegna, in Corsica, e nel continente, è statisticamente significativo e suggerisce che esistevano diversi meccanismi di scambio locale, regionale e con il continente. È possibile che i commercianti del Mediterraneo occidentale possano aver trasportato il tipo di ossidiana SA direttamente nel Golfo di Oristano dove navi hanno navigato verso Nord, passando per la Corsica verso la costa toscana. Il tipo di ossidiana SC presente sulla parte orientale del Monte Arci potrebbe essere stato trasportato verso il Golfo, ma è stato distribuito principalmente attraverso un estensivo network sulla terraferma. Anche se il tipo di ossidiana SB era usato solo localmente in Sardegna era accessibile ai commercianti marittimi e probabilmente per questo motivo l'uso di questo tipo di ossidiana è aumentato in Corsica. Le proprietà meccaniche e visuali dei giacimenti di ossidiana potrebbero aver influenzato lo sfruttamento dei giacimenti individuali.

5. I cambiamenti cronologici della distribuzione di ossidiana sono esaminati attraverso l'analisi di materiale archeologico che include siti con lunghi periodi di occupazione. Il cambiamento di certi modelli a livello regionale e nel Mediterraneo occidentale è contemporaneo ad altri cambiamenti, per esempio all'introduzione di animali domestici e di piante, e alla circolazione di nuove idee architettoniche e credenze religiose. È stato ipotizzato che a livello locale entro l'Età del Bronzo Medio, l'accesso ai giacimenti di ossidiana era sotto il controllo di comunità locali.

Western Mediterranean Obsidian Distribution and the European Neolithic

Patricia Phillips

Introduction

Obsidian's special composition as a volcanic glass makes it particularly suitable both for sharp-edged and piercing tools, and this property has been exploited wherever the material has been found in suitably sized blocks. In the European Neolithic period, obsidian artifacts were distributed hundreds and sometimes over a thousand km from source areas. Archaeologists have regarded obsidian as a material likely to be utilized by independent specialists (Brumfiel and Earle 1987: 5).

The geological sources of obsidian can be determined by chemical analysis, so that the origin of material can be identified in zones with several possible sources. Obsidian samples have been analyzed most successfully by neutron activation analysis, X-ray fluorescence and potassium-argon, strontium isotope, and fission-track dating (e.g. Dixon 1976; Gale 1981; Mackey and Warren 1983). Dixon (1976) identified four stages in characterization efficiency for the study of European obsidian sources. Most obsidian sources have now been located, except for possible sources within the western U.S.S.R., and it could be argued that scientific identification of Carpathian, Aegean and west Mediterranean obsidians has now reached the routine stage (Fig. 1).

The aim of this article is to consider the distribution of Sardinian and west Mediterranean obsidian from a European perspective, using calibrated BC dates. Three aspects will be considered: chronological controls, assemblage analyses and distribution and acquisition mechanisms. The starting point is Perlès's (1990) valuable interpretation of the distribution of Melian obsidian and other lithic raw materials around the Aegean from pre-Neolithic times to the Bronze Age. In the western Mediterranean the multiplicity of sources involved, as well as varying analytical schemes to describe obsidian assemblages, make interpretations more difficult (cf. Tykot, this volume). The situation in Eastern Europe is compared in a brief section.

The Aegean

1. Chronological Controls from Quarry to Use Area

The main quarry sites supplying the Neolithic populations of the Aegean are Sta Nychia and Demengaki on the Cycladic island of Melos. Although a few examples of obsidian have been noted from the Anatolian coastal island of Giali, 'we can now be reasonably confident that the vast majority of the obsidians found on the other Cycladic islands and on the Greek mainland are Melian in origin' (Shelford *et al.* 1982: 120). Surface survey of part of Melos has identified seven Neolithic sites consisting of scatters of obsidian artifacts, mainly Late Neolithic in date (Cherry and Torrence 1982). Perlès (1990) assumes that the island was not permanently inhabited until the Late Neolithic, and that exploitation of the obsidian before this period was undertaken from outside. Cherry (1985: 22-23), quoting studies of sea-level rise in the post-glacial period, has indicated that the Cycladic islands were larger than today in the pre-Neolithic and Early Neolithic periods, so that intervisibility was easier and intervening water stretches less broad.

In the absence of settlement evidence from the island itself, the dating of obsidian exploitation on Melos has been fixed by the radiocarbon chronology for the Franchthi cave in the southern Argolid (Table 1, after Perlès and Vaughan 1983: 220). The Late and Final Neolithic span two millennia in this southern Greek chronology.

2. Assemblage Analyses

The Aegean area is unique in that technological analyses have been made of the Melian quarry sources (Torrence 1986, and references therein) as well as of island and mainland settlements where obsidian was distributed (Torrence 1979; reviewed and partially re-analyzed by Perlès 1990). Much of the quarry debitage analyzed by Torrence related to the extensive Bronze Age

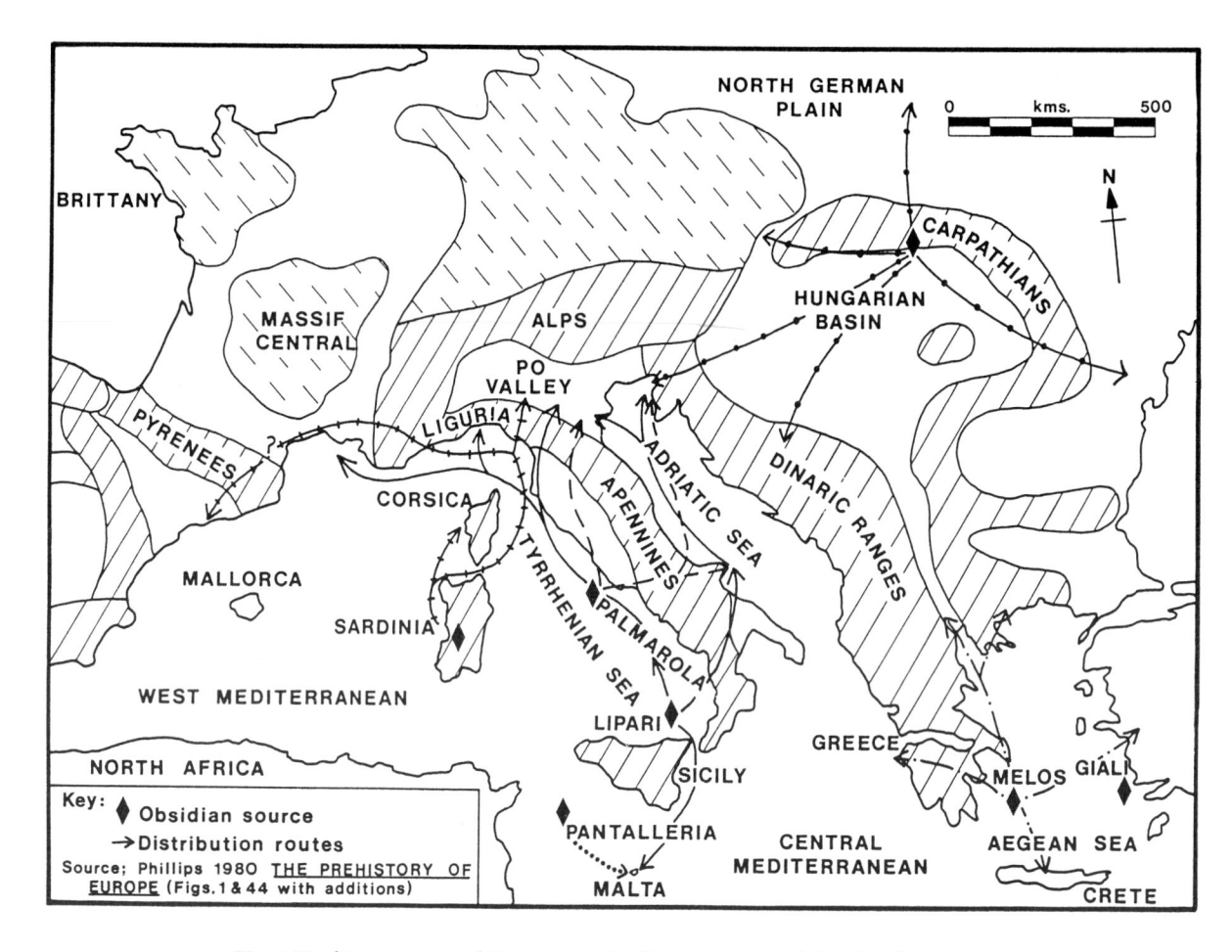

Fig. 1 Mediterranean and European obsidian sources and distribution routes.

exploitation of the obsidian and thus to the very preliminary stages of block reduction (Perlès 1990: n. 17). Only a few areas with tertiary flakes and chips and artifacts, or small cores, could be safely dated to the Neolithic period (Cherry and Torrence 1982). By contrast Perlès's (1990: 5) analysis of the Franchthi cave Neolithic levels, and re-analysis of a number of other mainland assemblages, was able to identify all the debitage stages involved in block reduction on Early and Middle Neolithic sites. On a more general level, Perlès (1988: 486) uses her analyses of Greek obsidian and flint assemblages to hypothesize a dual pattern of neolithization in Greece. The reduction sequence of the Franchthi cave obsidian and flint is illustrated by Perlès and Vaughan (1983: 218) in an article also covering the use-wear on the obsidian (12% of total chipped stone) and flint. The reduction sequence, or *chaîne opératoire*, at the cave in the Early and Middle Neolithic started with pre-form cores, reduced by pressure flaking to blades and bladelets, which were used to cut up plants (but not necessarily food plants). Perlès (1985) also has re-analyzed the Argissa Early Neolithic assemblage, with 50% obsidian artifacts, demonstrating the similarity of the blade part of the technology to that at Franchthi Early Neolithic Level X, although Argissa lacked the substantial Franchthi substrate of Mesolithic type *gros outillage* (notched and denticulated flakes, etc.). Perlès's (1985: 8) re-analysis showed that earlier morphological descriptions contained errors such as butts being identified as end-scrapers.

In the Late Neolithic, obsidian was imported to Franchthi in the form of unworked blocks and during the Late and Final Neolithic there were frequent changes in knapping techniques and assemblage composition at the site (Perlès 1990: 14). Torrence mentions the production of pressure-flaked as opposed to percussion-flaked blades from cores in the final Neolithic on Melos (Cherry and Torrence 1982). Perlès (1990) emphasizes the increased numbers of obsidian artifacts and the variability of knapping techniques and completed forms on Late Neolithic sites of the Greek mainland.

3. Distribution and Acquisition Mechanisms

Perlès (1990: 27) argues convincingly that the Early and Middle Neolithic acquisition of obsidian from Melos was a product of specialized trading, either by groups specializing in all phases of extraction, distribution, and production, or by two groups: sailors involved in extraction, and village craftsmen involved in production. Cherry (1985) suggests there was an improvement in ship technology in the Early Neolithic, and Perlès follows this argument, particularly since the sudden rise in obsidian at Franchthi in Level X is accompanied by an increase in large fish bones. Torrence (1986: 219), following Binfield, had previously argued for obsidian being acquired as a form of 'embedded procurement' during fishing expeditions. Bloedow (1987) disputes the link with tunny fishing and is strongly against any argument for trade in obsidian without also offering any clear mechanism for obsidian distribution. Perlès (1990: table 3) demonstrates from the numbers of pieces found on contemporary mainland sites and the distance from their source that the mechanism involved is not simple 'down-the-line' exchange. Obsidian found at Knossos, Crete, would also have been obtained directly from Melos and other sources.

There is a change in the Late Neolithic when Melos and other Cycladic islands are occupied (Cherry and Torrence 1982). On the basis of widespread variations in the form of the imported nodules or cores, the reduction sequence, typology, and use at different sites, Perlès (1990: 28) argues that obsidian acquisition becomes 'de-specialized', with nearer groups directly obtaining their own raw material in what Renfrew (1984) called 'freelance trade'. Differences in the proportions of obsidian in assemblages in the south and north of the mainland suggest nonetheless that areas most distant from the source (e.g., Thessaly and west Macedonia) were supplied by craftsmen in a manner more closely resembling the earlier pattern (Perlès 1990: 33).

4. Conclusions Regarding Aegean Obsidian in the Neolithic Period

The attraction of obsidian varied through time, as the break in acquisition of this raw material at Franchthi cave in the Late Mesolithic reveals. Perlès and Vaughan (1983: 217) discuss the use of obsidian and fine-grained flint for plant working in the Early and Middle Neolithic: plant-working does not correlate with the availability of grain at the site, and the authors think the blades were used on basketry, thatch and other materials associated with a sedentary life.

The role of obsidian changes from extensive use for cutting and piercing tasks in the Early and Middle Neolithic to a more general role in the Late Neolithic. As Torrence's (1979) work has shown, however, despite the increasing use of metal, a demand continued to exist for this cutting material well into the Bronze Age, although by this time it was also being used for mirrors, vases and other prestige items.

Given the high degree of sophistication by stone-using peoples in recognizing the working properties of different lithologies, the long-distance procurement of obsidian and fine-grained flint for difficult (e.g. plant fiber) cutting tasks is understandable. The changes in obsidian procurement from the Early/Middle to the Late Neolithic, are demonstrated by Perlès to reflect changes in settlement pattern (island occupation) and economic activity (primarily fishing). The supposed Neolithic–Bronze Age trajectory towards specialization is seen here as more cyclical than directional.

The Western Mediterranean

1. Chronological Controls from Quarry to Use Area

Four islands with obsidian sources were exploited during the west Mediterranean Neolithic: Lipari, Sardinia, Palmarola and Pantelleria. Initial dates for quarrying have to be extrapolated from radiocarbon determinations at use-sites, just as in the Aegean. In the case of the two main sources, Lipari and Sardinia, there is some dispute about the use-site dates. For instance, a recent publication of survey evidence from southeast Italy (Milliken and Skeates 1989) identified obsidian, assumed to be from Lipari, in otherwise Final Epigravettian/Mesolithic artifact collections. Sardinian obsidian from an Early Neolithic context at Corbeddu Cave (Olièna) in Sardinia may date from as early as the mid-7th millennium cal BC (Klein Hofmeijer *et al.* 1987–88: fig. 4), but detailed publication is still pending.

Obsidian artifacts occur in the second phase of occupation at the Uzzo cave, northwest Sicily, in Levels F7, 8, and 9, dated to the early to mid-6th millennium cal BC (Costantini *et al.* 1987: 398; Meulengracht *et al.* 1981: 230-31). Characterization studies identify both Liparian and Pantellerian obsidian at this time (Francaviglia and Piperno 1987). It is not clear which obsidian was used in the earlier neolithic Levels F10-12 at Uzzo; these are undated but according to the excavators may be as early as the mid-7th millennium cal BC.

Tinè (1990) argues from ceramic evidence that the earliest use of Liparian obsidian pre-dated the Late Stentinello settlement of Lipari. Liparian obsidian was exploited and transferred both to nearby Sicily and to Calabria on the Italian peninsula, where the Piana di Curinga Stentinello site is dated by a single radiocarbon determination to the mid-6th millennium cal BC (Ammerman 1985: 59).

The earliest dated use of Sardinian obsidian is at Basi (Corsica) where a single radiocarbon date recalibrates to around the mid-7th millennium cal BC. The date appears a little early given the close typological parallels between pottery from Basi and Late Impressed Ware from the Tuscan site of Pienza (Calvi Rezia 1980). Guilaine (1987: 750) suggests a slightly later uncalibrated dating of the Early Neolithic in Corsica and Provence (c. 5300–5200 uncal BC), while Binder (1989: 219) and Bagolini and Biagi (1990) date the Ligurian Impressed Ware sites with obsidian in their assemblages to c. 5500–5000 uncal BC. This would mean that Sardinian obsidian was probably exploited by the beginning of the 6th millennium cal BC. The obsidian hydration dating of between 5548 and 4875 BC for artifacts from Su Carroppu de Sirri in southwest Sardinia (Michels *et al.* 1984: 98) fits well into this scheme.

Between the early and middle parts of the 6th millennium BC obsidian use-sites occur on the islands of Lipari (Castellaro Vecchio) and Sardinia (Filiestru cave Level 7). Palmarolan obsidian was also probably exploited at this time, but no definite settlements are known on the island. Both Pantellerian and Liparian obsidian were utilized on Malta. Camps (1990: 138) has theorized, without radiocarbon evidence, that Pantellerian obsidian was used in North Africa as early as the mid-7th millennium cal BC.

From the mid-6th to early 5th millennia BC obsidian was being used along the Ligurian and French coast, throughout Italy, and in Dalmatia (Williams Thorpe *et al.* 1979; Tinè 1990; Bagolini and Biagi 1990; Barfield, pers. comm.). In the 5th millennium cal BC both Liparian and Sardinian obsidian reached northern Italy and southern France, with the majority of obsidian from French Middle Neolithic Chasseen contexts coming from Sardinia (Williams Thorpe, Warren and Courtin 1984). Palmarolan obsidian was distributed east and west from its source, through central Italy as far as Dalmatia, and up the Tyrrhenian coast to Liguria (Williams Thorpe *et al.* 1979).

Obsidian continued to be exchanged in the 4th millennium cal BC, with Sardinia acting as the main supplier to southern France and, less certainly, to northern Italy; and Liparian obsidian being traded to south and peninsular Italy. Obsidian distribution declined sharply from the beginning of the 3rd millennium BC.

2. Assemblage Analyses

Assemblages of Neolithic chipped stone tools in the west Mediterranean have been analyzed according to different techno-typological methods, for instance the *chaîne opératoire* method in France (e.g. Binder and Perlès 1990), and the Laplace method in Italy (e.g. Depalmas 1989). There is an overall fall-off in the significance of obsidian within chipped stone tool assemblages from south to north with increasing distance from sources (Lipari, Sicily, southern Italy, Sardinia, as opposed to Corsica, northern Italy, Dalmatia and southern France).

No numerical estimates have been made of either pre-cores or indeed of the different categories of debitage produced at the different sources. Similarly, few estimates have been made of the numbers of artifacts on sites close to obsidian outcrops, though Hallam *et al.* (1976) refer to 'enormous quantities of cores and of waste flakes recovered from the Neolithic villages in the Aeolian islands'. On Sardinia, Puxeddu (1958) located thousands of blades and other artifacts near the island's Monte Arci source. At Filiestru cave, northwest of Monte Arci, the small-scale excavations produced c. 1000 pieces of obsidian from all the Neolithic and Copper Age levels, and c. 3000 pieces of flint and other chipped stone raw materials (Trump 1983: table 6). Microwear studies of a sample of flakes and blades from Filiestru Levels 5 and 6 demonstrate a limited function for obsidian in cutting meat and flesh (Hurcombe in press, and this volume).

Further away from the sources, as for example at Basi (Corsica), Courtin (1989) has reported large quantities of debitage as well as finished artifacts, and sites near the Straits of Bonifacio produced large numbers of blade cores and bladelets. On Sicily there are numerous sites with a considerable amount of debitage, some 250 items from Barcellona in north Sicily as an example (Tinè 1990). Near the house at Piana di Curinga 225 artifacts were found (Ammerman *et al.* 1988), and relatively large numbers are known from other secondary workshops in north Calabria/Crotone (Tinè 1990).

In northern Italy the Pescale assemblage, with its 950 pieces, has been uniquely large for a number of years, but now the Faenza PEEP site has also produced a considerable amount of obsidian, and Ammerman *et al.* (1990) calculate that the 99 pieces found in surface survey at Gaione might mask a total of at least 2000 upon excavation. The recently excavated site of Giribaldi near Nice (Courtin 1989; Binder and Perlès 1990) has produced large quantities of obsidian, increasing the number of workshop sites in southern France to six (Phillips 1982: fig. 15). However, obsidian artifacts in southern France previously totalled only about 160 (Phillips 1982: 27).

Ammerman and his colleagues (Ammerman *et al.* 1976: table 7) have played an important role in first identifying a large number of sites in Calabria as having participated in the obsidian 'traffic', and in encouraging other researchers (Malone 1985; 1986; Tinè 1990) to develop and extend the information for Calabria. Study of the reduction sequences indicated the presence of workshops (division of the assemblages into cores, core trim, blades and large shattered pieces; e.g. Ammerman and Andrefsky 1982: fig. 7.9). Ammerman (1985: 65) identified two sites as particularly involved in Early Neolithic (Stentinello) obsidian reduction, mainly from imported pre-cores, and emphasized the large size of blades and lack of retouch. Microscopic study of striations showed that cutting and shaving actions had been performed, some of them on plants (Diamond and Ammerman 1985; Ammerman *et al.* 1988). Ammerman's techno-typological analyses are dynamic, but less rigorous than the *chaîne opératoire* method employed by Perlès in the Aegean and Binder (1989) in southeast France.

In an article identifying the sources of obsidian artifacts found in France, the pieces were mainly defined in terms of cores, flakes and blades (Courtin, in Williams Thorpe, Warren and Courtin 1984). More recently, in a brief appendix concerning chipped stone artifacts from the Giribaldi site, Binder (and Perlès 1990) indicates that for the obsidian all the reduction stages are there, including a core, cortical flakes and bladelets made by pressure flaking.

Barfield has only categorized north Italian obsidian artifacts as worked or unworked, including cores (Williams Thorpe *et al.* 1979: table 1), but more details are given in the report's appendix. Some Italian archaeologists employ the Laplace system of analysis when publishing chipped stone assemblages (e.g. Depalmas 1989, for a Sardinian site near Oristano). The Laplace system is applicable to assemblages of all periods, but its static categories do not easily lend themselves to a reconstruction of the reduction technology and function of chipped stone tools, including obsidian.

More detailed studies are currently under way in northern Italy. Ammerman (pers. comm.) is investigating with colleagues both the sources and reduction states of artifacts found in Liguria and the Po Valley. The Gaione site in the Po plain (Ammerman *et al.* 1990) is of considerable interest, with three sources (Lipari, Sardinia and Palmarola) represented, and the suggestion of a different distribution mechanism from the furthest source. Only finished blades are made of Liparian obsidian, whereas tools, cores and knapping debris occur in the other two source materials.

In southern France in the late 1980s an Action Thématique Programme funded by the C.N.R.S. permitted the testing of a large number of obsidian artifacts by X-ray diffraction analysis, carried out by G.M. Crisci of Calabria University, Cosenza. The program included techno-typological identification by Courtin of both the southern French material and of Corsican collections. The results of this program are being prepared for publication (Ricq-de Bouard, pers. comm.).

3. Distribution and Acquisition Mechanisms

While the earliest dates for obsidian acquisition from the west Mediterranean islands are still uncertain, all four island sources were being utilized by the mid-6th millennium cal BC at the latest. The earliest acquisition of obsidian in the west Mediterranean may have been via visits to unoccupied islands, as argued vigorously by Tinè (1990) for Lipari. This seems to have been true for Pantelleria, and possibly also for Palmarola. Sardinia may prove to have been occupied at the time obsidian was first being exploited. Good seamanship was required to transfer obsidian to use-sites beyond the islands. Most writers concur in regarding these sailors as 'specialists'.

Binder and Perlès (1990) emphasize that specialized raw materials, like obsidian, would be transported in many forms, both prepared and unmodified. In the case of Lipari, Ammerman and Andrefsky (1982) argue that pre-cores were knapped at the source and distributed in southern Calabria. Tinè (1990) identifies the passes used across the narrow mountain ridge of southern Calabria that enabled the obsidian to reach the east coast in the early Neolithic period. In the case of Sardinia, sailors acquired Monte Arci obsidian, possibly while anchored in the Cabras lagoon to the west of the mountain sources, and transported it in the forms of stream-transported blocks, unmodified chunks, or pre-cores—the study remains to be done—as far as southwest Corsica.

Tinè (1990) argues that the occupation of Lipari was an important step, particularly in the Middle Neolithic Serra d'Alto period, linking the island with the mainland in the northern part of Calabria. From here obsidian was distributed eastwards over mountain passes, reaching the eastern side of the peninsula and the villages of the Tavoliere plain. Tinè has plotted the likely routes for obsidian exchange across the hills of north Calabria, but it is not clear by what land or sea routes it reached north Italy and Dalmatia. Palmarolan obsidian was carried across the mountainous spine of central Italy to reach east and north Italian sites, and ultimately Dalmatia. The strength of the exchange mechanism is demonstrated, according to Tinè (1990) and Malone (1986), by the presence of southeast Italian and Dalmatian ceramics on Lipari. Along the Tyrrhenian coast, in Liguria, and as far west as Peiro Signado (Portiragnes-Hérault), Liparian obsidian reached its furthest westward expansion.

During the earliest period of Neolithic settlement on Sardinia, the volcanic glass is found as 17% of the chipped stone artifacts, together with flint and other raw materials, in the lowest levels of the Filiestru cave in northwest Sardinia. Other Impressed Ware sites are known from the same region, from the southwest peninsula, and from the Bay of Cagliari (Tanda 1982; Atzeni 1983). Of these, at least the southwestern site of Su Carroppu, with a 100% obsidian assemblage, is regarded as being as early as Filiestru (Tanda 1982). Given these distributions, it is possible that obsidian was carried overland both north and south across the relatively flat western side of the island. The most accessible route for Sardinian obsidian to reach Corsica is via the narrow 10 km Straits of Bonifacio, connecting northeast Sardinia with southeast Corsica, although broader crossings are also possible. The Bonifacio straits are not far from the Perfugas flint sources, also exploited and exported to Corsica.

Although Tanda (1982) also draws typological connections between the pottery of Filiestru Level 7 and Su Carroppu, the distribution map of Neolithic sites on Sardinia suggests the possibility that Sardinia was colonized from more than one island or continental area. The north–south differences in obsidian usage in Early Neolithic Sardinia could be due to colonization by separate groups: those in the south with no access to flint or chert and thus exclusively dependent on obsidian, and others in the north, possibly coming from Corsica or Tuscany, aware of flint sources and thus less dependent on obsidian. A hint of this appears in Lewthwaite's (1985) figure 3c.

During the maximum expansion of the obsidian trade in the 5th millennium cal BC, west Mediterranean obsidian is found at numerous inland sites in its most distant distribution zones, northern Italy and southern France. Sardinian obsidian may have reached Provence direct from the island or via the Ligurian coast, or overland from the Po Valley, probably all three (Phillips 1982: fig. 15). Research on other raw materials (jadeite axes, fine flint, etc.) has demonstrated widespread distribution of these products at the same time period and among the same cultural groups (users of Chasseen and Lagozzan pottery: Phillips 1982; Barfield 1981). Either by partial mobility of these Middle Neolithic groups, particularly to seasonal meeting places, or by exchange from a few small 'workshop' sites, obsidian pressure-flaked blades were distributed from hand to hand. In northern Italy, the location of several different large stocks of obsidian (e.g. Faenza PEEP, Pescale) demonstrate the passage of obsidian blocks and pre-cores along mountain passes and river valleys from the Tuscan coast. Obsidian only reached these distant inland areas after Neolithic groups were well established in all geomorphological zones of the west Mediterranean.

Obsidian is not definitely known west of the Ebro valley in Spain, where agriculturally-based groups linked to the French Chasseen populations were active from the early 5th millennium cal BC. Chapman (1990; Chapman and Muller 1990) has recently suggested that agriculture was a very late phenomenon in most of Iberia and in the Balearic islands, and the lack of obsidian in these most westerly parts of the Mediterranean may be linked with that situation.

By the end of the 4th millennium BC different settlement and exchange systems caused the cessation of much of the obsidian traffic. An indication of the continued widespread exchanges taking place, mainly in different raw materials, occurs with the find dating from the beginning to the middle of the 3rd millennium BC, when two fine arrowheads in Pantellerian obsidian occur in a Provençal megalithic tomb (Williams Thorpe, Warren and Courtin 1984).

4. Conclusions Regarding Western Mediterranean Obsidian in the Neolithic

The distribution of obsidian in the west Mediterranean postdates the distribution of Melian obsidian in the Aegean, and seems to occur at much the same time from the four island sources. Current evidence indicates that some of the source islands lacked permanent settlements when obsidian was first acquired from them. The lower sea level affected intervisibility as much in the west Mediterranean as in the Aegean, and reduced navigational distances out of sight of land. Nevertheless, great distances were covered by sea, as in the Early Neolithic by Maltese sailors acquiring Pantellerian obsidian and a range of products including obsidian from Lipari and Sicily, and in the Middle Neolithic by sailors from Sardinia and Corsica directly to the French coast.

Obsidian distribution, particularly in the form of blade cores and blades, coincides with the expansion of village farming along the coasts of the Adriatic (Chapman and Muller 1990) and in southeast Italy (Tinè 1990) in the mid-6th millennium cal BC. At a slightly later date it coincides with the spread of farming to the Po Valley and Liguria (Binder 1989), and in the 5th millennium cal BC it coincides with the definite expansion of farming in southern France (Phillips 1982; Williams Thorpe, Warren and Courtin 1984). Binder and Perlès (1990) link this specialized knapping and raw material situation—with flint, hyalin quartz and many other lithic materials also being transported over long distances—to an alteration in skills from general knapping ability among hunter-gatherers to specialized knappers serving agricultural populations. They emphasize that raw material from distant sources could travel either completely unaltered or in pre-knapped forms: the reduction sequence might only commence after a long sea or overland journey (Binder and Perlès 1990).

The finely pressure-flaked blades and bladelets obtained at distant use-sites like Giribaldi from Liparian obsidian, and at Chasseen sites throughout Provence and Languedoc from Sardinian obsidian, demonstrate high ability in knapping and identical techniques to those used on fine quality flint. Obsidian has been demonstrated as useful for cutting meat and flesh (butchery knives at Filiestru cave, Sardinia), and for cutting plant materials (Piana di Curinga hut, Calabria). Further work under way by Ammerman (pers. comm.) may add more detail about use-actions, but more work is needed on use-materials, along the line of Hurcombe's study.

Eastern Europe

East European obsidian distribution will only be mentioned briefly. Obsidian is found in eastern Europe in the Carpathian mountains, in southeast Czechoslovakia, and in northeast Hungary. Characterization studies using neutron activation analysis have demonstrated the overwhelming importance of the first resource area, Carpathian 1, over the second, Carpathian 2 (Williams Thorpe, Warren and Nandris 1984). There is also the possibility that further sources were used such as Orasu Nou in Rumania and Khust in the U.S.S.R. (Muraru 1987).

Extensive studies have been carried out on both the raw materials and the typology and technology of lithic assemblages in eastern Europe (e.g. Bíró 1985; Bíró 1988; Chapman 1987, for Hungary; and Lech 1987, with references for Poland).

If Binder and Perlès are correct in their belief that obsidian distribution correlates closely with changes in skills in village farming societies, the fact that obsidian sources in eastern Europe are continental rather than on islands should not alter the general thesis. In fact, using a three-stage division of the east European Neolithic period into pioneer, regional interaction and inter-regional interaction phases, Sherratt (1987) demonstrates increasingly wide distribution and use of obsidian from 5000–3500 uncal BC (early 6th millennium to mid-to-late 5th millennium cal BC). Obsidian is only one of many widely distributed raw materials (mainly lithic, but including spondylus shell, pottery, etc.) and Lech (1987: 243) refers to the 'vast multidirectional distribution of raw materials' seen in Danubian settlements in east central Europe. Sherratt and Lech regard lithic raw material distribution as a deliberate strategy, rather than embedded procurement, as does Reid (1977). Reid, using a series of simulation studies, suggested that the Early Neolithic Bukk communities, which controlled the obsidian source, traded obsidian north in what he called 'administered trade'. In contrast Bogucki (1988: 13, 126), discussing the Primary Neolithic (5400–4400 cal BC) in north-central Europe, regards the items exchanged as necessary for daily life, rather than as part of deliberate trade.

During Bogucki's Consequent Neolithic (4400–3300 cal BC), and Sherratt's period of inter-regional distribution, the scale of obsidian distribution reduces. Sherratt (1987: 204) interprets the changes in distribution of obsidian and other lithic materials as 'the mass circulation of everyday items' giving way 'to a concentration on specific exotic materials and types with a more explicit social status'.

General Conclusions

The Mediterranean island sources of obsidian appear to have lacked permanent settlement at the time of initial Neolithic exploitation of the obsidian. Large sea distances were covered to acquire the raw material, proving there must have been adequate ships and navigational capacity. The distribution of different types of obsidian in the west Mediterranean, and the movement of other lithic raw materials in all three of the areas discussed, demonstrate the multistrand movements that took place over centuries and millennia, in particular during the middle phase of the Neolithic. Sea crossings, coastal cabotage, movement along rivers, and crossings of mountain passes and inland plains were all involved.

Obsidian's visibility and easy identification has placed it in a prime position for studying exchange and distribution in the Early Neolithic. Obsidian can cut through fibrous material, including meat, more effectively than flint, and it is also useful for work on plants such as reeds, although fine-grained flints appear to have been used preferentially on raw plant materials in several cases. Although probably a multi-purpose material near to the source, obsidian forms a minute percentage of chipped stone assemblages far from the source (e.g. 0.2% in Ligurian sites: Maggi and Garibaldi 1987), and was probably used for specific purposes. Hypothetically, in its furthest use-zones, where an obsidian core and a few blades are found, in caves and rock-shelters for instance, it may have been used for ritual purposes such as facial or bodily scarring, and during initiation rituals.

Binder and Perlès (1990) have provided a most useful model which explains acquisition of obsidian, amongst other raw materials, from the west Mediterranean to the Indus during the Neolithic. It was an inherently insecure resource system, which broke down at the end of the Neolithic period, though obsidian continued to be used for limited purposes near its sources. Sherratt (1987) and Bloedow (1987) claim that obsidian was not sufficiently attractive to remain among widely-exchanged items during the Bronze Age, since it could not carry sufficient prestige value, and it is significant that the latest distributed obsidian products included heavily retouched, highly visible bifacial arrowheads. Bogucki (1988: 200) provides a contrasting explanation and argues that the exchanges did not break down accidentally, but that unstable social relationships were replaced by more stable ones, with increasing regional integration and more sociopolitical significance. These considerations may apply to the west Mediterranean equally as well as to Central Europe and the eastern Mediterranean/Near East.

This article has attempted to show the status of west Mediterranean obsidian studies in a European perspective, while accepting that obsidian was only one of many raw materials intensively used and exchanged during the Neolithic. Future work will continue to concentrate on sourcing, especially in the west Mediterranean, and on reduction stages and functions. Obsidian assemblages from good contexts provide the key to interpreting changing patterns of distribution and exchange. Research programs on manufacture and function hold great promise for a more complete understanding of obsidian's role in its use-sites.

Acknowledgment

This article is offered to Miriam Balmuth in token of her unremitting work on behalf of Sardinian archaeology during the past two decades. Miriam's energy and initiative led in the mid-1970s to the Ortu Còmidu excavations, on which she invited me to act as excavation director. I learned to admire her wide and enquiring intelligence, her capacity for friendship, and her sense of fun. Miriam's yearly conferences on Sardinian archaeology, and their prompt publication, have spearheaded wider understanding of Sardinian archaeology. This article is offered in affection and respect.

Table 1

Calibration dating of Melian obsidian distribution

	*Uncalibrated**	*Calibrated***
Aceramic Neolithic	6000–5700 bc	early to mid-7th millennium cal BC
Early Neolithic—1st half of Middle Neolithic	5700–5000 bc	mid-7th to early 6th millennium cal BC
Middle Neolithic—2nd half	5000–4700 bc	early 6th millennium cal BC
Late Neolithic	4700–? bc	early/mid-6th millennium cal BC–?
Final Neolithic	?–3000 bc	?–early 4th millennium cal BC

*   (after Perlès and Vaughan 1983: 220)
**   (after Kromer *et al.* 1986, and B.S. Ottaway, pers. comm.)

Table 2
Dating of west Mediterranean obsidian distribution

Cal BC	Lipari	Sardinia	Palmarola	Pantelleria
mid-7th mill.	Uzzo, Sicily?	Corbeddu?	-	Uzzo?
early 6th mill.	Castellaro Vecchio Sicily S. Italy	Filiestru Basi (Corsica) Liguria	-	Sicily
mid-6th mill.	Sicily S. Italy C. Italy Corsica?	Sardinia Corsica Liguria	-	Sicily
early 5th mill.	Sicily S. Italy C. Italy N. Italy Dalmatia Malta	Sardinia Corsica Liguria S. France NE Spain?	C. Italy Dalmatia	Malta N. Africa?
mid/late 5th mill.	Sicily S. Italy C. Italy N. Italy Malta	Sardinia Corsica Liguria S. France	C. Italy N. Italy	Malta N. Africa?
early 4th mill.	Sicily S. Italy C. Italy	Sardinia Corsica N. Italy S. France	C. Italy	?
end 4th mill.	Sicily S. Italy C. Italy	Sardinia Corsica N. Italy S. France	C. Italy?	?
3rd mill.	---- END OF MAIN OBSIDIAN DISTRIBUTION -----			S. France

References

Ammerman, A.J.
1985 *The Acconia Survey: Neolithic Settlement and the Obsidian Trade*. Institute of Archaeology Occasional Publication 10. London: Institute of Archaeology.

Ammerman, A.J., & W. Andrefsky, Jr
1982 Reduction sequences and the exchange of obsidian in neolithic Calabria. In J.E. Ericson and T.K. Earle (eds.), *Contexts for Prehistoric Exchange*, 149-71. London: Academic Press.

Ammerman, A.J., S. Bonardi & M. Carrara
1976 Nota preliminare sugli scavi neolitici a Piana di Curinga (Catanzaro). *Origini* 10: 109-33.

Ammerman, A., A. Cesana, C. Polglase & M. Terrani
1990 Neutron activation analysis of obsidian from two neolithic sites in Italy. *Journal of Archaeological Science* 17(2): 209-20.

Ammerman, A., G. Shaffer & N. Hartmann
1988 A Neolithic household at Piana di Curinga, Italy. *Journal of Field Archaeology* 15(2): 112-41.

Atzeni, E.
1983 Cagliari preistorica (nota preliminare). In *S. Igia. Storia, ambiente fisico e insediamenti umani nel territorio di S. Gilla (Cagliari)*. Pisa: ETS Editrice.

Bagolini, B. & P. Biagi
1990 The radiocarbon chronology of the Neolithic and Copper Age of northern Italy. *Oxford Journal of Archaeology* 9(1): 1-23.

Barfield, L.H.
1981 Patterns of north Italian trade 5000–2000 BC. In G. Barker and R. Hodges (eds.), *Papers in Italian Archaeology II: Archaeology and Italian Society*, 127-51. BAR International Series 102. Oxford: British Archaeological Reports.

Binder, D.
1989 Aspects de la néolithisation dans les aires padane, provençale et ligure. In O. Aurenche and J. Cauvin (eds.), *Néolithisations*, 199-225. BAR International Series 516. Oxford: British Archaeological Reports.

Binder, D. & C. Perlès
1990 Strategies de gestion des outillages lithiques au néolithique. *Paleo* 2: 257-83.

Bíró, K.T.
1985 Neogene rocks as raw materials of the prehistoric stone artifacts in Hungary. In *Neogene Mineral Resources in the Carpathian Basin. Historical Studies on their Utilization. VIIIth RCMNS Congress, Hungary*, 383-96. Budapest: Hungarian Geological Survey.

1988 Distribution of lithic raw materials on prehistoric sites. *Acta Archaeologica Academiae Scientiarum Hungaricae* 40: 251-74.

Bloedow, E.F.
1987 Aspects of ancient trade in the Mediterranean: Obsidian. *Studi Micenei ed Egeo-Anatolici* 26: 59-124.

Bogucki, P.I.
　1988　*Forest Farmers and Stockherders: Early Agriculture and its Consequences in North-Central Europe.* Cambridge: Cambridge University Press.

Brumfield, E.M., & T.K. Earle
　1987　Specialization, exchange, and complex societies: An introduction. In E.M. Brumfield and T.K. Earle (eds.), *Specialization, Exchange, and Complex Societies*, 1-9. Cambridge: Cambridge University Press.

Calvi Rezia, G.
　1980　La ceramica impressa di Pienza (Toscana) e quella di Basi (Corsica). *Rivista di Studi Preistoriche* 35: 323-34.

Camps, G.
　1990　Les relations entre l'Europe et l'Afrique du Nord pendant le Néolithique et le Chalcolithique. *Navigations et Migrations en Méditerrannée. De la Préhistoire à nos Jours*, 137-64. Paris: Editions du Centre National de la Recherche Scientifique.

Chapman, J.
　1987　Technological and stylistic analysis of the Early Neolithic chipped stone assemblages from Mehtelek, Hungary. In *International Conference on Prehistoric Flint Mining and Lithic Raw Material Identification in the Carpathian Basin*. II: 31-52. Budapest: Hungarian Geological Survey.

Chapman, J., & J. Muller
　1990　Early farming in the Mediterranean basin: The Dalmatian evidence. *Antiquity* 64: 127-34.

Chapman, R.
　1990　*Emerging Complexity: The Later Prehistory of South-East Spain, Iberia and the West Mediterranean.* Cambridge: Cambridge University Press.

Cherry, J.F.
　1985　Islands out of the stream. In A.B. Knapp and T. Stech (eds.), *Prehistoric Production and Exchange*, 12-29. UCLA Institute of Archaeology Monograph 25. Los Angeles: Institute of Archaeology, UCLA.

Cherry, J.F., & R. Torrence
　1982　The earliest prehistory of Melos. In C. Renfrew and M. Wagstaff (eds.), *An Island Polity: The Archaeology of Exploitation in Melos*, 24-34. Cambridge: Cambridge University Press.

Costantini, L., M. Piperno & S. Tusa
　1987　La néolithisation de la Sicile occidentale d'après les resultats des fouilles à la grotte de l'Uzzo (Trapani). In J. Guilaine, J. Courtin, J.-L. Roudil and J.-L. Vernet (eds.), *Premieres Communautes Paysannes en Mediterranee Occidentale*, 397-405. Paris: C.N.R.S.

Courtin, J.
　1989　Recherches sur l'obsidienne dans le néolithique du midi de la France. In *Rapport Scientifique ATP Archeologie Metropolitaine. Origine et Diffusion des Differentes Matieres Premieres dans la France Mediterraneene et ses abords au Néolithique (Responsable M. Ricq-de Bouard)*, 26-28. Valbonne: C.N.R.S.

Depalmas, A.
　1989　L'insediamento preistorico di Sorralia (Norbello-Oristano). *Quaderni della Soprintendenza Archeologica per le Provincie di Cagliari ed Oristano* 5: 7-20.

Diamond, G.P., & A.J. Ammerman
　1985　Lithic material. In A.J. Ammerman, *The Acconia Survey: Neolithic Settlement and the Obsidian Trade*, 60-82. Institute of Archaeology Occasional Publication 10. London: Institute of Archaeology.

Dixon, J.E.
　1976　Obsidian characterization studies in the Mediterranean and Near East. In R.E. Taylor (ed.), *Advances in Obsidian Glass Studies. Archaeological and Geochemical Perspectives*, 288-333. Park Ridge, NJ: Noyes Press.

Francaviglia, V., & M. Piperno
　1987　La repartition et la provenance de l'obsidienne archeologique de la grotta dell'Uzzo et de Monte Cofano (Sicile). *Revue d'Archeometrie* 11: 31-39.

Gale, N.H.
　1981　Mediterranean obsidian source characterisation by strontium isotope analysis. *Archaeometry* 23(1): 41-51.

Guilaine, J.
　1987　Expressions culturelles dans le Néolithique ancien mediterraneen. In J. Guilaine, J. Courtin, J.-L. Roudil and J.-L. Vernet (eds.), *Premieres Communautes Paysannes en Mediterranee Occidentale*, 749-52. Paris: C.N.R.S.

Hallam, B.M., S.E. Warren & A.C. Renfrew
　1976　Obsidian in the western Mediterranean: Characterisation by neutron activation analysis and optical emission spectroscopy. *Proceedings of the Prehistoric Society* 42: 85-110.

Hurcombe, L.
　in press　The restricted function of neolithic obsidian tools at Grotta Filiestru, Sardinia. In S. Beyries (ed.), *Les Gestes Retrouves: Traces et Fonctions*. Proceedings of the 1990 Conference, Liege.

Klein Hofmeijer, G., F. Martini, M. Sanges, P. Sondaar & A. Ulzega
　1987–88　La fine del Pleistocene nella Grotta Corbeddu in Sardegna. Fossili umani, aspetti paleontologici e cultura materiale. *Rivista di Scienze Preistoriche* 41(1-2): 29-64.

Kromer, B., M. Rhein, M. Bruns, H. Schon-Fischer, K.O. Muller, M. Stuiver & B. Becker
　1986　Radiocarbon calibration. Data for the 6th to the 8th millennia BC. *Radiocarbon* 28(2B): 954-60.

Lech, J.
　1987　Danubian raw material distribution patterns in eastern central Europe. In G. de G. Sieveking and M. Newcomer (eds.), *The Human Uses of Flint and Chert. Proceedings of the 4th International Flint Symposium, Brighton 1983*, 243-48. Cambridge: Cambridge University Press.

Lewthwaite, J.
　1985　From precocity to involution: The neolithic of Corsica in its west Mediterranean and French contexts. *Oxford Journal of Archaeology* 4(1): 47-68.

Mackey, M., & S.E. Warren
　1983　The identification of obsidian sources in the Monte Arci region of Sardinia. In A. Aspinall and S.E. Warren (eds.), *Proceedings of the 22nd Symposium on Archaeometry, University of Bradford, Bradford, U.K. March 30th—April 3rd 1982*, 420-31.

Maggi, R., & P. Garibaldi
　1987　Reports on the raw materials exploited for chipped stone artefacts by the Mesolithic and Neolithic communities of eastern Liguria. In *International Conference on Prehistoric Flint Mining and Lithic Raw Material Identification in the Carpathian Basin*. II: 91-96. Budapest: Hungarian Geological Survey.

Malone, C.
1985 Pots, prestige and ritual in Neolithic southern Italy. In C. Malone and S. Stoddart (eds.), *Papers in Italian Archaeology IV: The Cambridge Conference*. II. *Prehistory*, 118-51. BAR International Series 244. Oxford: British Archaeological Reports.
1986 Neolithic exchange and ritual networks in the central Mediterranean 5000-3000 BC. *The Neolithic of Europe*. In The World Archaeological Congress. London: Allen and Unwin.

Meulengracht, A., P. McGovern & B. Lawn
1981 University of Pennsylvania radiocarbon dates XXI. *Radiocarbon* 23(2): 227-40.

Michels, J.W., E. Atzeni, I.S.T. Tsong & G.A. Smith
1984 Obsidian hydration dating in Sardinia. In M.S. Balmuth and R.J. Rowland, Jr (eds.), *Studies in Sardinian Archaeology*, 83-113. Ann Arbor: University of Michigan Press.

Milliken, S., & R. Skeates
1989 The Almini Survey: The Mesolithic–Neolithic transition in the Salerno Peninsula (S.E. Italy). *Institute of Archaeology Bulletin, London* 26: 77-98.

Muraru, A.
1987 Preliminary petrographic considerations of the lithic materials used in the Neolithic of Moldavia, Rumania. In *International Conference on Prehistoric Flint Mining and Lithic Raw Material Identification in the Carpathian Basin*, II, 109-22. Budapest: Hungarian Geological Survey.

Perlès, C.
1985 Les industries du Néolithique 'preceramique' de Grece: Nouvelles études, nouvelles interpretations. In J. Kozlowski (ed.), *The Chipped Stone Industries of Early Farming Cultures in Europe*. Cracow.
1990 L'outillage de pierre taillée néolithique en Grece: Approvisionnement et exploitation des materiéres premiéres. *Bulletin de Correspondance Hellenique* 114(1): 1-42.

Perlès, C., & P. Vaughan
1983 Pièces lustrées, travail des plantes et moissons a Franchthi, Grece (Xe—IVe mill. B.C.). In M. Cauvin (ed.), *Traces d'Utilisations sur les Outils Néolithiques du Proche-Orient*, 209-24. Travaux de la Maison de l'Orient 5. Lyon: Maison de l'Orient.

Phillips, P.
1982 *The Middle Neolithic in Southern France. Chasseen Farming and Culture Process*. BAR International Series 142. Oxford: British Archaeological Reports.
1986 Sardinian obsidian and neolithic exchange in the west Mediterranean. In M.S. Balmuth (ed.), *Studies in Sardinian Archaeology, Volume II: Sardinia in the Mediterranean*, 203-209. Ann Arbor: University of Michigan Press.

Reid, P.
1977 An analysis of trade mechanisms in European prehistory. PhD dissertation, SUNY Buffalo. Ann Arbor: University Microfilms.

Renfrew, C.
1984 Trade as action at a distance. In *Approaches to Social Archaeology*, 86-134. Edinburgh: Edinburgh University Press.

Shelford, P., F. Hodson, M. Cosgrove, S. Warren & C. Renfrew
1982 The obsidian trade: The sources and characterisation of Melian obsidian. In C. Renfrew and M. Wagstaff (eds.), *An Island Polity: The Archaeology of Exploitation in Melos*, 182-92. Cambridge: Cambridge University Press.

Sherratt, A.
1987 Neolithic exchange systems in central Europe 5000–3000 BC. In G. de G. Sieveking and M. Newcomer (eds.), *The Human Uses of Flint and Chert. Proceedings of the 4th International Flint Symposium, Brighton 1983*, 193-204. Cambridge: Cambridge University Press.

Tanda, G.
1982 Il neolitico antico della Sardegna. In *Le Néolithique Ancien Mediterranéen. Archeologie en Languedoc*, 333-37. Sète: Fédération Archéologique de l'Hérault.

Tinè, V.
1990 La valle del Lao, la Calabria e l'ossidiana nel Neolitico. *Individuazione et Catalogazione di Beni Archeologici in Calabria. Finitalia Servizi, Regione Calabria*.

Torrence, R.
1979 A technological approach to Cycladic blade industries. In J.L. Davis and J.F. Cherry (eds.), *Papers in Cycladic Prehistory*, 66-86. UCLA Institute of Archaeology Monograph 14. Los Angeles: Institute of Archaeology, UCLA.
1986 *Production and Exchange of Stone Tools: Prehistoric Obsidian in the Aegean*. Cambridge: Cambridge University Press.

Trump, D.
1983 La Grotta Filiestru a Bonu Ighinu, Mara (SS). *Quaderni* 13. Sassari: Dessi.

Williams Thorpe, O., S.E. Warren & L.H. Barfield
1979 The distribution and sources of archaeological obsidian from Northern Italy. *Preistoria Alpina* 15: 73-92.

Williams Thorpe, O., S.E. Warren & J. Courtin
1984 The distribution and sources of archaeological obsidian from Southern France. *Journal of Archaeological Science* 11: 135-46.

Williams Thorpe, O., S.E. Warren & J. Nandris
1984 The distribution and provenance of archaeological obsidian in Central and Eastern Europe. *Journal of Archaeological Science* 11: 183-212.

Riassunto

La distribuzione d'ossidiana da fonti del Mediterraneo occidentale è da considerare come parte di un più ampio fenomeno Neolitico europeo. L'Autrice, usando dati comparativi dall'Egeo e dall'area dei Carpazi in Cecoslovacchia ed in Ungheria, esamina tre aspetti degli studi sull'ossidiana ed i loro contributi per una migliore comprensione dell'uso dell'ossidiana nella preistoria: (1) cambiamenti cronologici nell'uso dell'ossidiana; (2) analisi di complessi litici (tecno-tipologico e 'use-wear'); e (3) meccanismi di acquisizione e distribuzione dell'ossidiana.

Nell'Egeo le cave di Sta Nychia e Demengaki sull'isola di Melos hanno fornito la maggior parte dell'ossidiana utilizzata nelle isole Cicladi e nella Grecia. Melos è stata colonizzata permanente solo nel tardo neolitico (V mill. a.C.), ma l'ossidiana di

Melos ha raggiunto la Grotta di Franchthi (nella Grecia meridionale) numerosi millenni prima. L'analisi di nuclei d'ossidiana, di utensili e di schegge di lavorazione sia dalle cave che dai siti archeologici suggerisce che:

1. nel Neolitico antico e medio, commercianti specializzati hanno distribuito blocchi non lavorati da Melos. Giunti a destinazione, i blocchi sono stati ridotti attraverso un processo di sfaldatura a pressione, e gli utensili sono stati usati per tagliare piante per paglia e per ceste.
2. durante il Neolitico recente e finale, l'ossidiana è stata sfaldata usando una varietà di tecniche, producendo diversi complessi litici. L'aumento in tipi funzionali è parallelo ad un cambiamento di modelli d'insediamento (occupazione permanente delle isole) e ad un cambiamento della attività di sussistenza (pesca, agricoltura).
3. durante l'Età del Bronzo, nonostante l'aumento dell'uso dei metalli, lo sfruttamento delle cave di Melos si è intensificato. Nuclei 'pre-formati' sono stati prodotti vicino alle cave e poi esportati verso insediamenti dove le lamine di ossidiana sono state sfaldate. Si è anche iniziato ad usare ossidiana per specchi ed altri oggetti pregiati.

Nel Mediterraneo occidentale, l'ossidiana è stata distribuita per la prima volta all'inizio del sesto millennio BC, in siti come la Grotta dell'Uzzo (Sicilia), Piana di Curinga (Calabria) e Basi (Corsica). A partire dal quinto millennio BC, era possibile trovare dell'ossidiana proveniente da Lipari e dalla Sardegna nell'Italia settentrionale e nella Francia meridionale. L'ossidiana di Palmarola è stata distribuita principalmente nell'Italia centrale; l'ossidiana di Pantelleria è stata usata a Malta e nell'Africa settentrionale. Durante il quarto millennio BC, il 'mercato' dell'Italia settentrionale e della Francia meridionale è dominato dall'ossidiana sarda, ma nel terzo millennio BC l'uso dell'ossidiana inizia a declinare rapidamente.

Nel Mediterraneo occidentale, l'uso di diversi metodi tecno-tipologici, la mancanza di studi di cave e officine, ed alcuni problemi nella datazione e individuazione delle fonti, hanno limitato l'interpretazione dei dati riguardanti la distribuzione d'ossidiana (ma cfr. Tykot, in questo stesso volume). Ricerche in corso effettuate da Ammerman, Binder, Hurcombe (in questo stesso volume) e da altri sono indirizzate allo stesso problema. Sembra che ossidiana sarda non lavorata sia stata esportata in Sardegna e nell'Italia settentrionale, e che nuclei d'ossidiana parzialmente sbozzati e provenienti da Lipari siano stati sfaldati e distribuiti in Calabria. Presso Gaione, nell'Italia settentrionale, l'unica ossidiana proveniente da Lipari è presente nella forma di lamine, mentre l'ossidiana sarda, e quella di Palmarola appaiono nelle forme di utensili, nuclei e di detriti. Alcune indicazioni mostrano che l'uso d'ossidiana sarda in Sardegna varia considerabilmente, mentre variazioni geografiche e cronologiche all'esterno della Sardegna potrebbero essere state causate da una parallela espansione di villaggi agricoli.

L'ossidiana proveniente dai Carpazi nella Cecoslovacchia meridionale e nell'Ungheria nord-orientale è stata distribuita per la prima volta all'inizio del sesto millennio BC, insieme a conchiglie, ceramiche e altri materie prime litiche. La distribuzione dell'ossidiana in questa regione è stata vista da alcuni come il risultato di una strategia di acquisizione deliberata anziché il risultato di una acquisizione avvenuta nel corso di altre attività di scambio. Nell'Europa orientale la distribuzione dell'ossidiana è declinata a partire dal quarto millennio BC, sostituita da materiali esotici più prestigiosi.

Come nell'Egeo, le fonti del Mediterraneo occidentale sono state sfruttate prima che esistessero insediamenti permanenti, ciò implica che in quel periodo esistevano già navi adeguate e tecniche di navigazione. È generalmente accettata l'ipotesi secondo la quale 'specialisti' hanno acquisito e sfaldato l'ossidiana, ma non ci sono abbastanza testimonianze che mostrino l'esistenza di un controllo dell'accesso alle fonti. In tutte e tre le regioni analizzate, l'ossidiana è stata distribuita almeno centinaia di chilometri dalla sua fonte, attraverso corsi d'acqua, lungo le coste, su fiumi, e attraverso passi di montagna. L'esistenza di una piccola percentuale d'ossidiana presso siti così distanti suggerisce che l'ossidiana veniva usata per particolari funzioni, fra cui attività rituali. Ulteriori ricerche soprattutto nell'area dell'analisi 'use-wear' offrirà una maggiore conoscenza del ruolo che questa importante risorsa materiale ha avuto nel Mediterraneo durante il neolitico.

New Contributions to the Study of the Function of Sardinian Obsidian Artifacts

Linda Hurcombe

Obsidian Use-Wear Analysis

Since the work of Semenov (1964) and Keeley (1980) it has been possible, though not inevitably so, to employ the technique of wear analysis to understand what flint tools were used for. As the function of a tool, be it social or utiliarian, is its ultimate reason for existing, this has been a key development for the study of stone tools in this century. This paper outlines the preliminary results from use-wear analysis of Sardinian obsidian artifacts. The method is similar to that used on flint, and a broad overview of the technique is presented before two case studies are explored. In each case, a group of artifacts seem to have a common function and so can be considered functional types. For both studies a variety of other materials are available to do the task and so the relationship between raw material, form and function is also considered.

All use-wear analysis employs experimental pieces used on a variety of materials as the framework for establishing the relationship between observed wear features and the function which caused them. Function can be seen as a combination of use-action, use-material and use-time. For archaeological material we try to identify use-material as specifically as possible, but this is usually more difficult than identifying the use-action. The latter is implied by the direction and location of striations, polish and edge damage, whereas the identification of the use-material uses all of this information plus changes in surface texture—all at a microscopic level. The technique is thus first time-consuming and skilled, relying on macro- and microscopic observations of surface change, and secondly will vary slightly according to the original surface texture of different lithic materials. For this reason the technique of obsidian microwear analysis differs from flint microwear analysis in detail but not in principle. By experimental work Vaughan (1981; 1985) showed that obsidian wear occurs and can be used to specify some worked materials.

More recently, my own work (Hurcombe 1992) has concentrated on obsidian from Sardinia and the refinement of the microwear technique to obsidian. The publication documents the results of investigations into the technique via an experimental programme varying use-actions and materials for a series of set times. This provides the framework for interpretation by standard recording procedures and links between condition variations and wear formation. For each used piece some 18 variables were recorded, grouped under polish (surface smoothing at 250× magnification), striations (linear arrangements of wear), attrition (surface roughening at 250× magnification), and residues (visually distinct at 250× magnification); each variable had coded descriptions of number, severity, extent, etc. (Table 1). Using this recording system and an explicit series of steps outlined elsewhere (Hurcombe 1992), some use-actions and materials could be identified. The material could be specified as *Gramineae*, plants (for which there were two subdivisions), hide, wood, antler/bone, flesh, softer materials and resilient materials. Not every tool, however, could have its function identified to a specific material in this way. Generally, weak use-actions, low use-times, and soft use-materials all cause less wear and so insufficient wear features may have developed to specify the worked material. For archaeological tools there are additional factors from post-depositional processes. These were experimented with and have to be taken into account before interpreting the wear traces on ancient artifacts.

From this brief outline the key aspects of the technique can be appreciated. It is neither easy nor quick, and the technique neither gives 100% accuracy nor inevitable results (Hurcombe 1988). The full description of the technique is given elsewhere (Hurcombe 1991) but the starting point is always the natural surface of the obsidian and changes to this surface (Fig. 1). Obsidian does not have polishes in the sense of bright surface areas against a grey background, but if

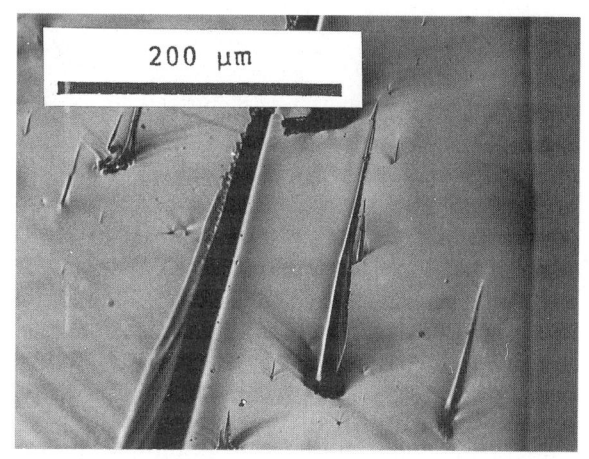

Fig. 1 Freshly flaked obsidian surface showing crystalline irregularities with stress fissures and ripple marks arising from them (original magnification 250×).

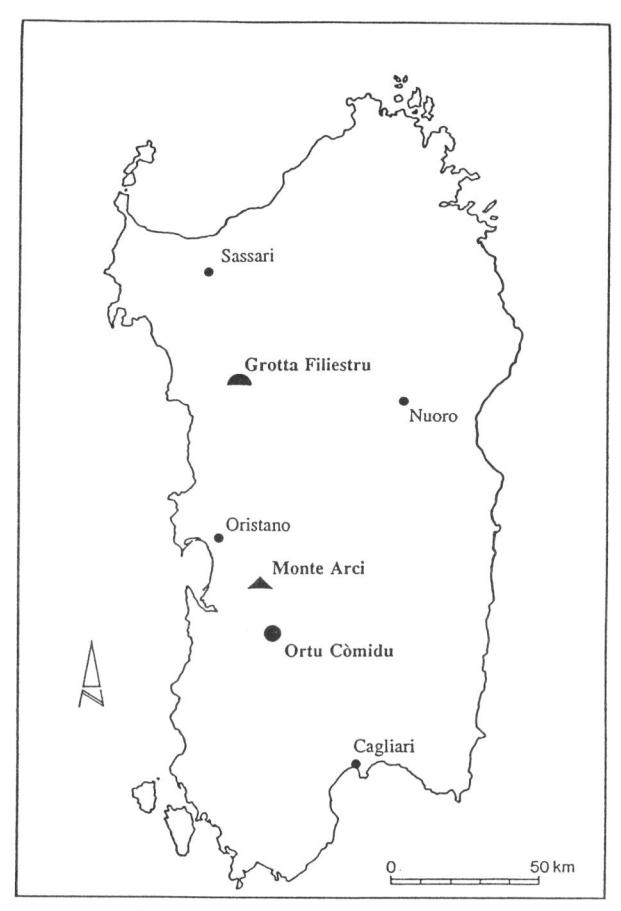

Fig. 2 Map of sites mentioned in the text.

polish is defined as smoothing, then it is a feature of wear on obsidian. Conversely, obsidian is better than flint for observing residues which show up clearly against the bright background. There is also evidence that residues from the use-material can survive in archaeological contexts and endure laboratory cleaning techniques (Anderson 1980; Mansur-Franchomme 1983; Hurcombe 1985; Hurcombe 1986a; Hurcombe 1986b). Hence, residue recognition plays an enhanced role in obsidian functional analysis. The two case studies presented in this paper both have residues interpreted as related to their original use.

Microwear research was really initiated by Keeley (1980; see also Semenov 1964) just over ten years ago. As such it is a very young technique which has not yet achieved its full potential. This is even more the case with obsidian. The two examples illustrated here should be seen as demonstrating the potential of this kind of work and very much as a preliminary survey for what could be achieved. The common theme is the concept of a functional type. Artifacts with a recognizably similar shape have been examined and shown to have very similar uses. The first example is from the Neolithic site of Grotta Filiestru (Mara-SS) where a group of broad and long flakes were used as knives. The second is from the Nuragic site of Ortu Còmidu (Sardara) where a group of lunate artifacts are interpreted as plant working tools (Fig. 2).

In each case full details of the wear and residue analysis and the reasoning behind the interpretations are available elsewhere (for Grotta Filiestru: Phillips and Hurcombe 1990; Hurcombe in press; for Ortu Còmidu: Hurcombe 1986a; Hurcombe 1986b; Hurcombe 1992: chap. 7); an overview is given here. In both cases raw materials other than obsidian were available and the shape, size and raw material chosen to conduct the task were cultural choices. For each case study there is a brief introduction to the site at which the artifacts were found, a discussion of the wear and residue analysis, and of the cultural choices that were made.

The Knives from Grotta Filiestru

The site is a limestone cave which was thought to be used as a residential base for at least part of its prehistoric occupation (Trump 1983). The stratigraphy spans the Early Neolithic 4760–75 uncal BC to the Chalcolithic Ozieri level. Levels 6 (Filiestru Level c. 4000 uncal BC) and 5 (Bonu Ighinu Level c. 3730 uncal BC) had sizeable lithic assemblages and were chosen for further study. A variety of lithic materials were employed, e.g., flint, obsidian and rhyolite. The flint assemblage included long blades and the obsidian assemblage contained some blades and arrowheads. Hence the technology and the objects produced differed slightly according to the lithic raw material. Of the lithic types found at the site, obsidian is the most brittle, produces the sharpest flake edges, and has the best conchoidal fracture properties. Moreover, the size of the raw material nodules available from the Conca Cannas and Perdas Urias sources on Monte Arci (12 cm in length is not uncommon) would not restrict the production of longer artifacts if the knapper were reasonably skilled. Obsidian is a good raw material for the knapping of precise shapes because it is predictable and easily flaked, and pressure-flakes well. Its use for producing the arrowheads and small blades is, therefore, not surprising. Instead, it demonstrates that the use of lithic materials was well suited to the tasks performed given the lithic variety available.

Given these properties of obsidian, the expected range of tasks the obsidian could perform as well as or better than the flint or rhyolite include the following: cutting meat, fish and hide where its sharp edge gives longevity and precision; reaping activities; working soft plant materials; working finer parts of woody plants, wood, bark and cork. The other lithic materials would be better for heavier tasks requiring more robust edges, for example, working wood, bone and antler. Furthermore, an unmodified obsidian edge is more effective for the slicing of flesh and hide, whereas retouch could increase the robustness of the working edge. All of the above comments stem from personal observation while knapping and using stone tools. There is, of course, no need for lithic materials to be used economically unless there is some pressure on the availability of raw materials, time, or at a more social and personal level the skill and quality of stone tool production or use. Bearing these factors in mind, the results of the functional analysis of the obsidian were in some ways not surprising.

Results

The study indicates that obsidian tools are strongly associated with flesh- and hide-related activities; a new tool category was identified as a knife with particular use for butchery; and some of the pieces were neither formal tool types nor retouched. These results are discussed in detail below, but for the total microwear sample the interpretations of use-material were dominated by the flesh and hide categories, representing 42.7% of the assemblage (Hurcombe in press).

The results identified a new tool type: a group of broad long flakes (Fig. 3) used for cutting. Where the use-material can be specified these show flesh (both fish and animal flesh are included in this category), butchery and hide traces (Figs. 4-5). It is tempting to call them butchery knives, but their use on dry hide and possibly other materials makes this slightly inaccurate (Table 2). Rather, they could be seen as 'knives' but used especially for carcass processing. The length (4.5-7.0 cm) and width (2-4 cm) make these flakes easy to hold in the hand. The most clearly recognizable examples of this group come from the later Level 5. The examples from Level 6 use more irregular shapes and in one case part of the dorsal surface is still cortex. One tool (D5+5.2) appears to be retouched at its proximal end to facilitate hafting, but in general the edge scars are use-related rather than deliberate retouch. Some have two usable sides increasing the amount of time the tools could have been used. Experimental work (Hurcombe 1992: 45, table 11) shows that wear traces are not distinct for cutting meat until after almost an hour of use, and a tool used for three hours was still cutting well. Thus, the artifacts in this knife class represent a considerable period of use. Their longevity as butchery tools would depend upon how the carcasses were cut up. For example, cutting meat into a number of shares or into small pieces for drying and storage would both result in higher processing time per carcass than simply removing skin, viscera, limb extremities and head.

The residues represented on the artifacts in Fig. 3 are interpreted to indicate holding arrangements as well as use and are worth discussing further. During experimental work sub-angular flat residues were noticed (Hurcombe 1992: 43-44) and interpreted as residues from skin (Fig. 6). These skin residues had a ridged surface texture and sometimes appeared to be folded. They were most evident on tools used to work hide, fish and animal flesh, and occurred in relation to the used edge but were also present from other activities where tools were hand-held. The distribution of this same residue type (Fig. 7) on the Filiestru material is schematically indicated by stippling in Fig. 3. There are clear indications of two distribution patterns on some tools. One relates to the used edge of the tool (e.g. the dorsal surface of D6+1.11), and hence is assumed to originate from the use-material; the other is on bulbar areas (e.g. D5+3.5) or mid-dorsal ridges and has been interpreted as residues from the hands which held the tools. Some further study of these via immunological and histological techniques are being investigated. Here, it is sufficient to present the residues and their distribution and to state that natural processes in the soil are unlikely to provide this type of patterned distribution nor are they similar in shape or texture to residues on experimental

86 *Sardinia in the Mediterranean*

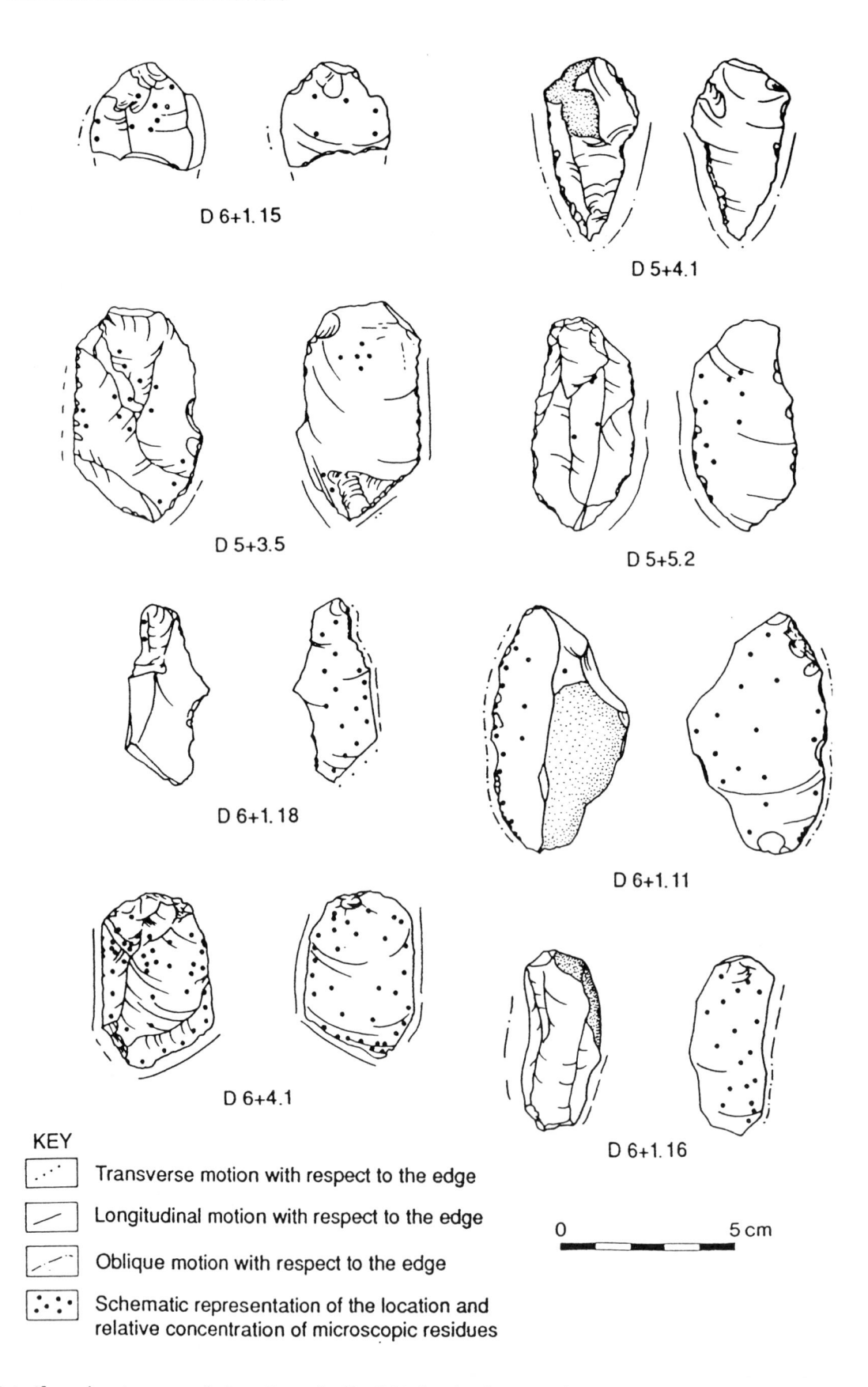

D 6+1.15

D 5+4.1

D 5+3.5

D 5+5.2

D 6+1.18

D 6+1.11

D 6+4.1

D 6+1.16

KEY

..·	Transverse motion with respect to the edge
/	Longitudinal motion with respect to the edge
⁄	Oblique motion with respect to the edge
:·:·	Schematic representation of the location and relative concentration of microscopic residues

0   5 cm

Fig. 3 Artifacts showing use as knives. From the Neolithic levels of Grotta Filiestru.

artifacts which have lain in a variety of contexts, including exposed to the elements, in agricultural soil, and in undisturbed soils. The interpretation of these residues as skin components best fits a variety of experimental data including the extraction from suede of similar residues (Hurcombe 1992: 45) (Fig. 8). Thus the residues documented here potentially offer animal and human remains from Neolithic Sardinia. A preliminary attempt to extract DNA has proved unsuccessful so far. It is not known whether the preservation of such residues is exceptional due to the site lying within a cave, but use-related residues have survived rigorous cleaning techniques on experimental tools and have been recorded on archaeological pieces from an open-air Bronze Age site in Sardinia (Hurcombe 1986a; 1992: chs. 4, 7). On present evidence it seems likely that the Filiestru residues may not be the result of exceptional preservation conditions.

Finally, it should be stressed that the use-wear analysis of material from Grotta Filiestru showed that unretouched edges were being used, and that the knives and the remainder of the obsidian component of the site lithic assemblage were strongly associated with the processing of flesh and animal carcasses. If these features can be demonstrated for a neolithic assemblage located only 75 km from the source of the obsidian, what more specific functional role might obsidian play further away from the source? As techniques improve, the residues on the Filiestru obsidian tools may allow the types of animal processed with obsidian to be determined, and may even document the genetic affiliations of both the Neolithic animals present in Sardinia and the people using the tools.

Fig. 4 Slight edge damage, very fine striations and faint polish on the edge of tool D6+1.11 (original magnification 250×).

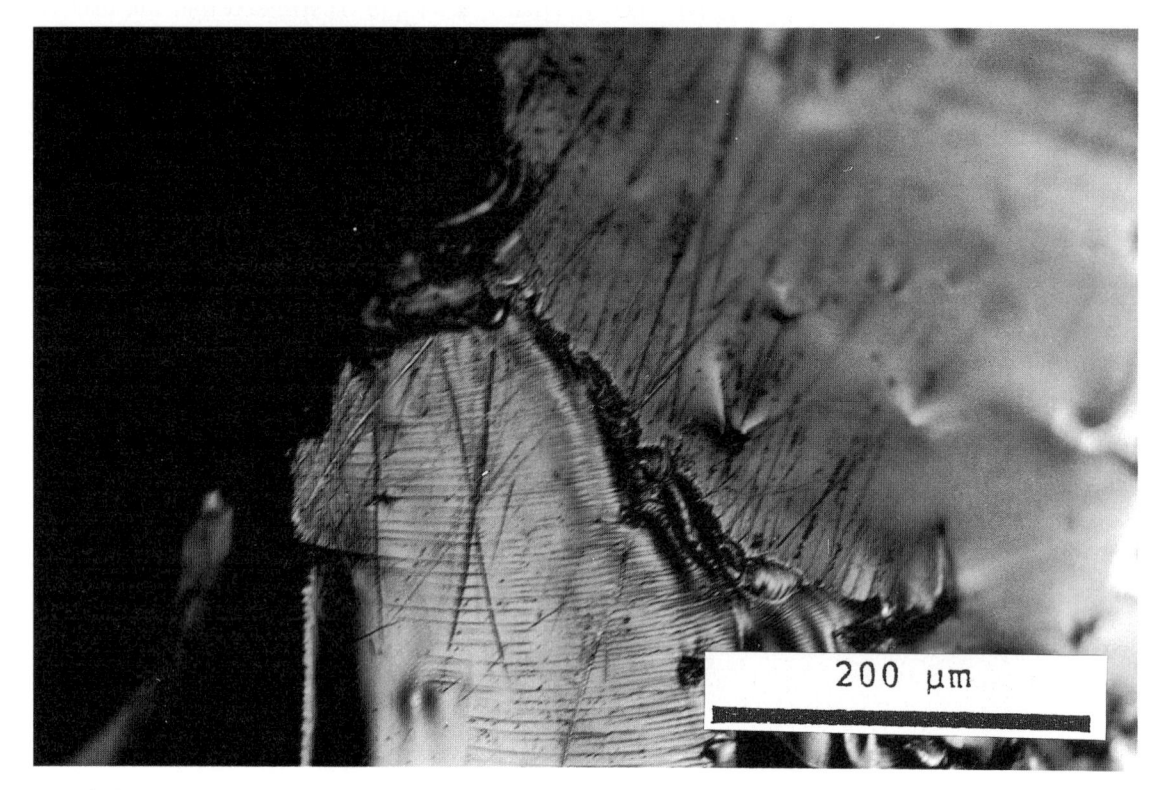

Fig. 5 Slight edge damage, very fine striations and polish on an experimental tool used to cut fish flesh (original magnification 250×).

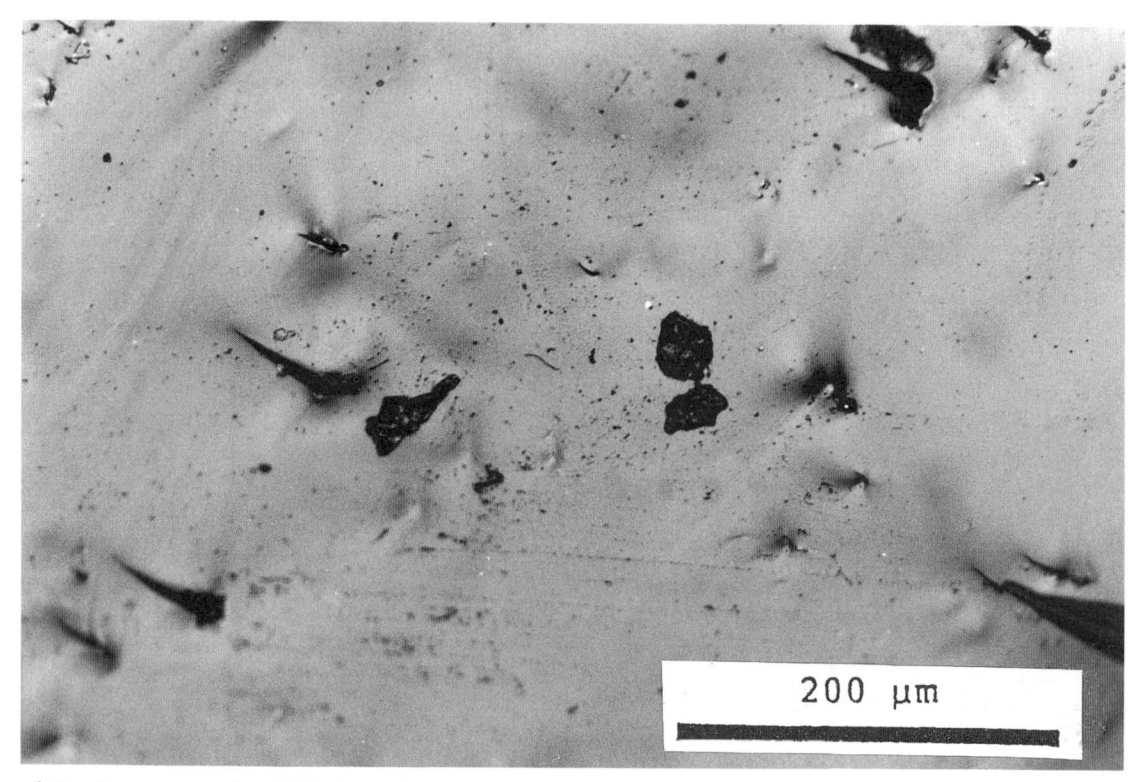

Fig. 6 Similar sub-angular, folded residues on the surface of an experimental tool used to scrape damp hide (original magnification 250×).

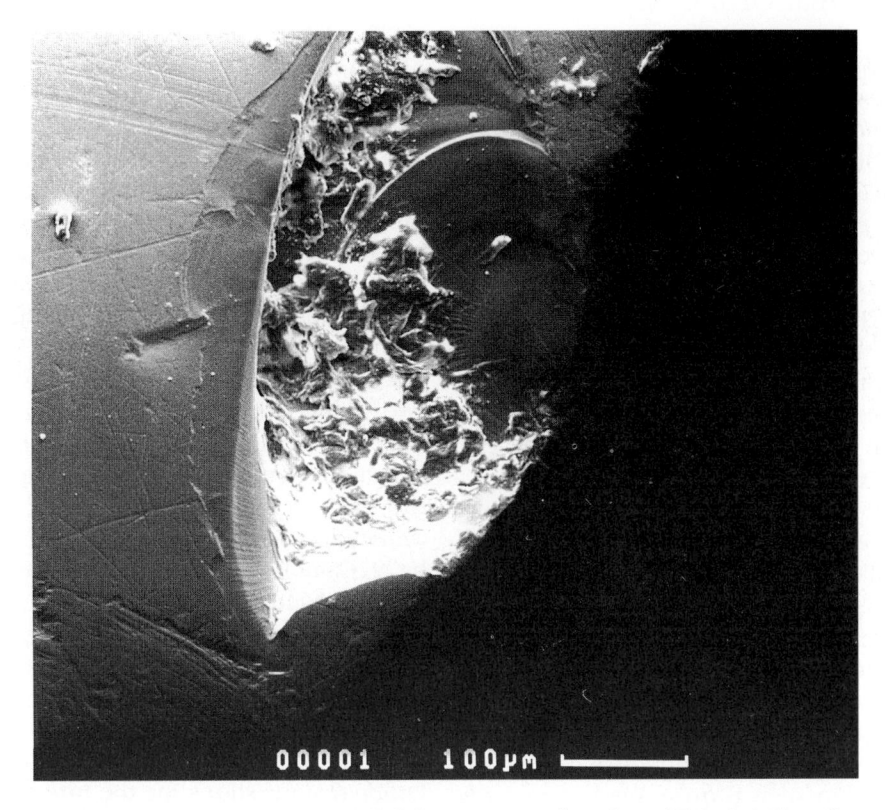

Fig. 7 Residues trapped in a small flake scar near the edge of D5+3.5. Very fine striations and surface smoothing are visible on the left of the photograph (scanning electron photomicrograph, scale bar on photo).

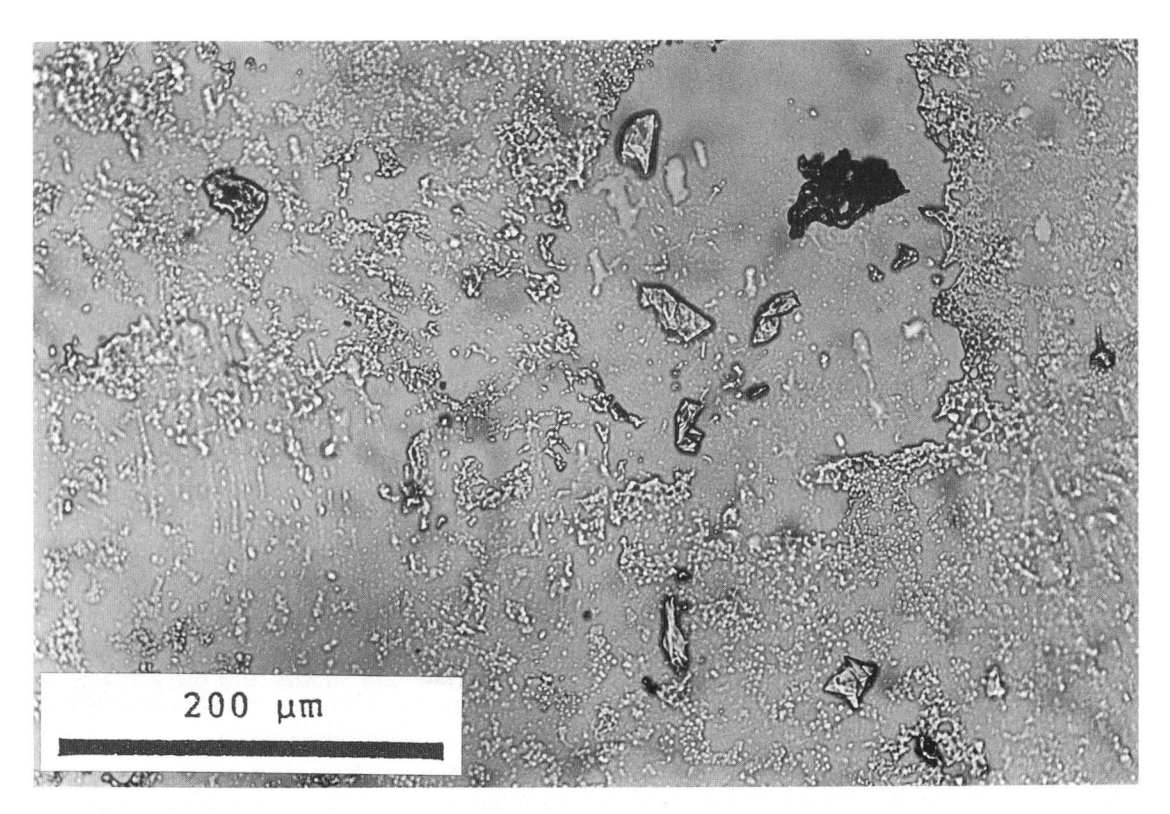

Fig. 8 Similar residues extracted from commercial suede boiled in distilled water, with the liquid allowed to evaporate on a glass slide (original magnification 250×).

The Lunates from Ortu Còmidu

Bronze Age stone tools have rarely been the subject of functional studies, although they are some of the most interesting artifacts from a functional point of view. There are various naturally occurring raw materials available for modification into tools to perform tasks. In Bronze Age contexts there is another material, metal, from which tools may be made. It is interesting, therefore, to understand what functions continued to be performed with stone tools when there was the option of using metal. Obviously, metal may be more precious, and has very different qualities from stone; it is exactly such influences in tool production that need to be understood.

The site of Ortu Còmidu (Sardara-CA) has Bronze Age deposits which contain some obsidian artifacts (Balmuth 1986). The retouched obsidian finds consisted only of blades and lunate (crescent-shaped) artifacts, of which the latter were most numerous. Blades may be used for a variety of cutting tasks and are a well-known tool type, but the lunate category is much more enigmatic. Despite an extensive literature search, no other reference to such Bronze Age lunate tools was found. Since the lunate tools were the most numerous of retouched tool types from Ortu Còmidu, even though they were apparently an unrecognized or unique tool class, their function is potentially interesting.

The lunates were examined for wear traces with three goals: (1) to see if artifacts which have the same shape were all used for the same task; (2) to discover what that task was; and (3) to elucidate why that particular task was undertaken. The relevance of these goals can only be perceived by understanding the archaeological background of their occurrence.

Ortu Còmidu was excavated by Balmuth with the collaboration of Phillips (Balmuth 1986). The site lies near the village of Sardara, 49 km NNW of Cagliari in the fertile Campidano plain (Fig. 2). At one stage there was a central tower, courtyard, plus at least three subsidiary towers. Radiocarbon dates indicate a timespan between 1500–1000 BC. Thus, there are the remains of a sequence of Bronze Age buildings with fairly complex structures.

The excavated finds include bronze, ceramic and stone artifacts. There were 214 obsidian pieces and 21 other stone artifacts (Phillips 1986). Most of the obsidian finds are extremely small flakes. These flakes are short and thick at the bulbar end with a round distal edge. There are two formal categories of obsidian tools: lunates (14) and blades (6). Phillips suggests that the flakes would have been a good 'preform' for the lunate tools. The obsidian artifacts were considered to form part of the Nuragic phase of occupation because on occasion they were found *in situ* with Nuragic pottery. The co-existence of stone and bronze artifacts on site is concluded. At Ortu Còmidu the main obsidian artifact type is the lunate, and its importance is enhanced if the flakes are seen as part of the production of the lunate tools. The lunates broadly conform to a semi-circular acute edge opposite a straight backed edge: this plan shape gives them their name (Fig. 9). They are made 'on squat flakes with the bulbar end reduced by steep backing retouch' (Phillips 1986). It should be noted that artifacts described as lunates because of this plan shape usually have the backed edge as the crescent form and the acute edge as the straight side (e.g. Clark 1980: 29, fig. 9; Campbell 1977: 3). These microlithic lunates are regarded as part of a range of microlithic types which are considered as components of composite, hafted tools (Clark 1980). Due to the reversed position of the acute and backed edge on the Ortu Còmidu lunates, it was not automatically assumed that they were composite tools. Original suggestions for the function of the Ortu Còmidu lunates were based on the very small size of the acute edge (average length 1.5 cm), and included shaving and surgery as possibilities (Phillips 1986).

Results

Before discussing the details of the results, it should be made clear that the microwear study revealed a major surprise. It had been assumed that the working edge was the acute, semi-circular one: the analysis showed that, while there were some instances of use-wear on this edge, in every case the backed straight edge had by far the greatest amount of wear. This inevitably led to the re-thinking of the proposed functions of shaving and surgery. Therefore, even a cursory assessment of function via wear analysis would have led to a fundamental alteration of the range of functions for this class of stone tools, because it would show that a small, straight scraping edge was the main working unit for the lunates.

The microscopic wear traces on individual lunates were very similar and the artifacts could be regarded as all having been utilized for the same purpose (Table 3). In every case the backed edge had the most polish, but the acute edge did have a similar polish to a lesser degree.

The use-action was implied by the distribution of wear traces in general and the orientation of

LUNATE 1, (3174)

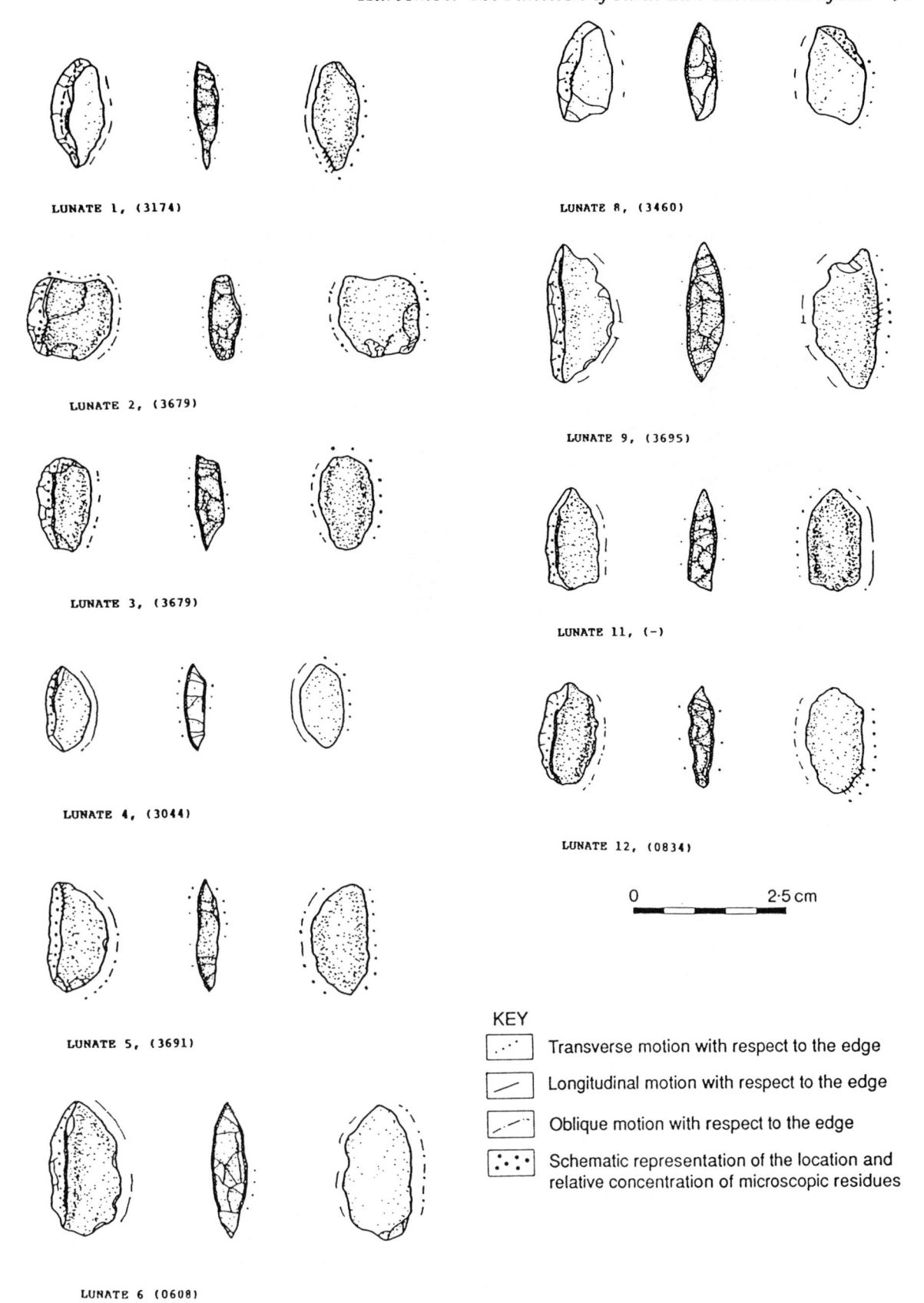

LUNATE 2, (3679)

LUNATE 3, (3679)

LUNATE 4, (3044)

LUNATE 5, (3691)

LUNATE 6 (0608)

LUNATE 8, (3460)

LUNATE 9, (3695)

LUNATE 11, (-)

LUNATE 12, (0834)

0   2·5 cm

KEY

- Transverse motion with respect to the edge
- Longitudinal motion with respect to the edge
- Oblique motion with respect to the edge
- Schematic representation of the location and relative concentration of microscopic residues

Fig. 9 Lunate artifacts from Nuraghe Ortu Còmidu.

the striae. The striations and wear on the backed edge suggested a very shallow scraping action. The angle of the bevel present on some lunates gave the working angle as c. 45-15° for the backed edge. The evidence for the use-action on the acute edge could have resulted from either a slicing/slitting action or slightly diagonal scraping but the length of the striations (up to 2 mm) makes the former action more likely.

Comparison with experimental results suggests the wear on the backed edges represents a minimum of 30 minutes use, but 60+ minutes is more likely. Since each piece has two backed edges as well as the acute edge, the lunates could have over an hour of use per tool and possibly three hours or more.

It is evident from Table 3 that the entire lunate group examined can reasonably be assumed to have worked plants (compare Figs. 10 and 11).

Fig. 10 Polish, striations and edge rounding, plus rod residues on Lunate 3 (original magnification 250×).

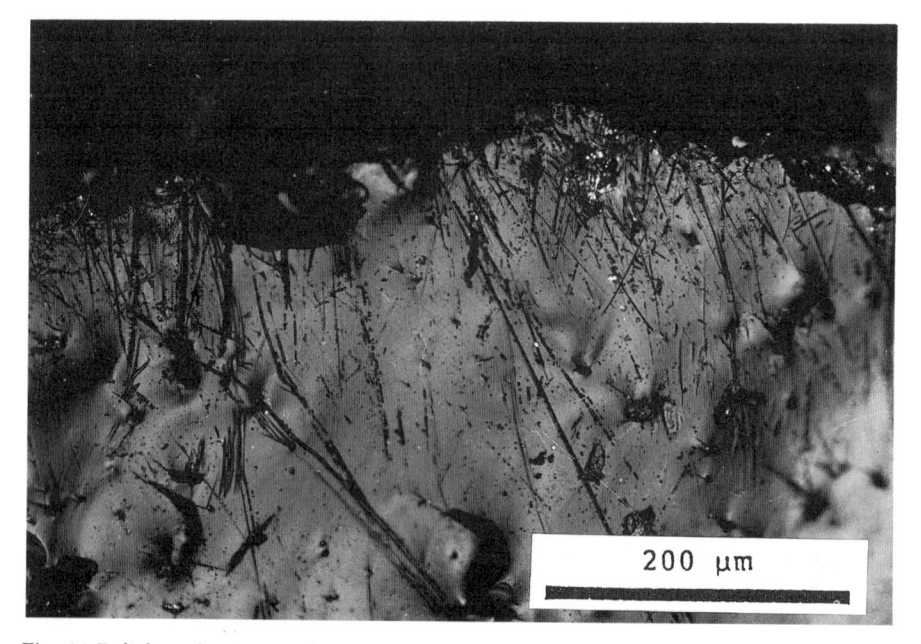

Fig. 11 Polish and striations from an experimental tool used to scrape *Juncus* (original magnification 250×).

The variation in attrition may be due to dirt on hands, or on the plants as mud or dust particles. There may be some variation in the actual plants being worked, as some of the tools have similar wear values to the wood-working experimental tools (Lunates 4, 5, 10 and 12). Some of the wear on the lunates was similar to that obtained from working soaked reeds. In general, the results suggest that reeds of some kind may be the use-material although the state of the use-material may be varied. The residues provided further evidence as they are best explained as being use-related. For example, the distribution of the residues is related to the used tool areas as can be seen in Figs. 9 and 10. There are various types of residue and all could originate from plant-working. The fragmentary nature of the rounded rod shapes seen in Fig. 10 are common on the tools and suggest that if they originate from plants, the activity performed by the tool results in the breaking apart of plant tissues. The full arguments and descriptions of these residues have been presented elsewhere (Hurcombe 1986a; 1986b).

The combined information obtained from the wear traces and residues gives a 'function' interpretation of scraping reed-like plants, probably involving the destruction and breakdown of some tissue. This interpretation is really only the primary analysis; what is needed is the purpose of the plant scraping. To achieve this level of interpretation, factors other than the wear traces are important, in particular, the size and shape of the tools plus ethnographic data reflecting practical details of similar processes.

The lunates could have been hafted to give a larger working edge, or to allow more force to be directed onto the tools. However, evidence of hafting was not apparent. Whatever plant was scraped, the residues from scraping are distributed over the whole tool. There is also the wear on the acute edge to account for, if the tools were hafted. If both acute and backed edges were designed to be used, as implied by the microwear evidence, holding the tool in the hand allows the edges to be interchanged very easily. This might have been an advantage in completing a task where both the backed and acute edge each had a role to play in relatively quick succession.

Even if the backed edges of the lunates mask some resharpening they were still small artifacts. Their small size, therefore, could be related to their function. The smallness may be due to a need for delicacy or precision in the task they performed. It may also imply that either the material being scraped was narrower in width than the backed edge, or that the space which was being scraped out was small. For this reason it has been assumed here that the small lunate scraping edge (21 mm max.) implies an even smaller size for whatever plant was being scraped. If the action of scraping out a stiff plant is considered, it is immediately apparent that a rounded scraping edge would be much easier to work with than a straight one. If the plant was tough but supple the straight scraping edge might flatten the plant slightly.

Three possible tasks suggested by ethnographic data may be evaluated considering the size and shape of the lunates plus the wear traces and residues:

1. Scraping plants to break down the fibers can involve softening the plant without necessarily breaking it. If the residues signify fragmented tissue, then this function is less likely because little fragmentation of plant tissue would be expected. The lunates could have been used for breaking each plant's fibers individually, but a larger tool could be used for this purpose with greater ease. Moreover, it might be possible to shred a bundle of plants at one time, in which case a lunate would be too small.

2. Slitting reeds and scraping out the pith would involve breaking into the internal plant structure and would require either a separate tool to slit the reed, or the use of the acute edge to perform this task. The shape of the lunates may have been convenient for performing a two-part task. The acute edge could have been used to slit the reed stem open, then the backed edge could be used to scrape the pith out of the narrow stems (c. 10 mm wide on *Juncus* sp. that grow in Britain). A further scrape could have increased the suppleness of the material by breaking some of the stiffer plant fibers. This may also have flattened the reed out slightly.

3. Scraping plants to separate the fibers from the fleshier plant parts would involve severe disruption of some soft plant tissues and might be better accomplished after a retting process. The latter might mean partial disintegration of some plant tissues would have occurred, rupturing the tissues along lines of weakness. Scraping the soft tissue from plant fibers could have been performed reed by reed with a lunate, but there is no reason why several plants could not be processed together if all that was required was a bundle of long fibers with the fleshy parts removed. In such a case a larger tool might be more efficient.

Although all three functions remain possible, on the basis of the residue hypotheses, the second and third tasks are more likely than the first. In addition, the size and shape of the backed edge make the second task easy to perform with a lunate with the extra use of the acute edge to split the reed. Experimental work replicating this task has shown the feasibility of this hypothesis (Hurcombe 1992: ch. 7). In conclusion, the lunates were all used for a similar function—scraping reed-type plants. They could have been employed to break plants down to fibers but there are more efficient tools for this than lunates. The more likely task was slitting and scraping reeds, for which the lunate shape is well suited. Some of the experimental reeds were scraped so thinly that the breakdown of secondary thickening of cell walls may have occurred. This process may be easier with damp or retted reeds.

Sardinian basketry work is still widespread and much of the work uses the coil technique. After watching a Sardinian basketmaker, it was obvious that the technique required two materials of very different qualities. Bundles of round-stemmed plants form the bulk of the coil (*Juncus* sp. on this occasion). The plants must be sufficiently supple to bend slightly, yet retain enough stiffness to hold their shape. A second material is wound around this group of stems to form the coil. In contrast, this phase requires a much softer, flaccid material. Today the wrapping material is a commercially available raffia, but in the past a local plant must have been employed.

Traditional basketry plants are given as *Juncus* sps., *Asphodelus ramosus* and *Chamaerops humilis* (Sardegna Guida 1981: 56). Of these plants, *Chamaerops humilis* has short leaves (c. 30 cm), while only the thick stem of *Asphodelus* is used (Sardinian basketmaker, pers. comm.). *Juncus* seems to be a good choice as it is relatively long and thin, and with the pith removed could be a good wrapping material for coil basketry. Atzori (1980: 28-30) describes the processing of *Juncus acutus*, a tall (sometimes above head height), stiff reed. The plant is broken into finer parts, soaked, then scraped with a knife on a wooden board. The plant is drawn past the stationary knife several times making it very flexible and thin. This material is then used to wrap around the coils, i.e. 'passive scraping'. The task the lunates performed may therefore be associated with basketry.

At higher levels of inference, these hypotheses are inevitably controversial but nonetheless worth stating. At a behavioral level, the lunates may have been re-sharpened, but in any event they are well-used, probably task-specific tools, made from a relatively near source of obsidian at Monte Arci (c. 20 km). They were probably kept for a single purpose and since they were the chief retouched obsidian artifact they could be interpreted as the cause of a particular trip or exchange transaction to obtain the raw material. This is not to say that these tools were conceived as important, because the procurement could have been embedded in other tasks. These ideas imply that a Bronze Age society of some cultural complexity was using stone tools to process plants for basketry or cordage. Metal tools of soft bronze could have worn too quickly or corroded too rapidly, especially if the plants were wet. It may also be that the task was not of sufficient importance to warrant the use of bronze. Thus, some attempt can be made to offer causal information on the role of the lunates within Nuragic society.

Finally, if the lunates were used to slit, and then scrape the pith from the center of reeds, they were likely to have had a part in the production of long flexible material for wrapping around coils and thus to have been involved in basketry production. The lunates may offer the opportunity to investigate a craft activity whose products do not survive well in the archaeological record.

Conclusion

Both case studies have shown how the wear and residue observations are really only the first step in arriving at an interpretation of what the tools were used for, and the cultural implications of this choice. Were the knives recognized in the first study gradually replaced by blades? Are the strong associations of the knives with flesh (meat and fish) and hide-working part of a more general use of obsidian for these activitities (Hurcombe in press), and should this be seen as using a raw material to its best advantage? For the lunate case study, was obsidian used for this plant activity because it performed the task better than other materials, or because it was easier to obtain? Were the lunate tools used to perform a novel task, perhaps signifying developments in plant craftwork or are earlier tools which performed this function still awaiting recognition? It should be evident from these questions that our understanding of function and its role within a society is at present cursory. Microwear analyses can augment our knowledge considerably.

Acknowledgments

The Soprintendenza Archeologica in Sassari, Sardinia, kindly gave its permission to export the material to Britain for the microwear analysis. The material was studied with the permission of the excavators Dr Trump and Professor Balmuth, using facilities at Sheffield University. The Science and Engineering Council funded the research on the technique of obsidian microwear. Exeter University provided additional resources. Christina Cattaneo arranged the preliminary genetic tests under the direction of Dr R. Sokal. The photographs were printed by Mike Roulliard, and the figures were the work of Sean Goddard, Don Henson and Barry Chandler. Lastly, thanks to Dr Patricia Phillips who encouraged and advised on many occasions.

Table 1

The variables and codes used to record microsopic wear on archaeological and experimental obsidian tools

	Variables		1	2	3	4	5	6
Polish	Brightness	1	intense	bright	fairly bright	fairly dull	dull	
	Texture	2	very smooth	smooth	slightly smooth	bumpy	rough	
	Relief on edge	3	bevelled	very rounded	rounded	slightly rounded		
	Location (edge)	4	0-25μm	26-250μm	243-485μm	>485μm	away from edge	
	Location (prominences)	5	0-25μm	26-250μm	243-485μm	>485μm	away from edge	
Striae	Striae type	6	sleek	rough-bottomed	intermittent	fern-like	flaked	crescent
	Width	7	<2μ	>2μ	both			
	Depth	8	deep	shallow	both			
	No. (in 485 × 365μm)	9	<25	>25	>50	>100		
	Orientation	10	longitudinal	transverse	one diagonal	crossed diagonal	rotary	
Attrition	Extent	11	slight	definite	pronounced	severe	bevelled	
	Debris	12	few	many				
	Part flaked	13	few	many				
	Cracks	14	few	many				
Residues	Share	15	present	definite				
	Texture	16	present	definite				
	Brightness	17	intense	bright	fairly bright	fairly dull	dull	
	Location	18	0-25μm	26-242μm	>243μm	all over	all over except edge	
	Observation point	19	BC = before chemical cleaning		AC = after chemical cleaning			

Table 2

The wear interpretations of artifacts from the Neolithic levels of Grotta Filiestru

Artifact No.	Used	Action	Material	Residues
5+3.5	yes	parallel	flesh/butchery	yes
5+4.1	yes	parallel	flesh	
5+5.2	yes	parallel	flesh/butchery/hide	yes
6+1.11	yes	parallel	flesh/butchery	yes
6+1.15	yes	parallel	flesh?	yes
6+1.16	yes	parallel	fresh hide/flesh	yes
6+1.18	yes	parallel	hide/flesh	yes
6+4.1	yes	parallel	fresh hide	yes

Table 3

The use-material interpretations of the lunate artifacts from Bronze Age Ortu Còmidu

Lunate	Use-material interpretation	Residues
1	soft—possibly plants	yes
2	soft—probably plants	yes
3	plants	yes
4	plants—probably tough sp.	yes
5	plants—probably tough sp.	yes
6	plants	yes
7	non-use surface alterations —interpretation impossible	no
8	plants—possibly very wet	yes
9	plants	yes
10	plants	yes
12	plants—probably tough sp.	yes

References

Anderson, P.C.
  1980 A testimony of prehistoric tasks: diagnostic residues on stone tool working edges. *World Archaeology* 12: 181-94.

Atzori, M.
  1980 Artigianato tradizionale della Sardegna. L'intreccio. Corbule canestri di Sinnai. *Quaderni Demologici* 2. Sassari.

Balmuth, M.S.
  1986 Sardara (CA)—Preliminary report of excavations 1975-78 of the Nuraghe Ortu Còmidu. *Notizie degli Scavi* 37: 353-410.

Campbell, J.
  1977 *The Upper Palaeolithic Of Britain: A Study Of Man And Nature In The Late Ice Age*, I. Edinburgh: Edinburgh University Press.

Clark, J.G.D.
  1980 *Mesolithic Prelude*. Edinburgh: Edinburgh University Press.

Hurcombe, L.
  1985 The potential of functional analyses of obsidian tools: a closer view. In C. Malone and S. Stoddart (eds.), *Papers in Italian Archaeology IV*, 50-60. BAR International Series 244. Oxford: British Archaeological Reports.
  1986a Residue studies on obsidian tools. *Early Man News* 9/10/11: 83-90.
  1986b Microwear analysis of obsidian chipped stone tools from the western Mediterranean. Unpublished PhD dissertation, Department of Archaeology, Sheffield.
  1988 Some criticisms and suggestions in response to Newcomer et al. 1986. *Journal of Archaeological Science* 15: 1-10.
  1992 *Use-wear Analysis and Obsidian: Theory, Experiments and Results*. Sheffield: J. Collis Publications.
  in press The restricted function of neolithic obsidian tools at Grotta Filiestru, Sardinia. In S. Beyries (ed). *Les Gestes Retrouvées: Traces et Fonction*. Conference proceedings, Liege December 1990.

Keeley, L.H.
  1980 *Experimental Determination of Stone Tool Uses*. Chicago: University of Chicago Press.

Mansur-Franchomme, M.E.
  1983 Scanning electron microscopy of dry hide working tools: the role of abrasives and humidity in microwear polish formation. *Journal of Archaeological Science* 10: 223-30.

Phillips, P.
  1986 Obsidian tools and waste from Ortu Còmidu. In M.S. Balmuth, Preliminary report of excavations 1975-1978 of the Nuraghe Ortu Còmidu. *Notizie degli Scavi* 37: 353-410.

Phillips, P., & L. Hurcombe
  1990 Archive report on the obsidian flaked material from levels 5 and 6 Grotta Filiestru (Mara, Sardinia): A Macroscopic and Microscopic Analysis. Unpublished archive report.

Sardegna Guida
  1981 *Sardegna Guida*. Genova: Sagep Editrice.

Semenov, S.A.
  1964 *Prehistoric Technology*. Trans. M. W. Thompson. London: Cory, Adams and Mackay.

Trump, D.
  1983 *La Grotta di Filiestru a Bonu Ighinu, Mara (SS)*. Quaderni 13. Sassari: Ministero per i Beni Culturali e Ambientali.

Vaughan, P.C.
  1981 Lithic microwear experimentation and the functional analysis of a lower Magdalenian stone tool Assemblage. PhD dissertation, University of Pennsylvania.
  1985 *Use-Wear Analysis of Flaked Stone Tools*. Tucson: University of Arizona Press.

Riassunto

Anche se l'esame microscopico di tracce di uso su utensili di pietra è una tecnica relativamente nuova, essa ha già contribuito a migliorare la conoscenza delle funzioni degli utensili di pietra. Per ciascun manufatto, l'Autrice, una specialista dell'analisi delle tracce d'uso sull'ossidiana, misura 18 variabili nelle categorie di lucidature, striature, attriti, e residui. Queste informazioni sono usate per identificare il materiale per cui gli strumenti sono stati usati; i materiali sono: erbe, altre piante (2 categorie), cuoio, legno, ossa, corna di cervo, carne, materiale più morbido, e materiale duttile.

In questo articolo l'Autrice presenta un sommario dei suoi studi di oggetti d'ossidiana provenienti da due siti in Sardegna, Grotta Filiestru (Mara-SS) e Nuraghe Ortu Còmidu (Sardara-CA).

Il complesso di ossidiane risalente al primo e medio Neolitico nei livelli 5-6 della Grotta Filiestru include punte di frecce, lamine larghe e lunghe, e anche selce e riolite. Analisi di tracce d'uso dell'ossidiana indicano che gli strumenti sono stati probabilmente usati per lavorare cuoio e per tagliare carne. Alcuni utensili possono essere considerati coltelli e probabilmente sono stati usati per un lungo periodo di tempo. Alcuni utensili presentano dei residui di pelle sia sul margine tagliente che sul margine d'impugnatura; l'Autrice suggerisce che è possibile raccogliere informazioni genetiche sia sugli animali mangiati che sugli esseri umani che hanno usato gli utensili. È da notare che anche margini non ritoccati sono stati usati.

Presso il Nuraghe Ortu Còmidu la maggior parte dei 214 oggeti d'ossidiana ritrovati sono estremamente piccoli e non ritoccati. Gli unici oggetti ritoccati sono lamine e semilunati: questi ultimi non sono stati scoperti in altri siti dell'età del Bronzo. È stato suggerito che potrebbero essere stati usati per radere o per scopi chirurgici, per il fatto che hanno dei margini taglienti piccoli, ma l'analisi delle tracce d'uso dell'Autrice dimostrano che il margine diritto è stato quello usato maggiormente. L'analisi indica anche che questi strumenti sono stati usati per raschiar materiali vegetali e che ciascuno di essi è stato usato almeno per un ora. Più specificamente, le analisi suggeriscono che le piante raschiate erano canne, e che il margine acuto degli strumenti veniva usato per aprire ciascuna canna e ottenere la polpa. La tecnica a molla per costruire cestini è una tecnica praticata ancora oggi in Sardegna, e l'Autrice conclude sostenendo che i semilunati di Ortu Còmidu erano usati principalmente per fabbricare cestini.

Questi risultati preliminari fanno emergere nuove domande. I coltelli di Filiestru sono stati poi sostituiti da lame? L'ossidiana è stata utilizzata specificamente per la lavorazione del cuoio e delle carne nel Neolitico? I semilunati sono stati costruiti specificamente per la lavorazione delle piante, e se è così, che tipo di strumenti sono stati impiegati prima che i semilunati apparissero? L'Autrice conclude che sono necessarie ulteriori ricerche per rispondere a queste domande e per dedurre i diversi comportamenti (procuramento, produzione, uso) associati con gli utensili d'ossidiana.

Elementi Architettonici e del Culto Funerario nella Domus de Janas di Su Littu (Ossi-Sassari)

Maria Luisa Ferrarese Ceruti

Fig. 1 Ossi, Sassari, loc. Su Littu: la facciata della tomba (a) e il particolare del dromos (b).

Alle ben note manifestazioni figurative offerte dall'arte preistorica della Sardegna del Neolitico Recente si aggiungono oggi una rappresentazione antropomorfa, delle figurazioni corniformi, una 'falsa porta' o 'porta inferi' e la riproduzione delle strutture lignee di una capanna rettangolare, nell'anticella della sepoltura di Su Littu o Monte Littu di Ossi.

La tomba (Figg. 1-2), del tipo a domus de janas, ubicata nel chiuso denominato *Su Montigiu 'e Sa Femmina*, in località Su Littu, in territorio di Ossi, si apre solitaria in uno spuntone calcareo che domina la valle del Mascari, a poche decine di metri dalla strada asfaltata, sulla sinistra di chi sale verso il paese. Si tratta di un ipogeo di modeste dimensioni, assai deteriorato nelle strutture sia a causa della notevole friabilità della roccia, che solo all'esterno è più compatta e solida, sia a causa della ripetuta frequentazione dell'uomo che vi ha trovato comodo rifugio dopo aver parzialmente abbattuto le pareti dell'anticella e delle celle interne, riconducendo i vari ambienti ad un unico grande vano.

In origine la sepoltura era costituita da un *dromos* che doveva avere pianta ellittica: il degrado della parte anteriore del dromos, oggi completamente mancante, mostra, sulle pareti laterali quanto residua di una raffigurazione cultuale costituita da bassorilievi piatti, riproducenti due paia di corna bovine iscritte l'una nell'altra (Figg. 3-5), dal profilo morbido ma fortemente erose, per cui la corretta lettura dell'una o dell'altra è impedita dai numerosi stacchi della roccia avvenuti soprattutto a causa dell'inquinamento dell'aria, imputabile ai fumi della non lontana cementeria di Scala di Giocca. Non si è salvata nemmeno la rappresentazione di un idolo, presumibilmente femminile, che sembra disposto al centro delle corna iscritte (Figg. 4-5).

A causa della totale assenza di tutta la parte anteriore del dromos, staccatosi in antico (Fig. 1), non ci è permesso di stabilire se la rappresentazione antropomorfa fosse ubicata o meno al centro di quella tauromorfa, sebbene appaia assai probabile la sua posizione centrale a causa dell'ampio sviluppo dei tratti di corna residui che non lascerebbe spazio sufficiente per un secondo idolo. In questo caso l'idolo, non essendo iterato, doveva costituire il fulcro dell'intera sintassi figurativa.

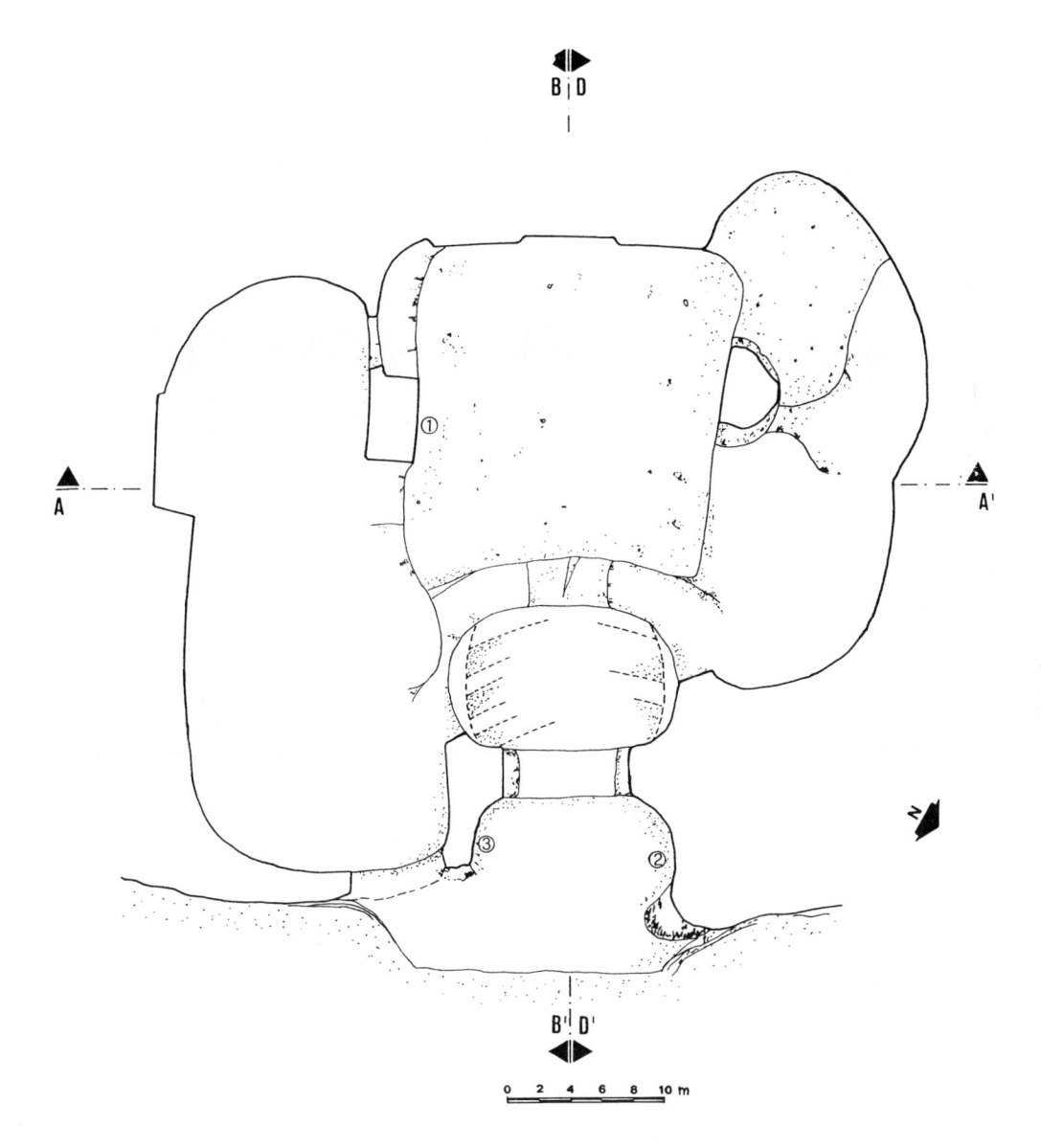

Fig. 2 Ossi, Sassari, loc. Su Littu: pianta della domus de janas.

Il piccolo rilievo è costituito da una ellisse, la testa, che è impostata su un busto, forse in origine di forma trapezoidale, di cui residua piccola parte sotto il collo, è ipoteticamente ricostruibile solo sulla base delle tracce degli stacchi sulla roccia.

Il forte degrado della parete sinistra del dromos non fornisce indicazioni certe sull'esistenza di simbolismi raffigurativi simmetricamente opposti a quelli descritti, ma l'estremità di due corna iscritte, identiche a quelle della parete destra, suggerisce questa ipotesi.

Nel dromos, attraverso un ingresso in antico rettangolare ma oggi allargato sino ad acquisire una forma circolare e di cui residua la soglia e la parte più bassa degli stipiti, si entra in una *anticella* di pianta ellittica. Il pavimento di questa anticella si trova su un piano più basso rispetto a quello del dromos dal quale emergono solo gli stipiti dell'anticella e della cella centrale. La copertura dell'ambiente ripropone, in negativo, le travature lignee di una capanna rettangolare con tetto a doppio spiovente.

Anche in questo caso i rilievi sono fortemente degradati ma non tanto da non consentire una lettura sicura (Fig. 2). Di particolare interesse risulta la disposizione delle travature rispetto alla pianta dell'ambiente. Infatti, mentre il trave di colmo si trova solitamente disposto parallelamente ai lati lunghi del vano, è perpendicolarmente all'ingresso, in questo caso esso è sullo stesso asse dell'ingresso, e quindi unisce tra loro i lati brevi, con i travetti che dal trave si allungano verso questi ultimi: sulla sinistra ne residuano sei mentre sulla destra soltanto tre. Il trave centrale è completamente eroso. Nulla residua di eventuali decorazioni o simboli del culto scolpiti nell'anticella.

SEZIONE A-A'

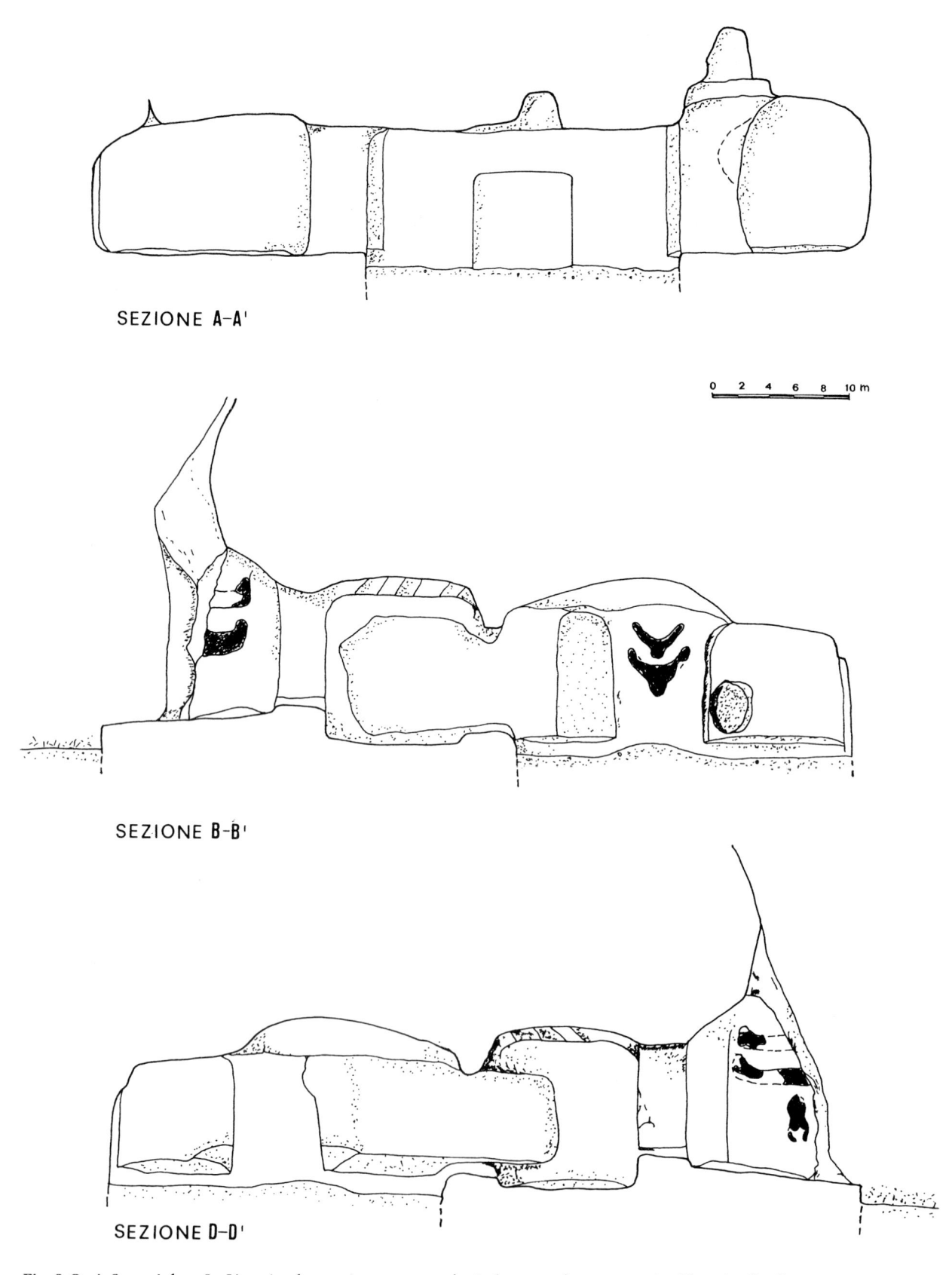

0 2 4 6 8 10 m

SEZIONE B-B'

SEZIONE D-D'

Fig. 3 Ossi, Sassari, loc. Su Littu: in alto, sezione trasversale; in basso e al centro, sezioni longitudinali.

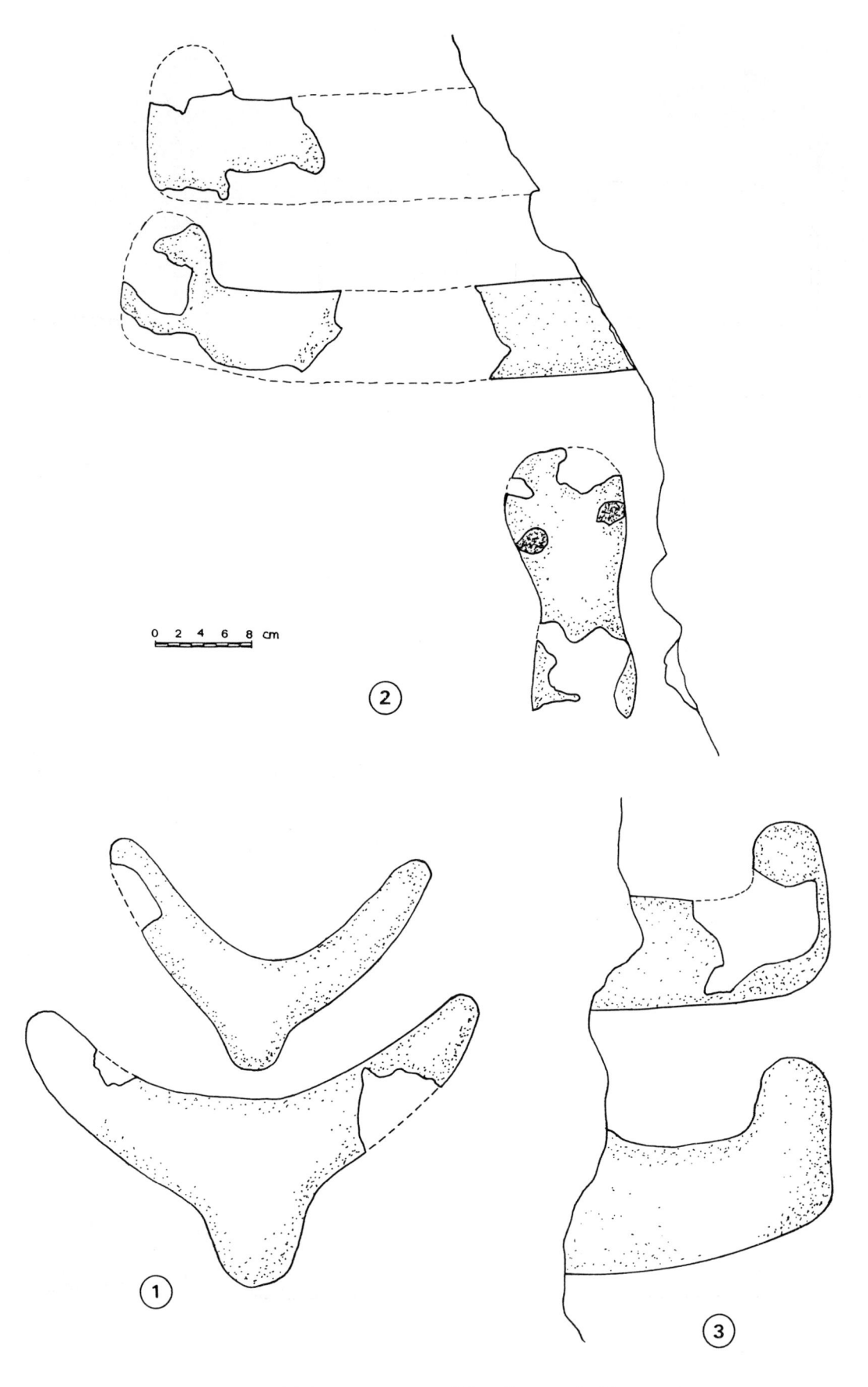

Fig. 4 Ossi, Sassari, loc. Su Littu: i rilievi del dromos (2 e 3), e della cella centrale (1).

Fig. 5 Ossi, Sassari, loc. Su Littu: la facciata della tomba (a) e il particolare del dromos (b).

Coassiale all'ingresso si trova un altro portello, anche questo individuabile solo dalla soglia. Esso introduce nella *cella centrale*, di pianta quadrangolare con il lato dell'ingresso fortemente concavo; il pavimento tende ad essere sempre più profondo man mano che si procede verso il fondo, secondo uno schema che è assai diffuso nelle aree circostanti il monumento di Monte d'Accoddi di Sassari, come nelle necropoli di Ponte Secco (Sassari) o di Su Crucifissu Mannu (Portotorres). La parete di fondo mostra, davanti all'ingresso della cella, una nicchia rettangolare perfettamente sagomata, probabilmente la rappresentazione di una 'falsa porta' o 'porta inferi,' la quale non presenta alcuna decorazione o simbolo del culto. Non è da escludere, però, che essa possa invece essere l'inizio dello scavo di una nuova cella, sebbene il tipo di rifinitura delle pareti farebbe propendere piuttosto per la prima ipotesi.

Due larghe e lunghe *celle*, di pianta subellittica, si aprono sulla sinistra e sulla destra della camera centrale; di difficile lettura l'impianto originario dei due ambienti, oggi mancanti di larga parte delle pareti che sono contermini al vano centrale; con ogni probabilità già in antico esso doveva presentare un impianto non particolarmente coerente.

È possibile che le due celle laterali siano state aggiunte in un momento secondario, mentre i due pilastri che fiancheggiano la camera centrale fanno parte del primo impianto della tomba. Sul pilastro di sinistra si notano, sovrapposti, due bucrani iscritti, di stile naturalistico, assai deteriorati e le cui condizioni di conservazione sono oggi assai più rovinate rispetto a come si presentavano quando li vidi la prima volta, a seguito della segnalazione dell'Avv. G. Spanedda di Ossi, nel 1967, come per altro anche i rilievi del dromos.

Se il problema dell'originario impianto della domus è allo stato attuale di difficile soluzione anche per l'assoluta assenza di dati di scavo (le celle laterali e l'anticella nonché il dromos mostrano la nuda roccia e la cella centrale è piena dei detriti dello sfaldamento del soffitto e delle pareti) altrettanto problematico appare, anche, quello dell'attribuzione cronologica dei vari rilievi o motivi cultuali. Assai diversi, sia da un punto di vista formale sia stilistico, i tauromorfi di Su Littu si presentano o tradotti con il simbolismo delle sole corna, come nel dromos, oppure con un netto rilievo e la rappresentazione dell'intera testa, come nella cella centrale. Questa diversa resa scultorea evidenzia in particolar modo anche il rilievo sottolineando suggestivi effetti chiaroscurali. Il rilievo piatto, assolutamente ben sagomato, quasi ritagliato dalla parete rocciosa crea infatti un gioco di ombre nette che sottolineano, evidenziandolo, il contorno del motivo decorativo. Come si è detto, anche l'idolo che completa questa scultura è realizzato con la stessa tecnica dei tauromorfi in un complesso assai armonico nel quale corna ed antropomorfo si fondono in una unica rappresentazione di indubbio valore sacrale.

La stessa valenza religiosa, legata al culto funerario, ha l'idolo che si trova sotto la doppia rappresentazione taurina. Si potrebbe ipotizzare che questa associazione rappresentasse una coppia divina legata al culto dei morti. L'interrogativo al quale appare oggi assai difficile dare una risposta è l'individuazione di queste divinità; inoltre è assai interessante il fatto che, mentre le rappresentazioni tauromorfe, nelle loro varie stilizzazioni sono assai frequenti, gli idoli trovano posto solo eccezionalmente nelle domus de janas. Gli unici esempi, infatti, ci riconducono alla necropoli di Montessu a Santadi, Cagliari, ove degli incavi sagomati secondo lo schema degli idoli di tipo cicladico si ritrovano nel dromos di alcune domus de janas, in prossimità dei portelli d'ingresso. Ora, se è pur vero che le raffigurazioni di idoli costituiscono una minoranza nel patrimonio figurativo scultoreo delle pareti delle domus de janas, è altrettanto vero che le figurine a tutto tondo sono frequentissime tra i corredi funerari, siano esse del tipo cicladico a placca, siano quelle a braccia traforate.

Pertanto l'associazione idolo femminile—rappresentazione tauromorfa si ripete anche in quelle sepolture nelle quali appaiono sulla parete le sole raffigurazioni dell'elemento bovino.

Per quanto riguarda i bucrani scolpiti sul pilastro della cella centrale, essi appartengono ad un tipo assai diverso da quelli notati nel dromos, poiché sono scolpiti con un rilievo morbido, convesso, più sfumato nella resa stilistica e con dei giochi chiaroscurali dovuti ad ombre lunghe e non nette prodotte dalla poca luce che penetra dal portello.

Vi è quindi un aperto contrasto stilistico tra i rilievi dal dromos e quelli della cella che, ad un primo esame, potrebbero far ipotizzare una cronologia dei medesimi tra loro assai distante nel tempo, rivelando così due interventi diversificati, imputabili a genti lontane tra loro per gusto e sensibilità artistica ma svoltisi, probabilmente, sempre nell'ambito della cultura di Ozieri, del Neolitico recente.

Certo l'ubicazione dei medesimi in due puntichiave dell'ipogeo (il dromos e l'interno della cella centrale, quella dove, almeno in origine, dovevano espletarsi cerimonie per il culto funerario) rende assai difficile determinare una sequenza cronologica degli stessi. L'andamento decisamente curvilineo dei bucrani della cella centrale potrebbe sembrare più antico rispetto alle più rigide raffigurazioni tauromorfe del dromos, assolutamente essenziali nella loro linearità, ma appare assai difficile pensare ad una loro aggiunta posteriore. Oggi è impossibile poter documentare il momento cronologico della ripresa muraria di quelle pareti e non ci è consentito precisare pertanto da chi siano state operate quelle trasformazioni che hanno modificato così radicalmente la sepoltura.

Ringraziamenti

Rilievi di A. Farina e G. Sulis; grafica di F. Ferrarese Ceruti. Fotografie di M.L. Ferrarese Ceruti.

Bibliografia

Antona Ruju, A.
1980   Appunti per una seriazione evolutiva delle statuette femminili della Sardegna prenuragica. *Atti della XXII Riunione Scientifica dell'Istituto Italiano di Preistoria e Protostoria nella Sardegna centrosettentrionale (21-27 ottobre 1978)*, 115-39. Firenze: Istituto Italiano di Preistoria e Protostoria.

Atzeni, E.
1975   Nuovi idoli della Sardegna prenuragica (Nota preliminare). *Studi Sardi* 23(1973–74): 3-51.
1978   La Dea-Madre nelle culture prenuragiche. *Studi Sardi* 24(1975–77): 3-69.

Atzeni, E., F. Barreca, M.L. Ferrarese-Ceruti, E. Contu, G. Lilliu, F. Lo Schiavo, F. Nicosia & E. Equini Schneider (eds.)
1981   *Ichnussa: La Sardegna dalle origini all'età classica*. Milano: Libri Scheiwiller.

Caprara, R.
1986   Due chiese rupestri altomedievali nella Sardegna settentrionale. *Nuovo Bullettino Archeologico Sardo* 1(1984): 301-22.

Contu, E.
1961a   Notiziario: Li Curuneddi (Sassari). *Rivista di Scienze Preistoriche* 16: 275.
1961b   Notiziario: Ponte Secco (Sassari). *Rivista di Scienze Preistoriche* 16: 276.
1962   Alcune osservazioni su 'domus de janas' edite ed inedite di Alghero e Sassari. *Studi Sardi* 17(1959–1961): 626-35.
1964   Tombe preistoriche dipinte e scolpite di Thiesi e Bessude (Sassari). *Rivista di Scienze Preistoriche* 19: 233-63.
1967   Ipogei con 'corna sacrificali' plurime di Brodu (Oniferi, Nuoro). *Rivista di Scienze Preistoriche* 21(1966): 195-200.

Demartis, G.
1985a   Alghero. Loc. Li Piani. In M.A. Fadda e F. Lo Schiavo (redattori), *10 anni di attività nel territorio della Provincia di Nuoro 1975-1985*, 237-40, 273. Nuoro.
1985b   Ossi. Loc. S'Adde 'e Asile. La Tomba Maggiore. In M.A. Fadda e F. Lo Schiavo (redattori), *10 anni di attività nel territorio della Provincia di Nuoro 1975-1985*, 307-309. Nuoro.
1985c   Ossi. Loc. S'Adde 'e Asile. La Tomba delle Finestrelle. In M.A. Fadda e F. Lo Schiavo (redattori), *10 anni di attività nel territorio della Provincia di Nuoro 1975-1985*, 306-307. Nuoro.
1986   Alcune osservazioni sulle 'domus de janas' riproducenti il tetto della casa dei vivi. *Nuovo Bullettino Archeologico Sardo* 1(1984): 9-19.

Demartis, G., & V. Canalis
1989   La tomba II di Mesu 'e Montes (Ossi-Sassari). *Nuovo Bullettino Archeologico Sardo* 2(1985): 41-47.

Ferrarese Ceruti, M.L.
1967   Domus de janas in località Molimentos (Benetutti, Sassari). *Bullettino di Paletnologia Italiana* 76: 69-98.
1988   Le necropoli di Su Crucifissu Mannu-Portotorres e di Ponte Secco-Sassari. In L.D. Campus (a cura di), *La Cultura di Ozieri. Problematiche e nuove acquisizioni*, 37-47. Ozieri: Il Torchietto.

Lilliu, G.
  1958 Religione della Sardegna prenuragica. *Bullettino di Paletnologia Italiana* 11(1957): 7-96.
  1988 *La Civiltà dei Sardi dal Paleolitico all'Età dei Nuraghi.* Torino: Nuova ERI.

Lo Schiavo, F.
  1985 Figurazioni antropomorfe nella grotta del Bue Marino, Cala Gonone (Dorgali, Nuoro). In M.A. Fadda e F. Lo Schiavo (redattori), *10 anni di attività nel territorio della Provincia di Nuoro 1975-1985*, 12-13. Nuoro.

Loria, R.
  1971 Figurette schematiche femminili nella ceramica eneolitica della Sardegna. *Rivista di Scienze Preistoriche* 26(1): 179-202.

Sanna, D. (a cura di)
  1980 *Nur. La misteriosa civiltà dei Sardi.* Milano: Cariplo.

Tanda, G.
  1977a *Arte Preistorica in Sardegna. Le figurazioni taurine scolpite dell'Algherese nel quadro delle rappresentazioni figurate degli ipogei sardi a 'domus de janas.'* Quaderni della Soprintendenza ai beni Archeologici per le Provincie di Sassari e Nuoro 5. Sassari: Dessì.
  1977b Le incisioni della 'domu de janas' di Tisiennari-Bortigiadas. *Archivio Storico Sardo di Sassari* 3: 199-211.
  1983 Arte e religione in Sardegna. Rapporti fra i dati monumentali e gli elementi di cultura materiale. *Valcamonica Symposium III. The intellectual expression of prehistoric man: Art and religion, 1979*, 259-79.
  1984 *Arte e religione della Sardegna preistorica nella necropoli di Sos Furrighesos, I-II.* Sassari.
  1985 *L'arte delle domus de janas.* Sassari.
  1988 A proposito delle figurine 'a clessidra' di Tisiennari, Bortigiadas. *Studi in Onore di Pietro Meloni*, 205-31. Sassari.
  1989 L'arte dell'Età del Rame in Sardegna. *Rassegna di Archeologia* 7(1988): 541-43.

Thimme, J. (ed.)
  1980 *Kunst und Kultur Sardiniens vom Neolithikum bis zum ende der Nuraghenzeit.* Karlsruhe: C.F. Müller.

Ugas, G., G. Lai & L. Usai
  1989 L'insediamento prenuragico di Su Coddu (Selargius-CA). Notizia preliminare sulle campagne di scavo 1981-1984. *Nuovo Bullettino Archeologico Sardo* 2(1985): 7-40.

Ugas, G., L. Usai, M. Nuvoli, G. Lai & M. Marras
  1989 Nuovi dati sull'insediamento di Su Coddu-Selargius. In L. Campus (a cura di), *La Cultura di Ozieri. Problematiche e nuove acquisizioni*, 239-75. Ozieri: Il Torchietto.

Usai, E.
  1981 Una domu de janas dipinta della necropoli di S'Acqua Salida di Pimentel-Cagliari. *Proceedings of the Second International Congress of Mediterranean Pre- and Protohistory. Interaction and Acculturation in the Mediterranean (Amsterdam, November 19-23, 1980)*, 31-35. Amsterdam.

Summary

The *domus de janas* tomb of Su Littu (Ossi-SS) offers several examples of prehistoric Sardinian art. Located on a rocky outcrop that dominates the Mascari valley, the tomb is thought to date to the Late Neolithic period. The tomb has a characteristic hypogean plan, including a *dromos* now partly destroyed. On its right side are sculpted in relief two pairs of bovine horns, with an idol, presumably female, located near their center. The Author asserts that this anthropomorphic representation was the focus of the reliefs. Two identical horns are also inscribed on the left wall, and it is suggested that the two reliefs were originally symmetrical.

The *anticella* of the tomb is elliptical in plan and its ceiling is carved to resemble the wooden beams of a rectangular hut with a sloping roof. Opposite the entry from the *dromos* is the door to the central chamber, which is of quadrangular shape. At the back of the central chamber is a 'false door' carved into the rock; subelliptical rooms open off both sides, and *bucrania* are carved on a pilaster on the left side. It is unclear whether the side chambers were part of the original tomb, or were added later.

While bulls'-horn motifs are common in Sardinian *domus de janas*, representations of idols are infrequently found except in funerary contexts. The Su Littu idol is carved in the same style as the horns in the *dromos*, but the complete *bucrania* of the central chamber are more curvilinear and perhaps more ancient. Today it is impossible to ascertain the exact chronology of the tomb and its reliefs, and the transformations that modified its use.

New Contributions to the Study of the Megalithic in Corsica*

Joseph Cesari

Introduction

On Corsica, Megalithic monuments are divided into three categories: tombs, menhirs (including statue-menhirs), and menhirs aligned with other architectural elements so that they make a spectacular display.

1. Tombs

Examples include funerary complexes made up of a group of coffer burials; the coffers are stone monoliths which may or may not be surrounded by one or more stone circles. It is possible that originally the tomb was protected by an actual tumulus. This first type, whose preserved remains can not be differentiated clearly from cists, bears the local name of *Bancali*, that is, 'large benches', alluding to their general appearance.

In the second type of Megalithic tombs we find true dolmens, 'houses for the dead' (Joussaume 1985: 259-75), that present an especially monumental appearance. The interior surface of these dolmens rarely exceeds 6m^2, and many times they are constructed above ground. Just as often, however, they can be found as subterranean chambers, enclosed within one or more large, peristyle, stone circles. This type is without doubt a transitional phase between the first coffer-type tombs and the large-scale dolmens. The local term generally used for the large-scale dolmens is *Stazzione*. The term *Tola*—literally 'table'—is used less frequently (Cesari 1985).

2. Menhirs and Statue-Menhirs

On Corsica, in contrast to other regions, menhirs are never just simple, rough stones. In all cases a menhir is a stone which, after its selection, has been regularized. These menhirs can have an anthropomorphic outline, and are then called *Stantara* (petrified). In popular belief, these are always thought of as people who have committed sexual transgressions and, in braving the wrath of heaven, were changed into stone statues. The statue-menhirs are called *Paladini*. Armed with daggers and swords, these statues refer in the collective cultural unconscious to an immortal Golden Age, wherein are mingled memories of pre-Christian antiquity and traditions from Medieval epic combats.

3. Menhirs (Stantari), Statue-Menhirs (Paladini), and Alignments (I Filarate)

These types, according to the number of elements making up the group, comprise a special manifestation of the Corsican Megalithic. Some graves in coffers or in cists (Fig. 1, Palaggiu-Sartène), but also some dolmens (Fig. 2, Rinaiu-Sartène; Stazzona of Taravo-Sollacaro: not shown) can be associated with menhir alignments.

Roger Grosjean (1967) has proposed a tentative chronological and cultural classification of the Corsican Megalithic. This work, starting from the morphology of the menhirs and the tombs, affirms an evolution and a permanence of the Corsican Megalithic phenomenon from the Final Neolithic period to the end of the Bronze Age.

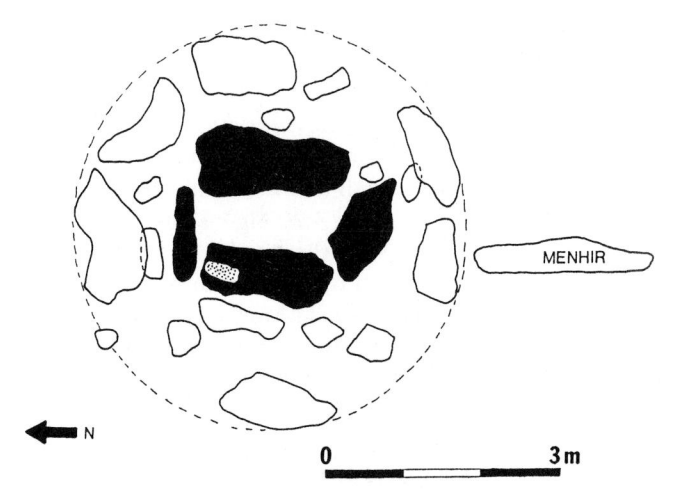

Fig. 1 Palaggiu (Sartène): megalithic coffer (after Grosjean *et al.* 1976).

---

* Translated from the French by G. Bates and T. Andrews.

106 *Sardinia in the Mediterranean*

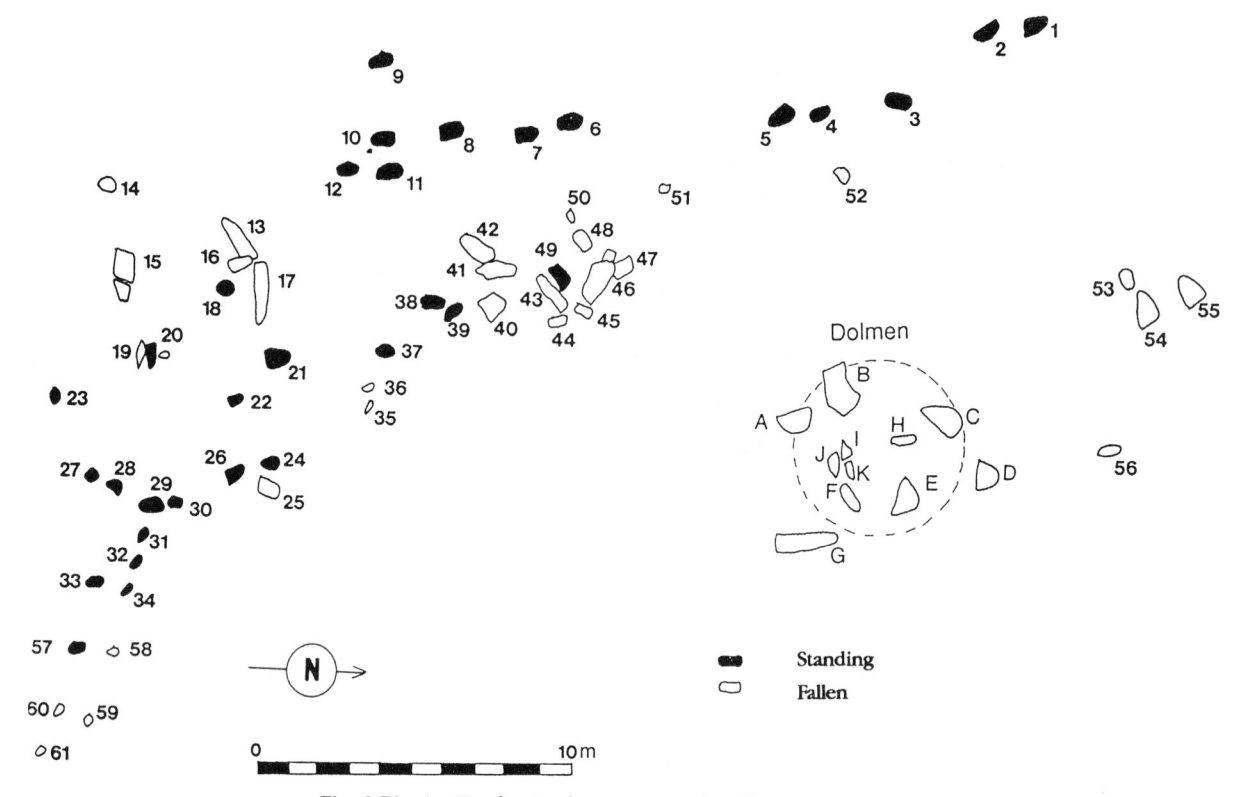

Fig. 2 Rinaiu (Sartène): alignment, and coffer or dolmen.

This explanation of the pre- and protohistoric societies of Corsica is understood primarily through the morphology of the menhirs which, by successive 'stages', pass from schematic and abstract designs to figurative work whose realism must have translated faithfully the living models on which they were based. Today, it is still acknowledged that evidence of the Megalithic is confined within this ample chronological horizon. The association of menhirs with graves in coffers (*Bancali*), even if this is not verified for all the monuments (often because of the poor conservation of the latter), is still attested for a sufficient number so that we can estimate that this association was a specific characteristic of this type of funerary architecture, common to Corsica and Gallura. We will recall that the tombs in the Porto-Vecchio region (Fig. 3.2, Fig. 4: necropolis of Tivolaggiu; Fig. 3.4: necropolis of Vascolaggiu) show analogies with the Sardinian necropoleis of Gallura, especially the Li Muri necropolis in the Arzachena region. Other graves in coffers, surrounded or not by stone circles (Fig. 3), could be compared to the Galluran monuments, as well as to those discovered in Cagliaritano on the Pranu Mutteddu plateau at Goni (Atzeni 1988; Atzeni and Cocco 1989).

Despite exactingly detailed excavations conducted on two new Megalithic funerary complexes, one at Poggiarella-Monte Rotondo (Sotta)

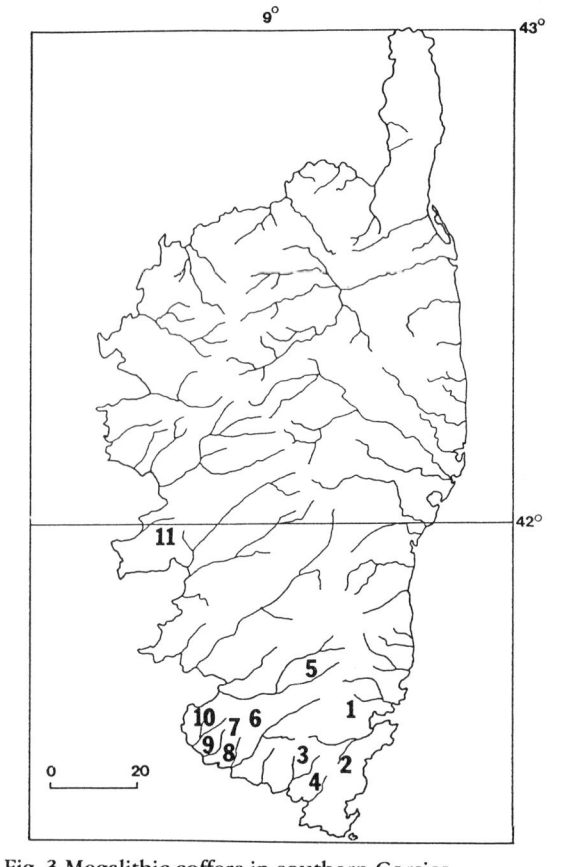

Fig. 3 Megalithic coffers in southern Corsica.
1. Palavese; 2. Tivolaggi 3. Poggiarella-Monte Rotondo; 4. Vascolaggiu; 5. Caleca; 6. Foce-Pastini; 7. Groupe de Cardiccia; 8. Coffre (?) de Rinaiu; 9. Palaggiu; 10. Venturosu; 11. Ciutulaghja.

(Fig. 3.3, Fig. 5), and the other at Ciutulaghja (Appietto) (Fig. 3.11, Fig. 6), the number of recovered artifacts remains rather small (for Sotta, Vascolaggiu and Tivolaggiu, cf. Grosjean and Liegeois 1964: 527-48; Lanfranchi 1980: 449-67; Lanfranchi and Weiss 1980: 469-73; for Ciutulaghja and Poggiarella, cf. Lanfranchi 1987: 305-18; 1989: 290-305). In the majority of these monuments, however, what appears to predominate is a lithic industry based on obsidian imported from Sardinia. If we refer to the chronology of comparable Sardinian monuments, we know that the peoples who erected these megaliths were confined within the horizon of the Final Neolithic (Atzeni 1981: xix-li; 1987: 381-400). In as much as we can establish certain typological parallels between Corsican and Sardinian megaliths, and perhaps other parallels on the basis of funerary artifacts, one should also emphasize the resemblances in site choices between the two areas. At Gallura, on the Pranu Mutteddu plateau, or in the region of Figari-Porto-Vecchio, we can see a similarity in potential for exploitation presented by these territorial ecosystems. Even though they present vast surface spaces, the quality of the soils remains mediocre. The native populations

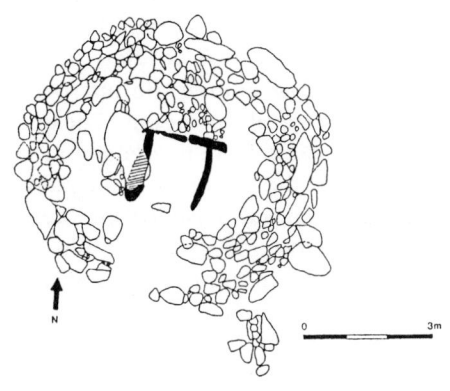

Fig. 6 Ciutulaghja I (Appietto-Ajaccio): megalithic coffer (after Lanfranchi 1987).

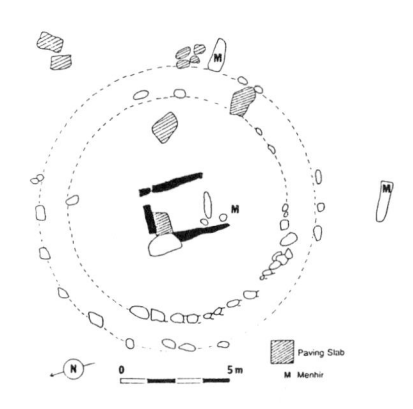

Fig. 4 Tivolaggiu (Porto-Vecchio): coffer B (after Grosjean and Liègeois 1964).

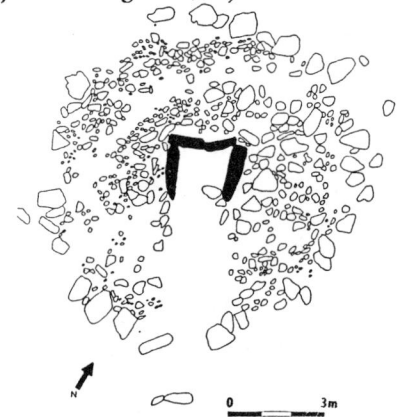

Fig. 5 Poggiarella (Sotta): megalithic coffer (after Lanfranchi 1989).

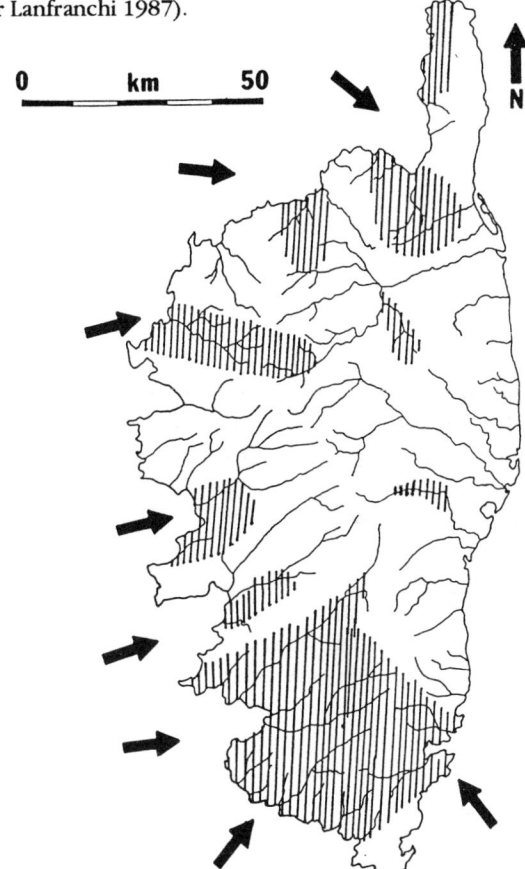

Fig. 7 Main concentrations of megaliths and probable directions of 'diffusion' (after Lanfranchi).

relied on a predominantly pastoral way of life rather than a true agriculture capable of meeting the dietary needs of a numerous population.

The geographic distribution of the different areas where Corsican megaliths are concentrated (Fig. 7) clearly shows the imbalance between the north and the south of the island. This inequality increases even more between the eastern and western island coasts, with far more numerous sites on the latter. It would seem that there was a Megalithic diffusion starting from the coastal zones and crossing the axis of the large valleys. This characteristic of the maritime origin for the Megalithic phenomenon is also verified in the site imbalance observable among the micro-areas in each large site-distribution region. These always show a significant monument density at coastal zones and plains at the outlets of principal valleys.

The still-unexplained absence of Megalithic monuments on the calcareous table-land of Bonifacio cannot be an argument for disassociating the Corsican–Sardinian cultures that, at the dawn of the 3rd millennium BC, produced the first funerary structures with great granite slabs inserted within stone circles. According to the current state of research, it appears probable that there were two most frequently used seaways between Corsica and Sardinia: one was the connection between the Gulf of Porto Torres and the mouth of the Ortolo, the Gulf of Tizzano, and the Gulf of Vallinco; the other was on the eastern coast at the Gulf of Arzachena, from which it was easy to reach the Gulf of Santa Manza and, especially, the Gulf of Porto-Vecchio. In both cases the difficult passage through the strait of Bonifacio is avoided.

I agree enthusiastically with Giovanni Lilliu's idea (Lilliu 1967: 30ff.) that sees in the geographic unity of Gallura and the nearby Corsican regions the crucible of a unique society. This holds true even today when we may suppose, thanks to important discoveries on the plateau of Pranu Mutteddu at Goni, that the powerful civilization of San Michele is indeed the dominant cultural foundation for Sardinian society during the second half of the 4th and part of the 3rd millennium BC. At Goni, exactly, we find a form of syncretism across the funerary architecture that connects here the great hypogeistic tradition with that of another vision of the sacred, linked to the raising of monoliths. Although we may find ourselves in a context at once less rich and more marginal, in a pastoral environment rather than an agricultural one, we may assume that these cultures in Cagliaritano, as well as in Gallura, directed their own religious values. Even if they wished to integrate the most potent aspect of their religiousness—as seen in their cult for the dead—with elements of the Ozieri culture, we cannot pass over the fact that they expressed this in a specific Megalithic architecture. The cultures of Gallura and southern Corsica seem to follow the same pathways. Even while they affirmed their uniqueness in architecture, they also seemed to integrate elements of powerful, dominant societies.

Chalcolithic Corsica and the Megalithic Phenomenon

1. The 'Terrinian' Facies

The work of Gabriel Camps (1988) has shed light on a new aspect of the civilizations of prehistoric Corsica, revealing a true Chalcolithic remarkably illustrated at the eponymous site of Terrina, near the ancient city of Aléria. This culture is recognized today in numerous other deposits on the island and fills a previous gap in our knowledge of Corsica's prehistory. The lack of information about the earliest Corsican metallurgy had created an unfortunate hiatus, uniquely complicating the explicative schema proposed for establishing cultural development from the Middle Neolithic (4th millennium) to the Bronze Age. The evidence from the second half of the 4th millennium and the 3rd millennium (in calibrated dates) of a cultural transformation around copper, without doubt from local deposits near Terrina, is the major reason for proposing a Corsican Chalcolithic.

By the same token, the earlier proposition by Grosjean (1965; 1966; 1967), that metallurgy had been introduced on the island by an immigrant population of warrior-sailors toward the beginning of the 2nd millennium BC, now becomes obsolete. These so-called 'sea peoples' were thought to have imported to Corsica not only bronze weapons, but also the technique of constructing turriform monuments surmounted by a cupola with false corbels. These *torri* are also subject to question because of the dating of the central monument at the site of Calzola-Castellucciu (Pila-Canale). The following C14 date (GIF-5117) is provided from a destruction level above the foundation level of the site: 3920 ± 200 BP (1970 ± 200 bc) or 2905–1950 cal BC.

Beyond these diverse considerations that serve to complete our knowledge of the Chalcolithic, it is important to add some supplementary information resulting from the study of the *taffoni* tombs.

2. The Association of Menhirs with Taffoni Tombs

Burials arranged within the interiors of natural rocks hollowed out by erosion into granite bowls—so-called *taffoni* burials—have been studied in several southern Corsican strata. The funerary *taffoni* in Corsica, as also in Gallura, comprise a special Megalithic group, even if they do not conform to the common definition of this monumental type because of the reduced human effort required to arrange them. From their appearance we can infer that they were chosen for a certain monumentality, deriving from a specific geological situation. In most instances these natural shelters have been reused; only rarely do they still contain undisturbed prehistoric funerary deposits. Nevertheless, excavations undertaken on several *taffoni* have produced significant results.

In the Cauria (Sartène) massif (Nebbia 1988), as at the site of Calanchi (Sollacaro) (Cesari 1987; 1988), it has been possible to connect the burials of some *taffoni* to the Terrinian facies of the Corsican Chalcolithic. The association of a small menhir with one of the largest *taffoni* at the site of Calanchi is significant for the close connection between this funerary mode and other manifestations of the Megalithic. *Taffonu* tomb no. 2 has a small monolith at the level of the threshold to the burial cavity. It has a roughly triangular shape and has been evened off; its face is planed flat and turned fully toward the south. The back of this monolith, nestled against the inner, concave wall of the rock, is less polished. The presence of this menhir in the architectural organization of the tomb connects us clearly to the symbolism of the baetyls and the 'dressed stones' in proximity to certain tombs (Lilliu 1977). A provisional conclusion can be hypothesized that there existed a certain diversity among funerary customs in the Terrinian Chalcolithic with the appearance of burials in *taffoni*. These seem to coexist with burials in trenches, as recovered from tumuli like that at Terrina, whereas coffer burials seem to fall off. Finally, if certain *taffoni* have associated menhirs, it is possible to include them in the range of Megalithic burials.

3. The Chronology of the Sartène Taffoni

In the case of *taffonu* no. 2 at Calanchi, the funerary artifacts associated with human remains from several individuals—including at least one infant—are poor. I have emphasized the presence of lithic material exclusively represented by a collection of rhyolite arrowheads (Cesari 1987: 345, fig. 14). Ceramic material is composed of the following: two-handled urns with flat bases, coarsely made; small single-handled cups; vases with perforations beneath the rim; and decorated bowls. The majority of the decoration is composed of arrangements of incised lines, grouped in interlocked chevrons that join the base and the rim of the vessels. This second category of vessels also has the best technical qualities. The surfaces have been burnished carefully by means of a tool, perhaps a pebble. The very somber color, sometimes frankly black, gives these vases a 'buccheroid' aspect, obtained by firing in a reduced atmosphere. The paste coheres successfully thanks to very finely crushed quartz that serves to remove grease. The decoration tends to differentiate clearly and sharply more important objects from those belonging to the common lot. These, in summary, are the principal characteristics of ceramic products in the Corsican Chalcolithic, especially Terrinian productions.

Concerning chronology, a *terminus ad quem* may be established by C14 dating (GIF-7153) of wood charcoal taken from the paste of a clay level deposited on the upper part of the tomb, making it watertight: 4080 ± 60 BP (2130 ± 60 bc) or 2890–2415 cal BC.

For other Sartène *taffoni*, excavated earlier by George Peretti (Grosjean *et al.* 1976: 644-53), I accept the opinion of Gabriel Camps (1988: 140) who sees in these decorated ceramics a reminder of the Terrinian decorated style. These ceramics could be included in a common Corsican–Galluran cultural environment. The cups with one handle, and those with raised and perforated feet, find interesting comparisons with ceramic production of the Bonnanaro culture (Ceruti 1981: esp. 68-72). These recall the cuts on the raised and perforated feet of ceramics from several Sardinian sites, in particular the cave of Coronggiu Acca II (Villamassargia).

Contributing to an improved chronological definition for these burials is the site of Calzola-Castellucciu where, in a rock-shelter located just below the monument summit, excavations have identified traces of a burial comprising a stone coffer within a rocky enclosure, sealed up by a thick wall. In a section of the archaeological stratum corresponding to the funerary level, a sherd of a single-handled cup was discovered. This ceramic piece is very reminiscent of cups found in the Murteddu 'hypogeum *taffoni*' (Fig. 8, no. 13 especially). These also find parallels with cups discovered on the floor of the burial chamber of the Settiva dolmen (Petreto-Bicchisano) (Grosjean 1972: 164; Jehasse 1974; Liegeois and Peretti 1976). In the Calzola-Castellucciu shelter, a very small quantity of wood charcoal was taken in the same stratigraphic horizon as the cup, and has been dated by C14 (GIF-5120): 3680 ± 120 BP (1730 ± 120 uncal bc). To this second, absolute chronology, we can add also a date (GIF-7154) from the upper funerary chamber of *taffonu* no. 3 at Calanchi-Sapar'Alta (Sollacaro): 3740 ± 60 BP (1790 ± 60 bc) or 2500–1965 cal BC.

The funerary chamber of *taffonu* no. 3 at Calanchi has yielded very burned human bones. Temperatures raised to the order of 650/750 °C had made the color of the bones very light, proving that the carbon had been burned. Also, it was evident that the bones had often splintered and were deformed from the effect of the heat.

110 *Sardinia in the Mediterranean*

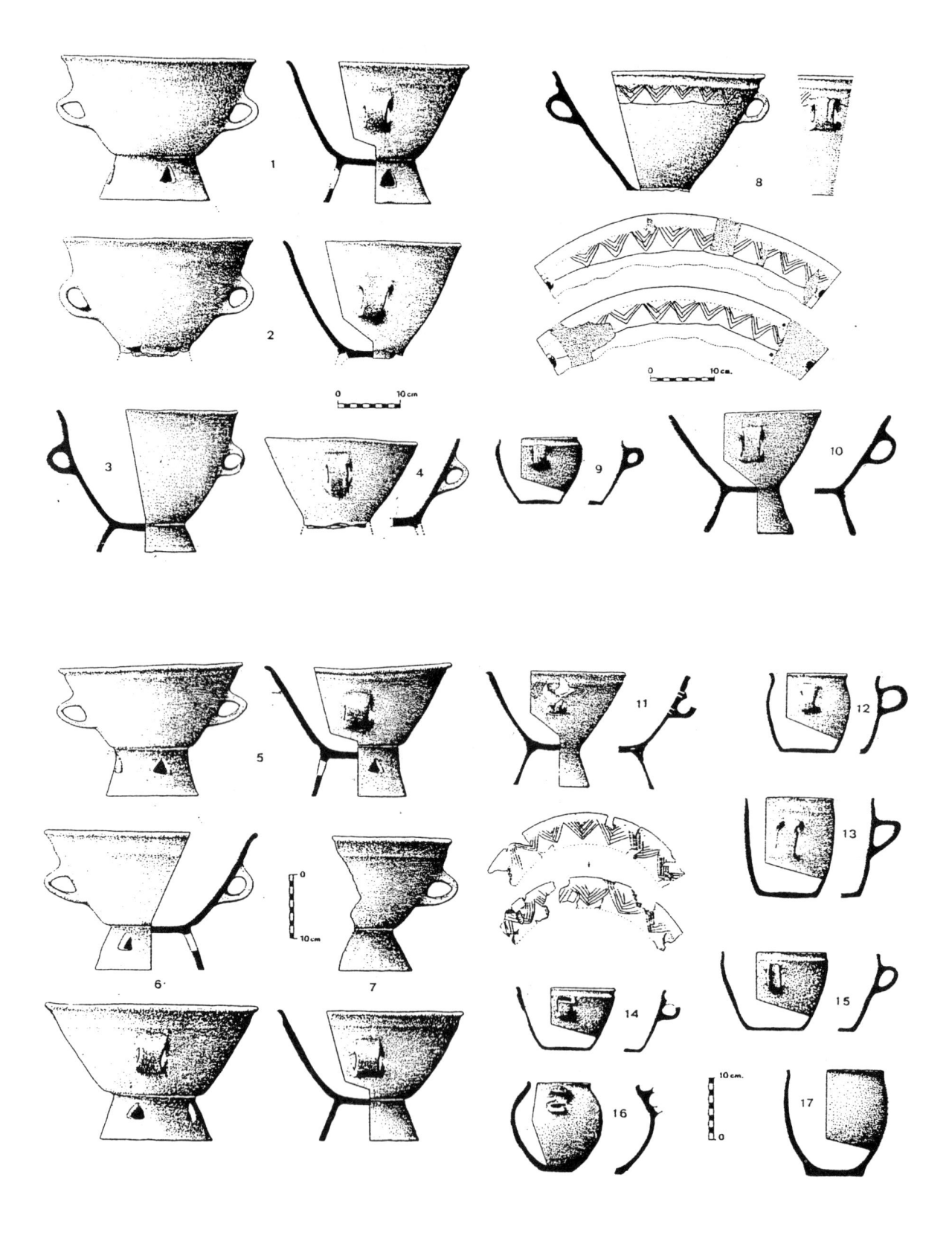

Fig. 8 Musée de Sartène: vases from tombs a taffoni (after Grosjean *et al.* 1976). 1-7: Castellucciu-Minza; 8-17: Murteddu.

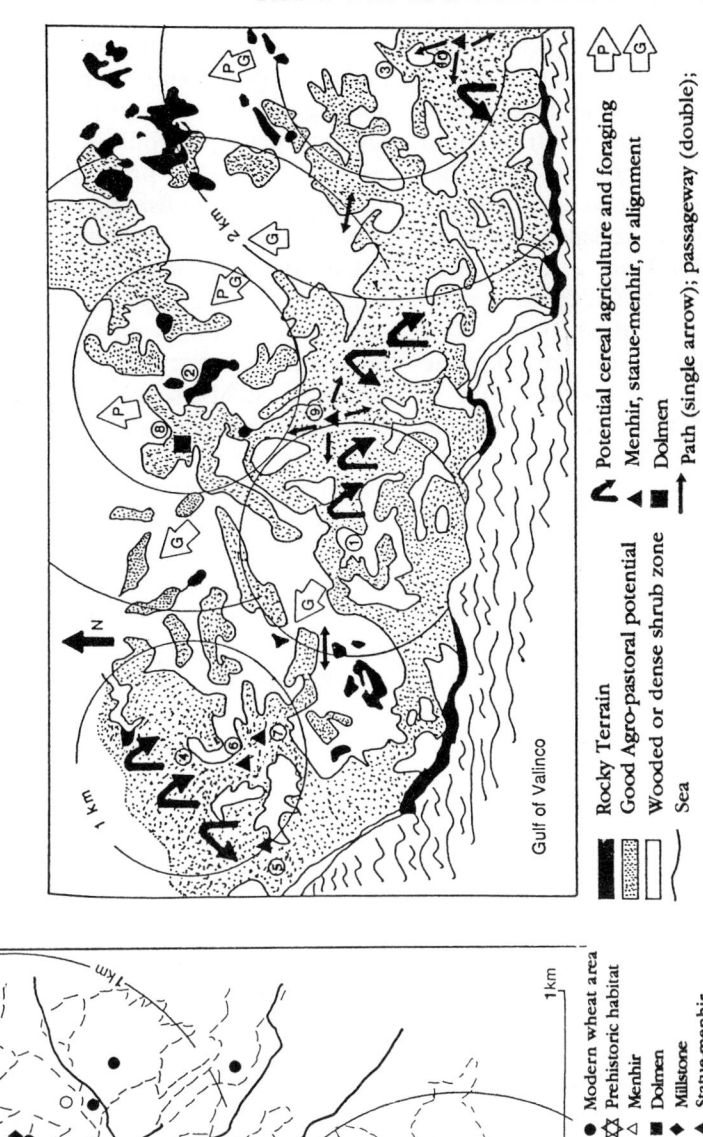

Cesari: *New Contributions to the Study of the Megalithic* 111

Fig. 9 Taravo Plain: principal settlements and megaliths. Modern divisions (dashed lines) and traditional zones of exploitation.

1. Eso; 2. Dolmen Tola di u turmentu; 3. Statue-menhir U Paladinu; 4. Statue-menhir Iesjola; 5. Menhir; 6. Statue-menhir Migalona; 7. Statue-menhir Sčalza Murta; 8. Menhir Fiurita; 9. Vurgonu; 10. Monument Salvaticu; 11. Dolmen Caudiano; 12. Menhir d'Austinaccia; 13/14. Statue-menhir and circular monument of Musolu; 15. Prehistoric site Calanchi-Sapar'Alta; 16. Statue-menhir d'Isula; 17/18. Dolmen, alignment and statue-menhirs Stazzona d'u Diavolu; 19. Petrajo.

Fig. 10 Gulf of Vallinco: subsistence potential of Bronze Age settlements and megaliths.

This type of cremation had been observed also on the human bones coming from the tomb in the 'hypogeum *taffonu*' of Minza-Castellucciu, near Sartène (Arnaud and Arnaud 1978). It could be supposed that these funerary customs that employed hollow rocks and showed incomplete incinerations evolved during the Chalcolithic. In the case of funerary *taffonu* no. 2, the human bones have been simply carbonized; the cremation had been stopped at around 300/350 °C. In a more recent period, datable to the Early Bronze Age, cremation is more advanced. I think that, in the first example, we are dealing with a technique aimed at the conservation of the greatest possible number of skeletel elements; in the second example, this no longer appeared to be more important than bringing about a true incineration.

If there is an evolution in the treatment of the dead, there is also a diversification of funerary architecture during the second half of the 3rd millennium BC. It is certainly possible to recover tombs paired with large monolithic slabs in the form of cists or coffers, generally associated with small standing stones. These latter, which seem to have been located away from burials in *tafffoni*, are found today, with the discovery of *taffonu* no. 2 at Calanchi, to be associated with tombs as well. It is not certain that such monoliths had not been present before the introduction of all these burials; their disappearance could be only the result of subsequent destruction and selective reutilization of the natural rocky cavities in the *taffoni*.

Menhirs and tombs are thus closely associated. It can be established that the majority of the large menhir alignments, some of which include statue-menhirs, are closely associated with dolmens or cist-tombs. It is not unusual to find funerary *taffoni* on the periphery of these monumental assemblages. This has been observed as much in the Cauria area as at Palaggiu (Peretti 1966); but the Taravo alignment with its celebrated dolmen, visited by Prospero Mérimée, is found closely associated with the site of Calanchi-Sapar'Alta.

Spatial Distribution of Settlements and Megaliths in Southern Corsica

1. Calanchi and the Taravo Plain Megaliths

Site aspects determined how the dwellings were set up: a windy hill—85 m a.s.l.—dominates the Canniccia road and the Taravo plain. The local geology, with its chaotic distribution of granite stones bored out with with numerous *taffoni*, and rich in shelter-potential under the rocks, offered generous hospitality. Fertile colluvials are connected in this area with the presence of the plain, the pond, and the river. Beyond the favorable agro-sylvo-pastoral potential, the region offers cynegetic possibilities appropriate to humid zones. Finally, the proximity to a river, a pond and the sea allows fishing.

The intensity of agricultural exploitation of the site is documented by the presence of numerous millstones and grinders. Several of these implements are localized on the border of vast areas favorable for cereal cultivation. These spaces, which can still be seen in the distribution of modern land divisions, were planted with wheat or barley up to recent times. The many areas of wheat still growing in the fields testify to this traditional agriculture that is only now on the verge of disappearing (Fig. 9).

On the periphery of Calanchi and at the edges of the prehistoric dwelling itself sacred spaces coexisted, bringing together the domains of the living and the dead. Within a radius of about 1 km (in my opinion, apparently corresponding to the maximum radius of the wheat fields around the site), there is a strong concentration of megaliths, including many statue-menhirs. Menhirs and statue-menhirs are sometimes associated with dolmens, like the Stazzona dolmen and its covered passage alignment which are associated with the Austinaccia menhir. The megaliths are often localized on the principal axes of travel leading toward other prehistoric habitation centers. One such organization of the territory's geography, whose main axes are apparently determined by the megaliths, is found in the micro-region delimited by the Taravo plain: a large portion of the northern bank of the Vallinco gulf, affording access between the Taravo and Baracci valleys.

2. The Northern Coast of the Gulf of Vallinco

The archaeological exploration of this territory is relatively recent. It began with the discovery of the beautiful statue-menhir at Santa Naria (Olmeto) (Grosjean 1974a; 1974b), situated at an ancient crossroads, in a lovely aspect of the land traditionally cultivated in vines and cereals. The presence near the statue of millstones fixed in vats signifies the agricultural exploitation of these lands since the prehistoric period.

The archaeological map (Fig. 10) clearly shows two kinds of dwellings: (1) a dwelling in a geographically dominant position, linked to a short summer residence; an example is Monte Barbatu, perched at more than 500 m above sea level; and (2) habitations at low altitudes, marking the ancient road from the Taravo plain to that of Baracci. These roads, following the northern shore of the gulf approximately from west to east, penetrate

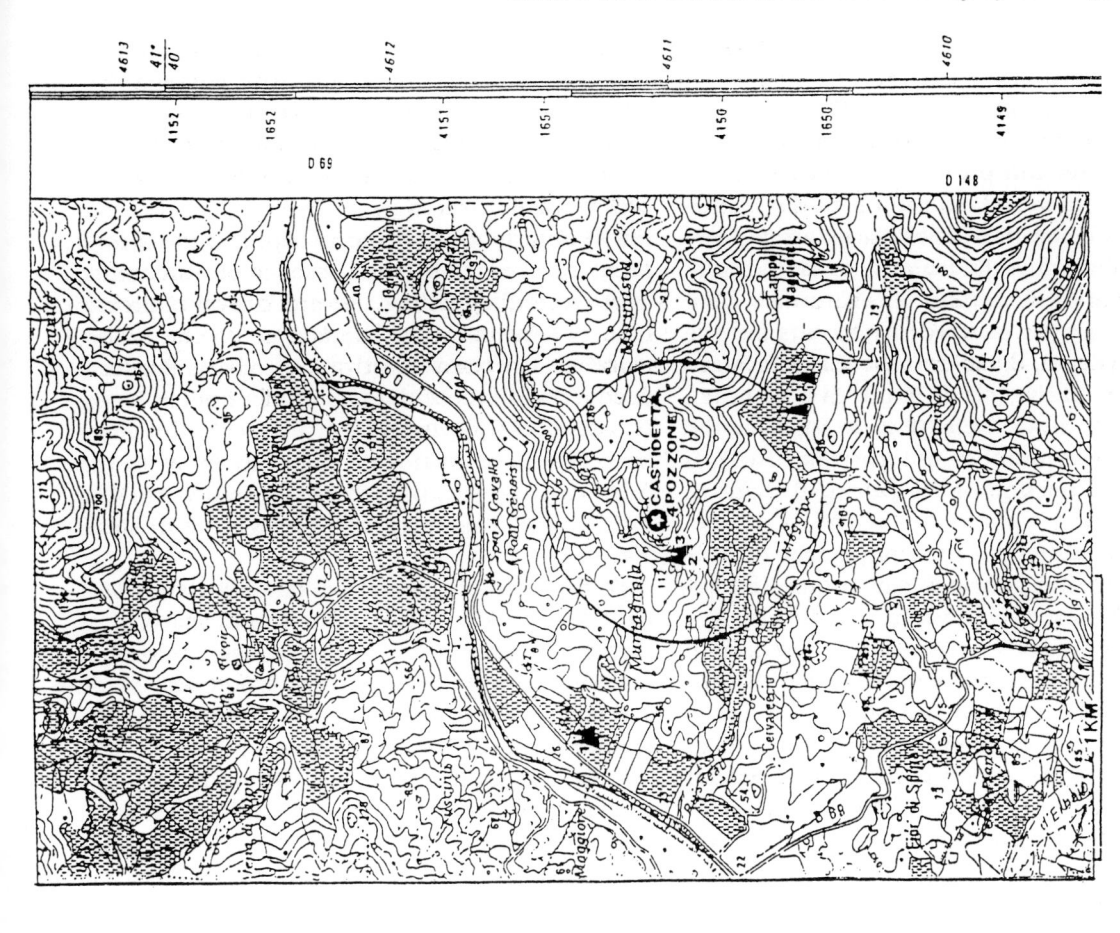

Fig. 12 Castello de Castidetta-Pozzone (Sartène): prehistoric settlement and associated megaliths.

1. Menhirs (2); 2. Statue-menhir of Muntagnola; 3. Menhir of Muntagnola; 4. Prehistoric site of Pozzone; 5. Menhirs (2) of CAMPO MAGGIORE.

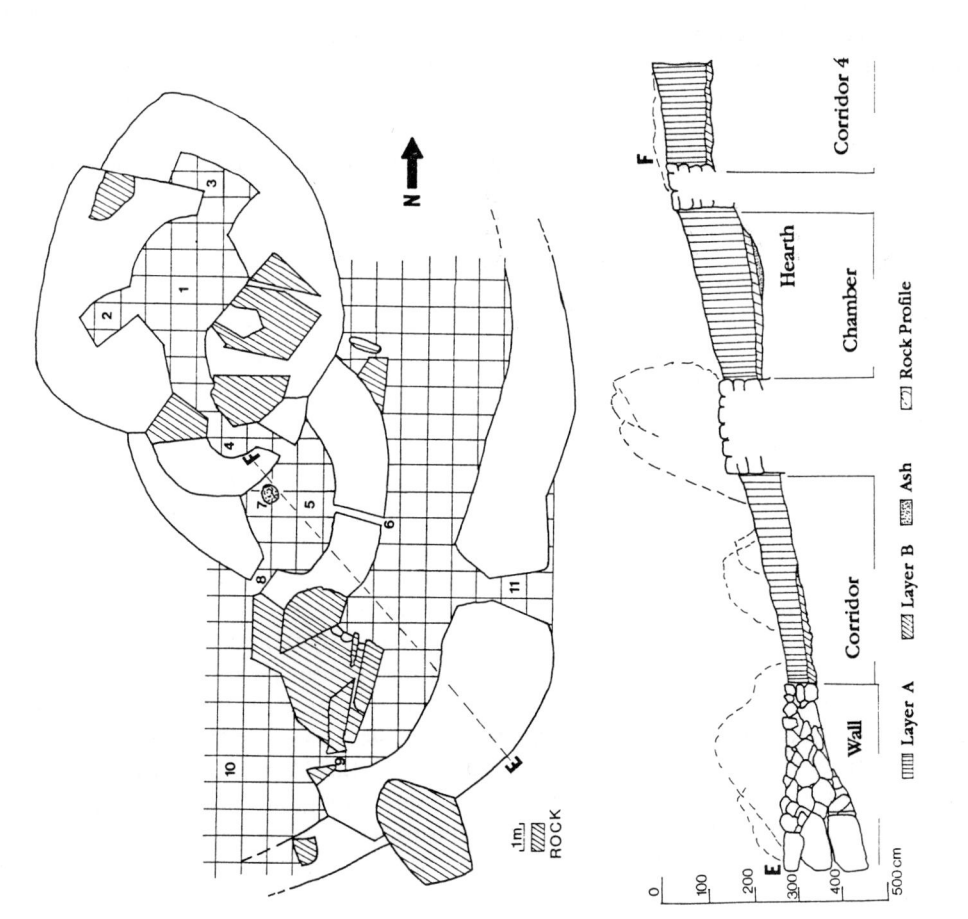

Fig. 11 Castello de Cuntorba (Olmeto): plan and section of the central monument.

the mountainous ridges separating the Taravo and Baracci plains.

The density of habitation sites and megaliths in this zone makes it possible to appreciate its importance to the pre- and protohistoric populations. There is a significant relationship between habitation space and megaliths. These latter are not distributed haphazardly; the majority mark the principal communication routes. Certain ones were set at strategic or noteworthy points in the countryside (Fig. 10.8: the dolmen at Figa la Sarra, at the level with the hill of Bocca di A Coppia). The alignment of Albitretu (Fig. 10.9), near the Bronze Age habitation of Cuntorba (Fig. 10.1), is located at the junction of the principal roads of this region.

All the megaliths in this zone are, in fact, directly associated with the principal habitations. The following show these relationships: the Bronze Age habitation of Torriciola (Fig. 10.3) is associated with the statue-menhir of Santa Naria (Fig. 10.10); the alignment of menhirs at Albitretu is directly linked to Castello de Cuntorba; the dolmen of Figa la Sarra is associated with Monte Barbatu (Fig. 10.2); the menhirs and statue-menhirs of Valle Chiara, Migalona (Fig. 10.5), Scalza Murta (Fig. 10.6) and Fiurita (Fig. 10.7) are closely related to several dwellings above the harbor of Taravo, one of which is Salvaticu (Fig. 10.4).

These diverse remarks on the close association between the distribution areas of habitats, some of which experienced an initial occupation phase in the Chalcolithic, and then became strongly structured by the building of enclosures and towers during the Bronze Age, lead me to revise Grosjean's thesis which proposed an antagonism between the people who created the various megaliths and those who built the habitations.

Through the archaeological results obtained from various habitations, I have tried to present new information that argues for an identification between the Bronze Age *castelli* and *torre* habitations, and the people represented by the statue-menhirs that are evidence of a final developmental phase of the Corsican Megalithic.

Bronze Age Relations between Settlements and Megaliths

I have underscored the extent to which the practice of metallurgy preceded the first half of the 2nd millennium BC. If the use of bronze definitely had been introduced to the island starting from this period, the autochthonous populations were already considerably disposed towards an experienced handling of metals. We know today that the weapons frequently portrayed on the statue-menhirs, especially the daggers, certainly had been produced locally. In the principal chamber of Castello di Cuntorba (Olmeto) (Fig. 11.1), there was discovered a bronze blade from a small riveted dagger. From the southern zone of the dwelling came a fragment of a crucible with some metal droplets, attesting to the melting and production of bronze objects here. At other habitations on the island, evidence has been found that supports the local production of these daggers. The mould at Marze (Corscia) (Acquaviva 1979), in the Niolo, must have produced blades or daggers similar to the ones discovered at Cuntorba, Torre (Grosjean 1959) and Tappa (Porto-Vecchio) (Grosjean 1962).

To this type of weapon we can associate a C14 date (GIF-1755), taken from wood charcoal at the edges of the foyer area of principal chamber no. 1 in Castello di Cuntorba, where the blade and dagger were found as well: 3110 ± 60 BP (1160 ± 60 bc) or 1660–1115 cal BC.

In the township of Sartène, the study of a new site at Castidetta-Pozzone, and a site at the level of a small hill at Muntagnola (Fig. 12.3-4), has resulted in establishing the marks of roads by the megaliths, and their incontestable association with a huge Bronze Age village. The hill at Muntagnola is dominated by a rocky crest, divided up by a vast complex of dwellings surrounded by enclosures. At its summit (168 m), a tower was built that dominates the Rizzanese valley below. It directly controls the confluence of the Campo-Maggiore and the Muntagnola hill, where one statue-menhir—the 77th in Corsica by recent count—and at least one menhir were erected.

Excavations in an out-building of the summit tower have brought to light traces of domestic activity. In a corner of the room, there was discovered a fragment from a valve-mould used for making daggers. This is the part that produces the solid handle with its curved pommel. I emphasize here the great significance of this unique room for the whole island. It confirms my hypothesis that it was the same people who built the villages and turriform monuments, and who sculpted the armed statue-menhirs. For the first time, in a discrete archaeological level, we have proof that weapons were made on a Corsican site itself. If we compare the curved—or semi-lunate—pommel area of the Castidetta-Pozzone mould with the pommel of the short sword of the Santa Naria statue-menhir (Grosjean 1974a; 1974b), and the dagger pommel of the so-called Filitosa 5 statue-menhir (Grosjean 1961; 1963), we can make a conclusive identification between pieces made from the mould, and the sculpted weapons of these statue-menhirs. Lastly, we can relate the Sartène mould to the beautiful bronze dagger discovered in a river-bed at Panchéraccia (Upper Corsica), now preserved at the Aléria archaeological museum (Bonifay *et al.* 1990: 91).

All these daggers exhibit the same model of curved—or semi-lunate—pommel and the same type of straight hilt. Typologically, they belong to the family of daggers with simple blades, including Rhodian and Italian types (Briard and Mohen 1983). The haft is solid metal. It could be useful to compare these with the miniature votive examples from Nuragic Sardinia (Lo Schiavo 1981: fig. 378).

The following C14 date (LGQ-272), taken from wood charcoal in the principal room of the Castidetta-Pozzone tower, and representing the same archaeological stratum as the one in the adjoining room which contained the mould, is added here in an effort to place these pieces with chronological precision: 2870 ± 140 BP (920 ± 140 uncal bc). For a chronological approach to the weapons represented on the Corsican statue-menhirs, and in other Mediterranean areas, a useful discussion is to be found in Chenorkian (1988).

Conclusion

By its monumental construction, and by its long development, the Megalithic phenomenon strongly marked the prehistoric civilizations of Corsica and became their dominant cultural expression. Megalithic production, as it seems to have evolved from its very earliest monuments—coffer tombs encircled by stones—towards the end of the 4th millennium, during a time of transition and rapid developments, exerted fundamental influences on metallurgy. The cultural unity of Gallura and southern Corsica is affirmed most of all through these first megalithic tombs which echo the powerful Ozieri culture. The insular Chalcolithic is marked above all by a precocious copper metallurgy at Terrina. The Terrinians developed a society whose dynamism is corroborated by population density and the powerful cultural unity evidenced by the decorations on ceramics. We may infer, however, certain cultural specifics, from north to south of the island, cutting across funerary customs that appeared diversified and adapted to the geological formations of the micro-regions in choice of architecture and certain rituals of skeletal cremation. The economic unity of Terrinian society is felt, above all, in the choice of sites which confirms the practice of rearing large livestock and an agriculture oriented towards cereals.

In the course of the second half of the 3rd millennium, the presence of bell-form ceramics is attested at *taffonu* no. 6 at Calanchi-Sapar'Alta in a Terrinian (C14 date LGQ- 279: 3910 ± 150 B P) context (Camps and Cesari 1991). Around this large site, where *taffoni* burials and built habitats were closely associated, an entire group of megalithic monuments divided up the territory. Even if all the megaliths were not built during the same period, it is certain that they bear witness to a continuity of sorts in the management of sacred space.

This continuity is also confirmed during the 2nd millennium, up to the beginning of the 1st millennium. Today, it is difficult to envision the cultures of the Bronze Age in terms of ethnic oppositions (Camps 1990, on the fragility of Grosjean's 'Shardane theory'). The always more precise identification between the builders of the villages and *torri*, and the sculptors of the statue-menhirs, marks a new stage in the confident identification of the Bronze Age Corsicans. The ostentation and the multiplication of weapons, paralleled by an organization of public architecture in which security was the dominant issue, disclose a picture of a bellicose society. If local hegemonies were possible, then the cultural unity of the island must have been maintained at the site of Rusumini (Castinetta), above the confluence of the Casaluna and the Golo. Here is a Bronze Age architecture that recapitulates in every way the entire architectural ensemble of southern Corsica.

References

Acquaviva, L.
    1979   Le castello de Marze à Corscia. *Archeologia Corsa* 4: 43-48.

Arnaud, G., & S. Arnaud
    1978   Os brûlés provenant de sépultures de Castellucciu (Sartene, Corse—Age du Bronze). *Archeologia Corsa* 3: 93-95.

Atzeni, E.
    1981   Aspetti e sviluppi culturali del neolitico e della prima età dei metalli in Sardegna. In E. Atzeni *et al.* (eds.), *Ichnussa: La Sardegna dalle origini all'età classica*, 21-51. Milano: Libri Scheiwiller.

    1987   Il neolitico della Sardegna. In *Atti della XXVI Riunione Scientifica, 'Il Neolitico in Italia,' novembre 1985, Firenze*, 381-400. Firenze: Istituto Italiano di Preistoria e Protostoria.

    1988   Megalitismo e arte. *Rassegna di Archeologia* 7: 449-56.

Atzeni, E., & D. Cocco
    1989   Nota sulla necropoli megalitica di Pranu Mutteddu-Goni. In L. Campus (a cura di), *La Cultura di Ozieri. Problematiche e nuove acquisizioni*, 201-16. Ozieri: Il Torchietto.

Bonifay, E., A. Gauthier, M.-C. Weiss, G. Camps, J. Cesari & F. de Lanfranchi
1990 *Préhistoire de la Corse*. Ajaccio: Centre Régional de Documentation Pédagogique.

Briard, J., & J.P. Mohen
1983 *Typologie des Objets de l'Age du Bronze en France. Fasc. II: Poignards, hallebardes, pointes de lances, pointes de flèches, armement défensif*. Paris: S.P.F.

Camps, G.
1988 *Préhistoire d'une Ile*. Paris: Errance.
1990 Statues-menhirs corses et Shardanes. La fin d'un mythe. *Revue Archéologique de l'Ouest* 2 (Supplement): 1-9.

Camps, G. (ed.)
1988 *Terrina et le Terrinien. Recherches sur le Chalcolithique de la Corse*. Collection de l'Ecole Française de Rome 109.

Camps, G. & J. Cesari
1991 Découverte d'un tesson campaniforme en Corse-du-Sud. *Bulletin de la Société des Sciences Historiques et Naturelles de la Corse* 659: 31-38.

Cesari, J.
1985 Les dolmens de la Corse. *Archéologia* 205 (September): 32-45.
1987 Le Néolithique et le Chalcolithique du gisement des Calanchi (Sollacaro, Corse-du-Sud), note de présentation. *Bulletin de la Société des Sciences Historiques et Naturelles de la Corse* 652: 319-58.
1988 Le Terrinien du Site des Calanchi (Sollacaro— Corse du Sud). In G. Camps (ed.), *Terrina et le Terrinien. Recherches sur le Chalcolithique de la Corse*. Collection de l'Ecole Française de Rome 109: 358-74.

Chenorkian, R.
1988 *Les Armes Métalliques dans l'Art Protohistorique Méditerranéen*. Marseille: C.N.R.S.

Ferrarese Ceruti, M.L.
1981 La cultura del vaso campaniforme. Il primo Bronzo. In E. Atzeni *et al.* (eds.), *Ichnussa. La Sardegna dalle origini all'età classica*, 53-77. Milano: Libri Scheiwiller.

Grosjean, R.
1959 Torre ... monument mégalithique du Bronze Moyen. *Revue Archéologique* 2: 15-40.
1961 Filitosa et son contexte archéologique. *Monuments et Mémoires Fond. E. Piot* 52(1). Paris.
1962 Le gisement fortifié de Tappa (Porto-Vecchio). *Bulletin de la Société Préhistorique Française* 59: 206-17.
1963 Les armes portées par les statues-menhirs de Corse. *Revue Archéologique* 2: 1-15.
1965 L'évolution culturelle et artistique de la civilisation mégalithique de Corse. In *C.R. du Congres Préhistorique de France, Monaco, XVIe sess. 1959*, 613-22. Paris.
1966 *La Corse avant l'histoire. Monuments et art de la civilisation mégalithique insulaire du debut du IIIe a la fin du IIe millenaire avant notre ère*. Paris: Editions Klincksieck.
1967 Classification descriptive du Mégalithique corse. *Bulletin de la Société Préhistorique Française* 3: 707-42.
1972 Le complexe mégalithique de Settiva (Petreto-Bicchisano, Corsica). *Bulletin de la Société Préhistorique Française* 69(6): 164.
1974a La statue-menhir de Santa Naria (Olmeto, Corse). *Bulletin de la Société Préhistorique Française* 70(8): 226.
1974b La statue-menhir de Santa Naria (Olmeto, Corse). *Bulletin de la Société Préhistorique Française* 71(2): 53-57.

Grosjean, R., & J. Liègeois
1964 Les coffres mégalithiques de la région de Porto-Vecchio. *L'Anthropologie* 68(5-6): 527-48.

Grosjean, R., avec la collaboration de J. Liègeois et G. Peretti
1976 Les civilisations de l'Age du Bronze en Corse. *La Préhistoire Française* 1(11): 644-53. Paris: C.N.R.S.

Jehasse, J.
1974 Informations archéologiques. Corse. *Gallia Préhistoire* 17(2): 701-709.

Joussaume, R.
1985 *Des dolmens pour les morts. Les mégalithismes à travers le monde*. Paris: Hachette.

Lanfranchi, F. de
1980 Les mégalithes corses et leur contexte. *Atti della XXII Riunione Scientifica nella Sardegna Centro-Settentrionale, ottobre 1978, Firenze*, 449-67. Firenze: Istituto Italiano di Preistoria e Protostoria.
1987 Le renouvellement de la recherche dans l'étude des dolmens de la Corse. *Bulletin de la Société des Sciences Historiques et Naturelles de la Corse* 652: 305-18.
1989 La nécropole mégalithique de Monte Rotondo à Sotta. *Bulletin de la Société des Sciences Historiques et Naturelles de la Corse* 656: 290-305.

Lanfranchi, F. de, & M.-C. Weiss
1980 Les chambres funéraires mégalithiques incluses dans un tumulus limité par des cercles de pierres ou dalles. *Atti della XXII Riunione Scientifica nella Sardegna Centro-Settentrionale, ottobre 1978, Firenze*, 469-73. Firenze: Istituto Italiano di Preistoria e Protostoria.

Liègeois, J., & G. Peretti
1976 Sites decouverts par Roger Grosjean. In J. Jehasse and R. Grosjean (eds.), *Sites Prehistoriques et Protohistoriques de l'Ile de Corse*, 101-104.

Lilliu, G.
1967 *La Civiltà dei Sardi. Dal neolitico all'età dei nuraghi*. Torino: ERI.
1977 *Dal 'Betilo' Aniconico alla Statuaria Nuragica*. Sassari: Galizzi.

Lo Schiavo, F.
1981 Economia e società nell'età dei nuraghi. In E. Atzeni *et al.* (eds.), *Ichnussa. La Sardegna dalle origini all'età classica*, 255-347. Milano: Libri Scheiwiller.

Nebbia, P.
1988 Le Chalcolithique Terrinien de Cauria, abris XX et XXI (Sartene Corse-du-Sud). In G. Camps (ed.), *Terrina et le Terrinien. Recherches sur le Chalcolithique de la Corse*, 374-79. Collection de l'Ecole Française de Rome 109.

Peretti, G.
1966 Une sépulture campaniforme en rapport avec l'alignement des menhirs de Palaggiu (Sartene-Corse). *Congrès de la Société Préhistorique Française Ajaccio, XVIIe Sess., 1966*, 230-42.

Riassunto

La maggiore espressione della preistoria Corsa si riferisce ad un fenomeno megalitico avvenuto grosso modo tra il Tardo Neolitico e la Età del Ferro. Esistono tre tipi di monumenti megalitici. Il primo tipo include ciste megalitiche chiamate *bancali*, e dolmens chiamati *stazzoni*. La seconda categoria include i *menhir* e le statue-*menhir*, pietre lavorate e che nella forma antropomorfica sono chiamate *paladini* e spesso recano rappresentazioni di spade o pugnali. I *menhir* e le statue-*menhir* sono chiamati *i filarate* se sono raggruppati in estesi allineamenti. Tombe a fossa, dolmens e allineamenti di *menhir* formano una distinta architettura funeraria corsa.

L'associazione di tombe a fossa con *menhir* è uno specifico tipo di complesso architettonico funerario tipico della Corsica e della Gallura nella Sardegna settentrionale, ed esempi paralleli includono tombe nella regione di Portovecchio e di Li Muri in Arzachena; c'è da aggiungere che le tombe a fossa nell'altipiano di Pranu Mutteddu presso Goni sono paragonabili ad alcuni monumenti della Gallura.

Presso gli scavi dei complessi funerari corsi la presenza di ossidiana sarda importata fra le industrie litiche locali mostra l'esistenza di un'associazione tra le due isole. C'è da aggiungere il fatto che sia in Sardegna che in Corsica i siti abitati sono localizzati in territori dove la pastorizia è più diffusa dell'agricoltura. L'Autore concorda con Lilliu nel sostenere che durante il IV e il III millennio a.C., la Gallura e la vicina regione corsa hanno formato un'unità culturale.

L'Autore sostiene (come Camps) che durante la seconda metà del IV millennio fino alla fine del III millennio a.C., è esistita una vera e propria cultura corsa calcolitica chiamata Terriniana (il nome deriva dal sito vicino all'antica Aléria). La principale caratteristica della cultura Terriniana è la metallurgia del rame, usando forse il minerale ottenuto dai depositi vicino a Terrina. Ulteriori testimonianze di un facies Terriniana del Calcolitico corso proviene dai 'taffoni': rocce cave di natura usate per sepolture e considerate monumenti megalitici. Nel 'taffonu' n. 2 a Sollacaro il corredo include ceramiche simili a quelle provenienti dai taffoni-ipogei di Murtedu (Sartène). Fra le forme sono: urne a biansate con basi piatte, tazze monoansate, vasi con orli perforati e scodelle decorate con galloni che connettono con le basi e gli orli. Questo stile ceramica, presente anche presso altri taffoni a Sartène, a Calzola-Castellucciu, e nel taffonu n. 3 a Calanchi-Sapar'Alta, è simile allo stile delle ceramiche di Bonnanaro. Dati C14 di materiali associati datano tutti allo stesso periodo.

L'Autore studia anche la relazione esistente tra la distribuzione spaziale delle abitazioni e dei megaliti nella Corsica meridionale. Particolarmente interessanti sono le relazioni esistenti tra i monumenti situati nella pianura di Taravo, le abitazioni all'interno e intorno al preistorico giacimento dei Calanchi, e la forte concentrazione locale di menhir e statue-menhir. Sono interessanti anche i rapporti nel golfo settentrionale di Vallinco, tra statue-*menhir*, allineamenti di *menhirs*, e siti abitativi. L'Autore conclude che esiste un'associazione tra i megaliti e gl'insediamenti d'abitazione. La maggior parte dei megaliti segnano le principali vie di comunicazione o altri punti strategici nella campagna, e i megaliti sono quasi tutti costruiti vicino a centri abitati.

L'Autore sostiene che gli abitanti dei castelli e delle torri durante l'Età del Bronzo sono le stesse persone raffigurate nelle statue-*menhir* del megalitico corso del II millennio. Questo è dimostrato dal fatto che alcune statue-*menhir* situate vicino a centri abitati, recano raffigurazioni di armi di tipologia corsa. Gli scavi di Castidetta-Pozzone sulla collina di Muntagnola (Sartène) hanno restituito una matrice con cui venivano prodotte pugnali con manici diritti solidi e con pomelli arcati. Questo tipo di pomello è presente su una spada corsa di una statua-menhir di Santa Naria, e sul pugnale della statua-menhir chiamata Filitosa 5. Dati C14, di carboni ritrovati a Castidetta-Pozzone, collocano la matrice del pugnale circa 920 ± 140 a.C. Un altro tipo di pugnale con manico a perno è attestato a Castello di Cuntorba (Olmeto), dove sono stati ritrovati un frammento di lama e un crogiolo per fondere metalli. Dati C14 di materiale associato collocano questi ritrovamenti circa 1160–1115 a.C. Questi ritrovamenti rivoluzionano la teoria di R. Grosjean secondo la quale coloro che hanno eretto le statue-menhir e coloro che hanno costruito i centri abitati erano in conflitto, e afferma l'esistenza di un'unità culturale nel megalitico corso.

The Megalithic Monuments of Corsica and Sardinia: A Comparative Study*

François de Lanfranchi

The archaeological riches of Sardinia, an island with an area of 24,089 km² and a population of 1,516,000 inhabitants, have resisted any comparison with Corsica, only 8681 km² with 250,000 inhabitants. Smaller and less populated, since Prosper Merimée's visit to Corsica in 1839 the smaller island has seemed characterized by a great cultural poverty in marked contrast to Sardinia. Over the last 50 years, however, progress in archaeological research has thrown these accepted ideas into question. It is now clear that Corsica has a singular prehistoric past within a Corsican–Sardinian geographic context. It is within this framework that the megalithic achievement common to both islands will be discussed.

A brief review of the first inhabitants of Corsica allows us to emphasize the great similarities between Corsica and Sardinia. The earliest Holocene (7th millennium BC) peoples of Corsica were hunters who established themselves in the south of the island at Bonifacio and Levie, and also in the north in the region of Nebbio. They were aceramic and pre-Neolithic, living by hunting, fishing and gathering. Their stone tools were fashioned from local quartz and rhyolite.

In the 6th millennium BC human habitation extended to all the coastal zones of Corsica. The presence of these Neolithic people is equally well attested in both rock-shelters and open-air settlements. Recent excavations conducted at Longone (Bonifacio) have made it possible to distinguish four successive cultural phases over approximately 1500 years:

First phase	= Cardial I (beginning in the mid-6th millennium BC). The pottery is decorated with *Cardium* shell impressions. Stone tools are of local rock or imported flint.
Second phase	= Cardial II (1st half of the 5th millennium BC). The pottery is still decorated with *Cardium* impressions. Quartz, rhyolite, flint, and obsidian were used for stone tools.
Third phase	= Cardial III (mid-5th millennium BC). This is apparently a transitional phase marked by the appearance of new pottery forms, especially vessels with numerous handles.
Fourth phase	= Punched Wares (middle to the end of the 5th millennium BC). Cardial impressed pottery becomes rare, whereas punch-decorated ceramics now appear, as well as a smooth-surfaced pottery. Stone tools made from obsidian are abundant. There are pieces in geometric shapes including segments of circles, triangles, trapezoids and rectangles.

The development of a Mediterranean Early Neolithic in four phases is a peculiarly Corsican—more precisely, southern Corsican—achievement. We should not fail to note, however, that this evolutionary process also concerns Sardinia. The Goulet Bonifacian ceramics and those of the Su Carroppu de Sirri (Carbonia) rock-shelter in southwest Sardinia are absolutely alike (Fig. 1). We may infer from this similarity that the same cultural stream that introduced Sardinian obsidian into Corsica for the first time during Phase II at Longone also carried the ceramics—or the ceramic technique—of Su Carroppu. By contrast, the pottery of Phase III of Longone is much closer to that of Grotte Verde (Alghero) in northwest Sardinia.

Finally, we note that Phase IV at Longone, where punched wares appear probably c. 4700/4400 cal BC, as well as at Araguina-Sennola (presumably at the same date as at Longone), reminds us of the later, Middle Neolithic, Bonu Ighinu culture in Sardinia. The two issues that arise are: (1) chronological, with a radiocarbon date of 3730 ± 160 uncal BC at Longone; and (2)

---

* Translated from the French by G. Bates and T. Andrews.

Fig. 2 Punched ware from Curacchiaghiu (above) and from the Goulet-Bonifacian rock-shelter (below).

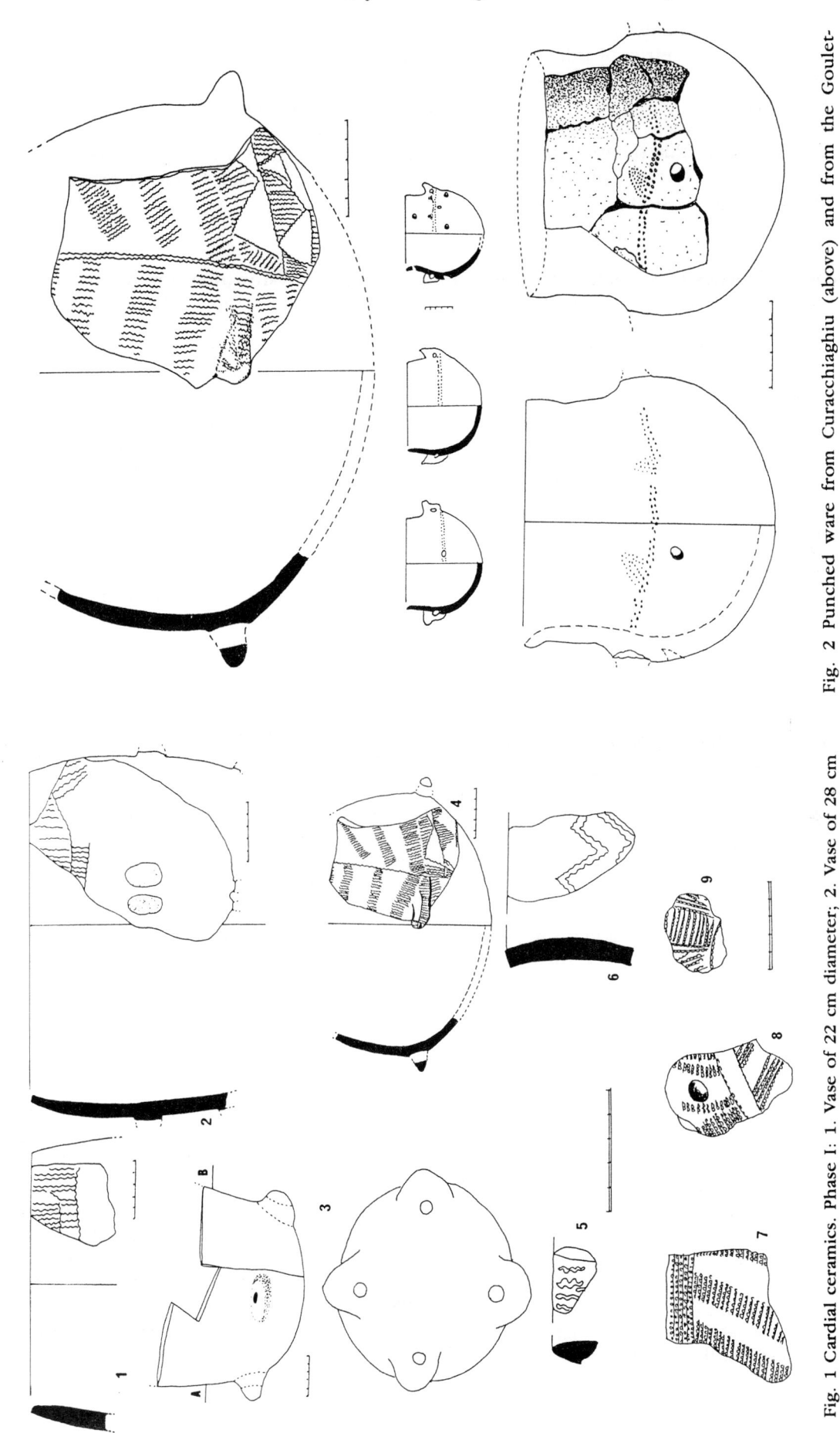

Fig. 1 Cardial ceramics. Phase I: 1. Vase of 22 cm diameter; 2. Vase of 28 cm diameter. Phase II: 3. Vase with four handles; 4. Vase from the Goulet-Bonifacian rock-shelter. Phase III: 5. Vase with normal impressions on the rim; Phase IV: 6. Decorated ceramic from the Araguina rock-shelter (level XVIIc); 7-9. Ceramics from Su Carroppu de Sirri.

cultural, with the presence alongside the Corsican Punched Ware of a geometric obsidian tool assemblage denoting a different cultural stream than the Cardial (Fig. 2).

The discontinuity between the end of the Mediterranean Early Neolithic (c. 4000 BC) and the beginning of the Late Neolithic, represented by the Basien culture (c. 3300 BC), for example, once posed a problem. Thanks to the discovery of the site of Presa-Tusiu in Alta Rocca, however, this hiatus has now been filled. The definition of the Middle Neolithic Presian culture, dating from 3870 to 3200 uncal BC,[1] rests in large part on an early pottery type: fine, polished, well-fired, of a dark color approaching a very deep brown. It is also in this period that the first villages appear in Corsica. The Presian culture, contemporary with that of Bonu Ighinu in Sardinia, bears no similarity to it.

In the Late Neolithic (end of the 4th/beginning of the 3rd millennium BC) we see a multitude of cultural groups virtually as numerous as the Corsican valleys themselves. The Basien (3300 BC), the culture of Curacchiaghiu (Level 5, 2980 BC), Levels 14 to 16 of Araguina-Sennola, the shelter of Scaffa Piana in the region of Saint-Florent Level 22, 3410 BC; Level 21, 3370 BC), Carcu (2690 BC), Monte Grosso at Biguglia, Monte Lazzu in the region of Cinarca, and others; all these reveal the numerous cultural divisions of Corsica in this period. The cultural uniformity of Sardinia in the Ozieri period (end of the 4th/beginning of the 3rd millennium BC) contrasts with contemporary Corsica where, on this smaller island, each micro-region exhibits a variety of ceramics and lithic implements, and therefore seems to have its own cultural development. There is evidence, however, of a certain unity of preference in some cultural aspects: settlements are frequently located on low hills near level ground, with numerous structures for grinding activities (mills, for example), and there is also a tendency towards uniformity of funerary rites with the adoption of the first megalithic monuments. These cultural characteristics, in evidence in the Corsican Late Neolithic and contemporary with the Sardinian Ozieri Culture, are affirmed and developed in the Corsican Final Neolithic–Chalcolithic. This, at least, is what I propose to demonstrate here.

The Megalithic Monuments of Corsica

The Corsican megalithic monuments can be organized into several classes, a fact that encourages us to propose from the outset a clear definition of the fundamental types. A typology can be based on several criteria, such as morphology or function; one must choose between these aspects, however, because we have found that in practice definitions based on both morphology and function are not acceptable. Morphological distinctions can be made between the megalithic coffer, the dolmen, the menhir, the statue-menhir and the stela. The classification of monoliths may also assume diverse terminologies: alignment, cromlech, etc. These classes have been variously defined as follows: *megalithic coffers* are chambers, greater than about 150 × 130 cm, closed on four sides by deeply-buried slabs placed sideways. This monumental type is not known to have a covering slab. Generally the coffer is bounded by a stone circle. *Cists* are nothing more than coffers smaller than about 150 × 130 cm. *Dolmens* are funerary chambers closed on three sides and protected on top by a covering slab. In a large number of cases the dolmen is bounded by a circle of stones (e.g. Settiva). *Menhirs* are dressed stones, either rough or shaped. *Statue-menhirs* are dressed stones carved to represent the human body. A *cromlech* is a circle of stones. An *alignment* is the linear juxtaposition of monoliths, usually with a north–south orientation.

The situation on Corsica, however, is much more complicated than these terms can describe, and these definitions often have only regional value where they are used. For this reason I have introduced the term 'megalithic complex', which I believe fits the circumstances more closely. Also, megalithic complexes may be found in Sardinia, where Puglisi and Castaldi (1966) have already identified two types of stone circles. I shall classify megaliths, therefore, into one of two groups.

---

1 Radiocarbon dating for the site of Presa-Tusiu, structure 1:

Level 4	(-72 cm)	5820 ± 130 BP
Level 3b/3c	(-70 cm)	5150 ± 130 BP
Level 2b/2c		4890 ± 130 BP

Level 2b/2c represents the Late Neolithic at Presa-Tusiu. This chronology is very important because it locates the beginning of megalithic constructions on this site between the end of the middle Neolithic, c. 3200 uncal BC, and the beginning of the Late Neolithic, c. 2940 uncal BC. Thus, the menhirs and the passage megalithic monuments of Presa-Tusiu are established at the end of the 4th–beginning of the 3rd millennium BC.

Fig. 4 Presa-Tusiu. Plan of structures 1-3.

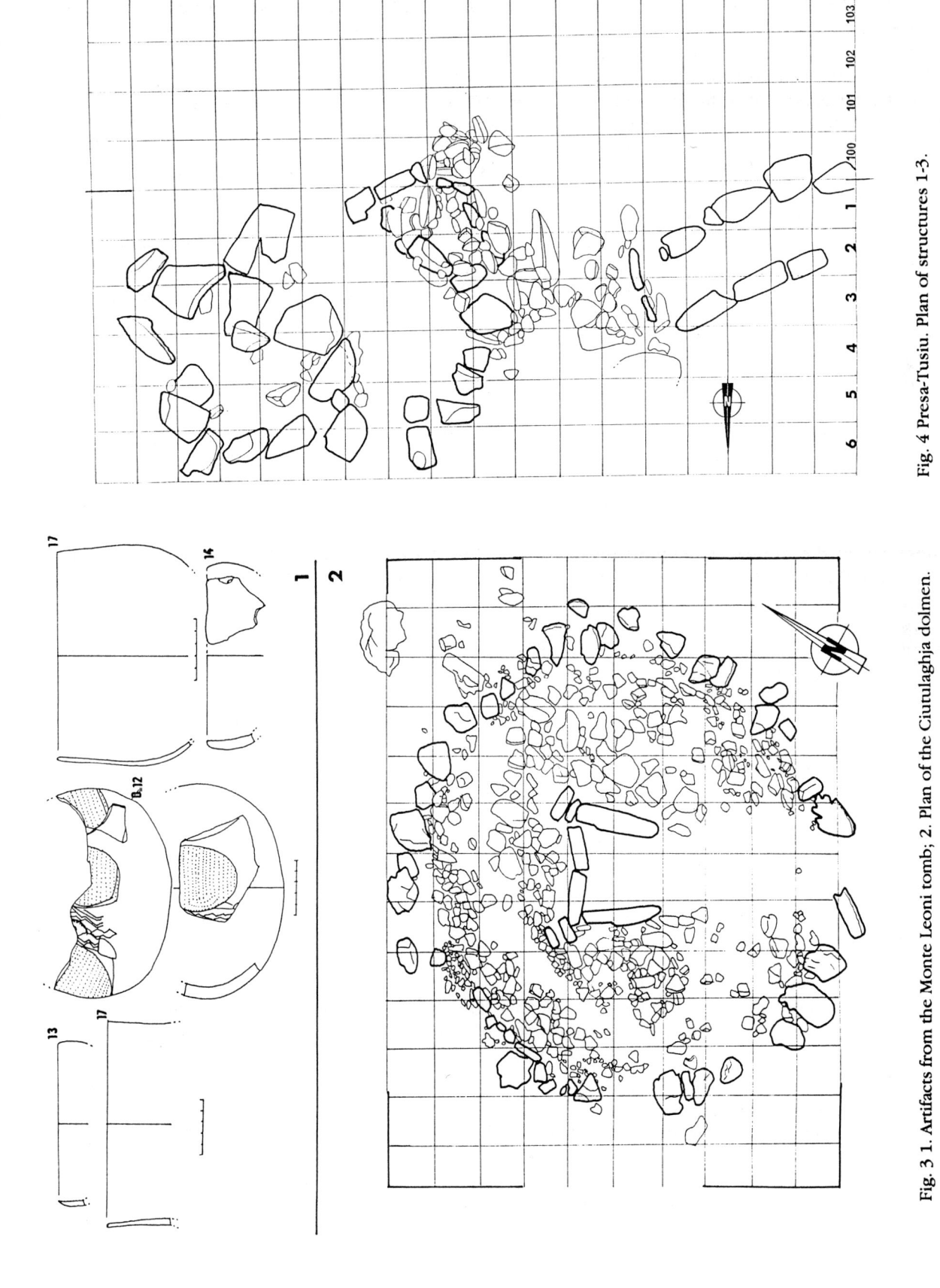

Fig. 3 1. Artifacts from the Monte Leoni tomb; 2. Plan of the Ciutulaghja dolmen.

Type A Dolmen Complex

This is a space of variable dimensions in which assemblages of monoliths are arranged in aspects of mutual orientation. In the best examples there are five components: (1) the dolmen tomb; (2) the stones surrounding the tomb; (3) one or more menhirs (raised stones); (4) an alignment of oblong stones (menhirs) or stone blocks; and (5) spaces of variable shape and dimension, demarcated by juxtaposed stones.

In general, the dolmen complex is Type A when it comprises all five components; this is the case at Ciutulaghia (Fig. 3) and Settiva. On other Type A sites some of these features may no longer be extant; Bizzicu Rosu, also a Type A complex, now comprises only components 1, 2, and 4.

Type B Megalithic Group

There are on Corsica concentrated groups of megaliths on the same site that do not include a dolmen tomb. Zoppo (Zonza), Cruci (Levie), and Porto Vecchio are all Type B megalithic group sites.

This typology seems, at first glance, to have the merit of precision. Our observation of the diverse constituent elements of these monumental complexes and their classification into Types A or B seems easy and natural. But in reality the situation is quite different since, for example, because of poor conservation, certain components of a megalithic complex may have disappeared. Further, the absence of anthropological documentation prevents us from stating in all cases whether a chamber, dolmen, or coffer actually served as a tomb, or as a place for offerings.

Cultural Aspects and Chronology

It goes without saying that it is important to understand the relationship between these architectural monuments and the local cultures that erected them. Nevertheless, the great rarity of artifacts found associated with the Corsican megalithic monuments usually limits us to the proposal of future directions of research rather than to the presentation of even meager evidence. Since my earlier study on the Corsican megalithic monuments (Lanfranchi 1987), a new monumental type, the megalithic passage, has been presented for consideration. It is represented by only a few examples: Musuleu (Casalabriva), Cumpulaghia (Santa Lucia di Tallà) and Presa-Tusiu (Altagène). I will concentrate here on the latter two sites, both elongated monuments, which have yielded abundant remains and much interesting scientific information.

Presa-Tusiu (Fig. 4) has a rectangular chamber 6×1.10 m (6.60 m^2). The northern alignment is made up of five slabs, the southern of six, and the small eastern side—actually the headstones—of two slabs. The narrow west side is open. These alignments overlie the upper part of an earlier occupation level on this site (Fig. 5). The sediment within this megalithic structure is composed of two levels. Level 2, the earlier, was radiocarbon dated to 2940 ± 130 uncal BC. This chronological measurement is extremely important since it dates the construction of the monument to which we assign the name 'megalithic passage' (uncovered type). This monument is contemporary with the Sardinian Ozieri sites of Grotta del Guano (2950 and 2880 ± 50 uncal BC; R-609 and R-609a) and Sa Ucca de su Tintirriolu (2990 ± 50 uncal BC; R-883a).

The artifacts from Level 2 of this structure comprise pottery decorated with impressed dots set in a line, and by lithic implements including a peduncular, notched obsidian arrowhead and a segment of a quartz circle (Fig. 6). This interesting assemblage had already been brought to light at the time the artifacts from Level 5 at Curacchiaghiu (dated to 2980 ± 140 uncal BC) were studied. Thus, in the light of these recent investigations, we can propose a date at the beginning of the 3rd millennium BC for the megalithic passage (uncovered type) as well as for the assemblage with the obsidian arrowhead and the quartz circle segment.

Elsewhere I have proposed a date for the Poggiarella dolmen (Fig. 7), part of the megalithic necropolis of Monte Rotondu at Sotta, in the first half of the 3rd millennium BC (Lanfranchi 1989). The circle segment and the unfinished arrowhead guided this calculation. This proposed date was confirmed by a sub-triangular transverse tranchet implement.

To summarize, in the history of Corsican megalithic monuments we can identify an early phase, dated to the end of the 4th/beginning of the 3rd millennium BC. It is then that the first megalithic monuments of elongated form and the first tombs bounded by stone circles were built. This cultural current has its parallel in Sardinia in the stone circles of Li Muri, of which the local aspect at Arzachena is only one part of the larger Ozieri culture.

On Corsica, a second megalithic phase developed. This is represented by the elongated monument at Cumpulaghia that could be called an 'arched' type, bounded by a stone circle, dating from the second half of the 3rd millennium BC. There are two parts to this monument: a corridor

Fig. 6 Artifacts from: 1. Presa-Tusiu, level 2; 2. Cumpulaghja; and 3. Nuciaresa.

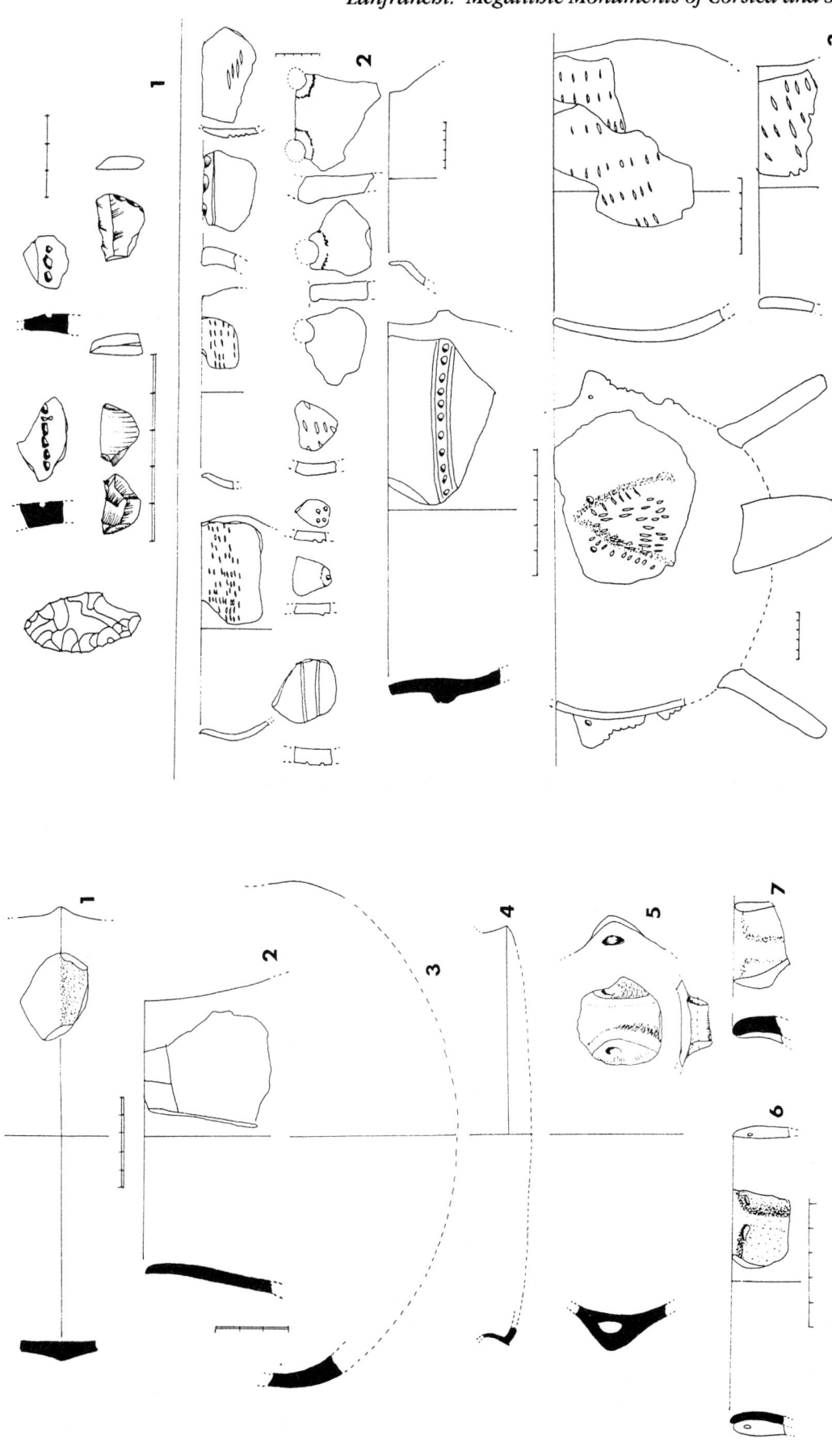

Fig. 5 Presa-Tusiu (level 3b). 1. Light cord in relief (diameter 25 cm); 2. Vase with 10 cm diameter at the rim; 3. Convex base of 19 cm maximum diameter; 4. Carenated vessel 23 cm in diameter; 5. Handle fragment with opening; 6. Vase with a horizontal band of perforations, 11 cm in diameter; and 7. Vase with a band of relief near the rim.

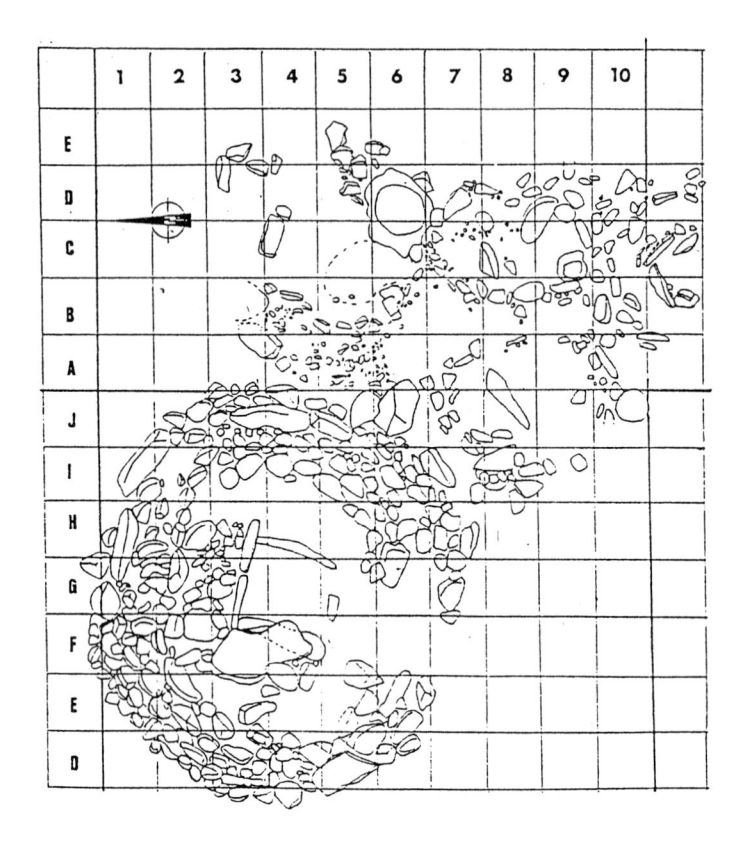

Fig. 7 Monte Rotundo (Sotta). Plan of the Poggiarella dolmen.

and a chamber. The corridor measures 6.2 × 2.0 m and leads to a rectangular chamber measuring 3.05 × 2.40 m. Both the north and south sides are made up of six stone slabs each. These stones rest on an enormous plaque of the emergent granite bedrock. In the chamber, a cup-shaped depressed area and hearths indicate two kinds of activities: the hearths indicate fires which produced a significant quantity of ashes; the other indicates grinding activity (the inner walls of the cavity are finely polished). The pottery is of the greatest interest since a large number of the sherds are decorated (Fig. 6.2). The decorative syntax is evocative of Late Neolithic production, but also of certain Terrinian elements. On the basis of these observations, I would date the ceramics to the second half of the 3rd millennium BC.

A chance find in the cliffs of Bonifacio proved to be a round-bottomed ceramic vessel decorated in a complex motif in which the dominant element is a field of impressed circles. Associated bones suggest the presence of a tomb in a natural grotto. Going by our chronological framework, this phase could be contemporary with the final Ozieri period on Sardinia. We should also recall that the pottery of Cumpulaghia has considerable affinity with the ceramics originating in the Nuciaresa-Capula (Levie) region (Fig. 6.3).

In the third phase, covering the 3rd millennium BC, the dolmens were developed. The monumental dolmen complex of Settiva (Petreto-Bicchisano) is the illustrative archetype. The ceramic artifacts from this tomb are comprised of cups with bent handles, not unlike ceramics from Polada (Italy), and of the Bonnanaro Culture of the Sardinian Bronze Age. In the fourth phase, we see the re-employment of megalithic monuments and funerary sites that were in use in the preceding period.

Having outlined the proposed phases of this megalithic cultural current, we will examine the preferred geographic areas where these monuments were introduced. A study of the distribution map of the Corsican megalithic monuments (Fig. 8) shows eight zones, unequally used: (1) Nebbiu and the Agriates zone; (2) the region of Galeria, although the only coffer from Susinu seems to belong to a sub-megalithic phase; (3) Cinarca; (4) Petreto-Bicchisano; (5) the lower and upper valley of the Taravu region; (6) the Sartenais region; (7) Alta Rocca; and (8) the Figari-Porto depression.

These regions are for the most part in western and southern Corsica, except for a few in the north. The east and the extreme south (the calcareous region of Bonifacio) seem to have been passed over by the megalithic cultural current. Establishing this archaeological fact is not sufficient; we must go beyond this and ask ourselves why there are no megalithic monuments in these two zones. Is the reason geological, religious or sociological? These questions, like so many others, still await answers.

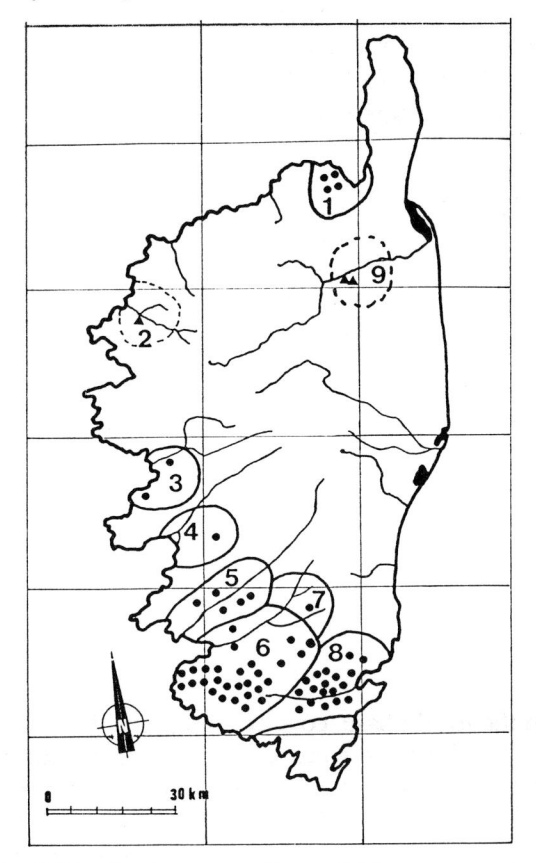

Fig. 8 Distribution map of megalithic monuments in Corsica.

One can see from a distribution map of the European megaliths that eastern Italy is bare, but also that the genesis of these monuments originates on the Atlantic coast, i.e. the coastal zones of France and Portugal. The map of Italy shows clearly that, with the exception of the 'heel' of the 'boot', there is no cultural involvement with these types of monuments. By contrast, the arrival from the west of megalithic cultural currents that, beginning in the low coastal river valleys of western Corsica, penetrated the high valleys and evolved further there, seems to me a secure fact. Furthermore, it is possible to pinpoint the very zone where this cultural influence was strongest: Valincu, Sartenais and above all the Figari/Porto Vecchio depression. Another fact confirms this analysis: the development in the Gallura, that area of Sardinia closest to Corsica, of the 'culture of circles' or Arzachena Culture. Here the cultural stream is so strong it succeeds in masking the most brilliant Neolithic civilization of the western Mediterranean, the Ozieri. In effect, in the region of Arzachena, there is formed a kind of small island that is no more than an aspect of the Ozieri. And finally, the distribution map of Sardinian megalithic monuments (Fig. 9) shows that the strongest concentration of monuments is located in the northern part of the island.

In conclusion, this recent work on the megalithic monuments of Corsica supports the idea (Lilliu 1967) that the origin of certain monuments on Sardinia may be located in southern France and Catalonia. More than a mere reinforcement of a theory, it demonstrates that this cultural current reached Corsica and Sardinia, then Malta and Apulia with the Bari-Taranto group, and also included coastal north Africa.

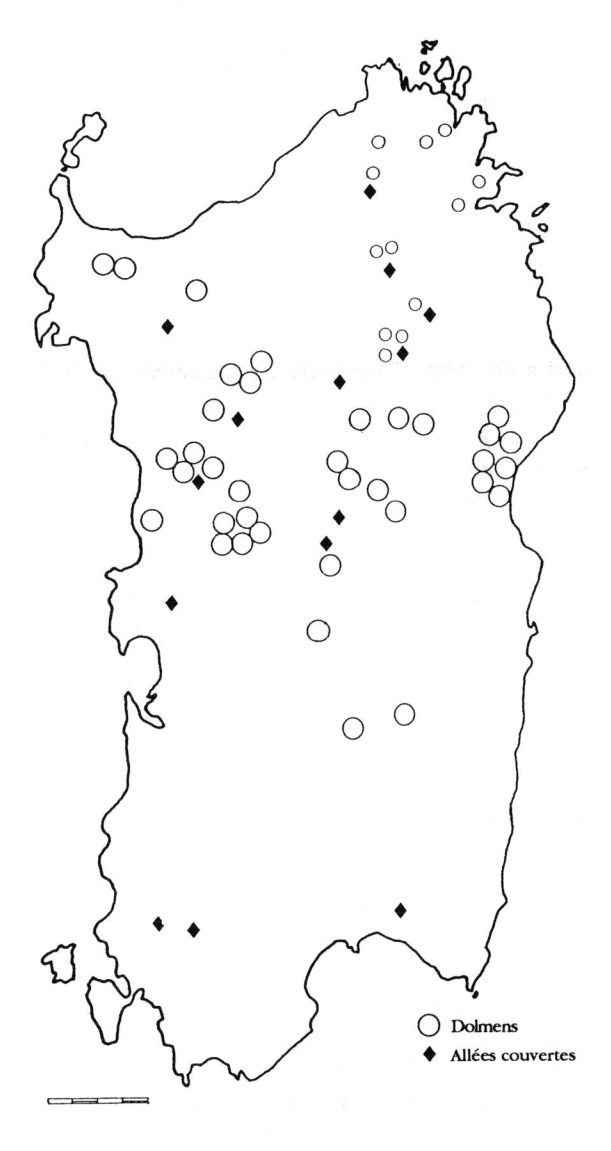

Fig. 9 Distribution map of megalithic monuments in Sardinia.

Table 1

Chronology of Megaliths in Corsica and Sardinia

Date BC	Period	Stone circles	Megalithic passages	Cave burials	Burials a tafoni	Dolmens	Sardinia
1st mill.	Iron Age / Late Bronze Age	----------	----------	Reuse of Sites	----------	----------	----------
2nd mill.	Bronze Age				Calanchi T3	Settiva	Bonnanaro / Polada
Late 3rd/ Early 2nd mill.		Palaghju	Cumpulaghja		Calanchi T2		Abealzu-Filigosa
2500 BC	Chalcolithic	Ciutulaghja			Nuciaresa		Monte Claro
2nd half of 3rd mill. 2600–2300 BC	Final Neolithic	Monte Rotondu				Poggiarella	
1st half of 3rd mill. BC	Late Neolithic	Vascolacciu		Presa-Tusiu			Ozieri & Arzachena
2940 3200		Tivulaghju					

References

Atzeni, E.
1975 Nuovi idoli della Sardegna prenuragica. *Studi Sardi* 23 (1973-74): 3-51.

Lanfranchi, F. de
1966 Coffre et structures funéraires mégalithiques de Caleca (Levie, Corse), communication préliminaire sur Caleca I. In *Congrès Préhistorique de France, Ajaccio 4-14 avril 1966*, 243-50.
1987 *Inventaire des Monuments Dolméniques de la Corse*. Thèse multigraphiée. Ecole des Hautes Etudes en Sciences Sociales.
1989 La nécropole mégalithique de Monte Rotondu à Sotta. *Cinquième Colloque d'Histoire et d'Archéologie de Bastia. Bulletin de la Société des Sciences Naturelles et Historiques de la Corse* 656(1-4): 291-305.

Lilliu, G.
1967 *La Civiltà dei Sardi dal Neolitico all'età dei Nuraghi*. Torino: ERI.

Puglisi,, S.M., & E. Castaldi
1966 Aspetti dell'accantonamento culturale nella Gallura preistorica e protostorica. *Studi Sardi* 19 (1964-65): 59-148.

Riassunto

Nuovi studi sulla preistoria corsa indicano che il Neolitico di quest'isola è ricco e complesso ed è caratterizzato dalla costruzione di monumenti megalitici. Il Neolitico corso ha dei paralleli con il Neolitico sardo e questo fatto potrebbe rispondere a domande riguardanti l'origine deimegaliti sardi. L'Autore riesamina lo sviluppo del Neolitico corso tenendo conto delle nuove scoperte fatte in proposito, e lo paragona alle culture sarde di Bonu Ighinu e Ozieri.

Recenti scavi presso Longone (Bonifacio) hanno rivelato l'esistenza di quattro fasi culturali neolitiche che si sono sviluppate nel corso di 1500 anni:

Prima fase = Cardiale I (all'inizio della metà del VI mill. a.C.). Il vasellame è decorato con impressioni fatte con conchiglie *Cardium*. Gli utensili di pietra sono di roccia locale o di selce importata.

Seconda fase = Cardiale II (prima metà del V mill. a.C.). Il vasellame è ancora decorato con conchiglie *Cardium*. Per gli utensili di pietra sono usati quarzo, riolite, selce, ed ossidiana.

Terza fase = Cardiale III (metà del V millennio a.C.). Questa è apparentemente una fase di transizione marcata dalla apparizione di nuove forme di vasellame, e in particolare dallo sviluppo di numerose anse sul vasellame.

Quarta fase = Vasellame puntato (dalla metà fino alla fine del V mill. a.C.). Il vasellame cardiale è diventato raro, ma appare il vasellame puntato, insieme a vasellame con superficie liscia; gli utensili di ossidiana sono abbondanti e alcuni hanno forme geometriche fra cui segmenti di cerchi, triangoli, trapezi, e rettangoli.

Il fatto che le ceramiche di Goulet-Bonifacien siano parallele a quelle del riparo sotto roccia di Su Carroppu de Sirri (Carbonia) in Sardegna, implica che c'è stata una influenza culturale comune. Le ceramiche della fase III di Longone sono simili a quelle di Grotta Verde di Alghero, e la fase IV di Longone è simile alla più tarda cultura di Bonu Ighinu in Sardegna.

In Corsica, la cultura di Presa-Tusia in Alta Rocca, datata 3870–3200 a.C., riempie il vuoto esistente tra la fine del primo Neolitico mediterraneo e l'inizio del Neolitico tardo. La cultura Presiana è definita dalle sue fini ceramiche brunescure, ed è alquanto differente dalla cultura Bonu Ighinu. Durante il tardo Neolitico corso assistiamo alla presenza di numerose culture in ciascun area dell'isola. Alcuni esempi includono le culture regionali di Basi, Curacchiaghiu, Araguina-Sennola, Scaffa Piana (Saint Florent), Carcu, Monte Grosso (Biguglia), Monte Lazzu (Cinarca), e altri. Questo è in contrasto con l'uniformità della contemporanea cultura Ozieri in Sardegna.

I monumenti megalitici corsi riflettono le stesse influenze culturali conosciute nella Sardegna neolitica. L'Autore riesamina i termini tradizionali che descrivono questi monumenti e li ritiene troppo semplicistici. Egli definisce le costruzioni corse come 'complessi megalitici' e li divide nel tipo A, complessi dolmen, e nel tipo B, gruppo megalitico. I complessi di tipo A includono uno spazio di dimensioni variabili in cui i complessi monolitici sono disposti secondo aspetti di mutuo orientamento. Un complesso di tipo A generalmente include cinque componenti: una tomba dolmen; le pietre che circondano la tomba, uno o più menhirs; un allineamento di pietre oblunghe (menhir) o blocchi di pietra; spazi di forme e dimensioni variabili demarcati da pietre giustapposte. Ciutulaghia e Settiva sono degli esempi. I complessi di tipo B sono complessi megalitici senza una tomba dolmen come ad esempio Zoppo (Zonza), Cruci (Levie), e Porto Vecchio.

Presso alcuni siti, come Musuleu, Cumpulaghia, e Presa-Tusiu, esiste un tipo di complesso megalitico, di forma allungata, chiamato 'allées couvertes'. Il complesso presso Presa-Tusiu è situato su sedimenti datati dal 2940 ± 130 noncal a.C. Questa data determina il *terminus post quem* per le allées couvertes, e per i materiali di Presa-Tusiu del livello 2 che includono ceramiche con punti impressi e con punte di freccia di ossidiana. Ciò conferma anche la data (terzo millennio) del dolmen all'interno di un circolo di pietra presso Poggiarella, una caratteristica delle necropoli megalitiche presso Monte Rotonda a Sotta. Per estensione, questa cronologia può essere applicata ai circoli di pietra sardi di Li Muri (Arzachena).

Una seconda fase megalitica corsa, che risale alla seconda metà del terzo millennio a.C., è rappresentata dal monumento allungato all'interno del circolo di pietra a Cumpulaghia. All'interno della camera troviamo una cavità usata per macinare, troviamo anche focolari, e ceramiche le cui decorazioni determinano la data del complesso architettonico. Una terza fase, quando i dolmen erano sviluppati, risale al terzo millennio a.C. Questa è rappresentata dal complesso dolmen di Settiva. I materiali di questa fase includono tazze con anse a gomito simili a forme della cultura italiana di Polada e della cultura sarda di Bonnanaro dell'Età del Bronzo.

Le mappe di distribuzione dei complessi megalitici della Corsica e della Sardegna mostrano che in Corsica i monumenti megalitici sono concentrati nella zone meridionali e in quella occidentale e alcuni sono stati ritrovati nella zona settentrionale. In Sardegna, la maggior parte dei monumenti megalitici sono concentrati nella metà settentrionale dell'isola. In Gallura, l'area sarda più vicina alla Corsica, esiste la stessa 'cultura di circoli di pietra'. Possiamo quindi concludere che durante il Neolitico le due isole sono state toccate dalle stesse influenze culturali.

The Megalithic in Sardinia, Southern France and Catalonia*

Jean Guilaine

The island of Sardinia, southern France, and Catalonia all have in common vigorous, diversified Megalithic civilizations. The relative geographic proximity of these three areas, the possible architectural parallels among some of their monuments, and the relationships—direct or indirect—that could have existed among these three areas from the Neolithic onwards (evidenced, for example, by the distribution of Sardinian obsidian from the Maritime Alps to Drôme and Aude) are all links that facilitated regional cultural interaction from an early period.

At the time when Mediterranean prehistory was being described in narrow, diffusionist terms, Sardinia was thought to be an obligatory way-station in the transmission to the west of a Megalithic culture conceived as a Near Eastern creation. Now that alternative explanations to such unilineal development over broad geographical areas are accepted, we can inquire instead about the emergence and reciprocal development of Sardinian architecture, and also that of Provence, Languedoc and Catalonia. The objective here is to compare certain architectural characteristics and the available chronological data for Sardinia, southern France and Catalonia, in order to understand better these three megalithic areas in their cultural and chronological contexts.

Corridor and Chamber Monuments

Some Sardinian megalithic monuments have one circular or polygonal chamber preceded by an access corridor. The finest example of this type is the dolmen of Motorra (Dorgali) (Fig. 1.1). Other tombs with circular chambers but no apparent access corridors, like the dolmen of Tanca Sar Bogadas (Birori), are members of the same architectural family since they might have originally had that element, but have lost it afterwards.

---

* Translated from the French by G. Bates and T. Andrews.

Some decorative elements among the ceramics from the Motorra dolmen are sometimes attributed to the Ozieri culture, and sometimes to a later period (Ferrarese Ceruti 1980). Masone Perdu, a tomb beneath a tumulus (Fig. 1.2), was excavated by Atzeni (1988) as part of a study of megalithic tombs in the Laconi region. The chamber of this monument is sub-trapezoidal. A kind of architraved, sub-circular passage serves as the entry between the access corridor and the chamber, and the surviving lower parts of the walls show a corbelled type of construction. The artifacts include Ozieri material as well as later material from a re-occupation of the site in the Abealzu period. In the necropolis of Pranu Mutteddu (Goni) (Atzeni and Cocco 1989), some tombs with a circular tumulus are characterized by the presence of a corridor and one of two types of chambers: a round chamber with a central coffer (Fig. 1.4), or a quadrangular chamber with an added antechamber (Fig. 1.3). Both monument types are attributable to the Ozieri culture.

This preliminary survey allows us to assign all Sardinian tombs with a round tumulus, a corridor, and a chamber to the San Michele (Ozieri) culture, dated between the horizon of Bonu Ighinu (the first half of the 4th millennium BC) and the Albealzu culture which starts around 2500 BC. The few available radiocarbon dates for the Ozieri culture cluster around 3200/2900 BC; the *termini ante* and *post quem* are not known with any precision.

In the same period the Chasseen civilization flourished in southern France. No tombs like those described above are associated with the Chasseen. At the Chasseen culture's territorial border in the Mediterranean Pyrenees, however, some tombs present morphological comparisons with the Sardinian types, especially those megaliths in the Haut Ampurdan. These are tombs with circular or polygonal chambers and a corridor, of which the best known example is Font del Roure at Espolla. The tomb with a sub-circular chamber and a corridor at Arreganyats in Espolla (Fig. 1.5) has been dated to 5400 ± 100 BP (3450 uncal BC—UGRA 148); and the dolmen with

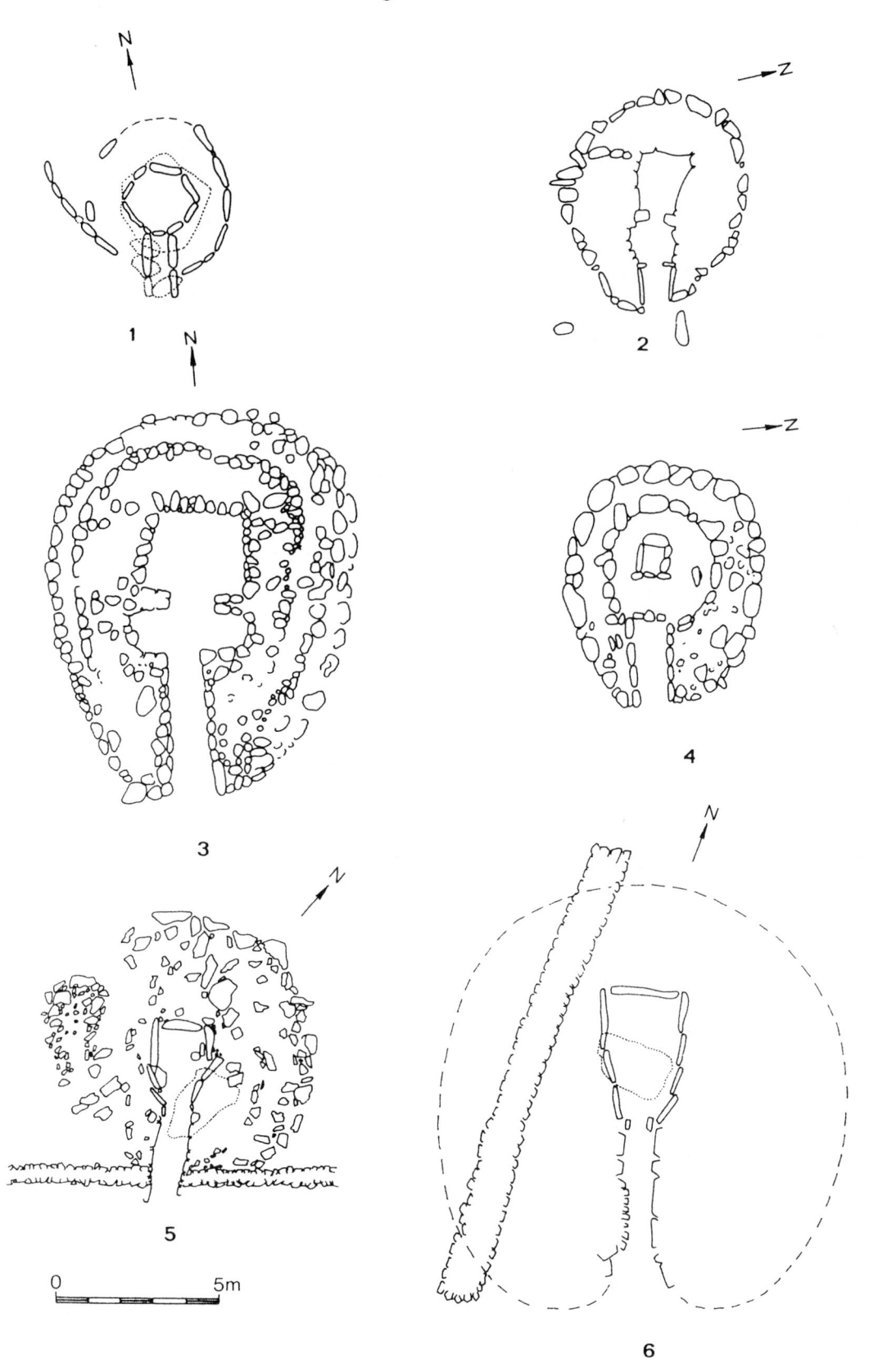

Fig. 1 Corridor monuments in Sardinia: 1. Motorra-Dorgali (after Atzeni 1981: 47); 2. Masone Perdu-Laconi (after Atzeni 1988: 527); and 3-4. Pranu Muttedu-Laconi (after Atzeni and Cocco 1989: 205 nn. 2-3). Corridor monuments in Catalonia (after Tarrus 1991); 5. Arreganyats, Espolla (Haut-Ampurdan); 6. Barranc, Espolla (Haut-Ampurdan).

Llargues in Sant Climent Sescebes in the same region has yielded a date of 5090 ± 160 BP (3140 uncal BC—GAK 12 162). These two radiocarbon dates then would also place these structures in the second half of the 4th millennium BC.

It might seem unwise to compare the Sardinian tombs with round or sub-circular chambers with tombs from the Catalonian Pyrenees; especially since contacts between the Ozieri and Chasseen cultures seem very limited, and certainly without reciprocal cultural influence, despite the circulation of obsidian between Sardinia and southern France (Guilaine 1990). The Catalonian group could be attributed to a branch of the Chasseen culture: the *sepulcros de fosa* of the Barcelona region, or some such contemporary aspect. It would appear more prudent, then, to stick to the idea of two distinct centers of origin for both megalithic and sub-megalithic monuments with corridors and chambers. Another western Mediterranean center of the same type, however, is indicated by some megalithic tombs in southeastern Iberia. The local origin of this third group might be found in the '*Rundgräber*' Neolithic monuments of the Almerian region. Thus, it seems that we are faced with three distinct and primary cultural centers, each resulting from the internal development of Middle Neolithic cultures: the Ozieri, the Catalonian *fosa* tomb group and the Almerian.

Long Dolmens with Rectangular Plan

Dolmens with a rectangular plan have been known on Sardinia for a long time; they are sometimes subdivided by internal separations as, for example, at Perda Lunga di Austis (Fig. 2.2) and Enna Sa Vacca at Olzai. These tombs have been called 'covered passage' monuments and at times associated with certain dolmen tombs in southern France, particularly in the Aude-Pyrenees region; but the Sardinian dolmens have always been difficult to place in a chronological-cultural framework. Corte Noa (Fig. 2.1), one of the monuments at Laconi, could be related to this category. It consists of an elongated rectangular chamber preceded by a corridor of the same width. Atzeni (1988) found numerous traces there of the Abealzu culture, and several artifacts 'of Ozieri-Filigosa type'. If these artifacts are contemporary with the construction of the monument they would date the complex to c. 2500 BC, i.e. the Final Neolithic.

Such a date would fit well with a cultural stream of the Mediterranean Megalithic which saw the progressive abandonment of monuments with chambers and diverse corridor types in favor of elongated, sometimes segmented, monuments of unchanging width. Again, although on Sardinia these monuments are narrow, this configuration is known in other western megalithic areas, such as Brittany and Andalusia, for example. The presence of rectangular monuments in the Final Neolithic, therefore, is not without any reference, as Lilliu has suggested, to certain tombs in the Pyrenees. Thus, some of the great corridor tombs of Aude fit into this global definition, although they often exhibit some inconsistency in height from the headstones to the stones at the entrance area. Some elongated Catalonian monuments (the dolmens of Llanera, Puig Ses Lloses and Cova d'En Daina) also fit into this same architectural order despite certain differences in details (Fig. 2.3). The majority of these east Pyrenean tombs contain the international-style bell-beaker ceramics, but also older artifacts that could be associated with at least the Final Neolithic, e.g., corded, spherical pottery from Boun Marcou, Saint-Eugène, and Jappeloup. A date in conventional terms of c. 2600–2500 BC could be proposed here, and an approximate chronological parallel could be made with Sardinian monuments of the same style if a Final Neolithic date is confirmed for them. Also notable are some unusual monuments with related architectural features in Provence, especially the Gauttobry dolmen at La Londe-les-Maures (Var) (Fig. 2.4). This tomb consists of a chamber, 6 m long by 1.5 m wide, preceded by a short corridor. Its associated artifacts can be dated to either the Final Neolithic or the Chalcolithic (Sauzade 1990).

It is difficult to find any further relationship between the megalithic architecture of southern France and Sardinia. To be sure, Sardinia has the so-called 'giants' tombs' (*tomba di giganti*), elongated chamber monuments covered with stone blocks and preceded by a facade of slabs arranged in a semi-circle. Even if the general plan of these chambers and their narrow widths can be compared with other western covered passage monuments, or with the elongated monuments in southern France, their chronologies do not match. The covered passage monuments on the continent appear first in the 3rd millennium, while the artifacts recovered in the giants' tombs hardly date back to the Early Bronze Age (Bonnanaro culture), i.e. no earlier than c. 1800 BC. However original they may be, the giants' tombs are not especially numerous and seem to be confined to Sardinia where they constitute a unique style of Late Megalithic architecture.

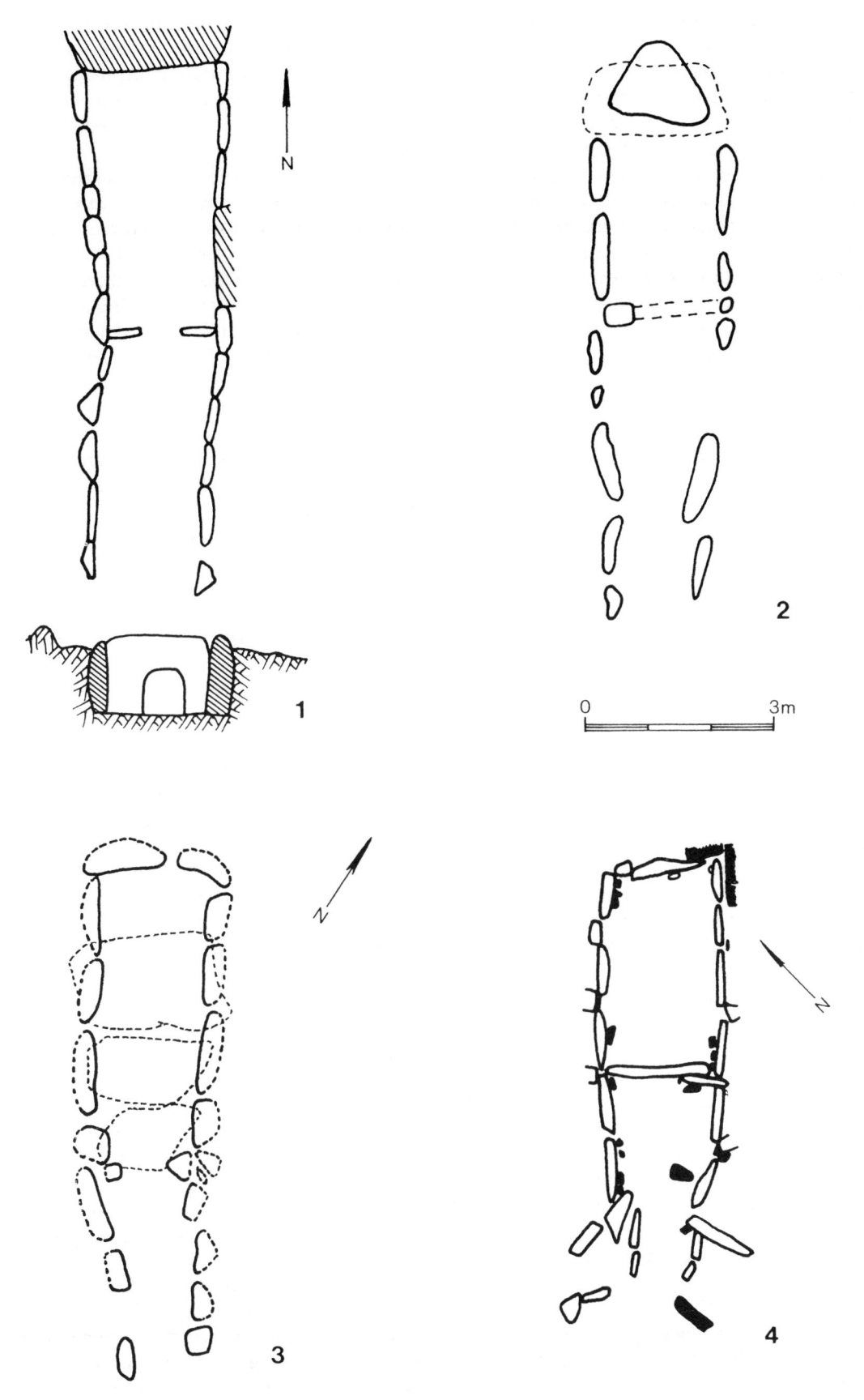

Fig. 2 Elongated, rectangular monuments from Sardinia, Catalonia and Provence: 1. Corte Noa-Laconi (after Atzeni 1988: 527); 2. Perda Lunga-Austis (after Atzeni 1981: 48); 3. Cova d'En Daina, Romanya de la Selva-Gérone (after Esteva Cruanas 1964); 4. Gauttobry, La Londe les Maures-Var (Sauzade 1991).

Monuments with a Simple Morphology

Megalithic (or perhaps sub-megalithic) development in both Sardinia and Corsica began with a very Mediterranean type of monument, of narrow width, often only partly subterranean, when they are not simply coffers or cists set into the ground. The age of these monuments can vary widely and, in Corsica for example, some of the coffers are without doubt no earlier than the Early Bronze Age (e.g. Pallaggiu). Some monuments are earlier, such as those on Sardinia in Arzachena (Gallura). The simple dolmens, or coffers, from the necropolis of Li Muri are surrounded by circular structures sometimes including dressed stones (Fig. 3). The artifacts recovered from these burial vaults are often attributed to a northern aspect of the Ozieri culture; these include numerous ornamental objects, flint blades and caches of perforated weapons, the last probably prestige objects. This high chronology seems to be confirmed by a steatite bowl found at Li Muri; another example in stone, with coiled handles, was found at Dolianova (Cagliari). These two pieces are morphologically parallel to the ceramics of the southern Italian Diana horizon for which radiocarbon dates, clustering around c. 3200–2900 BC, coincide with the available dates for the Ozieri culture. From one tomb at Li Muri and another at Li Muracci, only a single skeleton each was brought to light; only two skeletons came from a tomb at San Pantaleo. It is clear these were not collective tombs.

There are some proto-megalithic coffers or cists in southern France starting in the Chasseen period. These are known especially in western Languedoc (including Najac à Siran-Hérault and Dela Laïga à Cournanel-Aude), in Roussillon and in Solsonès on the southern slope of the Pyrenees. There is also the noteworthy example of the Sec tomb at Lozère. Although this area is generally without tumuli, these coffers were sometimes inserted into a mound, as at Arca de Calahons à Cattla in the eastern Pyrenees. Some monuments of this type may be even older, as in Catalonia where coffers recently were found embedded in tumuli, often very large—up to c. 30 m in diameter—and dating to the beginning of the Middle Neolithic (Montbolo horizon). This is also the case for the tombs at Font de la Vena (Tavertet, Osona) and Padro II where the radiocarbon dates vary between 3900 and 3600 BC. These monuments, although of great size, are nevertheless only individual tombs. In southern Catalonia, in the Amposta region, some burials in coffers are attributable to the Epicardial Period. Clearly these early Catalonian tombs with large mounds are important for understanding the genesis of the megalithic phenomenon in the Pyrenees. Their monumentality is already somewhat megalithic, but the change from passage grave to collective burial monument has not yet been realized.

By contrast, starting in the Chasseen some coffer burials might contain two or three bodies, for example, at Dela Laïga (Najac); or even up to six, for example, at Bordasse à Conilhac-de-la-Montagne (Aude). These specific cases should not be described as dolmens, because of their reduced character and the fact that most are set in the ground. Nevertheless, the transition from a coffer burial with one, two, or several bodies, to a spacious, partly above-ground chamber—representing an emergence from the underworld—serving the needs of collective entombment, must have taken place rapidly. Without doubt the link between coffer burials and chamber tombs will be found eventually. Nevertheless, in southern France the first identifiable megalithic forms of the Final Neolithic do not correspond to the 'simple dolmen' type which should constitute the logical development of the Middle Neolithic coffers. The passage monuments of Aude, the corridor dolmens of eastern Languedoc and Provence, and the 'Bas-Rhodanien' dolmens with dry-stone walls correspond directly to the architectural models already discussed at length above. Certainly there exist in the Pyrenees numerous 'simple dolmens' of which the coffers of the Middle Neolithic could be the archetypes. For the most part, however, these Pyrenean monuments are dated to the Chalcolithic or Early Bronze Age, and are thus separated in time from their predecessors. On the Causses in southern France there are other simple dolmens (if they are not monuments which have lost their vestibule) which are not earlier than the evolved Artenacien Period (Copper Age). These present the same problems of chronological relationship with earlier prototypes.

On Sardinia itself simple dolmens of indeterminate age are also known. This is the case with the most beautiful example on the whole island, the dolmen of Sa Coveccada (Mores) (Fig. 4). It is likely, however, that this monument may have gradually lost complementary structures such as a tumulus, and an access area in front of the entry cut into the *cella*. If this type of entrance is also known on the continent (cf. the dolmen at Gramont à Soumont-Hérault), it must be understood without doubt as a convergent phenomenon and not as indicating any precise chronological–cultural connection. The later giants' tombs, moreover, also bring to mind this

Fig. 3 Tombs at Li Muri (Arzachena-Sardinia).

134 *Sardinia in the Mediterranean*

type of entrance, cut flush with the ground to permit—with difficulty—the introduction of the dead into the chamber.

Finally, I should point out that on Corsica some monuments with a simple chamber can have late chronologies; thus the ceramic deposits from the dolmen of Settiva at Petreto-Bicchisano—which has a small vestibule—can only be associated with difficulty to the Sardinian Bonnanaro culture. If this evidence is in fact contemporary with the construction of the monument, it must be dated to the Early Bronze Age, or the beginning of the 2nd millennium BC.

Fig. 4 Dolmen of Sa Coveccada (Mores-Sardinia).

Hypogea at Arles, Giants' Tombs and Hypogea in Sardinia and the Balearic Islands

In this article, dedicated as it is to the megalithic phenomenon, it has not yet been possible to discuss the problem of the hypogea, monuments which represent a special phenomenon of the social response to death. The hypogea of Cordes Mountain, near Arles (Bouches-du-Rhône), merit special attention (Fig. 5). These are unusual in having a flat roof of juxtaposed slabs, and resemble architecturally some other megalithic constructions. These monuments might well be called 'semi-hypogea' or 'semi-megalithic', the latter impression reinforced by the placement of each tomb beneath a protective mound.

The question of which cultural influences were responsible for the production of these monuments has been discussed frequently in the past, and again recently (Sauzade 1991). First of all, these are the only monuments in France of this particular architectural type. They have long,

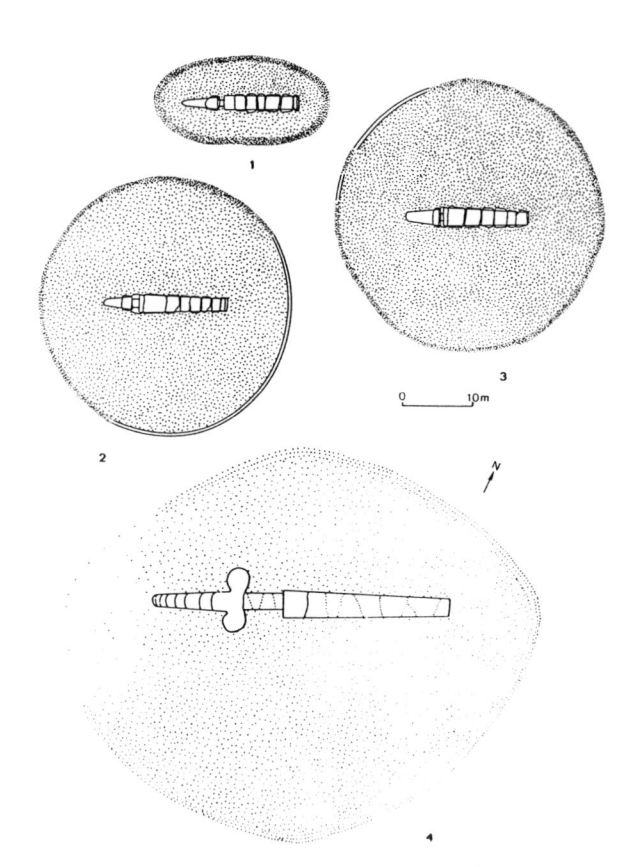

Fig. 5 Hypogea in Arles (after Arnal *et al.* 1953); 1. Castellet; 2. Bounias; 3. La Source; 4. Grotte des Fées.

narrow galleries, accessed by stairs marked by doorways cut into the living rock; small facing chambers have been added to the antechamber of the largest of these monuments, the Grotto of the Fairies (Grotte des Fées—Fig. 5.4). The age of these tombs can be deduced from a discovery made in one (Arnaud-Castellet—Fig. 5.1) of sherds decorated with chevrons of the Ferrières style (Cazalis de Fondouce 1878; Arnal *et al.* 1953). Thus, we may propose at the least a Final Neolithic date of c. 2600–2200 BC in order to come within range of the Ferrières radiocarbon date.[1] Of course, it is important to remember that these monuments too were re-utilized in the Chalcolithic Period.

There exist some broad similarities with some hypogea in the Balearic Islands, although the latter may date only from the Late Bronze Age (pre-Talayotic). Various groups of Chalcolithic hypogea from peninsular Italy, for example,

---

1 A debate has arisen over the possibility of a Chasseen dating of these monuments, defended most notably by J. Arnal. According to Arnal, a handle of a Pan flute must have come from the hypogeum; those who disagree say it came from an earlier habitation of the site. Another argument centers on a bowl decorated with radiating grooves, found in the Bounias hypogeum (Figure 5.2), that is not without similarity to some Neolithic bowls with sun-ray decoration from St. Léonard (Valais) and from Villeneuve-Tolosane (Haute-Garonne). But such bowls are equally common in bell-beaker contexts.

Laterza, Gaudo and Rinaldone, have completely different morphologies than those at Arles; the same may also be said of the Andalusian tombs. As for Sardinia, it does not seem that the hypogea of the Ozieri culture can be considered indisputably like these prototypes; some of them are merely sub-circular 'pockets', whereas the more elaborate examples do not correspond closely to the plan of the Arles tombs. Thus the monuments at Anghelu Ruju, occasionally embellished with peripheral chambers, follow different plans. In the same way the tombs that provide access to one—or several—central chambers surrounded by satellite alcoves (e.g. Sant'Andrea Priu), follow a completely different model than that of the Provence monuments. Finally, if the chronology of the Arles tombs fits well in the Final Neolithic, the Ozieri tombs would certainly be older by at least several centuries. Does this mean that there was no possible Sardinian influence on the hypogea of Arles? It is difficult to say. We may simply assert that for one period, corresponding roughly to the Final Neolithic, there is one similar general evolution: the elongation of the tombs, sometimes excessively, at the expense of the cella/access–gallery separation. In Aude and Catalonia there was an interest at that time in the development of long, rectangular monuments. The covered-passage monuments of Aquitaine, Armorique and the Paris basin conform to an identical principle. On Sardinia, the tradition prior to the tombs with multiple independent chambers faded away in favor of hypogea hollowed out along their whole length (cf. the tombs on the eponymous site of Filigosa at Macomer). The giants' tombs constitute a perfect manifestation of this tendency, of which they are the latest among this type of construction.

I cannot find, outside of Provence, any indisputable prototypes for the Arles tombs. I content myself, however, by noting certain broad parallels among all the monuments—dolmens and hypogea—in the west Mediterranean, especially the interest in an ever-greater lengthening of the monuments, a process occasionally carried out at the expense of the access corridors.

Finally, the plans of the Arles hypogea show closer affinities with those of the Sardinian giants' tombs than with those of the Balearic Islands. Were these architectural developments reciprocal or convergent? We have seen that the Arles tombs produced the earliest artifacts. Thus there is no close contemporaneity among these diverse tomb styles, unless we admit that the island monuments have been dated too late, and were re-utilized again and again. This problem, then, will remain intractable until new information can lead to a refinement of the chronology for these diverse types of funerary monuments.

References

Ambert, P.
1991   Reflexions concernant l'architecture des dolmens 'larges' de l'aire pyrénaïque. In *Autour de Jean Arnal*, 291-303. Montpellier: Premières Communautés Paysannes.

Arnal, J.
1963   *Les Dolmens du Département de l'Hérault*. Préhistoire 15. Paris: PUF.

Arnal, J., J. Latour & R. Riquet
1953   Les monuments et stations néolithiques de la région d'Arles en Provence. *Etudes Roussillonnaises* 3(1): 27-69.

Atzeni, E.
1981   Aspetti e sviluppi culturali del neolitico e della prima età dei metalli in Sardegna. In E. Atzeni *et al.* (eds.), *Ichnussa: La Sardegna dalle origini all'età classica*, 21-51. Milano: Libri Scheiwiller.

1988   Tombe megalitiche di Laconi (Nuoro). *L'Eta del Rame in Europea. Rassegna di Archeologia* 7: 526-27.

Atzeni, E., & D. Cocco
1989   Nota sulla necropoli megalitica de Pranu Mutteddu-Goni. In L.D. Campus (a cura di), *La Cultura di Ozieri. Problematiche e nuove acquisizioni. Atti del I convegno di studio, Ozieri, gennaio 1986-aprile 1987*, 201-16. Ozieri: Il Torchietto.

Castells, J., W. Cruells & M. Molist
1991   Una necropolis de cambres neolitiques am tumol complex del quart milleni a la Catalunya interiore. *El Neolitic a Catalunya. IXe Colloque de Puigcerda*. In press.

Cazalis de Fondouce, P.
1873–78   *Allées Couvertes de la Provence*. Montpellier-Paris: Coulet et Delahaye.

Chevalier, Y.
1985   *L'Architecture des Dolmens entre Languedoc Méditerranéen et Centre-Ouest de la France*. Saarbrücker Beitrage zur Altertumskunde 44.

Cura, M. & J. Castells
1977   Evolution et typologie des mégalithes de Catalogne. *Colloque sur l'Architecture Mégalithique*, 71-97. Vannes.

Esteva Cruanas, L.
1964   Los sepulcros megaliticos de la Gabarras I. *Corpus de Sepulcros Megaliticos* 3. Barcelona.

Ferrarese Ceruti, M.L.
1980   Le domus de janas di Mariughia e Canudedda e il dolmen di Motorra. In *Dorgali, Documenti Archeologici*, 57-65. Sassari.

Foschi Nieddu, A.
1986   *La Tomba I di Filigosa (Macomer-Nuoro)*. Nuoro.

Guilaine, J.
1981   *Premiers Bergers et Paysans de l'Occident Méditerranéen*. 2nd edition. Paris: Mouton.

1990   Ozieri et le Néolithique français. *Colloque 'La Cultura di Ozieri', Ozieri, ottobre 1990*. In press.

Lilliu, G.
1988   *La Civiltà dei Sardi dal Paleolitico all'Età dei Nuraghi*. 3rd edition. Torino: Nuova ERI.

Pericot Garcia, L.
1950   *Los Sepulcros Megaliticos Catalanes i la Cultura*

Santoni, V.
1976 Nota preliminare sulla tipologia delle Grotticelle funerari in Sardegna. *Archivio Storico Sardo* 30: 3-49.

Sauzade, G.
1991 Le dolmens de Provence orientale et la place des tombes de Fontvieille dans l'architecture mégalithique méridionale. In *Autour de Jean Arnal*, 305-34. Montpellier: Premières Communautés Paysannes.

Tarrus, J.
1991 Les dolmens anciens de Catalogne. In *Autour de Jean Arnal*, 271-89. Montpellier: Premières Communautés Paysannes.

Whitehouse, R.
1981 Megaliths of the Central Mediterranean. In *Antiquity and Man, Essays in Honour of Glyn Daniel*, 106-27. London: Thames and Hudson.

Riassunto

La Sardegna, la Francia meridionale e la Catalogna hanno in comune il fatto di aver avuto civiltà megalitiche sviluppate e diversificate. Il fatto che le tre regioni siano relativamente vicine e che i loro monumenti siano comparabili, mostra che a partire dal Neolitico ci sono state alcune relazioni culturali tra le tre regioni sopra menzionate. L'Autore esamina le caratteristiche architettoniche e i dati cronologici della Sardegna, della Provenza, del Languedoc e della Catalogna per meglio capire le culture megalitiche regionali ed interregionali.

L'Autore inizia con l'esaminare i monumenti sardi che hanno una camera preceduta da un corridoio d'accesso e talvolta un tumulo rotondo. Alcuni esempi di questo tipo di monumento sono Mottora (un dolmen) e Masone Perdu (una tomba a tumulo). In entrambi i casi le ceramiche sono databili alla cultura di Ozieri (Tardo Neolitico).

La cultura di Chassey nella Francia meridionale si è sviluppata contemporaneamente alla cultura sarda di Ozieri, ma gli stili delle tombe non sono simili. Ci sono delle eccezioni come i megaliti del Haut Ampurdan, come la Font del Roure a Espolla che ha una camera circolare ed un corridoio d'accesso, e come il dolmen con corridoio e camera sub-circolare presso Tires Llargues à Sant Climent Sescebes. I sepulcros de fosa vicino a Barcellona potrebbero essere un aspetto parallelo alla cultura di Chassey. L'Autore conclude sostenendo che i megaliti di Ozieri e le tombe a fossa catalane rappresentano due distinti centri di origine dei monumenti con corridoi e camere. Un terzo centro indipendente è riconoscibile nei megaliti *Rundgräber* nella regione di Almeria nell'Iberia sudorientale.

L'Autore esamina i dolmen a pianta rettangolare talvolta chiamati *allée couverte*. Questi monumenti, difficili da datare, sono stati ritrovati in Sardegna, per esempio a Perda Lunga di Austis, e nelle regioni degli Aude-Pyrenees nella Francia meridionale. Presso Corte Noa (Laconi), una camera rettangolare allungata ha restituito tracce della cultura Abealzu e dei manufatti di tipo Ozieri-Filigosa; i ritrovamenti fanno quindi riferimento ad una data appartenente al Neolitico Finale. Questo tipo di megaliti si trova anche nella Francia meridionale dove monumenti con camere e diversi tipi di corridoi sono stati progressivamente sostituiti da monumenti allungati con lati paralleli. Esempi di monumenti a pianta allungata sono stati ritrovati anche in Bretagna ed in Andalusia. Le tombe dei giganti in Sardegna rappresentano invece uno stile megalitico unico.

Alcuni megaliti sardi e corsi presentano uno stile mediterraneo: essi sono stretti ed hanno frequentemente una camera sotterranea. Le date, a cui i megaliti sopra menzionati risalgono, variano: alcuni sono riferibili all'inizio dell'Età del Bronzo, mentre la necropoli sarda di Li Muri appartiene al periodo di Ozieri. Nella Francia meridionale, tombe protomegalitiche appartenenti al periodo Chassey sono state ritrovate presso Najac à Siran, e tombe a tumulo sono state ritrovate ad Arca de Calahons à Cattla; tutti questi ritrovamenti risalgono a date diverse. Alcune tombe contenevano più corpi, e l'Autore afferma che c'è stato un rapido sviluppo dalla tomba con alcuni corpi verso una tomba più spaziosa usata per sepolture collettive.

L'Autore conclude l'articolo con una discussione riguardante i megaliti ipogei. I megaliti nelle Montagne di Cordes (Arles) sono alquanto insoliti, perchè hanno una copertura megalitica con lastre giustapposte, e potrebbero risalire al Neolitico Finale. Non è ancora chiaro quale sia stata l'influenza culturale che potrebbe aver causato questo fenomeno architettonico. Gli ipogei del Calcolitico peninsulare italiano, le tombe dell'Andalusia e gli ipogei sardi del periodo di Ozieri sono completamente differenti (morfologicamente) da quelli di tipo Arles. Possiamo solo dire che durante il Neolitico Finale c'è stata una evoluzione generale verso un allungamento delle tombe a spese delle gallerie di accesso. Questa tendenza sembra manifestarsi anche in Sardegna, come a Filigosa presso Macomer. Le piante degli ipogei di Arles mostrano più similitudini con le tombe dei giganti della Sardegna che con gli ipogei delle Isole Baleari, ma non sappiamo dire se si tratta di influenze reciproche o di un fenomeno di convergenza.

Paleosardi e Protosardi dal Paleolitico all'Età del Bronzo Recente (tentativo di analisi dell'avvicendarsi di forme umane nell'isola di Sardegna)

Franco Germanà

Generalità e metodi di indagine

La Sardegna è stata frequentata nella più remota Preistoria, al tempo dei glaciali Mindel e Riss, dall'uomo non ancora sapiens, anche se già abbastanza progredito nel suo processo di ominazione. In tempi successivi la presenza umana si è realizzata nell'isola in maniera eccezionale e discontinua per quanto riguarda il restante periodo paleolitico, mentre ha avuto il carattere di continuità dal Neolitico antico fino ai nostri giorni. Già in passato alcuni Autori avevano tentato, me compreso, una sintesi delle morfologie umane paleo- e protosarde (Maxia 1961; 1963; 1967; Maxia e Floris 1961; Germanà 1980b; 1983; 1990). Si trattava soltanto di semplici elenchi di gruppi umani non sempre ben collocati dal punto di vista cronologico-culturale e, d'altra parte, il fluitare delle datazioni e delle definizioni culturali di alcuni altri gruppi umani non aveva certo contribuito a facilitare il compito degli Antropologi. L'analisi attuale dal punto di vista cronologico e culturale si allinea alle vedute in merito di Lilliu (1988).

Peraltro la presente indagine non ha certamente la pretesa di essere conclusiva a riguardo, anche perché la numerosità di alcuni campioni, utilizzati per le stime, è minima (addirittura ridotta a poche unità) e le forme umane associate ad alcune culture paleo- e protosarde o sono in fase di analisi o sono addirittura ancora ai nostri giorni sconosciute. Quello presente resta pur sempre un volenteroso tentativo di analisi antropologica, risultando entro i limiti di una rigorosa scelta dei vari tipi umani (omologati e selezionati dal punto di vista sia morfometrico che culturale) raggruppati in campioni ben caratterizzati dal punto di vista cronologico-culturale in base alle più recenti acquisizioni sulla Preistoria della Sardegna (Lilliu 1982; 1988). Gruppi umani di incerta origine e collocazione sono stati pertanto scartati.

Per la presente analisi sono stati costruiti 8 campioni (vedi i riff. bibliografici nella prima parte della presente indagine) così distinguibili fra loro:

a. Campione del Neolitico medio, risultante da due subcampioni coevi: quello della Grotta Rifugio di Olièna e quello di Cuccuru s'Arriu (o Arrius), entrambi di Cultura Bonu Ighinu;
b. Campione del Neolitico finale, risultante da tutti i subcampioni di Cultura Ozieri, fino a ora noti e determinati;
c. Campione eneolitico, risultante da tutti i subcampioni di Cultura Monte Claro, fino a ora pubblicati;
d. Campione eneolitico campaniforme di Padru Jossu;
e. Campione di Anghelu Ruju (generica età dei primi metalli; più probabilmente tardo Eneolitico-Bronzo antico);
f. Campione del Bronzo antico, comprendente tutti i subcampioni fino a ora noti e connessi con la fase A della Cultura di Bonnanaro;
g. Campione del Bronzo medio, comprendente tutti i subcampioni della fase B della Cultura di Bonnanaro e gli altri subcampioni presumibilmente coevi; e
h. Campione del Bronzo recente, comprendente soltanto i subcampioni galluresi dei tafoni e delle tombe di giganti, fra loro morfologicamente affini.

Non è stato possibile costruire campioni cronologicamente precedenti (paleo-epipaleolitici e del Neolitico antico) e successivi (età del Ferro) per l'attuale grave carenza e incompletezza di materiale osteologico necessario per le varie stime.

Di ogni campione, costituito da individui ovviamente al termine dell'accrescimento, sono stati presi in considerazione i parametri più caratterizzanti (almeno 10 diametri cranio-facciali—rilevati secondo la metodica di Martin e Saller (1958) e classificati secondo E. Hug (1940)—10 indici cranio-facciali caratterizzanti, i valori staturali medi maschili e femminili, ricavati con il metodo di Manouvrier 1893; per il vivente). Dei 10 diametri e dei 10 indici cranio-facciali di ogni campione sono stati calcolati: la numerosità, la media aritmetica, il limite fiduciale con P=95% entro cui si presume cada la 'media vera', il campo di variabilità della classe (empiricamente espresso dai suoi valori estremi) e il sigma (calcolato per N-1, trattandosi di piccoli campioni). La significatività o meno della distanza fra medie omologhe (relative ai soli valori lineari) è stata saggiata con il metodo del t Student con P = 5% (indicato con * e ritenuto sufficientemente valido per la buona significatività del fattore distanza) e quando significativo, anche con P = 1% (indicato con **): differenza fra le due medie divisa per la deviazione standard media e moltiplicata per il fattore di dimensione (Cavalli-Sforza 1970). I risultati di una tale indagine formano l'oggetto della presente pubblicazione, che dedico molto volentieri alla Prof. Miriam Balmuth.

Parte Prima: Culture, cronologie e gruppi umani

Secondo le più recenti vedute in merito e usate nella presente analisi (Lilliu 1988) con qualche non sostanziale modifica, la cronologia della Preistoria e Protostoria della Sardegna può essere così distinta, anche i riferimenti agli otto campioni in esame:

Paleolitico inferiore (o antico)	industrie clactoniane dell'Anglona: 200.000–150.000 a.C.
Paleolitico medio	80.000–50.000 a.C. (?)
Mesolitico (o Preneolitico)	Grotta Corbeddu: 13.730–13.450 a.C. (Spoor e Sondaar 1986)
Neolitico antico	Cultura della ceramica impressa e di Filiestru: 6.000–3.730 a.C.
Neolitico medio	Cultura di Bonu Ighinu: 3.730–3.330 a.C. «campione a»
Neolitico recente	Cultura di Ozieri: 3.300–2.480 a.C. «campione b»
Calcolitico (o Eneolitico)	Culture di Abealzu-Filigosa, di Monte Claro e Campaniforme: 2.480–1.855 a.C. «campione c — campione d—campione e»
Età del Bronzo antico	Protonuragico, o Nuragico arcaico: fase A della Cultura di Bonnanaro: 1.855–1.490 a.C. «campione e—campione f»
Età del Bronzo medio	Medionuragico: fase B della Cultura di Bonnanaro: 1.490–1.200 a.C. «campione g»
Età del Bronzo medio	Medionuragico; inizio dell'Età protostorica in Sardegna: 1.200–900 a.C. «campione h»
I Età del Ferro	Tardonuragico: 900–500 a.C.
II Età del Ferro	Nuragico della sopravvivenza: 500–238 a.C.

□ = Preneolitico ● = Neolitico antico
✶ = Neolitico medio ○ = Neolitico recente

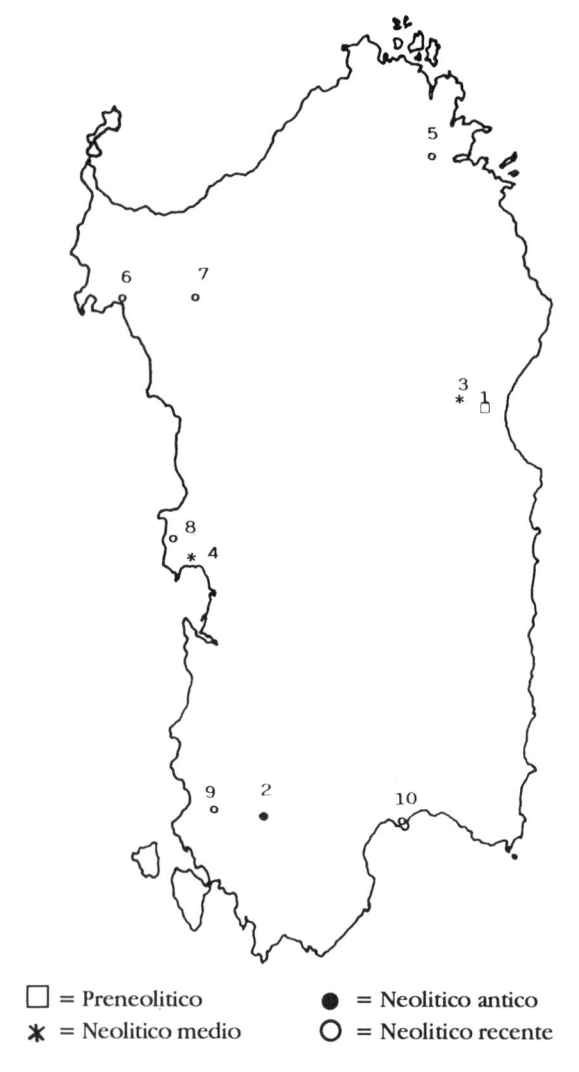

Fig. 1 Depositi funerari paleosardi preneolitici e neolitici. 1. Grotta Corbeddu (Olièna-NU) Preneolitico; 2. Riparo di Su Carroppu (Sirri-CA) Neolitico antico; 3. Grotta Rifugio (Olièna-NU) Neolitico medio; 4. Necropoli di Cuccuru s'Arriu o Arrius (Cabras-OR) Neolitico medio; 5. Circoli di S. Pantaleo (SS) Neolitico recente; 6. Grotta di Lu Maccioni (Alghero-SS) Neolitico recente; 7. Grotta Sa Ucca de su Tintirriolu Mara (SS) strato Neolitico recente; 8. Grotta Is Aruttas (Cabras-OR) Neolitico recente; 9. Domu di S. Benedetto (Iglesias-CA) Neolitico recente; 10. Domus di Capo S. Elia (CA) dal Neolitico antico alla Età del Bronzo.

Così stando le cose, i campioni a-g sono di età preistorica e, pertanto, i gruppi umani connessi vengono chiamati 'Paleosardi,' mentre il campione h è di età protostorica e i gruppi connessi vengono chiamati 'Protosardi,' là dove Maxia aveva usato la denominazione generica di 'Protosardi' per tutti i sardi di età pre- e proto-storica e Parenti (1967) aveva usato la denominazione di 'Paleosardi' in senso generico.

1. Il Paleolitico

Le morfologie paleosarde del Paleolitico inferiore sono ancora sconosciute, anche se con una certa approssimazione si può pensare che esse potessero essere simili alle tipologie di Montmaurin, di Steinheim, di Ehringsdorf, di Swanscombe e di Castel di Guido (Mallegni et al. 1982), tanto per citare quelle coeve più note.

2. Il Mesolitico (Figura 1)

Dalla Grotta Corbeddu (Nuoro) proviene un resto mascellare caratterizzato da una conformazione piuttosto arcaica dell'arcata dentaria e da una sensibile 'discontinuità morfologica' rispetto a forme umane paleosarde neolitiche successive (Spoor e Germanà 1987). Da una sepoltura 'preneolitica' priva di corredo funebre della Corsica meridionale (Araguina Sennola-Bonifacio) proviene lo scheletro di un individuo adulto di sesso femminile, morfologicamente riconducibile a tipologie di Téviec e di Hoedic, tipologie dolicomorfe, tendenti alla mesocrania (Duday 1975). Si può con certa cautela concludere che il Mesolitico dell'area corsa (e presumibilmente pure dell'area sarda, ancorché attualmente non conosciuta) è caratterizzata da forme umane non più robuste, ma già gracilizzate.

3. Il Neolitico (Figura 1)

Anche il Neolitico sardo dal punto di vista antropologico è caratterizzato da una netta gracilizzazione somatica delle forme umane coeve, forme evolutesi in tal senso non sappiamo se in territori estrainsulari, o se nella stessa area isolana. Da una tale gracilizzazione nell'Europa mediterranea erano venute fuori fin dalle prime fasi del Neolitico antico almeno due prevalenti morfologie (Riquet 1970):

  a. una tipologia mediterranea orientale, o danubiana, più antica e caratterizzata da conformazione corporea gracile con statura bassa, ma non pigmoide e da un neurocranio dolicomorfo ovoide o pentagonoide con faccia piccola tendenzialmente prognata e fenozica, orbite alte e cavità nasale mesorrina;
  b. una tipologia mediterranea occidentale, o afromediterranea, caratterizzata da una conformazione corporea più robusta, statura un po' più elevata e neurocranio dolicomorfo ellissoide con faccia tendenzialmente macroprosopa, criptoziga con cavità orbitarie e nasale più basse.

Appunto queste due morfologie più o meno pure, più o meno fra loro ibridate, caratterizzeranno—come vedremo—le varie fasi del Neolitico sardo.

1. *Il Neolitico antico.* Di questo periodo, pur diffusamente rappresentato in Sardegna dal punto di vista industriale, non si conoscono resti scheletrici umani, salvo due resti facciali (peraltro di insicura collocazione stratigrafica e -di conseguenza- cronologica), rinvenuti nel riparo di Su Carroppu di Sirri-Cagliari (Atzeni 1972) e di morfologia attendibilmente afromediterranea (Germanà 1990).

2. *Il Neolitico medio.* Resti scheletrici umani di questo periodo provengono dalla Grotta Rifugio di Olièna-Nuoro (Agosti et al. 1980; Germanà 1981) e da tre ipogei (il n. 384, il n. 386 e il n. 387) della necropoli di Cuccuru S'Arriu (o Arrius) presso Cabras-Oristano (Santoni 1982; comunicazione personale inedita; Germanà, inedito). Nel primo caso trattasi di una grotta-ossario, che ha restituito i resti di almeno 11 individui di ogni età e di entrambi i sessi in deposizione secondaria. Nel secondo caso si tratta di tombe monosome, tranne la n. 386, che conteneva una deposizione primaria di un individuo adulto e un resto cranico di un individuo juvenilis, probabilmente di sesso femminile. In entrambi i casi le tipologie umane, emerse dall'analisi (Germanà 1981; Germanà, inedito), erano dolicomorfe ellissoidi e ovoidi, di corporatura discretamente robusta e di statura medio-bassa, prevalentemente euroafricana. Il Campione a risulta, appunto, da questi due gruppi umani e sul piano craniologico si può così sintetizzare (Tabella 1).

3. *Il Neolitico recente.* Questo periodo della storia sarda è caratterizzato dalla diffusione peninsulare della Cultura di Ozieri (Lilliu 1988; Campus 1989). I resti scheletrici umani coevi provengono da quattro siti: due della provincia di Sassari (Grotta funeraria di Lu Maccioni-Alghero; Grotta Sa ucca de su Tintirriolu-Mara), uno della provincia di Oristano (Grotta di Is Aruttas-Cabras) e il quarto della provincia di Cagliari (Domu de janas di S. Benedetto-Iglesias). Il campione 'Ozieri' che ne vien fuori (Campione b) si può considerare significativo sia per la sua numerosità, che per la sua relativa omogeneità, che per la sua dislocazione geografica.

Il gruppo umano di Lu Maccioni-Alghero (Maxia e Fenu 1962) era composto da una quarantina di individui in deposizione secondaria, ma l'indagine antropologica venne condotta soltanto su 19 resti cranici (13 maschili e 6 femminili) e su 57 ossa lunghe. Il neurocranio era in tutti i casi dolicomorfo sia gracile che robusto, dolicocranico, acrocranico nella componente maschile, metricranico in quella femminile. La faccia risulta variabile: camerrini gli uomini, lepto-mesorrine le donne, tutti mesoconchi, ortognati e criptozighi. I valori staturali medi di gruppo (Manouvrier-vivente) risultano negli uomini attorno ai cm 163,1 (174,1-153,2) e cm 150,8 (157,5-140) nelle donne.

Tre resti cranici provengono dallo strato 'Ozieri' della Grotta Sa Ucca de su Tintirriolu-Mara (Loria e Trump 1978). Si tratta di tre individui (un uomo robusto e due donne gracili) dai neurocrani dolicomorfi, dolicocranici molto lunghi, di larghezza variabile, tutti discretamente alti. La faccia maschile è macroprosopa, leptena, con orbite basse e cavità nasale allungata, decisamente ortognata e fenoziga. Le due facce femminili sono più basse, più strette e microprosope, anch'esse leptene e leptorrine, però mesoconche (Germanà 1984a; 1989).

Da una grotticella naturale del Sinis, Is Aruttas-Cabras provengono i resti umani di almeno 25 individui, presumibilmente in deposizione secondaria, di ogni età e di entrambi i sessi, tutti dolicomorfi tanto gracili, che robusti, in prevalenza dolicocranici con il neurocranio in massima parte oomorfo, ma in minor misura anche ellissomorfo e pentagonoide, lungo, stretto e alto. Variabile per la faccia. Stature medie (Manouvrier-vivente) per gli uomini cm 161,4 (165,2-158,6) e per le donne cm 152,4 (157,3-148,1) (Germanà 1979–80; 1982).

Il quarto gruppo umano 'Ozieri' proviene da una domus de janas della necropoli di S. Benedetto-Iglesias; esso risultava composto da circa 35 individui in deposizione secondaria. Le forme craniche sono tutte dolicomorfe sia gracili che robuste. Non sostanziale differenza quantitativa fra oomorfi, ellissomorfi e pentagonoidi. Una faccia maschile è leptena; camerrina la componente maschile del gruppo, mesorrina quella femminile; cameconca la componente maschile, mesoconca quella femminile ma con qualche esemplare cameconco. I profili facciali sono mesognati con qualche esemplare ortognato. I valori staturali medi maschili si aggirano attorno ai cm 160,5 e quelli femminili attorno ai cm 151 (Maxia e Atzeni 1964).

Non sono stati presi in considerazione i resti scheletrici delle Grotte Cagliaritane di Capo S. Elia (Maxia 1951–52) per la loro insicura collocazione cronologico-culturale (Lilliu 1988: 168-69).

Il campione 'Ozieri', che scaturisce dalla fusione di questi gruppi umani coevi, è caratterizzato (stando almeno alle attuali conoscenze) da ricorrente dolicomorfia, prevalente dolicocrania con fronte larga e buona capacità cranica. Variabile la conformazione generale della faccia e di alcuni suoi particolari: prevalente l'ortognatismo e la criptozighia, ma alcune facce sono anche in minima parte fenozighe e mesognate, proponendo schemi negroidi. Lo scheletro post-craniale è caratterizzato da spalle il più delle volte larghe, tronco lungo, prevalente brachicherchia e arti superiori relativamente più sviluppati degli inferiori. I valori staturali si collocano nella classe delle

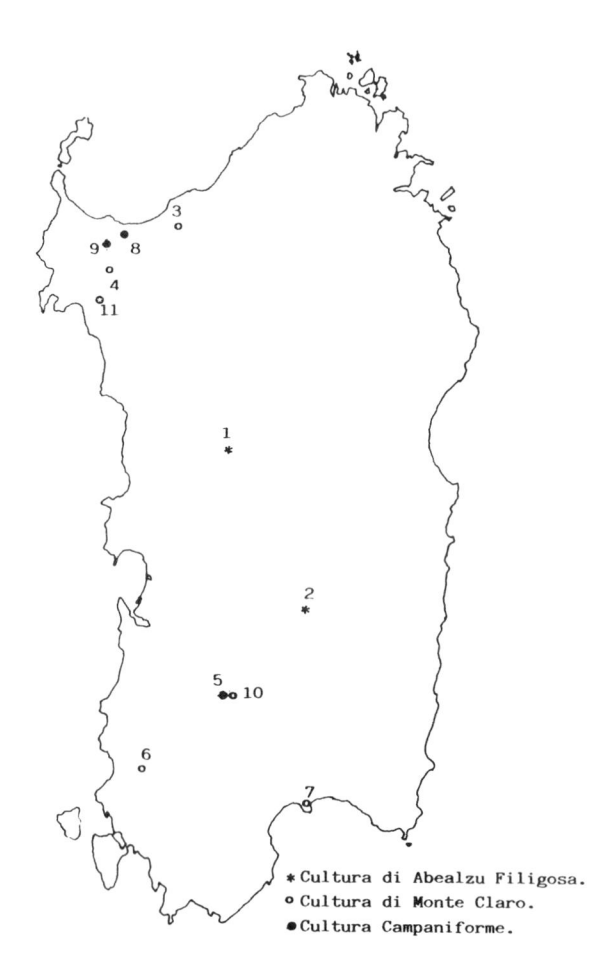

Fig. 2 Depositi funerari paleosardi eneolitici.
1. Necropoli di Filigosa (Macomer-NU); 2. Grotta Fromosa (Villanovatulo-NU); 3. Domu di Serra Crabiles (Sennori-SS); 4. Necropoli di La Crucca (SS); 5. Ipogeo di Padru Jossu (Sanluri-CA); 6. Grotta di Tanì (Villamassargia-CA); 7. Grotta di S. Bartolomeo (Capo S. Elia-CA); 8. Necropoli di Su Crucifissu Mannu (Porto Torres-SS) 9. Tomba di Marinaru (SS); 10. Ipogeo di Padru Jossu (Sanluri-CA); 11. Necropoli di Anghelu Ruju (Algherto-SS).

stature medio-base con valori estremi di stature alte (mai altissime) e basse (mai bassissime, ma talune-eccezionali-nanoidi): si tratta di stature squisitamente 'neolitiche'. In alcune rappresentazioni antropomorfe vascolari di questo periodo sono infatti raffigurate sagome umane con queste caratteristiche somatiche.

Nella morfologia 'Ozieri' sembra convergano, fra loro ibridate, le due prevalenti correnti mediterranee neolitiche: la danubiana e l'afromediterranea. Tale ibridazione è già documentata in Sardegna fin dal Neolitico medio, nelle forme umane che compongono il 'campione a', ma la fissazione genetica dei caratteri 'nuovi' deve essersi realizzata durante il Neolitico recente, caratterizzato appunto dal momento culturale agglutinante 'Ozieri' (Tabella 2).

4. L'Eneolitico (Figura 2)

Questo periodo, che in Sardegna si realizza nell'arco di 700 anni, è caratterizzato da tre culture, che Lilliu (1988) chiama 'di transizione': la Cultura di Abealzu-Filigosa, quella di Monte Claro e la Cultura Campaniforme. Poco e niente sappiamo delle forme umane connesse con la Cultura di Abealzu-Filigosa: un resto cranico è dolicomorfo, riconducibile a morfologie 'Ozieri' (Germanà 1971), e si conoscono due valori staturali rispettivamente maschile (cm 162 circa) e femminile (cm 150 circa) (Germanà, inedito).

1. *Gli uomini di Cultura Monte Claro.* Le forme umane connesse con la Cultura di Monte Claro sono circa una trentina, di cui il 50% maschili e il restante 50% femminili. Esse provengono da quattro siti: due del Nord della Sardegna (Serra Crabiles e La Crucca) e due del centro-Sud (Tanì e Padru Jossu). Il gruppo umano di Serra Crabiles-Sennori (Germanà 1980a) è costituito da almeno sei individui al termine dell'accrescimento, di conformazione gracile, riferibili a morfologie danubiane di statura medio-bassa (cm 162,9 la componente maschile; cm 147,7 quella femminile). Da una domu de janas di La Crucca-Sassari (Germanà e Fornaciari 1991) provengono due forme craniche dolicomorfe di media robustezza, entrambe trapanate in vivo. Il gruppo umano più numeroso proviene dalla Grotta di Tanì-Carbonia, altrimenti nota con i nomi di 'Su Cungiareddu de Serafini', o 'Baieddus de sa Sedderenciu' (Maxia e Fenu 1963): si tratta di 26 resti cranici ovoidi per il 50%, ellissoidi per il 29,2%, pentagonoidi per il 12,5% e sferoidi per il restante 8,3%. Le forme craniche sono prevalentemente dolicomorfe con due forme brachimorfe curvoccipitali (le prime in ordine cronologico segnalate nell'isola). Dall'ipogeo di Padru Jossu-Sanluri, dallo strato 'Monte Claro', proviene un resto cranico dolicomorfo robusto, ovo-pentagonoide di grande capacità cranica e di morfologia 'Ozieri'. Da tutte queste forme craniche è costituito il 'campione c', a seguito riportato (Tabella 3).

2. *I portatori del vaso campaniforme.* Nell'ambito del Campaniforme europeo (AA.VV. 1984) il momento campaniforme sardo si può inserire fra i 'gruppi derivati o tardivi'; esso è stato cronologicamente riferito al periodo eneolitico non tanto per datazioni assolute, quanto per paragoni estrainsulari (Lilliu 1988). Resti umani connessi alla Cultura del vaso a campana isolano provengono dalla tomba di Marinaru-Sassari e si tratta di forme umane dolicomorfe non ulteriormente definite dall'Antropologo che le ha esaminate: (Maxia in Lilliu 1988), dalla necropoli di Su Crucifissu Mannu-Sassari (tomba 15: Germanà, inedito; si tratta di due resti cranici brachimorfi, però giovanili), dalla necropoli di Anghelu Ruju-Alghero (Sergi 1906; Germanà 1984c) e si tratta di crani dolicomorfi e brachimorfi, però mescolati a resti umani di Cultura Bonnanaro e da una tomba ipogeica di Padru Jossu-Sanluri (Ugas 1982; Germanà 1987b). Dallo strato campaniforme di Padru Jossu-Sanluri proviene un campione umano composto da poco meno di una ventina di resti cranici, riferibili sia al momento A (ornato), che al B (inornato). I due subcampioni non presentano particolari differenze morfometriche, ancorché riferiti a due successivi momenti d'uso della tomba. Si tratta di forme tanto gracili, che robuste, dolicomorfe nell'84,6% delle osservazioni e brachimorfe nel restante 15,4%. Prevalgono le forme ovoidi (76,9%) sulle altre in egual misura ellissoidi, sfenoidi curvo- e plano occipitali (rispettivamente 7,7%). Variabili sono i dettagli facciali, la cui costante sembra una ricorrente criptozighia. Un valore staturale femminile provvisorio è nel vivente cm 146,1. Questo gruppo umano (saggio) costituisce il 'campione d', a seguito riportato (Tabella 4).

3. *La necropoli di Anghelu Ruju-Alghero.* La necropoli di Anghelu Ruju-Alghero merita cenno a parte non soltanto per la sua indiscussa importanza nella Preistoria della Sardegna (Taramelli 1904; Taramelli 1909; Lilliu 1988; etc.), ma anche per il ricco materiale osteologico umano restituito, materiale riferito sia alla Cultura Campaniforme, che alla Cultura di Bonnanaro-fase A. Molto di questo materiale è andato disperso e quello residuo fu analizzato (Sergi 1906) senza che si potesse tenere conto della sua associazione culturale nei singoli ipogei (Germanà 1984b). La sua incerta collocazione culturale dai tempi della

Cultura Campaniforme a quelli del Bonnanaro A (dall'Eneolitico all'età del Bronzo antico) ne impone lo studio globale. Le forme neurocraniche sono dolicomorfe (gli 'eurafricani' di sergiana memoria) per l'84,1% e branchimorfi (gli 'eurasiatici') per il restante 15,9%: prevalgono le forme ellissoidi (42,9%) sulle ovoidi (23,8%), sulle beloidi (3,2%) e vi è pure una forma definita da Sergi 'platicefala' (1,6%). Le facce sono variabili dalla leptenia alla eurienia; la maggior parte dei profili facciali sono ortognati con rare facce mesognate e una sola faccia (femminile) prognata. La criptozighia è regola nelle facce femminili e predomina nelle maschili con un solo esemplare subfenozigo e due fenozighi. Un tentativo di sintesi razziale (Germanà 1984a) ha evidenziato forme grimaldoidi, mediterranee antiche, cordate, acquitano-mediterranee, mesogrimaldoidi, alpino-grimaldoidi, neomediterranee, iberiche, dinaroidi e alpinoidi (classificazione sec. Charles 1960), senza però una netta prevalenza dell'una o dell'altra forma. Le stature, calcolate a partire da 78 omeri, oscillano nella componente maschile attorno ai cm 160,8 (168,7-156,2) e nella femminile attorno ai cm 149,7 (154,8-106,7) (Bruni 1924–25; calcoli di Germanà 1984b) e si tratta di valori fra i più bassi fra le serie neo-eneolitiche mediterranee. Il 'campione e' dalla tavola 5 riassume le caratteristiche cranio-facciali dei resti umani di Anghelu Ruju.

5. L'Età del Bronzo (Figura 3)

1. *Il Bronzo antico e i diffusori della Cultura di Bonnanaro A.* Sul piano della produzione industriale la fase A della Cultura di Bonnanaro presenta affinità tipologiche sia con il Campaniforme, che con la Polada (Ferrarese Ceruti 1981; Lilliu 1988; etc.). Alcuni Autori vogliono includere questa fase della cultura in esame nel 'Nuragico arcaico' (Lilliu 1988), mentre altri la ritengono estranea allo spirito della Cultura Nuragica (Ferrarese Ceruti, comunicazione personale). Dal punto di vista antropologico i resti scheletrici connessi con tale fase della Cultura di Bonnanaro provengono da almeno 7 siti funerari (tutti in deposizione secondaria), di cui 5 in provincia di Sassari (grotta di Palmaera-Sassari, Domu 2 di Monte d'Accoddi-agro di Sassari, necropoli di Su Crucifissu Mannu-Porto Torres, domu di S'Isterridolzu-Ossi e domu di Taulera-Alghero) e 2 nel Cagliaritano (domu di Pedralba-Sardara e Grotta Concali Corongiu Acca-Villamassargia).

La Grotta di Palmaera-Sassari (Frassetto 1907a; Frasseto 1907b; Facchini 1987) ha restituito 4 resti cranici dolicomorfi e almeno 2 brachiformi (uno sfenoide e uno sferoide). La domus n. 2 di Monte d'Accoddi (Tanda 1976) conteneva 8 resti cranici in maggior parte dolicomorfi (5 ovoidi e 1 pentagonoide) e 2 sfenoidi (Germanà 1984b). Da una domus de janas di S'Isterridolzu-Ossi (Ferrarese Ceruti e Germanà 1978; Germanà 1980c) provengono i resti di una quarantina di individui, di cui il 68% dolicomorfi (ovoidi per il 52%; ellissoidi per l'8% e pentagonoidi pure per l'8%) e il 32% brachimorfi (sfenoidi per il 16% e sferoidi per il restante 16%). Le tombe 1, 16, 21, e 22 della necropoli di Su Crucifissu Mannu-Porto Torres (Ferrarese Ceruti 1972–74) contenevano oltre una ventina di resti cranici (Germanà 1971; 1972–74; 1975; 1984b), di cui il 41,7% ovoidi, 41,7%, sfenoidi, il 4,2% ovosfenoidi e non determinabile l'8,2%. Un valore staturale maschile si aggira

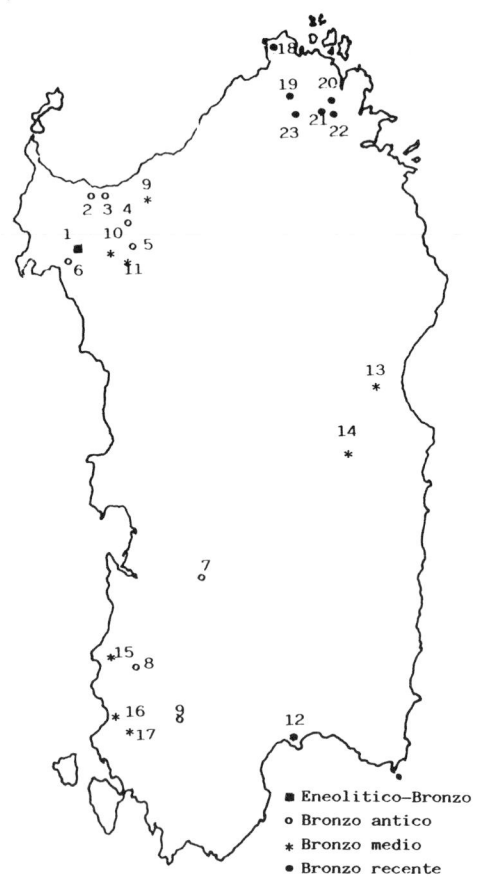

Fig. 3 Depositi funerari paleo- e protosardi dell'Età del Bronzo.

1. Necropoli di Anghelu Ruju (SS); 2. Necropoli Su Crucifissu Mannu (SS); 3. Domu di Monte d'Accoddi (SS); 4. Domu di Palmaera (SS); 5. Domu di S'Isterridolzu (SS); 6. Domu di Taulera (SS); 7. Domu di Pedralba (CA); 8. Domu di S'Orreri (CA); 9. Concali Corongiu (CA); 10. S'Iscia e sas Piras (SS); 11. Ena e Muros (SS); 12. Domus di Capo S. Elia (CA); 13. Grotta Sisaia (NU); 14. Grotticelle Seulo (NU); 15. Grotta Capo Pecora (CA); 16. Nicolai Nebida (CA); 17. Nuraxi Figus (CA); 18. Lu Brandali (SS); 19. Bassacutena (SS); 20. Li Muri (SS); 21. Donnicaglia (SS); 22. Malchittu (SS); 23. Balaiana (SS).

attorno ai cm 165,5 (Manouvrier-vivente). I resti cranici della tomba 16 si presentano in preda a un processo di brachicefalizzazione in atto. Le tombe 1 e 16 hanno inoltre restituito ognuna un cranio trapanato in vita. Un altro cranio dolicomorfo e trapanato proviene da una domus di Taulera-Alghero (Germanà 1971). Una domus di Pedralba-Sardara restituì 10 resti cranici dolicomorfi, di cui 6 ovoidi, 3 ellissoidi e 1 beloide; un cranio era inaltre trapanato in vivo (Maxia 1951-52). Dalla Grotta Concali Corongiu Acca-Villamassargia provengono rari e frammentari resti cranici e 5 ossa lunghe integre, da cui vennero ricavati alcuni valori staturali medi (Manouvrier-vivente) maschili cm 161,8 e femminili cm 159,3 (Maxia e Floris 1961).

In sintesi, le forme umane connesse con la fase A della Cultura di Bonnanaro presentano una concentrazione di branchimorfi nell'area nord-occidentale della Sardegna per un complessivo 35%, mentre la dominante dolicomorfia (65%) è distribuita in tutta l'isola. Le facce sono variabili con una dispersione dei valori singoli nelle varie classi. Nella Tabella 6, che rappresenta il 'campione f' sono riassunti i più significativi valori cranio-facciali dei Paleosardi del Bronzo antico.

2. I diffusori delle culture paleosarde del Bronzo medio. I siti funerari coevi, che hanno restituito materiale osseo umano, utilizzati per la presente indagine, sono almeno 8: 2 nel Sassarese (Oridda-Sennori; S'Iscia e sas Piras-Usini), 2 nella provincia di Nuoro (Grotta di Sisaia-Dorgali e Grotticelle di Seulo) e 4 nel Cagliaritano (Domu di Nuraxi Figus-Gonnesa, Grotta di Capo Pecora-Arbus, Grotta di Nicolai e Nebida-Iglesias e Grotta S'Orreri-Fluminimaggiore). Questi siti sono culturalmente riferibili alla fase B della Cultura di Bonnanaro. La domu con prospetto architettonico di Oridda-Sennori (Castaldi 1969) ha restituito i resti di una ventina di individui adulti, 6 bambini e 1 feto. Fu però possibile analizzare solo un resto cranico di donna adulta dolicomorfa e si ha un valore staturale di circa 150 cm (Messeri, in Castaldi 1969: 139-56).

Altra domu con prospetto architettonico è quella di S'Iscia e sas Piras-Usini (Castaldi 1975), che ha restituito i resti di almeno 14 individui di entrambi i sessi e di tutte le età. Tra i resti cranici (tutti dolicomorfi) vennero riferiti a tipologie cordata, aquino-mediterranea e mediterranea recente (sec. Charles 1960); i valori staturali medi (vivente-Manouvrier) maschili si aggiravano attorno ai cm 167,7 (173-163) e quelli femminili sui cm 155,5 (157,9-154) (Germanà 1975).

Uno scheletro quasi intero in deposizione primaria semirannicchiata di donna adulta è stato rinvenuto nella Grotta Sisaia-Dorgali: il cranio è dolicomorfo ellissoide con faccia euriena e microprosopa. La statura nel vivente doveva aggirarsi intorno ai 150 cm. Sul parietale di destra si nota una trapanazione cranica in vivo con autoinnesto (riuscito) della rondella in precedenza prelevata (Germanà 1972-74; Ferrarese Ceruti e Germanà 1978). Dalle Grotticelle di Seulo-Nuoro provengono 11 resti cranici e 68 ossa lunghe, analizzate prima sommariamente da Businco (1933) e successivamente in dettaglio da Maxia (1951-52). Dieci crani sono dolicomorfi (almeno 6 ellissoidi, 1 ovoide, 1 pentagonoide e 1 beloide) e uno brachimorfo (maschile, sfenoide). Le facce variano dalla mesenia alla leptenia e sono tutte ortogognate, 3 criptozighe e 1 subfenoziga. I valori staturali medi (Manouvier-vivente) sono cm 165,9 (167,5-164,5) e femminili cm 155,1 (158,3-152,8). I rapporti fra segmenti corporei indicano brachicnemia negli uomini e dolicocnemia nelle donne. Un esemplare cranico dolicomorfo venne trapanato in vivo (Maxia *et al.* 1972).

Un resto cranico con ben quattro trapanazioni in vivo proviene da una domu di Nuraxi Figus-Gonnesa: si tratta di una forma dolicomorfa, ellissoide, leptena e metrioprosopa (Germanà 1972-74; 1987a). Da una Grotta di Capo Pecora-Arbus provengono i resti di una ventina di individui, di cui sono stati analizzati 13 resti cranici dolicomorfi (almeno 8 ovoidi e 3 pentagonoidi) con facce variabili, tutte con profilo mesognato. Stature medie (vivente-Manouvrier) maschili cm 164,1 e femminili cm 151,4 (Maxia *et al.* 1972). Nella Grotta di Nicolai e Nebida-Iglesias venne rinvenuto un resto cranico dolicomorfo ellissoide con faccia di media altezza, mesoconco e mesorrino (Cosseddu *et al.* 1983). La Grotta S'Orreri-Fluminimaggiore restituì in un contesto Bonnanaro A e B resti scheletrici, da cui Rahon (in Jssel 1884) ricavò un valore staturale medio di 167,6 cm. Nella Tabella 7 sono stati sintetizzati i più importanti valori medi maschili e femminili dei Paleosardi del Bronzo medio (campione g).

3. Il Bronzo finale. Questo periodo fa parte del 'Medionuragico' e si colloca tra il 1200 e il 900 a.C. (Lilliu 1988). Alle forme umane coeve, ormai di età protostorica, noi abbiamo dato il nome di Protosardi. I resti scheletrici analizzati di questo periodo provengono soltanto dall'area nord-orientale della Sardegna, dalla Gallura (tafoni e tombe di giganti). Poichè le morfologie umane dei tafoni non differiscono sensibilmente da quelle delle tombe di giganti, entrambe sono state utilizzate per costruire il campione h.

I tafoni che hanno restituito il materiale scheletrico d'indagine sono almeno 8: Lu Brandali-

S.Teresa di Gallura, tomba 13; Balaiana-Luogosanto, tomba 1; Malchittu-Arzachena, tombe 1, 3 e 5 (Germanà, inedito); Li Muri-Arzachena (determinazioni di Maxia e Floris). La tomba di giganti è quella di Lu Brandali-S.Teresa di Gallura (Antona Ruju 1981; Germanà, saggio inedito). I Protosardi galluresi avevano il neurocranio di conformazione generale dolicomorfa, anche se si notano alcune forme larghe e corte, evolutive verso la brachicrania. Nel 74,1% la forma è ovoide, nel 14,8% pentagonoide e nell'11,1% ellissoide. Le facce variano dalla mesenia alla leptenia in assenza di facce euriene. Prevale la criptozighia con una eccezionale faccia fenoziga e i profili facciali sono prevalentemente ortognati con una sola osservazione di mesognatismo. I valori staturali medi (Manouvrier-vivente) maschili oscillano intorno ai cm 116,3 (173,7-160) e quelli femminili attorno ai cm 155,5 (157,6-144,6). Nella Tabella 8 sono sintetizzati i valori craniofacciali medi dei Protogalluresi.

Un gruppo umano protocorso, proveniente da un tafone di S. Vincente-Sartène ha restituito tre resti cranici, di cui due dolicomorfi e uno brachimorfo. Valori staturali maschili cm 164,6 (170,3-161) e femminili cm 149,3 (153,6-145) (Germanà 1970).

6. L'Età del Bronzo-Ferro

Di questo periodo conosciamo (e in forma lacunosa) soltanto due campioni scheletrici umani, provenienti da altrettanti siti del centro-sud dell'isola. Dal poliandro di Motrox e Bois-Usellus provengono i resti di oltre una ventina di individui, determinati da Maxia (Contu 1958; Maxia e Floris 1961). Le forme neurocraniche sono in 'maggioranza' ellissoidi e ovoidi; una faccia maschile è mesena, ortognata. La tomba T3 del sepolcreto di Antas-Fluminimaggiore conteneva i resti di un individuo adulto, robusto e di statura medio-bassa con neurocranio dolicomorfo di 'tipologia generale mediterranea' (Ugas e Lucia 1987).

Parte Seconda: la variabilità dei campioni paleosardi e protosardi

1. Il campione a (Cultura di Bonu Ighinu—Neolitico medio)

Il campione a è caratterizzato da un'esigua numerosità, soprattutto per quel che riguarda lo scheletro craniale, ma fino ai nostri giorni questo è, purtroppo, tutto quanto ci offre la situazione attuale e su questo bisogna lavorare, naturalmente con le dovute riserve. Sul piano morfologico i diffusori di questa cultura medioneolitica sono prevalentemente euroafricani (Germanà 1981), specie gli individui delle tre tombe di Cuccuru s'Arriu (Germanà, inedito).

I confronti fra le sue medie e quelle corrispondenti del campione b (Ozieri-Neolitico recente), condotti -come già detto in premessa- con il metodo del t Student, hanno evidenziato nella componente maschile distanze significative (e quindi sostanziali differenze) per la misura 51 con un t =3,699** e nella componente femminile per le misure 9, 51 e 52 con un t rispettivamente di 4,024**; 2,794* e 2,58*. Le più significative differenze, dunque, interessano alcuni dettagli della fronte e della faccia, mentre non sono significative le differenze dei dettagli del neurocranio. Il t medio (media aritmetica dei singoli t Student) maschile è uguale a 1,1 e quello femminile =1,8. Ulteriori significative differenze si hanno con il subcampione femminile di Monte Claro (misure 9** e 52** con un t medio = 1,9), mentre si hanno differenze significative fra i subcampioni maschili (t medio = 0,9). Nella componente maschile dei diffusori della Cultura Monte Claro evidentemente prevalgono le forme eurafricane. Il campione eneolitico di Padru Jossu (campione d) diverge sensibilmente dal campione paleosardo medioneolitico per misura 8 maschile (t =2,4 *) e 9 femminile (t= 4,2*) con un t medio maschile = 1,0 e femminile = 1,3. In effetti, rispetto alle forme indigene dolicomorfe, i Campaniformi di Padru Jossu presentano una importante percentuale di crani brachimorfi (23,1%). Le differenze aumentano significativamente con il campione di Anghelu Ruju (campione e) per le misure 8* e 9* maschili e le misure 9**, 51** e 52** femminili. Riguardo al campione f del Bronzo antico (Bonnanaro A) persistono le differenze per le misure 8* e 9* maschili (t medio = 0,7) e le misure 9** e 51* femminili (t medio = 1,8). Persistono le differenze con il campione g (Bonnanaro B) per la misura 51** maschile (t medio = 1,0) e 9** femminile (t medio = 1,6) e le distanze sembrano in parte diminuite, forse perchè in questo campione si nota la quasi totale scomparsa delle forme craniche brachimorfe. Ma anche fra le due componenti dolicomorfe si notano dissimiglianze non indifferenti. Con il campione gallurese del Bronzo recente (campione h) le distanze non sono significative per la componente maschile (in cui tuttavia si nota un t medio = 1,0), mentre nelle due componenti femminili si nota una distanza significativa per la misura 9**, con un t medio = 1,6.

Le forme umane paleosarde del Neolitico medio presentano pertanto una morfologia a se stante, forse dovuta al fatto che, essendo di recente acquisizione isolana e geneticamente non ancora consolidata, si presenta più affine a morfologie estrainsulari (si tratta infatti di forme sia danubiane che afromediterranee), che a quelle che si realizzeranno in tempi successivi nell'ambito del suolo sardo.

2. Il campione b (Cultura Ozieri-Neolitico recente)

Il campione b presenta un coefficiente di variazione (s.100/M) medio di 6,0 per la componente maschile e di 5,0 per la componente femminile, rivelando nel particolare una buona variazione intragruppale. In effetti come già accennato, nel campione 'Ozieri' confluiscono, fra loro ibridandosi, due morfologie neolitiche: la danubiana e l'afromediterranea. È questa l'Etnia Ozieri, che costituisce il substrato antropico del popolamento della Sardegna fino ai nostri giorni. Etnia biologica favorita sia dalla particolare conformazione geografica dell'isola (isolamento geografico), sia dalla durata millenaria della Cultura di Ozieri, periodo che ha consentito la fissazione a livello genetico dei caratteri morfologici specifici.

Rispetto al campione c (Monte Claro-Eneolitico) il campione Ozieri presenta una distanza significativa per le misure 8* e 17** della componente maschile e 17* della componente femminile. Una tale differenza è probabilmente dovuta al fatto che nel contesto umano Monte Claro già cominciano a realizzarsi quelle variazioni morfometriche (larghezza e altezza del cranio) che porteranno alla brachicefalizzazione più caratteristica dell'età del Bronzo. Nel campione Monte Claro, infatti, già figurano le prime due forme brachiforme della Prestoria sarda.

Le distanze si fanno più significative nei confronti del campione d (Campaniformi di Padru Jossu) nella componente maschile per le misure 1*, 8** e 17**, nella componente femminile per le misure 17* e 51*. Lo stesso t medio è per la componente maschile = 1,4 e per la componente femminile = 1,3. Il campione e (Anghelu Ruju-Eneolitico-I Bronzo) differisce significativamente nella componente maschile per le misure 8** e 51.* e nella componente femminile per le misure 8**, 17* e 45* con un t medio rispettivamente di 1,5 e 1,3. Se poi dal campione di Anghelu Ruju si isolano le forme dolicomorfe, le distanze con questo subcampione non sono più significative. Lo stesso fenomeno pure si osserva a proposito dei paragoni con il campione seguente.

Il campione f (Bonnanaro A-I Bronzo) presenta distanze statisticamente significative sia nella componente maschile (misure 1*, 8**, 10* e 17*) che in quella femminile (misure 45* e 48*) con un t medio di 1,3 in entrambe le componenti. Ed è sintomatico che nei confronti del campione g (Bonnanaro B-Bronzo medio) le distanze non risultano più significative e il t medio è = 0,8 per entrambe le componeneti: infatti in questo periodo le forme craniche brachimorfe scompaiono quasi completamente e le forme dolicomorfe indigene tornano a prevalere. Con il campione h (Galluresi del Bronzo recente) i confronti evidenziano significative distanze nella componente maschile a proposito della misura 51** e in quella femminile per la misura 9* con un t medio rispettivamente di 0,9 e 0,8. Tali differenze riguardano la forma delle orbite e della fronte, senza interessare la conformazione generale del neurocranio e del massiccio facciale. Dall'analisi di questi confronti si può dedurre come la morfologia Ozieri, nonostante l'inquinamento brachimorfo del periodo eneolitico-I Bronzo, persista nell'isola, ben meritando anche per questo motivo la denominazione di 'Etnia Ozieri'.

3. Il campione c (Cultura di Monte Claro-Eneolitico)

Il coefficiente medio di variazione del campione c è per la componente maschile 5,8 e per quella femminile 3,9 il che dimostra una variabilità intragruppale minore rispetto al campione Ozieri. In seno alle prevalenti (91,7%) forme umane dolicomorfe, che caratterizzano questo gruppo, si nota la comparsa dei primi crani brachimorfi sferoidi (8,3%).

Rispetto al campione d (Padru Jossu-Campaniforme) quello di Monte Claro diverge significativamente nella componente maschile per la misura 17* (t medio = 1,0) e nella componente femminile per le misure 17* e anche 45* (t medio = 1,2). Con il campione e (Anghelu Ruju) le differenze fra medie sono significative nella componente maschile per la misura 17* (t medio = 0,8) e in quella femminile per la misura 8** (t medio = 1,0). Il campione f (Bonnanaro A- Bronzo antico) nella componente maschile presenta differenze statisticamente valide per le misure 1** e 55* (t medio = 0,8) e in quella femminile per la misura 48* (t medio = 1,0). Nei confronti del campione g si hanno differenze significative negli uomini per la misura 55* (t medio = 1,2) e nelle donne per le misure 10* e 52* (t medio = 1,1). Il campione Monte Claro diverge significativamente dal campione h (Protogalluresi del Bronzo recente) nella componente maschile per la misura 17** (t medio = 1,1) e in quella femminile per le misure 9* e 45* (t medio = 1,2), presentando soltanto una occasionale identità per la misura 54 femminile.

4. Il campione d (Padru Jossu-Cultura campaniforme-Eneolitico)

Nel campione d il coefficiente medio di variazione

è per gli uomini 5,2 e per le donne 3,1. Rispetto al campione e (Anghelu Ruju) quello in esame diverge nella componente maschile per le misure 9** e 17** (t medio = 1,8) e in quella femminile per le misure 17*, 45* e 51** (t medio = 1,3). Col campione f (Bonnanaro A-Bronzo antico) si hanno differenze significativamente nella componente maschile per la misura 9* (t medio = 1,0) e nella femminile per le misure 17* e 45* (t medio = 1,3). Il campione g (Bonnanaro B-Bronzo medio) diverge fra le componenti maschili per le misure 8* e 17* (t medio = 1,4) e le femminili per la misura 8* (t medio = 1,4).

5. Il campione e (Anghelu Ruju-Eneolitico-Bronzo Antico)

Il campione di Anghelu Ruju, nel quale convergono morfologie eneolitiche campaniformi e del Bronzo antico-Bonnanaro A, presenta un coefficiente di variazione medio sia nella componente maschile, che in quella femminile = 4,6. Rispetto al campione f (Bonnanaro A) quello in esame diverge significativamente nella componente maschile per la sola misura 55* (t medio = 1,0) e in quello femminile per la misura 48* (t medio = 0,9) con identità della misura 51 femminile. Aumentano, come atteso, le divergenze nei confronti del campione g (Bonnanaro B) nella componente maschile per le misure 8*, 51*, 52* e 55** (t medio = 1,5) e in quello femminile soltanto per la misura 8** (t medio = 1,3). Il campione h (Protogalluresi del Bronzo recente) diverge nella componente maschile per le misure 8** e 9* (t medio = 1,2) e in quella femminile per la misura 45* (t medio = 1,0).

6. Il campione f (Bonnanaro A-Bronzo antico)

Il campione in esame—che ricordiamolo—è composto da poco meno del 70% di forme craniche dolicomorfe e da poco più del 30% da forme brachimorfe, presenta il più alto indice di variazione rispetto agli altri campioni sardi (7,1 negli uomini e 5,6 nelle donne). Le più significative differenze rispetto al campione g riguardano la misura 8* di entrambe le componenti con un t medio che varia da 0,7 negli uomini a 0,9 nelle donne. Fra queste ultime poi si nota l'identità della misura 55. La quasi completa scomparsa dall'isola delle forme umane brachimorfe spiega un tal fenomeno statistico, riconducibile alla netta prevalenza dei crani più stretti. Rispetto al campione h (Protogalluresi del Bronzo recente) il campione in esame presenta sensibili divergenze nella componente maschile per le misure 5** e 8** (t medio = 1,5) e in quella femminile per la misura 45* con una occasionale identità per la misura 52 (t medio = 1,2).

7. Il campione g (Bonnanaro B-Bronzo medio)

Questo campione del Bronzo medio presenta un coefficiente di variazione di 5,4 per la componente maschile e di 4,7 per quella femminile. Nei confronti del campione h (Protogalluresi) il campione in esame diverge nella componente maschile per la misura 51** con identità della misura 1. (t medio = 1,2) e in quella femminile per le misure 8*, 9** e 10* (t medio =1,4).

8. Il campione h (Galluresi del Bronzo recente)

Questo campione (che potrebbe diventare un subcampione il giorno in cui la mappa antropica della Sardegna del Bronzo recente dovesse venire completata) presenta un coefficiente di variazione medio per la componente maschile = 5,8 e per quella femminile = 4,4. I suoi paragoni con gli altri sette campioni dimostrano come anche esso sia caratterizzato dalla mistione di forme paleosarde (dolicomorfe) con forme nuove, nelle quali l'incipiente brachimorfia non presenta gli stessi caratteri della brachimorfia campaniforme o di quella 'Bonnanaro', ma prelude alle morfologie caratterizzanti i contesti galluresi più recenti e forse anche contemporanei.

Parte Terza: conclusioni provvisorie possibili

1. Morfologie paleosarde e protosarde

Una prima generica osservazione demografica sul popolamento della Sardegna preistorica e protostorica può scaturire dall'osservazione che tanto nella maggior parte dei gruppi umani esaminati, che degli otto campioni qui presentati, la componente maschile è quasi sempre numericamente superiore a quella femminile. Ma un tale fenomeno, oltre che essere reale, può risultare imputabile anche al fatto che gli elementi scheletrici femminili sono più gracili e pertanto più disgregabili rispetto a quelli maschili. Esaminando poi i vari campioni nelle due loro componenti (maschile e femminile), ci si accorge come dall'analisi emergano variazioni riferibili non soltanto alle immancabili differenze intersessuali, ma anche a più sostanziali variazioni morfologiche, da imputare addirittura a diversa etnogenesi. Inoltre il coefficiente di variazione è nella componente maschile sempre maggiore che nella corrispondente componente femminile, tranne che nei due subcampioni di Anghelu Ruju, dove le due componenti si eguagliano (Tabella 9). Un tal fenomeno molto probabilmente è da riferire al fatto che nei contesti umani paleo- e protosardi proprio la componente maschile è la più variabile e perciò stesso la maggiormente responsabile della variabilità antropica paleo- e protosarda.

Il fatto è che nella Preistoria i movimenti di popolazioni si realizzavano a carico soprattutto delle componenti maschili; queste ultime in seno alle popolazioni indigene trovavano i partners femminili e un tale fenomeno doveva verificarsi anche nell'isola di Sardegna, in cui le esogamie erano un fatto frequente, già messo in evidenza a livello di vari gruppi umani paleo- e protosardi sia da Maxia che da me in molti nostri lavori antropologici. In questa sede basterà sottolineare l'importante variazione nel tempo e nei due sessi soprattutto della larghezza (misura 8) e dell'altezza del cranio (misura 17), della larghezza frontale minima (misura 9), oltre che della larghezza orbitaria (misura 51).

Nell'ambito delle morfologie preistoriche della Sardegna le forme relativamente robuste sembrano prevalere in ogni tempo su quelle gracili con percentuali che variano dal 60% (Ozieri, Protogalluresi, Bonnanaro A e B, Campaniformi) addirittura al 79% (Anghelu Ruju, Bonu Ighinu). Una morfologia gracile (danubiana) è stata inoltre segnalata nel gruppo umano 'Monte Claro' di Serra Crabiles-Sassari.

Il neurocranio dei Paleosardi e dei Protosardi è prevalentemente dolicomorfo: percentualmente in quasi tutti i campioni si nota un'elevata incidenza delle forme ovoidi, salvo che in quelle di Bonu Ighinu e di Anghelu Ruju, dove sembrano prevalere le forme ellissoidi. Queste ultime forme negli altri campioni detengono il secondo posto dei singoli valori percentuali. Le forme pentagonoidi sono presenti in tutti i campioni salvo che in quello medioneolitico e in quello campaniforme. Sono anche state segnalate una forma birsoide (Ozieri) ed eccezionali forme beloidi (Anghelu Ruju, Bonnanaro A e Bonnanaro B). Delle morfologie brachimorfe prevalgono quelle sfenoidi, presenti nel campione di Padru Jossu (15,4%), di Anghelu Ruju (14,3%), Bonnanaro A (23,8%) ed eccezionalmente anche nel campione Bonnanaro B (3,4%). C'è da dire che sono rare le forme pure planoccipitali, mentre sembrano prevalere le forme curvoccipitali. Scarsa incidenza percentuale presentano le forme sferoidi, presenti soltanto nel campione Monte Claro (8,3%) e in quello Bonnanaro A (6,3%). Sembra utile ricordare come le poche forme brachicraniche protogalluresi abbiano conformazione generale dolicomorfa, indicando nel particolare forme evolutive verso la brachicrania.

Per quanto riguarda la capacità cranica (che può fornire qualche indiretta indicazione sul volume dell'encefalo) le medie maschili nei vari campioni oscillano dalla prevalente euencefalia (Bonu Ighinu, Monte Claro, Padru Jossu, Bonnanaro A) alla eccezionale aristencefalia (Ozieri, Anghelu Ruju, Bonnanaro B e Protogalluresi). Le corrispondenti medie femminili oscillano pure esse dall'aristencefalia (Padru Jossu, Anghelu Ruju, Protogalluresi) alla euencefalia (Ozieri, Monte Claro, Bonnanaro A e B). L'oligoencefalia (eccezionale) si osserva soltanto in alcuni esemplari maschili (Ozieri, Padru Jossu e Bonnanaro A).

Il cranio facciale risulta nella maggior parte dei campioni abbastanza variabile in tutte le sue componenti, anche se l'altezza facciale superiore (misura 48) nei vari campioni sembra essere il più delle volte medio-alta negli uomini e bassa nelle donne. Le facce maschili oscillano dalla macroprosopia (Bonu Ighinu, Ozieri, Monte Claro, Anghelu Ruju, Bonnanaro A e B) alla metrioprosopia (Bonu Ighinu, Monte Claro, Anghelu Ruju) e la microprosopia (Ozieri, Padru Jossu, Bonnanaro A e B, Protogalluresi). I valori medi dell'indice facciale superiore (48/45) nei vari campioni maschili oscillano dalla mesenia (Bonu Ighinu, Ozieri, Monte Claro, Anghelu Ruju) alla moderata leptenia (Padru Jossu, Bonnanaro A e B, Protogalluresi).

La conformazione delle orbite è il più delle volte subquadratica con maggior asse spesso obbliquo con valori medi oscillanti in ogni tempo dalla mesoconchia alla cameconchia (Ozieri maschile e Bonnanaro B). La ipsiconchia si riscontra come valore medio femminile a Padru Jossu e come valore estremo di gruppo fra gli uomini di Padru Jossu, di Anghelu Ruju, Bonnanaro A e Protogalluresi, oltre che fra le donne Ozieri, di Anghelu Ruju, Bonnaro B, Protogalluresi e, naturalmente, di Padru Jossu.

I valori medi dell'indice nasale (54/55) maschili oscillano dalla mesorrinia (Ozieri, Monte Claro, Padru Jossu) alla leptenia (Bonu Ighinu, Anghelu Ruju, Bonnanaro A e B, Protogalluresi) con valori estremi di camerrinila (Ozieri, Monte Claro, Padru Jossu, Anghelu Ruju, Bonnanaro A e B). Più varie le cavità nasali femminili, che oscillano dalla camerrinia alla leptorrinia.

Il profilo facciale (espresso dai valori dell'indice gnatico 40/5) negli uomini oscilla dal mesognatismo (Monte Claro, Padru Jossu) al più frequente ortognatismo (Ozieri, Anghelu Ruju, Bonnanaro A e B, Protogalluresi) con rare facce prognate (Ozieri e Monte Claro); queste ultime ripropongono schemi negroidi. Nella componente femminile dei vari campioni si verificano le stesse oscillazioni: il mesognatismo del gruppo Ozieri e Bonnanaro A, l'ortognatismo nei restanti campioni, con rarissime facce prognate (Ozieri, Anghelu Ruju).

L'indice cranio-facciale trasverso (45/8) negli uomini oscilla dalla prevalente criptozighia (Monte Claro, Padru Jossu, Anghelu Ruju, Bonnanaro A e B, Protogalluresi) alla subfenozighia (Ozieri e Monte Claro) con meno frequenti facce fenozighe nei campioni Bonu Ighinu, Ozieri, Monte Claru, Anghelu Ruju, Bonnanaro A e Protogalluresi. Nella componente femminile prevalgono decisamente i valori medi di criptozighia in tutti i campioni, tranne che in quello Monte Claro (subfenozigo) con eccezionali valori estremi di fenozighia nei campioni Ozieri e Monte Claro.

2. Le variazioni staturali di Paleosardi e Protosardi

Nonostante esistano per alcuni gruppi umani della Sardegna determinazioni staturali ricavate con metodologie diverse e forse più perfette, abbiamo preferito usare in questa indagine il metodo di Manouvrier (1893) sia per la sua vasta diffusione, sia perché esso è stato desunto da materiale scheletrico euromediterraneo, perciò stesso più affine ai resti scheletrici della Sardegna. Le tavole che seguono riassumono la situazione staturale dei vari campioni, distinti nella componente maschile (Tabella 10a) e in quella femminile (Tabella 10b). La significatività dei valori medi di ogni campione è espressa dal numero di ossa lunghe (o.l.) da cui sono stati ricavati i valori stessi: sono molto significativi i valori dei campioni Ozieri, Anghela Ruju, e Bonnanaro B; discretamente significativi quelli dei campioni Bonuighino e Protogalluresi; scarsamente significativi quelli dei campioni di Serra Crabiles, di Padru Jossu e Bonnanaro A.

Paragonando fra loro soltanto i valori 'molto e discretamente' significativi, ci si accorge come le stature paleosarde neolitiche (metricamente analoghe a quelle mediterranee coeve) subiscono un minimo decremento nel campione di Anghelu Ruju. Ma un tal fenomeno, oltre che essere reale, molto probabilmente è anche dovuto al fatto che queste ultime stature sono state calcolate soltanto a partire dagli omeri epertanto, esso va considerato con estrema precauzione. Ma nei campioni Bonnanaro B e Protogallurese si nota un effettivo incremento dei valori staturali medi sia rispetto ai campioni neolitici, che a quello di Anghelu Ruju. E non deve trattarsi di fenomeno auxologico casuale, data l'elevata numerosità dei segmenti scheletrici, usati per le stime. Un tal fenomeno può essere ricondotto ad almeno due fattori: a- le migliorate condizioni di vita della Sardegna nuragica (Lilliu 1982; 1988); b- il fenomeno del lussureggiamento degli ibridi da imputare a un rimescolamento di razze, avvenuto nel suolo sardo ai tempi dei nuraghi (cfr. letteratura in Germanà 1975).

Si possono trarre da questi dati conclusioni almeno provvisorie? Indubbiamente si e non poche:

> Innanzitutto si può affermare che in ogni tempo della sua Preistoria e Protostoria l'isola di Sardegna venne popolata da genti di morfologia mediterranea tanto antica, che recente nel senso di Charles (1960): conformazione somatica nella maggior parte degli individui di media robustezza con evidente dimorfismo sessuale e statura media, ma anche, e in min minor misura, gracile con attenuato dimorfismo sessuale e statura medio-bassa.
>
> La conformazione del cranio è di regola dolicomorfa, prevalentemente ovoide, ellissoide e anche pentagonoide durante il periodo neolitico, ma già nel successivo periodo eneolitico si notano forme brachimorfe: queste ultime eccezionali nel campione Monte Claro, con discreta incidenza percentuale nel campione campaniforme di Padru Jossu. Nello stesso campione di Anghelu Ruju (e riferibili non sappiamo a quale suo momento culturale) le forme brachimorfe incidono percentualmente in misura del 14,3% accanto alle sempre prevalenti forme dolicomorfe.
>
> La brachimorfia paleosarda presenta la sua massima incidenza (circa il 30%) però localizzata nell'area nord-occidentale dell'isola (Sassarese e Algherese), accanto a una sempre prevalente percentuale di dolicomorfi (circa il 70%), questi ultimi al contrario diffusi in tutta l'isola. In una tomba del Sassarese (la n. 6 della Necropoli di Su Crucifissu Mannu) ho poi creduto di scorgere un esempio di brachicefalizzazione in atto (Germanà 1984b).
>
> La brachicrania protogallurese non ha più lo stesso carattere morfologico dei brachimorfi precedenti: in norma superiore tali crani sono ovoidi o addirittura ellissoidi! La sua origine è di conseguenza diversa da quella eneolitica o delle precedenti età del Bronzo: probabilmente si tratta anche in questo caso di brachicefalizzazione.
>
> Ma le forme dolicomorfe di ogni tempo, dal Neolitico fino addirittura ai nostri giorni, sono morfologicamente (e probabilmente anche sul piano razziale) riconducibili a schemi 'Ozieri', tanto è vero che mi è stato possibile parlare già in passato di una 'Etnia Ozieri', geneticamente consolidatasi in un'isola (quale è la Sardegna) durante l'arco millenario agglutinante della cultura omonima.

Tabella 1
Il campione a (Neolitico medio-Bono Ighinu)

		medie maschili			valori femminili		
1.	(3)	mm	182,7	(194–170)	–	–	
8.	(3)	mm	131,7	(135–125)	–	–	
9.	(3)	mm	92,7	(98–88)	(1)	mm	80
10.	(3)	mm	123,0	(144–110)	–	–	
20.	(1)	mm	111		–	–	
45.	(2)	mm	130,0	(130–130)	(1)	mm	127,7
48.	(1)	mm	69		(1)	mm	66
51.	(3)	mm	38,8	(42–35)	(1)	mm	34
52.	(2)	mm	32,0	(33–31)	(1)	mm	26,5
54.	(1)	mm	24		(1)	mm	21,5
55.	(1)	mm	55		(1)	mm	47,5
8/1.	(3)		72,4	(79,4–64,4)	–		–
9/8.	(2)		71,8	(78,4–65,2)	–		–
9/10.	(3)		76,6	(85,2–61,1)	–		–
48/45.	(1)		53,1		(1)		51,7
52/51.	(1)		78,1	(78,6–77,5)	(1)		77,9
54/55.	(1)		43,6		(1)		45,3
45/8.	(1)		104		–		–

Tabella 2
Il campione b (Neolitico recente-S. Michele)

			medie maschili						medie femminili			
1.	(13)	mm	191,1 ± 4,5	(205–177)	σ	7,4	(8)	mm	179,5 ± 4,0	(185–170)	σ	4,7
5.	(11)	mm	105,6 ± 4,7	(121–98)	σ	6,9	(4)	mm	94,5	(100–91)		
8.	(13)	mm	133,5 ± 3,0	(143–124)	σ	5,0	(9)	mm	131,2 ± 2,8	(136–125)	σ	3,6
9.	(12)	mm	97,3 ± 3,3	(107–88)	σ	5,2	(8)	mm	93,2 ± 2,6	(98–89)	σ	3,1
10.	(12)	mm	112,6 ± 4,3	(120–99)	σ	6,8	(8)	mm	112,6 ± 4,7	(121–102)	σ	5,6
17.	(12)	mm	137,6 ± 4,3	(149–125)	σ	6,8	(4)	mm	118,7	(128–100,8)		
20.	(19)	mm	117,4 ± 4,6	(135–103)	σ	9,2	(11)	mm	108,8 ± 6,1	(125–96)	σ	8,9
38.ba	(12)	cc	1450,5 ± 56,0	(1581–1277)	σ	89,1	(3)	cc	1256,8	(1290–1204)		
45.	(12)	mm	129,5 ± 4,0	(138–117)	σ	6,3	(7)	mm	117,4 ± 5,7	(125–108)	σ	6,3
48.	(11)	mm	70,4 ± 3,2	(79–62)	σ	4,8	(7)	mm	65,1 ± 1,8	(68–62)	σ	2,0
51.	(8)	mm	42,2 ± 1,2	(45–41)	σ	1,4	(6)	mm	39,0 ± 1,7	(41–37)	σ	1,7
52.	(10)	mm	31,5 ± 0,9	(33,3–29)	σ	1,3	(7)	mm	31,0 ± 1,5	(33,7–28,8)	σ	1,7
54.	(13)	mm	25,1 ± 1,7	(31–22)	σ	2,8	(14)	mm	23,9 ± 1,2	(28–21)	σ	2,
55.	(13)	mm	52,4 ± 3,1	(63–43)	σ	5,2	(13)	mm	48,1 ± 1,9	(52–40)	σ	3,1
8/1.	(13)		69,9 ± 1,9	(77,4–63,4)	σ	3,1	(8)		73,1 ± 2,8	(77,1–67,6)	σ	3,3
17/1.	(12)		72,3 ± 2,3	(77,4–64,4)	σ	3,7	(3)		70,1	(72,0–67,4)		
17/8.	(12)		103,6 ± 3,3	(114,6–94,7)	σ	5,3	(4)		94,5	(96,2–93,3)		
9/8.	(12)		73,2 ± 2,3	(78,6–68,4)	σ	3,7	(8)		71,2 ± 3,4	(78,4–65,9)	σ	4,0
9/10.	(12)		86,7 ± 3,8	(98,1–78,5)	σ	6,0	(8)		83,2 ± 4,2	(91,6–76,0)	σ	5,0
48/45.	(11)		54,1 ± 2,3	(58,1–46,3)	σ	3,4	(6)		55,6 ± 4,6	(61,1–49,6)	σ	4,5
52/51.	(10)		75,4 ± 3,4	(80,2–68,9)	σ	4,8	(7)		79,9 ± 4,2	(86,5–73,7)	σ	4,6
54/55.	(14)		47,9 ± 3,4	(63,9–39,5)	σ	6,3	(13)		47,9 ± 2,0	(53,6–40,4)	σ	3,3
40/5.	(10)		92,9 ± 6,4	(108–75)	σ	9,1	(4)		99,4	(107,7–90)		
45/8.	(10)		97,4 ± 4,8	(106,2–93)	σ	6,8	(6)		89,2 ± 6,9	(100–80)	σ	6,7

Tabella 3
Il Campione c (Eneolitico-Monte Claro)

		medie maschili					*medie femminili*		
1.	(15)	mm	191,1 ± 4,8	(207–179)	σ 8,7	(12)	mm	178,3 ± 3,1	(185–170)	σ 5,0
5.	(14)	mm	102,2 ± 2,9	(111–93)	σ 5,0	(9)	mm	96,8 ± 3,3	(106,5–92)	σ 4,3
8.	(15)	mm	138,7 ± 3,1	(148–132)	σ 5,7	(11)	mm	131,7 ± 3,0	(138–124)	σ 4,4
9.	(15)	mm	97,9 ± 3,1	(107–86)	σ 5,7	(14)	mm	94,1 ± 1,4	(98–89,5)	σ 2,4
10.	(15)	mm	118,4 ± 5,4	(128–90)	σ 9,9	(13)	mm	115,6 ± 2,7	(123–105)	σ 4,4
17.	(14)	mm	130,3 ± 2,6	(136–122)	σ 4,4	(9)	mm	129,7 ± 2,5	(134–124,5)	σ 3,3
38.ba	(14)	cc	1440,3 ± 41,5	(1572–1318)	σ 71,1	(8)	cc	1286,9 ± 24,6	(1326–1243)	σ 29,1
45.	(8)	mm	131,7 ± 4,7	(139–126,5)	σ 5,6	(5)	mm	124,0 ± 4,7	(128–119)	σ 3,7
48.	(8)	mm	68,4 ± 4,2	(77–61)	σ 5,8	(7)	mm	65,8 ± 3,1	(69–59)	σ 3,4
51.*	(3)	mm	40,3 ±	(42–39)		–	–	–	–	–
52.	(11)	mm	31,9 ± 1,4	(35–29)	σ 2,1	(10)	mm	32,3 ± 1,1	(36–31)	σ 1,5
54.	(9)	mm	23,9 ± 1,8	(28–21)	σ 2,3	(8)	mm	23,3 ± 1,2	(25–21)	σ 1,4
55.	(9)	mm	49,8 ± 1,6	(52,5–46,5)	σ 2,1	(8)	mm	47,5 ± 2,5	(51–42)	σ 3,0
8/1.	(15)		72,7 ± 2,2	(81,5–67,8)	σ 3,9	(11)		73,7 ± 2,2	(78,5–69,3)	σ 3,3
17/1.	(14)		68,4 ± 2,0	(74,1–62,1)	σ 3,5	(9)		72,7 ± 2,1	(77,0–69,5)	σ 2,7
17/8.	(14)		94,1 ± 3,3	(102,6–83,2)	σ 5,6	(8)		99,1 ± 2,1	(102,7–95,9)	σ 2,5
9/8.	(15)		70,6 ± 2,5	(79,2–66,4)	σ 4,5	(11)		71,2 ± 2,1	(75,5–66,9)	σ 3,1
9/10.	(15)		82,7 ± 3,0	(95,6–74,7)	σ 5,4	(13)		81,4 ± 1,8	(88,4–77,6)	σ 3,0
48/45.	(8)		51,9 ± 3,0	(57,0–49,0)	σ 3,5	(4)		53,7	(56,3–50,4)	
52/51.	(11)		76,0 ± 3,9	(83,5–67,8)	σ 5,8	(9)		78,8 ± 2,6	(84,3–74,4)	σ 3,3
54/55.	(9)		48,1 ± 3,3	(54,9–41,2)	σ 4,3	(8)		49,2 ± 3,0	(55,6–42,9)	σ 3,6
40/5.	(10)		98,9 ± 3,3	(105,7–92,7)	σ 4,7	(4)		93,5	(95,9–90,2)	
45/8.	(8)		94,5 ± 5,1	(102,2–85,5)	σ 6,0	(4)		96,1	(101,1–90,2)	

* La esigua numerosità della classe relativa alla misura 51 è dovuta al fatto che gli esemplari della Grotta di Tani sono stati misurati con la misura 51.a (C. Maxia *et al.* 1963).

Tabella 4
Il campione d (Eneolitico—Campaniforme)

		medie maschili					*medie femminili*		
1.	(6)	mm	182,7 ± 7,9	(195–178)	σ 7,7	(7)	mm	175,1 ± 8,2	(190–160)	σ 9,0
5.	(3)	mm	96,7	(100–95)		(6)	mm	103,8 ± 13,7	(124–92)	σ 13,4
8.	(6)	mm	143,0 ± 7,1	(151–135)	σ 6,9	(7)	mm	138,0 ± 8,2	(155–128)	σ 9,1
9.	(6)	mm	94,0 ± 3,1	(100–92)	σ 3,0	(7)	mm	94,4 ± 2,9	(99,5–89)	σ 3,2
10.	(5)	mm	113,7 ± 9,7	(126–107)	σ 7,7	(7)	mm	115,1 ± 4,9	(121–106)	σ 5,4
17.	(4)	mm	124,0	(133–117)		(6)	mm	136,8 ± 7,5	(145–126)	σ 7,3
20.	(6)	mm	107,7 ± 7,8	(116–94,9)	σ 7,6	(7)	mm	111,1 ± 7,3	(119,8–96,7)	σ 8,1
38.ba	(4)	cc	1377,6	(1449–1277)		(6)	cc	1331,5 ± 41,8	(1364–1264)	σ 40,6
45.	(2)	mm	123,3	(126,5–120)		(3)	mm	115,0	(122–108)	
48.	(2)	mm	68,3	(75–61,5)		(3)	mm	66,5	(71–62)	
51.	(3)	mm	40,5	(45–37)		(4)	mm	35,6	(39,3–32)	
52.	(3)	mm	30,8	(34,5–26)		(3)	mm	31,5	(33,5–29)	
54.	(2)	mm	23,5	(24–23)		(3)	mm	21,7	(23–20)	
55.	(2)	mm	49,8	(54,5–45)		(3)	mm	49,2	(50,5–47)	
8/1.	(6)		78,3 ± 2,8	(82,0–74,9)		(7)		79,2 ± 8,2	(96,9–68,4)	σ 9,1
17/1.	(4)		68,6	(74,7–60,5)		(6)		78,5 ± 5,6	(86,9–73,9)	σ 5,4
17/8.	(4)		88,4	(98,5–78,2)		(6)		98,2 ± 7,6	(108,5–89,7)	σ 7,4
9/8.	(5)		66,7 ± 3,0	(69,3–63,0)	σ 2,4	(7)		68,1 ± 4,0	(73,8–61,3)	σ 4,4
9/10.	(5)		83,2 ± 4,4	(86,9–79,4)	σ 3,5	(7)		81,5 ± 2,4	(84,1–78,5)	σ 2,6
48/45.	(2)		55,3	(62,5–48,0)		(3)		58,1	(65,7–50,8)	
52/51.	(3)		76,2	(87,3–70,3)		(3)		86,4	(91,4–82,4)	
54/55.	(2)		47,6	(51,1–44,0)		(3)		44,1	(46,0–42,6)	
40/5.	(2)		100,6	(101,1–100)		(3)		94,2	(97,5–90,0)	
45/8.	(2)		90,0	(91,0–88,9)		(3)		85,5	(93,9–78,8)	

Tabella 5
Il campione e (Anghelu Ruju: Eneolitico-Bronzo)

		medie maschili					*medie femminili*		
1.	(27)	mm	188,4 ± 3,3	(207–170)	σ 8,4	(23)	mm	179,4 ± 2,4	(193–170)	σ 5,6
5.	(7)	mm	103,4 ± 5,1	(112–97)	σ 5,6	(7)	mm	99,4 ± 3,8	(104–93)	σ 4,2
8.	(27)	mm	140,6 ± 2,2	(151–128)	σ 5,5	(22)	mm	137,4 ± 1,7	(143–132)	σ 3,9
9.	(22)	mm	98,7 ± 1,5	(106–94)	σ 3,3	(23)	mm	95,0 ± 1,9	(103–88)	σ 4,4
17.	(14)	mm	134,4 ± 2,9	(130–120)	σ 5,0	(14)	mm	129,5 ± 3,5	(138–121)	σ 6,0
38.ba	(14)	cc	1473,6 ± 39,3	(1588–1317)	σ 64,7	(14)	cc	1311,7 ± 21,8	(1406–1251)	σ 37,3
45.	(8)	mm	130,5 ± 3,4	(140–128)	σ 4,0	(9)	mm	124,8 ± 3,6	(133–120)	σ 4,7
48.	(10)	mm	69,0 ± 2,5	(77–65)	σ 3,6	(10)	mm	65,6 ± 2,5	(72–60)	σ 3,5
51.	(10)	mm	40,4 ± 1,1	(44–39)	σ 1,6	(11)	mm	40,0 ± 1,1	(43–38)	σ 1,7
52.	(11)	mm	30,7 ± 1,3	(34–29)	σ 1,9	(11)	mm	31,1 ± 1,3	(35–29)	σ 1,9
54.	(10)	mm	23,2 ± 0,8	(25–21)	σ 1,2	(10)	mm	23,6 ± 1,1	(26–21)	σ 1,5
55.	(10)	mm	49,4 ± 2,3	(56–46)	σ 3,2	(10)	mm	48,7 ± 2,3	(54–43)	σ 3,3
8/1.	(25)		74,9 ± 2,9	(85,4–65,3)	σ 5,4	(22)		76,9 ± 1,1	(82,2–72,1)	σ 2,5
17/1.	(14)		71,4 ± 1,5	(76,4–68,0)	σ 2,6	(14)		72,3 ± 2,6	(81,2–65,1)	σ 4,1
17/8.	(14)		95,7 ± 3,5	(106,3–82,2)	σ 6,0	(14)		93,9 ± 3,0	(103,8–87,3)	σ 5,2
9/8.	(21)		70,0 ± 1,6	(79,7–65,6)	σ 3,5	(22)		69,0 ± 1,5	(75,0–61,5)	σ 3,5
48/45.	(7)		52,9 ± 1,7	(55,1–50,7)	σ 1,8	(9)		52,7 ± 2,2	(56,2–47,0)	σ 2,9
52/51.	(10)		77,5 ± 2,2	(87,2–67,5)	σ 6,1	(11)		77,4 ± 3,8	(89,7–67,4)	σ 5,7
54/55.	(10)		46,7 ± 2,5	(52,2–42,0)	σ 3,5	(10)		48,6 ± 2,6	(52,2–41,2)	σ 3,7
40/5.	(7)		93,5 ± 3,6	(101,0–88,7)	σ 3,9	(7)		95,1 ± 3,9	(103,2–91,2)	σ 4,3
45/8.	(8)		93,5 ± 4,4	(101,4–86,7)	σ 5,2	(8)		91,1 ± 2,1	(94,8–87,8)	σ 2,5

Tabella 6
Il campione f (Bronzo antico; Bonnanaro A)

		medie maschili					*medie femminili*		
1.	(36)	mm	184,5 ± 2,8	(208–165)	σ 8,6	(24)	mm	175,4 ± 3,0	(187–165)	σ 7,0
5.	(12)	mm	102,5 ± 5,5	(118–92)	σ 8,7	(7)	mm	97,4 ± 6,3	(110–90)	σ 6,9
8.	(38)	mm	141,1 ± 2,2	(155–126)	σ 7,1	(27)	mm	135,5 ± 2,5	(149–122)	σ 6,3
9.	(27)	mm	98,3 ± 1,6	(108–90)	σ 4,0	(22)	mm	94,8 ± 2,3	(106–86)	σ 5,0
10.	(29)	mm	119,4 ± 3,5	(140–102)	σ 9,1	(24)	mm	115,2 ± 3,3	(130–100)	σ 7,8
17.	(15)	mm	131,7 ± 4,2	(146–117)	σ 7,7	(9)	mm	127,1 ± 6,1	(139–117)	σ 7,9
38.ba	(15)	cc	1419,2 ± 61,2	(1696–1260)	σ 111,3	(9)	cc	1282,7 ± 38,8	(1353–1193)	σ 50,5
45.	(14)	mm	131,1 ± 5,4	(150–117)	σ 9,3	(4)	mm	127,0	(132–122)	
48.	(15)	mm	70,0 ± 2,8	(75–59)	σ 5,1	(4)	mm	61,3	(63–60)	
51.	(15)	mm	41,4 ± 2,3	(51–32)	σ 4,2	(3)	mm	40,0	(41–39)	
52.	(16)	mm	32,4 ± 1,7	(38–27)	σ 3,1	(5)	mm	31,0 ± 2,6	(34,5–29)	σ 2,1
54.	(10)	mm	24,2 ± 0,9	(26,5–22)	σ 1,3	(4)	mm	23,5	(24–22)	
55.	(10)	mm	53,8 ± 3,5	(60–47,5)	σ 4,9	(4)	mm	46,4	(49–41,5)	
8/1.	(36)		76,4 ± 1,7	(87,8–65,0)	σ 5,3	(24)		77,4 ± 1,9	(87,1–71,4)	σ 4,6
17/1.	(15)		72,1 ± 2,6	(79,4–63,5)	σ 4,8	(9)		71,9 ± 3,4	(78,8–65,0)	σ 4,4
17/8.	(15)		94,7 ± 2,6	(102,3–87,4)	σ 4,8	(9)		93,9 ± 4,2	(104,0–88,1)	σ 5,4
9/8.	(27)		69,8 ± 1,4	(75,2–63,9)	σ 3,6	(20)		70,2 ± 1,7	(77,6–65,9)	σ 3,6
9/10.	(27)		82,4 ± 2,5	(95,2–73,6)	σ 6,3	(21)		82,7 ± 1,8	(93,0–75,8)	σ 4,0
48/45.	(13)		55,1 ± 1,3	(59,1–51,8)	σ 2,2	(3)		49,2	(50,4–48,1)	
52/51.	(15)		80,2 ± 3,5	(95,0–71,1)	σ 6,4	(3)		77,8	(84,4–74,4)	
54/55.	(14)		46,8 ± 2,7	(53,3–39,5)	σ 4,6	(4)		50,8	(53,0–50,0)	
40/5.	(12)		92,0 ± 5,2	(98,9–72,9)	σ 8,3	(4)		94,3	(101,1–83,3)	
45/8.	(12)		92,2 ± 4,0	(106,2–81,4)	σ 6,4	(4)		91,5	(95,3–89,6)	

Tabella 7
Il campione g (Bronzo medio; Bonnanaro B)

		medie maschili					medie femminili		
1.	(18)	mm 188,6 ± 4,0	(203–165)	σ 8,0	(5)	mm 177,4 ± 4,9	(183–174)	σ 3,9
5.	(10)	mm 101,0 ± 4,5	(115–95)	σ 6,3	(4)	mm 95,9	(100–94)	
8.	(18)	mm 136,3 ± 3,0	(150–126)	σ 6,0	(8)	mm 129,5 ± 4,3	(136–120)	σ 5,1
9.	(18)	mm 97,1 ± 2,3	(105–86)	σ 4,6	(8)	mm 92,1 ± 2,5	(96–88)	σ 2,9
10.	(17)	mm 117,6 ± 3,3	(130–104)	σ 6,4	(8)	mm 111,0 ± 4,1	(119–106)	σ 4,9
17.	(11)	mm 132,9 ± 2,8	(142–128,5)	σ 4,2	(6)	mm 128,8 ± 2,5	(131–125)	σ 2,4
38.ba	(11)	cc 1430,5 ± 45,2	(1597–1342)	σ 67,0	(6)	cc 1269,3 ± 42,8	(1298–1222)	σ 33,9
45.	(10)	mm 129,0 ± 3,5	(140–122)	σ 5,0	(3)	mm 122,2	(126,5–120)	
48.	(11)	mm 70,2 ± 2,0	(74–65)	σ 3,0	(5)	mm 63,2 ± 3,4	(67–61)	σ 2,7
51.	(6)	mm 42,7 ± 1,5	(44,5–41)	σ 1,5	(5)	mm 39,3 ± 5,4	(44,4–33)	σ 4,4
52.	(11)	mm 32,6 ± 1,5	(37–30)	σ 2,2	(5)	mm 30,2 ± 2,5	(32–26,8)	σ 2,0
54.	(10)	mm 24,0 ± 2,4	(31–18)	σ 3,4	(5)	mm 23,9 ± 1,8	(25–21,5)	σ 1,4
55.	(10)	mm 53,6 ± 1,6	(57–49)	σ 2,3	(5)	mm 46,4 ± 3,2	(48,5–43)	σ 2,5
8/1.	(17)	72,6 ± 2,3	(81,8–64,0)	σ 4.4	(5)	73,6 ± 5,0	(78,2–68,6)	σ 4,4
17/1.	(11)	71,5 ± 2,9	(83,6–67,2)	σ 4,3	(5)	72,7 ± 2,1	(75,3–71,0)	σ 1,7
17/8.	(11)	95,7 ± 3,7	(105,2–86,7)	σ 5,5	(5)	99,1 ± 4,3	(100,4–95,6)	σ 3,4
9/8.	(17)	71,0 ± 2,3	(78,5–66,9)	σ 4,4	(6)	71,0 ± 2,3	(75,0–67,1)	σ 2,2
9/10.	(18)	82,6 ± 2,5	(92,9–74,8)	σ 5,0	(8)	83,1 ± 1,3	(85,2–80,7)	σ 1,5
48/45.	(9)	54,8 ± 2,2	(59,0–54,4)	σ 2,8	(2)	51,2	(54,2–48,2)	
52/51.	(8)	74,2 ± 2,8	(78,2–69,8)	σ 3,3	(6)	76,0 ± 9,6	(94,0–69,7)	σ 9,3
54/55.	(10)	44,7 ± 4,0	(56,4–34,6)	σ 5,7	(2)	50,8	(51,5–50,0)	
40/5.	(8)	94,5 ± 3,3	(99,0–90,5)	σ 3,9	(3)	98,8	(100,0–97,4)	
45/8.	(10)	94,2 ± 3,0	(98,8–86,5)	σ 4,3	(2)	91,0	(93,7–88,2)	

Tabella 8
Il campione h (i Galluresi del Bronzo recente)

		medie maschili					medie femminili		
1.	(15)	mm 188,6 ± 2,6	(196–182)	σ 4,8	(10)	mm 180,3 ± 4,3	(190–170)	σ 6,1
5.	(4)	mm 104,0	(109–103)		(2)	mm 90,0	(100– 80)	
8.	(15)	mm 135,1 ± 3,7	(152–126)	σ 6,7	(11)	mm 135,6 ± 3,8	(145–125)	σ 5,6
9.	(14)	mm 95,8 ± 3,0	(106–89,5)	σ 5,2	(11)	mm 97,6 ± 2,6	(104– 93)	σ 3,9
10.	(14)	mm 114,7 ± 4,4	(127,5–102)	σ 7,5	(11)	mm 117,4 ± 4,9	(127–107)	σ 7,2
17.	(6)	mm 138,8 ± 9,3	(152–128)	σ 9,0	(2)	mm 131,0	(133–129)	
38.ba	(6)	cc 1457,0 ± 85,4	(1562–1342)	σ 83,2	(2)	cc 1299,6	(1371–1288)	
45.	(7)	mm 124,9 ± 8,5	(140–110)	σ 9,4	(2)	mm 116,5	(118–115)	
48.	(3)	mm 68,0	(73– 65)		(2)	mm 64,3	(65,5–63)	
51.	(6)	mm 39,2 ± 2,3	(41,5–36)	σ 2,2	(2)	mm 37,3	(38,5–36)	
52.	(6)	mm 31,0 ± 2,1	(32– 28)	σ 2,0	(2)	mm 31,0	(31,5–30,5)	
54.	(6)	mm 24,5 ± 1,5	(27,5–23)	σ 1,6	(2)	mm 23,3	(24–22,5)	
55.	(3)	mm 51,3	(52– 50)		(2)	mm 48,8	(50,5–47)	
8/1.	(15)	71,7 ± 2,4	(80,4–65,3)	σ 4,3	(10)	75,3 ± 2,7	(80,1–69,3)	σ 3,8
17/1.	(6)	74,0 ± 4,0	(80,0–69,6)	σ 3,9	(2)	74,7	(76,0–73,3)	
17/8.	(6)	103,3 ± 6,9	(112,6–92,8)	σ 6,7	(2)	96,5	(101,5–91,5)	
9/8.	(14)	71,1 ± 2,0	(79,0–65,2)	σ 3,4	(10)	72,3 ± 1,8	(77,0–68,3)	σ 216
9/10.	(14)	83,8 ± 2,7	(96,4–78,7)	σ 4,6	(11)	83,3 ± 2,4	(89,7–78,0)	σ 3,6
48/45.	(3)	57,1	(60,0–53,3)		(2)	55,2	(55,5–54,8)	
52/51.	(6)	79,3 ± 4,8	(86,1–73,7)	σ 4,7	(2)	83,4	(87,5–79,2)	
54/55.	(3)	46,5	(49,0–44,2)		(2)	47,9	(51,1–44,6)	
40/5.	(3)	94,9	(98,0–93,2)		(2)	93,3	(94,0–92,5)	
45/8.	(7)	93,1 ± 5,6	(101,4–82,1)	σ 6,2	(1)	87,4		

Tabella 9
Medie maschili (m) e femminili (f) dei coefficienti di variazione distinti per campione

campione b:	m	6.,0	f	5,0
campione c:	m	5,8;	f	3,9
campione d:	m	5,2;	f	3,1
campione e:	m	4.,6;	f	4,6
campione f:	m	7,1;	f	5,6
campione g:	m	5,4;	f	4,7
campione h:	m	5,8;	f	4,4
medie totali:	m	5,8;	f	4,5

Tabella 10a
Stature maschili paleo- e protosarde (Manouvrier-vivente)

campione a	Bonu Ighinu (Neolitico medio)	(13 o.l.)	cm 162,2	(164,6-156,4)
campione b	Ozieri (Neolitico recente)	(60 o.l.)	cm 162,2	(174,7-153,2)
campione c	Serra Crabiles (Eneolitico)	(4 o.l.)	cm 162,9	(164,2-162,7)
campione e	Anghelu Ruju (Eneo.-I Bronzo)	(36 omeri)	cm 160,8	(168,7-156,2)
campione f	Bonnanaro A (Bronzo antico)	(4 o.l.)	cm 161,8	
campione g	Bonnanaro B (Bronzo medio)	(78 o.l.)	cm 165,6	(179,1-153,6)
campione h	Protogalluresi (Bronzo recente)	(9 o.l.)	cm 166,3	(173,7-160,0)

Tabella 10b
Stature femminili paleo- e protosarde (Manouvrier-vivente)

campione a	Bonu Ighinu (Neolitico medio)	(6 o.l)	cm 150,4	(154,0-147,3)
campione b	Ozieri (Neolitico recente)	(51 o.l.)	cm 151,8	(157,5-140,0)
campione c	Serra Crabiles (Eneolitico)	(2 o.l.)	cm 147,7	(154,4-141,0)
campione d	Padru Jossu (Eneolitico)	(1 o.l.)	cm 146,1	
campione e	Anghelu Ruju (Eneol.-I Bronzo)	(40 omeri)	cm 149,7	(154,8-106,7)
campione f	Bonnanaro A (Bronzo antico)	(2 o.l.)	cm 159,3	
campione g	Bonnanaro B (Bronzo medio)	(51 o.l.)	cm 152,9	(166,6-141,5)
campione h	Protogalluresi (Bronzo recente)	(8 o.l.)	cm 155,5	(157,6-144,6)

Bibliografia

AA.VV.
    1984   *Manual de Historia Universal, 1, Prehistoria.* Madrid: Najera.

Agosti, F., P. Biagi, L. Castelletti, M. Cremaschi & F. Germanà
    1980   La Grotta Rifugio di Oliena (Nuoro): Caverna ossario neolitica. *Rivista di Scienze Preistoriche* 35(1-2): 75-124.

Antona Ruju, A.
    1981   Notiziario, Santa Teresa di Gallura. *Rivista di Scienze Preistoriche* 36(1-2): 356-58.

Atzeni, E.
    1972   Su Carroppu di Sirri (Carbonia), Notiziario. *Rivista di Scienze Preistoriche* 27(2): 478-79.
    1977   Riparo sotto roccia di 'Su Carroppu' (Sirri-Carbonia), Notiziario. *Rivista di Scienze Preistoriche* 32(2): 357-58.

Bruni, E.
    1924-25   Gli omeri eneolitici di Anghelu Ruju. *Rivista di Antropologia* 1924-25: 235-50.

Businco, L.
    1933   Scheletri protosardi rinvenuti in recenti scavi in Campidano e in Barbagia. *Atti della Società Italiana Anatomica* 44: 323-26.

Campus, L. (a cura di)
    1989   *La Cultura di Ozieri. Problematiche e nuove acquisizioni. Atti del I convegno di studio (Ozieri, gennaio 1986—aprile 1987).* Ozieri: Il Torchietto.

Castaldi, E.
    1969   Tombe di giganti nel Sassarese. *Origini* 3: 1-132. Roma.
    1975   *Domus Nuragiche.* Roma: De Luca.

Cavalli Sforza, L.
    1970   *Analisi Statistica per Medici e Biologi.* Torino: Boringhieri.

Charles, R.
    1960   Le peuplement de l'Europe Méditerranéen pendant les IIIe et les IIe Millènaire avant Jèsus-

Christ. *Bulletin et Mémorie de la Société d'Anthropologie de Paris* 11(2): 3-176.

Contu, E.
1958 Argomenti di cronologia a proposito delle tomba a poliandro di Ena 'e Muros (Ossi-Sassari) e Motrox 'e Bois (Usellus-Cagliari). *Studi Sardi* 14-15.

Cosseddu, G., A. Fenu, G. Floris, G. Lucia & G. Vona
1983 Stato attuale dei reperti cranici protostorici sardi. *Archivio per l' Antropologia e la Etnologia* 113: 249-61.

Duday, H.
1975 *Le Squelette du Sujet Féminin de la Sepolture Prenéolithique de Bonifacio (Corse)*. Lab. Ass. 220 du C.N.R.S. n. 1. St. Peres: Laboratoire d'Anatomie.

Facchini, F.
1987 Note antropologiche su antichi reperti della Grotta Palmaera (Sassari). *Antropologia Contemporanea* 10(1-2): 97-110.

Ferrarese Ceruti, M.L.
1972-74 La tomba XVI di su Crucifissu Mannu e la Cultura di Bonnanaro. *Bullettino di Paletnologia Italiana* 81: 113-210.
1981 La cultura del Bonnanaro. In E. Atzeni *et al.* (eds.), *Ichnussa. La Sardegna dalle origini all'età classica*, 67-77. Milano: Libri Scheiwiller.

Ferrarese Ceruti, M.L., & F. Germanà
1978 *Sisaia. Una deposizione in grotta della Cultura di Bonnanaro.* Quaderni 6. Sassari: Dessi

Frassetto, F.
1907a Contributo alla paleoantropologia della Sardegna. Materiale scheletrico e paletnologico della Grotta di Palmaera (Sassari). *Atti del Congresso Naturale Italiano, settembre 1906*, 796. Milano.
1907b Grotta eneolitica di Palmaera (Sassari). *Bullettino di Paletnologia Italiana* 1907: 189.

Germanà, F.
1970 I resti umani delle tombe in tafoni galluresi. *Archivio per l'Antropologia e la Etnologia* 100: 197-244.
1971 Elementi di Paleopatologia umana in Provincia di Sassari. *Bollettino della Società Sarda di Scienze Naturali* 5(8): 23-64.
1972-74 Il brachimorfo trapanato di Su Crucifissu Mannu (Porto Torres-Sassari). *Bullettino di Paletnologia Italiana* 81: 219-51.
1975 Il gruppo umano nuragico di S'Iscia e sas Piras (Usini-Sassari), Antropologia e Paleopatologia. *Studi Sardi* 23: 53-124.
1979-80 I Paleosardi di Is Aruttas (Cabras-Oristano). Nota I. *Archivio per l'Antropologia e la Etnologia* 109-110: 343-91.
1980a Forme umane preistoriche di Serra Crabiles (Sennori-Sassari) nel contesto antropologico paleosardo. *Atti del XXII Riunione Scientifica, Firenze, 1978*, 305-30. Firenze: Istituto Italiano di Preistoria e Protostoria.
1980b L'Uomo. In D. Sanna (a cura di), *Nur. La misteriosa civiltà dei Sardi*, 60-77. Milano: Cariplo.
1980c Crani della seconda età del Bronzo da S'Isterridolzu (Ossi-Sassari) nel contesto umano paleosardo recente (Antropologia e Paleopatologia). *Atti del XX Congresso Internazionale di Antropologia e Archeologia Preistorica, Cagliari, 9-12 ottobre 1980*, 377-94.
1981 Forme umane medioneolitiche dalla grotta Rifugio di Olièna (Nuoro), Antropologia e Paleopatologia. *Quaderni delle Scienze Antropologiche* 6: 5-68.
1982 I Paleosardi di Is Aruttas (Cabras-Oristano). *Archivio per l'Antropologia e la Etnologia* 112: 233-80.
1983 Paleosardi arcaici e recenti. *Antropologia Contemporanea* 6(1): 41-42.
1984a Contesti umani paleosardi arcaici. In E. Anati (opera diretta di), *I Sardi. La Sardegna dal paleolitico all'età romana*, 330-41. Cagliari: Jaca Book.
1984b Paleosardi di Cultura Bonnanaro. *Rivisti di Scienze Preistoriche* 39(1-2): 181-221.
1984c La necropoli di Anghelu Ruju e i suoi problemi antropologici. *Nuovo Bullettino Archeologico Sardo* 1: 323-60.
1987a Un cranio trapanato da Nuraxi Figus (Cagliari. *Archivio per l'Antropologia e la Etnologia* 117: 135-51.
1987b Alcuni resti cranici di Padru Jossu, Sanluri (Cagliari). Saggio preliminare. *Quaderni della Soprintendenza Archeologica per le Provincie di Cagliari e Oristano* 4(1): 49-57.
1989 Forme umane di Cultura Ozieri. Sintesi craniologica. In L. Campus (a cura di), *La Cultura di Ozieri. Problematiche e nuove acquisizioni*, 295-308. Ozieri: Il Torchietto.
1990 Tentativo di sintesi della frequentazione umana nella Sardegna preistorica. *Nuovo Bullettino Archeologico Sardo* 3: 279-92.

Germanà, F., & G. Fornaciari
1991 Trapanazioni, craniotomie e traumi cranici nell'Italia antica. *Collana Studi Paletnologia della Sezione di Paleontologia Umana, Paletnologia e Etnologia del Dipartimento di Scienze Archeologiche, Università di Pisa*. Pisa.

Hug, E.
1940 Die Schädel der frühmittelalterlichen cräber aus dem solstfurnischen Aaregebit in ihrer Stellung zur Reifengiabervölkerung Mitteleuropas. *Zeitchrot der Morphol. Anthrop* 38: 402-407.

Jssel, A.
1884 Esame sommario di avanzi d'uomo e d'animali raccolti nella grotta degli Orreri in Sardegna. *Bullettino di Paletnologia Italiana* 1884: 9-12.

Lilliu, G.
1982 *La Civiltà Nuragica*. Sardegna Archaeologica: Studi e Monumenti 1. Sassari: Carlo Delfino.
1988 *La Civiltà dei Sardi dal Paleolitico all'Età dei Nuraghi*. 3rd edition. Torino: Nuova ERI.

Loria, R., & D. Trump
1978 Le scoperte a Sa 'Ucca de Su Tintirriolu e il neolitico Sardo. *Monumenti Antichi Lincei* 49: 115-253.

Mallegni, F., R. Mariani-Costantini, G. Fornaciari, E. Longo, G. Giacobini & A. Radmilli
1982 New European fossil hominid material from an Acheulean site near Rome (Castel di Guido). *American Journal of Physical Anthropology* 62.

Manouvrier, L.
1893 La détermination de la taille d'après les grands os des membres. *Mémorie de la Société d'Anthropologie de Paris* 4: 347-402.

Martin, R., & K. Saller
1958 *Lehrbuch der Anthropologie*. Stuttgart: Verlag.

Maxia, C.
1951-52 Sull'Antropologia dei Protosardi. Sinossi iconografica. *Rivista di Antropologia* 39: 133-78.
1961 Sugli insediamenti umani in Sardegna dalla preistoria ai tempi attuali. *L'Universo* 41(6): 1072-1108. Torino: Istituto Geografico Militare.

1963 Luci e ombre sugli insediamenti preistorici e protostorici nell'isola di Sardegna secondo i ritrovamenti degli ultimi dieci anni. *Atti del VII Riunione Scientifica, Firenze, 2-3 febbraio, 1963.* Firenze: Istituto Italiano di Preistoria e Protostoria.

1967 Nuovi ritrovamenti neo-enolitici in Sardegna. *Atti del XI e XII Riunione Scientifica, Firenze, 11-12 febbraio 1967, Sicilia 22-26 ottobre 1967,* 151-54. Firenze: Istituto Italiano di Preistoria e Protostoria.

Maxia, C., & E. Atzeni
1964 La necropoli eneolitica di San Benedetto di Iglesias. *Atti VIII e IX Riunione Scientifica, Firenze, 11-12 febbraio 1967, Sicilia 22-26 ottobre 1967,* 151-54. Firenze: Istituto Italiano di Preistoria e Protostoria.

Maxia, C., & A. Fenu
1962 Sull'Antropologia dei Protosardi. Sinossi iconografica. Nota II. *Rendiconti Seminario della Facoltà di Scienze, Università di Cagliari* 3-4(32): 1-26.

1963 Sull'antropologia dei protosardi e dei sardi moderni. Sinossi iconografica. Nota IV. *Rendiconti Seminario della Facoltà di Scienze, Università di Cagliari* 2(44): 1-84.

Maxia, C., A. Fenu, G. Lucia, E. Saiu, G. Floris & G. Cosseddu
1972 Sull'antropologia dei Protosardi e dei Sardi moderni. Nota VII. Sinossi iconografica. *Rendiconti Seminario della Facoltà di Scienze, Università di Cagliari* 3-4(42): 199-212.

Maxia, C., & A. Floris
1961 Osservazioni e rilievi sull'antropologia e l'etnografia dei Protosardi dal Neolitico al periodo nuragico secondo i ritrovamenti degli ultimi dieci anni. *Atti del I Congresso della Società di Antropologia, Etnologia e di Folklore, Torino,* 91-154.

Parenti, R.
1967 Gli scheletri umani di Ponte S. Pietro (Cultura Rinaldone) nel contesto antropologico della Provincia tirrenica, all'epoca dei primi metalli. *Archivio per l'Antropologia e la Etnologia* 97(1-2): 17-34.

Riquet, R.
1970 *Anthropologie du Néolithique et du Bronze Ancien.* Poitiers: S.F.I.L. & I.M. Texier.

Santoni, V.
1982 Il mondo del sacro in età neolitica. *Le Scienze* 170: 70-80.

Sergi, G.
1906 Crani antichi della Sardegna. *Atti della Società Romana di Antropologia* 13: 13-17.

Spoor, C.F., & F. Germanà
1987 Proportions of the neolithic human maxillae from Sardinia. *Bulletin et Mémoire de la Société d'Anthropologie de Paris* 14(2): 143-50.

Spoor, C.F., & P.Y. Sondaar
1986 Human fossils from the endemic island fauna of Sardinia. *Journal of Human Evolution* 15: 399-408.

Tanda, G.
1976 Monte d'Accoddi, Tomba II (Sassari). *Nuove Testimonianze Archeologiche della Sardegna Centro-Settentrionale,* 35-60. Sassari: Dessi.

Taramelli, A.
1904 Scavi della necropoli a grotte artificiali di Anghelu Ruju. *Notizie degli Scavi* 1904: 301-51.

1909 Alghero. Nuovi scavi nella necropoli preistorica a grotte artificiali di Anghelu Ruju. *Monumenti Antichi dei Lincei* 29: 397-540.

Ugas, G.
1982 Padru Jossu. Tomba ipogeica ed elementi di cultura materiale delle fasi campaniformi A e B. *Ricerche Archeologiche nel Territorio di Sanluri,* 19-26. Sanluri.

Ugas, G., & G. Lucia
1987 Primi scavi nel sepolcreto nuragico di Antas. In G. Lilliu, G. Ugas & G. Lai (a cura di), *La Sardegna nel Mediterraneo tra il Secondo e il Primo Millennio a.C. Atti del II convegno di studi 'Un millennio di relazioni fra la Sardegna e i Paesi del Mediterraneo,' Selargius-Cagliari, 27-30 novembre, 1986,* 255-77. Cagliari: Amministrazione Provinciale di Cagliari.

Summary

The morphology of human skeletal collections from Sardinia, ranging in date from the Middle Neolithic to the Late Bronze Age, is examined for sexual and ethnic characteristics. Chronological changes in morphology may be due to the settlement of new populations in various parts of the island and to changes in the standard of living in certain time periods. For each of eight cultural periods, cranio-facial and long-bone measurements were taken and represent most of the available Sardinian collections.

The earliest human remains in Sardinia are from Mesolithic levels of Corbeddu Cave (Olièna-NU) and have been studied elsewhere (cf. Klein Hofmeijer and Sondaar, this volume); a single skeleton is also known from a pre-Neolithic burial at Araguina-Sennola (Bonifacio) in Corsica. For the Early Neolithic period, the two facial remains from Su Carroppu di Sirri (CA) are of uncertain stratigraphic origin.

The Middle Neolithic is represented, on the other hand, by the skeletal remains of 13 individuals from Grotta Rifugio (Olièna-NU) and Cuccuru S'Arriu (Cabras-OR). These individuals were dolichomorphic and of medium-short stature. Even more data are availabe for the Late Neolithic Ozieri culture, with some 40 individuals from Lu Maccioni (Alghero-SS), 3 from Sa Ucca de su Tintirriolu (Mara-SS), 25 from Is Aruttas (Cabras-OR), and 35 from S. Benedetto (Iglesias-CA). As with the earlier Neolithic remains, the Ozieri sample is characterized by individuals with dolichomorphic crania; males averaged about 162 cm in height, and females about 151 cm. The Author sees some Negroid features in a few facial remains, and reaffirms the 'hybridization' of both 'Danubian' (Eastern) and 'Afro-Mediterranean' (Western) elements in the Ozieri population.

The Eneolithic or Chalcolithic of Sardinia comprises three cultures, the Abealzu-Filigosa, Monte Claro, and Beaker. Few Abealzu-Filigosa remains are known, but about 30 individuals come from

Monte Claro contexts at Serra Crabiles (Sennori-SS), La Crucca (Sassari), Grotta di Tani (Carbonia-CA), and Padru Jossu (Sanluri-CA); Padru Jossu also has about 20 individuals of Beaker date. Two brachymorphic crania from Grotta di Tani are the earliest known on Sardinia; 23% of the Beaker period remains from Padru Jossu are also brachymorphic. 16% of the individuals from the necropolis of Anghelu Ruju (Alghero-SS), perhaps transitional between the Beaker and Bonnanaro cultures, are brachymorphic; males average 161 cm in height, and females 150 cm.

Early Bronze Age Bonnanaro remains come from seven sites (Grotta di Palmaera-SS, Monte d'Accoddi, S'Isterridolzu-Ossi, Su Crucifissu Mannu-Porto Torres, Taulera-Alghero, Pedralba-Sardara, and Concali Corongiu Acca-Villamassargia), and represent as many as 75 individuals. The sites in northwest Sardinia are about 35% brachymorphic, while all the identified cranial forms from this period in the south are dolichomorphic. Individuals from three sites were trepanated while living.

Eight Middle Bronze Age (Bonnanaro Phase B) sites contain some 70 human individuals (Oridda-Sennori, S'Iscia e sas Piras-Usini, Grotta Sisaia-Dorgali, Seulo-Nuoro, Nuraxi Figus-Gonnesa, Capo Pecora-Arbus, Nicolai e Nebida-Iglesias, and S'Orreri-Fluminimaggiore). Again, three sites have trepanated remains, including one individual from Nuraxi Figus with four successful trepanations.

For the Late Bronze Age, skeletal remains come only from the Gallura in northeast Sardinia, and include eight from *tafoni* and 1 from a *tomba di gigante*. The predominant dolichomorphic skulls and average heights of 166 cm (male) and 156 cm (females) compare well with the remains from a *tafone* at Sartène in Corsica.

For each chronological period, individual skeletal features are compared statistically with the other sample groups, and significant differences noted at the 1% and 5% confidence levels. The Author concludes that: (1) in the Middle Neolithic, there are morphological affinities with extra-insular populations, perhaps due to the relatively recent settlement of Sardinia; (2) by the Late Neolithic, a hybridization of these Danubian and Afro-Mediterranean features resulted in the characteristic Ozieri *ethnos*, still recognizable in Sardinia today; (3) brachycephalic characteristics were introduced in the Eneolithic, and in some areas represented a significant percentage of the population. However, this trait disappears by the Middle Bronze Age, and there is no significant difference between any Late Neolithic Ozieri skeletal values and those of the Bonnanaro Phase B remains; (4) although males are more frequently represented in the skeletal record for all the periods examined, this may be due to their greater robusticity and survival rate, rather than to any social factors; (5) there is, however, consistently higher morphological variation among the male population than in the female, a difference probably related to the greater importance of males in population movements; and (6) finally, there is a notable increase in average stature of both males and females, beginning in the Early Bronze Age Bonnanaro period. This is attributable at least in part to an improved way of life in Nuragic Sardinia.

Cuccuru S'Arriu (Cabras).
L'Orizzonte Eneolitico Sub-Ozieri

Vincenzo Santoni

Come è noto, i settori A ed F di Cuccuru S'Arriu e quelli immediatamente contigui e interposti (Santoni 1989: 170, 189 fig. 1; 1989b: 51-56) hanno restituito una ricca e varia documentazione materiale sub-Ozieri, caratterizzata dal venir meno, graduale e definitivo, della ornamentazione classica tipo San Michele e dell'affermazione marcata della metallurgia, come elemento peculiare e innovativo dell'intervenuto mutamento culturale. In altra sede, si è già sottolineato il rapporto di gemmazione dell'insediamento abitativo tardo-Ozieri, da quello originario e contiguo di ambito San Michele: la separatezza topografica, oltremodo evidente, proprio in corrispondenza dei settori A ed F, è accentuata dall'omogeneo color cinerino chiaro dei depositi antropici dei relativi fondi di capanne sub-Ozieri, di contro alla colorazione più scura, tendente al grigio nerastro, propria delle 'sacche' San Michele. Tali fondi di capanne sub-Ozieri sono escavate artificialmente nel paleosuolo sabbioso-arenaceo, secondo stesure planimetriche sub-ovali, a otto o variamente polilobate, per modeste profondità, mediamente poco più di circa mezzo metro; lungo il perimetro esterno non vi è traccia di buche per pali, né a distanza dal relativo deposito (Santoni *et al.* 1982: 109-11).

Si propone, ora, una compendiaria esemplificazione dei contesti materiali della sacca n. 38 e del quadro più generale del settore A e di aree contermini privilegiando di questi ultimi, in particolar modo, il repertorio fittile decorato, in quanto meglio chiarificatore del mutamento formale rispetto alle corrispondenti fogge decorate San Michele. La sacca n. 38 si colloca nel tratto medio-alto del settore A, prossimale alla linea sud-occidentale dello stagno di Cabras: il relativo deposito, escavato nel bancone sabbioso, descrive una forma rotondeggiante, sub-ovale, con assi trasversi di m 6,00 × 4,50 × 0,80 di profondità massima. Sull'asse longitudinale di maggiore ampiezza, la sacca presenta un andamento del fondo irregolare, marcatamente accidentato e discontinuo. Sulla base dei numerosi depositi malacologici presenti, per lenti stratigrafiche sovrapposte, e, in minore misura, di resti ossei animali, il fondo di capanna può aver assunto anche la funzione di 'sacca-rifiuti', nel settore A, per tale funzione distinguendosi dagli altri contesti, con l'accentuazione del colore grigio-nerastro del medesimo deposito, nella sua intera potenza; sono peraltro decisamente numerose e frequenti le lenti di ceneri che, in maggiore misura, concorrono alla restituzione di tale colorazione.

La proposta di esemplificazione del contesto materiale della sacca n. 38 tra lo spunto da una recente analisi di studio specifica, in sede di documentazione di tesi di Laurea avente come argomento dell'indagine proprio la sacca n. 38 del settore A (Cacciatori 1989–90). Il repertorio in esame è riferito a forme e oggetti fittili, per lo più frammentari (Fig. 1: 1-10; 12-15; Fig. 2: 1, 4-10; 12-15) e a strumenti in ossidiana (Fig 1: 11), in osso (Fig. 2: 2), in rame (o bronzo?) (Fig. 2: 3), in pietra (Fig. 2: 11). Fra gli oggetti in ceramica, sono distinti e integri una ghianda missile (Fig. 2: 5) e due piastre discoidali (Fig. 2: 6, 14).

Tra il restante repertorio fittile, si hanno una forma biconica, verosimilmente a collo indistinto, provvista di anse a tunnel, alla massima espansione (Fig. 2: 1) e varie sagome carenate (Fig. 1: 2, 3, 6, 7; Fig. 2: 4), di cui una con doppio foro passante verticale alla carena (Fig. 1: 3) ed una decorata da triplici file parallele di minuti trattini impressi sotto l'orlo e sotto la carena, dove si associano a festoni, pur essi otttenuti in analoga tecnica (Fig. 1: 7); vi figurano poi vasi a cestello, di cui uno miniaturistico (Fig. 1: 8), uno recante l'incisione interna parallela all'orlo (Fig. 1: 9), il terzo, a profilo rigidamente troncoconico, con orlo provvisto di lobo, interessato da doppie e quadruplici file di segmentini impressi a semini (Fig. 1: 13), un quarto con orletto everso, a parete sottile (Fig. 2: 12); si hanno altresì due frammenti di tegami, di sagoma troncoconica (Fig. 1: 10, 14), uno miniaturistico con orletto assottigliato e fondo appena distinto a scarpa (Fig. 1: 14), due ollette, plausibilmente provviste di doppie prese a bozza forata orizzontalmente, una sub cilindroide, a

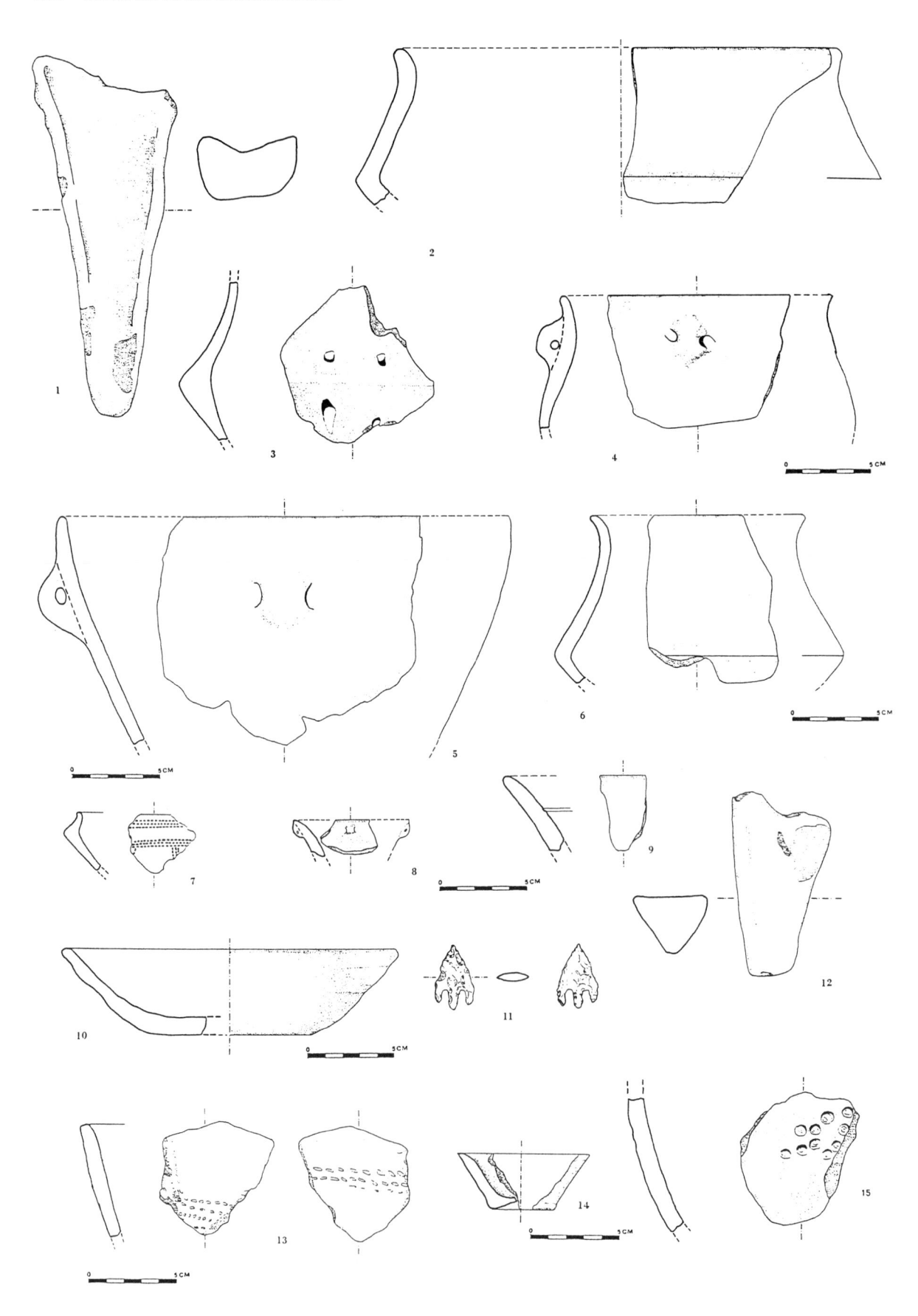

Fig. 1 Cuccuru S'Arriu (Cabras): Forme e oggetti fittili, e strumenti in ossidiana.

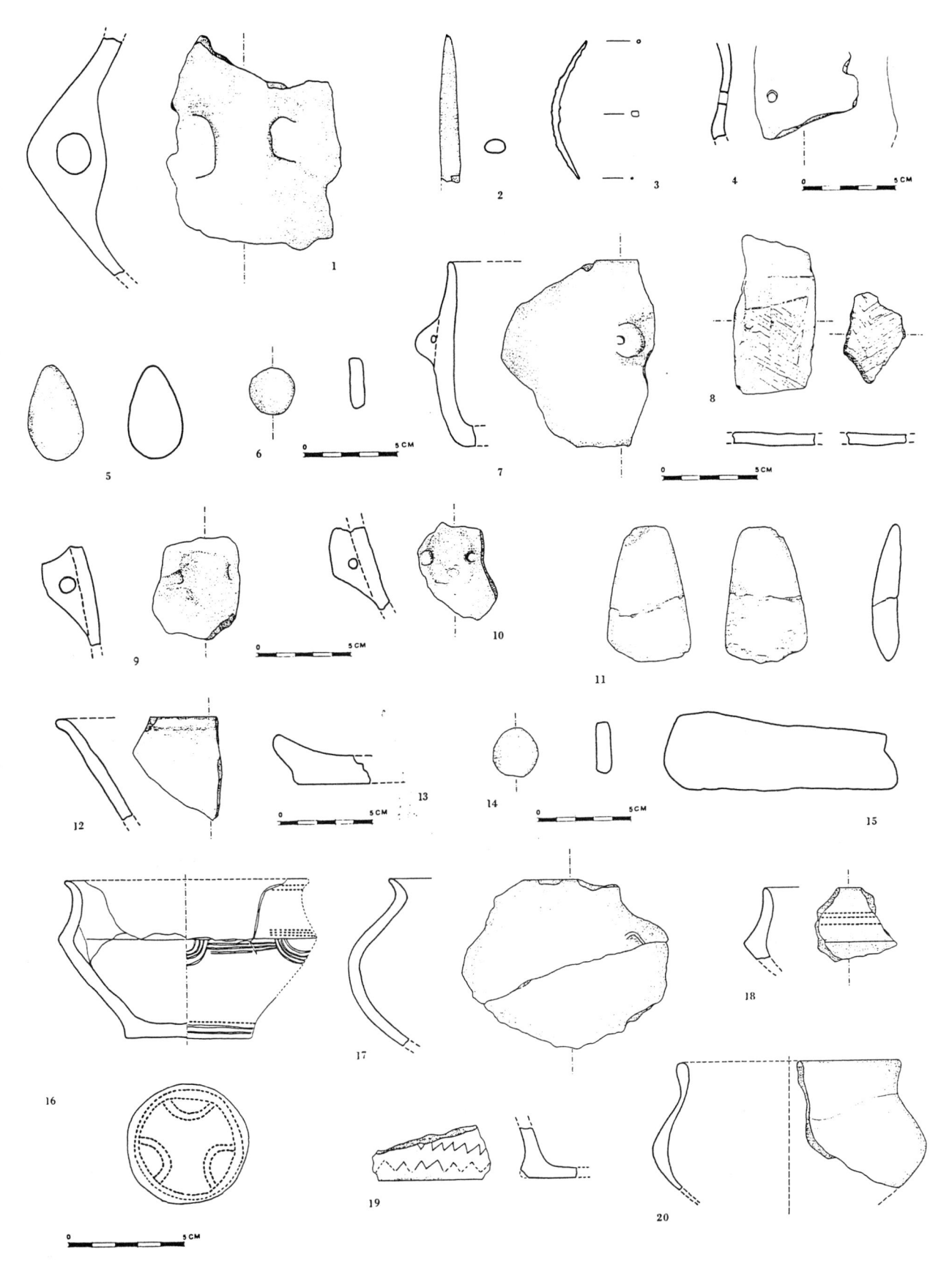

Fig. 2 Cuccuru S'Arriu (Cabras): Forme e oggetti fittili di ceramica, di pietra, di ossa, e di metallo.

160 *Sardinia in the Mediterranean*

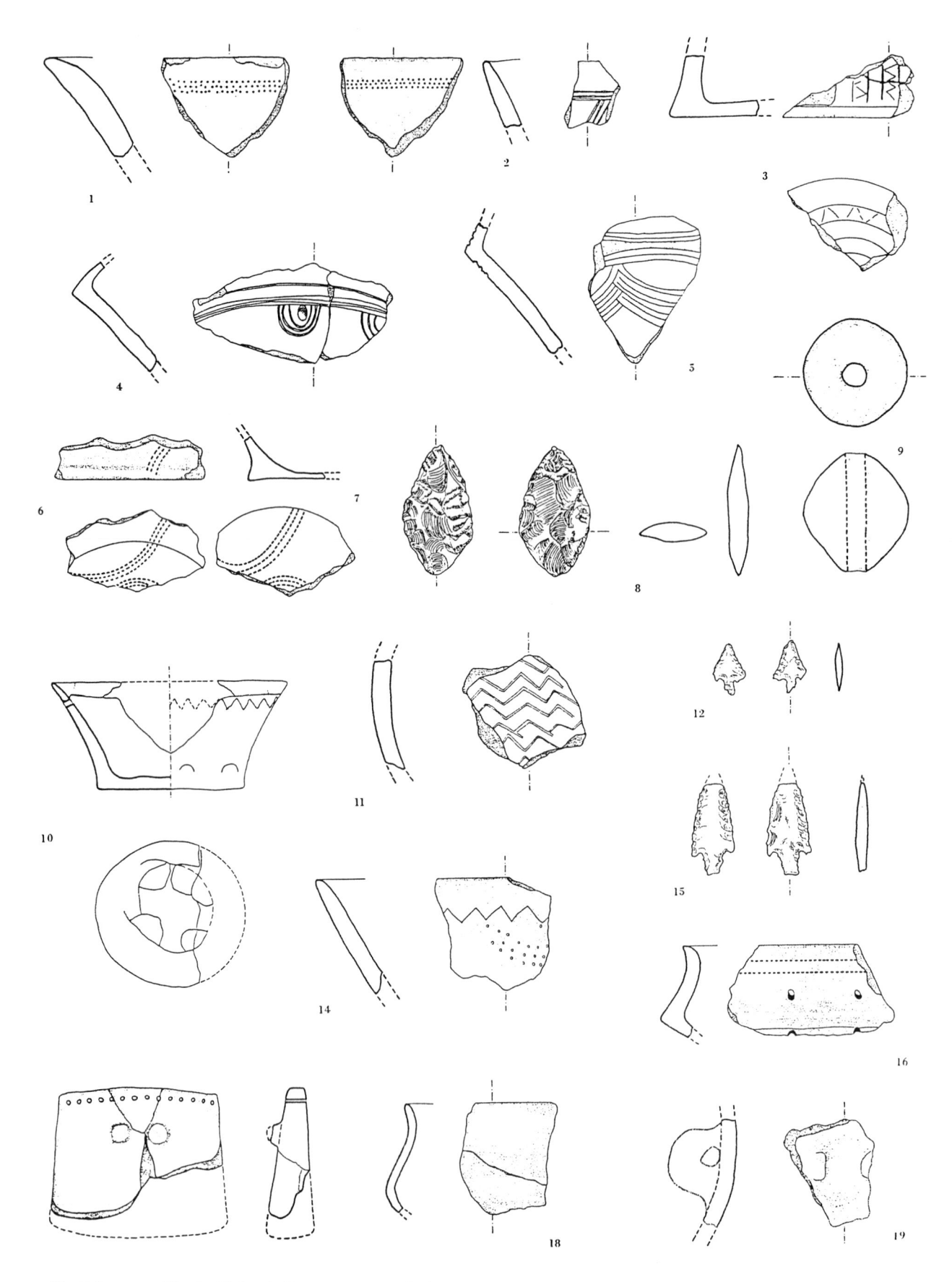

Fig. 3 Cuccuru S'Arriu (Cabras): Forme e oggetti fittili, e strumenti in ossidiana e di pietra.

fondo piano (Fig. 2: 7), la seconda panciuta a linea flessuosa, con orletto everso (Fig. 1: 4), un vaso troncoconico con orlo rientrante, provvisto di presa a bozza forata orizzontalmente (Fig. 1: 5) e infine due frammenti di spiane, a robusto disco piatto (Fig. 2: 15) o con orletto distinto, everso, su breve fondo a scarpa (Fig. 2: 13). Sono pertinenti a forme vascolari indeterminate un frammento di parete decorato da coppelline impresse (Fig. 1: 15) e due presine a bozza forata orizzontalmente, con accenno di gomito nel profilo sommitale (Fig. 2: 9-10); a scodellone troncoconico biansato sono invece riferibili i due frammenti sottili di fondo, interessati da impressione del tipo a stuoia (Fig. 2: 8).

Il restante repertorio materiale del settore A e di aree contermini è pur esso prevalentemente composto da frammenti fittili (Fig 2: 16-20; Fig. 3: 1-6; 8-10; 13-17); risultano invece in ossidiana una cuspide ovalare (Fig. 3: 7) e due punte di freccia triangolari peduncolate (Fig. 2: 12, 15). Eccezion fatta per talune forme inornate (Fig. 2: 17, 20; Fig. 3: 15, 17) e per una fusaiola (Fig. 3: 8), i restanti frammenti fittili sono tutti decorati (Fig. 2: 16, 18, 19; Fig. 3: 1-6; 9-10; 13, 16). È invece interessato da doppie bozze mammillari, quale motivo decorativo schematico, un peso fittile da telaio, frammentario (Fig. 3: 17).

Tra i reperti fittili inornati, si hanno ollette cipolliformi, a breve colletto everso (Fig. 2: 17) e a fettuccia verticale ispessita (Fig. 2: 20) e un bicchiere bitroncoconico, con collettino appena everso (Fig. 3: 15). L'ansa a bozza forata orizzontalmente di Fig. 4: 17 è pertinente a sagoma di olletta panciuta a linea flessuosa del tipo rappresentato dalla foggia della sacca 38 (Fig. 1: 4). Fra i reperti decorati, sono due le forme ricomposte totalmente nelle rispettive sagome: la ciotola carenata della sacca 226/settore H (Fig. 2: 16) e la sagoma di vaso a cestello della sacca 102/settore B (Fig. 3: 9). I restanti frammenti fittili risultano rispettivamente connessi con altre fogge vascolari a cestello (Fig. 3: 1, sacca 59/settore A; Fig. 3: 2, sacca 58/settore A), o troncoconica (Fig. 3: 13, settore A); sono decisamente frequenti le sagome a carena medio-bassa (Fig. 2: 18, settore A; Fig. 3: 16, sacca 47 bis/settore A) o a carena alta (Fig. 3: 4, sacca 44/settore A; Fig. 3: 5, sacca 53/settore A).

A fogge di vasi indeterminati, plausibilmente del tipo a cestello (o carenati?), sono attribuibili i due frammenti di fondi piani pronunciati a spigolo vivo (Fig. 2: 19; settore A; Fig. 3: 6; sacca n. 47/settore A); è altresi verosimile l'attribuzione ad una pisside del frammento di fondo piano, pur esso pronunciato esternamente a spigolo vivo, di Fig. 3: 3 (sacca 44/settore A). Il frammento di parete di Fig. 3: 10 (settore A) è attribuibile a forma panciuta indeterminata.

La peculiarità del repertorio fittile in argomento consiste, vuoi nell'innovazione dei temi esornativi adottati, vuoi nel rapporto di stringente continuità della sintassi decorativa rispetto al quadro San Michele, elementi entrambi che si esprimono in parallelo con il mutamento delle sagome vascolari già di pertinenza del medesimo orizzonte culturale San Michele. Al riguardo, è di particolare interesse la ciotola della sacca 226/settore H (Fig. 2: 16) interessata da motivi a file parallele e ad archi e cerchi concentrici, ottenuti da minuti trattini lineari impressi, sulle pareti e sul fondo, e a cui si associano, sotto la carena, motivi incisi a festoni, alternati a fasce di segmenti orizzontali, pur essi incisi. La decorazione per minuti trattini impressi, disposti per file orizzontali e per festoni, è analoga a quella già evidenziata per la sagoma, pur essa carenata, della sacca 38 di Fig. 1: 7. Con parziali differenze, evidentemente connesse con la stecca d'uso diversificata, la decorazione per file doppie o triplici si ripropone sulle fogge carenate (Fig. 2: 18; Fig. 3: 16), sui fondi di plausibile sagoma a cestello (o carenata?) (Fig. 3: 6), e sotto la linea di un frammento di vaso a cestello, internamente ed esternamente (Fig. 3: 1). L'ornamentazione a festoni incisi, sotto la linea di carena, di cui alla ciotola della Fig. 2: 16, si ripropone modificata nella sintassi grafica nelle fogge carenate di Fig. 3: 4-5, e nella sagoma di cestello di Fig. 3: 2; i festoni vi sono associati alle fasce di linee orizzontali, pur esse incise.

Su altro piano, va osservato come l'incisione, soprattutto nelle forme carenate, sia intervenuta in maniera apparentemente discontinua e incerta: ciò come se l'operazione grafica sia stata operata in termini sbrigativi, ma di proposito, con sufficiente autoconsapevolezza. Tale sorta di disordine esornativo apocrifo ben si coglie e si apprezza nella decorazione attestata nel vaso a cestello della sacca 102/settore B (Fig. 3: 9): al modulo lineare inciso a zig-zag, parallelo all'orlo, di garbata ed elegante fattura e, in linea di massima, innovativo nel quadro della sintassi decorativa del San Michele classico, soprattutto in rapporto con la sagoma vascolare, fa riscontro, sul fondo, il motivo degli archetti, pur essi incisi, inscritti al cerchio, in quadruplice ordine geometrico, ancor meglio e più decisamente mutuati dalla cultura-madre, ma realizzati in apparente disordine propositivo, essendo venuta meno l'adesione convinta al tema, assunto dunque in chiave strutturalmente e meramente memorialistica. In definitiva, una scelta consapevole e partecipe è invece sottesa ai moduli grafici innovativi (Fig. 2: 19; Fig. 3: 1, 3, 6, 10, 13) che, ancor più dei primi, si delineano come segno specifico del mutamento.

Alla varietà delle forme vascolari corrispondono superfici e impasti diversificati in stretto e ovvio rapporto con la relativa sagoma. Al riguardo, in un quadro di rapida sintesi, si possono individuare ceramiche fini, semifini e grezze. Le ceramiche fini sono pertinenti alle sagome carenate con doppi fori verticali alla carena (Fig. 1: 3), alle ciotole ed ai vasi pur essi carenati, per lo più interessati da decorazione (Fig. 1: 7; Fig. 2: 16, 18; Fig. 3: 3-6, 16) o a forme supposte tali, anche se decorate (Fig. 2: 19; Fig. 3: 6), a frammenti di pissidi (Fig. 3: 3), a vasi a cestello miniaturistici (Fig. 1: 8, 14), a bicchieri carenati (Fig. 2: 4; Fig. 3: 15) e cilindroidi (Fig. 2: 7) o a sagome cipolliformi (Fig. 2: 17, 20). Nel quadro complessivo di tali ceramiche e in specifico riferimento alla sacca 38, si apprezzano poi varie tonalità degli impasti, bruni (Fig. 1: 3; Fig. 2: 4), nero-carboniosi (Fig. 1: 7, 8; Fig. 2: 1), grigi (Fig. 1: 14; Fig. 2: 7) e delle superfici, brune (Fig. 1: 3, 7, 8; Fig. 2: 7), grigie (Fig. 2: 4) e nerastre (Fig. 1: 14).

Le ceramiche semifini danno luogo a fogge carenate (Fig. 1: 2, 6), ad una supposta forma biconica, verosimilmente a collo indistinto (Fig. 2: 1), a forme troncoconiche (Fig. 1: 13), vasi a cestello (Fig. 1: 9; Fig. 2: 12; Fig. 3: 9, 13), forme panciute indeterminate (Fig. 1: 15; Fig. 3: 10), una fusaiola (Fig. 3: 8), una ghianda missile (Fig. 2: 5), due piastre discoidali (Fig. 2: 6, 14), un peso da telaio (Fig. 3: 17). In questo sottogruppo di ceramiche si hanno impasti bruni (Fig. 1: 2, 9, 15), scuri e di cottura ineguale (Fig. 1: 9), nero-carboniosi (Fig. 2: 1), nocciola (Fig. 2: 12), bruno-rossiccio (Fig. 2: 5, 6), grigio-scuro (Fig. 2: 14); le superfici variano a loro volta dal colore bruno (Fig. 1: 2, 4; Fig. 2: 14) al grigio-scuro (Fig. 1: 6, 9) e al bruno-rossiccio (Fig. 2: 1, 5, 6), al rossiccio (Fig. 2: 12), al color arancio (Fig. 1: 15).

Le ceramiche grezze, infine, sono in rapporto con vasi tripodi (Fig. 1: 1, 12) e troncoconici (Fig. 1: 5), con tegami (Fig. 1: 10), tegamoni (Fig. 2: 8), con vasi indeterminati (Fig. 2: 9, 10) e con spiane (Fig. 2: 13, 15). In quest'ultimo sottogruppo si hanno impasti rossicci (Fig. 1: 1), nero-carboniosi (Fig. 1: 12; Fig. 2: 9), bruni (Fig. 1: 10; Fig. 2: 10), bruno-rossicci (Fig. 2: 13) e grigi (Fig. 2: 15); le superfici variano poi dal colore bruno-uniforme (Fig. 1: 1, 5, 10; Fig. 2: 13), con chiazze rossicce (Fig. 1: 12) al bicolore, nocciola e arancio rispettivamente interna ed esterna (Fig. 2: 9, 10), al grigio esterno ed al bruno interno (Fig. 2: 15).

L'insieme dei contesti della sacca n. 38 (Fig. 1: 1-15; Fig. 2: 1-15) e dei restanti del settore A e zone immediatamente contermini (Fig. 2: 16-20; Fig. 3: 1-17) evidenzia un orizzonte materiale sub-Ozieri assimilabile, come termine di paragone prioritario, al repertorio posto in luce nei fondi di capanna nn. 3-4 del sito di Is Arridelis di Uta (Sanna 1989: 231-38). Nelle due sacche di Is Arridelis si ripropongono, infatti, le forme carenate di Fig. 1: 3, 6 (Sanna 1989: 237 fig. 4, 6, 8: sacca n. 4), il vaso troncoconico con orlo rientrante, provvisto di presa a bozza forata orizzontalmente, di Fig. 1: 5 (Sanna 1989: 235 fig. 2, 17: sacca n. 3; 237 fig. 4, 19: sacca n. 4), l'ansa a tunnel di Fig. 2: 1 (Sanna 1989: 237 fig. 4, 17: sacca n. 4), il frammento di vaso troncoconico (tegame?), a parete medio alta, con orletto everso di Fig. 2: 12 (Sanna 1989: 238 fig. 5, 3: sacca n. 4), il tipo di presa a bozza forata di Fig. 1: 4 (Sanna 1989: 238 fig. 5, 16: sacca n. 4) e, meglio chiarificatrici del riscontro comparativo proposto fra i due siti, l'ornamentazione a festone inciso di Fig. 2: 16 e di Fig. 3: 2, 4, 5 (Sanna 1989: 234 fig. 1, 4, 5, 7, 9, 10: sacca n. 3) e a segmentini impressi, che compongono motivi rettilinei disposti a fasce parallele, ad archi di cerchio e a festoni, di cui alle Figg. 1: 7; 2:16, 18; 3: 1, 6, 16 (Sanna 1989: 234-35 fig. 1, 1, 2, 3; fig. 2, 1: sacca n. 3), così pure l'incisione a zig-zag, sotto la linea dell'orlo del vaso a cestello della sacca 102 di Fig. 3: 9 e di foggia troncoconica del settore A, di Fig. 3: 13 (Sanna 1989: 235 fig. 2, 5: sacca n. 3). Ulteriori elementi comuni, che ampliano il riscontro comparativo reciproco tra i due contesti di Is Arridelis e di Cuccuru S'Arriu, sono infine dati dal frammento di punteruolo in osso di Fig. 2: 2 (Sanna 1989: 236 fig. 3, 23: sacca n. 3) e dal peso da telaio della sacca n. 48, di Fig. 3: 17 (Sanna 1989: 235 fig. 2, 4: sacca n. 3).

Un secondo contesto materiale di rilevante interesse, verso cui indirizzare le comparazioni, è altresì individuabile nella necropoli di Su Crucifissu Mannu di Porto Torres (Ferrarese Ceruti 1989: 37-47). In tale deposito sono cioè riconoscibili temi esornativi per segmentini impressi di sposti per file parallele e a festoni, peculiari del contesto sub-Ozieri di Cuccuru S'Arriu (Ferrarese Ceruti 1989: 46 fig. 4, 4, 5, 8, 12, 13, 15). Fra le sagome fittili sono altresì attestate forme carenate su piede, con decorazione incisa e non (Ferrarese Ceruti 1989: fig. 4, 2, 6), assimilabili con ampia verosimiglianza alle fogge ornate di Fig. 2: 19 e di Fig. 3: 4, 5, 6. A Su Crucifissu Mannu sono pure presenti un vaso a carena bassa (Ferrarese Ceruti 1989: 46 fig. 4, 10) e una olletta biansata a profilo rotondeggiante e orletto everso (Ferrarese Ceruti 1989: 46 fig. 4, 5), che trovano riscontri in varianti di sagoma, rispettivamente della sacca n. 38 e della n. 16 (Figg. 1: 6; 2: 17).

In merito a quest'ultima foggia (Fig. 2: 17) ed alle parallele varianti di Su Crucifissu Mannu (Ferrarese Ceruti 1989: 46 fig. 4, 5, 15) è utile precisare come, a loro volta, si possano confrontare con la sagoma di ciotola bassa a profilo sinuoso, parete convessa e orletto everso, a virgola, pertinente a vaso tripode post-Ozieri di Viale Colombo di Quartu S. Elena (Atzeni 1966: 123 fig. 12, H). È interessante osservare, infine, come quest'ultima ciotola a profilo sinuoso possa trovare riscontro in foggia analoga, apoda, dell'insediamento neo-eneolitico di Podere Casanuova (Pontedera-Pisa) (Aranguren e Perazzi 1984: 305-306 fig. 2, 9), peraltro caratterizzato dalla presenza di un frammento fittile di peso reniforme (Aranguren e Perazzi 1984: 308-309 fig. 4, 1), del tipo lagozziano, attestato nel fondo di capanna n. 5 di Terramaini-Pirri (Cagliari) (L. Usai 1987: 184 fig. 16, 1) e nell'insediamento Ozieri, sub-Ozieri e Monte Claro di Su Cungiau de Is Fundamentas-Simaxis (Atzori 1960: 267-83, tav. II, 13). Il raccordo comparativo di Su Crucifissu Mannu con Cuccuru S'Arriu/sub-Ozieri, è infine proponibile per la parallela attestazione, in entrambi i contesti, della statuina femminile del tipo cicladico a traforo (Ferrarese Ceruti 1989: 39 fig. 5, 3; Atzeni e Santoni 1989: 53).

Ai riscontri già sottolineati con i repertori materiali di Is Arridelis e di Su Crucifissu Mannu sono da aggiungere diversi altri variamente caratterizzati per il relativo interesse scientifico. Due di essi assumono rilevanza di ordine stratigrafico; il primo è riferito alla grotta di Sa Ucca de su Tintirriolu di Mara, il secondo, alla tomba dei vasi tetrapodi di Santu Pedru di Alghero. Nella grotta di Mara, fatta salva la possibilità di ulteriori verifiche autoptiche tra il repertorio materiale, le comparazioni di principale risalto sono date dal riproporsi della peculiare decorazione a trattini impressi, disposti in sintassi lineare e geometrica, su vaso globulare indeterminato (Loria e Trump 1978: 145-46 fig. 21, 8, tav. XX, 5) e su due sagome carenate, di cui una rapportabile all'esemplare della sacca 226 (Fig. 2: 16) (Loria e Trump 1978: 142-43 fig. 18, 1, 6, tav. XVII, 1, 8). Nello strato di base dell'anticella b della domus di Santu Pedru, alcuni frammenti fittili decorati da motivi punteggiati disposti in ordine lineare, entro riquadri geometrici incisi o apparentemente disaggregati (Contu 1966: col. 55, tav. XIV, b VII, 303-310, tav. L), così pure altri frammenti di vasi a collo, interessati da singoli motivi ad ampi zig-zag (Contu 1966: col. 54, tav. XVI, b, 297-300, tav. LI, b VII, 299) non possono non richiamare i corrispondenti frammenti fittili decorati a zig-zag e punteggiato di Fig. 3: 13 e a zig-zag di Fig. 3: 9, della sacca 102.

Rimane altresì da osservare come i restanti motivi a zig-zag più serrati, in tecnica graffita, degli strati b VII-VI del medesimo ipogeo algherese, trovino il riscontro più prossimo nel motivo di cui alla Fig. 2: 19, evidentemente da riconoscersi come antesignano della specifica ornamentazione Filigosa. Al momento attuale delle conoscenze pare infatti legittimo interporre sul piano culturale i motivi richiamati, a zig-zag (Figg. 2: 19; 3: 9, 13), così pure quello pertinente a frammento di pisside, della sacca 44 (Fig. 3: 3), tra le tematiche esornative del San Michele classico (S. Gemiliano di Sestu: Atzeni 1962: 85 fig. 17, 14; Sa Ucca de su Tintirriolu-Mara: Loria e Trump 1978: 142-43 fig. 18, 5, tav. XVII, 7; Su Pirastu-Ussana: A. Usai 1985: 50-51 fig. 7, 3; 61, 63 fig. 10, 15) e quelle successive, dell'orizzonte Filigosa, meglio esplicitate dai depositi dell'ipogeo di Santu Pedru (Contu 1966: coll. 52-55, tavv. XV-XVI) e dagli strati di base di S. Giuseppe di Padria (Galli *et al.* 1988: 123), oltre che, sia pure con minore risalto, nello stesso ipogeo di Filigosa-Macomer (Foschi Nieddu 1986: 23, tav. 3, 2) e nella Tomba III di Anghelu Ruju (Manunza 1990: tav. IV, 36).

Come è noto, il decorativismo grafico lineare, a zig-zag, è ben documentato nell'architettura ipogeica e nell'artigianato mobiliare di pregio. Nel primo caso, mentre non si ha difficoltà a ritenere congruo all'ambito San Michele il prospetto esornativo della domus di Corongiu-Pimentel (Atzeni 1962: 189-90 fig. 32), ad orizzonte sub-Ozieri può invece ascriversi l'ornamentazione a zig-zag, successiva all'impianto San Michele, documentata sulle pareti della Tomba II di Mesu 'e Montes-Ossi (SS) (Demartis e Canalis 1989: 60-63): per tale riguardo, è utile tenere presenti i moduli grafici di cui alle Figg. 2: 19 e 3: 9, 13.

Su pari piano di valutazione, il prospetto esornativo per i quadri zonali a zig-zag, alternati a campi lisci paralleli, sulla parete del frammento di pisside di Fig. 3: 3, riproposto poi sul fondo con altro ordine grafico, consente anch'esso di ascrivere ad orizzonte sub-Ozieri analogo motivo decorativo graffito, presente sulla parete di fondo dell'anticella della domus di Is Gannaus di Giba (CA) (Atzeni 1987: 23, tav. IV, 3): in analogia con quanto proposto per la Tomba II di Mesu 'e Montes, è da ritenere plausibile, salvo prova difforme, che il motivo grafico possa essere stato realizzato in un momento successivo di escavazione della stessa domus, la cui attribuzione ad orizzonte San Michele è invece documentata dai relativi reperti materiali di scavo (Atzeni 1987: 23). A ben valutare, la contestualità specifica di Is Gannaus mostrerebbe quanto sia intensa la linea di continuità formale fra i due orizzonti San Michele e sub-Ozieri, così da far insorgere anche plausibili perplessità in ordine all'attribuzione proposta, per quanto ben legittimi e congrui i due piani comparativi.

Non minori incertezze attributive persistono in merito a due prodotti dell'artigianato mobiliare di pregio; trattasi delle pisside in trachite, l'una tripode, l'altra tetrapode, con parete decorata da singolo tema a zig-zag ricoprente l'intera parete, provenienti entrambe dal sito di Su Cungiau de Is Fundamentas-Simaxis (OR) (Atzeni 1978: 17 tav. IX; 1975: tav. XVIII, 3-6). Pur tuttavia, il contesto della stazione di Simaxis, l'unicità del motivo grafico e la sottolineatura dell'orlo, che accenna ad un morbido rigonfiamento, come in esemplare di pisside fittile della Tomba III di Anghelu Ruju, dal profilo a semplice tronco di cono (Manunza 1990: 61 tav. IV, 31) orientano di fatto per un ambito culturale post-Ozieri, non ancora evoluto al quadro Filigosa. Su altro piano di verifica, è da osservare come analogo tema grafico a zig-zag occupi, in maniera pervasiva, l'intera parete di vaso tripode, su ciotola a profilo sinuoso, della grotta A.C.A.I. di Carbonia (Atzeni 1987: 35, 37 fig. 8, 2), ben assimilabile, a sua volta, al vaso pur esso tripode della stazione di Viale Colombo-Quartu S. Elena (CA) (Atzeni 1966: 123 fig. 12, h). Su parallelo piano di analisi, è da osservare come il singolo modulo grafico a zig-zag sia attestato, a sottile linea incisa su ciotola troncoconica e, con incisione più larga, come a solcatura, sul campo verticale di piede a nastro triangolare di vaso tripode della stazione di Is Arridelis di Uta (Sanna 1989: fig, 2, 5: sacca n. 3; fig. 5, 10: sacca 4); ciò, secondo un gusto esornativo, per piani orizzontali e verticali, ben confermato su un secondo vaso tripode della medesima grotta A.C.A.I., precedentemente richiamata (Atzeni 1978: 35, 37 fig. 8, 3).

Il riscontro comparativo proposto con i depositi di Sa Ucca de su Tintirriolu di Mara e con la Tomba dei vasi tetrapodi di Alghero pone in risalto due situazioni stratigrafiche differenziate, tra loro complementari. Nel primo contesto di Mara è dato osservare come l'orizzonte sub-Ozieri risulti essere ragionevolmente interposto tra l'Ozieri classico e la cultura Monte Claro, senza l'interposizione del repertorio materiale Filigosa. Si riproporrebbe cioè la linea di continuità fra San Michele e Monte Claro, già sottolineata nel contesto insediativo di San Gemiliano di Sestu (Atzeni 1962) e ribadita indirettamente dai ritrovamenti di superficie a Conca Illonis di Cabras, a Su Cungiau de is Fundamentas di Simaxis, a Serra 'e sa Furca di Mogoro.

Nel contesto ipogeico di Santu Pedru insorge il quesito legittimo se i reperti dell'Ozieri classico associati al sub-Ozieri negli strati VII-VI dell'anticella b (Contu 1966: coll. 50, 55, tav. XIV, 234, 302) e documentati nel dromos a (Contu 1966: coll. 28-33, tav. XIV, 38, 87, 88, 26, 43) siano da ricollegare al medesimo orizzonte sub-Ozieri o se, invece, non siano autonomi, in tal modo consentendo l'attribuzione dell'impianto originario dell'ipogeo alla relativa cultura madre San Michele e non invece all'aspetto seriore sub-Ozieri. Al momento dell'analisi non mancano argomentazioni a favore dell'una o dell'altra possibilità.

In evidente significativa continuità diacronica si collocano invece i riscontri proponibili con il quadro materiale eneolitico di Terramaini-Pirri (L. Usai 1987: 175-92). Come già osservato per talune fogge e ornamentazioni incise di Cuccuru S'Arriu (Figg. 2: 16; 3: 4-5) così, anche nel sito di Terramaini perdurano tematiche esornative ancora impregnate degli esiti formali del San Michele classico (L. Usai 1987: 181 fig. 13, 1-2). In entrambi i siti, si propongono altresì la sintassi e le tecniche decorative a motivi impressi, innovativi rispetto all'orizzonte Ozieri (Figg. 1: 7; 2: 16; 3: 1, 6) (L. Usai 1987: 177-81 fig. 13, 4); parallelamente, ai motivi a chevrons incisi di Fig. 3: 10, corrispondono a Terramaini pressoché analoghi temi decorativi, però espressi nel segno dell'impressione segmentata lineare (L. Usai 1987: 177-81 fig. 13, 4).

Su pari orizzonte comparativo, per alcuni versi, potrebbe essere leggibile il riscontro tra i motivi incisi a zig-zag del frammento fittile di Fig. 2: 19 e quelli corrispondenti, dipinti a zig-zag, di Terramaini, strutture nn. 2, 3 (L. Usai 1987: 180 fig. 15, 1, 7). Le analogie fra i contesti di Cabras e di Pirri si ribadiscono ulteriormente per la comune presenza sia di piastre fittili (Fig. 2: 6, 14) (L. Usai 1987: 184-85 fig. 16, 2, 3), sia di punteruoli in osso (Fig. 2: 2) (L. Usai 1987: 185 fig. 16, 6-13). Non sono altresì trascurabili i confronti formali proponibili tra la ciotola carenata di Fig. 2: 18 e la corrispondente sagoma della cap. n. 3 di Terramaini (L. Usai 1987: 180 fig. 12, 3); di non minore interesse si configura pure il confronto fra l'olletta di Fig. 3: 15 e il vasetto triansato della cap. n. 6 (L. Usai 1987: 179 fig. 11, 4). La 'diversificazione' fra i due contesti oltre che su specifici piani comparativi di dettaglio dei quali si avrà modo di perfezionare la relativa analisi, pare al momento enucleabile, in principale misura, sulla base della decisa presenza della decorazione dipinta a Terramaini, eccezionalmente attestata invece a Cuccuru S'Arriu con esemplare sporadico di vaso a fiasco, tutt'ora inedito (Atzeni e Santoni 1989: 54).

Il collegamento fra l'orizzonte della cultura-madre Ozieri e l'aspetto evoluto sub-Ozieri è rimarcato e apprezzabile in altri reperti fittili decorati e non. Procedendo nell'analisi comparativa, è utile osservare come il motivo dell'impressione ad intreccio angolare di fibre vegetali (Fig. 2: 8) sia ben noto in stanziamenti abitativi neolitici, quale quello di Puisteris-Mogoro (Puxeddu 1962: 239 tav. III a/1) e di S. Gemiliano di Sestu (Atzeni 1962:

83 tav. XIV, 13-14), nel complesso neo-eneolitico di Monte d'Accoddi-Sassari (Contu 1953: 202), in strato Ozieri classico, alla grotta Filiestru di Mara (SS) (Trump 1983: 51 fig. 17, n), nella sacca n. 21 di Su Coddu-Selargius (Ugas et al. 1989: 255 fig. 4, 1), in contesto immediatamente successivo, assimilabile al quadro culturale Filigosa, della stazione di Fenosu-Palmas Arborea (Lugliè 1989: 76, 84 fig. 1, 2) e negli strati di base Filigosa di S. Giuseppe-Padria (Galli et al. 1988: 123).

La foggia vascolare di riferimento per tali frammenti è individuabile, da un lato, nelle spiane di cui alla Fig. 2: 13 (è utile al riguardo il riferimento proposto con l'esemplare di Su Coddu), dall'altro nei tegamoni a pareti medio-alte, con anse subcilindroidi a nastro largo, insellato, del tipo già noto a Su Ucca de su Tintirriolu-Mara (Loria e Trump 1978: 149-50 fig. 25, 12, 13) e variamente attestate nell'orizzonte materiale dela medesima sacca n. 38 di Cuccuru S'Arriu (Cacciatori 1989–90: 251-53 tav. 41, 147-150). Quest'ultima foggia di tegamone risulta attestata anche a Terramaini (L. Usai 1987: 177 fig. 4, 1); tende invece a venir meno nei successivi contesti Filigosa di Macomer, sito eponimo, e di S. Giuseppe di Padria.

Fra i due frammenti di spiane, il tipo con contorno perimetrale rimarcato a scarpa e con orletto distinto obliquo (Fig. 2: 12) mostra di essere evidentemente derivato dai modelli dell'Ozieri classico, documentati a S. Gemiliano di Sestu e a Monte Olladiri di Monastir (Atzeni 1962: 66 fig. 14, 4; 128 fig. 24, 13); il secondo esemplare, a piastra discoidale (Fig. 2: 15), può considerarsi una ulteriore esemplificazione di spiana discoidale del San Michele classico (Cuccuru s'Arriu, sacca 340: Atzeni e Santoni 1989: 172 tav. 4, 1), il cui esito tardivo è da individuarsi in foggia a piastra dell'ipogeo di Filigosa I di Macomer (Foschi Nieddu 1986: 72 tav. 51, 2), erroneamente interpretato come peso fittile da telaio (Foschi Nieddu 1986: 72).

Una evidente linea di continuità formale fra l'orizzonte classico San Michele e il quadro sub-Ozieri è altresì ben leggibile nell'analisi comparativa connessa con le sagome di vasi a cestello e forme derivate (Figg. 1: 8-10, 13-14; 2: 12; 3: 9) delle quali ultime, alcune mostrano e sottolineano l'intervenuto mutamento ormai portato a maturazione (Figg. 1: 10; 2: 12; 3: 9). Il raccordo con l'Ozieri classico è particolarmente accentuato nel frammento di vaso a cestello della sacca n. 38 (Fig. 1: 9), sia per il profilo, sia per l'incisione sotto l'orlo, elementi entrambi che consentono il raccordo con esemplari canonici di cestelli dell'orizzonte San Michele (Sa Ucca de su Tintirriolu-Mara: Loria e Trump 1978: 140-41 fig. 15; Cuccuru s'Arriu: Santoni 1989: 172-73 fig. 3, 2).

Nella versione coeva di vaso a cestello di Is Arridelis-Uta (Sanna 1989: 231-38 fig. 1, 1) l'incisione sotto l'orlo tende a venir meno, mentre la foggia vascolare, a sua volta, mostra di irrigidirsi nel puro profilo troncoconico (Sanna 1989: figg. 1, 4, 11; 2, 1, 5; 4, 1-3), soluzione entro la quale si inquadrano alcune varianti dello stesso contesto di Cuccuru S'Arriu (Figg. 1: 10, 13, 14; 2: 12).

Fra queste ultime, si delinea distinto il frammento di plausibile 'vaso a cestello', con orlo sormontato da un lobo triangolare e pareti interna ed esterna decorate da semini lanceolati impressi, disposti per triplici linee parallele all'orlo e per fascia quadruplice, con risvolto angolare verso l'alto. Per la peculiarità del lobo, la foggia vascolare si ricollega con altre sagome dell'orizzonte classico San Michele (Santoni 1989: 180: Cuccuru s'Arriu-Cabras; Loria e Trump 1978: 151-53 fig. 26, 2; fig. 14, 6, 10; 138-39 fig. 13, 6: Sa Ucca de su Tintirriolu). Per vero, tale caratteristica variata nelle soluzioni è già nota su forme fittili del neolitico antico corso e sardo (Weiss e Lanfranchi 1976: 432-35 fig. 1, 18; Trump 1983: 38-46 fig. 10 y), nel neolitico medio peninsulare (Broglio e Fasani 1975: 25 fig. 21, 4, 6: Persegaro presso Molino di Casalotto; Cremonesi 1976: 187-218 fig. 19, 27: Grotta dei Piccioni di Bolognano) e nel neolitico medio e superiore delle Arene Candide (Bernabò Brea 1956: 126 fig. 52; 72, tav. XIV, 2-8, 14 fig. 6).

Nell'isola, al momento, l'unico utile termine comparativo da tenere presente, come parallela foggia vascolare attribuibile pur essa con plausibile verosimiglianza al quadro sub-Ozieri, è dato dall'esemplare di vaso a cestello decorato a festoni incisi dello str. VI della Trincea XXIII di Monte d'Accoddi (Tinè e Traverso 1990: 4 tav. XXV, 12). La decorazione a festoni incisi è del tipo già individuato come pertinente all'orizzonte tardo-Ozieri (Figg. 2: 16; 3: 4-5); essa risulta peraltro del tutto inusuale nei vasi a cestello del quadro classico Ozieri che prediligono, invece, la decorazione a bande tratteggiate. È altresì utile osservare come altri due reperti fittili del medesimo str. VII di Monte d'Accoddi, un frammento di parete di vaso a cestello e un verosimile piede di tripode nastriforme a lingua (Tinè e Traverso 1990: 4 tav. XXV, 13, 19), siano pur essi riconducibili, ragionevolmente, a pari ambito tardo-Ozieri.

I due reperti sono entrambi decorati da fasce di segmenti incisi in ordine parallelo, discontinui e regolari, quasi a tremolo, secondo una tecnica ed una sintassi zonale affatto improprie all'orizzonte classico San Michele. I tre segmenti a tremolo disposti a comporre una fascia a morbido andamento angolare in zona prossimale al fondo del frammento di vaso a cestello (Tinè e Traverso 1990: tav. XXV, 13), episodio grafico in sè del tutto eccezionale, ripropongono di fatto, un gusto esornativo analogo a quello a fascia angolare del frammento di cestello lobato in argomento (Fig. 1: 13).

D'altro canto, la stessa sagoma a parete sottile con graduale rigonfiamento del fondo verso l'orlo, ben si accorda con il profilo di vasi troncoconici della stazione di Is Arridelis di Uta (Sanna 1989: fig. 1, 4, 11); ciò secondo una peculiarità distintiva di altre fogge vascolari del medesimo contesto insediativo (Sanna 1989: figg. 1, 7, 9; 4, 13; 5, 9, 16). Non casualmente, il rigonfiamento dell'orlo viene registrato anche nell'olletta cipolliforme a colletto di Cuccuru S'Arriu/settore A (Fig. 2: 20).

Parallelamente, il piede di tripode nastriforme a lingua è ben raccordabile con esemplare analogo della struttura 43 di Su Coddu-Selargius (Ugas *et al.* 1989: 261-67 fig. 2, 3), la cui attribuzione all'orizzonte sub-Ozieri, a sua volta, si configura pur essa decisamente legittima. Tale struttura infatti, pur recependo elementi fittili ancora impregnati delle tecniche e delle tematiche esornative dell'Ozieri classico (motivi a festoni e a cerchi concentrici, bande tratteggiate) (Ugas *et al.* 1989: fig. 2, 5, 8, 12, 14: motivi a festoni e a cerchi concentrici, bande tratteggiate), ne contiene insieme altri marcatamente 'rivelatori' del trapasso intervenuto. Tali elementi sono cioè costituiti dalla ceramica dipinta o decorata da motivi di rombi incisi associato a doppie linee parallele, da taccheggiature di segmentini obliqui, da tavolinetto tripode, da olla bi o triansata, da vaso tripode e da teglia (Ugas *et al.* 1989: 261-62, figg. 2, 2-4, 7, 9, 10, 13; 3, 1, 2, 6), relativamente rapportabili con corrispondenti fogge e motivi esornativi, del medesimo sito di Su Coddu (Struttura 12: Ugas *et al.* 1989: 269-75 fig. 2, 17; fig. 3, 1) e di Terramaini-Pirri (L. Usai 1987: 177-86 figg. 4, 2; 5, 2; 6, 3; 12, 1-5).

Altra foggia vascolare provvista di lobo prosegue in uso nel contesto della Tomba I di Filigosa-Macomer (Foschi Nieddu 1986: 24, tav. 4, 7), mentre, fuori dall'isola, si conoscono episodi analoghi nell'eneolitico medio della Tomba I Capaci-Palermo (Quoiani 1975: 241, 252 figg. 19, 5; 20, 5) e di Piano Conte (Bernabò Brea e Cavalier 1957: 139-40; 1980: 501 fig. 87, A, tav. CVIII, 1 a, 1 b), così pure nell'eneolitico superiore di Piano Quartara (Bernabò Brea e Cavalier 1960: 66, 70-71 tav. XXIII, 9, 10) e di Chiusazza-Malpasso (Tinè 1965: 186 tav. XX, 13). La transizione del vaso a cestello verso le soluzioni troncoconiche in argomento (Fig. 1: 13) e di Fig. 1: 10, 14, trova conferma indiretta nella contestuale presenza delle fogge di Fig. 3: 1, 9, ancora legate al modello di origine nel relativo profilo concavo delle pareti, ma ormai innovate nei rispettivi temi esornativi.

Queste ultime due forme mostrano di venir meno nei contesti di Terramaini-Pirri e di Filigosa I di Macomer, dove invece si affermano le soluzioni formali di tipo troncoconico (L. Usai 1987: 178 fig. 6, 4; 183 fig. 9, 3; 180 fig. 14, 8; Foschi Nieddu 1986: 31, tav. 8, 3; 36, tav. 12, 1; 38, tav. 14, 1-3, 5, 6; 40, tav. 19 A, 1; 54, tav. 32 A, 1; 64, tav. 46 A, 4). Come già il contesto di Cuccuru S'Arriu, così anche la struttura n. 21 di Su Coddu di Selargius documenta la gradualità della transizione formale della foggia del vaso a cestello (Ugas *et al.* 1989: 253-60 fig. 2, 1, 5-6, 8, 9) a quella del vaso troncoconico (Ugas *et al.* 1989: fig. 2, 7) che, peraltro, ripropone taluni elemento esornativi del vasetto di Fig. 3: 9.

In questo quadro di lettura, anche nella struttura 43 di Su Coddu è possibile cogliere la gradualità della evoluzione formale della sagoma vascolare: nella versione rigida, assimilabile alla foggia di Fig. 3: 13 di Cuccuru S'Arriu, si conserva il modulo grafico a bande tratteggiate dell'Ozieri classico (Ugas *et al.* 1989: 261, 267 fig. 2, 14); inversamente, nella variante a profilo flessuoso, si recepisce l'innovazione grafica a doppie linee parallele e a rombi incisi, sotto l'orlo (Ugas *et al.* 1989: fig. 2, 9). In questa ottica di analisi, potrebbe per vero costituire un obiettivo elemento di anomalia la presenza di frammento di vaso a cestello a parete sottile dello strato IV della Trincea XXIII di Monte d'Accoddi attribuito all'orizzonte Filigosa (Tinè *et al.* 1989: 27-29; Tinè e Traverso 1990: 4-5, tav. XXVI, 6), in quanto assimilabile nel profilo tettonico d'insieme a foggia della sacca n. 3 di Is Arridelis-Uta, decorata nello stile sub-Ozieri di Cuccuru S'Arriu (Sanna 1989: 231-33 fig. 1, 1).

In verità, e parallelamente, è da osservare come altre forme del medesimo strato IV di Monte d'Accoddi ben si comparino pur esse con sagome di ambito sub-Ozieri, così da far sospettare che il contesto materiale dello stesso strato IV possa delinearsi ancora pertinente a tale orizzonte o, eventualmente, quale prima espressione materiale di Filigosa, ai limiti con il sub-Ozieri. Come utile conferma di tale proposta di lettura, si richiama in evidenza il riscontro fra le sagome carenate di Fig. 1: 3, 6, i fondi di supposte pissidi o vasi carenati delle Figg. 2: 19 e 3: 3, 6, questi ultimi assenti nei contesti Filigosa, e le corrispondenti forme di Monte d'Accoddi (Tinè e Traverso 1990: 4-5 tav. XXVI, 1, 7, 5).

Di converso, è altresí utile osservare come il vaso a collo con anse a tunnel di Monte d'Accoddi (Tinè e Traverso 1990: tav. XXVI, 8) possa trovare i legittimi riferimenti comparativi nelle varianti formali dell'anfora dipinta della cap. 160 di Monte Olladiri di Monastir (Ugas *et al.* 1989: 239-43 fig. 1, 1) e anche, plausibilmente, del vaso a collo acromo e di quello dipinto, pur esso a collo, provvisto di tre anse a tunnel, della cap. 5 di Terramaini (L. Usai 1987: 177 fig. 5, 1; 179-180 fig. 11, 1). Per quanto concerne l'anfora di Monte Olladiri, come è noto, insieme ad altra ceramica dipinta, essa è associata con un articolato repertorio fittile inciso e impresso decisamente distinto dall'orizzonte classico San Michele e perciò correttamente classificato entro il quadro sub-Ozieri (Ugas et al. 1989: 239-43). Tra gli altri reperti del secondo gruppo è utile richiamare il frammento di vaso troncoconico decorato sotto la linea dell'orlo da una fascia di segmentini orizzontali impressi (Ugas et al. 1989: fig. 2, 6), ben ricollegabile, nel gusto di insieme del motivo decorativo, ai corrispondenti frammenti vascolari rispettivamente pertinenti alle sacche 59 e 38 di Cuccuru S'Arriu (Figg. 3: 1; 1: 13).

Nello stesso contesto, i motivi triangolari a tratteggio lineare interno e quelli a spina di pesce (Ugas et al. 1989: fig. 2, 9-10), consentono di assimilare al medesimo orizzonte sub-Ozieri il repertorio complessivo della struttura 27 di Su Coddu (Ugas et al. 1989: 245-51) per l'attestazione delle corrispondenti tematiche esornative (Ugas et al. 1989: fig. 3, 4, 5), così pure del motivo a coppelline (Ugas et al. 1989: fig. 3, 6), ben noto a Terramaini (L. Usai 1987: fig. 13, 6, 8). Non dovrebbe costituire ostacolo per tale inquadramento la presenza di altra ceramica invece attribuita all'orizzonte dell'Ozieri classico (Ugas et al. 1989: 245-51; Ugas, Lai e Usai 1989: 36-38) proprio in quanto, nota associativa costante, nelle diverse strutture di Su Coddu (Ugas et al. 1989: 239-78; Ugas, Lai e Usai 1989: 7-40), là dove il mutamento qualitativo verso il fronte sub-Ozieri può essere espresso anche da testimoni pur limitati, sul piano della frequenza numerica, ma significativi nel senso dell'innovazione e delle relazioni comparative di pertinenza.

È oltremodo indicativo, al riguardo, il contesto della struttura n. 4 (Ugas, Lai e Usai 1989: 20-22). L'elemento innovativo e trainante del mutamento, oltre che utile e rivelatore dell'orizzonte cronologico di pertinenza, è dato dal vaso biconico dipinto a riquadri zonali e da motivi a tremolo verticali. La sagoma vascolare in parte e soprattutto la quadripartitura grafica del prospetto rimandano, infatti, in termini ben esemplificativi, all'orizzonte dell'eneolitico antico del Conzo, con riferimento specifico allo strato IV, livelli inferiore e medio, della grotta della Chiusazza presso Siracusa (Tinè 1965: 145-76 tavv. II, 1, 3, 6; IV, 1, 5; V) con cui, peraltro, sono stati già istituiti puntuali riscontri comparativi (L. Usai 1987: 184 fig. 11, 3; Tinè 1965: 160-61, 250, tav. II, 5).

A ben guardare, in questo quadro specifico di connessioni relative che vanno chiarendosi e confermandosi reciprocamente, sono altresì rapportabili, al medesimo orizzonte del Conzo, i motivi dipinti a doppia fila parallela di triangoli, con vertici rivolti verso l'alto, quali compaiono sul colletto e sulla spalla dell'anforetta della capanna 160 di Monte Olladiri di Monastir, precedentemente richiamata (Ugas et al. 1989: 240 fig. 1, 1). La pertinenza dei termini comparativi che si vanno proponendo viene ulteriormente confermata da altri riscontri integrativi che, di fatto, fungono, per così dire, da 'verifiche incrociate'.

La foggia di vaso tripode della struttura 4 di Su Coddu (Ugas, Lai e Usai 1989: 20-22 fig. 8, 2) associato al vaso biconico dipinto (Ugas, Lai e Usai 1989: fig. 8, 1) si configura del tutto analoga ad una dei vasi tripodi della capanna n. 5 di Terramaini (L. Usai 1987: fig. 2, 2), in cui è attestato un vaso triansato dipinto, con fascia parallela all'orlo del colletto e con motivo serpentiforme (L. Usai 1987: 184 tav. 11, 1); quest'ultimo, a sua volta, ben si raccorda con i noti motivi ondulati o serpentiformi incisi della cultura della Conca d'Oro (Marconi Bovio 1944: Contrada Colli, col. 26, tav. IV, 1; Valdesi, col. 31, tav. IV, 7), nello stile di San Cono Piano Notaro-Cala Farina documentato nel medesimo strato IV, livelli inferiore e medio della grotta della Chiusazza (Tinè 1965: tav. VI). I riscontri puntuali già affacciati da Terramaini, in direzione delle fogge vascolari dello stesso deposito della Chiusazza e delle parallele forme vascolari della Conca d'Oro (L. Usai 1987: 183-84) si propongono quale ulteriore sottolineatura di conferma.

D'altro canto, e in parallelo, è da osservare come i due frammenti di ollette di Fig. 1: 4 e di Fig. 3: 8 di Cuccuru S'Arriu possano, a loro volta, confrontarsi, nello stesso strato IV della Chiusazza, con talune fogge dello stile Cala Farina (Tinè 1965: tav. IX, 1, 6-12), del quale si coglie una eco parziale, non trascurabile, nel profilo del vaso tripode di Terramaini, cap. 3 (L. Usai 1987: fig. 3, 2). Sul versante culturale post-Ozieri, è altresì utile tenere presente come il motivo inciso serpentiforme della Conca d'Oro prosegua a manifestarsi, in attestazioni pur sporadiche, nel complesso eponimo di Filigosa (Foschi Nieddu 1986: 23, tav. 3, 3; 39, tav. 17, 1).

Sulla base delle connessioni comparative proposte (cap. 160 di Monte Olladiri; strutture 4, 21, 27, 43 di Su Coddu-Selargius), non si ha difficoltà a prendere atto della reale coesistenza, per graduale progressione temporale, di elementi grafici ornamentali e delle relative sagome vascolari della tradizione dell'Ozieri classico, in contesti ormai pertinenti all'orizzonte culturale evidentemente innovato, sub-Ozieri, a sua volta, pur esso gradualmente preparatorio, nei diversi segmenti contestuali, del definitivo passaggio all'orizzonte Filigosa.

In questa cornice, è da osservare altresì come la medesima produzione fittile, individuabile come meglio pertinente alla tradizione dell'Ozieri classico, mostri di aver perso taluni connotati salienti originari, per assumerne invece altri marcatamente barocheggianti e pervasivi dell'intero campo vascolare, talvolta pasticciati, i quali elementi tutti, insieme con la forma irrigidita o appesantita, rivelano non casualmente il reale mutamento intervenuto e, dunque, la posizione culturale di merito.

A titolo esemplificativo si può richiamare la struttura n. 14 di Su Coddu, con contesto attribuito all'Ozieri classico. Il frammento di ciotola emisferica con orlo ingrossato piano rientrante (Ugas, Lai e Usai 1989: 22 fig. 8, 6), decisamente inusuale nell'orizzonte classico Ozieri, richiama almeno in parte, da un lato una parallela sagoma a piattello dello strato VI della Trincea XXIII di Monte d'Accoddi (Tinè e Traverso 1990: tav. XXV, 14) caratterizzata pur essa da un orlo ingrossato rientrante, e in associazione con elementi formali individuati come pertinenti al sub-Ozieri (cfr. supra), dall'altro, un secondo esempio di piattello, della Tomba V di Pranu Mutteddu-Goni (Cocco 1989: fig. 3, 3) pur esso con orlo ingrossato piano rientrante e in associazione con elementi di collana in argento e con industria litica in selce di tipologia remedelliana (Atzeni e Cocco 1989: 201, 211-12 fig. 4, 1).

Su altro piano, l'ornamentazione del piattello di Goni, non a caso, ben rieccheggia, pur divergendo la sintassi grafica, l'ornamentazione a semini lanceolati impressi di Cuccuru S'Arriu, sacca 38 (Fig. 1: 13), e anche quella presente su vaso troncoconico della cap. 160 di Monte Olladiri (Ugas *et al.* 1989: fig. 2, 6) e su frammento di pisside della Tomba III di Anghelu Ruju (Manunza 1990: tav. IV, 1). In parallelo, l'incisione anomala a fasce di segmentini paralleli sull'orlo piano della forma emisferica della struttura 4 di Su Coddu (Ugas, Lai e Usai 1989: fig. 8, 6) ben richiama, a sua volta, le incisioni 'pasticciate' e irregolari di Littoslongos-Ossi (Moravetti 1989: 86-87 fig. 6, 1-4, 6-9, 14) il cui repertorio vascolare di pertinenza è da supporre in plausibile associazione contestuale, sia con la ceramica a bande tratteggiate del San Michele, sia con gli esemplari di idoli a traforo (Moravetti 1989: 87-88 fig. 4, 1-4, tav. I, 2-3), come peraltro propone lo stesso Autore, da un angolo visuale differenziato di analisi (Moravetti 1989: 91).

Tale associazione di quadri materiali sub-Ozieri con gli idoli a traforo richiama, per analogia, la situazione contestuale documentata nella necropoli di Su Crucifissu Mannu di Porto Torres (Ferrarese Ceruti 1989: 37-47) dove si propongono reperti e temi decorativi tipici dell'orizzonte sub-Ozieri di Cuccuru S'Arriu (cfr. supra), l'ornamentazione incisa pasticciata presente a Littoslongos (Ferrarese Ceruti 1989: fig. 4, 11, 14), la decorazione impressa a segmenti dentellati di festoni multipli o di cerchi concentrici peculiari della sintassi grafica San Michele (Ferrarese Ceruti 1989: fig. 4, 1, 3), elementi tutti, in plausibile associazione culturale con gli esemplari di idoli in marmo, negli schemi a traforo e a placchetta, del tipo Sa Turriga-Senorbì (Ferrarese Ceruti 1989: fig. 5). Una situazione contestuale analoga, con evidenti elementi sub-Ozieri, viene registrata nelle tombe I e III di Ponte Secco-Sassari (Ferrarese Ceruti 1989: 37-38 figg. 1-2) e, in parte, anche nella domus di località Oredda-Sassari (Antona Ruju e Lo Schiavo 1989: 49-63 figg. 6, 1, 2, 5).

Fra i diversi complessi citati, quello di Littoslongos emerge ulteriormente, e in primo piano, in considerazione del fatto che il contesto materiale così configurato potrebbe essere unitariamente connesso con l'escavazione originaria dell'ipogeo, il cui impianto volumetrico è caratterizzato dalla presenza delle corna rigide inscritte in bassorilievo, in numero di diversi esemplari, sopra il portello di accesso del dromos e verso la cella E (Moravetti 1989: 83-84 figg. 1-3, tav. I, 1). Da ciò deriva, di conseguenza, la possibilità di istituire un organico collegamento formale con il contesto materiale sub-Ozieri e del San Michele classico (pur esso collocabile sul medesimo orizzonte culturale) della Tomba dei vasi tetrapodi di Santu Pedru-Alghero (cfr. supra); anche in questo caso, emergerebbe, dunque, la eventuale associazione tra repertori sub-Ozieri e corna rigide inscritte (Contu 1966: coll. 24-26 fig. 21, tav. VI, 1, 3).

Nell'impianto planovolumetrico di insieme, ben caratterizzato dall'anticella semicircolare ad uno spiovente seguito da vano rettangolare a pilastri, intorno a cui gravitano altri ambienti minori a sviluppo centripeto, si proporrebbero altresì, come ulteriori elementi di valutazione, la plausibile contestuale associazione dei medesimi repertori materiali sia con i motivi della falsa-porta (Contu 1966: coll. 16-17 fig. 22, tav. V, 2) e degli architravi in rilievo (Contu 1966: coll. 19-22, figg. 18-19, tavv. III, V, 3, VI, 2, 5), sia con i pilastri a sezione rettangolare (Contu 1966: coll. 15-17 fig. 20, tavv. III-IV) e con i setti divisori all'interno di celle laterali (Contu 1966: coll. 19-22, tav. IV: cellette f, h). Senza entrare nel merito di approfondimenti comparativi di dettaglio, relativi ai diversi elementi di natura architettonica e rituale, stante l'economia della presente analisi, è comunque utile richiamare, per analogia di principale interesse e di natura esemplificativa, da un lato, la Tomba dell'emiciclo di Sas Concas (Contu 1965: 91-98; Santoni 1976: 13-14 fig. 3, 1), dall'altro, con specifico riferimento alle corna plurime, la domus IV di Brodu, con anticella quadrangolare ad uno spiovente (Contu 1966: coll. 196-200,; Santoni 1976: 13 fig. 3, 3).

Come già per il vaso a piattello emisferico della Tomba V di Pranu Mutteddu-Goni (cfr. supra), così anche per le due fogge vascolari della Tomba II della medesima necropoli (Atzeni e Cocco 1989: 201-16 fig. 1, 2, tav. I fig. 3, 1-2) sussistono i termini congrui per l'attribuzione ad analogo quadro culturale. Sulla base delle osservazioni analitiche introdotte precedentemente in merito alla graduale elaborazione formale del vaso a cestello, l'esemplare documentato nella Tomba II in argomento (Atzeni e Cocco 1989: fig. 3, 1) mostra di riflettere, nella relativa sagoma troncoconica, tozza e goffa, e nella decorazione ricoprente tutte le superfici, ivi compreso il fondo, per una sorta di horror vacui in eccesso, la pertinenza ad un momento culturale successivo, rispetto allo stile canonico del San Michele. Non a caso il vaso troncoconico si raccorda per la sagoma, con l'esemplare inornato di Fig. 1: 14 della sacca 38, per la decorazione a semini lanceolati impressi, econ il vaso a piattello della Tomba V di Goni (cfr. supra).

Pari attribuzione è pure valida per il vaso a pisside (Atzeni e Cocco 1989: fig. 3, 2) decorato pur esso con analoga tecnica e secondo una sintassi grafica perfettamente corrispondente a quella del vasetto troncoconico. La foggia vascolare si richiama infatti alle sagome di Fig. 3: 4-5 di Cuccuru S'Arriu e ad esemplari già noti dell'Antiquarium Arborense di Oristano (Atzeni e Santoni 1989: 19 fig. 7) e, in parte, della grotta di Sa Ucca de su Tintirriolu-Mara (Loria e Trump 1978: 141-42 fig. 1, 16) in cui è documentato l'orizzonte sub-Ozieri.

Come già per il repertorio vascolare, anche per parte dell'industria litica (Atzeni e Cocco 1989: fig. 4, 3-5), stante l'evidente raccordo con quella documentata nella Tomba V, è ovviamente proponibile il medesimo inquadramento tardo-Ozieri. Allo stesso contesto è attribuibile, con ampia verosimiglianza, il frammento di pomo sferoide restituito dalla Tomba II (Atzeni e Cocco 1989: fig. 4, 7) per quanto, in questo caso, si possa sospendere il giudizio definitivo, in attesa di più compiuti termini di valutazione comparativa, considerato che lo strumento preesiste alla cultura Ozieri, in tomba a cista di Arzachena (Lilliu 1967: 30-41 fig. 4, 4) e perdura in orizzonte San Michele in grotta di Terreseu-Santadi (Atzeni 1978: 18 fig. 9, 8).

Così perfezionata l'analisi, si possono certamente apprezzare, con lente individuativa più pertinente, l'intreccio delle correlazioni esistenti nei contesti materiali ancora fortemente legati all'impronta formale ed esornativa dell'Ozieri classico, in una fase ormai mutata di rapporti culturali. Risalta fra gli altri, il contesto della strutture 27 di Su Coddu-Selargius, non casualmente caratterizzato dalla presenza della statuina femminile a placchetta trapezoidale schematica del tipo Senorbì (Ugas et al. 1989: 250 fig. 2, 2), pure attestata a Su Crucifissu Mannu di Porto Torres, in associazione con statuina a traforo (Ferrarese Ceruti 1989: fig. 5, 2).

Sulla base dell'analisi comparativa sinora prospettata, si può ribadire certamente che le ceramiche dipinte attestate negli strati VI-IV della Trincea XXIII di Monte d'Accoddi (Tinè et al. 1989: 19-36; Tinè e Traverso 1990: 4-5) e le evidenze parallele della cap. 160 di Monte Olladiri (Ugas et al. 1989: 239-243), del contesto abitativo di Su Coddu-Selargius (Ugas, Usai et al. 1989: 239-75; Ugas, Lai e Usai 1989: 7-40) e di Terramaini-Pirri (L. Usai 1987: 175-92), con gradualità diversificata, contesto per contesto, si configurino quale fossile-guida nella interposizione o nella sovrapposizione, rispettivamente, del mutamento in corso o dell'avvenuto superamento del repertorio materiale del San Michele classico.

Ad integrazione di questo dato di evidente 'risalto cromatico', il vaso tripode, forma fittile peculiare del San Michele classico, accompagna e ribadisce nel mutamento fittile, i modi della innovazione sub-Ozieri. La sacca n. 38 non restituisce forme integre (Fig. 1: 1, 12) (Cacciatori 1989–90: 106-109). Sulla base dei frammenti di piedi disponibili, possiamo ricomporre idealmente le sagome originarie, tenendo presenti i profili vascolari compiuti e definiti di alcuni dei contesti sub-Ozieri già noti, quali Sa Corona di Villagreca (Atzeni 1966: 123 fig. 12, D), Viale Colombo-Quartu S. Elena (Atzeni 1966 fig. 12, H), grotta A.C.A.I. di Carbonia (Atzeni 1987: 35, 37 fig. 8, 2, 3), strutture nn. 33, 42 di Su Coddu-Selargius (Ugas, Lai e Usai 1989: 24-30 fig. 10, 2; fig. 12, 2), strutture n. 12 e n. 43 del medesimo sito (Ugas et al. 1989: 269-75 fig. 3, 1-2; Ugas et al. 1989: 261-67 fig. 3, 6), Terramaini-Pirri (Atzeni 1966: 123 fig. 12, G; L. Usai 1987: fig. 2, 1-4; fig. 3, 1-2; fig. 4, 1-3) e, infine, lo stesso sito di Cuccuru S'Arriu (Depalmas 1989a: 11; Fig. 2: 14).

In alcune sagome di vasi tripodi si avverte graduale il superamento delle fogge vascolari carenate di tipologia chasseana (Atzeni e Santoni 1989: 175-76 fig. 5, 2; 1989b: 45-48 fig. 25, 1), proprie dell'orizzonte classico San Michele. Sembra essere del tutto assente la foggia a piattello emisferico del tipo documentato a Sa Ucca de su Tintirriolu-Mara e a Cuccuru S'Arriu (Atzeni e Santoni 1989: 175-76 fig. 5, 1) né quelli a vasca emisferica e parete rientrante a gola marcatamente concava del tipo San Gemiliano di Sestu (Atzeni 1962: 76 fig. 16, 9) nei quali è forse rimarcato l'influsso delle sagome a pissidi.

Nei contesti sub-Ozieri non parrebbero altresì documentati anche gli esemplari di profilo carenato, invece presenti nella Tomba III di Anghelu Ruju (Manunza 1990: 49-51 tav. IV, 34), in verosimile associazione con la ceramica graffita (Manunza 1990: tav. IV, 36) e perciò ipotizzabile come meglio pertinente al successivo orizzonte Filigosa, anche per le obiettive comparazioni proponibili con le corrispondenti fogge carenate degli strati VII-VI di Santu Pedru-Alghero (Contu 1966: coll. 49-53, tav. XV, 229, 275). Al riguardo di questa particolare foggia, è altresì utile tenere presenti due sagome analoghe, ma apode, attestate nella stessa Tomba III di Anghelu Ruju (Manunza 1990: tav. IV, 45-46), la cui ornamentazione a metope irregolari di riquadri punteggiati e incisi si ricollega significativamente a temi simili presenti nel contesto culturale di Ortucchio (Radi 1988: 370-77 fig. 18, 6, 12).

A perfezionamento dell'analisi della produzione vascolare, restano da esaminare altri reperti fittili. Più specificatamente trattasi di due rondelle (Fig. 2: 6, 14), di una ghianda missile (Fig. 2: 5) e di un peso da telaio a piastra tronco-piramidale (Fig. 3: 17), di una fusaiola (Fig. 3: 8) e, infine, di alcuni frammenti di anse, per le quali è indeterminabile la foggia vascolare di pertinenza (Figg. 2: 9-10; 3: 17). Per il frammento di ansa di Fig. 2: 10 è plausibilmente pertinente il confronto con il frammento di ansa aculeata della domus dell'Ariete di Perfugas (Lo Schiavo 1982: 144-49, 162-63 fig. 7, 1-2), mentre, per quanto concerne il frammento di Fig. 3: 17, la possibile forma vascolare di pertinenza è individuabile nel reperto di Fig. 1: 4.

Le rondelle o piastre fittili, di forma discoidale sono ben note nei diversi contesti insulari neo-eneolitici, quali Monte d'Accoddi (Contu 1953: 201), Sa Ucca de su Tintirriolu (Loria e Trump 1978: 161 fig. 36, 10), Corte Auda-Senorbì (L. Usai 1986: 149-50 fig. 3, 8), Terramaini (L. Usai 1987: 184-85 fig. 16, 2, 3), Santu Pedru di Alghero (Contu 1966: coll. 151-52, tavv. XXXVI, LVII, b VII, 377) e in ambito culturale Monte Claro (Santu Pedru ed Enna Pruna di Mogoro: Contu 1966: coll. 44, 51-152, tavv. XIV, L, b I, 152). Il tipo di reperto è stato indicato come possibile gettone per gioco, a larga diffusione nei diversi paralleli contesti neo-eneolitici della penisola e, fuori di essa, con ampia ambientazione mediterranea ed europea (Contu 1966: coll. 151-152). Tra i contesti di più congrua pertinenza comparativa, è utile citare gli strati Lagozza delle Arene Candide e di Ripoli della Grotta dei Piccioni (Cremonesi 1976: 200).

Per quanto attiene le ghiande missili, esse sono note, in esemplare unico, nella Tomba III di Anghelu Ruju (Taramelli 1904: 327; Manunza 1990: tav. III, 25), in altri esemplari, pur essi fittili, nel complesso neo-eneolitico di Monte d'Accoddi (Contu 1953: 201) e, in numero di cinque esemplari litici, nella torre capanna Sa Corona di Villagreca (Atzeni 1966: 122 fig. 9, a, 1, 3-6). La fusaiola di Fig. 3: 8 si inserisce entro il quadro variamente attestato nei contesti di Su Coddu (Ugas, Lai, e Usai 1989: 20-22 fig. 8, 3), di Terramaini (L. Usai 1987: fig. 16, 4), di Cuccuru S'Arriu (Atzeni 1978: 5, 8; Depalmas 1989a: 11 tav. III, 17) e dei successivi sviluppi di Fenosu-Palmas Arborea (Lugliè 1989: 95-96 fig. 7, 6-7), di Serra Cannigas di Villagreca (Atzeni 1985: 22-24 tav. II, 4-5), di Filigosa I di Macomer (Foschi Nieddu 1986: 72 tav. 51, 4, 5) e dei collaterali sviluppi di ambito culturale Monte Claro, a Biriai (Castaldi 1981: fig. 20, 18) o ad Isca Maiori-Cabras (Depalmas 1989b: 42-44 fig. 3, 11).

L'esemplare di peso fittile di Fig. 3: 17 si richiama per la forma e per la sezione trapezoidale, pur se irrigidita nel 'passaggio' intervenuto, al peso da telaio fittile con figura schematica incisa, proveniente dalla stazione Ozieri di Conca Illonis-Cabras (Atzeni 1978: 15, 17 tav. VIII). Il rapporto di derivazione diretto è rinforzato dal comune segno al femminile, presente in entrambi i pesi fittili, l'uno segnato dalla figura umana, associata ai motivi abetiformi e ad anelli tratteggiati, l'altro da motivo semiconico, compendiario, dato da due bozze mammillari. Su un piano di collateralità formale e culturale, in quanto attribuibile, con ampia verosimiglianza al quadro sub-Ozieri, dovrebbe invece collocarsi il frammento di peso da telaio a piastra fittile, decorato da motivi antropomorfi schematici, derivato pur esso dalla stazione di Conca Illonis (Atzeni 1988: 449-56 fig. 4, 8).

Altro utile riscontro comparativo è dato dal frammento di peso fittile dell'orizzonte sub-Ozieri di Is Arridelis-Uta (Sanna 1989: fig. 2, 3): esso è rapportabile all'esemplare in argomento, sia per la forma, sia per la sezione trasversa, di profilo trapezoidale, ciò in analogia ai due esemplari di Conca Illonis (cfr. supra), con i quali, peraltro, condivide l'indicazione della cornice incisa entro cui circoscrivere ed evidenziare il tema grafico e in bassorilievo, di plausibile valenza cultuale, che sviluppi paralleli o immediatamente successivi tendono a specializzare nel segno semianiconico di bozze mammillari (peso da telaio di Serra

Cannigas-Villagreca: Atzeni 1985: 22-24 fig. 6, 1) o di coppelle, pur esse di analogo significato (Nuraxinieddu, loc. sconosciuta: Ferrarese Ceruti 1967: 28 fig. 42).

Il segno materno, in positivo e in negativo, quale è sottolineato in forma compendiaria e simbolica nei due pesi da telaio di Serra Cannigas e di Nuraxinieddu (cfr. supra) si ripropone, parallelamente, anche nella nota statua-stele di Serra is Araus di S. Vero Milis (Lilliu 1957: 20 ss.; Atzeni 1962: 194 fig. 33, 26; 1975: 22 fig. 1, 10, tav. XI, 1). Infatti, diversamente dalla versione semiiconica proposta dal Lilliu (1957: 22), ad una lettura più attenta del campo esornativo della statua-stele, si individuano tre coppelline e non due, lungo lo stesso piano orizzontale in cui sono espressi gli 'occhi' della supposta divinità polimazone: la testa si dispone cioè sull'asse verticale del primo rilievo a pastiglia, in alto, verso sinistra, per chi guardi frontalmente la statua-stele; rimarrebbe su un piano inferiore la coppella maggiore individuata come bocca (Lilliu 1957: 22 ss.).

Al tipo di peso da telaio in argomento (Fig. 3: 17) e a variante del coevo contesto sub-Ozieri di Su Coddu-Selargius (strutture n. 33: Ugas, Lai e Usai 1989: 25-30 fig. 11, 2) fanno seguito, con elaborazioni immediatamente successive, gli esemplari a piastra inornata, di attribuzione culturale incerta (sub-Ozieri, Filigosa o Monte Claro?), dei contesti di Campu 'e Cresia-Simaxis (Atzori 1960: fig. 13, 4) e di Molimentos-Benetutti (Ferrarese Ceruti 1967: 110 fig. 29, 1) e di ambito culturale Monte Claro variamente decorato (Biriai-Oliena: Castaldi 1981: fig. 18, 14-15). Su un piano di valore diversificato, si colloca invece il noto peso da telaio, decorato da motivi ad oscilla puntinati, dell'orizzonte culturale Abealzu, da Monte d'Accoddi (SS) (Atzeni *et al.* 1988: 441-48 fig. 2, 12-13). Dal punto divista formale esso mostra di essere una elaborazione parzialmente modificata del tipo di Cuccuru S'Arriu in argomento.

Lo stringente quanto evidente raccordo del motivo simbolico ad oscilla con quelli più noti, dipinti e pendenti dalle corna a fascia orizzontale che sovrastano la falsa porta dell'ipogeo di Mandra Antine-Thiesi (Contu 1965), pone il tema figurato di Monte d'Accoddi in ragionevole rapporto di derivazione diretta dall'episodio di Thiesi, nell'ambito di un comune quadro culturale, che mostra di superare anche in termini diacronici le eventuali interposizioni di stratigrafia materiale.

Fra la restante industria materiale, il frammento di punteruolo in osso di Fig. 3: 2 si ricollega agli esemplari del contesto di Terramaini-Pirri (L. Usai 1987: 185 fig. 16, 6, 8, 9), del sito di Is Arridelis-Uta (Sanna 1989: 232 fig. 3, 14, 23), del nuraghe o torre-capanna di Sa Corona di Villagreca (Atzeni 1966: 122 fig. 8, a), così pure, di Sa Ucca de su Tintirriolu-Mara (Loria e Trump 1978: 160-61, tav. XXXVIII, 11). Fra l'industria litica, l'accettina levigata di Fig. 2: 11 ripropone una foggia trapezoidale di larga diffusione nei contesti San Michele di Ozieri (San Gemiliano di Sestu: Atzeni 1962: 46-47 fig. 11, 5; a Sa Ucca de su Tintirriolu: Loria e Trump 1978: 157-58 fig. 32, 15; Su Pirastu-Ussana: A. Usai 1985: 39-40 fig. 5, 9). Essa perdura poi in uso in ambito sub-Ozieri con esemplari sporadici (cap. 51, Su Coddu-Selargius: Ugas, Lai e Usai 1989: 22-23 fig. 16; Littoslongos-Ossi: Moravetti 1989: 88, 99 fig. 5, 12; Sa Corona-Villagreca: Atzeni 1966: 122 fig. 9, 2). Sembrerebbe venir meno, invece, nell'orizzonte Filigosa, almeno sulla base di quanto sinora noto sull'argomento; ciò diversamente dal parallelo quadro materiale Monte Claro (cfr. Biriai-Oliena: Castaldi 1981: 204-207 fig. 24, 3).

Fra lo strumentario in ossidiana, la cuspide foliacea di Fig. 3: 7 ben si confronta con esemplare affatto analogo della struttura 16 F di Su Coddu (Ugas, Lai e Usai 1989: 34 fig. 15, 2) e con un altro strumento foliaceo di Sa Ucca de su Tintirriolu (Loria e Trump 1978: 158-59 fig. 33, 6) dove, peraltro, ripropone ulteriori riferimenti comparativi la punta di freccia triangolare peduncolata a base concava di Fig. 3: 12 (Loria e Trump 1978: figg. 33, 7; 34, 12), pure presente a Monte Olladiri (Atzeni 1962: 119-20 fig. 21, 2, tav. XXVI, 2). Diversamente dal quadro di relazioni generiche istituibili, tra i contesti insulari, per la punta di freccia di Fig. 3: 12, l'esemplare triangolare con alette ricurve, a base concava, di Fig. 1: 11 è invece affatto analogo agli esemplari in selce bruna della cella E della Tomba XVII di Anghelu Ruju (Taramelli 1909: col. 446 fig. 49, 1) e a quello, in ossidiana(?) della Tomba dipinta di Mandra Antine di Thiesi (Contu 1964: 241-43 fig. 7, 2).

In riferimento al primo esemplare algherese, è utile evidenziare come dalla medesima Tomba XVII, di planimetria a T, pluricellulare (Taramelli 1909: col. 442 fig. 28), provengano anche tre punteruoli in rame, di sezione rettangolare (Taramelli 1909: col. 445 fig. 31, 7, 9) del tipo di Cuccuru S'Arriu (Fig. 2: 3) e alcuni vasi tripodi con 'piedi a lunga lingua acuminatissima' (Taramelli 1909: col. 443), peraltro collegabili al frammento di Fig. 1: 1. Da ultimo, il punteruolo in rame di Fig. 2: 3, che si aggiunge agli esemplari noti del settore F di Cuccuru S'Arriu (Atzeni 1981: XL, n. 105) e della Tomba A di Serra Cannigas-Villagreca (Atzeni 1985: 28-30 fig. 7, 14) si richiama alla produzione metallurgica analoga, del primo orizzonte eneolitico occidentale interno ed esterno all'isola (Lo Schiavo 1989: 286), con più vicino termine comparativo nell'ambito della cultura di Remedello (Acanfora 1956: 348-56, 9 fig. 7).

A conclusione dell'analisi, è possibile trarre talune indicazioni di larga massima, non certo esaustive e idonee a risolvere e a chiarire il quadro complessivo del fenomeno sub-Ozieri quanto piuttosto per lasciare traccia più dei punti interrogativi, che non invece delle certezze. D'altro canto, è pur vero che a fronte della unitarietà del fenomeno quale venuto in luce in alcuni contesti distinti (Cuccuru S'Arriu, Is Arridelis, Terramaini), fanno riscontro situazioni meno definite e ancora in progress, sia in ordine all'apprezzamento delle relazioni interne ai singoli contesti, sia in merito al quadro conoscitivo delle relative documentazioni di scavo (Su Coddu, Monte d'Accoddi, Monte Olladiri, Su Crucifissu Mannu).

Le indicazioni di relazione con altri contesti possono trovare i limiti nella frammentarietà delle informazioni sui depositi stratigrafici. Tuttavia, sulla base dei dati disponibili e delle correlazioni connesse, sembra di riconoscere come pertinente all'orizzonte sub-Ozieri l'insieme dell'architettura palaziale del tipo Santu Pedru di Alghero e della Tomba dell'Emiciclo di Sas Concas di Oniferi, così pure di quelle domus con elaborazione planimetrica a sviluppo longitudinale, evidentemente influenzate dal megalitismo funerario subaereo delle allées, quale è dato di riconoscere, in particolar modo, nell'esemplare della Tomba IV di Brodu di Oniferi caratterizzata dalla presenza delle corna rigida inscritte.

Non è improbabile che il fenomeno possa abbracciare altri termini dell'evoluzione funzionale corrispondente alla II fase dell'ipogeismo, quale fu individuata per linee generali, in anni passati (Santoni 1976). L'episodio monumentale di Monte d'Accoddi dà piena legittimità formale al coinvolgimento entro questo ambito culturale della Tomba Branca o Moreddu di Cheremule, in quanto essa propone, nella sostanza, analogo schema iconografico, accogliendo poi, i toni innovativi dei petroglifi schematici, antropomorfi, a braccia alzate, pure presenti nella Tomba dell'Emiciclo di Sas Concas (Contu 1965).

Fra le planimetrie ipogeiche di particolare distinzione, idonee a far parte di questo momento culturale, sono altresì da comprendere il tipo cruciforme (Littoslongos; Molimentos?) in quanto caratterizzato dai motivi scolpiti delle corna rigide, quale parallela elaborazione formale corrispondente, nel segno di origine, alle statuine cicladiche. Rimangono incerti, invece i confini di pertinenza di taluni tipi ipogeici a T o a sviluppo centripeto, già attribuiti alla II fase dell'ipogeismo (Santoni 1976) (Tombe III, XVII, Anghelu Ruju; Tomba dipinta di Mandra Antine) per quanto la presenza massiccia del segno del colore e del relativo disegno grafico possa coinvolgere nel mutamento anche taluni importanti episodi di questo quadro San Michele, sinora attribuito al suo orizzonte classico. Emerge in tutta evidenza lo stringente rapporto con l'elaborazione megalitica subaerea (Pranu Mutteddu-Goni).

Rimangono invece da definire i confini areali di merito con il successivo quadro di elaborazione materiale Filigosa, quale è sinora meglio noto nel deposito stratigrafico di Santu Pedru di Alghero, di San Giuseppe di Padria e nel sito eponimo di Filigosa, nel quale ultimo, si apprezzano più evidenti interferenze e connessioni formali con il quadro Monte Claro. Per vero di quest'ultimo si individuano avvisaglie e parallelismi legittimi già dal pieno dell'orizzonte sub-Ozieri.

Sono incontri e raccordi tutti da meglio comprendere e circoscrivere con successive analisi. Sulla base dei riscontri esterni proposti, si può ritenere che i tempi di maturazione dell'orizzonte sub-Ozieri (anche quelli ancora legati alla matrice Ozieri) tendano ad assestarsi, con ampia verosimiglianza, nei primi momenti dell'eneolitico peninsulare e siciliano, ciò determinando una possibile dilatazione del quadro classico Filigosa verso momenti dell'eneolitico medio, in possibile raccordo con le parallele fasi Piano Conte-Serraferlicchio, così da porre la fase conclusiva di Abealzu-Monte d'Accoddi in sicronia con l'orizzonte di Rinaldone e delle culture di Malpasso-Piano Quartara (Santoni e Usai in stampa).

Bibliografia

Acanfora, O.
1956   Funtanella Mantovana e la cultura di Remedello. *Bollettino di Paletnologia Italiana* 10(55): 321-85.

Antona Ruju, A., & F. Lo Schiavo
1989   Oredda-Sassari, la domus delle doppie spirali. In L.D. Campus (a cura di), *La Cultura di Ozieri. Problematiche e nuove acquisizioni*, 49-74. Ozieri: Il Torchietto.

Aranguren, B., & P. Perazzi
1984   L'insediamento preistorico di Podere Casanuova (Pontedera, Pisa): Nota preliminare, con Appendice di G. Cellai e P. Paoli. *Rivista di Scienze Preistoriche* 39(1-2): 301-19.

Atzeni, E.
1962   I villaggi preistorici di San Gemiliano di Sestu e di Monte Olladiri di Monastir preso Cagliari e le ceramiche della 'facies' di Monte Claro. *Studi Sardi* 17(1959-61): 3-216.
1966   Il nuraghe 'Sa Corona' di Villagreca (Cagliari). *Atti del XIII Congresso di Storia dell'Architettura (Sardegna), Cagliari 6-12 aprile 1963*, 119-26.
1975   Nuovi idoli della Sardegna prenuragica. *Studi Sardi* 23(1973-74): 3-51.

1978 La dea-madre nelle culture prenuragiche. *Studi Sardi* 24(1975–77): 3-69.
1981 Aspetti e sviluppi culturali del neolitico e della prima età dei metalli in Sardegna. In E. Atzeni *et al.* (eds.), *Ichnussa: La Sardegna dalle origini all'età classica*, 19-51. Milano: Libri Scheiwiller.

Atzeni, E., & D. Cocco
1989 Nota sulla necropoli megalitica de Pranu Muttedu-Goni. In L.D. Campus (a cura di), *La Cultura di Ozieri. Problematiche e nuove acquisizioni, Ozieri 1989*, 201-16. Ozieri: Il Torchietto.

Atzeni, E., E. Contu & M. Ferrarese Ceruti
1988 L'età del rame nell'Italia peninsulare: La Sardegna. *Rassegna di Archeologia* 7: 441-65.

Atzeni, E., & V. Santoni
1989 L'età prenuragica. Il Neolitico. L'Eneolitico. *Il Museo Archeologico Nazionale di Cagliari*, 31-56. Milano.

Atzori, G.
1960 Stazioni prenuragiche e nuragiche di Simaxis (OR). *Studi Sardi* 16(1958–59): 267-83.

Bernabò Brea, L.
1956 *Gli Scavi nella Caverna delle Arene Candide (Finale Ligure). Parte I: Gli strati con ceramiche. II. Campagne di scavo 1948-1950.* Bordighera.

Bernabò Brea, L., & M. Cavalier
1960 Stazioni preistoriche delle isole Eolie. *Bollettino di Paletnologia Italiana* 11(66): 97-152.
1980 *Meligunis Lipara IV. L'acropoli di Lipari nella preistoria*. Palermo.

Broglio, A., & L. Fasani
1975 Le valli di Fimon nella preistoria. 5-59.

Cacciatori, A.
1989–90 La cappanna n. 38 dell'abitato preistorico di Cuccuru S'Arriu—Cabras (Oristano). Tesi di Laurea, Università degli Studi di Firenze.

Castaldi, E.
1981 Villaggio con santuario a Biriai (Oliena-Nuoro). II relazione preliminare. *Rivista di Scienze Preistoriche* 36(1-2): 153-221.

Contu, E.
1953 Costruzione megalitica in località Monte d'Accoddi (Sassari). *Rivista di Scienze Preistoriche* 8: 199-202.
1964 Tombe preistoriche dipinte e scolpite di Thiesi e Bessude (Sassari). *Rivista di Scienze Preistoriche* 19: 233-63.
1965 Nuovi petroglifi schematici della Sardegna. *Bollettino di Paletnologia Italiana* 16(74): 69-122.
1966 La tomba dei vasi tetrapodi. *Monumenti Antichi* 47: 1-196.

Cremonesi, G.
1976 *La Grotta dei Piccioni di Bolognano nel Quadro delle Ceramiche dal Neolitico all'Età del Bronzo in Abruzzo*. Pisa.

Demartis, G., & V. Canalis
1989 La tomba II di Mesu 'e Montes (Ossi-Sassari). *Nuovo Bullettino Archeologico Sardo* 2(1985): 41-74.

Depalmas, A.
1989a I materiali fittili di Cuccuru S'Arriu nella Collezione Falchi di Oristano. *Quaderni della Soprintendenza Archeologica per le Provincie di Cagliari ed Oristano* 6: 5-18.
1989b Il materiale preistorico di Isca Maiori nella collezione Falchi di Oristano. *Studi Sardi* 28: 37-59.

Ferrarese Ceruti, M.L.
1967 'Domus de janas' in località Molimentos (Benetutti-Sassari). *Bollettino di Paletnologia Italiana* 18(76): 69-135.
1989 La necropoli di Su Crucifissu Mannu-Porto Torres e di Ponte Secco-Sassari. In L.D. Campus (a cura di), *La Cultura di Ozieri. Problematiche e nuove acquisizioni*, 37-47. Ozieri: Il Torchietto.

Foschi Nieddu, A.
1986 *La Tomba I di Filigosa (Macomer-Nuoro). Alcune considerazioni sulla cultura di Abealzu-Filigosa nel contesto eneolitico della Sardegna*. Nuoro.

Galli, F., V. Santoni & G. Tore
1988 Padria. *L'Antiquarium Arborense e i Civici Musei Archeologici della Sardegna*, 117-28. Milano.

Lilliu, G.
1957 Religione della Sardegna prenuragic. *Bollettino di Paletnologia Italiana* 66: 7-96.
1967 *La Civiltà dei Sardi. Dal neolitico all'età dei nuraghi*. Torino: ERI.

Lo Schiavo, F.
1982 La domus dell'Ariete (Perfugas-Sassari), con appendice di G. Pitzalis. *Rivista di Scienze Preistoriche* 37(1-2): 135-86.
1989 Le origini della metallurgia ed il problema della metallurgia nella cultura di Ozieri. In L.D. Campus (a cura di), *La Cultura di Ozieri. Problematiche e nuove acquisizioni*, 279-91. Ozieri: Il Torchietto.

Loria, R., & D. Trump
1978 Le scoperte a Sa 'Ucca de Su Tintirriolu e il neolitico Sardo. *Monumenti Antichi* 49: 115-253.

Lugliè, C.
1989 Ceramiche eneolithice dall'insediamenti di Fenosu-Palmas Arborea (Oristano). *Studi Sardi* 28: 73-100.

Manunza, M.
1990 La tomba III di Anghelu Ruju-Alghero (Sassari). *Quaderni della Soprintendenza Archeologica per le Provincie di Cagliari ed Oristano* 7: 43-61.

Marconi Bovio, J.
1944 La cultura tipo Conca d'Oro della Sicilia Nord-occidentale. *Monumenti Antichi*.

Moravetti, A.
1989 La tomba ipogeica di Littoslongos-Ossi. In L.D. Campus (a cura di), *La Cultura di Ozieri. Problematiche e nuove acquisizioni*, 83-101. Ozieri: Il Torchietto.

Puxeddu, C.
1962 Nota preliminare sulla stazione prenuragica e nuragica di Puisteris-Mogoro (Cagliari). *Studi Sardi* 17(1959–61): 217-59.

Quojani, F.
1975 Indagini nella necropoli di Capaci. Nuovi aspetti l;ocali e loro connessioni con la cultura della Conca d'Oro. *Origini* 9: 225-71.

Radi, G.
1988 L'eneolitico in Abruzzo. *Rassegna di Archeologia* 7: 370-77.

Sanna, R.
1989 Il villaggio di Is Arridelis-Uta. In L.D. Campus (a cura di), *La Cultura di Ozieri. Problematiche e nuove acquisizioni*, 231-41. Ozieri: Il Torchietto.

Santoni, V.
1976 Nota preliminare sulla tipologia delle grotticelle funerarie in Sardegna. *Archivio Storico Sardo* 30: 3-49.
1977 Cabras (Prov. di Oristano). Cuccuru S'Arriu, Notiziario. *Rivista di Scienze Preistoriche* 32(1-2): 350-53.

1982   Il mondo del sacro in età neolitica. *Le Scienze*, ottobre, 70-80.

1989   Cuccuru S'Arriu-Cabras. Il sito di cultura San Michele di Ozieri. Dati preliminari. In L.D. Campus (a cura di), *La Cultura di Ozieri. Problematiche e nuove acquisizioni*, 169-200. Ozieri: Il Torchietto.

Santoni, V., E. Atzeni, R. Forresu, S. Giorgetti, M. Mongiu, S. Sebis, A. Siddu & G. Tore

1982   Cabras, Cuccuru S'Arriu. Nota preliminare di scavo (1978, 1979, 1980). *Rivista di Studi Fenici* 10(1): 103-27.

Taramelli, A.

1904   Scavi nella necropoli preistorica a grotte artificiali di Anghelu Ruju. *Notizie degli Scavi* 1904: 301-51.

1909   Alghero. Nuovi scavi nella necropoli preistorica a grotte artificiali di Anghelu Ruju. *Monumenti Antichi* 19: 317-540.

Tinè, S.

1965   Gli scavi nella grotta della Chiusazza. *Bollettino di Paletnologia Italiana* 16(74): 123-286.

Tinè, S., S. Bafico, G. Rossi & T. Mannoni

1989   Monte d'Accoddi e la cultura di Ozieri. In L.D. Campus (a cura di), *La Cultura di Ozieri. Problematiche e nuove acquisizioni*, 19-36. Ozieri: Il Torchietto.

Tinè, S., & A. Traverso

1990   Relazione preliminare al colloquio sul santuario di Monte d'Accoddi: 10 anni di nuovi scavi. Sassari 18-20 ottobre 1990: ciclostilato.

Trump, D.

1983   La Grotta Filiestru a Bonu Ighinu, Mara (SS). *Quaderni* 13. Sassari: Dessì

Ugas, G., G. Lai & L. Usai

1989   L'insediamento prenuragico di Su Coddu (Selargius-CA). *Nuovo Bullettino Archeologico Sardo* 2(1985): 7-40.

Ugas, G., L. Usai, M. Nuvoli, G. Lai & M. Marras

1989   Nuovi dati sull'insediamento di Su Coddu-Selargius. In L.D. Campus (a cura di), *La Cultura di Ozieri. Problematiche e nuove acquisizioni*, 239-75. Ozieri: Il Torchietto.

Usai, A.

1985   La stazione preistorica di Su Pirastu (Ussana-Cagliari). *Almanacco della Sardegna* 1985: 27-78.

Usai, L.

1986   Tracce di insediamenti dalla preistoria al medioevo in loc. Corte Auda di Senorbì (Sardegna). *Studi per l'Ecologia del Quaternario* 8: 147-67.

1987   Il villaggio di età eneolitica di Terramaini presso (Pirri) Cagliari. *Atti del IV Convegno Nazionale di Preistoria e Protostoria—Pescia 8-9 dicembre 1984*, 175-92. Pescia.

Usai, L., & V. Santoni

In stampa   La domus XII di Cannas di Sotto—Carbonia e l'eneolitico in Sardegna. *Carbonia e il Sucis. Archeologia e territorio*.

Weiss, M.-C., & F. de Lanfranchi

1976   Le civilisations neolithiques en Corse. *La Prehistoire Française, Tome II*, 432-42.

Zanardelli, T.

1899   Le stazioni preistoriche e lacumaresi nel Campidano di Oristano. *Bullettino di Paletnologia Italiana* 25: 8-177.

Summary

Cuccuru S'Arriu (Cabras-OR), an open-air site well known for its Middle and Late Neolithic levels, also contains a sub-Ozieri component which is transitional between the classic San Michele and the mature Chalcolithic period. Sectors A and F have clearly separate settlements of sub-oval, partly sunken huts, from which the sacca 38 finds are examined in detail. The Author reviews the finds from this refuse area in order to clarify the differences between Ozieri, sub-Ozieri, Abealzu and Filigosa, and relates them to objects found at other Sardinian sites.

Among the finds are ceramics, mostly fragmentary, and tools in obsidian, stone, bone and copper (bronze?). The ceramics include biconical, tronconic and carenated forms, basket-vases, pans, plates, jars and tripods. These are almost always decorated, with incised festoons, zig-zag lines, or with bands of dots, in some cases clearly made by impressing seeds and mats. While clearly continuing the decorative syntax of the classic Ozieri culture, some of these elements are innovative, particularly the use of curves and circles.

These decorative motifs are comparable to those from Is Arridelis di Uta, another open-air site, the necropolis of Su Crucifissu Mannu di Porto Torres, Terramaini-Pirri (Cagliari), and Su Cungiau de Is Fundamentas-Simaxis, among others. Parallels among loom-weights, bone tools and Cycladic-type figurines at these sites are also noted.

The Author connects the sub-Ozieri horizon at Cuccuru S'Arriu with the architecture exhibited at Santu Pedru (Alghero), the Tomba dell'Emiciclo di Sas Concas (Oniferi), the elongated tombs apparently influenced by the *allèes couvertes*, and especially with the megalithic elaboration of sites like Pranu Mutteddu. Inscribed bulls' horn reliefs are also associated with sub-Ozieri sites.

Finally, it is suggested that the sub-Ozieri is contemporary with the early chalcolithic of Sicily and the Italian mainland, with the subsequent Filigosa period possibly coinciding with the Piano Conte-Serraferlicchio phase, and Abealzu-Monte d'Accoddi with the Rinaldone horizon.

PART II

Nuragic Architecture and Settlement

Tipologie Nuragiche:
I Protonuraghi con Corridoio Passante

Lucia Manca Demurtas e Sebastiano Demurtas

Distribuzione geografica

Il tipo di nuraghe che viene qui esaminato rientra nella classe dei 'Protonuraghi' di cui si è ritenuto di poter enucleare una varietà specifica per schema planimetrico interno (Manca Demurtas e Demurtas 1984a: 635; 1984b: 174) e si è denominato con 'corridoio passante' (Manca Demurtas e Demurtas 1991).

L'indagine, tutt'ora in corso, ha portato all'individuazione di 280 protonuraghi, distribuiti in tal modo: 70 nella provincia di Sassari, 100 nella provincia di Nuoro, 65 nella provincia di Oristano e 45 in quella di Cagliari. In una superficie di km^2 24.090 dell'intera Sardegna si calcola la densità media di un protonuraghe ogni km^2 86. La provincia di Oristano è quella che presenta il valore più alto di un protonuraghe ogni km^2 40,5 in rapporto alla sua estensione territoriale di km^2 2.630; segue la provincia di Nuoro con un protonuraghe ogni km^2 70,4 in un'estensione di km^2 7.044, poi la provincia di Sassari con un protonuraghe ogni km^2 107,4 in un'estensione di km^2 7.520 ed infine la provincia di Cagliari con un protonuraghe ogni km^2 153,2 con un'estensione di km^2 6.896.

Rispetto alla tipologia individuata si hanno i seguenti dati (Fig. 1A):

Tipo I	Pieno	(n=1:	0,4%)
Tipo II	a) a rampa esterna avvolgente	(n=1:	2,5%)
	b) corridoio a rampa interna diretta	(n=6:	25,%)
Tipo III	Corridoio passante	(n=55:	19,6%)
Tipo IV	Corridoio contenuto	(n=36:	12,9%)
Tipo V	Naviforme	(n=20:	7,1%)

Non determinabili: (n=161: 57,5%) per l'impossibilità di un rilevamento corretto ma facilmente individuabili.

Del tipo III si contano 9 nella provincia di Sassari, 21 nella provincia di Nuoro, 20 nella provincia di Oristano e 5 in quella di Cagliari (cf. Fig. 2 e Appendice). La provincia di Nuoro presenta il valore di 38,2%, segue Oristano con 36,4%, Sassari con 16,4% e Cagliari con 9,1% (Fig. 1B). Per un quadro conoscitivo più ampio si ripropone la distribuzione dei protonuraghi di tale tipo per referenti non più di tipo 'amministrativo' come le provincie, ma per ambiti geografici differenziati, per regioni storico-geografiche, per altimetria e rispetto all'idrografia. Al momento si notano presenze isolate nella Sardegna settentrionale in Gallura (S. Francesco d'Aglientu; Tempio); nel Monte Acuto (Ittireddu); nel Meilogu (Thiesi; Torralba; Bonorva). Una forte concentrazione nella Sardegna centro-occidentale nella Planargia (Suni; Sagama); nel Marghine (Bolotana; Macomer; Birori; Bortigali; Dualchi); nella Media Valle del Tirso (Aidomaggiore; Sedilo); nell'Altopiano di Abbasanta (Norbello; Ghilarza; Paulilatino; Bauladu); nel Montiferro (Bonarcado; Seneghe; Milis); nel Barigadu (Fordongianus). Ancora presenze isolate nella Sardegna centrale, nel Nuorese (Orotelli; Mamoiada; Fonni); nella Marmilla (Genoni); nel Sarcidano (Nurri); nella Trexenta-Parteolla (Donori); nelle pendici occidentali del Sarrabus-Gerrei (Sinnai) e nell'Iglesiente (Gonnesa).

Il materiale usato è di provenienza locale e risulta prevalente l'uso del basalto in quanto le regioni interessate dalla presenza dei protonuraghi presentano in superficie strati rocciosi di origine vulcanica (Meilogu, Monte Acuto, Planargia, Marghine, Montiferro, Media Valle del Tirso) mentre risulta minoritario l'utilizzo del granito (Gallura, Marghine, Nuorese, Marmilla, Sarrabus). Per quanto riguarda le altimetrie (Fig. 3), tali monumenti si dislocano preferibilmente tra i m 300 e i 400 s.l.m. in corrispondenza di aree collinari e ad altopiano. Abbastanza numerosi anche tra 0 e m 300, mentre si riducono notevolmente nelle aree che superano i m 400. L'altezza massima di m 885 s.l.m. si raggiunge con il protonuraghe Hastru Longu-Fonni (Nuoro) e la minima di m 68 col nuraghe Finucchiaglia-San Francesco d'Aglientu (Sassari).

I protonuraghi con corridoio passante si

ATTESTAZIONE TIPOLOGIE PROTONURAGHI (280)

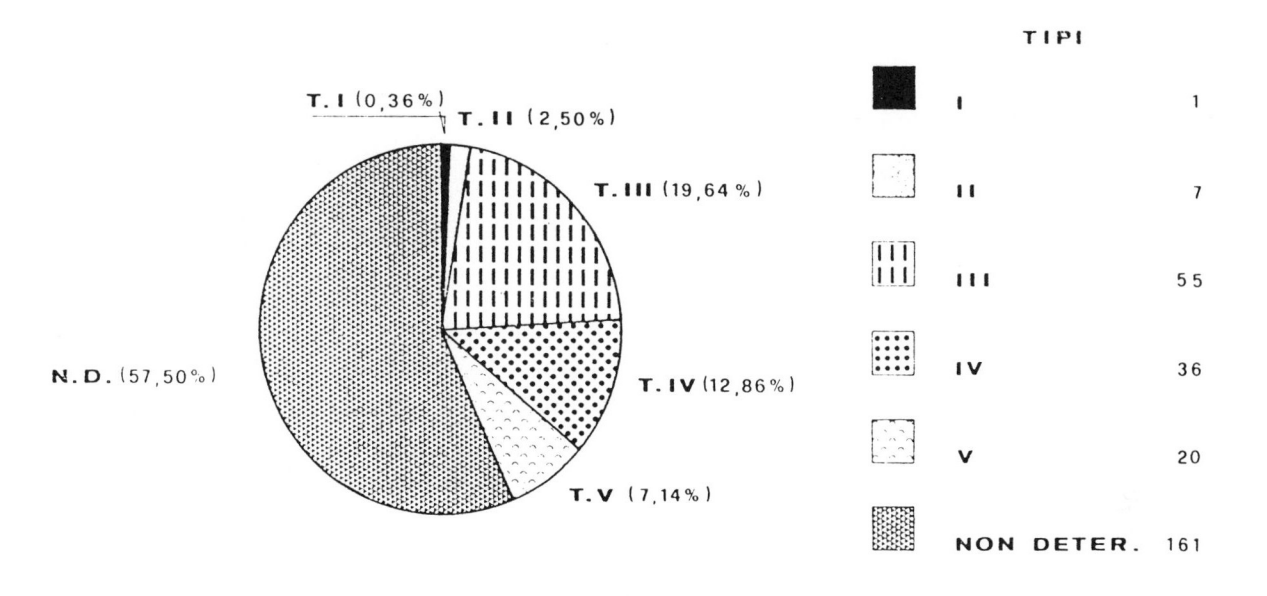

TIPI		
I		1
II		7
III		55
IV		36
V		20
NON DETER.		161

T.I (0,36%)
T.II (2,50%)
T.III (19,64%)
T.IV (12,86%)
T.V (7,14%)
N.D. (57,50%)

A

PROTONURAGHI CON CORRIDOIO PASSANTE (55)

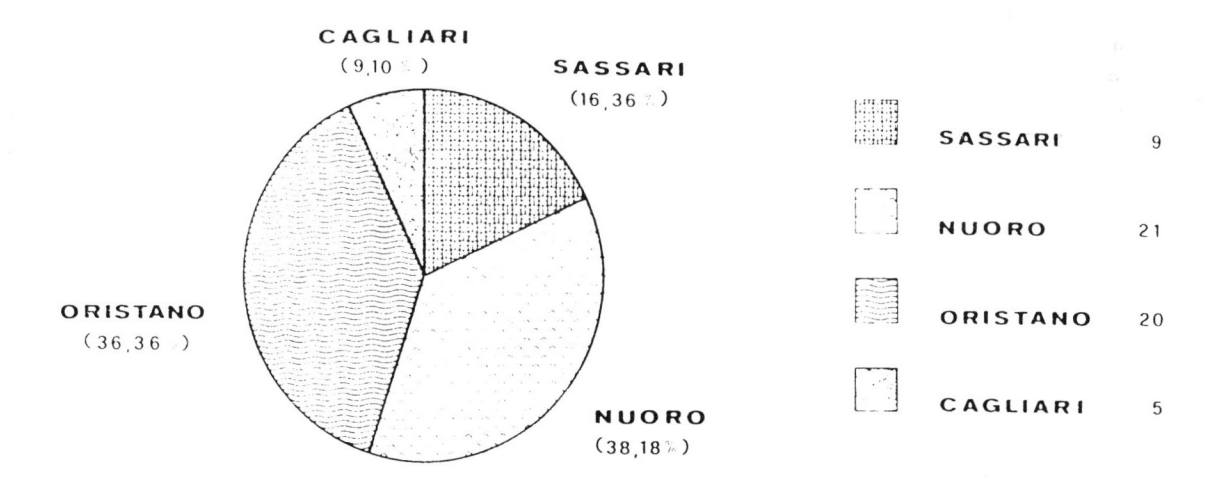

CAGLIARI (9,10)
SASSARI (16,36)
ORISTANO (36,36)
NUORO (38,18)

SASSARI		9
NUORO		21
ORISTANO		20
CAGLIARI		5

B

Fig. 1 (A) Grafico sulla tipologia dei protonuraghi; (B) Grafico illustrativo sulla distribuzione in percentuale dei protonuraghi con corridoio passante per provincia.

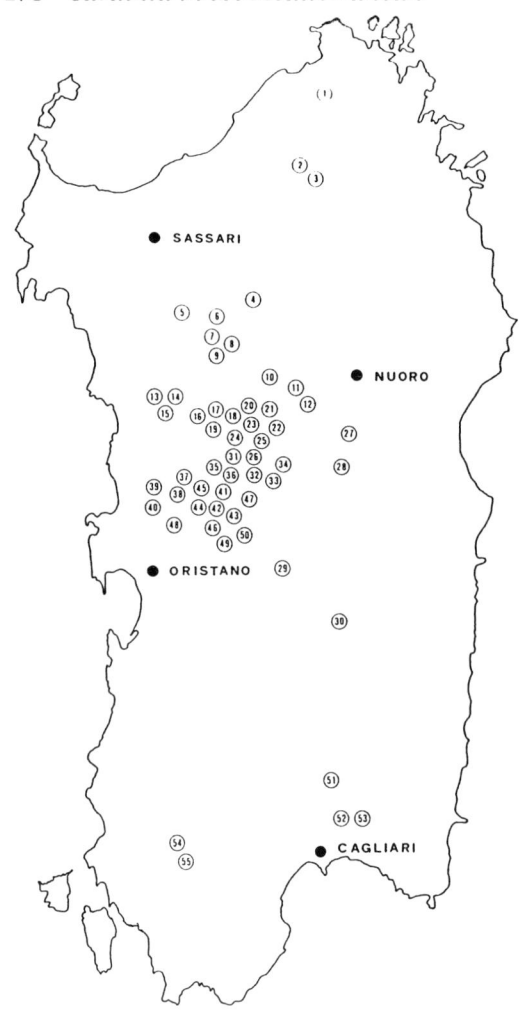

Fig. 2 Distribuzione dei protonuraghi con corridoio passante (guardare l'appendiche).

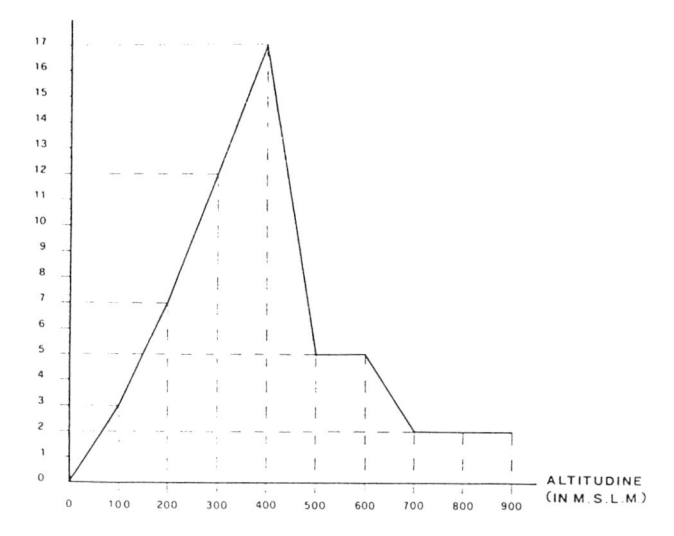

Fig. 3 Diagramma di distribuzione dei protonuraghi con corridoio passante in funzione dell'altitudine.

Problematica

Viene presentata una tipologia nuragica, quella dei 'Protonuraghi', modello architettonico di monumentalità specifica della Sardegna che con gli esempi di Sa Corona (Villagreca-CA) (Atzeni 1966: 121; 1981: xlv; 1985: 41; Lilliu 1982: 13) e del Brunku Madugui (Gesturi-CA) (Lilliu 1982: 13) sono stati ritenuti nella letteratura archeologica un elemento unificante per lo sviluppo progressivo verso il nuraghe a 'tholos' o 'vero' nuraghe (Dessi 1922: 12; Lilliu 1988: 181) accentuatamente sviluppatosi nell'Isola nell'età del Bronzo (1800–1400 a.C.). Ma il termine 'protonuraghe' ha, oggi, interpretazioni differenti corrispondenti alla soggettività di lettura architettonica. A nostro parere, l'uso puntuale del termine 'protonuraghe' (Manca Demurtas e Demurtas 1984a: 631; 1984b: 167) per indicare un monumento completo di corridoio, spazi interni e copertura con lastre in giacitura orizzontale, ha costituito una differenziazione. Infatti, datisi momenti di acquisizione di una preparazione tecnica mediante elementi fruiti precedentemente nel Calcolitico (Manca Demurtas e Demurtas in stampa C), si ebbe successivamente lo sviluppo della copertura 'voltata.'

Protonuraghe, è quindi, come svolgimento architettonico verso la 'tholos', il risultato finale di un processo di innalzamento di un vuoto costruito in funzione di un sistema di copertura; nuraghe a tutti gli effetti e non forma deviante e sconnessa di un processo evolutivo che si suppone autoctono (diversamente, con la definizione di pseudonuraghe: Dessi 1922: 12; Santoni 1980:

situano alternativamente o su un bassopiano con vicini corsi d'acqua (Ponte Etzu, S'Ena S. Juanni) o su un altopiano con sorgenti (Funtana Suei, Mura Fratta, Scarlozza, Ulinu) o su una pendice collinare con vicino un torrente (Galla, Liori, Canchedda, Mene, Pruna). Alcuni della stessa tipologia ma complessi (Abbaia A, Biriola, Frontelizzos) su un bassopiano, sempre in prossimità di corsi d'acqua. Molti, comunque, sembrano prediligere come posizione topografica il margine o parti interne di altopiani; altri si dislocano lungo pendii talvolta terrazzati di versanti vallivi o, meno frequentemente, sulla sommità di piccoli rialzi collinari e sul fondo di una vallata. Si riscontra, pertanto, un'effettiva scelta in prossimità di corsi d'acqua o sorgenti, di vie naturali con funzione di controllo di un territorio limitato. Insediamenti che sorgono in rapporto a linee di comunicazione; come epicentri, invece, quelli di maggiore mole e complessità, come simbolo di una forma di difesa collettiva per i beni di una società che si ipotizza in condizioni non conflittuali.

Sebastiano Demurtas

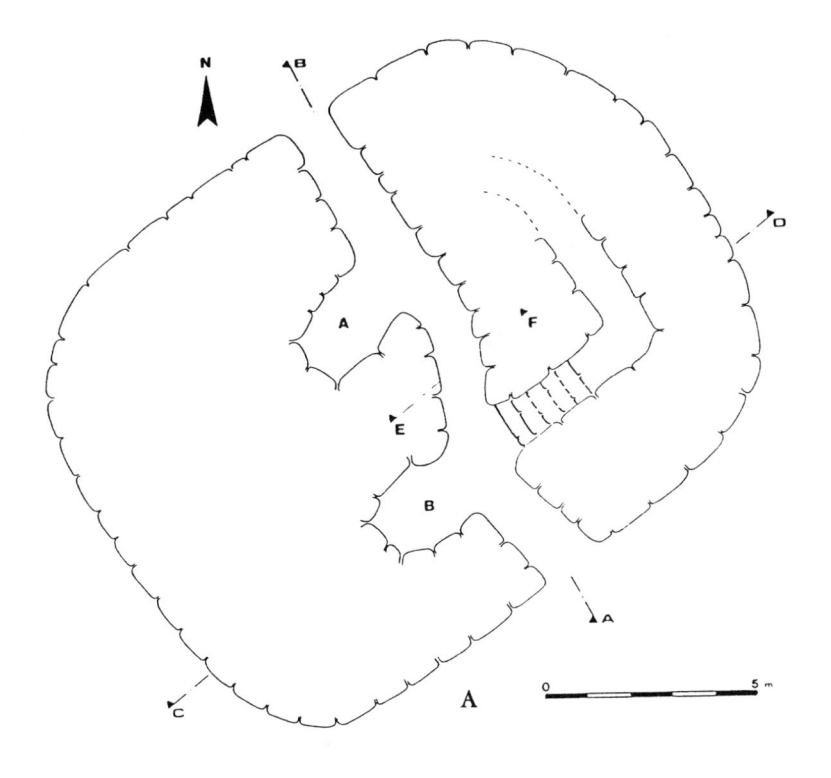

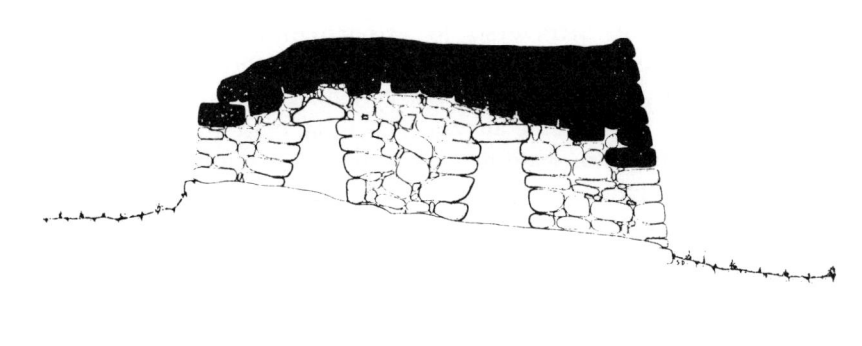

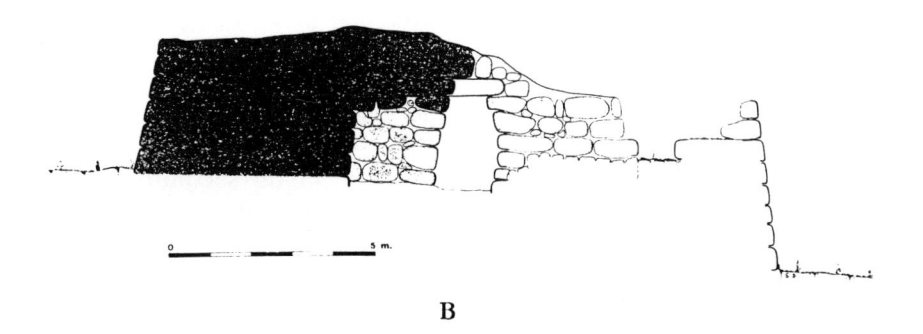

Fig. 4 Protonuraghe Funtana Suei (Norbello-OR). (A) Pianta; (B) Sezioni.

154 o di nuraghe a corridoio: Contu 1981: 45; Lilliu 1982: 30). I dati attuali (Manca Demurtas e Demurtas 1984a: 640; 1984b: 187; 1987: 497; Ugas 1987: 78-79) portano a localizzare l'inserimento dei protonuraghi già a partire dal Bronzo antico e nelle fasi del Bronzo medio. Tuttavia, non può essere formulato in senso assoluto un dato cronologico dal momento che tale tipo di monumento, se per certi aspetti architettonici parrebbe costituire il precedente del tipo a 'tholos', nello stesso tempo non può esserne esclusa una certa contemporaneità vista la presenza di materiali di una stessa cultura (Sub-Bonnanaro) (Lilliu 1988: 318) in monumenti ad uso civile (protonuraghi, nuraghi a 'tholos' e villaggi) (Manca Demurtas e Demurtas 1984a: 639; 1984b: 184; Ugas 1987: 78, 104; Sebis 1986: 19) e funerario (tombe di giganti a struttura ortostatica e a stele centinata) (Lilliu 1988: 318-19).

Escludendo una frattura nella elaborazione dei due differenti prodotti, si evidenzia la potenzialità del protonuraghe che delinea modelli in planimetrie varie come risultato di tecnica costruttiva a filari ciclopici quale sviluppo terminale del paramento a filari. Espressione, questo, di un sistema di innalzamento di muri che nel Calcolitico si documenta a circoscrivere aree di frequentazione con scopo di difesa e di controllo di risorse. Pertanto, i costruttori hanno maturato gradatamente l'espressione 'Nuraghe' attraverso lo sviluppo di fattori di validità per una forma elevantesi. Ciò ottenendosi con paramenti (esterno ed interno) fino ad una certa presumibile altezza media di m 5-6, corridoi di transito, scale per la parte alta del monumento, sistema di copertura: struttura poliedrica a filari irregolari di massi al naturale, connessi dal sistema di incastro. Tale tipologia non raggiungendo un'unità definita, si manifesta con la varietà planimetrica. Costituisce, quindi, un termine di confronto con la classe dei nuraghi a 'tholos.' Questa, pur nella varietà delle composizioni (torre singola o plurima), rappresenta l'unità architettonica, utilizzo di un'unica soluzione architettonica che è la 'tholos', in quanto punto conclusivo di una forma funzionale in altezza.

In base ai dati di ricerca, in corso, si riscontra un alto indice di diffusione di protonuraghi. Tale alto rapporto di densità-spazio potrebbe esplicarsi nella proposta di lettura di un momento basico, preliminare al successivo sviluppo del nuraghe a camera 'voltata' ('tholos') come fase intermedia di strutture all'origine difensive (muraglie) verso soluzioni più complesse di natura mista (abitativa-difensiva) con presumibile preminenza (o quanto meno equilibrio) fra le due funzioni suddette della prima sulla seconda, ma contenute ambedue nella natura del monumento stesso (al suo interno) rispetto alla muraglia in cui tale funzione (abitativa) è sussidiaria ma non esplicata al suo interno. Datosi che l'una racchiude soluzioni di insediamento, plausibilmente anche varie, l'altra le individua esclusivamente in rapporto alla sua massa.

In tale dinamica l'equilibrio delle forze è determinante per la staticità dell'insieme. Essa risulta dall'applicazione di un principio funzionale (ma non semplice) di controllare la larghezza di base del monumento con l'altezza. Con il protonuraghe con 'corridoio passante' Funtana Suei (Demurtas 1984) si attua un 'impegno' costruttivo di rilevante intensità da porsi in relazione alla capacità dei costruttori nuragici di creare all'interno di una massa spazi funzionali (Fig. 4). Il tema del corridoio, seppure con svolgimento diversificato: rettilineo (Ponte Etzu), curvilineo (Fruscos, Galla, Liori, S'Ena S. Juanni, Mura Fratta), sinuoso (Funtana Suei), ad L rovescia (Ono, Perka 'e Pazza, Sa Domu 'e S'Orku) finisce per prevalere e si concretizza, in un primo momento, con l'apertura dei due ingressi contrapposti. Nel contempo, la distribuzione dei vani ai lati del corridoio, in schema a transetto più o meno vario (Manca Demurtas e Demurtas 1984a: 635; 1984b: 174), dimostrerebbe l'abilità tecnica a ricavare spazi, in rapporto, sempre, alla ripartizione delle forze (Manca Demurtas e Demurtas 1984a: 638; 1984b: 180), in funzione di carichi soprastanti la copertura, sempre a piattabanda, e ad innalzare l'altezza del monumento dall'ingresso fino al punto di raccordo tra i bracci del corridoio e la scala. Ne ricava una doppia falda dalla linea obliqua in direzione degli ingressi (Canchedda, Fruscos, Funtana Suei, Galla, Liori, Mene, Mura Fratta, Ponte Etzu, Pruna, S'Ena S. Juanni, Scarlozza, S'Ulivera).

Piani abitativi sono ottenuti con l'edificazione di vani utilizzando il piano alto (Coattos, Mura Fratta, Seneghe). Le difficoltà statiche e la necessità dell'utilizzo di supporti di roccia naturale sembrerebbe poter spiegare la varietà degli schemi planimetrici. Questo, in funzione del concretizzare gradualmente, attraverso il decentramento dell'asse del corridoio (Manca Demurtas e Demurtas 1984a: 638; 1984b: 173), lo sviluppo degli spazi nella parte piena e, in un secondo momento, si avrebbe come risultato finale il controllo della forma di base.

Pertanto, lo sviluppo si attuerebbe da una forma di base già evoluta rispetto ai monumenti del tipo I (Monte D'Accoddi-SS) e del Tipo II (Monte Manzanu-Macomer-NU; Peppe Gallu-Uri-SS [Contu 1959]; Gazza e S. Caterina-Bolotana-NU; Corongiu Marxi e Su Iriu-Gergei-NU; Brunku

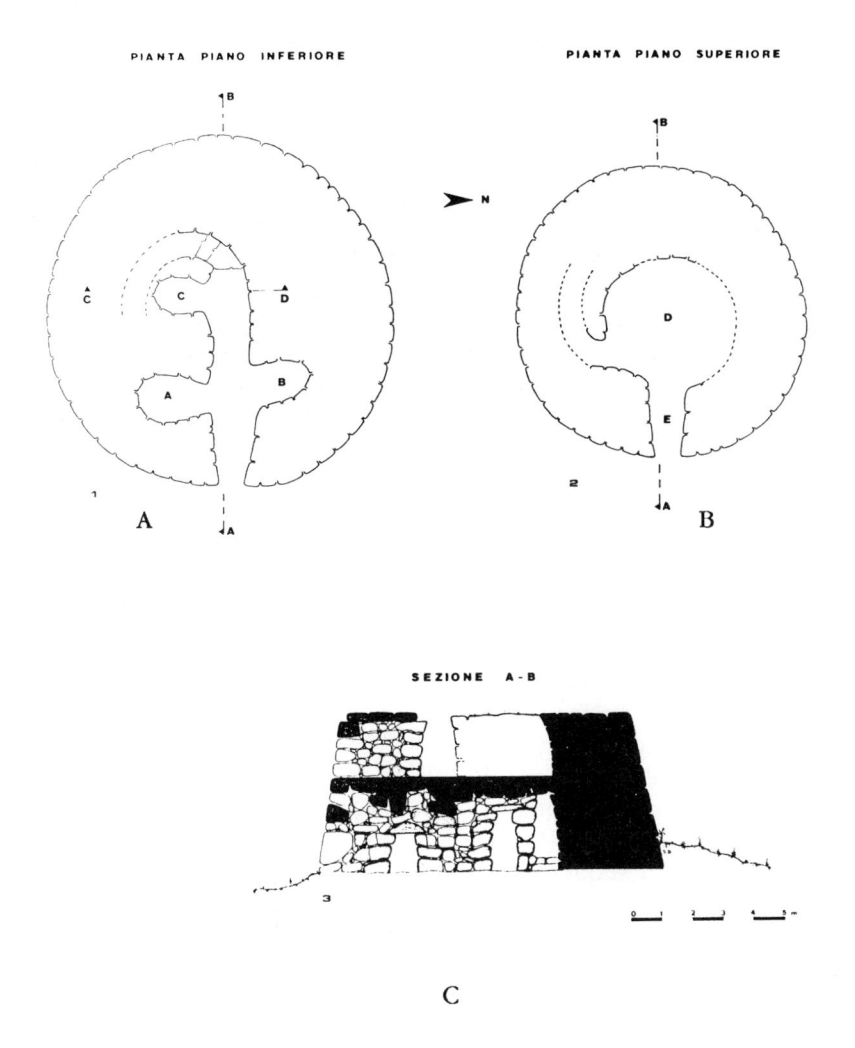

Fig. 5 Protonuraghe Sumboe (Ghilarza-OR). (A) Pianta piano inferiore; (B) Pianta piano superiore; (C) Sezione.

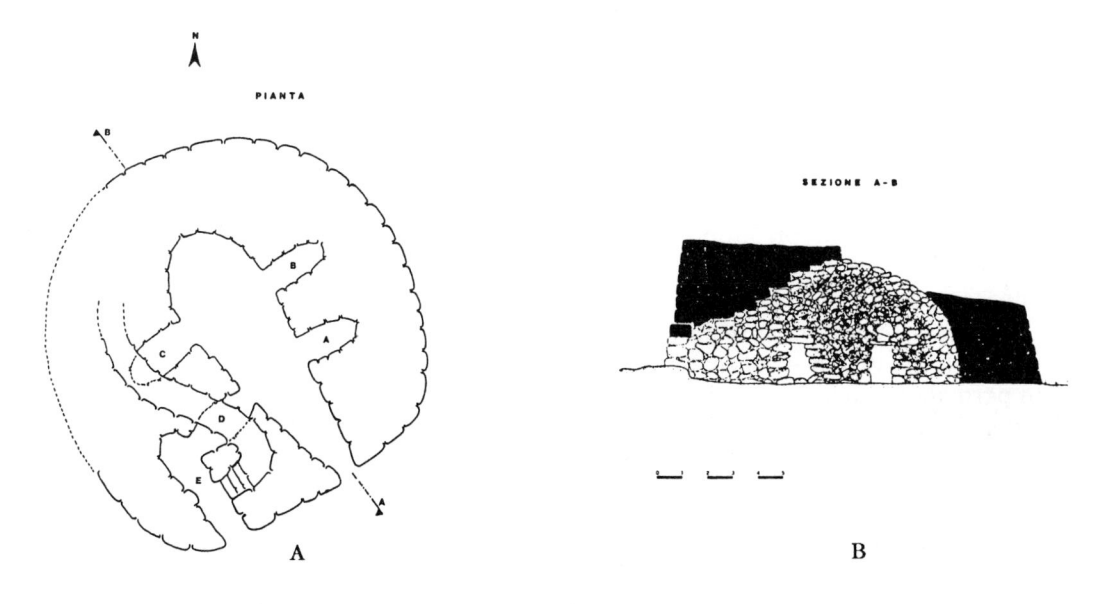

Fig. 6 Naviforme: Crastu A (Soddì-OR). (A) Pianta; (B) Sezione.

Madugui-Gesturi-CA) fino alla successiva del Tipo IV (Fonte Mola-Thiesi-SS; Lighedu-Suni-NU; Bilippone-Dualchi-NU; Cunculu-Scano Montiferro-OR; e Sumboe-Ghilarza-OR) col corridoio con un solo ingresso rappresentante lo stacco rispetto alle esperienze precedenti (Fig. 5). Infatti la distribuzione del rapporto massa-spazio conosce con questa fase uno squilibrio a favore dello spazio come riduzione di massa che si svilupperà ancor più nelle forme successive, così si attua il passaggio dal corridoio contenuto verso il naviforme (Manca Demurtas e Demurtas 1992), Tipo V, sia con ambiente unico (Crastu A-Soddì-OR: Manca Demurtas e Demurtas in stampa) (Fig. 6) o con ambienti multipli (Friarosu-Mogorella-OR) (Manca Demurtas e Demurtas 1984b: 180-81 fig. 9; Manca Demurtas 1984) dove la copertura tende a chiudere ad ogiva tronca per concludersi, poi, con la 'giro–volta' in un ambiente unico, di forma circolare.

Il rilevare delle varianti attraverso la tipologia proposta arricchisce il quadro delle conoscenze sulla classe del protonuraghi. Ma il nostro studio non definisce periodi precisi all'interno di questo processo. Al momento, si rileva l'alta densità di protonuraghe con corridoio passante, tuttavia, non possiamo determinare il rapporto tra singole aree e modelli di sviluppo sia per sequenzialità (il tipo di sviluppo proposto) che per collegamento specifico aree e fasi. Cioè manca la possibilità, non possedendosi riscontri oggettivi, di connettere i due elementi suddetti in un quadro conoscitivo dettagliato e individuabile in ogni sua parte.

L'accostamento dei due filoni costruttivi (protonuraghi e a'tholos') che si ritrova o per addizione orizzontale (Kuau e Serra Crastula-Bonarcado-OR; Biriola-Dualchi-NU) o per sovrapposizione verticale (Orgono e Sumboe-Ghilarza-OR; S'Ulivera-Dualchi) (Manca Demurtas e Demurtas 1984a: 638) può non solo esplicarsi come anteriorità dell'uno rispetto all'altro, dato il rapporto che si istituisce che ne presuppone la preesistenza del primo rispetto al secondo, ma potrebbe anche introdurre un'ulteriore distinzione. La sovrapposizione in orizzontale potrebbe far pensare ad una fase di sviluppo intermedio con permanenza parziale o globale o comunque funzionale del modello più antico in presenza di un utilizzo coevo del nuovo, nell'altro invece (a sovrapposizione verticale) la negazione della sua funzione autonoma. Sostanzialmente, il riconoscimento della sua funzione di supporto statico e quindi, paradossalmente, nell'abbandono dell'utilizzo a piano abitativo si ha l'evoluzione definitiva della struttura originaria verso la forma finale del nuraghe a 'tholos.' In questa fase si avrebbe il definitivo superamento del modello primitivo e quindi la sua cessazione del suo pieno utilizzo funzionale.

Lucia Manca Demurtas

Bibliografia

Atzeni, E.
1966   Il nuraghe Sa Corona di Villagreca (Cagliari). In *Atti del XIII Congresso di Storia dell'Architettura (Sardegna), Cagliari 6-12 aprile 1963*, 1, 119-24. Roma.
1981   Aspetti e sviluppi culturali del neolitico e della prima età dei metalli in Sardegna. In E. Atzeni *et al.* (eds.), *Ichnussa. La Sardegna dalle origini all'età classica*, 21-51. Milano: Libri Scheiwiller.
1985   Le premesse: il mondo prenuragico. In E. Arslan, F. Barreca e F. Lo Schiavo (eds.), *Civiltà Nuragica*, 19-44. Milano: Electa.

Contu, E.
1959   I più antichi nuraghi e l'esplorazione del nuraghe Peppe Gallu (Uri, Sassari). *Rivista di Scienze Preistoriche* 14(1-4): 59-121.
1981   L'architettura nuragica. In E. Atzeni *et al.* (eds.), *Ichnussa. La Sardegna dalle origini all'età classica*, 5-175. Milano: Scheiwiller.

Demurtas, S.
1984   Norbello (Oristano), loc. Funtana Suei. In E. Anati (ed.), *I Sardi. La Sardegna dal Paleolitico all'età romana*, 160-61. Milano: Jaca Book.

Dessi, C.
1922   *Singolari Nuraghi in Gallura*. Sassari.

Lilliu, G.
1962   *I Nuraghi. Torri preistoriche della Sardegna*. Verona: La Zattera.
1982   *La Civiltà Nuragica*. Studi e Monumenti 1. Sassari: Carlo Delfino.
1988   *La Civiltà dei Sardi. Dal Paleolitico all'età dei nuraghi*. Terza edizione. Torino: Nuova ERI.

Manca Demurtas, L.
1984   Mogorella (Oristano), loc. Friarosu. In E. Anati (ed.), *I Sardi. La Sardegna dal Paleolitico all'età Romana*, 157-59. Milano: Jaca Book.

Manca Demurtas, L., & S. Demurtas
1984a   I protonuraghi (nuovi dati per l'Oristanese). In W. Waldren, R. Chapman, J. Lewthwaite e R.-C. Kennard (eds.), *Early Settlement in the Western Mediterranean Islands and Their Peripheral Areas. The Deya Conference of Prehistory*, 629-70. BAR International Series 229(ii). Oxford: British Archaeological Reports.
1984b   Observaciones sobre los protonuragues de Cerdeña. *Trabajos de Prehistoria* 41: 165-204. Madrid.
1987   Di un tipo architettonico mediterraneo (Talaiot Rafal-Roig-Mercadal) (Minorca). In G. Lilliu, G. Ugas, & G. Lai (a cura di), *La Sardegna nel Mediterraneo tra il Secondo e il Primo Millennio a.C. Atti del II Convegno di Studi 'Un millennio di relazioni fra la Sardegna e i paesi del mediterraneo,' Selargius-Cagliari 27-30 novembre 1986*, 493-503. Cagliari: Amministrazione Provinciale di Cagliari.
1991   Analisi dei protonuraghi nella Sardegna centro-occidentale. In B. Santillo Frizell (ed.), *Arte*

Militare e Architettura Nuragica. Nuragic Architecture in its Military, Territorial and Socio-economic Context. Proceedings of the First International Colloquium on Nuragic Architecture at the Swedish Institute in Rome, 7-9 December, 1989. Acta Instituti Romani Regni Sueciae, Series In 4°, 48: 41-52. Stockholm: Svenska Institutet i Rom.

1992   Protonuraghi a camera naviforme. In *La Sardegna nel Mediterraneo tra il Bronzo medio e il Bronzo recente (XVI-XIV sec. a.C.). Atti del III Convegno di Studi, 'Un millennio di relazioni fra la Sardegna e i paesi del mediterraneo, Selargius-Cagliari 19-22 novembre 1987,* 107-25. Cagliari.

in stampa   I complesso fortificato di Crastu-Soddì (Oristano). Saggio di analisi sulle strutture di fortificazioni in Sardegna. In *Le Chalcolithique en Languedoc. Ses Relations Extra-Regionales. Hommage au Dr. Jean Arnal (Colloque International—Saint-Mathieu-de Treviers—20-22 settembre 1990).*

Santoni, V.
1980   Il segno del potere. In D. Sanna (a cura di), *Nur. La misteriosa civiltà dei Sardi,* 141-86. Milano: Cariplo.

1990   Il territorio in epoca nuragica. In *La Provincia di Oristano. L'orma della Storia,* 27-40. Milano: Cinisello Balsamo.

Sebis, S.
1986   Villaggio di età del Bronzo a Montegonella (Nuraxinieddu, OR). *Studi Sardi* 26(1981–85): 17-30.

Ugas, G.
1987   Un nuovo contributo per lo studio della tholos in Sardegna. La fortezza di Su Mulinu-Villanovafranca. In M.S. Balmuth (ed.), *Studies in Sardinian Archaeology III: Nuragic Sardinia and the Mycenaean World,* 77-128. BAR International Series 387. Oxford: British Archaeological Reports.

Appendice:
Distribuzione dei protonuraghi con corridoio passante (Fig. 2)

Provincia di Sassari

1.	Finucchiaglia	San Francesco D'Aglientu
2.	Budas	Tempio
3.	Contrapiana	Tempio
4.	Sa Domu 'e S'Orku	Ittireddu
5.	Sa Caddina	Thiesi
6.	Cassaros	Torralba
7.	Ena e Leperes	Bonorva
8.	Gagai	Bonorva
9.	Fenosu	Bonorva

Provincia di Nuoro

10.	Perka 'e Pazza	Bolotana
11.	Piscapu	Orotelli
12.	Pulighitta	Orotelli
13.	Fraigada	Suni
14.	Seneghe	Suni
15.	Mulineddu	Sagama
16.	Mene	Macomer
17.	Pruna	Macomer
18.	Arbu	Birori
19.	Pedra Oddetta I	Birori
20.	Aidu Arbu	Bortigali
21.	Carrarzu Iddia A	Bortigali-Mulargia
22.	Coattos	Bortigali
23.	Tusari	Bortigali
24.	Biriola	Dualchi
25.	Ono	Dualchi
26.	S'Ulivera	Dualchi
27.	Sarde Melas	Mamoiada
28.	Hastru Longu	Fonni
29.	Pobulus	Genoni
30.	Corongiu 'e Maria	Nurri

Provincia di Oristano

31.	Ulinu	Sedilo
32.	Frontelizzos	Aidomaggiore
33.	Mura Fratta	Aidomaggiore
34.	Scarlozza	Aidomaggiore
35.	Funtana Suei	Norbello
36.	Canchedda	Ghilarza
37.	Aurras	Bonarcado
38.	Genna Uda	Bonarcado
39.	Connau Piscamu	Seneghe
40.	Narva	Seneghe
41.	Abbaia A	Paulilatino
42.	Fruscos	Paulilatino
43.	Galla	Paulilatino
44.	Liori	Paulilatino
45.	Perdosu	Paulilatino
46.	Ponte Etzu	Paulilatino
47.	S'Ena Santu Juanni	Paulilatino
48.	Tronza	Milis
49.	Urasa	Bauladu
50.	Putzola	Fordongianus

Provincia di Cagliari

51.	Sa Domu e S'Orku	Donori
52.	Nuraxi Longu	Sinnai
53.	Funtana e Landiri	Sinnai
54.	Bangius	Gonnesa
55.	Moru Nieddu	Gonnesa

Summary

Some 280 protonuraghi are known in Sardinia, with most occurring in the northwest-central part of the island. The Authors subdivide the protonuraghi into 5 types: (1) full (n = 1); (2) with a ramp (n = 7); (3) corridor passage (n = 55); (4) internal corridor (n = 36); and (5) naviform (n = 20). The remaining 161 are of indeterminate type.

The protonuraghi *a corridoio passante*, the most numerous type, are most common in west-central Sardinia, in the Planargia, Marghine, Montiferro, and Barigadu regions, in the Tirso Valley, and in the Altopiano of Abbasanta. Usually built of local basalts and granites, they frequently are situated at altitudes greater than 300 m asl, on or near plateaus, and usually near sources of water. It is suggested that the protonuraghi served as lines of communication, and as symbols of collective defense of limited territorial areas (cf. also Trump, this volume, and Bonzani, this volume).

The protonuraghi (e.g. Sa Corona-Villagreca and Brunku Madugui-Gesturi) are now recognized as Early and Middle Bronze Age precursors (and in some cases contemporaries) to the true tholos nuraghi, but they must also be understood as successful attempts at constructing an enclosed space in their own right.

The Authors hypothesize that the corridor nuraghi had a dual function—habitation and defense. The balance between the two can be seen in the relative importance of height (defense) and horizontal/internal space (habitation); when necessary, additional rooms have been added to the central passage, and the top of the platform has also been utilized. The naviform protonuraghi reflect a much greater emphasis on space with a reduction in the massiveness of the construction, a development which must signify at least a partial change in function.

At the moment it is not yet possible to describe functional developments for individual regions in specific time periods, but this is the Authors' goal. Sites with classic nuraghi either adjacent to or superimposed on corridor nuraghi require particular investigation to determine their relative (and perhaps contemporaneous) functions, and what this tells us about changes in Nuragic society.

Sui Protonuraghi del Marghine e della Planargia[*]

Alberto Moravetti

Il Territorio (Fig. 1)

L'area di riferimento è data da due regioni storiche della Sardegna centro-occidentale—il Marghine e la Planargia—che si dispongono da Est a Ovest, dall'interno sino alla costa di Bosa e Magomadas, per una profondità di circa 50 km, una larghezza massima di 12 km ed una minima di 4 km con una superficie complessiva di 774,88 kmq. Il paesaggio naturale del territorio risulta formato dai rilievi trachitici del Marghine che, verso Est, si raccordano a quelli del Goceano e quindi ai Monti di Alà, mentre più ad Ovest giungono ad attestarsi nel Montiferru, costituendo una displuviale di maggiori altitudini tra i bacini imbriferi del Tirso e del Temo.

Il bacino del Temo è separato da questa dorsale montana dagli altopiani basaltici della Campeda (da 600-700 m s.l.m.) e della Planargia (da 300-500 m s.l.m.), che poi con taglio netto delimitano la valle incassata dal Temo. Il territorio risale ancora verso Nord la valle del fiume sino ai Monti di Montresta e alla catena costiera (M. Mannu, m 802; M. Sa Pattada, m 788) che con parete rocciosa scende sul mare tra Capo Marrargiu e l'insenatura di Poglina. Nel bacino del Tirso, invece, i terrazzamenti di valle (da 170-400 m s.l.m.) si raccordano ai pendii scoscesi della catena del Marghine (Punta Palai, m 1200; Punta Iameddari, m 1118; Monte Santu Padre, m 1028) (AA.VV. 1985: 33 ss.).

L'aspetto geomorfologico della regione è stato ampiamente studiato da A. Aru cui si deve una Carta pedologica del territorio nella quale, in unità cartografiche (U.P.1—U.P.2—U.P.3—U.P.4a—U.P.4b—U.P.5—U.P.6—U.P.7—U.P.8), sono stati classificati i suoli predominanti, le litologie principali, le morfologie, le attitudini e le potenzialità produttive.[1]

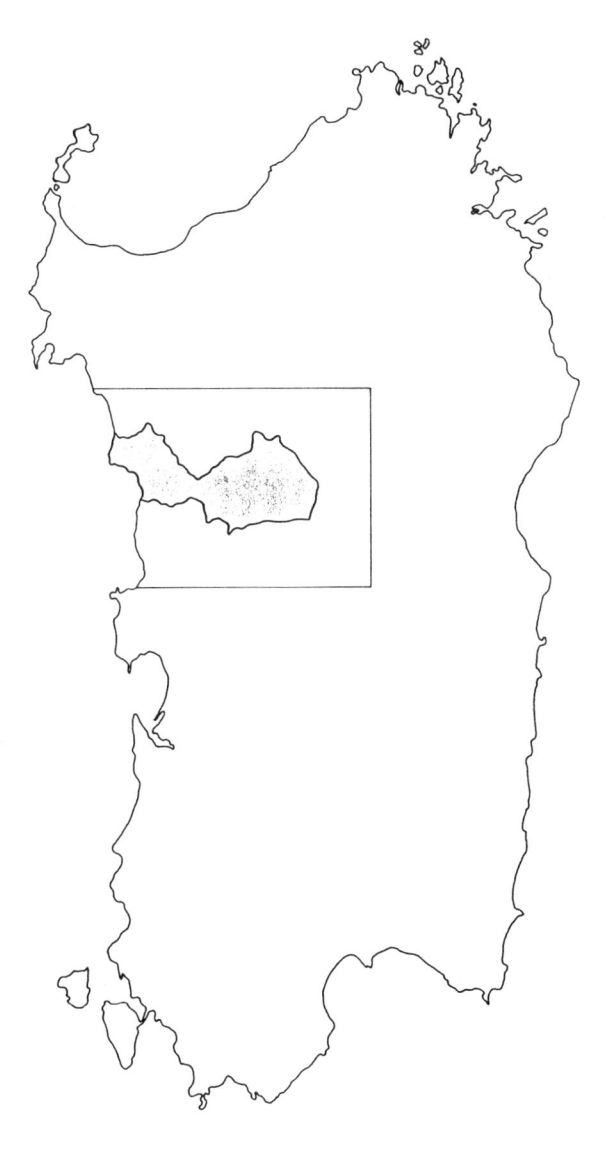

Fig. 1 La Sardegna con il territorio del Marghine-Planargia.

---

[*] Ringrazio vivamente il dott. Paolo Melis, dell'Istituto di Antichità e Arte, per l'elaborazione informatica dei dati.

[1] L'indagine pedologica è stata effettuata nell'ambito del Piano di sviluppo socio-economico voluto dalla Comunità Montana n. 8 (cfr. AA.VV., *Piano di Sviluppo Socio-economico. Atti della pianificazione integrata*, Macomer 1982; AA.VV. 1985: 20 ss.). Per il territorio di Macomer, cfr. Aru e Baldaccini 1985: 13-18.

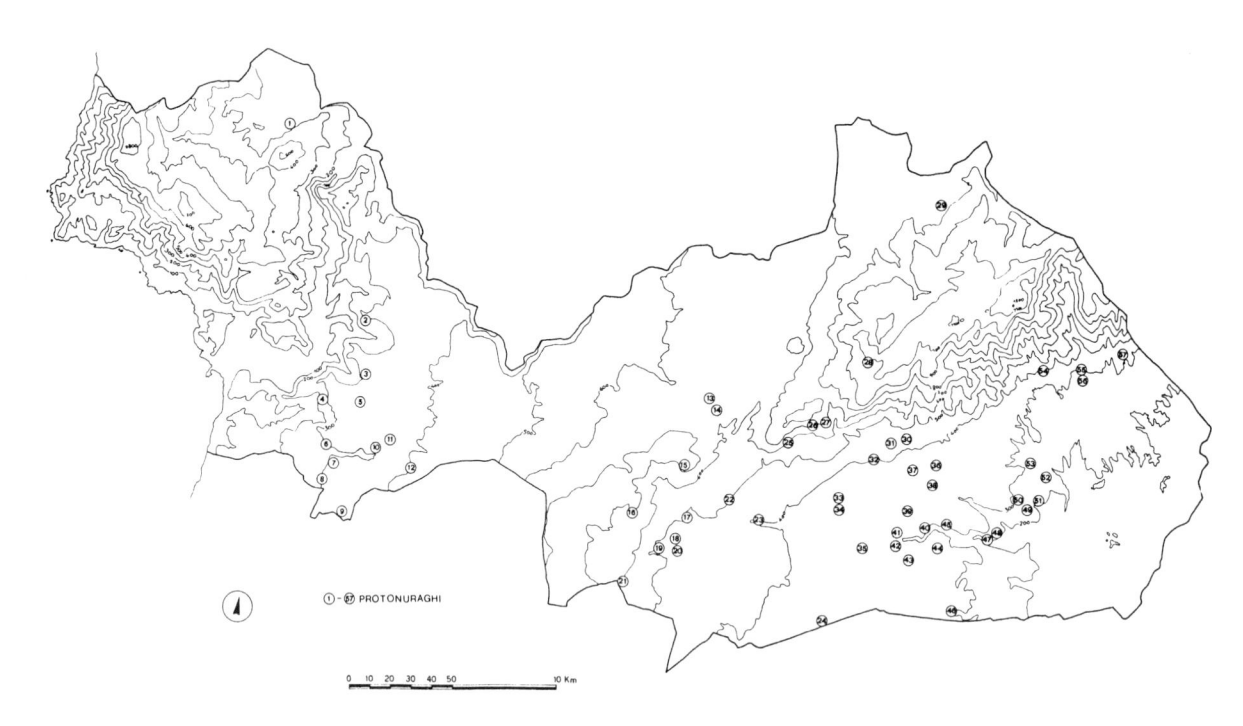

Fig. 2 Carta di distribuzione dei protonuraghi nel Marghine-Planargia.
01. Bena Ghiu-Montresta; 02. Sa Idda Bezza-Suni; 03. Lighedu-Suni; 04. Seneghe-Suni; 05. Sa Fraigada-Suni; 06. Caddaris-Flussio; 07. Murciu-Flussio; 08. Santa'Arvara-Magomadas; 09. Carcheras-Flussio; 10. Funtanedda-Sagama; 11. Mulineddu B-Sagama; 12. Pascialzos-Magomadas; 13. Monte Manzanu-Macomer; 14. Su Nou de Tiriani-Macomer; 15. Monte Putzolu-Macomer; 16. Monte Sara-Macomer; 17. Mandras-Macomer; 18. Mene-Macomer; 19. Prunas-Macomer; 20. Tottori-Macomer; 21. Oschera-Borore; 22. Orbentile-Macomer; 23. Su Salighe-Macomer- 24. Arghentu-Borore; 25. Bullittas-Birori; 26. Coattos-Bortigali; 27. Carrarzu Iddia A-Bortigali; 28. Perca 'e Pazza-Bolotana; 29. Su Nou de Pedramaggiore-Bortigali; 30. S. Martino-Bortigali; 31. Berre-Bortigali; 32. Seriale-Bortigali; 33. Pedra Oddetta A-Birori; 34. Pedra Oddetta B-Birori; 35. Arbu-Birori; 36. Ortu-Silanus; 37. Tusari-Bortigali; 38. Aidu Arbu-Bortigali; 39. Mura Elighe Bortigali; 40. Cubas-Dualchi; 41. Frenugarzu-Dualchi; 42. Bardalatzu-Dualchi; 43. Uana-Dualchi; 44. Bilippone-Dualchi; 45. Crabas-Dualchi; 46. Biriola-Dualchi; 47. Ono-Dualchi; 48. S'Ulivera-Dualchi; 49. S'Elilogu-Silanus; 50. Mura s'Inzaimo-Silanus; 51. Sorighes-Silanus; 52. Sa Mura 'e S'Ulumu-Silanus; 53. Sa Itria-Silanus; 54. Gazza-Bolotana; 55. Cannas-Bolotana; 56. Figu-Bolotana; 57. S. Caterina-Bolotana.

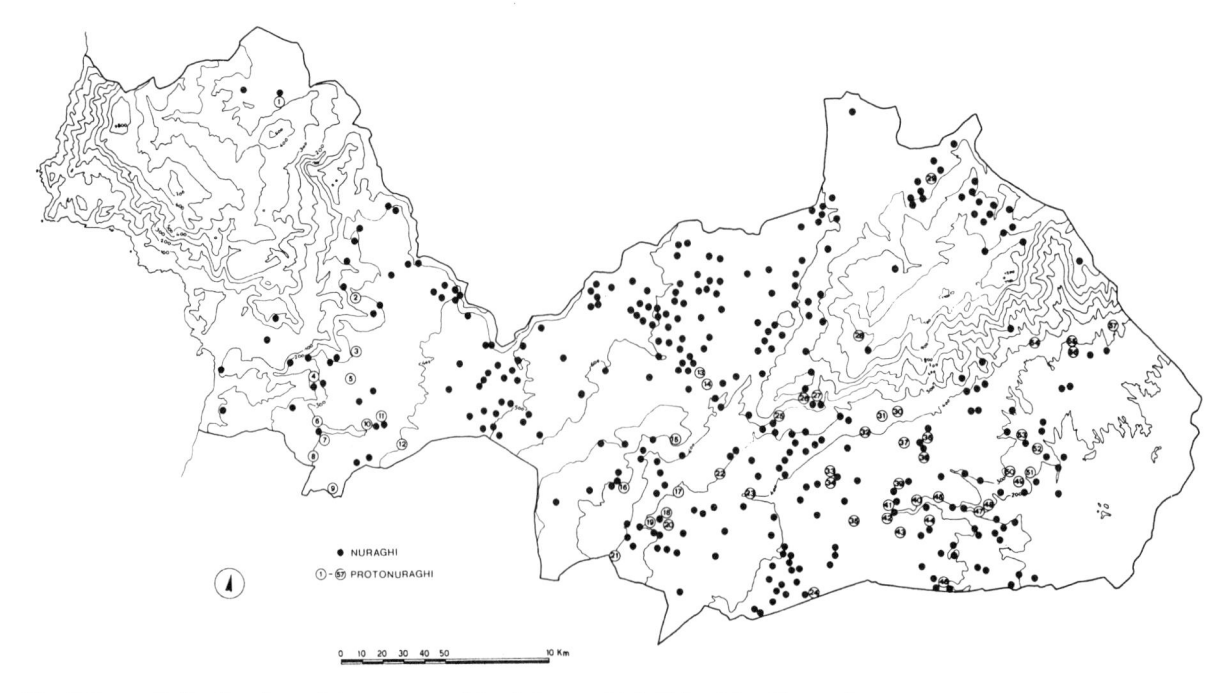

Fig. 3 Carta di distribuzione dei protonuraghi e dei nuraghi del Marghine-Planargia.

Rapporto nuraghi/protonuraghi nel Marghine-Planargia

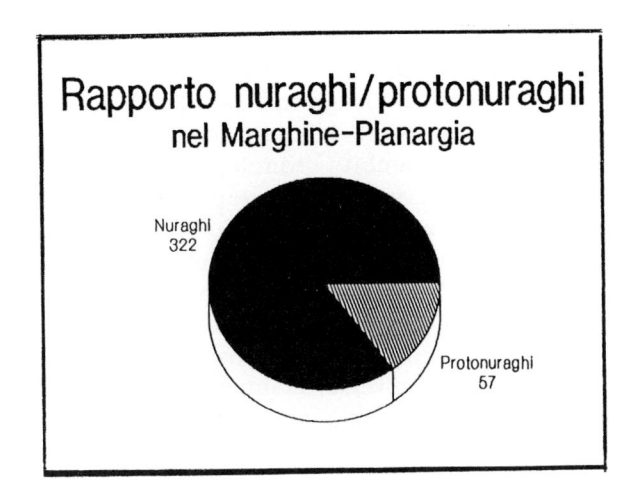

Nuraghi 322
Protonuraghi 57

Grafico 1 Rapporto nuraghi-protonuraghi nel Marghine-Planargia.

Pertanto, il quadro geo-pedologico del Marghine-Planargia si presenta in sintesi nel modo seguente:

U.P.1—costituita da basalti, trachiti, graniti, scisti e quarziti. Litosuoli, morfologie accidentate, con tratti di forti pendenze alternate ad aree pianeggianti o subpianeggianti. Suoli idonei a colture boschive naturali o artificiali, con alta attitudine per i pascoli naturali data l'ottima composizione floristica sotto l'aspetto pabulare.

U.P.2—Basalti e tufi vulcanici con morfologia a tratti dolci ma talora con forti pendenze. Roccia affiorante, suoli erosi e poco profondi. Elevata attitudine al pascolo.

U.P.3—Basalti, talora affioranti, con aree a morfologia ondulata, subpianeggiante e con qualche tratto a forti pendenze. Suoli erosi e di scarso spessore. Attitudine al pascolo.

U.P.4a—Basalti ed altre rocce vulcaniche. Morfologia generalmente pianeggiante o subpianeggiante, roccia affiorante. Elevata attitudine per i pascoli e a tratti anche per le attività agricole (cereali, erbai, etc.).

U.P.4b—Si differenzia dalla precedente per una più alta percentuale di rocciosità e pietrosità.

U.P.5—Rioliti, trachiti e altre rocce vulcaniche. Morfologia generalmente montana con tratti a forte pendenza ed altri pianeggianti. Roccia talora affiorante, suoli erosi e di scarso spessore. Attitudine al pascolo ed anche all'agricoltura nelle aree tabulari e con terreni profondi.

U.P.6—Calcari e calcareniti miocenici. Morfologia con aree a forti pendenze ed altre più dolci nella sommità delle colline e nei fondi valle.

U.P.7—Alluvioni antiche e conglomerati. Morfologia pianeggiante ed ondulata con incisioni e scarpate ad elevata pendenza. Suoli a tessitura argillosa in profondità. Fertilità generale molto bassa.

U.P.8—Alluvioni recenti con superfici pianeggianti o in lieve pendenza. Falda freatica talora superficiale. Elevata attitudine all'agricoltura.

I Monumenti

Indagini topografiche condotte in questo territorio da A. Moravetti a partire dal 1972,[2] hanno consentito di individuare emergenze archeologiche di varia epoca—dal Neolitico alla tarda età romana— e di rilevare, in gran parte, un centinaio di grotticelle artificiali, 32 tombe dolmeniche, 4 muraglie megalitiche, 8 fonti/pozzi sacri, 64 tombe di giganti, 322 nuraghi di varia tipologia ed infine i 57 protonuraghi che costituiscono l'oggetto della presente nota (Fig. 2, Grafico 1).[3]

Si tratta, come è noto, di monumenti variamente definiti nel tempo—*nuraghi abnormi, falsi*

---

2 Le ricognizioni di superficie nel Marghine-Planargia sono state condotte da chi scrive in tempi diversi e nell'ambito della pianificazione del territorio, promossa dalle amministrazioni comunali e soprattutto da parte della Comunità Montana n. 8: *Piano Regolatore Intercomunale dei Comuni di Birori, Borore, Bortigali, Macomer e Sindia*, a cura del Consorzio Industriale di Macomer, nel 1972; *Piano socio-economico*, della Comunità Montana n. 8, del 1982; *Piano urbanistico del Comune di Birori*, del 1982; *Piano di sviluppo della Montagna di S. Antonio*, del 1986; *Piano di sviluppo della Montagna del Marghine*, 1986; *Piano paesaggistico-ambientale della fascia costiera di Bosa*, 1988. Inoltre, in questi stessi anni, la Comunità Montana n. 8 ha finanziato il rilevamento grafico e fotografico della quasi totalità dei monumenti individuati nel corso del censimento. Mi è grato, per questo, ringraziare gli amministratori tutti per la loro sensibilità culturale, ed in particolare il Presidente, rag. Romano Benevole, che sempre ha favorito queste ricerche. Per una breve sintesi del patrimonio archeologico delle regione, cfr. Moravetti 1985b: 49-52. Per i monumenti del territorio di Birori, vedi Moravetti 1985a: 3-63.

3 Fra questi 57 monumenti non sono compresi i nuraghi Aladorza-Birori; S'Iscra de Abbasanta-Birori; Nurattolu-Birori; Serbine-Birori (Moravetti 1985a: 5); Orreddo-Silanus e Turre-Montresta (Manca-Demurtas e Demurtas 1984b: 192 n. 2; 194 n. 52), già segnalati come nuraghi a corridoio, ma di difficile definizione in assenza di un intervento di scavo.

nuraghi, pseudonuraghi, nuraghi a galleria, nuraghi-nascondiglio, nuraghi a corridoio/i, protonuraghi—ad indicare un rapporto di somiglianza/diversità rispetto al più classico nuraghe a tholos, oppure ad esprimere di volta in volta un giudizio di tipo funzionale, strutturale o cronologico.[4]

In realtà, questa molteplicità di termini per una classe monumentale che appare sempre più diffusa ed articolata in tutta l'Isola—non architettura episodica e casuale, quindi, ma consapevole e ben definito fenomeno culturale—deriva dal fatto che raramente questi monumenti sono stati oggetto di indagine stratigrafica esaustiva, seguita, poi, dalla edizione completa dei materiali di scavo.[5] Pesa, pertanto, su di essi, come una condanna, 'l'assenza dei dati di scavo' che viene sempre invocata, come se una architettura non contenesse essa stessa chiavi di lettura per una sua definizione cronologica e culturale.

Fra le varie espressioni sopra citate, tutte inadeguate o comunque riduttive, quella di protonuraghe sembra più delle altre giustificata per il fatto che pur nella carenza di sequenze stratigrafiche significative, non mancano, tuttavia, elementi utili per stabilire l'alta antichità di questi monumenti, dei quali sembra cogliersi la premessa già nella cultura eneolitica di Monte Claro, in particolare nel recinto a ferro di cavallo di Monte Baranta (Moravetti 1981: 288).

Inoltre, se i materiali di superficie raccolti in prossimità di questi edifici costituiscono solo labili indizi e possono essere fuorvianti,[6] e se i dati provenienti dai pochi protonuraghi scavati sono contradditori sul piano cronologico e non aiutano alla soluzione del problema legato alla genesi di questi monumenti, non può essere ignorato che dal protonuraghe Brunku Madili di Gesturi—a voler tralasciare la datazione al C14 (1820 ± 250), perchè effettuata su lastre di sughero e quindi poco attendibile—provengono ceramiche di tradizione Monte Claro ed altre con decorazione metopale riferibili ad un arco cronologico compreso fra il Bronzo antico e medio.[7]

Al Bronzo antico Lilliu (1988: 180) riferisce pseudonuraghi, nuraghi a corridoio e i monumenti di Sa Korona-Villagreca e Brunku Madugui-Gesturi, i soli ad essere definiti protonuraghi, così come allo stesso ambito cronologico V. Santoni (1980: 150) ascrive protonuraghi e pseudonuraghi, mentre il Contu (1985: 85) rifiuta la definizione di protonuraghe per l'implicito giudizio di maggiore antichità rispetto a quelli a tholos 'spesso non chiaramente documentato' e ritiene che queste costruzioni siano dovute 'più che a tempi o a funzioni diverse, all'urgenza', trattandosi di un tipo di costruzione indubbiamente più semplice (Contu 1981: 46).

F. Lo Schiavo (1986: 69) ipotizza che il tipo monumentale sia del tutto contemporaneo ai più diffusi nuraghi a tholos e che la scelta di pianta obbedisca a criteri di opportunità o di gusto, mentre per M.A. Fadda (1984: 409-10) lo schema planimetrico di questi monumenti, più che da momenti cronologici differenti, è determinato 'dalla morfologia del terreno e dalla volontà dei costruttori di utilizzare posizioni di avvistamento particolarmente importanti.' Più convincenti, a mio parere, le linee di sviluppo tracciate da Manca-Demurtas e Demurtas (1984a: 6 ss.; anche in questo volume) nello svolgimento formale di questa architettura, sia sul piano del processo evolutivo che su quello cronologico (Bronzo antico).

Una serie di ipotesi, come si vede, che in sintesi sembrano privilegiare quella della maggiore antichità del tipo monumentale, perchè più motivata rispetto a quella di una generica contemporaneità oppure di un casuale determinismo geomorfologico.

Pertanto, se riteniamo che tutti i 'nuraghi' che non rientrano nello schema classico del nuraghe a tholos—un modello che risponde ad un preciso e consolidato modulo architettonico, accettato e diffuso nei suoi caratteri tipologici in tutta l'Isola—siano 'altro' rispetto a quelli 'anomali', credo che, ad evitare confusione e in attesa di ulteriori elementi di giudizio, si possa accogliere per queste costruzioni la valenza cronologica di protonuraghe, come peraltro già proposto da Manca-Demurtas e Demurtas (1984a: 3).

In via preliminare, data l'economia della presente nota e in considerazione del fatto che oltre ai protonuraghi sono stati censiti e rilevati anche i nuraghi (Fig. 3), è parso opportuno tralasciare i confronti e l'analisi strutturale e tipologica di

---

4 Per la storia degli studi e delle problematiche legate a questi monumenti, cfr. Manca-Demurtas e Demurtas (1984: 2 ss., e in questo volume).

5 I monumenti di questo tipo oggetto di scavi, editi in misura più o meno ampia, ma in nessun caso esaustiva, sono soltanto i seguenti: Peppe Gallu-Uri (Contu 1959); Fonte Mola-Thiesi (Maetzke 1961); Albucciu-Arzachena (Ferrarese Ceruti 1962); Bruncu Madugui-Gesturi (Lilliu 1988); Sa Jacca-Busachi (Santoni 1980).

6 In particolare, i materiali raccolti in prossimità dei protonuraghi Fruscos-Paulilatino e Friarosu-Mogorella (Manca-Demurtas e Demurtas 1984: 12 ss.).

7 Sulle ceramiche di Cultura o di tradizione Monte

Claro, vedi Lilliu (1988; 1982: 14). Per la ceramica con decorazione metopale, cfr. Lilliu (1988); Contu (1978: 49); Ugas (1981: 9 ss.); Moravetti (1986: 94).

Fig. 5 Planimetria di protonuraghi del Marghine-Planargia; 1. Murciu-Flussio; 2. Bilippone-Dualchi; 3. Tottori-Macomer; 4. S'Elilogu-Silanus; 5. Prunas-Macomer.

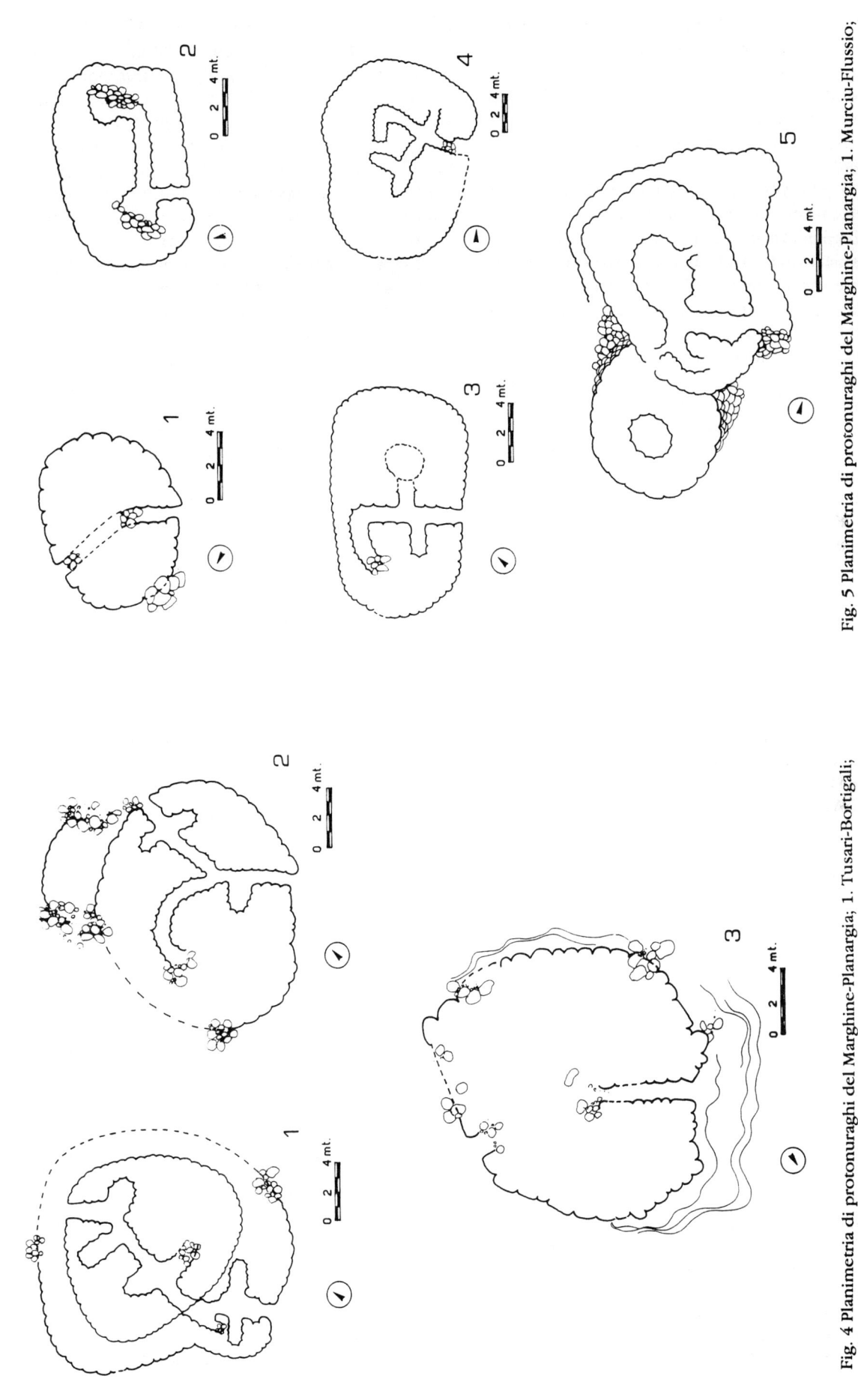

Fig. 4 Planimetria di protonuraghi del Marghine-Planargia; 1. Tusari-Bortigali; 2. Frenegarzu-Dualchi; 3. Gazza-Bolotana.

190 Sardinia in the Mediterranean

queste costruzioni del Marghine-Planargia (Fig. 4-10); si è preferito, invece, inserire i monumenti nel territorio fisico per cogliere, ove possibile, l'esistenza o meno di una diversa strategia d'insediamento fra le due classi monumentali, senza tuttavia applicare i vari modelli di *'spatial archaeology'* che si lasciano ad altra sede.

I 57 protonuraghi rilevati nel Marghine-Planargia costituiscono, al momento, il 31,66% di tutti gli analoghi monumenti censiti nell'Isola, con una densità dello 0,073 per kmq rispetto a quella generale che è dello 0,0074.[8] Un dato, questo, destinato ad essere ovviamente modificato dalla ricerca, ma pur indicativo della notevole presenza di questi monumenti nel territorio in esame ed anche della necessità di ricognizioni topografiche rigorose e di rilevamenti puntuali, mirati in particolare alla distinzione dei due tipi architettonici che talora è resa difficoltosa dal loro pessimo stato di conservazione.

Infatti, riferendoci ai dati pubblicati a suo tempo da Manca-Demurtas e Demurtas, nell'Oristanese, ove gli Autori hanno condotto estese ed approfondite indagini, la densità risulta dello 0,014 per kmq, mentre rimane molto bassa nel territorio delle province di Nuoro (0,008 per kmq)—più elevata, ora, con i dati di questo lavoro—di Sassari (0,007 per kmq) e di Cagliari (0,003 per kmq) ove finora sono mancate ricerche sistematiche (Manca-Demurtas e Demurtas 1984a: 4 ss; 1984b: 168 ss.), anche se non sfugge che l'area di maggiore diffusione di questi monumenti resta sempre la fascia centrale dell'Isola.

Tuttavia, l'alto numero di protonuraghi presenti nel Marghine-Planargia risulta assai modesto se riferito ai 322 nuraghi a tholos rilevati nello stesso territorio: il 15,04% rispetto all'84,96%. Complessivamente 379 monumenti equivalenti ad una densità di 0,41 per kmq, superiore a quella regionale, tipologicamente indifferenziata, che è dello 0,27 per kmq. In quanto alla ubicazione nel territorio (Tabella 1, Grafici 2-5), questi protonuraghi si dispongono di preferenza nella U.P.4a (26, pari al 45,61%), su rocce vulcaniche (basalti e trachiti) con morfologie caratterizzate da terreni pianeggianti o subpianeggianti segnati da litosuoli ed emergenze rocciose. In terreni generalmente accidentati, a forte pendenza, su rilievi o pianori dai fianchi ripidi sorgono 16

---

[8] Manca-Demurtas e Demurtas 1984: 4. In realtà la percentuale indicata nel testo è stata ottenuta sulla base di 180 monumenti che non rientrano tutti nella classe monumentale in esame. Su alcuni di essi, infatti, pesano delle riserve (vedi nota 3), mentre altri ancora non sono palesemente dei protonuraghi (si veda, ad esempio, Monte d'Accoddi, Monte Baranta, Nuraghe Sfundadu, etc.).

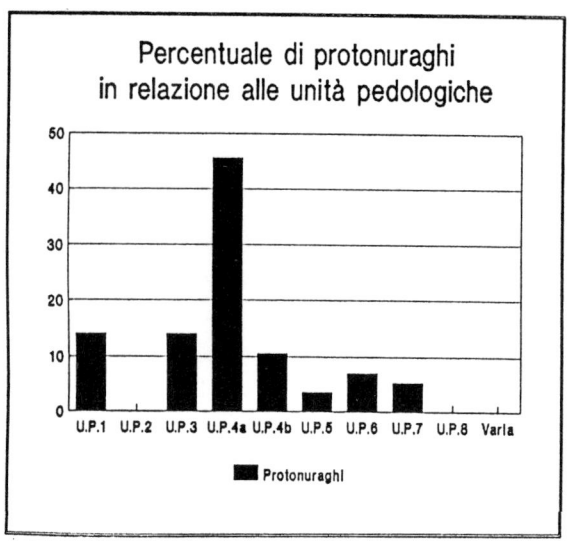

Grafico 2 Istogramma delle percentuali di protonuraghi in relazione alle Unità pedologiche.

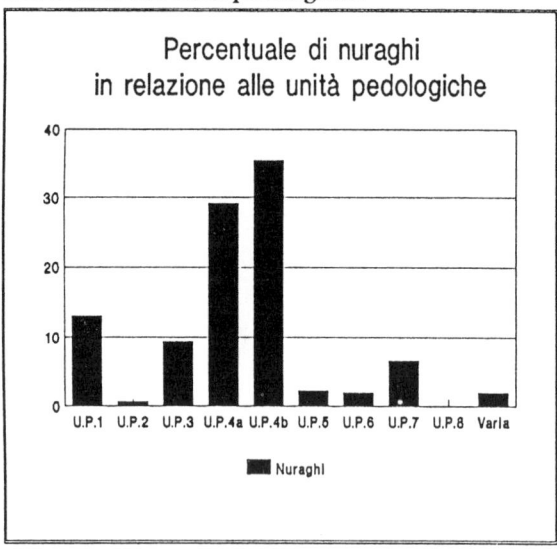

Grafico 3 Istogramma delle percentuali di nuraghi in relazione alle Unità pedologiche.

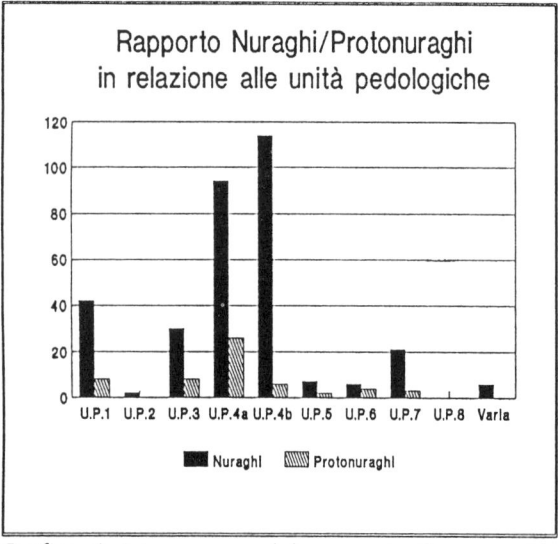

Grafico 4 Istogramma del rapporto fra nuraghi e protonuraghi in relazione alle Unità pedologiche.

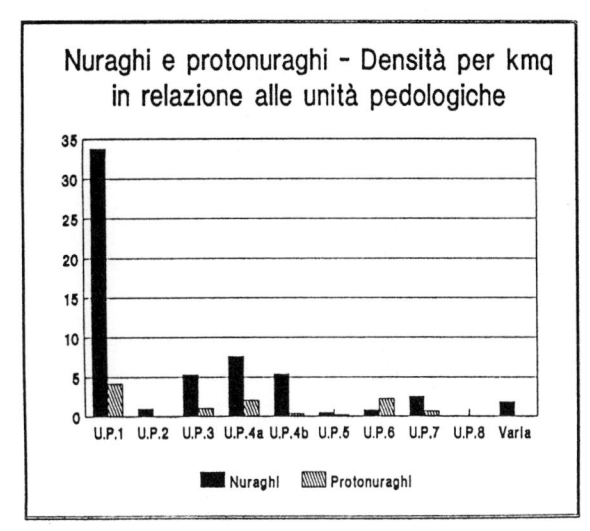

Grafico 5 Istogramma della densità dei nuraghi-protonuraghi in relazione alle Unità pedologiche.

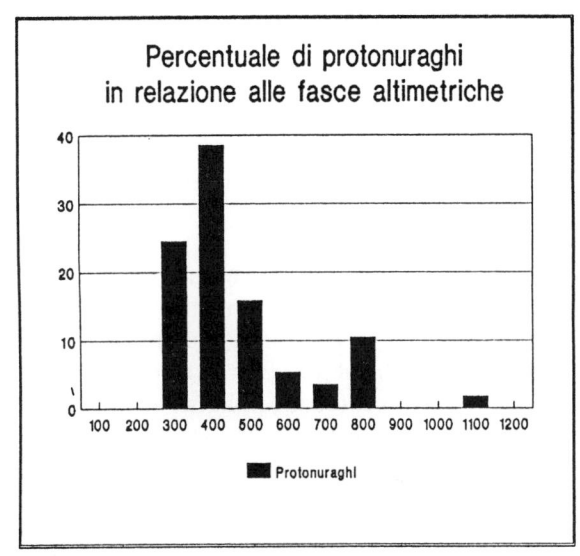

Grafico 6 Istogramma delle percentuali di protonuraghi in relazione alle fasce altimetriche.

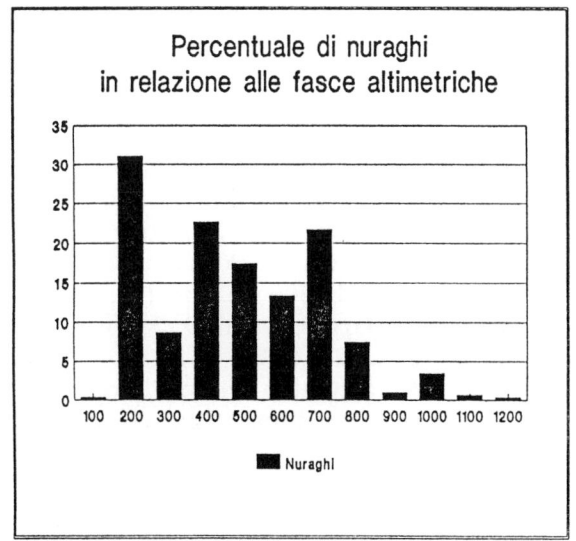

Grafico 7 Istogramma delle percentuali di nuraghi in relazione alle fasce altimetriche.

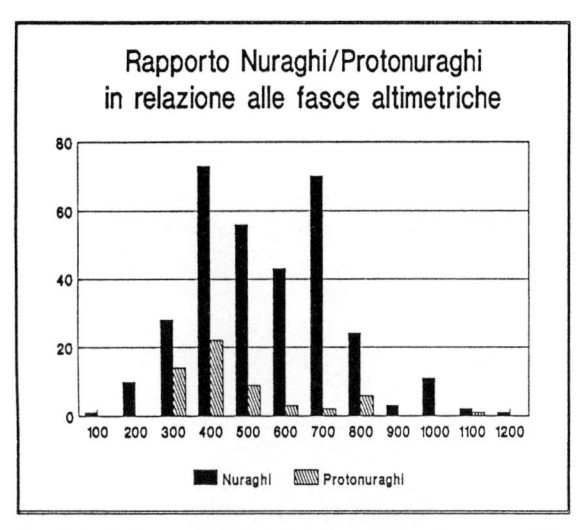

Grafico 8 Istogramma del rapporto fra nuraghi e protonuraghi in relazione alle fasce altimetriche.

costruzioni, 8 nella U.P.1 (14%) e 8 nella U.P.3 (14%). In misura minore, invece, vengono occupati i suoli della U.P.4b (6, pari al 10,52%), in genere pianeggianti ma pietrosi e con roccia affiorante, quelli della fascia montana U.P.5 (2, pari al 3,50%), o delle zone calcaree a morfologia ondulata, talora con forti pendenze, della U.P.6 (4, pari al 7,01%). Irrilevante, infine, la loro presenza nei terreni alluvionali a morfologia pianeggiante o subpianeggiante della U.P.7 (3, pari al 5,26), mentre nelle U.P.2 ed U.P.8 non sono documentati protonuraghi.

I nuraghi sorgono soprattutto nelle U.P.4b (114, pari al 35,40%) e U.P.4a (94, pari al 29,19%), quindi nella U.P.1 (42, pari al 13,04%) e nella U.P.3 (30, pari al 9,31%): percentuali minori si registrano nelle altre Unità pedologiche ove in tutte, comunque, essi sono presenti. Vi è quindi fra i due tipi di costruzione piena corrispondenza per quanto riguarda le U.P.4a, mentre esiste una netta divergenza fra l'alto numero di nuraghi nella U.P.4b e la presenza del tutto marginale di protonuraghi nella stessa area.

Per quanto riguarda l'altitudine (Tabella 2, Grafici 6-8), i protonuraghi si pongono ad una quota media di m 420 s.l.m., con valori compresi fra un minimo di m 270 (Funtanedda-Sagama) ed uno massimo di m 1024 (Su Nou de Pedramaggiore-Bortigali). La maggiore concentrazione si ha soprattutto fra i 300-400 metri, quindi nelle fasce altimetriche poste fra i 200-300 metri e i 400-500 metri. A parte il già citato Su Nou de Pedramaggiore, oltre i 769 metri del protonuraghe di Monte Putzolu non si segnalano monumenti, così come fra 0-200 metri.

I nuraghi a tholos, invece, sono presenti in tutte le fasce altimetriche, ad una quota media di m 508, da una altitudine minima di appena 4 metri (S. Lò-

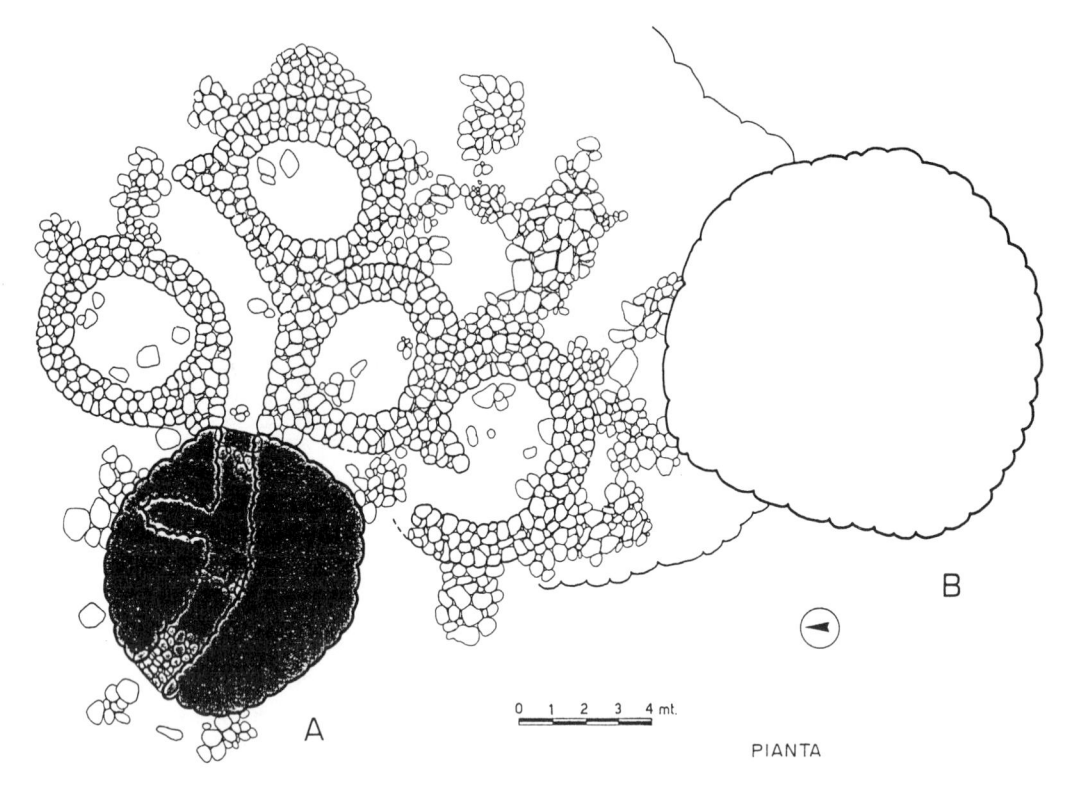

Fig. 6 Complesso di Carrarzu Iddia-Bortigali con protonuraghe (A) e probabile nuraghe a tholos (B).

Bosa) ad una massima di 1106 (Nodu de Sale-Bolotana). La fascia altimetrica preferita sembra anche per questi monumenti quella fra i 300-400 metri, ma con uguale predilezione per quelle successive fino a 800 metri, oltre la quale si contano, tuttavia, 19 nuraghi.

Quindi, pur se la distribuzione dei nuraghi riflette in qualche misura una superiorità numerica che consente loro di occupare il territorio in modo più capillare rispetto ai protonuraghi, sembrano emergere, tuttavia, scelte insediative differenziate fra i due tipi di costruzione, che, come si è detto, si presumono non contemporanei. Infatti, mentre i protonuraghi tendono a disporsi soprattutto nella fascia Sud-Sudest della regione, in particolare nelle aree subpianeggianti, quelle incise, però, e mosse da emergenze rocciose sulle quali sono di preferenza costruiti, i nuraghi sono ubicati in tutto il territorio, nelle più diverse tipologie geo-morfologiche, ad indicare un nuovo assetto territoriale degli insediamenti.

Questa diversa organizzazione dello spazio connessa ai nuraghi, oltre a suggerire una forte crescita demografica, maggiore adattamento all'ambiente e la capacità di sfruttare anche le aree meno favorevoli alla vita, sembra rivelare non solo l'esigenza di usare il territorio, ma soprattutto di possederlo. Ed è per questo che non vengono trascurate nemmeno quelle zone aspre e tormentate, povere di risorse ma di alto valore strategico per il controllo delle vie naturali, dei corsi d'acqua, etc.

In quanto allo schema di pianta (Figg. 4-10), questi protonuraghi del Marghine-Planargia mostrano la stessa varietà formale comune al tipo monumentale (circolare, ellittica, triangolare, quadrangolare, trapezoidale, poligonale, etc.), così come la tessitura muraria, la presenza di più ingressi (da uno a quattro) o l'articolazione degli spazi interni (corridoi, nicchie, cellette circolari, vani scala, etc.) non sembrano presentare, apparentemente, caratteri di particolare originalità rispetto a quelli già noti, mentre il rilevamento di 52 di questi monumenti sui 57 individuati fornisce dati significativi sulle loro dimensioni, soprattutto in relazione a quelle dei nuraghi dello stesso territorio.

Si registra, per i protonuraghi, una superficie media di mq 245,49, con misura massima di 1680 mq (Biriola-Dualchi) e minima di mq 51,40 (Carrarzu Iddia-Bortigali). La dimensione più frequente è quella compresa fra 100-200 mq (24, pari al 46,15%), seguita da 200-300 mq (14, pari al 26,92%), oltre 300 mq (10, pari al 19,23%) e quindi fra 50-100 mq (4, pari al 7,69%).

In quanto ai nuraghi, il valore medio ottenuto su 89 monumenti risulta di 150,59 mq, con estremi che vanno da un massimo di mq 635 (Tolinu-Noragugume) a un minimo di mq 73,50 (Prida C-Bolotana). Va detto che fra questi monumenti sono compresi quasi tutti i nuraghi complessi, vale a dire quelli di maggiori dimensioni: Miuddu-Birori

Fig. 8 Planimetria di protonuraghi del Marghine-Planargia: 1. S. Caterina-Bolotana; 2. Funtanedda-Sagama; 3. Uana-Dualchi; 4. Crabas-Dualchi.

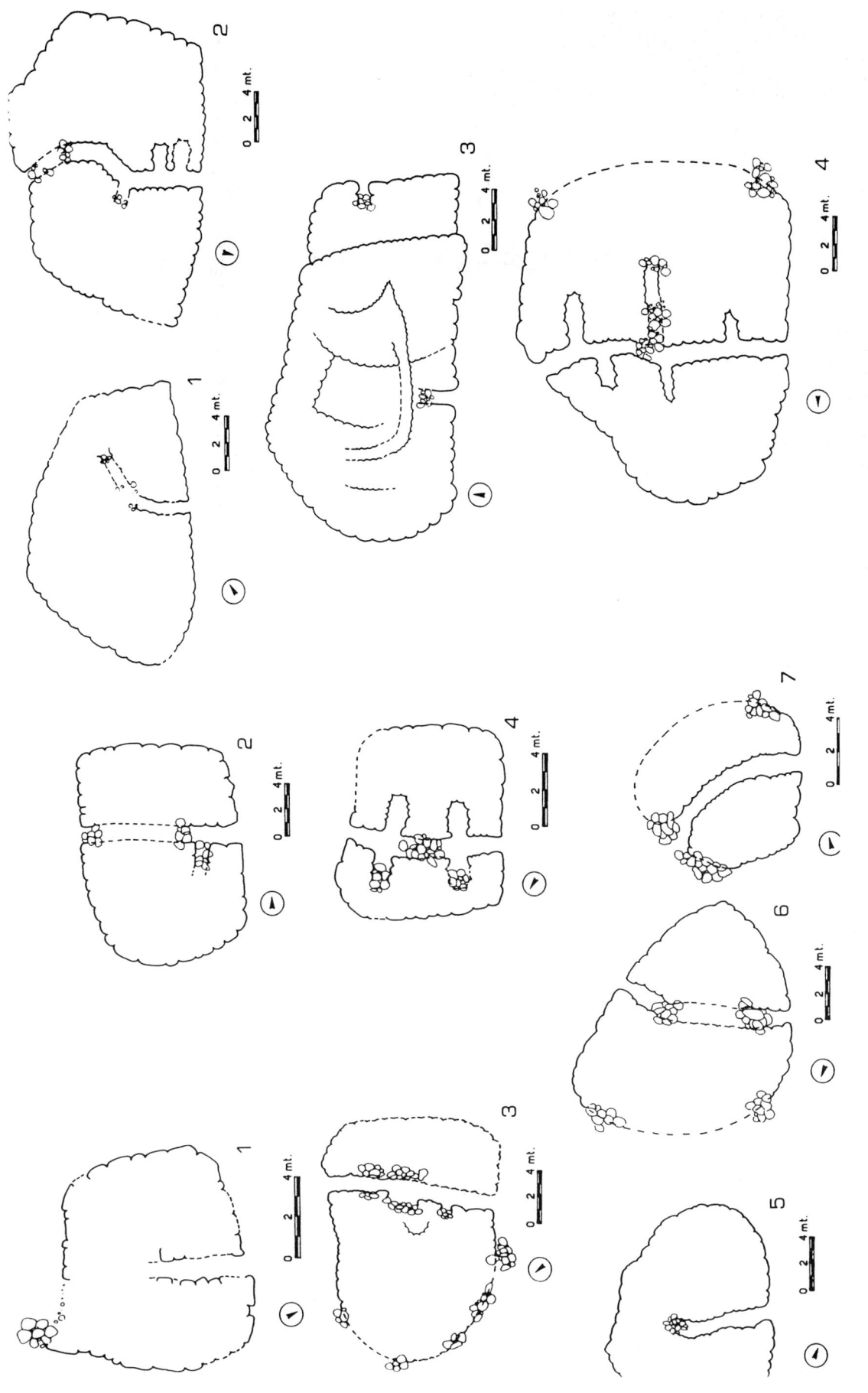

Fig. 7 Planimetria di protonuraghi del Marghine-Planargia: 1. Bena Ghiu A-Montresta; 2. Mulineddu-Sagama; 3. Sorighes-Silanus; 4. Coattos-Bortigali; 5. Ortu-Silanus; 6. S'Ena 'e S'Ulumu-Silanus; 7. Mura Elighe-Bortigali.

194 *Sardinia in the Mediterranean*

Fig. 10 Protonuraghi del Marghine-Planargia: 1. S. Martino-Bortigali; 2. Sa Itria-Silanus; 3. Mene-Macomer; 4. Bardalazzu-Dualchi.

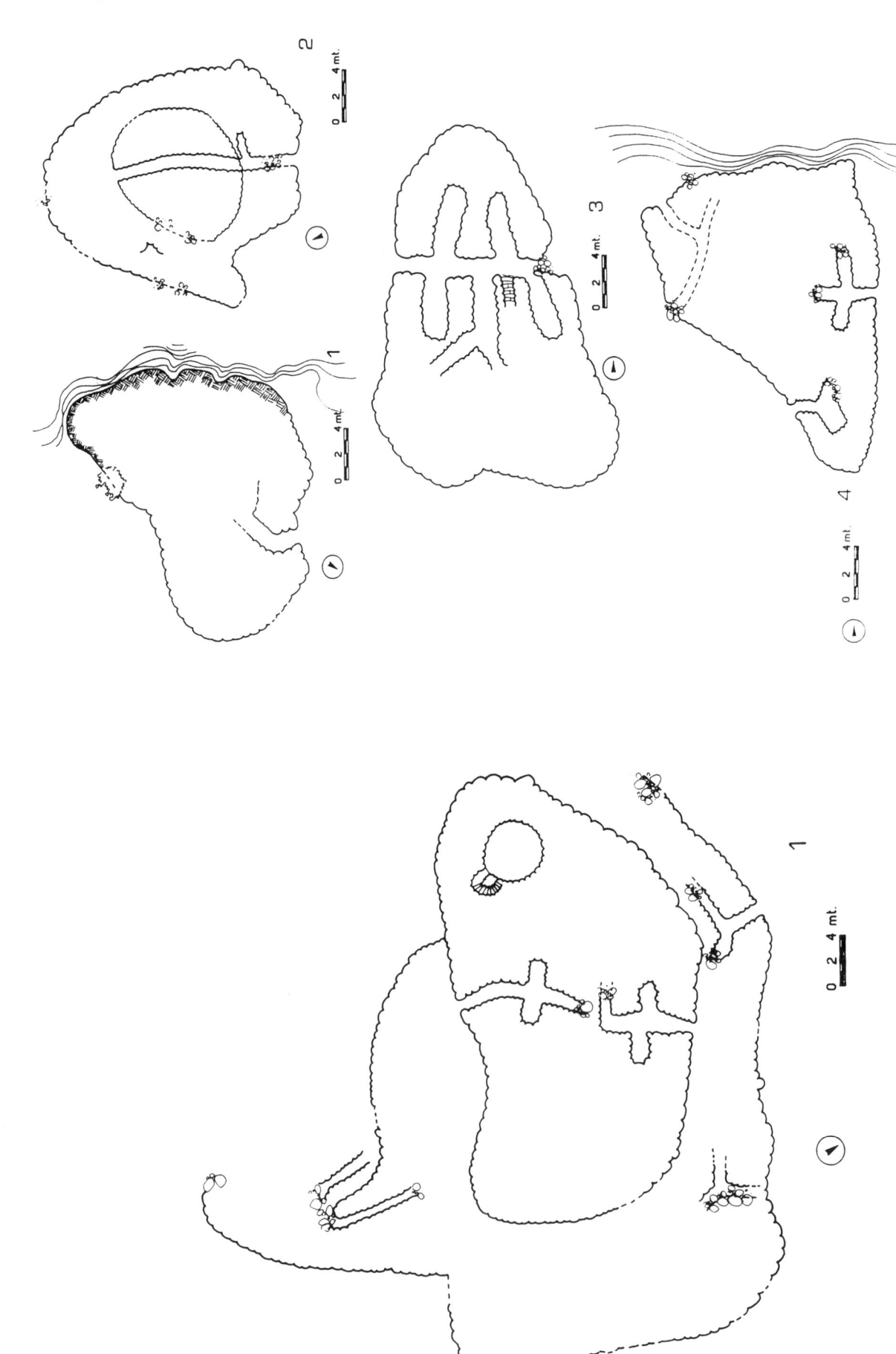

Fig. 9 Protonuraghe di Biriola-Dualchi.

(mq 451); Nuraddeo-Suni (mq 373); Bidui-Birori (mq 346); Mura 'e Coga-Sindia (mq 316); Mannu-Suni (282,60); Orolo-Bortigali (mq 260); S. Barbara-Macomer (mq 220); Funtana Mela-Macomer (mq 211). Anche per i nuraghi la maggiore concentrazione di monumenti si ha fra 100-200 mq (65, pari al 73,86%), seguita poi da quelle comprese fra 0-100 mq (12, pari al 13,63%), 200-300 mq (6, pari al 6,81%) e 300-700 (6, pari al 6,81%).

Se mettiamo a confronto le superfici dei protonuraghi e dei nuraghi, si nota che fra i nuraghi vi è una fascia dimensionale—quella compresa fra i 100-200 mq—molto ampia (73,86%) seguita da altre con valori del tutto marginali, ad indicare la scelta diffusa di un modulo costruttivo attento ai precisi parametri di una architettura ormai matura.

Nei protonuraghi, al contrario, pur convergendo la percentuale più alta di costruzioni nella stessa fascia dimensionale (46,15%), si assiste ad una maggiore variabilità dei valori con una tendenza verso superfici più ampie. Questa maggiore stesura planimetrica dei protonuraghi, più che ad una architettura ancora incerta e alla ricerca di un canone architettonico—è più facile, certamente, costruire in ampiezza che in elevato—si giustifica soprattutto con la destinazione abitativa che il terrazzo sembra avere avuto nei protonuraghi: la necessità, quindi, di uno spazio maggiore che invece non era indispensabile per il terrazzo dei nuraghi la cui funzione era esclusivamente di avvistamento e di difesa.

In conclusione, ad una analisi dei protonuraghi del Marghine-Planargia, legati al territorio e rapportati ai nuraghi della stessa regione, si avverte sempre di più il carattere distintivo che anima ciascun tipo monumentale, non soltanto nelle ben note differenze architettoniche, ora documentate anche da un diverso ordine di grandezza, ma nel modo stesso in cui viene 'vissuto' il territorio. Si ha l'impressione di trovarsi di fronte a concetti architettonici e spaziali diversi, tanto che l'acquisizione della torre circolare, troncoconica e con camera centrale ad ogiva sembra costituire una 'rivoluzione', più che l'esito finale del graduale sviluppo architettonico del protonuraghe.

Tabella 1

Protonuraghi—Nuraghi in relazione alle Unità pedologiche

	Protonuraghi	Nuraghi
U.P.1	8 = 14,03%	42 = 13,04%
U.P.2	–	2 = 0,62%
U.P.3	8 = 14,03%	30 = 9,31%
U.P.4A	26 = 45,61%	94 = 29,19%
U.P.4B	6 = 10,52%	114 = 35,40%
U.P.5	2 = 3,50%	7 = 2,17%
U.P.6	4 = 7,01%	6 = 1,87%
U.P.7	3 = 5,26%	21 = 6,52%
U.P.8	–	–
Varia	–	6 = 1,86%

Tabella 2

Protonuraghi—Nuraghi in relazione alle fasce altimetriche

	Protonuraghi	Nuraghi
0-100	–	1 = 0,31%
100-200	–	10 = 3,10%
200-300	14 = 24,56%	28 = 8,69%
300-400	22 = 38,59%	73 = 22,67%
400-500	9 = 15,78%	56 = 17,39%
500-600	3 = 5,26%	43 = 13,35%
600-700	2 = 3,50%	70 = 21,73%
700-800	6 = 10,52%	24 = 7,45%
800-900	–	3 = 0,93%
900-1000	–	11 = 3,41%
1000-1100	1 = 1,75%	2 = 0,62%
1100-1200	–	1 = 0,31%

Bibliografia

AA.VV.
1985　*Marghine-Planargia*. Cagliari.

Aru, A., & P. Baldaccini
1985　Ricerca sui parametri che determinano la capacità d'uso dei suoli. Correlazioni fra tipologia pedologica e marginalità. L'area di Macomer. *Risorse Agro-Forestali e Sviluppo nella VII Comunità Montana Marghine-Planargia*, 13-18. Macomer.

Contu, E.
1959　I più antichi nuraghi e l'esplorazione del nuraghe Peppe Gallu (Uri, Sassari). *Rivista di Scienze Preistoriche* 14: 59-121.
1978　*Il Significato della Stele nelle Tombe di Giganti*. Quaderni della Soprintendenza Archeologica per le Provincie di Sassari e Nuoro 8. Sassari.

Contu, E.
1981　L'architettura nuragica. In E. Atzeni *et al.* (eds.), *Ichnussa: La Sardegna dalle origini all'età classica*, 5-175. Milano: Libri Scheiwiller.
1985　Il nuraghe. In E. Arslan, F. Barreca e F. Lo Schiavo (a cura di), *La Civiltà Nuragica*, 45-110. Milano: Electa.

Fadda, M.A.
1984　Notiziario. *Rivista di Scienze Preistoriche* 39: 408-10.

Ferrarese Ceruti, M.L.
1966　Nota preliminare alla I e alla II campagna di scavo nel nuraghe Albucciu (Arzachena, Sassari). *Rivista di Scienze Preistoriche* 18: 161-204.

Lilliu, G.
1955　Il nuraghe di Barumini e la stratigrafia nuragica. *Studi Sardi* 12-13(1952-54): 90-469.
1968　Rapporti tra la cultura 'torreana' e aspetti pre e protonuragici della Sardegna. *Studi Sardi* 20(1966-67): 3-47.
1981　*Monumenti Antichi Barbaricini*. Quaderni della Soprintendenza Archeologica per le Provincie di Sassari e Nuoro 10. Sassari.
1982　*La Civiltà Nuragica*. Sardegna Archaeologica: Studi e Monumenti 1. Sassari: Carlo Delfino.
1988　*La Civiltà dei Sardi dal Paleolitico all'Età dei Nuraghi*. Terza edizione. Torino: Nuova ERI.

Maetzke, G.
1961　Scavi e scoperte nelle province di Sassari e Nuoro. *Studi Sardi* 17: 651-53.

Manca Demurtas, L., & S. Demurtas
1984a　I protonuraghi (Nuovi dati per l'Oristanese). In W. Waldren, R. Chapman, J. Lewthwiate e R.-C. Kennard (eds.), *Early Settlement in the West Mediterranean Islands and their Peripheral Areas. The Deya Conference of Prehistory*, 629-70. BAR International Series 229. Oxford: British Archaeological Reports.
1984b　Observaciones sobre los protonuragues de Cerdeña. *Trabajos de Prehistoria* 41: 165-204.

Moravetti, A.
1981　Nota agli scavi nel complesso megalitico di Monte Baranta (Almedo Sassari). *Rivista di Scienze Preistoriche* 36: 281-90.
1985a　*Il Patrimonio Archeologico del Comune di Birori*. Cagliari.
1985b　I beni archeologici. *Marghine-Planargia*, 3-60. Cagliari.
1986　La tomba di giganti di Palatu (Birori). *Nuovo Bullettino Archeologico Sardo* 1(1984): 69-96.
1990　Nota preliminare agli scavi del nuraghe S. Barbara di Macomer. *Nuovo Bullettino Archeologico Sardo* 3(1986): 49-113.

Santoni, V.
1980　Il segno del potere. In D. Sanna (a cura di), *Nur. La misteriosa civiltà dei Sardi*, 141-88. Milano: Cariplo.

Ugas, G.
1981　La tomba megalitica di San Cosimo-Gonnosfanadiga (Cagliari): Un monumento del Bronzo medio (con la più antica attestazione micenea in Sardegna). Notizia preliminare. *Archeologia Sarda* 2: 7-30.

Summary

The protonuraghi found in the Marghine and Planargia regions of west-central Sardinia are discussed in relation to the classic tholos nuraghi in the same regions, and to the local geography, pedology, geology and topography. The chronological development and function of both protonuraghi and classic nuraghi may be better understood through an understanding of their relative use of the Sardinian landscape (cf. Manca Demurtas and Demurtas, Trump, Bonzani and Becker, this volume).

Approximately 32% of all the protonuraghi so far identified on Sardinia are found in the Marghine and Planargia regions, a density ten times the island average. In these two regions, 322 nuraghi and 57 protonuraghi occupy 7 of the 9 geomorphological zones identified, at altitudes up to 1106 m asl. Nearly half of the protonuraghi are located over volcanic (basalt and trachyte) substrates on relatively level ground (zone U.P.4A); this zone contains 29% of the classic nuraghi. The major difference in location is found in zone U.P.4B, similar in characteristics to U.P.4A yet even rockier, which contains 35.4% of the classic nuraghi and only 10.5% of the protonuraghi. Protonuraghi are found at an average elevation of 420 m, classic nuraghi at an average elevation of 508 m; although 1 protonuraghe is found at 1024 m, only 12 (21%) are located above 500 m, where 154 (48%) of the classic nuraghi are found. Spatially, the protonuraghi are concentrated in the south-southeast area of the Marghine-Planargia regions, while classic nuraghi are found throughout the territory.

The Author, assuming chronological differences in the construction of the two types of nuraghi, interprets the differences in location to a change in subsistence adaptation, namely the exploitation of areas more marginal to agriculture and animal husbandry. Furthermore, the Author asserts that territorial control is necessary to explain the location of nuraghi in harsh zones deprived of resources but with strategic value.

In the Marghine-Planargia regions, classic nuraghi average 150.6 m² in area, ranging from 73.5 to 635 m², with 74% between 100 and 200 m²; protonuraghi average 245.5 m², ranging from 51.4 to 1680 m², with 46% between 100 and 200 m². The protonuraghi are clearly larger on average, yet more variable in size; the construction methods used facilitated the erection of large, instead of tall, monuments. The primary purpose of the terrace for occupation (protonuraghi) rather than defense (classic nuraghi) may have been a result of these architectural limitations.

The Author, in emphasizing these differences in geomorphology, altitude, location, and architecture, concludes that the emergence of classic tholos nuraghi was a revolutionary development, rather than the result of gradual architectural evolution from the protonuraghi.

Militarism in Nuragic Sardinia

David H. Trump

The Nuragic culture of Sardinia has always been recognized as a warlike society. The evidence of the great Nuragic fortresses like Su Nuraxi (Barumini-CA), Santu Antine (Torralba-SS), and Palmavera (Alghero-SS), and of the armed warriors shown in the bronze statuettes is both famous and incontrovertible. But both these phenomena belong to a comparatively late phase in the culture's history, how late still being a matter of some controversy. There has been too great a readiness to apply this same interpretation to the earlier monuments, seeing them as the castle keeps of local warring, or more specifically cattle-raiding, barons. Since this culture has its origins many centuries, or even a millennium earlier, this view is perhaps overdue for reconsideration, as I have already suggested (Trump 1990; 1991a; 1991b).

The nuraghi can be divided into three major (and apparently successive) groups: corridor nuraghi, simple towers (*monotorri*), and the complex fortress-nuraghi (Lilliu 1982; Lilliu 1988; Contu 1981). If we examine these in turn, without letting later developments influence our interpretation of earlier phenomena, alternative interpretations become possible.

Corridor Nuraghi (Protonuraghi)

After early controversies, the corridor nuraghe is now generally accepted as the ancestral form, not a late and degenerate version, of the typical nuraghe (Manca Demurtas and Demurtas 1984). These protonuraghi are solid blocks of masonry, commonly square or oval in plan, and typically contain only narrow passages or corridors. Their height is modest and, while the view that they were designed to be inconspicuous may be somewhat overstated (Balmuth 1991), it is true that they do not appear to be deliberately sited so as to be seen from a distance. In this respect they are different from classic nuraghi. The function of the corridor nuraghi appears to be raised platforms for domestic huts of slight construction, traces of which rarely survive (Lewthwaite 1985). Their internal passages may best be explained as storage chambers.

Had no later monuments been found, it is unlikely that the corridor nuraghi would have been interpreted as defensive structures. To take just one example, the Nuraghe Bonu Ighinu (Mara-SS) (Trump 1990: 29-30) was built on a slope, although there are numerous sites nearby that are better defended naturally. Its original height on the uphill side, as shown by the surviving pavement on its upper surface, was a mere 1 m above ground level. Its internal passages could hardly have been the main route of access to structures on its top. The paving left little space for any but a light screening wall around the lip of the platform. Although known from other sites on the island (e.g. Nuraghe Tilariga, Nuraghe Albucciu), no corbel supports (*mensoloni*) survived to suggest a projecting parapet. Raised artificial platforms are known elsewhere in the world, notably the ziggurats of Mesopotamia and the temple mounds of Central America, but they are virtually unknown in the Mediterranean area, apart from the famous earlier example from Sardinia itself, Monte d'Accoddi (Tinè 1989).

Classic Nuraghi (*monotorri*)

The classic, single-tower nuraghi are obviously much more effective militarily than the corridor nuraghi. Their massive battered walls, with only a single opening to the outside, clearly would serve well in a defensive role. A niche inside the front door, nearly always on the right side, seems designed as a guard chamber to control access to both the central vault and the spiral stairway which leads to the upper storeys and the roof. The roof itself would have been a magnificent fighting and lookout platform. Although none survives in position, fallen corbel supports show that projecting parapets were frequent, a conclusion reinforced by their presence in contemporary models of nuraghi (Moravetti 1980). Siting shows a very marked preference for prominent topographical features which, in extreme forms, are almost inaccessible crags. The intervisibility of many nuraghi might also argue for military use, though in a slightly different context from that usually assumed, that is, mutual support rather than mutual hostility.

These features appear to make a convincing case for the military function of classic nuraghi. Each of these characteristics, however, is open to alternative explanation. Unpierced walls are hardly surprising in Cyclopean masonry where wall thickness is determined by the need to stabilize the great vaulted cupola of the central chamber (Cavanagh and Laxton 1987; Santillo Frizzell 1987), and to accommodate the staircase within the wall itself. Window openings would be almost impossible to achieve under these constraints. The niche by the entrance could as well house a porter as a guard. The height of the monument, well beyond functional needs, could be to make it more obvious—to be seen rather than to see out from. This is particularly emphasized in many of the models of nuraghi, which have deliberately exaggerated proportions (Moravetti 1980). These models also show the elegance of the parapet projecting over the in-sloping walls of the tower. Both of these features suggest that these monuments were meant to be seen and admired, hence the preference for locating them on prominent sites, often deliberately in view of neighboring nuraghi.

Two other factors would seem to argue strongly against the conventionally held view. The large central chamber makes no sense in a military context. Defenders could retreat up the stairs to continue the fight from an upper storey, but the closed chamber on the ground floor would hardly be defensible. A smoke-producing missile would rapidly overcome any defenders inside. Secondly, the very numbers of nuraghi, and the density of their distribution, make the idea of their being the seats of mutually warring communities untenable, for reasons to be explained shortly.

If the corbelled chamber cannot be explained in military terms, one need not look far for an alternative explanation. Since its size is surely meant to be impressive, it is much more likely that neighbors were invited in to admire it than barred from entry by force. Feasting, storage, or both together are offered as more plausible explanations.

In many Sardinian communes, nuraghi occur at a density above 0.6 per sq km (Contu 1981: 162). In some smaller areas, the figure can rise to 1.1, 1.3, or even 2.2 per sq km (Trump 1990: 28-32; Webster 1991; Gallin 1991). For example, within the 10 sq km of the Bonu Ighinu Valley, 11 nuraghi were found: 10 *monotorri*, and 1 corridor nuraghe. It is worth noting that only four of these had been previously recorded, suggesting that estimates for areas not studied in detail, and especially figures for the island as a whole (6000-7000 is often quoted), are probably serious underestimates. What does this imply in practical terms?

The Bonu Ighinu basin is fixed by topographical limits (Trump 1985), and its resources are in no way exceptional. Assuming its nuraghi were in a general sense contemporary, each would be supported by a square kilometer or less of territory. If each had to be defended constantly against aggressive neighbors less than a kilometer away, it would seem quite impossible for the land around each to produce the agricultural subsistence required for its inhabitants. An even greater difficulty would be raising the resources necessary for the building of a monument like a nuraghe (Webster 1991). On economic grounds, constant mutual hostility would simply be impossible. However, mutual defense of the valley as a whole by a community dispersed between the farmsteads represented by the Nuragic towers remains possible. This point is examined further elsewhere (Trump 1990: 47-48), where it is suggested that the nuraghi could have been built by cooperative effort, the only way of explaining the scale of labor investment they imply.

This interpretation would, of course, be incompatible with the strictly military role. Instead, I have proposed that the motive for nuraghe construction was a social one, to demonstrate ownership and status within the community (Trump 1990: 45-48). None of the evidence in support of warfare excludes this interpretation. This does, however, lead us to reconsider the later, complex nuraghi.

Complex Nuraghi

There can be no reasonable doubt that these were indeed primarily military fortresses. Their narrow, sometimes elevated, entrances, subsidiary reinforcing towers with numerous arrow-slits (*feritoie*), curtain walls, together with those elements already noted like guard chambers and projecting parapets, all lead to this inescapable conclusion. If the simple towers were not military in function, how did this change come about? The problem must be approached from two directions: architectural and social.

It is patently obvious that the complex nuraghi developed from the simpler ones. With very few exceptions—S'Uraki (San Vero Milis-OR) seems to be one—the initial structure at the heart of each was a simple *monotorre*, as their plans clearly show. Complexity came from accretion, by the addition of extra towers and connecting walls. Sometimes these stages of growth seem to have been planned all at once, at one moment in time, as at Nuraghe Santu Antine. Other nuraghi developed in stages over a period of time, as at Su Nuraxi, Barumini; this often meant blocking off earlier features like the arrow-slits.

A word of caution is in order here. While always interpreted as arrow-slits, some openings seem far too small on the inside to operate a bow the size of those shown in the statuettes. Others are dangerously close to ground level outside the tower. An alternative use would be to admit light, but if so, there are places like the stairways where light would seem much more important than in these corner towers. Whatever their function, these external openings must have been important at the time of construction, though on occasion they were sealed off by later additions.

While variation in the form of the *monotorri* was slight, confined in effect to its dimensions, the complex nuraghi occur in a bewildering variety of plans. This is no more than one would expect of sites designed with military considerations paramount, strongly influenced by topography and, even more, resources.

To understand how the complex nuraghi developed from the simple *monotorri*, some general observations may be helpful. An impression obtained from published plans (Lilliu 1962), which needs much wider statistical verification, is that the central towers of complex nuraghi are on average both larger in diameter and have more storeys than those which did not develop further. While tower diameters are easily determined from the ground plans, later destruction often prevents precise measurement of the number of storeys.

A second observation is that the complex nuraghi rarely occur on sites with strongly marked natural defenses, Santa Barbara (Macomer-NU) and Genna Maria (Villanovaforu-CA) being among the few that spring to mind. Many, like Santu Antine, Losa (Abbasanta-OR), and Palmavera are on more or less level ground. Contrast these with a group of *monotorri*, like those of the Bonu Ighinu Valley, where six are on strong sites, five on modest prominences, and none on flat land.

Thirdly, only a small proportion of nuraghi developed into complex ones, and then not randomly. It is clearly noticeable how the great nuraghi of Sardinia are widely spaced across the island, as if each had its own supporting territory.

While all these arguments are circumstantial, they are consistent with the following theory of development: if the simple nuraghi represented local status and land ownership, over time one can envision certain families increasing their status into some sort of overlordship in their neighborhood. Ownership of land, and so wealth, is likely to have been more influential here than occupation of the best-defended site. Those families which controlled the greater resources at the time of the initial nuraghe-building, and who therefore probably built the largest *monotorri*, were more likely to have increased their wealth and power at the expense of their neighbors. Such developments are unlikely to have been universal, for dynastic, historic, or even purely accidental reasons.

By this model, in each area, after a certain amount of jockeying for position among competing neighbors—and the first *monotorri*, if not the first corridor nuraghi, strongly imply competition for status at least—one family edges ahead. It acquires the influence to persuade or coerce other families to contribute the labor force to enlarge, beautify and fortify that family's seat against other claimants. With the complex nuraghi, the increasing emphasis on the military strength of the monument implies that status is now backed by force. Note that this is also the period when the warrior statuettes appear. Just as the later complex nuraghi find their closest architectural parallels in medieval castles, it is suggested that the social background to the two could offer close parallels (Trump 1990: 45-46; Andrews 1991).

This hypothesis has several implications which should be testable from the archaeological evidence:

1. Complex nuraghi developed by elaboration of *monotorri*, probably those of above average size. Statistical analyses of large numbers in both classes should corroborate or refute this.
2. Complex nuraghi would be expected to lie alongside more extensive or more fertile agricultural land to supply the resources which allowed their owners to forge ahead and dominate the less well-endowed. For this, some sort of site catchment analysis would be required, bearing in mind environmental change since the period of interest. Again, a statistically valid sample size would be needed.
3. The building of complex nuraghi should be matched by a decline in the building, perhaps even the maintenance, of the *monotorri*, as limited resources were concentrated. Here, more precise dating of Nuragic material is called for than is yet generally

available, though continuing research will improve this situation.
4. Environmental research on colluvial deposits in the Bonu Ighinu Valley showed that its Nuragic Period was marked by a major phase of soil erosion (Trump 1990: 23). That may have been a purely local phenomenon, but if wider research could demonstrate that soil erosion was more widespread, that would explain the increased competition for land implied by the increasing military role of the nuraghi.

Although the complex nuraghi clearly imply militarism, no external threat need be involved to account for this; local competition for control of resources, above all land, would be quite sufficient. That could explain successively the appearance of classic nuraghi in the mid-second millennium BC, and their development into complex nuraghi early in the first millennium BC. That this is roughly the period when Phoenician settlements first appeared along the southern and western coasts of Sardinia could be no more than coincidence. The Phoenicians were traders rather than empire builders, and did not threaten the independence of native peoples inland. The nuraghi S'Uraki, Losa, Genna Maria and Su Nuraxi might have been built to discourage Phoenician encroachment, but it is hard to explain the nuraghi Santu Antine, Santa Barbara, or Orrubiu (Orroli-NU) in these terms. Alternatively, the residents of these nuraghi may have strengthened their position among their neighbors by controlling the trade between inland Nuragic settlements and the Phoenician cities on the coast.

Dates for these developments are unlikely to be very precise, or even very meaningful, since we are looking at evolutionary changes which may have taken long periods of time to show themselves, and have acted at different rates in different parts of the island. Indeed, for comparative purposes it would be interesting to look also at areas where no complex nuraghi are known. In the Gallura, for example, the thinly distributed *monotorri* might imply reduced competition, and thus a lack of incentive for the development of hierarchically stratified sites. This can hardly be the case in areas like the Bonu Ighinu Valley, however, where local densities of nuraghi exceed 1.1 per sq km.

The medieval analogy can also show, as archaeology can never do, the effects of historical chance. For example, if no family succeeded in winning a preeminent position, or failed to produce a male heir before securing it, a hierarchical society such as that implied by the complex nuraghi might never have developed. We can and should look for general trends and the factors which contributed to them, but cannot fill in historical detail until written sources allow us to do so.

References

Andrews, D.
1991   Tower building and upwardly mobile elites in Medieval Italy. In R. Whitehouse and J. Wilkes (eds.), *The Archaeology of Power: 4th Conference of Italian Archaeology*. Forthcoming.

Balmuth, M.S.
1991   Nuragic camouflage. In B. Santillo Frizell (ed.), *Arte Militare e Architettura Nuragica. Nuragic Architecture in its Military, Territorial and Socio-economic Context. Proceedings of the First International Colloquium on Nuragic Architecture at the Swedish Institute in Rome, 7-9 December, 1989.* Acta Instituti Romani Regni Sueciae, Series In 4°, 48: 19-22. Stockholm: Svenska Institutet i Rom.

Cavanagh, W.G., & R.R. Laxton
1987   Notes on building techniques in Mycenaean Greece and Nuragic Sardinia. In M.S. Balmuth (ed.), *Studies in Sardinian Archaeology III. Nuragic Sardinia and the Mycenaean World*, 39-56. BAR International Series 387. Oxford: British Archaeological Reports.

Contu, E.
1981   L'architettura nuragica. In E. Atzeni *et al.* (eds.), *Ichnussa: La Sardegna dalle origini all'età classica*. Milano: Libri Scheiwiller.

Gallin, L.
1991   Architectural evidence for the defensibility of the territory of Sedilo (Oristano). In B. Santillo Frizell (ed.), *Arte Militare e Architettura Nuragica. Nuragic Architecture in its Military, Territorial and Socio-economic Context. Proceedings of the First International Colloquium on Nuragic Architecture at the Swedish Institute in Rome, 7-9 December, 1989.* Acts Instituti Romani Regni Sueciae, Series In 4°, 48: 65-71. Stockholm: Svenska Institutet i Rom.

Lewthwaite, J.
1985   Colonialism and nuraghismus. In C. Malone and S. Stoddart (eds.), *Papers in Italian Archaeology IV: The Cambridge Conference*, 220-51. BAR International Series 243. Oxford: British Archaeological Reports.

Lilliu, G.
1962   *I Nuraghi. Torri preistoriche della Sardegna*. Verona.
1982   *La Civiltà Nuragica*. Sardegna Archeologica: Studi e Monumenti I. Sassari: Carlo Delfino.
1988   *La Civiltà dei Sardi dal Paleolitico all'Età dei Nuraghi*. 3rd edition. Torino: Nuova ERI.

Manca Demurtas, L., & S. Demurtas
1984   I protonuraghi (Nuovi dati per l'Oristanese). In W. Waldren, R. Chapman and J. Lewthwaite (eds.), *Early Settlement in the West Mediterranean Islands and the Peripheral Areas*, 629-70. BAR International Series 229. Oxford: British Archaeological Reports.

Moravetti, A.
    1980   Nuovi modellini di torri nuragiche. *Bollettino d'Arte* 7: 65-84.

Santillo Frizzell, B.
    1987   The true domes in Mycenaean and Nuragic architecture. In M.S. Balmuth (ed.), *Studies in Sardinian Archaeology III. Nuragic Sardinia and the Mycenaean World*, 57-76. BAR International Series 387. Oxford: British Archaeological Reports.

Santillo-Frizzell, B. (ed.)
    1991   *Arte Militare e Architettura Nuragica. Nuragic Architecture in its Military, Territorial and Socio-economic Context. Proceedings of the First International Colloquium on Nuragic Architecture at the Swedish Institute in Rome, 7-9 December, 1989.* Acta Instituti Romani Regni Sueciae, Series In 4°, 48. Stockholm: Svenska Institutet i Rom.

Tinè, S.
    1989   Monte d'Accoddi e la cultura di Ozieri: L'architettura. In L.D. Campus (a cura di), *La Cultura di Ozieri. Problematiche e nuove acquisizioni. Atti del I convegno di studio (Ozieri, gennaio 1986—aprile 1987)*, 19-26. Ozieri: Il Torchietto.

Trump, D.
    1985   Bonu Ighinu, site and setting. In C. Malone and S. Stoddart (eds.), *Papers in Italian Archaeology IV: The Cambridge Conference*, 185-99. BAR International Series 243. Oxford: British Archaeological Reports.
    1990   *Nuraghe Noeddos and the Bonu Ighinu Valley.* Oxford: Oxbow.
    1991a   Nuraghi as social history: A case study from Bonu Ighinu, Mara (SS). In B. Santillo Frizell (ed.), *Arte Militare e Architettura Nuragica. Nuragic Architecture in its Military, Territorial and Socio-economic Context. Proceedings of the First International Colloquium on Nuragic Architecture at the Swedish Institute in Rome, 7-9 December, 1989.* Acta Instituti Romani Regni Sueciae, Series In 4° 48. Stockholm: Svenska Institutet i Rom.
    1991b   The nuraghi of Sardinia, territory and power. In R. Whitehouse and J. Wilkes (eds.), *The Archaeology of Power: 4th Conference of Italian Archaeology*. (Forthcoming)

Webster, G.
    1991   Monuments, mobilization and Nuragic organization. *Antiquity* 65: 840-56.

Riassunto

La cultura nuragica della Sardegna è sempre stata considerata una cultura bellica. Questa interpretazione è basata sulle evidenze del periodo più tardo come di bronzetti guerrieri, e le grandi fortezze come Su Nuraxi-Barumini. L'Autore afferma che l'immagine dell'antica cultura nuragica non deve derivare da ritrovamenti archeologici riguardanti periodi successivi, quindi i nuraghi più antichi non devono essere visti come castelli-fortezze abitati da baroni bellicosi. Se noi esaminiamo questi monumenti più antichi senza lasciarci influenzare dagli avvenimenti storici successivi, noteremo che sono possibili altre interpretazioni dei monumenti sopra citati. L'Autore rivede i tre tipi di nuraghi e suggerisce funzioni non militari per quelli che non sono chiaramente fortezze.

I nuraghi a corridoio sono considerati forme antiche del tipico nuraghe a monotorre. Sono costruiti con una muratura solida, sono quadrati od ovali e generalmente contengono solo passaggi stretti o corridoi. La loro altezza è modesta ed essi sono poco appariscenti nel territorio da loro occupato. Il nuraghe a corridoio può essere interpretato come piattaforma elevata per l'erezione di capanne domestiche e i corridoi stessi potrebbero avere avuto la funzione di magazzini. Se non si fossero trovati monumenti riguardanti periodi successivi è molto probabile che i nuraghi a corridoio non sarebbero stati interpretati come strutture militari.

Il classico nuraghe a multitorri sembra giustificare una interpretazione militare. Le mure sono massicce e spioventi con una sola porta. La nicchia esistente all'interno della porta potrebbe essere stata una stanza da guardia per controllare l'accesso alla volta centrale e alla scala a chiocciola che conduce ai piani superiori ed al tetto. Il tetto stesso potrebbe essere stato un appostamento di guardia e di attacco. Questi tipi di nuraghi sono situati in modo da essere visibili l'uno dall'altro, questo forse sta ad indicare l'esistenza di un 'network' di difesa reciproca; in ogni caso è anche possibile interpretare queste caratteristiche come non militari. Le mure massicce e spioventi sarebbero potute essere state costruite per sostenere il peso della muratura; la nicchia 'da guardia' sarebbe potuta essere servita ad un portiere. L'altezza prominente dei nuraghi e la loro posizione sarebbe potuto servire a soddisfare bisogni estetici o di status. Le camere a falsavolta potrebbero essere servite come aree di immagazzinaggio o per grandi feste. Il numero di nuraghi e la loro scala sembrano mostrare l'esistenza di una cooperazione sociale. Considerando la loro densità, l'esistenza di una continua e reciproca guerra sembra economicamente impossibile.

I nuraghi complessi sono principalmente fortezze militari. Essi sono derivati da forme non militari—dal semplice nuraghe a monotorre—e attraverso l'aggiunta di torri e muri, essi hanno acquistato una grande varietà architettonica. In che modo si sono sviluppati i nuraghi complessi dai nuraghi a monotorre? L'Autore inizia la sua spiegazione notando che i nuraghi complessi tendono ad avere torri centrali con diametri larghi e più piani che i nuraghi a monotorre e che sono raramente situati in luoghi con marcate difese naturali. Solo pochi nuraghi sono divenuti nuraghi di tipo complesso e questi sono situati con spazi estesi tra l'uno e l'altro, come se ognuno di loro avesse il proprio territorio di sostegno. L'Autore ipotizza che questi fattori sono il risultato di competizione per lo status tra le famiglie. I nuraghi a monotorre più grandi sono stati probabilmente costruiti da famiglie che hanno acquistato territori e potere a spese dei loro vicini. Le famiglie più prominenti erano in competizione tra di loro, finché la più potente è emersa come la 'vincitrice'. La famiglia 'vincitrice' ha poi persuaso o obbligato le altre famiglie a contribuire all'imbellimento ed al rinforzamento del suo nuraghe che è conseguentemente divenuto un nuraghe con forme architettoniche più complesse. L'evidente funzione militare dei nuraghi complessi, mostra che l'uso della forza e delle armi è stato adottato per la conquista di uno status maggiore.

Ricerche archeologiche future dovrebbero essere fatte per confermare o smentire queste ipotesi: i nuraghi complessi sono derivati dai nuraghi a monotorre; i nuraghi complessi sono situati su territori più estesi e fertili, rispetto ai nuraghi a monotorre; nel momento in cui i nuraghi complessi sono stati costruiti, i nuraghi a monotorre sono declinati; durante il periodo dei nuraghi complessi, l'aumento di competizione per la conquista di nuovi territori era dovuto al diffuso fenomeno di erosione del suolo. Tutto questo ha portato alla conquista di nuovi territori attraverso la forza militare.

Cultural Uniformity during the Italian Iron Age: Sardinian Nuraghi as Regional Markers

Marshall Joseph Becker

Introduction

Stone towers, called nuraghi, are so widely distributed throughout Sardinia that they have come to characterize the prehistoric landscape of the island. Considerable effort is now being expended to determine their origins and functions, and to understand their significance in the cultural history of this large territory. Until recently the existence of the nuraghi throughout Sardinia has been taken as a sign of a homogeneous island culture transcending any regional anomalies. But data now emerging from central Italy suggests that the presence of nuraghi need not indicate cultural uniformity throughout the territory in which they are found. It will be the purpose of this paper to present this new evidence and examine its impact on the cultural interpretation of the nuraghi.

An interesting and instructive parallel to the Sardinian nuraghi are the hut urns of Late Iron Age central Italy. Hut urns were used as containers for cremations and enjoyed widespread distribution throughout the region. Recent studies suggest, however, that even though the various peoples employing this distinctive type of cinerary container may have shared some characteristic elements of material culture, local diversity can be inferred in the way each village or district structured these material elements within their specific behavioral systems. This new understanding of the use of hut urns in central Italy provides a cautionary tale for those seeking to interpret Sardinia's stone towers: the cultural uniformity implied by the wide distribution of Sardinian nuraghi must serve only as a working model for conducting research, and cannot be interpreted as proof that only a single cultural tradition is represented by these architectural aspects of the prehistory of Sardinia.[1]

The use of urns in the shape of thatched huts for cremation burials, a characteristic 'trait' known from central Italian archaeological sites in the Late Iron Age, is only a single element within a complex of traits which have yet to be examined in detail (by 'trait' I mean a specific element within a 'trait complex' or series of related features). The evidence from bones in these urns and other related archaeological data suggest that in central Italy numerous distinct cultures shared the hut urn complex. The specific identity of each culture, bounded by a village or other political unit, has yet to be determined, but clearly significant diversity exists within the region from which this urn form is known. This interpretation of the hut urn evidence has implications for the Nuragic complexes found throughout Sardinia, which also include a great number of traits reflecting localized differences. More detailed studies of the multiple elements associated with each nuraghe should reveal patterns enabling investigators to identify the cultural boundaries and political forms which once existed on Sardinia.

Nuraghi

Surveys and excavations associated with individual nuraghi on Sardinia increasingly reveal the island's cultural development during the Iron Age (see Lilliu 1982). Theories of developing social stratification, essential to the emergence of the 'state', have been suggested (Lo Schiavo 1981), and are being reviewed in the light of increasingly rich data (Webster 1990). Recent excavations are being directed toward answering the many questions relating to these processes of culture change and the ability to recognize them in the archaeological record. As the evidence from Sardinia expands, caution is needed in its interpretation as uniformly applicable to the entire area over

---

1 Also found on Sardinia are gallery graves called 'giants' tombs', as well as dolmens and other varieties of tombs. These probably vary in form and chronology, and also should be regarded with the same interpretive caution.

which these ancient stone towers are distributed. Nuraghi often are considered as a single class of artifacts, sometimes with two or three temporal subsets (see below). Modern excavations of these structures, as well as their associated sites (e.g. Michels and Webster 1987), now provide a good archaeological database, but these examples cannot be used as more than heuristic models for understanding the prehistory of the entire island.

The recognition of cultural or ethnic variations within Sardinia is the focus of the present archaeological question. Similarly-shaped stone towers are known from the Balearic Islands, Corsica and elsewhere in the western Mediterranean. These towers, as well as the Mycenaean tholos tombs, have been distinguished from the Sardinian nuraghi by careful comparison of architectural details. Gallin (1987; 1989) offers fundamental data needed in making comparisons within the complex of cultural traits relating to Nuragic architecture, but much more needs to be done to expand this particular database and to define the divergent aspects of settlement associated with each of these towers.

As an island, Sardinia certainly has clear geographical boundaries. The near saturation of the island with stone towers (see Balmuth 1984) gave earlier investigators the impression that the entire region was culturally uniform during the period when the nuraghi were built (Lilliu 1982). One problem in Nuragic research concerns the delineation of the period of construction for each type. An effective summary of temporal variation in earlier Sardinian cultures, which has implications for the Nuragic period, is provided by Lewthwaite (1986: 20-22). Lewthwaite (1986: 22-25) reviews some of the spatial variation to be found on Sardinia in the Copper Age, which helps to set the scene for examining later periods. Even more significant are Lewthwaite's attempts to correlate these variations with cultural behaviors.

Extremely noteworthy is Lewthwaite's (1986: 25) suggestion that the corbelled nuraghi and the less frequent, simpler, and probably earlier corridor-variant constructions may derive from Copper Age prototypes. These observations provide an avenue by which the problem may be effectively approached. Considerations of temporal variation in the development and occupation of nuraghi may be expected to reveal a *lack* of cultural uniformity throughout the territory in which they are found. This warning derives from findings in other archaeological as well as ethnographic circumstances in which similar materials may be present, but the patterns or organization of specific traits may differ considerably. These different 'patterns' of organization of artifacts in time and space are critical to the recognition of cultural differences and cultural boundaries.

The Hut Urn Analogy

As stated above, data now emerging from central Italy suggest that the use of hut urns as containers for cremations is not by itself a sufficient indicator of cultural boundaries. Ceramic traits, as the concept relates to hut urns or any other class of vessel, include the clay from which the vessel was made, the temper, the many elements of form or shape, surface decoration, painting or glaze, and also function. Hut urns are generally identified in terms of shape and function, with less attention paid to other associated variables.

The central Italian hut urn complex may be considered a regional marker, completely unrelated to the similar funerary containers known from Yugoslavia (Gregl 1988). Although used as cinerary containers, the Yugoslavian examples are very different in shape, perhaps representing storage buildings rather than houses. Also important is the fact that they date much later than the Italian hut urns, from the first and second centuries AD according to Gregl, based on his studies at the Archaeological Museum in Zagreb. Cinerary chests with saddle roofs common in Etruria from about the 5th-4th centuries BC also may be a related form of ash container. While closer in time and space to the central Italian hut urns, variations in shape indicate that there is no direct relationship.

The central Italian hut urn region, an area defined only by the presence of hut urns, now is known to have major internal variations based on differences in many other aspects of material culture. Significant in recognizing the cultural boundaries *within* this region are variations which occur in the trait complex associated with hut urns, as well as in other aspects of behavior such as ceramic use or domestic architecture in this part of central Italy. Possible temporal variations in use within the Iron Age also are critical factors. The data recovered from recent excavations at Osteria dell'Osa, now within the borders of modern Rome, reveal that cremation burials declined in popularity during the Iron Age, a change characteristic of the cultures of this region. By the 9th and 8th centuries BC only a relatively small number of cremations were still appearing among the increasingly common inhumations at Osteria dell'Osa. Cremations, placed both in hut urns and other containers, were reserved only for males. The extensive Osteria dell'Osa evidence is comparable to other sites throughout Latium which have a similar or parallel material culture, in particular the use of hut urns for cremations. But to what degree can we predict that the non-material aspects of all these cultures, and in particular mortuary customs, may be similar simply because they include the use of hut urns to hold the remains of some of their dead? Many hut urns were excavated at a time when minimal field records were kept, just as on Sardinia archaeologically detailed records of the numerous nuraghi are available from only limited numbers of sites. How much less then, in the face of incomplete material records, are we justified in drawing broad cultural conclusions for Iron Age central Italy or Nuragic Sardinia?

The presence of cremated bones in association with these hut urns provides another means by which we can examine the cultural behaviors of these people (cf. Chapman 1987). Bietti Sestieri (1985) has demonstrated that cremation at Osteria dell'Osa during the period from c. 900–740 BC was a mortuary ritual reserved primarily, if not exclusively, for males (Bietti Sestieri *et al.* in press; see also Becker and Salvadei in press). Cremation in central Italy had been common prior to 900 BC, with this custom lingering at Osteria dell'Osa only in limited contexts. This suggests a normal pattern of survival of the formerly traditional mortuary ritual of cremation. Such cultural survivals tend to linger with the higher status members of a community (adult males).

I would suggest that such males, particularly those of higher status in an increasingly class stratified community (Bietti Sestieri *et al.* in press), continued to be buried using more traditional forms of interment (cf. Becker MS). Bartoloni and De Santis (in Bartoloni *et al.* 1987: 207-17) also have gathered related data on hut urns, or their counterparts, from a wide area, thereby providing suggestions regarding variations in function over a considerable geographical range.

The evidence from sites contemporary with Osteria dell'Osa (Bartoloni *et al.* 1987) suggests that Bietti Sestieri's data might apply to all sites where hut urns are found. However, entirely different cultural patterns may have operated at each of these sites, as suggested by the historical record in this area. Therefore, a study of these site-specific examples should be made within each context, treating each site as a unique constellation of traits rather than inferring homogeneity for all sites from the evidence of a single shared trait. Assuming that there are vast similarities in culture just because all of these polities (villages, or other political units to be identified) had one small constellation of traits (hut urns) in common can only lead to making false assumptions regarding cultural uniformity.

The study of human remains and mortuary programs from archaeological contexts also provides significant information about the inhabitants of ancient sites (Becker 1982). The treatment of the dead provides us with an indication of how the living members of society conceptualized their universe, and how they viewed the passage of one of their number from this world into the next (cf. D'Agostino 1985).

Study of cremated human remains is an important way to differentiate hut urn functions from site to site, or even different points of time at the same site. The excavations at Osteria dell'Osa provide the tight chronological controls needed to achieve order in these hut urn data (Bietti Sestieri 1980; 1985). These data may be compared with information from the urns excavated at Veii in the 1960s (Close-Brooks 1965; Toms 1986). In addition to the extensive studies being carried out in central Italy, scholars from Sicily (Di Salvo 1986) to Spain (Reverte 1984) have focused their attentions on this subset of the human biological record as a trait intrinsically related to the study of hut urns.

Osteological data reveal important information on fundamental traits associated with Italian Iron Age hut urns such as the age and gender of the occupant. Trace element data from the bones, providing another set of traits, are discussed by Runia (1987: 125-29). Such studies (Bowmer and Molleson 1986; Becker 1987; 1988) suggest that significant variations existed in the mortuary practices at various sites where hut urns are found. While adult males appear to be the rule at Osteria dell'Osa (Becker and Salvadei in press), Cassoli and Taglicozza (in Bartoloni *et al.* 1987) believe that very young children predominate in the hut urns now in the Pigorini Museum. Such differences may *not* be reflections of different practices at the several ancient villages, but may reflect variations in the methods used by the evaluators (see Becker and Ginge 1990: tables 1 and 2). The data at present, however, suggest that Ridgway (1990) is correct in noting that the Osteria dell'Osa evidence 'cannot be extended automatically to all other centers'. In just the same way this caution should apply to the study of the Sardinian nuraghi: the evidence from a single Nuragic excavation cannot automatically be applied to all the others.

Discussion

Just as detailed examination of the central Italian hut urns and their associated skeletal remains have revealed site-specific variations within what appears to be a large region, so can we expect that parallel studies of nuraghi will yield information enabling us to establish boundaries and to differentiate areas of cultural cohesion within the region of Sardinia. As noted earlier, previous studies of nuraghi have enabled scholars to recognize temporal variations. Other traits such as size and configurations of associated structures, which can be revealed only through intensive archaeological excavation, should tell us a great deal about the ways in which the many peoples of Sardinia variously organized their social and political lives before the island came under Roman control.

Nuraghi, unlike hut urns, are very large, complex in their construction and expensive to excavate. Even detailed drawings are far more difficult to produce than the section drawings and photographs needed to understand and evaluate a hut urn. Thus the progress of understanding the prehistory of Sardinia during the Nuragic Period will continue to be restricted by the daunting scale of each complex. A single nuraghe and its associated structures requires a major excavation by a large team of archaeologists. Some focus can be brought to this research through architectural studies such as those conducted by Gallin (1989) which concentrate on the main Nuragic tower(s). These alone may provide the most significant evidence for variations within the general region.

Other approaches to the problem include testing for ceramic materials (see Webster et al. 1987) or for obsidian samples (see Michels 1987), both of which may be used to establish chronologies needed for temporal control. The excavation of two nuraghi has enabled Webster and his colleagues to generate important ceramic evidence for one portion of Sardinia; this will serve as an important reference for the kinds of studies suggested here. Nuraghe Toscono, from which has come a major sample, has been found to be ceramically identical to Nuraghe Urpes, as would be expected from the pottery remains of two nearly proximal sites in the Marghine region of west-central Sardinia. What is needed now are comparative studies with ceramic materials from other Nuragic complexes in other parts of the island (see Weiss Grele, this volume).

These studies from Toscono and Urpes are critical for providing a data base from which we can establish time–space considerations fundamental to working out effective strategies for future research. At that point other sets of traits can be studied, focusing on ceramic evidence or metallurgical data (cf. Balmuth and Tylecote 1976) or human skeletal studies, with the goal of confirming or negating ideas concerning cultural realms which have been postulated through fundamental studies such as those provided by Michels and Webster (1987). Each of these aspects of research will be an important addition to our current knowledge of the island's prehistory.

The presence of nuraghi as regional markers is not to be confused with the concept of cultural borders. The reconstruction of culture histories requires the identification of boundaries of specific peoples. The recognition of particular subsets of behavior through the archaeological record requires that we look beyond the gross regional responses to life, and seek to understand how each village or polity developed its individual means of self identity and self expression.

Acknowledgments

Sincere thanks are due Ann Brown, Andrew G. Sherratt, Professor Francis E. Johnston, Michael Vickers, and William Anderson for assistance in various aspects of the study. Special thanks are due Robert H. Tykot and Tamsey K. Andrews, as well as to Pamela Scheifele, for their considerable editorial assistance. Thanks also are due to Anna Maria Bietti Sestieri for her aid in related programs of research. The ideas and interpretations presented here as well as any errors which may appear are the responsibility of the author alone.

References

Balmuth, M.S.
    1984   The nuraghi of Sardinia: An introduction. In M.S. Balmuth and R.J. Rowland, Jr (eds.), *Studies in Sardinian Archaeology*, 23-52. Ann Arbor: University of Michigan Press.

Balmuth, M.S., & R.F. Tylecote
    1976   Ancient copper and bronze in Sardinia: Excavation and analysis. *Journal of Field Archaeology* 3: 195-201.

Bartoloni, G., F. Buranelli, V. D'Atri & A. De Santis (eds.)
    1987   *Le Urne a Capanna Rinvenute in Italia*. Roma: Giorgio Bretschneider.

Becker, M.J.
    1982   Anthropological appendix [to M. Gualtieri, Cremation among the Lucanians]. *American Journal of Archaeology* 86: 479-81.

    1987   Appendice I. Analisi Antropologiche e Paleontologiche: Soprintendenza di Roma. In G. Bartoloni, F. Buranelli, V. D'Atri and A. De Santis (eds.), *Le Urne a Capanna Rinvenute in Italia*, 235-46. Roma: Giorgio Bretschneider.

1988   The contents of funerary vessels as clues to mortuary customs: Identifying the *Os exceptum*. In J. Christiansen and T. Melander (eds.), *Proceedings of the 3rd Symposium on Ancient Greek and Related Pottery (Copenhagen, 1987)*, 25-32. Copenhagen: Nationalmuseet.

MS   Excavations at the Montgomery Site (36CH60), the burial area for the Brandywine Band of Lenape, c. 1720–1733.

Becker, M.J., & B. Ginge
1990   Cremations in Italic hut urns: an evaluation of the evidence together with the analysis of the remains found in an example in the Ashmolean Museum, Oxford, England. *Antropologia Contemporanea* 13: 371-81.

Becker, M.J., & L. Salvadei
in press   *Osteria dell'Osa, An Iron Age Cemetery in Central Italy* by A.M. Bietti Sestieri. Volume II: *The Human Remains* [working title]. Rome: Soprintendenza per Archeologia.

Bietti Sestieri, A.M.
1980   *Ricerca su una comunità del Lazio protostorico*. Il sepolcreto dell'Osteria dell'Osa sulla via Prenestina. Rome: De Luca Editore.

1985   The Iron Age cemetery of Osteria dell'Osa, Rome: Evidence of social change in Lazio in the 8th century BC. In C. Malone and S. Stoddart (eds.), *Papers in Italian Archaeology IV: The Cambridge Conference*. Part III: *Patterns in Protohistory*, 111-44. BAR International Series 245. Oxford: British Archaeological Reports.

Bietti Sestieri, A.M., A. De Santis & L. Salvadei
in press   The Iron Age cemetery of Osteria dell'Osa (Rome): An integrated anthropological and cultural study. *Proceedings of the German Archaeological Conference* (Frankfurt, May 1989). Demographic Section.

Bowmer, M., & T. Molleson
1986   Identification of human remains from the hut urns. Appendix to: G. Bartoloni, Le urne a capanna ancora sulla prime scoperte nei Colli Albani. In J. Swaddling (ed.), *Italian Iron Age Artefacts in the British Museum*, 238-39. London: Trustees of the British Museum.

Chapman, R.
1987   Mortuary practices: society, theory building and archaeology. In A. Boddington, A.N. Garland and R.C. Janaway (eds.), *Death, Decay, and Reconstruction: Approaches to archaeology and forensic science*, 198-216. Manchester: Manchester University Press.

Close-Brooks, J.
1965   Proposta per una divisione in fasi. *Notizie degli Scavi* 1965: 53-64. Reprinted in English in D. Ridgway and F. Ridgway (eds.), *Italy before the Romans* (1979).

D'Agostino, B.
1985   Società dei vivi, comunità dei morti: un rapporto difficile. *Dialoghi di Archeologia* 1: 47-58.

Di Salvo, R.
1986   Analisi dei resti umani incinerati (edificio 'Triolo Nord': LM 19) [santuario della Malophoros a Selinunte]. *Sicilia Archeologica* 19(60–61): 77.

Gallin, L.J.
1987   Appendix E. Nuraghe Toscono: An architectural study. In G.S. Webster and J. Michels (eds.), *Studies in Nuragic Archaeology: Village Excavations at Nuraghe Urpes and Nuraghe Toscono in West-Central Sardinia*, 163-69. BAR International Series 373. Oxford: British Archaeological Reports.

1989   *Architectural Attributes and Inter-site Variation: A Case Study: The Sardinian Nuraghi*. PhD dissertation, UCLA. Ann Arbor: University Microfilms International.

Gregl, Z.
1988   Antike hausurnen aus kroatien. *Rivista di Archeologia* 2: 54-59.

Lewthwaite, J.
1986   Nuragic foundations: An alternate model of development in Sardinian prehistory, c. 2500–1500 BC. In M.S. Balmuth (ed.), *Studies in Sardinian Archaeology, Volume II: Sardinia in the Mediterranean*, 19-37. Ann Arbor: University of Michigan Press.

Lilliu, G.
1982   *La Civiltà Nuragica*. Sardegna Archaeologica: Studi e Monumenti 1. Sassari: Carlo Delfino.

Lo Schiavo, F.
1981   Economia e società nell'età dei nuraghi. In E. Atzeni et al. (eds.), *Ichnussa: La Sardegna dalle origini all'età classica*, 255-347. Milano: Libri Scheiwiller.

Michels, J.W.
1987   Appendix A. Obsidian hydration dating and a proposed chronological scheme for the Marghine region. In J.W. Michels and G.S. Webster (eds.), *Studies in Nuragic Archaeology: Village Excavations at Nuraghe Urpes and Nuraghe Toscono in West-Central Sardinia*, 119-25. BAR International Series 373. Oxford: British Archaeological Reports.

Michels, J.W., & G.S. Webster (eds.)
1987   *Studies in Nuragic Archaeology: Village Excavations at Nuraghe Urpes and Nuraghe Toscono in West-Central Sardinia*. BAR International Series 373. Oxford: British Archaeological Reports.

Reverte, J.M.
1984   Prehistoric cremations in Spain [abstract]. *Papers on Paleopathology* presented at the Fifth European Members Meeting, 3-4 September, Siena, Italy, 13.

Ridgway, D.
1990   Review of G. Bartoloni, F. Buranelli, V. D'Atri and A. De Santis, *Le Urne a Capanna Rinvenute in Italia* (Roma: Giorgio Bretschneider, 1987). *American Journal of Archaeology* 94: 354-56.

Runia, L.T.
1987   *The Chemical Analysis of Prehistoric Bones: A paleodietary and ecoarcheological study of Bronze Age West-Friesland*. BAR International Series 363. Oxford: British Archaeological Reports.

Toms, J.
1986   The relative chronology of the Villanovan cemetery of Quattro-Fontanili at Veii. *Archeologia e Storia Antica* 8: 42-97.

Webster, G.S.
1990   Labor control and emergent stratification in prehistoric Europe. *Current Anthropology* 31(4): 337-66.

Webster, G.S., J.W. Michels & D. Hudak
1987   Ceramics. In J.W. Michels and G.S. Webster (eds.), *Studies in Nuragic Archaeology: Village Excavations at Nuraghe Urpes and Nuraghe Toscono in West-Central Sardinia*, 45-67. BAR International Series 373. Oxford: British Archaeological Reports.

Riassunto

Numerosi nuraghi sardi sono presenti in tutta l'isola e caratterizzano il suo paesaggio preistorico. La vasta distribuzione di nuraghi sembra implicare il fatto che tutta la preistoria sarda sia stata caratterizzata da una sola cultura. L'Autore afferma che questa uniformità culturale serve solo come un modello di lavoro per il compimento di ricerche. La scoperta e il riconoscimento di variazioni etniche e culturali nella Sardegna antica deve ricevere maggior attenzione. Gli studi di Gallin, Balmuth, e Lewthwaite offrono importanti dati che sottolineano l'esistenza di variazioni temporali e localizzate nello sviluppo e nell'occupazione dei nuraghi. Ulteriori ricerche in questo campo sono destinate a rivelare una mancanza di uniformità culturale associata con l'uso dei nuraghi, una volta che si è compreso che l'uso di quest'ultimi è parte di un complesso di caratteristiche sociali che variano all'interno degli antichi 'gruppi sociali' dell'isola. Questi studi indicano che anche se i materiali ritrovati in una vasta area sono simili, i modelli d'uso all'interno di organizzazioni sociali possono variare considerevolmente. Questi diversi modelli di uso nello spazio e nel tempo sono importanti per riconoscere le differenze culturali e i legami esistenti.

Un interessante e istruttivo esempio del fatto che anche se i nuraghi appaiono numerosi in diverse aree, essi hanno funzioni locali diverse, è l'urna a capanna. Esso è un contenitore usato per le ceneri, ed lo ritroviamo durante la tarda Età del Ferro nell'Italia centrale. L'uso dell'urna deve essere visto come una parte di un complesso di tratti sociali, così come deve esserlo l'argilla e la tempra di cui è fatta, e le sue decorazioni. Il complesso di urne a capanna dell'Italia centrale era un tempo utilizzato per definire una regione culturalmente uniforme. Ora, grazie all'attenzione prestata ai dettagli dei tratti dei complessi, il cui uso rappresenta solo uno dei suoi aspetti, le variazioni culturali all'interno della vasta regione in cui essi appaiono non sono più mascherate. Questa recente scoperta è basata sul paragone dei dati riguardanti le ossa cremate ottenute dagli scavi di Osteria dell'Osa con i dati di altri siti contemporanei. L'analisi di Bietti Sestieri di ossa cremate provenienti da urne a capanna di Osteria dell'Osa mostrano che esse provengono da uomini adulti. Ma Cassoli e Tagliacozza credono che ossa di bambini molto giovani predominano nelle urne a capanna del museo Pigorini. Le testimonianze di Osteria dell'Osa non possono essere estese automaticamente a tutti gli altri siti con urne a capanna, così come le testimonianze di un nuraghe non possono essere applicate a tutte le torri di pietra dell'antica Sardegna.

Territorial Boundaries, Buffer Zones and Sociopolitical Complexity: A Case Study of the Nuraghi on Sardinia

Renée M. Bonzani

Introduction

The following paper relates the spatial configurations of nuraghi found on the island of Sardinia to the broadly defined sociopolitical and economic structures of egalitarian, stratified pre-state and state societies. To do this, the link between geographical spatial distribution and the sociobiological concept of territoriality is defined. Emphasis is placed less on the actual location of settlements (the core area) than on the spacing (range) found between settlements. This spacing, variously called the boundary, periphery, border, 'neutral' area (Root 1983), no-man's-land (Myers 1976), or the buffer zone (DeBoer 1981), is expected to change and reflect the overlying sociopolitical and economic structure of the inhabitants of the land. Evidence in support of this basic outline is drawn from ethnographic and archaeological cases. A similar explanatory model applied to the location and potential occupation of nuraghi is then developed with a call for future testing.

Territoriality

The concept of territory has been defined as 'an area occupied more or less exclusively by animals or groups of animals by means of repulsion through overt defense or advertisement' (Wilson 1971: 195). By extrapolation, the concept of territoriality as applied to humans involves those behaviors of an aggressive or more symbolic nature which act to demarcate a particular area for more or less exclusive use by an individual or group. Territoriality, then, might involve direct aggression, and 'territory' would be defined as any physically defended area (Brown 1964). In this case a 'perimeter defense' of the actual border of a group's territory is expected (Peterson 1972; Cashdan 1983: 49). This may occur for environmental reasons, for example, the abundance and predictability of resources (Dyson-Hudson and Smith 1978) or for political reasons, for example, control over a territory's resources. However, although defense easily incorporates acts of direct aggression, it may also take on less overt manifestations (Wittenberger 1981: 250-51) and the type of territoriality may revolve around more symbolic means of defense, as in the case of 'social boundary defense' (Peterson 1972; Cashdan 1983: 49). For human groups who defend 'the boundaries of the social group rather than the perimeter of the territory itself' (Peterson 1972), defense at the borders is not necessary because the outside group comes to the inside group to ask permission to use the territory. Outside groups may pass across the border of another group's territory and the rites of entry may be ritualized and take the form of elaborate greeting ceremonies (Peterson 1975: 62).

Other definitions of territory have focused not on the behavioral means of defense but on the degree to which an area is exclusively utilized by its occupants. More ecological than behavioral in orientation, this definition brings up the varying degrees in which an individual, group, or species utilizes its surrounding habitat. Two aspects of this use of space are the home range and the core area. The home range is generally defined as the circumscribed area in which an animal spends its life. It is the area where the animal becomes intimately familiar with its surroundings, and includes areas that are utilized intensively and those that are not (Wittenberger 1981: 247-51). The part of the home range that is most important because it contains the best feeding, drinking, and resting places is the core area (Ewer 1968: 64-65). Home ranges may overlap in that neighboring individuals or groups utilize similar pathways; core areas generally do not overlap (Wittenberger 1981: 249). Applied to settlement pattern analysis, the core area can be seen as the actual settlement location of a group and the range as that area commonly used by a group but which is found among various settlement loci. The concepts of 'no man's land' and buffer zone can then be seen as special cases of the concept of range.

Accounting for both behavioral means of defense and exclusivity of the use of space is the link which ties social relationships to geographical spatial distributions. If coterminous autonomous territorial groups are related or have close historical ties, they will most likely practice 'social boundary defense' in that members of other groups can with some degree of freedom cross the boundary of another group's territory. Each group's home range will not be exclusively utilized by that group alone and borders between territories might be termed fluid as various parties of individuals cross the territorial boundaries at various times. For instance, groups that have recently split will have members in each group that are related and that occasionally visit the natal group (Kelly 1985: 182-83). Such visits are important for the maintenance of social ties and mutual reciprocity. These ties distribute risk over the population and establish a network of exchanges (Wiessner 1982: 66). The groups should have a similar language or dialect and relatively similar cultural practices. Further, these groups are expected to be relatively close together with contiguous borders, though each group would maintain its own territory (Sahlins 1967: 100).

Boundary defense suggests acts of overt aggression against groups outside of one's own territory. Exclusive use of the core area and range are concomitant with this occurrence. Social ties and other forms of interaction across boundaries are not maintained; the boundary itself becomes highly delineated. Defensive structures may occur and usually there are distinctive geographic areas separated by 'no man's land' or buffer zones in which settlement is devoid and individuals of either group tend not to enter (DeBoer 1981; Soja 1971). Differences in language or dialect (Barnard 1979: 137; Myers 1976: 35) might develop, while differences in cultural practices and their archaeological manifestations are expected to be found.

Hypothetical Constructs of Spatial Form

Seen as an open system (Root 1983; Green and Perlman 1985) since movement and information-flow between groups is not restricted, hunter-gatherer or egalitarian groups are expected to have a fluid pattern of settlement location and spacing. Ranges of different groups are expected to overlap. Although boundaries and spacing between settlements occur, their placement and defense should not be 'excessively' demarcated. In this case the terms buffer zone or 'no man's land' are not applicable in that regions between settlements will not be completely uninhabited or unused as the latter name implies. Indeed, the occurrence of such zones in association with egalitarian groups may be an indicator of changing sociopolitical relations, such as the intrusion of an unrelated group into the territory of an egalitarian tribal entity, or of resource scarcity (see Kelly 1985; Smith 1976: 321). Given the reciprocal, economic nature of egalitarian sociopolitical structures, frequent interaction between groups in different areas or territories and sharing of resources to minimize risk are expected (Smith 1976: 324; Wiessner 1982). Well-defined buffer zones and large concentrations of resources are not expected (Root 1983; Paynter 1982: 38-39). Examples of such a 'fluid local organization' (Peterson 1975: 59-60) have been noted for the Aborigines of Australia (see Stanner 1965; Radcliffe-Brown 1918; Pink 1936).

Stratified societies, on the other hand, are broadly defined as those which restrict resources (Fried 1967). The restriction of resources occurs both within the social group and in relation to others outside the group. Within the social group not all members will have equal access to resources. Elite persons will have control of surplus resources which must be extracted from others. The procurement of resources often is accompanied by mechanisms for reduction of the costs associated with their extraction. One means of cost reduction is the clustering or nucleation of settlements within a specified distance from a controlling elite. This is the most cost-efficient means of controlling and defending a particular area while keeping distance to be traveled at a minimum. Furthermore, 'such concentration of dependents would be encouraged by the wealthy since it provides enhanced opportunities for still further acquisition of wealth. This process would eventually involve the incorporation of existing small neighboring villages into the system or the founding of additional small villages by people from the emergent center so as to increase the resource base for wealth accumulation' (Drennan 1987: 314). Settlement clustering is predicted.

The restriction of resources requires not only controlling those within a territory (Webster 1975) but also keeping others outside it. Free access by unrelated groups to resources within a territory is a contradiction in terms and not expected to occur. Instead, indications of hostilities or defense are expected (Rowlands 1972; Brown 1977: 299). Such indications would include specific, well-defined boundaries between settlement clusters. Very specific areas devoid of settlements are also expected to occur in the space between cluster boundaries. This land may not be marginal in resource terms (DeBoer 1981). Natural geographic boundaries can be utilized for boundary defense as can human-made structures on the borders of settlement groupings, or internally where outlying populations can take refuge. With settlement clustering, then, well-defined buffer zones are expected to exist between stratified societies as elites attempt to maintain unequal access to resources in their territory. Just such settlement clustering and occurrence of buffer zones is evidenced during the Middle Classic period between the chiefdoms of Kaminaljuyu and Frutal in the Valley of Guate–mala, Guatemala (see Brown 1977; Michels 1977).

The sociopolitical nature of the state requires an intensification of both centrality and territoriality (Mann 1986). Here the focus is mainly within the state boundaries and not on interactions at such boundaries (see Green and Perlman 1985). Centrality in the early state is manifested by the disproportionate growth of one settlement above all others within the region. This occurrence is clearly depicted by Johnson's (1980) rank-size rule for a study area containing a complete, well-integrated settlement system (see Paynter 1983: 239-40). However, it is also apparent that the other settlements within the region remain or become relatively small (Adams 1988: 35; Kowalewski 1990). This is not to say that population remained dispersed and could come and go (fusion and fission) as it pleased. As is necessary for political enforcement and the extractive/redistributive economic nature of the state (i.e. through taxation, tribute or corvée labor), populations had to be tied to a specific piece of land which was their 'territory' and the land would become divided into quadrants, sections, or some type of imposed geometric 'accounting' system. Thus native populations could be left in the territory they had previously occupied while semi-nomadic groups would be encouraged or forced to concentrate into more well-defined, evenly spaced towns developed by the state (Kuznesof 1979). The important element here is that the state is superimposed over a pre-existing spatial structure, which in the process may be compartmentalized. This superimposition requires the suppression of the local government or chiefdom's autonomy and results in a reversion to a more 'egalitarian' spatial and economic pattern of dispersed settlements (Kuznesof 1979: 202-203; Yoffee 1988: 53).

Beyond an increase in individual settlement size as outlying groups are brought into towns and the resultant clarification or compartmentalization of spatial zones, settlement clustering is not expected to occur. A more evenly spaced, state-determined pattern of settlements of approximately the same size is predicted. Traditional settlement spacing may remain the same or settlements may be reallocated to fit the needs of the state. This dual pattern of a state-built system of settlements arranged in a relatively systematic way over a traditional settlement pattern, both somewhat compartmentalized and indicative of a loss of indigenous control of power, is evidenced in Peru during the Inca empire (see Murra 1975; Murra 1980; Morris 1985; Menzel 1959; Morris and Thompson 1985; Hyslop 1984; Hastorf 1990).

This return to the more 'egalitarian' spatial pattern is apparently tied to the evidence that the state does not redistribute subsistence goods, at least for the majority of the population (see Murra 1980; Gailey and Patterson 1987; cf. Service 1975). In this sense it would be quite hard to imagine a state that could survive by taking the majority of the food away from the food producers only to have to redistribute it back to them at a later date. Self-sufficiency of food producers through traditional means may be the most cost-effective way for an early state to maintain itself and its food producing populations. On the other hand, states are not all the same. The state is of necessity redistributive to those not involved in primary food production (Mann 1986: 121) and thus a person can move to the territorial center or city, becoming more dependent on the state. If further centralization occurs (i.e. one city dominates the entire state territory), the majority of the persons in the state are expected to have lost their self-sufficiency to some degree, and innovative as opposed to traditional kin–egalitarian means of resource acquisition and risk minimization should occur. For instance, these means may involve the establishment of a market economy (e.g. the Aztec: see Smith 1976). The expected settlement pattern and range/boundary characteristics for these three sociopolitical units are summarized in Table 1.

It must be stressed that boundaries or buffer zones are means of controlling energy and information flow as well as means of defense (see Adler and Wilshusen 1990; Renfrew 1984; Paynter 1989; Peebles and Kus 1977; Oyuela-Caycedo 1990). The ability to control the energy/material exchange of a society and the ability to maintain channels of information flow to persons outside of one's own territory or range can be used to define an autonomous, self-sufficient group (see Smith 1976 for a similar discussion on exchange and stratification). Keeping spatial boundaries in mind, economic autonomy is maintained if a

Table 1

Expected settlement pattern and range/boundary characteristics for entities of varying sociopolitical complexity

Sociopolitical complexity	Settlement pattern	Range/boundary characteristics
Egalitarian	dispersed	fluid
Chiefdom (pre-state stratified)	nucleated	discrete (buffer zone present)
State (within borders)	dispersed	discrete (single large center)

group controls what is produced within its own boundaries as well as what can or cannot be exchanged across boundaries. Political autonomy is maintained if decision-making remains at the level of the local group as well as if information flow across boundaries is maintained. As discussed, in egalitarian societies ranges are fluid and discrete boundaries or buffer zones are not maintained. The local group retains control over what is produced within its territory as well as what it can exchange with others. Economic exchanges and information flow are not restricted at boundaries and the system is open (Wiessner 1982; Peebles and Kus 1977: 430). Decision-making remains in the hands of the local group and, as such, these groups are economically and politically autonomous.

In chiefdoms or pre-state stratified societies, discrete boundaries occur in the form of unoccupied buffer zones and defensive accoutrements. As well-defined boundaries help for the defense of a territory (Carneiro 1970; Webster 1975), they also cut back on social interactions across such boundaries (Oyuela-Caycedo 1987; Root 1983). Rowlands (1972: 459) notes, 'The erection of fortifications is, in fact, the antithesis of communication and tends to impose limitations on social activities and alter the arrangement of dwellings that might be found in undefended settlements'. Both economic exchange and information-flow across ranges has been curtailed. As such, discrete buffer zones promote the loss of both economic and political autonomy at the local kinship level.

State societies can vary in the amount of energy exchange and information-flow that occurs across boundaries. Externally, information-flow and energy exchange is required if encroachment on outlying groups is to be successful, and if one of the tenets of early states, that of expansion, is to occur. However, the underlying purpose for such exchange is to enact the opposite of localized economic autonomy, in that the state requires control of such energy exchanges (Gailey 1987). Once a group is incorporated into the state, economic autonomy of localized kin groups is lost in that local control over the production of surplus is no longer viable. Borders between groups are either enforced or accentuated as freedom of movement between groups is discouraged (Kuznesof 1979; Murra 1980: 42, 110). On the other hand, in early tribute-based states (see Gailey and Patterson 1988), the local kin community is still responsible for its own subsistence, and traditional networks of energy exchange and information flow must remain viable for this to occur. Organization of spatial patterning would continue to reflect this kinship-based network of exchanges.

Internally, information-flow in the early state is also apparently more open at the local level than is found between pre-state stratified societies. Large, discrete clusters of settlements with intervening buffer zones are not developed by the state for native populations. If anything, such discrete spatial entities are dissolved where they occur (Hastorf 1990). Traditional networks of contact and information are maintained (Murra 1980). Information-flow within the state is concurrently hierarchical in nature as, indeed, road systems are maintained by state-built administrative centers to facilitate things like information-flow.

Sardinia: Spatial Model of Nuragic Location and Occupation

The nuraghi of Sardinia are a pervasive feature of the landscape and more than 6500 towers can be identified on the island (Balmuth 1984: 23). Problems in settlement pattern studies with this number of nuraghi on an island about 150 miles north–south and 75 miles east–west (Guido 1964: 23) revolve around the fact that it is very difficult to determine when a nuraghe was actually built and used. Nuragic construction in Sardinia is divided into three Bronze Age phases of three hundred years each (1800–900 BC) and two Iron

Age phases (900–500 BC; 500–238 BC) (Lilliu 1982). To propose that all the nuraghi in one region were occupied simultaneously could lead to serious biases in settlement pattern studies as well as in studies of prehistoric demography.

One approach to settlement studies and the topic of this paper was taken by Gallin (1989). Her research design involved 'the identification of clusters of nuraghi in which architectural heterogeneity had potential significance for understanding inter-site relationships and, on a higher level, Nuraghic social organization' (Gallin 1989: 204). Although not yielding chronological determinations, this approach does outline functional differences between Nuragic types that may indicate the development of sociopolitical, hierarchical relationships and concomitant spatial patterning of Nuragic sites.

Defined Nuragic types of particular importance here include the corridor type, the single 'classic' or corbelled tower, and the multi-towered 'classic' type (Balmuth 1984: 25-29; Gallin 1989: 88-200). An unknown category was also included in Gallin's (1989: 220-23) study due to the collapsed nature of some of the Nuragic features. Although the debate concerning the relative chronology of the corridor versus corbelled nuraghe now favors the corridor type as the earlier of the two developments, both forms are believed to have coexisted throughout Nuragic times (see Lewthwaite 1986: 25; Manca Demurtas and Demurtas, Trump, and Moravetti, this volume). No such debate focuses on the chronology of the multi-towered 'classic' type as the addition of numerous subsidiary towers and general larger scale are seen as indications of later, more advanced monument building (see Gallin 1989: 198-200; Trump 1980: 217; Renfrew 1982: 4; also see Bonanno *et al.* 1990). These multi-towered nuraghi have also been associated with a primarily defensive function (Balmuth 1984: 29; Lilliu 1959: 65-67; King 1975: 38).

Given that single-towered nuraghi of the corridor or corbelled type preceded the development of the multi-towered type, the numerous and widespread occurrence of the former throughout most of the island is accountable in terms of the 'egalitarian' pattern outlined above. In this sense one single-towered nuraghe (and accompanying hut structures) can be seen as the settlement locus for a small kin-based group (Balmuth 1984: 29; Webster 1988: 471). Fissioning of one group would lead to the development of settlement loci at some distance from the natal group but still potentially within communicating range. Initially a clustered pattern of 'aggregate groupings', as population grows, single-towered nuraghi would be expected to fill the total area of a region and 'the end result of this process is a systematic or regular pattern of farms in the region' (Gallin 1989: 239). A regular pattern in this sense is not one that follows a predetermined placement of settlement loci but rather one that illustrates random settlement placement and spacing throughout a region without noticeable patterns of settlement clustering. The earliest types of Nuragic constructions, then, should exhibit somewhat random settlement loci placement, each with its own territorial range separating it from the next.

This, of course, does not mean that single-towered nuraghi could not have been constructed at later times in Nuragic prehistory, but rather that when they were, they are expected to follow a different pattern of settlement placement and spacing. This pattern would be one more in line with the evidence of the occurrence of chiefdom societies in Late Bronze Age–Iron Age Sardinia (c. 1200–500 BC) (Balmuth 1984: 30; Webster 1988). Tentatively, this dispersed 'egalitarian' pattern for single-towered nuraghi is contrasted against site clusters involving multi-towered nuraghi. As Gallin (1989: 241) explains for the Sedilo territory in the Tirso valley, 'unlike the single-towered nuraghi which appear in random aggregates, these seven multi-towered nuraghi are located on the edges of the plateau surrounding clusters of 29 corridor and single tower classic nuraghi'. Further, Gallin (1989: 248) indicates that 'If only those nuraghi on the periphery were amplified by the construction of subsidiary towers, one explanation may involve nucleation of the population at the sites of certain multi-towered nuraghi from an earlier pattern of dispersed settlement in scattered groups of simple [single-towered] nuraghi'.

With increased competition as land becomes scarce and fissioning of groups less viable, contact between groups increases and the ability or need to form alliances is hypothesized. In Sardinia various lines of evidence are beginning to point to the development of chiefdom sociopolitical divisions during the later Nuragic periods (1200–500 BC) of Sardinian prehistory. Specifically, recent excavation (Webster 1988) has begun to develop population estimates for the Iron Age (c. 900 BC) Borore polity (Marghine region) which fall easily within the size range of defined African petty-chiefdoms. Development of hierarchical relationships among Borore communities, including the large, heavily-fortified Nuragic complex at Nuraghe Porcarzos (Webster 1988: 469), also indicate a pre-state level of stratification for Nuragic complexes in Sardinia at this time.

Turning back to Gallin's study (1989) on the settlement pattern of nuraghi in the territory of

Sedilo, the development of a high degree of sociopolitical complexity beyond that of egalitarian tribal societies is evidenced. This study will be utilized here to address further the applicability of spatial patterning in differentiating sociopolitical complexity. Specifically as outlined above, with the occurrence of pre-state stratified societies settlement loci should show noticeable patterns of site clustering and clearly definable ranges where settlement is lacking and which individuals of different groups tend to avoid (Barnard 1979: 138; DeBoer 1981; Myers 1976; Soja 1971).

In her study Gallin (1989: 220-26) was able to identify a closely grouped cluster of nuraghi in the territory of Sedilo. Out of a total of 55 nuraghi in the Sedilo territory, 41 were found to cluster within an area of approximately 19 sq km (Gallin 1989: 224). Interspersed at the borders of this area, eight multi-towered nuraghi surround the cluster (Gallin 1989: 221 figs. 5-12). Of the 14 remaining nuraghi, ten are on the other side of the Tirso River, a potentially defensive natural boundary. This leaves four nuraghi, three of the single 'classic' type and one unknown, in what would otherwise be a very well-defined buffer zone within the territory of Sedilo (see Gallin 1989: 79 figs. 3-4).

The potential that the four nuraghi in this zone were unoccupied during the habitation of the Sedilo cluster and the use of the multi-towered nuraghi is a distinct but as yet unproven possibility. The clustering of the remainder of the sites and the clear boundary defense function of the multi-towered nuraghi do lend support to the hypothesized association between sociopolitical complexity and spatial settlement patterning (see Gallin 1989: 237-53). Excavation at the nuraghi in the tentative buffer zone of the Sedilo cluster may be the only way to determine if indeed these nuraghi were occupied prior to the development of the Sedilo cluster and then abandoned or if they were occupied contemporaneously with those of the Sedilo cluster. One should keep in mind Trump's (1986: 14) foresight that 'Restricted length of occupation may be part of the answer to the quite extraordinary number of nuraghi throughout the valley [of Bonu Ighinu], and indeed throughout the island'. Further study along these lines in the Tirso Valley and elsewhere in Sardinia (see Webster and Michels 1987) should prove important for delimiting the relationship between settlement pattern/spatial distributions and sociopolitical complexity in prehistoric Sardinia.

Since nuraghi continued to serve as viable habitations for the populations of Sardinia into the historic period, their reuse led to some of the difficulties in dating (Balmuth 1984: 24). Noting that the reoccupation of once abandoned nuraghi can occur, this practice during periods of state domination may be evidence of the spatial structure and economic policies of state-level societies. Sardinia appears to be a perfect test case for the hypotheses that upon dominating a new area state societies break down local autonomous chiefdoms, disperse clustered settlements into the more 'egalitarian' pattern, and establish an overarching pattern of compartmentalized or evenly spaced state-emplaced settlement loci.

Preliminary evidence for the breakdown of local-level chiefdoms occurs at Nuraghe Toscono, a multi-towered nuraghe located at the border of the Borore aggregate (Webster *et al.* 1987b). Excavation at the nuraghe has indicated that approximately at the time of Carthaginian control over the island the nuraghe was abandoned by its inhabitants and not reoccupied until 260 years later (238 BC, a Punico-Roman phase component; Webster *et al.* 1987b: 19-20). Similar abandonment appears to have occurred at the Nuraghi Urpes, San Sergio and Duos Nuraghes during this period (c. 500-238 BC) with resumption of occupation following the Roman conquest of Sardinia in 238 BC (Webster 1988: 469). Nuraghe Urpes is a multi-towered construction while San Sergio and Duos are single-towered with complex-chambered components. Complex-chambered corbelled nuraghi are thought to be architectural improvements over archaic nuraghi of the corridor or simple chamber corbelled type (Webster 1988: 469; Balmuth 1984: 25-28). One nuraghe that does show continued occupation throughout the 5th to 2nd centuries BC is Nuraghe Serbine. This nuraghe, 2 km northeast of Duos, is tentatively identified as a corridor type (Webster 1988: 469).

Although preliminary in nature, these determinations are exactly what are expected to occur when a state-level society gains control over a particular territory. In the Sardinian case Nuragic clusters, especially their multi-towered or more complex components representing chiefdom level polities, should show some signs of abandonment indicating the loss of autonomous power. Not all nuraghi in the cluster are expected to be abandoned (e.g. as in the case of Nuraghe Serbine); however, the cluster 'polity' (Renfrew 1986) itself should no longer be demonstrated.

There are other indications of the abandonment and reoccupation of nuraghi during the Phoenician, Carthaginian and Roman periods on Sardinia. Rowland (1984: 288), listing numerous Roman occupations, including that of nuraghi, for the Sardinian countryside, notes that 'not infrequently we find nuraghic sites (both with and without remains of the Punic period) either continuously in use into the Roman period or reutilized in that era...' However, the location of these nuraghi are not placed in the context of settlement clustering and buffer zones, and one cannot determine if those that were reoccupied tended to be located in chiefdom polity buffer zones or were more complex in nature. At this point site abandonment and reutilization cannot be addressed in the terms I have hypothesized here.

Regarding state-controlled settlement patterns, studies indicate that the Phoenicians established inland garrisons at strategic positions 'to assure rule over the hinterland' and that many inner settlements founded by the Phoenicians and Carthaginians were connected by a road network (Barreca 1986: 154-55). Also, Carthage organized the occupied territory of Sardinia 'by applying the notion of colonization through far-reaching settlements, with families living in isolation or small groups in the countryside near the smaller urban settlements, which tended to be closer to the major settlements' (Barreca 1986: 151). Immigrants, and perhaps natives, were established throughout the Sardinian countryside in 'small groups scattered in agricultural, wooded or mining areas, away from major and minor urban settlements' (Barreca 1986: 151).

Upon establishing control over Sardinia in 238 BC, Rome appears to have utilized the existing Phoenician and Carthaginian patterns of inland settlement and colonization. Tronchetti (1984: 245) notes that the archaeological record at least in the agricultural zones 'shows no break in continuity between the Punic and the Roman periods'. Indeed, reference to Roman practices of colonization in northern and central Italy point to a similar pattern of evenly spaced state-sponsored settlements occurring along the system of centuriation (Garnsey 1979: 15). The expansion of rural settlements, however, had the effect of creating dispersed habitations in the form of small villages, hamlets and open farmsteads. Cities became less residential and more administrative in nature, and the basic structure of the traditional rural community appears not to have been greatly altered (Garnsey 1979: 4-13, 16-17).

Clearly, testing of the outlined locational and spatial models is required before their definitive relevance to Sardinia can be ascertained. Future study may test more explicitly if nuraghi found in areas defined as buffer zones were abandoned during the period of adjacent cluster occupation, if nuraghi occupied during the Phoenician/Carthaginian and Roman periods were dispersed in nature, and, concomitantly, if some nuraghi reoccupied during times of state intervention included those in previously abandoned buffer zones. Further, the abandonment of nuraghi within clusters during the initial periods of state domination might also be predicted as local chiefdom-level autonomy is lost.

Conclusion

In conclusion, the nuraghi of the island of Sardinia offer a good case study in which to test the models developed above. Specifically, the earliest nuraghi should exhibit a somewhat dispersed, random settlement pattern. Clustering of these nuraghi should be minimal. Upon the emergence of chiefdom-level societies, construction and habitation of nuraghi should exhibit indications of clustering. Multi-towered nuraghi with evident defensive functions should be dated to approximately this time and should be intimately associated with single-towered nuragic clusters. Also, nuraghi found in possible buffer zones between clusters should exhibit signs of abandonment. Upon intrusion by outside states, the discrete occupation of Nuragic clusters should dissolve. In this way nuraghi previously located in buffer zones should show signs of reoccupation during times of state influence. This reoccupation would be random so that some nuraghi would remain abandoned. Abandonment of other nuraghi in clusters should occur while the construction of new nuraghi is not expected to follow the chiefdom-level pattern of site clustering. Indeed, nuraghi which may have 'represented' the indigenous power structure, i.e., the multi-towered nuraghi, are expected to be abandoned or at least to be without evidence of social control during the times of state influence.

This model points to the need for a regional study approach (Kowalewski 1990). Further surveys as conducted by Gallin (1989) and Webster and Michels (1987) are required to define Nuragic clusters and potential buffer zones. Emphasis also must be placed on refining the chronology of Nuragic occupation. Household-level archaeology will help define the diachronic relationships between nuraghi. In turn this should add to the understanding of the processes of sociopolitical change that occurred on the island of Sardinia.

Acknowledgments

My deepest appreciations go to Professor Miriam Balmuth for establishing the foundations upon which my current and future studies in archaeology are based. The concept for this paper originated through discussions with Augusto Oyuela-Caycedo. Appreciation is also extended to Dr Alan McPherron for various insights and help and to Dr James Zeidler, both of the University of Pittsburgh, and James J. Bonzani for comments on various drafts of the paper.

References

Adams, R.M.
1988 Contexts of civilizational collapse: A Mesoamerican view. In N. Yoffee and G. Cowgill (eds.), *The Collapse of Ancient States and Civilizations*, 20-43. Tucson: University of Arizona Press.

Adler, M., & R. Wilshusen
1990 Large-scale integrative facilities in tribal societies: Cross-cultural and Southwestern US examples. *World Archaeology* 22(2): 133-46.

Balmuth, M.S.
1984 The nuraghi of Sardinia: An introduction. In M.S. Balmuth and R.J. Rowland, Jr (eds.), *Studies in Sardinian Archaeology*, 23-52. Ann Arbor: University of Michigan Press.

Barnard, A.
1979 Kalahari Bushman settlement patterns. In P. Burnham and R. Ellen (eds.), *Social and Ecological Systems*. New York: Academic Press.

Barreca, F.
1986 The Phoenician and Punic civilization in Sardinia. In M.S. Balmuth (ed.), *Studies in Sardinian Archaeology, Volume II: Sardinia in the Mediterranean*, 155-86. Ann Arbor: University of Michigan Press.

Bonanno, A., T. Goulder, C. Malone & S. Stoddart
1990 Monuments in an island society: The Maltese context. *World Archaeology* 22(2): 190-205.

Brown, J.
1964 The evolution of diversity in avian territorial systems. *Wilson Bulletin* 76: 160-69.

Brown, K.
1977 The Valley of Guatemala: A highland port of trade. In W. Sanders and J. Michels (eds.), *Teotihuacan and Kaminaljuyu: A Study in Prehistoric Culture Contact*, 205-395. University Park, PA: The Pennsylvania State University Press.

Carneiro, R.
1970 A theory of the origin of the state. *Science* 169: 733-38.

Cashdan, E.
1983 Territoriality among human foragers: Ecological models and an application to four Bushman groups. *Current Anthropology* 24(1): 47-66.

DeBoer, W.
1981 Buffer zones in the cultural ecology of aboriginal Amazonia: An ethnohistorical approach. *American Antiquity* 46(2): 364-77.

Drennan, R.
1987 Regional demography in chiefdoms. In R. Drennan and C. Uribe (eds.), *Chiefdoms in the Americas*, 307-24. Lanham, MD: University Press of America.

Dyson-Hudson, R., & E. Smith
1978 Human territoriality: An ecological reassessment. *American Anthropologist* 80: 21-41.

Ewer, R.F.
1968 *Ethology of Mammals*. New York: Plenum.

Fried, M.
1967 *The Evolution of Political Society: An Essay in Political Anthropology*. New York: Random House.

Gailey, C.
1987 Culture wars: Resistance to state formation. In T. Patterson and C. Gailey (eds.), *Power Relations and State Formation*, 35-56. Washington, DC: American Anthropological Association.

Gailey, C., & T. Patterson
1987 Power relations and state formation. In T. Patterson and C. Gailey (eds.), *Power Relations and State Formation*, 1-26. Washington, DC: American Anthropological Association.
1988 State formation and uneven development. In J. Gledhill, B. Bender and M. Larsen (eds.), *State and Society: The Emergence and Development of Social Hierarchy and Political Centralization*, 77-90. Boston: Unwin Hyman.

Gallin, L.J.
1989 Architectural attributes and inter-site variation: A case study: the Sardinian nuraghi. PhD dissertation, UCLA. Ann Arbor: University Microfilms International.

Garnsey, P.
1979 Where did Italian peasants live? *Proceedings of the Cambridge Philological Society* 205(25): 1-25.

Green, S., & S. Perlman (eds.)
1985 *The Archaeology of Frontiers and Boundaries*. Orlando: Academic Press.

Guido, M.
1964 *Sardinia*. New York: Frederick A. Praeger.

Hastorf, C.
1990 The effect of the Inka state on Sausa agricultural production and crop consumption. *American Antiquity* 55(2): 262-90.

Hyslop, J.
1984 *The Inka Road System*. New York: Academic Press.

Johnson, G.
1980 Rank-size convexity and system integration: A view from archaeology. *Economic Geography* 56: 234-47.

Kelly, R.
1985 *The Nuer Conquest: The Structure and Development of an Expansionist System*. Ann Arbor: University of Michigan Press.

King, R.
1975 *Sardinia*. Harrisburg: David & Charles; Newton Abbot; Stackpole Books.

Kowalewski, S.
1990 Merits of full-coverage survey: Examples from the Valley of Oaxaca. In S. Fish and S. Kowalewski (eds.), *The Archaeology of Regions: A Case for Full-Coverage Survey*, 33-85. Washington, DC: Smithsonian Institution Press.

Kuznesof, E.
1979 Clans, the militia and territorial government: The articulation of kinship with polity in eighteenth-century Sao Paolo. In D. Robinson (ed.), *Social Fabric and Spatial Structure in Colonial Latin America*, 181-226. Ann Arbor: University Microfilms International.

Lewthwaite, J.
1986 Nuragic foundations: An alternate model of development in Sardinian Prehistory c. 2500–1500 BC. In M.S. Balmuth (ed.), *Studies in Sardinian Archaeology, Volume II: Sardinia in the Mediterranean*, 19-37. Ann Arbor: University of Michigan Press.

Lilliu, G.
    1959   The proto-castles of Sardinia. *Scientific American* 1959: 63-69.
    1982   *La Civiltà Nuragica*. Sardegna Archaeologica: Studi e Monumenti 1. Sassari: Carlo Delfino.

Mann, M.
    1986   The autonomous power of the state: Its origins, mechanisms and results. In J. Hall (ed.), *States in History*, 109-36. New York: Basil Blackwell.

Menzel, D.
    1959   The Inca occupation of the south coast of Peru. *Southwestern Journal of Anthropology* 15: 125-42.

Michels, J.
    1977   *The Kaminaljuyu Chiefdom*. University Park, PA: The Pennsylvania State University Press.

Morris, C.
    1985   From principles of ecological complementarity to the organization and administration of Tawantinsuyu. In S. Masuda, I. Shimada and C. Morris (eds.), *Andean Ecology and Civilization: An Interdisciplinary Perspective on Andean Ecological Complementarity*, 477-90. Tokyo: University of Tokyo Press.

Morris, C., & D. Thompson
    1985   *Huánuco Pampa: An Inca City and Its Hinterland*. London: Thames and Hudson.

Murra, J.
    1975   *Formaciones Economicas y Politicas del Mundo Andino*. Lima: Instituto de Estudios Peruanos.
    1980   The economic organization of the Inka state. In G. Dalton (ed.), *Research in Economic Anthropology, Supplement 1*. Greenwich: JAI Press.

Myers, T.
    1976   Defended territories and no-man's-lands. *American Anthropologist* 78: 354-55.

Oyuela-Caycedo, A.
    1987   Implications of local and regional sequences for the Tairona Culture. In R. Drennan and C. Uribe (eds.), *Chiefdoms in the Americas*, 213-28. Lanham, MD: University Press of America.
    1990   La Redes de Caminos Prehispánicos en la Sierra Nevada de Santa Marta. In S. Mora (ed.), *Ingeniería Prehispánica*, 47-72. Bogotá: Fondo Fen Colombia-Colcultura.

Paynter, R.
    1982   *Models of Spatial Inequality: Settlement Patterns in Historic Archaeology*. New York: Academic Press.
    1983   Expanding the scope of settlement analysis. In J. Moore and A. Keene (eds.), *Archaeological Hammers and Theories*, 233-75. New York: Academic Press.
    1989   The archaeology of equality and inequality. *Annual Review of Anthropology* 18: 369-99.

Peebles, C., & S. Kus
    1977   Some archaeological correlates of ranked societies. *American Antiquity* 42(3): 421-48.

Peterson, N.
    1972   Totemism yesterday: Sentiment and local organization among the Australian aborigines. *Man* 7: 12-32.
    1975   Hunter-gatherer territoriality: The perspective from Australia. *American Anthropologist* 77: 53-68.

Pink, O.
    1936   The landowners in the Northern Division of the Aranda Tribe, central Australia. *Oceania* 6(3): 275-305.

Radcliffe-Brown, A.
    1918   Notes on the social organization of Australian tribes. *Journal of the Royal Anthropological Institute* 48: 222-53.

Renfrew, C.
    1982   Socio-economic change in ranked societies. In C. Renfrew and S. Shennan (eds.), *Ranking, Resources, and Exchange: Aspects of the Archaeology of Early European Society*, 1-12. Cambridge: Cambridge University Press.
    1984   *Approaches to Social Archaeology*. Edinburgh: Edinburgh University Press.
    1986   Introduction: Peer polity interaction and sociopolitical change. In C. Renfrew and J.F. Cherry (eds.), *Peer Polity Interaction and Sociopolitical Change*, 1-18. Cambridge: Cambridge University Press.

Root, D.
    1983   Information exchange and the spatial configurations of egalitarian societies. In J. Moore and A. Keene (eds.), *Archaeological Hammers and Theories*, 193-219. New York: Academic Press.

Rowland, R.J., Jr
    1984   The countryside of Roman Sardinia. In M.S. Balmuth and R.J. Rowland, Jr (eds.), *Studies in Sardinian Archaeology*, 285-300. Ann Arbor: University of Michigan Press.

Rowlands, M.
    1972   Defence: A factor in the organization of settlements. In P. Ucko, R. Tringham and G. Dimbleby (eds.), *Man, Settlement and Urbanism*, 447-62. Cambridge: Schenkman Publishing Company.

Sahlins, M.
    1967   The segmentary lineage: An organization of predatory expansion. In R. Cohen and J. Middleton (eds.), *Comparative Political Systems: Studies in the Politics of Pre-Industrial Societies*. New York: The Natural History Press.

Service, E.
    1975   *Origins of the State and Civilization: The Process of Cultural Evolution*. New York: W.W. Norton.

Smith, C.
    1976   Exchange systems and the spatial distribution of elites: The organization of stratification in agrarian societies. In C. Smith (ed.), *Regional Analysis. Volume II: Social Systems*, 309-74. New York: Academic Press.

Soja, E.
    1971   *The Political Organization of Space*. Commission on College Geography Resource Paper No. 8. Washington, DC: Association of American Geographers.

Stanner, W.
    1965   Aboriginal territorial organization: Estate, range, domain and regime. *Oceania* 36(1): 1-26.

Tronchetti, C.
    1984   The cities of Roman Sardinia. In M.S. Balmuth and R.J. Rowland, Jr (eds.), *Studies in Sardinian Archaeology*, 237-83. Ann Arbor: University of Michigan Press.

Trump, D.H.
    1980   *The Prehistory of the Mediterranean*. New Haven: Yale University Press.
    1986   Beyond stratigraphy—The Bonu Ighinu project. In M.S. Balmuth (ed.), *Studies in Sardinian Archaeology, Volume II: Sardinia in the Mediterranean*, 8-17. Ann Arbor: University of Michigan Press.

Webster, D.
　1975　Warfare and the evolution of the state: A reconsideration. *American Antiquity* 40: 464-70.

Webster, G.S.
　1988　Duos Nuraghes: Preliminary results of the first three seasons of excavation. *Journal of Field Archaeology* 15: 465-72.

Webster, G., & J. Michels
　1987　Introduction. In J. Michels and G. Webster (eds.), *Studies in Nuragic Archaeology*, 1-10. BAR International Series 373. Oxford: British Archaeological Reports.

Webster, G., J. Michels & C. Marean
　1987　Detailed description of the excavations. In J. Michels and G. Webster (eds.), *Studies in Nuragic Archaeology*, 11-37. BAR International Series 373. Oxford: British Archaeological Reports.

Wiessner, P.
　1982　Risk, reciprocity, and social influences on !Kung San economics. In E. Leacock and R. Lee (eds.), *Politics and History in Band Societies*, 61-84. Cambridge: Cambridge University Press.

Wilson, E.
　1971　Competitive and aggressive behavior. In J. Eisenberg, W. Dillon and S. Ripley (eds.), *Man and Beast: Comparative Social Behavior*, 180-217. Washington, DC: Smithsonian Institution Press.

Wittenberger, J.
　1981　*Animal Social Behavior*. California: Wadsworth, Inc.

Yoffee, N.
　1988　The collapse of ancient Mesopotamian states and civilization. In N. Yoffee and G. Cowgill (eds.), *The Collapse of Ancient States and Civilizations*, 44-68. Tucson: University of Arizona Press.

Riassunto

L'Autrice di quest'articolo definisce e rivede le correnti teorie riguardanti le strutture sociopolitiche ed economiche in tre tipi di società: società egualitarie, società stratificate (con classi sociali) ed infine società-stato. Le configurazioni spaziali dei nuraghi sardi sono studiate tenendo conto delle tre teorie sopra menzionate con lo scopo di investigare possibili relazioni tra la distribuzione geografica dei nuraghe e i concetti socio-biologici di territorialità. La posizione dei nuraghi, in questo caso, è meno importante dello spazio esistente tra i nuraghi stessi, in quanto questo illustra i principi socio-biologici secondo i quali gli abitanti utilizzano lo spazio esistente tra i nuraghi stessi e lo spazio del territorio circostante. Secondo le correnti teorie, lo spazio esistente tra gli insediamenti—definito come confine, periferia, area neutrale o 'buffer zone'—dovrebbe riflettere le strutture sociali, politiche ed economiche degli insediamenti. Ritrovamenti archeologici ed etnografici ottenuti dagli scavi sono discussi per provare la loro corrispondenza con la distribuzione dei nuraghi nello spazio e nel tempo, basate sulle correnti teorie.

L'Autrice inizia definendo il concetto socio-biologico di territorialità, come atteggiamento chiaramente aggressivo che l'essere umano adotta per delimitare un'area per uso esclusivo. La difesa dei confini territoriali, l'esclusione di estranei dal territorio e la creazione di regolamenti riguardanti l'accesso al territorio, sono i primi comportamenti tipici di questo concetto. Questa serie di comportamenti riflettono i legami esistenti tra disposizioni sociali, politiche ed economiche ed i modelli spaziali della distribuzione degli insediamenti in un determinato territorio.

Successivamente l'Autrice definisce tre ipotetici modelli di territorialità socio-politica e le loro caratteristiche. Il modello di società egualitaria o 'cacciatore-coltivatore' è contrassegnato da tipi di insediamento oserei dire fluidi, non rigidi. Le disposizioni economiche sono reciproche con frequenti contatti all'interno del gruppo e le risorse vengono egualmente spartite.

Nelle società con classi sociali (società stratificate) le risorse sono distribuite inequamente. In questo tipo di società il controllo dei confini territoriali è molto rigido, e questo tipo di insediamento è caratterizzato da piccoli agglomerati di villaggi con aree ben definite tra un villaggio e l'altro, dette anche '*buffer zones*'.

Nel terzo tipo di società, lo stato, è riscontrabile un centro emergente che ha la responsabilità di distribuire le risorse esistenti attraverso il sistema di amministrazione sociale, politico ed economico. In questo modello di società esiste una gerarchia. Lo stato può imporre modelli d'insediamento all'interno del territorio e decidere quali tipi di risorse produrre. I confini dello stato e i suoi 'vicini' sono chiaramente definiti e certamente rispettati. Le zone esistenti tra i diversi stati—buffer zones—sono estese e non abitate.

L'Autrice applica questi modelli di territorialità socio-politici, al caso dei nuraghi e allo spazio esistente tra un nuraghe e l'altro. Questo studio segue le opere di Gallin, e Webster e Michels, e cerca di identificare agglomerati di nuraghi e di capire meglio le relazioni esistenti tra un agglomerato e l'altro e la loro organizzazione sociale.

I diversi tipi di nuraghi sono riveduti: il nuraghe a corridoio, il nuraghe a monotorre, e il nuraghe a multitorri. Rimangano ancora problemi nel definire le cronologie relative del nuraghe a corridoio e del nuraghe a monotorre, e i precisi *termini post e ante quem* dei singoli nuraghi sono ancora sconosciuti. In compenso le cronologie relative dei nuraghi multitorri sono più chiare in quanto sono leggibili grazie all'aggiunta di torri sussidiarie ed espansioni a carattere architettonico che sono ovviamente più recenti delle torri e cui si sono aggiunte.

Sovrapponendo cronologie relative al nuraghe a corridoio, con quello multitorre e monotorre, l'Autrice prevede uno sviluppo socio-politico parallelo dei modelli d'insediamento dei nuraghi. I modelli più antichi, saranno quelli meno difensivi, saranno spaziati fortuitamente e ci saranno pochi agglomerati. Questo indica l'esistenza di una società nuragica egualitaria in questo periodo. Nel momento in cui una società stratificata (con classi sociali) emerge nell'isola, nuraghi a multitorri sono eretti e coesistono con i precedenti nuraghi a monotorre. I nuraghi trovati in aree esistenti tra gli agglomerati di nuraghi (*buffer zones*) dovrebbero mostrare segni di abbandono. Quando gli stranieri colonizzano la Sardegna, la discreta occupazione degli agglomerati di nuraghi dovrebbe cessare e i nuraghi abbandonati e situati nelle '*inter-polity buffer zones*' dovrebbero essere rioccupati in modo casuale. Ogni nuovo nuraghe costruito in questo periodo dovrebbe riflettere la mancanza di un controllo socio-politico indigeno sotto il dominio di uno stato straniero.

L'Autrice conclude sollecitando ulteriori ricerche regionali, come hanno fatto Gallin, e Webster e Michels. Ulteriori studi dovrebbero essere fatti nel definire gli agglomerati nuragici e le '*buffer zones*' e nel trovare più precise cronologie relative ed assolute dei complessi nuragici. Attraverso questi studi è possibile migliorare la capacità di capire i cambiamenti politici e sociali avvenuti nella Sardegna antica.

Considerazioni sullo Sviluppo dell'Architettura e della Società Nuragica

Giovanni Ugas

Quando ci si chiede quale fosse la struttura sociale nell'età dei nuraghi, non si può fare a meno di sottolineare le difficoltà che si incontrano nel rispondere al quesito, sia per la sviluppata e tutt'altro che uniforme articolazione della cultura nuragica, sia per l'incertezza sul suo stesso inizio.

Come si evince dalle diverse edizioni del volume *La civiltà dei Sardi* (Lilliu 1963; 1967; 1988a) e dal saggio su *La civiltà nuragica* (Lilliu 1982), le indagini del Lilliu sono fedeli testimoni del grande dinamismo dell'archeologia sarda nell'ultimo quarantennio, favorito dalla possibilità di fruire delle datazioni al C14 (Contu 1992), e dal moltiplicarsi delle ricerche e delle indagini stratigrafiche.

Non c'è da meravigliarsi se la rapida crescita dell'archeologia sarda abbia determinato continui mutamenti di pensiero, talora anche sensibili, tra coloro che hanno affrontato il tema, sempre affascinante e sempre *in fieri*, della civiltà dei nuraghi. Si assiste infatti a una pluralità di orientamenti sull'arco cronologico, sulle periodizzazioni e definizioni terminologiche interne che si avvicinano ora più ora meno al quadro basilare tracciato dal Lilliu sull'evolversi della cultura nuragica (tra gli altri: Atzeni 1980; Ferrarese Ceruti 1981; Ferrarese Ceruti 1989; Lo Schiavo 1981; Ugas 1981a; Ugas 1987b; Ugas 1989; Ugas 1990; Santoni 1989; Contu 1981; Contu 1990).

Chi scrive preferisce una ripartizione in fasi della cultura nuragica aderente agli avvenimenti dell'Italia peninsulare, secondo il seguente prospetto:

FASE I: **Bronzo medio (BM)** (1600–1300 a.C. circa). Ripartito in due sottofasi: BM I, correlabile sul piano cronologico e culturale con il Protoappenninico B I e II (XVI-XV secolo); BM II, legato allo sviluppo della cultura appenninica (XIV sec. a.C.) e alle culture siciliane di Thapsos, del Milazzese, nonché al Mic. IIIA2;

FASE II: **Bronzo recente (BR)** (1300–1150), correlabile con il Sub-appenninico, con l'Ausonio I, coevo del Mic. III B;

FASE III: **Bronzo finale (BF)** (1150–850), parallelizzabile con il Protovillanoviano e l'Ausonio II;

FASE IV: **Iª Età del Ferro** (850–510) comprendente le seguenti sottofasi: A, I° Ferro o età geometrica (850–730); B, Età orientalizzante (730–580 circa); C, Età arcaica (580–510);

FASE V: **IIª Età del Ferro** (510–238 a.C. e oltre, per le zone interne dell'isola).

La prima fase nuragica, caratterizzata dai nuraghi a corridoi (o protonuraghi), cade tra la fine del Bronzo antico e la prima parte del Bronzo medio (Bronzo Medio I), tra lo scorcio del XVII e i secoli XVI e XV (Ugas 1989: 79; 1990: 134 n. 19, cap. IV e n. 33, cap. VI), e si sviluppa per la prima parte in sincronia con il Protoappenninico B della penisola italiana (Lo Porto 1963: 317, ss.; Lo Porto 1964; Bernabò Brea e Cavalier 1980: 691, ss.; Peroni 1983: 217-27; Kilian 1983: 61-64; Damiani *et al.* 1984: 1-38, figg. 1-9) e con il Mic. I-II.

Durante il Bronzo Medio II (XIV secolo), in sincronia con la cultura appenninica (Puglisi 1959; Peroni 1967) e le *facies* di Thapsos e del Milazzese (Bernabò Brea 1960: 119-34; Tusa 1983: 389-442), i nuraghi a corridoi tendono ad acquisire le caratteristiche che sono proprie delle fortezze turrite con camera a *tholos*. Ma l'apogeo dell'età dei nuraghi, col fiorire degli straordinari castelli dalle alte torri, si colloca nel Bronzo recente, prima del declino senza ritorno dei tempi del Bronzo finale.

Come del precedente orizzonte Bonnanaro I del Bronzo antico (Ferrarese Ceruti 1989: 76), la formazione e l'aggregazione degli insediamenti e delle strutture abitative del XVI-XV secolo sono assai mal note e con limitatissime testimonianze. Le nostre conoscenze sugli abitati si riducono ai dati di Sa Turricola-Muros (Ferrarese Ceruti 1981: 63; Lilliu 1988a: 276 ss., 319), Costa Tana-Bonarcado e Abini-Teti (Lilliu 1988a: 276). L'unica capanna di questa età indagata con scavo stratigrafico è pertinente all'abitato di Sa Turricola: di pianta rettangolare, è in parte risparmiata sulla roccia e in parte costruita con uno zoccolo in muratura. Il tetto viene ipotizzato a un solo spiovente, di frasche. La datazione del deposito archeologico, valutata col C14 al 1510 a.C., s'intona con la tipologia del vasellame. Sono invece del XIV secolo le restanti testimonianze dell'edilizia abitativa del Bronzo medio II: le capanne circolari dell'insediamento di Muru Mannu di Tharros-Cabras (Santoni 1985: 33-140). Come le precedenti, esse sono ubicate in un sito diverso, anche se non distante, da quello del nuraghe. Per la loro forma gli edifici di Muru Mannu vanno considerati i prototipi delle capanne circolari nuragiche del Bronzo recente e del Bronzo finale. Ben diversamente consistenti sono le nostre cognizioni sulle fortezze e sulle tombe dello stesso periodo. Queste categorie dell'architettura, con le loro straordinarie manifestazioni offrono utili indicazioni per tracciare i contorni della società protosarda tra il Bronzo medio e il Bronzo recente.

Sulla scorta delle esperienze occidentali e specificamente iberiche (Los Millares: Almagro e Arribas 1963: 203 ss.; fig. 10, tavv. V-XIII; Zambujal: Sangmeister e Schubart 1969: 34s.; figg. 6-7 tavv. I-VIII; 1981) si potrebbe essere indotti a ritenere che le fortificazioni turrite abbiano fatto la loro comparsa nell'isola sin dallo scorcio del Calcolitico e abbiano interessato tutto il Bronzo antico. Tuttavia sino ad oggi non c'è alcun edificio protosardo, identificato come fortezza, che abbia restituito vasellame della cultura Bonnanaro I.

I materiali più antichi rinvenuti in strati archeologici connessi con la frequentazione dei nuraghi non superano la soglia del Bronzo medio. Infatti, sebbene da alcuni nuraghi provengano dei frammenti di vasellame M. Claro, la loro sporadicità e le modalità di ritrovamento non vanno in favore dell'attribuzione di tali edifici al Calcolitico. È il caso, ad esempio, della fortezza di Su Mulinu di Villanovafranca, nel quale un coccio M. Claro è stato palesemente reimpiegato nella massa muraria del bastione di II fase, pertinente al Bronzo medio (Ugas e Paderi 1990: 476 n. 4).

I protonuraghi già individuati sulla base della planimetria e di altre caratteristiche (rapporto pieno/vuoto della massa e degli spazi, planimetrie e tagli dei corridoi e dei vani), sono oramai diverse centinaia ed il loro numero è destinato a crescere. Alla cinquantina di nuraghi arcaici segnalati dal Lilliu (1988a: 181) ed ai 180 enumerati dai Demurtas (Manca Demurtas e Demurtas 1984: 173, e questo volume) e dal Contu (1990: 62), vanno aggiunti i 23 individuati nel Campidano centrale e nel Guspinese (Paderi e Ugas 1988: 200) oltre quelli della Marmilla e di altre aree del Campidano (Ugas 1989: 79) e del Sarrabus. Relativamente a quest'ultima regione R. Ledda (1985: 64 ss.) enumera 53 protonuraghi, 5 pseudo-nuraghi e 2 soli nuraghi classici, ma a giudicare dagli schizzi planimetrici un buon numero dei monumenti indicati come protonuraghi rientra tipologicamente tra i nuraghi classici con torre. Il numero di questi edifici è, in ogni caso, destinato rapidamente a crescere poiché, diversamente dalle fortezze contraddistinte dalle *tholoi*, molto spesso non sono riportati come nuraghi nelle carte dell'IGM (Istituto Geografico Militare) ed in quelle catastali.

I protonuraghi sottoposti ad indagine stratigrafica hanno restituito tutti indistintamente vasellame assegnabile al Bronzo medio: Trobas di Lunamatrona (Lilliu 1982: 24 ss.; 1988a: 277 s.), la cui edificazione è stata attribuita al Bronzo antico, ma può essere ricondotta alle prime fasi del Bronzo medio; Peppe Gallu di Uri (Contu 1959: 59-121 e 1981: 60 tav. 4,b,q; Lilliu 1988a: 318); Su Mulinu di Villanovafranca (Ugas 1987b: 77-84, figg. 5.4-5.7; Ugas e Paderi 1990: 475-77); Sa Jacca di Busachi (Santoni 1980: 164,168); Brunku Madugui di Gesturi (Lilliu 1982: 24s., fig. 2 e 1988a: 130, 321-22). Suppellettili del Bronzo medio provengono dalle vicinanze di altri protonuraghi: Argiddas di Samassi (Ugas 1981a: 10 e 1981b: 84); Friarosu di Mogorella e Fruscos di Paulilatino (Manca Demurtas e Demurtas 1984: 184 figg. 14-15); Trattasi di Villanovafranca (inedito); Faurras di Villamar (Ugas 1981a: 10).

Tra i nuraghi arcaici scavati scientificamente, sia pure in modo non sistematico, merita un'attenzione particolare il Brunku Madugui di Gesturi. Giustamente il Lilliu (1988a: 180) sottolinea che la genesi di questo edificio dovrebbe essere in sincronia con quella delle altre costruzioni megalitiche che comunemente vengono chiamate pseudo-nuraghi. Nonostante la datazione al C14 del monumento indichi il 1820 ± 250 a.C., le ricerche più recenti assegnano il complesso dei materiali del Brunku Madugui ad uno stadio avanzato del Bronzo medio. Infatti le olle biconiche con orlo a tesa interna e ad ornamenti plastici rinvenute in questo edificio, già riferite comprensibilmente alla *facies* calcolitica per la somiglianza con il repertorio Monte Claro, vanno attribuite al Bronzo medio (Ugas 1981a: 9). Pertanto una datazione dell'edificio intorno al XV secolo appare più plausibile e consona con le caratteristiche dei reperti. L'assenza di relazioni tra i materiali Bonnanaro I e l'architettura megalitica viene confermata anche nell'ambito funerario. Infatti, mentre la ceramica e le altre suppellettili Bonnanaro I sono ben documentate nelle strutture sepolcrali ipogeiche, sia naturali che artificiali, diversamente in modo del tutto complementare l'architettura aerea delle *tombe di giganti* è accompagnata dalla ceramica e dagli altri manufatti del Bronzo medio, e più oltre del Bronzo recente, e mai da suppellettili Bonnanaro I.

I materiali più antichi sinora trovati in tombe megalitiche sono quelli di Aiodda (Atzeni 1982: 30

ss. fig. 7, tav. XVI; Lilliu 1988a: 288 fig. 89), che non vanno oltre la I[a] fase del Bronzo medio, così come i reperti delle *allées* di Li Lolghi (Castaldi 1969: 2 ss.) e Coddu Vecchiu di Arzachena (Castaldi 1968: 8 figg. 1-10), nonché di Monte de S'Ape-Olbia (Castaldi 1968), le quali precedono i sepolcri monumentali con stele centinata. Infatti alcuni pezzi fittili, talora ritenuti emblematici del Bronzo antico, quali le anse a gomito e ad ascia, persistono ancora nella *facies* di San Cosimo-Gonnosfanadiga (Ugas 1989), così come i vasi polipodi sono oramai riconducibili agli inizi del Bronzo medio (Ferrarese Ceruti 1981: 73).

La cultura di Bonnanaro I chiude un lungo ciclo di esperienze maturate tra il Neolitico e il Calcolitico: al suo tramonto si apre un nuovo corso, che però trova terreno fertile in un *humus* culturale pronto a cogliere i fermenti e le sollecitazioni esterne. Dalle ceneri di questa cultura scaturisce il più macroscopico fenomeno del megalitismo sardo, connotato in senso numerico e monumentale dai nuraghi e dalle 'tombe di giganti', e che relega in secondo piano anche le già rilevanti testimonianze del megalitismo prenuragico, caratterizzato in modo precipuo dai *menhir*, dai *dolmens* e dai circoli. Durante il Bronzo medio il megalitismo non è più limitato, come nel Calcolitico, alla sfera del sacro (es. Monte d'Accoddi-Sassari, Biriai-Olièna), salvo il caso ancora da chiarire, sul piano cronologico e funzionale, dell'edificio di Sa Corona-Villagreca (Nuraminis), ma è esteso anche ad altre realtà del mondo civile. Ora l'arte del costruire in grande, con la pietra, compare nelle fortezze e nelle case, oltre che nei templi.

Purtroppo, a causa della limitatezza delle indagini, non è possibile stabilire quali siano i rapporti spaziali, gerarchici e di natura politica tra i protonuraghi e gli insediamenti. L'avvento dell'architettura monumentale nuragica implica un profondo mutamento sul piano delle gerarchie interne in seno alle comunità protosarde. I segni di un radicale cambiamento sociale, che porta ad una struttura gerarchica fondata sulle armi e sugli edifici di difesa traspaiono, in primo luogo, dalle sepolture di un gruppo di guerrieri, appartenenti ad un *ghenos* e databili tra la fine del XVII secolo e la prima metà del XVI, per le quali fu riutilizzato un ipogeo neolitico nel sito di Sant'Iroxi-Decimoputzu (Cagliari). Connotano lo *status* dell'elevato rango sociale dei defunti le tredici spade massicce a larga lama e a base semplice (lunghezza compresa tra cm 33 e cm 72), oltre ai sei pugnali in rame arsenicale (Ugas 1990: 105-11, *passim*, tav. XXVIII-XXXI, XXXVb-XXXVI).

Le armi di Sant'Iroxi consentono di comprendere meglio anche la posizione cronologica e funzionale del gruppo di spade corte, simili, seppure non identiche di fattura e di poco più recenti, rinvenute in una località sconosciuta della Sardegna, verosimilmente Siniscola (Lo Schiavo 1978: 85-87; Lilliu 1988a: fig. 144; Ugas 1990: 108, tav. LXIII: c). Non v'ha dubbio che la circolazione di nuove e più efficaci armi implica l'insorgere, in ambiti territoriali non molto ampi, di turbolenti capi locali, che per ampliare e difendere il loro territorio, hanno necessità di adeguate apparecchiature di difesa, innanzitutto di poderose fortificazioni: i protonuraghi.

Il numero di oltre 300 protonuraghi finora accertato (come detto, suscettibile di un consistente incremento) è già sufficiente per intravedere una struttura organizzativa e politica che prelude a quella imperniata sui castelli turriti del Bronzo recente. Restano da definire i rapporti tra la fortezza e l'insediamento, tra insediamento principale e insediamenti secondari, tra sede egemonica e sedi subalterne, senza sottovalutare i possibili condizionamenti di etnie di matrice diversa (Libi, Iberi, Corsi, Tirreni, ecc.) di cui parlano le fonti letterarie antiche (Pais 1881; Meloni 1945; Dunbabin 1948; Bérard 1963: *passim*; Mastino 1980: 61-274; Ugas 1980: 31; Ugas 1981a: 12 ss; 77-81; Ugas 1987b; Ugas 1990; Lilliu 1988a).

Sono già state più volte evidenziate le differenze che intercorrono fra i nuraghi a corridoi e quelli a *tholos*. Semplificando, i principali elementi strutturali dei nuraghi arcaici sono i seguenti:

1. *Corridoi aggettanti coperti a piattabanda* e *Corridoi ad ogiva gradonata*, che sostituiscono man mano i più antichi corridoi dolmenici a pareti verticali e a copertura piattabandata di tradizione neolitica e calcolitica;
2. *Piccoli vani* di pianta irregolarmente circolare e più spesso ellittica, con ingresso decentrato rispetto all'asse della camera e con copertura a *tholos* troncogivale o gradonata;
3. *Grandi camere ellissoidi* a volta troncogivale (a nave rovescia).

Sul piano della litotecnica, si osserva: a) l'impiego di massi poligonali o irregolarmente squadrati di grande e media pezzatura nel paramento esterno della muratura; b) l'uso di pietrame di pezzatura media e piccola, sotto forma di lastre, nel paramento interno dei vani; c) l'utilizzo di pietrame più minuto connesso con malta di fango, nella zona mediana tra i due paramenti.

Nel bastione della fortezza, non si palesa ancora la distinzione tra le torri e le cortine. Si ha un contorno continuo nei corpi circolari ellittici e quadrangolari (Contu 1981: 45 ss.; Lilliu 1982: 17

224 *Sardinia in the Mediterranean*

A

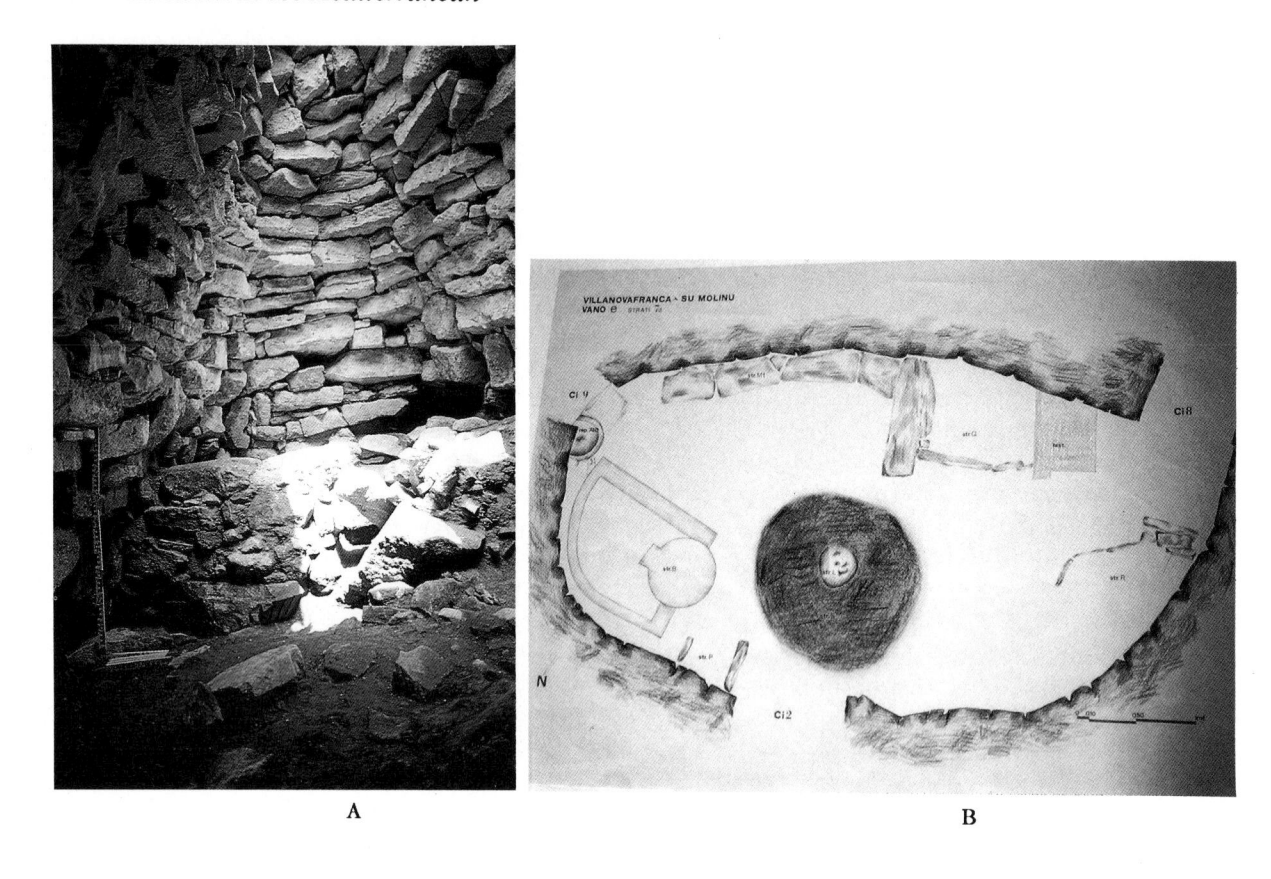

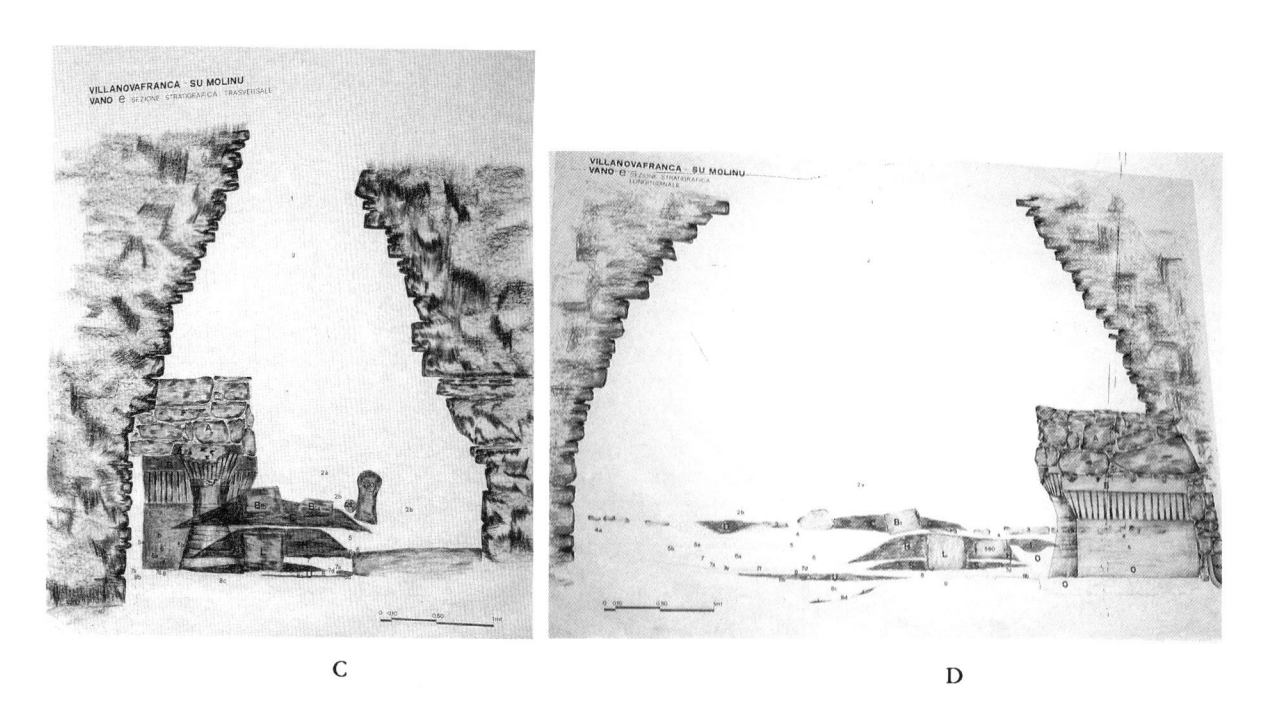

B

C

D

Fig. 1 Villanovafranca (CA). Nuraghe Su Mulinu, vano *e* (Bronzo medio): a) veduta della volta su un lato corto; b) planimetria; c) sezione longitudinale; d) sezione trasversa.

ss.; Lilliu 1988a: 176-86) o un profilo sinuoso o concavo-convesso negli edifici più complessi. La distinzione perimetrale tra le torri e le cortine si osserva nelle cinte murarie esterne a partire almeno dal XIV secolo a.C., quali, ad es., S'Aurrecci-Guspini (Lilliu 1962a: 49, in particolare 180-81 e *passim*, tav. LXXXVI ss.; Ugas 1987a: 91), primo e secondo impianto di Su Mulinu di Villanovafranca (Ugas 1987b: 77 ss.). Il profilo di queste cinte è sinuoso e lo stacco tra cortine e torri poco accentuato.

Mentre i piccoli vani ellittici che preludono alle camere circolari dei nuraghi a *tholos* assolvono a un ruolo sussidiario, ben altra rilevanza rivestono le grandi camere di forma ellittica, a nave rovescia, caratterizzate dalla volta aggettante. È di questa forma il vano *e* nel bastione di Su Mulinu (lungh. 6.20 m; largh. 3 m; h. 4.20 m), scavato per intero (Ugas e Paderi 1990: 475-79, tav. I; Ugas 1992) (Fig. 1) e una camera del protonuraghe Crastu A di Ghilarza (Manca Demurtas e Demurtas 1984: fig. 202).

Nell'ambito dell'architettura nuragica del Bronzo medio e recente è la fortezza che meglio esprime le relazioni sul piano tecnico-formale con le regioni egee. Nell'articolo relativo al nuraghe di Su Mulinu (Ugas 1987b) è stata prospettata la possibilità di un percorso evolutivo sincronico, fra il XVI e il XIII secolo, delle camere e dei corridoi di edifici sia della Sardegna che elladici e, più in generale, egei. In particolare è stato ipotizzato un graduale passaggio dalla copertura a sezione quadrangolare o a trilite a quella di taglio troncoconico e infine alla volta ogivale continua, prima a conci semplicemente squadrati e poi a conci isodomi.

Riguardo specificamente all'evoluzione parallela dei corridoi delle fortezze, in ambito sia egeo che sardo, colma un vuoto il taglio tronco-ogivale del *train culvert* della cinta muraria di Ayia Irini, a Keos (Davis 1986: tav. 39f,g e 40a), riferita al periodo VI° di Ayia Irini, correlato con il LC I e collocato intorno al XVI secolo a.C. Questa data coincide con quella dei primi corridoi a taglio troncoconico delle fortezze e delle tombe protonuragiche. Potrebbe forse non essere casuale il fatto che proprio Keos sia una tappa del cammino di Aristaios e con lui di un 'primo' Daidalos verso la Sardegna, come riferiscono alcune fonti letterarie antiche (Pausania 10.17.3; Sallustio 2.6,7; Diodoro 4.82).

Con straordinaria coerenza l'architettura delle tombe di giganti segue lo stesso sviluppo che si osserva nelle fortezze. Semplificando, nei sepolcri di Aiodda-Laconi (con stele) e di San Cosimo (senza stele) la camera, allungata e con rigonfiamento mediano, mostra una copertura troncogivale con lastre piattabandate terminali. Stessi schemi iconografici e in elevato, ma in una situazione di maggiore spazialità, si colgono negli ipogei con stele scolpita di Campu Lontanu-Florinas e nella T. IV di Sa Figu di Ittiri (Contu 1978: 15-21 figg. 1-5), le cui celle sono prossime a quelle a nave rovescia del vano *e* di Su Mulinu e del nuraghe Crastu A di Ghilarza.

La collocazione cronologica del complesso funerario di Ittiri emerge anche dalla presenza di un altro ipogeo con prospetto architettonico, che mostra una cella circolare con *dromos* sub-rettangolare o trapezoidale (Lilliu 1988a: 283-85, Tomba IV, fig. 86) e ripropone lo schema delle tombe a *tholos* micenee e siciliane (Tomasello 1986: 93-100 figg. 1-10). Anche negli ipogei di San Giorgio e Ladrofurti a Sassari oltre che di Ittiàri-Osilo (Lilliu 1988a: fig. 82: 1-3), le celle circolari sono precedute dalla stele centinata scolpita, e in esse non a caso appare la copertura a volta sia pure ribassata. Certo non è privo di significato il fatto che gli ipogei con prospetto architettonico a stele centinata documentino, oltre che la soluzione della cella circolare, anche planimetrie allungate, oblunghe, quadrangolari e rettangolari precedute da corridoi d'accesso e talora da una sorta di embrionale *dromos* rettangolare (Corona e Sa Figu di Florinas-Sassari, Chercos di Usini-Sassari e Pascialzos I di Cargeghe-Sassari) (Moravetti 1990: fig. 176 di p. 154; fig. 177 di p. 155). Sulla camera di queste tombe si affacciano una o talora più celle laterali ellittiche o quadrangolari quasi sempre ricavate sulle pareti laterali. Le architetture ipogeiche con prospetto architettonico hanno un unico denominatore comune: la rigorosità e la regolarità delle linee, frutto di una nuova concezione dello spazio che viene misurato e sentito 'geometricamente' e che consente di superare le angustie proprie dell'ipogeismo. È palese soprattutto la ricerca della spazialità aerea evidenziata dall'aumento sensibile delle altezze degli ambienti.

Sul tema dell'ipogeismo assume un ruolo importante, per la comprensione di tale processo, in ambito mediterraneo centro-occidentale, la tomba di S. Vito dei Normanni in Puglia (Lo Porto 1963), riferita al Protoappenninico B. Questo sepolcro ripropone lo schema delle più antiche tombe micenee con *dromos* rettangolare, corridoio o *stomion*, camera circolare con volta aggettante (*tholos*) e cella sussidiaria aperta su un fianco. Interessa rilevare in questa sede che la sezione della camera dell'ipogeo di San Vito, a *tholos* troncogivale con sommità chiusa da una lastra posta a piattabanda, rispecchia un modello di *tholos* che precede il tipo a ogiva piena. Infatti il disegno dell'ipogeo di San Vito riappare con qualche

226 *Sardinia in the Mediterranean*

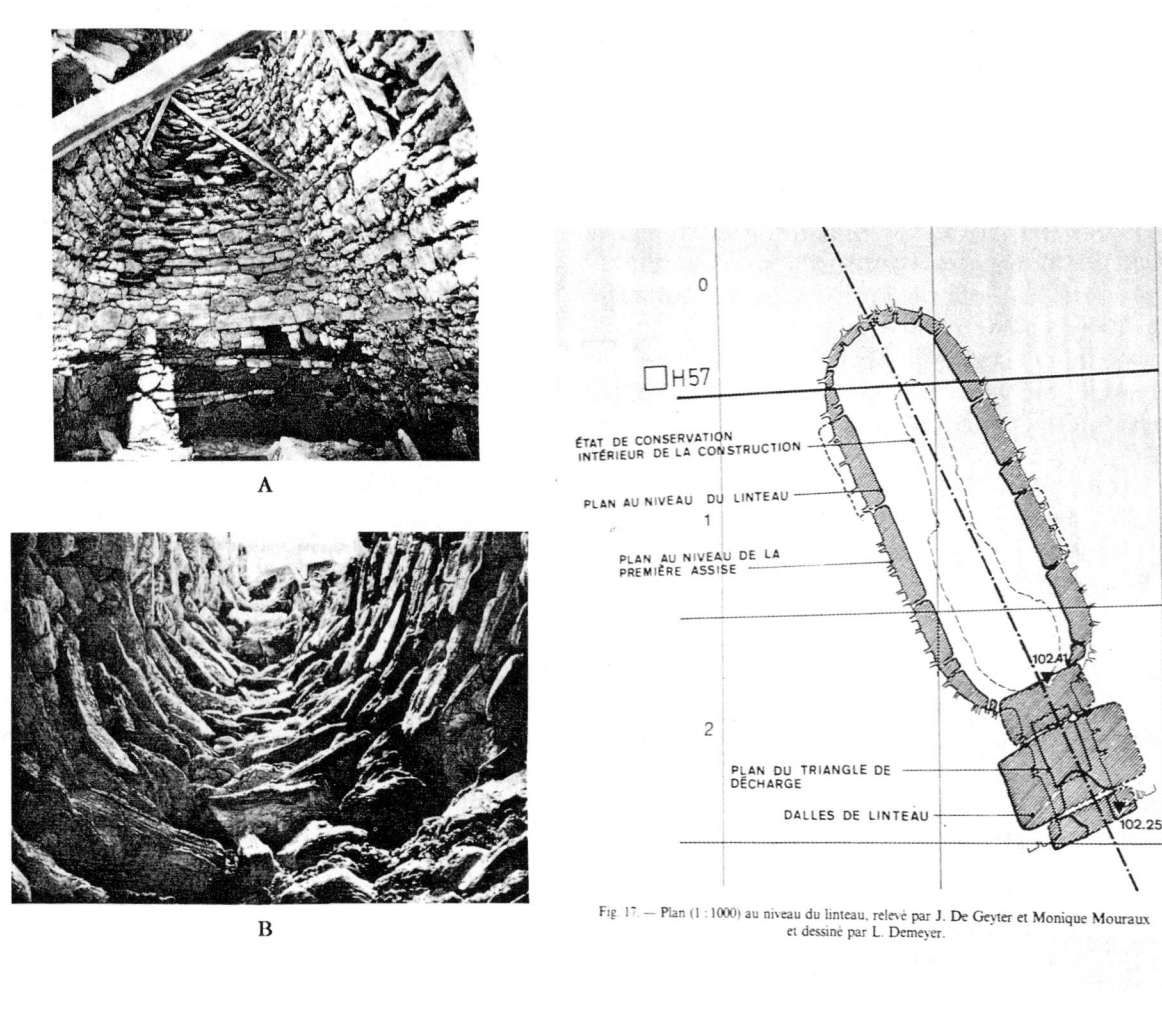

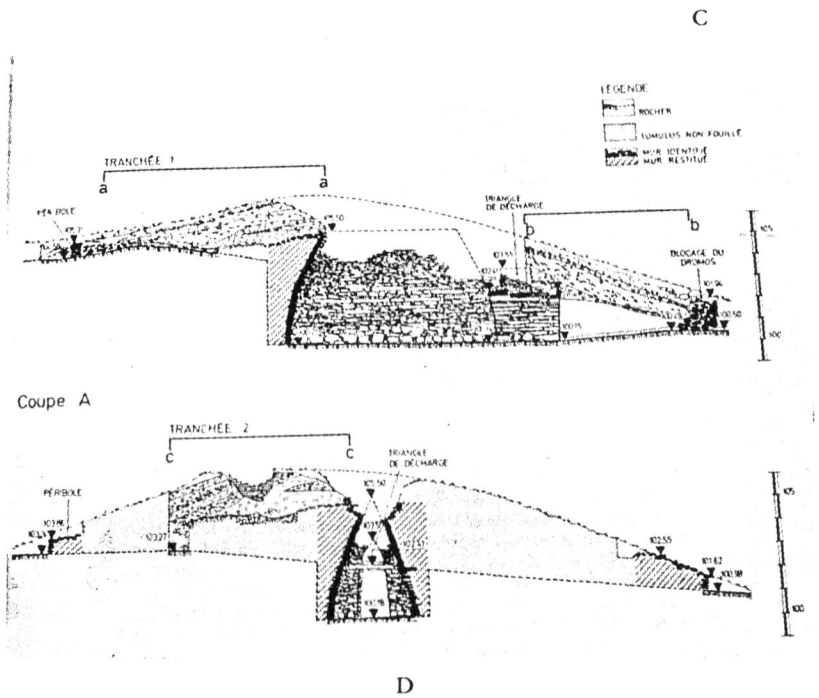

Fig. 2 Thorikos (Attica), Tomba IV: a) veduta della camera, parete interna (da Mussche *et al.* 1984: figg. 22, 25.8-9); b) veduta della camera, zona sommitale; c) planimetria; d) sezioni longitudinale (sopra) e traversa (sotto).

significativa differenza nelle tombe di Molinello-Augusta (Tusa 1983: 402 ss. figg. 13-14), Cozzo del Pantano-Matrensa (Tusa 1983: 408 fig. 18) e di altre località siciliane (Tomasello 1986: 93-100 figg. 1-10) che hanno restituito ceramiche di importazione del Mic. III A2. Negli ipogei ascritti alla cultura di Thapsos (XIV secolo a.C.), la camera circolare mostra, oramai, un taglio pienamente ogivale. In qualche esemplare, forse più antico, è ribassata, così da far pensare all'imitazione di prototipi con copertura a *tholos* ribassata anziché con la linea più slanciata e più regolare, propria delle tombe a *tholos* più evolute e armoniose, quali il Tesoro di Atreo.

Per quanto concerne l'architettura delle fortezze protonuragiche, finora sono state colte delle relazioni esclusivamente con gli edifici megalitici occidentali, quali i *talaiots* balearici e le torri corse (Lilliu e Schubart 1967: 11-180; Contu 1990: 72). Qui invece vengono prospettati rapporti non meno palesi, sia pure su piani funzionali differenti, con edifici del Mediterraneo orientale. È di quest'ambito geografico, infatti e precisamente dell'Attica, la camera oblunga a *tholos* della tomba IV di Thorikos (Fig. 2), una vera e propria nave rovescia, che è stata ritenuta più antica delle altre tombe a camera circolare della stessa necropoli datate all'Elladico recente II A (Mussche *et al.* 1984: 16-46 figg. 1-25). È questo uno dei più antichi esempi di possibili relazioni tra l'architettura egea e quella protonuragica ed è pienamente coerente con la linea di sviluppo dianzi prospettata. Nel contesto della necropoli di Thorikos va citata anche la tomba I che, seppure di dimensioni più ridotte, ripropone la stessa pianta oblunga della precedente.

Per quanto concerne altre aree esterne all'Attica vanno prese in considerazione le architetture delle *tholoi* di Palaiochori e di Keri a Zante per le quali però non viene intravisto un rapporto diretto con le *tholoi* oblunghe I e IV di Thorikos (Pelon 1976: 413; Mussche *et al.* 1984). Così sul piano stilistico e formale non pare potersi istituire alcun rapporto con le tombe di Ugarit con camera allungata e volta ogivale (Mussche *et al.* 1984: 45), datate al XIV-XIII sec. a.C., come le altre simili di Ibn Hani (Saliby 1982: 37-42 figg. 1-15), sia per la pianta rettangolare, sia per la tecnica più evoluta (impiego di conci isodomi), affine a quella del Tesoro di Atreo in Micene, sia infine, per l'ogiva completa.

D'altro canto è verosimile che le tombe di Ugarit e di Ibn Hani, nonostante gli ambienti a base rettangolare, abbiano i loro prototipi proprio nelle camere oblunghe di Thorikos o in altre che possono aver svolto funzioni di tramite. A questo proposito non va trascurato che anche in ambito protosardo, pressoché coevo, alcuni dei già citati ipogei a prospetto architettonico, con stele centinata, siano caratterizzati da una grande e larga camera rettangolare o quadrangolare, tipo Malafà e Ladrofurti b di Sassari (Lilliu 1988a: 180 fig. 87.5-6), pertinenti allo stesso contesto delle tombe con camera allungata e a lati corti ricurvi, tipo Campu Lontanu-Florinas (Contu 1978: 15-21 figg. 1-5), e a pianta circolare, tipo la tomba IV di Sa Figu-Ittiri (Lilliu 1988a: 283-85 fig. 86).

È probabile, pertanto, che le tombe a *tholos* circolari e quelle oblunghe abbiano avuto un cammino tutto sommato parallelo, anche se disarticolato e con specifiche varianti regionali, sia nell'Egeo che nell'area levantina. Un percorso ugualmente parallelo va ipotizzato per l'ambito occidentale sia nei sepolcri monumentali sardi (tombe di giganti e ipogei a prospetto architettonico) e balearici come le *navetas*, sia nei coevi edifici d'uso civile, sardi (protonuraghi) e balearici, quali le costruzioni di tipo pretalaiotico e talaiotico (Lilliu e Schubart 1967: 127-35, 138-46; Contu 1959: 59-121; Contu 1981: 73-75; Manca Demurtas e Demurtas 1987: 493-500; Plantalamor Massanet 1987: 533-46; Rita Larrucea 1987: 547-55). È in ogni caso sorprendente e non può essere dovuta a casuali convergenze la somiglianza tra la tomba IV di Thorikos e il vano e di Su Mulinu-Villanovafranca sia per il taglio a chiglia rovescia, sia per la pianta a lati corti ricurvi, sia, infine, per l'impiego di pietre tagliate a lastre e non a blocchi. Tenuti nella debita considerazione anche i disegni a chiglia rovescia delle strutture tombali sarde e baleariche, non va negata una base di esperienze comuni, derivate dalla percorrenza di rotte mediterranee da Est verso Ovest e viceversa, determinate in primo luogo dallo sfruttamento delle risorse minerarie della Sardegna (Ugas 1990) e, suo tramite, della penisola iberica.

Al numero ormai consistente degli insediamenti nuragici indagati non corrisponde una pari quantità di dati sugli abitati e sulle singole abitazioni del Bronzo recente, così che è assai limitata la conoscenza delle forme e delle strutture edilizie di questo periodo. Nonostante ciò è improbabile che la rilevata, iterata, assenza di abitazioni di questa età in vicinanza dei nuraghi, sia dovuta solo alla carenza delle ricerche. Si può pensare infatti che i castelli e gli abitati non occupassero gli stessi siti, come si evince dalle indagini condotte nel territorio di Dorgali-Nuoro, dove dei 78 villaggi individuati, 67 appaiono privi di fortezza e solamente 11 sono connessi con nuraghi dei quali 4 complessi (Fadda 1990: 102). Nell'ambito del Campidano di Cagliari risultano simili i dati forniti dall'indagine sul territorio di Decimoputzu dove solo 3 insediamenti su 10 sono

228 *Sardinia in the Mediterranean*

A

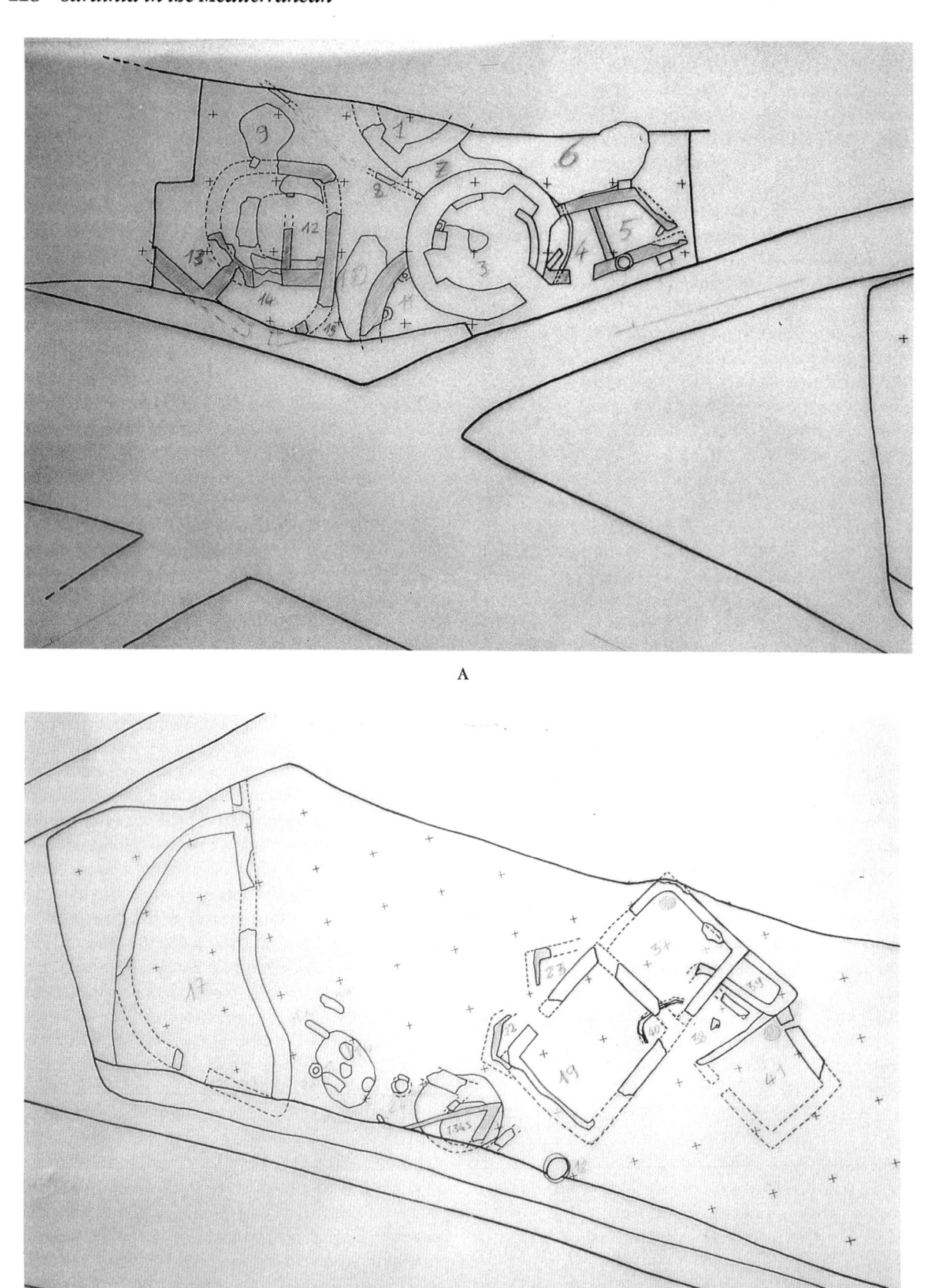

B

Fig. 3 Insediamento nuragico di Monte Zara (Monastir-CA): 1) settore A, nella zona centrale capanna circolare 3 (Bronzo recente); b) settore B, a destra, edificio plurivano ad ambienti rettangolari e quadrangolari (Bronzo finale).

in rapporto diretto col nuraghe, mentre per contro altri 7 nuraghi risultano isolati (Ugas 1990: 275 tab. B). Per prudenza occorrerà attendere riferimenti cronologici più precisi per risalire ai tempi in cui sorsero questi abitati ma i dati già acquisiti fanno prevedere fin d'ora che i villaggi senza nuraghe possono essere contemporanei con i nuraghi isolati (cioè senza villaggi attorno) e che i villaggi con nuraghi non siano coevi ma posteriori alla costruzione e all'uso primario delle fortezze.

La situazione topografica e strategica induce ad assegnare al castello un ruolo egemone nei confronti dell'insediamento che appare isolato e non difeso direttamente quando non sia ubicato in cima o a ridosso di un luogo elevato. Dai dati finora acquisiti parrebbe che il villaggio sia in stretta relazione con il nuraghe solo a partire dal Bronzo finale (es. Su Nuraxi-Barumini, in Lilliu 1982: fig. 120) e dagli inizi del I° Ferro (es. Genna Maria-Villanovaforru, in Badas 1987: 133-46; Atzeni 1988: 15-24). Purtroppo sono piuttosto limitate anche le nostre cognizioni sulle abitazioni dei villaggi senza nuraghe. Ciò discende dal fatto che le indagini sono state indirizzate prevalentemente sugli insediamenti adiacenti alle fortezze.

Al riguardo, il dubbio che le capanne circolari di Su Nuraxi di Barumini non documentino i livelli di frequentazione del Bronzo recente solo per una non completa edizione dei dati sui materiali dell'abitato tende a svanire con la constatazione che sono pertinenti al Bronzo finale anche le capanne circolari dei villaggi di Santa Vittoria di Serri e di Sant'Anastasia di Sardara (Capanna 1) connessi con santuari, oltre quelle di S'Urbale-Teti nel nuorese (Taramelli 1931: 63 ss.; Fadda 1990: 102 ss., 108 ss.). Non mancano, tuttavia, i casi accertati di capanne circolari risalenti al Bronzo recente. Dei pochi abitati soggetti ad indagine che hanno restituito strutture in muratura del periodo in argomento si ricorda in primo luogo quello di Monte Zara-Monastir nell'*hinterland* di Cagliari (Ugas 1987b: 119 s.; 1992). Le capanne circolari nn. 1, 3 del settore A di questo sito, provviste di zoccolo in muratura e di nicchie rettangolari, hanno restituito ceramiche grigio-ardesia. In particolare l'edificio n. 3, scavato per intero, mostra due nicchie disposte a triangolo con l'ingresso (Fig. 3a), come nelle camere delle torri centrali di diversi bastioni nuragici quadrilobati e trilobati (Su Nuraxi-Barumini, Lilliu 1982: fig. 73,2). Il bancone interno a giro, il focolare centrale, il canaletto e il seggio distinto nella panchina, fanno però di questo ambiente di Monte Zara il prototipo delle più tarde sale del consiglio come la capanna n. 5 di Sant'Anastasia di Sardara (Ugas e Usai 1987: 171-80), capanna 80 di Su Nuraxi-Barumini (Lilliu 1955: 284 ss., tavv. 39-40) e la grande capanna con altare a torre di Palmavera-Alghero (Moravetti 1977: 227-80 fig. 12; 1980: 74 figg. 25-26).

Sempre nello stesso sito di M. Zara, accanto all'utilizzo di edifici in muratura, continua l'uso di ambienti scavati profondamente sul terreno, di antica tradizione neolitica e calcolitica (strutture 32S e 34S), le quali hanno restituito, insieme alle solite ceramiche grigio-ardesia, anche dei pezzi di vasellame di importazione del Mic. III B (Ugas 1987a: 119). Analoghi ambienti seminterrati sono stati ipotizzati negli insediamenti di M. Olladiri di Monastir, San Gemiliano di Sestu (Atzeni 1961). Il fatto che nel sito di Monte Zara il nuraghe, diversamente dal villaggio, non sia ubicato sulle pendici ma sulla sommità del rilievo, in una posizione strategica funzionalmente assai diversa, induce ancora una volta a riconoscere una dicotomia nel rapporto castello-villaggio.

Da quanto detto emerge che nel Bronzo finale, allorché nuraghe e abitato coesistono fianco a fianco, va ipotizzato un processo di avvicinamento e di integrazione dei ruoli politici tra la fortezza e il villaggio, determinato dall'esigenza di una maggiore protezione del villaggio in un periodo di crisi che porta al tracollo del sistema politico imperniato sulle stesse fortezze.

Il ruolo primario, militare e politico ad un tempo, dei castelli (i nuraghi complessi polilobati) è indicato dal loro numero limitato in rapporto all'insieme dei nuraghi monotorri (Lilliu 1988b: 9). Pertanto il numero elevato dei nuraghi semplici fa sì che non sia accettabile, oltre che per ragioni di natura stilistica, l'ipotesi che essi (e il discorso vale anche per le torri centrali dei bastioni) precedano sul piano cronologico i nuraghi complessi. Le differenze tra i nuraghi monotorri e quelli polilobati sono piuttosto funzionali e legate al diverso ruolo nella tutela del territorio. Ai nuraghi monotorri va attribuito il compito di vedetta territoriale. Le migliaia di torri e castelli che nel corso del Bronzo recente controllano capillarmente il territorio dell'isola, offrono un chiaro indizio della struttura politica che si intuisce formata da una rete assai articolata di piccoli reami: i cantoni (Lilliu 1982; Lilliu 1988a; Ugas 1989; Contu 1985; Contu 1990).

Quale ruolo assume il tempio nel rapporto tra il castello e il villaggio nello stesso periodo? Bisogna innanzitutto conoscere quali luoghi sacri appartengono al Bronzo recente. Per certo sono di questa età diversi santuari in grotta, come quello di Su Benatzu di Santadi che ha il suo esordio già nel Bronzo medio (Lilliu 1988a; Ugas 1989), ubicati lontano sia dai castelli che dai villaggi, anche se vanno visti legati più a questi che non ai primi. Finora non è stata documentata alcune formazione stratigrafica che consenta di attribuire con sicurezza i templi a pozzo al

Bronzo recente. Per ragioni strutturali tuttavia il loro esordio va fissato proprio in questa fase, se non già nel Bronzo medio, in parallelo con lo sviluppo dei nuraghi (Santoni 1989: 169), ma difficilmente per ragioni stilistiche può essere riportato al Bronzo medio il nuraghe di Sisini-Senorbì che ripropone lo stesso schema planimetrico del tempio a pozzo. L'armonia della costruzione e l'accuratezza nella disposizione dei massi si addice più all'architettura evoluta del Bronzo recente piuttosto che a quella più 'arcaica' del Bronzo medio.

È perciò verosimile che già nel corso del Bronzo recente così come è evidente più tardi nel Bronzo finale, ci sia stata una relazione stretta tra il villaggio e il tempio a pozzo e non già tra il nuraghe e il tempio a pozzo. Nei casi di associazione in uno stesso sito del nuraghe e del tempio a pozzo, come a Santa Vittoria di Serri (Taramelli 1922; 1931), e a Cuccuru Nuraxi-Settimo S. Pietro (Atzeni 1987: 279-88 tavv. 1-9), si è di fronte a situazioni di sovrapposizioni stratigrafiche e cronologiche del tempio sul nuraghe, evidenziando un processo di sostituzione fisica e funzionale. Stando così le cose il sacerdote rappresenta la massima autorità del villaggio e funge da tramite nelle relazioni tra quest'ultimo e il principe che dimora nel castello. Anche i templi a *megaron* dell'isola, che per ragioni di tecnica edilizia potrebbero essere coevi con i templi a pozzo, noti a Serra Orrios-Dorgali, Cuccureddì-Esterzili e Sos Nurattolos di Alà dei Sardi (Lilliu 1988a: 393-96 figg. 135-37), sono in relazione con l'insediamento e non già col nuraghe e assumono, nell'ambito dell'abitato, lo stesso ruolo del tempio a pozzo.

È nel Bronzo recente che il castello raggiunge l'apice sia sul piano stilistico che funzionale. I bastioni pentalobati, quadrilobati e trilobati, con cortine ben distinte dalle alte torri angolari e muniti di cinte turrite esterne, sono l'epressione di un'architettura estremamente razionale. I loro disegni rappresentano lo sbocco logico dei vari tentativi di accorpamento delle torri mediante le quali venivano superati gli impianti dei protonuraghi, più compatti ma poco funzionali per i limiti oggettivi nell'utilizzo degli spazi in senso orizzontale e verticale. I tagli ogivali sempre più slanciati delle camere consentirono alle torri dei nuraghi di raggiungere altezze affatto inconsuete (anche oltre i 25 metri) per l'architettura preistorica e protostorica dell'Europa centro-occidentale.

Sul piano della monumentalità le fortezze del Bronzo recente trovano un loro parallelo nell'epressione più nota dell'architettura funeraria: 'le tombe di giganti'. Queste mantengono le stesse caratteristiche degli esempi del Bronzo medio, modificando solo i tagli dei corridoi, ora decisamente ogivali, e operando sul piano stilistico ed estetico mediante una accurata sovrapposizione dei filari ed un perfetto taglio dei massi, sviluppo che diventerà compiuto nei momenti conclusivi del Bronzo recente e nel Bronzo finale, quando verranno impiegati i conci isodomi. Un altro elemento di raccordo, forse non casuale, tra le esperienze architettoniche dei due opposti Mediterranei si coglie nel *wall of tunnel leading from sally port to city* di Ras Shamra (Hult 1983: tav. 19), dove i caratteristici conci ad 'L' raccordano ad angolo due differenti segmenti murari. L'uso di conci ad 'L', per rendere l'angolo d'incontro tra due diversi tratti murari, si osserva analogamente nell'attacco tra le cortine di una torre (Torre C) del nuraghe Addeiu di Gesturi (Lilliu 1962a: 93, ss. n. 6 tavv. 12-13; C. Lilliu e Puddu 1985: 39-41) dove i tipici conci ad 'L' servono a staccare e a distinguere il filo murario della cortina da quello della torre.

Una particolare attenzione in rapporto al periodo in argomento merita infine l'edificio formato da un corridoio-scala e da una camera sotterranea circolare coperta con una volta a *tholos*, che ripropone lo stesso schema, in pianta e in elevato, del tempio a pozzo nuragico: il pozzo circolare con scala d'accesso di Gjarlo (Bulgaria) studiato da Dmitrina Mitova-Dzonova (1983; 1992). Questo esempio di architettura balcanica esprime in modo chiaro la diffusione e la dispersione di forme architettoniche tra l'Occidente e l'Egeo, tanto più se si pensa che il tempio a pozzo nuragico, al di là delle specifiche funzioni, sul piano formale è un diretto parente delle tombe a *tholos* micenee, come osserva il Contu (1992). Infatti, come queste, il tempio nuragico è formato da un atrio rettangolare, un corridoio (o *stomion*) e una camera circolare ipogeica coperta a *tholos*.

Ai già richiamati elementi di raccordo tra le esperienze costruttive protosarde ed egee, occorre aggiungere per i tempi del Bronzo finale il particolare raggruppamento di vani nel settore B di M. Zara di Monastir (strutture 37, 19, ecc.: Ugas 1987b: 119 s.). Nella netta rigidezza del disegno geometrico, fondato sul tema del quadrato e del rettangolo, questo complesso architettonico (Fig. 3b) ripropone schemi di edifici siciliani e micenei, che non trovano riscontro in altri ambiti nuragici coevi. Nell'insediamento di M. Zara è stato documentato l'uso dei mattoni di fango sopra gli zoccoli degli edifici in muratura e soprattutto l'impiego di basi di pilastri, alcuni dei quali culminanti con capitelli a gola (due esemplari a base quadrata e uno rettangolare). Per questi ultimi si può stabilire un confronto col capitello frammentario, di base quadrangolare, del Tesoro di Atreo (Hult 1983: 125 fig. 83).

Ringraziamenti

Un pensiero di stima e di riconoscenza va rivolto a Klaus Kilian per la sua generosa e cortese disponibilità nell'indirizzarmi in quel cosmo ancora per me poco noto dell'architettura micenea e, più in generale, egea. Un sentito ringraziamento va al dr. R.H. Tykot. Alla sua cortese insistenza si deve questo omaggio al grande amore che Miriam S. Balmuth ha manifestato a più riprese nei confronti dell'archeologia sarda e, in particolare, della civiltà dei nuraghi. A questo tema la professoressa M.S. Balmuth ha offerto significativi contributi sia attraverso la rilettura del nuraghe Ortu Còmidu di Sardara, sottoposto a nuova indagine di scavo, sia con l'organizzazione di convegni dedicati alla metallurgia sarda e alle relazioni tra la civiltà nuragica e le culture dell'Egeo. Si ringraziano ancora Salvatore Mura per la collaborazione nella documentazione fotografica, Claudio Porta per i disegni di Su Mulinu e Luciano Pilia per la planimetria di Monte Zara.

Bibliografia

Almagro, M., & A. Arribas
1963 *El Poblado y la Necrópolis Megalitica de Los Millares*. Madrid.

Atzeni, E.
1961 I villaggi preistorici di San Gemiliano di Sestu e di Monte Olladiri di Monastir presso Cagliari e le ceramiche della 'facies' di Monte Claro. *Studi Sardi* 17: 1-216.
1980 Vornuraghenzeit. In J. Thimme (ed.), *Kunst und Kultur Sardiniens vom Neolithikum bis zum Ende der Nuraghenzeit*, 17-43. Karlsruhe: Verlag C.F. Müller.
1982 *Menbirs Antropomorfi e Statue-Menhirs della Sardegna*. In *Annali del Museo Civico di La Spezia*.
1987 Il neolitico della Sardegna. *Atti della XXVI Riunione Scientifica 'Il Neolitico in Italia,' Firenze, 7-10 novembre 1985*. Firenze: Istituto Italiano di Preistoria e Protostoria.
1988 Il nuraghe Genna Maria. *L'Umana Avventura* 3(8): 15-24.

Badas, U.
1987 Genna Maria-Villanovaforru (Cagliari). I vani 10-18. Nuovi apporti allo studio delle abitazioni a Corte Centrale. *La Sardegna nel Mediterraneo tra il Secondo e il Primo Millennio a.C. Atti del 2 Convegno di Studi 'Un millennio di relazioni fra la Sardegna e i Paesi del Mediterraneo, Selargius-Cagliari, 27-30 novembre 1986*, 133-46. Cagliari: Amministrazione Provinciale di Cagliari.

Bérard, J.
1963 *La Magna Grecia. Storia delle colonie greche dell'Italia meridionale*. Roma.

Bernabò Brea, L.
1960 *La Sicilia prima dei Greci*.

Bernabò Brea, L., & M. Cavalier
1980 *Meligunis Lìpara IV*. Palermo: Flaccovio.

Castaldi, E.
1968 Nuove osservazioni sulle tombe di giganti. *Bollettino Paletnologia Italiana* 19: 7 ss.
1969 Tombe di giganti nel Sassarese. *Origini*, 2ss. Sassari.

Contu, E.
1959 I più antichi nuraghi della Sardegna e l'esplorazione del nuraghe Peppe Gallu (Uri, Sassari). *Rivista di Scienze Preistoriche* 14(1-4).
1978 Il significato della stele nelle tombe di giganti. *Quaderni della Soprintendenza Archeologica per le Provincie di Sassari e Nuoro* 8. Sassari.
1981 L'architettura nuragica. In E. Atzeni *et al.* (eds.), *Ichnussa: La Sardegna dalle origini all'età classica*, 5-175. Milano: Libri Scheiwiller.
1990 Il nuraghe. In *La Civiltà Nuragica*. Milano: Electa.
1992 L'inizio dell'età nuragica. In G. Lai, G. Ugas e G. Lilliu (a cura di), *La Sardegna nel Mediterraneo tra il Bronzo medio e il Bronzo recente (XVI-XIII sec a.C.). Atti del 3 Convegno di Studi 'Un millennio di relazioni fra la Sardegna e i Paesi del Mediterraneo', Selargius-Cagliari, 19-22 Novembre 1987*, 13-40. Cagliari: Edizioni Della Torre.

Damiani, I., A. Pacciarelli & C. Saltini
1984 Le facies archeologiche dell'isola di Vivara e alcuni problemi relativi al Protoappenninico B. *Archeologia e Storia Antica* 6: 1-38. Napoli: Istituto Orientale Napoli.

Davis, J.
1986 Ayia Irini: Period V. *Keos*. Mainz am Rhein: Philipp von Zabern.

Dunbabin, T.
1948 *The Western Greeks*. Oxford.

Fadda, M.A.
1990 Il villaggio. In *La Civiltà Nuragica*, 100-19. Milano: Electa.

Ferrarese Ceruti, M.L.
1981 Documenti micenei nella Sardegna meridionale. In E. Atzeni *et al.* (eds.), *Ichnussa: La Sardegna dalle origini all'età classica*, 605-12. Milano: Libri Scheiwiller.
1989 L'età prenuragica. L'eneolitico finale e la prima età del bronzo. In V. Santoni (a cura di), *Il Museo Archeologico Nazionale di Cagliari*, 57-78. Sassari: Banco di Sardegna.

Hult, G.
1983 *Bronze Age Ashlar Masonry in the Eastern Mediterranean. Cyprus, Ugarit and Neighbouring Regions*. Göteborg: Paul Aström's Forlag.

Kilian, K.
1983 Civiltà micenea in Grecia: Nuovi aspetti storici ed interculturali. *Magna Grecia e Mondo Miceneo. Atti XXII Convegno Studi sulla Magna Grecia, Taranto, 7-11 ottobre 1982*, 53-96. Napoli.

Ledda, R.
1985 *Monumenti Megalitici della Sardegna Sud-orientale. Censimento archeologico nel territorio del comune di Muravera*. Quartu S. Elena.

Lilliu, C., & M.G. Puddu
1985 Le pendici orientali e sud-orientali della Giara. In C. Lilliu (a cura di), *Territorio di Gesturi: Censimento Archeologico*, 28-43. Cagliari.

Lilliu, G.
1955 Il nuraghe di Barumini e la stratigrafia nuragica. *Studi Sardi* 12-13(1952-54): 90-469.
1962 *I Nuraghi. Torri preistoriche della Sardegna*. Verona.

1982 La Civiltà Nuragica. Sardegna Archeologica: Studi e Monumenti 1. Sassari: Carlo Delfino.
1988a La Civiltà dei Sardi dal Paleolitico all'Età dei Nuraghi. Terza edizione. Torino: Nuova ERI.
1988b La bella età dei nuraghi. L'Umana Avventura 3(8): 6-14.

Lilliu, G., & H. Schubart
1967 Civiltà Mediterranee.

Lo Porto, F.
1963 Leporano (Taranto). La stazione preistorica di Porto. Notizie degli Scavi 17: 280-380.
1964 La tomba di San Vito dei Normanni e il Protoappenninico B in Puglia. Bollettino di Paletnologia Italiana 73: 109-42.

Lo Schiavo, F.
1978 Complesso d'armi in bronzo da Ottana. In R. Caprara, F. Lo Schiavo, A. Moravetti, e F. Nicosia (a cura di), Sardegna Centro-Meridionale dal Neolitico alla fine del Mondo Antico, 75-79. Sassari: Dessì.
1981 Economia e società nell'età dei nuraghi. In E. Atzeni et al. (eds.), Ichnussa: La Sardegna dalle origini all'età classica, 255-347. Milano: Libri Scheiwiller.

Manca Demurtas, L., & S. Demurtas
1984 Observaciones sobre los protonuragues de Cerdeña. Trabajos de Prehistoria 41.
1987 Di un tipo architettonico mediterraneo (Talaiot Rafal Roig-Mercadal) (Minorca). In G. Lilliu, G. Ugas e G. Lai (a cura di), La Sardegna nel Mediterraneo tra il secondo e il primo millennio a.C. Atti del 2 convegno di studi 'Un millennio di relazioni fra la Sardegna e i Paesi del Mediterraneo, Selargius-Cagliari, 27-30 novembre 1986. Cagliari: Amministrazione Provinciale di Cagliari.

Mastino, A.
1980 La voce degli antichi. In D. Sanna (a cura di), Nur. La misteriosa civiltà dei Sardi, 261-77. Milano: Cariplo.

Meloni, P.
1945 Gli Iolei ed il mito di Iolao in Sardegna. Studi Sardi 6(1): 43-66.

Mitova-Dzonova, D.
1983 Megalithischer Brunnentempel protosardinischen Typs vom Dorf Garlo. Sofija: Bez. Pernik.
1992 Elementi architettonici protosardi nella penisola balcanica. In G. Lai, G. Ugas e G. Lilliu (a cura di), La Sardegna nel Mediterraneo tra il Bronzo medio e il Bronzo recente (XVI-XIII sec. a.C.). Atti del 3 Convegno di Studi 'Un millennio di relazioni fra la Sardegna e i Paesi del Mediterraneo', Selargius-Cagliari, 19-22 Novembre 1987, 587-606. Cagliari: Edizioni Della Torre.

Moravetti, A.
1977 Nuove scoperte nel villaggio nuragico di Palmavera-Alghero (Sassari). Rivista di Scienze Preistoriche 32: 277-91.
1980 Nuovi modellini di torri nuragiche. Bollettino d'Arte 7: 65-84.
1990 Le tombe e l'ideologia funeraria. In La Civiltà Nuragica, 120-68. Milano: Electa.

Mussche, H., J. Bingen, J. Servais & P. Spitaels
1984 Rapport preliminaire sur les 9e, 10e, 11e et 11e campagnes de fouilles. Thorikos 8 (1972/1976).

Paderi, M.C., & G. Ugas
1988 Sardara. In G. Lilliu (a cura di), L'Antiquarium Arborense e i Civici Musei Archeologici della Sardegna, 199-214. Sassari: Banco di Sardegna.

Pais, E.
1881 La Sardegna prima del dominio romano. Studi storici archeologici di Ettore Pais. Memorie della R. Accademia dei Lincei 1880-81. Memorie della classe di scienze morali, storiche e filologiche, 7: 259-378.

Pelon, O.
1976 Tholoi Tumuli et Cercles Funéraires. Recherches sur les monuments funéraires de plan circulaire dans l'Egée de l'âge du Bronze (IIIe et IIe millenaire a.J.-C.). Paris.

Peroni, R.
1967 Per una revisione critica della stratigrafia di Luni sul Mignone e della sua interpretazione. Atti I Convegno di Protostoria, Orvieto, 167 ss.
1983 Presenze micenee e forme socio-economiche nell'Italia protostorica. Magna Grecia e Mondo Miceneo. Atti XXII Convegno Studi sulla Magna Grecia, Taranto 1982, 211-84. Napoli.

Plantalamor Massanet, L.
1987 El santuario de So na Caçana y las relaciones con el Mediterraneo Central y Occidental. In G. Lilliu, G. Ugas e G. Lai (a cura di), La Sardegna nel Mediterraneo tra il secondo e il primo millennio a.C. Atti del 2 convegno di studi 'Un millennio di relazioni fra la Sardegna e i Paesi del Mediterraneo', Selargius-Cagliari, 27-30 novembre 1986, 533-46. Cagliari: Amministrazione Provinciale di Cagliari.

Puglisi, S.
1959 La Civiltà Appenninica. Firenze.

Rita Larrucea, M.
1987 Evolucion de la cultura pretalayotica menorquina a traves de los yacimientos de Morellet y Son Mercer de Baix. In G. Lilliu, G. Ugas e G. Lai (a cura di), La Sardegna nel Mediterraneo tra il secondo e il primo millennio a.C. Atti del 2 convegno di studi 'Un millennio di relazioni fra la Sardegna e i Paesi del Mediterraneo', Selargius-Cagliari, 27-30 novembre 1986, 547-55. Cagliari: Amministrazione Provinciale di Cagliari.

Saliby, N.
1982 Restauration du caveau du palais Nord d'Ibn Hani. La Syrie au Bronze Récent, 37-42. Protohistoire du Levant. Paris: Recherches sur les Civilisations.

Sangmeister, E., & H. Schubart
1969 Grabungen in der kupferzeitlichen Befestigung von Zambujal/Portugal. Madrider Mitteilungen 10: 11ff.

Santoni, V.
1980 Il segno del potere. In D. Sanna (a cura di), Nur. La misteriosa civiltà dei Sardi, 141-88. Milano: Cariplo.
1985 Tharros. Il villaggio nuragico di Su Muru Mannu. Rivista di Studi Fenici 13(1).
1989 L'età nuragica. Dal Bronzo finale all'età orientalizzante. In V. Santoni (a cura di), Il Museo Archeologico Nazionale di Cagliari, 93-128. Sassari: Banco di Sardegna.

Taramelli, A.
1922 Serri. Nuovi scavi nel santuario nuragico presso la chiesa di Santa Maria della Vittoria sull'altopiano della Giara. Notizie degli Scavi 1922: 296-334.
1931 Nuove ricerche nel santuario di Santa Vittoria di Serri. Monumenti Antichi dei Lincei 34: 1-122.

Tomasello, F.
1986 L'architettura funeraria in Sicilia tra la media e tarda età del Bronzo. Le tombe a camera del tipo

a tholos. In M. Marazzi, S. Tusa e L. Vagnetti (eds.), *Traffici Micenei nel Mediterraneo. Problemi storici e documentazione archeologica*, 93-104. Taranto: Istituto per la Storia e l'Archeologia della Magna Grecia.

Tusa, S.
1983 *La Sicilia nella Preistoria*. Palermo.

Ugas, G.
1980 Le scoperte e gli scavi lungo i secoli. In D. Sanna (a cura di), *Nur. La misteriosa civiltà dei Sardi*, 298-304. Milano: Cariplo.
1981a La tomba megalitica di San Cosimo-Gonnosfanadiga: Un monumento del Bronzo medio (con la più antica attestazione micenea in Sardegna). Notizia preliminare. *Archeologia Sarda* 2: 7-30.
1981b Notiziario, s.v. Samassi-Argiddas. *Archeologia Sarda* 2: 84.
1987a Indagini ed interventi di scavo lungo la S.S. 131 tra il km. 15 e il km. 32. Breve notizia. *Quaderni della Soprintendenza Archeologica per le Provincie di Cagliari ed Oristano* 4(1): 117-28.
1987b La fortezza di Su Mulinu-Villanovafranca (CA). Un nuovo contributo per lo studio della tholos in Sardegna. In M.S. Balmuth (ed.), *Studies in Sardinian Archaeology III*, 77-128. BAR International Series 387. Oxford: British Archaeological Reports.
1989 L'età nuragica. Il Bronzo medio e il Bronzo recente. In V. Santoni (a cura di), *Il Museo Archeologico Nazionale di Cagliari*, 79-92. Sassari: Banco di Sardegna.
1990 *La Tomba dei Guerrieri di Decimoputzu*. Norax 1. Cagliari: Edizioni della Torre.
1992 Note su alcuni contesti del Bronzo medio e recente nella Sardegna meridionale. In G. Lai, G. Ugas e G. Lilliu (a cura di), *La Sardegna nel Mediterraneo tra il Bronzo medio e il Bronzo recente (XVI-XIII sec. a.C.). Atti del 3 Convegno di Studi 'Un millennio di relazioni fra la Sardegna e i Paesi del Mediterraneo', Selargius-Cagliari, 19-22 Novembre 1987*, 201-27. Cagliari: Edizioni Della Torre.

Ugas, G., & M. Paderi
1990 Persistenze rituali e cultuali in età punica e romana nel sacello nuragico del vano 'e' della fortezza di Su Mulinu-Villanovafranca (Cagliari). *L'Africa Romana* 7: 475-86.

Ugas, G., & L. Usai
1987 Nuovi scavi nel santuario nuragico di Sant'Anastasia di Sardara. In G. Lilliu, G. Ugas e G. Lai (a cura di), *La Sardegna nel Mediterraneo tra il secondo e il primo millennio a.C. Atti del 2 convegno di studi 'Un millennio di relazioni fra la Sardegna e i Paesi del Mediterraneo', Selargius-Cagliari, 27-30 novembre 1986*, 167-218. Cagliari: Amministrazione Provinciale di Cagliari.

Summary

In Sardinia, the increasing amount of research over the last 40 years, especially the number of scientific excavations, has provided much information about the Nuragic civilization, if not about its social organization and development. The Author reviews the chronological development of Nuragic society, paying particular attention to the Bronze Age phases.

The Middle Bronze I period (c. 1600–1400 BC) is characterized by corridor or protonuraghi, and is contemporary with the Protoappennine B culture of the Italian mainland (and Mycenaean I-II). The second part of the Middle Bronze Age (1400–1300 BC) corresponds to the Appennine culture and to the Thapsos and Milazzese cultures of Sicily and Lipari, respectively. It is in this second subphase that true tholos nuraghi become common.

Few village settlements dating to the Middle Bronze I period are known, among them Sa Turricola-Muros, Costa Tana-Bonarcado and Abini-Teti; only the hut at Sa Turricola has been scientifically excavated. More data come from the nuraghi themselves, and from funerary contexts. Unlike other parts of the Mediterranean, there seem to be no other fortress-like antecedents to the nuraghi. Of the hundreds of protonuraghi known, only Middle Bronze Age materials are found; and notwithstanding the C14 date of 1820 ± 250 uncal BC at Brunku Madugui (Gesturi), the ceramics from that site are now attributed to the 15th century BC. Bonnanaro and Monte Claro ceramics, occasionally found at nuraghi, do not indicate earlier use of these structures; rather, they indicate a pre-Nuragic use of the same site.

In the Middle Bronze Age, the megalithic phenomenon of pre-Nuragic Sardinia, previously limited to sacred-religious architecture (menhirs, dolmens, circle tombs), is extended to the domestic sphere (nuraghi and village settlements). Perhaps the best evidence for an accompanying change in social structure is the Tomb of the Warriors (17th/16th cent. BC) at Sant'Iroxi-Decimoputzu, which indicates elevated social status with its rich grave goods (swords and daggers in arsenical copper). The weaponry also suggests the need for defense among local groups, a need manifested in Nuragic architecture as well.

The Author has proposed before that the transition from corridor to tholos nuraghe may have some relationship with architectural developments in the Aegean, for example at Keos, where the legendary Aristeus stopped on his way to Sardinia (cf. Lilliu, this volume). There also seem to be parallels between some Sardinian hypogea (e.g. Sa Figu di Ittiri) and the Mycenaean and Sicilian tholos tombs (e.g. Treasury of Atreus, Tomb IV at Thorikos, S. Vito dei Normanni-Puglia). The Author asserts that the similarity between Tomb IV of Thorikos and Room e of Su Mulinu-Villanovafranca cannot be due to casual convergence, but rather to the maritime contacts between East and West.

Despite the paucity of excavations and

chronometric data, it appears that in the Late Bronze Age many Nuragic villages did not have their own fortress-nuraghe, yet may have been contemporary with isolated nuraghi without villages. It seems, then, that only with the Final Bronze Age and Early Iron Age were villages constructed around a central fortress (e.g. Genna Maria-Villanovaforru, Su Nuraxi-Barumini). The site of Monte Zara-Monastir is noteworthy in that the nuraghe is located in a strategic position, whereas the associated village is not. This suggests a functional dichotomy between the two, and reflects their diverse origins in the Late Bronze Age. In the Final Bronze and Iron Ages, the political role of the nuraghi and the villages converged and new constructions were architecturally integrated.

Nuragic well-temples appear to be associated with village sites rather than with fortress-nuraghi in the Late and Final Bronze Ages. These circular wells with access stairs have their own comparanda outside Sardinia, for example, the well at Gjarlo in Bulgaria (cf. also Belli, this volume). Such connections require further attention, with confirmation by additional scientific excavation and chronometric dating.

Aegean Architectural Links with the Central Mediterranean: Sardinian Sacred Wells and Lipari's Thermal Tholos

Paolo Belli

One of the most controversial problems concerning prehistoric Sardinia is the possible Aegean influence in the vaulted architecture of the nuraghi, which are often compared with Mycenaean tholos tombs (Taramelli 1918; Lilliu 1958; Contu 1981; Bernardini 1983; Gras 1985; Ugas 1987). This comparison, however, is in many ways inappropriate: in Sardinia the nuraghi are free-standing, often multi-storeyed structures, with no subterranean component; in the Aegean, the tholos tombs are semi-subterranean, with a different developmental history and function.

This problem has been recently reexamined by several scholars. Santillo Frizell and Santillo (1984; Santillo Frizell 1987) have stressed the independent origin of cupola structures around the Mediterranean, while Cavanagh and Laxton (1981; 1982; 1985; 1987a; 1987b), after a detailed study of selected Mycenaean and Cretan monuments, went on to study a small group of Sardinian nuraghi using the same methods. Their conclusion, based on mathematical and statistical analysis, is that no parallel can be traced between the Aegean hypogaea and the Nuragic towers. Only a small number of monuments were considered, however, and they have not examined one group of vaulted structures with round plans—the *pozzi sacri*. The 'sacred wells' are not as numerous as the nuraghi, but are equally distributed throughout Sardinia (Lilliu 1958; Lilliu 1982; Contu 1981; Santoni 1985). They are built underground and covered with a beehive vault, and their function is always related to sources of water.

At the time of their first discovery, the sacred wells or 'well-temples' had been dated to no earlier than the mid-9th century BC, according to the late Nuragic chronology accepted at that time. They were also forcibly considered of late date for stylistic reasons, since they were often constructed in ashlar blocks, in contrast to the 'cyclopean' aspect of most Nuragic tower construction. Recently, however, stratigraphic excavation, more careful consideration of the material recovered inside the wells, together with a general revision of Nuragic chronology, have combined to push back the dating of the sacred wells several centuries to the Final, if not the Late, Bronze Age (Lo Schiavo 1981; 1986).

Without entering into the details of the varied typology of these monuments, the reader is reminded that the sacred wells usually have a staircase that descends to the level of the spring, which is enclosed by a well-shaft and covered by a cupola structure. The staircase is preceded by a slab-paved hall, often flanked by stone benches on both sides. A courtyard or an enclosure, often paved and sometimes also flanked by benches, surrounds the entire complex. The wells represent different levels of technical achievement, with some built of extremely fine ashlar masonry (Fig. 1). The subject of this small contribution—in honor of Miriam Balmuth, whose special interest has been in the relationship between prehistoric Sardinia and the Mediterranean world—is not a specific study of the Sardinian sacred wells, but an attempt to relate them to other examples of water-related beehive architecture in the Mediterranean region.

An outstanding example of this kind of architecture is the recently recognized thermal bath of S. Calogero on Lipari. It is a round, corbelled structure that L. Bernabò Brea and M. Cavalier, after a careful cleaning, date to an earlier phase of the local Bronze Age (Capo Graziano culture; contemporary with Aegean LH I-II). The bath at first revived the long-debated question of Aegean and eastern Mediterranean relations and influence on monumental architecture in the Central Mediterranean during the 2nd millennium BC (Cavalier 1988), and a detailed archaeological study of the San Calogero Tholos and the surrounding area has now appeared (Bernabò Brea and Cavalier 1990). The measurement of the plan and elevation of the structure were done by the present writer, who has also added some remarks on the architectural techniques used in the tholos (Belli 1990) (Fig. 2).

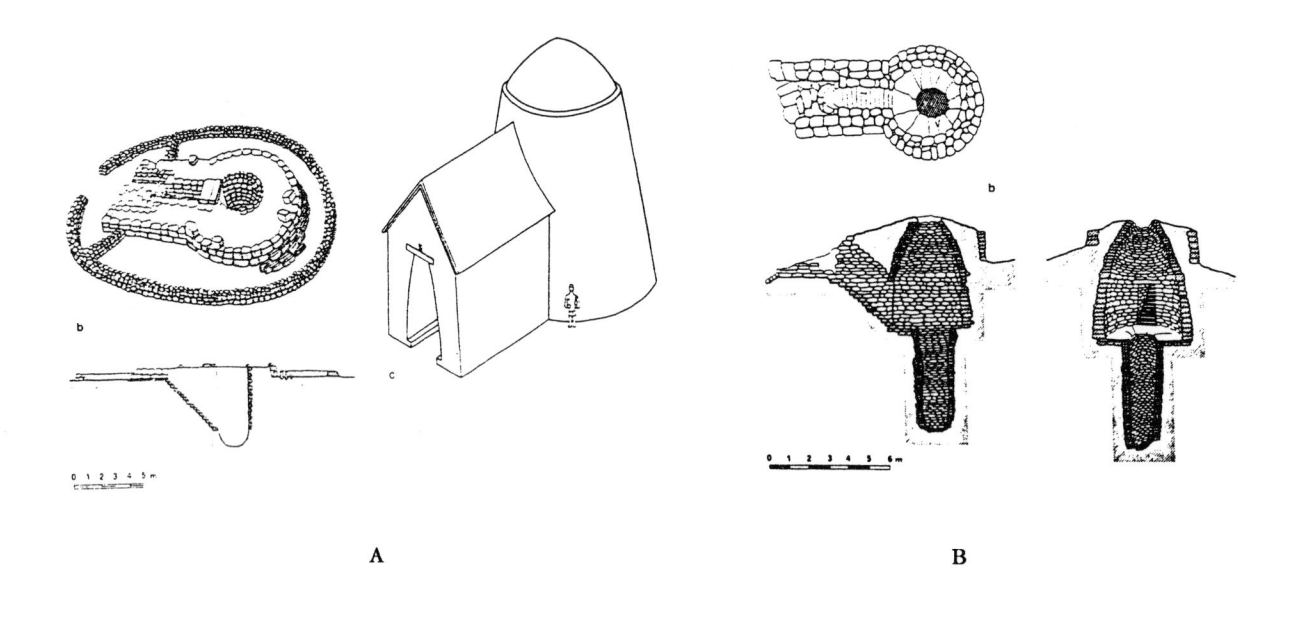

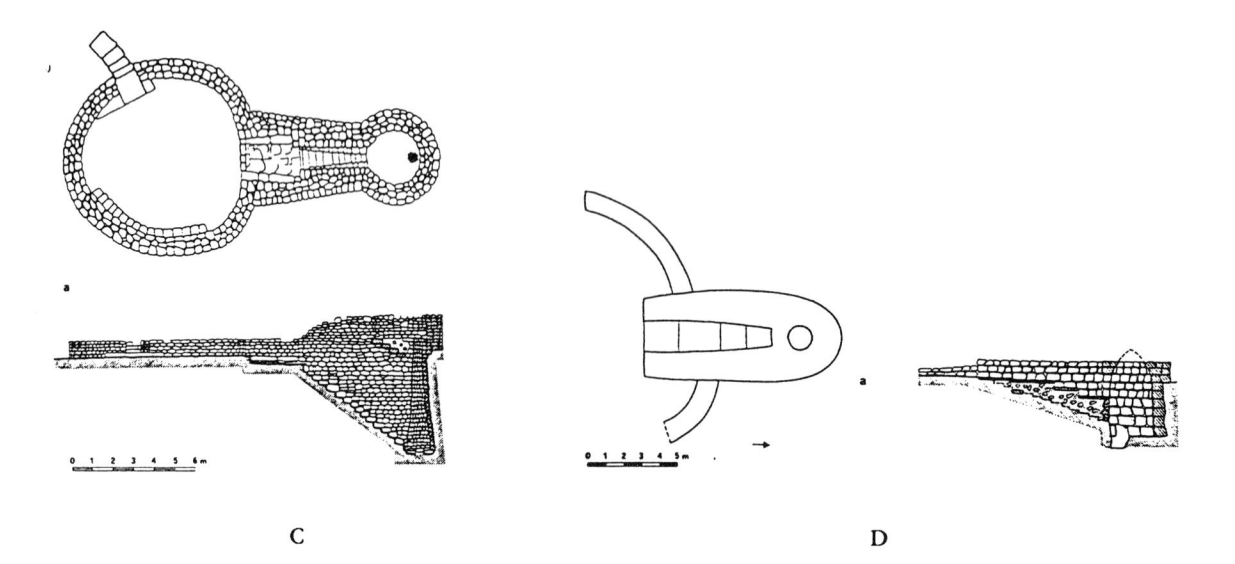

Fig 1 (a-d) Sardinian sacred wells: a. Serri (NU), Santa Vittoria; b. Ballao (CA), Funtana Coperta; c. Olbia (SS), Sa Testa; d. Orroli (NU), Su Putzu.

Fig. 1 (e-i) Sardinian sacred wells: e. Noddule (NU); f. Orune (NU), Su Tempiesu; g. Bonorva (SS), Rebeccu; h. Alà dei Sardi (SS), Sos Nuratolos; i. Alà dei Sardis (SS), So Posidu. After Contu (1981).

The round structure is part of a very large thermal complex. The so-called Terme di San Calogero are located against a natural slope of the mountain on the western side of Lipari. The principal thermal spring (c. 45-50°C) is channeled through a built drain which abuts a round chamber built of blocks of two kinds (one reddish, one yellowish) of local volcanic stone. The chamber has an internal diameter of 4.20-4.40 m and a cupola-like roof with regular courses of blocks reaching a height of about 2.50 m. This bath, used continuously over the centuries as a *stufa*, was flanked by a Roman thermal chamber which was fed by the same water source, and which has now disappeared. The ancient structures were concealed by a large building of the last century that housed various facilities for those who frequented the thermal bath to obtain relief from rheumatism and other ailments. When Lipari's municipality, responsible for the management of the installations, decided in 1983 to thoroughly reorganize and restore the complex, the round chamber was eventually emptied of the thick and moist vapor and examined by Bernabò Brea and Cavalier, who immediately understood its importance.

Running hot water has always been channelled into the room through a drainage system, which should be properly investigated; the high temperature of the water, and the ever-present moisture have eroded much of the stones' surface, so that it is almost impossible to see now how the original blocks looked. Traces of the tools used to dress the stone could have provided us with some useful information about the technology used, and perhaps the chronology of the structure. One of the two original door-jambs, and the original lintel, although very much worn, are still readable.

The entry to the small cupola-chamber consists of three monolithic slabs: there are four circular courses of worked stone blocks below the lintel, and five above. The circular courses form a corbelled structure whose top was completed after the remodelling of the uppermost courses; this restoration has partially reshaped what originally would have been a more ogival vault. At ground level, a modern bench runs around the perimeter of the chamber, and served also as a channel for the hot water. Opposite the door, there is an opening, a sort of window, in the northeastern side of the wall, through which the water enters. The center of this small room is occupied by a shallow round basin, surrounded by a modern iron fence resting on a masonry ring; the mud on the floor could be mixed with the hot water for therapy.

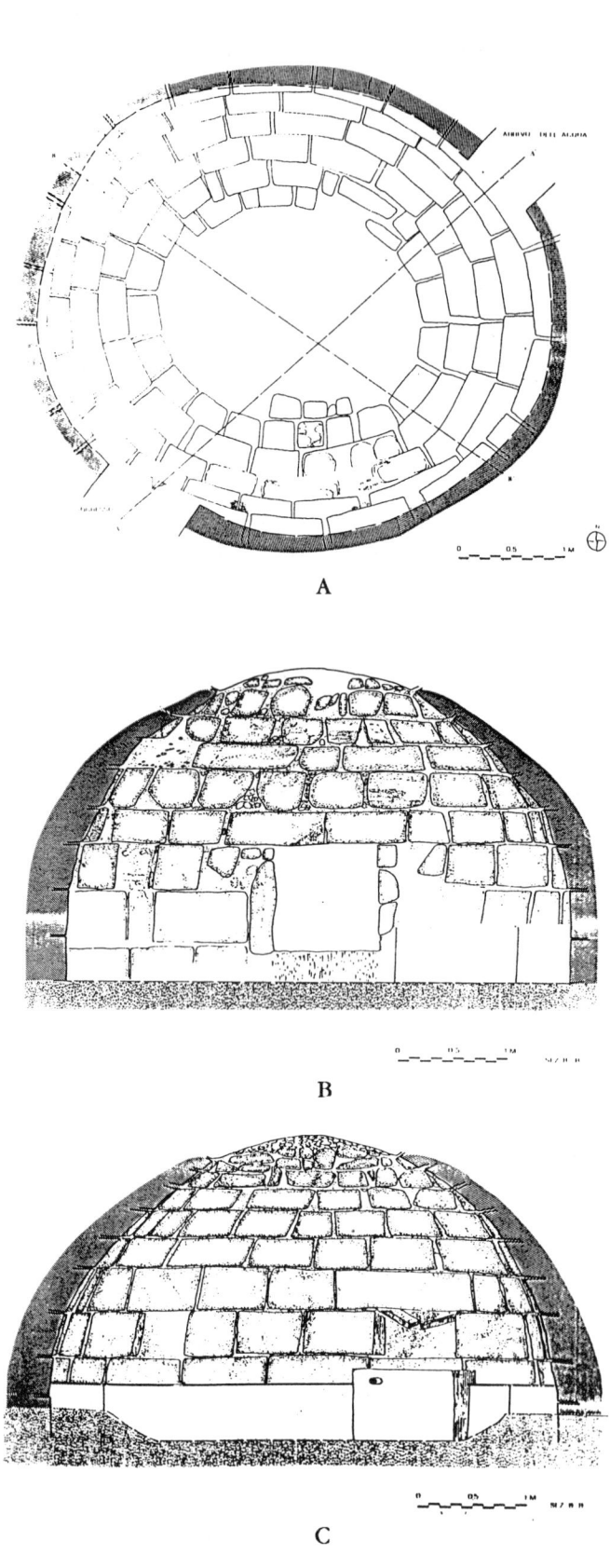

Fig. 2 Lipari (ME), Terme di San Calogero: a. tholos plan; b. tholos section B'-B; c. tholos section B-B' (drawing by P. Belli).

The inner aspect of this small chamber must have been altered both in plan, which appears to be shifted from the original circle—probably due to the slipping action of natural surface clays—and in the elevation, where many of the original courses in lavic stone are lacking; some of them have evidently been replaced. The upper part, as noted above, has been completely remodelled. Thus, the general shape of the section through this vault has become rather flat and certainly different from its original profile. Nevertheless, one can envision an ideal restoration, in order to trace some architectural comparisons with other Mediterranean structures.

A long series of possible comparisons in the protohistoric Central Mediterranean is made by the excavators, including examples from Sicily, Malta, southern Italy, Sardinia, Etruria and Latium. They find the most satisfactory parallel to the thermal tholos, however, in the well-known Aegean tholos tombs, one of the most impressive achievements of Mycenaean architecture (Bernabò Brea and Cavalier 1990).

Although the thermal function of the S. Calogero tholos and its small dimensions make such a parallel not entirely satisfactory, there are at least 30 examples of Aegean tholoi whose inner diameter ranges between 3.5 and 5.5 m (Pélon 1976) (Table 1). As far as the problem of function is concerned, I have examined the existing Aegean architectural installations related to waterworks in order to see if some parallels with both structural and functional value could be traced at the same time.

Starting with Minoan Crete, the earliest structure related to water storage is the so-called Early Hypogaeum under the southern porch of the palace at Knossos (Evans 1921) (Fig. 3a). This is a large round rock-cut chamber dug in the *kouskouras* (the local bedrock) and is usually dated to the pre-palatial period, and is a unique example of hydraulic skill. In the Second Palatial Period (MM III–LM I) a number of fountains and cisterns, all of round shape, are known, including two examples at Mirtos-Pyrgos (Cadogan 1976; 1977–78), and others at Zakros (Platon 1971) and Archanes (Evans 1921) (Figs. 3b-c).

The Archanes spring is the most interesting of the series. It is built of large blocks and the upper visible row curves inwards slightly. The quantity of fallen stones found inside led Sir Arthur Evans to conclude that it would have been a tholos structure. Other examples at Tylissos (Hatzidakis 1934) and Karphì (Pendlebury 1937-38) are of later date (LM III) (Figs. 3d-e); there is also the unique example of the LM II-III Kephala tholos tomb at Knossos, which is similar to the Lipari tholos in its dimensions and the very accurate dressing of its masonry (Hutchinson 1956) (Fig. 3f).

An interesting underground fountain has been identified at Aghia Irini on Kea (Caskey 1971; Davis 1986) (Fig. 4a). A short staircase leads to a subterranean, subrectangular chamber; the ceiling over the staircase is constructed of stone slabs in such a way as to form inverted steps. This small and unpretentious building is, however, very significant because it could be considered a prototype of the more sophisticated waterworks characteristic of several Mycenaean citadels. The fountain is dated to the Middle Minoan III period, and is related to the fortification of the site. The small Kea spring is therefore a first attempt at relating a hydraulic work with the defensive system of a fortified settlement.

The Perseia fountain at Mycenae is the most famous of its type (Karo 1934; Wace 1949; Mylonas 1983) (Fig. 4b). The water chamber is located outside the citadel's walls, but was accessible through a series of corridors and landings covered with carinated vaults. Other examples at Tiryns (Verdelis 1963; Kilian 1988), Athens (Broneer 1939; Iakovidis 1983), and Corinth (Hodge Hill 1964: 46-48 fig. 24) complete the range of examples with similar features (Figs. 4c-e). All of these fountains are dated to the LH IIIB and LH IIIC periods.

In this view, one can also very briefly trace two main models or 'streams' of potential inspiration for this type of water-related building in the Aegean world. The first, associated with mainland Greece, shows an elaborate knowledge and skill of making rock-cut tunnels. It finds its nearest parallels in the Hittite citadels of Anatolia (von Gall 1967; Neve 1970). The second is associated with Crete and the Levant, where examples can be found for instance at Megiddo, and where other types of hydraulic structures seem more comparable with the Cretan cisterns (Thomsen 1925; Pritchard 1961; Wright 1985).

Before concluding this survey, I would like to draw attention to a neglected monument, the so-called Burinna Spring near the town of Cos on the same island (Ross 1850; Maiuri 1921-22; Neppi Modona 1933) (Fig. 5a). It is a building with a tholos roof, built entirely underground, with a very long dromos. It is sunk into the mountain's slope and its deep circular chamber reaches a spring of water. The Burinna Spring has never been properly published; in fact it is still used for supplying water to the town of Cos, and this has prevented any real archaeological exploration.

The chamber is 7 m high, oblong in shape, almost cylindrical in its lower part; the walls

240 *Sardinia in the Mediterranean*

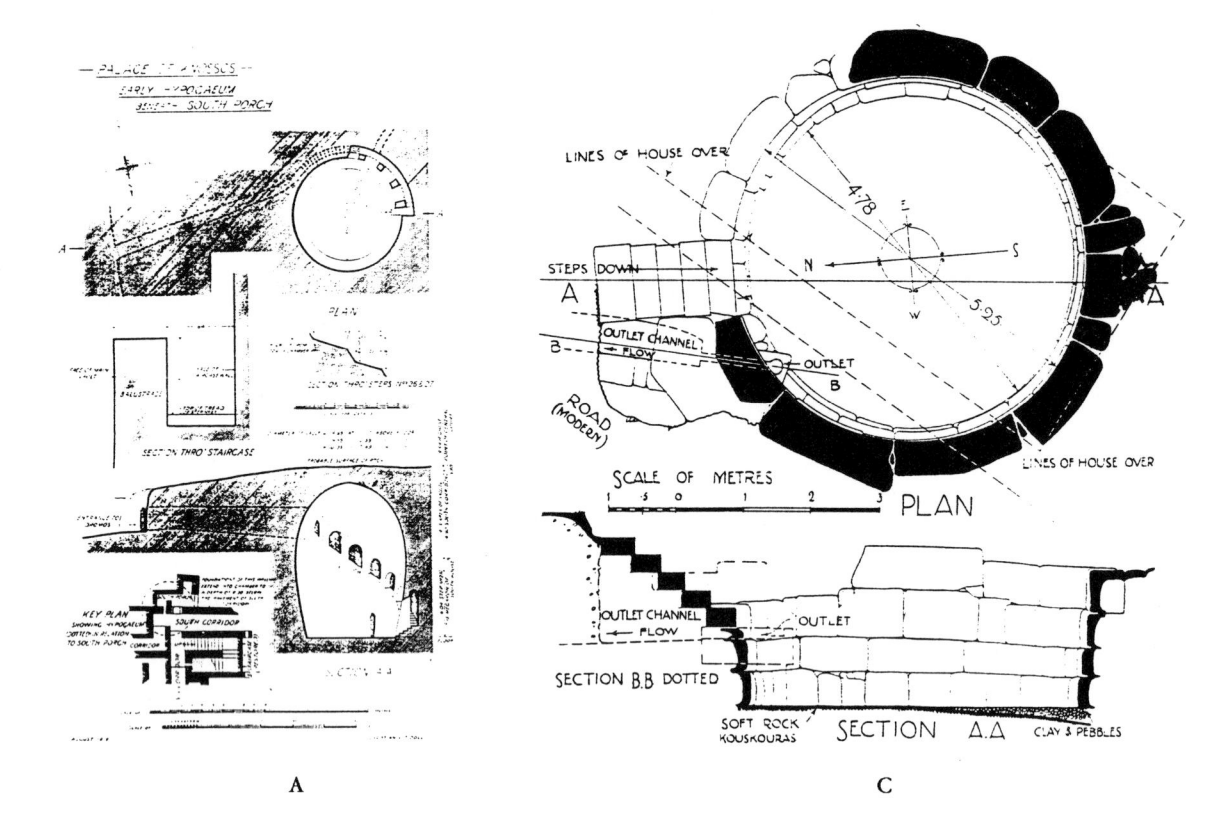

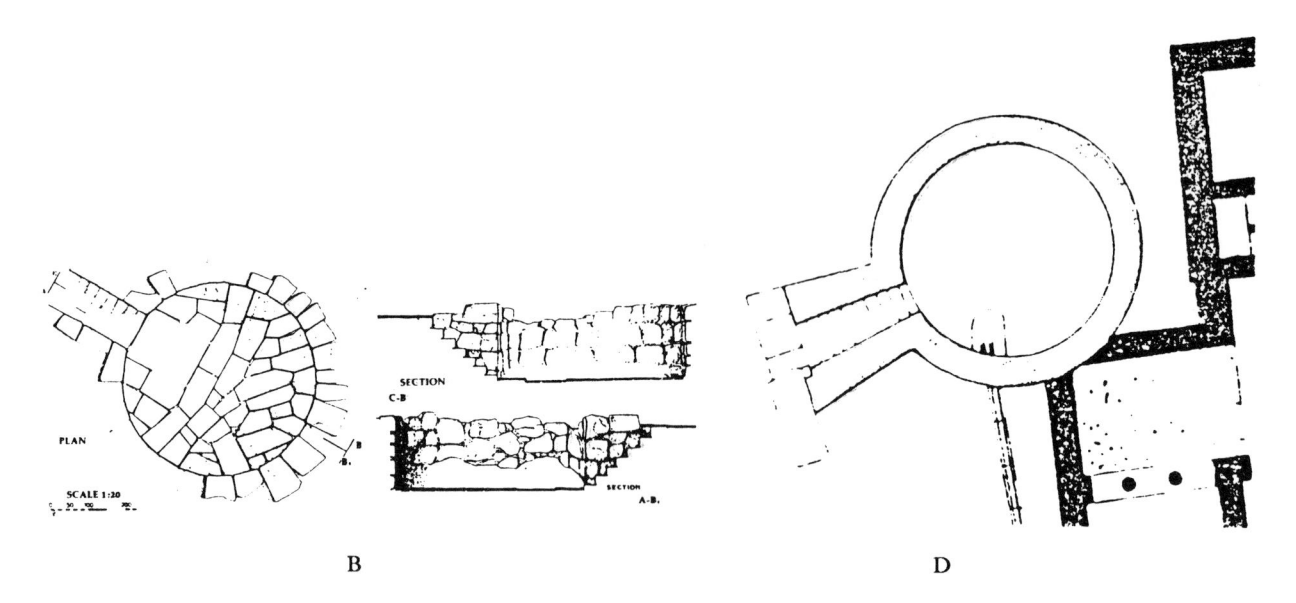

Fig. 3 (a-d) Minoan water-related architecture: a. Palace at Knossos, Early Hypogaeum. Plan and section after Evans (1921); b. Palace at Zakros, circular cistern in the Hall of Cisterns. Plan and sections after Platon (1979); c. Archanes, Circular Spring Chamber. Plan and section after Evans (1928); d. Tylissos, cistern to the north of the Minoan Villa. Plan after Hatzidakis (1935).

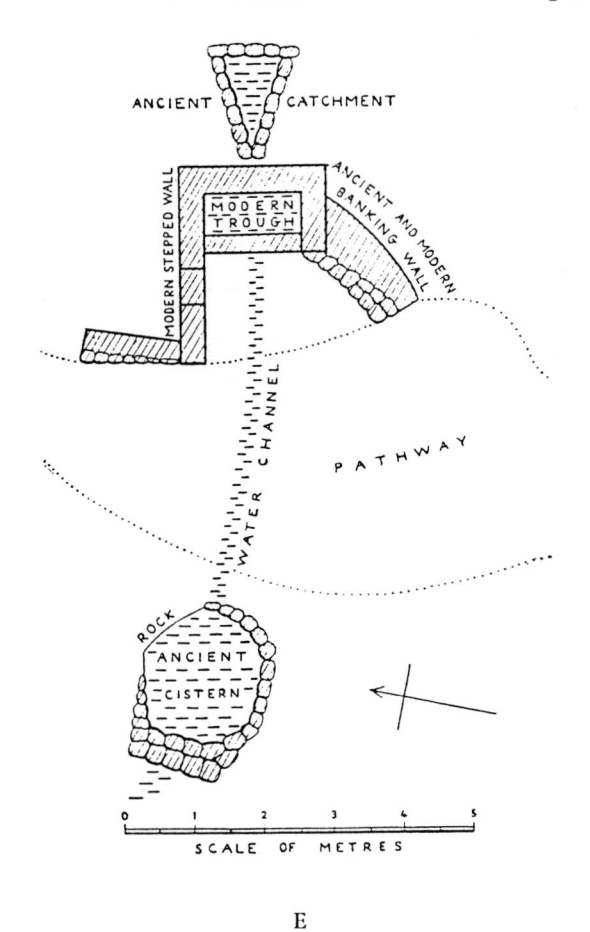

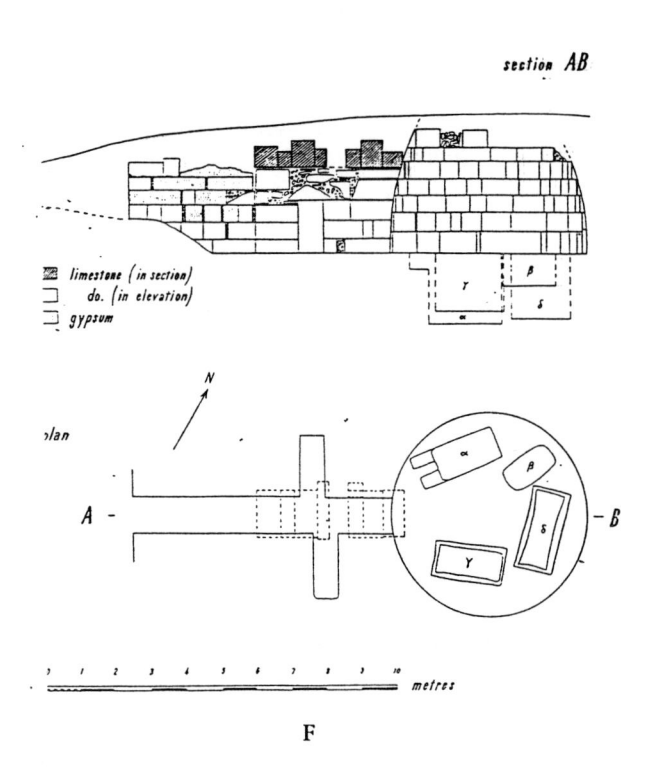

Fig. 3 (e-f) Minoan water-related architecture: e. Karphì, Vitzelovrysi Spring. Plan after Pendlebury (1937–38); f. Kephala (Knossos) LM II-III tholos tomb. Plan and section after Hutchinson (1956).

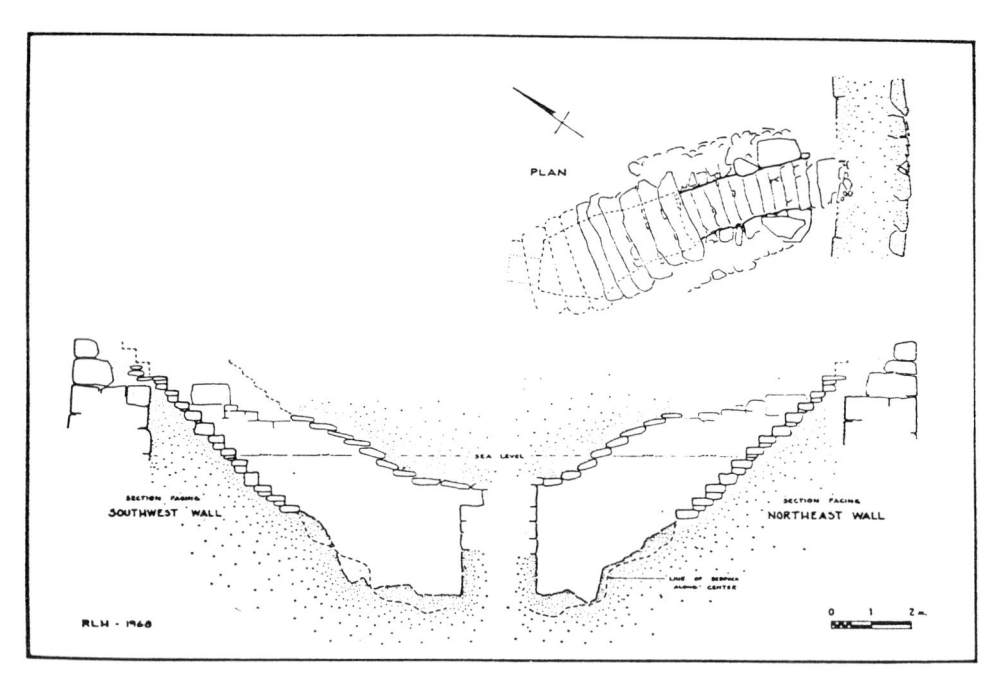

Fig. 4a Mycenaean water-related architecture: Ayia Irini (Kea), Spring Chamber. Plan and sections after Caskey (1971).

consist of 18 courses of finely-worked blocks of gray limestone. The inner diameter of the chamber is 2.75 m at the bottom, and starts decreasing above the level of 2 m; the size of the blocks varies from 30 × 60 to 50 × 90 cm. The upper 12 courses lean progressively inward and form a corbel-like and elongated, ogival vault. Above the vault there is an *opaion* built of regular blocks (at least 5 courses) that provide ventilation and light. The very narrow dromos is not rectilinear, but forms two strong curves; it is 35 m long and 2.5 m high, but only 0.60-0.70 m wide. The water is drained through the dromos since there is no reservoir inside the chamber to collect it; it is now difficult to judge how the water was channeled and exploited, since modern use has partially modified the ancient system.

The dromos opens into the chamber through a passage. Above the inner part of the dromos there is a sort of side chamber that communicates with the main cistern through a small opening—actually just a missing block in the masonry. The chronology of this peculiar monument has not been well-established. Although its technical details seem in favor of a date not earlier than the classical period, it shows clear continuity from a type of building with roots in the Bronze Age.

Finally, we must recall another monument, the so-called *Brunnentempel* discovered in the vicinity of Garlo in Bulgaria, 40 km southwest of Sofia (Mitova-Džonova 1983; 1984) (Fig. 5b). It has been attributed to Aegean influence in Thrace, but its characteristics put it very close to the sacred wells of Sardinia. It lies in the upper valley of the river Strymon, in southwest Thrace, and is located on the steep slope of a hill; its northern part is dug into the rock, and its southern part is actually built.

The building is entered from the East through a partially-covered dromos 7 m long that leads to the chamber through a staircase of 13 steps. At a depth of 2.60 m there is a vestibule, and then a round chamber—with a diameter of 4.15 m—covered with a corbelled vault. A circular well 6.50 m deep is located in the middle of the chamber. The tholos was provided with an *opaion* which has recently been destroyed. The building technique is very interesting in that the dromos and the tholos rest on a large platform built of monolithic slabs; the walls are built with smaller slabs. The tholos chamber itself is cylindrical in its lower part and is covered with a cupola of hemispheric shape.

This monument is dated by the excavator to the Bronze Age, although no diagnostic artifacts were found during the excavations. A fragmentary stone axe and animal bones of various kinds are the only finds from inside the building, to which a Bronze Age sherd found near the entrance can be added. Turning again to the Central Mediterranean, we must stress that the more striking similarity of the Garlo *Brunnentempel* with the Sardinian *pozzi sacri* rather than with Aegean monuments is still awaiting a satisfactory explanation.

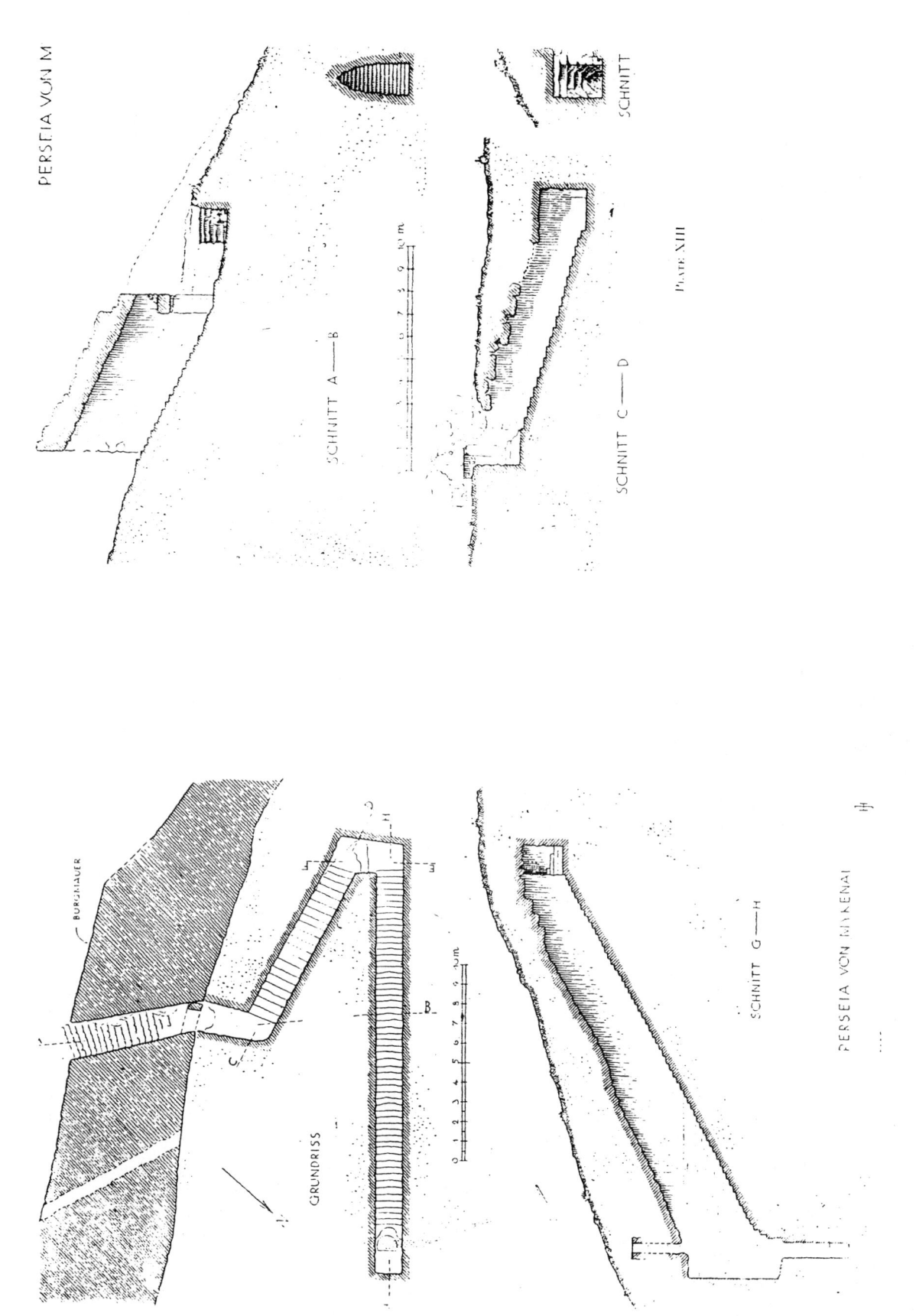

Fig. 4b Mycenaean water-related architecture: Mycenae, Perseia. Sections after Karo (1934).

244 *Sardinia in the Mediterranean*

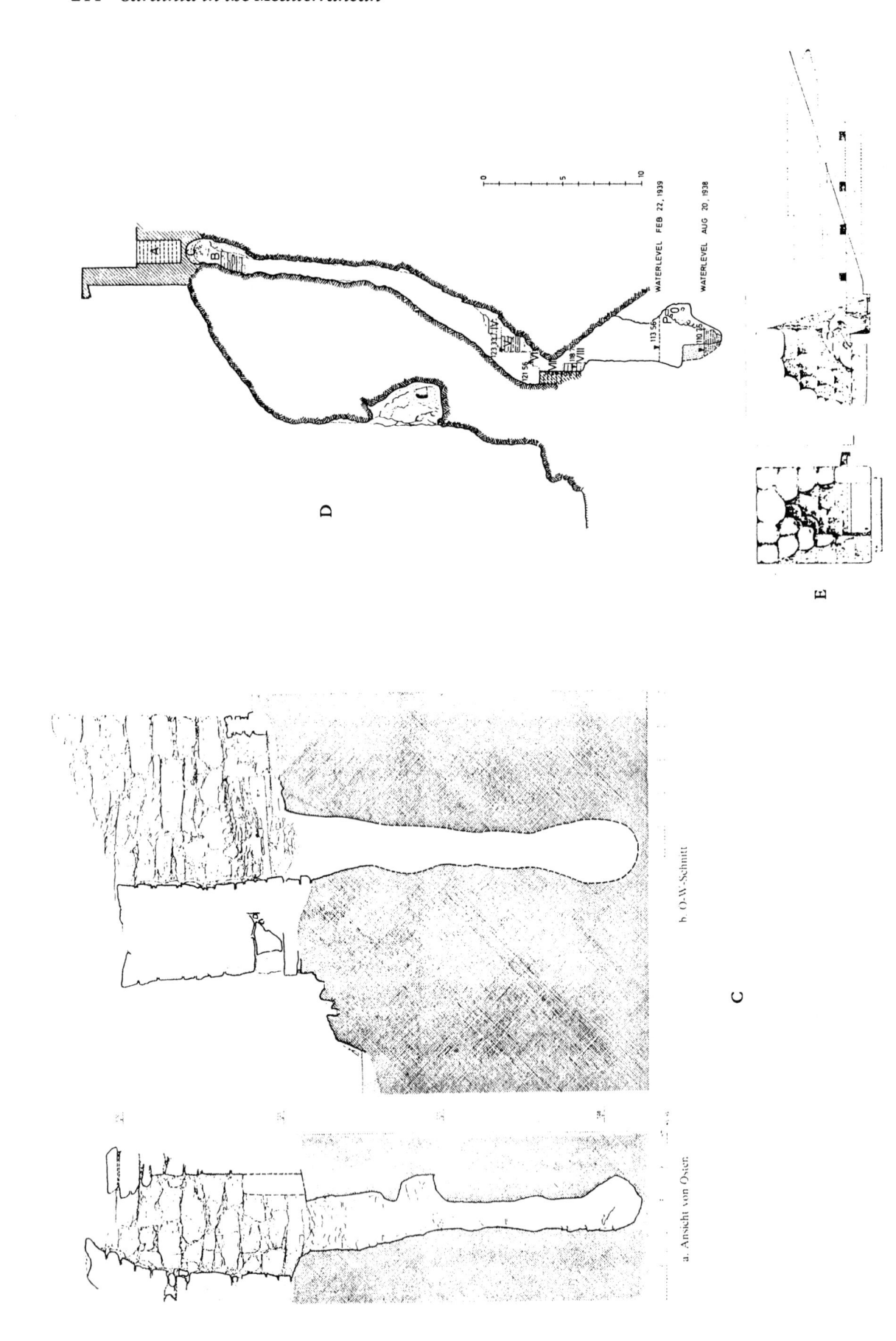

Fig. 4 (c-e) Mycenaean water-related architecture: c. Tiryns, Spring under room 14. Sections after Kilian (1988); d. Athens, North Fountain. Section after Iakovidis (1983); e. Corinth, Peirene. Section and restoration after Hodge Hill (1964).

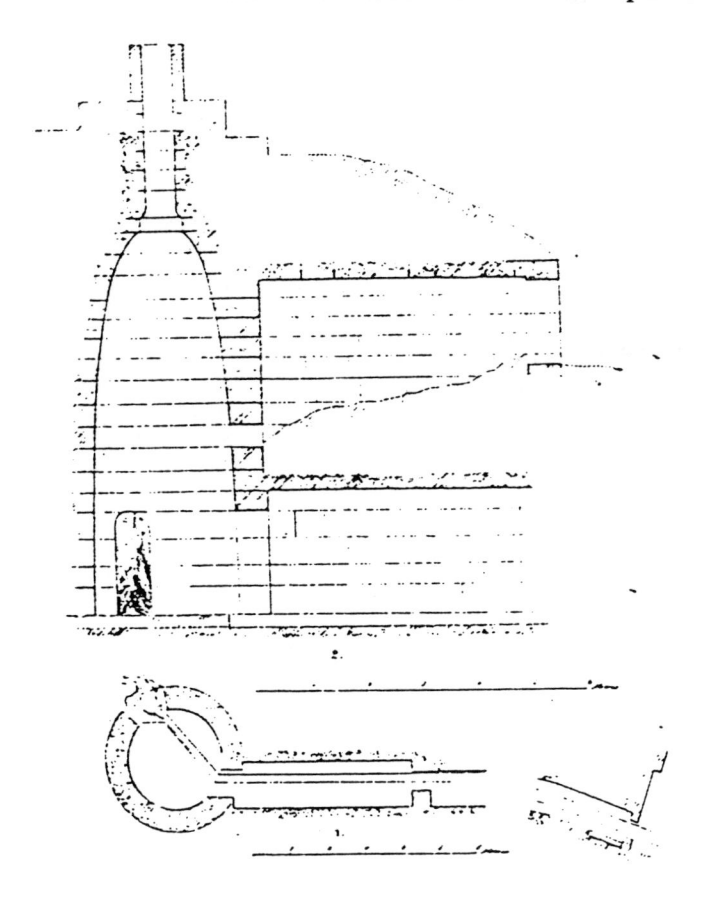

Fig. 5a Cos. The Burinna Spring. Plan and section after Ross (1850).

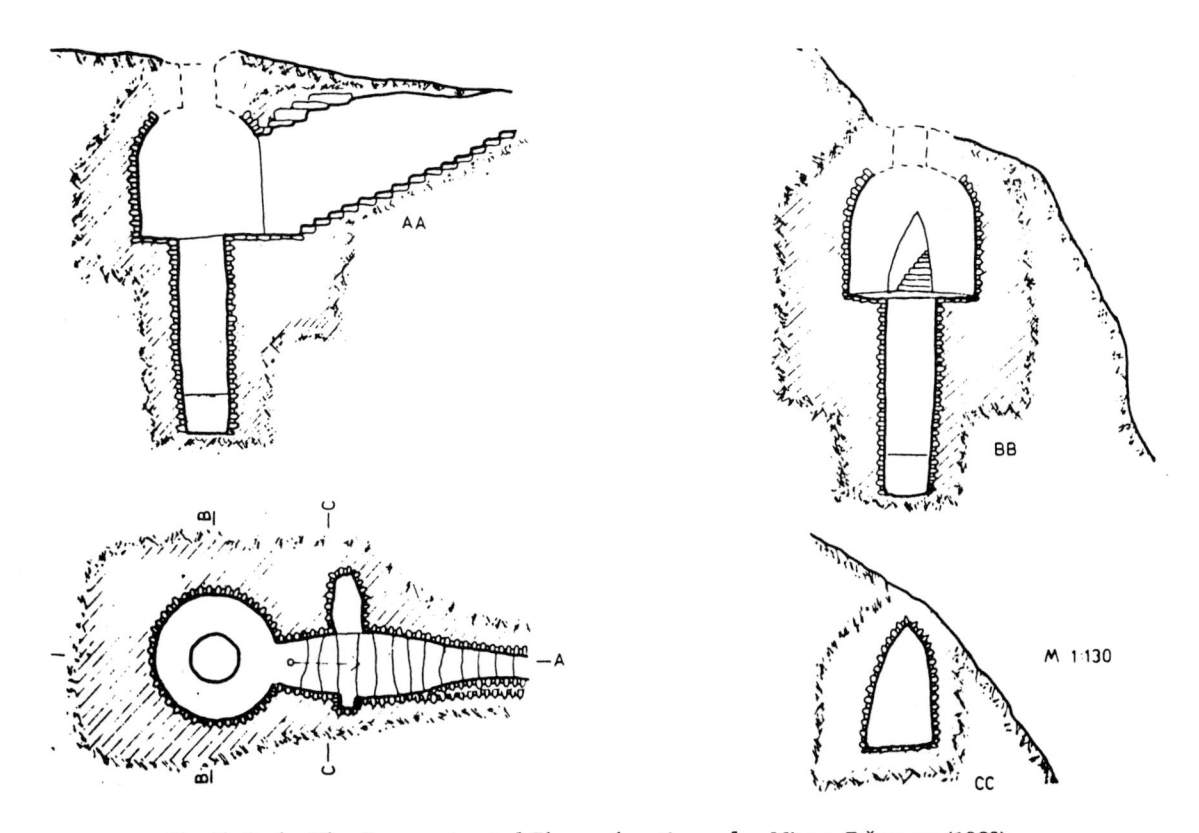

Fig. 5b Garlo. The *Brunnentempel*. Plan and sections after Mitova-Džonova (1983).

The architectural parallels discussed here were proposed in order to trace the type of building rather than a strict formal similarity. The most valid example as a prototype for the S. Calogero tholos seems to be the Archanes fountain which is similar in size, has a complex system of water supply and drainage, and could have been covered with a corbelled vault.

Although the S. Calogero tholos is an *apax* in the prehistoric architecture of the central Mediterranean, for its hydraulic system and for its exploitation of a thermal spring clearly used for health (and cult?) reasons, we should not rule out its possible role as a link between the Aegean and Sardinia in the development of a particular technical solution to the problem of collecting water from natural sources and protecting such a precious element with a suitable architectural shelter-system. In light of the preceding considerations, and while attempting to retrace a network of relationships that are not easy to figure out simultaneously, we can conclude saying that for the moment, a reconsideration of architectural relationships between the Aegean world and the Central Mediterranean should not be entirely rejected. It is certainly acceptable that at a given point, prehistoric peoples pressed by similar necessities often solved the same problems in analogous ways; and it is also undoubted that the frequent commercial exchange of ceramics and metalwork between East and West (Vagnetti 1982; Ferrarese Ceruti et al. 1987), could have been accompanied by the circulation of ideas, technologies and craftsmen. Among these, master builders could have occasionally introduced new models which, later on, could have been accepted and re-elaborated according to local traditions, the availability of materials, and individual technical skill.

Acknowledgments

Figs. 3a, 3c, 3e, and 3f are courtesy of the British School at Athens; Figs. 4a and 4e are courtesy of the American School of Classical Studies at Athens.

References

Belli, P.
    1990   Note strutturali sulla tholos di S. Calogero a Lipari. *Studi Micenei ed Egeo-Anatolici* 28.

Bernabò Brea, L., & M. Cavalier
    1990   La tholos termale di S. Calogero nell'isola di Lipari. *Studi Micenei ed Egeo-Anatolici* 28.

Bernardini, P.
    1983   Tholoi in Sardegna: Alcune considerazioni. *Studi Etruschi* 51: 43-54.

Broneer, O.
    1939   A Mycenaean fountain on the Athenian Acropolis. *Hesperia* 8: 317-430.

Cadogan, G.
    1976   *Palaces of Minoan Crete*. London.
    1977-78   Pyrgos, Crete, 1970-77. *Archaeological Reports* 1977-78: 74.

Caskey, J.
    1971   Investigations in Keos. Part I: Excavations and explorations 1966-70. *Hesperia* 40: 365-67.

Cavalier, M.
    1988   Lo scavo intorno alla Tholos di S. Calogero. In E. Acquaro, L. Godart, F. Mazza and D. Musti (eds.), *Momenti Precoloniali nel Mediterraneo Antico, Roma, 1985*, 109-11. Roma.

Cavanagh, W.W., & R.R. Laxton
    1981   The structural mechanics of the Mycenaean tholos tombs. *British School at Athens* 76: 109-40.
    1982   Corbelling in Late Minoan tholos tombs. *British School at Athens* 77: 65-77.
    1985   Vaulting in Mycenaean tholos tombs and Sardinian nuraghi. In C. Malone and S. Stoddart (eds.), *Papers in Italian Archaeology IV*, 413-33. BAR International Series 245. Oxford: British Archaeological Reports.
    1987a   Notes on building techniques in Mycenaean Greece and nuragic Sardinia. In M.S. Balmuth (ed.), *Studies in Sardinian Archaeology III. Nuragic Sardinia and the Mycenaean World*, 39-55. BAR International Series 387. Oxford: British Archaeological Reports.
    1987b   An investigation into the construction of Sardinian nuraghi. *Papers of the British School at Rome* 55: 1-74.

Contu, E.
    1981   L'architettura nuragica. In E. Atzeni et al. (eds.), *Ichnussa: La Sardegna dalle origini all'età classica*, 5-175. Milano: Libri Scheiwiller.

Davis, J.
    1986   *Ayia Irini: Period V (Keos, volume V)*. Mainz am Rhine: Verlag Philipp von Zabern.

Evans, A.J.
    1921   *The Palace of Minos, I*. London.
    1928   *The Palace of Minos, II*. London.

Ferrarese Ceruti, M.L., L. Vagnetti & F. Lo Schiavo
    1987   Minoici, micenei e cipriotti in Sardegna nella seconda metà del II millennio a.C. In M.S. Balmuth (ed.), *Studies in Sardinian Archaeology III. Nuragic Sardinia and the Mycenaean World*, 7-38. BAR International Series 387. Oxford: British Archaeological Reports.

Glaser, F.
    1983   *Antike Brunnenbauten in Griechenland*. Denkschr. Ost. Akad. Wiss. 162. Wien.

Gras, M.
    1985   *Trafics thyrréniens archaïques*. Bibliothèque des Ecoles françaises d'Athènes et de Rome 258. Rome: Ecole française de Rome.

Hatzidakis, J.
    1934   *Les Villas Minoennes de Tylissos*. Paris.

Hodge Hill, B.
    1964   *Corinth, Vol. I, Part VI, The Springs*. Princeton.

Hutchinson, R.
    1956   A tholos tomb on the Kephala. *British School at Athens* 51: 74-80.

Iakovidis, S.
    1983   *Late Helladic Citadels on Mainland Greece*. Leiden: Brill.

Karo, G.
1934   Die Perseia von Mykenai. *American Journal of Archaeology* 38: 123-27.

Kilian, K.
1988   Ausgrabungen in Tiryns 1982/3. *Archäologische Anzeiger*.

Lilliu, G.
1958   Nuovi templi a pozzo della Sardegna nuragica. *Studi Sardi* 14-15 (1955–1957) Parte I: 197-288.
1982   *La Civiltà Nuragica*. Sardegna Archeologica: Studi e Monumenti 1. Sassari: Carlo Delfino.

Lo Schiavo, F.
1981   Economia e società nell'età dei nuraghi. In E. Atzeni et al. (eds.), *Ichnussa: La Sardegna dalle origini all'età classica*, 255-347. Milano: Libri Scheiwiller.
1986   L'età dei nuraghi. In F. Lo Schiavo (a cura di), *Il Museo Sanna in Sassari*, 63-109. Sassari: Banco di Sardegna.

Maiuri, A.
1921-22   Viaggio di esplorazione in Caria. Parte II. *Annuario della Scuola di Atene* 4-5: 458-60.

Mitova-Džonova, D.
1983   *Megalitischer Brunnentempel protosardinischen typs von Dorf Garlo, Bez. Pernik*. Sofia.
1984   Ein megalithischer Brunnentempel aus Südwestthrazien. *Actes du 3 Congrès Internazionale de Thracologie, Sofia 1984*, 58-61.

Mylonas, G.
1983   *Mycenae Rich in Gold*. Athens.

Neppi Modona, A.
1933   L'isola di Coo nell'Antichità classic. *Istituto di Studi Archeologici di Rodi* 1: 161-63.

Neve, P.
1970   Eine hethitische Quellengrotte in Boghazköy. *Ist. Mitteilungen* 19-20: 97-107.

Pelon, O.
1976   *Tholoi Tumuli et Cercles Funéraires. Recherches sur les monuments funéraires de plan circulaire dans l'Egée de l'âge du Bronze (IIIe et IIe millenaire a.J.-C.)*. Paris.

Pendlebury, J.
1937–38   Excavations in the plain of Lasithi, III. *British School at Athens* 38: 98-100.

Platon, N.
1971   *Zakros. The Discovery of a Lost Palace of Ancient Crete*. New York.

Pritchard, J.
1961   *The Water System of Gibeon*. Philadelphia: The University Museum.

Santillo Frizzell, B.
1987   The true domes in Mycenaean and Nuragic architecture. In M.S. Balmuth (ed.), *Studies in Sardinian Archaeology III. Nuragic Sardinia and the Mycenaean World*, 57-76. BAR International Series 387. Oxford: British Archaeological Reports.

Santillo Frizzell, B., & R. Santillo
1984   The construction and structural behaviour of the Mycenaean tholos tomb. *Opuscula Atheniensia* 15: 45-52.

Santoni, V.
1985   I templi di età nuragica. In E. Arslan, F. Barreca and F. Lo Schiavo (eds.), *Civiltà Nuragica*, 181-207. Milano: Electa.

Taramelli, A.
1918   Il tempio nuragico di Sant'Anastasia in Sardara (Provincia di Cagliari). *Monumenti Antichi dei Lincei* 25.

Thomsen, P.
1925   Bewässerung und Wasserversorgung (D. Palästina-Syrien). In R. Ebert (ed.), Volume II.

Ugas, G.
1987   La fortezza di Su Mulinu-Villanovafranca (CA). Un nuovo contributo per lo studio della tholos in Sardegna. In M.S. Balmuth (ed.), *Studies in Sardinian Archaeology III. Nuragic Sardinia and the Mycenaean World*, 77-128. BAR International Series 387. Oxford: British Archaeological Reports.

Vagnetti, L. (ed.)
1982   *Magna Grecia e Mondo Miceneo. Nuovi Documenti*. Taranto: Istituto per la Storia e l'Archeologia della Magna Grecia.

Verdelis, N.
1963   Anaskaphe Tirynthos: Apokalpysis dyo neon syringon. *Arch. Delt.* 18: 66-73.

von Gall, H.
1967   Zu den kleinasiatische Treppentunneln. *Archäologische Anzeiger* 84: 504-27.

Wace, A.
1949   *Mycenae. An Archaeological History and Guide*. Princeton.

Wright, R.
1985   *Ancient Buildings in South Syria and Palestine, I-II*. Leiden: Brill.

Riassunto

Si sono osservate da tempo affinità costruttive tra i nuraghi sardi e le tholoi micenee: alcune caratteristiche di queste strutture sono state anche di recente oggetto di indagini dettagliate, p. es. da Santillo Frizell e da Cavanagh e Laxton. Questi studiosi hanno posto l'accento sull'origine indipendente delle strutture a cupola, osservando fra l'altro che alcuni fra i primi nuraghi potrebbero più antichi di qualche secolo dei monumenti egei comunemente considerati.

I pozzi sacri (o templi a pozzo) sardi non sono così numerosi, né così antichi come i nuraghi: essi sono però delle costruzioni sotterranee ed hanno copertura realizzata con volta ad ogiva. Inoltre spesso presso di essi sono stati trovati depositi di offerte, e si ritiene che avessero una funzione religiosa. I pozzi hanno spesso la camera interna costruita con blocchi isodomi, e molti di essi risalgono alla fine dell'età del Bronzo (c. 1200–900 a.C.). È quindi possibile configurare una relazione fra pozzi sacri ed altre strutture simili nell'area mediterranea.

Un nuovo contributo al problema viene dato ora dalla recente 'riscoperta' della tholos termale di S. Calogero presso Lipari. Una camera rotonda a tholos con diametro di ca. m. 4,20 è coperta con una cupola che raggiunge l'altezza di ca. m. 2,50; una sorgente d'acqua calda, convogliata da una condotta, si riversa nel lato nordorientale della tholos in una vasca. Restauri di epoca romana, ed il continuo uso delle terme attraverso i secoli ne hanno parzialmente alterato la pianta e l'alzato originali.

Gli archeologi L. Bernabò Brea e M. Cavalier hanno notato delle somiglianze tra S. Calogero e le tombe a tholos egee, specie quelle di Micene, anche se la funzione dei monumenti è diversa. A Creta, in ogni caso, esistono delle architetture a pianta circolare destinate alle acque: un ipogeo del Palazzo di Cnosso, le cisterne del Palazzo di Zakros e della villa minoica di Tylissos, e le sorgenti presso Archanes e Karphì.

La fonte sotterranea di Aghia Irini, a Kea, e quelle presso le cittadelle di Micene, Tirinto, Atene e Corinto, sono tutte raggiunte attraverso tunnel, corridoi, scalinate ed ospitate in camere con coperture di tipo vario, prevalentemente con volte di tipo ogivale; anche la c.d. fonte Burinna presso Coo, risalente al periodo classico, ha pure una copertura a tholos, con una camera alta ca. m. 7 e 18 filari di pietre ben lavorate.

Infine vicino a Garlo, in Bulgaria, troviamo un 'Brunnentempel'. Situato sulla pendice di un colle, esso ha un dromos lungo ca. m. 7, ed una scalinata di 13 gradini, alla cui base c'è un vestibolo ed una camera rotonda, del diametro di ca. m. 4, coperta con volta emisferica. Il monumento potrebbe risalire all'età del Bronzo, anche se poco è il materiale significativo ritrovato in esso.

I paralleli esposti mostrano che durante l'Età del Bronzo indiverse parti del Mediterraneo furono adottate delle strutture simili per ospitare fonti, sorgenti, bagni termali. Tali monumenti rappresentano soluzioni simili al problema analogo di raccogliere l'acqua e di proteggerla con una copertura architettonica. D'altra parte il frequente scambio di manufatti ceramici ed in metallo fra Oriente ed Occidente può essere stato il tramite di scambio di idee, tecnologia ed anche di artisti-artigiani. Le soluzioni architettoniche, elaborate a seconda delle tradizioni locali e dei materiali costruttivi disponibili, avrebbero dunque potuto essere il frutto di questo tipo di relazioni fra Egeo e Mediterraneo centrale durante l'età del Bronzo: ulteriori studi potranno dare conferma a questa ipotesi.

Table 1
Selected Aegean tholoi of small dimension (after Pélon 1976)

Tholos tombs (Pélon: TTCF)	Room diameter	Room height	Room pavement	Stomion height	Stomion width	Stomion thickness	Stomion lintel	Dromos orientation	Special features	Chronology	Bibliography
ARKINES (Laconia): cat. 9a	4.70			1.16/1.30	0.78	2.80	3 elem.	South-East		LH III	PAE/EA 1889
NICHORIA: Akones (SE Pelop.): cat. 13a	5.10							South-West		LH IB/II-IIIB	AD 23 1968
—: Tourkokivoura 3: cat. 13b	3.40							South-West		LH III A-B	AD 25 1970 2
—: Tourkokivoura 4: cat. 13c	3.40							South (?)		MH/LH I-IIIA	AD 25 1970 2
—: Tourkokivoura 5: cat. 13d	5.20									LH I (?)	AD 25 1970 2
—: Tourkokivoura 6: cat. 13e	3.00							South		LH III B-C (PG)	AD 25 1970 2
ENGLIANOS: Vagenas: cat. 14c	5.50									MH/LH I-II/III	AJA 62 1958
ROUTSI: Myrsinochori: cat. 17a (Th.1)	5.50			2.30	1.50	2.30	2 elem.	North-NW		LH II-III	Ergon 1956–57
—: Myrsinochori: cat. 17b (Th.2)	5.00		nat. rock		1.30	1.50		North-NW	stomion closing	LH I-III A1	id. + PAE 1956
KATARRAKTIS (Achaia): Th. A: cat. 29a	3.90				1.05	0.40		South	threshold	?	Ergon 1956–57
—: Th. B: cat. 29b	5.20		stucco		1.57		3 elem.	West		LH III A (?)	Ergon 1956–57
MEDEON (Focis): Th. A1: cat. 34a	5.00						1, or >1	West	lateral chamber + threshold	LH III A-B	BCH 91 1967
BELLOUSSIA (Eubea): cat. 35	4.20			1.65		2.75	5 elem.	South		LH III	PAE 1907
KATAKALOU (Eubea): cat. 36	5.60				0.80	3.30	4 elem.		stomion closing (tiang.)	LH III	PAE 1907
OXYLITHOS (Eubea): cat. 37	4.60				0.80					LH III A-B	PAE 1907
PTELEON (Thessaly): Gritsa, Th. A: cat. 41a	4.06	4.50 (?)		1.85	1.20/1.02		2 elem.	South-East	stomion closing	LH III A-C	PAE 1951–52
—: Gritsa, Th.C: cat. 41c	5.20						1 elem.	North		LH III C	PAE 1952
—: Aghil Theodori: cat. 41e	3.54	3.40(?)		1.15	0.84	0.40	4 elem.	West	stomion closing + threshold	LH III C	PAE 1951–52
AGHIOS ILIAS (Acarnania): Seremeti: cat. 45a	5.27		clay					South-West	threshold	LH II-III C	Ergon, PAE 1963
—: Marathia, Th. 1: cat. 45b	4.14		worked rock					South		LH III A	Ergon, PAE 1963
—: Marathia, Th. 2: cat. 45c	4.17		clay				4 elem.	South		LH III B-C	Ergon, PAE 1963
MAVRATA (Cefalonia): cat. 49	4.00				0.70			South		LH III C	BCH 60 1936
MAZARAKATA (Cefalonia): cat. 52	3.60				0.80			South		LH III C (?)	PAE 1912
ALIKES (Zakinthos): cat. 533	5.00							East		LH III	BSA 32 1931–32
SPHAKIA (Crete): cat. 55	4.00	4.00					3 elem.		st. closing + false side cham. + threshold	LM III B	Ergon, PAE 1955
ACHLADIA (Crete): cat. 56	4.00			2.05	1.06/0.80		1 elem.		side chamber	LM III B	KChr, PAE 1952
ARCHANES (Crete): Th. A: cat. 59	4.30/4.40			2.26	0.95	3.8	8 elem.	South-West		LM III A	AD 21 1966 PAE 1970
KNOSSOS (Crete): Kephala: cat. 60	5.50									LM II	BSA 51 1956
STYLOS (Crete): cat. 62	4.30	4.80	nat. rock	2.3	1.05	1.8	3 elem.	South	stomion closing	LM III B	AD 17 1961–62
KOLOPHON (Anatolia occ.): cat. 63	3.87							North-NE		LH III B (or C?)	Hesperia 1978

Le Tecniche Edilizie del Periodo Nuragico nell'Architettura delle Acque, Presenti nel Territorio della Barbagia

Maria Ausilia Fadda, Caterinella Tuveri e Giuseppe Murru

Numerosi scavi condotti nel territorio della provincia di Nuoro hanno consentito una più chiara definizione tipologica dell'architettura dei luoghi di culto della Sardegna nuragica che in questo territorio viene meno ai canoni architettonici documentati nel restante territorio della Sardegna. Le anomalie di carattere architettonico risultano all'analisi più interessanti se vengono esaminati i materiali lapidei utilizzati dalle popolazioni nuragiche per costruzioni di monumenti cultuali, che come verrà chiarito più avanti, in alcuni casi assumono una dimensione e una valenza di grandi santuari che sembrano sommare al potere religioso anche un potere di carattere economico. Per poter sviluppare, in modo organico l'argomento dell'architettura templare è stato creato dai geologi Caterinella Tuveri e Giuseppe Murru un quadro generale della geologia dei siti dove sorgono i monumenti e le relative distanze dai possibili punti di cava dei materiali vulcanici impiegati per la loro costruzione (Tavola 1). L'obiettivo da raggiungere con questo studio è quello di stabilire se l'uso delle rocce vulcaniche sia legato a motivi di carattere strettamente religioso che in qualche modo giustificherebbero lo sforzo economico e fisico sostenuto per procurarsi i materiali o se l'uso delle rocce laviche sia determinato soltanto dalla sua funzionalità per la realizzazione di architetture di tipo isodomo. In questo lavoro vengono quindi presi in esame soltanto i pozzi sacri e le fonti costruite con materiale lapideo effusivo in zone con assenza totale di colate laviche. I monumenti che verranno presi in esame sono: il pozzo sacro del santuario di Abini (Teti-NU) (Taramelli 1931: 323; 1913a: 167); Coni o Santu Milanu di Nuragus (NU) (Taramelli 1913b: 275); la fonte di Noddule di Nuoro (Contu 1974; Lilliu 1982); la fonte di Su Lidone di Orune (NU) (Taramelli 1919: 120-126); Su Tempiesu di Orune (NU) (Davoli 1950; Lilliu 1958: 244 ss.; Fadda 1982: 284 ss.; Fadda 1985: 208; Fadda 1988); il santuario di Nurdole di Orani (NU) (Fadda 1986: 308; Fadda 1990: 260; Fadda e Madau in stampa); il complesso di fonti Gremanu di Fonni (NU) (Fadda in stampa); la fonte Funtana 'e Deu di Lula (NU).

Gran parte dei monumenti citati sono stati oggetto di ampie pubblicazioni, perciò in questa sede verranno inserite delle brevi schede descrittive che evidenziano le caratteristiche architettoniche e soprattutto la tecnica di lavorazione e la tecnica edilizia documentata nei singoli monumenti.

La Fonte del Santuario di Abini

La fonte di Abini (Taramelli 1931: 323) è inserita in un grande recinto di forma ellittica, compreso tra le numerose capanne di un villaggio nuragico costruito con blocchi di granito a filari regolari. L'area interna del vano era in origine pavimentata con ciottoloni e la base dello stesso muro era segnata da un sedile che si adattava alla circonferenza del recinto. All'interno dello stesso recinto si delineava un secondo ambiente delimitato da un muro ad andamento curvilineo costruito con conci di trachite rosa lavorati a martellina. Il muro di conci di trachite era attraversato alla base da una canaletta che trasportava le acque che sgorgavano da una fonte adiacente al muro sul lato esterno. Della fonte rimangono i conci di trachite con la faccia interna sagomata a sezione di cerchio che in origine formavano una copertura a tholos. L'acqua del pozzo, attraverso una canaletta tracciata sul pavimento, si versava in un secondo pozzetto scavato sotto il piano di calpestio e delimitato da una ghiera di pietre appena sbozzate. I diversi interventi condotti in modo improprio a partire dal 1865 e fino al 1931 non offrono elementi sufficienti per ricostruire l'intero complesso ed inoltre la planimetria pubblicata dal Taramelli (1931: 323) non trova riscontri con i nuovi rilievi. I lavori di diserbo effettuati dalla scrivente nel 1982 hanno riportato alla luce gran parte dei conci di trachite accumulati all'esterno del recinto riferibili alla copertura a tholos, ma soprattutto ad un paramento murario composto da conci con la faccia a vista rettilinea alcuni dei quali presentano una cornice in rilievo. I blocchi di trachite di Abini hanno strettissime analogie con quelli rinvenuti a Su Tempiesu (Orune) e Gremanu (Fonni) a Nurdole (Orani) per la forma dei conci, il tipo di lavorazione a martellina e gli incastri. Soltanto uno scavo sistematico potrà consentire una restituzione grafica attendibile dell'edificio cultuale che costituiva nel periodo nuragico uno dei centri religiosi più importanti del territorio più interno della Sardegna. L'uso esclusivamente religioso della fonte di Abini è attestata dal rinvenimento di centinaia oggetti in bronzo di carattere votivo.

Pozzo Sacro di Coni o Santu Millanu (Nuragus)

Il pozzo di Coni o Santu Millanu sorge ai piedi della giara di Gesturi vicina all'omonimo nuraghe posto in cima ad una collina in un'area interessata da numerose preesistenze di epoche diverse. Parte del monumento è scavato su uno strato di calcari marmosi miocenici mentre la struttura architettonica è stata realizzata con conci di pietra vulcanica ben lavorati e disposti a filari regolari. La fonte conserva una scala di 5 gradini che raggiungono la conca emisferica che raccoglie l'acqua sorgiva e sette filari della tholos, lacunosa della parte superiore. Dal pozzo proviene una statuina in bronzo raffigurante una sacerdotessa orante con mantello. I conci della tholos hanno la faccia a sezione di cerchio e la parte interna con appendici a coda che ancoravano solidamente la muratura, anche senza malta cementizia, ed una massicciata di pietre calcaree. Davanti alla scala si conservano i resti di un dromos di forma rettangolare (m 4 × 5) pavimentato con lastre di calcare lamellare messe in opera in modo regolare. Il Taramelli nel dare notizia del risultato dello scavo evidenzia il fatto che i numerosi monumenti di epoca nuragica presenti nella zona sono tutti costruiti con un calcare compatto presente sul posto, mentre la pietra impiegata per la costruzione del pozzo è stata trasportata da una distanza non inferiore ai 10 km. Lo stesso Taramelli ritiene che l'uso della pietra lavica sia da attribuire al carattere sacro della costruzione.

Fonte di Noddule (Nuoro)

A qualche centinaio di metri dal nuraghe è ubicata la fonte sacra che, nella primavera del 1961, venne esplorata dalla Soprintendenza Archeologica delle provincie di Sassari e Nuoro. Il monumento è costituito da un ampio vestibolo quadrangolare provvisto di panchine e dal pozzetto che raccoglieva l'acqua sorgiva. Il pozzetto di forma cilindrica è costruito con conci di trachite lavorati a martellina e disposti a filari regolari a tenuta perfetta. Nel fondo piano, anch'esso in trachite, è stata scavata una fossetta di decantazione di forma circolare regolare. Il pozzo ha una copertura a tholos chiusa da un concio che presenta un foro conico impervio. Il parametro esterno del pozzo delimita un vano di forma rettangolare con fondo absidato che presenta un leggero aggetto nei filari della parte più alta.

La facciata della fonte ha un andamento rettilineo e si conserva, in altezza per m 3,30 a partire dalla soglia del pozzetto; è costruita per un'altezza di m 1,60 con otto filari di conci trachitici lavorati con cura, mentre la parte superiore è costituita di conci di granito locale di varia grandezza e disposti a filari molto irregolari. Un portello architravato, rettangolare, con una piccola nicchia sopra l'architrave, immette nel pozzo attraverso una breve rampa di scale strombata verso l'esterno, composta da quattro larghe pedate formate da lastre di granito locale e da tre piccoli gradini messi in opera con conci squadrati di trachite. Questa scala è delimitata da un muro di blocchi granitici disposti a filari irregolari a chiudere un'area interna di forma trapezoidale, lunga metri 3,60; larga all'ingresso m 1,70 e metri 1,30 sul fondo. Sulla sinistra del muro che racchiude la scala, si apre, in corrispondenza del terzo filare, una piccola nicchia di forma trapezoidale. Alla base dello stesso muro e in corrispondenza del terzo gradino sono visibili due panchine costituite da due blocchi di forma rettangolare, in granito, usate forse come piano d'appoggio per oggetti di uso cultuale o come sedili. Ai muri rettilinei si innestano i muri di un emiciclo irregolare, pavimentato parzialmente con lastre di granito, con ingresso esposto a Nord e decentrato rispetto all'asse della scala. Dei sedili sono visibili alla base dei muri del vestibolo; sul lato Sud rimane un focolare circolare irregolare. Il tempietto è racchiuso da un recinto di forma irregolare che probabilmente costituiva l'area sacra destinata alle funzioni religiose.

Fonte di Su Lidone (Orune)

Non lontano dal nuraghe Santa Lulla, in una zona chiamata Su Lidone, si conserva una modesta fonte nuragica. Il monumento risulta addossato ad una piccola parete di roccia di scisto donde scaturisce la vena d'acqua. È costruito con conci di lava basaltica lavorati a martellina, con la faccia a vista tagliata in modo obliquo ed aggettanti gradualmente verso l'alto fino a chiudere con una lastra piattabandata.

L'acqua è incanalata in una celletta rettangolare (largh. m 0,45; lungh. m 0,90) all'interno della quale è stata scavata una piccola conca circolare che risulta ad un livello più basso rispetto al piano di campagna; l'altezza complessiva, alla base della copertura è di m 1,30. Al momento della sua scoperta e dalla descrizione fattane da A. Taramelli, nel 1919, la fonte conservava un piccolo piazzale lastricato, di forma trapezoidale e delimitato da banconi laterali, che, attualmente, sono stati distrutti durante lavori di scasso nel tentativo di deviare le acque in un sottostante abbeveratoio. Poiché la piccola fonte presenta le stesse caratteristiche architettoniche del tempio a pozzo di Su Tempiesu, essa può essere attribuita allo stesso momento culturale, tra il XII e il IX sec. a.C.

La Fonte Sacra di Su Tempiesu di Orune (Fig. 1)

Il monumento risulta addossato all'incisione interposta tra due ripide pareti di roccia di scisto dove è stata captata ed incanalata la vena d'acqua che alimenta il pozzo sacro. L'edificio è costituito da un vestibolo a pianta rettangolare, leggermente strombato verso l'esterno e con pavimento in lieve pendenza realizzato con grandi lastroni di trachite che si congiungono perfettamente. Ai lati del vestibolo si conservano due banconi composti da vari blocchi affiancati; sopra di essi si aprono due stipetti rettangolari ricavati nello spessore murario dei due pedritti, che si ergono per un'altezza di m 2,76, adattandosi alla conformazione della roccia naturale, usata come base per le fondazioni delle strutture portanti. I muri portanti si sviluppano in altezza con un andamento obliquo nella parete interna e un rilevante restringimento verso l'alto, evidenziato dal taglio obliquo dei conci leggermente aggettanti uno sull'altro che creano una linea di contorno dentellato. Il vestibolo è coperto da due archetti monolitici ad arco ribassato, inseriti, come puri elementi decorativi, in una incastellatura a triangolo acuto che continua il restringimento verso l'alto della parete interna delle due spalle murarie, chiuse in origine con uno stretto concio posto a piattabanda. Dall'atrio, attraverso una piccola scala, miniaturistica, trapezoidale e strombata verso l'interno—composta da quattro piccoli gradini ancorati tra loro con conci ad incastro, mentre sottili verghe di piombo alle giunture impediscono la dispersione delle acque—si arriva al vano a tholos che raccoglie e custodisce la vena sorgiva.

La tholos ha un diametro di base di m 0,90 e con undici filari perfettamente connessi sviluppa un'altezza massima di m 1,82 ove si misura il diametro minore di cm 26. La base del pozzetto ha un lastricato a tenuta perfetta, costruito con una leggera pendenza in direzione dell'ingresso che presenta, decentrata sul lato sinistro, una fossetta di decantazione di forma circolare che raccoglie le impurità e mantiene le acque sempre limpidissime. Le acque che traboccano dal pozzo scorrono in un solco, praticato al centro della soglia modanata, che versa l'acqua su una piccola conca sottostante che a sua volta la convoglia in un canaletto tracciato sul lastricato del vestibolo, attraversandolo per tutta la lunghezza in senso obbliquo, da sinistra verso destra. Al momento della scoperta, tutti i blocchi dei pilastri, i conci dei banconi laterali e il lastricato del vestibolo erano saldati da verghe di piombo. Una singolare copertura a doppio spiovente, che nasce dalla parete della roccia, ricopre il monumento e termina con

Fig. 1 Su Tempiesu (Orune). Veduta generale.

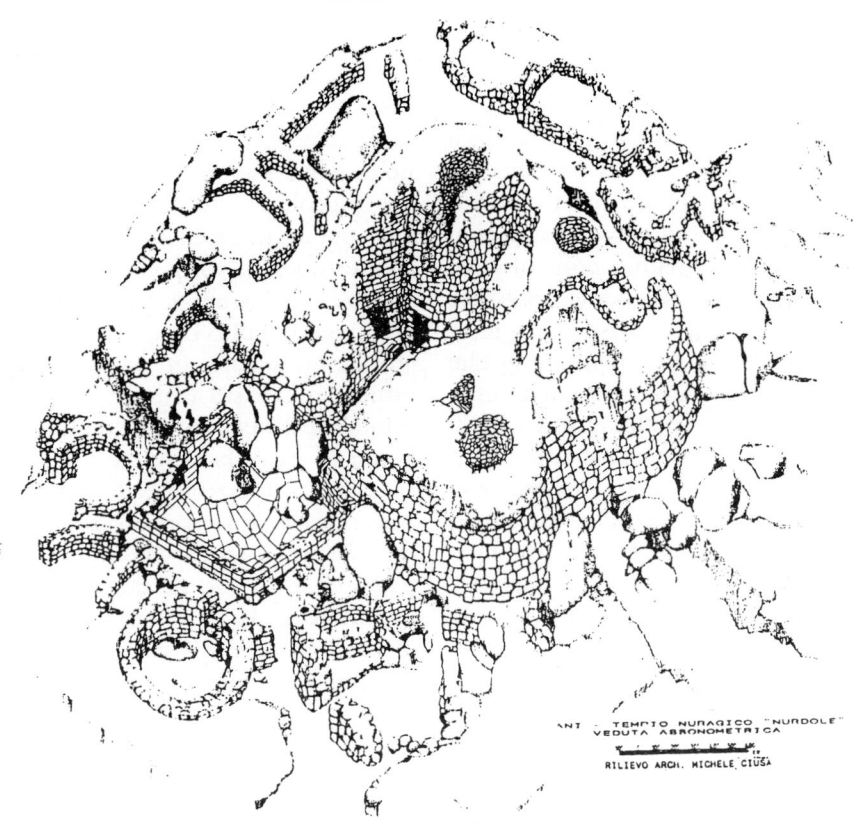

Fig. 2 Nurdole di Orani. Veduta assonometrica.

una doppia gronda magistralmente scolpita nella roccia vulcanica. L'interno della copertura è costituito da un riempimento di lastrine di scisto locale sovrapposte che ne allegeriscono la struttura.

La facciata che in origine si ergeva in altezza per m 6,85, ha un timpano a triangolo acuto messo in risalto da una doppia cornice che termina alla base ripiegando verso l'interno del timpano stesso a formare un angolo ottuso. Il timpano originariamente terminava con un fastigio costituito da un concio troncopiramidale che rappresentava in prospetto l'apice della cornice del timpano, mentre nella parte superiore piana aveva infisse 20 spade votive in bronzo, fissate negli incavi con colate di piombo. L'area antistante il tempio è delimitata da un muro curvilineo molto irregolare, costruito, nei filari di base, con blocchi di basalto, simili a quelli del tempio, mentre nella parte superiore la muratura è costituita da filari di scisto locale. Nel muro sono ricavate due piccole nicchie, mentre nella parte più alta del medesimo si conservano ancora due lastre sporgenti sistemate come mensole. Sotto il recinto, gli scavi più recenti hanno portato alla luce un pozzetto di raccolta delle acque del pozzo maggiore che riproduce nella forma e nella tecnica costruttiva, ma in scala più piccola. Questo pozzetto, che ha un'altezza complessiva di m 0,90 e un diametro di m 0,65, raccoglie le acque che defluiscono dal pozzo maggiore attraverso una canaletta scavata in blocco di basalto al quale si adatta una seconda canaletta in steatite verde con gocciolatoio semicircolare finemente lavorato, che risulta in asse alla già nota canaletta tracciata nei lastroni del pavimento del vestibolo. Anche in questo pozzetto è presente una fossetta di decantazione analoga a quella del pozzo più grande; l'imboccatura è sovrastata da un archetto monolitico ad arco ribassato, anch'esso in trachite, fortemente degradato dall'acqua. All'interno del pozzetto sono stati rinvenuti numerosi oggetti votivi: bronzi figurati, spilloni, braccialetti, anelli, stiletti votivi, spade, bottoni etc. offerti dai fedeli alla divinità delle acque.

L'esplorazione stratigrafica dell'area circostante il monumento ha portato alla luce, sul lato sinistro del tempio, un vano posto in una posizione molto più elevata rispetto all'attuale piano di calpestio; è delimitato da un muro costituito da due filari di grossi conci appena sbozzati che poggiano sulla roccia naturale, mentre il suo sviluppo in altezza è dato da filari di lastre di scisto che aggettano verso lo spiovente della copertura dell'edificio sacro. Anche sul lato destro gli scavi hanno evidenziato un altro vano, ricavato da una naturale rientranza della parete di scisto con profondità diverse a causa dell'irregolare conformazione della roccia; il vano è delimitato, per una lunghezza di 14 metri, da un muro di blocchi granitici e di scisto molto irregolari.

Il Santuario di Nurdole in Orani
(Fig. 2)

In agro di Orani su un'altura a 700 m s.l.m. sorge il nuraghe Nurdole. Nella fase edilizia più antica il nuraghe si presentava con un impianto planimetro più semplice composto da un mastio centrale e due torri, costruite con blocchi appena sbozzati che si adattavano alla irregolare conformazione della roccia di base. In questa fase, intorno al 1500 circa a.C. il nuraghe che inglobava una vena sorgiva, usata probabilmente per il fabbisogno quotidiano, volgeva funzioni di controllo e di difesa dell'abitato circostante. L'uso della sorgente è attestato da una canaletta tracciata sotto l'attuale lastricato del cortile e del lungo corridoio d'accesso che fuoriesce sotto la rampa lastricata posta davanti all'ingresso del nuraghe.

Nel bronzo recente il nuraghe subì profonde modifiche di carattere planimetrico e architettonico e venne trasformato in luogo di culto. Intorno alla sorgente venne costruito un muro di blocchi squadrati di trachite, fino ad un'altezza di m 1,30. Su questo muro si pare l'ingresso della fontana sacra che, analogamente ad altre fonti di tipo isodomo della Sardegna, presenta una copertura costruita da tre architravi scalati ancorati allo spessore dei muri laterali della fonte. La parte esterna della fonte è delimitata da una soglia modanata che poggia sul lastricato del cortile. In corrispondenza dell'ingresso della fonte si conserva un basamento (0 metri 1,24 alt. res. m 0,73), ottenuto da due filari di conci a coda in trachite con la faccia a vista a sezione di cerchio. I conci ritrovati intorno al basamento consentono di ricostruire una cupola con un concio terminale attraversato da un foro passante nel quale probabilmente veniva versata l'acqua. Dalla base circolare parte un altro basamento rettangolare anch'esso in conci di trachite, che si inserisce nello spessore murario del cortile sul lato Sud. La base sosteneva una canaletta composta da più elementi che si incastrano perfettamente tra loro. La canaletta per una lunghezza di m 5,50 attraversa due ambienti di forma trapezoidale costruiti con una muratura a filari di piccoli conci di trachite con un aggetto molto accentuato, che in origine erano coperti da lastre piattabandate. L'acqua versata nella canaletta raggiungeva una grande vasca rettangolare (m 6,50 × 7,40), realizzata con conci di tufo e trachite perfettamente squadrati. Nella muratura perimetrale della vasca e nel lastricato di pavimentazione sono state inglobate numerose rocce granitiche naturali. Nel lastricato della vasca sono stati realizzati nelle connessure perfette numerosi fori, alcuni dei quali facilitavano l'inserimento di leve nella messa in opera, altri, fatti nei punti di maggiore pendenza, facilitavano la fuoriuscita dell'acqua. In corrispondenza della vasca e nell'area esterna sono state rinvenute numerose basi in pietra di forme diverse con fori nella parte superiore, nei quali venivano fissati con piccole colate di piombo i bronzi votivi. Le basi per le offerte, una base d'altare rinvenuta all'interno della torre centrale e una straordinaria quantità di bronzi votivi attestano l'importanza del luogo di culto capace di attirare folle di fedeli che deponevano in prossimità della fonte e intorno alla vasca lustrale, spade votive, punte e puntali di lancia, pugnali, stiletti e farette votive, fibule ad arco ribassato etc.

La funzione rituale dell'acqua e la trasformazione architettonica della fonte sacra ha modificato l'intera architettura del nuraghe che si è arricchito di cortine murarie che raccordano le quattro torri. Le parti architettoniche aggiunte nel bronzo recente presentano differenze evidenti nell'impiego di pietre piccole appena sbozzate e disposte a filari irregolari. Nell'area esterna intorno al nuraghe lo scavo ha portato alla luce numerosissimi conci in trachite e tufo lavorati a scalpello con la faccia a vista decorata da motivi decorativi, prevalentemente geometrici finora sconosciuti altrove.

Il Complesso di Fonti di Gremanu di Fonni
(Figg. 3a-b)

In agro di Fonni in località Madau, in prossimità del passo di Caravai posto oltre 1000 m s.l.m. è stato portato alla luce un complesso di fonti di epoca nuragica costruita all'interno di un'area semicircolare delimitata da un muro di blocchi di granito locale disposti a filari regolari. Le fonti risultano inserite sotto un bosco fittissimo e disposte su un forte pendio che degrada verso la valle sottostante attraversata dal Rio Gremanu. Lungo le sponde del fiume si conservano i resti di un villaggio nuragico e di un nuraghe. L'acqua è stata captata nella parte alta del monte e incanalata in una fonte principale con copertura a tholos con una base composta da due blocchi semicircolari in basalto, con una larga cornice in rilievo. L'acqua captata dalla parete rocciosa passa nella conca circolare attraverso cinque scanalature ricavate in modo radiale nella circonferenza della cornice (ϕ max cm 88 ϕ min 55). Nel punto di unione tra i due blocchi della base è stata scavata una piccola fossetta circolare di decantazione che raccoglie, con una leggera pendenza, le impurità dell'acqua. I due blocchi della base del pozzetto conservano all'esterno due appendici mammelliformi, lasciate in origine per

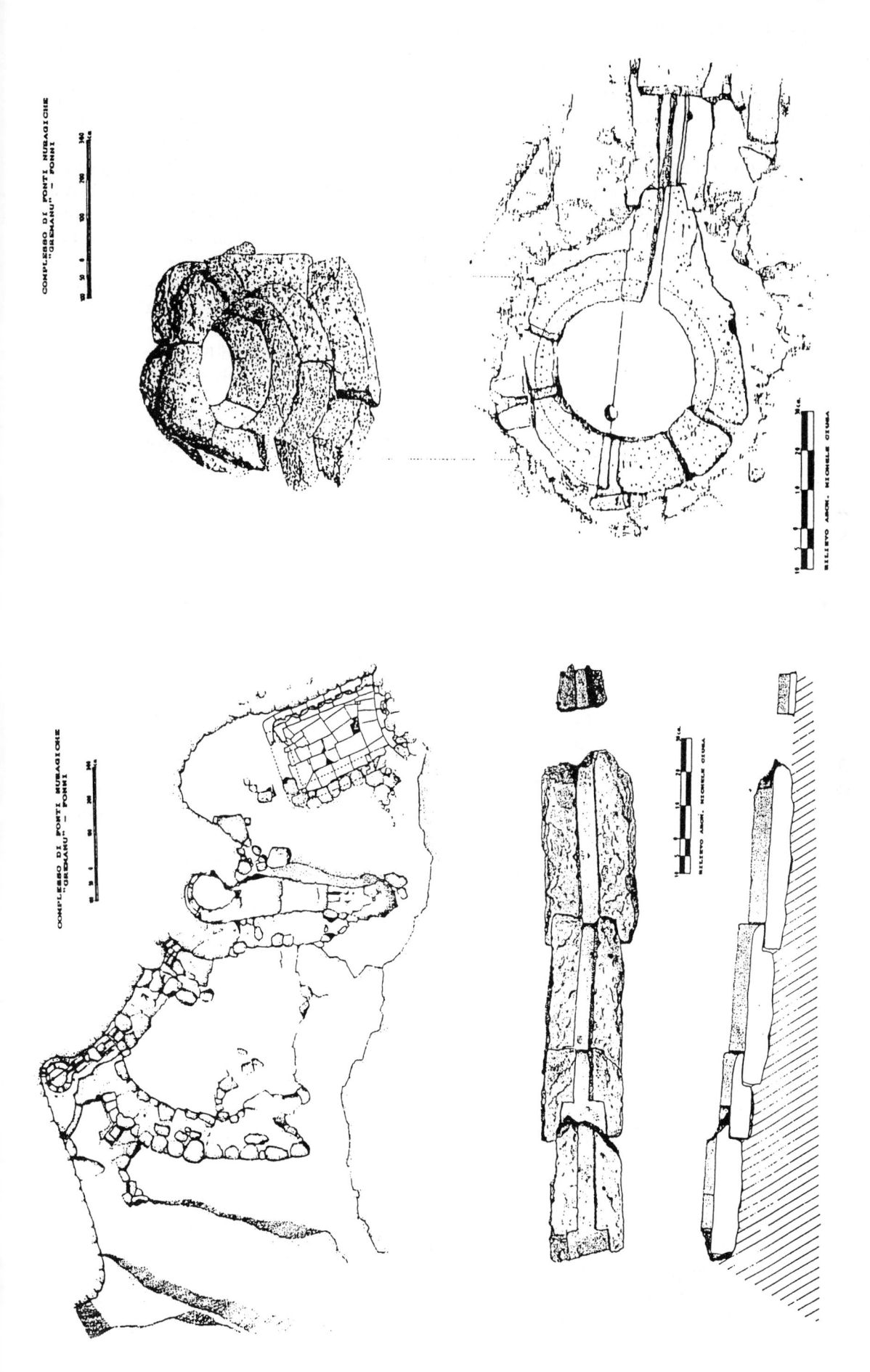

Fig. 3 Gremanu di Fonni. (A) Complesso di fonti e canaletta; (B) Il primo pozzo e cupola.

facilitare la messa in opera e per ancorare più saldamente i blocchi alla roccia in disfacimento dalla quale sgorga l'acqua. In corrispondenza della prima fonte sono stati raccolti 12 blocchi di basalto che, nella parte esterna, presentano una forma a sezione di cerchio, e congiungendosi compongono circonferenze di diametri diversi. I blocchi che all'interno hanno un taglio obbliquo costituivano in origine i filari aggettanti di una piccola tholos che conteneva l'acqua sorgiva. Dal primo pozzetto passa attraverso una canaletta (lungh. m 6,20, largh. m 0,60) costituita da diversi conci in basalto che si incastrano tra loro, coperta da altri conci che si sovrappongono perfettamente per formare un canale a sezione circolare. La canaletta in basalto a sua volta è coperta da 5 lastre di scisto locale disposte a piattabanda che si adattano gradualmente alla pendenza del terreno. La difficoltà di tenere saldamente i vari elementi della canaletta iu un terreno di forte pendenza, è stata risolta predisponendo incastri perfetti e inserendo dei cunei di trachite che tengono saldamente ancorati tra loro i blocchi pur non conservando la stessa linea di posa in opera. La doppia canaletta risulta infine contenuta tra due muri realizzati con blocchi iregolari che aggettano vistosamente e che in origine chiudevano probabilmente con una copertura a dorso piattabandata.

Le acque attraverso la canaletta passano in un secondo pozzo circolare (0 max 1) costruito con piccoli conci squadrati di granito degradato, disposti a filari regolari. I blocchi hanno la faccia interna a vista a sezione di cerchio di grandezze diverse, che vanno dai 45 ai 20 cm di lunghezza. Dal secondo pozzetto parte un'altra canaletta, contenuta all'interno di un vano rettangolare delimitato da due muri di conci di granito disposti a filari irregolari che si conserva per una lunghezza di m 3,50. La canaletta visibile all'esterno è scavata in un blocco di scisto, in origine probabilmente veniva coperta con la stessa tecnica del pozzetto soprastante. Le acque raccolte nelle due fonti già scavate e in quelle adiacenti non ancora esplorate, venivano convogliate in un punto di raccolta in corrispondenza di uno sbarramento sottostante costruito in un terreno molto scosceso, la canaletta sviluppa dalla prima fonte fino allo spianamento una lunghezza di m 14,40. Lungo il pendio si conservano in mezzo al crollo numerosi conci a T, in trachite, con la faccia a vista aventi su un lato una cornice in rilievo, che trovano strette analogie con quelli rinvenuti nella vasca del tempio di Nurdole e nel timpano del tempio di Su Tempiesu di Orune. Sul lato destro del parametro murario a emiciclo che racchiude le fonti, lo scavo ha portato alla luce una vasca di forma rettangolare con il muro di fondo convesso soltanto all'interno (Fig. 3b). La vasca ha una lunghezza interna di m 3,5 e una larghezza di m 1,75 è costruita con conci di basalto a T lavorati con scalpelli con la punta di larghezza diversa impiegati per rifinire e lisciare le superfici che rimanevano a vista. I blocchi si legavano tra loro con verghe metalliche e lignee inserite negli incastri che venivano scolpiti nelle code o nelle estremità dei conci, con tacche contrapposte, oppure in senso longitudinale.

L'interno della vasca è pavimentata da lastre di trachite e di tufo legate tra loro da incastri perfetti. I filari dei blocchi che delimitano il perimetro della vasca poggiano invece su un basamento di lastre di scisto. La vasca non risulta collegata alle canalette degli altri pozzetti e soltanto la prosecuzione dello scavo potrà stabilire l'esistenza di un canale, non visibile, che consentiva il riempimento della vasca. Nelle vicinanze della vasca lo scavo ha portato alla luce una testina di ariete in trachite spezzata in corrispondenza del collo. La mancanza di materiale fittile significativo e i pochi frammenti di bronzo rinvenuti nello scavo non danno chiari indizi nell'uso delle fonti esclusivamente religioso. La presenza della vasca rituale, molto simile a quella presente nel tempio di Nurdole e soprattutto la presenza di numerose basi per offerte rinvenute nel villaggi sottostante, in corrispondenza di un edificio a pianta rettangolare che ricorda la planimetria dei templi a megaron, costituiscono dei chiari esempi della sacralità del luogo. L'ultima campagna di scavo ha portato alla luce un terzo pozzo, che si apre all'interno di un ambiente con copertura a filari aggettanti e risulta adiacente al lato concavo della vasca. All'interno della tholos lungo la circonferenza e sopra un piano lastricato, poggiavano pugnali e spilloni in bronzo, elementi di collana in ambra con scanalature parallele. Dall'interno del pozzo provengono diverse olle a colletto con anse a nastro a gomito rovesciato, brocche piriformi e piccoli contenitori che si inquadrano nelle fasi finali dell'età del bronzo. Il complesso delle fonti collegate tra loro da un elaborato progetto idraulico costituisce l'unico esempio in Sardegna di acquedotto, funzionale alla raccolta delle acque delle sorgenti della montagna e utilizzate probabilmente per il fabbisogno ordinario delle genti del villaggio sottostante e per riti religiosi.

La Fonte Funtana 'e Deu di Lula

Su un canalone posto in forte pendio si conservano i resti di una fonte di epoca nuragica che facevano parte di un complesso di fonti che attualmente risultano poco leggibili a causa di una devastazione operata da scavatori clandestini. Soltanto un'attenta indagine archeologica potrà consentire la ricostruzione di tutto il complesso architettonico. Le strutture della fonte ancora visibili risultano contenute da un paramento murario curvilineo costruito con blocchi di calcare poliedrici, appena sbozzati, e disposti a filari irregolari che si adattano alla roccia affiorante. La fonte che sorge alla base del muro è costruita con blocchi di trachite con la faccia a vista curvilinea e la faccia interna con grandi e profonde appendici di incastro sagomate con larghi colpi di scalpello. I blocchi si riferiscono alla copertura a tholos della fonte che è andata distrutta e che sicuramente era collegata attraverso diverse canalette, ad altre fonti di raccolta che si adattavano nel terreno scosceso. La tipologia delle fonti di Lula trova analogia con il complesso di fonti di Gremanu (Fonni) poiché entrambe risultano racchiuse in un parametro murario che oltre a contenere il terreno in forte pendio sembra voler delimitare o separare l'area cultuale. Nonostante non sia stato effettuato alcun intervento di scavo stratigrafici, la presenza di un braccialetto e di una lamina in bronzo, e alcuni frammenti ceramici consentono di inquadrare le fonti di Lula nel Bronzo Finale e inoltre gli stessi materiali possono indicare l'uso cultuale del monumento.

Discussione

Dalle descrizioni dei monumenti risulta evidente la varietà tipologica delle architetture legate al culto delle acque ma soprattutto le varie soluzioni tecniche adottate dalle popolazioni nuragiche in condizioni geomorfologiche accidentate in zone di difficile accesso, nel territorio del Nuorese o della Barbagia. L'elemento comune dei monumenti presi in esame è l'impiego di rocce vulcaniche per la realizzazione di architetture isodome costruite con conci a coda o a T lavorate a martellina.

Dalla tavola geologica risulta che i punti di cava di pietre laviche, distano dai monumenti presi in esame da un minimo di 3 km in linea d'aria ad un massimo di 20 km. Tali distanze riportate su possibili strade di penetrazione possono aumentare sensibilmente, perciò considerando la difficoltà dei trasporti, l'uso di tale materiale nell'architettura religiosa assumeva un significato particolare, che va al di là dei criteri di durevolezza e lavorabilità della roccia che può aver condizionato le scelte dei costruttori nuragici. Risultano determinanti nell'impiego di rocce vulcaniche la lavorabilità ovvero l'attitudine delle rocce a spaccarsi nella forma e dimensioni volute e soprattutto la durevolezza determinata dalla scarsa azione dell'idrolisi che attacca soprattutto il granito e il calcare. I pozzi sacri costruiti con conci di rocce vulcaniche presentano pareti e filari regolari con le giunture perfettamente aderenti dovute anche alla lavorazione delle pareti a vista a sezione di cerchio. Diversi tipi di incastri laterali e longitudinali consentivano l'inserimento di verghe di piombo, di ferro e cunei di legno che ancoravano saldamente i blocchi tra loro anche senza malta di coesione. L'obiettivo principale nell'architettura cultuale era dunque quello di impedire la dispersione ed il trasudamento delle acque quale elemento sacro ed espressione di una divinità ctonica che assume valenza di divinità nutrice ed elemento essenziale nei fenomeni di riproduzione della natura. La perfetta conservazione dell'acqua in alcuni monumenti veniva assicurata dall'inserimento di verghe di piombo che saldavano i giunti dei diversi filari di conci delle pareti interne.

A Su Tempiesu di Orune le verghe metalliche saldavano anche i filari esterni dei piedritti che delimitano il vestibolo coperto e nello stesso tempio le verghe di piombo sono ancora visibili nei gradini della scala trapezoidale. L'estrazione dei conci ed il trasporto comportavano sicuramente un notevole sforzo economico ed anche la costruzione dei pozzi, con architetture complesse non escludono l'esistenza di maestranze specializzate che progettavano i templi adattandoli alle diverse conformazioni geologiche. I diversi esempi di architettura templare documentati nel territorio nuorese e barbaricino si discostano dai modelli canonici realizzati nelle altre zone della Sardegna. Si aggiunge che nei monumenti presi in esame sono stati rinvenuti numerosissimi oggetti in bronzo di carattere votivo deposti nelle apposite basi o accumulati in prossimità dei pozzi. Nei casi specifici dei santuari di Abini (Teti) e Nurdole (Orani) dove il numero degli oggetti in bronzo raggiunge diverse migliaia non è azzardato ipotizzare la presenza di un edificio cultuale intorno al quale il potere economico si somma a quello religioso.

I problemi relativi ai rapporti tra i santuari e i nuraghi sono di difficile soluzione anche in considerazione del fatto che all'interno dei nuraghi difficilmente si rinvengono elementi sufficienti che dimostrino la presenza di un potere economico espresso attraverso l'accumulo dei beni. Nel santuario di Nurdole oltre all'immensa quantità di materiale bronzeo è documentato un notevole accumulo di derrate contenute in grandi doli e in contenitori di sughero e legno accumulati nelle capanne adiacenti l'area cultuale. La presenza di un edificio religioso che gestisce grandi disponibilità economiche può giustificare lo sforzo necessario sostenuto per la costruzione degli edifici cultuali realizzati con materiale lapideo proveniente da molto lontano. Si sottolinea inoltre che tali edifici sono nella gran parte nel territorio nuorese e barbaricino che finora, sono stati considerati come luoghi di attardamenti culturali. I dati, al contrario, rivelano la presenza di una centralità del potere, espresso attraverso un imponente accumulo di beni economici che fanno ipotizzare l'esistenza di gruppi emergenti che gestivano il potere religioso e quello temporale.

Maria Ausilia Fadda

Aspetti Geologici e Tecnici

I monumenti archeologici della Sardegna sono costruiti con materiale roccioso di varia natura proveniente dall'ambito geologico isolano. La notevole varietà dei litotipi utilizzati rappresenta, unitamente alle diverse tipologie, un elemento fondamentale nella definizione e comprensione del sito archeologico (Murru 1990). Si nota l'utilizzo di blocchi rocciosi sia allo stato naturale che dopo opportune trasformazioni più o meno rilevanti, queste ultime tendenti a modificare la realtà naturale per usi particolari. I monumenti nuragici nel loro complesso dimostrano la ricerca, la scelta e l'utilizzo dei materiali rocciosi sulla base di diverse considerazioni: l'impiego specifico al quale erano destinati, la disponibilità o meno di idoneo litotipo nelle vicinanze del sito di costruzione, dotato di caratteristiche tecniche opportune, la morfologia del sito medesimo, le tradizioni costruttive, l'importanza della costruzione dal punto di vista sociale e culturale. L'utilizzo di materiali litoidi estranei al contesto geolitologico del sito, è evidente nelle architetture religiose dedicate a particolari culti delle acque.

I dati emersi nel corso del presente lavoro consentono di evidenziare un duplice ordine di fattori, che sembrano influire sulla scelta dei materiali rocciosi: in primo luogo è evidente una conoscenza, seppur empirica, delle principali proprietà tecniche delle rocce (Desio 1989; Ippolito *et al*. 1975), cioè di quella somma di pregi e di difetti in relazione all'impiego al quale erano destinate, deducibili da parte delle maestranze nuragiche sulla base di osservazioni del mondo geologico che li circondava e probabilmente su sperimentazioni e valutazioni qualitative, affinate nel corso di esperienze diversificate e prolungate nel tempo. In secondo luogo non è azzardardato affermare che dalla ricerca e dalla scelta di materiali particolari, non presenti in loco e talvolta provenienti da rilevanti distanze e/o particolarmente rari o di difficile prelievo, emerge la volontà di sottolineare l'importanza della costruzione stessa, dal punto di vista sociale e religioso, proprio attraverso l'elevazione degli standard qualitativi in senso lato richiesti ai materiali geologici per l'opportuno impiego.

Fonti e pozzi sacri possono essere definiti come murature speciali, nelle quali sono presenti conci sbozzati e lavorati non solo sulla faccia a vista, ma anche sulle altre, modellate secondo forme e dimensioni variabili nell'ambito della stessa costruzione. Dall'esame dei monumenti emerge un dato interessante: la costante presenza di conci di basalto[1] opportunamente lavorati e di medie dimensioni. La varietà litoide comunemente utilizzata si presenta fornita di ridotto peso di volume[2] fino a 1/3-1/4 in meno rispetto ai valori normalmente riscontrabili (circa 3 grammi a cmc) il motivo è riconducibile alla struttura vacuolare del litotipo in oggetto, cioè la massa rocciosa è interessata da una fitta rete di cavità di diametro da 1 cm a 5 cm, distribuite in maniera omogenea. Questa varietà di basalto, definibile come bolloso-scoriaceo, si rinviene sui livelli più superficiali delle colate, dovuto alla rapida e turbolenta degassificazione della lava; lo spessore di questi livelli particolari è assai variabile e può arrivare fino ad alcuni metri. Nello stesso tempo si mantengono elevate le caratteristiche di resistenza a sollecitazioni meccaniche,[3] necessarie in strutture sviluppatesi in senso verticale, talvolta aggettanti e con spinte laterali e dal basso sia litostatiche che idrostatiche. Il materiale basaltico si presenta altresì a ridotta o nulla capacità d'imbibizione,[4]

---

1 Roccia ignea effusiva del ciclo plio-quaternario, presente in Sardegna sotto forma di altopiani, denominati 'Giare' nel settore centrale, 'Gollei' nella zona del golfo di Orosei: si presenta compatto, oppure vacuolare a struttura porfirica o vitrofirica, fessurato in affioramento con sistemi regolari che individuano prismi o parallelepipedi.

2 Peso dell'unità di volume della roccia (gr/cmc) completamente essicata: quanto meno la roccia è compatta, ossia quanto più è fornita di interstizi, vuoti, cavità, tanto più è ridotto il peso di volume: es. granito 2,55/2,85; basalto compatto 2,75/3,10; tufi vulcanici 1,80/2,00; gneiss 2,65/2,90.

3 Resistenza che la roccia oppone a forze esterne che tendono a romperla per schiacciamento, per urto, per trazione, per flessione, per usura. I valori di resistenza variano a seconda delle direzioni lungo le quali vengono esercitate: i valori di resistenza a trazione e flessione sono molto più bassi di quelli che esprimono la resistenza a compressione, variando da 1:15-1:40. Resistenza alla compressione (kg/cmc): granito 1600-2400, basalto 2500-4000, tufi 200-300, gneiss 1600-2800.

4 Capacità d'imbibizione: attitudine della roccia di

durevole[5] e a facile lavorabilità. Quest'ultima proprietà, corrispondente in parte con la divisibilità per fessurazione, dovuta al raffreddamento della lava, giustifica la relativa facilità di approvvigionamento di blocchi o di parallelepipedi o di prismi, presenti in fronti di colate e bordi di altopiano. Questi siti sono eccellenti fonti di materiale roccioso dell'idonea varietà e si presentano località adatte per l'imposta di piccole cave.

L'ulteriore lavorazione del concio, mediante operazioni manuali tendenti a ridurlo alle forme e dimensioni volute, era facilitata dalla tessitura isotropa ed omogenea della componente microcristallina e vetrosa. Elementi di copertura, rivestimenti, pavimentazioni, sono costituiti da rocce divisibili in lastre, leggere, impermeabili e durevoli, requisiti presenti in alcune rocce metamorfiche come filladi, gneiss micacei, micacisti etc. a spiccata tessitura orientata. Nel caso di conci scolpiti o incisi, si rinvengono litotipi a struttura minuta ed uniforme, come alcuni tufi.[6]

Elementi particolari delle costruzioni come architravi, scalini, canalette, presentano di volta in volta caratteristiche litologiche autonome in base all'utilizzo cui erano destinati: le canalette si rinvengono in roccia vulcanica (tufo o lave acide), metamorfiche (steatite e filladi), nelle quali prevalevano evidentemente le proprietà di facile lavorabilità, dovute alla bassa durezza dei singoli costituenti cristallini della roccia, alla tessitura isotropa e struttura omogenea. Il passaggio all'utilizzo di blocchi naturali a conci squadrati, spesso incisi e scolpiti, segna due momenti della civiltà nuragica, non necessariamente separati temporalmente, ma anche compenetrati in senso orizzontale, tali da rappresentare variazioni di facies culturali contemporanee.

Tavola 1
Materiali da Costruzione dei Monumenti Nuragici

Toponimo	Comune I.G.M.	Coordinate Geografiche*	Quota s.l.m.	Litologia dell'Area	Materiali Principali e Secondari	Distanza dei Probabili Punti di Cava
Abini	Teti 207 III NE	Lat. N 40° 08' 43" Long. W ° 21' 58"	300	Granito	Granito e Trachite	Lave trachitiche 5-8 km
Santu Millanu	Nuragus 218 III NO	Lat. N 39° 46' 31" Long. W 3° 23' 35"	370	Calcari	Basalto	Basalto 5-6 km
Noddule	Nuoro 194 II SO	Lat. N 40° 22' 29" Long. W 3° 09' 57"	680	Granito	Granito e Trachite	Lave trachitiche 8-13 km
Su Lidone	Orune 194 II SE	Lat. N 40° 24' 12" Long. W 3° 02' 16"	405	Gneiss e	Basalto Filladi	Basalto 10-14 km
Su Tempiesu	Orune 194 II SE	Lat. N 40° 24' 38" Long. W 3° 02' 22"	300	Gneiss e	Basalto—Scisto Filladi	Basalto 10-14 km Filladi
Nurdole	Orani 194 II SO	Lat. N 40° 20' 06" Long. W 3° 14' 19"	687	Granito	Granito e Tufi	Tufi vari colori 3-6 km
Gremanu	Fonni	Lat. N 40° 06' 26" Long. W 3° 06' 47"	950	Granito	Basalto Tufi Filladi	Basalto 25-30 km Filladi Tufi 23-30 km
Funtana 'e Deu	Lula Calcari	Lat. N 40° 30' 38" Long. W 2° 53' 32"	575	Gneiss-	Dolomie-Trachite Dolomie	Trachite 30 km

* Rispetto a Monte Mario (Roma)

---

assorbire acqua, si misura mediante la relazione: peso roccia umida meno peso roccia secca, diviso peso roccia secca.

5 Durevole: si dice di una roccia resistente all'alterazione da parte degli agenti fisico-chimici.

6 Tufo: roccia effusiva, caratteristica di un vulcanismo di tipo esplosivo a prevalente chimismo acido, presente in bancate nei sistemi vulcanici terziari della Sardegna.

Bibliografia

Contu, E.
- 1974 La Sardegna dell'età nuragica. *Popoli e Civiltà dell'Italia Antica.*

Davoli, G.
- 1950 Saggio di Catalogo Archeologico, Foglio 194 I.G.M. Tesi di Laurea, Anno Accademico 1949-50.

Desio, A.
- 1989 *Geologia Applicata all'Ingegneria.* Milano: HOEPLI.

Fadda, M.A.
- 1982 Il tempio a pozzo di Su Tempiesu (Orune, Nuoro). *Rivista di Scienze Preistoriche* 36: 284ss.
- 1985 Il tempio a pozzo di Su Tempiesu—Orune (Nu). In E. Arslan, F. Barreca e F. Lo Schiavo (eds.), *Civiltà Nuragica,* 208. Milano: Electa.
- 1986 Il complesso nuragico di Nurdole (Orani, Nuoro). *Nuovo Bullettino Archeologico Sardo* 3: 308-14.
- 1988 *La Fonte Sacra di Su Tempiesu.* Guide ed Itinerari della Sardegna 8: 13-31. Sassari: Carlo Delfino Editore.
- 1990 Orani (NU), loc. Nurdole. Il nuraghe santuario. *Bollettino di Archeologia del Ministero per i Beni Culturali e Ambientali* 1/2 (Gennaio-Aprile): 260.
- in stampa Il complesso di fonti di Gremanu (Fonni, NU). *Bollettino di Archeologia del Ministero per i Beni Culturali e Ambientali.*

Fadda, M., & M. Madau
- in stampa Un tempio nuragico in Barbagia, punto di incontro di grandi civiltà. *Rivista di Studi Fenici.*

Ippolito, F., P. Nicotero, P. Lucini, M. Civita & R. De Rita
- 1975 *Geologia Tecnica.* Torino: ISEDI.

Lilliu, G.
- 1958 Nuovi templi a pozzo della Sardegna nuragica. *Studi Sardi* XIV-XV(1955-1957)Parte I: 197-288.
- 1982 *La Civiltà Nuragica.* Sardegna Archaeologica: Studi e Monumenti 1. Sassari: Carlo Delfino.

Murru, G.
- 1990 Proposta di indagine sui materiali da costruzione dei monumenti archeologici. *Geologia Tecnica—Rivista Trimestrale O.N.G.* (Roma) 1/90: 23-28.

Taramelli, A.
- 1913a Nuragus. Statuetta in bronzo di età preromana, rappresentante una sacerdotessa, rinvenuta in regione Coni o Santu Millanu. *Notizie degli Scavi* 1913: 167.
- 1913b Nuragus. Pozzo votivo di età preromana, scoperto in regione Coni o Santu Millanu. *Notizie degli Scavi* 1913: 275.
- 1919 Orune, fonte sacra in regione S. Lulla e pozzo sacro in regiona Lorana. *Notizie degli Scavi* 1919: 120-26.
- 1931 Teti. Esplorazione del santuario nuragico di Abini. *Monumenti Antichi* 34.

Summary

The building materials used in the construction of Nuragic cultic architecture are identified and compared with those used in domestic structures. Eight sacred wells (Coni o Santu Milanu di Nuragus), springs (Noddule, Su Lidone di Orune, Su Tempiesu di Orune, Gremanu di Fonni, Funtana 'e Deu di Lula), and sanctuaries (Abini-Teti, Nurdole di Orani) in the province of Nuoro all utilized building materials brought from 3 to 30 km away.

The sanctuary of Abini (Teti), located within a Nuragic village built of granite, was originally covered by a tholos dome, of which some blocks of worked trachyte still remain. The exclusive religious use of the spring is attested by the hundreds of votive bronze objects found there. Trachytic lavas occur some 5-8 km from Abini.

The Coni o Santu Millanu (Nuragus) well is located on a bed of limestone, but is constructed of well-worked basalt. Five steps and several courses of the tholos remain, and a bronze figurine was found there. The dromos in front of the stairs is constructed of local limestone, while the basalt for the well must have come from 5-6 km away.

The spring at Noddule (NU), located a few hundred meters from the nuraghe, has a cylindrical-shaped well which is covered by a tholos. The well itself is constructed of worked blocks of trachyte originating 8-13 km away, while the other parts of the complex are made of local granites. The Nuragic well of Su Lidone (Orune) is also constructed of basalts transported 10-14 km.

The well-preserved sacred well-temple of Su Tempiesu (Orune), where a number of votive bronzes have been recovered, consists of a large structure with a vestibule in front of the tholos chamber, and a smaller well under the surrounding stone wall. The vestibule is paved with perfectly-fitting slabs of trachyte, while part of the roof is made of local schist. Much of the temple itself is of basalt, from 10-14 km away. The channel running from the main well to the small well is carved out of basalt and terminates in a steatite spout.

The Nuragic complex of Nurdole (Orani) was transformed into a cult place in the Late Bronze Age. In the courtyard next to the nuraghe is a wall of squared trachyte blocks which serves as the entry to the spring. Parts of the cupola remain, also in trachyte, and a channel runs to a large rectangular basin of tufa and trachyte. A great number of votive bronzes attest to the importance of this sanctuary. The tufa is found in various colors 3-6 km from Nurdole.

Gremanu di Fonni features a series of Nuragic springs connected by an acqueduct and flowing into a basin in a rectangular room. Parts of the spring and its tholos, the water channel, and the basin in the rectangular room are made of basalt occurring some 25-30 km from Fonni. Local schists and granites are also used in the complex, while the basin is paved with slabs of tufa brought from 23-30 km away. Numerous bases for offerings show that the site was used for religious rites.

The spring Funtana 'e Deu di Lula is actually part of a complex of springs mostly destroyed by clandestine activity. A surrounding wall is constructed of local limestone. The spring itself is constructed of trachyte blocks brought from 30 km away.

The selection of lavic rocks for religious architecture may be due in part to criteria such as durability and workability. The use of basalt in particular must be due to the recognition of its superior mechanical properties, specifically its density, strength, absorption of water, and resistance to wear. It is suggested that the use of non-local materials enhanced the importance or significance of these structures, while the transport of building materials over great distances demonstrates a notable economic effort. Finally, the presence of these monuments in the Nuorese and Barbaricino regions suggests that these zones were culturally and economically equal to less remote parts of Sardinia.

Phoenician Echoes in a Nuragic Building

Barbro Santillo Frizell

> Tyre, you used to say: I am a ship perfect in beauty. Your frontiers stretched far out to sea; those who built you made you perfect in beauty. Cypress from Senhir they used for all your planking. They took a cedar from Lebanon to make you a mast. From the tallest oaks of Bashan they made your oars (Ezekiel 27).

In this article I intend to raise a question which I have asked myself several times during my study of Nuragic architecture, namely, if certain distinctive features in some buildings could be related to the Phoenician presence on the island.

As I have argued elsewhere (Santillo Frizell 1989), I do not accept the idea of a Mycenaean influence on Nuragic architecture, seen by some scholars particularly in the evolution of domes in the nuraghi and the sacred wells. Nuragic architecture should not be understood as a result of diffusion, that is, the spreading of a building type, or constructional features, or certain architectural elements from one culture to another in diverse geographical areas; instead it should be perceived in its entirety as a wholly Sardinian creation. This, however, does not necessarily imply that the buildings were untouched by developments or innovations caused by external factors; in Sardinia, as elsewhere, interactions generated new interests, inciting mutual responses. Foreign influence on indigenous architecture could be the result or consequence of interaction and/or acculturation, affecting an architecture based on a construction technique which was already mature and consolidated before the peoples in question came into contact.

Interaction in architecture, which one would expect in buildings with a military function such as the complex nuraghi, does not necessarily require a permanent presence of intrusive people on the island; it could also be a response to repeated aggression from people living outside the area. This response then promotes innovations born of a new necessity. Mycenaean contacts as well as the earliest Phoenician presence on Sardinia were of a commercial nature and concentrated on the coast where the good harbors are located. It is against this background that we should try to understand some specific structural developments of the complex Nuragic bastions.

Acculturation as reflected in architectural construction is, however, quite a different matter. Acculturation intended as the acquisition of material goods can be a fairly rapid process, but still requires permanent habitation and/or continuous contact. Cognitive acculturation, however, is an extended process and is a consequence of a more enduring presence which slowly penetrates into the individual and collective mind. In Sardinia this latter process first becomes explicit with Phoenician colonization. In the following discussion I will explore this phenomenon in the field of architecture and attempt to relate certain remarkable features of Nuragic architecture to Phoenician culture and mentality.

Since little is known of Phoenician architecture from its homeland, in order to understand the nature of Phoenician influence on Nuragic building we must first look at other, indirect evidence. From the Biblical account of the construction of the temple and palace of King Solomon we learn that the Phoenicians were skilled in building, carpentry, and furnishing (1 Kings). But they were also a seafaring people with highly developed skills in shipbuilding and related crafts, such as rope, sail, and tent-making, of which little is left in the archaeological record due to the rapid decomposition of these organic artifacts. We can also cite their reputation for the production and export of textiles, which is well documented in literary sources such as the Bible (Ezek. 27.27) and the Homeric epics (*Iliad* 6: 285-305). Phoenician textile production, although we have no material remains, may well be reflected in ceramic decorations of the Greek Orientalizing period (Murray 1980: 82-84). If so, we have here a reflection, an echo, of an important craft, direct evidence of which is now lost to us, that exerted a profound influence on other crafts in different media. I think we can see this same principle at work in another form of material culture in a remarkable piece of Nuragic architecture, namely the sacred well of Santa Cristina at Paulilatino.

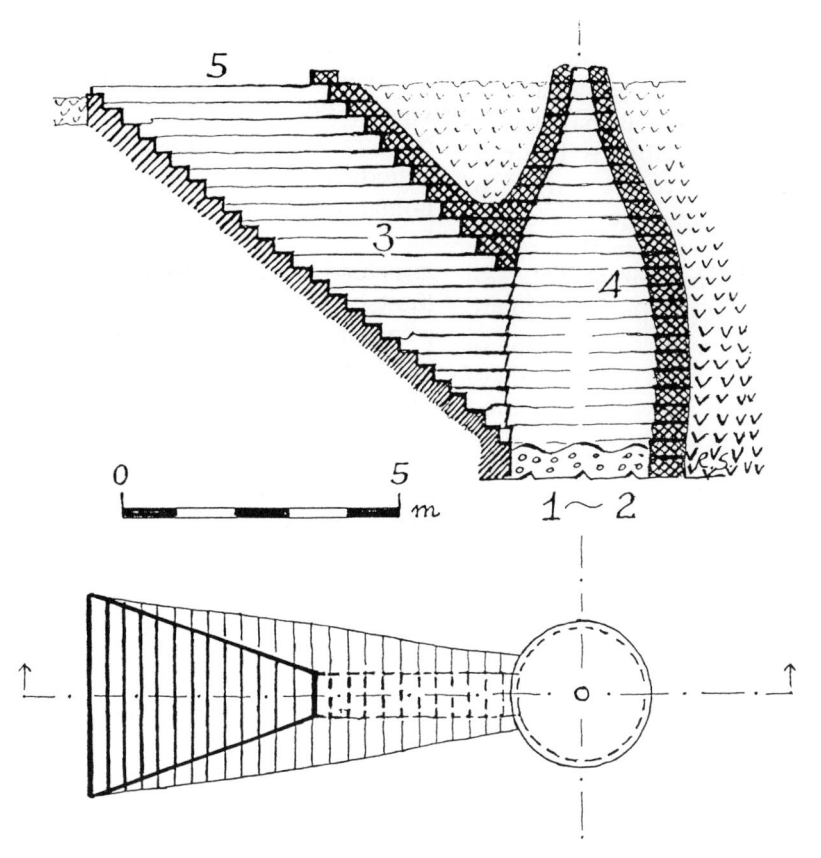

Fig. 1 Sketch plan and axial section of the sacred well of Santa Cristina at Paulilatino.

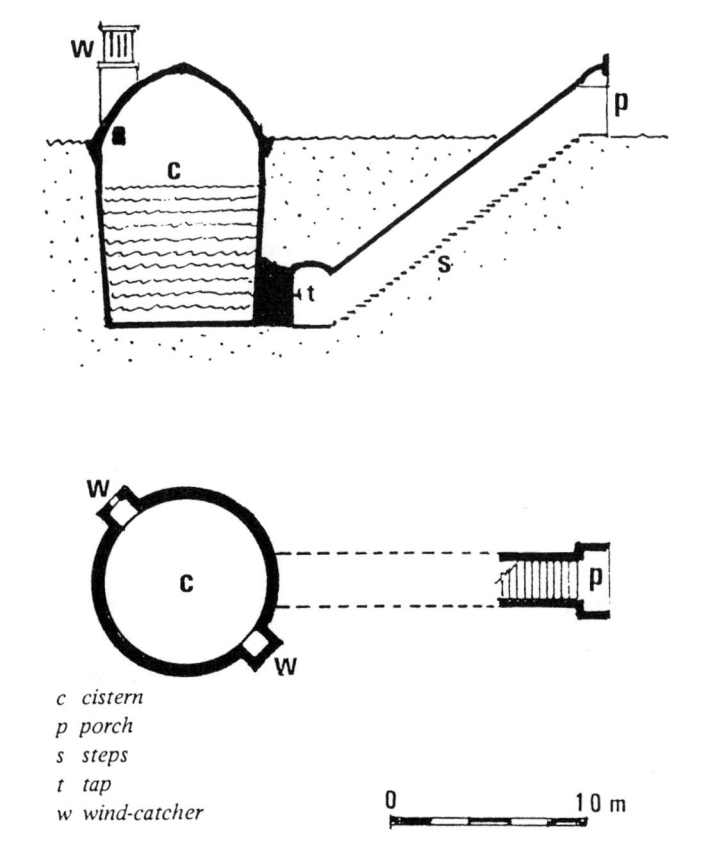

c cistern
p porch
s steps
t tap
w wind-catcher

Fig. 2 Iranian water cistern (after Beazley and Harverson 1982: 41).

The Sacred Well

After the nuraghe, the most important type of indigenous architecture in Nuragic Sardinia is the so-called sacred well. About 50 have been identified so far, but this number is likely to increase greatly given the prolific nature of archaeology in Sardinia today. The origin and development of this structure, like that of the nuraghi, should be considered indigenous and understood in that context (Santillo Frizell 1989). In its fundamental conception the construction of the well is purely utilitarian, being an evolution of wells with a cylindrical shaft, a type that existed in many cultures long before the Sardinian examples. The sacred well can be described as consisting of five main parts (Fig. 1):

1. well for picking up water;
2. shaft for collecting and storing water;
3. *dromos*, which consists of the covered ramp with stairs leading down to the bottom of the water chamber;
4. dome, which, binding the parts together into an organic entity, has the primary multiple function of protecting the water from dirt, from animals falling in and of reducing evaporation;
5. porch, often built in front of the *dromos*, and which in some cases became subject to elaborate architectural decoration.

The development of this type of building into cult places is not surprising considering the scarcity of water in Sardinia; the sacred connotation of fresh water sources of any kind must have been primordial. This is a common phenomenon in ancient societies, and in the Mediterranean even today many ancient cult places are named after saints, as are many of the Nuragic well sanctuaries (e.g. Santa Vittoria, Santa Cristina, Sant'Anastasia).

Similar systems for water collecting have been invented by peoples living in analogous conditions. In modern-day Iran similar constructions are built and still used, fed by water from *qanats*, man-made underground water tunnels with a long tradition, stretching back at least to the time of ancient Persia and presumably earlier (Beazley and Harverson 1982: 34-39). The structural and functional typology of the cisterns shows striking similarities to the Sardinian wells (Fig. 2).

It is understood that environmental and economic conditions combined with the inventive capacity of local artisans create the prime mechanism for similar responses in the creative human mind, and that these factors are independent of time and space. Variations appear, as is obvious, in the finishing process, and in the execution of details which reflect the artistic sensibilities of a culture. In this context the Iranian well example is very interesting. Some of its primarily functional aspects differ from those of the Sardinian wells. It collects water not from a spring but from an aqueduct and is in that respect closer to the Roman *castellum*. But its architectural features have more in common with the Sardinian buildings. The harsh environmental conditions in both these countries have, in each case, brought these primarily utilitarian edifices into the sphere of ritual and cult by creating an additional architectural element: a porch. Beazley and Harverson (1982: 41), in their book on Iranian buildings in the desert, make the following perceptive comment: 'This porch is reminiscent of an *aiwan* in a mosque; both share a sense of sanctity and sanctuary'.

Santa Cristina at Paulilatino

The Nuragic sanctuary at Santa Cristina (Paulilatino) was excavated and partly restored in the 1960s but still awaits final publication. Consequently, it is difficult to determine the chronology of the building since most of the data are not available; but its dating has provoked conflicting opinions among scholars. The four bronze figurines, clearly of Phoenician origin, found on the stairs of the *dromos*, are very important for the dating of the sacred well (Barreca 1985: 316). The dating of these bronze figurines, however, varies from the Late Bronze Age, 12th–9th centuries BC (Santoni 1985: 199) to the Iron Age, 9th–8th centuries BC (Tore 1983). Since the main issue here is to establish possible examples of acculturation reflected in the architecture, it is the context of these figurines, rather than their exact chronology, which is significant for this discussion.

The figurines represent Phoenician divinities and at least one is a goddess identified as a possible representation of Astarte (Tore 1983). It is the figurines' *ex-voto* function and their relation to the building which is important for this discussion, specifically the appearance of Phoenician cult-related objects in this Nuragic sanctuary.

Photographs of the sacred well of Santa Cristina appear in all general books and publications on Nuragic architecture and society, but no drawings are available except for a sketch of the plan and section by Spano which was made already in the middle of the last century (Lilliu 1958: tav. XII). This is an important piece of information showing its state of preservation

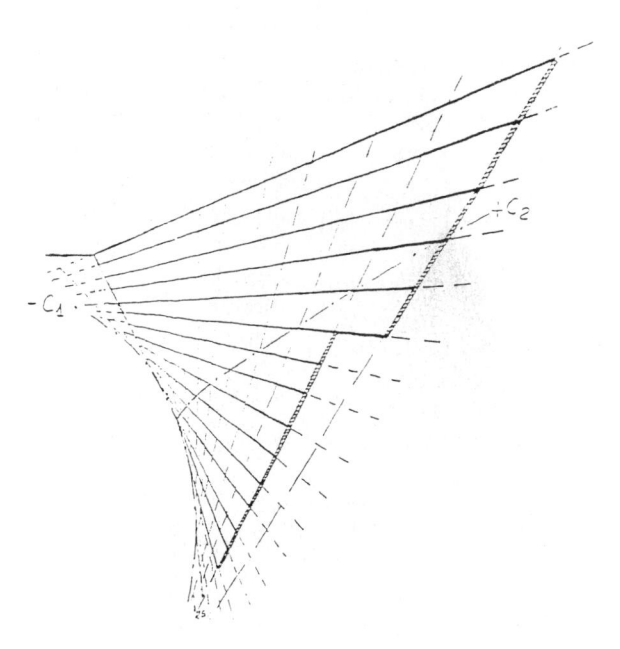

Fig. 3 The geometric net of a generic sector of hypar. Turning the page all around, circa 90 degrees each time, one easily recognizes forms appearing in modern architecture.

Fig. 4 The northern *dromos* wall seen from the bottom of the stairs.

266 *Sardinia in the Mediterranean*

Fig. 5 The twisting of the *dromos* walls visible by the fan-like net on the left and the curved zig-zag shadow on the right.

Fig. 6 Exterior of the well embodying the sign of Tanit. Compare the abstract proportions of the metrical plan (Fig. 1) with the real perspective view (projective)

before the restoration work. Its formal and exceptional beauty is usually remarked upon—but what are the features that impress and fascinate the visitor so profoundly?

There are two specific features in the geometrical configuration of the internal space which call for attention. The first is the shape of the facing walls of the *dromos* leading down to the well: they consist of two twisted (fan-like) surfaces (Fig. 3), in technical terms known as sectors of hypar (Santillo 1992). This geometric property, a subchapter within the discipline of differential geometry, would tell us archaeologists little, were it not for its appearance in another type of construction, namely ships. This geometric configuration resembles that of the sheathing of a ship's hull. This feature is clearly not the fortuitous result of a mistake made during construction; neither is it to due to any secondary causes such as the shifting or movement of the ground. It was intentional, the result of a premeditated design. Both the creative imagination and the practical execution reflected in these walls belong to the skills of the craft of shipbuilding (Figs. 4-5). The plots and templates devised for the general layout, the tracing of the stone profiles, and the geometrical vision behind them are typical of this professional art. That craftsmen who specialized in shipbuilding should also be involved in building structures other than boats was not a unique situation in this period; on the contrary, it may have been rather common during antiquity. A well-known example is the construction of the roofing system of the Roman Colosseum by part of the fleet of Misenum, stationed in Rome for that purpose. Moreover, even today the craftsmanship of naval architecture is called for in certain refinements of building in concrete (Santillo 1992).

The second remarkable feature in the geometry of the building is clearly visible in the plan drawing of the hopper-shaped *dromos* (Figs. 1 and 6). Here the standard key-hole shape which normally occurs in other sacred wells is turned into a very clear trapeziform or triangular configuration which, together with the circular top hole of the dome, shows a striking similarity to the Phoenician sign of Tanit (Figs. 7 and 8a-b).

The symbol of Tanit is usually depicted as a triangle topped by a disk separated by a horizontal cross-bar. There are, however, many variations of this symbol: sometimes the cross-bar is turned into raised arms, while in other cases it is completely omitted (Fig. 7). I believe that the visual similarity between the sign of Tanit and the Santa Cristina well structure is not fortuitous, but that it has been consciously incorporated into the geometry of the building and thus has a specific

Fig. 7 'Sign of Tanit' depicted on stelae (after Bisi 1967: fig. 7).

reason for being there. One might object that this configuration, which is clearly visible from above in the present state of conservation, especially from an air photograph, is difficult to perceive standing on the ground. This, however, does not seem to be the case; on the contrary, looking into the *dromos*, its anomalous shape is emphasized as a result of viewing it from a distance. The perspective effect shortens the object so that the increasing visual distance gradually makes the shorter base of the trapeziform *dromos* appear even shorter in relation to the longer base facing the observer, thus increasing the convergence of the sides of the key-hole and accentuating still more the 'Tanit-effect'.

Tanit

In the absence of archaeological evidence from the Phoenician homeland, it has long been believed that the goddess Tanit originated in the Phoenician settlements of North Africa, since representations, inscriptions and the Tanit design had been found only in the western Mediterranean area and not in the east. In the last 20 years, however, the symbol of Tanit has been identified in several find contexts, appearing in various

Fig. 8a-b Ship and Tanit on stelae (after Bartoloni 1979).

media, including glass (Pritchard 1978) and terracotta (Dothan 1974), and on figurines (Linder 1973) along the Syro-Palestinian coast. The first inscription from the Phoenician homeland where the name of the goddess Tanit occurs connected with Astarte was found at the harbor town of Sarepta. This find not only proves an eastern origin for Tanit, but also indicates a much earlier date than previously thought, the excavator having attributed it to the 7th century (Pritchard 1982). However, even prior to the appearance of these finds which explicitly mention or depict Tanit, Yadin (1970) had already proposed the presence of the goddess at Hazor as early as the 14th or 13th centuries BC.

The evidence suggests, therefore, that on Sardinia we are seeing the importation of a Phoenician cult into a Nuragic sanctuary, namely a Phoenician cult of Tanit or perhaps Tanit–Astarte since there seems to have been a syncretism of the two goddesses at an early stage in their Phoenician homeland (Carter 1987: 373). That Tanit was associated with the sea is clear from the numerous marine symbols connected with her: on the many stelae and figurines from the Shave-Ziyyon ship-wreck she is represented with the dolphin, a symbol which also occurs on Carthaginian stelae. On the latter, ships are frequently depicted together with the symbol of Tanit (Figs. 8a-b).

It is the interweaving of both these features, ships and Tanit, that makes this Nuragic sanctuary so distinctive and not only gives it an artistic quality superior to the other known sacred wells, but also invites us to reflect on the meaning expressed through its forms.

The Significance of the Symbols

If my interpretation is correct, we have a foreign element, due to Phoenician craftsmen, integrated architecturally into a building which is purely Nuragic in origin.

As Barreca (1981) has pointed out, the Phoenician contribution to Nuragic society is most evident in the religious sphere. He also observed some Phoenician influence in military architecture, as in the Nuraghe Losa (Barreca 1983), and I think that further studies in this field would probably reveal more evidence of this phenomenon. Phoenician influence is particularly evident in house building, as in the domestic quarters at Barumini and Santa Vittoria. But it is Nuragic religious architecture, especially the sacred wells, that seems to have been of particular interest to the Phoenicians, probably because these sanctuaries echoed the Phoenicians' own religious response to water as a sacred element. Similar phenomena of religious acculturation in Nuragic sacred wells has been observed at Sardara, in the sanctuary of Sant'Anastasia, where a lustral basin for ritual ablutions was placed outside the ramp leading down to the well. The same phenomenon is seen at the hypogeum of San Salvatore at Cabras, which was constructed above a Nuragic sacred well. The placement of a lustral basin is significant since it was an element foreign to Nuragic cult but always present in Semitic ritual (Barreca 1981).

What does Santa Cristina tells us? How should we interpret the intervention of Phoenician architects at Paulilatino? And what is the message conveyed by these phenomena? Such questions are, of course, completely open to speculation. Here I have tried to make the point that there is a deliberately expressed symbolic meaning embedded in the design and finishing of these buildings. There are several examples of Phoenician influence and presence in religious contexts, not only in Sardinia, but also in other contemporary cultures in the Mediterranean such as the Phoenician tri-pillar shrine at Kommos in southern Crete (Shaw 1989) which, however, is purely Semitic in origin. The sanctuary of Santa Cristina at Paulilatino apparently has no parallels in the east since the situation on Sardinia is completely different. The craftsmen engaged in this building project had to work in the indigenous Nuragic tradition, which must have been a challenge for them since sacred wells are complex edifices. Did the Phoenicians at this early stage of colonization bring architects or master-builders (as we use the word today) with them? This is something that we cannot know with certainty, although I think it is unlikely. What we do know is that they brought with them craftsmen, highly specialized and skilled in shipbuilding, for maintenance and repair work and the building of new ships if necessary. It should not have been a problem for them to transfer their shipbuilding and designing skills from wood to stone when the need arose. To hire skilled local craftsmen to quarry and cut the stone in Sardinia was surely no problem.

In conclusion, I interpret the evidence at Paulilatino as a deliberate transmission of symbolic meaning reflecting aspects of Phoenician civilization in a more durable material than wood. This was performed through the architectural incorporation of symbols important to them, the ship and the sign of the goddess Tanit, in the sacred well at Santa Cristina. This integration, and the continuity of the religious importance of water, gives this unique piece of Nuragic architecture a new dimension.

Acknowledgments

My warm thanks to the 'Fondazione Famiglia Rausing' for a travel grant covering part of the expenses of the preparative field work in Sardinia. The drawings in Figs. 1, 3, and 8a have been prepared by Raffaele Santillo who also took the photographs for Figs. 4-6.

References

Barreca, F.
    1981   La Sardegna e i Fenicia. In E. Atzeni *et al.* (eds.), *Ichnussa. La Sardegna dalle origini all'età classica*, Milano: Libri Scheiwiller.
    1983   L'archeologia fenicio-punica in Sardegna. Un decennio di attività. In *Atti del I Congresso Internazionale di Studi Fenici e Punici, Roma, 5-10 novembre 1979*. Rome: C.N.R.
    1985   Sardegna nuragica e mondo fenicio-punico. In E. Arslan, F. Barreca and F. Lo Schiavo (eds.), *Civiltà Nuragica*, 308-28. Milano: Electa.

Bartoloni, P.
    1979   Le figurazioni di carattere marino rappresentate sulle più tarde stele di Cartagine. II. Le imbarcazioni minore. *Rivista di Studi Fenici* 7.

Beazley, E., & M. Harverson
    1982   *Living with the Desert. Working Buildings of the Iranian Plateau*. Warminster.

Bisi, A.M.
    1967   Le stele puniche. *Studi Semitici* 27.

Carter, J.B.
    1987   The masks of Ortheia. *American Journal of Archaeology* 91(3): 355-84.

Dothan, M.
    1974   A sign of Tanit from Tel 'Akko'. *Israel Exploration Journal* 24: 44-49.

Lilliu, G.
    1958   Nuovi templi a pozzo della Sardegna nuragica. *Studi Sardi* 14-15(1955–1957)Parte I: 197-288.

Linder, E.
    1973   A cargo of Phoenician-Punic figurines. *Archaeology* 26: 182-87.

Murray, O.
    1980   *Early Greece*. Brighton: Harvester Press.

Pritchard, J.B.
    1978   *Recovering Sarepta, a Phoenician City*. Princeton: Princeton University Press.
    1982   The Tanit inscription from Sarepta. In H.G. Niemeyer (ed.), *Phönizier im Westen. Die Beiträge des Internationalen Symposiums uber 'Die Phönizische Expansion im Westlichen Mittelmeerraum' in Koln vom 24. bis 27. April 1979*, 83-92. Madrider Beiträge 8. Mainz am Rhein: Verlag Philipp von Zabern.

Santillo, R.
    1992   Hyperbolic paraboloids and conoids in prehistoric Sardinia. *Edilizia Militare*. Corps of Engineers Review. Forthcoming.

Santillo Frizell, B.
    1989   The autonomous development of dry masonry domes in the Mediterranean area. Some considerations. *Opuscula Romana* 17(11): 143-61.

Santoni, V.
    1985   I templi di età nuragica. In E. Arslan, F. Barreca and F. Lo Schiavo (eds.), *Civiltà Nuragica*, 181-207. Milano: Electa.

Shaw, J.W.
    1989   Phoenicians in Southern Crete. *American Journal of Archaeology* 93: 165-83.

Tore, G.
1983 I bronzi figurati fenicio-punici in Sardegna. *Atti del I Congresso Internazionale di Studi Fenici e Punici, Roma, 5-10 novembre 1979.* Vol. II: 449-61.

Yadin, Y.
1970 Symbols of deities at Zinjirli, Carthage and Hazor. In J.A. Sanders (ed.), *Near Eastern Archaeology in the Twentieth Century. Essays in Honor of Nelson Glueck*, 199-224. New York.

Riassunto

L'Autrice si domanda se la presenza di certi caratteri distintivi del pozzo sacro di Santa Cristina (Paulilatino) può essere riferita alla presenza fenicia in Sardegna. Il pozzo mostra alcuni elementi di forma geometrica che indicano l'intervento di architetti estranei all'architettura nuragica, ma che sono invece esperti nella costruzione di navi. L'Autrice propone l'ipotesi secondo la quale questa può essere la conseguenza di un'acculturazione operata dai dominatori fenici a Paulilatino. Secondo questa ipotesi i colonizzatori avrebbero incorporato aspetti della loro religione riguardo all'acqua, nel simbolismo strutturale del pozzo di Santa Cristina.

Dopo il nuraghe, il pozzo sacro nuragico è il più importante esempio di architettura indigena. La sua struttura fondamentale è divisibile in cinque parti: il fondo con la sorgente, il fusto, il *dromos*, la cupola, e il portico. Il pozzo è stato costruito per scopi utilitari, ma il fatto che esso sia diventato un luogo sacro è dovuto al fatto che la fonte di acqua fresca ha delle connotazioni sacre. Questo è un fenomeno diffuso nel Mediterraneo nelle zone fenici come in Sardegna.

Quando nel 1960 il santuario nuragico di Santa Cristina è stato scoperto, nel *dromos* sono state ritrovate quattro statuine di bronzo *ex-voto* fenicie. Sembra che ognuna di esse rappresenti una divinità, e almeno una di queste potrebbe essere la dea Astarte. Com'è possibile che oggetti di culto fenicio siano stati ritrovati in un santuario nuragico? Per rispondere a questa domanda l'Autrice esamina la geometria dell'interno del santuario. All'interno del *dromos*, i due muri opposti sono intrecciati, sono strutture a forma di ventaglio chiamate settori di paraboloide iperbolico. Lo stesso tipo di configurazione è usato per fasciare l'intelaiatura di una nave. Il progetto di questa difficile costruzione, il tracciamento dei suoi profili di pietra e la visione geometrica dietro l'architettura, sono intenzionali. Un'altra caratteristica insolita è la forma dell'entrata del *dromos*. Qui la forma di buco di chiave è stata sostituita da una forma trapezoidale che, con il buco circolare della cupola, forma uno dei simboli della dea fenicia Tanit. Questa forma insolita, è enfatizzata se si guarda nel *dromos* in lontananza, cosicché la prospettiva accorcia la base stretta del trapezio in relazione alle base lunga. Nel pantheon fenicio Tanit è associata con Astarte e con il mare. I suoi simboli includono conchiglie, delfini e navi. Per questo motivo in Santa Cristina assistiamo all'intervento di costruttori fenici di navi che hanno adornato il pozzo con simboli rappresentanti le navi che li hanno portati in Sardegna e Tanit che li ha protetti durante il viaggio. Questa analisi conferma ciò che ha detto Barreca, ossia che il contributo fenicio alla società nuragica è stato notevole soprattutto nella sfera religiosa. In Sardegna questo può essere visto più chiaramente nella risposta fenicia al pozzo sacro nuragico.

A Temporal Analysis of the Ceramic Industry at Duos Nuraghes: A Step toward Chronology

Aviva Weiss Grele

Introduction

As the oldest continuously occupied nuraghe settlement presently under investigation on Sardinia (Webster 1988: 465-72), Duos Nuraghes provides a unique opportunity to study Nuragic village formation processes over the entire known history of this culture and to shed new light on the evolution of Nuragic civilization. One of the obstructions encountered in the investigation of these questions at Duos Nuraghes and other Nuragic sites is the lack of a well-established ceramic chronology (Webster *et al.* 1987: 46; Balmuth 1984: 23). In the absence of such a chronology it is often difficult to interpret the stratigraphy at a site. Problems such as vertical mixing, and the 'curse of the *terminus post quem*' in dating by imports, are familiar to the Sardinian archaeologist.

This paper initiates an evaluation of temporal variation in the Nuragic ceramic record for the Late Eneolithic through Roman periods (c. 2300 BC–456 AD) based on the analysis of 1396 diagnostic sherds from the well-stratified and well-dated contexts of Nuraghe Tower A at Duos Nuraghes. Apart from its utility in dating architectural features, both at this site and at others within the Borore polity, the establishment of a chronologically controlled ceramic sequence would also provide the necessary framework for analyzing patterns of territoriality, social and political organization, and trade/exchange based upon the analysis of the distribution of pottery types on the island during specific periods. Such inquiries are currently areas of considerable debate among scholars of Sardinia.

Duos Nuraghes

The site of Duos Nuraghes occupies c. 4600 m^2 and is located on the NE edge of the small town of Borore in the province of Nuoro. It is one of a group of 40 nuraghe settlements in the Marghine plateau under investigation by the Pennsylvania State University's Sardinia Research Program (directed by Gary S. Webster). The site comprises the standing ruins of two tholos nuraghi surrounded by a small village of circular huts. Tower A, to the south, is a single-storey structure of simple-chamber design. It dates from the Late Eneolithic/Early Bronze Age (c. 2000–1800 BC) and was occupied virtually continuously up through Medieval times. Nuraghe Tower B, c. 10 m to the north, is a collapsed multi-storey structure with a complex-chamber design and dates from the Middle Bronze Age (c. 1500 BC). A stone circuit wall of Iron Age date (c. 900 BC) encloses the two nuraghi and the surrounding village of stone-walled huts which date from the Late Bronze Age (c. 1250 BC) (Webster 1988: 465-66).

The Ceramic Data Set

During the 1985, 1987 and 1988 excavation seasons some 29,800 ceramic sherds were recovered from the entire site. Of these sherds, a much smaller quantity identified as diagnostic sherds (i.e., lips, bases, handles, and decorated sherds) were classified according to fabric and vessel form attributes including paste, temper, surface treatment, decorative technique and motif, lip form, lip orientation, base form, and handle form as well as other traits. All of these attributes were then recorded, for each diagnostic sherd, as a series of 36 attribute codes, for later analysis by computer (see Webster *et al.* 1987 for further description of initial sherd classification criteria). This computer-based multiple attribute approach to pottery classification was chosen over more traditional methods because of its potential for great flexibility in generating detailed quantitative data in a variety of groupings permitting the data to be used in the investigation of a wide range of research problems.

The data presented here are based on the analysis of 1396 sherds from three trenches in

Nuraghe Tower A, excavated in 1985 and 1988. The reasons for this restriction are threefold: Nuraghe Tower A dates initially from an earlier period than Tower B, has four radiocarbon dates (Table 1), and was occupied almost continuously until Medieval times, thereby providing a more chronologically complete sample of the Nuragic ceramic record than material from other sections of the site.

The Research Problem and Research Technique

The primary research problem addressed in this paper is the identification and evaluation of temporal variation in the Nuragic ceramic record. In pursuing this goal individual ceramic attributes were investigated as well as groupings of attributes for temporal variation. Some of these groupings define major ceramic types at Duos Nuraghes and may be compared to findings for other nuraghi in the Borore aggregate (Webster *et al.* 1987: 45-68), while others are simple pairings and do not represent in themselves major ware groups. Since the primary interest here is temporal variation, the listing of ware groups identified through computer analysis has not been exhaustive. A comprehensive listing shall be the subject of future reports.

After the raw attribute data was entered into the computer, each sherd was given one of seven period designations (Table 1) based on its trench and stratigraphic level. These designations by period, rather than by level numbers, were used in all subsequent analyses, and served two functions: first, to make it possible to combine data from different trenches since the level dates were not equivalent across trenches; and secondly, to sharpen any temporal effect in the data since the total number of sherds was not very large.

Since the focus of interest was the indigenous Nuragic ceramic industry it was necessary to exclude imported or non-Nuragic wares from the analysis when possible. This was done by including only sherds which were hand-made rather than wheel-thrown, and resulted in the exclusion of 80 sherds from the working database. Although it is a common assumption that native Nuragic wares were hand-made, whereas imports to Sardinia were wheel-thrown or moulded, the possibility that Nuragic potters also made some use of the wheel cannot be discounted, especially in the later Punic and Roman periods. For the purposes of this preliminary study, however, it seems sufficient to exclude wheel-thrown and moulded wares as imports without concern over the potential exclusion of a rare example of a Nuragic wheel-thrown vessel.

The technique used in analysis of the data was cross-tabulation. Initially, single attributes were cross-tabulated to show changes in attribute frequency over time. In a cross-tabulation of temper against period, for example, the change in frequency of fine, medium and coarse-tempered sherds would be charted through time. In a later stage of analysis attributes were combined in pairs, and subsequently in related groups, which were used to define major ware fabrics and major vessel form 'types'. These 'types' were themselves cross-tabulated in order to demonstrate change in ware fabrics and vessel forms over time. It should be noted that the vessel types defined by this method have been related here, in a general way, to traditional Nuragic pottery typologies (cf. Table 7). It is a future goal of this project that these typologies should be related and compared in some detail so that the computer analysis could be more accessible and useful to a broad spectrum of scholars.

A Note about Limitations of the Data

The distribution of total numbers of sherds by period in the data set is extremely uneven (see Tables 2-13) with the Late Eneolithic (LE) especially poorly represented. Any analysis of the data must take this uneven distribution into consideration. For the current purposes it was considered that the Late Eneolithic sample was too small to make statistically generalized statements with any degree of confidence. For completeness, however, the Late Eneolithic data has been included in all charts and reference is made to this data in the text whenever the presence of an attribute, even in small quantity, may be considered relevant.

Temporal Variation in Ceramic Attributes

1. Temper (Table 2)

To describe temper, one of four designations was used for each sherd: fine, medium, coarse and organic. No instances of organic temper were recorded in this data set. For the remaining three categories an interesting temporal pattern was observed. In all periods medium temper was predominant, exceeding the frequency of fine- and coarse-tempered sherds by a considerable percentage. Fine-tempered wares began a steady increase in the Early Bronze Age which continued through the Late Bronze Age, while medium-tempered wares underwent a commensurate decline over the same period. The percentage of fine wares dropped in the Iron Age while the popularity of medium wares rose at that time. Coarse wares were present in small percentages during all periods except the Early Bronze Age. A large increase in coarse wares was observed for the Punic–Roman and Medieval periods.

A pattern of regular growth in an attribute's frequency through the Bronze Age, followed by a fairly large decrease in the Iron Age—in this case the attribute of fine temper—also seems to be the case for a number of other attributes/attribute groupings. A complementary pattern of decrease through the Bronze Age followed by an increased frequency of occurrence during the Iron Age (e.g. medium temper) suggests that, as some wares increased in popularity, their production was replacing that of a commensurate percentage of another ceramic type or types. In no case, however, did the growth in popularity of one attribute or type appear to supplant another completely. An overall trend in the ceramic record at Duos Nuraghes appears to be an increasing diversity coupled with a remarkable temporal continuity.

2. Paste (Table 3)

Paste color, or the color of the baked ceramic core of the vessel, is not subject to as much variation within the same pot as is surface color. This makes paste color a particularly useful diagnostic for the ceramics from Duos Nuraghes, which are known to vary in surface color considerably within the same vessel (Webster, pers. comm.).

The characteristic diversity and temporal continuity found in the Duos Nuraghes ceramic record is well exemplified by the chronological patterning of paste color. There is a trend toward an increasing number of paste colors rather than replacement of one by another. The greatest change occurs between the Middle Bronze Age and the Late Bronze Age where the number of paste colors almost doubles, rising from seven to thirteen. Primarily responsible for this increase is the introduction of a group of five pastes (light orange, red, dark red, red-yellow and buff) which, although always occurring in small frequencies, appear overall to rise in popularity through the Punic–Roman period. The sherds in this group were not uniform in their other fabric characteristics. They possessed fine or medium tempers, with the exception of red paste, which occurred only in medium and coarse tempers. Their surfaces were treated in a variety of ways including smoothing, roughening, a plain matte, and low burnish, and their surface colors closely matched their paste color. Most appear to have comprised a relatively fine ware group while the red paste sherds represent a somewhat coarser ware.

Dark-colored pastes such as brown, black, red-brown and red-orange appear to have been consistently preferred, and all occur in most periods. Grey, also occurring in all periods, is the only lighter paste color that was consistently represented. Its popularity peaked in the Middle Bronze Age and slowly declined in subsequent periods. In the Late Eneolithic and the Early Bronze Age dark brown paste was the most common, but in the Middle Bronze Age black paste occurred in the highest frequencies and continued to do so into the Medieval–Modern period. The second most popular paste color from the Early Bronze Age through the Punic–Roman period was consistently red-brown.

3. Exterior Surface Treatment (Table 4)

Several patterns of temporal interest emerged from the data collected on exterior surface treatment. In the Early Bronze Age almost 71% of the sherds were finished with a high burnish. That was the highest percentage observed for any one surface treatment in any single period. Following a precipitous decrease in the Middle Bronze Age, high-burnished sherds continued a gradual decline in frequency through the Iron Age, recovering slightly in the Punic–Roman period. Sherds with low-burnish and streak-burnish, as well as those that were smoothed, roughened, or left unsmoothed, increased in frequency in the Middle Bronze Age, making up for the decreased production of highly-burnished pottery. These types of surface treatments, then, either continued to appear more frequently, or maintained approximately the same frequencies through the Iron Age. In the Punic–Roman period there was another shift in which low-burnished, streak-burnished, and smoothed pottery occurred slightly less often, and high-burnished and roughened pottery occurred somewhat more often. The temporal patterning of this attribute demonstrates once again an emphasis on both diversity and continuity in Nuragic pottery. Rather than one newly popular surface treatment replacing another, most finishes, once introduced, were evident in all subsequent periods.

4. Other Ceramic Fabric Attributes

A number of other ceramic fabric attributes were

analyzed for temporal variation. These attributes were not ultimately used in establishing ware-fabric types but their investigation, nonetheless, yielded useful information.

Exterior surface color, as previously mentioned, was found to be somewhat variable within the same pot. It was partly for this reason that this attribute was not used in the definition of ware-fabric type. In looking at a cross-tabulation of this attribute by period, however, several patterns already well-established in the investigation of the ceramic data were clearly evident. First, the preference for dark colors which appeared in the paste color tabulation was obvious here as well. Although there were a number of other surface colors represented, brown, dark brown, black and red-brown sherds taken all together total slightly more than 80% of the sherds analyzed. These four colors account for the bulk of sherds in all periods emphasizing the continuity and similarity of the Duos Nuraghes ceramics through time. Although temporal patterning was somewhat obscure for surface color overall, the data suggests that brown enjoyed increasing popularity from the Late Eneolithic through the Iron Age and then dropped off sharply in the Punic–Roman period. Also clear was a peak of popularity for a red-brown surface color in the Early Bronze Age followed by a slow decline which continued through the Punic–Roman period.

The number of decorated sherds in the data set is extremely small and is therefore not a suitable sample for statistical analysis (Table 5). Some useful information can be gained, however, by the very fact that sherds decorated in a certain style are present, even in very small quantities, in a given period. In Tower A, ceramics decorated with curvilinear designs in the *a pettine impresso*, or comb-punctate, technique appear in well-dated Middle Bronze, Late Bronze and Iron Age contexts. Comb-decorated (*a pettine*) ware has traditionally been considered a Middle–Late Bronze Age diagnostic (see Bafico and Rossi 1988; Fadda 1984; and Moravetti 1984, for contrasting viewpoints) and its continued presence in the Iron Age at Duos Nuraghes brings the conventional view into question. This finding will be especially significant if the increasing use of chronometric dating techniques on Sardinia will, in the future, lead to more instances of *a pettine* ceramics dated to the Iron Age.

From the Bronze Age levels in Tower A comes a distinctive fine, dark burnished ware with exterior streak-incised decorations which has been referred to as Duos A Ware (Webster 1988: 467). This pottery is highly diagnostic for the Early and Middle Bronze periods at Duos constituting 100% of all decorated sherds in the Early Bronze Age and 66% of the decorated sherds in the Middle Bronze Age (Table 5: streak-incised). Examples closely comparable to Duos A Ware have not yet been identified elsewhere on the island (Webster 1988: 467), but as more nuraghi with Early Bronze Age contexts are identified and excavated it should become evident whether Duos A comprises a localized ware or represents instead a more generalized Early Bronze Age type.

5. Nuragic Fabrics (Table 6)

Ware-fabric types were determined using the attributes of temper texture/size, paste color, and exterior surface treatment. Since the purpose was to see whether these wares underwent a differential cycling of popularity, only two possible designations for temper and exterior surface treatment were used in order to enhance temporal clarity. Fine and medium temper were merged under the category of fine temper while the designations of burnished or not burnished were used for the attribute of exterior surface treatment (Table 6).

The patterns of diversity, continuity and the preference for dark colors, which was identified in the analysis of single attributes, remained clearly evident in this multi-variate analysis. A simple and consistent pattern is revealed by looking at the most popular wares for each period. Fine dark-brown unburnished wares were the most popular wares in the late Eneolithic followed by fine dark-brown burnished wares in the Early Bronze Age and fine red-brown unburnished wares in the Middle Bronze Age. For the remaining Late Bronze Age through Medieval periods fine black burnished wares consistently had the highest frequencies; this ware was also a close second in popularity during the Middle Bronze Age.

Many of the fabric types showed a sudden rise and peak in frequency followed by a more gradual decline. In no case did a fabric disappear totally from the record once it made its initial appearance (with the exception of some fabric groups represented by only 10 sherds or less).

Fine dark brown burnished and fine red-brown burnished wares both rise suddenly to their peak of popularity in the Early Bronze Age, dropping off fairly dramatically (red-brown less so) in the Middle Bronze Age and following periods. Fine brown burnished ware maintained its highest frequency through both the Early and Middle Bronze Ages and then underwent a substantial decline over the subsequent periods. Fine grey burnished, fine brown unburnished, and fine red-brown unburnished all peaked in the

Middle Bronze Age, and declined in the Late Bronze Age. Fine red-brown unburnished had a second peak of popularity in the Iron Age and fine brown unburnished a second peak in the Punic–Roman period. In the Late Bronze Age fine black burnished and unburnished, fine red-orange unburnished, and fine grey unburnished all reached their highest frequencies of popularity and all declined slightly in the Iron Age, with the exception of fine black burnished ware which maintained the same level through the Iron Age. In the Punic–Roman period these fabrics either continue or commence a decline in frequency except for fine red-orange unburnished ware which had begun to rise in popularity again. Fine cinnamon ware, which made its first appearance in the Middle Bronze Age, had its peak in the Iron Age but it was not a particularly popular Iron Age ware overall.

The last group that should be mentioned comprises four wares consisting of a fairly small number of sherds. All four fabrics—fine buff unburnished, fine red unburnished, fine light orange unburnished, and coarse red-orange unburnished—made their first appearance in the ceramic record during the Late Bronze Age, increased in frequency slightly in the Iron Age, and three of four continued to increase in the Punic–Roman period (Table 6). This group of four fabrics is similar to each other, but fairly dissimilar in color both to earlier Nuragic fabrics and to other Late Bronze Age, Iron Age and Punic–Roman fabrics. Whether they were made of local clay or imported from elsewhere, either on or off the island, is not known but is a question that certainly merits further investigation.

What is to be understood from this welter of information? Primarily it seems evident that there was a high level of continuity through time in the types of ceramics preferred by the residents of Tower A. Although a fabric may have varied widely in its frequency, it seldom disappeared completely, and most periods saw a large range of types. It was not possible to associate any one type of pottery fabric with one or two periods. One group of pottery which was somewhat temporally restricted was the group of four fabrics that first appeared in the Late Bronze Age.

Nuragic Vessel Forms

General vessel types were defined based on variations in rim form, rim orientation, wall form, type of base-wall articulation and an 'in-field' general form designation. Before discussing the vessel forms, however, it would be useful to look at the temporal patterning of some individual and paired vessel form attributes.

1. Vessel Form and Temper

An 'in-field' form designation was made by the excavators for each sherd whenever possible. These designations are extremely broad and a number of traditional types are subsumed under each form category (Table 7). The data were examined to determine how individual forms (Table 8) and their temper size (Tables 9-11) varied through time. Bowls and dishes were the most common pottery types overall, while jars occurred much less frequently, cups even less often, and basins, vases and platters extremely rarely (Table 8). Bowls were present in all periods but peaked in popularity in the Early Bronze Age, decreased in the Middle Bronze Age, and thereafter maintained a fairly constant percentage. Dishes, also present in all periods, were not well represented in the Early Bronze Age but increased in subsequent periods. Cups appeared in small, relatively constant quantities in the Middle Bronze, Late Bronze and Iron Ages; jars, also occurring in small quantities, enjoyed an increase in frequency over the same period.

By looking at form broken down by temper, it was possible to determine whether there had been shifts in preference for fine, medium, or coarse wares within each form over time. Such a shift was evident for bowls (Table 9), where a strong Early Bronze Age preference for fine temper was dramatically reversed in favor of medium temper in the Middle Bronze Age. Coarse-ware bowls first appeared in small quantities in the Late Bronze Age and increased in frequency through the Punic–Roman period.

Dishes were primarily a medium-tempered ware in all periods (Table 10). The frequency of fine-tempered dishes increased slightly between the Middle and Late Bronze Ages, only to drop again in the Iron Age, while coarse-ware dishes, after appearing for the first time in the Middle Bronze Age, remained a steady 10-14%.

Jars were not sufficiently well represented in the Middle Bronze Age, Punic–Roman, or Medieval periods to form any conclusions. A strong preference for medium-tempered jars was evident, however, in the Late Bronze Age, and this preference continued through the Iron Age (Table 11).

Cups also occurred in statistically insignificant numbers, appearing first in the Middle Bronze Age and continuing through the Iron Age (Table 8). There were more than twice as many fine-tempered as medium-tempered cup sherds, and although it could be predicted that cups were primarily a fine ware, there were not enough sherds in the sample to fully support this conclusion.

2. Handle Form

The total number of handle sherds recovered was small (97), making it difficult to draw conclusions about temporal patterning (Tables 12a-b). Strap handles were the most common finds, occurring on jars, bowls, and dishes. Strap-handled jars, or water jugs (*brocche askoidi*), were found mainly in Late Bronze Age through Iron Age levels. Ledge handles were the second most frequent type, spanning the same range of vessel forms. Loop handles occurred in limited numbers on bowls and cups, and tubular handles appeared on jars and bowls. Of the 97 handles recovered from the site, 57 were given no vessel form designation in the field (e.g. jar, bowl). This group of sherds demonstrated the same pattern of diversity as most handle forms occurred in a number of different periods.

3. Vessel Types

Vessel types were created by using only sherds for which the attribute of form had been coded, and cross-tabulating these with the attributes of wall, lip and lip orientation. Sherds which were classified neither as walls or lips were excluded from this analysis. A large number of categories were created (93), many represented by three or fewer sherds. This profusion of types could be interpreted in several ways. Nuragic potters may have been producing pottery which conformed to generalized vessel forms, but varied greatly in certain details (note the simultaneous popularity of several types of convex-walled bowls with different rim types/orientations, as described below). Alternatively, the data might be interpreted as suggesting a very large quantity of rigorously defined types, and this relatively small ceramic sample was simply inadequate in providing multiple examples of only the most popular vessel form types. It will be assumed here, however, that the sample is adequate and discussion will be primarily limited to temporal patterning among the better represented types 1-7. Table 13 provides information on 36 types comprised of three or more sherds.

During the Early Bronze Age, a period for which the total number of sherds analyzed was quite small, there was a very strong preference for carinated bowls with simple, excurvate lips (type 4) and little diversity in types (7). Type diversity increased in the Middle Bronze Age (18) and almost doubled in the Late Bronze Age (34), falling off slightly in subsequent periods. The popularity of carinated bowls (types 4 and 6) is described by a simple fall-off curve. Type 4 peaks in the Early Bronze Age, type 6 in the Middle Bronze Age, and both decline steadily in the following periods. Bowls with convex walls and varying lip shape/orientation (types 1, 7, 8 and 11) were present in most periods, but were especially popular in the Middle and Late Bronze Ages, and the Punic–Roman period. In the Iron Age there were numerous small-scale frequency changes; about a dozen types increased slightly and an equal number decreased slightly (see Table 13). Straight-walled dishes with straight lips peaked during this period, while straight-walled dishes with excurvate lips were at their lowest frequency. Lastly, during the Punic–Roman period, straight-walled bowls rose in frequency and convex-walled bowls regained their previous popularity.

A final cross-tabulation was made using the vessel types just described and the ware fabrics discussed earlier. The results demonstrated that individual vessel types were rendered in a very large range of ware fabrics. In other words, individual vessel types were not produced preferentially in a restricted range of ware fabrics. Ware-fabric preferences varied with time, but not with vessel type.

Discussion

One of the greatest problems in the interpretation of this data is that of comparability to data organized by other systems. The relationship of the traditional classificatory system on Sardinia to that used at Duos Nuraghes and other Borore aggregate sites has already been touched on in this paper (see above and Table 7). It is easier to make comparisons with other sites in the Borore aggregate (Nuraghi Toscono and Urpes, Webster *et al.* 1987), where the same classificatory and attribute coding system was used.

The analysis of the ceramic material from Nuraghi Toscono and Urpes was designed primarily to create preliminary classifications of ware fabrics and vessel types at these sites rather than to explore temporal variation. Chronological comparisons with Duos Nuraghes are further limited by the late date of the excavated portions of Toscono/Urpes, since their earliest phases are Iron Age. Nevertheless, there are a number of useful comparisons that can be made.

Nuraghi Toscono and Urpes are located close to each other and to Duos Nuraghes. The Duos Nuraghes sample derives from the interior of a tower, whereas the Toscono/Urpes sample comes from the village areas surrounding the nuraghi. All three are likely to have had access to similar, if not the same, clay beds, and their inhabitants might easily have interacted with each other. Under such conditions a high degree of correspondence among the ceramics of these sites might be expected, and in fact, that was found to be the case.

Limiting the comparison to Duos Nuraghes and Toscono (the Urpes sample was quite small), a comparable degree of diversity in Nuragic fabrics was identified at both sites. The complete range of fabric and color types were comparable at the two sites but the frequency of occurrence was, in some cases, markedly disparate. Both sites were dominated by Nuragic fine wares and both had a higher total proportion of fine unburnished wares than fine burnished wares. At Toscono, however, the single most frequent ware fabric in the Iron Age, Punic–Roman and Roman periods was fine black unburnished, whereas a fine black burnished ware was the most popular in all but the Late Eneolithic and Early Bronze Age periods at Duos Nuraghes. Similarly, the fine cinnamon burnished wares which were popular at Toscono were almost non-existent at Duos, whereas fine red-brown burnished and unburnished wares, a frequent find at Duos, were poorly represented at Toscono.

When comparing the vessel types at Duos Nuraghes and Toscono a higher degree of variation was evident than had existed between the ware fabrics of the two sites. There was a greater diversity of vessel form represented at Duos Nuraghes and a greater variation in the distribution of types. Convex-walled bowls were the most frequent types overall at both sites, but did not correspond in frequencies during the same periods where comparisons were possible. Carinated bowls were well represented at both sites and had similar frequency curves. Strap-handled jugs occurred during different periods and more frequently at Toscono (Iron Age, Punic-Roman, Roman) than at Duos (Late Bronze Age, Iron Age). Dishes were slightly more common at Duos Nuraghes than at Toscono and were more varied in style. Jars and cups were more frequent at Toscono than at Duos Nuraghes; cups clustered in the Punic–Roman/Roman periods at Toscono and in the Middle Bronze, Late Bronze and Iron Ages at Duos, with none occurring in the Punic–Roman phase. It would be premature to do more than venture a guess as to the reasons for this inter-site variation. There is a high degree of correspondence overall between the two sites and it seems quite possible that the greater degree of variation in the vessel form distribution, as well as the burnished/unburnished dichotomy, might be accounted for by functional differences between the excavated parts of the two sites: the interior of a nuraghe versus the surrounding village.

Aside from the Toscono/Urpes and Duos Nuraghes analyses, quantitative studies of Nuragic ceramic material have been almost entirely lacking, a notable exception existing in Bafico and Rossi's (1988: 61-188) analysis of the Nuragic ceramics from Santu Antine (Torralba). Bafico and Rossi found ten vessel types/attributes which presented 'battleship curves' of rising and falling frequency along a time dimension represented by depth (in centimeters). Although their study was not tied to absolute or radiocarbon dates, as the Duos Nuraghes analysis is, it nevertheless used quantitative techniques to establish stratigraphic/temporal patterns which can be compared with those found at Duos Nuraghes. Bafico and Rossi (1988: 136-67, 174-79) identified at Santu Antine the same tendency we encountered for a pottery type, once established, to continue in production for a very long time. A number of the Santu Antine ceramic types followed a frequency pattern similar to that of their counterparts at Duos Nuraghes. Bowls (*ciotole*) were extremely popular in all periods, with a slight rise in frequency at the end of the Iron Age; carinated bowls (*ciotole carenate*) peaked early and gradually dropped off in the following periods; strap-handled jugs existed in small numbers over a restricted period of time (Iron Age 900–500 BC) as they did at Duos Nuraghes, though at the latter they occurred in the Late Bronze Age as well as the Iron Age (Table 12). While decoration in the *a pettine* style followed a pattern similar to that found at Duos Nuraghes (Table 5), at Santu Antine it did not continue into the Iron Age. Decorations in the form of small concentric circles (*decorazione a cerchielli*) occurred in the later Iron Age (Lilliu's Phase IV 900–500 BC) at Santu Antine, while only a single example was recovered from Punic/Roman levels at Duos Nuraghes. Two categories of handles which appeared in the Iron Age and Late Bronze Age, the *ansa a bastoncello* and the *ansa a gomito rovescio*, respectively, were considered highly diagnostic by Bafico and Rossi. Despite the many excellent illustrations of these handle types (Bafico and Rossi 1988: 119 fig. 29; 79 fig. 9), it was not possible to equate them with the categories used in the Duos Nuraghes data. This was thought to be the result of insufficiently sensitive distinctions in the attributes used for coding handles in the Duos Nuraghes system, one of several correctable shortcomings found in the attribute coding system overall.

Conclusions and Suggestions for Future Research

The analysis of temporal patterning in the Duos Nuraghes ceramic data, although preliminary in nature, has identified a number of potentially useful temporal elements in the Nuragic ceramic record. The degree of continuity through time of ware fabrics and many vessel types was striking at Duos Nuraghes and was reflected also, to the extent that the shorter time span of occupation/analysis permitted, at Toscono and Santu Antine. Comparison with these sites also suggests that many of the same vessel forms and decoration styles were popular contemporaneously across a wide geographic area and in some cases described similar temporal patterns of frequency distribution.

Also identified were a number of ceramic elements which may find use as chronological indicators or diagnostics. Duos A Ware, a distinctive fine dark burnished ware with exterior streak-incised decorations (see Table 5) was a strong Early Bronze Age diagnostic at Duos Nuraghes and was also present (in very small quantity) during the Late Eneolithic. Although as yet it has no close comparisons on the island, as more Nuragic sites with Early Bronze Age occupations are excavated, Duos A Ware may turn out to be of more than isolated significance.

Decorations in the *a pettine* and *a cerchielli* styles may be of some use as chronological indicators, though there has been a great deal of disagreement over the dating of *a pettine* style decorations (see for example, Fadda 1984; Moravetti 1984; Bafico and Rossi 1988). Within this context, the Iron Age Duos Nuraghes *a pettine* finds (Table 5) can only serve to make a restricted Middle/Late Bronze Age date less likely and so reduce the usefulness of *a pettine* style decorations as a chronological indicator.

Some handle forms may also prove to be useful chronological indicators, as Bafico and Rossi (1988: 146-88) found in several cases. It was not possible to confirm their conclusions, or to provide any further insight on the topic due to insufficient sensitivity in the Duos Nuraghes coding system for handle forms/attributes. Since this is easily correctable, useful handle attribute data should be forthcoming from future excavation in the Borore aggregate.

In conclusion, the preliminary nature of this study must be stressed; much work remains for the future. Several limitations and shortcomings in the computer-based multivariate attribute coding system have been highlighted, not least of which is the difficulty in comparing traditional and multivariate systems. Far more work needs to be done utilizing the same or similar computer-based systems before their usefulness can be maximized. The system employed at Duos Nuraghes and Toscono/Urpes has proven far more flexible and adaptable to the varying aspects of ceramic analysis than traditional ceramic typologies could ever be alone. It is hoped that this demonstration will in the future encourage a more general use of such systems in Sardinian archaeology.

Acknowledgments

Grateful acknowledgment is made to Professor Gary S. Webster for support and advice during the preparation of this manuscript as well as for the use of data from his ongoing excavations at Duos Nuraghes. I am also grateful to Professor Miriam S. Balmuth for introducing me to the beautiful and fascinating island of Sardinia.

Table 1

Sardinian chronology and Duos Nuraghes Tower A

Period	Dates	Cal C14 ranges	Uncal C14 dates
Medieval–Modern	456 AD–Present		
Punic–Roman	500 BC–456 AD		
Iron Age	900–500 BC		
Late Bronze Age	1250–900 BC	1130–900 BC	2830 ± 90 BP (I-14775)
		1250–930 BC	2880 ± 80 BP (I-15466)
Middle Bronze Age	1500–1250 BC	1510–1270 BC	3110 ± 90 BP (I-15465)
Early Bronze Age	1800–1500 BC		
Late Eneolithic Age	2300–1800 BC	3300–2340 BC	4180 ± 320 BP (I-14774)

Table 2

Relative abundance of temper types

Percentage of each type in each period

	Late Eneolithic	Early Bronze Age	Middle Bronze Age	Late Bronze Age	Iron Age	Punic–Roman	Medieval–Modern
Fine	37.9	19.0	23.0	25.8	18.1	18.8	16.1
Medium	55.2	81.0	73.4	68.2	75.3	70.9	67.8
Coarse	6.9	0	3.6	6.0	6.6	10.3	16.1
Total number of sherds in each period	29	58	165	559	303	165	31

Table 3

Relative abundance of paste colors

Percentage of each type in each period

	Late Eneolithic	Early Bronze Age	Middle Bronze Age	Late Bronze Age	Iron Age	Punic–Roman	Medieval–Modern
Black	31.0	15.2	29.1	38.9	34.0	31.1	25.8
Dark brown	41.4	43.1	13.9	8.6	7.9	8.5	0
Red-brown	13.8	20.7	26.1	14.4	18.1	16.5	19.3
Brown	10.3	13.8	16.4	13.7	10.2	10.4	12.9
Dark grey	3.4	1.7	12.1	9.6	8.2	4.9	9.7
Red-orange	0	5.2	1.2	6.6	5.9	10.4	19.3
Cinnamon	0	0	0.6	2.7	3.3	3.0	0
Buff	0	0	0	2.5	5.9	1.2	0
Light orange	0	0	0	0.9	1.6	4.8	3.2
Red	0	0	0	1.1	2.6	4.9	9.7
Dark red	0	0	0	0.5	0.3	0.6	0
Red yellow	0	0	0	0.4	1.6	2.4	0
Cream	0	0	0	0	0	1.2	0
Green	0	0	0.6	0	0	0	0
Pink	0	0	0	0.2	0	0	0
Total sherds	29	58	165	561	303	164	31

Table 4

Exterior surface treatment

Percentage of each type in each period

	Late Eneolithic	Early Bronze Age	Middle Bronze Age	Late Bronze Age	Iron Age	Punic–Roman	Medieval–Modern
High burnish	29.6	70.7	24.4	14.9	14.3	16.3	3.3
Smoothed	25.9	5.2	19.5	29.0	26.0	17.6	10.0
Roughened	22.2	12.1	20.7	17.5	23.0	26.4	26.7
Low burnish	14.8	5.2	18.3	19.5	18.7	13.2	36.7
Unsmoothed	7.4	1.7	7.3	9.9	12.7	15.1	6.7
Plain matte	0	3.4	3.0	6.0	0	5.7	16.7
Streak burnish	0	1.7	6.1	3.0	4.7	3.1	0
Slipped matte	0	0	0	0.2	0.7	1.3	0
Glazed	0	0	0	0	0	1.3	0
Pattern burnish	0	0	0.6	0	0	0	0
Total sherds	27	58	164	537	300	159	30

Table 5
Decoration technique

Percentage of each type in each period

	Late Eneolithic	Early Bronze Age	Middle Bronze Age	Late Bronze Age	Iron Age	Punic–Roman	Medieval–Modern
Incised	100	0	9.4	16.1	18.2	21.4	0
Streak-incised	0	100	65.6	3.2	0	0	0
Punctation	0	0	15.6	54.8*	72.7*	21.4	50
Grooved	0	0	3.1	16.1*	0	21.4	0
Modeled	0	0	3.1	3.2	0	7.1	0
Channeled	0	0	3.1	0	0	0	0
Applique	0	0	0	6.4*	18.2*	0	0
Ridged	0	0	0	3.2	0	0	0
Molded	0	0	0	3.2	0	0	0
Plain	0	0	0	0	0	7.1	50
Excised	0	0	0	0	0	7.1	0
Stamped	0	0	0	0	0	7.1	0
Waved rim	0	0	0	0	0	7.1	0
Total sherds	3	31	32	31	11	14	2

* These contain sherds which utilized a different decoration technique on the inside and the outside.

Table 6
Ware-fabric types

Percentage of each type in each period

	LE	EBA	MBA	LBA	IA	P–R	M–M
Fine black burnished	27.5	15.5	14.5	19.9	19.8	16.3	16.0
Fine black unburnished	3.4	0	12.7	16.4	13.5	10.3	9.6
Fine red-brown unburnished	10.3	3.4	15.1	10.7	15.5	11.5	6.4
Fine brown unburnished	6.9	8.6	10.9	9.4	6.2	9.7	9.6
Fine dark-brown unburnished	34.4	8.6	4.8	5.8	3.3	3.6	0
Fine dark-brown burnished	6.9	34.4	8.4	2.6	4.2	4.2	0
Fine red-orange unburnished	0	1.7	1.2	6.0	4.6	6.6	12.9
Fine red-brown burnished	3.4	17.2	10.3	2.8	2.6	3.6	12.9
Fine grey burnished	0	1.7	8.4	4.6	2.9	3.6	6.4
Fine brown burnished	0	5.1	5.4	3.3	2.3	0.6	3.2
Fine grey unburnished	0	0	3.0	4.1	3.3	0.6	3.2
Fine cinnamon unburnished	0	0	0.6	2.1	3.3	3.0	0
Coarse black unburnished	0	0	1.8	2.3	0.6	3.0	0
Fine buff unburnished	0	0	0	1.4	3.9	1.2	0
Fine red unburnished	0	0	0	0.7	2.3	3.6	0
Fine light-orange unburnished	0	0	0	0.7	0.9	4.8	3.2
Coarse red-orange unburnished	0	0	0	0.3	0.6	3.6	6.4
Coarse brown unburnished	3.4	0	0	0.8	1.3	0	0
Fine red-yellow unburnished	0	0	0	0	1.3	2.4	0
Coarse grey unburnished	0	0	0.6	0.7	0.6	0.6	0
Fine buff burnished	0	0	0	0.8	0.6	0	0
Coarse red-brown unburnished	0	0	0.6	0.5	0	1.2	0
Fine red-orange burnished	0	3.4	0	0.1	0.6	0	0
Fine dark-red unburnished	0	0	0	0.5	0.3	0.6	0
Coarse grey burnished	3.4	0	0	0	1.3	0	0
Coarse red unburnished	0	0	0	0.3	0	0	9.6
Fine light-orange burnished	0	0	0	0.1	0.6	0	0
Fine red burnished	0	0	0	0	0.3	1.2	0
Fine red-yellow burnished	0	0	0	0.3	0.3	0	0
Coarse buff unburnished	0	0	0	0.1	0.6	0	0
Coarse black burnished	0	0	0	0.1	0	1.2	0
Coarse dark-brown burnished	0	0	0.6	0	0.3	0.6	0
Fine cream unburnished	0	0	0	0	0	1.2	0
Fine cinnamon burnished	0	0	0	0.3	0	0	0
Coarse buff burnished	0	0	0	0	0.6	0	0
Fine green burnished	0	0	0.6	0	0	0	0
Coarse brown burnished	0	0	0	0	0.3	0	0
Coarse cinnamon unburnished	0	0	0	0.1	0	0	0
Coarse red-brown burnished	0	0	0	0.1	0	0	0
Coarse pink unburnished	0	0	0	0.1	0	0	0
Total	29	58	165	559	303	145	31

Table 7

Relationship of Duos Nuraghes ceramic forms to traditional ceramic typologies on Sardinia

Duos Nuraghes general form	Traditional ceramic category
Bowl	ciotola, ciotolone
Carinated bowl	ciotola carenata
Dish	tegame/spiana
Cup	ciotolina
Jar	brocca askoide
	olla (all types)
	ziro (all types)

Table 8

Relative abundance of pottery forms

Percentage of each type in each period

	Late Eneolithic	Early Bronze Age	Middle Bronze Age	Late Bronze Age	Iron Age	Punic–Roman	Medieval–Modern
Bowl	40.0	73.3	47.1	41.6	35.1	50.0	31.6
Dish	40.0	26.7	45.6	40.6	42.9	42.6	52.6
Jar	20.0	0	5.9	13.4	14.9	7.3	15.8
Cup	0	0	1.5	1.3	5.2	0	0
Basin	0	0	0	2.0	0	0	0
Platter	0	0	0	0.7	0.6	0	0
Vase	0	0	0	0.3	0.6	0	0
Spindle whorl	0	0	0	0	0.6	0	0
Total number of sherds in each period	5	14	68	298	154	68	19

Table 9

Relative abundance of bowl tempers

Percentage of each type in each period

	Late Eneolithic	Early Bronze Age	Middle Bronze Age	Late Bronze Age	Iron Age	Punic–Roman	Medieval–Modern
Fine	50.0	90.9	28.1	38.7	27.8	23.5	16.7
Medium	50.0	9.1	71.9	58.1	66.7	61.8	83.3
Coarse	0	0	0	3.2	5.6	14.7	0
Total number of sherds in each period	2	11	32	124	54	34	6

Table 10

Relative abundance of dish tempers

Percentage of each type in each period

	Late Eneolithic	Early Bronze Age	Middle Bronze Age	Late Bronze Age	Iron Age	Punic–Roman	Medieval–Modern
Fine	0	0	6.4	15.0	6.1	6.9	20.0
Medium	100	100	83.9	75.0	80.3	82.8	70.0
Coarse	0	0	9.7	10.0	13.6	10.3	10.0
Total number of sherds in each period	2	4	31	120	66	29	10

Table 11

Relative abundance of jar tempers

Percentage of each type in each period

	Late Eneolithic	Early Bronze Age	Middle Bronze Age	Late Bronze Age	Iron Age	Punic–Roman	Medieval–Modern
Fine	100	*	50.0	20.0	21.7	60.0	0
Medium	0	*	50.0	77.5	69.6	20.0	100
Coarse	0	*	0	2.5	8.7	20.0	0
Total number of sherds in each period	1	0	4	40	23	5	3

Table 12A

Handle forms

Percentage of each type in each period

	Late Eneolithic	Early Bronze Age	Middle Bronze Age	Late Bronze Age	Iron Age	Punic–Roman	Medieval–Modern
Ledge	1	0	1	7	7	3	1
Strap	2	0	6	27	8	5	1
Loop	1	0	0	4	3	1	0
Tubular	0	1	0	16	0	1	0
Lug	0	0	0	0	1	0	0
Total	4	1	7	54	19	10	2

Table 12B

Breakdown of handle forms by vessel type

Percentage of each type in each period

	Late Eneolithic	Early Bronze Age	Middle Bronze Age	Late Bronze Age	Iron Age	Punic-Roman	Medieval Modern
Bowl handle types							
Ledge	1	0	1	4	4	1	1
Strap	0	0	1	1	0	0	0
Loop	0	0	0	2	0	0	0
Tubular	0	0	0	4	0	0	0
Jar handle types							
Ledge	0	0	0	0	1	0	0
Strap	0	0	0	6	4	0	0
Loop	0	0	0	0	0	1	0
Tubular	0	0	0	1	0	0	0
Dish handle types							
Ledge	0	0	0	1	0	1	0
Strap	0	0	1	2	1	0	0
Cup handle types							
Loop	0	0	0	0	1	0	0
Handles with no form designation							
Ledge	0	0	0	2	2	1	0
Strap	2	0	4	18	3	5	1
Loop	1	0	0	2	2	0	0
Tubular	0	1	0	11	0	1	0
Lug	0	0	0	0	1	0	0

Table 13
Vessel types

Vessel type	Late Eneolithic Age	Early Bronze Age	Middle Bronze Age	Late Bronze Age	Iron Age	Punic-Roman	Medieval Modern	Pottery form	Quantity
1	20.0	9.0	9.2	13.0	6.6	9.4	15.3	Convex bowls with a simple straight lip	51
2	0	0	1.8	9.0	13.2	9.4	0	Straight-walled dishes with a simple straight lip	42
3	0	9.0	5.5	7.6	2.4	13.2	0	Straight-walled bowls with a simple straight lip	31
4	0	36.3	12.9	4.5	4.1	1.8	7.6	Carinated bowls with a simple excurvate lip	28
5	0	0	11.1	6.3	2.4	7.5	7.6	Straight-walled dishes with a simple excurvate lip	28
6	0	0	12.9	5.8	3.3	1.8	0	Carinated bowls with a simple straight lip	25
7	0	18.1	0	4.0	4.9	1.8	0	Convex bowls with a simple incurvate lip	18
8	0	0	5.5	1.3	3.3	11.3	0	Convex bowls with no lip extant	16
9	0	0	0	3.6	5.7	1.8	0	Concave dishes with a simple excurvate lip	16
10	20.0	0	0	1.8	6.6	0	0	Convex jars with a simple excurvate lip	13
11	0	0	3.7	2.2	2.4	1.8	0	Convex bowls with a simple excurvate lip	11
12	0	9.0	0	2.2	0.8	3.7	15.3	Concave bowls with a simple excurvate lip	11
13	0	0	1.8	1.8	2.4	3.7	7.6	Straight-walled bowls with a simple excurvate lip	11
14	0	0	0	0.9	3.3	0	15.3	Convex dishes with no lip extant	8
15	0	0	1.8	1.8	2.4	0	0	Convex dishes with a simple straight lip	8
16	0	0	1.8	1.3	0	5.6	0	Straight-walled dishes with no lip extant	7
17	0	0	0	1.3	1.6	3.7	0	Straight-walled jars with a simple straight lip	7
18	0	0	1.8	0.9	2.4	0	0	Concave bowls with a simple straight lip	6
19	0	0	0	1.3	1.6	1.8	0	Carinated bowls with no lip extant	6
20	0	0	1.8	0.9	0	5.6	0	Straight-walled dishes with a bolstered excurvate lip	6
21	0	0	0	1.8	0.8	0	0	Bowls with a simple straight lip	5
22	20.0	0	0	1.3	0	1.8	0	Bowls with a simple excurvate lip	5
23	0	0	0	0.9	2.4	0	0	Convex dishes with a simple excurvate lip	5
24	0	0	0	1.8	0.8	0	0	Concave dishes with a simple straight lip	5
25	0	0	1.8	1.8	0	0	0	Jars with a thickened straight lip	5
26	0	9.0	1.8	0.4	0	1.8	0	Straight-walled bowls with a bolstered straight lip	4
27	0	0	0	1.8	0	0	0	Convex jars with no lip extant	4
28	0	0	1.8	0.4	0	1.8	0	Convex bowls with a bolstered excurvate lip	3
29	0	9.0	0	0.9	0	0	0	Carinated bowls with a Simple incurvate lip	3
30	0	0	0	0.4	1.6	0	0	Concave dishes with no lip extant	3
31	20.0	0	1.8	0	0	0	7.6	Concave dishes with a flanged excurvate lip	3
32	0	0	0	0.9	0.8	0	0	Cups with a simple straight lip	3
33	0	0	1.8	0.4	0.8	0	0	Convex jars with a simple straight lip	3
34	0	0	0	0.4	0.8	0	7.6	Convex jars with a bolstered excurvate lip	3
35	0	0	0	0.4	1.6	0	0	Convex jars with a thickened excurvate lip	3
36	0	0	0	0	2.4	0	0	Straight-walled jars with a simple excurvate lip	3
Total	5	11	54	222	121	53	13		

References

Bafico, S., & G. Rossi
1988 Il Nuraghe S. Antine di Torralba. Scavi e materiali. In A. Moravetti (a cura di), *Il Nuraghe S. Antine nel Logudoro-Meilogu*, 61-188. Sassari: Carlo Delfino.

Balmuth, M.S.
1984 The nuraghi of Sardinia: An introduction. In M.S. Balmuth and R.J. Rowland, Jr (eds.), *Studies in Sardinian Archaeology*, 23-52. Ann Arbor: University of Michigan Press.

Fadda, M.A.
1984 Il nuraghe Monte Idda di Posada e la ceramica a pettine in Sardegna. In W.H. Waldren (ed.), *Early Settlement in the Western Mediterranean Islands and the Peripheral Areas*, 671-702. BAR International Series 229. Oxford: British Archaeological Reports.

Moravetti, A.
1984 La tomba di giganti di Palatu (Birori). *Nuovo Bullettino Archeologico Sardo* 1: 69-96.
1986 Nota preliminare agli scavi del Nuraghe S. Barbara di Macomer. *Nuovo Bullettino Archeologico Sardo* 3: 49-113.
1988 Il Nuraghe S. Antine di Torralba: Brocche askoidi, pintadere, lisciatoi. In A. Moravetti (a cura di), *Il Nuraghe S. Antine nel Logudoro-Meilogu*, 189-206. Sassari: Carlo Delfino.

Santoni, V., & G. Bacco
1987 L'isolato A del villaggio nuragico di Serucci-Gonnesa (CA). Lo scavo della capanna 5. In G. Lilliu, G. Ugas and G. Lai (a cura di), *La Sardegna nel Mediterraneo tra il Secondo e il Primo Millennio a.C. Atti del 2 convegno di studi 'Un millennio di relazioni fra la Sardegna e i Paesi del Mediterraneo'*, *Selargius-Cagliari, 27-30 novembre 1986*, 313-36. Cagliari: Amministrazione Provinciale di Cagliari.

Webster, G.S., J. Michels & D. Hudak
1987 Ceramics. In J. Michels and G. Webster (eds.), *Studies in Nuragic Archaeology: Village Excavations at Nuraghe Urpes and Nuraghe Toscono in West-Central Sardinia*, 45-68. BAR International Series 373. Oxford: British Archaeological Reports.

Webster, G.S.
1988 Duos Nuraghes: Preliminary results of the first three seasons of excavation. *Journal of Field Archaeology* 15: 465-72.

Riassunto

Il programma di ricerca in Sardegna della Pennsylvania State University (diretta da G.S. Webster) ha scoperto una lunga occupazione nuragica presso il sito di Duos Nuraghes (Borore-SS) che risale al tardo periodo eneolitico. L'attento scavo stratigrafico della Torre A e del villaggio circostante, accompagnato da date radiocarboniche, e da datazione derivate dal metodo di idrazione d'ossidiana, e la lunga occupazione del sito, forniscono un'opportunità unica per studiare e rifinire la cronologia delle ceramiche nuragiche.

1396 cocci diagnostici (orli, fondi, anse) nuragici sono stati esaminati secondo 36 '*attributi*' (tempra, pasta, trattamento della superficie, decorazione, forma dell'orlo, forma del fondo, forma dell'ansa, ecc.) e i dati sono stati inseriti in un computer. Ciascun *attributo* è stato analizzato per vedere come esso è cambiato relativamente al tempo. Gli attributi sono stati analizzati prima ad uno ad uno, poi a coppie, e finalmente come '*tipi di impasto*' e '*fogge di vasellame*'. Le fogge del vasellame definite dall'Autrice sono simili, ma non identiche a quelle di tradizionale tipologia nuragica; i '*tipi di vasellame*' sono più specifici e incorporano attributi del 'fabric' e attributi della forma.

Queste sono alcune delle scoperte dell'Autrice:

1. *Tipi di impasto*, definiti dalla combinazione di attributi di tempra, pasta e della lavorazione della superficie, mostrano una forte continuità nel tempo. Per esempio il vasellame brunito nero non è mai sceso al di sotto del 15%, e soltanto nel tardo Eneolitico ha superato il 20%. Non è stato possibile associare un tipo di '*fabric*' con un particolare periodo di tempo. *Tipi di vasellame* erano spesso costituiti da diversi *impasti*. Questi sono variati a seconda del tempo, ma non sono variati insieme al tipo di vasellame.

2. La decorazione a '*striature-incise*' è tipica dell'età del Bronzo Medio e Antico presso Duos Nuraghes. Questo tipo non è stato ancora identificato presso altri siti, ed è stato chiamato 'Duos A Ware'.

3. Le ceramiche 'a pettine', che sono tradizionalmente considerate tipiche del Bronzo Medio e Recente, continuano ad esistere a Duos Nuraghes nell'età del Ferro. Presso Duos Nuraghes, le brocche askoidi appaiono sia nel Bronzo Recente che nell'età del Ferro.

4. La più grande diversità nella *foggia di vasellame* avviene durante il Bronzo Recente e durante l'età del Ferro. Infatti sembra che nei *tipi di vasellame* c'è una crescente diversità con il passare del tempo, accompagnata dalla continuazione di certi attributi. Un notevole aumento di diversificazione è avvenuto con l'introduzione di cinque nuovi colori di pasta durante il Bronzo Recente.

Anche se il complesso di Duos Nuraghes è sommariamente paragonabile a quello del vicino nuraghe Toscono, tra i due complessi ci sono delle differenze significative. L'Autrice suggerisce che le differenze possono essere state causate dalla differenza funzionale delle aree di scavo presso ciascun sito. Numerose conclusioni dell'Autrice sono simili a quelle di Bafico e Rossi per il nuraghe Santu Antine (Torralba). In quest'ultimo scavo era evidente che una volta che un tipo di vasellame è stato stabilito, esso è continuato ad esistere per un lungo periodo.

Gli studi preliminari dell'Autrice hanno sottolineato il bisogno di una sequenza di ceramiche ben controllata in Sardegna. Tale sequenza è essenziale per gli studi dei modelli di insediamento e di territorialità (cf. Bonzani, in questo volume), per lo studio dello sviluppo socio-politico (cf. Trump, Ugas, Becker, in questo volume), per lo studio sull'attività economica locale e regionale (cf. Bartoloni, Tronchetti, Will, in questo volume) e per una conoscenza atttendibile della preistoria sarda nel suo vasto contesto Mediterraneo.

Vertebrate Faunal Remains at the Nuragic Village of Santa Barbara, Bauladu (OR)

Lenore J. Gallin and Ornella Fonzo

Excavations at Nuraghe Santa Barbara, Bauladu (OR) yield important new evidence about two poorly understood aspects of the palaeoeconomy of a Late Bronze/Early Iron Age Sardinian village. On the one hand, the discovery of terracotta moulds used in bronze casting provides large-scale and uncontestable evidence of lost-wax investment casting at a Nuragic site (Gallin and Tykot, in press). On the other, the analysis of a portion of an unusually large assembly of faunal material from good Nuragic contexts permits preliminary interpretations relating to both ancient Sardinian diet and stock-raising practices.

The Nuraghe and Village of Santa Barbara

Nuraghe Santa Barbara sits on a hill 635 m above sea level at the edge of a rich agricultural zone near the River Mannu, an area densely occupied during the Nuragic Period, where at least 24 nuraghi are located within a zone of 22 sq km. The site of Santa Barbara is distinguished by a monumental stone wall enclosing five acres around a polylobate nuraghe (Fig. 1). Preliminary investigations reveal evidence of an extensive village within the walls, verified in 1986–89 by the excavation of a multi-functional precinct to the west of the nuraghe (Fig. 2).

The main Nuragic tower at Santa Barbara is well-preserved at its lower level, with a large central chamber (diameter 5 m), three niches, and a high corbelled dome (height over 10 m) (Gallin and Sebis 1989; Gallin 1989). A winding staircase from the first floor is collapsed, and the original number of floors is unknown. Two subsidiary towers on the eastern side of the nuraghe are collapsed and partially buried. A third was uncovered on the north side in 1986, and a possible fourth tower is believed buried on the west side.

The west village at Santa Barbara is organized around a large paved courtyard with entries to the north and south, and a stone 'sidewalk' flanking its western half. Opening onto the eastern and southern sides of the courtyard are small sub-rectangular stone houses, each with its own entry leading down from the sidewalk into a single room. Two large round structures dominate the eastern side, one resembling the 'casa di riunione' seen at other Nuragic sites, with a low stone bench or ledge constructed around the interior periphery. To the north are several specialized areas, including another structure typical of Nuragic villages: a room containing a circular stone bench of well-dressed blocks with pieces of a round basin in the center. Adjacent to this structure is a large double stone basin, two ovens (one with a thick layer of ash in which numerous bone fragments are imbedded), and a low stone platform on which a stone model may have stood.

Three millennia of almost continuous occupation complicates the investigation and interpretation of Santa Barbara's Nuragic village. The Nuragic occupation, represented by the structural remains and dated by ceramic evidence, is attributed to the Late Bronze Age/Early Iron Age (12th to 8th centuries BC). This phase followed the partial destruction of the nuraghe as evidenced by village huts constructed with blocks from the upper sections of the nuraghe. The nature of the archaeological remains suggests that the site was abandoned peacefully, with residents carrying away most of their valuable belongings. The remaining artifacts and structures are not well preserved, and have been disturbed by successive occupations in the Punic, Roman and Medieval periods. During the last century, the hillside was extensively plowed. Nevertheless, ceramic, lithic, faunal and metallurgical remains document a range of activities, including cooking, baking, butchery, spinning and weaving, pottery repair, and metallurgy.

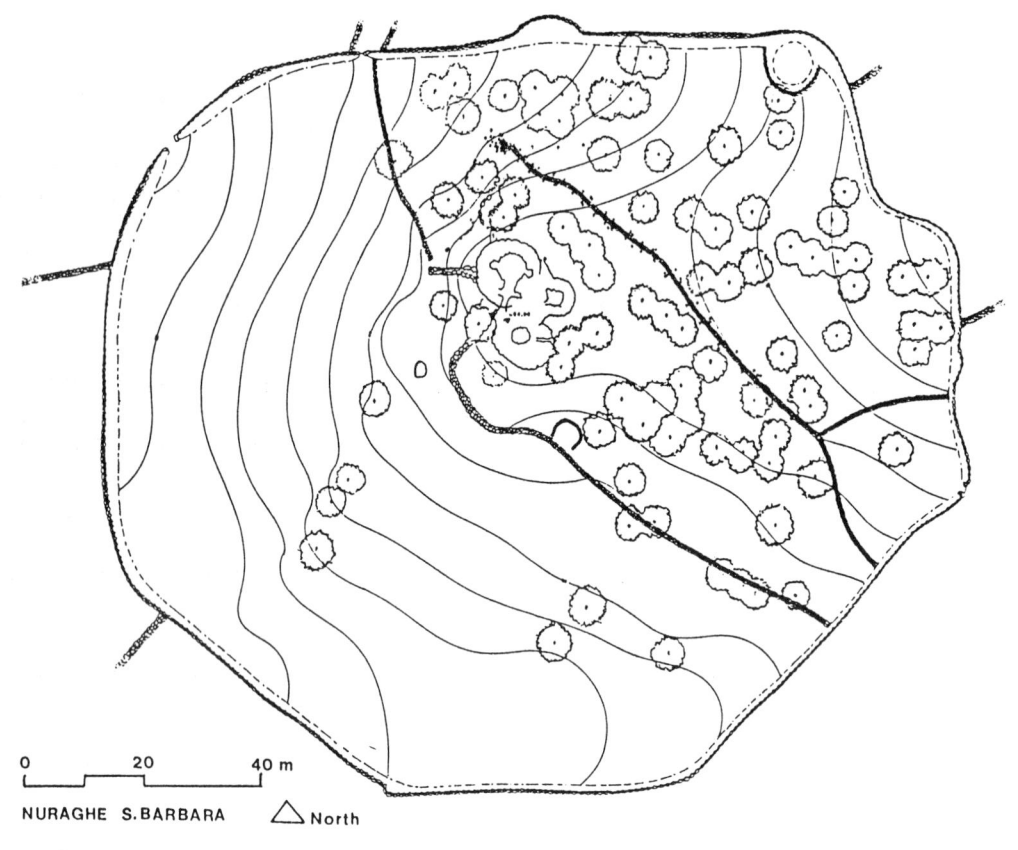

Fig. 1 Plan of the site of Nuraghe Santa Barbara within the monumental enclosing wall.

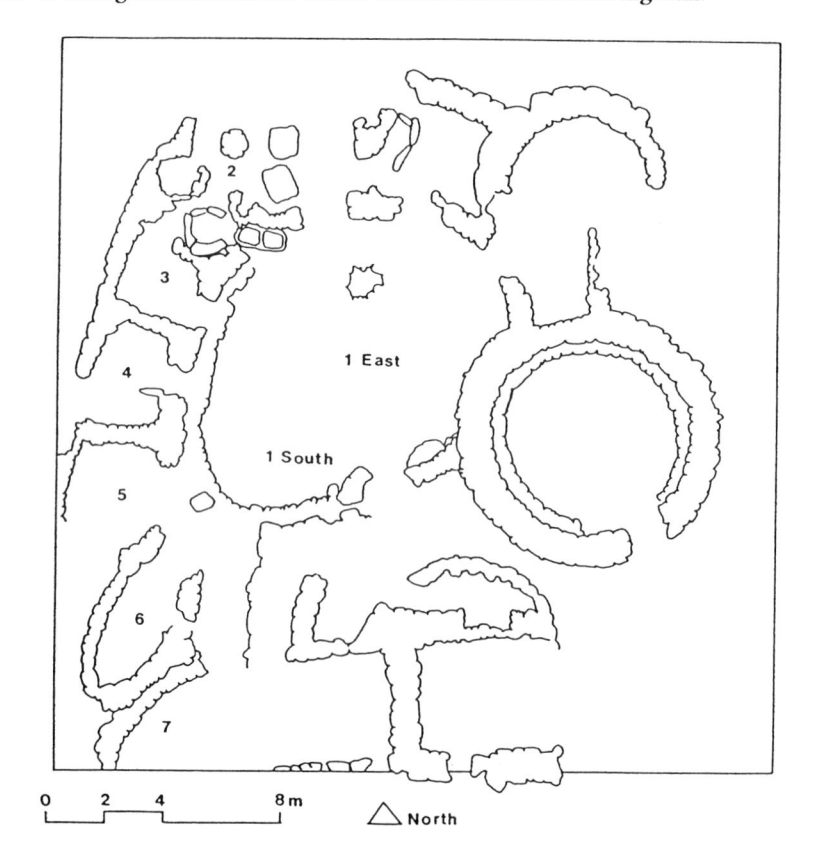

Fig. 2 Plan of west village.

Faunal Remains at Santa Barbara

Sardinian prehistorians are beginning to piece together a picture of the Nuragic diet and ancient stock-raising practices from recent analytical studies of faunal material from controlled excavations. Faunal material from Nuragic sites in the Marmilla and Campidano (Fonzo 1987), from Nuraghe Ortu Còmidu-Sardara (CA) (Balmuth 1986), and from the Nuraghi Toscano, Urpes, and Duos Nuraghes in the territory of Borore (NU) (Webster 1988; Webster 1987; Webster and Michels 1986), and data from Corsica (Vigne 1988; Lewthwaite 1981) have contributed to this emerging picture. The analysis of faunal remains from Nuraghe Santa Barbara confirms certain patterns reflected in these studies.

While the residents of ancient Santa Barbara carried off most of their worldly possessions when they abandoned the village in the 8th century BC, they left behind a considerable amount of faunal remains. More than 21 kg of animal bone fragments were recovered in the Nuragic levels of the west village so far excavated (Fig. 2). Despite the poor state of preservation of this material, 40% of the bone was identifiable. Due to the large quantity of bone, analytical priority was given to 5 kg of bone fragments coming from undisturbed Nuragic strata within identifiable contexts: the east and south sides of the courtyard, a multi-purpose activity area (area 2) to the north, and five houses (numbers 3-7) flanking the courtyard on its western side.

The majority (94%) of the bones represent domesticated animals (Table 1). The largest number of bones (c. 38%) come from domesticated cows (*Bos taurus*, L.). Almost as numerous (37%) are sheep (*Ovis aries*, L.), possibly mouflon (*Ovis musimon*, P.), and goat (*Capra hircus*, L.). Pigs (*Sus scrofa*, L.), including wild boar, constitute 19% of the material. The remaining 6% includes wild game: the Sardinian deer (*Cervus elaphus corsicanus*, Erx.); a small now-extinct mammal (*Prolagus sardus*, W.); and porcupine (*Erinaceus europaeus*, L.), still eaten in rural parts of the island. Bird and fish bones were also found, but are not yet classified.

Evidence for Nuragic Stock-raising

Hypotheses regarding Nuragic stock-raising can be advanced through the analysis of the minimum number of individuals (MNI) and their age when killed. In the Mediterranean, where one cow is equivalent in economic value to five sheep or one-and-one-half pigs (Miege 1977; Vigne 1988), the importance of various species of animals found at Santa Barbara appears to vary with the sector of the village in which they were found. For example, in houses 3-6, activity area 2, and the southern border of the courtyard, the faunal remains indicate that pork was eaten to a far greater extent than beef, lamb, goat, or the other represented game (Tables 1 and 4). In contrast, material coming from house 7 and the eastern courtyard suggests that cattle was the most economically important species, followed by pig, sheep, and goat (Tables 2 and 3).

The descending economic value of *Bos* > *Sus* > *Ovis* > *Capra* represents the dominant pattern established by the end of the Sardinian Neolithic. This equilibrium replaced the more primitive formula of *Sus* > *Ovis* > *Capra*. Such distinctions are notable at Santa Barbara, since the archaeological evidence suggests that activity area 2 was the most ancient nucleus of the west village.

The faunal remains examined so far indicate that the economy of Santa Barbara was based essentially on stock-raising. Wild game was used only minimally. The remains of deer, found only in house 7, constitute 0.37% of the studied sample (7 bone fragments). The relatively young age at which swine and caprines were slaughtered suggests that the animals were raised primarily for the production of meat (Tables 1-5), leaving a few older individuals for reproduction. In the case of caprines, older individuals may have been used for milk and wool. This is substantiated by the large number of excavated spindle whorls and loom weights in the same Nuragic context. Half of the identified cattle were slaughtered at an advanced age, suggesting their use as draught animals.

The fact that all sections of the animal skeletons are present suggests that each unit butchered its meat. Only a few long bones were missing, those favored for tool manufacture. This is in contrast to the findings at Nuraghe Toscano, which suggest preliminary butchering before the carcasses were brought into the village (Webster 1987: 83). No bone implements have as yet been found at Nuraghe Santa Barbara, and are rare at other Nuragic sites. The absence of these long bones, desirable for making bone tools, together with the light weight and portability of such tools, could easily account for this absence at sites known to have been abandoned peacefully.

Cut marks on the bones and signs of burning identify ancient butchering techniques used at Nuraghe Santa Barbara. For example, the butchering of sheep and goats involves the disarticulation of the foot from the leg bone, while in cows, the foot is completely severed. Questions quickly come to mind as to the existence of two different butchering techniques at Santa Barbara, and whether one prevailed over the other. The analysis of the entire sample may shed more light on this situation.

Another butchering technique is illuminated by a fragment of the lumbar vertebra of a caprine found in the vicinity of houses 2-6. The bone shows a definite cut along the spinal column where the carcass has been divided in two halves.

General Impressions

The study of vertebrate faunal remains at Nuraghe Santa Barbara helps to focus on the problems of faunal analysis at archaeological sites in Sardinia (Rowland 1987). The biggest problem is lack of material necessary to substantiate trends suggested by a relatively small group of data. Poor preservation of bone material and disruption of strata by reoccupation of Nuragic sites further complicate the analysis of faunal material.

Preliminary results from Santa Barbara verify stock-raising as an important aspect of the ancient Nuragic economy. Changes in the valuation of certain species of domesticated animals, already hinted at other sites, call for additional research to: (a) substantiate evolving patterns on a regional basis; and (b) isolate and explain factors precipitating the change in utilization of domesticated animals. Perceived differences in distribution and consumption of stock may be related to other than chronological factors. Variation may be indicative of differential usage among groups of households, an hypothesis difficult to prove at Santa Barbara due to the difficulty in isolating material from individual houses. Continued excavation at Nuraghe Santa Barbara is expected to clarify this situation and provide new evidence for the palaeoeconomy of a Nuragic village.

Acknowledgment

The authors wish to thank Dr Vicenzo Santoni, Superintendent of Archaeology for the Provinces of Cagliari and Oristano, for his permission to collaborate on this material.

Table 1

Activity area 2 and houses 3-6

Type of individual	No. total finds	% total finds	Min. no. indiv.	% min. no. indiv.	Weight grams	% weight grams	Burn	% burn	Age
Cow	52	22.51	1	6.66	370	48.18	3	23.08	10 yrs
Sheep/Goat	94	40.70	4	26.67	170	22.13	6	46.15	4-5, 2.5 yrs 8, 3 mos
Pig	68	29.44	4	26.67	210	27.34	4	30.77	2yrs, 2 yrs, few mos, newborn
Prolagus	7	3.03	2	13.34	5	0.65	/	/	---
Porcupine	1	0.43	1	6.66	3	0.40	/	/	---
Birds	5	2.16	2	13.34	5	0.65	/	/	---
Fish	4	1.73	1	6.66	5	0.65	/	/	---
Total	231	100	15	100	768	100	13	100	

	Total finds	% total finds	Weight grams	% weight grams	Burn	% burn
Determined	231	39.22	768	51.61	13	2.20
Undetermined	358	60.78	720	48.39	/	/
Total	589	100	1488	100	13	2.20

Table 2

House 7

Type of individual	No. total finds	% total finds	Min. no. indiv.	% min no. indiv.	Weight grams	% weight grams	Burn	% burn	Age
Cow	148	52.11	3	15.79	2670	77.37	3	25	12+, 2+, 1.5–2 yrs
Sheep/Goat	70	24.64	5	26.32	360	10.43	3	25	4, 2+, 1.5–2 yrs, 3 mos (2)
Pig	40	14.09	4	21.05	340	9.85	3	25	3.5, 2 yrs, few mos (2)
Prolagus	13	4.58	3	15.79	10	0.09	1	8.33	---
Deer	7	2.47	1	5.26	60	1.74	2	16.67	2 yrs
Birds	5	1.76	2	10.53	10	0.29	/	/	---
Fish	1	0.35	1	5.26	1	0.03	/	/	---
Total	284	100	19	100	3451	100	12	100	

	Total finds	% total finds	Weight grams	% weight grams	Burn	% burn
Determined	284	35	3451	64.80	12	1.47
Undetermined	528	65	1875	35.20	34	4.18
Total	812	100	5326	100	46	5.65

Table 3

East courtyard

Type of individual	No. total finds	% total finds	Min. no. indiv.	% min. no. indiv.	Weight grams	% weight grams	Burn	% burn	Age
Cow	17	18.48	1	25	60	26.67	/	/	8.5 yrs
Sheep/Goat	71	77.17	2	50	140	62.22	/	/	4, 2.5 yrs
Pig	4	4.35	1	25	25	11.11	/	/	---
Total	92	100	4	100	225	100	/	/	

	Total finds	% total finds	Weight grams	% weight grams	Burn	% burn
Determined	92	60.53	225	84.90	/	/
Undetermined	60	39.47	40	5.10	3	1.97
Total	152	100	265	100	3	1.97

Table 4
South courtyard

Type of individual	No. total finds	% total finds	Min. no. indiv.	% min. no. indiv.	Weight grams	% weight grams	Burn	% burn	Age
Cow	51	52.53	1	16.67	330	80.19	2	33.33	1.5–4.5 yrs
Sheep/Goat	26	26.26	2	33.33	35	8.54	2	33.33	<5, 22+ mos
Pig	21	21.21	2	33.33	40	9.76	2	33.34	very young, 22+ mos
Prolagus	1	1.01	1	16.67	5	1.21	/	/	---
Total	99	100	6	100	410	100	6	100	

	Total finds	% total finds	Weight grams	% weight grams	Burn	% burn
Determined	99	33.90	410	55.16	6	2.05
Undetermined	193	66.10	320	43.84	24	8.20
Total	292	100	730	100	30	10.25

Table 5
Summary of faunal material from activity area 2, houses 3-7, and east and south sectors of the courtyard

Type of individuals	No. total finds	% total finds	Min. no. indiv.	% min no. indiv.	Weight grams	% weight grams	Burn	% burn
Cow	268	37.96	6	13.64	3430	70.66	8	25.81
Sheep/Goat	261	36.97	13	29.54	705	14.53	11	35.48
Pig	133	18.84	11	25	615	12.67	9	29.03
Prolagus	21	2.97	6	13.64	20	0.41	1	3.23
Deer	7	0.99	1	2.27	60	1.24	2	6.45
Porcupine	1	0.14	1	2.27	3	0.06	/	/
Birds	10	1.42	4	9.09	15	0.31	/	/
Fish	5	0.71	2	4.55	6	0.12	/	/
Total	706	100	44	100	4854	100	31	100

	Total finds	% total finds	Weight grams	% weight grams	Burn	% burn
Determined	706	38.26	4854	62.15	31	1.68
Undetermined	1139	61.47	2955	37.85	61	2.05
Total	1845	100	7809	100	92	3.73

References

Balmuth, M.S.
   1986   Sardara (Cagliari). Preliminary report of excavations 1975–1978 of the Nuraghe Ortu Còmidu. *Notizie degli Scavi di Antichità* 37(1983): 353-410.

Fonzo, O.
   1987   Reperti faunistici in Marmilla e Campidano nell'età del Bronzo e nella prima età del ferro. In G. Lilliu, G. Ugas e G. Lai (a cura di), *La Sardegna nel Mediterraneo fra il Secondo e il Primo Millennio a.C. Atti del II Convegno di studi, Selargius-Cagliari, 27-30 novembre 1986*, 233-42. Cagliari: Amministrazione Provinciale di Cagliari.

Gallin, L.J.
   1989   Architectural attributes and inter-site variation: a case study: the Sardinian nuraghi. PhD dissertation, UCLA. Ann Arbor: University Microfilms International.

Gallin, L.J., & S. Sebis
1989 Bauladu (Oristano)—Villaggio Nuragico di Santa Barbara. *Nuovo Bullettino Archeologico Sardo* 1989: 271-75.

Gallin, L.J., & R.H. Tykot
in press Metallurgical activity at the Nuragic village of Santa Barbara (Bauladu), Sardinia, Italy. *Journal of Field Archaeology*.

Lewthwaite, J.
1981 Plain tails from the hills: Transhumance in Mediterranean archaeology. In A. Sheridan and G. Bailey (eds.), *Economic Archaeology*, 57-66. BAR International Series 96. Oxford: British Archaeological Reports.

Miege, J.
1977 Problems botaniques de l'eleveur Mediterraneen. *L'Elevage en Mediterraneen Occidentale*, 9-22. Paris: C.N.R.S.

Rowland, R.J., Jr
1987 Faunal remains in prehistoric Sardinia: The current state of the evidence. In J.W. Michels and G.S. Webster (eds.), *Studies in Nuragic Archaeology*, 147-61. BAR International Series 373. Oxford: British Archaeological Reports.

Vigne, J.-D.
1988 *Les Mammiferes Post-glaciaires de Corse. Etude archeozooligique.* Gallia Préhistoire Supplement 26. Paris: CNRS.

Webster, G.S.
1987 Vertebrate faunal remains. In J.W. Michels and G.S. Webster (eds.), *Studies in Nuragic Archaeology*, 69-91. BAR International Series 373. Oxford: British Archaeological Reports.
1988 Duos Nuraghes: Preliminary results of the first three seasons of excavation. *Journal of Field Archaeology* 15: 465-72.

Webster, G.S., & J.W. Michels
1986 Paleoeconomy in west-central Sardinia. *Antiquity* 60: 221-29.

Riassunto

Gli scavi effettuati presso il Nuraghe Santa Barbara (Bauladu) hanno fornito testimonianze importanti riguardo la dieta e l'allevamento delle popolazioni dell'antica Sardegna. Gli scavi presso questo sito così ben preservato e così vasto sono stati complicati dal fatto che Santa Barbara è stata occupata quasi ininterrottamente per tre millenni. Secondo le ceramiche ritrovate, il periodo di occupazione nuragica risale al XII-VIII secolo BC, e sembra che sia declinato pacificamente. Numerosi resti di ossa di animali sono stati analizzati selettivamente e l'importanza relativa degli animali domestici è la seguente: 38% bue (*Bos taurus*, L.); 37% pecora (*Ovis aries*, L.), muflone (*Ovis musimon*, P.), e capra (*Capra hircus*, L.); 19% suino (*Sus scrofa*, L.); e il rimanente 6% include selvaggina come il cervo sardo (*Cervus elaphus corsicanus*, Erx.), l'estinto *Prolagus sardus*, W., e il porcospino. Gli Autori notano che l'importanza relativa delle specie varia da settore a settore all'interno del villaggio.

Il modello dominante esistente durante la fine del Neolitico sardo è rappresentato dal valore delle *Bos*>*Sus*>*Capra*, che ha sostituito i valori primitivi della *Sus*>*Ovis*>*Capra*. La distinzione è visibile presso Santa Barbara stessa dal momento che l'area di attività 2 del villagio, che ha restituito resti di ossa di animali, è il nucleo più antico del villaggio occidentale presso questo sito e presenta la più antica formula economica.

I risultati di queste analisi indicano che l'economia di Santa Barbara era basata principalmente sull'allevamento ed era completata solo in minima parte da selvaggina. Suini e caprini venivano macellati in giovane età, ciò indica che venivano allevati per utilizzare la loro carne. Il ritrovamento di numerose fusaiole e resti di pesi per telaio indica la conservazione di animali più vecchi per utilizzare la loro lana e probabilmente il loro latte.

Lo studio di resti di vertebrati presso Santa Barbara fa luce su problemi di analisi di fauna presso altri siti sardi. Gli Autori concludono l'articolo sostenendo che è necessario che ulteriori ricerche siano effettuate per verificare i modelli regionali di allevamento e di dieta e per spiegare i fattori che hanno causato il sorgere di cambiamenti nell'uso degli animali domestici in Sardegna.

PART III

Sardinia and the Mediterranean World

Un'Altra Fibula 'Cipriota' dalla Sardegna

Fulvia Lo Schiavo

Il Nuraghe-Santuario di Nurdole (Orani-NU). Circostanze del recupero

La fibula in esame fa parte di un gruppo di bronzi sequestrati dalla Guardia di Finanza di Nuoro nel luglio 1990 in uno dei tanti episodi che segnano, dal 1988 ad oggi, una vera e propria battaglia che ha al centro la difesa dell'eccezionale nuraghe-santuario di Nurdole, in agro di Orani, al confine con il comune di Nuoro. Ogni campagna di scavo infatti (1987, 1988, 1989, 1990), tutte dirette da Maria Ausilia Fadda, incaricata della direzione dell'Ufficio Operativo di Nuoro, è stata preceduta, seguita e accompagnata da danneggiamenti gravissimi, che hanno infine portato alla parziale demolizione del lato Sud.

La causa di questo accanimento dei 'tombaroli' è anche uno dei motivi del grande interesse scientifico del monumento: si tratta infatti di un nuraghe a pianta complessa includente una fonte ed altre strutture, utilizzato come santuario e perciò letteralmente gremito di offerte di armi, ornamenti, strumenti e statuine di bronzo, oltre ad oggetti d'ambra, d'argento e di ferro e ad una notevole quantità di vasellame d'impasto.

I depositi votivi si presentano concentrati in alcune aree privilegiate: il corridoio di ingresso, la torre orientale, le adiacenze della vasca lustrale, eccetera, ed anche dispersi nel villaggio intorno al perimetro del monumento. Il numero di reperti finora recuperati è incalcolabile e solo di bronzi si contano diverse migliaia di pezzi. È dunque comprensibile che oltre al materiale rinvenuto nelle campagne di scavo, molto sia stato rintracciato e sequestrato durante le indagini a carico di scavatori clandestini e ricettatori; uno di questi lotti è appunto quello di cui fa parte la fibula oggetto di questo articolo. Non vi sono dubbi, per i motivi esposti, sulla sua provenienza dal nuraghe Nurdole, anche se purtroppo non sono precisabili il punto esatto e le condizioni di giacitura.

Il nuraghe ha pianta complessa, costituita da una torre centrale e quattro torri ad addizione concentrica. Da un lungo corridoio si accede al cortile dove, di fianco alla torre centrale, si apre una fonte, ora priva di acqua. Adiacente al lato Sud del cortile, una sorta di monumentino gradonato con la funzione di sostenere una canaletta, comunica con due vani trapezoidali ricavati nello spessore del rifascio murario, attraverso i quali l'acqua sgorgava a caduta in una vasca lastricata a pianta irregolarmente rettangolare, adattata alla roccia naturale ed alla parete del nuraghe. Il monumento, che sorge sulla sommità di un'altura di 700 m slm, è delimitato da NO a SE da un possente antemurale all'interno del quale si trova un vasto villaggio che circonda tutto il nuraghe.

La cronologia del monumento è da collocare dall'età del Bronzo Medio alla prima età del Ferro (XVI–X sec. a.C.), ma la maggiore frequentazione si registra con la trasformazione del nuraghe in santuario nell'età del Bronzo Recente e Finale. Il luogo sacro ha poi continuato ad essere visitato, come attestano materiali votivi anche di importazione, almeno fino all'età Orientalizzante ed Arcaica (fine VIII–VI sec. a.C.).

Da segnalare è la presenza di reperti ceramici di cultura Monte Claro e Bonnanaro, al di sotto dello strato di fondazione del nuraghe, pertinenti ad una occupazione dell'altura—un vero nido d'aquila, eccellente per il largo raggio di avvistamento—già nell'Eneolitico Maturo e nella prima età del Bronzo (circa metà III e prima metà II millennio a.C.) (Fadda 1986: 308-14; 1990; 1991; in stampa). Molto di più si potrà dire quando sarà completata la documentazione e lo studio della enorme quantità di materiali, abbinati alla singolarità delle strutture ed alla successione stratigrafica riscontrata durante gli scavi.

Descrizione ed Analisi Tipologica

Fibula a gomito con nodo centrale allungato ed incavo a goccia sui due lati; la parte anteriore dell'arco ha sezione piano-convessa, con allargamento centrale, quasi a placchetta rettangolare, marginata da due motivi incisi a spina di pesce, e con quattro costolature per parte; quattro costolature si trovano all'inizio della parte posteriore dell'arco (Fig. 1.1). Si conserva solo un frammento che comprende la parte anteriore dell'arco con

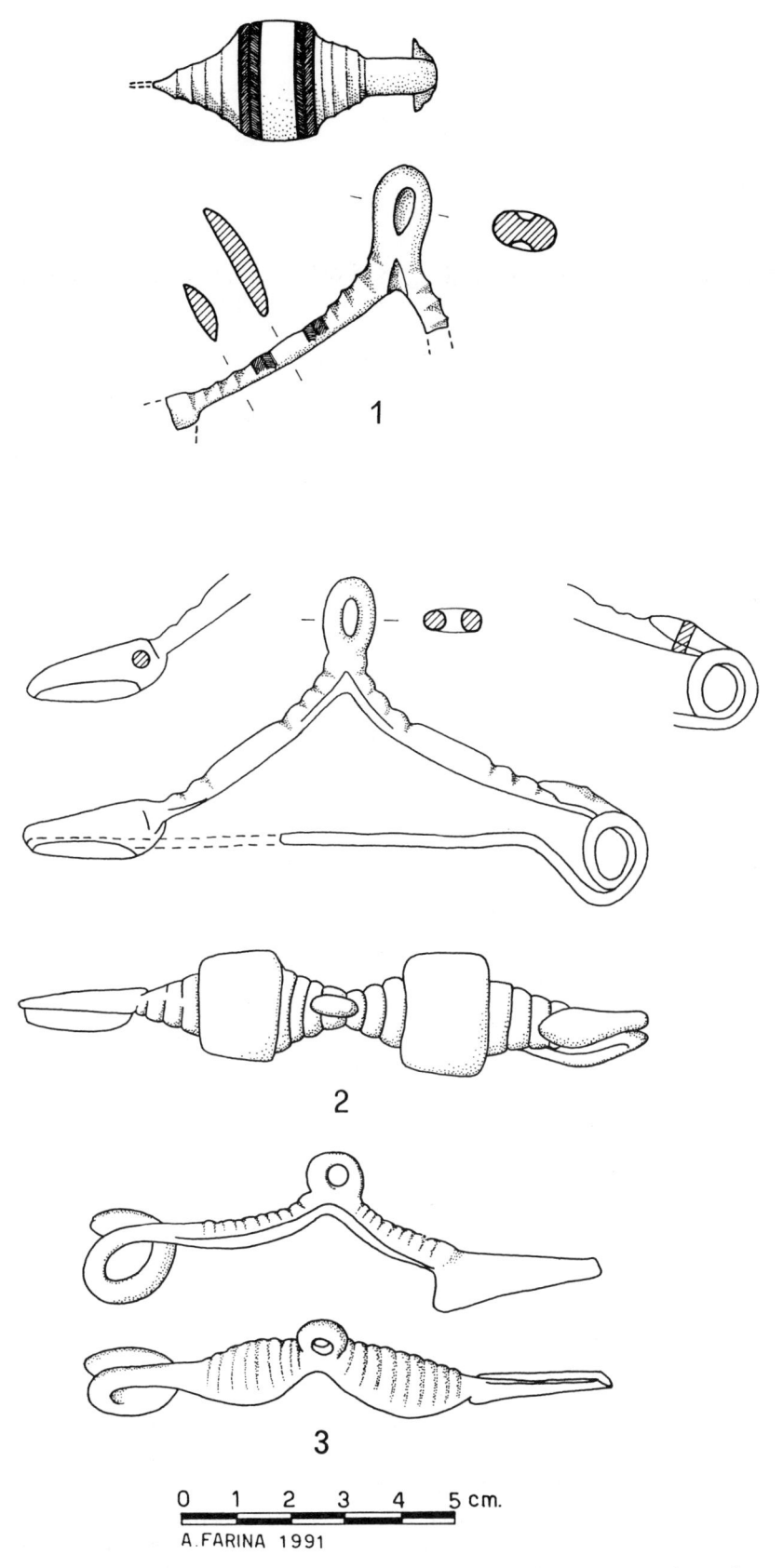

Fig. 1 Fibule 'cipriote' in Occidente: 1. Orani (Nuoro), nuraghe Nurdole; 2. Beaume-les-Créancey (Côte-d'Or) (da Cunisset Carnot *et al.* 1971); 3. 'Meseta' (da Almagro 1966).

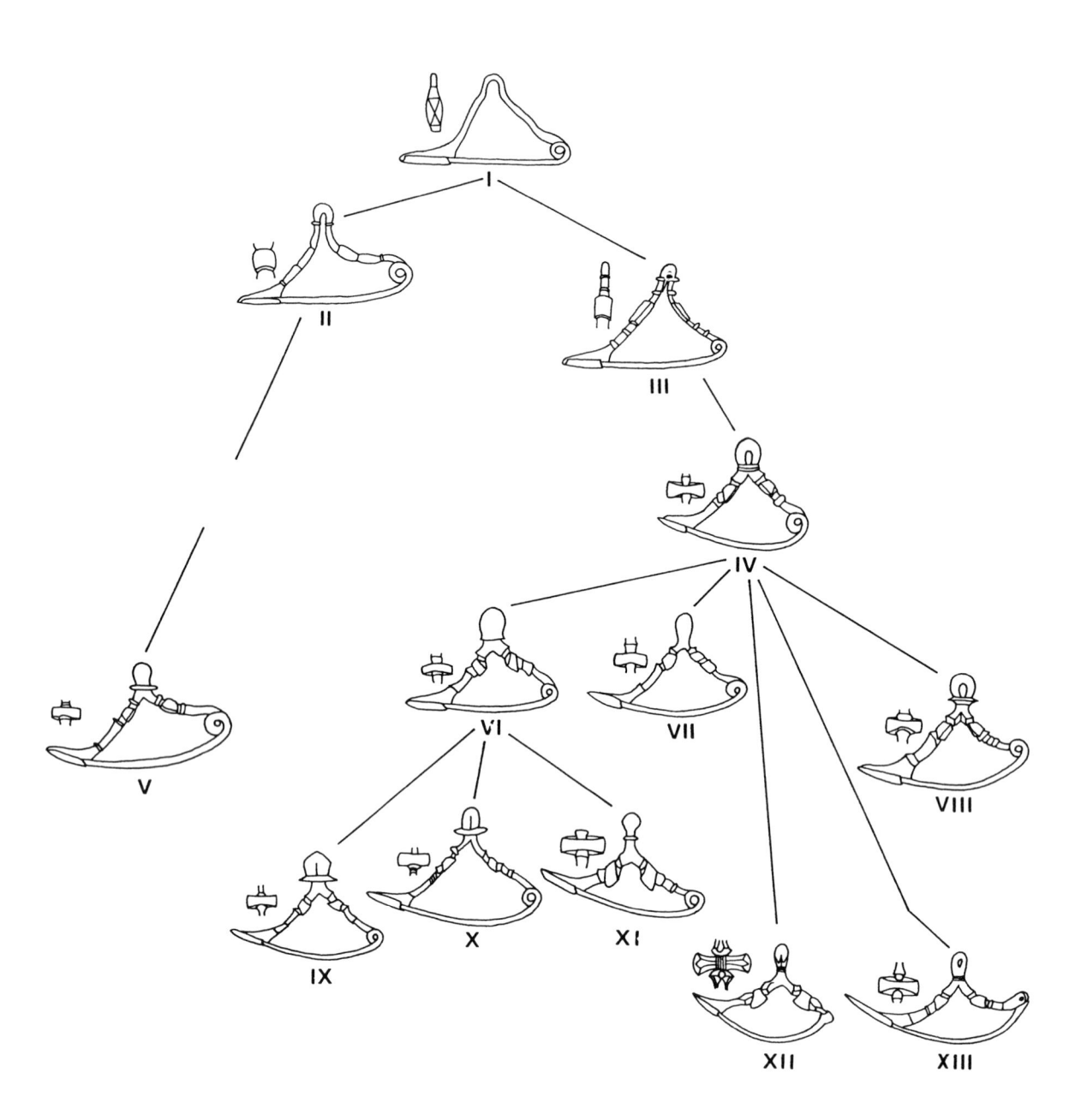

Fig. 2 Schema tipologico delle fibule cipriote (da Buchholz 1986).

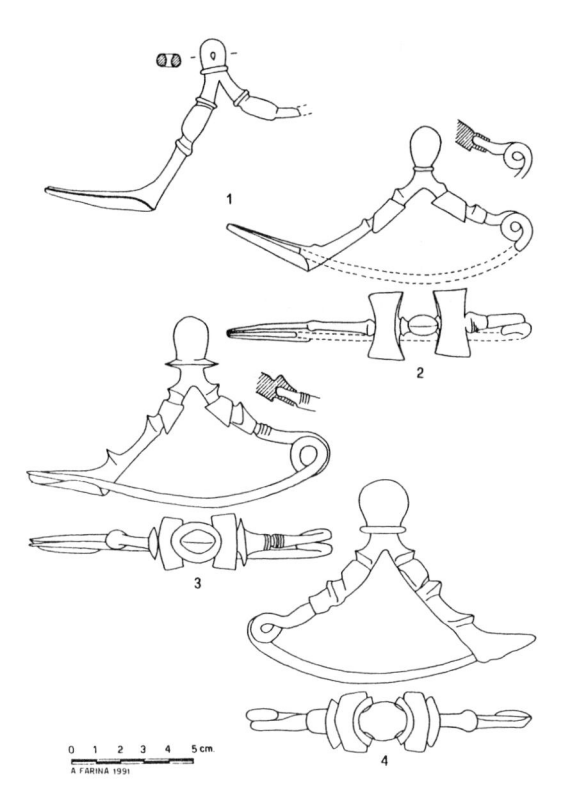

Fig. 3 Fibule cipriote in Occidente: 1. Barumini (Cagliari), Su Nuraxi (da Lo Schiavo 1978); 2-3. 'Italia' (da Cunisset Carnot *et al.* 1971); 4. Baune, Museo Archeologico (da Cunisset Carnot *et al.* 1971).

un piccolo tratto della staffa, il nodo centrale e l'inizio della parte posteriore, che appare leggermente contorta. Lunghezza 5.3 cm; altezza 4.8 cm; larghezza massima 2.2 cm.

Nonostante lo stato del frammento, la tipologia della fibula è perfettamente definibile: si tratta infatti di una fibula 'cipriota,' per la presenza del gomito con nodo centrale, del profilo triangolare dell'arco e della elaborata decorazione plastica. Di recente questa categoria di fibule è stata riesaminata a fondo da H.-G. Buchholz (1986) che ha ripreso ed ampliato gli studi di J.L. Myres (1910) e di J. Birmingham (1963), raccogliendo tutti gli esemplari attribuibili ad essa che assommano a circa un'ottantina. Esposizioni parziali si devono a Ch. Blinkenberg (1926: 247-53, types chypriotes XIII, 14 e 15) nell'ambito del suo catalogo *Fibules Grecques et Orientales*. In riferimento con esemplari occidentali affini, l'argomento è stato trattato da Martin Almagro in più occasioni (1949: 138-41; 1957; 1957–58; 1966: 182-88), da P.G. Guzzo (1969), da P. Cunisset Carnot, J.P. Mohen e J.P. Nicolardot (1971) e, in sintesi, da F. Lo Schiavo (1978: 42-44).

Da Buchholz conviene dunque partire, perchè non solo è l'opera più recente ma anche la più estesa, il maggior difetto della quale consiste proprio nel fatto che, pur analizzando e descrivendo accuratamente una serie di fibule di questa categoria, ne illustra solo una trentina. Ne consegue che trattandosi di una forma complessa, articolata in molti tipi ed in un ampio arco cronologico, non si ha la possibilità di verificare lo schema tipologico che l'autore denomina '*Stammbaum*,' caricandolo dunque di una precisa valenza evolutiva (Buchholz 1986: fig. 9) (Fig. 2). La seriazione è stata costruita sulla base della struttura generale dell'arco, prima a gomito (tipo I), poi a gomito assai accostato, a profilo asimmetrico (tipo II) e a profilo simmetrico (tipo III), poi a gomito legato e costituente un occhiello (tipo IV), e infine a nodulo (tipi V-XIII). Grande attenzione è stata dedicata agli aspetti tecnici: al bimetallismo, ovvero all'impiego di un ago di ferro su di un arco di bronzo, alla lavorazione in parti separate della staffa, dell'arco e della molla, alla sostituzione della molla con la cerniera. Per ammissione dello stesso autore, altri particolari strutturali, pur esaminati, non sono stati considerati determinanti per un diverso schema di raggruppamento: l'arco simmetrico o asimmetrico, l'ago dritto o curvo, la decorazione plastica a foggia di placchetta rettangolare (che poi, per la sua forma caratteristica, diviene il *Doppelaxtzierelement*) disposta in senso longitudinale o perpendicolare rispetto all'arco. I tredici tipi distinti si distribuiscono fra il

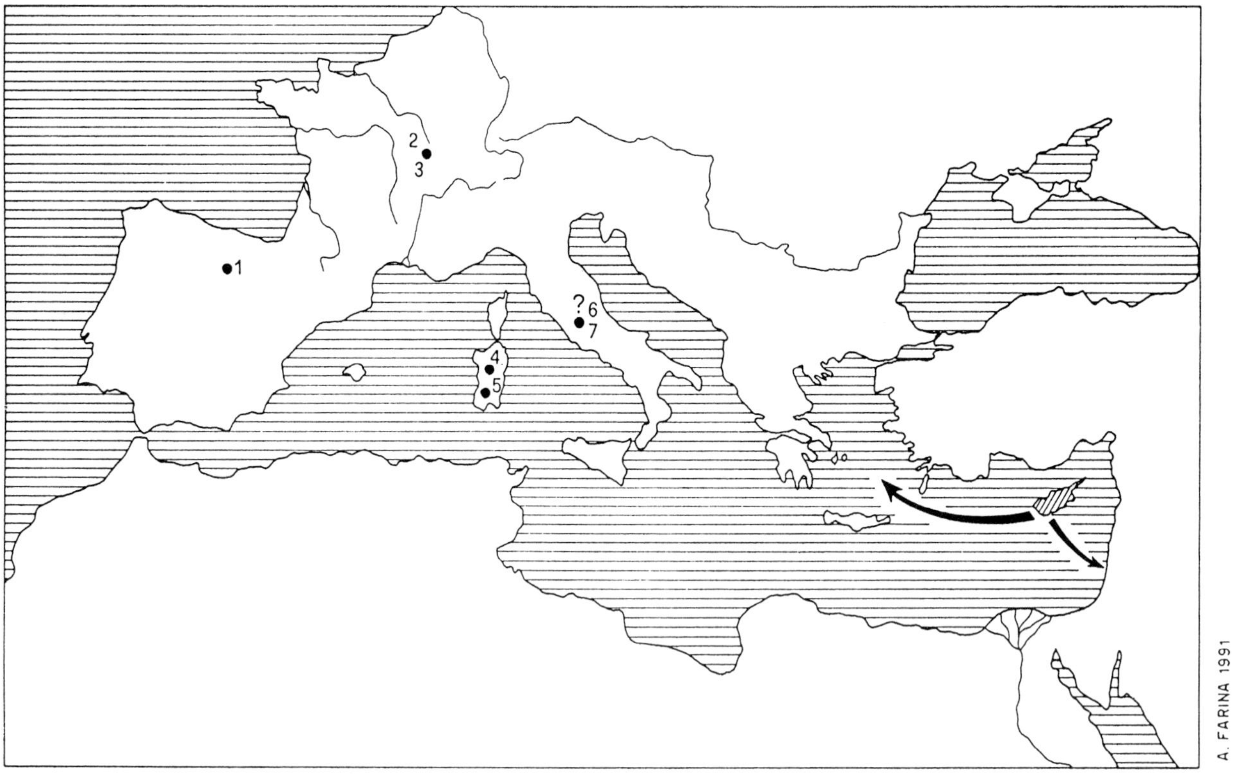

300 *Sardinia in the Mediterranean*

Fig. 4 Carta di distribuzione delle fibule cipriote in Occidente: 1. 'Mesata' (Spagna); 2. Beaume-les-Créancey (Francia); 3. Museo Archeologico di Baune (Francia); 4. Orani (Nuoro), nuraghe Nurdole (Sardegna); 5. Barumini (Cagliari), Su Nuraxi (Sardegna); 6-7. 'Italia'.

1200 e il 700 (tipi I-IV) e dalla seconda metà del VII a parte del VI secolo (tipi V-XIII). Buchholz riconosce che la scarsità di dati archeologici obiettivi rende dubbio il quadro cronologico, e questo è senz'altro un fatto innegabile. Non stupisce, invece, che pochi tipi rappresentati da pochi esemplari si collochino in un grande spazio di tempo, perchè questo è un fenomeno che si riscontra, in genere, in tutte le fibule nelle fasi più antiche. Successivamente, nell'età del Ferro inoltrata ed in particolare nel periodo Orientalizzante, le tipologie si arricchiscono e la produzione diviene quasi di serie. A commento del lavoro di Buchholz, si può dire che sarebbe stato preferibile non insistere su criteri evolutivi che restano, come si è visto, ampiamente soggettivi, mentre è basilare cercare di identificare i diversi tipi con la maggior precisione possibile; in tal modo alcuni dei fenomeni di imitazione, influenza, distribuzione risaltano in tutta evidenza.

Confronti e Relazioni sulle Lunghe Distanze

Questa veloce sintesi critica era necessaria per poter inquadrare in modo completo la problematica della fibula in esame, anche se poi l'esemplare più simile al nostro viene da Buchholz escluso dalla seriazione delle fibule cipriote:

> Auch Bildungen, die zwar als 'kyprisch' apostrophiert wurden, sich jedoch in den Details als westliche Arbeiten zu erkennen geben, müssen mit Huelvaformen in verbindung gebracht werden, so etwa ein Stück aus der Mesetaregion Spaniens (Almagro 1966: 187, fig. 6) und ein anderes aus Frankreich' (Cunisset Carnot *et al.* 1971) (Fig. 1.2).

Per quest'ultima è opinione di Buchholz (1986: 243) che si tratti di una esportazione iberica in Francia. Appunto una fibula di Beaume-les-Créancey (Côte-d'Or) rinvenuta in superficie sul fronte di taglio di una cava in località Larrey de Corton, è il più preciso confronto per le dimensioni (11,2 cm integra, altezza 5,2 cm) e le proporzioni, per la forma e orientamento delle placchette ornamentali, per la sezione schiacciata piano-convessa, per la sagoma in generale e nei suoi particolari costitutivi. Le differenze sono: la presenza, nell'esemplare della Sardegna, di una decorazione incisa sul bordo della placchetta (peraltro non ignota a fibule di questa categoria: cfr. Buchholz 1986: fig. 6c) ed il fatto che il nodo centrale (*Schlaufen*) non presenti un foro passante ma due incavi contrapposti; inoltre non sembra, dal frammento residuo, che la staffa fosse lavorata a parte, come invece è accertato nella fibula dalla Francia. Per tutti e due gli esemplari è dunque incontestabile tanto l'appartenenza alla classe delle fibule 'cipriote,' quanto la fattura locale. Non fosse per l'occhiello forato a Beaume-les-Créancey e non forato a Nurdole, si potrebbe sostenere la fattura in una medesima officina; comunque appare assai probabile la provenienza da un'unica zona di produzione. Per la fibula dalla Francia gli autori pensavano a relazioni dirette fra la Gallia e il bacino orientale del Mediterraneo, pur senza precisarne la natura esatta e la direzione; con prudenza, a motivo della carenza di notizie sulla provenienza, viene ricordata la presenza di una seconda fibula cipriota di tipo canonico (apparentemente ascrivibile al tipo VI di Buchholz) (Cunisset Carnot *et al.* 1971: 607) (Fig. 3.4); Buchholz invece riferisce gli esemplari francesi ai rapporti con la Penisola Iberica, anche per la somiglianza—invero non strettissima—con un esemplare dalla Meseta, come riportato sopra (Fig. 1.3).

La fibula del nuraghe Nurdole pone un problema ancora più complesso. Nessuna difficoltà risiede nell'ammissione di una relazione diretta con Cipro, accertata e ben documentata a partire almeno dall'età del Bronzo Finale ed alla quale è certamente dovuto l'esemplare di Barumini (Buchholz tipo IV per la presenza dell'occhiello pervio) (Lo Schiavo 1978: fig. 6.3) (Fig. 3.1). Si potrebbe addirittura avanzare l'ipotesi che dalla Sardegna provengano, in antico o di recente, anche le due fibule 'dall'Italia,' conservate nel Museo di St. Germain-en-Laye (Cunisset Carnot *et al.* 1971: fig. 2.2-3) (Fig. 3.2-3) che invece Buchholz (che le inquadra nei suoi tipi VII e X) ritiene indicazione troppo generica da essere affidabile e che attribuisce direttamente a Cipro (Buchholz 1986: 235 n. 41).

Per questo secondo esemplare da un contesto nuragico, invece, l'indipendenza dalle tipologie cipriote e la decorazione a spina di pesce potrebbe anche suggerire una fabbricazione locale, come per tanti altri materiali di ispirazione orientale liberamente rielaborati, mentre più difficile resta proporre un qualche contatto con la Borgogna, sia pure per il tramite dell'Italia Peninsulare (Fig. 4). Esiste ancora un'altra ipotesi possibile: che ambedue le fibule provengano da un'area meseteña della Penisola Iberica, dove appunto è documentato un esemplare simile. Anche in questo caso, vi sono sufficienti elementi che riconnettono saldamente questa vasta regione e soprattutto le sue coste atlantiche con la Sardegna; proprio nel nuraghe Nurdole è stata rinvenuta un'ascia piatta a tallone ristretto di derivazione da modelli iberici (Lo Schiavo e D'Oriano 1990: 110 n. 48). Questa seconda ipotesi evidenzierebbe l'"internazionalità' delle relazioni transmarine della Sardegna e la sua familiarità con le rotte sia dall'Occidente che dall'Oriente (Lo Schiavo 1991). Non si può escludere, in tal caso, che la decorazione incisa ai lati della placchetta sia stata aggiunta in un secondo momento per meglio adattare l'oggetto al gusto locale.

Riferimenti Cronologici e Conclusioni

Il problema della datazione delle fibule cipriote, come si è detto, resta aperto, per il fatto che per la maggioranza di esse non si sono conservate notizie attendibili sul contesto di provenienza, dopo l'estrapolazione e le vicende, in parte anche clandestine, del commercio antiquario. I pochi esemplari databili servono così a costruire uno schema generale (Buchholz 1986: 223-29) in base al quale, ad esempio, la fibula di Barumini (tipo IV) rientrerebbe nel periodo dal 1200 al 700 e le due fibule 'dall'Italia' (tipi VII e X) tra la seconda metà del VII e la prima parte del VI secolo a.C. Per la fibula da Barumini si ha una conferma stratigrafica, data dalla presenza di frammenti di brocche askoidi e di vasi piriformi con decorazione geometrica nel battuto sabbioso-argilloso del vano 135 su cui posava, nel villaggio di Su Nuraxi (Lilliu 1955: 464-68, tav. LXXVI, 12); ciò consente, alla luce delle nuove acquisizioni in merito alle relazioni fra il mondo nuragico ed il mondo villanoviano, di inquadrare il livello forse ancora entro la prima età del Ferro. Ben diversa è la situazione della fibula di Beaume-les-Créancey—e, per la sua stringente somiglianza, per quella del nuraghe Nurdole—che Buchholz ritiene una evoluzione del tipo Huelva ('*Huelvatypus mit Bügelzier*').

Lasciando da parte ogni criterio evoluzionista, le fibule di Huelva trovano oggi la loro corretta collocazione cronologica, nell'ambito del riesame dell'intero complesso di bronzi di cui fanno parte, all'850 circa a.C. e forse anche prima, soprattutto se si tiene conto della ricalibrazione, conformemente alla datazione attribuibile al frammento di fibula tipo Cassibile ad esse associato (Almagro Gorbea 1977: 182, 524-25, 542-43). Perciò, accertata la fattura locale, anche se non estranea a fenomeni di imitazione e di gusto tanto cipriota quanto siciliano (Guzzo 1969: 306; Delibes de Castro 1978: 245), ancora meno facile riesce attribuire una datazione ad altri tipi a loro volta ricettivi di influssi locali ed esterni e parzialmente modificati. Cunisset Carnot, Mohen e Nicolardot (1971: 606-607) datano la fibula dalla Francia al VII secolo sulla base di confronti non del tutto soddisfacenti e basati sulla presenza dell'occhiello. A titolo orientativo e con tutte le riserve già espresse, si può accettare anche per l'esemplare della Sardegna questa indicazione, ma nel frattempo attendiamo che il completamento delle ricerche nella località di provenienza e lo studio di tutto l'insieme dei materiali rinvenuti consenta di precisare ed argomentare maggiormente le considerazioni ed i suggerimenti qui formulati.

Ringraziamenti

Ringrazio Maria Ausilia Fadda non solo per avermi segnalato il recupero della fibula e per aver cooperato per la pronta riconsegna alla Soprintendenza ai fini della documentazione e dello studio, ma anche per aver dato sollecite notizie preliminari sullo scavo del nuraghe Nurdole, che ne hanno consentito l'inquadramento. Grazie alla sua generosa disponibilità, una notizia con relativa documentazione fotografica è stata pubblicata da David Ridgway (1988–89: 131 fig. 2a-c) ed un'altra, nelle more dell'edizione nel *Nuovo Bullettino Archeologico Sardo* 3 (1986 della serie ma pubblicato nel 1990 e distribuito nel 1991), nel *Bollettino di Archeologia* 4 (1990): 123-25, e nella *Rivista di Studi Fenici* (1991). Ringrazio anche Antonio Farina che ha realizzato le illustrazioni per questo lavoro.

Bibliografia

Almagro, M.
    1949   El hallazgo de la ria del Huelva y el final de la Edad del Bronce en el Occidente de Europa. *Ampurias* 2: 85-143.
    1957   Las fibulas de Codo de la Ria de Huelva. Su origen y cronologia. *Cuadernos Trabajos Escuela Española Roma* 9: 7-46.
    1957–58   A proposito de la fecha de las fibulas de Huelva. *Ampurias* 19-20: 198-207.
    1966   *Las Estelas Decoradas del Suroeste Peninsular*. Biblioteca Praehistorica Hispana 8. Madrid.

Almagro Gorbea, M.
    1977   *El Bronce Final y el Periodo Orientalizante en Extremadura*. Biblioteca Praehistorica Hispana 14. Madrid.

Birmingham, J.
    1963   The development of the fibula in Cyprus and the Levant. *Palestine Exploration Quarterly* 95: 80-112.

Blinkenberg, C.
    1926   *Fibules Grecques et Orientales*. Lindiaka 5. Kobenhavn.

Buchholz, H.-G.
    1986   Ein kyprischer Fibeltypus und seine auswärtige Verbreitung. In *Cyprus Between the Orient and the Occident. Acts of the International Archaeological Symposium, Nicosia 8-14 Sept. 1985*, 233-44. Nicosia.

Cunisset Carnot, P., J. Mohen & J. Nicolardot
    1971   Une fibule 'chypriote' trouvée en Côte-d'Or. *Bulletin de la Société Préhistorique Française* 68: 602-609.

Delibes de Castro, G.
    1978   Una inhumaciòn triple de facies Cogotas I en San Romàn de la Hornija (Valladolid). *Trabajos de Prehistoria* 35: 225-50.

Fadda, M.
    1986   Orani (Nuoro)—Il tempio nuragico di Nurdole. *Nuovo Bullettino Archeologico Sardo* 3: 308-14.
    1990   Orani (Nuoro)—Località Nurdole. Il tempio nuragico. *Scavi e Scoperte. Bollettino d'Archeologia* 4: 123-25.
    1991   Nurdole: Un tempio nuragico in Barbagia, punto d'incontro nel Mediterraneo. *Rivista di Studi Fenici* 19 (1): 107-19.
    in stampa   L'arte decorativa nell'architettura templare del periodo nuragico—Nota preliminare. *L'Arte Italiana dal Paleolitico Superiore all'età del Bronzo. Atti della XXVIII Riunione Scientifica Istituto Italiano di Preistoria e Protostoria, Firenze, 20-22 novembre 1989*. Firenze.

Guzzo, P.
    1969   Considerazioni sulla fibula del ripostiglio di Huelva. *Rivista di Scienze Preistoriche* 24(2): 299-309.

Lilliu, G.
    1955   Il nuraghe di Barumini e la stratigrafia nuragica. *Studi Sardi* 12-13(1952–54): 90-469.

Lo Schiavo, F.
    1978   Le fibule delle Sardegna. *Studi Etruschi* 46(2): 25-116.
    1991   La Sardaigne et ses relations avec le Bronze Final Atlantique. *L'Age du Bronze Atlantique. Actes du 1er Colloque du Parc Archéologique de Beynac, 10-14 sept. 1990*, 213-24. Beynac-et-Cazenac.

Lo Schiavo, F., & R. D'Oriano
    1990   La Sardegna sulle rotte dell'Occidente. *Magna Grecia ed il lontano Occidente. Atti XXIX Convegno di Studi sulla Magna Grecia, Taranto 6-11 ott. 1989*, 99-161. Taranto.

Myres, J.
    1910   A type of fibula of the Early Iron Age, apparently peculiar to Cyprus. *Annals of Archaeology and Anthropology* 3: 138-44.

Ridgway, D.
    1988-89   Archaeology in Sardinia and South Italy. *Archaeological Reports* 35: 130-47.

Summary

Recent excavations at the Nuragic sanctuary of Nurdole (Orani-NU) have produced a vast array of offerings, including tools, weapons, bronze figurines, and objects in amber, silver, and iron. Unfortunately, the scientific excavations directed by M.A. Fadda have been accompanied by clandestine activities which have resulted in irreparable damage to this important site. The nuraghe itself is of complex plan, with four towers and a courtyard with well, and is surrounded by an extensive village. The nuraghe was first constructed in the Middle Bronze Age, on a site already occupied in the Monte Claro and Bonnanaro periods. The complex was transformed into a sanctuary in the Late/Final Bronze Age, and continued in use until the 6th century BC.

The focus of this paper is a single bronze fibula, actually confiscated from *clandestini*, but certainly coming from Nuraghe Nurdole. Although fragmentary, the fibula is identifiable as a 'Cypriot' type, of 'local' manufacture. Its characteristic features are a central node, the triangular profile of the arc, and its elaborate plastic decoration. A large corpus of fibulae have recently been studied by Buchholz, and the Nurdole example seems to fall within his evolutionary typological scheme. Buchholz's typology has 13 forms, ranging in date from c. 1200–600 BC, but the utility of his scheme is limited because of the insecure dating of many fibulae.

The closest comparison to the Nurdole fibula is an example from the Côte-d'Or in France; that fibula has been associated by Buchholz with Iberian examples. A Cypriot-type fibula is also known from Barumini, from an Iron I context, and has been accepted as further evidence of Sardinian contact with the eastern Mediterranean in the Bronze and Iron Ages. The Author explores the possibility, however, that both Sardinian fibulae may come from Spain; a flat axe apparently of Iberian derivation was also found at Nurdole. If the Iberian connection for these items is correct, then this is a new element of an already well-documented long-distance trade, involving Sardinia in 'international' commercial activities in the Late Bronze and Iron Ages—in both the eastern and western Mediterranean.

Nuragic Sardinia and the Mediterranean: Metallurgy and Maritime Traffic

Claudio Giardino

In prehistoric times, Sardinia played a role of prime importance among the world's maritime routes due to its special geographical position between the eastern and western Mediterranean. Sardinia is the most distant of the Mediterranean islands from the mainland and, with its long stretches of coastline which point towards both the Italian and Iberian peninsulas, represents a sort of natural stepping stone to what was considered the far west in ancient times. The island possesses, in addition to this eminently strategic role, considerable metal resources. In the Bronze Age, such wealth contributed decisively to an increase in Sardinia's involvement in the maritime trade network over both medium and long distances.

The mythical traditions that have reached us on a piecemeal basis through various classical authors recall an interwoven pattern of legendary associations between Sardinia and other Mediterranean countries, associations that have continued ever since remote times. Despite the difficulties entailed in a critical interpretation of these literary and historical sources (Nicosia 1981: 421-41), the personalities of Iolaüs, Daedalus, Aristaeüs son of Cyrene, as well as the Thespiad sons of Heracles and Norax, nevertheless suggest the establishment of a series of transmarine contacts taking place in a mythical past between Sardinia and Sicily, the eastern Mediterranean, North Africa and Iberia (Bondì 1975: 49-66).

According to Diodorus Siculus (4.82), Aristaeüs, son of Apollo and the nymph Cyrene, the Queen of Libya, is supposed to have reached Sardinia from northern Africa before proceeding onwards to Sicily. Diodorus also relates that Heracles dispatched his Thespiad sons and Iolaüs, his brother's son, to Sardinia with the aim of colonizing the Island. Iolaüs is then reported to have arranged for Daedalus to arrive there from Sicily. Silius Italicus (12.355-369) relates how several Trojan survivors also reached Sardinia following the destruction of their city. One particularly substantial description is given by Pausanias (10.17.1-7). He relates that the first navigators to land in Sardinia were the Libyans under the leadership of Sardus. The Greeks, headed by Aristaeüs, were to follow later. Next to arrive were the Iberians, with Norax as their leader. Pausanias then states that other Greeks subsequently reached the island with Iolaüs at their head. Last of all were some Trojans who arrived there after the Trojan War. Solinus (4.1-2) brings to light the belief that Norax originated from Tartessus, a Spanish locality famous in ancient times for its rich metallic mineral deposits. Thus Sardinia and Iberia, two of the main sources of western Mediterranean metal supplies, had mythical associations.

The numerous archaeological findings of both metals and ceramics are evidence of contact between Sardinia and other cultural zones of the central and western Mediterranean during the Later Bronze and Early Iron Ages. At that stage in history, there developed a considerable amount of medium-range and long-distance overseas traffic in a westerly direction. Sardinia was to play a leading part in this traffic, both as an indispensable navigational reference point, and as a supply source of metallic minerals.

It is well known that there are numerous copper, lead and iron deposits located in various areas of Sardinia (Marcello *et al.* 1978). These deposits differ from each other in terms of richness, origin and ore deposition (Cello and De Vivo 1988: 626-37). The exploitation of these natural sources by local communities dates back to very ancient times. Metallic objects first appear in Sardinia in the Ozieri culture, in a Late Neolithic context (Fig. 1). Not only copper articles (necklace beads: Grotta Sa Korona di Monte Majore-SS; a disk: Montessu-CA; several pins and a dagger: Cuccuru Arrius-OR), but also objects made of silver have been documented. Two necklace beads of this metal originate from Pranu Mutteddu (CA), while a small ring was discovered in Montessu (CA), in funerary contexts of the Ozieri culture (Lo Schiavo 1989: 282-83).

Silver is found in its natural state in the cementation zone of mineral deposits containing silver salts below the oxidation gossan (Bertolani 1972: 61-63) at a depth which was inaccessible by prehistoric mining techniques. It was thus necessary to extract it from the minerals that surround it (mainly galena) by way of metallurgical processes. The discovery of slags from silver and copper smelting in huts dating back to the Ozieri period at Su Coddu (Selargius-CA) (Lilliu 1986: 8; Lo Schiavo 1989: 283) is of considerable importance. This is direct evidence of complex metallurgical skills enabling them to extract silver from galena by desulphurization and cupellation.

Metal objects become relatively more frequent in later contexts belonging to the Abealzu-Filigosa (Early Eneolithic) and Monte Claro (Later Eneolithic) cultures. The most ancient examples of lead finds in Sardinia also date back to the Eneolithic. Galena fragments, metallic lead and short-handled terracotta crucibles similar to those found at Terrina IV in Corsica have been found at Monte d'Accoddi in a Filigosa context (Lo Schiavo 1984: 21-22; Lilliu 1986: 8; Lilliu 1988: 299). A lead fragment from the *allée couverte* of Sa Corte Noa (Laconi-NU) has also been found in a Filigosa-Abealzu context (Atzeni 1988: 526-27), and a cup restored with lead clamps has been found in the Cuccuru Tiria cave (Iglesias-CA) in a Monte Claro context (Atzeni 1981: XLIII).

Some authors have observed that Late Eneolithic (Beaker Culture) metalwork in Sardinia does not have specific shape characteristics; all the more so in the Early Bronze Age (Bonnànaro Culture). This feature is especially obvious when previous production is compared (Ferrarese Ceruti 1981: lxii-lxiii, llxxiii-lxxiv; Lo Schiavo 1984: 26-27; Lo Schiavo 1989: 285-87). Metal articles in the Bonnànaro horizon are rare, about 30 having been found, mainly pins or awls (Lilliu 1986: 8). This lack is especially surprising in light of the flourishing metallurgy in Continental Europe and on the Italian peninsula in this period. It may be due to a period when the island's mineral resources were exploited less or not at all.

The situation changed completely in the Middle Bronze Age. At this time, Sardinia became an important point of reference in maritime routes and the metal trade. There was a new impulse to metallurgy on the island, perhaps also due to outside influence. The bronze weapons complex discovered in the Ottana area shows similarities with Cypriot finds dating to the middle of the 3rd millenium BC and with the horizons found in the western Middle Bronze Age, especially with cultures of southern England and northern France (Lo Schiavo 1978a: 342-56; 1984: 31). This is valuable evidence of the numerous influences on Sardinian metallurgy in that period.

Copper oxhide ingots were introduced at a certain point during the Middle Bronze Age which has not yet been identified, but probably dating to the building of the Nuragic towers, i.e. about the 15th century BC or afterwards. Oxhide ingots seem to have been found under the floor of the central room of the Nuragic tower at S. Antioco di Bisarcio (Lo Schiavo 1990: 20-21, 36-37). Some have marks in the Cypriot-Minoan alphabet (Lo Schiavo 1984: 32). This ingot type, widespread in Sardinia (Lo Schiavo 1990: 18-31) (Fig. 2), undoubtedly links the island with the eastern Mediterranean; this issue is separate from the complex and controversial problem of whether the metal comes from local or imported sources (Balmuth and Tylecote 1976: 198-201; Gale and Stos-Gale 1987: 161-62; Muhly and Stech 1990: 202; Gale 1991: 212-24; Muhly 1991: 189-91; Stos-Gale and Gale, this volume).

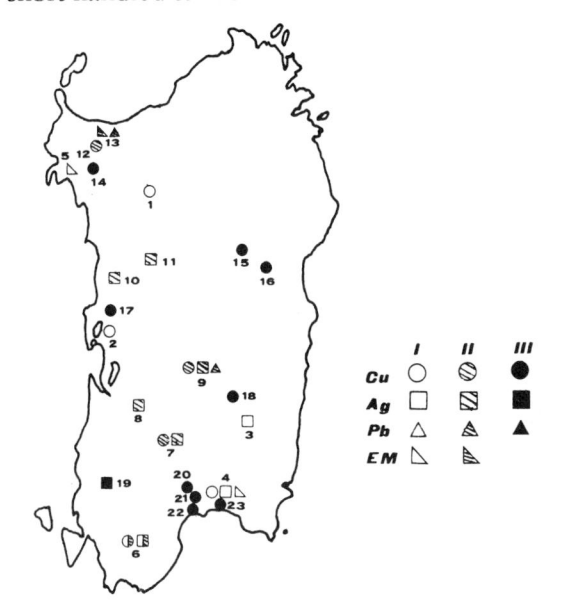

Fig. 1 Early metallic finds in Sardinia.
Key: I: Neolithic; II: Early Eneolithic; III: Late Eneolithic; Cu: copper; Ag: silver; Pb: lead; EM: evidence of metallurgy
1. Grotta Sa Korona di Monte Majore (Thiesi); 2. Cuccuru Arrius (Cabras); 3. Pranu Mutteddu (Goni); 4. Su Coddu (Selargius); 5. Anghelu Ruju (Alghero); 6. Montessu (Villaperucciu); 7. Serra Cannigas (Villagreca); 8. Scaba 'e Arriu (Siddi); 9. Sa Corte Noa (Laconi); 10. S. Caterina di Pittinuri (Cuglieri); 11. Filigosa (Macomer); 12. Cabula Muntones (Sassari); 13. Monte d'Accoddi (Sassari); 14. Monte Baranta (Olmedo); 15. Janna Ventosa (Nuoro); 16. Biriai (Oliena); 17. Serra Is Araus (S. Vero Milis); 18. Su Monti (Orroli); 19. Grotta di Cuccuru Tiria (Iglesias); 20. Cresta Is Cuccurus (Monastir); 21. Sa Duchessa (Cagliari); 22. Via Basilicata—Cagliari; 23. Simbirizzi (Quartu S. Elena).

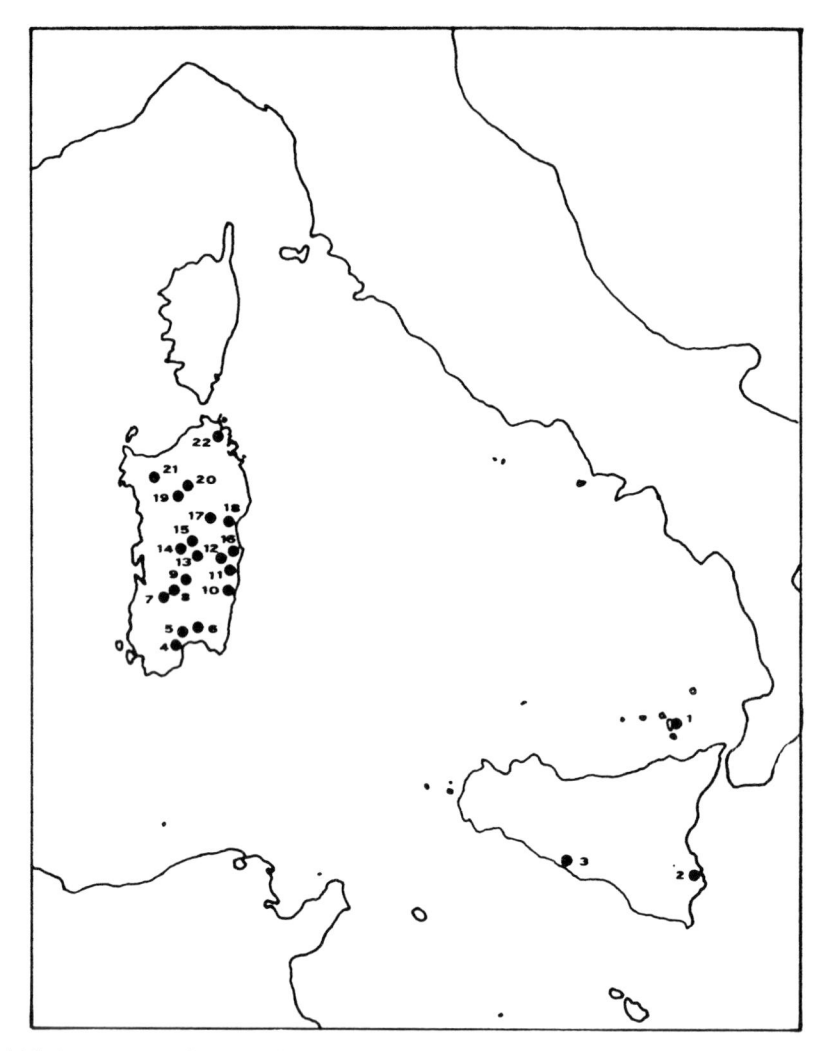

Fig. 2 Copper oxhide ingots in and near Italy.
1. Lipari; 2. Thapsos (Siracusa); 3. Cannatello (Agrigento); 4. Capoterra; 5. Assemini; 6. S'Arenagiu (Soleminis); 7. S. Anastasia (Sardara); 8. Baccu Simeone (Villanovaforru); 9. Serra Ilixi (Nuragus); 10. Nuraghe Nastasi (Tertenia); 11. Perda 'e Floris (Lanusei); 12. Nuraghe Corte Maceddos and S'Arcu 'e is Forras (Villagrande Strisaili); 13. Ocile (Belvì); 14. Funtana 'e Cresia (Ortueri); 5. Abini (Teti); 16. Nuraghe Bau Nuraxi (Triei); 17. Nuoro province; 18. Valle dell'Isalle (Dorgali); 19. Nuraghe Funtana (Ittireddu); 20. S. Antioco di Bisarcio and S. Luca (Ozieri); 21. Sa Mandra 'e Sa Giua (Ossi); 22. Nuraghe Albucciu (Arzachena)

The discovery in the mid-1970s of Aegean-type pottery in Sardinia has highlighted the island's Late Bronze Age role in the Eastern Mediterranean (Lo Schiavo and Vagnetti 1980: 371-79; Ferrarese Cerruti 1980: 391-93). The sequence of levels at Nuraghe Antigori (Sarroch) enables us to date the beginning of systematic trade with the island to the Late Bronze Age. Most of the Aegean-type material can be attributed to LH IIIB, except a fragment from room *n* dating to early LH IIIC (Ferrarese Cerruti *et al*. 1987: 14-16). It is significant that physical and chemical analyses of the clays have shown many pieces to be of local production (Jones and Day 1987: 257-63).

During the Later Bronze Age there were especially significant contacts between Sardinia and the eastern Mediterranean, resulting in the importation of items (e.g., tripod-stands) which later inspired Nuragic production (Lo Schiavo 1983: 309-14; Lo Schiavo *et al*. 1985: 35-51, 62-63). The massive double-axes with round shaft-holes closely recall characteristic Cypriot types. In other cases, such as the double-axes with vertical blades, big picks, and axe-adzes, a general Cypriot influence on local culture rather than direct imitation of foreign models is more likely (Lo Schiavo *et al*. 1985: 14-22). It should also be pointed out that these tools may have been used in mining (Giardino 1987a: 199).

Cyprus was one of the major Mediterranean copper producing centers in the Bronze Age, and there is abundant archaeological evidence of copper ore mining and processing (Muhly 1976: 90-92; Muhly 1983: 214; Karageorghis 1977: 29-31; Constantinou 1982: 18-22; Weisgerber 1982: 25-28). There must have been frequent contact in the field of metallurgy between the two Mediterranean islands, which have in common the exploitation of their rich mineral deposits; this can also be seen in the strong Cypriot influence on Nuragic foundry tools (Lo Schiavo 1982: 291-300; Lo Schiavo et al. 1985: 62). This is also related to the early appearance of iron in Sardinia, found at various Nuragic sites in the Later Bronze Age (Ferrarese Ceruti et al. 1987: 24-25; Lo Schiavo 1988: 86-89). An iron fragment from Nuraghe Antigori, associated with a wishbone handle of the Late Cypriot II period, probably dating to the 13th century BC, is a significant find in this context (Ferrarese Ceruti et al. 1987: 17-24).

Slags from the Nuragic period have been found in the past at Funtana Raminosa (Taramelli 1923: 67; Lo Schiavo 1982: 273 fig. 2), and in the Forraxi Nioi hoard (Nissardi 1882: 308-11; Tylecote et al. 1984: 133-38). More recently, slags have been found at the Nieddue site (Nurallo-NU) (Zwicker et al. 1980: 138, 141), and at the Genna Maria complex at Villanovaforru (Atzeni et al. 1987: 150). Bronze and iron slags have also been found at the Nuragic foundry of Sa Sedda 'e Sos Carros (Olièna-NU), together with a large amount of fragmentary artifacts and bronzes with casting defects (Lo Schiavo 1976a: 69-71; 1978b: 99-101). It should be pointed out that the quantity of slag found is not very great, suggesting that Sardinia also, as may have been the case for other parts of Europe, used smelting techniques different from those used in the Middle East, and were characterized by essentially non-slagging processes (Craddock and Meeks 1987: 190-93; Craddock in press).

The intensive metallurgical production in Sardinia may be indicated not so much by slag findings as by the large number of hoards, about 50, and the production of thousands of different types of articles with different characteristics. Other evidence of this type includes the more than 100 bun ingots found, as well as the moulds which have been found at various sites on the island (Birocchi 1934; Lo Schiavo 1982: 273-75 fig. 3; Becker 1984; Gallin and Tykot in press). Lead isotope analysis performed on Sardinian bronze objects from the S. Maria in Paulis (SS) hoard (Macnamara et al. 1984) have shown that the metal originates from Cambrian ore deposits in southwestern Sardinia, thus providing further proof of native exploitation of the island's copper resources (Gale and Stos-Gale 1987: 154-55).

The correlation of ore deposits and the distribution of some nuraghi, and the discovery of Nuragic-age mining tools, such as hammer-stones and pottery lamps, inside the Iglesiente mine, as well as similar findings at Masua and Planu Dentis, are especially significant (Giardino 1987a: 193-99) (Fig. 3). Early in this century, short mine shafts were found near the mouth of the Rio Sarraxinus with pestles, mortars, heaps of charcoal and scorified stones, probably the residue from fires used to break up the rock; in one case a stack of mineralized oak wood was also found. In the Gadoni mine, at the bottom of a vertical pit following the ore deposits, the skeleton of a Nuragic miner crushed by a millstone was found next to the collected ore (Rellini 1923: 59-60).

While recent studies have increasingly highlighted the importance of metallurgy in the Nuragic culture and economy, it is still not easy to establish how much metal was exported from the island and through which channels. It has been pointed out that the numerous metallic (as well as some in ceramic) votive models of rigid hull boats could be a significant clue to the existence of local seamanship, as well as Nuragic interest in navigation (Ferrarese Ceruti 1987: 434).

Evidence in this respect may be found in the contacts between Sardinia and Sicily, the other major island of the central Mediterranean, located less than 300 km from the southern coast of Sardinia. Nuragic pottery finds in the Ausonian II levels of the Lipari Acropolis (Contu 1980; Ferrarese Ceruti 1987), consisting mainly of askoi and large storage jars used as food containers, are clear evidence of trade with Sicily. This discovery must be associated with other Sicilian evidence of imports from Nuragic Sardinia dating to the Later Bronze Age, consisting of metal objects from several sites in Sicily. Unfortunately, since these finds come from old collections, their provenience is not known, except for the axe-adze from Taormina now housed at the Pigorini Museum in Rome. This is the problem with the two double-axes housed in the Biscari Museum in Catania (Libertini 1930: 115, pl. LVIII: 406-407), and an axe with a raised edge and wide blade housed in the Palermo Archaeological Museum; the latter is perhaps a more ancient find (Giardino 1987: 419) (Fig. 4a-b). The absence of contemporary Sicilian artifacts in Sardinia seems to indicate that trade was a one-way process.

The oxhide ingot fragments discovered up to now in Sicily, in the Lipari hoard (Bernabò Bernabo Brea and Cavalier 1980: 756-57, 785-86), at Cannatello (Mosso 1906: 524; 1908: 669), and at Thapsos (in the Paolo Orsi Museum in Syracuse), present a special problem. Until modern metallurgical analyses are conducted, it can only be observed that together with the Sardinian finds they represent the most westerly evidence of this type of ingot, which is not found on the Italian mainland (Fig. 2). Looking at the number of the Sardinian oxhide ingots, it would be interesting to consider the hypothesis of whether the Sicilian finds, and therefore copper imports, are the products of direct trade with the eastern Mediterranean or of links with Sardinia.

The Later Bronze Age seems to have been the most flourishing period of trade between Sicily and Sardinia; in contrast, there is little evidence of links between the two islands during the Early Iron Age. A small Nuragic askos from tomb 81 in the SE acropolis of Pantalica, decorated with circular imprints, can be dated by the associations to the 9th century BC (Orsi 1912: 317 tav. IX, 66).

From the early 9th to the mid-8th century BC there is a lot of evidence of Nuragic finds in Tyrrhenian Etruria (Bartoloni and Delpino 1975: 40-45; Gras 1985: 113-62; Lo Schiavo and Ridgway 1987: 392-95). These include figurines, model quivers, votive boats, 'buttons', daggers, pins and askoi, often found at Villanovan and Orientalizing sites, usually in burials. These articles, therefore, were probably votive, prestige items. The quality of the finds indicates considerable trade. It is likely that information and experience in metallurgical and mining techniques were exchanged together with the products themselves. Etruria has important metal ore deposits, including those in southern Tuscany and in the Monti della Tolfa area. At the end of the 2nd millennium BC the north coast of Etruria (Elba, Populonia, Vetulonia), easily accessible from Sardinia, was the main point of contact between the Villanovan and Nuragic peoples. It can therefore be proposed that the more advanced Sardinian metallurgical knowledge was exported to Etruria; individuals with Nuragic-type artifacts in their tombs may have been involved in this process (Gras 1985: 144-47, 159-62; Lo Schiavo and Ridgway 1987: 400-404; Ridgway 1989: 120-26).

The period spanning the end of the Late Bronze Age and the beginning of the Early Iron Age in Sardinia was characterized by considerable metallurgical activity, as shown by the hoards dating from this period: Monte Sa Idda (Taramelli 1921), Monte Arrubiu di Sarroch (Lo Schiavo 1981: fig. 359), and the Abini complex at Teti (Pais 1884). The Forraxi Nioi hoard (Nissardi 1882), as well as older material, also contains later items (Giardino 1987b: 421).

Researchers have long been interested in Sardinia's role in Mediterranean trade at this time, over both medium and long distances, testified to mainly, but not exclusively, by bronze objects resembling the 'western' type artifacts found on the island (Almagro Bash 1940; Bernabò Brea 1953–54; Hencken 1956; Coffyn 1985: 147-59; Lo Schiavo 1976b; Lo Schiavo 1985; Lo Schiavo and Ridgway 1987; Giardino 1986; Giardino 1987b; Lo Schiavo, this volume). Metalwork of the Western Area type, especially recalling the Iberian Peninsula, has been found at various sites. Examples include swords of the Huelva (Siniscola) and Vénat types (Monte Sa Idda); flat axes with lateral loops (Monte Arrubiu and Flumenelongu); palstaves with lateral loops (Monte Sa Idda, Monte Arrubiu, Forraxi Nioi); socketed axes with one (Monte Sa Idda) or two loops (Monte Sa Idda and Funtana Janna); socketed barbed arrowheads (Torralba); socketed sickles (Sarule and Forraxi Nioi-Nuragus); articulated spits (Monte Sa Idda); and *doble resorte* fibulae (Pirosu-Su Benatzu and Bithia).

Besides the parallels among metal artifacts, there is also some similarity between the Iberian Peninsula and Nuragic Sardinia in the pottery. A particular kind of decorative technique, with burnishing patterns on the surface of the pottery, appears at some Nuragic sites, and is comparable to Iberian material. In Sardinia, this pottery dates from the Final Bronze to Early Iron Age, with both open and closed forms typical of the Nuragic culture, such as carinated bowls, askoi, and jugs, having a type of geometric decoration highlighting the shape of the pot (Fig. 5). Examples have been found at several sites on the island (Bidistili-Fonni, Villanovaforru, Barumini, Sardara, Settimo S. Pietro, Ossi) (Lo Schiavo 1981: figg. 342-45; Lilliu 1982: 102-103; Ferrarese Ceruti 1987: 432; Badas 1987: tavv. IV-V). Some examples have been found with other Nuragic material at Lipari in an Ausonian II context (Ferrarese Ceruti 1987: 431-32).

In the Iberian Peninsula there are two types of burnished ware: the *Lapa di Fumo* of central and southern Portugal, and the *reticula bruñida* of southwestern Spain. Iberian burnished ware, like the Nuragic, dates to around the 10th–8th centuries BC, with some surviving up to the 7th century BC (Almagro Gorbea 1977: 125-32, 495-96 fig. 53; Lopez Roa 1978; Chamorro 1987: 208-11). Although this decoration appears in both geographical areas on pottery linked to local cultural traditions, the presence of this technique, and sometimes, the resemblance of decorative patterns, do not seem to be a coincidence; this could be expected from the previously mentioned close links between Sardinia and Iberia in the distribution of metal artifacts.

Fig. 3 Masua (Iglesias) mine: ceramic lamps.

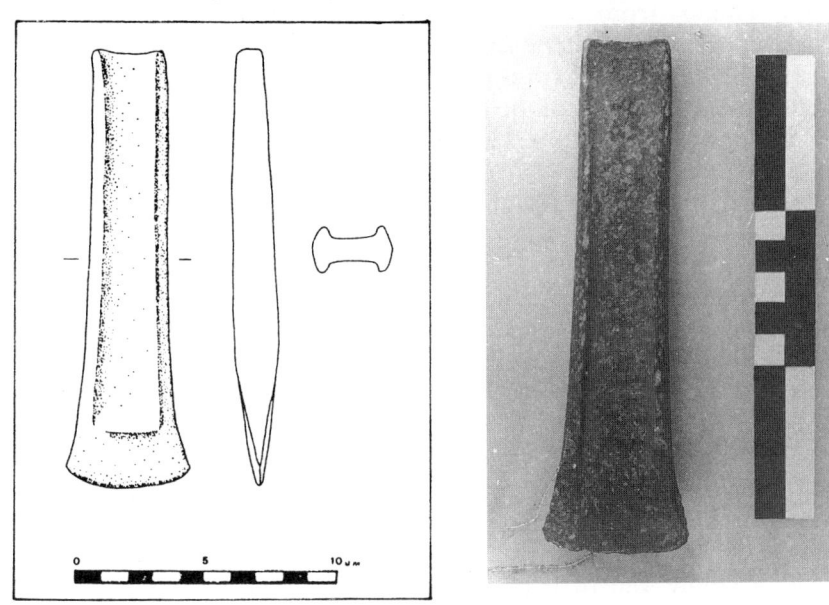

Fig. 4 Palermo Archaeological Museum: Sardinian axe.

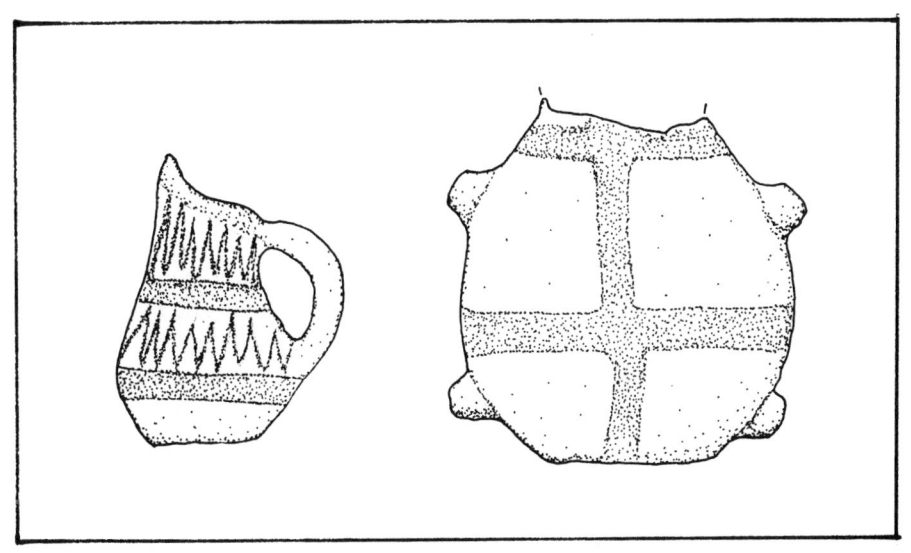

Fig. 5 Villanovaforru: Sardinian burnished ware (after Badas 1987).

It should be pointed out that the complex phenomenon of Phoenician 'pre-colonial' expansion dates to the period between the 11th and 9th centuries BC. This involved active trade links extending from the Syrian and Palestinian coast to the central and western areas of the Mediterranean, including Sardinia, the strategic point between east and west (Moscati 1983: 3-7; Moscati 1988: 13-16; Bisi 1988: 223-25; Godart 1988: 295-97).

These many-sided influences and contacts may also be associated with the bronze figurines found at Nuragic sites and having characteristics recalling those found in the Levant. Some figurines of a particularly archaic model have been recognized as imports from the Syrian, Palestinian and Cypriot area. The Flumenelongu figurine probably comes from the Syrian-Palestinian area, while the bronze figurine from S. Cristina di Paulilatino, dating to the 11th century BC, and the Galtellì figurine, probably of the same age, are probably Cypriot (Barreca 1986: 134-35; Bisi 1977: 919-21; Lo Schiavo *et al.* 1985: 52-56).

Archaeological evidence seems to show that in the Later Bronze and Early Iron Ages not only goods, but also ideas and experiences, were exchanged in the Mediteranean. In order to understand this complex phenomenon an analysis should be made in terms of the means of transport, in order to identify the sea routes used by these mariners. Unfortunately there is very little evidence regarding the technical characteristics of the boats used at the end of the 2nd millennium BC. The evidence mainly includes quotations from Homeric verse, and stylized representations which are not very accurate and hard to interpret. Up to now, little information has been available from underwater archaeological excavations regarding the structure of Bronze Age ships, although in some cases extremely interesting data has been supplied on the type of cargo carried, such as in the shipwrecks of Cape Gelidonya and Hof ha-Carmel (Bass 1967; Galili *et al.* 1986). Researchers are now awaiting the results from the investigation currently under way on the shipwreck of Ulu Burun, near Kaş, Turkey, involving a vessel with a very rich cargo (Bass 1986; Bass 1987; Pulak 1988; Bass *et al.* 1989).

By the 14th century BC, round-hull ships were common in Cyprus and the Levant, as can be seen from the Egyptian painting in tomb 162 of the Theban necropolis (Davies and Faulkner 1947) depicting some of these ships. The clothing worn by the crew enables us to identify them as coming from the Syrian area. The downward-curved mast holds the single large sail (Casson 1971: 35-36). Mycenaean ships also had square sails, and differed from Levantine vessels mainly in the shape of the hull, which was straight with a raised bow and stern, as can be seen on the Phaestos goblet and pitharaki, and on the stirrup jar from Asine (Laviosa 1972: 9-13, 24-25 fig. 1, 3, 23). According to the Odyssey, these ships carried from 20 to 50 oarsmen (Guglielmi 1971: 420 n. 3). The same source states that the mast at the center of the ship could be raised and lowered (*Odyssey* 2.424-426; 5.254, 318). It has been pointed out that this system was used because of the poor stability of the vessel and the limitations of the single square sail, which permitted only a limited exploitation of the wind. It could only be used to its best with a moderate wind blowing over the ship's bow (Guglielmi 1971: 422-23).

In prehistoric and proto-historic times, sailing was mainly along coastal routes with frequent landings for getting supplies of food and drink. We find an indication of this in the *Odyssey* (12.289-290), where the sailors are said to be accustomed to landing to spend the night. In the Mediterranean, mainly coastal routes oblige the ships to make frequent changes of angle with respect to the wind, since the coastline is often irregular. Changes in wind patterns in areas quite near to each other is also caused by local weather phenomena which influence the strength and direction of the wind. These conditions were a limitation on the use of single square sails, which were therefore not very efficient for long voyages. Oars were therefore used for the propulsion of the ship, especially for shorter stretches, along with surface currents. The integrated and often interacting use of the three systems enabled vessels to cover the medium and long distance routes for which there is evidence from archaeological and literary sources.

Since it was difficult to sail against the current, the direction of the current was exploited instead. The study of permanent and seasonal surface currents (Metallo 1955; 1962), therefore, may enable us to identify some possible routes followed by ancient sailors (Fig. 6). With regard to Sardinia, the western coast is washed by currents from Catalonia and Languedoc, especially during certain months of the year: October, December, March, June, July, September. These currents could be a useful aid to navigation from Iberia, alternating with the routes along the North African coast. The latter could be reached by exploiting other currents flowing from southern Sardinia directly to the Tunisian coast. From western Sardinia, the Tyrrhenian current can be utilized to reach the northwestern coast of Sicily, and from there, through the Straits of Messina to the eastern Mediterranean.

MARCH

JUNE

SEPTEMBER

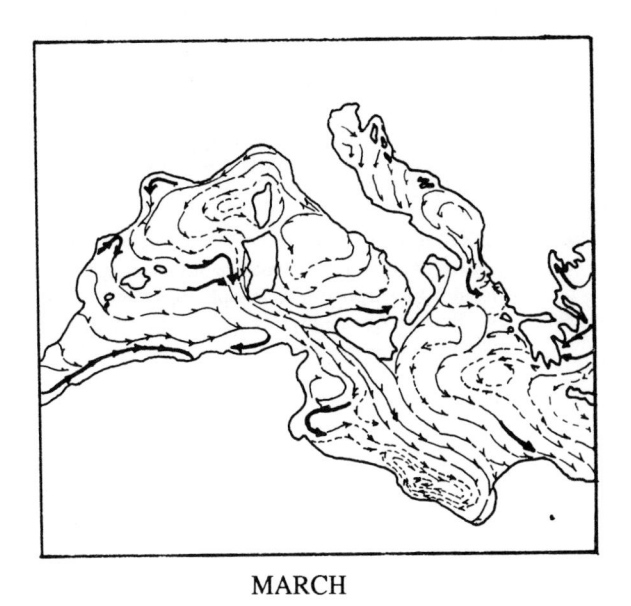

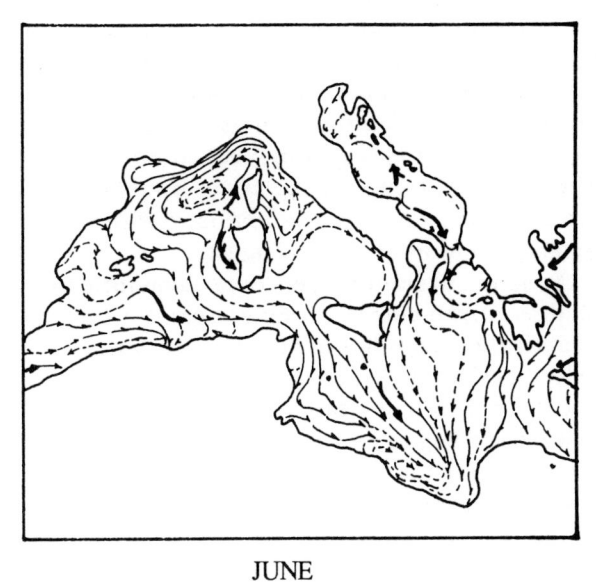

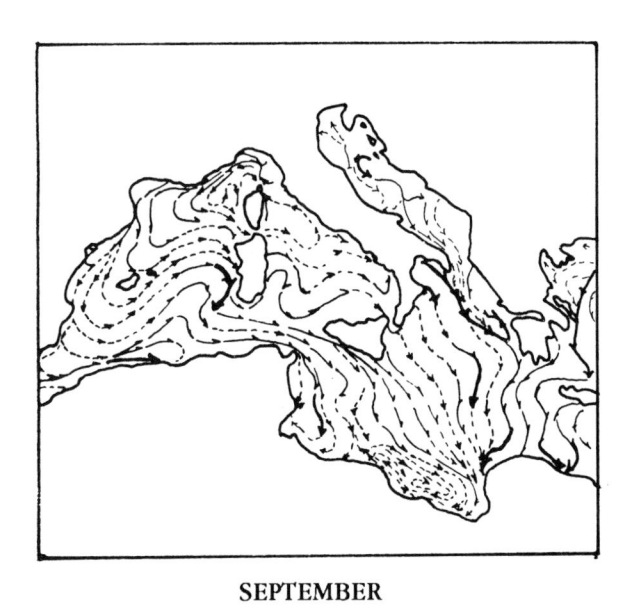

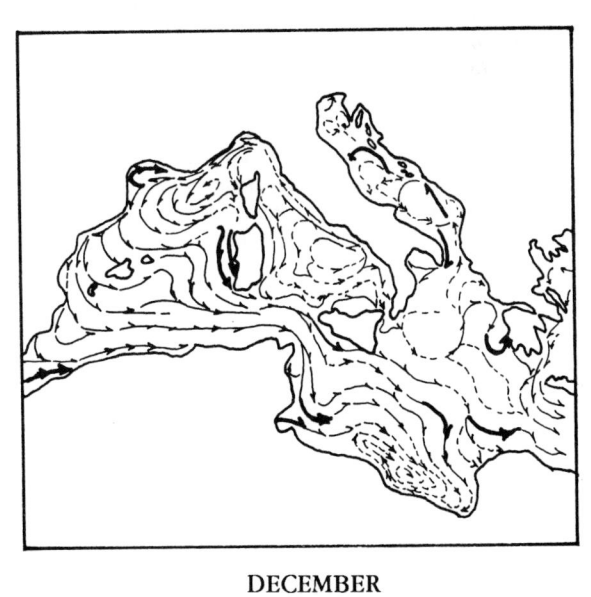

DECEMBER

Fig. 6 Seasonal surface sea currents.

There is also another system of currents flowing towards the Italian Peninsula. Some of these currents reach the Latium coast between March and October, while more northerly currents flow towards the Tuscan islands and northern Etruria between the months from December to March, from May to July, and in September. The opposite route can be taken by using currents flowing towards Sardinia from November to March, and from May to August.

On the basis of the data available on Mediterranean currents, one can try not only to identify the routes taken, but also the most favorable times of the year for making the voyage to and from Sardinia. Maritime trade had to take place according to an exact schedule which takes into account the seasonal weather conditions. The study of surface currents can therefore contribute to our knowledge about maritime links which, as we have seen, played an essential role in the proto-historic cultural evolution of Sardinia.

References

Almagro Bash, M.
1940   El hallazgo de la ria de Huelva y el final de la Edad del Bronce en el Occidente de Europa. *Ampurias* 2: 85-143.

Almagro Gorbea, M.
1977   *El Bronce Final y el Periodo Orientalizante en Extremadura*. Biblioteca Praehistorica Hispana 14. Madrid: C.S.I.C.

Atzeni, C., L. Massidda, U. Sanna & P. Virdis
1987   Archeometallurgia nuragica nel territorio di Villanovaforru. In G. Lilliu, G. Ugas and G. Lai (a cura di), *La Sardegna nel Mediterraneo tra il secondo e il primo millennio a.C. Atti del II convegno di studi 'Un millennio di relazioni fra la Sardegna e i Paesi del Mediterraneo', Selargius-Cagliari, 27-30 novembre 1986*, 147-65. Cagliari: Amministrazione Provinciale di Cagliari.

Atzeni, E.
1981   Aspetti e sviluppi culturali del neolitico e della prima età dei metalli in Sardegna. In E. Atzeni *et al.* (eds.), *Ichnussa: La Sardegna dalle origini all'età classica*, 21-51. Milano: Libri Scheiwiller.
1988   Tombe megalitiche di Laconi (Nuoro). *L'Eta del Rame in Europea. Rassegna di Archeologia* 3: 526-27.

Badas, U.
1987   Genna Maria—Villanovaforru (Cagliari). I vani 10/18. Nuovi apporti allo studio delle abitazioni a corte centrale. In G. Lilliu, G. Ugas and G. Lai (a cura di), *La Sardegna nel Mediterraneo tra il secondo e il primo millennio a.C. Atti del II convegno di studi 'Un millennio di relazioni fra la Sardegna e i Paesi del Mediterraneo', Selargius-Cagliari, 27-30 novembre 1986*, 133-46. Cagliari: Amministrazione Provinciale di Cagliari.

Balmuth, M.S., & R.F. Tylecote
1976   Ancient copper and bronze in Sardinia: Excavation and analysis. *Journal of Field Archaeology* 3: 195-201.

Barreca, F.
1986   Phoenicians in Sardinia: The bronze figurines. In M.S. Balmuth (ed.), *Studies in Sardinian Archaeology, Volume II: Sardinia in the Mediterranean*, 135-54. Ann Arbor: University of Michigan Press.

Bartoloni, G., & F. Delpino
1975   Un tipo di orciolo a lamelle metalliche: Considerazioni sulla prima fase villanoviana. *Studi Etruschi* 43: 3-45.

Bass, G.F.
1967   *Cape Gelidonya: A Bronze Age Shipwreck*. Transactions of the American Philosophical Society 57/8. Philadelphia: American Philosophical Society.
1986   The Bronze Age shipwreck at Ulu Burun (Kaş): 1984 campaign. *Journal of Field Archaeology* 90: 269-96.
1987   Oldest known shipwreck reveals Bronze Age splendors. *National Geographic* 172(6): 692-733.

Bass, G.F., C. Pulak, D. Collon & J. Weinstein
1989   The Bronze Age shipwreck at Ulu Burun: 1986 campaign. *Journal of Field Archaeology* 93: 1-29.

Becker, M.
1984   Sardinian stone moulds: An indirect means of evaluating bronze age metallurgical technology. In M.S. Balmuth and R.J. Rowland, Jr (eds.), *Studies in Sardinian Archaeology*, 163-208. Ann Arbor: University of Michigan Press.

Bernabò Brea, L.
1953-54 La Sicilia prehistorica y sus relaciones con Oriente y con la Peninsula Iberica. *Ampurias* 15-16: 137-235.

Bernabò Brea, L., & M. Cavalier
1980   *Meligunis Lipara IV. L'acropoli di Lipari nella preistoria*. Palermo: Flaccovio.

Bertolani, M.
1972   Elementi nativi. *Enciclopedia Italiana delle Scienze, Minerali e Rocce I*, 60-70. Novara: Istituto Geografico de Agostini.

Birocchi, E.
1934   I ripostigli nuragici e le Panelle di rame grezzo. *Studi Sardi* 1: 37-108.

Bisi, A.M.
1977   L'apport phénicieen aux bronzes nouragiques de Sardaigne. *Latomus* 36: 909-32.
1988   Modalità e aspetti degli scambi fra Oriente e Occidente fenicio in età precoloniale. *Momenti precoloniali nel Mediterraneo antico. Questioni di metodo—Aree d'indagine. Evidenze a confronto, Atti del Convegno Internazionale (Roma, marzo 1985)*, 205-26. Roma: C.N.R.

Bondì, S.
1975   Osservazioni sulle fonti classiche per la colonizzazione della Sardegna. *Saggi Fenici* 1: 49-66. Roma: C.N.R.

Casson, L.
1971   *Ships and Seamanship in the Ancient World*. Princeton: Princeton University Press.

Cello, G., & B. de Vivo
1988   Cenni sulle mineralizzazioni metallifere italiane. In C. Park and R. MacDiarmid (eds.), *Giacimenti Minerari*, 626-76. Napoli: Liguori.

Chamorro, J.
1987   Survey of archaeological research on Tartessos. *American Journal of Archaeology* 91: 197-232.

Coffyn, A.
1985   *Le Bronze Final Atlantique dans la Péninsule Ibérique*. Paris: Publications du Centre Pierre Paris.

Constantinou, G.
1982 Geological features and ancient exploitation of the cupriferous sulphide orebodies of Cyprus. In J.D. Muhly, R. Maddin and V. Karageorghis (eds.), *Early Metallurgy in Cyprus, 4000–500 BC*, 13-24. Nicosia: Pierides Foundation.

Contu, E.
1980 Ceramica sarda di età nuragica a Lipari. In L. Bernabò Brea and M. Cavalier (eds.), *Meligunìs Lipàra IV: L'acropoli di Lipari nella preistoria*, 827-36. Palermo: Flaccovio.

Craddock, P.T.
in press The inception of extractive metallurgy in western Europe. *Archeologia delle Attività Estrattive e Metallurgiche, V Ciclo di Lezioni sulla Ricerca Applicata in Campo Archeologico (Pontignano-Campiglia Marittima 1991).*

Craddock, P.T., & N.D. Meeks
1987 Iron in ancient copper. *Archaeometry* 29(2): 187-204.

Davies, N., & R. Faulkner
1947 A Syrian trading venture to Egypt. *The Journal of Egyptian Archaeology* 33: 40-46.

Ferrarese Ceruti, M.L.
1980 Micenei in Sardegna!, postilla a F. Lo Schiavo e L. Vagnetti, Micenei in Sardegna? *Rendiconti Accademia Lincei* 35(5-6): 391-93.
1981 La cultura del vaso campaniforme. Il primo Bronzo. In E. Atzeni, F. Barreca, M.L. Ferrarese-Ceruti, E. Contu, G. Lilliu, F. Lo Schiavo, F. Nicosia and E. Equini Schneider (eds.), *Ichnussa: La Sardegna dalle origini all'età classica*, 55-77. Milano: Libri Scheiwiller.
1987 Considerazioni sulla ceramica nuragica di Lipari. In G. Lilliu, G. Ugas and G. Lai (a cura di), *La Sardegna nel Mediterraneo tra il secondo e il primo millennio a.C. Atti del II convegno di studi 'Un millennio di relazioni fra la Sardegna e i Paesi del Mediterraneo', Selargius-Cagliari, 27-30 novembre 1986*, 431-42. Cagliari: Amministrazione Provinciale di Cagliari.

Ferrarese Ceruti, M.L., L. Vagnetti & F. Lo Schiavo
1987 Minoici, micenei e cipriot014 in Sardegna nella seconda metà del II millennio a.C. In M.S. Balmuth (ed.), *Studies in Sardinian Archaeology III. Nuragic Sardinia and the Mycenaean World*, 7-38. BAR International Series 387. Oxford: British Archaeological Reports.

Gale, N.H.
1991 Copper oxhide ingots: their origin and their place in the Bronze Age metals trade in the Mediterranean. In N.H. Gale (ed.), *Bronze Age Trade in the Mediterranean*. Studies in Mediterranean Archaeology 90: 197-239. Jonsered: Paul Åströms Förlag.

Gale, N.H., & Z.A. Stos-Gale
1987 Oxhide ingots from Sardinia, Crete and Cyprus: New scientific evidence. In M.S. Balmuth (ed.), *Studies in Sardinian Archaeology III. Nuragic Sardinia and the Mycenaean World*, 135-78. BAR International Series 387. Oxford: British Archaeological Reports.

Galili, E., N. Shmueli & M. Artzy
1986 Bronze Age ship's cargo of copper and tin. *The Journal of Nautical Archaeology and Underwater Exploration* 15(1): 25-37.

Gallin, L.J., & R.H. Tykot
in press Metallurgical activity at the Nuragic village of Santa Barbara (Bauladu), Sardinia, Italy. *Journal of Field Archaeology.*

Giardino, C.
1986 Il Mediterraneo occidentale durante la Tarda età del Bronzo e la prima età del ferro: Rapporti fra le varie aree, metallurgia, sfruttamento delle risorse minerarie. Tesi di Dottorato di Ricerca presso l'Università di Roma.
1987a Sfruttamento minerario e metallurgia nella Sardegna protostorica. In M.S. Balmuth (ed.), *Studies in Sardinian Archaeology III. Nuragic Sardinia and the Mycenaean World*, 189-222. BAR International Series 387. Oxford: British Archaeological Reports.
1987b Sicilia e Sardegna fra la tarda età del Bronzo e la prima età del ferro. Aspetti di contatti nel Mediterraneo centro-occidentale nell'ambito della metallurgia. In G. Lilliu, G. Ugas and G. Lai (a cura di), *La Sardegna nel Mediterraneo tra il secondo e il primo millennio a.C. Atti del II convegno di studi 'Un millennio di relazioni fra la Sardegna e i Paesi del Mediterraneo', Selargius-Cagliari, 27-30 novembre 1986*, 419-29. Cagliari: Amministrazione Provinciale di Cagliari.

Godart, L.
1988 Conclusioni. *Momenti precoloniali nel Mediterraneo antico. Questioni di metodo—Aree d'indagine. Evidenze a confronto, Atti del Convegno Internazionale (Roma, marzo 1985)*, 291-97. Roma: C.N.R.

Gras, M.
1985 *Trafics Thyrréniens Archaïques*. Bibliothèque des Ecoles françaises d'Athènes et de Rome 258. Rome: Ecole française de Rome.

Guglielmi, M.
1971 Sulla navigazione in età micenea. *La Parola del Passato* 26: 418-35.

Hencken, H.
1956 Carp's Tongue Swords in Spain, France and Italy. *Zephyrus* 6: 125-78.

Jones, R.E., & P.H. Day
1987 Late Bronze Age Aegean and Cypriot type pottery on Sardinia: Identification of imports and local imitations by physico-chemical analysis. In M.S. Balmuth (ed.), *Studies in Sardinian Archaeology III. Nuragic Sardinia and the Mycenaean World*, 257-69. BAR International Series 387. Oxford: British Archaeological Reports.

Karageorghis, V.
1977 *Archaeologia Mundi. Cipro*. Ginevra: Nagel.

Laviosa, C.
1971 La marina micenea. *Annuario della Scuola Archeologica di Atene* 47-48: 7-40.

Libertini, G.
1930 *Il Museo Biscari*. Milano, Roma: Bastetti e Tumminelli.

Lilliu, G.
1982 *La Civiltà Nuragica*. Sardegna Archeologica: Studi e Monumenti 1. Sassari: Carlo Delfino.
1986 Le miniere dalla preistoria all'età tardo-romana. In F. Mannoni (ed.), *Le Miniere e i Minatori della Sardegna*, 7-18. Cagliari: Consiglio Regionale della Sardegna.
1988 *La Civiltà dei Sardi dal Paleolitico all'Età dei Nuraghi*. Torino: Nuova ERI.

Lo Schiavo, F.
1976a Fonderia Nuragica in loc. 'Sa Sedda 'e Sos Carros' (Oliena, Nuoro). In *Nuove Testimonianze*

Archeologiche della Sardegna Centro-Settentrionale, 69-78. Sassari: Dessì.

1976b *Il ripostiglio del nuraghe Flumenelongu (Alghero-Sassari). Considerazioni preliminari sul commercio marittimo nel Mediterraneo occidentale in età protostorica*. Quaderni 2. Sassari: Dessì.

1978a Complesso di armi di bronzo da Ottana. *Sardegna Centro-Orientale dal Neolitico alla Fine del Mondo Antico*, 75-79. Sassari: Dessì.

1978b Complesso nuragico di 'Sa Sedda 'e Sos Carros'. *Sardegna Centro-Orientale dal Neolitico alla Fine del Mondo Antico*, 99-101. Sassari: Dessì.

1981 Economia e società nell'età dei nuraghi. In E. Atzeni et al. (eds.), *Ichnussa: La Sardegna dalle origini all'età classica*, 255-347. Milano: Libri Scheiwiller.

1982 Copper metallurgy in Sardinia during the Late Bronze Age: New prospects on its Aegean connections. In J.D. Muhly, R. Maddin and V. Karageorghis (eds.), *Early Metallurgy in Cyprus, 4000-500 BC*, 271-82. Nicosia: Pierides Foundation.

1983 Le componenti Egea e Cipriota nella metallurgia della tarda età del Bronzo in Italia. *Magna Grecia e Mondo Miceneo. Atti del XXII Convegno di Studi sulla Magna Grecia (Taranto 1982)*, 285-320. Taranto: Istituto per la Storia e l'Archeologia della Magna Grecia.

1984 Appunti sull'evoluzione culturale della Sardegna nell'età dei metalli. *Nuovo Bullettino Archeologico Sardo* 1: 21-40.

1985 La Sardegna nuragica e il mondo mediterraneo. In E. Arslan, F. Barreca and F. Lo Schiavo (eds.), *Civiltà Nuragica*, 255-84. Milano: Electa.

1988 Il primo ferro in Sardegna. *The First Iron in the Mediterranean—Il primo ferro nel Mediterraneo (Populonia/Piombino 1983)*, 83-89. PACT 21. Strasbourg: Council of Europe.

1989 Le origini della metallurgia ed il problema della metallurgia nella cultura di Ozieri. In L.D. Campus (a cura di), *La Cultura di Ozieri. Problematiche e nuove acquisizioni. Atti del I convegno di studio (Ozieri, gennaio 1986—aprile 1987)*, 279-92. Ozieri: Il Torchietto.

1990 Copper oxhide and plano-convex ingots in Sardinia. In *Metallographic and Statistical Analyses of Copper Ingots from Sardinia*, 14-40. Quaderni 17. Ozieri.: Il Torchietto.

Lo Schiavo, F., E. Macnamara & L. Vagnetti
1985 Late Cypriot imports to Italy and their influence on local bronzework. *Papers of the British School at Rome* 53: 1-71.

Lo Schiavo, F., & D. Ridgway
1987 La Sardegna e il Mediterraneo occidentale allo scorcio del II millennio a.C. In G. Lilliu, G. Ugas and G. Lai (a cura di), *La Sardegna nel Mediterraneo tra il secondo e il primo millennio a.C. Atti del 2 convegno di studi 'Un millennio di relazioni fra la Sardegna e i Paesi del Mediterraneo', Selargius-Cagliari, 27-30 novembre 1986*, 391-418. Cagliari: Amministrazione Provinciale di Cagliari.

Lo Schiavo, F., & L. Vagnetti
1980 Micenei in Sardegna? *Rendiconti della Accademia Nazionale dei Lincei* 8(35): 371-93.

Lopez Roa, C.
1978 Las ceramicas alisadas con decoracion bruñida. *Huelva Arqueologica* 4: 145-80.

Macnamara, E., D. Ridgway & F.R. Serra Ridgway
1984 *The Bronze Hoard from S. Maria in Paulis, Sardinia*. British Museum Occasional Paper 45. London: British Museum.

Marcello, A., S. Pretti & I. Salvadori
1978 *Carta Metallogenica della Sardegna*. Firenze: Servizio Geologico d'Italia.

Metallo, A.
1955 Il sistema meteo-oceanografico del Mediterraneo. *Rivista Marittima* 88(5): 288-303.

1962 L'onda portante meteo-oceanografica del Mediterraneo. *Rivista Marittima* 95: 59-67.

Moscati, S.
1983 Precolonizzazione greca e precolonizzazione fenicia. *Rivista di Studi Fenici* 11(1): 1-7.

1988 Momenti precoloniali nel Mediterraneo antico. *Momenti precoloniali nel Mediterraneo antico. Questioni di metodo—Aree d'indagine. Evidenze a confronto, Atti del Convegno Internazionale (Roma, marzo 1985)*, 11-18. Roma: C.N.R.

Mosso, A.
1906 Le armi più antiche di rame e di bronzo. *Memorie dell'Accademia Nazionale dei Lincei* 12: 490-575.

1908 Villaggi preistorici di Caldare e Cannatello presso Girgenti. *Monumenti Antichi* 18: 573-684.

Muhly, J.D.
1976 *Supplement to Copper and Tin*. Hamden, Connecticut: The Connecticut Academy of Arts and Sciences.

1983 Lead isotope analysis and the Kingdom of Alashiya. *Report of the Department of Antiquities, Cyprus* 1983: 210-18.

1991 The development of copper metallurgy in Late Bronze Age Cyprus. In N.H. Gale (ed.), *Bronze Age Trade in the Mediterranean*, 180-96. Studies in Mediterranean Archaeology 90. Jonsered: Paul Åströms Förlag.

Muhly, J.D., & T. Stech
1990 Final observations. In *Metallographic and Statistical Analyses of Copper Ingots from Sardinia*, 200-21. Quaderni 17. Ozieri: Il Torchietto.

Nicosia, F.
1981 La Sardegna nel mondo classica. In E. Atzeni et al. (eds.), *Ichnussa. La Sardegna dalle origini all'età classica*, 421-76. Milano: Scheiwiller.

Nissardi, F.
1882 Nuragus. *Notizie degli Scavi* 1882: 305-11.

Orsi, P.
1912 La necropoli sicula di Pantalica, e la necropoli sicula di M. Dessueri. *Monumenti Antichi* 21: 301-408.

Pais, E.
1884 Il ripostiglio di bronzi di Abini presso Teti. *Bullettino Archeologico Sardo* 5-10: 67-179.

Pulak, C.
1988 The Bronze Age shipwreck at Ulu Burun, Turkey: 1985 campaign. *Journal of Field Archaeology* 92: 1-37.

Rellini, U.
1923 Miniere e fonderie d'età nuragica in Sardegna. *Bullettino di Paletnologia Italiana* 43: 58-67.

Ridgway, D.
1989 La 'Precolonizzazione.' *Un secolo di ricerche in Magna Grecia, Atti del XXVIII Convegno di Studi sulla Magna Grecia (Taranto 1988)*, 111-26. Taranto: Istituto per la Storia e l'Archeologia della Magna Grecia.

Taramelli, A.
1921   Il ripostiglio dei bronzi nuragici di Monte Sa Idda di Decimoputzu (Cagliari). *Monumenti Antichi* 27: 5-108.
1923   Appendix to U. Rellini, Miniere e fonderie d'età nuragica in Sardegna. *Bullettino di Paletnologia Italiana* 43: 67-72.

Tylecote, R.F., M.S. Balmuth & R. Massoli-Novelli
1984   Copper and bronze metallurgy in Sardinia. In M.S. Balmuth and R.J. Rowland, Jr (eds.), *Studies in Sardinian Archaeology*, 115-62. Ann Arbor: University of Michigan Press.

Weisgerber, G.
1982   Towards a history of copper mining in Cyprus and the Near East: Possibilities of mining archaeology. In J.D. Muhly, R. Maddin and V. Karageorghis (eds.), *Early Metallurgy in Cyprus, 4000–500 BC*, 25-32. Nicosia: Pierides Foundation.

Zwicker, U., P. Virdis & M.L. Ferrarese Ceruti
1980   Investigations on copper ore, prehistoric copper slag and copper ingots from Sardinia. In P.T. Craddock (ed.), *Scientific Studies in Early Mining and Extractive Metallurgy*. British Museum Occasional Paper No. 20: 135-64. London: British Museum.

Riassunto

La Sardegna ha svolto un ruolo di primaria importanza nelle rotte marittime pre- e protostoriche grazie alla sua posizione geografica nel Mediterraneo ed alle sue ricchezze minerarie. Vari autori classici ci hanno tramandato il ricordo, sfumato nel mito, di antichissimi contatti con l'Egeo, la Sicilia, il Nord Africa e l'Iberia. Ormai alquanto numerose sono le testimonianze archeologiche che attestano l'esistenza di rapporti fra la Sardegna ed altre aree mediterranee durante il periodo compreso fra la tarda età del Bronzo e la prima età del ferro. L'isola dovette rappresentare un indispensabile punto di appoggio per la navigazione ed una importante fonte di approvvigionamento di metalli.

Assai precoce è in Sardegna la presenza di oggetti metallici. Sia il rame che l'argento sono stati utilizzati durante la cultura di Ozieri, nel Tardo Neolitico, come dimostrano i rinvenimenti di Grotta Sa Korona (Monte Majore-SS), Montessu (CA), Cuccuru Arrius (OR) e Pranu Mutteddu (CA). Residui di fusione di rame ed argento provengono dalle capanne del periodo di Ozieri di Su Coddu (Selargius-CA). Poiché l'argento si rinviene allo stato nativo al di sotto del cappellaccio d'ossidazione dei giacimenti, ad una profondità irraggiungibile con le tecniche estrattive preistoriche, per ottenerlo era indispensabile la conoscenza di complessi processi metallurgici. Il piombo che, come l'argento, era estratto dalla galena è attestato in contesti eneolitici, a Monte d'Accoddi (SS), Sa Corte Noa (Laconi-NU) e nella grotta di Cuccuru Tiria (Iglesias-CA). In particolare da Monte d'Accoddi provengono anche frammenti di galena e crogioli in terracotta.

Mentre nel Bronzo antico (cultura di Bonnànnaro) si osserva una relativa scarsezza di manufatti metallici—forse connessa con un mancato o ridotto sfruttamento delle risorse minerarie, nel Bronzo medio l'isola diviene un punto cruciale nel commercio marittimo dei metalli. Nel periodo in cui vennero edificate le torri nuragiche—e quindi intorno o dopo il XV sec. a.C.—va collocata l'introduzione dei lingotti di rame ox-hide: sembrano dimostrarlo i lingotti di questo tipo che sarebbero stati rinvenuti sotto il pavimento di un nuraghe a S. Antioco di Bisarcio. Indipendentemente dalla provenienza del metallo i lingotti ox-hide testimoniano contatti con il Mediterraneo orientale. I rapporti con tale area mostrano uno speciale sviluppo durante la tarda età del Bronzo: la maggior parte del vasellame di tipo egeo rinvenuto nel nuraghe Antigori (Sarroch-CA) può essere attribuita al T.E. IIIB. Particolarmente significativi i contatti con il mondo cipriota, da cui si hanno sia importazioni dirette di manufatti (tripodi), che influenze sulla produzione metallurgica locale (doppie asce e picconi). Va rilevato come le due isole siano accumunate dalla presenza di ricchi giacimenti metalliferi.

Scorie di fusione di età nuragica sono state rinvenute in varie località (presso Funtana Raminosa, nel ripostiglio di Forraxi Nioi, a Nieddu, a Genna Maria di Villanovaforru, a Sa Sedda 'e sos Carros), ma in quantità alquanto limitata. Si ipotizza perciò l'impiego in Sardegna di tecnologie fusorie a bassa produzione di scorie, diverse da quelle note per il Vicino Oriente. L'esistenza di una produzione metallurgica nuragica è comunque indicata dal gran numero di lingotti, matrici di fusione e manufatti metallici disseminati nell'isola. I rapporti isotopici del piombo di oggetti sardi indicano una provenienza locale del rame. Del resto non mancano attestazioni dirette di antiche coltivazioni: mortai, pestelli, teste di mazza, lucerne e finanche resti umani rinvenuti all'interno di miniere.

Indizi di una marineria indigena sono offerti dai numerosi modellini nuragici di imbarcazioni, realizzati in terracotta ed in metallo. La scoperta di ceramica nuragica nei livelli dell'Ausonio II di Lipari e la presenza in Sicilia di asce di bronzo sarde testimoniano l'esistenza di scambi fra le due isole durante la tarda età del Bronzo. L'assenza di reperti siciliani in Sardegna sembra tuttavia suggerire che tali scambi avessero un carattere unidirezionale. Con la prima età del ferro, mentre divengono assai scarsi i rapporti con la Sicilia, l'Etruria diviene il punto focale del commercio sardo. Fra gli inizi del IX e la metà dell'VIII sec. a.C. si moltiplicano le attestazioni di materiali nuragici in contesti villanoviani. È verosimile che con le merci venissero anche scambiate esperienze ed informazioni nel campo della metallurgia e delle tecniche estrattive, anche in considerazione degli importanti giacimenti metalliferi posseduti dall'Etruria settentrionale tirrenica.

Fra lo scorcio del Bronzo finale e l'inizio della prima età del Ferro la produzione metallurgica sarda è particolarmente intensa, come indicano, tra l'altro, gli importanti ripostigli di Monte Sa Idda, Monte Arrubiu di Sarroch ed il complesso di Abini presso Teti. In questo momento la Sardegna partecipa attivamente ai traffici con il Mediterraneo occidentale, di cui si hanno attestazioni non solo nei numerosi bronzi di fogge 'occidentali' rinvenuti nell'isola (spade, asce, fibule, falci), ma anche nell'ambito della ceramica. L'Autore rileva una singolare comunanza fra la Sardegna e la Penisola Iberica in un particolare gusto di ornato vascolare, ottenuto con la tecnica dello stralucido; in esso la somiglianza talora si estende anche alla sintassi decorativa.

Nonostante si abbiano testimonianze di scambi di materie prime, di prodotti finiti, di conoscenze tecnologiche e di informazioni culturali, la documentazione di cui si dispone sulla navigazione e sulle imbarcazioni della fine del secondo millennio a.C. è assai scarsa. Navi a scafo arrotondato erano caratteristiche dell'area cipriota-levantina già intorno al XIV secolo a.C., come rilevabile dalle raffigurazioni rimaste; il pennone, curvato verso il basso, sosteneva l'unica vela, grossa e quadrata. La vela quadra era anche caratteristica delle navi micenee, che differivano da quelle levantine soprattutto per la forma dello scafo. Tale velatura consentiva soltanto uno sfruttamento limitato del vento. In una navigazione prevalentemente costiera quale quella protostorica i frequenti mutamenti dell'asse del vento riducevano le possibilità d'impiego della vela quadra, che quindi non risultava molto efficiente nelle lunghe traversate. Per la propulsione la nave doveva quindi avvalersi anche, durante la navigazione, oltre che dei venti, dell'impiego integrato dei remi e delle correnti superficiali marine.

La necessità di non dirigere la nave in senso contrario alla corrente, ma anzi di sfruttarne vantaggiosamente la forza, permette di ottenere una chiave di lettura delle possibili rotte seguite dagli antichi navigatori, tenendo conto delle correnti superficiali, sia a carattere permanente che stagionale. Si può osservare ad esempio come le correnti favoriscano in alcuni periodo dell'anno la navigazione diretta dalla Catalogna e dalla Linguadoca verso la Sardegna occidentale, facilitando così rotte provenienti dall'Iberia alternative a quelle che costeggiano il Nord Africa. Dalla Sardegna orientale un circuito di correnti dirige verso la Sicilia e da qui verso il Mediterraneo orientale. Un altro circuito collega invece, in particolari mesi, la Sardegna alla penisola italiana.

Lo studio delle correnti permette, oltre che di ipotizzare le antiche rotte, anche di individuare i periodi dell'anno in cui poteva aver luogo la navigazione.

New Light on the Provenience of the Copper Oxhide Ingots Found on Sardinia

Zofia A. Stos-Gale and Noël H. Gale

Introduction

We are greatly honored and very pleased to have been asked to contribute to this Festschrift in honor of Professor Miriam S. Balmuth and her outstanding contributions to Sardinian archaeology. Sardinia has hitherto not figured in the history of the Mediterranean in the same way as mainland Italy, Greece, Crete, or Cyprus. It has had no Schliemann or Evans, it has no Greek temples, malaria was not eradicated until the 1940s of our era, and it was noted mostly as a pestilential place of exile both by the Romans (in the time of Tiberius) and by Mussolini. It is largely in the last 30 years that Sardinia has truly risen from obscurity, in one direction with the development of the Costa Smeralda in the 1960s by the Aga Khan, and in another by the systematic work on the archaeology of the island by a handful of scholars, notably Lilliu, Barreca, Contu, Ferrarese Ceruti, Atzeni, Balmuth and Lo Schiavo. The work of these scholars has of course forced us to realize that the notion of obscurity in relation to Sardinia is a modern one; in the Neolithic, Copper, Bronze and Iron Ages (not to mention the Phoenician prospecting and colonizing ventures of the 9th and 8th centuries BC) an island as large as Sardinia, at the crossroads of the Western Mediterranean, and well endowed with obsidian, metal ores, grain, wool, and men, was not obscure. Recent discoveries of direct evidence of contacts in the Late Bronze Age with the Mycenaean, Minoan and Cypriot worlds (see Balmuth 1987, and references cited therein) have emphasized this, while the international exhibition in Karlsruhe (Thimme 1980) and the book *Ichnussa* (Atzeni *et al.* 1981) revealed to the world at large the sophistication and complexity of the pre-Nuragic and Nuragic peoples. Sardinia has now begun to take its place in the prehistory of the Mediterranean. That it has done so is in no small degree due to the tireless activity of Miriam Balmuth, who was not only the first American excavator in Sardinia but also the organizer of the series of Tufts University Symposia in Sardinian Archaeology which, since 1979, have brought the dynamically evolving state of Sardinian archaeology to the English-speaking world.

Copper Oxhide Ingots and Sardinian Metallurgy

The subject of the copper oxhide ingots found on Sardinia, and more generally of ancient metallurgy on Sardinia, is of course one of the many aspects of Sardinian archaeology to which Miriam Balmuth has herself made important contributions (Balmuth and Tylecote 1976; Tylecote, Balmuth and Massoli-Novelli 1983; 1984), and it is a pleasure to acknowledge her encouragement of our own work in this field. Our research forms part of a broader programme of study on the copper oxhide ingots which have been found throughout the Mediterranean; other aspects of this work at Oxford have been reported by Gale and Stos-Gale (1986; 1987; 1988; 1991) and by Gale (1989b; 1991). Where the ingots found on Sardinia are concerned our work forms part of a group effort directed by Fulvia Lo Schiavo and which involves also John Merkel, James Muhly, Tamara Stech and Robert Maddin. The present paper is but a short progress report of the Oxford work, with some amplification of the archaeological aspects, in the spirit of the rather longer account of the American work which appeared recently (Lo Schiavo *et al.* 1990).

Copper oxhide ingots (known also as *talenta*, *keftiubarren, kissenbarren*, double-axe ingots, etc.) have been most comprehensively discussed by Buchholz (1959), Bass (1967), Muhly *et al.* (1988), and Gale (1989b; 1991). These ingots, apparently confined to the Aegean Late Bronze Age, are found on land all over the Mediterranean, approximately from Cyprus through Crete and Greece to Sardinia and Sicily (see the distribution maps in Muhly *et al.* 1988:

282 fig. 1; and Gale 1991: 201 fig. 2). The large number of such ingots found in the two Late Bronze Age shipwrecks of Cape Gelidonya (Bass 1967) and Ulu Burun (Bass 1986; Bass 1987; Pulak 1988a; Pulak 1988b) corroborate the assumption from the distribution of land-based finds, that oxhide ingots were traded by sea. The find-spots on land are dominated by those on the three great islands of the Mediterranean: Cyprus, Crete, and Sardinia; the earliest, dating to LM I (c. 1550–1450 BC), have so far been found only in Crete, though they are depicted in contemporary Egyptian tomb paintings (Bass 1967: 62-63). All examined oxhide ingots dated to the later part of the Aegean Late Bronze Age have been proven by scientific means to have been made of copper extracted from Cypriot copper ores including, unsurprisingly, those ingots found on Cyprus itself (Gale and Stos-Gale 1986; Gale 1989b; Gale 1991). On the other hand, the earlier LM I copper oxhide ingots found on Crete at Hagia Triadha and Tylissos have been proven *not* to have been made of copper from Cyprus; these LM I oxhide ingots have Palaeozoic, especially Precambrian, lead isotope ratios which cannot be related to the younger copper ore deposits of the Mediterranean or Turkey, but point probably to ore sources in Afghanistan, Iran, or Central Asia (Gale and Stos-Gale 1986; Gale 1991; the same is true of the geologically old lead found in many EB II bronzes from Troy IIg and Kastri in Syros: Stos-Gale *et al.* 1984; Gale *et al.* 1985). That the ingots excavated in Crete are not made from copper ore deposits in Crete itself is no surprise, since copper ores are rare and scanty in Crete (Stech Wheeler *et al.* 1975; Gale and Stos-Gale 1986).

This article is primarily devoted to the most recent evidence about the provenience of those copper oxhide ingots which have been discovered on Sardinia. Our discussion is based chiefly on objective assessment of the scientific evidence bearing on the geological ores which were smelted for the copper metal used in casting the Sardinian oxhide ingots. Especially important is the new evidence about the lead isotope composition of copper ores from Tuscany, suggested by some as a possible source of copper for Sardinian oxhide ingots, and about sources of copper used to make Nuragic period copper alloy objects which may be contemporary with (or somewhat later than) the appearance of copper oxhide ingots on Sardinia.

Archaeological Introduction

It will be apparent that a large and necessarily expensive research programme has been mounted to examine the Sardinian ingots and to attempt to establish their provenience. This is an important endeavor both for Sardinian archaeology *per se* and within the larger framework of a project sponsored by the British Academy to examine Bronze Age trade in the Mediterranean (Knapp and Cherry 1990; Gale and Stos-Gale 1991). The very first copper oxhide ingots to be found at all were the five found in 1857 (Spano 1858) at Serra Ilixi (Nuragus-NU) in Sardinia, of which three now remain and are displayed in the Cagliari Museum. These were followed in the 1890s by Tsountas's discovery of an ingot at Mycenae (Svoronos 1906; 1910: plate II), in 1896 by discoveries at Enkomi on Cyprus (Murray *et al.* 1900: 15, 17 plate 1535), and in 1903 by the discovery of the ingots at Hagia Triadha on Crete (Paribeni 1903: 20-21; Carratelli 1945: 433, 455-458; Halbherr *et al.* 1977). Against this background Pigorini (1904) found it natural (perhaps influenced by notions of *ex oriente lux*) to think of the examples found in Sardinia as having come from the Aegean; other scholars thought of them as having been made from Cypriot copper, though perhaps with no more evidence than the fact that by then copper oxhide ingots had been found in Cyprus itself, not only at Enkomi but also at Mathiati and Skouriotissa. More recently some scholars, influenced it seems chiefly by the fact that copper deposits exist on Sardinia and by the flourishing Nuragic metal industry, have suggested explicitly or implicitly that the oxhide ingots found in Sardinia were made on the island from copper metal extracted from local copper ores, perhaps under Cypriot influence (Balmuth and Tylecote 1976: 195; Lo Schiavo and Vagnetti 1980; Lo Schiavo *et al.* 1985; Muhly *et al.* 1988; Lo Schiavo 1989). Muhly (1991) and Cherry and Knapp (1991) have gone so far as to speculate about ore deposits in Spain, Tuscany, the Negev, or Oman as a possible source for the copper from which the Sardinian ingots were made. Clearly it is crucial to our understanding of an important part of the Bronze Age metals trade in the Mediterranean to discover the copper source used for the Sardinian oxhide ingots.

Although we place most reliance on the scientific evidence, clearly we must also take into account the archaeological evidence. Concerning the oxhide ingots found on Sardinia the most familiar are the whole ingots from Serra Ilixi; they are conveniently illustrated by Lo Schiavo (1981: fig. 281), together with fragments of oxhide ingots excavated from Nuraghe Albucciu, Arzachena (Lo Schiavo 1982: 271-72). The whole ingots have no archaeological context, but the fragments from Albucciu are thought to date to the end of the Italian Late Bronze Age (Ferrarese Ceruti 1985: n. 18), c. 1200–1000 BC according to the chronology of Lilliu (1982). If this is correct, this is among the latest known contexts for oxhide ingots (others which may be in similar contexts include those from Villanovaforru and Sardara), though of course these fragments may well be from an oxhide ingot or ingots made rather earlier. Since 1857, and especially in recent years, a great many copper oxhide ingot fragments have been found in Sardinia. Figure 1 shows some of the more than 20 find spots for oxhide ingots now known on Sardinia, recently reviewed by Lo Schiavo (1980; 1985; 1989). A feature of the Sardinian oxhide ingots is that they are not infrequently found together with bun (plano-convex) copper ingots (Lo Schiavo 1989: 36), for example, at Villanovaforru (Baccu Simeone), Villagrande Strisaili (Vagnetti and Lo Schiavo 1989), Ittireddu (Galli 1984; 1985), etc. It should be noted that the Bronze Age shipwrecks of Cape Gelidonya and Ulu Burun also had both oxhide and bun ingots as part of their cargo. Superficially this might be taken as consistent with the view that bun ingots and oxhide ingots came together as 'imports' to Sardinia on a similar ship from the east, but it is equally possible that the Sardinian bun ingots are of local manufacture while the oxhide ingots were imported. At any rate the association together on shipboard or on land of both types of ingot, since they are both raw material for bronze-smithing, should occasion no surprise. It is clearly important to compare and contrast scientific analyses of both types of ingot, both from Sardinia and from the two Bronze Age shipwrecks.

We pause here to consider an objection by Vagnetti and Lo Schiavo (1989: 238 n. 3) to considering the oxhide ingots found on Sardinia as 'imports'. They write:

> If, for example, all the oxhide ingots are accepted as imports, what can be said about their wide—indeed, ubiquitous—distribution in Sardinia? The hypothesis that they were all carried to and round the island on one ship cannot be accepted. What is the rationale behind this distribution pattern?

To us there seems to be no reasonable objection at all to the possibility that these ingots might have arrived in Sardinia on one ship, if we just consider the more than 200 whole oxhide ingots on the Ulu Burun ship. It is *not* necessary, nor is it reasonable, to assume that they were carried round the island by one ship. We can instead think in terms of the suggestion made by Jones and Vagnetti (1991: 137) of: 'the circulation of exotic goods along local trade networks that do not necessarily imply a direct connection of the findspot area with the Aegean or Cyprus'. Examples quoted by these authors of such a pattern within Sardinia are based upon imported material known at inland sites such as Decimoputzu (Mycenaean ivory head, probably LH IIIA-B: Ferrarese Ceruti *et al.* 1987: 12-14 fig. 2.3) or Orroli (alabastron fragment; chemical analysis classifies it with the White Ware from Chania in West Crete: Jones and Vagnetti 1991: 131). Oxhide ingot fragments, though the original ingots may have come into Sardinia through coastal 'emporia' such as Antigori, might well have circulated along the same local trade networks, which then provide the underlying rationale for the observed distribution.

In most cases the Sardinian oxhide ingots and fragments do not have an archaeological context which allows firm dating, though it has been suggested by Stech (1989) that they begin in the 13th century BC. Those oxhide ingots that do come from excavations have been assigned to the Italian Late Bronze Age (thought to extend from the 13th to the 10th century BC) either on the basis of associated pottery (or, say, Iberic bronze objects such as axes) or because they came from nuraghi of complex plans. These include the ingots found at Nuraghi Albucciu, Funtana, Bau Nuraxi, and Nastasi and at Baccu Simeone. The absolute dating of the Italian Late Bronze Age continues to elude us, which makes comparison with dates in Cyprus or the Aegean difficult; confidence is not increased by recent controversies about Aegean chronology itself (Manning 1988).

Distribution of Oxhide Ingots

We must clearly consider the Sardinian examples in the context of the other oxhide ingots found in the Mediterranean. For the finds on land, which often consist only of fragments, it is difficult to estimate the number of whole ingots represented, but it is very approximately 130, with about 20 on Cyprus, 37 on Crete, 50 on Sardinia, 22 in Greece (chiefly Mycenae and Kyme), and 1 each in Sicily, Lipari, Anatolia and off the coast of Bulgaria. There were 38 ingots on the Cape

320 *Sardinia in the Mediterranean*

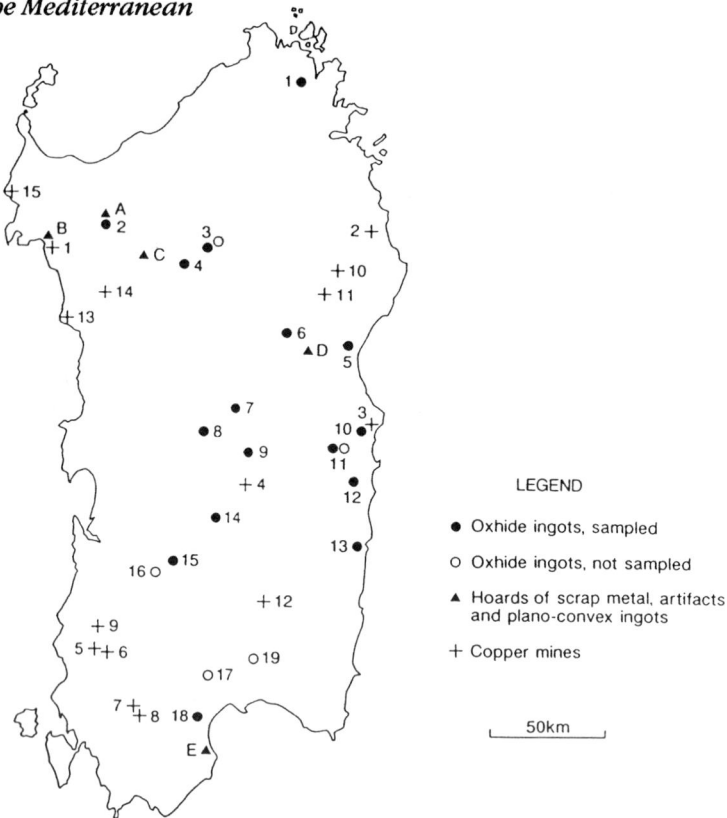

Fig. 1 Map of Sardinia showing some of the sites where oxhide ingot fragments have been found and the location of some copper ore deposits. **Ore deposits**: 1-Calabona, Alghero; 2-Torpe, Canale Barisoni; 3-Genna Olidoni; 4-Funtana Raminosa; 5-Arenas; Tiny; 6-Sa Duchessa; 7-Rosas; Truba Niedda; 8-Sa Marchesa; 9-Perda s'Oliu; 10-Gozzura; 11-Sos Enattos; 12-Pranu e Sanguini; 13-Capo Marargiu; 14-Castello di Bonvei; 15-Argentiera. **Oxhide Ingots**: 1-Arzachena; 2-Ossi; 3-Ozieri; 4-Ittireddu; 5-Dorgali; 6-Nuoro; 7-Teti; 8-Ortueri; 9-Belvi; 10-Triei; 11-Villagrande Strisaili; 12-Lanusei; 13-Tertenia; 14-Nuragus; 15-Villanovaforru; 16-Sardara; 17-Assemini; 18 Capapoterra; 19-Solominis. **Hoards**: A-Ossi; B-Alghero; C-Bonnanaro; D-Oliena; E-Sarroch.

Gelidonya wreck and more than 200 on the Ulu Burun wreck, so that about 65% of all known ingots have been found on only two shipwrecks.

That indicates the scale of the trade in copper in just the oxhide ingot form (or at least that *intended*; how many ships foundered with their cargoes, how many voyages were successful?), with at least 6 metric tonnes of copper as oxhide ingots on the Ulu Burun ship alone. The distribution of find-spots on land suggests that these ingots were almost exclusively transported by ship. They have been found overwhelmingly either on islands or at mainland sites not far from the sea; sites (such as Kommos in Crete: Shaw 1984) which generally have other evidence for international trade.

A clear feature of the distribution of oxhide ingot find-spots on land is the prominent role played by the three great islands of the Mediterranean, Cyprus, Crete and Sardinia. About 80% of all ingots discovered on land have come from these three islands; the Ulu Burun and Cape Gelidonya ships, with their cargoes of oxhide ingots, may well have been sailing to the west with Cyprus as their last port of call before disas-

ter struck. What are the relative potentials of these three islands as sources of copper ores? Crete can be dismissed more or less out of hand; our own surveys (Stos-Gale *et al.* 1986) have shown the copper deposits on that island to be few, low grade, and to contain far too little ore to have supported the Minoan copper industry (a position with which Stech Wheeler *et al.* 1975 concur); moreover, lead isotope analyses show that no copper oxhide ingot yet analyzed was made of Cretan copper (Gale and Stos-Gale 1986; Stos-Gale *et al.* 1986; Gale 1989b). In contrast copper ore deposits are of course abundant on Cyprus (Bear 1963), though considerably less so on Sardinia (Zuffardi 1980). Sardinia is in fact not noted for its reserves of copper, but rather for its deposits of lead. For example, the total production of copper concentrates from Sardinia in the period 1851–1948 was 75,000 tonnes, compared with 3,147,000 tonnes of lead minerals in the same period (Società Elettrica Sarda 1949: 59). That the reserves of copper in Cyprus are overwhelmingly larger is shown by the fact that in Cyprus one mine (Mavrovouni) exported 131,093 tons of copper concentrates in the year 1938 alone (Bear

1963: 58). Moreover there are only about six small copper mines (Calabona, Funtana Raminosa, Sa Duchessa, Rosas, Sa Marchesa, Canale Barisoni) of any account at all in Sardinia (though there are a number of smaller deposits), while in Cyprus there are more than 30 cupriferous ore bodies, each vastly larger than any in Sardinia (Constantinou 1980; 1982). The probability of ancient discovery of copper in Cyprus, and of an excess for export elsewhere, is enormously larger than in Sardinia. Such arguments do not, however, rule out the possibility, indeed probability, that Nuragic metallurgy made use of Sardinian copper ores, while leaving open the possibility that the oxhide ingots came to the island from abroad.

The Copper Trade

If we are to use the oxhide ingots to contribute to our studies of Bronze Age trade we need to discover where they were made, which copper sources were used, how they were transported, what were their destinations, and what were the nationalities of the people who made them, sold them, and transported them. It will also be interesting to discover how and where they were cast, whether bun and slab ingots formed part of the copper trade at the same time that oxhide ingots were in use, and the relative quality of the copper used for the different types of ingot. Can we also discover the extent to which copper imported as oxhide ingots competed with other sources of copper, local or foreign, at a particular site in a particular period?

Who Controlled the Trade?

In considering the Sardinian ingots we should also consider the evidence regarding the possible identity of the people who operated the trade in oxhide ingots. In the past it has been almost universally assumed that such trade was in late Minoan, Mycenaean, or at least Aegean (perhaps Cycladic) hands (e.g. Vercoutter 1956; and the general use of the term *Keftiubarren* by Buchholz 1959). The careful studies of representational evidence made by George Bass (1967), and recently confirmed by Shelley Wachsmann (1987), throw considerable doubt on that.

Their examination of the Egyptian evidence from tomb paintings and reliefs suggests that it is in only one tomb, that of Rechmire at Thebes, dating to about 1470 to 1410 BC, where oxhide ingots may definitely be associated with Aegeans, from Keftiu (Bass 1967: 63 fig. 67). Even here (Bass 1967: 64 fig. 68) Syrian chiefs present similar ingots, and when the ingots are seen in the hands of porters bringing them to Egyptian bronze workers in the same tomb (Bass 1967: 64 fig. 70), they are identified as Asiatic copper from Retnu, that is, Syria. Wachsmann (1987: 50) goes as far as to write: 'It would seem, therefore, that in the case of the oxhide ingots of Rechmire's Aegeans they have been transferred from the source scene of Syrian tribute.' As Bass (1967: 62-67) has written, in 11 other representations we may be certain that the Egyptians considered the ingots to be in the hands of Syrians. An example is from the tomb of Huy at Thebes (Bass 1967: 67 fig. 82), whilst from the tomb of Amenemopet (Wachsmann 1987: plate LIIB) the porters, carrying both copper oxhide and lead ingots, have been identified by Wachsmann (1987: 50) as an example of hybrid Aegean/Syrians. It is not uncommon in Egyptian art for human figures and objects to be composed by uniting elements originally belonging to two or more separate entities. We should note however that the Egyptian representations of Syrians bringing oxhide ingots to Egypt date no later than 1350 BC. Also these records do not by themselves necessarily tell us who traded oxhide ingots to the west, or in whose hands the trade was in later times.

There are at least two pieces of evidence which do seem to indicate a Syrian connection with the production of copper oxhide ingots in later times. The most positive is the excavation by Elisabeth and Jacques Lagarce (Lagarce *et al.* 1983: 277-90; for an illustration see Gale 1989b: fig. 29.19) of the only mould for an oxhide ingot yet discovered, from the Late Bronze Age palace at Ras Ibn Hani just south of Ugarit. It was found in *atelier* 17 of the North Palace and the excavators (Lagarce *et al.* 1983: 287-89) have noted that this may indicate that the metal working was a royal franchise. Scattered around the ingot were a number of copper metal droplets which presumably splashed out when the mould was used to cast an ingot; lead isotope analyses of these droplets (Gale 1989b: 255-57 fig. 29.18) are consistent with these oxhide ingots at Ras Ibn Hani having been cast from Cypriot copper. In Ugarit itself two possible oxhide ingot fragments were found by Schaeffer (1936: 99; 1956: 269, 260 fig. 224: 19, 262 fig. 226).

Another, perhaps less certain, piece of evidence linking copper oxhide ingots with the Syrians is the well-known bronze stand from Kourion in Cyprus (Catling 1969: figs. 1, 17; and Tatton-Brown 1987: 19), now in the British Museum (BM 1920/12-20/1), dating to the 12th century BC. Scholars debate the ethnic identity of the man carrying the Type 2c ingot, but parallels have been drawn with figures on contemporary North Syrian sculptural reliefs.

Finally, we must mention the evidence from the Cape Gelidonya shipwreck. It carried much to associate it with Near Eastern merchants, such as a merchant's seal, religious talismans, Near Eastern weights, stone hammers, mortars, a lamp, and bronzes more than half of whose prototypes are found in the Near East (Bass 1967). It is true that the probable ethnic mix in contemporary Cyprus, making it difficult to distinguish a Syrian from a Cypriot merchantman, does not rule out the possibility that the ship was Cypriot; but it can hardly have been Aegean. There is nothing in the archaeological record to suggest that the Nuragic people were engaged in the transshipment of copper, though that in itself would not necessarily preclude their making ingots in the oxhide form destined to be traded abroad by others.

The Chronology of the Copper Trade in the Mediterranean

Archaeological evidence suggests that bulk trade in copper developed in the Levant and Eastern Mediterranean only in the Late Bronze Age; by that time the large-scale bronze industry of Late Minoan Crete (as witnessed by sites such as Knossos, Hagia Triadha, Zakros, Malia, Tylissos, the Arkalochori cave, Gournia, Palaikastro, Armenoi, etc.), which depended entirely on imported copper and tin, was in full swing. Indeed the earliest copper oxhide ingots are so far attested only at sites in Crete such as Hagia Triadha, Gournia and Zakros (perhaps all dating to LMIB, though formerly dated to LMIA) and in Egyptian tomb paintings dating to the reigns of Hatshepsut and Tuthmosis III (perhaps 1504–1450, following the 1976 chronology of the Oriental Institute of Chicago). Later depictions of oxhide and other ingots occur successively in tombs dating to the reigns of Amenhotep II (1453–1419), Tuthmosis IV (1419–1386), Akhenaten (1350–1334), and Ramesses III (1182–1151) (Bass 1967: 62-68) to which we may add the evidence of the ingots on the Ulu Burun ship (c. 1300 BC), the Cape Gelidonya wreck (c. 1240–1200 BC), and the ingots on Cyprus, Crete, Sardinia, and the Mycenaean world, discussed earlier. None of this evidence reveals precisely where the ingots came from or the ore deposits which were exploited to provide the copper metal from which they were made.

Links between Sardinia and the Eastern Mediterranean

The most exciting new development to emerge from the recent work of such scholars as Maria Ferrarese Ceruti, Fulvia Lo Schiavo, Lucia Vagnetti and Ellen Macnamara is the evidence for eastern contacts with Sardinia from about the early 13th century BC to the 10th century BC. Evidence for contacts with Cyprus lies partly in detailed comparisons of such metal types as heavy smithing tools and tripod-stands, partly in the recognition of Cypriot and Mycenaean pottery in Sardinian sites, and partly in scientific analysis which has related a pithos sherd from Antigori to a southern Cypriot source and to similar pithos sherds from Kommos in Crete, and has proved that in Sardinia there are significant quantities (Jones and Vagnetti 1991) of coarseware stirrup jars (cf. stirrup jars on the Ulu Burun wreck, Pulak 1988a; Pulak 1988b; Bass *et al.* 1989) and imported Mycenaean wares (Lo Schiavo *et al.* 1985; Ferrarese Ceruti *et al.* 1987; Vagnetti and Lo Schiavo 1989; Jones and Day 1987). In discussing how this evidence might relate to the question of the origin of the copper oxhide ingots found in Sardinia it may be useful to do so in relation to some views advanced recently by Muhly (1991):

> The presence of heavy smithing tools in Sardinian bronze hoards parallels the situation in Cyprus, indicating that both islands were copper-producing regions whereas Minoan Crete and Mycenaean Greece, without such tools in any of the surviving hoards, were copper importing regions...Why then would a local Sardinian metal industry be making use of imported Cypriot copper?

Here it seems to us that the inference does not necessarily follow from the facts; there seems to be an alternative possibility. Muhly simply *assumes* that the heavy smithing tools found in Sardinia were made there from copper extracted from Sardinian copper ores. We hope to show that conventional archaeological arguments can easily lead to a quite different conclusion. First, we know that a sherd of a LH IIIB:1 Cypro-Mycenaean rhyton has been excavated at Nuraghe Antigori (Lo Schiavo *et al.* 1985: 7; Ferrarese Ceruti 1981: fig. M4; Ferrarese Ceruti 1982: pl. 63,5) and Muhly himself draws attention to the Cypriot pithos sherds (Vagnetti and Lo Schiavo 1989: 221) from the same nuraghe, which scientific analyses (Jones and Day 1987) suggest was made at Kalavasos-Ayios Dhimitrios or Maroni-Vournes in Cyprus, both sites with known metallurgical associations (copper slags and fragments of copper oxhide ingots at both sites). These Cypriot sherds and other Aegean pottery found at Antigori (Ferrarese Ceruti *et al.* 1987) would not be out of place among the Aegean wares aboard the Cape Gelidonya or Ulu

Burun ships, which were of course also carrying oxhide ingots. The Ulu Burun ship also carried a sword suggested to have been of Italian or Sicilian manufacture (Vagnetti and Lo Schiavo 1989: 222), possibly left over from a previously successful voyage to the Western Mediterranean. Moreover it has been concluded that several tripod-stands found in or associated with Sardinia were Late Cypriot III in date, of Cypriot manufacture, reaching Sardinia towards the end of the second millennium BC (Lo Schiavo *et al*. 1985: 35-51); a few fragments of Cypriot tripods were also found in the Cape Gelidonya wreck (Bass 1967: 107-109). Perhaps most telling is the presence of heavy smithing hammers and shovels (Bass 1967: 84-110) and probably part of a pair of smithing tongs (Catling 1964: 99, 292) on board the Cape Gelidonya ship; thus there seems every reason to suppose that the smithing tools found in Sardinia came from Cyprus together with Aegean pottery. Indeed Lo Schiavo *et al*. (1985: 27-28), in their study of Cypriot imports to Italy, conclude that:

> Concerning the smithing tools as a whole, there must be noticed the association of similar forms in Cyprus and Sardinia, as opposed to the absence of similar forms elsewhere. Sledge-hammers, 'Levantine' tongs and charcoal shovels are totally unknown in the Aegean and otherwise in the west; raising hammers and shovels are different from the examples known in Italy and Greece; and in the Levant only 'Levantine' tongs and charcoal shovels are documented. It seems difficult to suggest a contemporary independent invention of the complete set of smithing tools in the two islands, even based on the argument of the mining activity of both of them. The few but distinctive imports also stand against this interpretation of the archaeological data, stressing, on the contrary, the general framework of imports and influences from Cyprus to the west and mostly to Sardinia.

It seems almost as difficult to see the oxhide ingots as an independent invention in both islands. If we are to apply Occam's razor and seek the simplest interpretation of the Cypriot pottery, Cypriot smithing tools, Cypriot tripod-stands (admitting that some may be copies of Cypriot models—a hypothesis which could be tested by lead isotope analysis) and oxhide copper ingots found in Sardinia, we should surely see them as forming a whole which cannot artificially be separated. In this view the whole represents 'imports' from Cyprus into Sardinia, an interpretation which is strengthened by the cargoes of the Cape Gelidonya and Ulu Burun ships which between them include all of these classes of Cypriot artifacts. Nevertheless we do not wish to rely solely on such arguments, however plausible, but instead seek evidence coming from the application of the methods of the natural sciences.

Lead Isotope and Trace Element Analyses

Clearly, if we are to be able to use the copper oxhide ingots to shed some light on the pattern of the Bronze Age Copper trade in the Mediterranean we have to find a way of being able to answer such questions as were the ingots found on Sardinia imported or were they made on that island from Sardinian copper ores?

The ordinary methods of archaeology are powerless to answer such questions. There has been no progress with attempts to understand the meaning of the signs on some oxhide ingots and in any case many bear no signs. Typological classification has given no certain information about their place of manufacture, nor have the Egyptian tomb paintings or the evidence from Bronze Age shipwrecks. A considerable effort has been put into trying to find a scientific technique which would enable the provenience of copper or bronze objects to be established. Most of that effort has been expended on the chemical analysis of objects, with the hope that at least the minor or trace element compositions would solve the problem. Very little effort was put into chemical analyses of ores or into the study of the relevant ore deposits and their geology. The end result has been a failure to make any progress along these lines with the provenancing problem properly so-called (see Coles 1982), i.e. the linking of copper alloy artifacts with the ore deposits which provided their copper metal. Much effort has been put into metallographic studies of oxhide ingots (e.g. Zwicker *et al*. 1980; Zwicker *et al*. 1985; Muhly *et al*. 1977; Muhly *et al*. 1980; Tylecote *et al*. 1984); this has yielded much of metallurgical interest but has not at all solved the problem of provenience.

The most promising approach seems to be the use of lead isotope analyses backed up by trace element analyses (e.g. Gale 1989a; Gale and Stos-Gale 1989; Gale and Stos-Gale 1991). At the first level of utility one can in this way link together oxhide ingots which appear to be made from the same copper metal source.

It is much more important that, by comparing lead isotope analyses of ingots with those of copper ore deposits, one can hope to link both oxhide ingots and manufactured bronze objects to the copper ore deposits whence came their copper metal. At the most basic level this method can succeed only if the lead isotope compositions of the different copper ore deposits in the

Mediterranean region can be distinguished from each other. This question and the underlying principles of the use of lead isotope analysis for provenancing have been examined in a number of papers (e.g. Gale 1989a; Gale and Stos-Gale 1991; Stos-Gale *et al.* 1991) and it has been concluded that those Mediterranean copper deposits which have so far been examined do have lead isotope 'fingerprints' which can be distinguished from each other.

Natural lead has four isotopes which vary in their relative proportions; mass spectrometry measures the three isotopic ratios which can be formed. It is necessary to use two ordinary bivariate diagrams to depict the three lead isotope ratios available. When this is done for a number of copper deposits one gets, for each normal ore deposit, a scatter of isotope compositions confined within a small region of the bivariate diagrams; these are the lead isotope 'fields' for the ore deposits, around which one can construct statistically based ellipses at a chosen confidence level (see Gale and Stos-Gale 1991 for examples). It is necessary to use both diagrams since it is often the case that the apparent overlap between some of the ore deposit fields disappears when all three isotope ratios are used.

The important principle of lead isotope provenience analysis is that if the isotopic composition of the trace of lead in an ingot falls well outside the field of isotopic compositions characteristic of a given ore deposit, then the copper used to make that artifact did not come from that ore deposit. Conversely, if the lead isotope composition for an ingot falls within the field for a particular ore deposit, then that ingot is consistent with having been made using copper extracted from those copper ores.

An important point to remember is that the lead isotope composition of an ore deposit is governed to first order by the geological age of that ore deposit, so that ore deposits widely different in age are likely to have quite different lead isotope compositions (see, e.g., Gale and Stos-Gale 1991). Second-order effects often conspire so that the converse is not necessarily true.

The geology of Sardinia and the setting of its ore deposits are quite complicated (see Gale and Stos-Gale 1987; Gale and Stos-Gale 1988; Garbarino *et al.* 1980; Zuffardi 1980; Marcello *et al.* 1978) and range quite widely in geological age, which helps considerably the scientific investigation of the ore sources used to make copper ingots found on Sardinia. Metal ore deposits in Sardinia are present in rock units ranging in age from the Cretaceous to the Cambrian periods; that is, from about 100 million years ago to 500 million years ago. By far the greatest concentration of ore deposits lies in the southwest of the island, in the Iglesiente-Sulcis district, where they date geologically chiefly between about 550 million years ago and 400 million years ago. More than 30 major lead-zinc and 3 medium-sized copper deposits lie in this district. There are, however, several other copper deposits scattered through Sardinia (including the important mine of Funtana Raminosa, Gadoni), and attention should particularly be drawn to that of Monte Sissini (Calabona: Frenzel *et al.* 1975) since this dates as recently as the Tertiary Period. The important point is that the range in geological age of the Sardinian copper ore deposits is a positive advantage for the method of characterizing ore deposits based on isotopic analysis of the trace lead which they contain.

Diagrams, Overlap and Statistics

The methods available for the display and analysis of lead isotope data have been discussed recently (Gale 1991; Gale and Stos-Gale 1991). We feel that it is now preferable to go beyond the use of bivariate scatter plots both for discriminating between different copper ore deposits and for associating copper alloy artifacts with copper from a particular deposit.

Another more quantitative approach is to use multivariate statistics to include all three lead isotopic ratios together at the same time. A technique which is ideally suited to situations which focus on a set of two or more groups of data, such as we have with lead isotope data from a number of different copper ore deposits, is discriminant function analysis (see, e.g., Manly 1986), which can be applied in a stepwise fashion. This method of statistical analysis, which is far superior for our purposes to principal components analysis or factor analysis, investigates how well it is possible to separate several groups of data and provides numerical assessments of the separation between groups. It subsequently provides a means of testing whether the lead isotope data of, say, an oxhide ingot belong to one of the copper ore groups, and gives an objective assessment of the probability that the ingot belongs to that group. Cluster analysis, in contrast, does not produce a quantitative measure of the degree of separation between groups, nor does it result in mathematical functions for classifying new objects to groups with a quantitative measure of group membership. Cluster analysis remains, however, a useful preliminary technique for investigating the grouping of data where one has no *a priori* indication as to what groups should exist; these groups should always subsequently be assessed by a proper multivariate technique such as discriminant function analysis.

As an example of the power of discriminant analysis, it has been shown (e.g. Gale and Stos-Gale 1989: fig. 3; Gale 1991: fig. 5) that for the Aegean copper deposits of Lavrion, Kythnos and Cyprus (which overlap in the bivariate plots) discriminant analysis gives a good separation of their lead isotope data. This can be visualized in the scatter diagram for the first two canonical functions which discriminant analysis produces as best separating these three groups. Such a scatter diagram is a useful pictorial summary of a discriminant analysis, but of course it does not tell the whole story. Discriminant analysis software, such as BMDP program 7M (Dixon 1990), also produces numerical information. On the one hand group centers are computed together with, for each data point, the Mahalanobis distances to the group center; if an observation is very significantly far from the center of its group on the basis of the chi-square distribution, then this brings into question whether that observation really comes from this group. The posterior probabilities of group membership are also computed for each observation. In the present example, the probabilities for Lavrion ores belonging individually to the Lavrion group are all over 98%; the same is true for the Kythnos ores except that for just one sample the probability of its belonging to the Kythnian group drops as low as 81%; for the Cypriot group the probabilities of group membership are all above 99%, save for one ore sample mis-classified with Kythnos at a probability of 88%. We shall henceforth use scatterplots for brevity in summarizing the results of discriminant function analysis. In such scatterplots, if the data follows a multivariate normal distribution with equal variances and covariances amongst groups, then each scatter of points would be ellipsoidal with approximately the same size and direction of tilt. The dissimilar 'ellipses' for the three copper deposits we have been considering suggest a departure from such assumptions, but the discriminant functions generated still divide the groups quite sharply. The same is true for the famous Fisher iris data (Fisher 1936), used as a test example by BMDP (Dixon 1990: 339-58). Further examples of the use of discriminant analysis to separate apparently overlapping lead isotope ore fields are given by Gale (1991).

Gale and Stos-Gale (1991) have investigated many other apparent cases of partial overlap of lead isotope fields for copper deposits in the Aegean, Anatolia, Tuscany, Sinai, etc. In every case but one, discriminant function analysis has been able to resolve the lead isotope fields. The one case where overlap cannot be completely unscrambled by multivariate statistical analysis of all three ratios is the copper deposits on Thasos and on Kythnos. Here, however, combined analytical and archaeological arguments (Gale and Stos-Gale 1991) show that copper was not exploited on Thasos in the Bronze Age, and could not therefore be a source of copper for the oxhide ingots studied in this paper.

Scientific Data for Oxhide Ingots from Cyprus

Before we turn to the data for lead isotope analyses of copper oxhide ingots, we wish to say a little about trace element data. Thermodynamic and geochemical arguments, together with the copper smelting experiments of Tylecote *et al.* (1977) and Merkel (1983), suggest that the trace metals in smelted copper which may most reliably reflect the level at which they are present in the copper ore are the platinum group metals and gold (Au), silver (Ag), cobalt (Co), nickel (Ni), antimony (Sb) and arsenic (As). There is no space here to discuss all our trace element data, so I will concentrate on the elements gold and silver since they seem to give us significant extra information for Late Cypriot copper. Stos-Gale *et al.* (1986: 131 fig. 8) showed that, in a plot of their gold and silver contents, all analyzed copper and tin-bronze artifacts from the Late Bronze Age sites of Hala Sultan Tekke and Ayios Dhimitrios in Cyprus plotted in a restricted region or 'field' of the Au–Ag diagram. All of these artifacts have lead isotope compositions falling into the field defined by Cypriot copper ores (Stos-Gale *et al.* 1986: 130 figs. 6-7). The sites now included for which this characteristic remains true range in date from Late Cypriot IIC (c. 1325–1260 BC) at Kalavasos-Ayios Dhimitrios (e.g. South 1980) to latest LCIIC (c. 1230 BC) at Pyla-Kokkinokremos (Karageorghis and Demas 1984) and at Maa-Palaeokastro (Demas 1984). Their geographical position is such that the different sites may well have drawn their copper from different ore deposits around the Troodos, but the gold and silver contents plot in a well-defined field of compositions. This gold/silver field seems to be a 'fingerprint' for Late Cypriot copper. Middle Cypriot copper artifacts from Alambra and elsewhere, and Early Cypriot artifacts from Lapithos do not have gold and silver contents falling into this field (unpublished data), so that it seems to be a fingerprint only for Late Cypriot copper metal.

Oxhide ingots and fragments have been known from Cyprus for a long time from Enkomi, Skouriotissa and Mathiati. The whole ingot and six fragments from the Enkomi Foundry Hoard, now in the British Museum, probably date from about 1200 BC, though they could be earlier (Knapp *et al.* 1988a). These ingots again span sites across Cyprus and perhaps extend to later times, but Fig. 2 shows that their gold/silver analyses all fall in the field defined by the Late Cypriot copper alloy artifacts. On this evidence the oxhide ingots found on Cyprus are indeed consistent with having been made of Cypriot copper. This conclusion is greatly reinforced by the lead isotope data for the oxhide ingots found on Cyprus. Stos-Gale *et al.* (1986: 129 fig. 5) showed, in an ordinary lead isotope diagram, that the ingot fragments from Skouriotissa and Mathiati fall within the field defined by Cypriot copper ores; they showed also (Stos-Gale *et al.* 1986: 130 figs. 6-7) that the Cypriot ore lead isotope field contains all the Cypriot artifacts from Kalavasos, Pyla and Hala Sultan Tekke whose gold/silver contents define the Late Cypriot Au–Ag field. Figure 3, a diagram resulting from stepwise discriminant function analysis, shows that the lead isotope data not only for the oxhide ingots from Skouriotissa and Mathiati, but also the data for the whole oxhide ingot and 6 fragments from Enkomi (from the British excavations, and housed in the British Museum), are all contained within the field defined by Cypriot copper ores. This diagram includes all three lead isotope ratios and allows a comparison of the grouping of the ingots with the ore deposits nearest in lead isotope composition to Cyprus, from which they are completely resolved.

There is no doubt that both the lead isotope data and the gold and silver concentrations support the conclusion that all analyzed oxhide ingots and fragments found on Cyprus were made from Cypriot copper ores. This is not a surprise, since we know that Cyprus possesses abundant copper ore deposits, and our own lead isotope data proves that Cypriot copper ores were used to make artifacts from the stratigraphic excavations at Vounous (Stos-Gale *et al.* 1991) which date as early as Early Cypriot IB (c. 2100 BC) and at the LCIIC (c. 1325–1225 BC) sites of Ayios Dhimitrios, Pyla, and Hala Sultan Tekke (Stos-Gale *et al.* 1986).

In considering the scientific evidence that we have accumulated about copper oxhide ingots we must remember one important fact: we have both a lead isotope and a gold/silver fingerprint for copper produced from Cypriot copper ores in the Late Bronze Age, fingerprints which we can use to trace the movement overseas of Cypriot copper in the form *inter alia* of oxhide ingots.

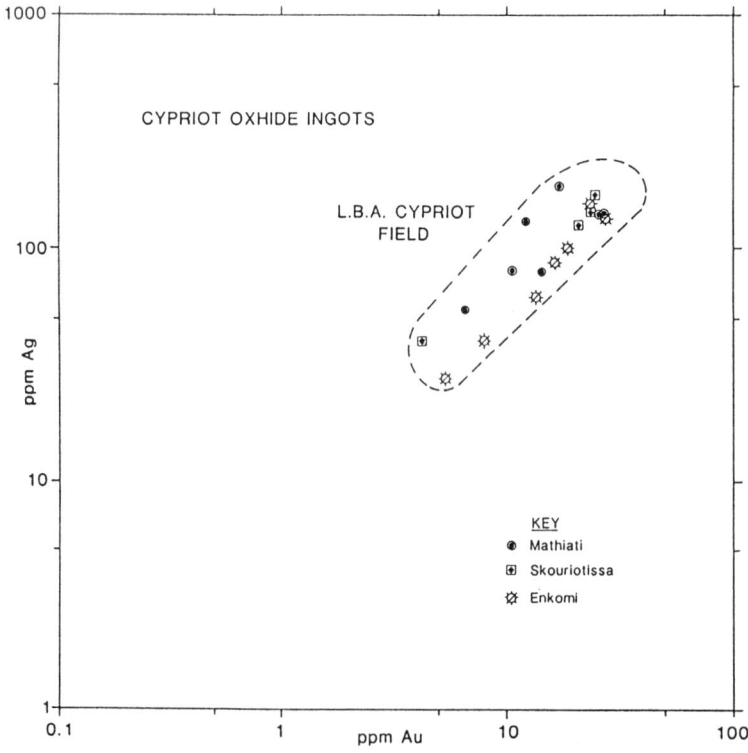

Fig. 2 A plot of the concentrations of gold (Au) and silver (Ag) in parts per million (ppm) for oxhide ingots found in Cyprus in relation to the field defined by the concentrations found in copper alloy artifacts from Late Bronze Age sites in Cyprus.

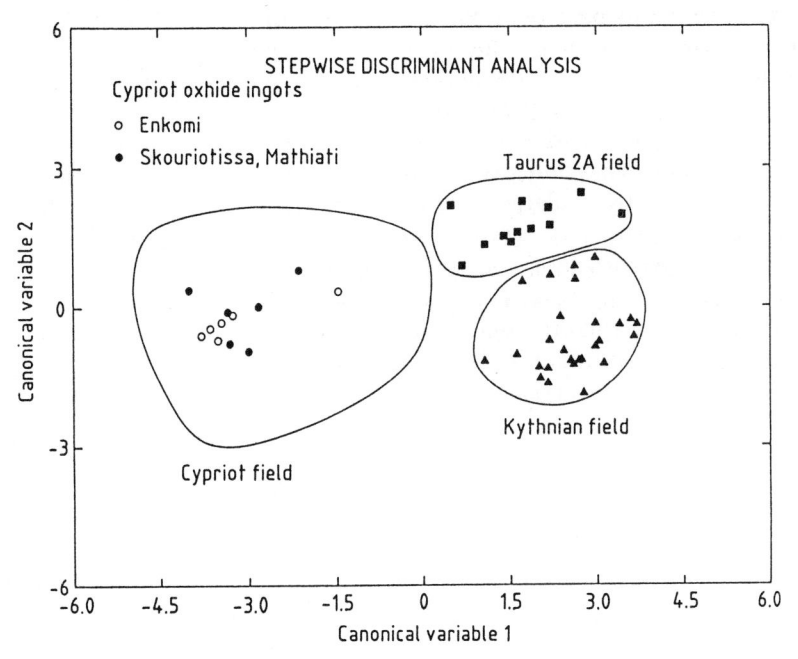

Fig. 3 Stepwise discriminant analysis of the lead isotope data for copper oxhide ingots found in Cyprus compared with data for copper ore deposits in Cyprus, the Cycladic island of Kythnos, and in the Taurus mountains, Turkey. The latter two deposits have lead isotope compositions close to those for Cypriot ore deposits.

Lead Isotope Analyses of Sardinian Copper Ores

Figure 1 shows the location of the major, and some minor, copper mines in Sardinia; we repeat that, according to the conventions of the Metallogenic Map of Europe about original size of ore deposits, even Funtana Raminosa is a deposit of only medium tonnage, while all the rest are classified as of small tonnage. The most accessible reviews of the copper ore deposits in Sardinia are those of Zuffardi (1980; 1989). It is of some importance as a first-order constraint on the possible lead isotope composition of the Sardinian ore deposits to place them into their geological/stratigraphical setting. It may be important also to consider briefly their tectonic setting, since major orogenic events are often connected with mineralization, or the remobilization of pre-existing mineralization. The oldest orogenic event known in Sardinia is the Caledonian orogeny (Sardinian phase), which is represented in southwestern Sardinia at the end of the Cambrian and during the Lower Ordovician (c. 510–470 million years [Ma] ago). The second orogeny is the Hercynian, in the Carboniferous (c. 360–300 Ma), which is represented in Sardinia as a first phase with intensive compressions; its second phase, with relaxations, has associated hydrothermal mineralization. The third orogeny is Alpidic (from Upper Cretaceous, through the Palaeogene and Neogene, c. 95–10 Ma) which, in Sardinia, took the form of normal faulting with partial rejuvenation of former fracture zones, producing a horst-and-graben structure.

From the point of view of stratigraphy, and starting with the oldest mineralization, we have the Cambrian system in the Iglesiente-Sulcis districts of southwestern Sardinia (of Georgian [Acadian] age, c. 530–10 Ma). The chief mineralized member of the Cambrian sequence has a carbonate composition with some interbedded volcanics, is traditionally known as the 'Metalliferous', and is host to large lead (Pb), zinc (Zn), pyrite, baryte and fluorite deposits, some very large, such as Monteponi, Campo Pisano and Masua. This member is also host to a number of small, pre-Hercynian, strata-bound, copper-bearing, skarn/saddle-reef mixed-sulphide deposits such as Rosas/Sa Marchesa, Monte Tamara and Truba Niedda. The 'Metalliferous' also hosts the quite different autochthonous, karstic, oxidised small copper deposit of Sa Duchessa. The 'Metalliferous' is overlain by the 'calc-schists', a thin, fossiliferous, in places ore-bearing transition zone to the barren 'Cabitza Slates' member.

Next in the sequences of metallogenic significance is the Silurian (partly Devonian) member of black graphitic shales and limestones with interbedded volcanics, which hosts stratiform, polymetallic, mixed sulphide deposits, among them Funtana Raminosa, Correboi, Pranu e Sanguini and Perda s'Oliu. These deposits have sedimentary features (though many have been affected by remobilization phenomena related to tectonics and/or porphyry dyke emplacement); they are also connected to syn-sedimentary volcanics.

A number of acidic/medium acidic plutonic rocks are related to the Hercynian orogenic and magmatic cycles; related to them are vein-type polymetallic ore deposits some of which, such as Montevecchio, are extremely rich and extensive. Much of the ore concentration related to this Hercynian plutonic and volcanic activity is believed to have been generated by the remobilization of metals in pre-existing rocks. These are polymetallic (Pb, Zn, Cu) deposits related to Hercynian granitoids and include the famous Pb-Zn deposits of the Arburese district (Montevecchio-Ingurtosu-Gennamari); some of them (Gozzura, Sos Enattos, Montevecchio) gave not-negligible production of copper. Another example is the small chalcopyrite/pyrite deposit of Torpe-Canale Barisoni, as is the Sn-Zn-Cu-Pb deposit of Monte Mannu-Canale Serci.

In the Jurassic-Palaeocene (c. 200-50 Ma) a large ophiolite complex was emplaced in Italy; in northwestern Sardinia this is evidenced by a small, poorly dated (between Cretaceous and early Oligocene, c. 130-30 Ma) dioritic mass (Calabona region) which contains a small, low-grade, porphyry copper deposit (Ridge 1990: 323-34). There are a number of other Tertiary/Quaternary mixed-sulphide, vein-type, copper deposits in northwestern Sardinia in a huge Tertiary flat-lying trachytic-andesitic complex. Most are in tuffaceous horizons, with a metal grade (Cu+Zn+Pb) which can be fairly high (up to 6-8%), but the individual ore bodies are small; the largest (pyrite/copper) vein is at Capo Marrargiu.

We have already mentioned that, to first order, the lead isotope composition of an ore deposit is governed by its geological age. Hence we would anticipate that we should easily be able to distinguish the older Cambrian (c. 500 Ma) Sardinian copper ore deposits from the Late Cretaceous Cypriot ore deposits, which date to about 80 Ma. We have measured lead isotope compositions for over 30 Sardinian ore deposits, including both copper and lead ores, and this discrimination is indeed easy to make (Gale and Stos-Gale 1987; 1988).

Our earlier lead isotope analyses did not include enough data from each copper ore deposit to allow the extent of the 'fields' to be defined; Table 1 gives new data for some of the Sardinian copper deposits whose locations are indicated in Fig. 1. Plotted in Fig. 4 are lead isotope data for the copper deposits of Sa Duchessa (CA), Perda s'Oliu (CA), Sa Marchesa (CA) and Rosas (CA) for which we now have more data. The diagrams show that good separation is obtained, except that the lead isotope data for Sa

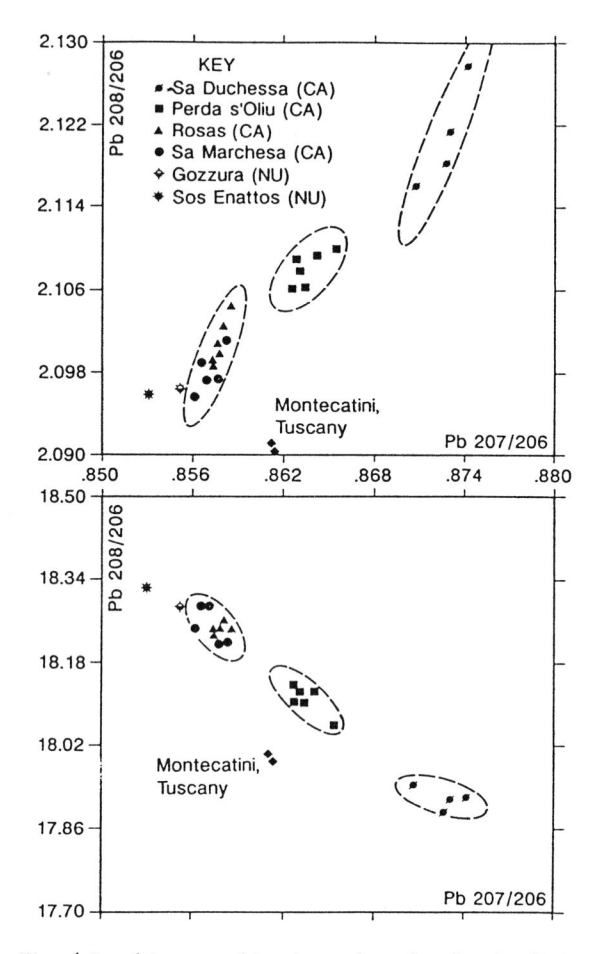

Fig. 4 Lead isotope bivariate plots for the Sardinian copper ore deposits of Sa Duchessa, Perda s'Oliu, Rosas, Sa Marchesa, Gozzura and Sos Enattos. Data for the large Tuscan copper deposit of Montecatini in Val di Cecina are also shown.

Marchesa and Rosas define a single field; this is geologically quite explicable, since these mines are together and are driven into the same ore deposit, which Zuffardi (1980) classifies as belonging to the skarn, saddle-reef, stock-work mixed-sulphide deposits in the Cambrian 'Metalliferous'. The deposit of Sa Duchessa, on the other hand, is classified as an autochthonous karstic oxidized deposit in the Cambrian 'Metalliferous', while Perda s'Oliu is a stratiform mixed-sulphide ore deposit in the Middle Silurian. Figure 4 also shows that two data points for the famous Tuscan copper ore deposit of Montecatini in Val di Cécina (related to intensely weathered pillow lavas, affected by Appeninic orogenesis and belonging to Mesozoic ophiolites) have lead isotope compositions quite different from the Sardinian ores.

Figure 5 depicts lead isotope data for the geologically similar ore deposits of Funtana Raminosa and Pranu e Sanguini, both hosted by the Silurian black shales, but which have lead isotopic compositions which, though similar, can be distinguished; Fig. 6 shows that both can be distinguished isotopically from the similarly hosted ores at Perda s'Oliu. The ore deposit at Arenas has an isotopic composition clearly different from Funtana Raminosa, Pranu e Sanguini, Rosas/Sa Marchesa, but which overlaps (see Fig. 6) that for

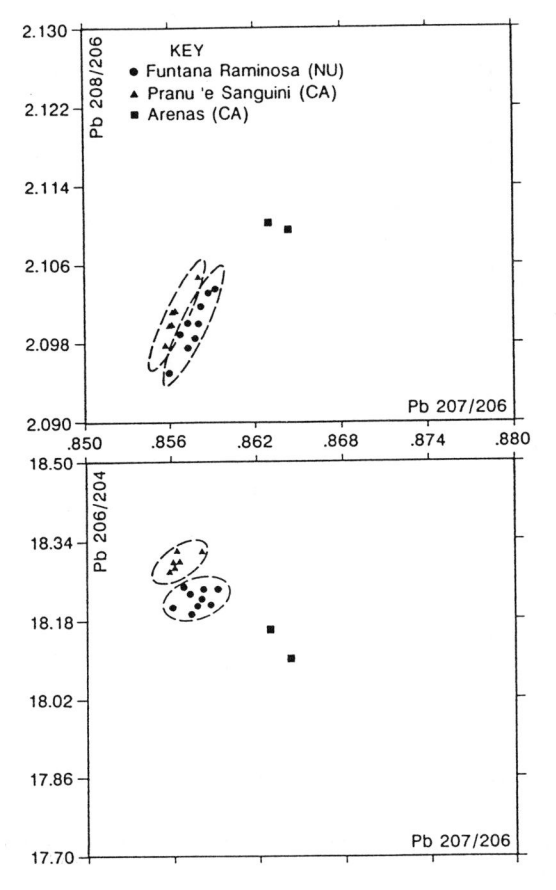

Fig. 5 Lead isotope bivariate plots for the Sardinian copper ore deposits of Funtana Raminosa, Pranu e Sanguini and Arenas.

Perda s'Oliu. Figure 6 shows that the isotopic composition of ores from Truba Niedda falls, as expected, within the geologically identical, metamorphosed syn-sedimentary, Cambrian skarn deposits of Rosas/Sa Marchesa; all are related to the transition zone between the 'Metalliferous' and the enclosing slate-silt complex. The lead isotopic composition for Arenas (NU) is similar to that for Pranu e Sanguini (CA), emphasizing that geology is the controlling factor, not geographical location.

Table 2 gives new lead isotope data for some of the copper mines in the Colline Metallifere, Tuscany; locations of some of these deposits are given in Fig. 7. Figure 8 plots the lead isotope fields based on the data of Table 2 in relation to the lead isotope field for Cyprus, from which the Tuscan ore deposits are clearly easily separated.

In this case there is certainly no need to use multivariate discriminant analysis. Some of the lead isotope fields for Sardinian ore deposits are also plotted in Fig. 8; this, and the comparison of Fig. 8 with Figs. 4, 5, and 6 (note the differences in scales) shows that all the Tuscan ore deposits are

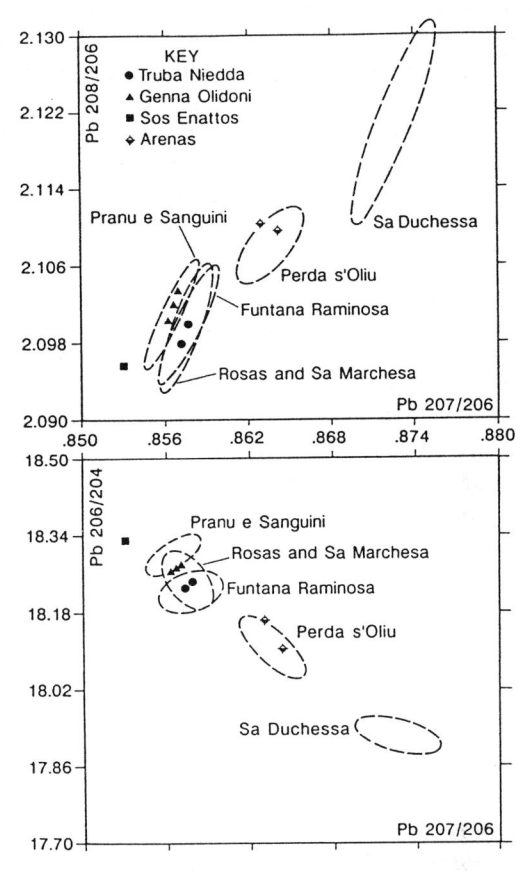

Fig. 6 Lead isotope bivariate plots for the Sardinian copper ore deposits of Truba Niedda, Genna Olidoni, Sos Enattos, and Arenas in relation to isotopic fields for some other Sardinian deposits.

easily separated from all of the Sardinian ore deposits whose lead isotope compositions are plotted in these diagrams.

Figure 9 shows some of the lead isotope data for Sardinian ores (including some for the Tertiary Sardinian copper ores) together with the field for the Tuscan ores of the Colline Metallifere; it depicts data from 22 analyzed Sardinian oxhide ingots (data given in Gale and Stos-Gale 1987: table 7.7) together with that from a number of Nuragic copper alloy objects from Santa Maria in Paulis. This hoard of Nuragic artifacts dates most probably around the 12th–11th or the 10th–9th centuries BC (Macnamara *et al.* 1984).

It is at once clear from Fig. 9 (together with Figs. 4, 5, 6 and the discussion of Gale and Stos-Gale 1987) that none of the 22 Sardinian oxhide ingots match the analyzed Sardinian copper ore

330 *Sardinia in the Mediterranean*

deposits, even though all the major and many minor Sardinian copper deposits have been analyzed. In contrast, the Nuragic bronzes have isotopic compositions which, while being completely different from those of the oxhide ingots, are consistent with having been made from the lead isotope compositions of this ore body.

Further lead isotope analyses have been made of both oxhide and bun ingots from the Nuragic hoard found by Ubaldo Badas at Villanovaforru (CA), Baccu Simeone (Gale 1989b: table 29.6, fig. 29.27) (N.B., some printing errors occurred in

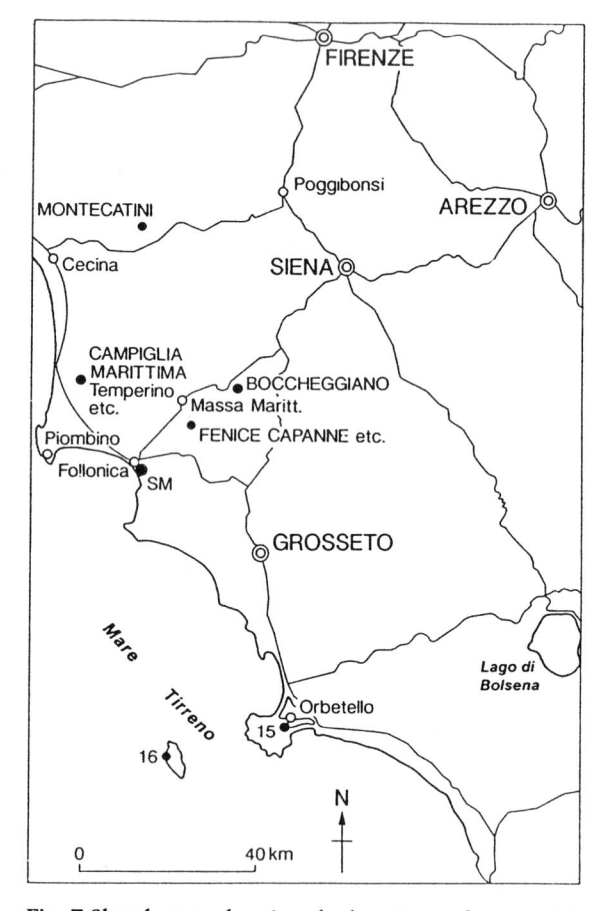

Fig. 7 Sketch map showing the locations of some of the mines in the Colline Metallifere, Tuscany.

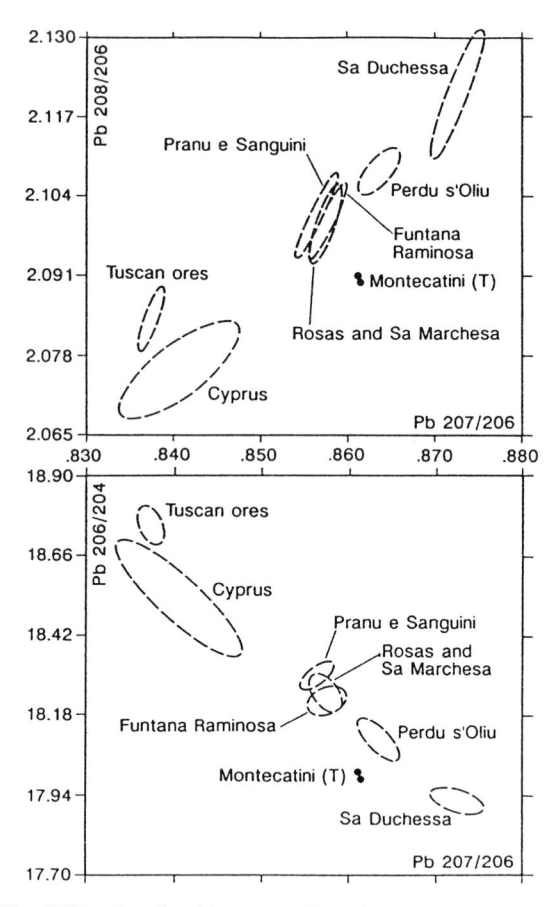

Fig. 8 Bivariate lead isotope plots showing the fields for the Tuscan copper ores in relation to lead isotope fields for copper ores from Cyprus and Sardinia.

copper extracted from the Sardinian ore deposit of Sa Duchessa (Domusnovas), in the southwest of Sardinia. We can deduce from the lead isotope compositions of the Sardinian oxhide ingots that they are made of copper coming from deposits dating to the Tertiary or Cretaceous periods, but the compositions do not match those of the analyzed Tertiary copper deposits in Sardinia (ores from Capo Marargiu and Castelli di Bonvei; see Gale and Stos-Gale 1987: table 7.8 fig. 7.18). Figure 9 also shows that the oxhide ingots found in Sardinia cannot have been made from the copper ores from the Tuscan Colline Metallifere district, whose lead isotope field is shown to be quite distinct from the isotopic compositions of the oxhide ingots. Suggestions made by Muhly (1991: 190-91) of a Spanish source have been shown by Gale (1991: 219, 221) to be completely unsupported by

table 29.6, which is repeated correctly for clarity here as Table 3). The nine analyzed oxhide ingot fragments from this hoard plot with the 22 already discussed, making 31 Sardinian oxhide ingot fragments analyzed so far which plot together in a small region which does not overlap with any analyzed Sardinian ore deposits. On the other hand four bun ingots from the same hoard have lead isotope compositions which are consistent with manufacture from Sardinian copper ores (Gale 1989b: fig. 29.27).

If the oxhide ingots do not match with Sardinian copper ores then it is clear that comparison should be made with the Cretaceous copper ores from Cyprus. Gale (1989b: 250 fig. 29.6) has given the evidence for the field of lead isotope compositions for Cypriot copper ores which derives from stepwise discriminant analysis

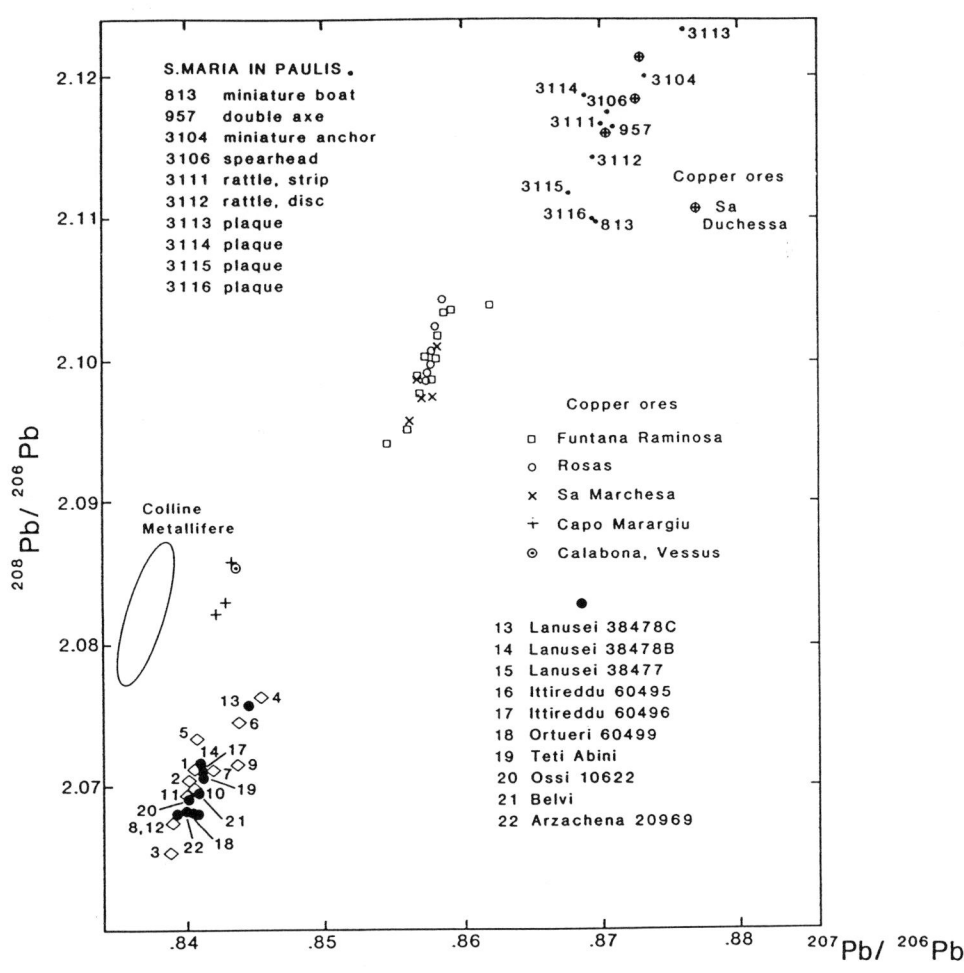

Fig. 9 One of the lead isotope bivariate plots for some Sardinian copper ores, copper oxhide ingots found in Sardinia, Nuragic oopper-based alloy objects from Santa Maria in Paulis, and the field for copper ores from the Colline Metallifere, Tuscany.

of all three isotopic ratios for each ore sample. Figure 10 shows that multivariate stepwise discriminant function analysis groups the Sardinian oxhide ingots (including the nine analyzed examples from Baccu Simeone, represented as solid circles) firmly in the field of Cypriot copper ores. Here we should mention that Muhly's comment (Muhly and Stech 1990: 203) is misleading in focusing on the fact that, in one of the bivariate lead isotope diagrams (Gale and Stos-Gale 1988: 375, 379 fig. 17) the Sardinian ingots lie towards the edge of the Cypriot lead isotope field, 'so the relationship (of the Sardinian ingots with Cyprus) cannot be taken as proved'. In fact all the lead isotope data for Late Cypriot artifacts and for Cypriot oxhide ingots lie in the same position with respect to the Cypriot copper ore field as do the Sardinian oxhide ingots in this bivariate plot. Moreover, the discriminant analysis of all three isotope ratios allots very high statistical probabilities (over 95%) that the analyzed Sardinian oxhide ingots belong to the Cypriot field.

Trace element analyses, including gold and silver contents, were given by Gale and Stos-Gale (1987: table 7.3) for 17 Sardinian oxhide ingots; Table 4 gives data for a further three Sardinian oxhide ingots from Baccu Simeone, together with data for five bun ingots from the same site. Figure 11 shows the gold/silver diagram for the 18 Sardinian oxhide ingots so far analyzed, in which the Sardinian oxhide ingots group in the field defined by Late Cypriot bronze artifacts and Cypriot oxhide ingots. In contrast the Nuragic bronze artifacts from Santa Maria in Paulis plot high up in the diagram, quite outside the Cypriot field. This agrees with the lead isotope evidence (see Fig. 9) that these particular Nuragic bronzes were made from Sardinian, not Cypriot, ores. Clearly these Nuragic bronzes and the oxhide ingots found on Sardinia were made from quite different sources of copper.

Figure 11 also plots the gold and silver concentrations for five bun ingots from Baccu Simeone and for eight objects from the Nuragic hoard of Forraxi Nioi. All of these Nuragic copper alloy objects have Au–Ag compositions which fall quite outside the Cypriot field, and are therefore quite different from the copper oxhide ingots found on

332 *Sardinia in the Mediterranean*

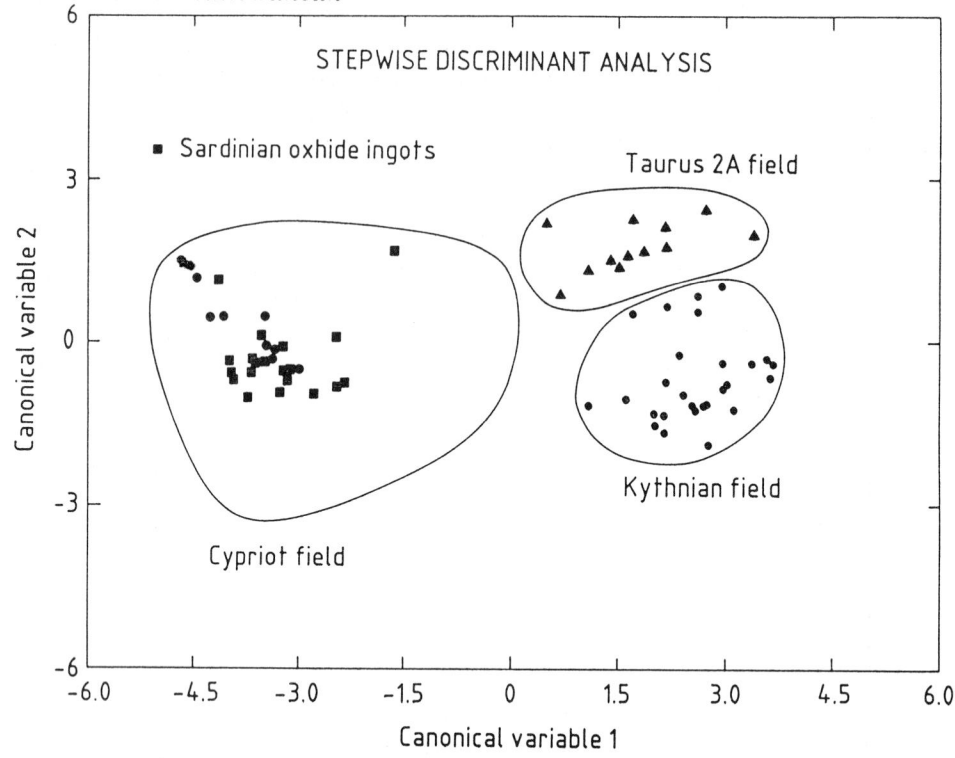

Fig. 10 Stepwise discriminant analysis of lead isotope data for copper ores in Cyprus, the Taurus and Kythnos, compared with oxhide ingots found in Sardinia. Analyses for nine oxhide ingots found at Villanovaforru are shown by filled circles.

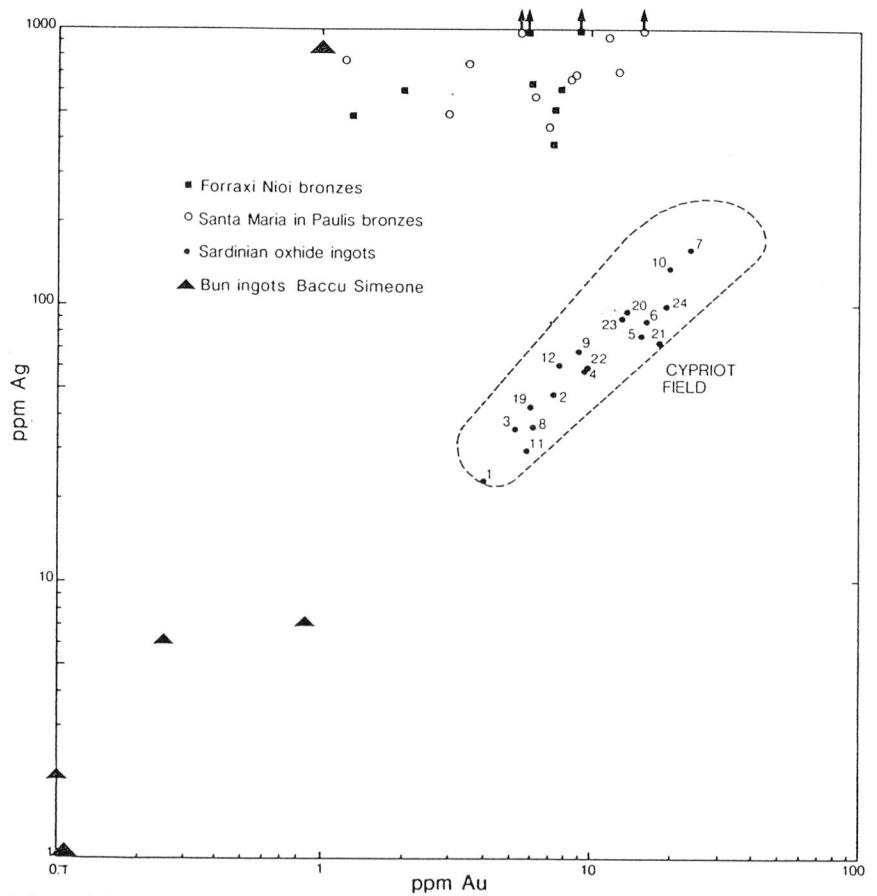

Fig. 11 Plot of the gold and silver concentrations in oxhide ingots found in Sardinia, in bun ingots from Baccu Simeone (Villanovaforru), in Nuragic bronzes from Forraxi Nioi and Santa Maria in Paulis, compared with the field for Late Bronze Age copper alloy artifacts from Cyprus.

Sardinia. These Forraxi Nioi objects are silver-rich and have gold–silver compositions similar to the objects from the Santa Maria in Paulis (SS) hoard; the bun ingots from Baccu Simeone (CA) are mostly silver-poor, but one is silver-rich.

It seemed important to investigate further whether there is a consistent difference between the lead isotope composition (and the Au–Ag composition) of Nuragic copper alloy objects and the oxhide ingots found on Sardinia. Beyond Baccu Simeone-Villanovaforru and Santa Maria in Paulis the sites (or hoards) of Forraxi Nioi, Teti, Bonnanaro, Ossi, Alghero and Olièna have at present been chosen for that purpose. In 1882 at Forraxi Nioi (Nuragus), F. Nissardi excavated a hoard of bronze weapons and tools; the account of the excavation by Fiorelli (1882) mentions a crucible filled with tin. Tylecote *et al.* (1983: 69-71) identified, among the material from Forraxi Nioi kept in the Cagliari Museum, tin crust, objects of bronze, bun ingots, bronze casting remains, copper slag and a number of objects made of iron. At Teti (NU) there is the Nuragic site of Abini, with a Nuragic village and sacred well, probably related to the sanctuary, where many bronze hoards have been excavated since 1865. Our samples from Teti and Forraxi Nioi came from the samples taken for the large German analytical programme and then held in Stuttgart; they were published with illustrations by Junghans *et al.* (1968). At Bonnanaro (SS) there was found in 1951 the large, Late Bronze Age Funtana Janna hoard, from which a few objects are preserved in the Sassari Museum; amongst them are four truncated conical ingots (Lo Schiavo 1982: fig. 5, top), a double-looped socketed axe of Iberic type, and three double axes. The Alghero (SS) hoard (said to date from the 10th century BC: Contu 1968) is from the Nuraghe Flumenelongu; it includes 32 bun ingots, a flat double-looped axe (similar to axes from Spain and Portugal), a trunnion celt, a maul and two bracelets. At Ossi (SS) two hoards have been found at the Nuragic village of Sa Mandra 'e Sa Guia; the second hoard had bun ingots, tools and weapons, while both hoards may be Late Bronze Age in date (Ferrarese Ceruti 1985: 52). At Olièna (NU) is the Nuragic complex of Sa Sedda 'e Sos Carros, which is believed to have started in the Late Bronze Age (Lo Schiavo 1989: 36); here there were found bun ingots, fragments of spearheads and swords, axes, bronze sheet, bars and rods. At Ortueri (NU) there was an isolated find at Funtana 'e Cresia of two oxhide ingot fragments together with a copper axe of archaic type (Lo Schiavo *et al.* 1985: 13 n. 8).

Lead isotope analyses for a selection of Nuragic objects from these sites, including Forraxi Nioi, are given in Table 5 (those for Santa Maria in Paulis have already been published in Gale and Stos-Gale 1987: table 7.6). Figure 12 plots this data in two bivariate lead isotope diagrams together with fields for some Sardinian copper ore deposits. Comparison of Fig. 12 with Figs. 8 and 9 (note the different scales) shows that no bun ingot, bronze scrap, tools or weapons from any of these eight Nuragic sites has a lead isotopic composition which falls anywhere near the Cypriot field; instead they are consistent with the fields for various Sardinian copper ore deposits. The gold–silver data for objects from Santa Maria in Paulis and Forraxi Nioi, and bun ingots from Baccu Simeone, plotted in Fig. 11, was also widely divergent from the small range of gold–silver concentrations characteristic of Cypriot Late Bronze Age copper. Our neutron activation analyses of Nuragic material from Olièna, Ossi, Bonnanaro, Alghero and Ortueri are not yet complete, but silver analyses (not gold) of these objects are given by Maddin and Merkel (1990: 43-199); these analyses show that at least 75% of these objects are as silver-rich as the objects from Santa Maria in Paulis and Forraxi Nioi; i.e. they are so argentiferous as completely to exclude their falling in the Cypriot field in a gold–silver plot. There is no doubt at all that all properly Nuragic copper alloy objects and bun ingots so far analyzed (for both their lead isotope and Au–Ag contents) are made of copper which did not come from Cyprus, but that rather they are consistent with having been made from copper smelted from Sardinian copper ores.

In contrast, two independent lines of evidence are consistent with the Sardinian oxhide ingots having been made of Cypriot copper; the gold/silver analyses for the Sardinian oxhide ingots show their copper metal to be of the type being produced in LCII-III times on Cyprus. It is quite certain that all the Nuragic objects so far analyzed were made from copper which came from completely different copper ore sources than those which supplied the analyzed copper oxhide ingots found on Sardinia. This conclusion is true even where fragments of bun ingots and oxhide ingots were found together, as they were at Villanovaforru (where they were discovered in a large Nuragic double-handled impasto pot). Figure 13 plots the lead isotope data for Olièna (Sa Sedda 'e Sos Carros) alone; all the analyzed objects are Nuragic, and the lead isotope diagrams point clearly to the use of at least two (possibly as many as four) different Sardinian copper ore sources for objects found at the same site. This is not an unusual situation; for instance, the LM III Poros Wall Hoard at Mycenae gives

334 *Sardinia in the Mediterranean*

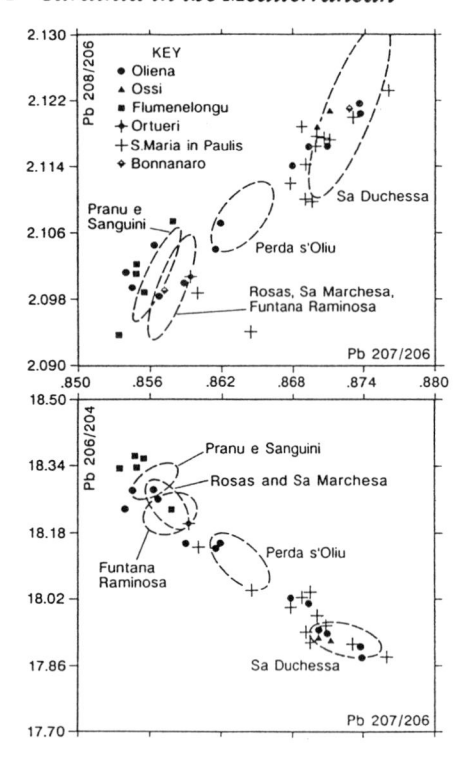

Fig. 12 Bivariate lead isotope plots for Nuragic copper-based alloy objects from Olièna, Ossi, Alghero (Flumenelongu), Ortueri, Bonnanaro and Santa Maria in Paulis, compared with the lead isotope fields for some Sardinian copper ore deposits.

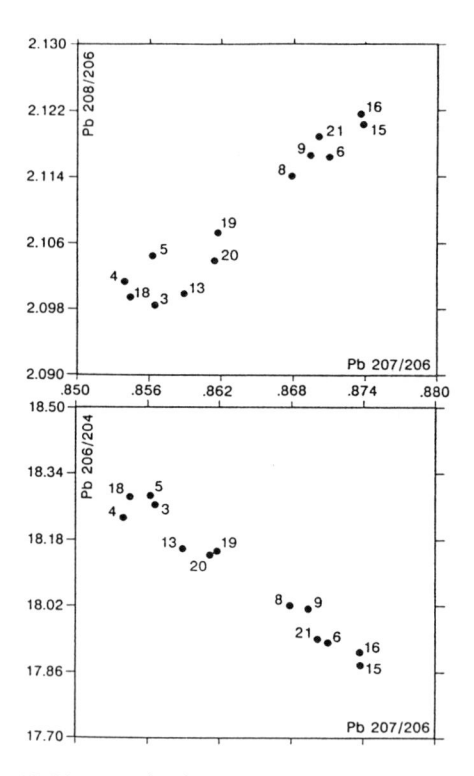

Fig. 13 Bivariate lead isotope plots for Nuragic copper-alloy artifacts from Olièna.

clear evidence that the copper oxhide ingots within it are made of Cypriot copper, while many of the artifacts are made of copper from Lavrion (Demakopoulou *et al.* 1991).

Here we should comment on remarks by Cherry and Knapp (1991: 100) to the effect that:

> On the other hand, if a series of artifacts or ingots contain isotopic traces of lead of approximately the same age as the lead in the Cypriot ore bodies—as, for instance, a number of oxhide ingots from Sardinia—it is only permissible to state that these ingots are consistent with Cypriot ores analysed thus far, and they will of course plot in the field defined for those ores...The problem remains that other ore sources (e.g., in Spain, in the Negev Desert, or in Oman) may have similar or overlapping ages, and therefore overlapping fields...

First, it is by no means certain that lead from an ore deposit of the same age as the Cypriot ores will overlap in isotopic composition with the Cypriot field, though it is likely to be near, since isotopic composition is controlled only to first order by geological age. Secondly, we have ourselves on many occasions emphasized the point about consistency rather than certainty, and the great power of lead isotope analyses to *exclude* ore sources (e.g. Stos-Gale *et al.* 1986: 128; Gale 1989b: 249, 254). Thirdly, for Late Cypriot copper we emphasize yet again that we have *two* independent fingerprints. One is certainly lead isotopic composition; the other is the gold/silver composition. We re-emphasize further that, while they retain the lead isotope signature, even Early to Middle Cypriot artifacts do not have the gold/silver signature which is probably telling us something about the copper ores and/or the extractive metallurgical technology used in Cyprus in Late Cypriot times, but not earlier (Gale 1989b: 252). It seems at the least rather unlikely that copper from elsewhere will have both of these characteristics, so that their possession by *all* the analyzed oxhide ingots which were found on Sardinia does seem rather compelling. The improbability that copper produced other than in Late Bronze Age Cyprus will have both of these 'fingerprints' argues against the suggestion by Cherry and Knapp (1991: 100) that copper ore deposits in Spain, in the Negev Desert, or in Oman may have to be taken into account as a possible source of copper for production of the oxhide ingots found on Sardinia. By 'the Negev', Cherry and Knapp presumably mean the Timna copper mines in the Arabah; the lead isotope compositions for the Timna deposits (and for Fenan in Jordan) are widely different from those for Cyprus (Gale and Stos-Gale 1985). For the copper deposits in the ophiolite sequence in Oman (Hauptmann 1985), Gale et al. (1981) have shown that their lead isotopic field is again quite distinct from that for Cyprus. The copper deposits in Cyprus and Oman are in fact examples of deposits with similar geological ages having easily separable lead isotopic compositions. We should emphasize at this point that, so far, there has been no analyzed copper deposit in Greece, Crete, the Cyclades, Anatolia, Sardinia, Italy, or Spain which has a lead isotope composition with a major overlap with the Cypriot field; 99% do not overlap at all.

The existing scientific evidence is fully consistent with the view that we should see the Sardinian ingots as the successful western extreme of the trade in Cypriot copper exemplified by the ill-fated Cape Gelidonya and Ulu Burun ships (Gale 1991). This would not be inconsistent with the Cypriot bronze artifacts found in Sardinia, like those recently published by Lo Schiavo et al. (1985), or with the Cypriot, Minoan and Mycenaean pottery recently excavated from Sardinian sites (Ferrarese Ceruti et al. 1987). These eastern Mediterranean artifacts, down to the heavy smithing tools, are all represented among the cargoes of the Cape Gelidonya and Ulu Burun ships.

Here we would part company with the views expressed by Muhly (1991) about the copper oxhide ingots found on Sardinia. First, he finds it difficult to accept that Cypriot copper might be imported into an island like Sardinia, 'with its own rich deposits of copper ore'. But, as discussed above, the copper deposits on Sardinia are really quite meager, and are quite insubstantial in comparison with those in Cyprus or even with those closer to hand in Tuscany (especially the large Tuscan copper mine of Montecatini Val di Cécina, see Dessau et al. 1975). Further, can we be sure that the motives driving trade in the Bronze Age were not at least as complex as those today, where some countries choose to conserve their own strategic reserves of certain materials while importing the same materials from overseas? Again Wiener (1991) has written that:

> A rational purchaser may elect to maintain a long-term relationship with a higher-cost supplier in order to insure access to a critical resource (such as metal in the Bronze age) while satisfying any increase in demand from a lower-cost source.

Moreover, we know that the Romans carefully distinguished copper from different mines as being of different quality (Pliny, *Natural History* 34.2) which, if it can be extended back into the Late Bronze Age, may add another degree of complexity. But we should also be careful about terminology; even if the oxhide ingots in Sardinia truly are made of Cypriot copper it is dangerous to speak of the *import* of Cypriot copper into Sardinia if by that word we understand a deliberate endeavor on the part of the Nuragic people to ensure that shiploads of such copper were to be delivered to Sardinia. It is difficult to see at present why the arrival off the coast of Sardinia of a Bronze Age ship from the eastern Mediterranean could not be a trading venture inspired wholly from the east, carrying copper oxhide ingots which were in surplus in the east but which, it would be hoped, might be welcome somewhere in the western Mediterranean. In that case, the presence of small copper deposits in Sardinia, probably not known in advance to the eastern traders, would be quite irrelevant. Nuragic people, if indeed at the time of arrival of the ship they knew anything at all about mining and smelting their own copper ore sources, might well nevertheless have been glad to receive copper metal in a state ready for making tools, etc., and might even have been induced to take it as part of a bargain for accompanying decorated pottery, tripods, smithing tools, etc., which they may have wanted more. Alternatively it might be that oxhide ingots were seen as a status symbol, and desirable just on that account.

Muhly's argument against a Cypriot origin for the Sardinian ingots—that oxhide ingots were in use down to the end of the 10th century BC in Sardinia while they are not known in Cyprus after the early 12th century BC—is not only a dangerous argument *ex silentio* (it is only in the last ten years that oxhide ingots have been excavated in sound contexts in Cyprus) but also has other difficulties. First, the absolute dating of the Italian Late Bronze Age (and the relative chronology between Italy and elsewhere in the Mediterranean) is not yet on so sound a basis as is dating in Greece or Cyprus; even in the latter there are still differences of opinion (see, e.g., French 1980: 269; Karageorghis and Demas 1984: 68-75; Manning 1988). Secondly, very few oxhide ingots from Sardinia have any sound archaeological context. Thirdly, for those fragments that do the latest can be ascribed only to a deposition 'not later than the end of the Italian Late Bronze Age' (Lo Schiavo 1989: 36). Fourthly, this does not necessarily mean that they were made as late as that; they could well have been made much earlier, subsequently broken up, and a few fragments later stored away for a use to which they were never put. One can easily hypothesize circumstances in which this might arise. On Crete, for instance, the 19 whole ingots from Hagia Triadha were stored in a basement room which was twice walled off from the other three basement rooms; the oxhide ingot room was accessible to rooms above only by a wooden ladder (Paribeni 1903: 334). If, after the LMIB(?) destructions of Hagia Triadha, the later LMIII inhabitants (Pernier and Banti 1947: 7, 29) had discovered them and broken them up for use but had not used all fragments, leaving some to be excavated today from LMIII strata, there would be roughly a 200-year gap between the date of their manufacture and the date of the strata in which the fragments were found.

If the oxhide ingots on Sardinia are indeed made of Cypriot copper and came there on a ship like those excavated by Bass, how can we set this into a picture of the relations between Sardinia and the eastern Mediterranean? Jones and Vagnetti (1991) have distinguished a number of phases in the development of contacts during the Late Bronze Age between the central and eastern Mediterranean. During the Aegean LH I-II period, finds of Aegean pottery are concentrated largely in the Aeolian and Phlegraean islands with only a few traces from sites on the south Italian coast on the sea route leading to these islands. During the LH IIIA period there is both an increase in the number of sites with Aegean pottery and a change in distribution to sites such as Scoglio del Tonno near Taranto, the many necropolises (such as Thapsos, where Mycenaean and Cypriot pottery are found together) around Syracuse in southeastern Sicily, and the Aeolian islands of the Milazzese phase; imports seem to constitute a large proportion of the known pottery. In the LH IIIB period the number of sites is much larger, with the Adriatic and Ionian coasts of Apulia, Basilicata and Northern Calabria densely settled. Scoglio del Tonno now becomes a very prosperous site, and important sites in southern Italy are Termitito, Broglio di Trebisacce and Torre Mordillo. Sicily and the Aeolian Islands seem to be less involved but Sardinia becomes fully involved, with the main Nuragic site of Antigori perhaps having the status of an 'emporium' for trade. During the LH IIIB period there seems to appear in Sardinia not only imported Aegean pottery but also pottery of Aegean technology and style made, however, of local clays (Vagnetti and Jones 1988); at the same time, metal objects seem to be exchanged from east to west, with a very strong Cypriot connection (Lo Schiavo et al. 1985). In the LH IIIC period this pattern seems to continue, but the number of known sites is smaller.

As we have emphasized, if oxhide ingots made from Cypriot copper came to Sardinia, this can possibly be seen not as a result of Nuragic entrepreneurs setting out to import copper, but rather as a speculative venture set up in the eastern Mediterranean. The evidence from the Ulu Burun and Cape Gelidonya ships shows that they carried a richly diverse range of goods of which copper and tin were only part; the eastern merchants may not always have been completely confident in advance about the Aegean or central Mediterranean ports at which particular items were to be unloaded. Some goods, less needed at a particular destination, may sometimes have been traded as part of a package with more desired goods. However, presumably there were goods desired in the central Mediterranean which inspired the ships to come from the east; what were the products of Sardinia which might have been of interest in the international market? Could Sardinia have been a way station on a western tin route (Gale and Stos-Gale 1988: 382)? Sardinia certainly produced tin bronzes in the Late Bronze Age, so it had access to a supply of tin. Sardinia has its own ore deposits containing tin (such are unknown in the Aegean) at Monte Mannu (Canale Serci) and Perdu Carra (near Fluminimaggiore); Monte Mannu had about 200,000 tonnes of ore and produced some hundreds of tonnes of tin concentrates during the Second World War (Zuffardi 1989: 254). The tin ore at Monte Mannu tends to be intergrown with chalcopyrite, sphalerite and galena, so that whether it was exploited in the Bronze Age remains unknown, but much more amenable tin ore (cassiterite, with concentrations up to 30% tin) exists across the sea at Monte Valerio in Tuscany (Zuffardi 1989: 259), where 1500 tonnes of metallic tin were produced between 1936 and 1937. Further afield of course are the tin deposits in Iberia, Brittany and Cornwall. Other products altogether might have been sought; apart from textiles there is alum (Jones and Vagnetti 1991: 139) and the important suggestion that the Sardinians may have been exchanging iron for eastern Mediterranean copper (Muhly and Stech 1990: 209-13).

We believe that it may be premature to go further with such speculations at this time. It would at present be presumptuous to make a final judgment about the origin of the oxhide ingots found in Sardinia, which should perhaps be reserved until the complete study directed by Fulvia Lo Schiavo is completed. In particular, more attention should be given to the copper deposits at Calabona, Alghero, and it is vital to make lead isotope analyses of a much wider range of

Sardinian oxhide ingots and of Nuragic bronze objects, of metal objects found on Sardinia but thought to be Cypriot imports (or copies of Cypriot objects), and of a wide range of the bronze objects from the Cape Gelidonya wreck, especially those thought to be of Cypriot manufacture.

Acknowledgments

This work would not have been possible without generous support from the Leverhulme Trust, the Science and Engineering Research Council, the University of Oxford, Nuffield College, and the British Academy, which we gratefully acknowledge. Our thanks are due to the Italian Ministry of Culture and to many colleagues, especially to Dr Fulvia Lo Schiavo, Professor Miriam Balmuth, Dr Vassos Karageorghis, Professors R. Maddin, J.D. Muhly, P. Zuffardi and U. Zwicker, Dr A. Panayiotou, Dr G. Constantinides, Dr A. Leonardelli, Dr Tamara Stech, Herr Walter Fasnacht, and many others.

Table 1

New lead isotope analyses of Sardinian copper ore deposits
(sphal. = sphalerite; chalco = chalcopyrite)

Sample no.	Mine	Mineral analysed	Pb208/206	Pb207/206	Pb206/204
ARN3	Arenas (CA)	galena	2.10958	0.86431	18.100
ARN1	Arenas	galena	2.11032	0.86298	18.161
ARN2	Arenas	galena	2.11672	0.87059	17.966
CB 1007A	Canale Barisone, Torpe	galena	2.09616	0.84785	18.452
X4	Canale Barisone, Torpe	galena	2.08999	0.84900	18.420
FR 1011A	Funtana Raminosa (NU)	galena, chalcopyrite	2.09895	0.85676	18.254
FR 1011B	Funtana Raminosa	galena	2.09758	0.85737	18.197
FRM	Funtana Raminosa	galena	2.10325	0.85870	18.214
SARD 10	Funtana Raminosa	chalcopyrite	2.10378	0.86196	18.103
SARD 40a	Funtana Raminosa	galena, sphalerite	2.09861	0.85773	18.212
SARD 41ca	Funtana Raminosa	galena, chalcopyrite	2.09502	0.85599	18.203
SARD 41d	Funtana Raminosa	malachite, azurite	2.10004	0.85808	18.225
SARD 43	Funtana Raminosa	chalcopyrite	2.10179	0.85814	18.244
SARD 50a	Funtana Raminosa	pyrite, chalcopyrite	2.10017	0.85732	18.236
SARD 9	Funtana Raminosa	chalcopyrite	2.10355	0.85919	18.243
GEO1	Genna Olidoni (NU)	galena	2.10207	0.85670	18.272
GEO2	Genna Olidoni	galena	2.10017	0.85648	18.265
GEO2	Genna Olidoni	galena	2.10328	0.85699	18.277
GO	Genna Olidoni	galena	2.10017	0.85648	18.265
PSO 100	Perda s'Oliu (CA)	galena	2.10894	0.86284	18.136
PSO 101	Perda s'Oliu	galena	2.10799	0.86311	18.124
PSO 1014A	Perda s'Oliu	galena	2.10618	0.86276	18.105
PSO 1015A	Perda s'Oliu	galena	2.11005	0.86536	18.059
PSO 1016A	Perda s'Oliu	galena	2.10625	0.86334	18.103
PSO 102	Perda s'Oliu	galena	2.10937	0.86418	18.123
PS 1013A	Pranu e Sanguini (CA)	galena	2.09782	0.85582	18.280
PS 1013D	Pranu e Sanguini	galena	2.10012	0.85611	18.290
PS 1013E	Pranu e Sanguini	galena	2.10007	0.85619	18.296
PS 1013F	Pranu e Sanguini	galena	2.10154	0.85637	18.300
PS 1013G	Pranu e Sanguini	galena	2.10156	0.85635	18.234
PS 1013H	Pranu e Sanguini	galena	2.10498	0.85813	18.321
R 1000A	Rosas, Narcao (CA)	galena	2.10075	0.85769	18.245
R 1000B	Rosas, Narcao	galena, sphalerite	2.10434	0.85856	18.243
R 1000C	Rosas, Narcao	galena, haematite	2.09861	0.85738	18.237
R 1000D	Rosas, Narcao	galena, haematite	2.09963	0.85769	18.247
R 1000E	Rosas, Narcao	galena	2.10240	0.85799	18.259
R 1000F	Rosas, Narcao	galena	2.09914	0.85740	18.246
SD 1006A	Sa Duchessa (CA)	malachite, azurite	2.11605	0.87063	17.946
SD 1006C	Sa Duchessa	malachite, azurite	2.12768	0.87412	17.926
SD 1006D	Sa Duchessa	malachite, azurite	2.11834	0.87269	17.900
SD 1006D1	Sa Duchessa	malachite	2.12137	0.87301	17.921
SM 1001A	Sa Marchessa	galena, sphal., chalco.	2.09738	0.85779	18.220
SM 1001B	Sa Marchessa	galena, sphal., chalco.	2.09564	0.85613	18.247
SM 1001C	Sa Marchessa	galena	2.09737	0.85698	18.290
SM 1001D	Sa Marchessa	galena, sphal., chalco.	2.10101	0.85822	18.221
SM 1001G	Sa Marchessa	galena, sphal., chalco.	2.09894	0.85667	18.288
TRB1	Truba Niedda (CA)	galena	2.09804	0.85742	18.232
TRB1	Truba Niedda	galena	2.10014	0.85767	18.250
GUZ1	Gozzura (NU)	galena	2.09644	0.85524	18.287
SE	Sos Enattos	galena	2.09597	0.85296	18.325

Table 2

New lead isotope analyses of ores from the Colline Metallifere, Tuscany
(mal. = malachite; az. = azurite)

Sample no.	Mine	Region	Mineral analysed	Pb 208/206	Pb 207/206	Pb 206/204
BACI 1A	Baciolo	Bocchegiano	galena	2.08428	0.83774	18.692
BACI 2A	Baciolo	Bocchegiano	galena	2.08505	0.83800	18.711
BAL 1A	Ballarino	Bocchegiano	galena	2.08462	0.83782	18.737
BAL 3A	Ballarino	Bocchegiano	galena	2.08539	0.83808	18.743
BAL 4A	Ballarino	Bocchegiano	galena	2.08533	0.83789	18.743
BAL 5A	Ballarino	Bocchegiano	galena	2.08470	0.83789	18.733
BAL 6A	Ballarino	Bocchegiano	galena	2.08773	0.83845	18.763
CAM 1A	Campiano	Bocchegiano	galena	2.08557	0.83814	18.735
CAM 2A	Campiano	Bocchegiano	galena	2.08490	0.83808	18.742
CAM 3A	Campiano	Bocchegiano	galena	2.08609	0.83802	18.748
CAM 4A	Campiano	Bocchegiano	galena	2.08497	0.83792	18.736
CAM 6A	Campiano	Bocchegiano	galena	2.08368	0.83772	18.726
CAM 7A	Campiano	Bocchegiano	galena	2.08451	0.83794	18.726
CAM 8A	Campiano	Bocchegiano	galena	2.08659	0.83823	18.763
CAPN 1A	Capanne Vecchie	Massa Marittima	galena	2.08355	0.83702	18.763
CAPN 2A	Capanne Vecchie	Massa Marittima	galena	2.08222	0.83659	18.756
CAPN 3A	Capanne Vecchie	Massa Marittima	galena	2.08306	0.83676	18.761
CAPN 4A	Capanne Vecchie	Massa Marittima	galena	2.08540	0.83709	18.788
CAPN 5A	Capanne Vecchie	Massa Marittima	galena	2.08610	0.83877	18.709
CAPN 6A	Capanne Vecchie	Massa Marittima	galena	2.08256	0.83675	18.760
CAPN 7A	Capanne Vecchie	Massa Marittima	galena	2.08229	0.83680	18.758
LP 1A	La Pesta	Massa Marittima	galena	2.08680	0.83761	18.795
LP 2A	La Pesta	Massa Marittima	galena?	2.08450	0.83714	18.775
LP 4A	La Pesta	Massa Marittima	galena	2.08341	0.83676	18.774
LZ 1A	Lanzi Mine	Campiglia Marittima	galena	2.08590	0.83800	18.811
LZ 3A	Lanzi Mine	Campiglia Marittima	galena	2.08053	0.83706	18.760
LZ 4A	Lanzi Mine	Campiglia Marittima	galena	2.07941	0.83670	18.756
LZ 5A	Lanzi Mine	Campiglia Marittima	galena	2.07857	0.83645	18.762
LZ 6A	Lanzi Mine	Campiglia Marittima	galena	2.07969	0.83672	18.768
Monas 4B	Montecatini	Val di Cécina	mal.; az.	2.08718	0.85675	18.144
Monas 4C	Montecatini	Val di Cécina	mal.; az.	2.09028	0.86138	17.994
Monas 5B	Montecatini	Val di Cécina	mal.; az.	2.09096	0.86121	18.004
TEM 1A	Temperino	Campiglia Marittima	galena	2.08162	0.83681	18.788
TEM 3A	Temperino	Campiglia Marittima	galena	2.07942	0.83681	18.752
TEM 4A	Temperino	Campiglia Marittima	galena	2.08774	0.84246	18.641

Table 3

Lead isotope analyses of copper oxhide and bun ingots from Baccu Simeone (Villanovaforu), Sardinia

Number	Ingot type	208Pb/206Pb	207Pb/206Pb	206Pb/204Pb
BS6	Bun	2.11849	0.86933	17.953
BS13	Bun	2.10231	0.85961	18.151
BS27	Bun	2.11106	0.86578	18.020
BS53	Bun	2.11560	0.86961	17.915
BS59	Bun	1.76992	0.74462	21.168
BS1	Oxhide	2.07138	0.84114	18.489
BS2	Oxhide	2.07258	0.84134	18.491
BS3	Oxhide	2.07395	0.84329	18.438
BS4	Oxhide	2.07858	0.84583	18.387
BS5	Oxhide	2.07025	0.84048	18.510
BS7	Oxhide	2.07526	0.84282	18.486
BS9	Oxhide	2.07686	0.84504	18.404
BS10	Oxhide	2.07408	0.84335	18.430
BS11	Oxhide	2.07169	0.84141	18.489

Table 4

Chemical analyses made by instrumental neutron activation of Nuragic copper bun ingots (B), of oxhide ingots (O) found in Sardinia, and of Nuragic copper alloy artifacts

Sample No.	Site	Au	As	Sb	Se	Te	Ag	Sn	Zn	Co	Fe
7943	Teti Abini	0.66	413	45	–		81	8.9 %	540	696	
7944	Teti Abini	7.39	2771	149	74		224	8.9 %	1130	223	
7944c	Teti Abini	10.6	3937	194	60		400	12.9 %	112	147	
7945	Teti Abini	3.56	3338	186	39		800	4.2 %	255	204	
7946	Teti Abini	43.70	699	192	35		93	11.6 %	212	107	
7947	Teti Abini	0.8	1336	4182			1689		267	16	
7948	Teti Abini	17.8	3413	47	134		21	13.9 %	427	55	
7951	Teti Abini	24.5	9116	210	37		557	9.15%	61	196	
7953	Teti Abini	6.8	2586	1031	54		545	9.8 %	524	232	
7955	Teti Abini	9.39	5863	591	51		254	5.6 %	674	302	
7956	Teti Abini	5.52	1828	67	120		38	12.9 %	452	99	
7957	Teti Abini	4.18	2395	115	120		31	9.1 %	119	52	
7958	Teti Abini	14.4	4620	81	102		72	8.8 %	183	580	
7959	Forraxi Nioi	1.3	3635	1497			488	6.1 %	305	20	
7960	Forraxi Nioi	5.64	4044	164	44		2221		503	307	
7961	Forraxi Nioi	9.04	1678	3808			1211	5.5 %		171	
7962	Forraxi Nioi	7.59	2687	1212	39		611	9.6 %	360	134	
7964	Forraxi Nioi	2.03	2332	1842	54		595	11.5 %	106	106	
7965	Forraxi Nioi	7.31	2186	1349			509	9.1 %		150	
7966	Forraxi Nioi	7.3	1923	1265	65		383	3.9 %	558	313	
7967	Forraxi Nioi	6.04	1636	400	49		615	6.4 %	236	223	
BS11	B. Simeone O	19.6	5694	137	91	123	98			224	
BS27	B. Simeone B?	0.1	648	2	3		1		378	331	2.1%
BS34	B. Simeone B?	0.88	77	3	41		7			6	602
BS53	B. Simeone B?	0.25	247	2			6	68	58	782	
BS59	B. Simeone B?	1.0	4647	6	14	28	868		24	3	875
BS6	B. Simeone B	0.07	406	2	1		2		588	823	1.6%
BS3	B. Simeone O	16.4	6333	96	67	79	88	–	46	1250	1245
BS5	B. Simeone O	5.83	3427	55	137	91	30	54	34	761	406

Table 5

Lead isotope analyses of artifacts from Nuragic sites (samples from Teti and Forraxi Nioi kindly provided by Dr H. Schichler, Stuttgart).

Inventory nos.	Site	Description	Pb 208/206	Pb 207/206	Pb 206/204
SS.G = 10710	Bonnanaro, F. Janna (SS)	bun ingot frag.	2.07434	0.83720	18.621
SS.L = 10715	Bonnanaro, F. Janna (SS)	double axe	2.12051	0.87319	17.898
SS.M = 10712	Bonnanaro, F. Janna (SS)	double axe	2.10739	0.86428	18.081
SS.N = 10713	Bonnanaro, F. Janna (SS)	double axe	2.09882	0.85696	18.214
7959	Forraxi Nioi (NU)	small droplet	2.09916	0.85522	18.198
7960	Forraxi Nioi (NU)	shaft; rim chisel	2.11400	0.86947	17.985
7961	Forraxi Nioi (NU)	dagger tip	2.09023	0.85087	18.391
7962	Forraxi Nioi (NU)	round metal tip	2.09817	0.85632	18.070
7964	Forraxi Nioi (NU)	dagger blade frag.	2.10885	0.86129	18.136
7965	Forraxi Nioi (NU)	round lump	2.11179	0.86470	18.101
7966	Forraxi Nioi (NU)	casting droplet	2.12316	0.86916	18.146
7967	Forraxi Nioi (NU)	casting droplet	2.10933	0.86483	17.946
SS.A2 = 10240	Nur. Flumenelongu (SS)	bar ingot frag.?	2.10249	0.85495	18.333
SS.A3 = 10260	Nur. Flumenelongu (SS)	bun frag.	2.09389	0.85352	18.335
SS.A4 = 10274	Nur. Flumenelongu (SS)	ingot handle frag.	2.10137	0.85491	18.360
SS.C = 10272	Nur. Flumenelongu (SS)	shaft hole axe	2.09906	0.85546	18.356
SS.D = 10273	Nur. Flumenelongu (SS)	axe edge, cutting	2.10761	0.85789	18.234
OL.3	Olièna (NU)	bun frag.	2.09853	0.85656	18.264
OL.4 = 41198	Olièna (NU)	spearhead frag.	2.10136	0.85404	18.236
OL.5 = 41153	Olièna (NU)	spearhead frag.	2.10460	0.85630	18.284
OL.6 = 41095	Olièna (NU)	sword votiv. frag.	2.11649	0.87105	17.934
OL.8 = 41286	Olièna (NU)	twisted bar frag.	2.11405	0.86793	18.024
OL.9 = 41063	Olièna (NU)	axe blade frag.	2.11651	0.86943	18.013
OL.13	Olièna (NU)	bun frag.	2.10010	0.85895	18.157
OL.15	Olièna (NU)	bun frag.	2.12039	0.87378	17.879
OL.16	Olièna (NU)	sword frag.	2.12160	0.87370	17.910
OL.18 = 59018	Olièna (NU)	cylind. rod frag.	2.09957	0.85455	18.285
OL.19 = 54484	Olièna (NU)	cylind. rod frag.	2.10726	0.86179	18.151
OL.20	Olièna (NU)	square sec. bar	2.10408	0.86147	18.145
OL.21	Olièna (NU)	square sec. bar	2.11895	0.87015	17.945
NU.1 = 60500	Ortueri, Funtana 'e Cresia	axe	2.10015	0.85927	18.204
SS.O	Ossi (SS)	PC(flat) ingot	2.11864	0.87021	17.929
SS.S	Ossi (SS)	PC(flat) ingot	2.12068	0.87132	17.921
SS.T	Ossi (SS)	PC(flat) ingot	1.95421	0.82028	19.146
SS.V	Ossi (SS)	oxhide ingot	1.91076	0.80357	19.557
7943	Teti Abini (NU)	dagger blade	2.11356	0.86530	17.930
7944	Teti Abini (NU)	dagger blade frag.	2.11201	0.86906	17.942
7945	Teti Abini (NU)	dagger blade frag.	2.11750	0.87153	17.973
7946	Teti Abini (NU)	dagger blade frag.	2.10345	0.86318	17.959
7948	Teti Abini (NU)	dagger blade	2.09365	0.86097	18.066
7950	Teti Abini (NU)	folded sheet	2.08399	0.83886	18.354
7951	Teti Abini (NU)	ringform bead	2.11105	0.86878	17.971
7953	Teti Abini (NU)	round needle	2.10344	0.85909	18.194
7955	Teti Abini (NU)	forked metal	2.07014	0.85055	18.259
7956	Teti Abini (NU)	dagger blade frag.	2.10312	0.85910	18.179
7957	Teti Abini (NU)	dagger blade frag.	2.10313	0.86101	18.129
7958	Teti Abini (NU)	dagger blade frag.	2.09537	0.85181	18.233

References

Atzeni, E., F. Barreca, M.L. Ferrarese-Ceruti, E. Contu, G. Lilliu, F. Lo Schiavo, F. Nicosia & E. Equini Schneider (eds.)
1981   *Ichnussa: La Sardegna dalle origini all'età classica*. Milano: Libri Scheiwiller.

Balmuth, M.S. (ed.)
1987   *Studies in Sardinian Archaeology III. Nuragic Sardinia and the Mycenaean World*. BAR International Series 387. Oxford: British Archaeological Reports.

Balmuth, M.S., & R.F. Tylecote
1976   Ancient copper and bronze in Sardinia: Excavation and analysis. *Journal of Field Archaeology* 3: 195-201.

Bass, G.F.
1967   *Cape Gelidonya: A Bronze Age Shipwreck*. Transactions of the American Philosophical Society 57/8. Philadelphia: American Philosophical Society.
1986   The Bronze Age shipwreck at Ulu Burun (Kaş): 1984 campaign. *American Journal of Archaeology* 90: 269-96.
1987   Oldest known shipwreck reveals Bronze Age splendors. *National Geographic* 172(6): 692-733.

Bass, G.F., C. Pulak, D. Collon & J. Weinstein
1989   The Bronze Age shipwreck at Ulu Burun: 1986 campaign. *American Journal of Archaeology* 93: 1-29.

Bear, L.M.
1963   *The Mineral Resources and Mining Industry of Cyprus*. Nicosia.

Buchholz, H.G.
1959   Keftiubarren und Erzhandel im zweiten vorchristlichen Jahrtausend. *Prähistorische Zeitschrift* 37: 1-40.

Carratelli, G.P.
1945   Le iscrizioni preelleniche di Haghia Triada in Creta. *Monumenti Antichi* 40: 428-591.

Catling, H.W.
1964   *Cypriot Bronzework in the Mycenaean World*. Oxford.
1969   The Cypriote copper industry. *Archeologia Viva* 2(3): 81-88.

Cherry, J.F., & A.B. Knapp
1991   Quantitative provenance studies and Bronze Age trade in the Mediterranean: Some preliminary reflections. In N.H. Gale (ed.), *Bronze Age Trade in the Mediterranean*, 90-119. Studies in Mediterranean Archaeology 90. Göteborg: Paul Åström's Forlag.

Coles, J.M.
1982   The Bronze Age in north western Europe: Problems and advances. In F. Wendorf and A.E. Close (eds.), *Advances in World Archaeology*, 265-321. Orlando: Academic Press.

Constantinou, G.
1980   Metallogenesis associated with Troodos ophiolite. In A. Panayiotou (ed.), *Ophiolites: Proceedings of the International Ophiolite Symposium, Cyprus 1979*, 663-74. Nicosia.
1982   Geological features and ancient exploitation of the cupriferous sulphide orebodies of Cyprus. In J.D. Muhly, R. Maddin and V. Karageorghis (eds.), *Early Metallurgy in Cyprus, 4000–500 BC*, 13-24. Nicosia.

Contu, E.
1968   Ripostiglio di bronzi e tracce di capanne presso il nuraghe Flumenelongu (Alghero, Sassari). *Rivista di Scienze Preistoriche* 23(2): 425.

Demakopoulou, K., E. Mangou, Z.A. Stos-Gale & N.H. Gale
1991   Synthesis on copper metallurgy in the Mycenaean epoch. In G.S. Korres (ed.), *Acts of the 6th International Colloquium on Aegean Prehistory (Athens 1987): The Prehistoric Aegean and its Relations to Adjacent Areas*.

Demas, M.V.
1984   Pyla-Kokkinokremos and Maa-Palaeokastro: Two fortified settlements of the End of the 13th century BC in Cyprus. PhD dissertation, University of Cincinnati. Ann Arbor: University Microfilms International.

Dessau, G., A. Leonardelli & L. Vighi
1975   Toscana: Minerali di rame: Montecatini Val di Cécina. In G. Castaldo and G. Stampanoni (coordinatori), *Memoria Illustrativa della Carta Mineraria d'Italia*, 106-107.

Dixon, W.J.
1990   *BMDP Statistical Software Manual* 1: 339-58. Berkeley: University of California Press.

Ferrarese Ceruti, M.L.
1981   Documenti micenei nella Sardegna meridionale. In E. Atzeni *et al.* (eds.), *Ichnussa: La Sardegna dalle origini all'età classica*, pp. 605-12. Milano: Libri Scheiwiller.
1982   Il complesso nuragico di Antigori. In L. Vagnetti (ed.), *Magna Grecia e Mondo Miceneo. Nuovi Documenti*, 167-76. Taranto: Istituto per la Storia e l'Archeologia della Magna Grecia.
1985   Un bronzetto nuragico da Ossi (Sassari). *Studi in Onore di G. Lilliu per il Suo Settantesimo Compleanno*, 51-69. Cagliari.

Ferrarese Ceruti, M.L., L. Vagnetti & F. Lo Schiavo
1987   Minoici, micenei e ciprioti in Sardegna nella seconda metà del II millennio a.C. In M.S. Balmuth (ed.), *Studies in Sardinian Archaeology III. Nuragic Sardinia and the Mycenaean World*, 7-38. BAR International Series 387. Oxford: British Archaeological Reports.

Fiorelli, S.
1882   Nota Scavi (July 15, 1882), 308-11.

Fisher, R.A.
1936   The use of multiple measurements in taxonomic problems. *Annals of Eugenics* 7: 179-88.

French, E.B.
1980   A colloquium on Late Cypriote III sites. *Report of the Department of Antiquities, Cyprus* 1980: 267-69.

Frenzel, G., J. Ottemann, M. Al-Tabaqchali & B. Nuber
1975   Calabona copper ore deposit of Alghero, Sardinia. *Neues Jahrbuch für Mineralogie, Abhandlungen* 125(2): 107-55.

Gale, N.H.
1989a   Lead isotope studies applied to provenance studies—A brief review. In Y. Maniatis (ed.), *Archaeometry*, 469-502. Amsterdam: Elsevier.
1989b   Archaeometallurgical studies of Late Bronze Age copper oxhide ingots from the Mediterranean region. In A. Hauptmann, E. Pernicka and G.A. Wagner (eds.), *Old World Archaeometallurgy*, 247-68. Der Anschnitt Beiheft 7. Bochum.
1991   Copper oxhide ingots: Their origin and their place in the Bronze Age metals trade in the Mediterranean. In N.H. Gale (ed.), *Bronze Age Trade in the Mediterranean*, 197-239. Studies in

Mediterranean Archaeology 90. Göteborg: Paul Åström's Forlag.

Gale, N.H., & Z.A. Stos-Gale
1985 Lead isotope analysis and Alashiya: 3. *Report of the Department of Antiquities, Cyprus* 1985: 83-99.
1986 Oxhide ingots in Crete and Cyprus and the Bronze Age metals trade. *Annual of the British School of Archaeology at Athens* 81: 81-100.
1987 Oxhide ingots from Sardinia, Crete and Cyprus: New scientific evidence. In M.S. Balmuth (ed.), *Studies in Sardinian Archaeology III. Nuragic Sardinia and the Mycenaean World*, 135-78. BAR International Series 387. Oxford: British Archaeological Reports..
1988 Recent evidence for a possible Bronze Age metal trade between Sardinia and the Aegean. In E.B. French and K.A. Wardle (eds.), *Problems in Greek Prehistory*, 349-84. Bristol: Bristol Classical Press.
1989 Bronze Age archaeometallurgy of the Mediterranean: The impact of lead isotope studies. In R. Allen (ed.), *Archaeological Chemistry IV*, 159-99. Advances in Chemistry 220. Washington, DC: American Chemical Society.
1991 Lead isotope studies in the Aegean (The British Academy Project). In M. Pollard (ed.), *New Developments in Archaeological Science. Oxford Journal of Archaeology.*

Gale, N.H., Z.A. Stos-Gale & G. Gilmore
1985 Alloy types and copper sources for Anatolian copper alloy artefacts. *Anatolian Studies* 35: 143-73.

Gale, N.H., E. Spooner & P. Potts
1981 The lead and strontium isotope and trace element geochemistry of metalliferous sediments associated with the Upper Cretaceous ophiolitic rocks of Cyprus, Syria and Oman. *Canadian Journal of Earth Science* 18: 1290-1302.

Galli, F.
1984 Scavi nel nuraghe Funtana di Ittireddu (Sassari). *Nuovo Bullettino Archeologico Sardo* 1: 115-22.
1985 Nota preliminare alla III e IV campagna di scava al nuraghe Funtana (Ittireddu, Sassari). *Nuovo Bullettino Archeologico Sardo* 2: 87-108.

Garbarino, C., L. Maccioni, N. Minzoni, G. Padalino, S. Tocco & M. Violo
1980 The strata-bound copper-lead-zinc mineralisation of the Sardinian microplate. In S. Jankovich and R. Sillitoe (eds.), *European Copper Deposits*, 251-60. Belgrade: University of Belgrade.

Halbherr, F., E. Stefani & L. Banti
1977 Haghia Triada nel periodo tardo palaziale. *Annuario della Scuola Archeologica di Atene* 55: 121-25.

Hauptmann, A.
1985 *5000 Jahre Kupfer in Oman*. Der Anschnitt Beiheft 4. Bochum.

Jones, R.E., & P.H. Day
1987 Late Bronze Age Aegean and Cypriot type pottery on Sardinia: Identification of imports and local imitations by physico-chemical analysis. In M.S. Balmuth (ed.), *Studies in Sardinian Archaeology III. Nuragic Sardinia and the Mycenaean World*, 257-69. BAR International Series 387. Oxford: British Archaeological Reports.

Jones, R.E., & L. Vagnetti
1991 Traders and craftsmen in the Central Mediterranean. In N.H. Gale (ed.), *Bronze Age Trade in the Mediterranean*, 125-45. Studies in Mediterranean Archaeology 90. Göteborg: Paul Åström's Forlag.

Junghans, S., E. Sangmeister & M. Schröder
1968 *Kupfer und Bronze in der Frühen Metallzeit Europas 1-3*. Studien zu den Anfängen der Metallurgie 2. Berlin.

Karageorghis, V., & M. Demas
1984 *Pyla-Kokkinokremos*. Nicosia.

Knapp, A.B., & J.F. Cherry
1990 The British Academy Group Research Project: An aspect of science and archaeology in Great Britain. *Society of Archaeological Sciences Bulletin* 13(1): 3-5.

Knapp, A., J.D. Muhly & P. Muhly
1988 To hoard is human: Late Bronze Age metal deposits in Cyprus and the Aegean. *Report of the Department of Antiquities, Cyprus* 1988: 233-62.

Lagarce, J., E. Lagarce, A. Bounni & N. Saliby
1983 Les fouilles à Ras Ibn Hani en Syrie (Campagnes de 1980, 1981 et 1982). *Académies des Inscriptions et Belles Lettres: Comptes Rendus*, Avril-Juin, 249-90.

Lilliu, G.
1982 *La Civiltà Nuragica*. Sardegna Archeologica: Studi e Monumenti 1. Sassari: Carlo Delfino.

Lo Schiavo, F.
1980 I lingotti di rame: Bibliografia ed analisi critica. *Rendiconti della Accademia Nazionale dei Lincei* 35(5-6): 379-88.
1981 Economia e società nell'età dei nuraghi. In E. Atzeni et al. *Ichnussa: La Sardegna dalle origini all'età classica*, pp. 255-347. Milano: Libri Scheiwiller.
1982 Copper metallurgy in Sardinia during the Late Bronze Age: New prospects on its Aegean connections. In J.D. Muhly, R. Maddin and V. Karageorghis (eds.), *Early Metallurgy in Cyprus, 4000-500 BC*, 271-82. Nicosia.
1985 *Nuraghic Sardinia in its Mediterranean Setting*. Department of Archaeology Occasional Paper 12. Edinburgh: University of Edinburgh.
1989 Early metallurgy in Sardinia. In A. Hauptmann, E. Pernicka and G. Wagner (eds.), *Old World Archaeometallurgy*, 33-38. Der Anschnitt Beiheft 7. Bochum.

Lo Schiavo, F., & L. Vagnetti
1980 Micenei in Sardegna? *Rendiconti della Accademia Nazionale dei Lincei* 8(35): 371-91.

Lo Schiavo, F., E. Macnamara & L. Vagnetti
1985 Late Cypriot imports to Italy and their influence on local bronzework. *Papers of the British School at Rome* 53: 1-71.

Lo Schiavo, F., R. Maddin, J. Merkel, J.D. Muhly & T. Stech (eds.)
1990 *Analisi Metallurgiche e Statistiche sui Lingotti di Rame della Sardegna/Metallographic and Statistical Analyses of Copper Ingots from Sardinia*. Soprintendenza ai Beni Archeologici per le provincie di Sassari e Nuoro, Quaderni 17. Ozieri: Il Torchietto.

Macnamara, E., D. Ridgway & F.R. Serra Ridgway
1984 *The Bronze Hoard from S. Maria in Paulis, Sardinia*. British Museum Occasional Paper 45. London: British Museum.

Maddin, R., & J. Merkel
1990 Metallographic and statistical analyses. In F. Lo Schiavo et al,. *Analisi Metallurgiche e Statistiche sui Lingotti di Rame della Sardegna/Metallographic and Statistical Analyses of Copper*

Ingots from Sardinia. 43-186. Soprintendenza ai Beni Archeologici per le provincie di Sassari e Nuoro, Quaderni 17. Ozieri: Il Torchietto.

Manly, B.
1986   Multivariate Statistical Methods. London: Chapman & Hall.

Manning, S.
1988   The Bronze Age eruption of Thera: Absolute dating, Aegean chronology and Mediterranean cultural interrelations. *Journal of Mediterranean Archaeology* 1(1): 17-82.

Marcello, A., S. Pretti & I. Salvadori
1978   *Carta Metallogenica della Sardegna*. Firenze: Servizio Geologico d'Italia.

Merkel, J.
1983   Reconstruction of Bronze Age copper smelting. Experiments based on archaeological evidence from Timna, Israel. PhD dissertation, Department of Archaeology, University of London.

Muhly, J.D.
1991   The development of copper metallurgy in Late Bronze Age Cyprus. In N.H. Gale (ed.), *Bronze Age Trade in the Mediterranean*, 180-96. Studies in Mediterranean Archaeology 90. Göteborg: Paul Åström's Forlag.

Muhly, J.D., & T. Stech
1990   Final observations. In F. Lo Schiavo et al., *Analisi Metallurgiche e Statistiche sui Lingotti di Rame della Sardegna/Metallographic and Statistical Analyses of Copper Ingots from Sardinia*, 201-22 Soprintendenza ai Beni Archeologici per le provincie di Sassari e Nuoro, Quaderni 17. Ozieri: Il Torchietto.

Muhly, J.D., T. Stech Wheeler & R. Maddin
1977   The Cape Gelidonya shipwreck and the Bronze Age metals trade in the Eastern Mediterranean. *Journal of Field Archaeology* 4: 353-62.

Muhly, J.D., R. Maddin & T. Stech Wheeler
1980   The oxhide ingots from Enkomi and Mathiati and Late Bronze Age copper smelting in Cyprus. *Report of the Department of Antiquities, Cyprus* 1980: 84-95.

Muhly, J.D., R. Maddin & T. Stech
1988   Cyprus, Crete and Sardinia: Copper ox-hide ingots and the Bronze Age metals trade. *Report of the Department of Antiquities, Cyprus* 1988: 281-98.

Murray, A., A. Smith & H. Walters
1900   *Excavations in Cyprus*. London.

Paribeni, R.
1903   Lavori eseguiti dalla missione archeologica italiana nel palazzo e nella necropoli di Haghia Triada. *Rendiconti della Accademia dei Lincei* 12(7-8).

Pernier, L., & L. Banti
1947   *Guida degli Scavi Italiani in Creta*. Roma.

Pigorini, L.
1904   Pani di rame provenienti dall'egeo e scoperti a Serra Ilixi in provincia di Cagliari. *Bollettino di Paletnologia Italiana* 10: 91-107.

Pulak, C.
1988a   The Bronze Age shipwreck at Ulu Burun, Turkey: 1985 campaign. *American Journal of Archaeology* 92: 1-37.
1988b   Excavations in Turkey: 1988 campaign. *Institute of Nautical Archaeology Newsletter* 15(4): 13-17.

Ridge, J.D.
1990   *Annotated Bibliographies of Mineral Deposits in Europe: Part 2, Western and Central Europe*. Oxford: Pergamon.

Schaeffer, C.
1936   *Missions en Chypre, 1932-1935*. Paris: Academie des Inscriptions et Belles-Lettres.
1956   Soixante-quatorze armes et outils en bronze avec dédicace au Grand-Prêtre d'Ugarit. *Ugaritica* (Paris) 3: 251-75.

Shaw, J.W.
1984   Excavations at Kommos (Crete) during 1982-1983. *Hesperia* 53: 251-87.

Società Elettrica Sarda
1949   La Sardegna: Miniere. *Il Gruppo Elettrico Sardo e gli Impianti dell'alto Flumendosa*, 59-101. Roma.

South, A.K.
1980   Kalavasos—Ayios Dhimitrios 1979: A summary report. *Report of the Department of Antiquities, Cyprus* 1980: 22-53.

Spano, G.
1858   Stele mortuarie di bronzo. *Bollettino Archeologico Sardo* 4(1): 11-15.

Stech, T.
1989   Nuragic metallurgy in Sardinia. In A. Hauptmann, E. Pernicka and G.A. Wagner (eds.), *Old World Archaeometallurgy*, 39-43 Der Anschnitt Beiheft 7. Bochum.

Stech Wheeler, T., R. Maddin & J.D. Muhly
1975   Ingots and the Bronze Age copper trade in the Mediterranean. *Expedition* 17(4): 31-39.

Stos-Gale, Z.A., N.H. Gale & G. Gilmore
1984   Early Bronze Age Trojan metal sources and Anatolians in the Cyclades. *Oxford Journal of Archaeology* 3(3): 23-44.

Stos-Gale, Z.A., N.H. Gale & U. Zwicker
1986   The copper trade in the south-east Mediterranean region. Preliminary scientific evidence. *Report of the Department of Antiquities, Cyprus* 1986: 122-44.

Stos-Gale, Z.A., C. MacDonald & N.H. Gale
1991   New studies of Final Chalcolithic and Early Bronze Age copper metallurgy in Cyprus. In C. Eluère (ed.), *La découverte du metal*, 341-56. Paris: Picard.

Svoronos, J.N.
1906   *Journal Internationale d'Archéologie Numismatique* 9: 161-89.
1910   *Leçons Numismatiques (Les Premières Monnaies)*. Brussels.

Tatton-Brown, V.
1987   *Ancient Cyprus*. London: British Museum Publications.

Thimme, J. (ed.)
1980   *Kunst und Kultur Sardiniens vom Neolithikum bis zum ende der Nuraghenzeit*. Karlsruhe: C.F. Müller.

Tylecote, R.F., H. Ghaznavi & P. Boydell
1977   Partitioning of trace elements between the ores, fluxes, slags and metal during the smelting of copper. *Journal of Archaeological Science* 4: 305-33.

Tylecote, R.F., M.S. Balmuth & R. Massoli-Novelli
1983   Copper and bronze metallurgy in Sardinia. *Journal of the Historical Metallurgy Society* 17: 63-78.
1984   Copper and bronze metallurgy in Sardinia. In M.S. Balmuth and R.J. Rowland, Jr (eds.), *Studies in Sardinian Archaeology*, 115-62. Ann Arbor: University of Michigan Press.

Vagnetti, L., & R.E. Jones
1988   Towards the identification of local Mycenaean pottery in Italy. In E.B. French and K.A. Wardle

(eds.), *Problems in Greek Prehistory*, 335-48. Bristol: Bristol Classical Press.

Vagnetti, L., & F. Lo Schiavo
1989 Late Bronze Age long distance trade in the Mediterranean: The role of the Cypriots. In E. Peltenburg (ed.), *Early Society in Cyprus*, 217-43. Edinburgh: Edinburgh University Press.

Vercoutter, J.
1956 *L'Égypte et le monde égéen préhellénique*. Cairo.

Wachsmann, S.
1987 *Aegeans in the Theban Tombs*. Orientalia Lovaniensa Analecta 20. Leuven.

Wiener, M.
1991 The nature and control of Minoan foreign trade. In N.H. Gale (ed.), *Bronze Age Trade in the Mediterranean*, 325-50. Studies in Mediterranean Archaeology 90. Göteborg: Paul Åström's Forlag.

Zuffardi, P.
1980 Copper deposits of Italy: Metallogenesis and evaluation. In S. Jankovic and R.H. Sillitoe (eds.), *European Copper Deposits*. Belgrade: Belgrade University Press.
1989 Italy. In F.W. Dunning, P. Garrard, H.W. Haslam and R.A. Ixer (eds.), *Mineral Deposits of Europe Volume 4/5: Southwest and Eastern Europe, with Iceland*, 221-77. London: Institute of Mining and Metallurgy.

Zwicker, U., P. Virdis & M.L. Ferrarese Ceruti
1980 Investigations on copper ore, prehistoric copper slag and copper ingots from Sardinia. In P.T. Craddock (ed.), *Scientific Studies in Early Mining and Extractive Metallurgy*, 135-64. British Museum Occasional Paper 20. London: British Museum.

Zwicker, U., H. Greiner, K.-H. Hofmann & M. Reithinger
1985 Smelting, refining and alloying of copper and copper alloys in crucible furnaces during prehistoric up to Roman times. In P.T. Craddock and M.J. Hughes (eds.), *Furnaces and Smelting Technology in Antiquity*, 103-21. British Museum Occasional Paper 48. London: British Museum.

Riassunto

Recenti scoperte che hanno rivelato contatti con il mondo miceneo, minoico e cipriota, hanno enfatizzato l'importanza della Sardegna durante l'età del Bronzo recente. Lingotti di rame del tipo 'oxhide' sono stati ritrovati in tutta la zona mediterranea ed in particolare nei relitti di Ulu Burun e Capo di Gelidonia. I lingotti sono stati ritrovati per la prima volta nel 1857 in Sardegna presso Serra Ilixi. Da allora sono stati localizzati 20 siti in Sardegna che presentano frammenti di almeno 50 lingotti del tipo oxhide, frequentemente associati con lingotti di forma piano-convessa. Il fatto che su affreschi di tombe egiziane siano raffigurati lingotti, che numerosi lingotti siano stati ritrovati a Cipro, a Creta e in Grecia, e che caratteri Cipro-Minoici siano raffigurati su numerosi lingotti, suggerisce che l'idea dei lingotti è originata nel Mediterraneo orientale. L'origine delle materie prime dei lingotti invece, ha provocato il sorgere di un dibattito. Alcuni studiosi, forse influenzati dalla presenza di depositi di rame in Sardegna e dalla fiorente industria metallurgica nuragica, hanno suggerito che i lingotti ritrovati in Sardegna siano stati fatti in Sardegna usando rame locale, anche se questo è avvenuto sotto un controllo o un'influenza cipriota. Le scoperte delle fonti minerarie del rame usato per fare i lingotti e la scoperta delle fonti minerarie dello stagno per fare oggetti di bronzo, è cruciale per la comprensione del commercio di metalli nel Mediterraneo nell'età del Bronzo.

L'analisi dei rapporti isotopici del piombo su oggetti di rame è la tecnica più promettetente per risolvere problemi archeologici come quello sopra menzionato. Se la composizione isotopica di un oggetto non corrisponde a quella di una fonte metallifera analizzata, ciò vuol dire che il metallo presente in quell'oggetto non proviene dalla fonte analizzata; se invece avviene il contrario ciò vuol dire che l'oggetto è compatibile con il metallo proveniente dalla fonte analizzata. Siccome la composizione isotopica del piombo di un deposito metallifero è determinata in gran parte dall'età del deposito, è possibile che più di un deposito metallifero abbia una composizione isotopica simile ad un altro. Effetti secondari fanno sì che tranne in due casi (Thasos e Kythnos), le fonti metallifere Mediterranee differiscono se si usano tecniche statistiche appropriate. È da ricordare anche il fatto che i manufatti di rame del periodo cipriota recente sono insoliti in quanto contengono una specifica proporzione d'oro e d'argento.

Gli Autori presentano una descrizione dettagliata dei depositi metalliferi sardi; essi li paragonano fisicamente e analiticamente ad altri depositi mediterranei di rame. Più di 30 depositi di rame e piombo in Sardegna sono stati sottoposti ad analisi isotopiche del piombo e ad analisi di attivazione di neutroni in numero sufficiente da determinare in quale 'gruppo' statistico ognuno di essi può essere collocato. Sono qui riportati anche i dati su depositi metalliferi in Toscana.

I risultati delle ricerche degli Autori sono i seguenti:

1. Tutte le fonti metallifere toscane sono distinguibili da tutti i depositi sardi, come lo sono i depositi di rame a Cipro, a Creta, nelle isole Cicladi, in Grecia, in Anatolia, in Spagna, nella Negev, in Giordania e in Oman.

2. Tutti i 31 lingotti del tipo oxhide provenienti dalla Sardegna fino ad ora analizzati non corrispondono a nessuna delle 30 fonti metallifere in Sardegna. Tutti i 31 lingotti, comunque, corrispondono indipendente-

mente al gruppo cipriota per quanto riguarda la composizione isotopica del piombo e per quanto riguarda il rapporto oro/argento.
3. I bronzi nuragici provenienti da Santa Maria in Paulis, da Forraxi Nioi (NU), dal nuraghe Flumenelongu (SS), da Bonnanaro (SS), da Ortueri (NU), da Olièna (NU), da Ossi (SS) e da Teti Abini (NU) e i lingotti di forma piano-convessa da Baccu Simeone (Villanovaforru-CA), hanno tutti composizioni isotopiche simili al rame estratto da una delle seguenti fonti: Sa Ducchessa (Domusnovas), Pranu e Sanguini, Perda s'Oliu, e Rosas/Funtana Raminosa/Sa Marchesa.
4. In alcuni casi almeno quattro diverse fonti minerarie sarde sono rappresentate tra gli oggetti di bronzo presso uno stesso sito.

Gli Autori concludono sostenendo che ciò indica che i lingotti del tipo oxhide ritrovati in Sardegna sono il frutto di un commercio di bronzo cipriota. Il fatto che oggetti [del artifatti] di bronzo e ceramiche minoiche e micenee sono stati ritrovati in Sardegna, dimostra che ci sono stati dei contatti tra queste popolazioni. Anche se l'industria metallurgica sarda era fiorente prima dell'arrivo di navi straniere, è possibile che i popoli nuragici abbiano accettato ulteriore rame già fuso pronto da essere utilizzato. Dovremmo pensare che questo scambio tra est ed ovest è stato iniziato da popolazioni orientali in cerca di risorse minerarie (Cu, Sn, Fe) o di altro genere nella zona del Mediterraneo centrale ed occidentale. Prima di considerare come definitiva l'origine dei lingotti sardi, è necessario che siano effettuate ulteriori analisi isotopiche del piombo sui pochi depositi metalliferi rimasti in Sardegna. L'analisi di una vasta gamma di [del oggetti] bronzi nuragici, includendo quelli di ispirazione o di origine cipriota, dovrebbe consentirci di approfondire le nostre conoscenze sullo sviluppo metallurgico in Sardegna e sulle relazioni economiche dell'isola con le civiltà mediterranee orientali.

Some Metallurgical Remarks on the Sardinian Bronzetti

C. Atzeni, L. Massidda, U. Sanna and P. Virdis

Introduction

The figurines known as *bronzetti* have long been recognized as one of the most characteristic features of prehistoric Sardinia. The majority of these *bronzetti* are recognized as being of indigenous inspiration. Their dating, however, is the object of some controversy; some leading specialists date them to between the 9th and 8th century BC, while others claim that at least some styles may belong to the late 2nd millennium BC (Lilliu 1988; Lilliu 1966; Barreca 1986; Bisi 1987). Currently there are few archaeometric studies of the *bronzetti*, which is unfortunate in view of their importance. Paradoxically, it is the very importance of these finds that has hindered investigations of this type. Up until 1990 only elemental chemical analyses of examples belonging to collections outside Italy were available (Craddock 1986; Tylecote *et al*. 1983; Riederer 1980; Balmuth 1978). Moreover, doubts had been raised concerning the authenticity of some of these finds. The market value of the *bronzetti* is often quite considerable; this has led not only to the trafficking of original pieces but also to the production of fakes, a practice which first began as far back as the early 1800s, and interferes with scientific research (Lilliu 1974; Lilliu 1982; Atzeni *et al*. 1992).

Archaeometric Analysis

Twelve of the more than 500 figurines housed in Sardinia's museums have now been analyzed (Atzeni *et al*. 1991a). All the figurines analyzed (Table 1) are from the National Archaeological Museum in Cagliari. Figurines with Y-shaped bases, which we interpret as the product of the pouring patterns, were selected for chemical, metallo-graphic and lead isotope analyses (the latter still in progress). Samples were removed from the bases (Fig. 1) in order not to spoil the body of the figurines. The experimental methods used have been described elsewhere (Atzeni *et al*. 1991a).

Casting Techniques

The 'one-piece' feature common to all the figurines suggests that they were produced by means of the lost-wax method, using clay moulds that were broken after casting to extract the artifact (Taylor *et al*. 1959).

A series of terracotta fragments (together with crucible remains and scraps from bronze and copper casting) unearthed in the Bronze Age levels at Nuraghe Santa Barbara, Bauladu (Gallin and Tykot in press; Atzeni *et al*. n.d.; Gallin and Sebis 1989) might well be the first recognizable remains of moulds used for this type of casting. Both the funnel-shaped pouring cup and the Y-shaped pouring pattern of the molten alloys can be seen in Fig. 2a. Figure 2b shows figurine no. 207 placed in what we believe to be the casting position. The remains of the pouring cup and the pouring pattern on this figurine clearly reflect the shape of the clay mould found at Nuraghe Santa Barbara.

Alloy Composition

The determination of the bulk chemical composition is the primary requisite for characterizing the alloy of a metal find. One must acknowledge the limitations of such results, however, since the lost-wax technique often affects the homogeneity of the cast object. Elements with a lower specific gravity may become concentrated in the upper part, in this case the base, from which our samples were removed. Riederer (1980: no. 96), for example, found that four samples taken from a single Nuragic figurine revealed variations of 80% in the Sn content, 50% in Ag, 37% in Pb and 135% in Fe. The frequent lack of provenience and the uncertain dating of the figurines in general further limits the interpretation of the analytical data.

The compositions of the 12 analyzed figurines are given in Table 2. Taking into account the above-mentioned limitations, the following observations can be made:

Fig. 1 Museo Nazionale di Cagliari: figurines no. 104 (left) and no. 116 (right) (from Abini-Teti). Arrows show where samples were removed.

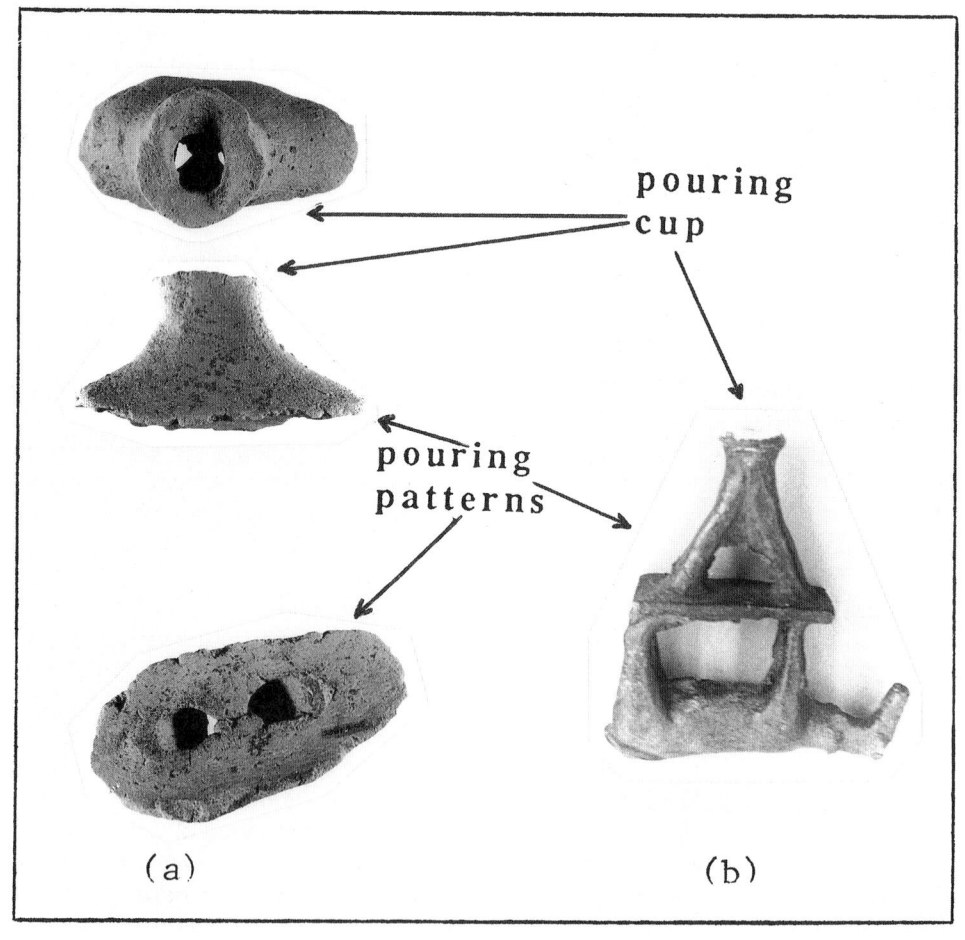

Fig. 2 Casting Technique: A. Ceramic fragment of funnel-shaped pouring cup with Y-shaped pouring pattern, from Nuraghe Santa Barbara (Bauladu); B. Figurine no. 207 (from Abini-Teti) in casting position. The remains of a funnel-shaped pouring cup with Y-shaped pouring pattern are evident.

1. With the notable exception of no. 116, the figurines were all made of tin-bronze. 10 of the 12 figurines examined had a tin content between 9 and 13%. Riederer (1980), however, reports half this amount in the finds he examined, and the same goes for those belonging to the British Museum (Tylecote et al. 1983). The availability of tin is indisputable but whether the craftsmen were able to control the actual composition of the alloy and/or kept up with a standard remains to be seen (contra Giardino 1987).
2. Lead was always the 'third element', usually amounting to less than 1%, but consisting of 6.5% in figurine no. 216.
3. Zinc was detected in all samples in amounts of less than 0.02%. This differs radically from the composition of the so-called 'Sardo-Phoenician idols', the long series of fake *bronzetti* produced during the last century and made of brass.
4. In figurine no. 116, the tin (0.27%) has been intentionally replaced with silver (6.5%). Though unusual, a similar composition has been observed for a small boat figurine (Riederer 1980, no. 194). There are at least two other figurines closely resembling no. 116, one of which is housed in the Cagliari museum. The second, for some much too similar not to be a fake, belongs to a private collection and is a true tin bronze (12.03% Sn, 0.02% Ag: Riederer 1980: no. 132).

Alloy Microstructure

The thorough technological evaluation of metal finds can no longer rely solely on microstructural examination by optical metallographic techniques but must be followed by electronic microanalysis which enables the composition of the individual phases to be rapidly and reliably determined.

The first general finding that emerged from the metallographic examination of the *bronzetti* was the heterogeneous distribution of the tin (which is typical for alloys of this composition) and the presence of almost pure copper grains (see Atzeni et al. 1991a). This suggests that the alloy was produced by the dissolution of tin (as metal or ore) in molten copper, but diffusion processes did not reach completion before casting. The metallographic section from figurine no. 128 (Fig. 3) clearly shows the presence of the intergranular alpha (α) and delta (δ) phases, lead metal and copper sulphide (Cu_2S) inclusions. The chemical composition maps shown in Fig. 4 (Sn, Pb, S; the matrix is Cu) are typical of an intergranular area.

Table 3 summarizes the (semi-quantitative) results of a series of microanalyses conducted on different points of the same figurine. The first two columns show the considerably different percentage of tin in two distinct points of the copper matrix. The third column gives the composition of a copper oxide inclusion; the fourth, an anglesite inclusion (lead sulphate, rather rare, originating from the oxidation of the sulphide); and the fifth point, a copper sulphide inclusion. Columns 6 and 7 are analyses of phases high in tin.

Figurine no. 116, made from a copper/silver alloy, has a phase composed mainly of silver (Fig. 5). Table 4 gives the (semi-quantitative) composition from two copper-phase (columns 1-2) and two silver-phase (columns 3-4) points, as well as from a copper sulphide inclusion. Of particular significance are those phases high in silver: the presence of lead (about 5%) suggests that the silver employed was obtained by cupellation.

Silver Metallurgy

The figurines examined here are composed of two distinct types of alloy. The majority were obtained by casting tin bronzes (6-13% Sn), and may be considered the product of quite advanced bronze working. The microstructural examination revealed that at least some of the copper used is of good quality (high purity grains were detected). The presence of inclusions of compositions similar to chalcocite and covellite minerals may provide some clues to the type and the provenience of the ore used. Other inclusions contain lead or, more rarely, zinc and iron. Consideration of the provenience of the ores from which the metals were extracted will only be possible once the lead isotope ratios, currently being evaluated, are available.

In contrast, the alloy used for figurine no. 116 differs considerably from those described above, containing 6.5% silver and only traces of tin (0.27%). There is little doubt that silver was used intentionally in place of tin and though this probably did not much alter the outward appearance, its preciousness could not be overlooked.

To this point, the studies that have been done on prehistoric Sardinian metallurgy have contributed to a better definition of the *problems* rather than providing *answers* to them. The data presented here, for instance, suggest a new problem: the development (or lack) of silver metallurgy in Sardinia. The relative absence of silver artifacts in Sardinia is unusual given that silver and gold artifacts began to appear in treasures hoarded by the most advanced civilizations of

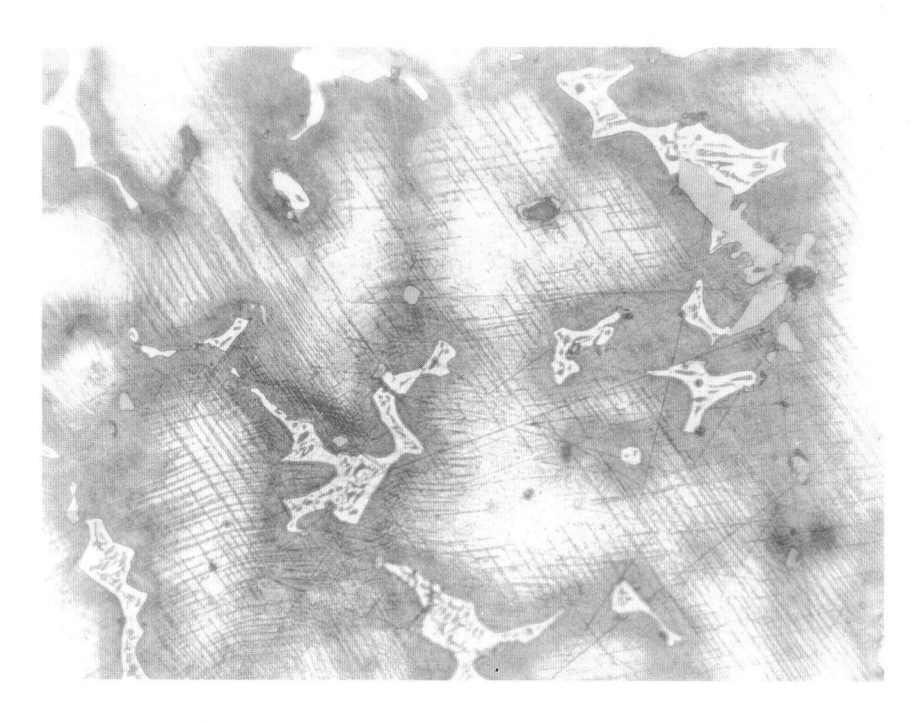

Fig. 3 Optical micrograph (400×) of sample from figurine no. 128, showing the presence of copper sulphide (light grey phase), lead (dark grey), and an intergranular phase ($\alpha + \delta$).

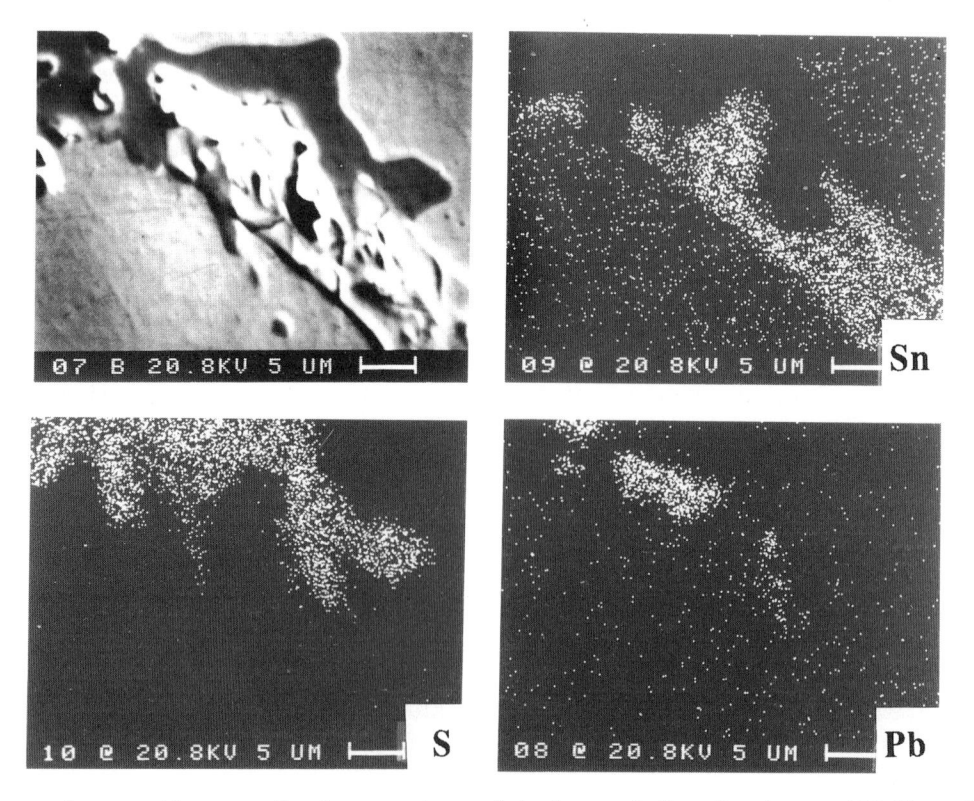

Fig. 4 Elemental composition maps (by electron microprobe) of a sample from figurine no. 128. Upper left: typical intergranular area. Clockwise: tin, lead, and sulphur (bright areas).

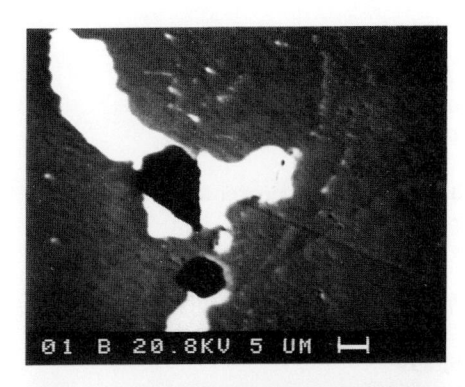

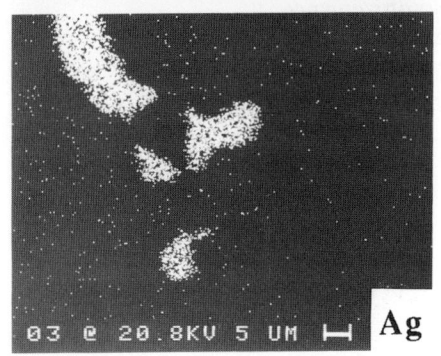

Fig. 5 Sample from figurine no. 116. Top: phase composed mainly of silver (bright areas).
Bottom: elemental composition map showing silver concentration.

the Near East and the Mediterranean very early. The cupellation process itself is described in a clay tablet found at Assur dated c. 2000 BC (Gale and Stos-Gale 1981; Krysko 1979; Tylecote 1976). This process was both time-consuming and fuel intensive since an enormous amount of lead had to be removed in the form of lead oxide, with the silver remaining in the cupel as a liquid residue. This process did not, however, require technology beyond the reach of Bronze Age cultures. Thus, this metal could not have escaped the attention of native Sardinians and the metal prospectors travelling the western Mediterranean in search of new sources of metal.

Silver artifacts, even those containing some silver like figurine no. 116, are rarely found at Nuragic sites of any age (Lilliu 1988). Lilliu (1987) explicitly rules out the possibility that early Sardinians mined silver ores and initiated its metallurgy. It is more likely that silver artifacts were used during the pre-Nuragic period, but so far no systematic studies have been carried out to test this possibility (Lo Schiavo 1987).

Data published so far on Nuragic finds of lead usually indicate a silver content too low to justify cupellation. The analysis of lead finds from Nuraghe Antigori (Sarroch-CA) detected silver in amounts ranging from 388 to 607 g/ton, while a find from Nuraghe Albucciu (Arzachena-SS) contained 560 g/ton (Gale and Stos-Gale 1987); other finds from Antigori had silver assays of between 30 and 230 g/ton (Atzeni et al. 1991b). Eleven pieces of lead discovered at Nuraghe Genna Maria (Villanovaforru-CA) contained between 60 and 320 g/ton (in one the silver content varied from 130 to 320 g/ton depending on the point sampled). Finally, in the six pieces tested from Nuraghe Santa Barbara (Bauladu-OR), 13 to 52 g/ton of silver were detected (Atzeni et al. 1991b).

Sardinian galenas are often argentiferous, with lodes of silver-bearing ores and even some metallic silver outcrops existing in the Sarrabus region, where for some years in the last century a flourishing extractive industry went on (Gouin 1867; Tangheroni 1985). Paradoxically, tin ores, which are much rarer in Sardinia and very likely imported, were much more widely used, particularly, as our data confirm, for the production of votive figurines.

Conclusion

While further field and laboratory research will be necessary to address fully the problem of silver metallurgy in Sardinia, many other figurines housed in the island's museums could be sampled without risk to their integrity. Such an investigation would enable a systematic study by typological classes, which could only result in a greatly improved understanding of the role of metallurgy in prehistoric Sardinia.

Table 1

Bronzetti in the National Archaeological Museum, Cagliari
(number and description after Lilliu 1966)
(from Abini-Teti unless marked otherwise)

No. 84	Warrior with shield hanging from his shoulder. No provenience
No. 93	Warrier with shield on his shoulder
No. 104	Hero with four eyes and four arms (Fig. 1a)
No. 110	Demonic being
No. 116	Supplicant with long braids of hair (Fig. 1b)
No. 121	Woman speaking
No. 128	Warrior with shield behind his shoulders
No. 144	Female offerer with a short cape. No provenience
No. 145	Priestess with a stole. No provenience
No. 163	Offerer with *focaccia*. No provenience
No. 207	Standing ox
No. 216	The joker

Table 2

Chemical composition (%) of bronzetti (analyses by atomic absorption spectroscopy)

Element	No. 84	No. 110	No. 98	No. 104	No. 121	No. 128	No. 116	No. 163	No. 207	No. 216	No. 144	No. 145
Sn	10.3	9.5	9.3	9.4	10.8	12.4	0.270	13.1	9.4	12.0	10.0	5.9
Ag	0.086	0.065	0.083	0.023	0.078	0.062	6.500	0.005	0.010	0.001	0.011	0.140
Pb	0.590	0.700	0.990	0.290	0.310	0.420	0.290	0.140	0.700	6.500	0.060	0.680
Zn	0.008	0.015	0.012	0.008	0.015	0.012	0.097	0.003	0.005	0.005	0.005	0.014
Fe	0.200	0.250	0.120	0.035	0.170	0.045	0.011	0.230	0.029	0.050	0.029	0.930
Ni	0.016	0.021	0.020	0.029	0.021	0.025	0.038	0.028	0.042	0.028	0.019	0.020
Co	0.014	0.020	0.016	0.017	0.015	0.004	< 0.004	0.016	0.01	0.028	0.008	0.015
Sb	< 0.06											
Bi	< 0.05											

Table 3

Semi-quantitative analysis (by electron microprobe) of metallurgical phases in figurine no. 128

Element %	1	2	3	4	5	6	7
S	0.010	0.020	0.010	9.500	16.060	0.392	0.270
Pb	0.03	0.15	0.06	65.3	0.25	1.954	2.9
Ag	nd	0.04	0.131	0.03	0.09	0	0.1
Sn	10.0	5.15	0.09	0	2.04	44.86	18.30
Cu	88.9	93.5	85.7	4.7	72.93	20.5	54.8
Zn	nd	nd	nd	nd	nd	nd	nd
Fe	0.050	0.050	0	0.009	0.009	0.250	0.230

Table 4
Semi-quantitative analysis (by electron microprobe) of metallurgical phases in figurine no. 116

Element %	1	2	3	4	5
S	0.008	nd	nd	nd	19.200
Pb	nd	0.04	5.03	4.80	0.60
Ag	4.854	5.600	88.200	86.900	0.500
Sn	0.12	0.12	0.75	0.60	nd
Cu	92.4	93.2	9.5	9.4	76.2
Zn	nd	nd	nd	nd	nd
Fe	nd	nd	nd	nd	nd

References

Atzeni, C., L. Massidda, U. Sanna & P. Virdis
   1991a   Struttura e composizione dei 'Bronzetti Nuragici' del Museo Archeologico Nazionale di Cagliari. *La Metallurgia Italiana* 83(6): 583-90.
   1991b   Notes on lead metallurgy in Sardinia during the Nuragic Period. *Journal of the Historical Metallurgy Society* 24(2): 97-105.
   1992   Chemical and metallographic study of 'Sardo-Phoenician' idols. *Journal of the Historical Metallurgy Society* (in press).
   n.d.   Bronze metalworking at the Nuragic site of S. Barbara (Sardinia, Italy). Submitted to *Journal of the Historical Metallurgy Society*.

Balmuth, M.S.
   1978   Sardinian bronzetti in American museums. *Studi Sardi* 24(1975-77): 145-56.

Barreca, F.
   1986   Phoenicians in Sardinia: The bronze figurines. In M.S. Balmuth (ed.), *Studies in Sardinian Archaeology, Volume II: Sardinia in the Mediterranean*, 135-154. Ann Arbor: University of Michigan Press.

Bisi, A.M.
   1987   Bronzi vicino-orientali in Sardegna: Importazioni ed influssi. In M.S. Balmuth (ed.), *Studies in Sardinian Archaeology III. Nuragic Sardinia and the Mycenaean World*, 225-46. BAR International Series 387. Oxford: British Archaeological Reports.

Craddock, P.
   1986   The metallurgy of Italic and Sardinian bronzes. In J. Swaddling (ed.), *Italian Iron Age Artefacts in the British Museum. Papers of the Sixth British Museum Classical Colloquium*, 143-50. London: British Museum Publications Ltd.

Gale, N.H., & Z.A. Stos-Gale
   1981   Cycladic lead and silver metallurgy. *Papers of the British School at Athens* 76: 169-224.
   1987   Oxhide ingots from Sardinia, Crete and Cyprus: New scientific evidence. In M.S. Balmuth (ed.), *Studies in Sardinian Archaeology III. Nuragic Sardinia and the Mycenaean World*, 135-78. BAR International Series 387. Oxford: British Archaeological Reports.

Gallin, L.J., & S. Sebis
   1989   Bauladu (Oristano)—Villaggio Nuragico di Santa Barbara. *Nuovo Bullettino Archeologico Sardo* 2: 271-75.

Gallin, L.J., & R.H. Tykot
   in press   Metallurgical activity at the Nuragic village of Santa Barbara (Bauladu), Sardinia, Italy. *Journal of Field Archaeology*.

Giardino, C.
   1987   Sfruttamento minerario e metallurgia nella Sardegna protostorica. In M.S. Balmuth (ed.), *Studies in Sardinian Archaeology III. Nuragic Sardinia and the Mycenaean World*, 189-222. BAR International Series 387. Oxford: British Archaeological Reports.

Gouin, L.
   1867   *Notice sur les Mines de l'Île de Sardaigne*. Cagliari.

Krysko, W.W.
   1979   *Lead in History and Art*. Stuttgart: Riederer-Verlag GmbH.

Lilliu, G.
   1966   *Le Sculture della Sardegna Nuragica*. Cagliari: La Zattera.
   1974   Un giallo del secolo XIX in Sardegna—gli idoli Sardo-Fenici. *Studi Sardi* 23: 1-53.
   1982   *La Civiltà Nuragica*. Sardegna Archeologica: Studi e Monumenti 1. Sassari: Carlo Delfino.
   1987   Le miniere dalla preistoria all'età tardo-romana. In F. Mannoni (ed.), *Le Miniere e i Minatori della Sardegna*, 7-18. Cagliari: Consiglio Regionale della Sardegna.
   1988   *La Civiltà dei Sardi dal Paleolitico all'Età dei Nuraghi*. 3rd edition. Torino: Nuova ERI.

Lo Schiavo, F.
   1987   Le origini della metallurgia ed il problema della metallurgia nella cultura di Ozieri. In L.D. Campus (a cura di), *La Cultura di Ozieri. Problematiche e nuove acquisizioni. Atti del I convegno di studio (Ozieri, gennaio 1986—aprile 1987)*, 279-92. Ozieri: Il Torchietto.

Riederer, J.
   1980   Metallanalysen sardischer bronze. In J. Thimme (ed.), *Kunst und Kultur Sardiniens vom Neolithikum zum Ende der Nuraghenzeit*, 156-60. Karlsruhe: C.F. Müller.

Tangheroni, M.
   1985   *La Città dell'Argento*. Napoli: Liguori.

Taylor, H., M.C. Fleming & J. Wulff
   1959   *Foundry Engineering*. New York: J. Wiley and Sons.

Tylecote, R.F.
   1976   *A History of Metallurgy*. London: The Metals Society.

Tylecote, R.F., M.S. Balmuth & R. Massoli-Novelli
1983   Copper and bronze metallurgy in Sardinia. *Journal of the Historical Metallurgy Society* 17: 63-78.

Riassunto

In Sardegna sono state ritrovate statuine che hanno mostrato di avere una notevole importanza artistica e metallurgica. Fino ad ora sono stati svolti soltanto alcuni studi archeometrici sulle suddette statuine, e in tutti i casi gli studi sono stati effettuati su collezioni non sarde. La datazione e lo stile dei bronzetti ha originato parecchie controversie: secondo la maggioranza degli studiosi esse risalgono al IX e all'VIII secolo a.C., ma alcuni tipi potrebbero risalire a periodi più antichi. Gli Autori hanno analizzato campioni ottenuti da 12 statuine conservate nel Museo Archeologico Nazionale di Cagliari, usando tecniche chimiche e metallografiche di tipo standard. Sono attualmente in corso ricerche sui dati riguardanti i rapporti isotopici del piombo.

Le basi delle figurine selezionate per l'analisi sono a forma di 'Y', ciò è dovuto alla forma dei bocchelli di colata adoperati appunto nel processo di colata. Le statuine sono state colate con la tecnica della 'cera perduta', in seguito le formelle di terracotta sono state rotte per estrapolare il metallo solidificato. Recentemente, durante gli scavi diretti da L. Gallin presso il nuraghe Santa Barbara (Bauladu), sono stati ritrovati frammenti delle suddetti formelle.

Analisi chimiche, effettuate tramite spettrofotometria di assorbimento atomico, hanno rivelato che 10 dei 12 'bronzetti' sono composti da leghe di stagno e rame (9-13% Sn); un bronzetto soltanto contiene solo il 6% Sn. La dodicesima statuina contiene 6.5% Ag e solo 0.27% Sn. Soltanto una delle statuine composte da bronzo contiene più del 1% di piombo (6.5% Pb, 12% Sn).

Queste composizioni chimiche sono simili a quelle determinate da Balmuth, Tylecote et al., Riederer, e Craddock durante l'analisi degli oggetti nuragici delle collezioni non sarde. Gli Autori, comunque, hanno notato che le statuine possono essere etereogenee per quanto riguarda la loro composizione chimica e spesso ciò dipende da dove il campione è stato ottenuto. Questo è probabilmente dovuto all'aggiunta di stagno al rame fuso che risulta in una diffusione incompleta dello stagno durante il processo di fusione.

L'analisi a microsonda elettronica di una sezione metallografica di una statuina composta da argento e rame, mostra la presenza sia di argento che di piombo. Ciò sta ad indicare che l'argento è stato ottenuto dalla coppellazione del minerale di piombo. Gli Autori affermano che non esistono dati che mostrano l'esistenza di una metallurgica dell'argento in Sardegna, una tecnologia che sarà stata certamente conosciuta dalle culture dell'età del Bronzo. Paradossalmente in Sardegna esistono numerosi giacimenti di argento, ma ovviamente questi vengono utilizzati raramente in questo periodo, mentre lo stagno, che è molto più raro e viene spesso importato è frequentemente usato per la costruzione di utensili ordinari e per la costruzione dei preziosi bronzetti. Gli Autori concludono l'articolo sostenendo che è importante svolgere ulteriori studi archeometrici sulle collezioni presenti nei musei dell'isola.

Sardinia and History

David Ridgway and Francesca R. Serra Ridgway

Reflecting on his own writings about early Italy, David Randall-MacIver once remarked that 'if there are still scholars who protest that such things are not worth knowing, they can no longer have any excuse for asserting them to be unknowable' (Randall-MacIver 1928: 12). Nothing less will serve as a summary of what Miriam S. Balmuth has achieved in Sardinia. By her magnificent example in the field, in the library, and at the editorial desk, she has made it inexcusable for scholars in the English-speaking world to ignore the Sardinian dimension of any aspect of Mediterranean archaeology. We are grateful for this opportunity to salute *unu grande personazu in s'archeologia de sa Sardigna*, and we await with trepidation her critique of the modest contribution that follows.

It is well enough known that Sardinia is an essentially anhellenic island. As such, it has long been passed over by Classical specialists in favor of the almost infinitely richer pickings to be found elsewhere in the West, at the head of the Adriatic, in Etruria, and in South Italy and Sicily. The last decade, however, has seen a growing interest in the possible nature and extent of Sardinian relations with the Greek world. The discovery of Mycenaean pottery in the Nuragic fortress of Antigori (Sarroch-CA) (Ferrarese Ceruti 1981; Balmuth 1987; Bietti Sestieri 1988) was followed by the tentative revival (Gras 1985: 77-91) and final demolition (Cavanagh and Laxton 1987) of the alleged causal relationship between the Mycenaean and Nuragic stone structures that incorporate corbelled domes of apparently similar beehive shape. Prior to this, a sturdy local catalogue of the Etruscan and Greek vases that reached Sardinia during the Archaic period (Ugas and Zucca 1984, usefully reviewed by Tronchetti 1985) accompanied a number of valiant attempts (Breglia Pulci Doria 1981; Davison 1984; Davison 1986) to unravel the Greek traditions concerning 'the biggest island in the world' (Herodotus 1.170; 5.106; 6.2; but see Rowland 1974–75).

More recently, the possibility of post-Mycenaean and pre-Archaic Greek contact with Sardinia (and even perhaps of a limited Greek presence there) has been greatly increased by the discovery of a handful of Late Geometric/Early Protocorinthian sherds in an urban context at Phoenician Sulcis (Bernardini 1981–82; 1988). They would be at home in the later 8th century at the Euboean emporium of Pithekoussai on the island of Ischia in the Bay of Naples, a demonstrable fact that accords well with the previous independent identification *de visu* by the excavator of Pithekoussai, Giorgio Buchner, of the well-known painted cinerary urn and its lid from the Sulcis *tophet* as 'Made at Pithekoussai' (Coldstream 1968: 388, 429; Tronchetti 1979; D. Ridgway 1986: 179-80). A second Euboean(izing) lid has since turned up at Sulcis (Bartoloni 1985: 170 fig. 2); and we are grateful to Professor Massimo Pallottino for drawing our attention to the existence of a close parallel for the Sulcis urn in tomb 1 of the Tumulo della Speranza at Caere (Cerveteri) in Southern Etruria, excavated in 1952 and inexplicably concealed for the best part of 40 years (Rizzo 1989: 29-38, with figs. 58-60). The precise context of the 'new' urn was not recorded at the time of excavation (and in any case may not have survived); this important piece is said to be among the earliest items in the chronological range, c. 690/680–630/620 (Rizzo 1989: 30 n. 70, 33), represented by the material associated with the unknown number of depositions in the tomb. The fabric is identified as Caeretan, an interesting hypothesis that deserves to be tested, along with the proposed Pithekoussan identity of the Sulcis urn, by the type of physical analysis that has been applied in recent years to other Geometric pottery in the West (Deriu *et al.* 1985; 1986).

Prior to the publication of the sherds from Sulcis (Bernardini 1988), other (admittedly tenuous) links between Euboean Pithekoussai and the Phoenicians in Sardinia had already joined the somewhat stronger hints of early Phoenician interest in Pithekoussai itself (Buchner 1982; Buchner and Ridgway 1983; D. Ridgway 1986: 178-79) to prompt the following suspicion on the part of one of the present writers: 'news of the West may well have been the most valuable commodity that the Euboeans acquired in the East' (D. Ridgway 1986: 175). Largely as the result of major advances in the appreciation of Sardinian metalwork and of its Late Cypriot affinities (Lo Schiavo *et al.* 1985, see below), he has since felt able to re-state this position more explicitly:

> [the] first chapter of Western Greek history should be read as the last chapter in a long story of contact between the Cypro-Levantine world and Sardinia that was in full working order throughout the period between the beginning of the Greek Dark Age and the despatch of the first Euboean pendent semicircle skyphoi to the East (Ridgway 1990: 69).

The main assumptions here are two: (1) an Age that was Dark in Greece was not necessarily so everywhere else; and (2) the demise of Mycenaean long-distance trade in the 12th century need not have been bad for business between other parties. In other words, the concept of the 'awakening of Greece' in the mid-9th century (Coldstream 1977: 55-72) should not be taken to imply that everyone else had been asleep too.

The now familiar symbol of Greek revival at the end of the Dark Age, namely the pendent semicircle skyphos of Euboean type, has a geographical distribution (Coldstream 1977: 94 fig. 29) that provides an effective general illustration of renewed Greek interest in a Near Eastern (Cypro-Levantine) world that had never lost touch with the far West. This reading of the evidence finds a substantial measure of confirmation in the individual distribution maps of the six overlapping but successive types of pendent semicircle skyphoi that have emerged from Rosalinde Kearsley's (1989) careful analysis of the category. The Greek mainland and island sites make up the main area of concentration for her types 1 (Kearsley 1989: 134 fig. 45), 2, and 3 (Kearsley 1989: 135 fig. 46). Cyprus is represented from type 2 onwards and scores well—as does the Levant—with types 4 and 5 (Kearsley 1989: 138 fig. 47), although Euboea and the Cyclades still constitute an important focus of interest. It is difficult to see the distribution maps of these five types as anything other than the outward and visible sign of the gradual extension of Euboean maritime trade (Desborough 1976): the steady progress beyond the limits of the immediately surrounding region suggests precisely the degree of growing optimism—and, of course, success— required to underpin renaissances. A highly significant stage is reached with pendent semicircle skyphoi of Kearsley's type 6 (Kearsley 1989: 139 fig. 48, 142-145): 20 specimens come from the Levant, mainly Al Mina (but still including Cyprus); 12 from Euboea (Eretria and Lefkandi); and, for the first time, two from the west (one from Villasmundo in eastern Sicily, and one from the Villanovan cemetery of Quattro Fontanili at Veii in southern Etruria [Kearsley 1989: 67-70 cat. nos. 229, 237]).

And now, after an unfortunate false alarm (Ridgway 1989), a pendent semicircle skyphos has been discovered in Sardinia during the ninth (1990) campaign directed by Susanna Bafico for the Sassari Archaeological Superintendency in the Nuragic village of Sant'Imbenia overlooking the Baia di Porto Conte (Alghero-SS). From the brief preliminary notice (Bafico 1991, with illustrations), it is already clear that this remarkable find is part of a coherent context that extends to chevron and one-bird skyphoi of Euboean type, Phoenician plates and other forms, and amphorae that find good parallels in Tyrrhenian Italy: one of them contained a hoard (c. 44 kg) of plano-convex (bun) copper ingots. Surely much will be heard of Sant'Imbenia in the future; for the moment, we gladly acknowledge the generosity of the excavator and of her Superintendent, Fulvia Lo Schiavo, in sending us a drawing within days of the discovery. This, in turn, enabled Kearsley, to whom our best thanks are due also, to express the provisional opinion that the Sant'Imbenia skyphos has more in common with certain Cypriot examples of type 5 from Cyprus than it does with type 6. At the time of writing, the earliest piece of Greek or Greek-type painted Geometric pottery in the west thus comes not from a Villanovan cemetery in southern Etruria (cf. Bartoloni 1989), but from a Nuragic village on the northwest coast of Sardinia that was clearly a nodal point in an international commercial network from at least the late 9th century. We wonder, too, if the Sant'Imbenia skyphos is the only piece of Geometric painted pottery in the West that might have reached the West from Cyprus or the Levant.

With this in mind, we turn to Sir John Boardman's (1990) new and authoritative assessment of old and new discoveries of Greek Middle to Late Geometric pottery along the Syro-Phoenician coast, principally (from north to south) Tarsus, Al Mina, Tell Tainat, Ras el Bassit (see Courbin 1990), Tell Sukas and Tyre. Even on the cautious analysis prompted by a variety of factors (not least selectivity in both excavation and publication), and in the absence of a report on the excavations at Tell Tainat, it emerges that the density of Greek finds at Al Mina (apparently the port of Tell Tainat) is markedly higher than that registered at Tarsus and the sites to the south (Boardman 1990: 175 table 1). This naturally has important implications for the diagnosis of Al Mina's crucial role in the dissemination of Oriental artifacts and ideas to the 8th-century Greek world and, ultimately, in the whole Orientalizing revolution of Greek culture at home and in the west. Boardman is firmly of the opinion that no 'Phoenician' Iron Age finds in the western Mediterranean can be securely dated before about 800 BC. He dismisses as 'noisy' Frank Cross's (1986) arguments in favor of a rather earlier date for the Nora and Bosa inscriptions, and, though admitting as 'probable' the early introduction of metallurgical ideas from Cyprus to Sardinia, he discards it as effectively irrelevant in the absence of any evidence for 'important' continuity of east–west contacts 'after...the Late Bronze Age and its immediate aftermath' (Boardman 1990: 177). In Greece, on the other hand, Boardman recognizes Phoenician finds in contexts that can be dated significantly earlier than 800 BC by the application of 'our yardstick' (i.e. the Greek pottery sequence); he explains the primary concentration of such finds in Euboea not by a Phoenician predilection for the Euboean centers and their allied or dependent islands, but rather in terms of 'the out-going character' of the early Euboeans themselves, well-attested by their subsequent exploits in the west during the 8th century—which for Boardman (1990: 179) is 'the first really busy period of traffic' to the farthest west.

The declared object of the paper baldly and inadequately summarized above is to 'bring us closer to a more balanced indication of what happened, and even to some degree of why it happened' (Boardman 1990: 186). Our own object here is to suggest that this approach is entirely compatible with a less pessimistic view than Boardman's of the possibly wider significance of certain recent developments in the archaeology of Sardinia—more particularly in the archaeology of Sardinian metalworking. We feel bound to point out, too, that the nature of the archaeological record in Sardinia prior to 800 BC is not at all like that in contemporary Greece. The 10th- and 9th-century north Syrian and Phoenician luxury items listed by Boardman (1990: 177-78) from Athens, Knossos and Lefkandi come from readily datable funerary contexts of a kind that simply do not exist in Sardinia. There, chronological yardsticks are non-ceramic and non-Greek, and are only rarely encountered in hermetically-sealed associations: the Nuragic *tombe di giganti* were used for collective multi-period burials—and clearly re-used too, like the nuraghi themselves. It follows that the available schemes of Sardinian chronology for the period with which we are concerned here (e.g. Lilliu 1982, whence Lo Schiavo 1985: 5 table) are considerably less sensitive and detailed than the neatly labeled Aegean 'chests of drawers' derived from, say, the settlement and cemeteries at Lefkandi (Popham *et al.* 1980: xiii) where Submycenaean (c. 1100–1050 BC), Protogeometric (Early, Middle and Late together c. 1050–900 BC), and Sub-Protogeometric (I, c. 900–875 BC; II, c. 875–850 BC; III, c. 850–750 BC), and Late Geometric (c. 750–700 BC) account for a period that is actually slightly shorter than the contemporary First Lower (c. 1200–900 BC) and First Upper (c. 900–700 BC) Nuragic periods in the structural history of the Nuraghe Su Nuraxi at Barumini, corresponding to most of phases III and IV in Lilliu's sequence for the whole island. Even so, it can of course be argued that if Phoenician faience, glass, jewelry and fine bronze vessels had reached Sardinia in the 10th and 9th centuries, they would surely have come to light by now, as they have not, in excavations or at least in the massive collections of unassociated artifacts assembled during the last century. True, many of the latter will long since have found anonymity outside the island, but the largest, that of the indefatigable Canon Spano, is virtually all in the public domain and includes the almost 5000 pieces that he bequeathed to the (now) National Museum in Cagliari (Ridgway 1979–80: 56). We can only plead that the Sardinian archaeological record currently abounds in new and previously unsuspected features, ranging from the native large-scale stone statuary from Monti Prama (Cabras-OR) (Tronchetti 1986) to the imported Mycenaean and Geometric pottery mentioned above. This apart, it seems reasonable to ask whether the pre-800 BC Levantine relationship with Sardinia was in fact the same as the contemporary Levantine relationship with Greece, and whether the denizens of Nuragic Sardinia were 'outgoing' in the same way and with the same ends in mind as their Euboean contemporaries.

In both cases, we think not. The early introduction of metallurgical techniques from Cyprus to Sardinia is, in our view, rather more than 'probable', and so is the extensive practical application of these techniques over a long period of time, corresponding to the greater part of the four centuries that make up the Italian Late Bronze Age (c. 1300–900 BC) and, in part, to Late Cypriot III (c. 1200–1050 BC). A great deal of the evidence for this uncompromising statement has been gathered in an important paper (Lo Schiavo *et al.* 1985; not cited in Boardman 1990), of which we would single out the substantial sections devoted to double-axes, smithing tools, and tripod-stands as particularly relevant to our present purposes. Sardinia being Sardinia, closed finds and independently dated archaeological contexts are conspicuous by their absence; but in these three artifact categories the visual comparisons between Cyprus and Sardinia (and in the west *only* Sardinia) are numerous and striking. Thus, of the 16 massive bronze double-axes assigned to Lo Schiavo's type 1 and its variants, 10 have Sardinian proveniences and 3 more are in Sardinian museums; they find their closest parallels in the 12th-century Enkomi Weapon and Foundry hoards (Lo Schiavo *et al.* 1985: 14-22 [Lo Schiavo]). The no-less-remarkable 'kits' of Cypriot smithing tools—sledgehammers, 'Levantine' tongs, and charcoal shovels, otherwise unknown not only in the west but also in Greece—are again firmly associated with Late Cypriot III contexts at home (Lo Schiavo *et al.* 1985: 22-28 [Lo Schiavo]); so too are the *comparanda* for a handsome imported tripod-stand, dated to the first half of the 11th century and now in a private collection in Oristano (Lo Schiavo *et al.* 1985: 36-40 [Macnamara]).

We accept the approximate date of 1050 BC as a *terminus ante quem* for the reasonable use of the term 'Syro-Palestinian' to refer to people or artifacts (including bronze figurines) from the Levant, and as a *terminus post quem* for the similar use of 'Phoenician' (Lo Schiavo *et al.* 1985: 51 n. 48 [Macnamara]). 1050 BC is also the round date after which no further actual imports from Cyprus to the west are known until the colonizing age (Lo Schiavo *et al.* 1985: 63). Not least in view of the considerable pre-1050 Cypriot commitment to Sardinia, however, we do believe there is a good case for accepting that Sardinian bronzeworking continued both to flourish and to imitate Late Cypriot models to a significant extent after that date. Particularly clear examples of the results are the sophisticated tripod-stands from the votive deposit in the Grotta Pirosu at Su Benatzu (Santadi-CA) (Lo Schiavo *et al.* 1985: 42-45 [Macnamara]) and from the hoard in the British Museum, said to have been found at Santa Maria in Paulis (Ittiri-SS) (Macnamara *et al.* 1984; Lo Schiavo *et al.* 1985: 46-47 [Macnamara]), both undoubtedly made in Sardinia. On the present state of the evidence, it would naturally be excessive to assume that skilled metalworkers from Cyprus continued to visit (or emigrate to) the other copper-rich island after 1050 BC; but we feel that it is no less excessive to assume that Sardinia was suddenly and decisively excluded *sine die* from the Cypro-Levantine world-view in the second half of the 11th century. In fact, evidence for Sardinian participation in the international scene around and after 1050 BC is by no means lacking. Three examples must suffice: (1) Nuragic pottery has been found on the Aeolian island of Lipari in a context of local Ausonian II date (c. 1125–850 BC; Contu 1980); (2) the bronze hoard from Monte Sa Idda (Decimoputzu-CA) provides one of only two non-Atlantic find-spots for a Portuguese type of bronze spit, or *obelos*— the associations of the other, from a tomb at Amathus in Cyprus excavated in 1986, have been assigned to the later part of Cypro-Geometric I, c. 1000 BC or soon after (Karageorghis and Lo Schiavo 1989); and (3) a common native type of Sardinian pottery *askos* has been identified in tomb 2 at Khaniale Tekke near Knossos, with several burials in the c. 850–680 BC range (Cretan Protogeometric B-Early Orientalizing; Vagnetti 1989). These may, of course, be regarded as straws in the wind, of no cumulative importance. The same can hardly be said of certain new findings that concern one of the best-known and most controversial categories of artifact encountered in Sardinia.

The importance rightly attached to the presence in Sardinia of Cypriot-type smithing tools leads naturally to the actual raw material worked by the smiths. The most familiar form in which it occurs in the archaeological record is that of the oxhide ingot of copper, whole or fragmentary examples of which are now known from no fewer than 18 different sites (latest map in Lo Schiavo *et al.* 1990: 16-17). The shape is notoriously 'international'; and the same must surely be true of the pressures that, long before Boardman's 'first really busy' period of east–west traffic, were responsible for extending this degree of physical standardization from the Levant to the central Mediterranean (Niemeyer 1984: 10 Abb. 5). The archaeological situations at the Sardinian find-spots, old and new, have recently been reviewed by Lo Schiavo (in Lo Schiavo *et al.* 1990: 14-40); she gives good reasons for supposing that the use of oxhide ingots in the island has a *terminus post quem* in the 15th century and a *terminus ante quem* around 900 BC. As to the source of the copper itself, we can only relay the two main points that so far have been made in the course of on-going scientific investigations. The results of lead isotope analysis have been taken to indicate that the origin of the Sardinian examples should be sought in Cyprus (Gale and Stos-Gale 1987: 156-61; 1988: 375-83; this volume); metallographic, elemental (atomic absorption spectrometry) and statistical (principal components) analyses have been combined independently to show that the 73 sampled copper oxhide ingots from Sardinia most likely were derived from a single source of raw material, while bun ingots were made of copper from several different sources (Lo Schiavo *et al.* 1990: 203 [Muhly and Stech]).

These hypotheses are currently provisional and subject to reconsideration, and for this reason alone it seems premature to combine them with the archaeological evidence and conclude without further ado that Cyprus was still, after something like half a millennium, sending regular supplies of homogeneous copper to Sardinia as late as 900 BC. It is, after all, not impossible that the specimens from the latest Sardinian contexts are the remnants—carefully husbanded because highly prized?—of early stockpiling. The fact remains that, for whatever reason (and whatever the source of the copper), the 'international' ingot type survived long after 1050 BC in Sardinia, to be employed alongside the ubiquitous bun; arguments against the contemporaneity of oxhides and buns (Gale and Stos-Gale 1987: 163) are now difficult to sustain. The different purposes for which the two ingot types were intended are not clear; in our view, the possibilities might have involved recognition by interested parties of the handsome (and sometimes monogrammed) oxhides as raw material of higher purity than the buns obtained from recycled scrap—whether or not the distinction included, and was known to include, that between imported and locally obtained material. In the present provisional state of the scientific evidence, we prefer to stress that during their currency in Sardinia oxhide ingots of copper could well have been seen to have international connotations, and that their distribution and use within the island was wide in both space and time. Incidentally, we are not unduly perturbed by the apparent survival of the oxhide type in the far west for well over two centuries after its seeming disappearance in Cyprus around 1150 BC (Lo Schiavo *et al.* 1990: 207 [Muhly and Stech]); after that date, as our Edinburgh colleague Edgar Peltenburg kindly advises us, non-funerary evidence is significantly thinner in Cyprus than it is in contemporary Sardinia.

The early and large-scale transfer of metalworking technology from Cyprus to Sardinia, followed by its prolonged application there, seems to us to be the result of a relationship between the two islands that is not at all the same as that suggested by the presence before 800 BC of Phoenician trinkets in rich Greek graves. We do not insist that Cypriot–Sardinian contact was necessarily deeper or broader in any sense than its Phoenician–Greek counterpart, nor can we shed any real light on the ethnic identity of those who were responsible for initiating and maintaining the far western operation. Boardman (1990: 177) prudently requires to be 'reassured about the role of Cypriots as seagoers'; we ourselves are encouraged by Hans Georg Niemeyer's (1990: 476) tacit acceptance of 'Phoenician traders of the ninth and eighth centuries...[on]...the ancient sea routes to the West', and by the same author's thoughtful proposal that 8th- and 7th-century Phoenician settlements 'were designed and established only to consolidate and secure...early trade relationships which were threatened by the new and aggressive colonization movement of the Greeks' (Niemeyer 1990: 488). All told, we find it difficult to believe that the existence of Sardinian natural resources and of on-going Sardinian metallurgical operations were unknown in Cyprus and the Levant generally during the period corresponding to the Greek Dark Age.

Prominent among the Sardinian natural resources in question is iron, which is rare in Cyprus. It has recently been announced that the earliest piece of worked iron in the western Mediterranean occurs in the Nuraghe Antigori, where it is associated with a characteristic 'wish bone' handle of imported Late Cypriot II base ring ware (earlier than 1200 BC; Vagnetti and Lo Schiavo 1989: 227 [Lo Schiavo]). This discovery surely increases the range of possible motives for the early and continuing Cypriot commitment to Sardinia. Indeed, now that the Sardinian oxhide ingots of copper may turn out to be of Cypriot origin, it conjures up a picture of transactions precisely similar to one described by no less an authority than Athena herself: we refer to the occasion when, disguised as Mentes, doge of the Taphians, (s)he told Telemachus that (s)he and her/his ship's crew had put in at Ithaca on their way to Temesa to exchange their cargo of iron for copper (*Odyssey* 1.184; Zancani Montuoro 1969; Maddoli 1982, reviewed by Ridgway 1984; Snodgrass 1989: 29-30). In addition, as Lo Schiavo suggests (in Vagnetti and Lo Schiavo 1989: 227), the search for and processing *in loco* of iron ore by Cypriots would provide a most appropriate technological context for the early introduction to Sardinia of the lost-wax method of casting bronze, already available in the Levant and indispensable to the production of many local Sardinian bronze types.

Among the latter are, naturally, the human and animal figurines in the well-known class of *bronzetti nuragici*. Much past and current discussion of these attractive and highly collectable (and thus nearly always unassociated) pieces has centered on their chronology and style. After some wildly diverging early assessments (summarized in Lilliu 1966: 29-31), they were usually seen as inevitably dependent on the Geometric and Orientalizing traditions of Greece and Etruria and hence produced in the 7th to 6th centuries (with more or less prolonged *attardamenti*). Then the Villanovan context of one of these Nuragic figurines was unimpeachably assigned to the late 9th century (Bartoloni and Delpino 1975: 36-42), a date that was accepted without enthusiasm as the starting point for the whole category (Lilliu 1982: *passim*): but the figurine concerned was attributed subsequently to an *advanced* stage in the Uta-Abini series (Tore 1986). Meanwhile, one of us, invited by Miriam Balmuth to establish a reliable cultural and historical framework for the *bronzetti* in the British Museum for the 1983 Tufts colloquium, was unable to find any precedent in Iron Age Italy or Geometric Greece for the aesthetic and technical accomplishment of the Uta-Abini figurines (Serra Ridgway 1986). Interestingly enough, analogous conclusions were reached independently on the same occasion with regard to the Monti Prama statues (Bonfante 1986; B. Ridgway 1986; both include the 7th and 6th centuries in their surveys).

And now, in spite of the continuing scourge of pseudo-scholarly collectors, modern excavations (references in Ridgway 1988-89: 134) are beginning to provide the long-awaited contextual evidence for the currency of *bronzetti* prior to 900 BC. Although not yet universally accepted (e.g. Bernardini 1985), the implication is that ideas and models need no longer be regarded automatically as reaching Sardinia from or through the Italian peninsula. Thus, it becomes possible to recognize that a cultural and ideological milieu suited to the large-scale production of sophisticated luxury items such as the *bronzetti* is hardly likely to be found in the 8th century, when the Nuragic communities were under increasing pressure from rapacious Phoenician incomers. A more appropriate setting is not far to seek: that created by the outward-looking, active, and lively Nuragic aristocracies who commissioned the great achievements of Sardinian Late Bronze Age architecture (Lo Schiavo *et al.* 1985: 51-62 [Macnamara]); Serra Ridgway 1987).

The putative early search for, and exploitation of, iron in Sardinia by Cypriots or Phoenicians is, finally, reminiscent of one element in the story of pre- and early colonial Greek trade with the west: the mineral, and especially ferrous, resources of northern Etruria and the almost literally magnetic attraction they are traditionally supposed to have exerted on the first western Greeks (e.g. Coldstream 1977: 224)—who are represented in the archaeological record of Southern Etruria by the painted Greek (or Greek-type) Geometric pendent semicircle, chevron, and one-bird skyphoi (the same combination as that attested now at Sant'Imbenia) in the Villanovan cemeteries at Veii (Descoeudres and Kearsley 1983) during the generation immediately preceding the establishment of Pithekoussai. Studies of Nuragic items in Villanovan Etruria and of Villanovan items in Sardinia (most recently in Lo Schiavo and Ridgway 1987, with earlier references) show a clear concentration of Sardinian interest in the Tuscan Colline Metallifere from the Italian Final Bronze Age onwards. This being the case, we do not yet see any reason to revise the following statement, made by one of us in 1987:

> It seems increasingly possible that the earliest external and mutually beneficial assessment of the metallurgical potential of Villanovan Etruria was not planned in the Aegean or the East, *but in the West itself* and no further away than Sardinia (Ridgway 1988: 496, emphasis in original).

If this bears any relation to what actually happened, one conclusion is inescapable: the first western Greeks were not averse either to useful precedents or to good advice. Both commodities were abundantly available in the island known in their world as Ichnussa.

References

Bafico, S.
   1991   Greci e Fenici ad Alghero. *Archeo* 74 (aprile): 18.

Balmuth, M.S. (ed.)
   1987   *Studies in Sardinian Archaeology III. Nuragic Sardinia and the Mycenaean World.* BAR International Series 387. Oxford: British Archaeological Reports.

Bartoloni, G.
   1989   Veio nell'VIII secolo e le prime relazioni con l'ambiente greco. *Atti, Secondo Congresso Internazionale Etrusco, Firenze 26 maggio—2 giugno 1985*, I, 117-28. Roma: Giorgio Bretschneider.

Bartoloni, G., & F. Delpino
   1975   Un tipo di orciolo a lamelle metalliche: considerazioni sulla prima fase villanoviana. *Studi Etruschi* 43: 3-45.

Bartoloni, P.
   1985   Nuove testimonianze arcaiche da Sulcis. *Nuovo Bullettino Archeologico Sardo* 2: 167-92.

Bernardini, P.
   1981–82   Pithekoussai-Sulci. *Annali della Facoltà di Lettere e Filosofia, Università degli Studi di Perugia* 19: 11-20.
   1985   Osservazioni sulla bronzistica figurata sarda. *Nuovo Bullettino Archeologico Sardo* 2: 119-66.
   1988   S. Antioco, area del Cronicario (campagne di scavo 1983-86): L'insediamento fenicio. *Rivista di Studi Fenici* 16: 75-89.

Bietti Sestieri, A.M.
1988 The 'Mycenaean Connection' and its impact on the central Mediterranean societies. *Dialoghi di Archeologia* 6(1): 23-51.

Boardman, J.
1990 Al Mina and History. *Oxford Journal of Archaeology* 9: 169-90.

Bonfante, L.
1986 The Etruscan connection. In M.S. Balmuth (ed.), *Studies in Sardinian Archaeology, Volume II: Sardinia in the Mediterranean*, 73-83. Ann Arbor: University of Michigan Press.

Breglia Pulci Doria, L.
1981 La Sardegna arcaica tra tradizioni euboiche ed attiche. *Nouvelle contribution à étude de la société et de la colonisation eubéennes*, 61-95. Cahiers du Centre Jean Bérard 6. Naples: Institut Français de Naples.

Buchner, G.
1982 Die Beziehungen zwischen der euböischen Kolonie Pithekoussai auf der Insel Ischia und dem nordwestsemitischen Mittelmeerraum in der zweiten Hälfte des 8. Jhs. v. Chr. In H.G. Niemeyer (ed.), *Phönizier im Westen: Die Beiträge des Internationalen Symposiums über 'Die Phönizische Expansion im Westlichen Mittelmeerraum' in Köln vom 24. bis 27. April 1979*, 277-98. Madrider Beiträge 8. Mainz am Rhein: Philipp von Zabern.

Buchner, G., & D. Ridgway
1983 Pithekoussai 944. *Annali, Istituto Universitario Orientale, Napoli: Archeologia e Storia Antica* 5: 1-9.

Cavanagh, W.G., & R.R. Laxton
1987 Notes on building techniques in Mycenaean Greece and Nuragic Sardinia. In M.S. Balmuth (ed.), *Studies in Sardinian Archaeology III. Nuragic Sardinia and the Mycenaean World*, 39-55. BAR International Series 387. Oxford: British Archaeological Reports.

Coldstream, J.N.
1968 *Greek Geometric Pottery: A Survey of Ten Local Styles and Their Chronology*. London: Methuen.
1977 *Geometric Greece*. London: Ernest Benn.

Contu, E.
1980 Ceramica sarda di età nuragica a Lipari. In L. Bernabò Brea and M. Cavalier (eds.), *Meligunìs Lipàra IV: L'acropoli di Lipari nella preistoria*, 827-36. Palermo: Flaccovio.

Courbin, P.
1990 Bassit-Posidaion in the Early Iron Age. In J.-P. Descoeudres (ed.), *Greek Colonists and Native Populations. Proceedings of the First Australian Congress of Classical Archaeology Held in Honour of Emeritus Professor A.D. Trendall, Sydney 9—14 July 1985*, 503-509. Oxford: Clarendon Press; Canberra: Humanities Research Centre.

Cross, F.M.
1986 Phoenicians in the West: the early epigraphic evidence. In M.S. Balmuth (ed.), *Studies in Sardinian Archaeology, Volume II: Sardinia in the Mediterranean*, 117-30. Ann Arbor: University of Michigan Press.

Davison, J.M.
1984 Greeks in Sardinia: the confrontation of archaeological evidence and literary testimonia. In M.S. Balmuth and R.J. Rowland, Jr (eds.), *Studies in Sardinian Archaeology*, 67-82. Ann Arbor: University of Michigan Press.
1986 Greek presence in Sardinia: Myth and Speculation. In M.S. Balmuth (ed.), *Studies in Sardinian Archaeology, Volume II: Sardinia in the Mediterranean*, 187-200. Ann Arbor: University of Michigan Press.

Deriu, A., F. Boitani & D. Ridgway
1985 Provenance and firing techniques of Geometric pottery from Veii: A Mössbauer investigation. *Annual of the British School of Archaeology at Athens* 80: 139-50.

Deriu, A., G. Buchner & D. Ridgway
1986 Provenance and firing techniques of Geometric pottery from Pithekoussai: A Mössbauer investigation. *Annali, Istituto Universitario Orientale, Napoli: Archeologia e Storia Antica* 8: 99-116.

Desborough, V.
1976 The background to Euboean participation in early Greek maritime enterprise. In *Tribute to an Antiquary: Essays Presented to Marc Fitch by Some of his Friends*, 25-40. London: Emmison and Stephens.

Descoeudres, J.-P., & R. Kearsley
1983 Greek pottery at Veii: another look. *Annual of the British School of Archaeology at Athens* 78: 9-53.

Ferrarese Ceruti, M.L.
1981 Documenti micenei nella Sardegna meridionale. In E. Atzeni et al., *Ichnussa: La Sardegna dalle origini all'età classica*, 605-12. Milano: Libri Scheiwiller.

Gale, N.H., & Z.A. Stos-Gale
1987 Oxhide ingots from Sardinia, Crete and Cyprus and the Bronze Age copper trade: new scientific evidence. In M.S. Balmuth (ed.), *Studies in Sardinian Archaeology III. Nuragic Sardinia and the Mycenaean World*, 135-78. BAR International Series 387. Oxford: British Archaeological Reports.
1988 Recent evidence for a possible Bronze Age metal trade between Sardinia and the Aegean. In E.B. French and K.A. Wardle (eds.), *Problems in Greek Prehistory: Papers Presented at the Centenary Conference of the British School of Archaeology at Athens, Manchester, April 1986*, 349-84. Bristol: Bristol Classical Press.

Gras, M.
1985 *Trafics Tyrrhéniens Archaïques*. Bibliothèque des écoles françaises d'Athènes et de Rome 258. Rome: Ecole française de Rome.

Karageorghis, V., & F. Lo Schiavo
1989 A West Mediterranean obelos from Amathus. *Rivista di Studi Fenici* 17(1): 15-29.

Kearsley, R.
1989 *The Pendent Semicircle Skyphos: A Study of its Development and Chronology and an Examination of it as Evidence for Euboean Activity at Al Mina*. Bulletin Supplement 44. London: Institute of Classical Studies.

Lilliu, G.
1966 *Sculture della Sardegna Nuragica*. Cagliari: La Zattera.
1982 *La Civiltà Nuragica*. Sardegna Archeologica: Studi e Monumenti 1. Sassari: Carlo Delfino.

Lo Schiavo, F.
1985 *Nuragic Sardinia in its Mediterranean Setting: Some Recent Advances* [Munro Lectures 1982]. Department of Archaeology Occasional Paper 12. Edinburgh: University of Edinburgh.

Lo Schiavo, F., E. Macnamara & L. Vagnetti
1985   Late Cypriot imports to Italy and their influence on local bronzework. *Papers of the British School at Rome* 53: 1-71.

Lo Schiavo, F., R. Maddin, J. Merkel, J.D. Muhly & T. Stech
1990   *Analisi Metallurgiche e Statistiche sui Lingotti di Rame della Sardegna/Metallographic and Statistical Analyses of Copper Ingots from Sardinia.* Soprintendenza ai Beni Archeologici per le provincie di Sassari e Nuoro, Quaderni 17. Ozieri: Il Torchietto.

Lo Schiavo, F., & D. Ridgway
1987   La Sardegna e il Mediterraneo occidentale allo scorcio del II millennio. *La Sardegna nel Mediterraneo fra il Secondo e il Primo Millennio a.C. Atti del II Convegno di Studi, Selargius-Cagliari 27-30 novembre 1986*, 391-418. Cagliari: Amministrazione Provinciale di Cagliari.

Macnamara, E., D. Ridgway & F.R. Serra Ridgway
1984   *The Bronze Hoard from S. Maria in Paulis, Sardinia.* British Museum Occasional Paper 45. London: British Museum.

Maddoli, G. (ed.)
1982   *Temesa e il Suo Territorio: Atti del Colloquio di Perugia e Trevi, 30-31 maggio 1981.* Taranto: Istituto per la Storia e l'Archeologia della Magna Grecia.

Niemeyer, H.G.
1984   Die Phönizier und die Mittelmeerwelt im Zeitalter Homers. *Jahrbuch des Römisch-Germanischen Zentralmuseums, Mainz* 31: 3-94.
1990   The Phoenicians in the Mediterranean: A non-Greek model for expansion and settlement in antiquity. In J.-P. Descoeudres (ed.), *Greek Colonists and Native Populations. Proceedings of the First Australian Congress of Classical Archaeology Held in Honour of Emeritus Professor A.D. Trendall, Sydney 9—14 July 1985*, 469-89. Oxford: Clarendon Press; Camberra: Humanities Research Centre.

Popham, M.R., L.H. Sackett & P.G. Themelis
1980   *Lefkandi I: The Iron Age. The Settlement; The Cemeteries.* The British School of Archaeology at Athens, Supplementary volume 11. London: Thames and Hudson.

Randall-MacIver, D.
1928   *Italy before the Romans.* Oxford: Oxford University Press.

Ridgway, B.S.
1986   Mediterranean comparanda for the statues from Monti Prama. In M.S. Balmuth (ed.), *Studies in Sardinian Archaeology, Volume II: Sardinia in the Mediterranean*, 61-72. Ann Arbor: University of Michigan Press.

Ridgway, D.
1979-80   Archaeology in Sardinia and Etruria, 1974-1979. *Archaeological Reports for 1979-80*: 54-70.
1984   Review of G. Maddoli (ed.), *Temesa e il Suo Territorio: Atti del Colloquio di Perugia e Trevi, 30-31 maggio 1981* (Taranto: Istituto per la Storia e l'Archeologia della Magna Grecia, 1982). *Classical Review* 34: 278-80.
1986   Sardinia and the first western Greeks. In M.S. Balmuth (ed.), *Studies in Sardinian Archaeology, Volume II: Sardinia in the Mediterranean*, 173-85. Ann Arbor: University of Michigan Press.
1988   Western Geometric pottery: new light on interactions in Italy. In J. Christiansen and T. Melander (eds.), *Proceedings of the Third Symposium on Ancient Greek and Related Pottery, Copenhagen 31 August—4 September 1987*, 489-505. Copenhagen: Nationalmusseet, Ny Carlsberg Glyptotek, Thorvaldsens Museum.
1988-89   Archaeology in Sardinia and South Italy, 1983-88. *Archaeological Reports for 1988-1989*: 130-47.
1989   Nota di rettifica sul frammento ceramico THT 81/6/6 da Tharros. *Rivista di Studi Fenici* 17: 141-44.
1990   The first western Greeks and their neighbours, 1935-1985. In J.-P. Descoeudres (ed.), *Greek Colonists and Native Populations. Proceedings of the First Australian Congress of Classical Archaeology Held in Honour of Emeritus Professor A.D. Trendall, Sydney 9—14 July 1985*, 61-72. Oxford: Clarendon Press; Canberra: Humanities Research Centre.

Rizzo, M.A.
1989   Ceramica etrusco-geometrica da Caere. *Miscellanea Ceretana* 1: 9-39. Quaderni del Centro di Studio per l'Archeologia Etrusco-Italica 17. Roma: C.N.R.

Rowland, R.J., Jr
1974-75   The biggest island in the world. *Classical World* 68: 438-39.

Serra Ridgway, F.R.
1986   Nuragic bronzes in the British Museum. In M.S. Balmuth (ed.), *Studies in Sardinian Archaeology, Volume II: Sardinia in the Mediterranean*, 85-101. Ann Arbor: University of Michigan Press.
1987   Commentary: some remarks on A.M. Bisi's paper/Osservazioni a proposito della relazione di A.M. Bisi. In M.S. Balmuth (ed.), *Studies in Sardinian Archaeology III. Nuragic Sardinia and the Mycenaean World*, 251-55. BAR International Series 387. Oxford: British Archaeological Reports.

Snodgrass, A.M.
1989   The coming of the Iron Age in Greece: Europe's earliest Bronze/Iron transition. In M.L. Stig Sørensen and R. Thomas (eds.), *The Bronze Age—Iron Age Transition in Europe: Aspects of Continuity and Change in European Societies c. 1200 to 500 BC*, 22-35. BAR International Series 483. Oxford: British Archaeological Reports.

Tore, G.
1986   Contribution to discussion at the colloquium Nuragic Sardinia and the Mycenaean World/Sardegna Nuragica e Il Mondo Miceneo, American Academy in Rome, September 22-24, 1986.

Tronchetti, C.
1979   Per la cronologia del *tophet* di S. Antioco. *Rivista di Studi Fenici* 7: 201-205.
1985   Review of G. Ugas and R. Zucca, *Il Commercio Arcaico in Sardegna: importazioni etrusche e greche (620-480 a.C.)* (Cagliari: Angelo Viali, 1984). *Annali, Istituto Universitario Orientale, Napoli: Archeologia e Storia Antica* 7: 209-19.
1986   Nuragic statuary from Monti Prama. In M.S. Balmuth (ed.), *Studies in Sardinian Archaeology, Volume II: Sardinia in the Mediterranean*, 41-59. Ann Arbor: University of Michigan Press.

Ugas, G., & R. Zucca
1984   *Il Commercio Arcaico in Sardegna: importazioni etrusche e greche (620-480 a.C.).* Cagliari: Angelo Viali.

Vagnetti, L.
1989 A Sardinian askos from Crete. *Annual of the British School of Archaeology at Athens* 84: 355-60.

Vagnetti, L., & F. Lo Schiavo
1989 Late Bronze Age long distance trade in the Mediterranean: the role of the Cypriots. In E. Peltenburg (ed.), *Early Society in Cyprus*, 217-43. Edinburgh: Edinburgh University Press.

Zancani Montuoro, P.
1969 Dov'era Temesa? *Rendiconti dell'Accademia di Archeologia, Lettere e Belle Arti di Napoli* 44: 11-23.

Riassunto

Riesaminando ultimamente (1990) il contributo di Al Mina alla diffusione del fenomeno orientalizzante nel mondo ellenico, John Boardman ha messo in rilievo l'assenza nel Mediterraneo occidentale di rinvenimenti 'fenici' certamente più antichi dell'800 a.C., sostenendo che mancano pertanto testimonianze di una continuità di contatti 'importante' fra Oriente ed Occidente dopo la Tarda Età del Bronzo. Nel presente articolo si prende in esame la dimensione sarda di tale ipotesi, con particolare riferimento a recenti studi dedicati al perdurare delle influenze tardo-cipriote nella cultura sarda.

Si considera come i rapporti fra Cipro e la Sardegna nel periodo 1050-800 a.C. siano diversi da quelli intercorrenti alla stessa epoca fra il Levante e l'Egeo. Questi ultimi sono infatti caratterizzati dalla presenza di oggetti di lusso fenici e nord-siriaci in contesti funerari di Atene, Knossos e Lefkandi particolarmente ricchi, sicuramente datati al decimo e nono secolo. Per la Sardegna viceversa le testimonianze archeologiche suggeriscono un modello di contatto specializzato Oriente-Occidente (Cipro-Sardegna) riguardante artigiani metallurghi e i loro presumibili committenti. Benché non si registrino effettive importazioni da Cipro in Sardegna dopo il 1050 a.C., la componente tecnologica e stilistica cipriota riconoscibile nella metallurgia sarda prima di tale data è unica, sia per ampiezza sia per profondità; in nessun altro sito fuori dell'Isola, nemmeno in Grecia, si ritrovano attrezzi da fonderia del Tardo Cipriota III (1200-1050 a.C.) come si incontrano in diverse località sarde. Gli Autori accettano l'opinione più volte espressa che le tradizioni metallurgiche di origine cipriota restarono in vita in Sardegna ben oltre il 1050: come è chiaramente dimostrato, per esempio, dai raffinati sostegni tripodi della Grotta Pirosu a Su Benatzu o di S. Maria in Paulis.

E se per la produzione di questi, come di altri manufatti presenti in Sardegna dopo il 1050, non è necessario invocare la presenza *in loco* di bronzisti ciprioti immigrati, gli Autori ritengono tuttavia ingiustificato presumere che dopo il 1050 la Sardegna sia semplicemente scomparsa dal campo visivo cipro-levantino. Da un lato infatti è da annoverare fra le risorse naturali dell'Isola il ferro (notoriamente raro in Cipro), di cui nel nuraghe Antigori si è trovato un frammento lavorato, in un contesto per il quale le associazioni cipriote indicano una data anteriore al 1200 a.C. La presenza sarda sulla scena internazionale palesemente non cessa, d'altronde, con il 1050: si fa riferimento a ceramica nuragica rinvenuta a Lipari in un contesto locale dell'Ausonio II (1125-850 a.C.); ad un *obelos* di bronzo del ripostiglio di Monte sa Idda appartenente ad un tipo rappresentato fuori dell'area atlantica solamente ad Amatunte, in un contesto del Geometrico Cipriota I (dal 1000 a.C.); e ad un *askos* fittile sardo recentemente identificato in una tomba collettiva di Khaniale Tekke presso Knossos datata nell'ambito 850-690 a.C. Si osserva inoltre che i lingotti di rame del caratteristico tipo 'internazionale' *oxhide*, importati o no da Cipro, circolano in Sardegna fino al 900 a.C.; e si mette in evidenza come tale data sia ormai dimostrata troppo bassa per fungere da *terminus post quem* per l'inizio della produzione dei noti bronzetti figurati nuragici.

Tutto considerato, non sorprende che sia stato recentemente (1990) rinvenuto nel villaggio nuragico di S. Imbenia uno skyphos a semicerchi pendenti di stile euboico, che non solo rappresenta il più antico esemplare di ceramica dipinta geometrica importato in Occidente, ma—ciò che è ancor più significativo—è stato anche riconosciuto come tipologicamente affine ad esemplari trovati in Cipro. Se ne conclude che il primo capitolo della storia dei Greci d'Occidente non rappresenta, come suggerisce Boardman, 'il primo periodo di intensa attività' nei traffici Oriente-Occidente, giacché esso fu preceduto da una lunga storia, di cui può anzi essere letto come capitolo conclusivo, di contatti fra il mondo cipro-levantino e la Sardegna, che erano in piena funzione durante il cosiddetto Medioevo ellenico, e nell'ambito dei quali è perfino pensabile che sia avvenuto il primo riconoscimento esterno, reciprocamente proficuo e originato in Sardegna, del potenziale metallurgico dell'Etruria stessa.

Osservazioni sulla Ceramica Attica di Sardegna

Carlo Tronchetti

Introduzione

Parlare della ceramica attica della Sardegna significa, sostanzialmente, parlare della Sardegna durante il periodo punico. Infatti, tranne un solo pezzo sicuramente databile in epoca fenicia (anteriore, cioé, alla metà del VI sec. a.C.), tutti gli altri possono assegnarsi alla fase storica caratterizzata dalla dominazione cartaginese dell'Isola.

Questo, naturalmente, a grandi linee. In realtà esiste una piccola serie di pezzi, databili fra il 550 ed il 520 a.C., la quale appartiene cronologicamente al complesso periodo che possiamo definire di interregno fra la Sardegna fenicia e la Sardegna punica. Non siamo ancora in grado di puntualizzare con esattezza quando avviene il momento di trapasso tra queste due fasi storiche, e probabilmente non lo saremo mai; così, convenzionalmente, si pone come elemento dirimente i due periodi la data del primo trattato fra Roma e Cartagine del 509 a.C. Dopo tale anno la Sardegna è sicuramente punica; prima del 550 a.C. i Fenici vi hanno una incontrastata presenza; nei decenni intermedi avvengono le lotte dei Cartaginesi per impossessarsi dell'Isola. Se i materiali attici importati durante quegli anni debbano assegnarsi alla componente fenicia ovvero a quella punica è problema non facile a risolvere e che, con ogni verosimiglianza, non può ridursi ad una soluzione univoca.

Il vasellame ateniese che giunge in Sardegna dal VI sino alla fine del IV sec a.C. si distribuisce nelle tre grandi categorie della ceramica attica, e cioè: vasi a figure nere; vasi a figure rosse; vasi a vernice nera. Attorno ad essi, con edizioni di materiali, considerazioni specifiche su singoli esemplari, esami più o meno generali su specifici centri o sull'intera isola, già è stato scritto in diverse sedi da diversi Autori, cui faremo riferimento in seguito, e pertanto abbiamo a disposizione una ampia messe di dati su cui basarci per tentare di proporre linee di interpretazione del significato della presenza di questo vasellame nel contesto della società punica sarda, o meglio dei significati e delle funzioni che la ceramica attica assume nei diversi centri punici dell'isola.

Per dare una certa omogeneità al lavoro, ci si è basati, nelle analisi, su alcuni centri principali (elencati appresso) che hanno restituito materiali significativi, tralasciando i ritrovamenti sporadici ed anche quelli di cui si hanno notizie solo ufficiose, senza edizione scientifica dei materiali, ovvero sui quali lo scrivente non ha potuto effettuare una verifica personale. Naturalmente, però, di tutti questi dati si è tenuto conto per le considerazioni di carattere generale.

Il periodo arcaico

Non molto di più che una citazione deve essere spesa per l'anfora tirrenica proveniente da Tharros attribuita al Pittore di Timiades. Nonostante siano sorti in merito pareri discordi (Carpenter 1984), continuo a ritenere i vasi tirrenici di produzione attica; la redistribuzione del vaso in Sardegna da una città costiera dell'Etruria meridionale mi pare, più che verosimile, certa. Il pezzo rientra così nell'ottica dei rapporti: Fenici di Sardegna-Etruria meridionale, già più volte delineata dallo scrivente (Tronchetti 1988: 41-88).

Già sopra, abbiamo accennato alla situazione dei materiali attici giunti in Sardegna nei decenni immediatamente posteriori alla metà del VI secolo. Questi sono pochissimi e concentrati in pochi punti. Come detto, non siamo in grado di sapere se siano dovuti al commercio fenicio ancora esistente ovvero a quello punico legato alla presenza delle truppe nell'isola. L'ipotesi che vede in questi materiali e negli altri attici tardo-arcaici la testimonianza delle teste di ponte puniche, da individuarsi in centri urbani fenici a loro favorevoli (se non addirittura alleati), può sostanzialmente essere accolta come ipotesi di lavoro, ma forse più per il periodo tardo-arcaico che per quello precedente. Così preferiamo lasciare sospeso il problema per quanto riguarda i pochi frammenti delle Coppe dei Piccoli Maestri. Questi, proprio per la loro frammentarietà, dimostrano la loro appartenenza a contesti di abitato, mentre l'anfora tirrenica precedente proveniva senz'altro da una sepoltura, dove si era conservata integra. Assai di più possiamo dire per il periodo tardo-arcaico, ormai sicuramente punico.

Esaminando dal punto di vista della distribuzione delle forme fra necropoli ed abitati, possiamo vedere come questi ultimi offrano una gamma di sette fogge in otto località rispetto alle dieci in cinque necropoli. Negli abitati predominano assolutamente le forme per bere (coppe e coppe-*skyphoi*) sia a figure nere che a vernice nera, presenti in sette degli otto siti, seguite dalle lucerne; esemplari di altre forme sono sporadici.

Anche nelle necropoli il vasellame per bere è in buon numero, con coppe (una delle quali a figure rosse), coppe-*skyphoi* e *skyphoi* in quattro siti, ed anche le lucerne sono ben presenti assieme a vasetti per contenere olio profumato (*lekythoi*, *aryballoi*, *alabastra*) ed alcuni esemplari di forme chiuse (anfore, *oinochoai*).

In generale, quindi, si può affermare che le importazioni attiche del periodo arcaico si riferiscono in misura precipua alla sfera del simposio (vasi per bere, per conservare e per versare) sia negli abitati che nelle necropoli; in queste ultime si trovano anche in misura rilevante vasetti di prevalente destinazione funeraria come le *lekythoi*; le lucerne, invece, sono attestate in buon numero in entrambe le situazioni.

Ancora, si può rilevare come l'incremento dei ritrovamenti porti al rafforzarsi della constatazione della sostanziale assenza della grande produzione attica a figure rosse tardo-arcaica. Solo una coppa è presente, e di qualità mediocre. Questo fattore, già notato in altra sede (Tronchetti 1985b), è tanto più peculiare in quanto, in periodo tardo-arcaico, con ogni verosimiglianza, la massima parte del materiale attico importato viene redistribuito in Sardegna ancora tramite le relazioni commerciali con le grandi città costiere dell'Etruria meridionale, delle quali è appena necessario ricordare la straordinaria ricchezza di capolavori della ceramica attica a figure rosse. Non è agevole trovare una spiegazione ad un tale fenomeno, per il quale, allo stato attuale dei fatti, forse conviene rifarsi al concetto di 'gusto', opportunamente tirato in ballo da Morel (1985: 36) proprio per la Sardegna.

Il V secolo

La carenza di vasellame figurato prosegue poi per quasi tutto il V secolo. Anche se i recenti ritrovamenti negli abitati dei centri punici (Zucca 1987: 191-99; Tronchetti 1990: *passim*) ci significano una presenza di vasi figurati sino a pochi anni or sono insospettata, essi sono pur sempre in larghissima minoranza rispetto a quelli a vernice nera. Allo scorcio del secolo si può rilevare un incremento dei vasi figurati, grazie al relativamente consistente arrivo delle *lekythoi* ariballiche decorate in diverse maniere, ma prevalentemente con una palmetta sul lato opposto all'ansa. Tali vasetti si propongono in quantità maggioritaria nelle necropoli, ma anche negli abitati se ne trovano esemplari. La larga diffusione delle *lekythoi* ariballiche e del loro contenuto di olio profumato si nota osservandone la presenza, sia pure con esemplari isolati, in centri interni, di non particolare rilevanza in questo periodo, come il villaggio sorto sopra le strutture nuragiche di Barumini e l'insediamento presso il nuraghe Ortu Còmidu di Sardara.

Anche se non in rilevante quantità, il vasellame attico inizia pure ad essere presente nella Sardegna settentrionale. Globalmente la ceramica di V secolo, sia a vernice nera che a figure rosse, si distribuisce in 15 fogge per 6 abitati, mentre 16 forme si rinvengono ancora in 6 necropoli.

Fra il vasellame da mensa predominano le coppe, fra cui la presenza più importante è data dalla *stemless inset-lip* dei decenni antecedenti la metà del secolo, mentre alla fine iniziano ad apparire i piatti da pesce. Pochi sono gli esemplari delle coppe appartenenti alla *delicate class*, anche se forse vi si possono assegnare alcuni frammenti di fondi decorati, mentre in misura maggiore si identificano le bolsal. Fra gli *skyphoi*, quelli decorati prevalgono su quelli interamente verniciati; una presenza importante è data dai pezzi della classe di Saint Valentin, rappresentata anche da *kantharoi*. Pressoché esclusivamente rinvenute in sepolture sono le *lekanides*, legate alla sfera muliebre. I vasi di grandi dimensioni non sembrano avere goduto di particolare fortuna. A parte le *oinochoai*, sono attestati crateri, ma sino ad ora, solo a Neapolis e Tharros.

Se le forme trovate negli abitati e nelle necropoli sono sostanzialmente le stesse, ben diverso è l'aspetto che abbiamo quando esaminiamo i rapporti proporzionali fra le singole fogge. Purtroppo, però, lo stato dei ritrovamenti non ci consente, per il V secolo, di effettuare una disamina approfondita delle varie *facies* dei singoli centri e così ci dobbiamo limitare a rilevare come il servito da mensa (coppe in senso lato, piatti, *oinochoai*) sia presente in maggior numero negli abitati, mentre le *lekythoi* e le *lekythoi* ariballiche e le *lekanides* lo siano nelle necropoli. Al solito le lucerne si distribuiscono equamente nelle due situazioni.

Possiamo notare l'elevata frammentazione in forme della ceramica importata. Complessivamente, fra abitati e necropoli, i vasi si distribuiscono in ben 19 fogge. Certamente alcune sono assimilabili per funzione (*lekythoi* e *lekythoi* ariballiche; coppe, coppe-*skyphoi*, *skyphoi*, *kantharoi*), ma il dato che ci significa una produzione così parcellizzata è significativo, non solo per i centri importatori, ma anche in relazione all'organizzazione produttiva del centro esportatore, Atene.

Un elemento costantemente rilevabile ovunque è l'accrescersi delle presenze di ceramica attica durante il corso del V secolo. Da un numero abbastanza limitato si passa via via a quantità sempre maggiori. La seconda metà del secolo vede un incremento che si può quantificare in circa quattro volte il numero dei pezzi attestati nel primo cinquantennio.

Ciò sembra andare di pari passo con la progressiva ellenizzazione che si intravede insinuarsi in diversi aspetti del mondo punico: dai culti, con l'introduzione della venerazione per Demetra e Kore, agli schemi iconografici, rilevabili in special modo nelle raffigurazioni delle stele dei *tophet* (Moscati 1986).

In sostanza ci pare di poter affermare che siamo dinanzi ad un diffondersi del consumo di sostanze profumate esotiche (il contenuto delle *lekythoi* ariballiche) e ad un affermarsi del vasellame attico come servito da mensa 'di lusso', con prevalenza dei vasi per bere (coppe, *skyphoi*, *kantharoi*) rispetto ai piatti per mangiare. Le bevande che venivano consumate dovevano essere, però, locali, dal momento che non abbiamo praticamente attestazioni dell'importazione di contenitori anforici greci.

Il IV secolo

Con il IV secolo prosegue l'accrescersi delle importazioni di ceramica attica in Sardegna. Certamente l'utilizzo delle *lekythoi* ariballiche continua nei suoi primi anni, a fianco di pochi altri pezzi decorati a figure rosse: *askoi*, coppe e *skyphoi*, in numero assai ridotto. La gran massa del vasellame è adesso a vernice nera. Possiamo riscontrare una notevole standardizzazione del repertorio delle forme vascolari: in totale sono 10, che si distribuiscono in 9 fogge per 7 abitati, mentre in 5 necropoli si trovano 8 forme.

Il repertorio si addensa ancora di più sul servito da mensa, per mangiare e bere. Le forme predominanti fra le coppe sono quelle denominate L. 21 (Tavola 1) e L. 22 (Tavola 2), quest'ultime in prevalenza, e le bolsal (Tavola 3), accompagnate dalle coppette L. 21/25 (Tavola 4); più specificatamente per la consumazione del cibo solido sono destinati i piattini (Tavola 5) ed i piatti da pesce (Tavola 6). A fianco di un notevole numero di lucerne si trovano gli *askoi-gutti*, destinati a contenere l'olio per riempirle.

Praticamente queste forme coprono la quasi totalità delle importazioni di ceramica attica, anche se non dobbiamo dimenticare altri tipi di coppette e di coppe, presenti in quantità ridottissime, così come gli *skyphoi*.

Anche solo osservando la situazione generale, prima di passare ad esaminare partitamente i singoli centri, si possono rilevare interessanti dati di *trend*. Scompaiono pressocchè interamente gli olii profumati esotici, ma non il consumo di olio straniero, utilizzato per le lucerne. Questo doveva avvenire, comunque, a fianco di un cospicuo utilizzo di risorse locali, fatto, questo, significatoci dall'alto numero di lucerne fabbricate *in loco* che dovevano bruciare combustibile prodotto nell'isola: olio di olivi sardi ovvero olio di lentischio.

Scompaiono anche i sia pur pochi esemplari di brocche e brocchette, mentre si affermano in modo notevole i piatti, in precedenza assenti. Le fogge del piattino con orlo arrotondato (*rolled-rim*) e del piatto da pesce (che trova significative concordanze strutturali con i piatti ombelicati fenici prima e punici poi) sono presenti in misura più o meno abbondante pressocché ovunque. In special modo il piatto da pesce gode di una fortuna incredibile, dando origine ad una lunga serie di imitazioni presso officine ceramiche sarde.

Fra le coppe un'analoga fortuna viene incontrata dalle L. 22. Anche se deve essere sfumata, con le nuove acquisizioni di scavo, la mia posizione che ne faceva un elemento assolutamente dominante e caratterizzante della *facies* delle importazioni ceramiche attiche nell'area punica sud-occidentale del Mediterraneo ed in special modo nella Sardegna (Bartoloni e Tronchetti 1981: 116-17), appare indubbio che la forma gode di una forte popolarità. Questa non si evince solo dal numero e dalla diffusione degli esemplari importati, ma, e potrei dire soprattutto, dalla quantità di imitazioni che vengono fabbricate in diversi opifici, e che iniziano durante lo scorcio del IV secolo per coprire poi tutto il III, quando la ceramica attica è ormai assente dai mercati sardi. È da riscontrare come queste imitazioni seguano abbastanza fedelmente l'evoluzione della forma originale, così come è stata individuata, e cioé con un progressivo inclinarsi esterno delle pareti rispetto al labbro. Sono piuttosto poche le coppe locali che conservano la parete con la curva ad arco di cerchio, tipica degli esemplari databili attorno alla metà del secolo, mentre la assoluta maggioranza mostra, appunto, una marcata obliquità della parte superiore della vasca, caratteristica, questa, dei pezzi assegnabili allo scorcio del IV secolo ed ai primi decenni del III (Thompson 1934: *passim*; Bats 1988: 86).

Del pari, dalle coppette di forma L. 21/25 ha origine una incredibile quantità di imitazioni e derivazioni, il cui utilizzo giunge sino allo scorcio del III sec. a.C. (Tronchetti 1985a: 103).

Per quanto attiene ai piattini, non si sono sinora rinvenute imitazioni della forma nel suo aspetto 'classico,' con le modanature ed il listello in parete; sono altresì presenti numerosi tipi assai più semplificati, con parete liscia ed orlo diritto appena rilevato, ma fabbricati con la stessa tecnica e nelle stesse officine che producevano le ceramiche di imitazione della vernice nera attica. Con ogni verosimiglianza dovremo assegnare questi vasi ad una traduzione nella tecnica della vernice nera locale di simili forme puniche, piuttosto che andare a cercare i prototipi nella evoluzione del piattino dei primi decenni del III secolo in Attica.

Quello che, infine, si può dire per concludere il tema delle produzioni locali 'di imitazione,' è che, con ogni evidenza, il vasellame attico a vernice nera ha avuto una diffusione tale nell'ambito punico di Sardegna da far nascere una notevolissima quantità di imitazioni e derivazioni in diverse officine. Per quanto possiamo constatare, esiste più di un opificio del genere nei centri maggiori: a Cagliari se ne possono individuare almeno quattro; a Sulci due; a Nora tre e così via. Questo vasellame, poi, dai centri produttori, si diffondeva e veniva commerciato nei centri minori dell'entroterra, costituendo un utile indizio per poter verificare le zone di influenza delle città maggiori.

Esaminando, infine, le tavole (1-6) ed i grafici dei diametri (presi al bordo interno dell'apertura) del vasellame da mensa attico, possiamo rilevare che i pezzi, generalmente, non hanno una grande varietà di misure.

Le coppe L. 21 (Tavola 1) si addensano in un arco di tre centimetri, da 12 a 15, con addensamento a 12/13; un solo pezzo misura cm 21. Le L. 22 (Tavola 2) coprono un arco di diametri più ampio, da cm 11 sino a 17, ed in questa forbice pare di poter individuare due punte di addensamento a cm 11/12 e cm 15/16; anche qui un esemplare isolato misura cm 21. Le coppette L. 21/25 (Tavola 4) offrono una omogeneità notevole: tranne un esemplare che si attesta sui cm 10, tutti gli altri pezzi variano dagli 8 ai 9 centimetri. Le bolsal (Tavola 3) sono anch'esse ristrette in pochi centimetri, da 9 sino a 15, ed in questa gamma la punta assolutamente più importante si colloca fra i cm 11 e 12. Del pari i piattini (Tavola 5) si articolano in un arco di 3 centimetri, da 13 a 16, con forte addensamento a cm 13. I piatti da pesce (Tavola 6) mostrano una punta rilevante a cm 17/19, andando dai cm 15 sino ai 20. Si può affermare che il piattino ed il piatto da pesce erano complementari fra loro, coprendo due gamme di misure diverse: più piccola il piattino, superiore il piatto da pesce, che si intrecciano in modo marginale agli estremi, rispettivamente superiore ed inferiore.

A livello di valutazioni generali, prendendo in esame anche i frammenti e le altre forme ceramiche sopra non considerate—fatta eccezione per le lucerne—, possiamo constatare come fra le coppe, ansate e non, la preminenza spetti alle bolsal seguite immediatamente dalle L. 22, mentre le L. 21 e le *incurving-rim* sono in misura assai minore (Tavola 7). Fra i piatti predomina palesemente il piatto da pesce che è, con la coppetta L. 21/25, la forma di vaso da mensa in assoluto più attestata. Una buona quantità è palesata anche dagli *askoi-gutti*.

Nel servito da tavola, riunendo le fogge dei vasi per tipo di recipiente, e prescindendo quindi dalle suddivisioni interne, acclariamo una attestazione maggioritaria delle coppe, seguite a distanza dai piatti, dalle coppette e dalle coppe ansate (Tavola 8). Questo può spiegarsi, probabilmente, con l'ambivalenza della funzione delle coppe, che potevano essere usate sia per cibi solidi che per liquidi, mentre i piatti e le coppe ansate erano limitati ad una soltanto di queste categorie; tale intercambiabilità può ben avere favorito una scelta prioritaria da parte del ceto punico che voleva connotare *graeco more* le proprie abitudini conviviali.

Altre interessanti osservazioni possono essere tratte dall'esame parallelo fra abitati e necropoli, accorpando i dati globali, anche se il diverso stato delle ricerche può portare ad imprecisioni e comporta il rischio di deduzioni parzialmente errate; comunque la quantità dei dati è tale da porsi come buona base, almeno per ipotesi propositive (Tavola 9).

Esaminando la tavola precedente saltano subito all'occhio alcune particolarità. Esistono delle forme che sono caratteristiche e peculiari dell'una situazione ovvero dell'altra. La coppa *incurving-rim*, ad esempio, sino ad adesso è stata individuata soltanto negli scavi e nelle ricognizioni superficiali in aree di abitato a Cagliari e Senorbì, ed è segnalata anche a Tharros nell'area del *topbet* (Madau 1989: 73). Anche le bolsal e sopratutto le coppe L. 22 si rinvengono in misura percentuale maggiore nei livelli di vita. Al contrario, trovano una presenza privilegiata nei corredi tombali gli *askoi-gutti*, concentrati per più del 90% nelle necropoli, ed anche il piatto da pesce si segnala per un'alta percentuale di attestazioni (oltre il

73%) nelle tombe. Le altre fogge si distribuiscono fra le case dei vivi e le case dei morti in misura più o meno equa, pur se dobbiamo riconoscere un *trend* di preferenza in quest'ultime per le coppette L. 21/25.

Certamente il diverso stato delle conoscenze dei singoli centri incide assai sulle valutazioni, inerenti al vasellame attico, che possiamo presentare, ma appaiono, sino ad ora, palesi alcune marcate differenziazioni fra città e città, nonché al loro interno, ove sia possibile istituire confronti, fra zone abitative e necropoli (Tavola 10) (Tronchetti 1989).

A Cagliari, ad esempio, le lucerne sono presenti in buona quantità sia nelle necropoli che nell'abitato, dove abbiamo anche un discreto numero di bolsal, che, al contrario, nelle tombe sono quasi del tutto assenti. Altresì le coppe L. 22, in piccolo numero rappresentate nei corredi tombali, sono in quantità maggiore nei livelli di vita. Il contrario, invece, come già detto sopra, si può rilevare per gli *askoi-gutti*, pochissimo diffusi nelle case ma ben presenti nelle tombe. Questo dato può far pensare che l'olio straniero fosse destinato prevalentemente al rituale funerario, in virtù della sua valenza di 'bene di lusso'. La *facies* di Cagliari trova una sostanziale concordanza con quella di Senorbì, centro da essa non distante e che da essa riceveva sia la ceramica attica che altri beni; in questo caso ci interessa rilevare la cospicua presenza di vasellame di imitazione, in stragrande maggioranza coppe di tipo L. 22, le cui caratteristiche ci inducono a collocarne una parte tuttora entro il IV sec. a.C. Si può ancora far notare che, mentre a Cagliari il vasellame a vernice nera prodotto localmente appare in massima prevalenza nel corso del III secolo, a Senorbì esso si pone come alternativo alla ceramica attica, la quale sembra caratterizzare non un diverso livello cronologico, come sostanzialmente avviene a Cagliari, bensì un diverso livello sociale.

Non appare adesso il caso di insistere sulle eclatanti differenze riscontrabili fra i corredi tombali di Cagliari, Nora e Sulci, già altrove fatte rilevare (Tronchetti 1989), e che, riassumendo brevemente, si possono sintetizzare nella totale assenza di vasellame attico a Sulci, dove si hanno solo lucerne; la quasi totale mancanza di lucerne a Nora di contro ad una fortissima presenza delle altre forme ceramiche ateniesi, e la posizione intermedia di Cagliari che ha un po' di tutto.

Per Tharros, nonostante recenti edizioni di materiali e sintesi generali, più o meno utili (Sparkes 1987; Madau 1989), non abbiamo dati analitici pienamente utilizzabili. Dal pregevole lavoro di Madau si ricavano notizie interessanti, quali, per quanto attiene i corredi tombali, la quasi assoluta prevalenza di bolsal fra le coppe, assieme alle L. 22 ed alle coppette L. 21/25, una forte presenza di *askoi* ed una modesta rappresentanza di lucerne. Negli scavi del terreno di colmata del *tophet*, proveniente con ogni verosimiglianza dall'adiacente abitato (Madau 1989: 77) le coppe sono in maggioranza, mancano gli *askoi* e le lucerne mantengono una presenza minoritaria. È poco rilevante il numero dei piatti, sia nell'abitato che nelle tombe, e questo viene individuato come un elemento caratterizzante la *facies* peculiare di Tharros (Madau 1989: 78). In sostanza viene confermata l'afferenza del vasellame attico alla sfera del simposio (Madau 1989: 79).

Per quanto attiene alla Sardegna settentrionale, i dati sono troppo pochi e sporadici per consentirci considerazioni di un qualche rilievo. È segnalata la presenza di coppette, bolsal, piatti da pesce e piattini ad Olbia (D'Oriano 1990: 489), di vasellame a vernice nera 'precampano' a Monteleone Rocca d'Oria (Madau 1986: 97); frammenti sono sparsi in altre località, ma l'indagine sulla punicizzazione della Sardegna settentrionale è ancora in fase di impostazione.

Conclusioni

Con la fine del IV secolo, i Punici di Sardegna proseguono ad utilizzare ancora per qualche anno la ceramica attica precedentemente importata e che viene progressivamente sostituita da altre ceramiche a vernice nera sia giunte dall'esterno (Atelier des Petites Estampilles, produzioni dell'Italia centrale e della penisola iberica), sia soprattutto fabbricate localmente.

La grande stagione dei vasi attici si è ormai conclusa, ma la sua importanza nell'Isola è stata notevolissima e tutte le problematiche cui le ceramiche ateniesi di Sardegna sono connesse risultano in tale abbondanza da offrire agli studi un vasto campo di indagine, iniziato soltanto adesso a dissodare.

Tavola 1

COPPA L. 21						
Diam.	CA ab.	CA nec.	Nora	Sulci	Senorbì	Totale
12	1	3				4
13		2		1		3
14			1			1
15	1					1
16						
17						
18						
19						
20						
21	1					1
Tot.	3	5	1	1		10

Tavola 2

COPPA L. 22						
Diam.	CA ab.	CA nec.	Nora	Sulci	Senorbì	Totale
11		1	2			3
12	1	1	2	1	1	6
13				1		1
14	1					1
15	1		3			4
16			1	1		2
17				1		1
18						
19						
20						
21	1					1
Tot.	4	2	8	4	1	19

Tavola 3

COPPETTA L. 21/25						
Diam.	CA ab.	CA nec.	Nora	Sulci	Senorbì	Totale
8		6	6	2	2	16
9			11	1	2	14
10					1	1
Tot.		6	17	3	5	31

Tavola 4

BOLSAL						
Diam.	CA ab.	CA nec.	Nora	Sulci	Senorbì	Totale
9			1			1
10						
11		2	8			10
12			3		1	4
13			1			1
14					1	1
15			1			1
Tot.		2	14		2	18

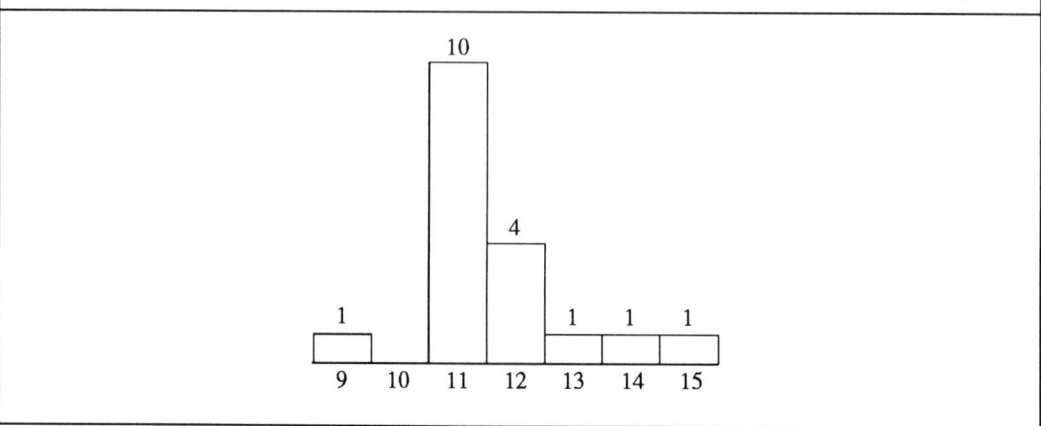

Tavola 5

			PIATTINO			
Diam.	CA ab.	CA nec.	Nora	Sulci	Senorbì	Totale
13	2	2	2		1	7
14		1			2	3
15	1			1	1	3
16	1					1
Tot.	4	3	2	1	4	14

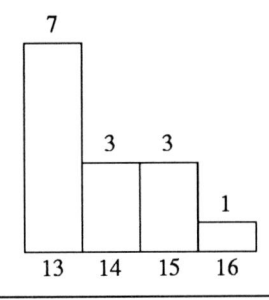

Tavola 6

			PIATTO DA PESCE			
Diam.	CA ab.	CA nec.	Nora	Sulci	Senorbì	Totale
15		1				1
16			1		1	2
17	1	3	3	1	1	9
18		6	4	1	1	12
19		3	7		1	11
20	3	1	1			5
Tot.	4	14	16	2	4	40

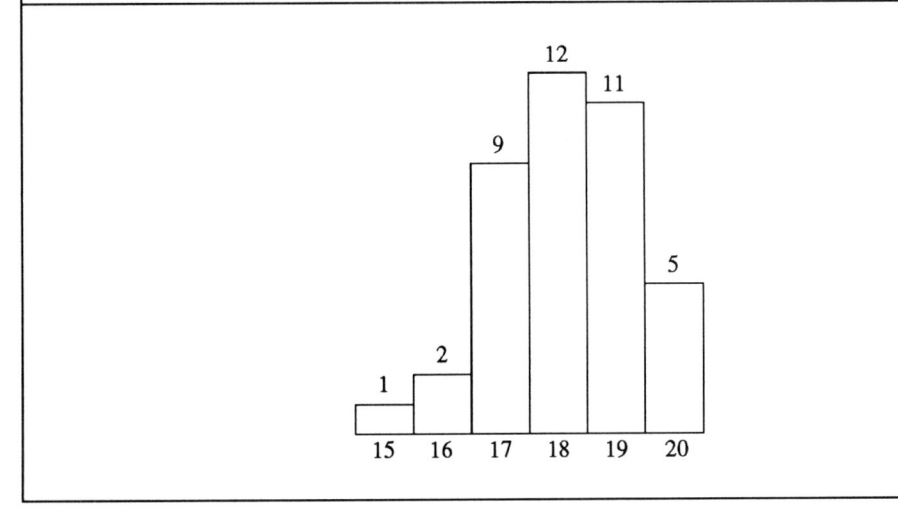

Tavola 7

Legenda:	A = CA ab.	B = CA nec.	C = Nora	D = Sulci	E = Senorbì ab.	F = Senorbì nec.		
Forma	A	B	C	D	E	F	Tot.	%
Coppa L. 21	7	11	1	2	5		26	7,62
Coppa L. 22	20	3	9	6	7	1	46	13,49
Incurving rim	19				8		27	7,92
Bolsal	15	1	15	14	6	2	53	15,54
Coppetta L. 21/25	15	20	17	12	5	5	74	21,70
Piattino	5	5	2	2	3	4	21	6,16
Piatto da Pesce	5	30	16	5	8	4	68	19,94
Askos-Guttus	1	15	4		1	5	26	7,62

Tavola 8

TAVOLA RIEPILOGATIVA PER TIPO DI RECIPIENTE
Comprendente anche forme non inserite nelle tavole precedenti

Coppe	131	29,11 %
Coppette	122	27,11 %
Coppe Ansate	86	19,11 %
Piatti	111	24,66 %
Totale	450	99,99 %

Tavola 9

	ABITATI			NECROPOLI		
Forma		% su totale forma	% su totale abit.		% su totale forma	% su totale necr.
Coppa L. 21	14	53,85	8,19	12	46,15	7,06
Coppa L. 22	33	71,74	19,30	13	28,26	7,65
Incurving rim	27	100,00	15,79			
Bolsal	35	66,03	20,47	18	33,96	10,59
Coppetta L. 21/25	32	43,24	18,71	42	56,76	24,70
Piattino	10	47,61	5,84	11	52,38	6,47
Piatto da Pesce	18	26,47	10,52	50	73,53	29,41
Askos-Guttus	2	7,69	1,17	24	92,31	14,11
Totali:	171		99,99	170		99,99

Tavola 10

	ETÀ ARCAICA — ABITATO									ETÀ ARCAICA — NECROPOLI								
	1	2	3	4	5	6	7	8	1	2	3	4	5	6	7	8
Alabastron													N			
Amphoriskos																
Anfora								N								N
Aryballos																V
Askos																
Askos-Guttus																
Brocchetta																
Coperchio				N												
Coppa	N	V		NV	NV	N	N	V	R	N						NV
Coppa-Kantharos																
Coppa-Skyphos	N	N	N	N				N							N	N
Coppetta																
Cratere																
Forma Chiusa		N														
Kantharos																
Lekanis																
Lekythos															N	N
Lekythos ar.																
Lucerna		V		V					V	V					V	V
Oinochoe																N
Pelike																
Phiale		V														
Piattino																
Piatto da Pesce																
Piatto su Piede													V			
Pisside		V														
Skyphos															V	N

1. Bithia
2. Cagliare
3. Monte Sirai
4. Neapolis
5. Nora
6. Senorbì
7. Sulci
8. Tharros

N = Figure Nere
R = Figure Rosse
V = Vernice Nera

Tavola 10
(continuata)

	V SECOLO — ABITATO								V SECOLO — NECROPOLI							
	1	2	3	4	5	6	7	8	1	2	3	4	5	6	7	8
Alabastron																
Amphoriskos		V		V												
Anfora													V			
Aryballos																
Askos		R														V
Askos-Guttus																
Brocchetta										V						
Coperchio				R												
Coppa		V		RV		RV	V	V		V	V		V	RV	V	V
Coppa-Kantharos																
Coppa-Skyphos				V		V							V			
Coppetta				V				V							V	V
Cratere				R				R								
Forma Chiusa		R														
Kantharos		R		R				V								
Lekanis													V		V	
Lekythos		N				RV		V					RV			V
Lekythos ar.				RV	RV		RV						R	V	R	R
Lucerna		V			V	V	V	V		V				V	V	V
Oinochoe		V				V							R		V	V
Pelike																V
Phiale																
Piattino																
Piatto da Pesce		V		V				RV								R
Piatto su Piede																V
Pisside																
Skyphos		R		RV		R	V	V		R			RV			V

1. Bithia
2. Cagliare
3. Monte Sirai
4. Neapolis
5. Nora
6. Senorbì
7. Sulci
8. Tharros

N = Figure Nere
R = Figure Rosse
V = Vernice Nera

Tavola 10
(continuata)

	IV SELOLO — ABITATO								IV SELOLO — NECROPOLI							
	1	2	3	4	5	6	7	8	1	2	3	4	5	6	7	8
Alabastron																
Amphoriskos																
Anfora																
Aryballos																
Askos													V			RV
Askos-Guttus		V			V					V			V	V		V
Brocchetta																
Coperchio																
Coppa		V		RV		V	RV	V		V			V	V		RV
Coppa-Kantharos		V														
Coppa-Skyphos				V												
Coppetta		V		V		V	V	V		V			V	V		V
Cratere																
Forma Chiusa																
Kantharos																
Lekanis																
Lekythos																
Lekythos ar.																
Lucerna		V		V		V	V	V		V			V	V	V	V
Oinochoe																
Pelike																
Phiale																
Piattino		V				V	V	V		V			V	V		V
Piatto da Pesce		V		RV		V	V	V		V			V	V		V
Piatto su Piede																
Pisside																
Skyphos			RV	R			V					V				

1. Bithia
2. Cagliare
3. Monte Sirai
4. Neapolis
5. Nora
6. Senorbì
7. Sulci
8. Tharros

N = Figure Nere
R = Figure Rosse
V = Vernice Nera

Bibliografia

Bartoloni, P. & C. Tronchetti
- 1981 *La Necropoli di Nora*. Collezione di Studi Fenici 12. Roma.

Bats, M.
- 1988 *Vaisselle et Alimentation a Olbia de Provence*. Revue Archeologique de Narbonnaise Supplement 18. Paris.

Carpenter, T.
- 1984 The Thyrrenian Group: Problems of provenance. *Oxford Journal of Archaeology* 3: 45-56.

D'Oriano, R.
- 1990 Olbia: Ascendenze puniche nell'impianto urbanistico romano. *L'Africa Romana. Atti del VII Convegno di Studio, Sassari, 15-17 dicembre 1989*, 487-95. Sassari.

Madau, M.
- 1986 Materiali d'importazione dalla Sardegna settentrionale. *Società e Cultura in Sardegna nei Periodi Orientalizzante e Arcaico (fine VIII sec. a.C.–480 a.C.). Rapporti fra Sardegna, Fenici, Etruschi e Greci. Atti del 1 convegno di studi 'Un millennio di relazioni fra la Sardegna e i Paesi del Mediterraneo', Selargius-Cagliari, 29-30 novembre-1 dicembre 1985*, 95-100. Cagliari: Amministrazione Provinciale di Cagliari.
- 1989 Importazioni attiche da Tharros. *SEAP* 4: 73-87.

Morel, J.P.
- 1985 I rapporti tra Sardegna, Fenicio-punici, Etruschi e Greci, visti dalla Gallia e da Cartagine. *Società e Cultura in Sardegna nei Periodi Orientalizzante e Arcaico (fine VIII sec. a.C.–480 a.C.). Rapporti fra Sardegna, Fenici, Etruschi e Greci. Atti del 1 convegno di studi 'Un millennio di relazioni fra la Sardegna e i Paesi del Mediterraneo', Selargius-Cagliari, 29-30 novembre-1 dicembre 1985*, 31-39. Cagliari.

Moscati, S.
- 1986 *Le Stele di Sulcis. Caratteri e confronti*. Collezione di Studi Fenici 23. Roma.

Senorbì
- 1990 *Senorbì. Museo Sa Domu Nosta*. Cagliari.

Sparkes, B.
- 1987 4b. Pottery: Greek and Roman. In R. Barnett and C. Mendleson (eds.), *Tharros. A Catalogue of Material in the British Museum from Phoenician and Other Tombs at Tharros, Sardinia*, 59-70. London: British Museum Publications.

Thompson, H.
- 1934 Two centuries of Hellenistic pottery. *Hesperia* 3: 311-480.

Tronchetti, C.
- 1985a Tomba punico-romana a S. Sperate (Cagliari). *Studi Sardi* 26: 101-11.
- 1985b I Greci e la Sardegna. *Dialoghi d'Archeologia* 1985: 17-34.
- 1988 *I Sardi. Traffici, relazioni, ideologia nella Sardegna areaica*. Milano: Longanesi.
- 1989 La ceramica attica nelle necropoli puniche di IV sec. a.C. della Sardegna meridionale. *Riti Funerari e di Olocausto nella Sardegna Fenicia e Punica. Atti dell'incontro di studio, Sant'Antioco, 3-4/10/1986*. Quaderni della Soprintendenza Archeologica di Cagliari e Oristano 6(Supplemento): 83-88. Cagliari.
- 1990 *Cagliari Fenicia e Punica*. Sardò 5. Sassari.

Zucca, R.
- 1987 *Neapolis e il Suo Territorio*. Oristano.

Summary

Most of the Attic Greek ceramics found in Sardinia may be dated to the period of Punic occupation (i.e. later than c. 509 BC); very few examples are earlier than c. 550 BC, and thus attributable to the Phoenician colonists. For the most part, then, the presence in Sardinia of black-figure, red-figure and black-glaze Attic wares must be understood in the context of Punic activity in Sardinia (but cf. Davison, this volume).

From the Late Archaic Period is a Tyrrhenian amphora attributed to the Timiades painter, which probably made its way to Sardinia in the course of Etrurian–Phoenician trade. There also exist a few fragments of cups attributed to the Little Masters. There are only a few examples of Attic wares to be found from the second half of the 6th century. Of the 7 shapes found at 8 habitation sites, cups, *skyphos*-cups, and lamps are the most common; 10 forms, including cups, lamps and perfume containers (*lekythoi*, *aryballoi* and *alabastra*), are known from five burial sites. The importance of drinking vessels and containers in both habitation and funerary contexts is significant, as is the near-absence of red-figure vases, which are so abundant in the coastal cities of Etruria.

During the 5th century BC, red-figure vases replaced the earlier black-figure style, but the frequency of black-glazed wares increased. Perfume containers also increased in frequency, and are found at inland as well as coastal sites; and, while cups still dominate, fish-plates begin to appear late in the 5th century BC. 15 vessel forms are known from 6 habitation sites, as are 16 forms from 6 cemeteries; the 20 forms represented overall are a small increase over the range of forms known from the Late Archaic period. More importantly, the quantity of Attic pottery found in Sardinia quadrupled from the 1st half to the 2nd half of the 5th century BC. The Author suggests that this explosion is due to the progressive Hellenization of the Punic civilization. Drinking vessels continued to be of major importance, and the absence of amphoras (cf. Will, this volume) suggests that the beverages consumed were locally produced.

By the 4th century BC, a notable standardization in the forms of Attic pottery may be found in Sardinia. Only 9 shapes are known from 7 habitation sites, and only 8 shapes come from 5 cemeteries. The most common forms are cups, lamps, plates, and the *askos-guttus*. By the end of the century the importation of Attic pottery ceased, although a flourishing industry in locally-made imitations continued through the 3rd century BC. It appears that the larger sites such as Cagliari,

Sulcis and Nora had at least two or three 'schools' producing imitations. The absence of containers for lamp-oil suggests that this product too was local, whereas perfumed oils were still imported.

Quantitative examination of the Attic vessels reveals that each vessel form is remarkably homogeneous in size, usually with diameters varying by no more than a few centimeters. The most significant variation seen is that between habitation and burial sites. Cups with incurving rims are found only at habitation sites, where both cup #L.22 and the *bolsal* are also much more common. The *askos-guttus* and fish-plates are more frequent in burial contexts.

Much more research needs to be done on this topic, particularly on the function these vessels served, and their significance to the Punic/Sardinian people who used them. This knowledge is important for understanding the extent of Greek cultural influence, and the economic and social relationships between the Carthaginians and the indigenous Sardinians.

Miti e Rituali nella Sardegna Preistorica

Giovanni Lilliu

Introduzione

Miti e rituali riguardanti la Sardegna preistorica ci sono stati tramandati dalla letteratura greco-romana. Per la verità sono scarsi e frammentari, confusi anche, ma sempre utili per la conoscenza del mondo leggendario più remoto.

Nel mito, per quanto prevalga l'elemento inventivo e fantasioso, non manca qualche eco di realtà storica e vi sono rispecchiate anche situazioni di volta in volta derivate da rapporti dell'isola con altre terre, in periodi di tempo diversi. La tradizione storiografica, di varia radice (greco-orientale, siceliota, attica), si è compiuta in massima parte tra il I secolo a.C. e il II dopo, ossia in età romana. Ma l'elaborazione di certi elementi mitografici risale almeno al VII-VIII secolo a.C., tempi comunque assai lontani da quelli nei quali si verificarono realmente taluni avvenimenti raccontati. Il racconto si incentra sulla storia di invasioni successive dell'isola, da parte di genti straniere, ciascuna delle quali è capeggiata e rappresentata da un eroe. Gli occupanti in armi vincono gli indigeni, li colonizzano, convivono infine. Al fondo del mito sta l'ideologia, sostanzialmente di matrice ellenica, che enfatizza la supremazia della civiltà (l'eroe straniero) sulla barbarie locale.

I Miti

Sallustio (I secolo a.C.) e Pausania (II secolo d.C.) riferiscono che Sardus, figlio di Ercole (detto Makeris dagli Egizi e dai Libi), fu il primo a occupare la Sardegna, con una grossa schiera partita dalla Libia. Egli diede il suo nome all'isola. I Libi non espulsero gli indigeni, ma coabitarono con essi sebbene poco disposti verso i colonizzatori. Né invasori né invasi costruirono città, ma vissero in ordine sparso in capanne e dentro grotte. Altri narrano che non solo i Libi, ma anche i Tirreni, rivendicavano il merito del nome nuovo 'Sardò', in luogo 'dell'antico isola delle vene d'argento', in onore della sposa dell'eroe Tirreno. È Pausania a ricordare che Sardus era un eroe divinizzato, nel far cenno di una sua statua di bronzo, donata al santuario di Delfi dai 'barbari' abitanti nell'occidente della Sardegna. Il simulacro avrebbe riprodotto l'originale custodito nel tempio del dio, il *Sardo patoris fanum*, situato da Tolomeo (*Geografia* 3.3.2) alle sorgenti del 'fiume sacro' (oggi identificato col riu Mannu di Fluminimaggiore) nei pressi di Antas, laddove una volta stava il cospicuo centro minerario e civile di Metalla. Nel tempio, di recente scavato e ricomposto dalle rovine, l'iscrizione monumentale della facciata ne commemora la restituzione fatta durante il regno di Caracalla (213 d.C.) e la dedica alla divinità: 'templum dei Sardi Patris bab' (da *babbai* o *abai* con significato di padre, avo o antenato). È la stessa denominazione del nome venerato in precedente sacello, costruito in età punica (V-IV secolo a.C.): il dio Sid detto *b'by*. Questo sacello, a sua volta, avrebbe sostituito un più antico luogo di culto indigeno in onore dell'eroe eponimo dell'isola, in vita almeno dal IX secolo a.C. come testimoniano oggetti votivi di bronzo di epoca nuragica, rinvenuti in prossimità del santuario. Sardus Pater figura poi, associato al culto imperiale romano, in monete, di conio sardo, di Atius Balbus (39–15 a.C.) e lo ricorda una targa ansata bronzea, ex-voto di certo Alessandro, 'servus regionarius' dell'Augusto, esposto nel tempio rinnovato di Antas agli inizi del III secolo d.C.

La tradizione storiografica di Sardus, dietro il cui personaggio si deve vedere il dio nazionale dei Protosardi, contiene un nucleo di verità storica che le fonti archeologiche confermano appieno (tempio, ex-voti, monete etc.). Invece il riferimento, da taluno supposto, di Sardus ai Sardina (uno dei popoli del mare che ebbero a che fare con Libi ed Egizi negli ultimi secoli del II millennio a.C.), è tutto da provare, anche se non manca di suggestione. Quello di Sardus è un vero mito perché ancorato a una certa realtà di immagine dell'isola che si identifica nella credenza e nel culto d'una figura ideale della stirpe immanente nella vicenda storica sarda dalla preistoria ad età bizantina (il *Sardopatoris fanum*, corrotto in *Sartiparias*, è ricordato ancora nel VII secolo d.C. dall'Anonimo Ravennate).

Altro mito eroico è quello di Aristeo, nato da Apollo e dalla ninfa Cirene, marito di Autonòe figlio di Cadme, il fondatore e primo re di Tebe. L'eroe tebano sarebbe fuggito dalla sua città, con uno stuolo di Greci della Beozia, sconvolto dalla perdita del figlio Atteone, cacciatore, mutato in cervo e morto dilaniato dai suoi cinquanta cani per avere attentato alla castità della vergine dea Artemis che si bagnava alla fonte Partenia. Il fuggiasco, alla fine di un lungo viaggio con tappe nell'isola di Ceo (Cicladi) e in Libia dalla madre Cirene, per suo consiglio sarebbe approdato in Sardegna, con l'intento di colonizzarla. Fu questa la seconda colonizzazione per Pausania e Diodoro Siculo; la terza per Solino (III-IV secolo d.C.) e per Silio Italico (I secolo d.C.) l'ultima.

Terra bellissima ma ancora selvaggia la Sardegna—scrivono gli autori—dove Aristeo introdusse l'agricoltura creando felicità e sviluppo, testimoniati dai nomi Charmo e Callicarpo dei figli natigli nell'isola. Benefattore, egli riuscì anche a far convivere Libi e Iberi. Una fonte nota a Sallustio connette ad Aristeo un eroe attico, l'artigiano Daidalos (Dedalo). Silio Italico fa arrivare Aristeo, per prima, 'ai golfi della Sardegna': l'eroe avrebbe regnato 'non lontano da quei luoghi' nella città di Cagliari: notizie confermate da Solino, rifiutate da Pausania che nega ad Aristeo il ruolo di ecista, ossia di fondatore di città. Aristeo, dunque, esplica anche in Sardegna quelle funzioni che gli riserva il mito più in generale: di inventore delle tecniche dell'allevamento e della caccia, soprattutto di inventore dell'apicultura. La tradizione pare molto antica, c'è chi la ritiene fissata nell'isola già dal VII secolo a.C., quando la condizione economica della società protosarda raggiunse effettivamente un elevato livello di progresso che la leggenda rispecchia e rappresenta con la figura tipica d'un eroe culturale. Gli elementi del racconto non sembrano avere un riferimento reale nei personaggi e negli avvenimenti, se si eccettua forse il riflesso lontano di contatti culturali tra area sarda ed aree egea ed elladica sulla fine dell'età del bronzo. Soltanto contatti, una presenza straniera effimera se Diodoro scrive di Aristeo che abbandonò la Sardegna per passare in Sicilia e di qui raggiungere la Grecia.

A dire di Pausania, la terza colonia nell'isola fu quella di Norace (Norax), figlio di Hermês e di Erizia, figlia a sua volta di Gerione, il mostro 'ruggente' di tre teste o di tre corpi, che viveva ad Eriteia, l'*isola rossa*, nel lontano Occidente al di là dell'Oceano, cui Eracle, dopo averlo ucciso con il mandriano Eurizione e il cane Orto, sottrasse i meravigliosi armenti portandoli a Tirinto o ad Argo. Per Sallustio e Solino Norax sarebbe arrivato con gli Iberi da Tartesso, nel sud della Spagna, dove fioriva un regno indigeno autonomo; avrebbe poi fondato Nora, il primo centro urbano nell'isola secondo Pausania. È chiara la natura eziologica del nome dell'eroe: da Nora e dalla radice *nur/nor* del nuraghe, presente anche nella Penisola iberica e nelle Baleari (Nura è l'antica denominazione di Minorca, la Balearis minor). La menzione di Norax, ecista eponimo di Nora (d'una città), dopo Sardus e Aristeo che non avrebbero fondato città, vorrebbe indicare, per gli autori del mito, una situazione urbana della Sardegna dopo quella rurale, selvaggia. Ma non ha un riferimento reale: la preistoria sarda conosce soltanto lo stadio di villaggio con tendenza all'urbanesimo negli ultimi tempi delle vicende storiche. L'ambientamento del racconto di Norax, risalente forse a dopo la fondazione di Gaddir (che prese il luogo di Tartesso) ad opera dei Tirii, è occidentale, fuori della tradizione greca. Taluno ha voluto vedere nella narrazione l'arrivo dei Fenici in Sardegna, se mai il mito potrebbe alludere a relazioni commerciali nella tarda età del Bronzo tra Protosardi e Tartessii, aventi comuni interessi in un clima di sovranità politica di entrambi.

Il racconto di Iòlaos, riferito alla quarta colonizzazione, è il più denso di contenuti, ma anche il più imbrogliato, perché la versione originale greco-orientale è stata manipolata, alla metà circa del V secolo a.C., in ambiente attico per favorire il disegno politico di espansione degli Ateniesi verso l'Italia meridionale e le coste provenzali e iberiche. Secondo Pausania, i Greci di Tespie (città della Beozia), e di Atene sarebbero giunti nell'isola capeggiati da Iòlaos, figlio di Iphiklês, fratello strettamente umano di Heraklês e di quest'ultimo nipote, scudiero e ausiliario inseparabile nei combattimenti, anche *eròmenos* (compagno d'amore) secondo una tradizione. Proprio Heraklês, per ordine dell'oracolo di Delfi, avrebbe inviato Iòlaos in Sardegna, ingiungendogli di recare con sé un valido, saldo e bellicoso gruppo di giovani: i Tespiadi, nati all'eroe dopo aver ucciso a Tespie il leone del monte Citerone, dalle cinquanta figlie del re Thespios, godute e fecondate in un lungo travaglio amoroso tra il calar del sole e il levare del giorno (un'impresa sessuale eroica al pari di quella cinegetica). Diodoro spiega questo particolare, aggiungendo che il re Thespios avrebbe offerto le sue figlie per avere come genero il più grande eroe dei tempi e a mo' di ricompensa per aver egli liberato le terre dalla feroce belva. Silio Italico precisa che dei cinquanta Tespiadi, arrivati all'età virile, solo quarantuno partirono per la Sardegna, sulle navi costruite da Heraklês: sette restarono a Tespie, e due si fermarono a Tebe (tre secondo lo Pseudo Apollodoro).

I Tespiadi, cui si unirono altri Greci (Cadmei, cioè Tebani, Locresi, Etoli ed Ateniesi, questi ultimi però—specifica Pausania—'a titolo particolare'), giunsero nella terra promessa dall'oracolo e, vinti in battaglia gli indigeni, presero a colonizzarla. Iòlaos divise in sorte tra i componenti della spedizione le regioni più fertili, prediligendo la pianura denominata 'Iolaion' che venne coltivata e piantata a frutteti. Furono costruite nobili città (Olbia ad opera dei Tespiadi, Ogryle con l'intervento autonomo degli Ateniesi e *alia graeca oppida*). Furono edificati grandi e sontuose palestre, tempii, nonché tribunali, cioè quanto era necessario al vivere civile e felice degli uomini. Si dovette all'arte di Dedalo che Iòlaos chiamò espressamente dalla Sicilia, se fu possibile realizzare tali opere e numerose altre di eccellente architettura, quali edifici fatti al modo arcaico greco e, in particolare, monumenti a volta (*tholoi*) di straordinarie proporzioni. Tutte queste prestigiose costruzioni, delle quali discorrono Pausania, Sallustio, Diodoro e l'autore ignoto dello scritto pseudoaristotelico 'De mirabilibus auscultationibus' di età adrianea, furono denominate 'dedalee' dal grande 'artista' ateniese.

A causa delle sue benemerenze demiurgiche i Tespiadi consentirono alla loro guida militare e morale Iòlaos di imporre il proprio nome agli abitanti dell'isola, detti così Iolei, e lo vollero chiamare 'Iòlaos padre'. E poiché, dopo morto, sulla tomba eressero un tempio, gli riservarono onori divini con offerte e sacrifizi. È questa una versione del mito. Secondo un'altra—seguita da Diodoro—Iòlaos (nome emblematico di guerra che significa 'popolo armato di freccia'), dopo aver ben sistemato le cose della colonia (la 'prima di quelle greche' annota Pausania), se ne tornò in patria, facendo breve tappa in Sicilia, insieme ad alcuni dei suoi compagni i quali vi si fermarono unendosi ai Sicani. I Tespiadi rimasero in Sardegna per lungo tempo, signori della terra, sino a quando ne furono espulsi e costretti a dirigersi verso l'Italia dove si stanziarono nella regione intorno a Cuma. I pochissimi scampati alla fuga, imbarbaritisi, si confusero con gli indigeni dei quali elessero i migliori come loro capi. La fertilità delle terre in loro possesso indusse molti popoli ad appetirle e, infine, i Cartaginesi a conquistarle in lunghe lotte. In conseguenza gli Iolei si ritirarono nelle zone montane, dove abitarono in case sotterranee e in grotte e si ridussero alla vita pastorale, cibandosi di latte, formaggio e carne e facendo a meno del grano. Pur tra le angustie seppero mantenere la libertà che l'oracolo di Apollo aveva garantito in eterno ai Tespiadi.

Dal tessuto intricato del racconto si sciolgono alcuni fili reali. Sono questi: l'esistenza del popolo indigeno (nuragico) degli Iolei, assoggettato da Cartagine e costretto alla fuga verso le zone interne dove le condizioni ambientali procurano il passaggio a una dura economia di pastori dalla felice civiltà contadina dei tempi liberi; il culto locale d'una divinità guerriera chiamata Iòlaos avente per motivo la forma d'una designazione etnica (gli Iolaeîs) oppure di toponimi (la pianura detta Iolaeîon e la radice *Iol/Ol* di altri luoghi dell'isola di sustrato protosardo). Ma dell'eroe-dio Iòlaos non si ha alcuna traccia archeologica (né la tomba, né il tempio, né oggetti di venerazione), a differenza del Sardus, per effetto dell'identificazione in un' unica divinità (quella di Sardus) dei due numi.

Con referente reale è anche la menzione nel mito dei monumenti costruiti nel modo arcaico greco, ossia cretese-micenea, le 'tholoi' in particolare nelle quali si possono riconoscere nuraghi e pozzi sacri. Invece l'accenno a palestre, ginnasi, alla tomba e al tempio di Iòlaos pare il calco di strutture urbane, connesse con l'eroe, in Grecia: tomba e santuario eroico davanti alle porte Pretidi, ginnasio, stadio e ippodromo a Tebe. Sono differenti le vicende, le culture e i tempi echeggiati nel racconto: saga degli Eraclidi (secolo XIII a.C.), imprese artistiche di Dedalo (XIV-XIII secolo), istanze di colonizzazione greca storica di varie parti, da quella beota più antica a quella attica più recente (IX-V secolo a.C.). Nell'insieme dalla leggenda di Iòlaos esce un'immagine della Sardegna, idealizzata, ambigua e, per la maggior parte degli aspetti, fuori dal tempo storico.

I Rituali

C'è una peculiarità nel mito sardo di Iòlaos, interessante perché fa conoscere un rituale caratteristico della civiltà indigena. Aristotile, in un passo della *Fisica*, convalida la morte dell'eroe e dei Tespiadi nell'isola. E aggiunge che era costume della gente di dormire presso la tomba eroica, per essere guarita dai deliri (*visiones*). Commentatori del filosofo di Stagira spiegano che la pratica incubatoria che durava cinque giorni, avveniva in prossimità della sepoltura di nove Tespiadi i quali, dopo la morte, avevano conservato intatto il loro corpo così che sembravano addormentati. Tertulliano, citando Aristotile, scrive d'un unico eroe della Sardegna che guariva dalle ossessioni coloro che entravano in sonno nel suo tempio (*fanum*).

Gli archeologi sono largamente consenzienti nell'individuare questa tomba mitica dei Tespiadi, o dell'eroe, nelle tombe dei giganti talune delle quali per la monumentalità delle strutture e per le ampie esedre dove presumibilmente si praticava il sonno terapeutico, sembrano veri templi della morte, *pantheon* di avi eroizzati. Pare che la società protosarda abbia prestato una particolare attenzione ai malati di mente. Alla cura ipnotica, di cui non sappiamo quale fosse il risultato, potevano attendere sacerdoti-stregoni i quali esercitavano, forse, una sorta di *training* che in qualche modo richiama al dovere degli psicanalisti dei nostri giorni, assoggettati essi stessi ad analisi per un corretto esercizio della professione. Non si esclude, poi, che nel rito degli eroi addormentati nelle tombe nuragiche, vi sia la traccia d'un mito di morte mistica, iniziatica, che calza a Iòlaos beneficiario, secondo qualche tradizione, d'un rituale di rinnovamento di giovinezza. Iòlaos muore e risuscita, come gli infermi (che egli, l'eroe ricordato da Aristotile, guarisce) passano nel sonno (la morte simbolica) dalla malattia alla salute. È un mondo d'incantesimo e di magia conveniente al mito e alla spiritualità irrazionale della remota civiltà dei Sardi.

Al rituale dell'incubazione, intesa in senso restaurativo di vita (salute) nuova, si può accostare un'altra cerimonia, improntata a rito di rinascita, riferita all'isola dallo scrittore siceliota Timeo. Egli riporta la consuetudine degli indigeni, consistente nell'uccisione dei padri vecchi. Questi, giunti ai settantanni, venivano uccisi dai figli in onore del dio Kronos (divoratore della propria prole), nel seguente modo: i figli li accompagnavano verso baratri, li bastonavano a morte e poi li gettavano nel vuoto tra risa feroci e disumane. Demone ed Eliano da Palestrina confermano la pratica, l'ultimo spiegando col riso sforzato e amaro del genitore e dei figli il detto del 'riso sardonico' di cui v'è cenno anche nel poeta Simonide di Ceo (556–467) e nell'autore dell'Odissea, nel declinare del Medioevo greco. Il rituale nel quale il riso funge da liberazione orgiastica dall'angoscia derivata dalla morte violenta dei genitori (agisce cioè come elemento rigeneratore di vita: 'dai morti viene il nutrimento' diceva Ippocrate di Ceo), ha numerosi riscontri in esempi di patricidi e, in genere, di uccisione di vecchi presso popoli primitivi e moderni, tra genti dell'età classica e medievale, in diversi paesi del mondo. Il costume si allinea anche con pratiche rituali analoghe di luoghi dove vigono (o vigevano) il cannibalismo o addirittura l'antropofagia del defunto. È questa una varietà di endocannibalismo connessa con l'obbligo rituale di identificarsi col trapassato addossandosene la morte, al fine della rigenerazione. Il costume che Timeo ricorda per la Sardegna, calza alla sfera psicologica di culture più remote della civiltà sarda prenuragica, e all'ambiente neolitico con stadio di economia rurale (e di raccolta) e di società matriarcale. Appunto la potenza della donna-madre, confusa con la natura vegetativa e creativa, unita alla forza magica del *totem*, cioè il vero padre genealogico, fa scadere il padre naturale sino a consentire di sopprimerlo per necessità. Il rituale, praticato fino alla totale consumazione, assolve a un obbligo morale inteso a procurare la liberazione dalla morte con la rimozione violenta di colui che dimostra più vicina la presenza della stessa morte: ossia dei padri giunti a tarda vecchiaia. La morte fatta subire coscientemente al *vivente* accelera la riproduzione della *vita*: di quella umana (discendenza) e di quella vegetale magicamente connesse nella spiritualità primitiva.

È stupefacente che il ricordo del rito dell'uccisione dei vecchi padri sia ancora vivo nella tradizione sarda. A Gàiro (Ogliastra), i ragazzini dicono solitamente: 'is béccius a sa babaieca', e cioè i 'vecchi alla babaieca', da *babai* (= padre naturale). All'invettiva scherzosa giovanile corrisponde il racconto circostanziato degli anziani sul luogo della *babaieca* e sulla relativa cerimonia. *Babaieca* è una roccia a picco alta circa trenta metri, appena a un chilometro da Gàiro vecchia. Una stradina muove dal paese e mette capo al burrone sotto il quale si apre una voragine ora ripiena di detriti e (si dice) anche di resti scheletrici umani. Qui i padri, arrivati all'età di settantanni, venivano buttati giù e sparivano dentro la caverna profonda più di otto metri. Era il figlio maggiore che prendeva sottobraccio il genitore, cosciente della sua fine, dopo aver salutato e abbracciato tutti i parenti convenuti alla sua casa. Poi lo accompagnava, lungo la strada della *babaieca*, fermandosi e riposandosi di tanto in tanto nel viaggio rituale. Giunti al burrone, il figlio buttava giù il vecchio, scoppiando in un riso convulso e amaro.

Del costume resta tradizione anche a Ovodda, dove la gente sa di vecchi padri e di malvagi precipitati dalla rupe porfirica detta 'Su nodu de Lopene'. Lo stesso si dice in Cossoìne (Sassari). A un chilometro a sud-ovest dell'abitato si apre nella roccia basaltica un inghiottitoio naturale chiamato *Su Mammuscone*. Il popolo vuole che dentro la fessura fossero gettati un tempo i genitori anziani e le mogli infedeli. Il nome della voragine, *Su Mammuscone*, il medesimo di *Mamuthone*, accenna a una divinità sotterranea o a un demone infernale e anche forse alle anime dei morti che sono qui le 'ombre' dei padri vecchi e delle adultere uccisi. Pare di cogliere nel costume elementi significativi di una società gerontocratica fondata sulla compattezza della famiglia che non accetta deviazioni morali. Le vicende della terra e il mutare dell'uomo, ucciso per rigenerarsi, sono accomunati da un ferreo destino. La tradizione popolare conservatasi tanto a lungo sino ad oggi, rivela, con la straordinaria persistenza, che il rito, per noi feroce, ma organico alla moralità neolitica, è remotissimo, in quanto riferibile alla più lontana preistoria sarda.

Note Bibliografiche

Per i miti, le gesta e le figure degli eroi sardi (*Sardus, Aristeus, Norax, Iòlaos*) nella letteratura classica: Pais (1881: 272, 355-60); Pettazzoni (1912: 67-92); Meloni (1945); Guido (1964: 30-33, 138, 205); Bondì (1975); Mastino (1980); Gras (1985: 22, 222, 251); Ugas (1985); Nicosia (1981); Lilliu (1988: 562). Per il tempio del Sardus Pater in località Antas-Fluminimaggiore, le sue fasi e il corredo votivo: Acquaro *et al.* (1969); Barreca (1986: 126-30, 296 figg. 78-83); Lilliu (1990). Per l'incubazione presso la tomba di Iòlaos e dei Tespiadi (le 'tombe di giganti'): Pettazzoni (1912: 12 s., 83 s.); Lilliu (1988: 563). Per il rituale dell'uccisione dei vecchi padri: Lilliu (1988: 259 s.)

Bibliografia

Acquaro, E., F. Barreca, S.M. Cecchini, D. Fantar, M.G. Amadasi Guzzo & S. Moscati
 1969 *Ricerche Puniche ad Antas. Rapporto preliminare delle campagne di scavi 1967 e 1968*. Roma: Istituto di Studi del Vicino Oriente, Università di Roma.

Barreca, F.
 1986 *La Civiltà Fenicio-Punica in Sardegna*. Studi e Monumenti 3. Sassari: Carlo Delfino.

Bondì, S.F.
 1975 Osservazioni sulle fonti classiche per la colonizzazione della Sardegna. *Saggi Fenici* 1: 49-66. Roma: C.N.R.

Gras, M.
 1985 *Trafics Thyrréniens Archaïques*. Bibliothèque des écoles françaises d'Athènes et de Rome 258. Rome: Ecole française de Rome, Palais Farnese.

Guido, M.
 1964 *Sardinia*. London: Thames and Hudson.

Lilliu, G.
 1988 *La Civiltà dei Sardi dal Paleolitico all'Età dei Nuraghi*. Torino: Nuova ERI.
 1990 Sopravvivenze nuragiche in età romana. *L'Africa Romana*, 'Atti del VII Convegno di Studi, Sassari, 15-17 dicembre 1989*, 443-46. Sassari: Gallizzi.

Mastino, A.
 1980 La voce degli antichi. In D. Sanna (a cura di), *Nur. La misteriosa civiltà dei Sardi*, 261-74. Milano: CARIPLO.

Meloni, P.
 1945 Gli Iolei ed il mito di Iolao in Sardegna. *Studi Sardi* 6(1): 43-63.

Nicosia, F.
 1981 La Sardegna nel mondo classico. In E. Atzeni *et al.* (eds.), *Ichnussa. La Sardegna dalle origini all'età classica*, 423-41. Milano: Libri Scheiwiller.

Pais, E.
 1881 La Sardegna prima del dominio romano. Studi storici ed archeologici di Ettore Pais. *Atti della R. Accademia dei Lincei* 1880-81. Memorie della classe di scienze morali, storiche e filologiche 7: 259-378.

Pettazzoni, R.
 1912 *La Religione Primitiva in Sardegna*. Piacenza.

Ugas, G.
 1985 Il mondo religioso nuragico. In E. Arslan, F. Barreca and F. Lo Schiavo (eds.), *Sardegna Preistorica: Nuraghi a Milano*, 209-12. Milano: Electa.

Summary

The legendary history of Sardinia derives mostly from Roman authors of the 1st century BC to the 2nd century AD, but contains elements dating back at least to the 7th–8th century BC. These accounts tell of successive invasions of the island by foreign peoples who defeat the natives, establish colonies, and ultimately live there together with the native Sardinians. The supremacy of civilized peoples over barbarians is rooted in Greek ideology.

According to Sallustius (1st cent. BC) and Pausanias (2nd cent. AD), the hero Sardus, son of Herakles, was the first to settle in Sardinia, giving his name to the island. Sardus was revered in the Punic period (Temple of Sardus Pater at Antas), and perhaps several centuries earlier by an indigenous cult at the same site.

Another myth has Aristeus, son of Apollo and Cyrene, fleeing to Sardinia from Boeotia, stopping along the way at Keos and in Libya; his was considered the second colonization of Sardinia by Pausanias and Diodorus. Connected to Aristeus is the Attic hero Daedalus, thought to be the founder and ruler of Cagliari.

Norax is said to have come from the west, perhaps Iberia, and founded the first urban center at Nora. The name Norax appears related both to *nuraghe* and to *Nure*, the ancient name of Minorca.

Iòlaos, representing the fourth colonization of Sardinia, led the Thespiades there at the request of Herakles, and oversaw the construction of great buildings and temples. Afterwards, the people of Sardinia kept the name Iolei, even after they fled to the mountains during the Carthaginian invasion. There is a ritual, recorded by Aristotle, in which native Sardinians slept near the tombs of the Thespiades, because their ills could be cured in their sleep; it has been suggested that the *exedra* in front of the *tombe di giganti* could have served this purpose.

For the most part, these myths have an idealized image of Sardinia, with some threads of truth; they are, however, mostly unsupported by archaeological evidence, and generally refer to events that would have occurred before the historical period. Likewise, there are reports by Timeus and other authors of the custom of sons killing their parents at the age of 70; this is said to be the origin of the 'Sardinian laugh'. A similar custom is today still recalled in parts of Sardinia (Gàiro-Ogliastra, Ovodda, Cossoìne-Sassari), and if true, may find its origins in prehistoric Sardinia.

Greeks in Sardinia: Myth and Reality

Jean M. Davison

It is a particular pleasure to contribute this paper in honor of Miriam S. Balmuth, because it was she who first introduced me to Sardinia and the problems of its appearance within the orbit of Greek archaeology and mythology.

As Holloway (1981: 99) points out with respect to Greek colonization in Italy and Sicily, many of the links claimed by the Greeks to their heroic Mycenaean past are simply the result of recognizing or appropriating elements of native cults reminiscent of their own mythical traditions (see also Pearson 1987: 42-43). In the case of Sardinia, however, there is no indication that the early Greeks ever had access to local traditions, so that the legends of colonization there had to be created from 'outside in' rather than 'inside out'. The progressive Hellenization of the island culture through commercial contacts (Madau 1988: 250) meant that the natives and the Carthaginian settlers in their turn accepted or adapted to their own traditions a view of their mythic history which was essentially Hellenocentric (Morel 1984: 129). The result of this more or less enthusiastic reception was that later writers could see, already in place, cults and practices that convinced them of the historical validity of the earlier legends. If there is a cult of Iolaos in Sardinia now, say Diodorus Siculus (4.30.2) and Pausanias (10.17.5), it is because Iolaos and the children of Herakles from Thespiae established a settlement there in the pre-Trojan war era.

The chief difficulties in assessing such literary references to a Greek presence in Sardinia include determining the possibility of an original historical event (Meloni 1945), the purposes for which a story might have been fabricated, and the initial impulse for its development. Recent finds and studies have helped to modify, refine, or confirm some of my own earlier speculations concerning the Greek presence in Sardinia (Davison 1984; 1986). The imprint of the Phoenicians, first in trade and then in actual presence, can be seen clearly on the island, where Phoenician settlement occurred as early as the middle of the 8th century BC (Bartoloni 1987: 220). Greek trade and/or presence has been harder to define; but over the last ten years an enormous amount of material has become accessible, both through continuing excavation and through the publication of material from earlier excavations and museum collections. An inventory and statistical study of Greek and Etruscan imports during the Archaic period (620–480 BC) has now appeared (Ugas and Zucca 1984), and the bibliography of analytical and interpretive studies has increased dramatically, especially concerning relationships of Phoenicians and Greeks within the wider confines of the Mediterranean (Fig. 1).

The present state of Greek contact with Sardinia down to the middle of the 4th century BC may be summarized as follows (see Moscati 1985; Moscati 1989: 137-38; Tronchetti 1985a: 32, and this volume; and Nicosia 1981, for fine illustrations of the range of local and imported products):

1. Greek pottery of Euboean/Pithecusan types appears in association with Phoenician wares (and Phoenician imitations of Greek Late Geometric designs and shapes) from the initial phase of Phoenician settlement at Sulcis (S. Antioco) in the second half of the 8th century BC (Bernardini 1988: 76-81). Neither the quantity nor the quality of the Greek material demands the assumption of an actual Greek presence at the site. Tronchetti (1985a: 19) entertains this possibility, but the evidence suggests instead that it was brought by Phoenicians in the normal course of trade along the metal route to Spain.

2. As Phoenician settlements spread during the 7th and 6th centuries, still more Greek ware appears, now in association with Etruscan material; both reached Sardinia from an Etruscan point of origin, especially Cerveteri and Vulci. Some scholars think that the Phoenicians were the purveyors (e.g. Moscati 1985), while others imply that Etruscans were responsible for this trade (Tronchetti 1985a: 23-24). In any case, there is a noticeable preponderance of

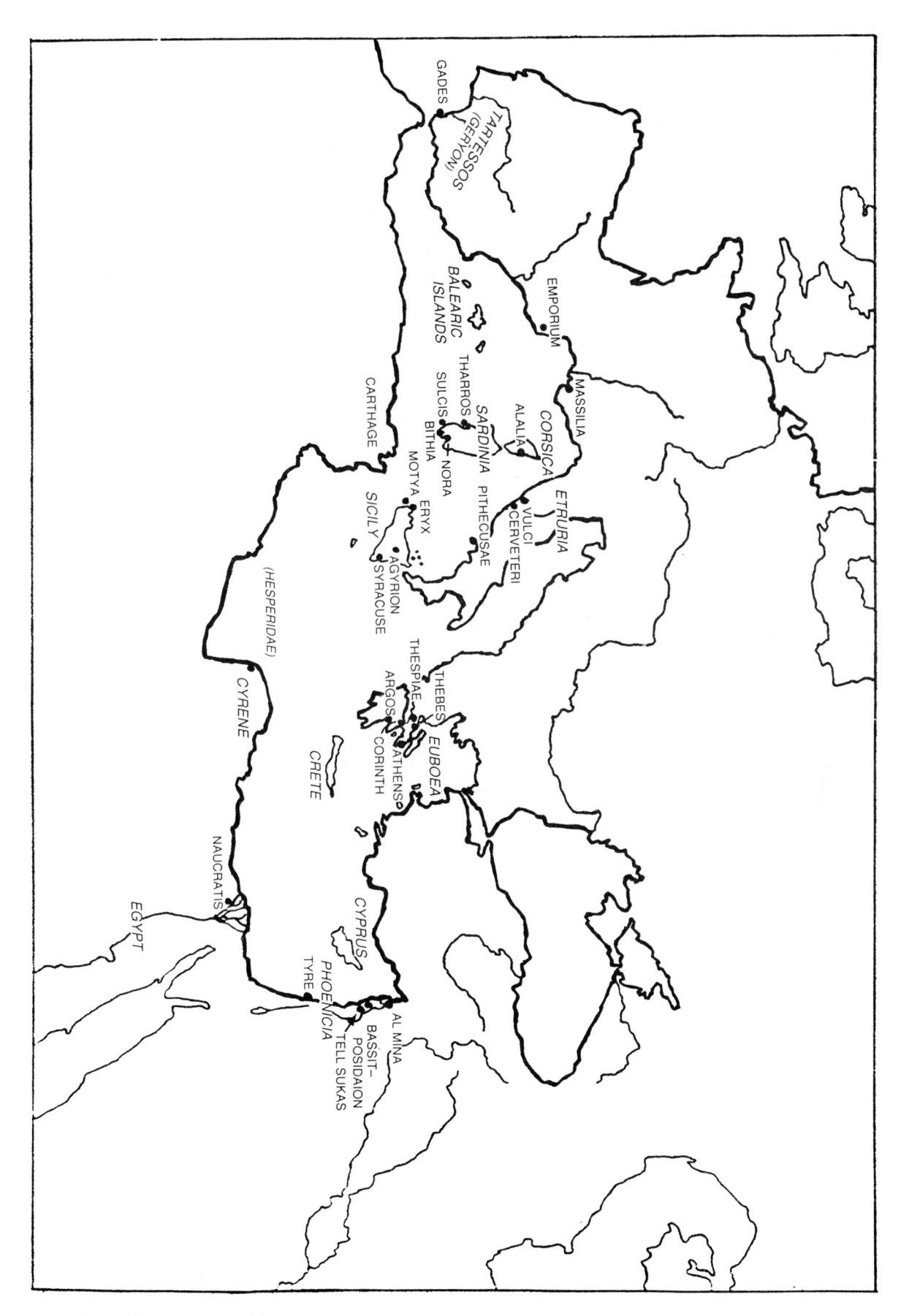

Fig. 1 The Mediterranean World.

Etruscan *bucchero* over the East Greek ware of the previous period. Tharros and Bithia are the centers of this new commerce in imported wares that spread from the coasts to inland Sardinian centers, where they appear in mixed contexts of Phoenician and native material (Tronchetti 1985a: 21-23).

3. Toward the end of the 6th century (c. 540-520/10), when Carthage begins to exercise control over Sardinia, there is a marked diminution of imported Etruscan and Greek wares. The Astarte plaques from Carthage now making their appearance on the island, especially at Tharros, soon begin to reflect Greek influence, probably deriving from Sicilian models (Barnett and Mendleson 1987: 42-43) making their way into Phoenician centers such as Motya (Bondì 1989: 165). The intermediary in this case is probably still Carthage, since there is no indication of direct contacts between Sardinia and Sicily; and the likely carriers are probably Phoenician–Punic ships (Moscati 1985). A local impulse toward Hellenization also appears in a series of scarabs with mythological subjects deriving from late Archaic Greek art. They have been found on both eastern and western Mediterranean sites, but mainly in the west (especially at Tharros, Ibiza and Carthage). Most are of green jasper and may in fact have been produced in Sardinia itself (Boardman 1982: 295; Barnett and Mendleson 1987: 42-43).

4. At the turn of the 5th century, and increasing dramatically throughout the 5th and to the middle of the 4th, there is a return of imported Greek pottery, now exclusively Attic and with a concentration on black-glaze ware. The proportion of black-glaze to figured ware may be fairly represented by the El Sec shipwreck recently discovered off the coast of Majorca (Arribas *et al.* 1987). Its cargo, dated to the second quarter of the 4th century, contained 101 fragments of Attic red-figured pottery and 358 pieces of black-glaze (Arribas *et al.* 1987: 47, 204). The Spanish excavators (Arribas *et al.* 1987: 123) suggest a continuation of an active Phoenician–Punic commerce in Attic pottery extending from the Archaic period to the mid-4th century. The consistent volume of Attic imports turning up at the ongoing excavations at Tharros has led to another, even stronger conclusion: at least from the 5th century there occurred a profound and progressive Hellenization of the Punic world; and this was the result of a direct connection with Athens and its commerce in the western Mediterranean (Madau 1988: 250; Tronchetti 1985a: 32). The 'Greco-Phoenician' scarabs of the earlier period continue to be produced; unlike the evidence of the pottery, however, they show no Athenian influence (Boardman 1982: 297).

The recent finds from Sulcis (Bernardini 1988) cast an intriguing light on the fluctuating trade routes of various periods and on the interaction of Phoenicians and Greeks in their use. In Bartoloni's (1986: 20) discussion of Sulcis, he finds evidence of an active commerce from the mid-8th through the 6th centuries BC, with an almost complete break in the 5th. Since the 5th century is the very period when Attic wares began to flood into Sardinia, apparently Tharros and Nora replaced Sulcis as the ports of entry. Inasmuch as the earliest strata show Phoenician pottery mixed with Greek imports of Euboeic/Pithecusan fabric, as well as the fragments of a Protocorinthian *kotyle* of Aetos 666 type dated to 750 BC (see a fine color reproduction in Bernardini 1990: 151 fig. 13), Sulcis may claim to be the earliest attested Phoenician settlement on the island. Bernardini (1988: 80, 83, 85) notes that the Phoenician imitations of Euboeic/Pithecusan shapes and decoration are particularly close to similar productions at Al Mina. Bartoloni (1986: 220-25; see also Buchner 1982) concludes from this and the close resemblances of material found both at Sulcis and Pithecusae that an intense commercial relationship existed between southwestern Sardinia and Pithecusae. This material includes commercial amphorae of the same make; grave goods in Pithecusae implying a nucleus of Phoenician inhabitants; and a Late Geometric *stamnos* of Pithecusan fabric found in the late 8th-century *tophet* at Sulcis. Because of the similarities of Phoenician and Euboeic material in both east and west, Bartoloni (1986: 226) suggests that the close commercial connection between Sardinia (i.e. Sardinian Phoenicians) and Euboea had begun in Syria-Palestine and Cyprus; its vigorous development (in Sardinia and Pithecusae) in the 8th and all of the 7th century was the result of a common push to the West of the two peoples.

This picture of Phoenicians and Greeks proceeding hand-in-hand (or rather prow-to-stern) in a joint or at least comradely venture to the west is by no means an unlikely one (see Meloni 1945: 45). The trading contact and probable cohabitation in Al Mina, Tell Sukas and Cyprus (and also the Egyptian Delta) must have led to the exchange of useful information along with goods (Ridgway 1990: 64). In Homer, the Phoenicians are praised for their craftsmanship (*Iliad* 6.288-95; Mazza *et al.* 1988: T1), deprecated as slave-traders (*Odyssey* 15.403-484; Mazza *et al.* 1988: T9 and S19), and considered untrustworthy in their dealings (*Odyssey* 14.287-98; Mazza *et al.* 1988: T7; Niemeyer 1990: 488). What has not been stressed often enough, however, is that despite their reputation for double-dealing and kidnapping, they never appear in Greek literature (with all the ill-will in the world) as either pirates or marauders, or in fact as *enemies* in any guise. It is not until the Persian Wars that the Greeks actually come to blows with (native) Phoenicians, when the Phoenician navy (like the Egyptian) was in service to the Persian Empire. Even at a time when the Greeks were actively hostile to the Phoenicians, they did not use that opportunity to ascribe deeds of piracy or the sacking of cities to earlier Phoenicians.

That the Phoenicians were capable of cooperative trading enterprises is clear from the biblical account concerning Solomon and Hiram of Tyre and their joint venture to Tartessos in the mid-10th century BC (1 Kgs 9.27-28; 10.11 and 22; Tsirkin 1986: 182). All the evidence of the 8th and 7th centuries points to peaceful coexistence of Greeks and Phoenicians in Cyprus, at various trading stations along the coast of Syria-Palestine, and throughout the western Mediterranean (cf. Ridgway and Serra Ridgway, this volume, for earlier contacts). Aside from the defensive engagement of the Sicilian Phoenicians to ward off the encroachment of Pentathlos into western Sicily in the early 6th century (Diodorus 5.9; Pausanias 10.11.3), it is not until the second half of the century, with the expansion of Carthaginian interests, that we see the beginning of actual hostilities between 'Phoenicians' and Greeks (the naval battle c. 540 BC of Carthaginians and Etruscans against the Phocaeans settled at Alalia on the island of Corsica: Herodotus 1.166). The shift from a Phoenician 'sphere of interest' in Sardinia and the western Mediterranean to Carthaginian dominion (Nicosia 1981: 473-74; Marras *et al.* 1989; Bondì 1989: 167-68; Bartoloni 1987) is clearly marked at Tharros, where by the end of the 6th century a new complex of fortifications has given it 'a new life as a Punic naval stronghold without renouncing its former role as a commercial port' (Barnett and Mendleson 1987: 27). Ridgway (1990: 69) appears quite right, then, in his felicitous description of Phoenicians and Greeks as partners or rivals in their initial voyages of exploration and trade in the west.

Even under Carthaginian dominion, however, the western Mediterranean was still open to Greek trade, now almost exclusively Athenian (cf. Tronchetti, this volume). Initial apprehension of Massilian encroachment in the north shifted east to include Greek pirates in the Tyrrhenian Sea and the Greek colonies in Sicily; but apparently the Greek mainland was safely distant and Athenian wares much prized, even though they now seem to have been mass-produced to satisfy the growing western market (Madau 1988: 250). The suggestion that this trade was now being carried on by the Athenians directly (Madau 1988: 250), without intermediaries, even if under the supervision of local Carthaginian 'customs agents', is a natural assumption given the nature of the goods and the historical situation during the 5th century. Etruscan control of the Tyrrhenian Sea had been crushed in the Battle of Cumae in 474; Euboea was a member of the Athenian Empire; Corinth's trade in the West had long since been usurped by Athens; and Phoenicia (and Egypt) had become part of the Persian Empire. The only long-distance carriers left were the Carthaginians and the Athenians.

This circumstance may help to explain a curious anomaly at Nora. Among the tombs containing imported ware is a unique example in which all but perhaps one of the grave goods are Attic (Tomb XXXI: Bartoloni and Tronchetti 1981: 115, catalogue 139-45, plates I-II). Imported wares in other tombs (not only at Nora but throughout the Phoenician–Punic area of the western Mediterranean) never occur as a majority of the grave goods but only as adjuncts within a thoroughly Phoenician–Punic cultural context. Another peculiarity of Tomb XXXI is that 10 of the 21 vases are red-figure ware (Bartoloni and Tronchetti 1981: 115), blatantly contradicting the preference for black-glaze indicated by the archaeological record everywhere else in this area (Arribas *et al.* 1987). The likelihood of Athenian carriers of Athenian wares to the west may provide an acceptable explanation for the idiosyncracies of Tomb XXXI, which may indicate the presence of a resident Athenian serving as a kind of commercial *proxenos* in the mercantile activities of Nora (Davison 1984: 75-76).

A consideration of earlier Greek trading practices at a site in the East may support this explanation of the isolated situation in Nora (see Fig. 1). The Syrian port of Bassit-Posidaion was for centuries the focus of lively trade with Phoenicia, Cyprus, East Greece, and eventually mainland Greece and Italy. Courbin (1990) assumes that Ionians had been resident there until they (and their pottery) were replaced by Athenians from the mid-6th century to 480 BC. He points out, however, 'It was never a Greek emporium in the proper sense of the term, not more than Sukas or Al Mina. Instead, we are dealing with a small group living together with the local population in a kind of *enoikismos*' (Courbin 1990: 509). Al Mina, Tell Sukas and Bassit-Posidaion, then, while remaining under the control of the local population (and the more remote supervision of the latest victor among the various Near Eastern empires), were open to 'world' trade and resident merchants (see Morel 1984: 148-50 for a discussion of such *emporia*, both east and west, as distribution centers). In this regard Courbin (1990: 503-11) has an interesting observation to make about a group of Attic imports: they were found 'in or around a house that was twice rebuilt...a residence either for Athenians or people with a close link to Attica, who lived in Bassit, faithfully keeping their own traditions for two or three generations'. This kind of *enoikismos* does not seem to have been tolerated by the Phoenicians in the areas under their control in Sardinia or anywhere else in the west, where both settlements and burials show a single, Phoenician, cultural stamp (Niemeyer 1990: 485-86, 488), and where the Phoenicians themselves evidently served as the sole carriers; unless Maluquer de Motes (1986: 206; see also Morel 1984: 144 and Shefton 1982: 353, 355, 359) is correct in suggesting that the Phocaeans were permitted to carry on commerce with Spain as clients of the Phoenicians.

But when control of the trade routes takes a different pattern in the 5th century, a situation analogous to that at Bassit-Posidaion earlier may have arisen in areas now controlled by Carthage. In light of all these considerations, a more flexible interpretation may be applied to the social and economic implications of Tomb XXXI at Nora. The range of Attic pottery in the burial covers the whole 5th century, with a concentration in the later decades. The nature of the majority of the vases (11 lekythoi out of 20 identifiable forms: Tronchetti 1985b: 29) and the presence of jewelry (Chiera 1978: 71-83 plate V) would suggest that this was a woman's grave, or the grave of the women of the family, and that the occupant(s) were associated with an Athenian merchant or commercial agent. Bartoloni and Tronchetti (1981: 19) do not consider this possibility, assuming that because of Carthage's jealous custody of the western Mediterranean, the presence of Attic ware is not the result of direct exchange; Moscati (1985: 271; 1989: 138) is in agreement: 'i Fenici (e più tarde i Punici) esercitassero, facendo capo alle basi sarde, un commercio che, in arrivo come in partenza, essi controllavano e condizionavano'. The fact, however, that Nora shows no signs of 'quella fase di cultura punica ellenizzata che è invece oltremodo cospicua a Sulcis e a Tharros nel IV-III sec. a.C.' (Chiera 1978: 166) would tend to give unusual significance to the collection of Attic wares in a single tomb of the late 5th century.

Whether or not the trade in Athenian wares was carried on directly or through Phoenician-Punic intermediaries, the Greeks in Sicily and mainland Greece shaped the *literary* record of the western Mediterranean world to agree with their own assumptions and aspirations. Aside from the Phoenician flavor of some of the earlier episodes in the settling of Sardinia (Davison 1984: 68; Davison 1986: 188; Breglia Pulci Doria 1981: 66), and the historical grounding of the foundation story of Carthage (Niemeyer 1990: 486), the whole area provided a field for Panhellenic enterprise, with later Athenian insertions.

The Panhellenic element in this legendary history is represented by Herakles in his circuit of the western Mediterranean in the course of his adventures with Atlas and the Hesperidae in North Africa, and with Geryon in Gades and Tartessos beyond the Pillars of Herakles (Page 1973; Brize 1980). Metaphorically, Herakles' journeyings, both west and east, complement those of Io from Greece through Scythia and a monster-ridden east to the Egyptian Delta, in that they both indicate an expansion of the space covered by mythical travel to correspond to the Greeks' expanding knowledge of their world through exploration and trade (Davison 1991: 54-55, 58, 60). Aside from such symbolic implications of Herakles' labors and incidental exploits, by the 5th century they were serving an overtly political purpose: to justify Greek claims to areas visited by Herakles. Bonnet (1988: 406-407) has suggested that some of Herakles' western adventures, especially in Sicily and Spain, may be explained by an early assimilation of Herakles and Melqart and the natural assumption that where cults of Melqart existed, there also Herakles must have gone. Pareti (1912–13: 1024-32) reverses the idea of Herakles' being used as a pretext or justification for later sorties, such as Pentathlos's and Dorieus's attempts to settle in Sicily in the early and late 6th century (Herakles having promised the area of Eryx to his descendants: Herodotus 5.43; Pearson 1987: 66). He suggests rather that Dorieus's historically attested action was responsible for the fabrication of an earlier attempt by Pentathlos and the creation of a mythic exploit of Herakles as justification for both ventures, abortive though they were. Dorieus's attempt, to be dated c. 510

BC, seems a little too late for the insertion of new episodes into the Herakles' canon; and in any case it was usually only the *successful* Greek colony or trading station that attempted to attach itself to an earlier tradition (Holloway 1981: 99; Courbin 1990: 505-506, 508).

Herakles himself is well attested in the earliest Greek literature; in Homer, Hesiod and the lyric poets (Galinsky 1972: 9-22), and in representations of the labors beginning as early as 700 BC (*LIMC* 5: 37, no. 2019). It is his nephew and companion, Iolaos, who is of particular interest in the legendary history of Greek presence in Sardinia, for he is supposed to have led an expedition of Herakles' sons from Thespiae (in Boeotia) to settle there. According to Meloni (1945: 44), this story reflects an actual historical event in very early times. The references to the expedition are late (Diodorus Siculus 4.29-30; 5.15; Pausanias 1.29.5; 7.2.2; 9.23.1; 10.17.5), but Iolaos appears in the literary and artistic tradition almost as early as Herakles himself. Hesiod (*Theogony* 317) says that he assisted Herakles in the killing of the Hydra, and in art he appears at least as a bystander in all the labors except those of the Augean Stables and the Horses of Diomedes (*LIMC* 5: 688-691). Iolaos appears with Herakles in a 700 BC representation against the Hydra on a bronze Boeotian fibula (*LIMC* 5: 37, no. 2019 = 690, no. 28), and his name is actually inscribed on Corinthian black figure vases showing the same scene c. 610–600 BC (*LIMC* 5: 690, nos. 24-26; no. 25 = 37, no. 2011 and figure: ϜΙΟΛΑϜΟΣ). He first occurs on Attic vases in the second quarter of the 6th century, and the popularity of Herakles accounts for his continued appearance on such wares during the second half of the 6th century and into the 5th (*LIMC* 5: 695). From the middle of the 5th century to 300 BC, Iolaos as a companion disappears from Herakles' labors (Vollkommer 1988: 1); and he occurs only rarely in other scenes, usually limited to South Italian vases (*LIMC* 5: 695; Vollkommer 1988: 49-73, *passim*). There are two stories involving Iolaos, known to us through Euripides, and these appear only in South Italian vase-painting: Herakles' madness (Euripides, *Hercules Furens*; *LIMC* 5: 695; 4: 1684; Vollkommer 1988: 61, no. 464) and the Herakleidai seeking Athenian protection (Euripides, *Herakleidai*; *LIMC* 5: 694.G). The Etruscan adoption of Iolaos is attested in his appearance as 'Vile' (adapted from the Doric spelling with a digamma) on a series of bronze mirrors dating from the late 5th to the 2nd century BC (*LIMC* 5: 700; Breglia Pulci Doria 1981: 94-95). If Iolaos makes his way into Etruria 'probably' from Sardinia and Magna Graecia (*LIMC* 5: 696), this lends greater credence to the likely existence of a popular cult in both places by the 5th century (or even earlier through Euboean influence), even though attested only in later literature (Pausanias 10.17.5: Sardinia; Diodorus 4.30.2-3: Sardinia, many cities in Sicily; 4.24.4: a sacred precinct established for Iolaos by Herakles in Diodorus's own hometown of Agyrion).

Iolaos, then, for all his well-established but modest standing in the body of Greek legend, became fairly ubiquitous in cult and art. His leadership of a colonizing expedition to Sardinia is attested by Diodorus and Pausanias; but only Pausanias includes a group of Athenians among the original settlers, the Thespian sons of Herakles. The 6th century provides the most appropriate moment for the creation of the original tale, with the insertion of the Athenians occurring logically within the second half of the 5th, when their political ambitions were at their height (Davison 1984: 77-88; Davison 1986: 190-95; Breglia Pulci Doria 1981: 69-70). One would expect Diodorus to have mentioned the Athenians, especially if, as Meister (1967: 28) insists and Pearson (1987: 66, and *passim*) agrees, his history of earlier periods is almost totally dependent upon Timaeus. Timaeus (mid-4th to mid-3rd century BC) spent 50 years of exile in Athens and might have had some enthusiastic comments or additions to make to enhance its political reputation (Pearson 1987: 43, 54-55). Meister (1967: 28) points out that Diodorus, in addition to his information from Timaeus, could have used a mythological handbook for additional details. Such handbooks or study-guides must have been in circulation at least as early as the first half of the 5th century, for an Athenian red figure cup (attributed to the Akestorides Painter, c. 460 BC) shows a schoolboy poring over a scroll which apparently refers to one of Herakles' exploits. The text begins with the heading 'Those with Herakles'; and the first (and only visible) name on the list of presumed companions is that of Iolaos himself (Immerwahr 1973: 143 plate 31.3; *LIMC* 4: 731, where it is mistakenly described as the start of a hymn to Herakles). Pausanias too would have had similar handbooks at his disposal; but even if he produced a trustworthy compendium of what was known about Sardinia in his own day, there is no certain evidence of when the Athenians come into the story. We must take what comfort we can in the fact that he himself certainly believed it, for he repeats it four times (Pausanias 1.29.5; 7.2.2; 9.23.1; 10.17.5).

One thing is certain, that besides the better known episodes of Herakles' birth in Thebes and his adventures in the Argolid, as a Panhellenic hero he has close connections with Athens as well. By the middle of the 5th century, the Athenians had turned Herakles into a popular cult figure (Holt 1989: 71), and were beginning to express a literary interest in both Herakles and Iolaos. In Euripides' *Herakleidai* (207-212), produced c. 430 BC, Iolaos and the Thespian children of Herakles can come to Athens as suppliants because of the ties between the royal families of Athens and Thebes. Diodorus (4.29) says that the Thespian children are the grandsons of Thespios, himself a grandson of Erechtheus, a legendary king of Athens. This claim, like that of Pausanias, may well hark back 'ad un periodo in cui certe tradizioni sono ancora abbastanza vive ed Atene non può permettersi di attribuire a se stessa in prima persona la colonizzazione, ma tenta per così dire di svuotarla all'interno' (Breglia Pulci Doria 1981: 76). The development of this aspect of the story may be dated more exactly to the first half of the 5th century, during the time of the Persian Wars when Athens and Thespiae were allied until 449 BC (Breglia Pulci Doria 1981: 76).

Iolaos is surely confirmed as a tenacious fixture in some form in the western Mediterranean by his appearance in the god-list of Hannibal's intended alliance with Philip V of Macedon in 215 BC, during the Second Punic War (Barré 1983). The Greek translation of the Punic original was captured by the Romans on its way back to Philip; thus it was available in the Roman archives to Polybius (7.9), who quotes it in full (Barré 1983: 1-2). The original Carthaginian gods, listed as divine witnesses to the agreement, were translated into what was obviously intended to be their equivalents in the Greek pantheon. Along with Zeus and Hera (Ba'al-Hamon and Astarte: Barré 1983: 57) appear Herakles and Iolaos. Because of their paired relationship, Barré (1983: 78) argues that if Herakles must represent Melqart, then Iolaos should stand for the Semitic 'Ešmun. Iolaos as a functioning figure in Carthaginian religion in the late 3rd century argues strongly for his having been absorbed at a considerably earlier time, especially since he never operated at this level at any time in the Greek world. He was the constant companion of Herakles, and he had cults in his honor in such geographically diverse places as Etruria, Sicily, Thebes, Athens and perhaps Sardinia; but he had never been a god to swear by.

Athens's diplomatic and literary efforts to cement relationships with the Thespians in both prehistoric and 'modern' terms (as relatives, fugitives and allies) imply a growing effort to insert herself into the larger world described in myth and experienced in fact (as Bondì points out in his discussion of Shefton 1982: 370). When Athens was planning the famous Sicilian Expedition of 415, Thucydides (6.15.2) says that right from the beginning Alcibiades had wider intentions: to conquer the Greek cities of Sicily and South Italy and then to attack the Carthaginian empire and finally Carthage itself. Using the resources and mercenaries resulting from this successful campaign, Athens would have achieved control of all the Hellenic people (Thucydides 6.90).

In Alcibiades' speech to the Spartans, where he gives all the details of Athenian plans in the west (Thucydides 6.90), he notes that the two generals in Sicily, Nicias and Lamachus, were aware of these plans and would carry them out if possible. Kagan (1981) feels that while Thucydides believes that this was *Alcibiades*' purpose in urging the Sicilian Expedition (and that he may in fact have had the opportunity to learn of it from Alcibiades himself while both were in exile), Nicias would never have accepted such an idea, if indeed he had ever heard of it. For Kagan (1981: 256, 254), this 'grand design' was invented by Alcibiades in order to provoke a reaction from Sparta. Nicias and the rest of Athens *had* in fact heard of an intended assault upon Carthage, even if it occurred within the context of comic drama. In Aristophanes' *Knights* (1302-1305), produced in 424, a project to send a fleet of 100 triremes against Carthage is ascribed to Hyperbolus, a prominent political opponent of both Alcibiades and Nicias. Such a number of ships goes far beyond the 20 normally required for a diplomatic mission, or even a military mission (Athens sent 20 ships to assist Leontinoi against Syracuse in 427: Thucydides 3.86.1; see also Sommerstein 1981: 212, note on line 1303). Even a joke at the expense of an unpopular radical by the conservative Aristophanes must have had some basis in real imperial aims (as Kagan 1981: 61 admits, though later deprecating the wider implications: Kagan 1981: 252-59).

The possibility that the widespread trade of Attic wares to the west during the 5th century may have involved direct Athenian contact with Sardinia; the actual literary references during the second half of the century to the fertility of Sardinia (Herodotus 1.170; 5.106, 124) and to Athenian imperial designs in the direction of Carthage; and the wide circulation of the cults not only of Herakles but also of Iolaos among Greek, Carthaginian and native areas of the western Mediterranean; all this may mean that the Greeks not only created a presence for themselves in Sardinia, but that they convinced the natives of it as well.

Abbreviation

LIMC = *Lexicon Iconographicum Mythologiae Classicae.* Zurich and Munich: Artemis Verlag. Volume 4 (1988), and Volume 5 (1990).

References

Arribas, A., M. Gloria Trías, D. Cerdá & J. De Hos
    1987   *El Barco de el Sec (Costa de Calviá, Mallorca). Estudio de los materiales.* Mallorca.

Barnett, R., & C. Mendleson (eds.)
    1987   *Tharros: A Catalogue of Material in the British Museum from Phoenician and Other Tombs at Tharros, Sardinia.* London: British Museum Publications.

Barré, M.
    1983   *The God-List in the Treaty between Hannibal and Philip V of Macedonia: A Study in Light of the Ancient Near Eastern Treaty Tradition.* Baltimore: Johns Hopkins University Press.

Bartoloni, P.
    1986   Orrizonti commerciali sulcitani tra l'VIII e il VII sec. a.C. *Atti della R. Accademia Nazionale dei Lincei, Rendiconti della classe di scienze morali* 41(7-12): 219-26.
    1987   Le relazioni tra Cartagine e la Sardegna nei secoli VII e VI a.C. *Egitto e Vicino Oriente* 10(1): 79-86.

Bartoloni, P., & C. Tronchetti
    1981   *La Necropoli di Nora.* Collezione di Studi Fenici 12. Roma: C.N.R.

Bernardini, P.
    1988   S. Antioco, area del Cronicario (campagne di scavo 1983-86): L'insediamento fenicio. *Rivista di Studi Fenici* 16: 75-89.
    1990   Abitato fenicio e necropoli punica di Sulcis. *Bollettino di Archeologia* 3: 149-52.

Boardman, J.
    1982   Greek myths on 'Greco-Phoenician' scarabs. In B. Von Freytag *et al.* (eds.), *Praestant Interna. Festschrift für Ulrich Hausmann zum 65. Geburtstag am 13. August 1982*, 295-97. Tübingen.

Bondì, S.
    1989   Mozia, tra i Greci e Cartagine. *Egitto e Vicino Oriente* 12: 165-73.

Bonnet, C.
    1988   *Melqart: Cultes et mythes de l'Héraclès tyrien en Mediterranée.* Studia Phoenicia 8. Leuven: Peeters.

Breglia Pulci Doria, L.
    1981   La Sardegna arcaica tra tradizioni euboiche ed attiche. *Nouvelle Contribution à l'Étude de la Société et de la Colonisation Eubéennes*, 61-95. Cahiers du Centre Jean Bérard 6. Naples: Institut Français de Naples.

Brize, P.
    1980   *Die Geryoneis des Stesichoros und die frühe griechische Kunst.* Beiträge zur Archäologie 12. Würzburg: Konrad Triltsch Verlag.

Buchner, G.
    1982   Die Beziehungen zwischen der euböischen Kolonie Pithekoussai auf der Insel Ischia und dem nordwestsemitischen Mittelmeerraum in der zweiten Hälfte des 8. Jhs. v. Chr. In H.G. Niemeyer (ed.), *Phönizier im Westen: Die Beiträge des Internationalen Symposiums über 'Die phönizische Expansion im westlichen Mittelmeerraum' in Köln vom 24. bis 27. April 1979*, 277-98. Madrider Beiträge 8. Mainz am Rhein: Philipp von Zabern.

Chiera, G.
    1978   *Testimonianze su Nora.* Collezione di Studi Fenici 11. Roma: C.N.R.

Courbin, P.
    1990   Bassit-Posidaion in the Early Iron Age. In J.-P. Descoeudres (ed.), *Greek Colonists and Native Populations. Proceedings of the First Australian Congress of Classical Archaeology Held in Honour of Emeritus Professor A. D. Trendall, Sydney 9-14 July 1985 (Humanities Research Centre, Canberra)*, 503-509. Oxford: Clarendon Press.

Davison, J.M.
    1984   Greeks in Sardinia: The confrontation of archaeological evidence and literary testimonia. In M.S. Balmuth and R.J. Rowland, Jr (eds.), *Studies in Sardinian Archaeology*, 67-82. Ann Arbor: University of Michigan Press.
    1986   Greek presence in Sardinia: Myth and speculation. In M.S. Balmuth (ed.), *Studies in Sardinian Archaeology, Volume II: Sardinia in the Mediterranean*, 187-200. Ann Arbor: University of Michigan Press.
    1991   Myth and the periphery. In D. Pozzi and J. Wickersham (eds.), *Myth and the Polis*, 49-63. Ithaca, NY: Cornell University Press.

Galinsky, K.
    1972   *The Herakles Theme. The Adaptations of the Hero in Literature from Homer to the Twentieth Century.* Oxford: Basil Blackwell.

Holloway, R.R.
    1981   *Italy and the Aegean 3000-700 B.C.* Archaeologia Transatlantica 1. Louvain: Publications d'Histoire de l'Art et de l'Archéologie de l'Université Catholique de Louvain.

Holt, P.
    1989   The end of the *Trachiniai* and the fate of Herakles. *Journal of Hellenic Studies* 109: 69-80.

Immerwahr, H.
    1973   More book rolls on Attic vases. *Antike Kunst* 16(2): 143-47.

Kagan, D.
    1981   *The Peace of Nicias and the Sicilian Expedition.* Ithaca, NY: Cornell University Press.

Madau, M.
    1988   Ceramica attica dalla campagna del 1987. *Rivista di Studi Fenici* 16(2): 245-52.

Maluquer de Motes, J.
    1986   La dualidad comercial fenicia y griega en Occidente. *Aula Orientalis* 4: 203-10.

Marras, L., P. Bartoloni & S. Moscati
    1989   Cuccureddus. *Atti della R. Accademia dei Lincei, Rendiconti della classe di scienze morali* 42(7-12): 225-48.

Mazza, F., S. Ribichini & P. Xella
    1988   *Fonti Classiche per la Civiltà Fenicia e Punic. I. Fonti letterarie greche dalle origini alla fine dell'età classica.* Collezione di Studi Fenici 27. Roma: C.N.R.

Meister, K.
    1967   *Die sizilische Geschichte bei Diodor, von den Anfängen bis zum Tod des Agathokles. Quellenuntersuchungen zu Buch IV-XXI.* Munich.

Meloni, P.
    1945   Gli Iolei ed il mito di Iolao in Sardegna. *Studi Sardi* 6(1): 43-66.

Morel, J.
1984 Greek colonization in Italy and in the west (Problems of evidence and interpretation). In R. R. Holloway et al. (eds.), *Crossroads of the Mediterranean. Papers Delivered at the International Conference on the Archaeology of Early Italy. Haffenreffer Museum, Brown University, May 1981*, 123-61. Providence and Louvain.

Moscati, S.
1985 Fenici e Greci in Sardegna. *Atti della R. Accademia Nazionale dei Lincei, Rendiconti della classe di scienze morali* 40: 265-71.
1989 *Tra Tiro e Cadice. Temi e problemi degli studi fenici*. Studia Punica 5. Roma: Università di Roma.

Nicosia, F.
1981 La Sardegna nel mondo classico.. In E. Atzeni et al. (eds.), *Ichnussa. La Sardegna dalle origini all'età classica*, 421-76. Milano: Scheiwiller.

Niemeyer, H.G.
1990 The Phoenicians in the Mediterranean: A non-Greek model for expansion and settlement in antiquity. In J.-P. Descoeudres (ed.), *Greek Colonists and Native Populations. Proceedings of the First Australian Congress of Classical Archaeology Held in Honour of Emeritus Professor A. D. Trendall, Sydney 9–14 July 1985 (Humanities Research Centre, Canberra)*, 469-89. Oxford: Clarendon Press.

Page, D.
1973 Stesichorus: *The Geryoneis. Journal of Hellenic Studies* 93: 138-54.

Pareti, L.
1912-13 Pentathlo ed Eracle nella Sicilia occidentale. *Atti della Accademia delle Scienze di Torino* 48: 1007-32.

Pearson, L.I.C.
1987 *The Greek Historians of the West. Timaeus and his Predecessors*. American Philological Association Philological Monographs 35. Scholars Press.

Ridgway, D.
1990 The first western Greeks and their neighbours, 1935–1985. In J.-P. Descoeudres (ed.), *Greek Colonists and Native Populations. Proceedings of the First Australian Congress of Classical Archaeology Held in Honour of Emeritus Professor A. D. Trendall, Sydney 9–14 July 1985 (Humanities Research Centre, Canberra)*, 61-72. Oxford: Clarendon Press.

Shefton, B.
1982 Greeks and Greek imports in the south of the Iberian peninsula. The archaeological evidence. In H.G. Niemeyer (ed.), *Phönizier im Westen: Die Beiträge des Internationalen Symposiums über 'Die phönizische Expansion im westlichen Mittelmeerraum' in Köln vom 24. bis 27. April 1979*, 337-68. Madrider Beiträge 8. Mainz am Rhein: Philipp von Zabern.

Sommerstein, A. (ed., trans., ann.)
1981 Aristophanes, *Knights (The Comedies of Aristophanes: Vol. 2)*. Warminster: Aris & Phillips.

Tronchetti, C.
1985a I Greci e la Sardegna. *Dialoghi di Archeologia* 3(2): 17-34.
1985b La necropoli punica: la ceramica di importazione. *Nora. Recente studi e scoperte*, 29-31. Pula: Amministrazione Comunale di Pula.

Tsirkin, J.B.
1986 The Hebrew Bible and the origin of Tartessian power. *Aula Orientalis* 4: 179-85.

Ugas, G., & R. Zucca
1984 *Il Commercio Arcaico in Sardegna: Importazioni etrusche e greche (620-480 a.C.)*. Cagliari: Angelo Viali.

Vollkommer, R.
1988 *Herakles in the Art of Classical Greece*. Oxford University Committee for Archaeology Monograph 25. Oxford.

Riassunto

In quest'articolo l'Autrice esamina le storie greche riguardanti la colonizzazione greca della Sardegna per determinarne l'origine. L'Autrice propone l'ipotesi secondo la quale la progressiva ellenizzazione della cultura sarda attraverso contatti commerciali, è risultata nel fatto che le popolazioni sarde hanno adattato i loro miti a quelli greci. Storici successivi come Diodoro Siculo e Pausania hanno affermato che le storie greche sono autentiche in quanto culti e pratiche religiose sarde riflettevano e celebravano le suddette storie. Diodoro e Pausania spiegano il culto di Iolaos in Sardegna come una conseguenza fatto che durante il periodo che precede la guerra di Troia, Iolaos ed i figli di Herakles provenienti da Thespiae si sono stabiliti in Sardegna.

Quanta verità si cela dietro i miti greci riguardanti la colonizzazione della Sardegna? L'Autrice riassume le attuali testimonianze che mostrano contatti greco-sardi fino alla metà del IV sec. a.C. Vasellame eubeo-pitecussano appare in associazione con vasellame fenicio dell'VIII secolo presso Sulcis. La presenza di vasellame greco, associato con materiale etrusco, sembra aumentare in Sardegna nel VII e nel VI sec. a.C., insieme agli insediamenti fenici. Nel tardo VI sec. assistiamo ad una diminuizione di vasellame greco; ma influenza ellenica è presente nelle placche cartaginesi di Astarte e negli scarabei di diaspro verde decorati con soggetti tipici della Grecia arcaica. Vasellame attico, specialmente a vernice nera, inonda la Sardegna durante il V sec. e l'inizio del IV sec. a.C. Gli scavi effettuati a Tharros indicano una profonda ellenizzazione del mondo punico dovuta all'esistenza di un commercio attivo tra Atene ed il Mediterraneo occidentale.

Durante l'VIII e il VII secolo, greci e fenici sono partners o rivali, ma non sono nemici per quanto riguarda i loro commerci diretti ad ovest; ciò è riflesso nella mescolanza delle loro ceramiche nello strato inferiore di Tharros. Il commercio greco con la Sardegna è continuato ad esistere anche dopo la dominazione cartaginese. È possibile che il vasellame attico del V secolo ritrovato a Tharros sia stato portato dagli atenesi stessi; un esempio è il fatto che il defunto della tomba 31 a Nora, è attorniato unicamente da vasellame attico. Anche se non è chiaro se i Greci commerciavano direttamente con la popolazione sarda, è evidente che il Mediterraneo occidentale è stato usato dai Greci non solo come un'area che ha ospitato le loro vicende commerciali, ma anche le loro vicende mitiche.

Le avventure occidentali di Herakles con Atlas e con gli Hesperidae sono metafore mitiche che rappresentano l'espansione greca attraverso i viaggi e il commercio. Questi miti sono stati usati anche per giustificare rivendicazioni greche su aree visitate da Herakles e dei suoi compagni. Iolaos—nipote e compagno di Herakles—ha condotto i figli di Herakles da Thespiae in Beotia verso la Sardegna. Diodoro ha riportato la leggenda originale, e Pausania l'ha estesa includendo un gruppo di ateniesi al gruppo d'insediamento originale. Considerando i reperti archeologici greci in Sardegna, il VI secolo è il periodo più logico per la creazione di questa leggenda, ed il V è il periodo più logico per l'aggiunta dell'elemento ateneo. La leggenda di Iolaos è divenuto un culto popolare tra i greci e le popolazioni del Mediterraneo occidentale.

PART IV

Interaction and Acculturation:
Phoenician, Punic and Roman Settlement in Sardinia

La Facies Orientalizzante in Sardegna: Problemi di Individuazione e di Metodologia

Paolo Bernardini

In anni recenti ed in seguito a importanti ricerche sul campo, vari studiosi hanno proposto di individuare sotto l'etichetta di 'fase orientalizzante' una serie di prodotti artigianali di ambito protostorico sardo, così come, più in generale, di definire con lo stesso termine una vera e propria temperie culturale che, come si verifica in vario modo in più aree dell'Occidente mediterraneo, caratterizzerebbe anche in Sardegna gli sviluppi della società locale tra l'VIII e il VII sec. a.C.[1] Tale proposta, nei modi sia pure necessariamente provocatori in cui talvolta è stata formulata e svolta, legittima reazione alla visione di un'astratta Sardegna preistorica sempre uguale a sè stessa, deve in ogni caso ancora emanciparsi, e sarà cosa lunga, da una notevole confusione e superficialità nei procedimenti e nei metodi di individuazione ad essa applicati.

Al di là della discussione sull'attribuzione cronologica di alcuni materiali e dell'opportunità di attribuire validità generale a contesti particolari e, in molti casi, noti in modo assai parziale e preliminare, la riserva più immediata, che sorge spontanea scorrendo le ultime discussioni sull'argomento, riguarda la tendenza, che spesso diventa vera e propria forzatura, a voler costringere e incanalare il percorso storico-sociale della Sardegna in questi duecento anni nei parametri di sviluppo ben noti e collaudati della cultura orientalizzante etrusca e laziale (Ugas 1986: 41, 49 n. 3). Non meno perplessi lascia l'atteggiamento metodologico di chi, per superare le ovvie dissonanze ed aporie emergenti dalla giustapposizione automatica di due realtà diversamente strutturate, si affida alla scarsità di contesti scavati e di informazioni disponibili per sostenere che tutto quello che manca o non è finora attestato nella Sardegna 'orientalizzante', vuoi i materiali specifici, vuoi i fatti organizzativi, politico-economici, del territorio, è semplicemente sotterra, quindi storicamente e archeologicamente presente ma a noi celato (Ugas and Zucca 1984: 58-61).

I secoli dell'orientalizzante scandiscono in Sardegna l'avvio e lo sviluppo del fenomeno della colonizzazione fenicia; il confronto con la nuova realtà coloniale è la griglia fondamentale di lettura e di verifica del mutare degli aspetti produttivi ed organizzativi indigeni in questo stesso periodo (Bernardini 1986: 106-108; Bondì 1988: 147-72). Ritornare su questo concetto potrà anche essere banale, ma non è certo scontato quando si osserva che l'identificazione di un orientalizzante sardo serve talvolta ad evocare una Sardegna dei Greci e degli Etruschi, alternativa a quella dei Fenici, proprio in una fase degli studi in cui viene rivalutato il ruolo di intermediari di prodotti orientalizzanti svolto dai Fenici nell'Occidente mediterraneo (Moscati 1988: 542-47; Martelli 1991: 1049-72). L'irradiazione fenicia in Iberia si accompagna in questi secoli allo sviluppo di una cultura orientalizzante, di prevalente ambito tartessico, a dir poco monumentale nelle sue componenti; diversa, e non soltanto per la frammentarietà dell'indagine, appare la situazione sarda (Almagro Gorbea 1991: 573-99).

È appunto in questi termini il nodo cruciale del problema: in età orientalizzante oggetti appartenenti a questa temperie culturale possono circolare, anche in quantità cospicua, in un dato ambito e in un certo ambiente, ma altra cosa è la

---

1 Se si è sollecitata da tempo la necessità di applicare alla produzione bronzistica figurata indigena metodi e termini di approccio impiegati nell'analisi della piccola plastica geometrica e orientalizzante (Nicosia 1981: 459) e se in questa direzione esiste ora un tentativo di inquadramento (Bernardini 1985), chi scrive ha proposto di estendere l'uso di questi parametri d'indagine allo svolgimento culturale dei quadri indigeni nel corso dei primi secoli della età del Ferro (Bernardini 1982). Più di recente si sono tentate presentazioni complessive degli aspetti artigianali e culturali dell'orientalizzante sardo (Ugas and Zucca 1984: 58-61; Ugas 1986: 41-49). Della Sardegna dall'età geometrica al tardo orientalizzante si propone un acuto quadro di insieme (Tronchetti 1988: 19-39), mentre si esprimono perplessità sulla convenienza di applicare nomenclature di questo tipo allo sviluppo culturale indigeno dell'età del Ferro (Lilliu 1986: 86-87).

formazione di una 'cultura' orientalizzante. Essa sottende e realizza l'assorbimento di repertori, anche sovrastrutturali, in una società indigena, la loro replicazione e rielaborazione come offerta-risposta ad una commmittenza locale profondamente condizionata e orientata nei gusti e nell'ideologia. Le osservazioni che seguono, impostazioni del tutto preliminari e parziali di alcune problematiche, si muovono nel paesaggio culturale della Sardegna di età orientalizzante, tentando di recuperare alcuni caratteri, specificità e limiti di una cultura orientalizzante locale.

La classificazione e la seriazione della ceramica indigena dell'età del Ferro sono ancora in pieno divenire, condizionate dalla mancanza di soddisfacenti edizioni di scavi vecchi e nuovi, dalla frammentarietà della ricerca e, dispiace dirlo, dal gran contendere degli specialisti indisponibili, complessivamente, a mediare, sincronizzare e verificare i propri parametri di giudizio discendenti da scavi parziali e settoriali con i risultati proposti e sostenuti dai 'concorrenti'.[2] Anche se molto poco, qualcosa di verosimilmente definito possiamo comunque affermare sulla produzione ceramica delle fasi mature dell'età del Ferro; si è proposto, ad esempio, di collocare la ceramica indigena decorata a falsa cordicella nella fase orientalizzante e, in dettaglio, nel periodo dell'orient-alizzante antico, tra la fine dell'VIII e gli inizi del secolo successivo. Tra il campionario formale identificato, le brocche askoidi a collo stretto documentate a Monte Olladiri di Monastir, S. Anastasia di Sardara e Monte Canu di Sorso (Ugas 1986: 41-42, tav. I-II) (Fig. 1.1), hanno di recente trovato un importante elemento di verifica per quanto attiene la loro attestazione nella seconda metà avanzata dell'ottavo secolo. Due esemplari della classe, uno dei quali decorato a falsa cordicella, provengono infatti dal contesto fenicio dell'abitato di Sulci, entrambi associati alla ceramica fenicia arcaica e ad elementi di importazione greca euboica e protocorinzia (Usai 1990: 114 fig. 8a-b) (Fig. 1.2). È opportuno sottolineare la natura di contesto della situazione sulcitana, poichè si è invece proposto di sottovalutarla, affermando l'esistenza di un supposto strato nuragico più antico, di cui i due oggetti sarebbero 'residui', strato di cui peraltro non vi è assolutamente traccia in tutte le stratigrafie disponibili per lo scavo sulcitano (Santoni 1989a: 87, 95 n. 143). La classe delle brocche askoidi, una serie ben consolidata e di sicura tradizione nella produzione locale, ci rivela, nel corso del suo proseguimento agli inizi del VII secolo a.C., alcuni indizi, anche se ridotti, di un adeguamento delle officine locali alla 'moda' orientalizzante; in questo senso va interpretata la testimonianza della brocca askoide bronzea proveniente dal Nuraghe Ruju di Buddusò, che presenta l'attacco inferiore dell'ansa foggiato a palmetta fenicia (Nicosia 1978: 587, tav. 98a-b; Lo Schiavo 1986: 104-105 fig. 139-140) (Fig. 1.3).

Un secondo indizio, meno sicuro nei suoi termini cronologici, può forse cogliersi in un'altra serie ceramica di salda tradizione locale, quella delle anfore piriformi, se i tipi distinti dall'applicazione di figurine antropomorfe rappresentano davvero l'evoluzione in età orientalizzante della categoria (Bernardini e Tronchetti 1985: 286, 294-95 n. 6b; Ugas 1986: 49 n. 13).

Un terzo indizio, stavolta svincolato da una documentabile seriazione ceramica locale, non è per questo meno importante nell'indicare l'adeguarsi di officine indigene alla nuova temperie culturale; si tratta della grande coppa in metallo rinvenuta nel Nuraghe Su Igante di Uri (Nicosia 1980: 208-209 nn. 36-38; Lo Schiavo 1986: 105 fig. 141) (Fig. 2.1). Questo pezzo è stato composto utilizzando porzioni di quattro vasi diversi: l'estremità inferiore di una oinochoe in lamina bronzea, un piede bronzeo appartenente ad un vaso non identificabile e due palmette in lamina d'argento che dovevano in origine far bella mostra di sè su due oinochoai di tipo fenicio. Bisogna intendersi sul significato da attribuire a questo '*collage*', che non è certo il barbaro incollaggio di rottami ripescati dalla spazzatura di un fonditore, nè tanto meno un 'commercio' di rottami (Nicosia 1980: 203); è invece un prodotto originale, elaborato da un'officina indigena, una maestosa coppa per bere, non dimentichiamolo, che si inquadra nell'ambito dei prodotti 'esagerati', ben attestati in ambito culturale orientalizzante, e non dissimile, peraltro, dal gusto che popola di un 'esagerato' bestiario la navicella indigena deposta nella tomba del Duce di Vetulonia (Lilliu 1966: 429-34 n. 321; Bernardini e Tronchetti 1985: 287, 296 n. 10) (Fig. 2.3).

Tra la fine dell'VIII secolo e la prima metà del secolo successivo le botteghe dei ceramisti indigeni registrano altri fondamentali elementi di novità; ci riferiamo alla presenza cospicua di ceramica subfigulina e figulina, spesso associata alla decorazione dipinta e con un repertorio in cui frequente è l'ispirazione a forme di tradizione greca, fenicia e di ambito orientalizzante etrusco-laziale; i dati da tempo noti per le località di Monte Olladiri di Monastir, S. Anastasia di Sardara,

---

2 Un panorama complessivo delle seriazioni ceramiche indigene tra la fine dell'età del Bronzo e l'Orientalizzante, sul quale ci si augura che finalmente si apra un dibattito costruttivo è in Santoni (1989b: 93-128).

Fig. 1.1

Fig. 1.2

Fig. 1.3

Fig. 1.4

Fig. 1 1. Monte Canu: brocca askoide; 2. Sulci: ceramica nuragica dall'area del Cronicario; 3. Nuraghe Ruju: brocca askoide ; 4. S. Anastasia: frammento di brocca con figura antropomorfa.

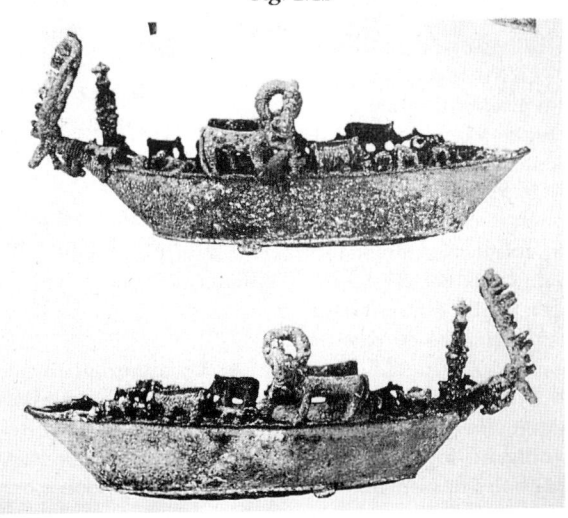

Fig. 2 1a-b. Nuraghe Su Igante: coppa bronzea; 2. Vetulonia: navicella nuragica.

Cuccuru Nuraxi di Settimo S. Pietro ed altri ricevono ora un'importante conferma e puntualizzazione dallo spaccato stratigrafico restituito da una capanna dell'insediamento del Nuraghe Piscu di Suelli (Ugas 1986: 42-45, tav. II.5-6; IV, IX-XI, XVI; Santoni 1989a: 76-82, tav. V-VIII, XI; Santoni 1989b: 126-27; Santoni 1991: 1242-44 fig. 6-7) (Fig. 3).

Non è opportuno, al momento, tentare seriazioni cronologiche di questa nuova produzione nelle fasi dell'orientalizzante medio e recente sulla base di dati ristretti, parziali e sovente editi in modo affrettato;[3] ciò che più importa, per il nostro discorso, è valutare in termini corretti il fenomeno come segnale di una trasformazione organizzativa delle botteghe indigene, legata evidentemente alla parallela evoluzione (ideologica, oltrechè socio-economica) della committenza locale. Va inoltre sottolineato come tutti gli elementi di derivazione esterna indicati nel repertorio stilistico e formale della ceramica indigena del 'nuovo corso' trovino ottimi ed esaustivi punti di riferimento, e di partenza, nelle composite esperienze artigianali che si elaborano nelle sedi coloniali fenicie; così le influenze euboiche, protocorinzie, fenicie stesse, particolarmente evidenti ora in ambito sardo coloniale dopo gli scavi dell'abitato arcaico di Sulci, sul versante dell'VIII-primo quarto del VII sec. a.C. (Bernardini 1988: 76-85; Bernardini 1990: 81-89; Bartoloni 1990: 39-56); così, nel prosieguo del settimo, i riferimenti alla produzione corinzia, etrusco-corinzia e di bucchero, di cui i centri fenici sono voraci consumatori e presumibilmente intermediari preferenziali (Tronchetti 1988: 47-62).

Il quadro delle importazioni che raggiungono le comunità indigene non contraddice le osservazioni esposte, anzi le rafforza; l'unico dato in qualche modo insolito, quello di Santu Brai di Furtei, con la sua straordinaria campionatura di bucchero (Ugas 1986: 44, tav. XIII), non può ancora seriamente compromettere l'opinione che il mutamento in senso orientalizzante della cultura materiale indigena tra l'VIII e il VII sec. a.C. dipenda sostanzialmente dal confronto-scontro con le città coloniali fenicie e dal loro moto di penetrazione interna.[4] Gli splendidi oggetti, i sontuosi 'doni' che danno lustro e prestigio al donatore e all'offerente, circolano in Sardegna in quantità certo non cospicua, tuttavia rimarchevole; la già ricordata composizione del vaso di Uri di per sè testimonia la non sporadicità di circolazione di oggetti di questo tipo nell'isola (Nicosia 1980; Bernardini 1982). I grandi santuari indigeni sono i contenitori più significativi di questi oggetti, dai calderoni bronzei di S. Anastasia di Sardara (Fig. 4.1) all'incensiere di S. Vittoria di Serri; anche se non si tratta di contesti esclusivi, come indica la presenza di altri due incensieri analoghi provenienti rispettivamente dal Nuraghe S'uraki di S. Vero Milis (Fig. 4.2) e dal ripostiglio di Tadasuni (Ugas and Usai 1987: 191-92; Tore 1987: 65-72). Se oggetti di questo tipo non sembrano, al momento, produrre echi immediati sulla produzione locale, non vi è dubbio che le botteghe indigene, in età orientalizzante, sono impegnate a produrre per una committenza interna opere di alto artigianato, in bronzo, ispirate a repertori di tradizione assai antica: i c.d. tripodi di tipo e derivazione ciprioti (Bernardini 1991: 22-24, in cui si discutono le cronologie alte, ad es. Lo Schiavo et al. 1985: 35-51). Anche se volessimo sospendere il giudizio sulla collocazione cronologica del manufatto della

---

3 V. anche Ugas (1986: 43), a proposito delle fasi dell'Orientalizzante medio. Non resta che attendere indicazioni stratigrafiche più puntuali per verificare il possibile attardamento all'Orientalizzante finale ed al Primo Arcaismo di alcuni tipi ceramici di M. Olladiri (ivi: tav. X-XI) ed è prematuro, anche se al momento più convincente, concentrare il grosso della produzione dipinta indigena tra il 730 e il 650 a.C. (Santoni 1989a: 89-90). Si propongono soltanto alcune brevissime osservazioni; è improbabile che le due *kotylai* di Furtei-Bangius (Ugas 1986: 42, tav. IV.6-7) possano essere importazioni alla luce dell'insolito motivo decorativo che le caratterizza; decorazioni analoghe a quelle presenti sulla ceramica definita dell'Orientalizzante medio (ivi: tav. IX, I.3-4) compaiono negli strati fenici sulcitani tra il 730 e il 670 a.C.; nelle stesse fasi cronologiche si registrano, nel repertorio fenicio, forme assai simili alle coppe di impasto di Monte Olladiri (ivi: tav. XVII.9 da San Sperate). Per quanto riguarda Suelli, il frammento CI-58 (Santoni 1989a: tav. VII) lascia qualche perplessità nella sua attribuzione a brocca con orlo a fungo, mentre l'ansa CI-195 (ivi: tav. VIII) è difficilmente inquadrabile in una seriazione tipologica e cronologica. Per quanto attiene la ceramica indigena, forme come il piattello CI-27 (ivi: tav. VII) e la coppetta su piede CI-432 (ivi: tav. VII) potrebbero scendere nella seconda metà avanzata del VII secolo. Non pertinente, infine, appare il confronto per l'*oinochoe* CI-52 (ivi: tav. VIII) con l'esemplare di Pontecagnano inserito in un contesto dell'Orientalizzante antico, da cui il pezzo di Suelli si differenzia notevolmente sia per la forma che per la decorazione.

4 Le ultime acquisizioni sembrano anzi indicare una più ricca e complessa gamma di suggestioni che dai Fenici vengono trasmesse al mondo indigeno a partire dalle fasi precoloniali. Per citare alcuni esempi di rilievo, si ricordi l'abbondante ceramica di importazione greca, euboica e protocorinzia, associata alla ceramica fenicia, che caratterizza il sito nuragico di Sant'Imbenia di Alghero (Bafico 1991: 18), le *oinochoai* 'fenicie' in lamina bronzea dallo stupefacente santuario di Nurdole (Madau 1991: 122), ed infine il *thymiaterion* ed il torciere bronzei di Santa Giusta (Nieddu and Zucca 1991: 56, tav. XVIII).

Fig. 3.1

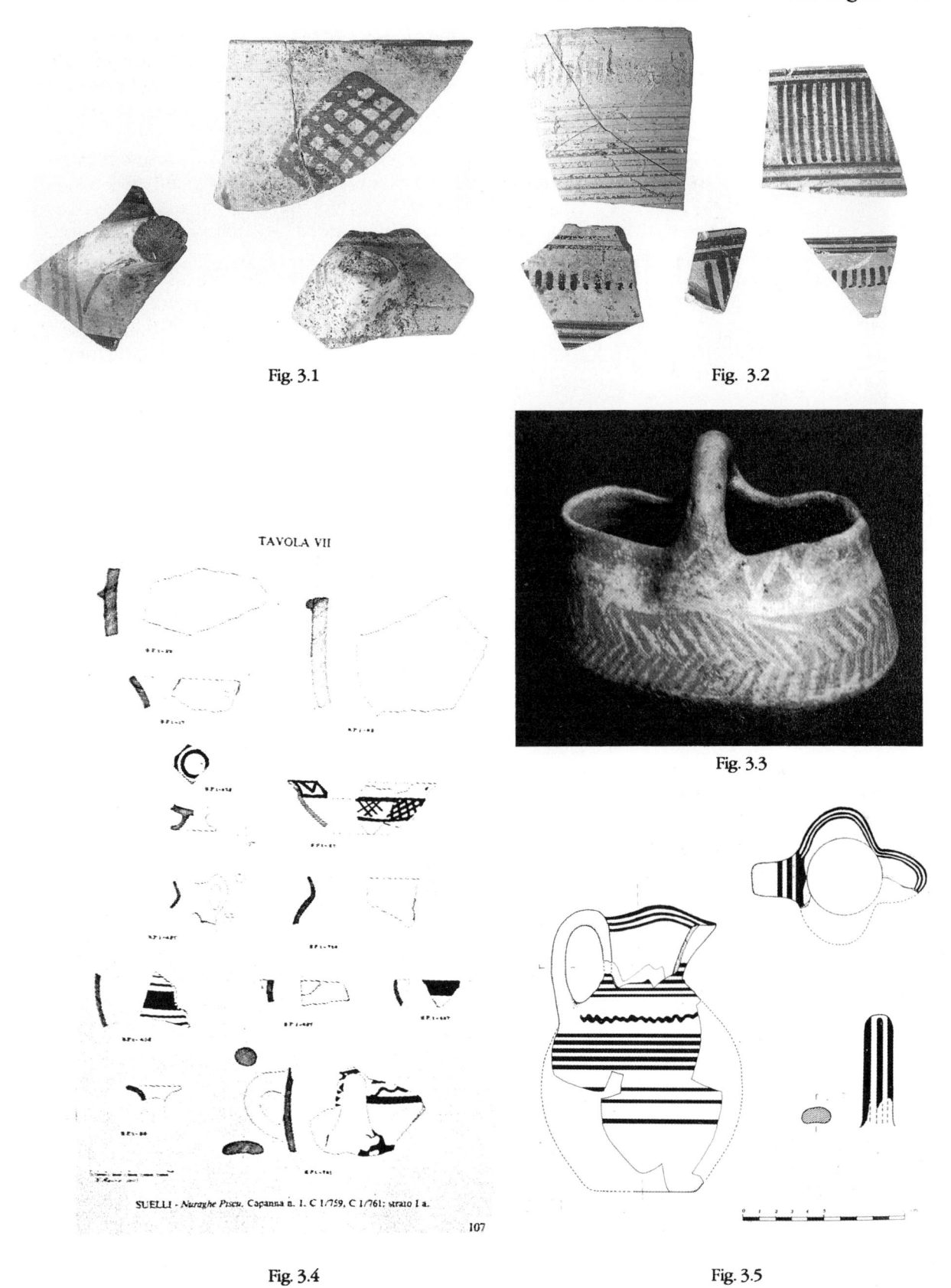

Fig. 3.2

Fig. 3.3

Fig. 3.4

Fig. 3.5

Fig. 3 1. Sulci: ceramica greca dall'area del Cronicario; 2. Sulci: ceramica greca dall'area del Cronicario;
3. S. Anastasia: cestello a chevrons; 4. Nuraghe Piscu: ceramica dipinta; 5. Nuraghe Piscu: oinochoe lobata.

402 *Sardinia in the Mediterranean*

Fig. 4.1

Fig. 4.2

Fig. 4.3

Fig. 4.4

Fig. 4 1. S. Anastasia: calderone bronzeo; 2. S'Uraki: incensiere bronzeo; 3. Su Benatzu: tripode miniaturistico; 4. Antas: bronzo di guerriero.

grotta di Su Benatzu di Santadi (Fig. 4.3), rimane evidente, per una circolazione complessiva di questi prodotti nelle fasi dell'Orientalizzante, la datazione al VII secolo dell'esemplare rinvenuto in un contesto funerario di area bolognese (Lo Schiavo *et al*. 1985: 45 n. 2; Bernardini 1991: 23).

Il tramite fenicio è stato indicato, ci pare giustamente, per i bacili sardaresi (Ugas and Usai 1987: 192; in precedenza Ugas 1986: 42, 50 n. 26), così come la classe degli incensieri è attestata in area fenicia coloniale, nella necropoli di Bitia (Tore 1987: 68); per quanto riguarda i tripodi di tipo cipriota ho osservato altrove come la lunga circolazione di oggetti di questo tipo, che nell'VIII e nel VII secolo sono replicati nelle botteghe locali su suggestione di originali evidentemente ancora circolanti, deve presumere un vettore uso ad una lunga frequentazione dei mercati indigeni che non può essere altro che quello fenicio (Bernardini 1991: 23). Non va però dimenticato che gli stimoli orientalizzanti, nelle botteghe dei bronzisti locali, si inseriscono nel solco di una lunga tradizione di contatti vicino-orientali ed egei che si abbina ad una compiuta acquisizione di tecnica, iconografie e repertorio, i quali caratterizzano la fiorente industria metallurgica indigena dalla fine dell'età del Bronzo. Sotto questo aspetto, certi esiti della produzione indigena si spiegano meglio come sviluppo, in ottavo e settimo secolo, di tematiche orientali da tempo saldamente assimilate più che come innovazioni *tout court* di cultura orientalizzante. Il caso della bronzistica figurata sarda rientra in pieno in questa problematica; se bronzi di importazione vicino-orientale anticipano, tra XI e IX sec. a.C., la nascita delle iconografie antropomorfe nell'isola (Bisi 1987: 225-39), mancano però fino ad ora le premesse iconografiche e stilistiche perchè tra le due produzioni si possa istituire in modo convincente un itinerario di derivazione, una continuità di sviluppo (Bernardini 1985: 131-40). I bronzi figurati indigeni, il cui sviluppo inizia nel corso della seconda metà del IX secolo a.C., si presentano fin dall'inizio come elaborazione del tutto originale, autonoma, figli di una temperie orientale pienamente assimilata.

È possibile, anzi probabile, che esemplari come il guerriero di Antas (Fig. 4.4), e più ancora, le nuove sorprendenti iconografie restituite dai santuari della Sardegna centro-settentrionale, quando edite nella loro interezza, forniscano alcuni tasselli mancanti e modifichino queste osservazioni (Ugas and Lucia 1987: 255-59; Rovina 1986: 42-46; Fadda 1991: 113-20), ma è difficile che il discorso sull'originalità della produzione sarda, nata da una rielaborazione antica di tradizioni orientali, fatte proprie e trasferite in un gusto ed in una iconografia peculiari, possa mutare in modo sostanziale. In questa situazione il linguaggio orientalizzante, che pure emerge a tratti nella produzione di ottavo e settimo secolo con nette cifre stilistiche (si pensi al già citato 'bestiario' della navicella vetuloniese o alla decorazione 'barocca' che si sviluppa nelle serie dei guerrieri e dei demoni) è nel suo complesso contenuto e meglio apprezzabile in termini di 'cultura' dell'Orientalizzante più che di stile, ricavabile cioè dai temi scelti, dagli eventi che si vogliono richiamare, dai concetti che si intendono celebrare (Fig. 5). Saranno le leggende,

Fig. 5.1 Nule: centauro.

404 *Sardinia in the Mediterranean*

Fig. 5.2a

Fig. 5.2b

Fig. 5.2a-b. Padria: guerriero.

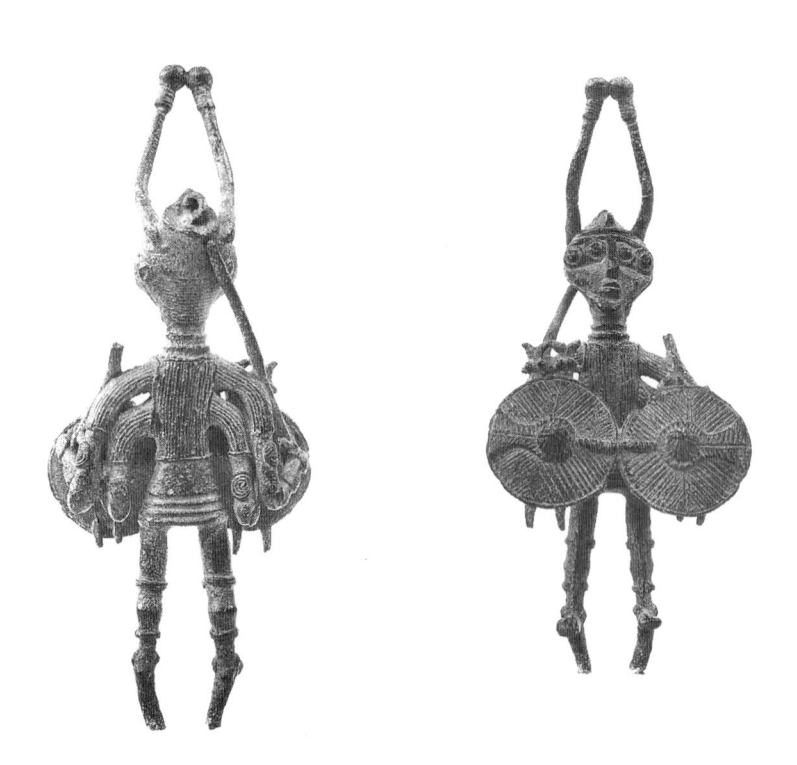

Fig. 5.3. Abini: essere demoniaco.

Bernardini: *La Facies Orientalizzante in Sardegna* 405

Fig. 6.1

Fig. 6.2

Fig. 6.3

Fig. 6.4

Fig. 6 Monte Prama:: 1-2. teste di guerriero; 3. braccio con arco; 4. mano e frammento di scudo.

le saghe degli antenati delle 'famiglie che contano', popolate di mostri come centauri e demoni bellicosi e superdotati; saranno i richiami, più terreni, al commercio marittimo, con i ricchi armenti del fortunato mercante che si accalcano presso le fiancate delle navi; sarà, ancora, l'indulgere nella rappresentazione accuratissima delle proprie fastose armature, segno del potere di una casta guerriera e militare che, dinanzi agli uomini e agli dei, rigenera e riproduce il proprio consenso e la propria legittimità alla supremazia (Bernardini 1985).

Le sculture di Monte Prama (Fig. 6) rappresentano uno dei momenti più significativi nel contesto dell'evoluzione delle botteghe locali, del loro diverso strutturarsi in risposta alle esigenze celebrative della committenza (Tronchetti 1986: 41-50); se possiamo concordare con chi afferma che questo importantissimo scavo è rimasto largamente incompiuto e che ogni sua interpretazione è fortemente limitata e precaria (Lilliu 1986: 127-28), è comunque assai problematico allontanare i colossi del Sinis da un contesto orientalizzante, più volte proposto e mai contestato con solide argomentazioni (Bernardini 1985: 140-48). Ben inserite nei modelli consolidati della piccola plastica bronzea, e riferibili in particolare alla serie iconografica del gruppo c.d. di Abini, le sculture di Monte Prama manifestano della comparsa e dell'elaborazione nelle botteghe artigianali indigene dei moduli stilistici e formali della plastica dedalica, ancora commisti al calligrafismo orientalizzante e forse mediati dall'ambiente artigianale etrusco. Dovremo verosimilmente pensare ai Fenici, in particolare ai Fenici di Tharros, quali tramiti per la diffusione in ambito indigeno di queste nuove sollecitazioni, le quali, presupponendo l'accoglimento di veri e propri modelli culturali, allignano in un gruppo umano che sempre più le analisi di dettaglio configurvano di fisionomia gentilizia (Tronchetti *et al.* 1991).

La presenza di gruppi egemoni, emergenti, di carattere aristocratico (Bernardini 1982; Lilliu 1986; Lilliu 1988: 356-417) ha ricevuto accoglienza positiva, nel complesso della sua impostazione, come plausibile e convincente proposta di lettura dei quadri socio-culturali sardi tra l'VIII e il VII sec. a.C. (Bondì 1988b: 143; Bisi 1991: 249-51), anche se valutata con perplessità e scetticismo da parte di alcuni studiosi di preistoria, i quali, peraltro, non hanno elaborato niente di più valido, in alternativa, della astratta teoria dei falsi contesti (sulla quale la più recente discussione in Bernardini 1991: 31-34, 55-66) oppure, superando il piano dell'interpretazione dei materiali, una sfumata aderenza ai principi polanyiani senza verifiche puntuali sulla situazione sarda (Lo Schiavo 1981:

304-42). Va in ogni caso detto con chiarezza che la nascita delle aristocrazie precede nel tempo la diffusione di elementi culturali orientalizzanti, i quali germogliano in un tessuto sociale già ampiamente stratificato e diversificato; da questo punto di vista, l'elemento più rilevante nel campo della produzione materiale resta l'affermazione, quindi la necessità, dell'esigenza celebrativa del proprio status attraverso l'iconografia antropomorfa, ormai funzionante, con ovvio richiamo ideologico, alla fine del IX sec. a.C. I gruppi emergenti locali hanno una lunga genesi di formazione, il cui itinerario possiamo ancora soltanto indicare a grandi linee: dall'avvio di fitti contatti commerciali con i *prospectors* egei e vicino-orientali alla fine della età del Bronzo sul versante del circuito occidentale dei metalli, al rafforzamento e regolarizzazione di questi scambi nell'età della precolonizzazione e con gli inizi della colonizzazione fenicia (Lo Schiavo *et al.* 1985; Bernardini 1986; Bernardini 1991), ai ben documentati contatti con l'ambiente tirrenico villanoviano e protoetrusco a partire dal IX secolo a.C. (da ultimo Tronchetti 1988b: 66-73).

Come la diffusione dei nuovi potentati modifichi gli assetti territoriali, innovando il sistema di 'popolamento a nuraghi', è ancora da comprendere; si rischia in ogni caso di generare confusioni e fraintendimenti facendo scomparire drasticamente il nuraghe dal paesaggio socio-economico della Sardegna dell'età del Ferro. Il '*new look*' più consono alle formule dell'associazionismo urbano ed alla divisione del lavoro, sia pure in dimensione sempre assai lontana dagli impianti urbani in senso proprio, quale emerge nella discussione sui caratteri dell'abitato di Barumini nel VII secolo a.C. (Lilliu 1986: 78-79), attende conferme areali e cronologiche, così come le situazioni protourbane di tipo 'fenicio' segnalate per l'area del Campidano e che sarebbe opportuno vedere finalmente edite in modo dettagliato (Ugas e Zucca 1984: 59; Ugas 1986: 42). Ancora, un'indagine sui gruppi gentilizi indigeni dell'età del Ferro non può prescindere da una corretta valutazione della compagine sociale che produce l'architettura e lo spazio del nuraghe, a sua volta ben lontano dall'associazionismo comunitario tribale (il mito del 'buon selvaggio' è duro a morire) e meglio aderente piuttosto alle organizzazioni di tipo 'omerico', dove l'*oikos* c.d. comunitario è la casa del re, dei compagni del re e, all'ultimo posto di una scala sociale complessa, della manodopera di tipo schiavile (Musti 1981: 39-46; Finley 1978: 49-76).

Tornando al problema che ci interessa più da vicino, l'evoluzione delle botteghe locali e la natura medesima di un certo tipo di documentazione materiale ci assicurano che, tra l'VIII e il

VII sec. a.C., è attestata nell'isola una committenza di tipo 'aristocratico', ormai consolidata, fruitrice di modelli orientalizzanti e potenzialmente in grado di riproporli in una solida 'cultura' orientalizzante locale. Detto questo, bisogna subito osservare come tale cultura realizzi soltanto in parte le potenzialità delle premesse: astraendo dalla circolazione del materiale importato, infatti, e concentrando la nostra attenzione sulle espressioni ed elaborazioni locali (del tipo che la nostra veloce ricognizione ha messo in rilievo: i vasi di Uri e Buddusò, la bronzistica figurata, la ceramica dipinta indigena) si ha l'impressione che la fisionomia orientalizzante della Sardegna sia da un lato limitata nelle sue espressioni, dall'altro ben delineata per le fasi alte dell'orientalizzante per poi sfumare ed indebolirsi quando ci si addentra nelle fasi mature ed avanzate di questo periodo, intorno allo scadere della prima metà del settimo secolo.

Alcune situazioni di carattere generale possono in parte dar conto di questi esiti: l'incapacità della società aristocratica di definire un proprio urbanesimo e la conseguente perdita di competitività con le nuove realtà urbane che fioriscono dappertutto nel bacino occidentale del Mediterraneo (Bernardini 1982: 95-98); l'impatto della colonizzazione fenicia, la quale, fin dall'VIII secolo a.C., è in fase di avanzata espansione territoriale, con effetti da presumere dirompenti disgreganti sui tradizionali assetti territoriali ed economico-produttivi indigeni. È chiaro che un discorso di questo tipo può essere accolto soltanto come impostazione generale di problemi, da verificare puntualmente per singoli centri ed aree geografiche, perchè i Fenici di Tharros e quelli di Sulci, per fare un esempio, hanno avuto con ogni evidenza storie diverse (per Sulci e il suo territorio v. ora Bernardini 1989: 48-50); pare arrivato in ogni caso il tempo di mettere in discussione l'impostazione romantica dell'idilliaco rapporto che unisce Fenici e indigeni nelle fertili pianure sarde e che nasconde, come tutte le integrazioni, una realtà ben diversa (ad es. Bartoloni 1983: 58-60). Il fascino della città produce, come è in parte documentabile per i siti di Tharros, Bitia e, forse, Sulci, l'inurbamento di indigeni nella nuova colonia (Zucca 1987: 124-25); mai però, a quanto finora è dato vedere, repliche dei modelli urbani nell'hinterland indigeno, il che la dice lunga sulla profonda crisi che il mondo indigeno si trova ad affrontare e che lo porterà al collasso in tempi relativamente brevi. Il progressivo indebolimento delle aristocrazie indigene, l'espansionismo fenicio, il concentrarsi dei traffici e degli scambi con le regioni circostanti nelle mani dei Fenici ci aiutano in definitiva a comprendere la natura particolare del fenomeno culturale orientalizzante nell'isola.

Si riconferma il dato della maggior validità e solidità di una linea portante, più antica, legata a tradizioni vicino-orientali ben assimilate (più che orientalizzanti) che corrisponde all'*exploit* della stessa committenza e che assume più specifiche connotazioni di tipo orientalizzante nella fase in cui i germi della prossima crisi sociale ed economica non hanno ancora incrinato gli assetti produttivi e organizzativi indigeni, per poi progressivamente perderle nell'avanzare ed evidenziarsi della crisi medesima. La società degli *aristoi*, la società dei Sardi, come di recente si è voluta definire (Tronchetti 1988), si presenta sostanzialmente convulsa, ricca di stimoli e di suggestioni, ma anche effimera e precaria nel suo svolgimento: i possenti guerrieri che si ergono sulle loro basi nel santuario di Monte Prama (tra il 650 e il 600 a.C.?) hanno davvero i piedi d'argilla.

Bibliografia

Almagro Gorbea, M.
    1991   El mundo orientalizante en la Peninsula Iberica. *Atti II Convegno Internazionale di Studi Fenici e Punici*, 573-99. Roma: C.N.R..

Bafico, S.
    1991   Greci e Fenici ad Alghero. *Archeo* 74: 18.

Bartoloni, P.
    1983   La ceramica fenicia di Bithia: Tipologia e diffusione areale. *Atti del I Congresso Internazionale di Studi Fenici e Punici*, 491-500. Roma: C.N.R.
    1990   S. Antioco. Area del Cronicario. I recipienti chiusi di uso domestico e commerciale. *Rivista di Studi Fenici* 18(1): 37-79.

Bernardini, P.
    1982   Le aristocrazie nuragiche nei secoli VIII e VII a.C. Proposte di lettura. *La Parola del Passato* 203: 81-101.
    1985   Osservazioni sulla bronzistica figurata sarda. *Nuovo Bullettino Archeologico Sardo* 2: 119-66.
    1986   Precolonizzazione e colonizzazione fenicia in Sardegna. *Egitto e Vicino Oriente* 9: 101-16.
    1988   S. Antioco, area del Cronicario (campagne di scavo 1983-86): L'insediamento fenicio. *Rivista di Studi Fenici* 16: 75-89.
    1989   Le origini di Sulcis e Monte Sirai. *Studi di Egittologia e di Antichità Puniche* 4: 45-59.
    1990   S. Antioco: Area del Cronicario (campagne di scavo 1983-1986): La ceramica fenicia: Le forme aperte. *Rivista di Studi Fenici* 18: 81-99.
    1991   *Micenei e Fenici. Considerazioni sull'età precoloniale in Sardegna*. Orientis Antiqui Collectio 19. Roma.

Bernardini, P., & C. Tronchetti
    1985   La Sardegna, gli Etruschi e i Greci. In E. Arslan, F. Barreca e F. Lo Schiavo (eds.), *Civiltà Nuragica*, 285-306. Milano: Electa.

Bisi, A.
    1987   Bronzi vicino-orientali in Sardegna: Importazioni ed influssi. In M.S. Balmuth (ed.), *Studies in Sardinian Archaeology III. Nuragic Sardinia and the Mycenaean World*, 225-46. BAR International Series 387. Oxford: British Archaeological Reports.

1991   L'economia fenicia tra Oriente e Occidente. *Atti II Congresso Internazionale di Studi Fenici e Punici*, 241-57. Roma: C.N.R.

Bondì, S.
1988a   La colonizzazione fenicia. *Storia dei Sardi e della Sardegna. I. Dalle origini alla fine della età bizantina*, 147-71. Milano.
1988b   La frequentazione precoloniale fenicia. *Storia dei Sardi e della Sardegna. I. Dalle origini alla fine dell'età bizantina*, 129-45. Milano.

Fadda, M.
1991   Scavi a Nurdole (NU). *Rivista di Studi Fenici* 19(1): 113-20.

Finley, M.
1978   *Il Mondo di Odisseo*. Bari.

Lilliu, G.
1966   *Le Sculture della Sardegna Nuragica*. Cagliari: La Zattera.
1986   Società ed economia nei centri nuragici. *Società e Cultura in Sardegna nei Periodi Orientalizzante e Arcaico*, 77-87, 123-28. Cagliari.
1988   *La Civiltà dei Sardi dal Paleolitico all'Età dei Nuraghi*. Terza edizione. Torino: Nuova ERI.

Lo Schiavo, F.
1981   Economia e società nell'età dei nuraghi. In E. Atzeni et al. (eds.), *Ichnussa: La Sardegna dalle origini all'età classica*, 255-347. Milano: Libri Scheiwiller.
1986   L'età dei nuraghi. In F. Lo Schiavo (a cura di), *Il Museo Sanna in Sassari*, 63-109. Sassari: Banco di Sardegna.

Lo Schiavo, F., E. Macnamara & L. Vagnetti
1985   Late Cypriot imports to Italy and their influence on local bronzework. *Papers of the British School at Rome* 53: 1-71.

Madau, M.
1991   Importazioni dal Nuorese e centralità delle aree interne. Nota preliminare. *Rivista di Studi Fenici* 19(1): 121-29.

Martelli, M.
1991   I Fenici e la questione orientalizzante in Italia. *Atti II Congresso Internazionale di Studi Fenici e Punici*, 1049-1072. Roma: C.N.R.

Moscati, S.
1988   L'arte orientalizzante. *I Fenici*, 542-47. Milano.

Musti, D.
1981   *L'Economia in Grecia*. Bari.

Nicosia, F.
1978   Scavi e scoperte. *Studi Etruschi* 46: 587-89.
1980   Etruskische zeugnisse und enflüsse. In J. Thimme (ed.), *Kunst und Kultur Sardiniens vom Neolithikum bis zum Ende der Nuraghenzeit*, 200-211. Karlsruhe: C.F. Müller.
1981   La Sardegna nel mondo classico. In E. Atzeni et al. (eds.), *Ichnussa. La Sardegna dalle origini all'età classica*, 421-76. Milano: Scheiwiller.

Nieddu, G., & R. Zucca
1991   *Othoca. Una città sulla laguna*. Oristano.

Rovina, D.
1986   Il santuario nuragico di Serra Niedda (Sorso). *Nuovo Bullettino Archeologico Sardo* 3: 37-47.

Santoni, V.
1989a   L'orientalizzante antico-medio della capanna n. I del Nuraghe Piscu di Suelli-Cagliari. *Quaderni della Soprintendenza Archeologica per le Provincie di Cagliari ed Oristano* 6: 73-110.
1989b   L'età nuragica. Dal bronzo finale all'orientalizzante. In V. Santoni (a cura di), *Il Museo Archeologico Nazionale di Cagliari*, 93-128. Sassari: Banco di Sardegna.
1991   Suelli (Cagliari). Nota preliminare sull'orientalizzante antico-medio della capanna n. I del Nuraghe Piscu. *Atti II Congresso Internazionale di Studi Fenici e Punici*, 1233-44. Roma.: C.N.R

Tore, G.
1987   Intorno ad un 'torciere' bronzeo di tipo cipriota da San Vero Milis (S'Uraki)-Oristano. *Società e Cultura in Sardegna nei Periodi Orientalizzante e Arcaico*, 65-74. Cagliari.

Tronchetti, C.
1986   Nuragic statuary from Monti Prama. In M.S. Balmuth (ed.), *Studies in Sardinian Archaeology, Volume II: Sardinia in the Mediterranean*, 41-59. Ann Arbor: University of Michigan Press.
1988a   *I Sardi: Traffici, relazioni, ideologie nella Sardegna arcaica*. Milano: Longanesi.
1988b   La Sardegna e gli Etruschi. *Mediterranean Archaeology* 1: 66-83.

Tronchetti, C., F. Mallegni & F. Bartoli
1991   Gli inumati di Monte Prama. *Quaderni della Soprintendenza Archeologica per le Provincie di Cagliari ed Oristano* 8 (in stampa).

Ugas, G.
1986   La produzione materiale nuragica. Note sull'apporto etrusco e greco. *Società e Cultura nei Periodi Orientalizzante e Arcaico*, 41-53. Cagliari.

Ugas, G., & G. Lucia
1987   Primi scavi nel sepolcreto nuragico di Antas. In G. Lilliu, G. Ugas e G. Lai (a cura di), *La Sardegna nel Mediterraneo tra il Secondo e il Primo Millennio a.C. Atti del II convegno di studi 'Un millennio di relazioni fra la Sardegna e i Paesi del Mediterraneo'*, Selargius-Cagliari, 27-30 novembre, 1986, 255-77. Cagliari: Amministrazione Provinciale di Cagliari.

Ugas, G., & L. Usai
1987   Nuovi scavi nel santuario nuragico di Sant'Anastasia di Sardara. In G. Lilliu, G. Ugas e G. Lai (a cura di), *La Sardegna nel Mediterraneo tra il secondo e il primo millennio a.C. Atti del 2 convegno di studi 'Un millennio di relazioni fra la Sardegna e i Paesi del Mediterraneo'*, Selargius-Cagliari, 27-30 novembre 1986, 167-218. Cagliari: Amministrazione Provinciale di Cagliari.

Ugas, G., & R. Zucca
1984   *Il Commercio Arcaico in Sardegna: Importazioni etrusche e greche (620-480 a.C.)*. Cagliari: Angelo Viali.

Usai, L.
1990   S. Antioco. Area del Cronicario. Ceramica preistorica dall'area del Cronicario. *Rivista di Studi Fenici* 18(1): 103-23.

Zucca, R.
1987   Bronzi nuragici da Tharros. In G. Lilliu, G. Ugas e G. Lai (a cura di), *La Sardegna nel Mediterraneo tra il secondo e il primo millennio a.C. Atti del II convegno di studi 'Un millennio di relazioni fra la Sardegna e i Paesi del Mediterraneo'*, Selargius-Cagliari, 27-30 novembre 1986, 117-29. Cagliari: Amministrazione Provinciale di Cagliari.

Summary

In the first millennium BC, Sardinia was not a static, abstract place, but rather an area of the western Mediterranean with a dynamic, evolving local culture. When the Phoenicians established colonies on the island in the 8th–7th centuries BC, Nuragic culture entered an Orientalizing phase which was both similar yet different from analogous developments in Etruria and Iberia, for example. Furthermore, even though Orientalizing objects may have circulated in conspicuous quantity, it is more difficult to speak of an Orientalizing 'culture'. It is thus an ambitious but necessary task to characterize and individuate this period in Sardinia, a situation not helped by incomplete publication of excavation data, and the fragmentary state of ongoing research.

Nevertheless, certain indigenous ceramics (with decoration *a falsa cordicella, brocca askoidi a collo stretto*) can be dated to the late 8th century BC, and local production may even have adopted an Orientalizing mode. This is supported by a bronze Nuragic jug with a Phoenician palmette handle from Nuraghe Ruju di Buddusò, and a large metal cup from Nuraghe Su Igante di Uri, which is a collage of four Phoenician and native Sardinian vases. In the first half of the 7th century BC, Greek, Phoenician and other Orientalizing features influenced Nuragic production, but again the chronological data are limited, and we cannot yet attempt a seriation of this new production. Instead, we must be sure to use the correct terms to describe this Orientalizing phenomenon, and not to obscure the evolving, multi-faceted, indigenous component.

Certainly, it was the presence of Phoenician cities on the coasts of Sardinia that resulted in the importation of Euboean, Protocorinthian, Etruscan, as well as Phoenician wares, and their ultimate distribution to native centers; this exchange may in fact have begun in the pre-colonial period. The initial circulation of foreign art objects as gifts, and the prestige associated with this exchange, undoubtedly spurred local production of the highest quality, even if imitation and adaptation of foreign motifs was not quickly adopted. The Sardinian bronze figurines exemplify this, with imports of the 11th–9th centuries BC reelaborated in local *bronzetti* by the 2nd half of the 9th century BC. The Author argues that the selection of Orientalizing traditions was not just an abstract, artistic process, but part of a deeper understanding of a foreign iconography and style, and probably of legends, myths and other aspects of eastern Mediterranean culture.

The presence of local, aristocratic groups seems a plausible medium for the adoption of Orientalizing 'culture', but it must be remembered also that Nuragic society was already complex and stratified before this period, still developing during the Late Bronze Age when Aegean and Villanovan commercial contacts were first established (cf. also Webster and Teglund, this volume). We must also reexamine the extent of urbanism on a local level, and the nature of Nuragic settlement and life, for example, at Barumini in the 7th century BC. The colonization of the island must have disrupted the territorial and economic *status quo* of the indigenous Sardinians, and the individual histories of each zone must be treated separately (cf. Peckham, and Tore, this volume). The romantic, ideal coexistence of Phoenicians and Sardinians cannot have been a universal reality. In fact, the progressive weakening of the indigenous aristocracy, Phoenician expansion, and the concentration of exchange in the coastal zones all characterized the Orientalizing phenomenon in Sardinia. These factors presage an economic and social crisis that results in the collapse of true Nuragic civilization in a relatively brief time.

The Phoenician Foundation of Cities and Towns in Sardinia

Brian Peckham

Lately, on the basis of accumulating archaeological evidence and under the impetus of refined historical interest, there has been an emphasis on the individuality of ancient Sardinian cities, on the particularity of their artistic traditions, on the exclusiveness of their commercial ties, and on their special contribution to a common Phoenician enterprise. Intricately involved in this burst of information and insight is a more accurate perception of the original diversity of the Phoenician explorers who arrived in the west, by different routes, for specific reasons, from competitive ports, at different times, and with various crews and companions. From the Sardinian perspective it is no longer useful or correct to suppose that some faceless and multifaceted Phoenician empire rolled indiscriminately and inexorably over the western Mediterranean from some indeterminate Cypriot base, for uniquely crass exploitative purposes, and with indistinguishable and predictable results. Sardinia, in its very complexity, has become exemplary in defining the meaning of the Phoenician world.

The Growth of the Mainland Phoenician City-States

From earliest times Phoenicia was known by its cities and their reach into the Mediterranean world. The Egyptians, in their maritime ventures, were familiar especially with Byblos; but they also dealt with Tyre and Sidon and, in governing their Asiatic possessions, understood the individual relations of the three cities with the northern coast of Amurru, with the interior Syrian dominions, and with the southern Palestinian ports. The Assyrians, from the inception of their Empire, recognized the value and delight of Arvadian ships and of the bounty provided by the great cities to the south. Homer could distinguish between Phoenicians and Sidonians; Herodotus knew more about Tyre's connections with Egypt and Africa than about Sidonian contacts with Europe; and later Greek writers regularly identified all Phoenicians with the merchants of Tyre. Even the Bible knew one from the other: it gave precedence to Sidon, associating it with the Northern Kingdom of Israel and with the alien culture of Canaan and the coastal cities of Amurru; Byblos was recognized as a source of materials, artisans and skilled laborers; and Tyre was identified as the resource of kingdoms, the ally of Egypt, and the model of the perfect Judaean state (Bunnens 1983b; Peckham 1992).

Byblos

Epigraphic evidence sets Byblos apart as an independent capital city throughout the first millennium. It had its own dialect, a distinctive script, and peculiar religious and artistic traditions. It routinely collaborated with Tyre and Sidon in their respective heydays. Also, Byblos repeatedly demonstrated an ability to submit to and still survive the domination of world powers (Cross 1979; Elayi 1985b; Peckham 1987).

Byblos was not a typical Phoenician city and it does not fulfill our expectations of the Phoenician stereotype. In artistic matters, at least in later times, it shows a critical interest in representations of the human form (Peckham 1987) but it does not conform to the usual artistic canons (Gubel and Bordreuil 1985; Gubel and Cavet 1987). In earlier times it may have been an influential source of the south Syrian style of carving in ivory and stone (Barag 1983; Winter 1981; Markoe 1990). This style was centered, perhaps, in Damascus from where it spread, with Aramaean imperial designs, to northern Syria where Byblian complicity in the enterprise was recognized and taxed by the Assyrians (Bunnens 1983a; Kestemont 1985). Byblian interests were modest and land-based, and the city is not known for its territorial expansion on the mainland or for its adventuresome spirit. Its affiliation with Phoenicians at Larnaka tis Lapethou in northwestern Cyprus and at Pyrgi in southwestern

Italy is attested in texts that have Cypriot components but adhere closely to the linguistic and religious traditions of the founding city (Gibson 1982: 134-41, 151-59).

Sidon

From the beginning Sidon is noted in Egyptian and Assyrian sources for its association with Arvad and Amurru and for its interference in northern affairs. In its Late Bronze Age relations with Egypt it protested fidelity to the Pharaoh but was engaged in sedition with Syrian and Anatolian states. It began to prosper after the advent of the Sea Peoples and took advantage of the decline of great cities such as Ugarit which had not survived the upheavals of the impending new age. Its ambition did not escape notice and, with Byblos and Arvad, it was the first of the seafaring cities to pay tribute to Assyria. For three centuries, throughout the Early and Middle Geometric periods, it was free to pursue its affairs and, at the inconsiderable cost of sporadic tribute to Assyria, was able to maintain its relations with the rich and powerful North Syrian and Neo-Hittite states. In the latter part of the 8th century, however, Sidon's network in the North began to unravel when Arvad, along with its affiliate coastal cities Arqa, Simirra and Siyannu, was incorporated into the Assyrian provincial system. By the end of the century Sidon's Syrian and Anatolian interests were lost to Assyria, the capital city itself came under Assyrian control, and its king, Ilu'ili, when he tried unsuccessfully to restore Sidon's preeminence and prevent Tyre from taking its place, unwisely fled to Cyprus where Tyrian loyalists put him to death. Early in the 7th century Sidon, with the help of its traditional Cilician allies, tried once more to reassert its dominion but its king was executed and the city was destroyed (Bunnens 1983a; Elayi 1985a; Kestemont 1983; Oded 1974; Peckham 1992).

Sidon's mainland possessions were not extensive but, to judge from its literary trademarks and from the Canaanite, Syrian and Anatolian features that mark its presence, its influence was profound and far-reaching. At the end of the 8th century, by right or in its desperate struggle to survive, it held cities in Tyrian territory as far south as Acco (Elayi 1982: 95). Sarepta, conversely, that had always belonged to it, was ceded to Tyre in the time of Esarhaddon (Elayi 1982: 95), and the transfer of power is clearly marked in the different ensembles of imported pottery (Koehl 1985). A late 9th-century tomb in the vicinity of the city contained local Canaanite and imported Geometric pottery with little that is peculiarly Phoenician (Saïdah 1977; Bordreuil 1977). Contemporary tombs at Khalde near Beirut, in the territory of Byblos but in the probable jurisdiction of Sidon, contained similar pottery (Saïdah 1966; 1983), a seal in the hybrid south Syrian style (Culican 1974), and a stela inscribed with the Luwian name *ptty* (Bordreuil 1982: 191; Houwink Ten Cate 1961: 158). Later inscriptions from the sanctuary at Amrit, in the region of Arvad, attest to the worship of Eshmun, the tutelary god of Sidon, according to the rituals of the southern metropolis (Bordreuil 1985; Puech 1986). The 9th-century Phoenician inscription of Kilamuwa from Zinjirli, before his kingdom and the entire region were overrun by the Aramaeans and Assyrians, argues for continued Sidonian involvement with the Danunians who had first lured them into Anatolia. The 8th-century inscription of Azitawadda from Karatepe reveals the prosperity that Danunians in Cilicia enjoyed through their relations with Sidon before the Assyrians destroyed their alliance. The distribution of ivories carved in the north Syrian style, from manufacturing centers in the Aramaean and Neo-Hittite states, through the Danunian kingdoms and to the Aegean and to Greece, are testimony to the broad sweep of Sidonian interests and influence (Barnett 1982; Winter 1976a; Winter 1976b; Winter 1983; Winter 1989; Herrmann 1989).

Tyre

Tyre is the maritime city that displays all the typically Phoenician characteristics. It flourished later than Sidon, in different directions, and with more lasting effects. It was interested in overland routes, in becoming the client of kings and commoners who relinquished territorial rights in return for its services, and in adjusting to the habits and traditions of the foreign lands where it had commerce. When it was delivered from the web of the Sidonian world it was proud to call its own all the best of its Sidonian and Byblian heritage.

Eclecticism is Tyre's chief characteristic. It was the creator and purveyor of ivories in the Phoenician style noted for their grace and refinement and regular Egyptian features (Winter 1976a). Its floruit coincides with the Orientalizing fever that swept the Mediterranean world. Its pantheon included Eshmun of Sidon and the terrestrial Baals of Byblos (Parpola and Watanabe 1988: 24-27), Egyptian, Greek and Cypriot gods (Müller 1988), and local syncretistic effigies like Melqart, Tanit and Milkastarte (Bordreuil 1987; Bodreuil 1990; Pardee 1988); its amalgam of ancestral traditions and alien beliefs merited special treatment in Philo's *Phoenician History* (Baumgarten 1981: 264).

Assyrian sources, the dedication to Melqart on the Bar Hadad stela, and two inscriptions and ivories in the Phoenician style from Arslan Tash attest to Tyrian presence in North Syria in the mid-9th and late 8th centuries; but Tyre's principal thrust was towards Cyprus. Byblians, certainly, and perhaps Sidonians, had occupied the northern coast of Cyprus (Peckham 1991), but Tyre concentrated on the south. By the 11th century, Tyrians had occupied the western part of the island near Palaepaphos (Bikai 1987; Bikai 1988; Wilson 1974), and the eastern part at Salamis (Karageorghis 1983; Sznycer 1980); still later, they settled at Kition and a city called Carthage (Lipinski 1983). They ended up nearly everywhere on the island, prominent in Amathus, predominant in places such as Kition, but most often content to live under local Greek and Cypriot rule.

On the mainland, Tyre had effective relations with Judah and with Philistia. Through them, as well as from Cyprus, it also maintained enduring links with Egypt. In Tyre itself most of the imported pottery is like the Greek products that were sold in Cyprus (Coldstream 1988) and the local pottery, apart from the typically Phoenician wares, can be compared with examples from the adjacent cities in Israel and from sites in Judah and Palestine (Bikai 1978). Along the coast, in the wake of the various Sea Peoples or with their agreement, Tyre had ports of entry at Achzib, Acco and Dor (Dothan 1986; Prausnitz 1982; Stern 1990) and, at various times, access to the harbors and facilities at Tell Abu Hawam, Athlit, Joppa, Yabneh Yam and Qasile (Raban 1985). Signs of Tyre's passage are found in the sea (Culican 1976; Linder 1973), and in the south the Philistines adopted their language and worshipped their gods. Inland there are traces of their habitation at Tell Keisan, Azor, Arad, Kuntillet Ajrud and Elath. They settled in Egypt at Daphne, were mercenaries at Abu Simbel, and lived with the exiled Judaeans in their colony at Elephantine.

Tyrian expansion partly overlaps with the age of Sidonian preeminence, although it took other directions with different results. Tyrian supremacy, on the other hand, coincided with the decline of Sidon, with the reorganization of the Neo-Assyrian empire, and with the development of the Greek colonial system. When Sidon was defeated and destroyed, Tyre and its Cypriot cities paid tribute. The Assyrians gave them control of the markets, and the king of Tyre assumed the ancient title of King of the Sidonians. When the king of Tyre submitted to Esarhaddon it was with the proviso that Tyre would maintain control of the seas. When the Assyrians went against Egypt the rules were changed, but Tyre maintained its hold on maritime commerce and overland routes. It was not until the mid-6th century that the world that Tyre had made and dominated came to an end. In the 5th century, weary from the debacle at Salamis, Tyre lost the plain of Sharon and its ports at Dor and Joppa to a new and vigorous Sidonian dynasty (Kelly 1987).

Phoenicians in the Emerging Western Mediterranean World

The phases of Phoenician growth and expansion are intimately linked with the development of the larger Mediterranean world. Sardinia had local age-old traditions and flourished long before the Phoenicians came to the island (Lo Schiavo 1981). This situation changed gradually as Sardinia was drawn into European, Asian and North African cultures and, with the expert help of non-Sardinians, both adventurers and immigrants, became active in the history of the west. The Phoenicians were not the least among these newcomers but their involvement was at first intermittent and varied with their place of origin and with their political, cultural and economic affiliations.

Mycenaeans went west and frequented Sardinia throughout the Late Bronze Age. When they were defeated and dispersed, Cyprus, where many of them had settled, was inspired to continue their traditions and became the predominant link between east and west. In the wake of the Mycenaeans, but independently of Cyprus, Sidon and Euboea became engaged in trade, commerce and exploration that brought them to each other's shores and westward along the routes that the Mycenaeans had first taken to Italy and Sardinia. Separately and at some remove, Tyrians who had settled in Cyprus followed the southern sea lanes past Palestine and Egypt to North Africa and the Atlantic, and then homeward via southern Sardinia. Later still, after the fall of Sidon and when its Cypriot colonies were subject to Assyria, Tyre exploited the westward routes and soon founded cities in southern and western Sardinia.

The Mycenaean presence in Italy and Sardinia is attested by imported pottery as well as local imitations, and is evident in the Mycenaean contribution to the mining and smelting of copper. Mycenaeans arrived in the Gulf of Cagliari but are known mostly in the eastern half and northern reaches of Sardinia, and seem to have followed the sea lanes between Italy and Sardinia around the northwestern part of the island as far south as Tharros (Lo Schiavo and Vagnetti 1980;

Ferrarese Ceruti *et al.* 1987). Incursions by Cypriots, accompanied by Tyrian captains or crews who had settled among them, at first followed the same routes; but they soon diverged and went along the southern coast of Sicily to the southern and western ports of Sardinia (Botto 1986). These strangers are distinguished by their metallurgical skills and artifacts and by their influence on indigenous Nuragic culture (Lo Schiavo 1985; Lo Schiavo *et al.* 1985). The presence among them of Phoenicians is evident from the statuette of a divinity lost off the coast of Selinunte (Bisi 1980), and from a late 11th-century inscription at Nora (Cross 1986). These two cultural waves may also be represented by the Mycenaean freighter that foundered off Ulu Burun and by the Cypriot ship that sank not far away, but about a hundred years later, off Cape Gelidonya (Muhly *et al.* 1988); the hiatus between their explorations was filled by the ships and exploits of the Sea Peoples, and among them maybe Sardinians, in the worn and susceptible East (Dayton 1984).

Sidonians reached Euboea and Attica by the 10th century and Euboeans, in their growing overseas business, had establishments at Al Mina and Sukas by the end of the 9th. The Sidonians were merchants and artisans who had travelled to Crete, Rhodes and Cos beginning in the 11th century (Coldstream 1969; Coldstream 1982; Bisi 1987a). They brought 9th-century Aramaean heirlooms to Samos and Eretria (Eph'al and Naveh 1989), and they instructed their friends and allies in the mysteries of the alphabet that they themselves used and in the system of spelling they had seen in north Syria. Euboeans and Sidonians together went to Italy where the Euboeans eventually settled in the 8th century (Amadasi Guzzo 1987). They followed the earlier Mycenaean routes along the instep of Italy through the straits of Messina to northwestern Sardinia where an inscription from Bosa (Cross 1986) and bronze figurines in an oriental but not quite Phoenician style (Bisi 1980; 1987b) attest to an early Sidonian presence.

The emigration of Tyrians from Cyprus to the west and their foundation of another Carthage is witnessed in legend and history and confirmed by a late 9th-century inscription from Nora. In it a sea captain in the service of Pygmalion, either the Cypriot god (Peckham 1972) or the legendary king of Tyre (Cross 1986), records that he and his crew found safe harbor in Sardinia after a stormy passage from Tarshish. Since the Greeks told stories of just such an Iberian adventurer who landed in Sardinia, and since this route from Spain was sailed in later times, the text throws an uncommon light on recorded events. There is no suggestion that Cypriots built cities at this time in either place, but they had founded Carthage on their way to the west, and rediscovered Nora on their homeward route; but they left the development of the towns to a later time when Tyrians and refugees from Cyprus (Krahmalkov 1981) and Sidon needed a place to settle and stay.

The final phases in Phoenician expansion are represented by late 8th- and 7th-century foundations in Sardinia, in places to which Mycenaeans, Cypriots, Sidonians, Euboeans and the Tyrians themselves had once sailed. In this period there is a clear Phoenician determination to settle among the indigenous populations in cities and towns, living by trade and commerce, working with local resources, and dealing with Greek, Etruscan, Iberian and Carthaginian supply and demand. All this involved homeland and foreign ports, staging areas in Malta and Sicily, and outposts along the way. It included other Phoenicians who wanted to join them, but it was clearly Tyrian and was marked by their characteristic eclecticism, adaptability, and flair. It soon turned Sardinia into a hub of oriental culture in the west.

The Phoenician Foundation of Cities and Towns in Sardinia

The urbanization of a diffused, densely but irregularly settled, mining, manufacturing and agricultural population was the principal contribution of the Phoenicians to the civilization of Sardinia (Bondì 1984). It was a gradual but radical change and with it came the regional diversification of the island and the specialized relations of individual sites along traditional routes with various people and places abroad. Above all it left the island open to constantly changing international influences as other markets and monopolies developed. It was not surprising in the end that Carthage had to interfere to assert its peculiar position in the western world.

The Phoenician cities, unlike the native Sardinian settlements around which they were built, were enclosed by walls and organized into sectors (Barreca 1978; de Socio 1983). The walls were originally designed for administrative and not for military purposes. This is suggested by the separation of religious, residential and commercial districts from cemeteries, farmland and sources of supply (Isserlin 1983). Each city had territory along the inland roads, where there is evidence of Phoenician presence among the Sardinian population, and settlements along the shore (Barreca 1965). The cities were cosmopolitan, judging from the variety of Nuragic (cf. Bartoloni, this volume), Etruscan and Greek products, but the population, however disparate, appears not to have been mixed (Moscati 1986a). The absence of signs of monarchic or autocratic government and the indistinction of residence and burial customs suggest that business was a civic enterprise based on ability and success rather than any monopoly by the government or guilds (Bondì 1981). The big cities, like their Levantine counterparts, soon became regional centers.

The cities and towns were founded in places frequented by the earlier explorers around the southwestern part of Sardinia, in evident agreement with the inhabitants who maintained their own sophisticated cultural traditions in the rest of the island (Lo Schiavo 1978; 1987) and who began to flourish almost as soon as the Phoenicians had settled among them (Bartoloni 1985). The most northerly was Tharros, originally a native settlement, where some early pottery and remnants of sculptured stones in a north Syrian style (Moscati 1986b) suggest it was on a route travelled in Mycenaean and Sidonian times. Further south was Sulcis which, as early imports indicate (Bartoloni 1987a), was the northern terminal on the route that started from Italy and extended along the southern coast of Sicily. In the Gulf of Cagliari, frequented by Cypriots over the centuries on travels that eventually brought them to North Africa, were the three towns of Bithia, Nora and Cagliari. Thus all of the new Phoenician emplacements were located where charts, tradition and opportunity dictated.

These Phoenician cities and towns were not founded simultaneously; nor, despite their individuality and autonomy, were they independent of one another. Tharros and Sulcis were the earliest settlements and their foundation can be traced to the fresh burst of Tyrian enterprise at the end of the 8th century when Assyrian needs, Egyptian ambition and an awakening Greek world impelled it toward the west. Cagliari, Nora and Bithia were founded toward the end of the 7th century (Barreca 1986), when the Assyrian empire had crumbled and Egypt and mainland Phoenicia were engulfed in war. We may see the founding of these cities as a reaction to increasing Phocaean control of the seas around northern Sardinia, or in the interests of promoting continued trade with Etruria and the Greek cities of Italy (Bartoloni 1987b), or as a response by Sulcis and Tharros to the emergence of a strong and ambitious Carthaginian state (Barreca 1986). Nora, a typical Phoenician town in the Cypriot tradition (Bondì 1978), had ties to Tharros (Moscati 1986c: 219) and commercial links to Carthage. Bithia was a Sardinian village before it was walled and became, perhaps, the port that linked Sulcis with Greek, Etrurian and North African markets (Bartoloni 1983; Moscati 1986c: 226-39). Cagliari was founded, perhaps jointly by Tharros and Sulcis, to facilitate relations with Carthage, whose people soon occupied the town, and its nearby outpost at Cuccureddus flourished as long as the town could maintain its independence (Marras et al. 1987). Monte Sirai was established by Sulcis at about the same time to protect or reaffirm its interests in the interior. The latest Phoenician site in Sardinia was Antas, between Tharros and Sulcis, where the Phoenician population, at least in classical and Roman times, came to honor the Almighty Sid, the patron of Sardinia and fabled ancestor of all the Sidonians (Ferron 1976).

The original Phoenician foundations at Tharros and Sulcis were also distinguished by their products and by their relations with the eastern and western Mediterranean. Tharros dealt mainly in precious stones and metals, some mined locally, some imported from Spain, France, Etruria and other parts of Europe. Sulcis was perhaps a producer and distributor of wine, oil and perfumes, and had preferential relations with the Greek world. Each belonged to complicated networks that resulted only rarely in direct contact with the cities and towns on the Phoenician mainland or in Cyprus. Both succumbed to the new barbarism that, beginning with the organization of the Carthaginian empire, soon wrapped the western world in its dismal uniformity.

Conclusion

The Phoenician foundation of cities and towns in Sardinia was the culmination of centuries of collaboration between Europe, Asia and Africa. It was neither necessary nor haphazard but the result of curiosity, experiment, and bold decisions by the people who created the Mediterranean world. The Phoenicians, among the latest of these explorers, came from Tyre, Sidon and Byblos and arrived in the west at various times and by separate routes. The most famous were the Tyrians who founded Tharros and Sulcis in the late 8th century and, from these cities, in the 7th century, established other towns along the coast and inland. They were different from the other visitors in their determination to stay and create with the Sardinians a special blend of east and west. They came from a city that basked in the accumulated glory of the Phoenician past and were ranked among the legendary heroes, or even imagined by some to be gods.

References

Amadasi Guzzo, M.G.
1987 Fenici o Aramei in Occidente nell'VIII sec. a.C.? *Studia Phoenicia* 5: 35-47.

Barag, D.
1983 Glass inlays and the classification and dating of ivories from the ninth-eighth centuries BC. *Anatolian Studies* 33: 163-67.

Barnett, R.D.
1982 *Ancient Ivories in the Middle East.* Qedem 14. Jerusalem: Israel Exploration Society.

Barreca, F.
1965 L'esplorazione lungo la costa sulcitana. *Monte Sirai II*, 141-75. Roma: Istituto di Studi del Vicino Oriente.
1978 Le fortificazioni fenicio-puniche in Sardegna. *Atti del 1 Convegno Italiano sul Vicino Oriente Antico, Roma 22-24 aprile 1976*, 115-28. Roma: Centro per le Antichità e la Storia dell'Arte del Vicino Oriente.
1986 *La Civiltà Fenicio-punica in Sardegna.* Sardegna Archeologica: Studi e Monumenti 3. Sassari: Carlo Delfino.

Bartoloni, P.
1983 La ceramica fenicia di Bithia: Tipologia e diffusione areale. *Atti del I Congresso Internazionale di Studi Fenici e Punici*, I, 491-500. Roma: C.N.R.
1985 Anfore fenicie e ceramiche estrusche in Sardegna. In *Il Commercio Etrusco Arcaico. Atti dell'Incontro di Studio 5-7 dicembre 1983*, 103-18. Roma: C.N.R.
1987a Orizzonti commerciali sulcitani tra l'VIII e il VII sec. a.C. *Rendiconti dell'Accademia Nazionale dei Lincei* 41: 219-26.
1987b Le relazioni tra Cartagine e la Sardegna nei secoli VII e VI a.C. *Egitto e Vicino Oriente* 10: 79-86.

Baumgarten, A.
1981 *The Phoenician History of Philo of Byblos: A Commentary.* Leiden: Brill.

Bikai, P.M.
1978 *The Pottery of Tyre.* Warminster: Aris & Phillips.
1987 Trade networks in the Early Iron Age: The Phoenicians at Palaepaphos. In D.W. Rupp (ed.), *Western Cyprus. Connections. An Archaeological Symposium held at Brock University, St Catherines, Ontario, Canada, March 21-22, 1986*, 125-28. Göteborg: Paul Aströms Förlag.
1988 The imports from the east. In V. Karageorghis (ed.), *Palaepaphos-Skales. An Iron Age Cemetery in Cyprus*, 396-405. Konstanz: Universitätsverlag.

Bisi, A.M.
1980 La diffusion du 'Smiting God' Syro-Palestinien dans le milieu phénicien d'Occident. *Karthago* 19: 5-14.
1987a Ateliers phéniciens dans le monde égéen. *Studia Phoenicia* 5: 225-37.
1987b Bronzi vicino-orientali in Sardegna: Importazioni ed influssi. In M.S. Balmuth (ed.), *Studies in Sardinian Archaeology III. Nuragic Sardinia and the Mycenaean World*, 225-46. BAR International Series 387. Oxford: British Archaeological Reports.

Bondì, S.F.
1978 Un tipo di inquadramento architettonico fenicio. *Atti del 1 Convegno Italiano sul Vicino Oriente Antico*, 147-55. Roma: Centro per le Antichità e la Storia dell'Arte del Vicino Oriente.
1981 Qualche appunto sui temi della più antica colonizzazione fenicia. *Egitto e Vicino Oriente* 4: 343-48.
1984 Per una caratterizzazione dei centri occidentali nella più antica espansione fenicia. *Egitto e Vicino Oriente* 7: 75-92.

Bordreuil, P.
1977 Epigraphe d'amphore phénicienne du 9e siècle. *Berytus* 25: 159-61.
1982 Epigraphes phéniciennes sur bronze, sur pierre et sur céramique. *Archéologie au Levant. Recueil à la mémoire de Roger Saïdah*, 187-92. Paris: Maison de l'Orient.
1985 Le dieu Echmoun dans la région d'Amrit. *Studia Phoenicia* 3: 221-30.
1987 Tanit du Liban. *Studia Phoenicia* 5: 79-85.
1990 A propos de Milkou, Milqart et Milk'ashtart. *Maarav* 5-6: 11-21.

Botto, M.
1986 I commerci fenici e la Sardegna nella fase precoloniale. *Egitto e Vicino Oriente* 9: 125-49.

Bunnens, G.
1983a Considérations géographiques sur la place occupée par la Phénicie dans l'expansion de l'empire assyrien. *Studia Phoenicia* 1-2: 169-93.
1983b La distinction entre Phéniciens et Puniques chez les auteurs classiques. *Atti del I Congresso Internazionale di Studi Fenici e Punici*, I, 233-38. Roma: C.N.R.

Coldstream, J.N.
1969 The Phoenicians of Ialysos. *Bulletin of the Institute of Classical Studies* 16: 1-7.
1982 Greeks and Phoenicians in the Aegean. In H.G. Niemeyer (ed.), *Phönizier im Westen: Die Beiträge des Internationalen Symposiums über 'Die phönizische Expansion im westlichen Mittelmeerraum' in Köln vom 24. bis 27. April 1979*, 261-75. Madrider Beiträge 8. Mainz am Rhein: Philipp von Zabern.
1988 Early Greek pottery in Tyre and Cyprus: Some preliminary comparisons. *Report of the Department of Antiquities, Cyprus* 1988: 35-43.

Cross, F.M.
1979 A recently published Phoenician inscription of the Persian Period from Byblos. *Israel Exploration Journal* 29: 40-44.
1986 Phoenicians in the West: the early epigraphic evidence. In M.S. Balmuth (ed.), *Studies in Sardinian Archaeology, Volume II: Sardinia in the Mediterranean*, 117-30. Ann Arbor: University of Michigan Press.

Culican, W.
1974 A Phoenician seal from Khaldeh. *Levant* 6: 195-98.
1976 A votive model from the sea. *Palestine Exploration Quarterly* 171: 119-23.

Dayton, J.E.
1984 Sardinia, the Sherden and Bronze Age trade routes. *Annali Istituto Orientale di Napoli* 44: 353-71.

de Socio, P.
1983 Appunti per uno studio sui materiali da costruzione nella Sicilia e Sardegna fenicio-puniche. *Atti del I Congresso Internazionale di Studi Fenici e Punici*, I, 97-106. Roma: C.N.R.

Dothan, M.
1986 Šardina at Akko? In M.S. Balmuth (ed.), *Studies in Sardinian Archaeology, Volume II: Sardinia and the Mediterranean*, 105-15. Ann Arbor: University of Michigan Press.

Elayi, J.
1982 Studies in Phoenician geography during the Persian Period. *Journal of Near Eastern Studies* 41: 83-110.
1985a Les relations entre les cités phéniciennes et l'empire assyrien sous le règne de Sennachérib. *Semitica* 35: 19-26.
1985b Byblos et la domination assyro-babylonienne. *Baghdader Mitteilungen* 16: 393-97.

Eph'al, I., & J. Naveh
1989 Hazael's Booty inscriptions. *Israel Exploration Journal* 39: 192-200.

Ferrarese Ceruti, M.L., L. Vagnetti & F. Lo Schiavo
1987 Minoici, Micenei e Cipriori in Sardegna alla luce delle più recenti scoperte. In M. S. Balmuth (ed.), *Studies in Sardinian Archaeology III. Nuragic Sardinia and the Mycenaean World*, 7-38. BAR International Series 387. Oxford: British Archaeological Reports.

Ferron, J.
1976 Sid: Etat actuel des connaissances. *Le Muséon* 89: 425-40.

Gibson, J.C.L.
1982 *Textbook of Syrian Semitic Inscriptions, III: Phoenician Inscriptions*. Oxford: Clarendon Press.

Gubel, E., & S. Cavet
1987 Un nouveau type de coupe phénicienne. *Syria* 64: 193-204.

Gubel, E., & P. Bordreuil
1985 Statuette fragmentaire portant le nom de la Baalat Gubal. *Semitica* 35: 5-11.

Herrmann, G.
1989 The Nimrud Ivories, 1: The Flame and Frond School. *Iraq* 51: 85-109.

Houwink Ten Cate, P.H.J.
1961 *The Luwian Population Groups of Lycia and Cilicia Aspera during the Hellenistic Period*. Leiden: Brill.

Isserlin, B.S.J.
1983 Phoenician and Punic rural settlement and agriculture: Some archaeological considerations. *Atti del 1 Congresso Internazionale di Studi Fenici e Punici*, I, 157-63. Roma: C.N.R.

Karageorghis, V.
1983 New Phoenician discoveries in Cyprus. *Atti del 1 Congresso Internazionale di Studi Fenici e Punici, Roma*, I, 173-76. Roma: C.N.R.

Kelly, T.
1987 Herodotus and the chronology of the kings of Sidon. *Bulletin of the American Schools of Oriental Research* 268: 39-56.

Kestemont, G.
1983 Tyr et les Assyriens. *Studia Phoenicia* 1-2: 53-78.
1985 Les Phéniciens en Syrie du Nord. *Studia Phoenicia* 3: 135-61.

Koehl, R.B.
1985 *Sarepta III. The Imported Bronze and Iron Age Wares from Area II, X*. The University Museum of the University of Pennsylvania Excavations at Sarafand, Lebanon. Beyrouth: Librairie Orientale.

Krahmalkov, C.R.
1981 The foundation of Carthage, 814 B.C. The Douïmès Pendant inscription. *Journal of Semitic Studies* 26: 177-91.

Linder, E.
1973 A cargo of Phoenician-Punic figurines. *Archaeology* 26: 182-87.

Lipiński, E.
1983 La Carthage de Chypre. *Studia Phoenicia* 1-2: 209-34.

Lo Schiavo, F.
1978 Le fibule delle Sardegna. *Studi Etruschi* 46 (2): 25-46.
1981 Economia e società nell'età dei nuraghi. In E. Atzeni *et al.* (eds.), *Ichnussa: La Sardegna dalle origini all'età classica*, 255-347. Milano: Libri Scheiwiller.
1985 *Nuragic Sardinia in its Mediterranean setting: Some Recent Advances [Munro Lectures 1982]*. Department of Archaeology Occasional Paper 12. Edinburgh: University of Edinburgh.
1987 Modellino di elmo in bronzo dal Nuraghe Picciu di Laconi (Nuoro). *Studi Etruschi* 53: 95-103.

Lo Schiavo, F., & L. Vagnetti
1980 Micenei in Sardegna? *Rendiconti della Accademia Nazionale dei Lincei* 8(35): 371-93.

Lo Schiavo, F., E. Macnamara & L. Vagnetti
1985 Late Cypriot imports to Italy and their influence on local bronzework. *Papers of the British School at Rome* 53: 1-71.

Markoe, G.E.
1990 The emergence of Phoenician art. *Bulletin of the American Schools of Oriental Research* 279: 13-26.

Marras, L.A., P. Bartoloni & S. Moscati
1987 Cuccureddus. *Rendiconti della Accademia Nazionale dei Lincei* 42: 225-51.

Moscati, S.
1986a Fenici e Greci in Sardegna. *Rendiconti della Accademia Nazionale dei Lincei* 40: 265-71.
1986b Due statue di Tell Halaf e i troni fenici. *Rendiconti della Accademia Nazionale dei Lincei* 41: 53-56.
1986c *Italia Punica*. Milano: Rusconi.

Muhly, J., R. Maddin & T. Stech
1988 Cyprus, Crete and Sardinia: Copper ox-hide ingots and the Bronze Age metals trade. *Report of the Department of Antiquities, Cyprus* 1988: 281-98.

Müller, H.-P.
1988 Pygmaion, Pygmalion und Pumaijaton. Aus der Geschichte einer mythischen Gestalt. *Orientalia* 57: 192-205.

Oded, B.
1974 The Phoenician cities and the Assyrian Empire in the time of Tiglath-Pileser III. *Zeitschrift der deutschen Palästinavereins* 90: 38-49.

Pardee, D.
1988 A new datum for the meaning of the divine name Milkashtart. In L. Eslinger and G. Taylor (eds.), *Ascribe to the Lord. Biblical and Other Studies in Memory of Peter C. Craigie*, 55-68. Sheffield: JSOT Press.

Parpola, S., & K. Watanabe
1988 *Neo-Assyrian Treaties and Loyalty Oaths*. State Archives of Assyria 2. Helsinki: Helsinki University.

Peckham, B.
1972 The Nora Inscription. *Orientalia* 41: 457-68.
1987 Phoenicia and the religion of Israel: The epigraphic evidence. In P.D. Miller, P.D. Hanson and S.D. McBride (eds.), *Ancient Israelite Religion. Essays in Honor of Frank Moore Cross*, 79-99. Philadelphia: Fortress Press.
1992 The history of Phoenicia. *Anchor Bible Dictionary of the Bible*. New York: Doubleday.

Prausnitz, M.W.
1982 Die Nekropolen von Akhziv und die Entwicklung der Keramik vom 10. bis zum 7. Jahrhundert v. Chr. in Akhziv, Samaria und Ashdod. In H. G. Neimeyer (ed.), *Phönizier im Westen. Die Beiträge des Internationalen Symposiums über 'Die Phönizische Expansion im Westlichen Mittelmeerraum' in Koln vom 24. bis 27. April 1979*, 31-44. Madrider Beiträge 9. Mainz am Rhein: Philipp von Zabern.

Puech, E.
1986 Les inscriptions phéniciennes d'Amrit et les dieux guérisseurs du sanctuaire. *Syria* 53: 327-42.

Raban, A.
1985 The ancient harbours of Israel in Biblical times. In A. Raban (ed.), *Harbour Archaeology. Proceedings of the First International Workshop on Ancient Mediterranean Harbours, Caesarea Maritima 24-28.6.83*, 11-44. BAR International Series 257. Oxford: British Archaeological Reports.

Saïdah, R.
1966 Fouilles de Khaldé. *Bulletin du Musée de Beyrouth* 19: 51-90.
1977 Une tombe de l'âge du fer à Tambourit (région de Sidon). *Berytus* 25: 135-46.
1983 Nouveaux éléments de datation de la céramique de l'âge du fer au Levant. *Atti del I Congresso Internazionale di Studi Fenici e Punici* 1: 213-16. Roma: C.N.R.

Stern, E.
1990 New evidence from Dor for the first appearance of the Phoenicians along the northern coast of Israel. *Bulletin of the American Schools of Oriental Research* 279: 27-34.

Sznycer, M.
1980 Salamine de Chypre et les Phéniciens. *Salamine de Chypre. Historie et archéologie: état des recherches*, 123-29. Paris: C.N.R.S.

Wilson, V.
1974 The Kouklia sanctuary. *Report of the Department of Antiquities, Cyprus* 1974: 139-46.

Winter, I.J.
1976a Phoenician and North Syrian ivory carving in historical context: Questions of style and distribution. *Iraq* 38: 1-22.
1976b Carved ivory furniture panels from Nimrud: A coherent subgroup of the North Syrian Style. *Metropolitan Museum Journal* 11: 25-54.
1981 Is there a South Syrian Style of ivory carving in the early first millennium B.C.? *Iraq* 43: 101-30.
1983 Carchemish *ša kišad puratti*. *Anatolian Studies* 33: 177-97.
1989 North Syrian ivories and Tell Halaf reliefs: The impact of luxury goods upon 'major' arts. In A.J. Leonard and B.B. Williams (eds.), *Essays in Ancient Civilization Presented to Helene J. Kantor*, 62-66. Chicago: The Oriental Institute of the University of Chicago.

Riassunto

Durante la Tarda Età del Bronzo e progressivamente durante l'Età del Ferro la Sardegna ha fatto parte di un mondo mediterraneo in espansione. I Fenici hanno fatto della Sardegna un centro di attrazione per esploratori, artigiani e imprenditori e hanno contribuito al fatto che l'isola sia diventata una fonte di prodotti d'artigianato, di materie prime e provviste.

I fondatori di città fenice in Sardegna facevano parte di un gruppo diversificato. Essi hanno raggiunto l'Ovest attraverso vie diverse e durante periodi diversi, per diverse ragioni e provenivano da città in competizione. L'Autore esplora questa complessità per correggere una visione semplificata che si ha dell'impatto fenicio sulla Sardegna.

L'Autore riesamina la nascita e l'espansione delle città-stato fenicie continentali. Byblo aveva una cultura particolare ed è stata una capitale indipendente durante il I millennio a.C. Non era conosciuta per estensioni territoriali nel continente, ma ha collaborato con Tiro e Sidone in altre imprese. Al contrario, gli interessi e l'influenza di Sidone erano largamente diffusi. La letteratura e l'arte sidoniana mostrano caratteristiche appartenenti all'arte siriana, anatolica e canaanita. Sidone aveva contatti politici con i Danuniani dell'Anatolia e questo è dimostrato dalle iscrizioni del IX secolo di Kilamuwa provenienti da Zinjirli e da un'iscrizione dell'VIII secolo di Azitawadda proveniente da Karatepe che rivela la prosperità dei Danuniani in Cilicia durante le relazioni con Sidone. C'è da aggiungere il fatto che durante l'VIII secolo Sidone controllava città nel territorio di Tiro.

Tiro mostra tutte le caratteristiche tipiche di una città fenicia marittima. La sua principale caratteristica è l'ecclettismo in arte e in politica. Essa ha infatti fornito al mondo mediterraneo incisioni su avorio note per la loro bellezza e grazia. Il suo pantheon include divinità tipiche dell'Egitto, della Grecia e di Cipro. Durante il IX e l'VIII secolo, Tiro ha stabilito contatti con la Siria settentrionale, ma i suoi contatti principali sono quelli con Cipro dove ha stabilito numerosi insediamenti tra cui Palaepaphos, Salamis, Kition, e Amathus. Nel continente Tiro ha mantenuto relazioni con la Giudea e la Palestina e ha avuto contatti indiretti con l'Egitto. Sulla costa, durante periodi diversi, ha avuto porti importanti come Achzib, Acco, Tell Abu Hawam, Joppa, e Qasile, *inter alii*. La supremazia di Tiro ha coinciso con il declino di Sidone. In seguito alla distruzione di Sidone operata dall'Assiria, Esarhaddon ha affidato il controllo del mercato di Sidone e delle sue rotte a Tiro. La situazione è rimasta così immutata fino alla risurrezione di Sidone durante il V secolo.

Gli abitanti di Sidone sono stati i primi ad avventurarsi verso ovest come artigiani e mercanti. Insieme agli Eubei essi hanno seguito le rotte marittime stabilite dai Micenei verso l'Italia occidentale e la Sardegna meridionale. La presenza sidoniana in Sardegna durante l'VIII secolo a.C. è attestata da un'iscrizione proveniente da Bosa.

Gli abitanti di Tiro hanno raggiunto l'ovest dopo Sidone partendo da Cipro e seguendo la rotta passante per la Palestina e l'Egitto verso il Nord Africa e l'Atlantico e tornando attraverso le rotte della Sardegna meridionale. In seguito alla distruzione di Sidone, quando l'Assiria controllava le colonie cipriote di Sidone, Tiro ha utilizzato le rotte verso ovest e ha fondato città nella Sardegna meridionale e occidentale. Le iscrizioni di Nora testimoniano la presenza di Tiro in Sardegna durante l'inizio del nono secolo a.C.

Durante l'VIII e il VII secolo, i Fenici hanno contribuito ad un'urbanizzazione in Sardegna con insediamenti irregolari e con la popolazione occupata in attività minerarie, agricole e di produzione. Ciò ha portato ad una diversificazione regionale e ha favorito il cambiamento costante di influenze e mercati internazionali. Le città fenice erano centri amministrativi, non militari; erano centri cosmopoliti e ciò e dimostrato dalla varietà dei prodotti nuragici, etruschi e greci. Tharros, sulla costa occidentale, e Sulcis, più a sud, sono state fondate da Tiro durante la fine dell'VIII secolo; Sulcis era il terminale settentrionale della rotta marittima che cominciava in Italia e che si estendeva lungo la costa meridionale della Sicilia. Bithia, Nora, e Cagliari, tutte situate nel Golfo di Cagliari, sono state fondate alla fine del VII secolo e sono state frequentate dai ciprioti durante i loro viaggi verso il Nord Africa. Attraverso queste città i Fenici hanno coinvolto la Sardegna in un network commerciale e culturale che ha legato l'Europa dell'Età del Ferro, l'Asia, l'Africa e il Mediterraneo.

Lucerne Arcaiche da Sulcis

Piero Bartoloni

La ricca messe di dati che ancora oggi ci è offerta dall'antica Sulcis e in particolare dal suo *tofet* consente al mondo degli studi di ricostruire purtroppo solo parzialmente, ma tessera per tessera, il complesso mosaico che la civiltà fenicia e punica ha tentato di tramandarci (Moscati 1988). Ciò che resta attualmente è costituito dalle testimonianze superstiti di questa civiltà, che non solo sono maltrattate dal tempo e dalla inconsapevolezza della vita quotidiana, ma che sono spesso anche insidiate fin dal loro interno attraverso l'ignava insipienza e la stolida malevolenza.

Vengono presentate in questa sede, con l'intento di rendere onore e omaggio a Miriam Balmuth e al suo proficuo e indefesso lavoro in Sardegna e nei luoghi a Lei cari, alcune lucerne di tipologia nuragica e fenicia rinvenute nell'area sacra sulcitana nel corso dei lavori effettuati durante le campagne tra il 1956 e il 1961 e tra il 1968 e il 1970. Le prime indagini di scavo sono state dirette da Gennaro Pesce (1961: 68-69), che ebbe l'indubbio merito di riconoscere immediatamente la natura del santuario, in un'epoca nella quale gli studi fenici erano stati posti decisamente al margine. Le successive campagne sono state condotte da Ferruccio Barreca, che valorizzò il santuario (Barreca 1986: 107-23), con il contributo scientifico dell'Istituto per la Civiltà fenicia e punica del Consiglio Nazionale delle Ricerche, tra cui è anche chi scrive. Non sono purtroppo disponibili per il mondo degli studi i dati di scavo riguardanti il susseguirsi delle indagini archeologiche condotte in quegli anni, ma sono state edite anche di recente alcune notizie sulla topografia dell'area sacra (Bartoloni 1989b: 50-56; Moscati 1986a; Tronchetti *et al.* 1989: 145).

Tuttavia, a parziale integrazione nel corso degli anni successivi sono stati editi numerosi lavori che riguardano i materiali mobili emersi durante gli scavi del *tofet* sulcitano: in particolare, si ricorderanno le stele (Bartoloni 1986; Moscati 1986b), gli amuleti (Bartoloni 1973) e alcune urne (Bartoloni 1983: 21-31; 1985; 1988b). Ciò ha permesso, per quanto riguarda soprattutto i materiali mobili, di disporre attualmente di un quadro di assieme abbastanza puntuale e sicuramente ricco di dati su questa caratteristica area sacra.

Le otto lucerne che vengono presentate in questa sede non sono mai state oggetto di studio specifico, anche se esistono alcune menzioni al riguardo (Pesce 1961: 70; Moscati 1972a: 205; Barreca 1979: 150; Bartoloni 1989a: 158), e non costituiscono probabilmente la totalità dei reperti di questo tipo rinvenuti nell'area sacra sulcitana. Le lucerne che vengono descritte rappresentano in questo caso una scelta che ha intenti tipologici e cronologici. Infatti si tratta di materiali arcaici, tutti attribuibili con certezza alla fase più antica del *tofet* (Bartoloni 1988b: 165-66; Tronchetti 1979: 205) e collocabili dunque non più tardi della seconda metà dell'VIII sec. a.C. In particolare, sono presenti e vengono illustrate tre piccole lucerne di tipologia nuragica e cinque lucerne di fabbrica fenicia.

Per quanto riguarda l'utilizzo e la matrice delle prime tre, non si tratta certamente di un esotismo o di una tesaurizzazione 'colta' da parte di offerenti fenici, bensì di una ulteriore conferma della presenza a Sulcis, fin dai primi anni della sua fondazione urbana fenicia, di elementi di stirpe nuragica. La presenza *in loco* delle tre lucerne testimonia evidentemente che gli elementi appartenenti alla popolazione di stirpe nuragica recentemente inurbati avevano un paritetico accesso ai riti dell'area sacra e, quindi, erano partecipi ed ecisti a pari diritto di una precoce urbanizzazione (Bartoloni 1985: 189-90).

Per quanto concerne invece le seconde cinque, ciò che ne caratterizza il maggior numero è la presenza di un singolo becco, che, oltre a permetterci di ascriverne almeno alcune ad ambienti orientali, costituisce una particolarità rara nel mondo fenicio di Occidente. Infatti, oltre ad alcuni esemplari sempre provenienti da Sulcis, ma dall'area dell'abitato (Bernardini 1990: 87), non molto numerose sono le lucerne ad un becco rinvenute nel bacino occidentale del Mediterraneo. Di certo, mentre l'insediamento sulcitano attualmente si presenta come il sito con il maggior numero di testimonianze, ulteriori attestazioni, numericamente non cospicue, provengono ad esempio dal *tofet* e dalla necropoli di Cartagine, da Toscanos,

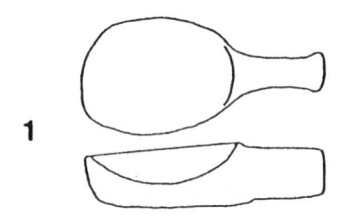

Fig. 1 Museo Communale di Sant'Antioco: lucerna nuragica 'a barchetta'.

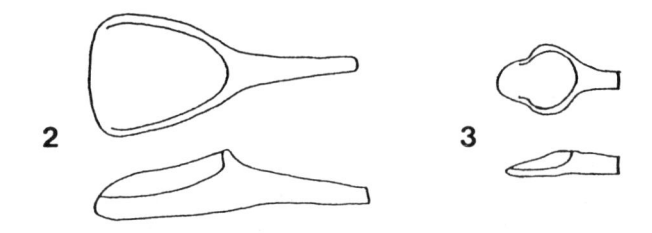

Figg. 2-3 Museo Communale di Sant'Antioco: lucerne nuragiche 'a paletta'.

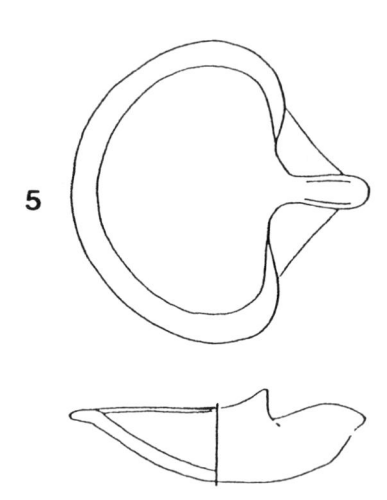

Figg. 4-5 Museo Nazionale di Cagliari: lucerna fenicia del tipo monolicne.

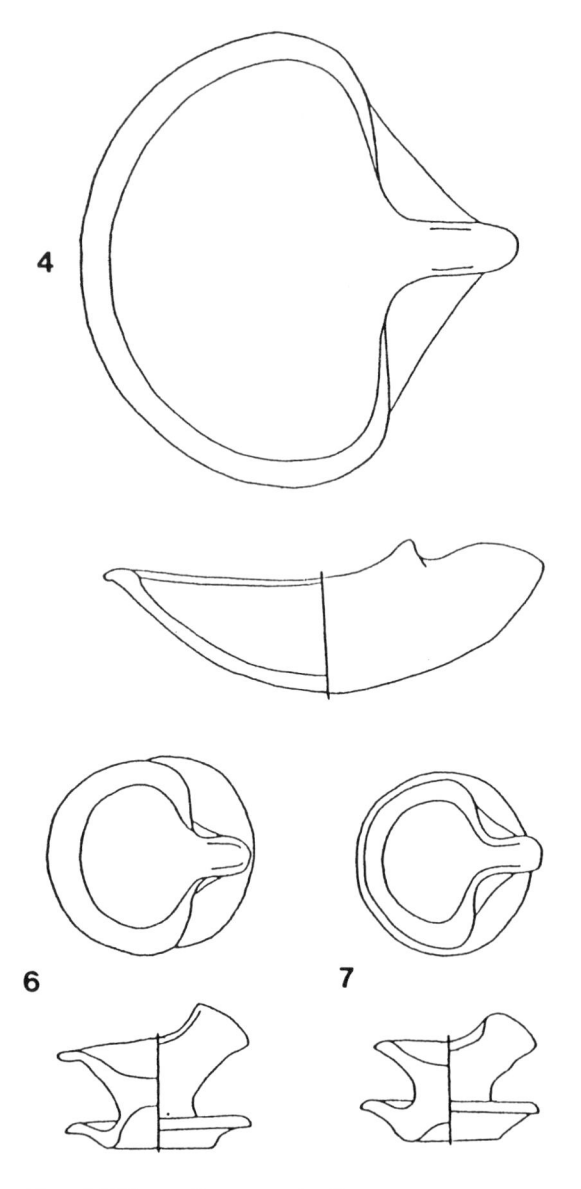

Figg. 6-7 Museo Communale di Sant'Antioco: lucerne monolicni su piattello.

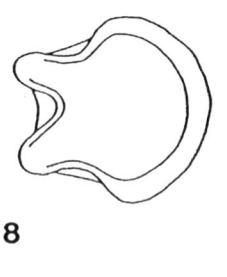

Fig. 8 Museo Communale di Sant'Antioco: lucerna fenicia con due becchi.

da Alcacer do Sal, dal Rio Tinto (Cintas 1970: pl. X; Cintas 1976: 306-17; Deneauve 1969: 23), da Mersa Madakh (Vuillemot 1965: 149) e da Chorreras (Aubet 1974: 88-89).

Le tre lucerne di tipologia nuragica, conservate presso il Museo Comunale di Sant'Antioco, appartengono tutte al tipo miniaturistico e ai due tipi, a barchetta (Fig. 1) e a paletta (Figg. 2-3). La tipologia, nota anche per il più o meno tozzo manico cilindrico, è testimoniata sia nelle dimensioni di uso comune (Lo Schiavo 1978: 94) che in quelle miniaturistiche, probabilmente di funzione votiva (Sanges 1978: 160), come del resto è da attendersi per il santuario sulcitano.

Per quanto riguarda le lucerne di fabbrica fenicia, sono anch'esse tutte visibili presso il Museo sulcitano, ad eccezione dell'esemplare maggiore (Fig. 4), che è conservato nel Museo Nazionale di Cagliari. Il tipo monolicne derivante dai piatti, è forse ispirato a conchiglie bivalvi del tipo *Glycimeris* ben noto in ambiente fenicio (Lancel 1982: 325, 328). Come è noto, la lucerna monolicne è frequentissima in area orientale, ove ha tratto origine fin dal III millennio (Bisi 1970: 55-56), e si presenta nelle tre varianti, cosmopolite in tutta l'area levantina, che sono rispettivamente con peduncolo di supporto o di infissione (Bikai 1987: 16), con base piatta (Bikai 1978: 18-20) e con fondo tondeggiante (Briend 1980: 212), che ne richiedeva l'utilizzo in associazione con le basi ad anello (Buhl 1983: 45-46; Anderson 1988: 233-34).

I due esemplari sulcitani (Figg. 4-5), entrambi con fondo tondeggiante e vasca profonda, ancorchè privi di dati contestuali, sembrano appartenere a un periodo di prima frequentazione e certamente non posteriore alla seconda metà dell'VIII sec. a.C. Ciò in virtù dell'orlo molto sottile, che caratterizza e scandisce l'antichità dei piatti fenici (Schubart 1982: 99), poichè, come è noto, le lucerne a uno o due becchi derivano direttamente dai piatti con breve orlo (Bartoloni 1981: 44). La cronologia alta, apparentemente non posteriore all'800 a.C., ci viene confermata dai caratteri formali del tutto particolari della vasca e del fondo, che negli insediamenti siro-palestinesi sono appunto ascrivibili al Ferro II A-B (Amiran 1969: 292-93).

Anche le inusitate caratteristiche della pasta, riferibili unicamente ai due esemplari presentati, sembrerebbero orientare il giudizio verso una loro importazione piuttosto che nel senso di una produzione locale, i cui caolini e digrassanti sono normalmente assai ben identificabili (Bartoloni 1988a: 92).

Seguono due piccole lucerne monolicni su piattello (Figg. 6-7), conservate come accennato nel Museo Comunale di Sant'Antioco, che appartengono palesemente alla categoria dei recipienti miniaturistici con valenza puramente votiva e dunque privi di funzionalità. La forma deriva latamente dai recipienti doppi con gambo di separazione, quali ad esempio le doppie patere, che hanno generalmente una funzione sacra o votiva (Bartoloni 1981: 51-53).

La loro presenza, soprattutto nella veste di lucerne, non costituisce una novità per le aree sacre simili, poiché si registra ad esempio anche nel *tofet* di Mozia, nella veste di lucerna bilicne singola o associata a figurine antropomorfe fittili (Moscati 1972b: 103-104; Uberti 1973: 78). Il tipo con piattello, illustrato in questa sede, concluderà il suo itinerario in età ellenistica con la ben nota e assai comune forma cosiddetta a 'bugia' (Acquaro 1978: 68), per altro già testimoniata in epoca arcaica ancorchè non cosmopolita nell'area di cultura fenicia (Niemeyer e Schubart 1975: 75). Nel caso specifico l'elemento superiore diviene passante e quindi semplice supporto, mentre quello inferiore acquista palesi funzioni di gocciolatoio, che nei nostri due esemplari sono unicamente intuibili.

I due oggetti erano probabilmente parte degli esigui corredi votivi, tra i quali soprattutto appunto ceramiche miniaturistiche o amuleti (Bartoloni 1987: 154), che spesso accom-pagnavano le urne, soprattutto in età arcaica. Infatti proprio nel santuario sulcitano si registrano numerosissime testimonianze, tra le quali soprattutto ceramiche miniaturistiche (Bartoloni 1991), alla cui categoria appartengono evidentemente le due lucerne in questione. Si notano infatti forme aperte e forme chiuse di tipo mono e biansato.

L'ultima lucerna presentata, anch'essa conservata nel Museo Comunale di Sant'Antioco, è fornita di due becchi (Fig. 8) ed è un esemplare che evidentemente, date le ridotte dimensioni, aveva funzioni puramente votive. Ben poco vi è da aggiungere poiché l'esiguità del recipiente, strutturalmente miniaturistico, non permette di attribuire una valenza assoluta alle caratteristiche riportate. La vicinanza dei due becchi sembrerebbe comunque ricondurci ad epoca arcaica (Maass-Lindemann 1982: 102).

Bibliografia

Acquaro, E.
    1978   Tharros—IV, lo scavo del 1977. *Rivista di Studi Fenici* 6: 63-68.

Amiran, R.
    1969   *Ancient Pottery of the Holy Land*. Jerusalem: Masada Press.

Anderson, W.P.
    1988   *Sarepta I. The Late Bronze and Iron Age Strata of Area II, Y*. Beyrouth: Université Libanaise.

Aubet, M.E.
    1974   Excavaciones en Las Chorreras (Mezquitilla, Malaga). *Pyrenae* 10: 79-108.
Barreca, F.
    1979   *La Sardegna Fenicia e Punica*. Sassari: Chiarella.
    1986   *La Civiltà Fenicio-Punica in Sardegna*. Sardegna Archeologica: Studi e Monumenti 3. Sassari: Carlo Delfino.
Bartoloni, P.
    1973   Gli amuleti punici del *tofet* di Sulcis. *Rivista di Studi Fenici* 1: 181-203.
    1981   La ceramica punica. In *La Necropoli di Nora*, 17-104. Roma: C.N.R.
    1983   *Studi sulla Ceramica Fenicia e Punica di Sardegna*. Roma: C.N.R.
    1985   Nuove testimonianze arcaiche da Sulcis. *Nuovo Bullettino Archeologico Sardo* 2: 167-92.
    1986   *Le Stele di Sulcis. Catalogo*. Roma: C.N.R.
    1987   La tomba 54 della necropoli arcaica di Monte Sirai. *Quaderni della Soprintendenza di Cagliari e Oristano* 4: 153-59. Cagliari: STEF.
    1988a   S. Antioco: area del cronicario (campagne di scavo 1983-86), Anfore fenicie e puniche da Sulcis. *Rivista di Studi Fenici* 16: 91-110.
    1988b   Urne cinerarie arcaiche a Sulcis. *Rivista di Studi Fenici* 16: 165-79.
    1989a   La civiltà fenicia e punica. La cultura materiale e l'epigrafia. In V. Santoni (a cura di), *Il Museo Archeologico Nazionale di Cagliari*. Sassari: Banco di Sardegna.
    1989b   *Sulcis*. Roma: Libreria dello Stato.
    1991   Ceramiche vascolari miniaturistiche dal *tofet* di Sulcis. *Quaderni della Soprintendenza Archeologica di Cagliari e Oristano* 8. Cagliari: La Torre.
Bernardini, P.
    1990   S. Antioco: area del cronicario (campagne di scavo 1983-1986): La ceramica fenicia: le forme aperte. *Rivista di Studi Fenici* 18: 81-99.
Bikai, P.M.
    1978   *The Pottery of Tyre*. Warminster: Aris & Phillips.
    1987   The Phoenician Pottery. In V. Karageorghis, O. Picard and Chr. Tytgat (eds.), *La Nécropole D'Amathonte. Tombes 113-367*, 1-19. Nicosia.
Bisi, A.M.
    1970   *La Ceramica Punica. Aspetti e problemi*. Napoli.
Briend, J.
    1980   Les Niveaux 9 à 11. *Tell Keisan (1971-1976). Une cité phénicienne en Galilé*. Friburg: Editions Universitaires.
Buhl, M.-L.
    1983   *Sukas VII. The Near Eastern Pottery and Objects of Other Materials from the Upper Strata*. Copenhagen: Munksgaard.
Cintas, P.
    1970   *Manuel d'archéologique punique I, Historie et Archéologie comparées (chronologie des temps archaïques de Carthage et des villes phéniciennes de l'Ouest*. Paris.
    1976   *Manuel d'archéologie punique II*. Paris: A. & J. Picard.
Deneauve, J.
    1969   *Lampes de Carthage*. Paris: C.N.R.S.
Lancel, S.
    1982   Les niveaux funéraires. *Byrsa II. Rapports preliminaires sur les fouilles 1977–1978: Niveaux et vestiges puniques*, 263-364. Rome: Ecole Française de Rome.

Lo Schiavo, F.
    1978   Nuraghe di 'S. Lulla', Orune. *Sardegna Centro-Orientale dal Neolitico alla Fine del Mondo Antico*, 93-94. Sassari: Chiarella.
Maass-Lindemann, G.
    1982   *Toscanos. Die Westphonikische Niederlassung an der Mundung des Rio de Velez*. Berlin: De Gruyter.
Moscati, S.
    1972a   *I Fenici e Cartagine*. Torino: U.T.E.T.
    1972b   Note sulle figurine punica. *Mozia—VII*. Roma: C.N.R.
    1986a   *Italia Punica*. Milano: Rusconi.
    1986b   *Le Stele di Sulcis. Caratteri e confronti*. Roma: C.N.R.
    1988   *Le Officine di Sulcis*. Roma: Università degli Studi.
Niemeyer, H.G., & H. Schubart
    1975   *Trayamar. Die Phonizischen Kammergraber und die Niederlassung an der Algarrobo-Mundung*. Mainz: Von Zabern.
Pesce, G.
    1961   *Sardegna Punica*. Cagliari: Fossataro.
Sanges, M.
    1978   La collezione Dino Giacobbe. *Sardegna Centro-Orientale dal Neolitico alla Fine del Mondo Antico*, 155-61. Sassari: Chiarella.
Schubart, H.
    1982   Asentamientos fenicios en la costa meridional de la peninsula iberica. *Huelva Arqueologica* 6: 71-99.
Tronchetti, C.
    1979   Per la cronologia del *tophet* di S. Antioco. *Rivista di Studi Fenici* 7: 201-205.
Tronchetti, C., P. Bartoloni & S. Moscati
    1989   Nuove stele sulcitane. *Quaderni della Soprintendenza Archeologica di Cagliari e Oristano* 6: 145-56. Cagliari: La Torre.
Uberti, M.L.
    1973   Note sulle figurine puniche. *Mozia—VIII*. Roma: C.N.R.
Vuillemot, G.
    1965   *Reconnaissances aux échelles puniques d'Oranie*. Autun: Musée Rolin.

Summary

The ancient Phoenician city of Sulcis is one of the most important sites in Sardinia. The first excavations, directed by Gennaro Pesce, began in 1956, and were continued until recently by Ferruccio Barreca and members of the Institute for Phoenician and Punic Civilization (CNR-Rome), including the Author. Perhaps the best known part of the site is the *tophet*, where a number of funerary stelae, urns, and amulets have been found.

Also associated with this sacred area are eight ceramic lamps datable to the earliest phase of the site, i.e., no later than the second half of the 8th century BC. Three of these are Nuragic; more significantly, all are miniatures, and must have served a votive rather than utilitarian function. The Author suggests that some of the Nuragic population must have had access to the sacred rites performed at Sulcis. Such access suggests that from the beginning of the Phoenician colony at Sulcis, there existed a Nuragic component in its formation and in its urbanization.

Two of the Phoenician lamps are of a type extremely rare in the western Mediterranean, with only one mouth; other examples of this rare type come from Carthage, Toscanos, Alcacer do Sal, Rio Tinto, Mersa Madakh and Chorreras. These lamps were probably inspired by the shape of the bivalve *Glycimeris*, well known in the eastern Mediterranean, and having their origins in the 3rd millennium BC. The two examples from Sulcis, both with rounded bases and a deep well for the oil, are datable to the second half of the 8th century BC or earlier. The color and quality of their paste suggest that they are imports from the Levant; if so, they would be among the earliest Phoenician imports known in Sardinia.

Two smaller lamps of the single-mouth type, but attached to a small saucer, and one lamp with two mouths, are also miniatures. Like the small Nuragic lamps, they too must have served a purely votive function. Miniatures of other ceramic shapes are also well attested at Sulcis.

These lamps from Sulcis, while only minor elements in the complex mosaic of the Phoenician culture, are important testimony to Phoenician ritual activity in Sardinia. The presence of Nuragic offerings in the *tofet* is instructive for our understanding of the intimate relationship between the Phoenician colonists and the indigenous Nuragic people.

I Gioielli Punici di Tharros

Enrico Acquaro

La frequentazione e la successiva colonizzazione dei Fenici in Sardegna hanno dato luogo ad un 'deposito' di cultura materiale, in cui i gioielli rivestono un posto di rilievo per il bene *simbol* che da sempre rappresentano. La presa di possesso dell'isola da parte di Cartagine e le più strette connessioni politiche ed economiche che si attivano nella nuova, più integrata, prospettiva nord-africana (Acquaro 1988: 47-49), aggiungono ulteriori valenze economiche e sociali al gioiello. Documento di una pietà funeraria strettamente dipendente dall'Egitto, da cui riprende simboli di magica profilassi (Acquaro 1984: 13-43), il gioiello delle tombe fenicie e puniche mantiene nei tipi e nelle figurazioni adottate i caratteri del più raffinato artigianato fenicio. Alta qualità e selezione di funzionalità funeraria permangono nei gioielli importati nell'isola sia dal centro dello stesso mondo punico, Cartagine, sia dalla Magna Grecia. Il tutto compone un quadro articolato in cui il 'gioiello' dei Fenici e dei Punici di Sardegna, se mai ebbe autonoma vita di civile quotidianità o invece non fosse già confezionato come arredo personale del defunto (Garbini 1989) o dei manufatti culturali che lo accompagnavano (Chérif 1987), non sembra avere alcun legame con la precedente e in parte parallela cultura protosarda. È innegabile, tuttavia, che tecniche, tipologia, simboli finiranno per entrare anche nel tessuto artigianale sardo, che li riprenderà nelle età successive a quella punica, sino alla codificazione bizantina (Serra 1987) e al *revival* ottocentesco.

L'antica città di Tharros, con la sua vita più che millenaria, custodisce ancora nelle sue rovine buona parte dei dati della propria storia monumentale e civile (Acquaro e Finzi 1983). Ciononostante, l'indagine antica e moderna sembra polarizzarsi con ricorrente attenzione, anche in questi ultimissimi tempi, su i gioielli che le sepolture fenicie e puniche hanno restituito (Pisano 1974; Pisano 1987; Acquaro 1984: 13-43; Moscati 1987: 81-127; Moscati 1988), alterando spesso la fisionomia del centro oristanese a discapito di un'organica lettura di una città che dovette avere una vita economica e commerciale delle più interelate fra oltremare e territorio paleosardo sino all'ultima età punica (Acquaro *et al.* 1990). Come che sia, è ormai dato ricorrente nella letteratura, e qui lo registriamo ben volentieri, indicare in Tharros fenicia e punica il centro produttore dei ricchi gioielli recuperati nelle sue tombe (Moscati 1988). Prescindendo quindi da divergenti valutazioni non ancora, a mio parere, tutte soddisfacentemente definite sulla fattura locale o sull'importazione degli ori e degli argenti tharrensi, è anche vero che gli stessi, per quantità e qualità, possono a buon diritto guidare l'esame sulla natura e i tipi della gioielleria utilizzati dai Fenici e dai Punici di Sardegna. I due musei nazionali della Sardegna, Cagliari e Sassari, insieme a numerose collezioni private e il British Museum di Londra conservano la maggior parte, nota, dei gioielli di Tharros (Pisano 1988: 23-53).

Diversi sono i procedimenti tecnici utilizzati per la realizzazione di orecchini, anelli crinali e digitali, bracciali, collane a diversi pendenti, astucci portamuleti, placche, che utilizzano come elementi di base la lamina, il filo e il getto (Pisano 1974: 16-19; 1988: 9-20). Sulla lamina interviene la lavorazione a sbalzo; la placcatura è tecnica ampiamente utilizzata. Il filo, di diametro variato, entra nella confezione di quasi tutti i gioielli, con impiego portante negli orecchini, in alcuni anelli e nelle collane. Il getto ripropone la colata di metallo fuso su matrice in materiale refrattario: filigrana, granulazione ed incisione concorrono alla decorazione dei gioielli di Tharros, che nella loro composizione utilizzano spesso contemp–oraneamente diverse tecniche e vari elementi poi assemblati. Gli orecchini, con corpo 'a sanguisuga' o a filo con uno o più pendenti, sono ampiamente debitori della simbologia magica egiziana, ben lontani dalla tipologia che figura ai lobi della testa femminile che appare al dritto delle monete puniche (Jenkins e Lewis 1963; Manfredi 1987) (Fig. 1.2), di evidente ambientazione magno-greca, o delle stesse terracotte figurate (Solanilla 1974: 465).

Orientano il giudizio dal punto di vista iconografico il falcone e la croce ansata. Mentre la croce ansata si limita alla funzione di pendente in alternative con grappoli di globetti di più antica tradizione vicino-orientale, ampio è l'impiego del

Fig. 1 1. Antiquarium Arborense, Oristano: frammenti di laminette in argento da Tharros; 2. Museo Nazionale, Cagliari: dritto di moneta punica con testa di Core; 3. Museo Nazionale, Calgliari: pendente in oro da Tharros; 4. Museo Nazionale, Cagliari: pendente in oro da Tharros; 5. Museo Nazionale, Cagliari: protome in calcare dalla necropoli occidentale di Cagliari.

falcone, che da solo o in combinazioni figurative di ambientazione glittica decora anche castoni di anelli, coperture di astucci portamuleti e si configura a pendente. Palmette e occhi di Horo decorano lamine di bracciali, castoni e placchette di diverso impiego; sfingi alate, dischi solari alati, 'simboli di Tanit' i castoni di anelli. La protome equina è tema che sembra al momento attestato su un solo castone di anello in oro (Pisano 1974: n. 111).

Le innegabili connessioni dell'anello tharrense, tipologiche ed iconografice, con anelli digitali di Ibiza (San Nicolàs Pedraz 1987) datati al IV secolo a.C. riaprono la possibilità di proporre, per questa categoria, anche a Tharros, in analogia con gli anelli di Monte Luna, una via magno-greca con probabile passaggio da Cartagine. Ma vera guida ed emblema dell'oreficeria di Tharros è il famoso bracciale in oro del Museo Nazionale di Cagliari (Pisano 1988: 32), costituito da cinque lamine con al centro uno scarabeo alato a testa di falco verso destra e palmette e fiori di loto nelle restanti. Lo schema, senza la lamina centrale, riappare su un bracciale sempre da Tharros del British Museum (Pisano 1987: 86, tav. 45c.8/23) ed ha diversi riscontri sardi in lamine d'oro e d'argento (Fig. 1.1) che dovevano far parte di gioielli di analoga impostazione. Nelle necropoli di Cartagine i resti di quattro gioielli in argento ed in argento dorato, tre di antichi scavi, uno di recenti interventi, hanno restituito una variante del motivo dello scarabeo alato tharrense: una testa femminile a sinistra è imposta sul corpo dello scarabeo, mentre altre laminette con palmetta, capitello protoeolico e fiore di loto dovevano con ogni probabilità affiancarlo nella composizione. Per i tre oggetti degli antichi scavi, due bracciali ed un diadema, la data proposta è rispettivamente del primo quarto del VI secolo a.C. e del V secolo a.C. (Lancel 1991). Per il bracciale di recente rinvenimento a Byrsa la data è del primo quarto del VI secolo a.C. (Lancel 1986).

Ci troviamo quindi per il bracciale di Tharros, come ha indicato giustamente S. Lancel, e per gli argenti di Cartagine davanti a due varianti di una medesima tradizione figurativa fenicia di Cipro, con possibile importazione di matrici. Il bracciale tharrense di Cagliari è di gran lunga superiore agli analoghi schemi cartaginesi sia per il materiale impiegato, l'oro, sia per la qualità della realizzazione, sia per l'eccellente stato di conservazione. I confronti cartaginesi finiscono, quindi, per valorizzare ancora di più il documento tharrense di Cagliari, cui si aggiunge quello del British Museum, lasciando aperta a tutt'oggi ogni ipotesi sull'individuazione di officine locali o no, ivi compresa quella dell'importazione della matrice dall'Oriente. Quest'ultima ipotesi non sarebbe del resto del tutto estranea al restante mondo fenicio di Occidente, che pur in epoca successiva (IV secolo a.C.) e in ambito geografico differente come quello gaditano ebbe con il Mediterraneo orientale contatti diretti e stimolanti (Perea Caveda 1985a; Perea Caveda 1985b; Pisano 1990).

Da ultimo, tre categorie di pendenti hanno originale e significativa attestazione a Tharros: i pendenti configurati a protome e busto di divinità femminile (Fig. 1.4), i pendenti a medaglione umbonato (Fig. 1.3) e rettangolare con arco ogivale e gli astucci portamuleti. I pendenti a protome e a busto nudo femminili riprendono due iconografie largamente presenti in tutto l'artigianato fenicio e punico. Il tipo inquadrato da pesante parrucca egiziana è, in sostanza, la riduzione dell'iconografia della protome femminile egittizzante in terracotta, diffusa in tutto l'Occidente, da Cartagine a Mozia e nella stessa Sardegna alla fine del VI secolo a.C. (Moscati 1980: 311-13) o, meglio, degli esemplari in calcare di Cartagine e di Cagliari (Moscati 1990: 63-68) (Fig. 1.5). I busti divini con le mani ai seni di Sassari e di Cagliari hanno significativo riscontro in un analogo pendente di Cartagine: l'iconografia si rifà a remote origini orientali, con riscontri in Occidente nelle stele votive e nella coroplastica (Moscati e Uberti 1985: 44).

Ancora due sono le varianti che si possono riconoscere nei pendenti a medaglione di oro e d'argento. Il tipo circolare e con bordo generalmente risalente in basso verso l'umbone sembra riempire con temi figurativi geometrici o di elementare simbolismo astrale uno spazio riservato un tempo ad iscrizioni di carattere funerario, mentre a Cartagine e ad Ibiza i medaglioni si caricano di composite iconografie proprie della glittica (Pisano 1974; Quillard 1979). Il tipo rettangolare, che solo raramente indulge al decorativismo geometrico del precedente, è sostanziale rappresentazione di un'edicola con 'idolo a bottiglia,' serpenti urei e base-altare a loro sostegno ed evidenza cultuale, secondo schemi noti da stele votive di Mozia, Nora e Tharros (Moscati e Uberti 1985: 44). Gli astucci portamuleti, con il loro corpo predisposto ad accogliere lamine magiche, come hanno dimostrato proprio rinvenimenti sardi, o papiri iscritti, come ha testimoniato un rinvenimento maltese (Gouder e Rocco 1975), costituiscono un esplicito riferimento al prestigio che il rituale funerario egiziano (Leclant 1980) ebbe nel mondo fenicio e punico. Protomi di animali anch'essi presenti nell'amuletistica di tradizione egiziana aggiungono rinnovata valenza al contenitore, che riprende anche soluzioni a cippo rettangolare o a semplice cilindro, liscio o scanalato.

I gioielli tharrensi sembrano dunque restituire nel loro insieme un coerente repertorio, iconografico e di ritualità magica che ha la propria unità, al di là della prevalenza dell'una o dell'altra ipotesi finora percorribili, da possibili interventi locali su matrici e temi d'importazione a realizzazioni integralmente locali, in un'adesione originale agli stilemi egizzizzanti dell'arte fenicia. Che i modelli abbiano già maturato la propria recezione di temi egiziani in contesto fenicio d'Oriente, con probabile ruolo trainante di Cipro, è ipotesi senz'altro praticabile. Ipotesi, tuttavia, che non esclude un apporto occidentale con probabile perno a Cartagine, mediatrice in più casi di importazioni magnogreche. Le botteghe tharrensi se intervennero nella manifattura dei gioielli lo fecero con ogni probabilità in presenza di un mercato in cui l'importazione 'di lusso' circolava senza problemi e l'"imitazione" e l'"invenzione" di temi e tipologie dovevano confrontarsi con questa realtà e da questa essere stimolati.

Bibliografia

Acquaro, E.
- 1984 *Arte e Cultura Punica in Sardegna*. Studi e Monumenti 2. Sassari: Carlo Delfino.
- 1988 *Gli Insediamenti Fenici e Punici in Italia*. Roma.

Acquaro, E., & C. Finzi
- 1983 *Tharros*. Sassari.

Acquaro, E., G. Manca di Mores, L.I. Manfredi & S. Moscati
- 1990 *Tharros: La Collezione Pesce*. Roma.

Chérif, Z.
- 1987 Les bijoux Carthaginois d'après les figurines en terre cuite. *REPPAL* 3: 117-150.

Garbini, G.
- 1989 Un'iscrizione fenicia su un anello d'oro. *Rivista di Studi Fenici* 18: 41-54.

Gouder, T., & B. Rocco
- 1975 Un talismano bronzeo contenente un nastro di papiro con iscrizione fenicia. *Studi Magrebini* 7: 1-18.

Jenkins, G., & R. Lewis
- 1963 *Carthaginian Gold and Electrum Coins*. London.

Lancel, S.
- 1986 Rapport sur les travaux d'une mission de courte durée. Fin juin-début juillet 1985. *CEDAC, Carthage Bulletin* 7 (Mars): 12-14.
- 1991 Un bracelet en argent doré de la nécropole archaïque de Byrsa, à Carthage. *Congresso Internazionale di Studi Fenici e Punici, Roma 1991*, 969-76. Roma: C.N.R.

Leclant, J.
- 1980 A propos des étuis porte-amulettes égyptiens et puniques. *Oriental Studies Presented to B.S.J. Isserlin*, 102-107. Leiden.

Manfredi, L.
- 1987 *Le Monete della Sardegna Punica*. Sassari.

Moscati, S.
- 1980 Due maschere puniche da Sulcis. *Rendiconti dell'Accademia Nazionale dei Lincei* 1980: 311-15.
- 1987 *Iocalia Punica*. Roma.
- 1988 *I Gioielli di Tharros*. Roma.
- 1990 *Techne Studi sull'Artigianato Fenicio*. Roma.

Moscati, S., & M. Uberti
- 1985 *Scavi al Tofet di Tharros: I Monumenti Lapidei*. Roma.

Perea Caveda, A.
- 1985a La orfebrería púnica de Cádiz. *Aula Orientalis* 3: 295-309.
- 1985b Piezas singulares de orfebrería Gaditana en el M.A.N. *Boletín del Museo Arqueológico Nacional (Madrid)* 3: 37-42.

Pisano, G.
- 1974 *I Gioielli Fenici di Tharros nel Museo Nazionale di Cagliari*. Roma.
- 1987 Jewellery. *Tharros. A Catalogue of Material in the British Museum from Phoenician and other tombs at Tharros, Sardinia*, 78-95. London.
- 1988 *I Gioielli Fenici e Punici in Italia*. Roma.
- 1990 I monili. *La Necrópolis Fenicio-Punica de Cádiz. Siglos VI-IV a. de C.*, 57-77. Roma.

Quillard, B.
- 1979 *Bijoux Carthaginois. I: Les colliers*. Louvain-La-Neuve.

Serra, P.
- 1987 Quartu S. Elena: Coppia di orecchini aurei con cestello a calice floreale (Orecchini di tipo I provenienti dalla Sardegna. *Quaderni della Soprintendenza Archeologica di Cagliari e Oristano* 4(3): 105-23.

Solanilla, V.
- 1974 La vestimenta púnica, a través de los exvotos hallados en Ibiza. *VI Symposium de Prehistoria Peninsula, Barcelona 1974*, 457-70.

Summary

The Phoenician colonization of Sardinia resulted in the introduction of Egyptian and Near Eastern religious symbols to the island, and is particularly well-represented by the gold and silver jewellery found in funerary contexts. This symbolism would later find its way into native production, for example, of decorative textiles.

Tharros, a major Phoenician and Punic city, is a major source of information, with jewellery found in many of its tombs. Imported mostly from Carthage and Magna Grecia, these finds are now conserved in the Cagliari and Sassari museums in Sardinia, in the British Museum in London, and in private collections.

Earrings, rings, bracelets, necklaces, pendants, scarabs, amulets and plaques were produced by various techniques and decorated with filigree, granulation and incision. Common motifs are the falcon, the anse cross, palmettes, the eyes of Horus, solar disks and Tanit symbols.

A bracelet in the Cagliari museum with a falcon head, palmette, and lotus decoration, has parallels in 6th-5th century BC Carthage, and in Phoenician Cyprus. Several types of pendants from Tharros also rely heavily on Egyptian motifs, but are well diffused in the west, at Carthage, Mozia and Cagliari. Whether local workshops in Sardinia produced fine jewellery, or if all such material was imported from the East, is a question which remains to be answered.

The jewellery from Tharros forms a coherent repertoire of iconography consistent with the Egyptian styles in Phoenician art. It is proposed that if some of the Tharros jewellery were made locally, it was nevertheless accompanied by a market of imported luxury goods. The availability of imports could have stimulated local production, but also would have constrained it to the familiar themes and types of the imported material.

Testimonianze Fenicio-Puniche nella Sardegna Centro-Settentrionale

Giovanni Tore

A partire dalla sistematizzazione del Pais (1881) ed il fondamentale contributo del Lilliu (1944), permangono ancor oggi da affrontare, nonostante l'intensificarsi dei trovamenti e alcuni contributi specifici attinenti sia al campo archeologico[1] che linguistico (Paulis 1990, ivi bibliografia anteriore), le implicazioni derivanti da due 'modelli di lettura' antitetici che si sono proposti per affermare o negare la presenza fenicio-punica nella Sardegna centro-settentrionale ed in particolare in quest'ultima.[2]

Da un lato (e si può citare *exempli gratia*, da ultima Lo Schiavo 1983b) si denega la presenza fenicia in età arcaica e si considera poco significativa quella punica, dall'altro (Barreca 1986) si tende ad integrare la documentazione archeologica pertinente le due fasi in un quadro storico più articolato (Fig. 1). Se l'una attribuisce, sulla scia della suggestiva ipotesi della Sardegna 'resistente' alla penetrazione allogena ed in particolare semitica (Lilliu 1988), una notevole capacità di autonomia e di persistenza culturale nei confronti di un contatto assai antico fra un popolo del Vicino Oriente (preceduto da Egei, Micenei e Ciprioti), i Fenici, portatori di cultura urbana e gli autoctoni, espressione di una civiltà sviluppata, pre- (o meglio) proto-urbana (Lilliu 1982; 1988: 416-579), l'altra (Barreca 1986) sottolinea e accentua la capacità, al di là del confronto, di una fusione ed evoluzione culturale originale, in Sardegna, dall'incontro dei Fenici e Nuragici, definita 'l'integrazione' (Barreca 1981: 377-416). Il quadro delle risultanze archeologiche è stato, di volta in volta adattato alle esigenze di lettura derivanti da queste due interpretazioni fondamentali.

A ciò si integra anche un ulteriore modello interpretativo che tiene conto dell'ambito geografico ove la natura delle coste, l'esistenza specialmente di favorevoli approdi su rotte transmarine (Barreca 1986: 16-18), l'esistenza di risorse naturali e di vie di penetrazione dalla costa all'interno (Barreca 1986: 89-90 fig. 40), hanno rappresentato elementi cogenti per lo sviluppo di contatti fra i Protosardi, definiti usualmenti Nuragici, e i Semiti. Per le coste fanno parte di questo quadro di lettura una serie di testimonianze assai antiche che si incentrano, assai significavamente, in zone corrispondenti ai requisiti suddetti. La notizia ottocentesca di due frammenti di iscrizioni fenicie provenienti da Bosa Vetus (*CIS* I: 162-63: 211, tav. XXXV), oggi disperse, di cui, la prima ritenuta assai antica e coeva della grande norense (Amadasi Guzzo 1987), cioè databile almeno al IX-VIII sec. a.C., individua una tappa significativa per un insediamento tipico fenicio,

---

[1] Oltre il saggio di Lilliu (1948) è di utile riscontro la bibliografia in Tore (1986: n. 52, 55, 57, 58, 61, 66-68, 72-75, 79, 81, 84, 87-88, 105, 128-30, 146, 160, 162, 176, 183-85, 187-89, 191, 195-96, 201-203, 205, 207, 338, 341, 368, 370, 372, 375, 392, 412, 467, 484, 494, 501-502, 505, 507, 520, 523-24, 530).

[2] Cf. Bafico (1986); Madau (1986; 1988a; 1988b); Zucca (1986); D'Oriano 1985; Tore (1990b, ivi aggiornamenti bibliografici). Per notizie sui trovamenti nei singoli siti cf. Cecchini (1969); Meloni (1985: 25); Barreca 1986: 279-325). Per il quadro storico cf. anche Mastino (1985) e Bondì (1988: 129-211). I risultati delle indagini del collega Paulis sono di estremo interesse. Nelle due illustrazioni (Figg. 4-5) che ripubblichiamo dal suo articolo (Paulis 1990: figg. 27-28), si evidenziano gli esiti che documentano nella prima, con la diffusione del termine semitico indicante la sorgente in sardo (*Mittsa*), un'area di contatto stabile con i fenicio-punici, mentre la seconda attesta un più vasto ambito di contatto non collegato a insediamento urbano antico, ma a presumibile presenza commerciale, documentato dall'attestazione dell'altro termine semitico *Tsippiri*, indicante in sardo il rosmarino. La sovrapposizione delle altre due cartine, tratte rispettivamente da Tore (1990b: fig. 25), pertinenti i sistemi fortificati punici, eretti da Cartagine nel V sec. a.C. e perfezionati nel IV sec. a.C., e le vie di penetrazione fenicio-puniche dalla costa all'interno (Fig. 3); e da Tore (1990b: fig. 24), con l'elenco delle influenze e interferenze nella Sardegna fenicio-punica (Fig. 2), fornisce di per sè facile lettura per l'immediato riscontro territoriale rilevabile. Ulteriore elemento di confronto è la cartina della diffusione dei rilievi funerari punici e di tradizione punica in Sardegna (Fig. 1) tratta da Tore (1990a: tav. II).

430   *Sardinia in the Mediterranean*

1. Cabras (OR)
2. S. Vero Milis (OR)
3. Riola (OR)
4. Milis (OR)
5. Santulussurgiu (OR)
6. Oristano (Fenosu)
7. Pau (OR)
8. Villanova S. Antonio (OR)
9. Allai (OR)
10. Sarule (NU)
11. Oniferi (NU)
12. Bortigali (NU)
13. Macomer (NU)
14. Bonorva (SS)
15. Alghero (SS)
16. Sorso (SS)
17. Ossi (SS)
18. Castelsardo (SS)
19. Tergu (SS)
20. Valledoria (Codaruina) (SS)
21. Viddalba (SS)
22. Gesturi (CA)
23. Nurri (NU)
24. Uras (OR)
25. Mogoro (OR)
26. Senorbì (CA)
27. Ozieri (SS)
28. Sennori (SS)

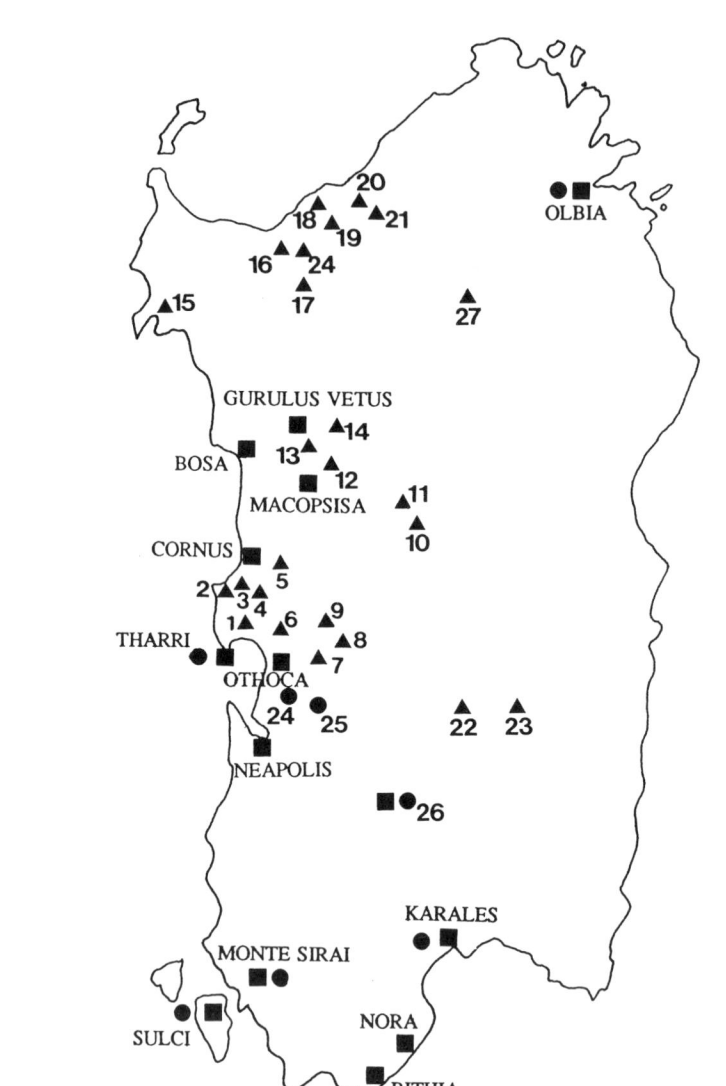

■   Principali siti fenicio-punici
●   *Karales*—siti con documentazione funeraria (rilievi, cippi, stele, altarini) di età punica (ambito urbano)
●   Siti con documentazione archeologica funeraria di età punica
▲   Siti con documentazione archeologica funeraria di tradizione punica

LOCALITÀ: 1 = Abitato (A); S. Salvatore (A); Sa Pedrera (A.1); Nuraghe Sa Tiria (A.2); 2 = Bidda Maiore (A.2, A.3, A.4, B, B.1/a, C); 3 = Sinis (A.2); 4 = S. Paolo (A.2); Nuraghe Cobulas (A); 5 = Procarzos (A); 6 = Fenosu (C); 7 = Pedra Pastori (B.1/a); 8 = Is Cresieddas (A.2); 9 = ? (A); 10 = Sa Morrica (A); 11 = agro (B); 12 = Nuraghe Ponte (B), (B.1/a); 13 = Foresta di Sauccu (A); Cunzadu de sa Pedra (A); 14 = calvias (A.2); 15 = Lazzaretto (A.2); S. Imbenia (a.1, A.1/a); 16 = Cani Malu (A); Santa Filitica (A.2); 17 = S. Antonio (A.1, A.1/a, A.2); 18 = lu Rumasinu (A.2); 19 = Monte Rizzu (A.1/a); 20 = Codaruina: Monte di Campo (A.1); la Muddizza (A.2); 21 = Campo Sportivo (A.1, A.b = A.1); 22 = Bruncu Suergiu, Giara (A); 23 = su Monte (A.2); 24 = S. Giovanni (A.1/a); 25 = S'Arxidda (A.1); 26 = Monte Luna (A?); 27 = Sa Costa (A.2); 28 = Badde Negolosu (A.1); OLBIA = B; THARRI = A, B, B.1, B.2, D.1, D.1/a, D.1/b, D.2/a = B.2, D.2/b; SULCI = A.1, A.5 = A.2, B.1, B.2 = D.2/a; MONTE SIRAI (Carbonia) = B.1/a; NORA = D.1; KARALES = A.2, D.1/a, D.1b.
ALTORILIEVI FUNERARI; *Sulci, Monte Sirai*
RILIEVI FUNERARI; *Tharri, Monte Sirai, Nora Karales*

Fig. 1 Principali siti della Sardegna fenicio-punica e distribuzione dei rilievi funerari punici e di tradizione punica (da Torre 1990a: tav. II).

sull'estuario di un fiume navigabile, il Temo, lungo la rotta per la Penisola Iberica e sussidiariamente per la zona delle Bocche del Rodano (Lo Schiavo 1981: 334-35; Barreca 1986: fig. 1). Al suo interno, il ritrovamento ottocentesco di un bronzetto fenicio nella zona di Bonorva (Tore 1983: 461 n. 15, tav. LXXXII) parrebbe segnare un possibile terminale di quella via di penetrazione, da Bosa verso la Campeda, di cui, in età punica, le fortificazioni di Padria (ritenute pertinenti Gurulis Vetus) e di San Simeone di Bonorva (Barreca 1986: 35, 36, 88 fig. 40), legate al sistema fortificato centro-settentrionale (Barreca 1986: 88), paiono confermare la persistenza, pur in un mutato quadro storico che presuppone la volontà di controllo dell'Isola, base e finalità della conquista cartaginese, a partire dal VI sec. a.C.

Nella zona di Alghero sono state ritrovate testimonianze, come i due bronzi fenici dal Nuraghe Flumenelongu e dal tempio a Pozzo di Olmedo (Tore 1983: 459 n. 1-2, tav. LXXXI; Gras 1985: 98-111). Recentemente si sono aggiunti ritrovamenti di ceramiche fenicie e greche sulla costa (Bafico 1986; Madau 1988b), dal villaggio nuragico di Sant'Imbenia, e il bronzetto greco proveniente dallo stesso tempio a pozzo nuragico di Olmedo (Gras 1985: 106), datato fra la fine del VII e l'inizio del VI sec. a.C. Sono anche da menzionare le importazioni coeve o di poco più tarde greche ed etrusche ritrovate sia sulla costa che all'interno (Madau 1988b; Tore 1990b). L'insieme di questi ritrovamenti indica l'esistenza di un lungo periodo di contatto sviluppatosi a partire dal IX-VIII sec. a.C., sotto la spinta di una più che presumibile 'vague' cipro-fenicia e persistente in un quadro di complesse interrelazioni mediterranee.

Testimonianze, queste, di esiti e della frequentazione di comodi approdi costieri, in funzione, ad Alghero come a Bosa, di tappa lungo rotte transmarine, ma anche di collettori delle risorse minerarie della zona, in particolare il ferro, l'argento ed il piombo della Nurra. Tale fenomeno abbraccia l'arco compreso fra la prima età del Ferro e la sua parte centrale (IX-VI sec. a.C.) con una netta censura avvertibile nella sua fase terminale attorno la seconda metà del secolo VI a.C., coerentemente con un mutato quadro internazionale. Esso si documenta in vari centri, secondo le categorie delle influenze e delle interferenze, lucidamente tratteggiate già dal Lilliu (1944: 324, 326 ss., 332 ss.) e aggiornate da lavori recenti (Barreca 1986; Madau 1988b; Tore 1990b). Essi sono Ittireddu (Monte Zuighe), Perfugas, Uri (nuraghe su Igante), Torralba (nuraghe Santu Antine) come interferenze di ambito greco, etrusco e fenicio (Fig. 2), a cui parrebbe collegarsi Bono (pressi nuraghe Eri Manzanu) per possibile documentazione etrusca.

Influenze di tipo orientalizzante e con più che plausibili referenze fenicio-cipriote ed etrusche si individuano, secondo una recente lettura (Gras 1985: 98-162), con anteriorità di collegamenti risalenti, per queste ultime, ad ambito villanoviano (Gras 1985: 114 ss.) e intessute ad elementi di scambio (interferenze) che vengono da un lato a confermare un quadro aperto sino almeno buona parte del secolo VII a.C., con larga autonomia degli autoctoni, legata forse anche a capacità di spinte propulsive all'esterno (Lo Schiavo e Ridgway 1987; Karageorghis e Lo Schiavo 1989; cf. in precedenza Lo Schiavo 1985), per tutta la parte settentrionale. Aperto è anche il dibattito sui vettori e sul valore da attribuire sia alla componente fenicia (o fenicio-cipriota *tout court*? cf. Tore 1983; Lo Schiavo *et al.* 1985), euboica che appare ora presente anche nella Sardegna settentrionale (Madau 1988b: 186) per la fase più antica (VIII-VII sec. a.C.), ed in proseguo di tempo per quella etrusca o greca o fenicia (cf. Selargius 1986; Lilliu *et al.* 1987; da ultimo Tronchetti 1985 e 1988a, nonché Moscati 1988 e 1989: 53-66). Per la fase più antica si potrebbe ipotizzare solo la Bosa come possibile centro stabile, nel quadro di quel fenomeno di colonizzazione per significativi punti costieri e sostanziale equilibrio con l'ambito locale (una fase di scambi senza necessità di uno stretto controllo territoriale) che si va documentando per vari centri fenicio-punici dell'Isola, quali Karales, Sulci e Tharri, costituiti attorno il secolo VIII a.C., in strutture urbane autonome (Tore 1990b: 108-109). Più probabili, invece, come scali, ancora oltre la fase costitutiva suddetta (anche se va rilevato che per la Bosa non vi sono sinora altri documenti arcaici se non l'iscrizione frammentaria), sono siti quali Porto Conte o Alghero medesima e, forse anche, Porto Torres, dove le testimonianze, sinora assai scarne, sono ritenute non univoche (Nicosia 1980: 208-209 n. 54, 133-34; Nicosia 1981: 450-51 figg. 484-85, 487; Zucca 1986: 56). Tale ipotesi permetterebbe di esplicare interferenze rilevate a Perfugas e le più tarde di Monti Cau-Sorso, e pure su Igante di Uri, presumibilmente coeve alle prime, come, anteriormente l'influsso 'cipriota' rilevato a Santa Maria di Paulis-Ittiri (Fig. 3).

Le tracce rilevate invece ad Uri e a Buddusò, di pretto ambito orientalizzante (cf., come per le menzioni precedenti, Tore 1990b: 108-109, ivi bibliografia anteriore), parrebbero gravitare in direzione della costa nord-orientale, rendendo ipotizzabile un punto d'approdo nella zona dell'odierna Olbia, ove le testimonianze possono

432 *Sardinia in the Mediterranean*

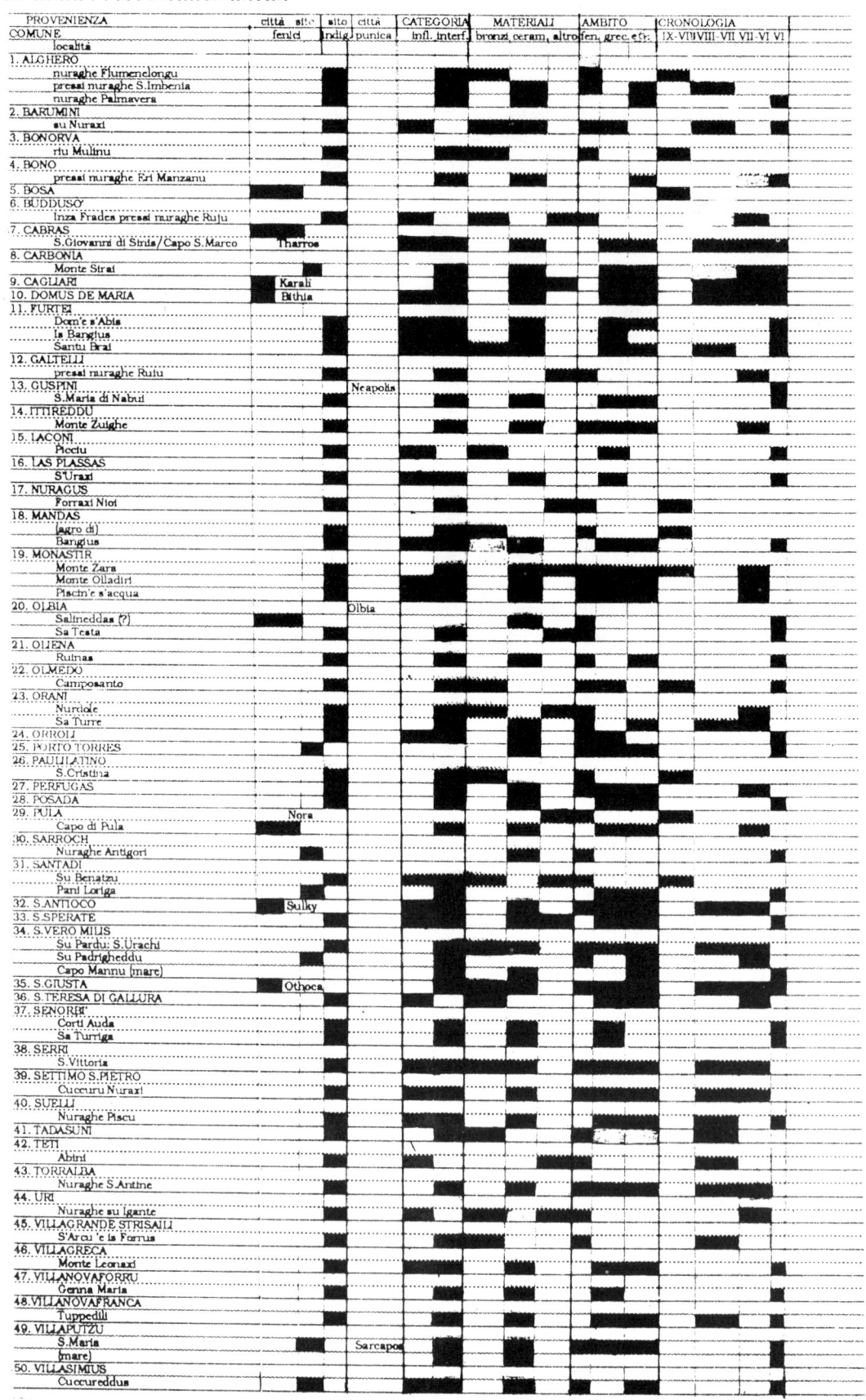

N.B. Per i rapporti con la penisola iberica, l'Italia centrale villanoviana e Cipre cfr. Tore 1981, pp. 285-95 e Gras 1985, pp. 98-162. Sugli elementi orientalizzanti in Sardegna cfr. in testo la nota 14 e Gras 1985, pp. 123-25.

Fig. 2 La Sardegna fenicio-punica: influenze e interferenze (da Tore 1990b: fig. 24). I numeri indicati nella tavola corrispondono alle località illustrate nella cartina geografica in Fig. 3.

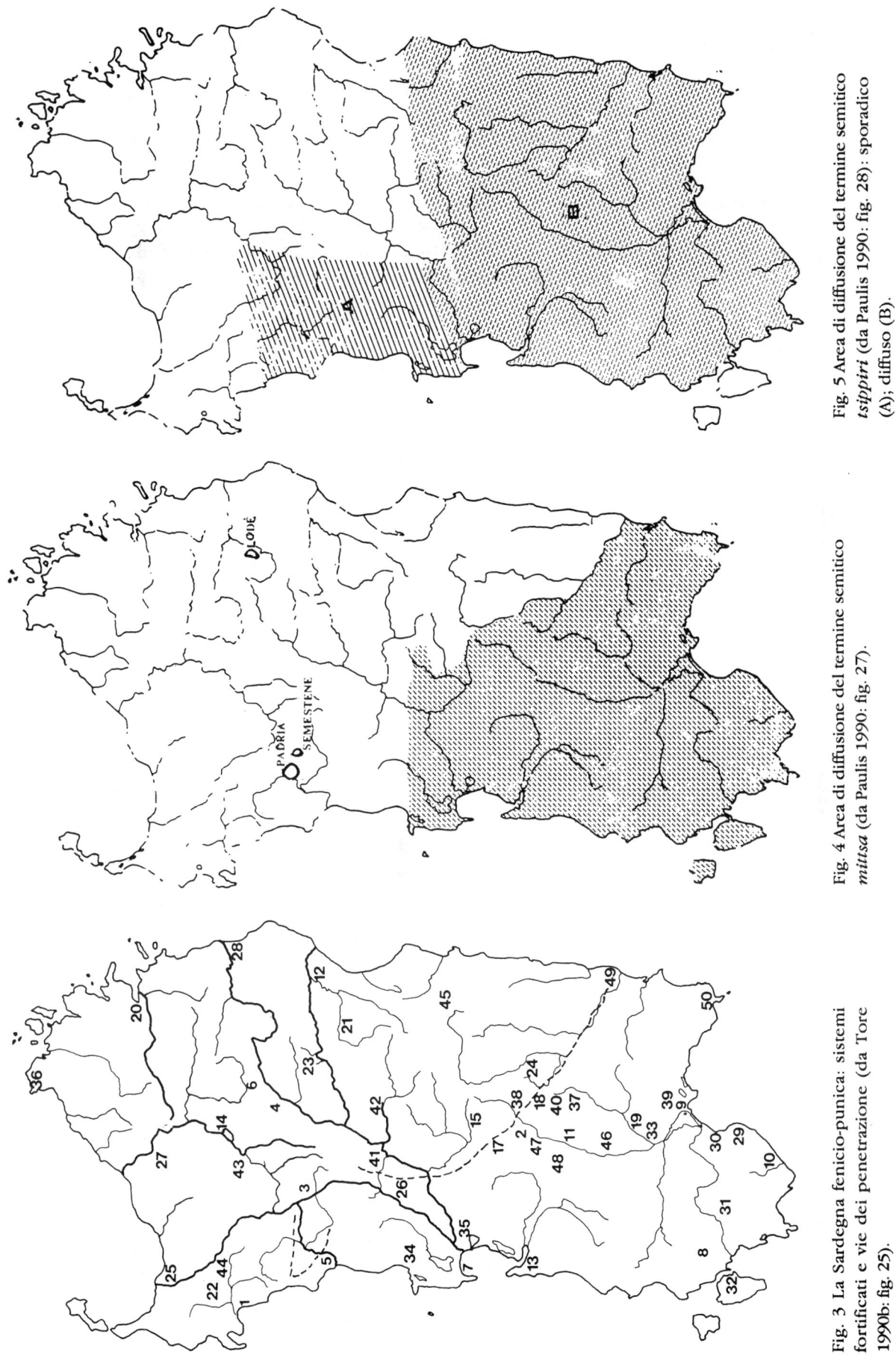

Tore: *Testimonianze Fenicio-Puniche nella Sardegna Centro-Settentrionale* 433

Fig. 5 Area di diffusione del termine semitico *tsippiri* (da Paulis 1990: fig. 28): sporadico (A); diffuso (B).

Fig. 4 Area di diffusione del termine semitico *mittsa* (da Paulis 1990: fig. 27).

Fig. 3 La Sardegna fenicio-punica: sistemi fortificati e vie dei penetrazione (da Tore 1990b: fig. 25).

ragionevolmente far pensare[3] a frequentazione semita pur in ambito aperto e concorrenziale,[4] almeno a partire dal secolo VI a.C., se non prima (per le diverse posizioni cf., da ultimi, Zucca 1986: 56; D'Oriano 1985: 238 n. 39). La costa settentrionale sembrerebbe avere anche, come si è notato, un rapporto se non privilegiato, almeno particolarmente stretto con l'Etruria villanoviana prima, ed etrusca poi, attraverso il ponte dell'arcipelago toscano (Gras 1985: 220), costituendo, insieme alla costa orientale il tramite di passaggio per le rotte da e per l'Etruria alla Sardegna attraverso il Tirreno. A questo traffico parrebbero riferirsi documenti già da tempo elencati (Tore 1981; 1990b: 108-109, ivi bibliografia anteriore) e ricondotti a contatti intensi e da ritenersi, in una prima fase dell'età del Ferro, se non esclusivi, almeno paritari fra le due sponde del Tirreno e con più che presumibile *partnership* nuragica viste le importazioni protosarde individuate nella penisola italiana (Lo Schiavo e Ridgway 1987; Gras 1985: 135-62). Le importazioni sono collegate a documenti di notevole interesse attestanti influenze parallele (Gras 1985: 147 ss.) in un arco di tempo che, abbracciando il passaggio dalla cultura villanoviana all'urbanizzazione etrusca, segna un rapporto profondo fra culture in possesso della metallurgia più avanzata dell'epoca, nell'Isola e nel continente, e delle risorse naturali ad essa connesse e che ad esse presiedono. Base economica che non può avere avuto risvolti di uno sviluppo parzialmente parallelo, ma con esiti diversi: urbanizzazione e civiltà egemone 'storica',

nella penisola, presumibile evoluzione interrotta e subalternità rispetto ad uno sviluppo urbano sì, ma non autoctono, ma d'importazione vicino-orientale (fenicia), forse anche più lento e strisciante, nell'Isola, con sostituzione progressiva, in ambito aperto ancora sino all'VIII sec. a.C., ma sempre più incalzante per il secolo successivo e da ritenersi conchiusa attorno la metà del sec. VI a.C., nel quadro di una mutata e complessa situazione internazionale,[5] di una variegata presenza fenicia (come parrebbero indicare recenti e affinate analisi linguistiche: Amadasi Guzzo 1987), distinta da Cartagine, ad una, più oppressiva e totalizzante, nell'ambito di una politica di controllo territoriale delle risorse locali realizzata attraverso le spedizioni militari promosse da questa e attuata con il sistema militare di fortificazioni (Barreca 1986) in fase conclusiva di tale articolata e differenziata presenza semita in Sardegna (Figg. 4-5). In tal modo si ha il passaggio di questa da un'autonomia derivante dalla peculiare (anche se integrata nel più vasto ambito mediterraneo nella sua caratteristica e storica oscillazione fra Oriente e Occidente) evoluzione autoctona già evidenziatesi dall'età del Bronzo e concretamente realizzatasi nella successiva età del Ferro, all'inserimento definitivo di un sistema di potere identificatosi con subalternità culturale, definita però da aspetti specifici (Barreca 1986) i cui deboli echi si avvertono infine in elaborazioni mitografiche di prevalente stampo classico (cf., da ultima, Breglia Pulci Doria 1981). Episodi di recessione e di abbandono sulla costa orientale paiono confermare la minore importanza di questo tratto di costa per il declinare dell'interesse 'continentale' in favore del controllo semita. Vicende quali quella della supposta colonia romana di Feronia (cf., da ultimo, D'Oriano 1985, ivi bibliografia anteriore) non paiono smentire tale quadro che, anzi, lo confermano proprio per la loro conclusione negativa, certo per solerte e potente intervento cartaginese, testimoniato, per altro, indirettamente dai vari trattati riportatici da Polibio (Meloni 1975: 7-19, 377-80). Non pare, pertanto sostenibile un conflitto interno tra Fenici già insediatisi nell'Isola e i Cartaginesi, almeno sulla base di evidenze archeologiche di interpretazione non meramente determinante (da ultimo, con ripresa forse un po' acritica di tali posizioni, cf. Bernardini 1989: 50, ivi bibliografia anteriore), anche se è possibile che gli

---

3 Spiace rilevare lo scomposto modo di presentare elementi ritenuti probanti a negare la validità di quanto da tutti sino al 1980 accettato (l'esistenza di fittili arcaici da Olbia, cf. Tore 1980, ivi bibliografia anteriore). Accertamenti condotti anche in seguito, mi portano a confermare l'esattezza delle informazioni fornitemi sia dal primo editore che dalle proprietarie (che non ebbero dubbi, nell'estate del 1984, a confermarmi quanto scritto e dettomi a voce), né speciose (e di tono personalistico e acrimonioso) argomentazioni contrarie mi portano a dubitare della mia e della altrui buonafede (e *de hoc satis*).

4 L'assenza di ulteriori testimonianze pertinenti la necropoli arcaica di Olbia è stata già ragionevolmente esplicata con la sua probabile distruzione per lavori di sbancamento dei primi del Novecento, come notava lo storico Ettore Pais (cf. Panedda 1953: 9 n. 16). Tale precisa indicazione, per altro, è assai di rado ripresa da chi discetta in materia. Del resto solo negli anni Ottanta si sono avuti materiali attestanti con chiarezza la fondazione arcaica di *Karales, Sulci e Tharri*. Da ciò può considerarsi la validità dell'*argumentum ex silentio*. Non pare inopportuno, pertanto, ritenere il problema aperto (e non solubile d'imperio), in assenza di ulteriori scoperte.

5 Cf. Liverani (1988: 642-56, 693-713). Per una recente e interessante rassegna delle fonti storiche cf. Botto (1990). Permangono di utile lettura Garbini (1966) e D'Agostino (1977: 44-51). Vedasi, infine, di recente, Aubet (1987) e Gras *et al.* (1989). Trattazione specifica in Moscati (1988; 1989). Sul tema in generale cf. Acquaro *et al.* (1988).

esiti di tale intervento possano anche non aver del tutto collimato con intenzioni e interessi dei centri urbani fenici della Sardegna.[6, 7] Del resto la costa orientale mostra, come si è rilevato, aperture anche precoci, ritenute pure prefenicie (cf. Lo Schiavo 1983a) comunque pertinenti ad una matrice vicino-orientale (o riduttivamente solo egea) cui l'ambito cananeo non sembra doversi ritenere antitetico o affatto antagonistico. Anzi, per il tramite cipriota l'uno sembra, significativamente, precedere l'altro, quasi in un comune divenire dello sviluppo storico del 'Lontano Occidente'. Di recente (da ultimo, Tore 1990b: 92 n. 15 e 16) si è rilevato tale fenomeno di persistenza nelle vie di penetrazione che dalla costa (Golfo di Orosei e bacino del Cedrino) portavano all'interno, andandosi poi a saldare con le altre che salivano dal golfo di Oristano, ove la fondazione tharrense conosce attestazioni di alta antichità (Acquaro 1989: 250; per le attestazioni, anche recentissime, su tali vie di penetrazione cf. Tore 1990b, specie alle pp. 87-88 e 92).

La situazione derivante dalla successiva conquista cartaginese (cf. Meloni 1984: 13-17), secondo gli schemi di lettura più correnti (Barreca 1986: 31-42), segnerebbe il riassetto di buona parte dell'Isola, sotto il diretto controllo punico, presumibile organizzazione a latifondo delle ampie pianure (Meloni 1984) e a monocolture cerealicole, a cui si lega una colonizzazione capillare che dovrebbe lasciare a sè, come specie di 'ridotti' (Lilliu 1988) le zone nord-orientali, specie di 'grandi riserve' *ante litteram*, ben note dall'esperienza anglossassone del Nuovo Mondo nel secolo XIX. Da esse i Cartaginesi attingeranno (Meloni 1985) mercenari, stabilendo un rapporto simbiotico tale da far schierare i discendenti dei Nuragici a fianco dei ribelli Sardopunici del 215 a.C. e motivare un cent'anni di guerriglia contro i Romani (Meloni 1985).

Per la zona centro-settentrionale la ricerca archeologica,[8] di questi ultimi anni in particolare, motiva, per recenti acquisizioni, in particolare dell'indagine linguistica (Paulis 1990), una parziale rilettura che, tenendo conto delle ipotesi già avanzate (Pais 1881: 328-32; Moscati 1967), tenga conto di un più che presumibile trasferimento forzato di popolazioni libiche nella parte della Sardegna controllata direttamente da Cartagine (per il quadro storico cf. Mastino 1985 e Bondì 1988). Ciò esplicherebbe diffuse testimonianze di rilievo funerario di età romana repubblicana ed imperiale (Tore 1990a, ivi bibliografia anteriore) come l'attestarsi di esiti di un filone secondario di tradizione semita, legato ad ambiti non aulici, ma di più ampia pertinenza popolare (e come tale più agevolmente omologabile anche da genti punicizzate).

Nell'interno, come proverebbero tesoretti monetali ed altri elementi (Meloni 1985: 24-25), la penetrazione culturale dell'elemento ormai culturalmente egemone ed economicamente e politicamente prevalente, deve aver progressivamente intaccato l'antico fondo 'mediterraneo' delle popolazioni autoctone favorendo la loro progressiva omologazione a modelli di vita di specifico riferimento urbano, in origine ad esse estranee. Non è facile pertanto veder in posizione di assoluto antagonismo queste due componenti culturali della Sardegna antica, la semita e la protosarda. Il lungo periodo di contatto deve avere interagito su diversi piani e con aspetti e sviluppi che, a mio parere, non sempre e (come da un po' con certa cursiva sufficienza di recenti addetti ai lavori, forse per l'eccessivo zelo dei neofiti) a piena ragione, si tendono a schematizzare e semplificare. Di fatto la struttura sociale e i rapporti di produzione della Sardegna fra la fine dell'età del Bronzo e l'inizio dell'età del Ferro (per non parlare degli aspetti successivi) non paiono così acclarati (e basicamente di fatto) e leggibili nei dettagli. Si lumeggia un quadro generale che sa di ripetizione meccanica, di realtà quali quelle della Etruria continentale diversamente e più accuratamente messe in luce, con un quadro non solo più definito, ma non per questo obbligatoriamente e d'imperio trasferibile a mo' di comoda semplificazione di stampo centralistico-diffusionista (e d'implicita, inconscia o meno, mentalità veterocoloniale). Basti pensare che analisi più corrette (e meglio fondate) sul piano metodologico tracciano una lettura più sfumata anche per zone più legate a tale interpretazione ricostruttiva (cf. Carancini *et al.* 1985: 53-54; Bietti Sestieri *et al.* 1987: 42-44, 57-58; quest'ultime pagine, inoltre di Bruno D'Agostino [1987] sembrano essere utili sotto il profilo di una maggiore prudenza metodologica). D'altra parte non si vuole considerare improponibile un simile schema se non come mera proposta, da vagliare e discutere un po' più approfonditamente, come del resto si va tentando di fare (Selargius 1986 e Lilliu *et al.* 1987 possono considerarsi un interessante metodo d'approccio come Cortona 1983) anche se appaiono comprensibili improrogabili esigenze di carriera.

---

6 Cf. già Pais (1881: 316, ivi bibliografia e fonti).

7 Sul trasferimento forzato di genti libiche in Sardegna cf. già Pais (1881: 328-32) ed anche Moscati (1967). Per il quadro di relazioni Africa-Sardegna cf. Mastino (1985).

8 La documentazione, in particolare le stele funerarie (cf. Tore 1990b: tav. II), rende plausibile l'ipotesi di centri di diffusione e irradiamento di una certa entità sulla costa: Porto Torres sul Golfo dell'Asinara e Ampurias per il bacino del Coghinas.

Bibliografia

Acquaro, E.
1989 Tharros XV-XVI. *Rivista di Studi Fenici* 17(2): 249-306.

Acquaro, E., L. Godart, F. Mazza & D. Musti
1988 *Momenti Precoloniali nel Mediterraneo Antico. Questioni di metodo. Aree d'indagine. Evidenze a confronto*. Roma: Academia Belgica, Istituto per la Civiltà fenicia e punica, C.N.R.

Amadasi Guzzo, M.G.
1987 Forme della scrittura fenicia in Sardegna. In G. Lilliu, G. Ugas and G. Lai (a cura di), *La Sardegna nel Mediterraneo tra il secondo e il primo millennio a.C. Atti del 2 convegno di studi 'Un millennio di relazioni fra la Sardegna e i Paesi del Mediterraneo', Selargius-Cagliari, 27-30 novembre 1986*, 377-90. Cagliari: Amministrazione Provinciale di Cagliari.

Aubet, M.
1987 *Tiro y las Colonias Fenicias de Occidente*. Barcelona: Ediciones Bellaterra.

Bafico, S.
1986 Materiale d'importazione dal villaggio nuragico di Sant'Imbenia. *Società e Cultura in Sardegna nei Periodi Orientalizzante e Arcaico (fine VIII sec. a.C.—480 a.C.). Rapporti fra Sardegna, Fenici, Etruschi e Greci. Atti del 1 convegno di studi 'Un millennio di relazioni fra la Sardegna e i Paesi del Mediterraneo', Selargius-Cagliari, 29-30 novembre-1 dicembre 1985*, 91-93. Cagliari: Amministrazione Provinciale di Cagliari.

Barreca, F.
1981 La Sardegna e i Fenici. In E. Atzeni *et al*. (eds.), *Ichnussa. La Sardegna dalle origini all'età classica*, 351-416. Milano: Libri Scheiwiller.
1986 *La Civiltà Fenicio-Punica in Sardegna*. Sardegna Archeologica: Studi e Monumenti 3. Sassari: Carlo Delfino.

Bernardini, P.
1989 Le origini di Sulcis e Monte Sirai. *Studi di Egittologia e di Antichità puniche* 4: 45-59.

Bietti Sestieri, A., A. Greco Pontrandolfo & N. Parise (a cura di)
1987 *Archeologia e Antropologia. Contributi di Preistoria e Archeologia classica*. Quaderni di Dialoghi di Archeologia 2. Roma: Edizioni Quasar.

Bondì, S.F.
1988 Capp. VI-IX. In S.F. Bondì *et al*., *Storia dei Sardi e della Sardegna. Vol. 1: Dalle origini alla fine dell'età bizantina*, 129-211. Milano: Jaca Book.

Botto, M.
1990 *Studi Storici sulla Fenicia. L'VIII e il VII secolo*. Pisa: Università degli Studi di Pisa.

Breglia Pulci Doria, L.
1981 La Sardegna arcaica tra tradizioni euboiche ed attiche. *Nouvelle contribution à l'étude de la société et de la colonisation eubéennes*, 61-95. Cahiers du Centre Jean Bérard 6. Naples: Institut Français de Naples.

Carancini, G.L., S. Massetti & F. Posi
1985 L'area tra l'Umbria meridionale e Sabina alla fine della protostoria. *Dialoghi di Archeologia* 3(2): 37-56.

Cecchini, S.
1969 *Ritrovamenti Fenici e Punici in Sardegna*. Roma: Università di Roma.

Cortona
1983 *Forme di Contatto e Processi di Trasformazione nelle Società Antiche. Atti del convegno di Cortona (24-30 maggio 1981)*. Pisa e Roma: Scuola Normale Superiore di Pisa e Ecole Française de Rome.

D'Agostino, B.
1977 Tombe 'principesche' dell'Orientalizzante antico di Pontecagnano. *Monumenti Antichi* 49 (ser. misc. II,1).
1987 Società dei vivi, comunità dei morti: un rapporto difficile. In A.M. Bietti Sestieri, A. Greco Pontrandolfo e N. Parise (a cura di), *Archeologia e Antropologia. Contributi di Preistoria e Archeologia classica*, 47-58. Quaderni di Dialoghi di Archeologia 2. Roma: Edizioni Quasar.

D'Oriano, R.
1985 Contributo al problema di Pheronia polis. *Nuovo Bullettino Archeologico Sardo* 2: 229-47.

Garbini, G.
1966 I Fenici in occidente. *Studi Etruschi* 34: 114-47.

Gras, M.
1985 *Trafics thyrréniens archaïques*. Bibliothèque des Ecoles françaises d'Athènes et de Rome 258. Rome: Ecole française de Rome.

Gras, M., P. Rouillard & J. Teixidor
1989 *L'univers phénicien*. Paris: Arthaud.

Karageorghis, V., & F. Lo Schiavo
1989 A West Mediterranean obelos from Amathus. *Rivista di Studi Fenici* 17(1): 15-29.

Lilliu, G.
1944 Rapporti tra la civiltà nuragica e la civiltà fenicio-punica in Sardegna. *Studi Etruschi* 18: 323-70.
1948 Tracce puniche nella Nurra. *Studi Sardi* 8: 318-27.
1982 *La Civiltà Nuragica*. Sardegna Archeologica: Studi e Monumenti 1. Sassari: Carlo Delfino.
1987 La Sardegna tra il II e il I millennio a.C. In G. Lilliu, G. Ugas e G. Lai (a cura di), *La Sardegna nel Mediterraneo tra il secondo e il primo millennio a.C. Atti del 2 convegno di studi 'Un millennio di relazioni fra la Sardegna e i Paesi del Mediterraneo', Selargius-Cagliari, 27-30 novembre 1986*, 13-32. Cagliari: Amministrazione Provinciale di Cagliari.
1988 *La Civiltà dei Sardi dal Paleolitico all'Età dei Nuraghi*. Terza edizione. Torino: Nuova ERI.

Lilliu, G., G. Ugas & G. Lai (a cura di)
1987 *La Sardegna nel Mediterraneo tra il secondo e il primo millennio a.C. Atti del 2 convegno di studi 'Un millennio di relazioni fra la Sardegna e i Paesi del Mediterraneo', Selargius-Cagliari, 27-30 novembre 1986*. Cagliari: Amministrazione Provinciale di Cagliari.

Liverani, M.
1988 *Antico Oriente. Storia, Società, Economia*. Bari: Laterza.

Lo Schiavo, F.
1981 Economia e società nell'età dei nuraghi. In E. Atzeni *et al*. (eds.), *Ichnussa: La Sardegna dalle origini all'età classica*, 255-347. Milano: Libri Scheiwiller.
1983a Un bronzetto da Galtellì. *Atti del I Convegno Internazionale di Studi Fenici e Punici (Roma, 5-10 novembre 1979)*, II, 463-69. Roma: C.N.R.
1983b Il primo millennio avanti Cristo. *La Provincia di Sassari. I secoli e la storia*, 38-49. Milano: Silvana Editoriale, Cinisello Balsamo.
1985 Vaso nuragico di bronzo da Badde Ulumu (Sassari). *Nuovo Bullettino Archeologico Sardo* 2: 109-18.

Lo Schiavo, F., E. Macnamara & L. Vagnetti
1985 Late Cypriot imports to Italy and their influence on local bronzework. *Papers of the British School at Rome* 53: 1-71.

Lo Schiavo, F., & D. Ridgway
1987 La Sardegna e il Mediterraneo occidentale allo scorcio del II millennio a.C. In G. Lilliu, G. Ugas e G. Lai (a cura di), *La Sardegna nel Mediterraneo tra il secondo e il primo millennio a.C. Atti del 2 convegno di studi 'Un millennio di relazioni fra la Sardegna e i Paesi del Mediterraneo', Selargius-Cagliari, 27-30 novembre 1986*, 391-418. Cagliari: Amministrazione Provinciale di Cagliari.

Madau, M.
1986 Materiali d'importazione dalla Sardegna settentrionale. *Società e Cultura in Sardegna nei Periodi Orientalizzante e Arcaico (fine VIII sec. a.C.—480 a.C.). Rapporti fra Sardegna, Fenici, Etruschi e Greci. Atti del 1 convegno di studi 'Un millennio di relazioni fra la Sardegna e i Paesi del Mediterraneo', Selargius-Cagliari, 29-30 novembre-1 dicembre 1985*, 95-100. Cagliari: Amministrazione Provinciale di Cagliari.
1988a Nuraghe S. Antine di Torralba. Materiali fittili di età fenicio-punica. In A. Moravetti (a cura di), *Il Nuraghe S. Antine nel Logudoro-Meilogu*, 243-71. Sassari: Carlo Delfino Editore.
1988b Nota sui rapporti tra mondo nuragico e mondo fenicio e punico nella Sardegna nord-occidentale. *Rivista di Studi Fenici* 16: 181-94.

Mastino, A.
1985 Le relazioni tra Africa e Sardegna: Inventario prelimnare. *L'Africa Romana. Atti del II convegno di studio, Sassari, 14-16 dicembre 1984*, 27-91. Sassari: Edizioni Gallizzi.

Meloni, P.
1975 *La Sardegna Romana*. Sassari: Chiarella.
1984 Cartaginesi e Romani in Sardegna: Latifondo e monocoltura. *Sardegna: L'uomo e la pianura*, 13-26. Sassari: Banco di Sardegna.
1985 Cartaginesi e Romani, lotta per la sopravvivenza. *L'Uomo e le Montagne*, 23-32. Sassari: Banco di Sardegna.

Moscati, S.
1967 Africa ipsa parens illa Sardiniae. *Rivista di Filologia e di Istruzione Classica* 95: 385-88.
1988 Dimensione tirrenica. *Rivista di Studi Fenici* 16(2): 133-44.
1989 *Tra Tiro e Cadice. Temi e problemi degli studi fenici*. Studia Punica 5. Roma: Università degli Studi di Roma.

Nicosia, F.
1980 Etruskische zeugnisse und enflüsse. In J. Thimme (ed.), *Kunst und Kultur Sardiniens vom Neolithikum bis zum Ende der Nuraghenzeit*, 200-11. Karlsruhe: C.F. Müller.
1981 La Sardegna nel mondo classico. In E. Atzeni et al., *Ichnussa. La Sardegna dalle origini all'età classica*, 421-76. Milano: Scheiwiller.

Pais, E.
1881 La Sardegna prima del dominio romano. Studi storici archeologici di Ettore Pais. *Memorie della R. Accademia dei Lincei 1880-81. Memorie della classe di scienze morali, storiche e filologiche*, VII, 259-378.

Panedda, D.
1953 *Olbia nel Periodo Punico e Romano*. Roma: Regione Autonoma della Sardegna.

Paulis, G.
1990 La penetrazione punica nella Sardegna centro-orientale alla luce dei dati linguistici. In G. Tanda (a cura di), *Ottana. Archeologia e territorio*, 113-23. Nuoro: Amministrazione Comunale di Ottana.

Rivò, R.
1985 Scavi a Monteleone Roccadoria. *Rivista di Studi Fenici* 13(3): 269-73.

Selargius
1986 *Società e Cultura in Sardegna nei Periodi Orientalizzante e Arcaico (fine VIII sec. a.C.–480 a.C.). Rapporti fra Sardegna, Fenici, Etruschi e Greci. Atti del 1 convegno di studi 'Un millennio di relazioni fra la Sardegna e i Paesi del Mediterraneo', Selargius-Cagliari, 29-30 novembre-1 dicembre 1985*, 95-100. Cagliari: Amministrazione Provinciale di Cagliari.

Tore, G.
1980 Elementi culturali semitici nella Sardegna centro-settentrionale. *Atti della XXII Riunione Scientifica dell'Istituto Italiano di Preistoria e Protostoria nella Sardegna centro-settentrionale, 21-27 ottobre 1978, Firenze*, 487-511. Firenze.
1981 Elementi sulle relazioni commerciali della Sardegna nella prima età del ferro. *La Sardegna nel Mondo Mediterraneo, 1 convegno internazionale di studi geografico-storici, Sassari, 7-9 aprile 1978*, I, 257-95. Sassari: Gallizzi.
1983 I bronzi figurati fenicio-punici in Sardegna. *Atti del I Congresso Internazionale di Studi Fenici e Punici, Roma, 5-10 novembre 1979*, II, 449-61. Roma: C.N.R.
1990a Cippi, altarini e stele funerarie nella Sardegna fenicio-punica (nota preliminare). *Quaderni della Soprintendenza Archeologica per le Provincie di Cagliari ed Oristano* 6 (supplemento): 109-22.
1990b L'età fenicio-punica (parte di G. Tore e A.M. Corda, Testimonianze fenicio-puniche e di età romana). In G. Tanda (a cura di), *Ottana. Archeologia e territorio*, 87-111. Nuoro: Amministrazione Comunale di Ottana.

Tronchetti, C.
1985 I Greci e la Sardegna. *Dialoghi di Archeologia* 3(2): 17-34.
1988 *I Sardi. Traffici, relazioni, ideologie nella Sardegna arcaica*. Milano: Longanesi.

Zucca, R.
1986 Elementi di cultura materiali greci e etruschi nei centri fenici. *Società e Cultura in Sardegna nei Periodi Orientalizzante e Arcaico (fine VIII sec. a.C.–480 a.C.). Rapporti fra Sardegna, Fenici, Etruschi e Greci. Atti del 1 convegno di studi 'Un millennio di relazioni fra la Sardegna e i Paesi del Mediterraneo', Selargius-Cagliari, 29-30 novembre-1 dicembre 1985*, 55-83. Cagliari: Amministrazione Provinciale di Cagliari.

Summary

There is some disagreement among scholars today regarding the influence of the Phoenicians and their successors on the indigenous people of Sardinia. Some feel that the Nuragic population was strongly resistant to outside influence, while others prefer a model of cultural integration, or fusion, caused by the encounter of these two

Mediterranean peoples. The available archaeological data has been used to support both of these hypotheses.

The existence of natural resources such as silver, iron and lead, the island's centrality in the Mediterranean, and its good harbors (e.g. Bosa, where two fragmentary Phoenician inscriptions were found in the 18th century), attracted foreigners to Sardinia. The first Phoenician colonies were established in the 8th and 7th centuries BC, mainly along the western coast, but also in the northern part of the island. Phoenician presence is attested near Alghero by Phoenician bronzes from several sites (Nuraghe Flumenelongu, Olmedo, Sant'Imbenia), while earlier Mycenaean, and later Greek, and Etruscan finds attest to the long and evolving interaction of Sardinia with other Mediterranean cultures. In fact, the presence of Phoenician, Greek and Etruscan material in Perfugas, at Monti Cau (Sorso), Monte Zuighe (Ittirreddu), and at the Nuraghi su Igante (Uri), Santu Antine (Torralba), and Eri Manzanu (Bono) demonstrates that Sardinia's participation in Mediterranean commerce was a complex phenomenon. It appears that the northern coast had particularly close ties with Villanovan Etruria, and the Author suggests that Olbia may have been a major port some centuries earlier than the current archaeological evidence would suggest (6th century BC).

The Carthaginian settlement of Sardinia, beginning in the 6th century, was quite different from the Phoenician colonization. The conquest by force of the indigenous people, and the establishment of a military system of fortifications, resulted in a different relationship between natives and colonists. In the Phoenician period, the Nuragic people maintained their autonomy, while during the Carthaginian domination, much of Sardinia's arable land and natural resources came under direct Punic control, although the northern and eastern parts of Sardinia seem to have been left to themselves. The indigenous Sardinians may have had difficulties adapting to the *latifundia* system and cereal monoculture presumed to have been introduced by the Carthaginians. Eventually, however, a peaceful, symbiotic relationship developed between the Carthaginians and the indigenous Sardinians, so that in the 3rd century BC they united against the Romans in a conflict that lasted 100 years.

We do not have a perfect understanding of the nature and extent of Mediterranean interactions between the end of the Bronze Age and the Iron Age; nor was the influence of Phoenicians and Carthaginians on the Nuragic people of Sardinia a simple process. Certainly the introduction of urban centers, and the continued contact between them and even the most remote parts of the island, must have led to a progressive homogenization of Sardinia's inhabitants. We know that absolute antagonism did not necessarily exist between the Semitic urbanites and the Sardinians of the interior. This interpretation results from generalizing the archaeological and historical data, and may not have been universally true. Furthermore, the development and evolution of interaction between Phoenicians, Carthaginians, and Sardinians was far more complex and intricate than the archaeological and historical evidence can ever fully reflect. Such evidence can and should be used to support hypotheses about the influence of Phoenician and Punic colonists on Sardinia, but one must always remember the limitations of the data when making schematic generalizations.

Divertimento 1991.[1] Ancora sulla Cartagine di Sardegna

Maria Giulia Amadasi Guzzo

Il nome di 'città nuova' è forse il primo che viene in mente a chi, lasciato il proprio paese e giunto finalmente su sponde ospitali, decida di stabilire qui la propria dimora. Nei tempi antichi come in quelli recenti, chi sceglie una nuova patria in luoghi ancora non abitati fonda una città nuova, la città nuova, dove costruisce per sé e per i suoi un'ugualmente nuova casa. È evidente così come le tante testimonianze antiche di toponimi con il significato di 'città nuova' non si identifichino sempre facilmente con uno specifico insediamento, in particolare quando queste siano isolate, prive di altri riscontri sicuri. È questa la situazione di almeno due fra le 'città nuove' di origine fenicia: quella di Cipro e quella attestata da due iscrizioni puniche di Sardegna (Amadasi 1967: Sard. 32, 34).

Tralasciando qui il problema dell'identificazione della 'città nuova' (qrtḥdšt) di Cipro, ampiamente trattato di recente (Masson e Sznycer 1972: 77-78; Masson 1985: 33-46; Lipiński 1983: 209-34), si riprende invece in esame la questione se si possa davvero supporre l'esistenza, nella Sardegna fenicio-punica, di un sito dal medesimo nome.

Dopo una prima proposta di attribuire il toponimo di QRTḤDŠT all'insediamento che porta oggi il nome di S. Maria di Nabui, e che corrisponde ad un precedente centro antico dal nome di Neapolis (Amadasi 1968; sull'antica Neapolis cf. Zucca 1987; Moscati e Zucca 1989), è stato supposto invece, in base alle due iscrizioni sopra citate, che 'Cartagine' fosse il nome antico sia di Tharros (Chiera 1982) sia di Olbia (Chiera 1983). Ora, messa da parte la questione della lingua originaria del nome tramandato come Neapolis dagli antichi geografi, tende a prevalere l'ipotesi che la menzione di QRTḤDŠT nei citati documenti punici si riferisca alla capitale africana (Huss 1977–78: 250 n. 8; 1985: 473 n. 58; Lipiński 1989).

Sembra opportuno sgombrare in prima luogo il campo da quanto non è direttamente pertinente all'identificazione di un eventuale centro di nome QRTḤDŠT in Sardegna, cioè dall'iscrizione di Olbia del III sec. a.C. circa (ritrovata fuori contesto, la datazione si basa su una valutazione approssimativa della forma delle lettere) (Fig. 1). Questa, rinvenuta nel 1911 (si conserva nel Museo G. A. Sanna di Sassari), è stata tempestivamente pubblicata da A. Taramelli (1911: 240-41) con l'interpretazione di I. Guidi e successivamente più volte ristudiata (Lidzbarski 1915: 281-83; Chabot 1916; *RES* 1216; *KAI* 68; Amadasi 1967: Sard. 34). Il toponimo QRTḤDŠT è conservato all'inizio della l. 2, dopo una prima linea per la maggior parte lacunosa. Si dà il testo dell'iscrizione, privo delle diverse integrazioni proposte per la l. 1:

1. Ĺ°...' MŠḤ... 'DN Ḥ...... NDR....(.)[2] 'M
2. QRTḤDŠT BN ḤNB'L BN ḤMLKT BN GRMLQRT B̊[N Ḥ]N̊B̊[']L BN
3. MHRB'L BN GR'ŠMN BN BDSD BN B'LŠM' BN 'BDTYWN BN
4. PT' BN 'RŠ BN GR' BN YM' BN ḤLBN BN ḤLṢB'L BN MLKṢD
5. K ŠM' QL' 'D P'MT BRBM

La riga iniziale conteneva la dedica (verbo NDR) ad una divinità che appare maschile (si possono riconoscere all'inizio i resti dell'espressione L'DN).[3] Dopo il verbo e una lacuna di 10 (al massimo 11) lettere,[4] è conservato, alla fine della

---

1 Il titolo deriva da G. Morselli, *Divertimento* 1889 (Milano: Adelphi, 1975, 5a edizione 1989), cf. p. 187: 'Cara Lettrice, la storia che hai avuto sott'occhio, arcaica e ingenua come questo mio rivolgermi a Te, non va pi in là di ciò che dice. Verosimile e inconsistente è circoscritta ...[a] un mondo di cose scomparse e ...che pure sono state, per me, motivo determinante, ben altro che decorazione'. Spero che questo mio 'Divertimento' piaccia a Miriam Balmuth, la Lettrice alla quale lo dedico.

2 Le lettere mancanti non sono state contate esattamente nella trascrizione di Amadasi 1968.

3 Guidi (in Taramelli 1911: 240-41) supponeva invece una divinità femminile, leggendo le lettere iniziali come LR̊[BT ...; così in seguito fino a Amadasi (1967: Sard. 34).

4 Si preferirebbe contarne 10, anche perché le lettere di l. 1 appaiono di dimensioni un po' maggiori rispetto a quelle delle linee successive; Guidi (in Taramelli 1911: 240) ne suppone 9, Lipiński (1989: 70), 11.

Fig. 1 Museo G.A. Sanna, Sassari: iscrizione punica di Olbia. Foto Museo Nazionale di Sassari.

Fig. 2 Museo Nazionale di Cagliari: iscrizione punica da Tharros. Foto C.N.R. Istituto per la Civiltà fenicia e punica (foto Petruccioli).

linea, il sostantivo 'M 'popolo'. Si è proposto (Amadasi 1967: Sard. 34) di riempirla con il nome del dedicante (di 7 lettere;[5] si ricorda che i nomi fenici più lunghi contano 8 lettere, ad es. il frequente 'BDMLQRT) seguito dal relativo 'Š e dalla preposizione B-, a formare l'espressione ['Š B]'M / QRTḤDŠT, 'che appartiene al popolo di Cartagine', qualifica etnica e sociale del dedicante (sull'espressione 'Š B'M accompagnata da un nome di città cf. Levi Della Vida 1963: 464-68; Moscati 1968; Garbini 1969: 323-27; Sznycer 1975: 47-48) del quale poi è data la genealogia. Questa è la più lunga nota nelle iscrizioni fenicie e puniche: comprende infatti 16 ascendenti trovando un confronto per ora solo nell'iscrizione da Cartagine *KAI* 78 (*CIS* I.3778; cf. ora Xella 1990).

La lunghezza della genealogia (con nomi sempre diversi: solo il nome ḤNB'L sembra attestato due volte) ha indotto alla supposizione che la dedica sia stata effettuata non da un singolo, ma da un insieme di famiglie: in tale caso BN sarebbe uno stato costrutto plurale, designante gli appartenenti a un gruppo ('i figli di'). Le famiglie elencate costituirebbero una specificazione dell'espressione 'M QRTḤDŠT 'il popolo di Cartagine', identificato in questo caso come il dedicante. Si deve supporre allora che al 'popolo', 'M, sia da attribuire il pronome suffisso singolare in QL' 'la sua voce' (L. 5), che la divinità ha ascoltato 'molte volte'.[6] Tale ipotesi, avanzata per la prima volta da J.B. Chabot (1916: 80-81) è stata ripresa da G. Chiera (1983) che ritiene così di poter identificare QRTḤDŠT con Olbia stessa. A parte il problema del pronome suffisso singolare, osta a questa spiegazione l'impossibilità di fornire un'integrazione di qualsiasi tipo per la lacuna che segue il verbo.

Una diversa soluzione è stata proposta da E. Lipiński (1989: 70-73). Supponendo una lacuna di 11 lettere, egli propone che dopo NDR fosse conservato un nome breve (3 lettere) seguito da una designazione di funzione, 'capo della flotta' o 'capo dell'esercito del popolo di Cartagine'; si avrebbe cioè 'Š NDR [ḤN' 'L 'NYT] 'M / QRTḤD o 'Š NDR [ḤN' RB ḤMḤNT] / 'M QRTḤDŠT. Tale capo viene identificato con Annone (ḤN') figlio di Annibale (il primo nome proprio conservato a L. 2 è ḤNB'L) comandante un esercito cartaginese nel corso della prima guerra punica, che vinse i Romani in Sardegna nel 258 a.C.[7] L'iscrizione consisterebbe dunque in un ex-voto, offerto come ringraziamento dopo la vittoria, da un generale cartaginese: QRTḤDŠT sarebbe perciò da identificare con la capitale africana. Tale voto sarebbe stato indirizzato a due divinità, la prima sconosciuta a causa della lacuna, la seconda forse ḤRN in base ai resti di lettere (una sicuramente Ḥ) visibilie a L. 1, noto in Sardegna da un'iscrizione di Antas (Fantar 1969, cui si riferiscono le iscrizioni denominate Antas + un numero romano; Garbini 1969; Sznycer 1969–70; Uberti 1978).

La proposta di Lipiński, per quanto ingegnosa, non è sostenuta da confronti esistenti:[8] un ex-voto eccezionale, compiuto da un eccezionale personaggio non può del resto trovare troppo diffusi paragoni. Nulla di veramente serio sembra tuttavia opporsi alla più banale integrazione che qui si ripropone. In particolare l'obiezione di Lipiński sulla ricostruzione qui dell'espressione 'Š B'M QRTḤDŠT perché verrebbe a trovarsi prima della genealogia, mentre negli esempi noti si trova dopo, è smentita come indica lo studioso stesso, da un esempio di Antas, nella stessa Sardegna, press'a poco contemporaneo della presente iscrizione (Antas II). Ribadendo tale integrazione sembra di poter anche migliorare la lettura d'insieme della l. 1 come segue:

L'DN [LṢD] MŠ ḤRN 'DN Ḥ.. 'Š NDR [.... 'Š B] 'M

Il nome della divinità è breve, forse solo di due lettere, della prima della quali si scorge la fine di un'asta lunga, mentre la seconda è priva di asta. Non si sfugge alla tentazione di integrare il nome di ṢD, che riceve in dono una 'statua' di Horon nell'iscrizione n. VI di Antas (si ricorda che nell'iscrizione XI lo stesso dio riceve un MŠ ṢDRP'). La lettura MŠ, già individuata anche se non interpretata nella prima edizione di Guidi, appare praticamente certa sulla fotografia; un esame diretto dell'iscrizione nel museo G.A. Sanna di Sassari (novembre 1991; l'iscrizione è esposta al pubblico) l'ha confermata. Si nota la grafia fenicia priva di alef, attestata sempre come tale anche ad Antas (in particolare proprio in Antas VI e in

---

5 Se è giusta questa ricostruzione, in base alla tracce conservate, il nome doveva iniziare con una lettera con asta lunga, cf. ad es. GRMLQRT, ma cf. in seguito.

6 L. 5: K ŠM' QL' 'D P'MT BRBM 'poiché ha ascoltato la sua voce molte volte;' per BRBM cf. Röllig (1974: 8).

7 Cf. Lipiński (1989: 72) che cita come fonte Zonara VIII.12 (in Dio's *Roman History* 1.418 [London: Loeb, 1914]). Da ricordare che Chabot (1916: 81) menziona una 'note anonyme' in *The Athenaeum*, 11 dicembre 1915: 444, col. 2, dove si identifica nel dedicante, che è BN ḤNB'L BN ḤMLKT il figlio del grande Annibale.

8 L'espressione 'Š 'L 'NYT non è attestata allo stato attuale; RB MḤNT 'capo dell'esercito' è attestato in neopunico per designare il 'console' (e RB THT RB MḤNT designa il 'proconsole') ed era verosimilmente una carica già esistente in periodo punico a Cartagine (cf. Levi Della Vida 1971).

Antas IX, ma anche Antas I, IV, VII). Come ad Antas si ha qui l'attestazione dell'immagine di un dio offerta ad un'altra divinità: tale consuetudine è stata documentata con certezza per la prima volta in ambito punico solo ad Antas, ma è certo più diffusa di quanto si sia finora supposto. Il fenomeno è in particolare ben noto in ambito greco dove gli sono stati dedicati studi analitici (cf. già Rouse 1902; in particolare Alroth 1987; Alroth 1989: 108-113; Alroth 1991).

Il nome del dio Horon sembra seguito dall'epiteto 'signore', cui poteva seguire un complemento di speficazione, forse un toponimo (come nell'iscrizione punica di Lepcis: Levi Della Vida e Amadasi 1986: n. 31; Shadrapa e Milkashtart ricevono l'epiteto RBT 'LPQY 'patroni di Lepcis'). Di nuovo perché tale designazione non trova precisi confronti e perché dopo Ḥ manca la parte superiore di due lettere ambedue provviste di lunga asta verticale (la seconda abbastanza lontana dalla prima, tale perciò da portare ad escludere che si tratti di un segno con occhiello a sinistra), non si può evitare di proporre l'identificazione dell'espressione 'BN ḤRṢ 'pietra scolpita' (interpretazione migliore rispetto a quella di 'pietra dorata', anch'essa possibile, cf. Garbini 1969: 322; Sznycer 1969–70: 69-70) che ricorre in Antas V (...MŠ 'BN ḤRṢ 'Š NDR BD 'ŠTRT BN... 'immagine di pietra scolpita che ha dedicato B.'); tuttavia dalet sembra ben chiara sulla nostra iscrizione: si dovrebbe supporre che la parte inferiore dell'asta sia così consunta da non essere più visibile.[9] Contro l'ipotesi proposta sembra inoltre il numero eccessivo di complementi retti da MŠ (MŠ ḤRN 'BN ḤRṢ); ma una uguale successione potrebbe presumersi anche nell'iscrizione VI di Antas, con l'aggiunta del frammento XIII.[10]

Il verbo NDR doveva essere seguito, come già proposto, da un nome di 7 lettere; come alternativa si può proporre un'espressione di dedica formata da due verbi e un soggetto di 3 lettere, come NDR [WṬ(Y)N'... 'ha dedicato e ha eretto...';[11] in questo caso diventa possibile, con E. Lipiński, proporre per il dedicante il nome di ḤN'.[12]

In conclusione, secondo quanto qui riproposto, il dedicante, che si qualifica come 'appartenente al popolo di QRTḤDŠT' non è senza dubbio di Olbia. Con simile specificazione infatti, si presentano gli 'stranieri' (sulla connotazione cf. supra) che vengono a dedicare in un santuario che non è della loro città, o fedeli che vengono in santuari extraurbani; in questi ultimi appunto tali designazioni si presentano più di frequente, come mostrano in Sardegna le iscrizioni del santuario di Antas (qui hanno dedicato persone di Karalis e di Sulcis: Antas I, II, III). Di nuovo si propone perciò il quesito da quale 'città nuova' provenisse il dedicante punico di Olbia (sul nome di Olbia cf. le notizie in Meloni 1975: 419-20), per noi ignoto, ma di ben antico lignaggio.

Si riprende perciò in esame il passo dell'iscrizione da Tharros dove è citato il toponimo (Fig. 2). Il documento—una lastra in marmo(?) nero—rinvenuto in luogo imprecisato intorno al 1900, e reso noto parzialmente nel 1901 da Ph. Berger (1901: 576-79; bibliografia successiva in Amadasi 1967: Sard. 32), consiste nella dedica a Melqart di un insieme importante di costruzioni (è datata approssimativamente al III-II secolo a.C.).[13] Per quanto il monumento sia disponibile agli studiosi, esposto com'è nel Museo Nazionale di Cagliari, il pessimo stato della superfice (mancante di un ampia porzione in alto a sinistra) incisa molto sottilmente, non ne ha mai consentito una pubblicazione adeguata. Oltre ad alcune frasi, soltanto la struttura d'insieme della dedica è stata riconosciuta (Amadasi 1967: Sard. 32; cf. ora, sulla parte finale, Lipiński 1989: 67-69; la data proposta è la prima metà del III sec. a.C.), mentre manca uno studio dettagliato compiuto sul

---

9 L'esame nel museo di Sassari mostra che davvero l'iscrizione presenta tratti della superficie consunta, specie in prossimità delle lacune; non si può perciò escludere una lettura 'BN che rimane tuttavia alquanto congetturale, anche perché l'occhiello di bet sembra avere una diversa inclinazione rispetto a quello di dalet.

10 Ll. 1-2 L'DN L[ṢD 'DR] B'BY MŠ / ḤRN '[BN ḤRṢ 'Š NDR]; a l. 3 era il nome del dedicante (MGN) seguito da un patronomico e dal nome del nonno (o dal solo patronomico lungo) + K che introduce la formula conclusiva (l. 4: ŠM' Q[L...). La restituzione proposta comprende però 16 lettere a l. 1 e solo 14 a l. 2.

11 L'asta lunga ben visibile dopo NDR potrebbe adattarsi a una waw. La formula NDR WṬYN' con mater lectionis per la forma piel è in restituita in *KAI* 119 = Levi Della Vida e Amadasi 1986: n. 31; si può altrimente proporre NDR [WYṬN...

12 Senza che ciò costringa tuttavia a identificarlo col generale cartaginese che combatté i Romani nel 258. Si ricorda di nuovo, con Chabot (1916), la frequenza dei nomi ḤN' e ḤNB'L a Cartagine; lo stesso Lipiński (1989: 71-72), ricorda almeno due 'Annone figlio di Annibale' menzionati dalle fonti classiche in rapporto con la Sardegna. La datazione approssimativa dell'iscrizione (e la lacuna solo in parte colmabile e in maniera congetturale) rende secondo me arbitraria ogni proposta di identificazione.

13 Di nuovo il contesto del ritrovamento è sconosciuto; la forma dei segni è difficile da analizzare per la cattiva conservazione, l'incisione molto sottile e le piccole dimensioni.

monumento stesso. Fin dalla prima pubblicazione, tuttavia, oltre alla dedica a Melqart (L. 1), è stata riconosciuta (ll. 9-10) l'espressione...Š]PṬM BQRTḤDŠT 'DN/B'L WḤMLKT W..., che ha aperto la discussione sull'attribuzione del toponimo.

Date le ampie lacune nel testo, non sembra possibile né opportuno fornire la trascrizione complessiva di quanto è leggibile. L'iscrizione consta di 11 righe, il cui contenuto si può così riassumere (cf. Amadasi 1967: Sard. 32). Le ll. 1-5 contengono la dedica: L'DN L'LM HQDŠ MLQRT 'L ḤṢR,[14] 'Al signore al dio santo Melqart, su Tiro', seguita dall'enumerazione dei lavori eseguiti: il primo è un portico, 'RPT (l. 1); a l. 2 si individua l'espressione 'D HGG 'L 'MDM 'fino al tetto sopra colonne'; prima della lacuna è forse leggibile QRṮ['città' (se non si tratta della prima parte del toponimo QRTḤDŠT); a l. 3 è nominato di nuovo 'il tetto' (HGG); un 'rivestimento o decorazione' (?) (MṬḤT);[15] una 'porta' (?) (Š'R).[16] Alle ll. 4 e 5 sono leggibili gruppi di lettere, ma non sembra di poter individuare espressioni di significato sicuro.[17] Alle ll. 6-7 sono una serie di nomi propri, per quanto distinguibile tutti accompagnati dal titolo di ŠPṬ e in rapporto di filiazione l'uno rispetto all'altro: erano verosimilmente qui contenuti il nome del dedicante (o dei dedicanti?)[18] e il motivo della dedica. Alla fine di l. 7 e alle ll. 8-9 erano nominati gli artigiani che avevano eseguito i lavori. Alle ll. 9 e 10 è fornita una cronologia; la seconda metà di l. 10 è illeggibile, a parte qualche lettera; la l. 11 sembra contenere un nome proprio. Della seconda parte del testo (ll. 6-11) si può dare la seguente trascrizione parziale:[19]

6. M̊[..(5 o 6 lettere)]ḤMY HŠPṬ BN[..(3 o 4 lettere)..]L̊ [H]ŠPṬ [B]N̊ MḤ̊[R]B'L HŠPṬ BN GRSKN [HŠ]
7. PṬ BN 'ZRB'L HŠPṬ BN ḤMY HŠPṬ K̊[..(5 o 6 lettere)..]B D̊Y YBR[..(ca. 9 lettere)]P'L 'YT H[MLK]
8. T Ż B'L[Š]LK HBN' '[Š B']M R[ŠML]Q̊RT W'ZR W'BDŠG̊[R..(ca. 6 lettere)]W̊ḤR[..(ca. 4 lettere)..]W̊['B]
9. DKŠR ḤM̊ṬḤ..B'T R̊/BD.. HŠPṬ BN ṬM̊[..(11 o 12 lettere).. Š]PṬM BQRTḤDŠT 'DN
10. B'L WḤMLKT W̊ [.................]
11. N 'D̊[N]B'L

a) Ammettendo che il dedicante fosse ḤMY, egli sembra presentare una genealogia che consta di 5 antenati, tutti sufeti: ciò è importante per quanto riguarda l'antichità del sufetato, poiché lo farebbe risalire indietro di circa 150 anni rispetto al presente documento (disgraziatamente non databile con sicurezza).[20] È inoltre da notare, se la lettura è corretta, che il capostipite ha lo stesso nome del presunto dedicante (gli altri antenati hanno invece nomi diversi).

b) Mentre il verbo (o i verbi) della dedica non sono identificati, nemmeno per quanto riguarda la loro collocazione sulla pietra (erano forse nella parte mancante di l. 5 e/o all'inizio di l. 6), il motivo della dedica e la possibile benedizione della divinità (accordata o richiesta) potevano essere contenuti nella l. 7, dopo il nome ḤMY: è infatti leggibile K̊, che si ritiene poter introdurre la motivazione; tuttavia non si possono leggere con sicurezza né il verbo ŠM' (si potrebbe individuare dopo K), né eventualmente l'espressione QL DBRY, di seguito a tale verbo, né, infine, una forma di BRK (eventualmente l'imperfetto: ma la lettera che segue resh non ha l'inclinazione di kaf).

c) Dalla fine di l. 7 sono riportati gli artigiani che hanno eseguito le opere, descritte all'inizio del testo. Tra questi (almeno quattro in base a quanto è leggibile), il primo e il più importante è l'architetto (HBN'): si deve notare la sua qualifica, identificabile con un buon grado di sicurezza come 'Š B'M RŠMLQRT 'che appartiene al popolo di Roshmelqart'. La stessa espressione identifica due individui che dedicano a Cartagine (KAI 86 = CIS I.264.4—la lettura corretta è in Sznycer 1975: 60 n. 4; CIS I.3707.4-5); la presente attestazione sembra dover dimostrare una volta per tutte che la legenda R(')ŠMLQRT della serie di monete

---

14 La lettura è sicura; l'espressione non è attestata altrove. Si deve supporre che il nome di Tiro sia provvisto dell'articolo, ciò che non è infrequente nei toponimi, cf. Segert (1976: §62.311.1); cf. ad es. Antas I, II, III: 'KRLY, HKRL', HSLKY̊.

15 Cf. KAI 137.2 dove è nominato un MLKT HMṬḤ 'lavoro di rivestimento, decorazione'. Non appare ora sicura l'identificazione di [Ḥ]ṢBT (ll. 2-3) proposta in Amadasi (1967: Sard. 32); l'identificazione del termine appare invece tuttora verosimile a l. 5.

16 Si legge...Š'RTKL..[..: piacerebbe individuare KL M̊N̊[M.., ma il femm. Š'RT non è attestato.

17 La l. 4 inizia con 'L' (ma 'sopra di esso' dovrebbe essere più correttamente 'LY); si legge anche chiaramente 'GL[..., forse 'GLT 'carro'?

18 Lipiński (1989: 67-68) individua il nome del dedicante all'inizio di l. 6: si tratterebbe di MGN: ma la lettura non è sicura, né il rapporto con quanto segue. Il nome ḤMY, di lettura sicura, non è certo preceduto da BN, né dall'eventuale congiunzione W, nel caso si trattasse del nome di un altro dedicante.

19 Parole o gruppi di parole sono separate da punti; non sono qui riportati perché non sono sempre distinguibili con sicurezza.

20 Sul problema dell'antichità della carica cf. in particolare Sznycer (1978: 567-76, con bibliografia precedente); Huss (1983); sulla funzione cf. anche Bacigalupo Pareo (1977); Teixidor (1979; in Fenicia); Huss (1985: 458-461).

siciliane coniate tra il 320 e il 306 a.C. si riferisce a un centro cittadino e non a funzionari templari.[21] Se Roshmelqart è una città della Sicilia (l'identificazione tradizionale è con Heraclea Minoa, cf. ad es. *CIS* I sub 3707), è da notare l'impiego di un costruttore siciliano per opere di ampio respiro compiute in Sardegna.

d) Una doppia cronologia è riportata dalla 1.9, dopo la menzione dell'ultimo artigiano (?). Già Ph. Berger (1901: 579) aveva supposto la presenza di una doppia datazione, mediante funzionari locali e mediante i sufeti cartaginesi.[22] L'ipotesi alternativa della menzione di una Cartagine di Sardegna è stata avanzata con esitazione da chi scrive (Amadasi 1967: Sard. 32, 34). Non era tuttavia pensabile che un'iscrizione redatta a Tharros fosse datata mediante i sufeti di un centro di non primaria importanza quale appare quello di Neapolis individuato nella zona.[23] È per questo che QRTḤDŠT nominata nell'iscrizione è stata identificata con Tharros stessa da G. Chiera (1982), mentre sia W. Huss (1977–78: 250 n. 8; 1985: 473 n. 58) sia E. Lipiński (1989) ritornano all'ipotesi della Cartagine d'Africa. Il primo insiste sulla presenza nell'iscrizione di una doppia datazione sufetale; il secondo fa notare che sarebbe strano precisare il luogo dove i sufeti esercitavano la loro autorità se questo coincidesse con il centro dove è stata eseguita l'iscrizione.[24]

Sembra opportuno riesaminare le formule di datazione qui presenti in quanto tali e in rapporto con quanto noto dalle altre iscrizioni fenicie e puniche, osservando già ora che conclusioni sicure sono impedite dal poco materiale di confronto e, soprattutto, dalle insufficienti conoscenze sul sistema di governo cartaginese e sulla cronologia della presente iscrizione. La prima espressione consiste nel sotantivo 'T preceduto da B-, forse seguito da R (la lettura ', da unire al nome che segue, facendone un composto con 'BD sembra tuttavia forse concordare meglio con le tracce conservate sulla pietra), seguito da un nome proprio con la qualifica di sufeta e da BN + i resti di due lettere del patronomico. Segue una lacuna di 11 o, al massimo, 12 lettere. In base a quanto supposto da Huss (datazione in base ai sufeti locali), si dovrebbe supplire la fine del patronomico (almeno 1 lettera), la congiunzione W, il nome del secondo sufeta (almeno 3 lettere), il titolo di sufeta (4 lettere), BN + il patronomico (almeno 3 lettere):[25] Mancherebbero perciò almeno 14 lettere (calcolando in tutti i casi nomi di tre lettere, cioè tra i più brevi esistenti in fenicio: è attestato qualche nome di due lettere, ma si tratta di casi rarissimi). Si deve perciò supporre o che fosse menzionato un secondo funzionario senza titolo di sufeta (è più difficile che fosse senza patronomico), o che fosse menzionato un solo funzionario con una genealogia risalente fino al nonno.[26] In ogni caso è verosimile supporre che il personaggio, o i personaggi, qui nominati non fossero i locali sufeti annuali. Tale conclusione pare da raggiungere anche sulla base della formula stessa impiegata: sembra a chi scrive che la datazione in base ai sufeti fosse introdotta o dalla menzione dell'anno (ŠT o BŠT) seguito o meno dal termine (H)ŠPṬM (cf. *CIS* I.179, 196, 3920, 4824, 5510; *KAI* 66, 77 [*CIS* I.143], 77 [*CIS* I.3921], 80 [*CIS* 175], 96 [*CIS* I.5523], 130; Levi Della Vida e Amadasi 1986: n.17); oppure dal semplice ŠPṬM 'essendo sufeti', cui seguivano i nomi propri (*KAI* 81 [*CIS* I.3914], 146; Mahjoubi e Fantar 1966). L'espressione 'T R non introduce certamente i sufeti nel caso della datazione 'doppia' in Mahjoubi e Fantar (1966: ll. 2-3): ŠPṬM ŠPṬ W'DNB'L 'T R 'DNB'L BN 'ŠMNḤLṢ BN B̂[....]

---

21 Sulla serie cf., da ultime, Cutroni Tusa (1983); Manfredi (1985), con l'ipotesi che R(')Š MLQRT sia un nome di funzione legata a un santuario, 'gli eletti di Melqart'.

22 Berger non riporta tuttavia altro che la trascrizione dell'espressione contenente i nomi dei due sufeti di 'Cartagine'.

23 La scrivente pensava, senza tenere nel dovuto conto le indicazioni dei cartografi, che il toponimo QRTḤDŠT, da attribuire originariamente a Tharros, si fosse nel tempo spostato poco più a sud e fosse sopravvissuto nell'epiteto Nabui della chiesa di S. Maria. Su Neapolis cf. soprattutto Zucca (1987); Moscati e Zucca (1989).

24 Huss (1985: 473 n. 58): 'zum einen haben wir keinen Anhaltspunkt für die Annahme, dass Tharros je den Namen Qrtḥdš't getragen hat, und zum anderen ist in der Inschrift nach *zwei* sufetalen Systemen datiert'; Lipiński (1989: 68): 'l'emploi de la tournure 'suffètes qui sont à Carthage' indique sans conteste qu'il s'agit de suffètes d'une ville distincte de Tharros'.

25 Cf. la datazione di *KAI* 69.1-2 (cf. 18-19) (*CIS* I 165): 'T [R' HLS]B'L HŠPṬ BN BDTNT BN BD['ŠMN WḤLSB'L] / HŠPṬ BN BD'ŠMN BN ḤLSB'L WḤ[BRNM]. Si ritiene di solito che si tratti qui dei sufeti (Sznycer 1978: 574, con l'ipotesi che ḤBRNM indichi un altro collegio 'qui assiste ceux-ci [i sufeti] dans l'exercice de certaines de leurs fonctions'; posizione diversa in Huss (1977: 250-51), con l'idea di rab che siano anche sufeti, ma senza collegare l'indicazione dei sufeti eponimi alla menzione di [B]ŠT). Chi scrive preferisce supporre una datazione in base a un collegio di rab che avevano rivestito (o rivestivano anche) la carica di sufeti, cf. n. 28 sotto.

26 Quando, nelle formule di datazione, il primo funzionario ha la genealogia, la ha sempre anche il secondo; quando invece, nelle datazioni sulla base dei sufeti eponimi, uno dei due è privo di genealogia, si tratta sempre del primo, cf. Huss (1977–78).

QRT BN ḤN' WḤBRNM.[27] La situazione è incerta negli altri casi: *KAI* 69 già citata (n. 25), dove i due personaggi hanno il titolo di sufeta;[28] *CIS* I.170 (l. 1) dove compare solo la formula 'T R + nomi propri (si tratta di una tariffa, come *KAI* 69); *CIS* I.3919, con la stessa espressione è frammentaria. È da ricordare anche l'iscrizione da Gozo *KAI* 62 (*CIS* I.132) dove l'espressione (l. 4) B'T R introduce il titolo 'DR 'RKT, funzione considerata come l'equivalente a quella del censore latino.

Se quanto finora esposto è valido, una sola era la cronologia mediante i sufeti eponomi, l'ultima. In questo caso è da esaminare se QRTḤDŠT si debba per forza applicare alla città d'Africa. È in primo luogo da osservare che città della Sardegna erano certo rette da sufeti locali, almeno dal III secolo a.C.; lo mostrano non solo formule di datazione (ad es. *KAI* 66 = *CIS* I.143, da S. Nicolò Gerrei, dove è difficile attribuire i sufeti ad una determinata città di Sardegna), ma in particolare le non rare menzioni di personaggi (e tra queste proprio la dedica a Melqart qui esaminata) che, con il titolo di ŠPṬ, mostrano di aver rivestito tale carica, certo in Sardegna stessa (cf. *KAI* 65.5 da Cagliari; Antas II.2; III.3.4; XII.2; da Sulcis, Bartoloni 1986: n. 1052 [forse] n. 1189, l. 1 [= Uberti 1983: 800-801]; *CIS* I.176 [se proviene da Sulcis, cf. Cecchini e Amadasi 1990]). D'altra parte la formula qui attestata, ŠPṬM BQRTḤDŠT, non esclude che il sito di Tharros si chiamasse così: si ricorda l'iscrizione da Cartagine *CIS* I.5632, la cui lettura è in parte discussa (cf. Krahmalkov 1976; Huss 1986, discutibili l'uno e l'altro; Sznycer 1978: 574-75), ma dove appare con sicurezza l'espressione ŠPṬM BQRTḤDŠT (l. 3): nella stessa capitale africana si poteva fornire una data mediante la specificazione che i sufeti erano 'a Cartagine'. La stessa specificazione si ha a Leptis Magna, dove l'unica iscrizione punica pervenutaci (Levi Della Vida e Amadasi 1986: n. 31 del II secolo a.C.) data mediante la formula: BYRḤ ḤYR ŠPṬM B'LPQY 'RŠ W'BDMLQRT 'nel mese di ḤYR, essendo sufeti a Lepcis Arish e Abdmelqart'.[29]

Se quanto osservato è esatto, l'iscrizione di Tharros, dopo la dedica, la descrizione delle opere eseguite, la menzione del dedicante e del motivo della dedica, avrebbe comportato la seguente struttura: (a) architetto e altri artigiani; (b) funzionario (o funzionari) non eponimo; (c) sufeti. Il pessimo stato della superficie della pietra dopo il nome del secondo sufeta non consente di conoscere la fine del testo (Huss 1977–78: 250 n.8 suppone la presenza di più sufeti—quattro?). Ciò che è ricostruibile permette comunque di notare che lo schema usato è inverso rispetto a quanto è noto più comunemente.

Quando infatti si abbiano o più di un'indicazione cronologica o la menzione di più funzionari fra i quali i sufeti, l'enumerazione parte in generale dalla funzione più importante, per scendere a quelle di ambito più ristretto. In formule di datazione doppie attestate in ambiente fenicio di epoca ellenistica si dà prima l'anno in base all'era seleucide, poi la corrispondenza con l'era locale (cf. ad es. *KAI* 19.6-8, 40.1-2 e 43.3-5). In ambito punico (prima del periodo romano)[30] non si hanno datazioni in base a ere diverse (a meno che l'unica attestazione non sia questa di Tharros); tuttavia quando si nominano più funzionari il criterio è in genere lo stesso: in primo luogo sono nominati i sufeti, poi eventuali altre categorie,[31] in particolare quella che è stata identificata con quella dei rab, forse una magistratura a carattere finanziario (così Huss 1977); alla fine sono nominati altri funzionari, come i 'soprastanti all'opera' (ṬN'M 'L HMLKT), l'architetto o altri artigiani. Naturalmente non sappiamo se iscrizioni frammentarie e che attualmente contengono una cronologia solo in base a funzionari che non appaiono come sufeti, potessero avere

---

27 Un'indicazione simile, con formula un po' diversa e con un solo rab (un caso perciò forse parallelo a quello di Tharros) compare in *KAI* 81, ll. 5-6: ...LMBYRḤ ḤYR ŠPṬM 'BDMLQRT W [.../]Y ŠPṬM ŠPṬ WḤN' BN 'DNB'L WRB 'BDMLQRT BN MGN B[N... (un'integrazione 'fino al mese X] dei sufeti' nella lacuna è proposta da Sznycer 1978: 573).

28 Il titolo appare portato da chi, almeno una volta, abbia esercitato la carica; cf. l'esempio *CIS* I.5510 dove, all'opposto, la data è fornita mediante l'espressione B ŠT seguita dai nomi di due personaggi che portano, ambedue, il titolo di RB (ll. 8-9: ...B ḤDŠ [P]'LT ŠT 'ŠMN'MS BN 'DNB'L HRB WḤN' / BN BD'ŠTR[T] BN ḤN' HRB): qui se non si vuole supporrre che i rab fossero anch'essi eponimi, si devono supporre due sufeti che abbiano esercitato (o che esercitino anche) la funzione di rab.

29 È da ricordare che non conosciamo la data, se non molto approssimativa, dell'iscrizione di Tharros e che non si può escludere che essa appartenga ad un periodo successivo l'occupazione romana della Sardegna (238 a.C.): una menzione dei sufeti cartaginesi sarebbe allora davvero fuori luogo.

30 In tale periodo l'iscrizione Levi Della Vida e Amadasi 1986: n.21, dell'8 a.C. fornisce la data prima in base all'anno dell'imperatore e di funzionari imperiali, poi quella in base ai sufeti locali.

31 Attestazioni delle formule in Huss (1977; 1977–78; 1979). Cf. in particolare Mahjoubi e Fantar 1966: ll. 1-2: ŠPṬM ŠPṬ W'DNB'L 'T R 'DNB'L BN...; inoltre 'ŠMNḤLṢ BN B[.../...]QRT BN ḤN' WḤBRNM; cf. anche, complicata per la presenza della lacuna e con l'indicazione di più di un anno, *KAI* 81.5-6 (cf. nota 27 sopra).

originariamente tale datazione, posta dopo il nome di questi, ad es., anche se con poca verosimiglianza, *KAI* 62 [= *CIS* I.132] e *CIS* I.170.

In conclusione, nonostante la struttura inversa rispetto ad altre iscrizioni con dedica di opere architettoniche, il formulario qui presente non vieterebbe, anzi indurrebbe, a identificare la stessa Tharros con il sito di QRTḤDŠT (del quale sarebbe originario il dedicante di Olbia). La difficoltà ad accogliere questa identificazione senza riserve viene non tanto dalle fonti epigrafiche indigene, ma da fonti classiche e da qualche iscrizione latina. Gli antichi geografi, e in primo luogo Tolomeo, quindi l'Itinerario di Antonino, l'Anonimo ravennate e Guidone, conoscono infatti un centro sardo di nome Tarrae, Tarri o Tharros che si deve localizzare proprio sul Capo S. Marco, dove sorgeva l'insediamento fenicio.[32] Tra le iscrizioni un miliario del tempo dell'imperatore Filippo trovato reimpiegato a Cabras ricorda la strada che conduce da Tharros a Cornus;[33] la grafia Tarrhos è su un'iscrizione ritenuta di autenticità dubbia.[34] Le testimonianze dei geografi sembrano inoltre concordi nel porre Neapolis, ben distinta da Tharros, a Sud del Golfo di Oristano, nella località di S. Maria di Nabui (cf. Meloni 1980; Zucca 1987: 99-113). In questa situazione, per mantenere l'ipotesi di una Cartagine sul Capo S. Marco si deve supporre una doppia denominazione dell'insediamento, legata a circostanze che non siamo, almeno per ora, in grado di chiarire (mentre resta aperto il problema del nome originario del centro chiamato Neapolis negli antichi itinerari). Le ingiurie del tempo ci hanno privato dei dati sufficienti a risolvere la questione; e la sorte maligna ha distrutto quel frammento dell'iscrizione a Melqart dove poteva essere nominata ancora una volta QRTḤDŠT (l. 2) (se non genericamente 'la città', come in Mahjoubi e Fantar 1966: l. 6: 'MQ QRT), in una posizione che non avrebbe lasciato dubbi all'identificazione.

---

[32] Sulle attestazioni antiche del toponimo cf. in particolare Meloni (1975: 418-19; 1980, su Tolomeo); F. Barreca (in Barnett e Mendleson 1987: 21); un riferimento a Tharros è anche individuato in Sallustio, *Historiae* I, fr. 74 ss. (ed. Maurenbrecher); sono inoltre citate le testimonianze dei grammatici Pseudo-Probo e M. Plautius Sacerdos (*Grammatici Latini*, a cura di H. Keil) che riferiscono il nome della città come esempio di plurale.

[33] *CIL* X.8009 (5. ...VIaM / QUAE DUCIT a thAR/ROS CornuS). Cabras è il centro abitato recente più vicino a Tharros; il sito stesso della città antica si chiama S. Giovanni di Sinis.

[34] *CIL* X.7951. Per altre attestazioni epigrafiche cf. Sotgiu (1961: n. 228): TARR[ ]; Sotgiu (1969: n. 53): TAR[ ], ambedue rinvenute a Tharros e di 'epoca imperiale'.

Bibliografia

Alroth, B.
1987 Visiting Gods—who and why. In T. Linders e G. Nordquist (edd.), *Gifts to the Gods. Proceedings of the Uppsala Symposium 1985*, 9-19. Uppsala.
1989–90 *Greek Gods and Figurines. Aspects of the Anthropomorphic Dedications.* Boreas 18. Uppsala.
1991 Visiting gods. *Scienze dell'Antichità* 3-4: 301-10.

Amadasi Guzzo, M.G.
1967 Le iscrizioni fenicie e puniche delle colonie in occidente. *Studi Semitici* (Roma) 28.
1968 Neapolis = qrtḥdšt in Sardegna. *Rivista degli Studi Orientali* 43: 19-21.

Bacigalupo Pareo, E.
1977 I supremi magistrati a Cartagine. *Contributi di Storia Antica in Onore di A. Garzetti*, 61-87. Genova.

Barnett, R., & C. Mendleson (edd.)
1987 *Tharros: A catalogue of material in the British Museum from Phoenician and other tombs at Tharros, Sardinia.* London: British Museum Publications.

Bartoloni, P.
1986 *Le stele di Sulcis. Catalogo.* Roma.

Berger, P.
1901 *CRAI* 576-579.

Cecchini, S.M. & M.G. Amadasi Guzzo
1990 La stèle C.I.S. I 176. *Carthage et son territoire dans l'antiquité. IVe Colloque International Strasbourg 1988*, I, 101-11. Paris.

Chabot, J.B.
1916 Inscription punique d'Olbia (Sardaigne). *Journal Asiatique* 1916: 77-81.

Chiera, G.
1982 Qarthadasht = Tharros? *Rivista di Studi Fenici* 10: 197-202.
1983 Osservazioni su un testo punico di Olbia. *Rivista di Studi Fenici* 11: 177-81.

Cutroni Tusa, A.
1983 Recenti soluzioni e nuovi problemi sulla monetazione punica della Sicilia. *Rivista di Studi Fenici* 11(supplemento): 37-42.

Fantar, M.
1969 Les inscriptions. *Ricerche Puniche ad Antas*, 47-93. Studi Semitici 30. Roma.

Garbini, G.
1969 Le iscrizioni puniche di Antas (Sardegna). *Annali dell'Istituto Orientale di Napoli* 29: 317-31.

Huss, W.
1977 Vier Sufeten in Karthago? *Le Muséon* 90: 427-33.
1977–78 Zu punische Datierungsformeln. *Die Welt der Orients* 9: 249-52.
1983 Der karthagische Sufetat. In H. Heinen, K. Stroheker e G. Walser (edd.), *Althistorische Studien: Hermann Bengston zum 70. Geburtstag dargebracht von Kollegen und Schülern*, 25-32. Wiesbaden.
1985 *Geschichte der Karthager.* Handbuch der Archäologie III/8. München.
1986 Eine republikanische Ära in Karthago? In H. Kalcyk, B. Gullath e A. Graeber (edd.), *Studien zur Alten Geschichte: Siegfried Lauffer zum 70. Geburtstag am 4. August 1981 dargebracht von Freunden, Kollegen, und Schülern*, II, 439-42. Roma.

Krahmalkov, C.
1976 Notes on the rule of the sōftim in Carthage. *Rivista di Studi Fenici* 4: 153-57.

Levi Della Vida, G.
1963 Frustuli neopunici tripolitani. *ANLR* Ser. 8(18): 463-82.
1971 Magistrature romane ed indigene nelle iscrizioni puniche tripolitane. *Studi in Onore di E. Volterra*, VI, 457-71. Milano.

Levi Della Vida, G. & M.G. Amadasi Guzzo
1986 *Iscrizioni Puniche di Tripolitania (1927-1967)*. Roma.

Lidzbarski, M.
1915 *Ephemeris für semitische Epigraphik III*. Giessen.

Lipiński, E.
1983 La Carthage de Chypre. In E. Gubel, E. Lipiński e B. Servais-Soyez (eds.), *Studia Phoenicia* 1-2: 209-34. Leuven.
1989 Carthaginois en Sardaigne à l'époque de la première guerre punique. In H. Devijver e E. Lipiński (eds.), *Studia Phoenicia* 10: 67-73. Leuven.

Mahjoubi, A., & M. Fantar
1966 Une nouvelle inscription carthaginoise. *ANLR* Ser. 8(21): 201-209.

Manfredi, L.I.
1985 RŠMLQRT, R'ŠMLQRT: Nota sulla numismatica punica di Sicilia. *Rivista Italiana di Numismatica* 87: 3-8.

Masson, O.
1985 La dédicace à Baal du Liban (Corpus Inscriptionum Semiticarum I, 5) et sa provenance probable de la région de Limassol. *Semitica* 35: 33-46.

Masson, O., & M. Sznycer
1972 *Recherches sur les Phéniciens à Chypre*. Genève-Paris.

Meloni, P.
1975 *La Sardegna romana*. Sassari: Chiarella.
1980 La geografia della Sardegna in Tolomeo. In *Miscellanea di Studi Classici in Onore di E. Manni*, 1531-53. Roma.

Moscati, S.
1968 Il popolo di Bitia. *Rivista degli Studi Orientali* 43: 1-4.

Moscati, S., & R. Zucca
1989 *Le Figurine fittili di Neapolis*. Accademia Nazionale dei Lincei. Memorie, ser. 8(22).

Röllig, W.
1974 Eine neue phönizische Inschrift aus Byblos. *Neue Ephemeris für semitische Epigraphik* 2: 1-15. Wiesbaden.

Rouse, W.H.D.
1902 *Greek Votive Offerings. An Essay in the History of Greek Art*. Cambridge. Repr. 1976, New York: Hildesheim.

Segert, S.
1976 *A Grammar of Phoenician and Punic*. München.

Sotgiu, G.
1961 *Iscrizioni latine della Sardegna I*. Padova.
1969 Nuove iscrizioni inedite sarde. *Annali della Facoltà di Lettere, Filosofia e Magistero dell'Università di Cagliari* 32: 5-72.

Sznycer, M.
1969-70 Note sur le dieu Sid et le dieu Horon d'après les nouvelles inscriptions puniques d'Antas (Sardaigne). *Karthago* 15: 68-74.
1975 L' 'assemblée' du peuple dans les cités puniques d'après les sources épigraphiques. *Semitica* 25: 47-68.

1978 Carthage et la civilisation punique. In C. Nicolet (ed.), *Rome et la conquête du monde méditerranéen*, II, 545-93. Paris: Genèse d'un Empire.

Taramelli, A.
1911 Terranova Pausania—Avanzi dell'antica Olbia rimessi in luce in occasione dei lavori di bonifica. *Notizie degli Scavi* 1911: 223-43.

Teixidor, J.
1979 Les fonctions de rab et de suffète en Phénicie. *Semitica* 29: 9-17.

Uberti, M.L.
1978 Horon ad Antas e Astarte a Mozia. *Annali dell'Istituto Orientale di Napoli* 36: 315-19.
1983 Dati di epigrafia fenicio-punica in Sardegna. *Atti del I Congresso Internazionale di Studi Fenici e Punici, Roma 1979*, 797-804. Roma: C.N.R.

Xella, P.
1990 KAI 78 e il pantheon di Cartagine. *Rivista di Studi Fenici* 18: 209-17.

Zucca, R.
1987 *Neapolis e il Suo Territorio*. Oristano.

Summary

The Author examines the epigraphical evidence for a Phoenician settlement in Sardinia, called simply 'New City' (QRTHDŠT), as the North African metropolis. Attested in two Punic inscriptions, one from Olbia, the second from Tharros, it has been variously identified as Neopolis, Olbia, Tharros, or perhaps the Carthage in Tunisia.

The inscription from Olbia is first examined in detail. Dated to the 4th/3rd century BC, it has been read as a dedication to one or two divinities by an individual 'belonging to the people of Carthage', by Carthaginian families, or by a Punic general. The lacunae in the text allow for alternative interpretations. The Author argues that it is a dedication to Sid and that the dedicant is a foreigner in Olbia. So the eventual Sardinian Carthage can only be Tharros.

The Tharros inscription, dated to the 3rd/2nd century BC, is even more fragmentary than the Olbia one. It records the offering to Melqart of a group of buildings, including a portico. The second half of the text lists the dedicant(s); the artisans (the architect came from a Sicilian town) and functionaries, in particular sufets 'of Carthage'. The Author suggests that there is no reason Carthage *could not* be identified as the local 'New City', in this case Tharros. Her hesitancy in doing so is based on the recognition by Latin inscriptions and ancient geographers of a Sardinian settlement called Tharros, and thus the need to accept also the possibility that this site had two names.

Toward the Study of Colonial–Native Relations in Sardinia from c. 1000 BC–AD 456

Gary S. Webster and Maud Teglund

> Although the Carthaginians made war upon them many times with considerable armies...the people remained unenslaved. Last of all, when the Romans conquered the island and oftentimes made war on them, they remained unsubdued...(Diodorus Siculus 5.15.4-5).[1]

Introduction

Within the past 10 years archaeologists have become increasingly interested in the nature of the colonial–native interactions which characterized cultural adaptations in many European regions during the late prehistoric and early historical periods. Most often these studies have dealt with the effects of Greek and Roman expansionism on native populations bordering the main cultural centers of the Mediterranean (e.g. Whitehouse and Wilkins 1989; Dietler 1989; Winter and Bankoff 1989; Bartel 1989; Fulford 1985; Haselgrove 1987; Hedeager 1987).

Sardinia during the Iron Age (1000–500 BC) and subsequent Punic (500–238 BC) and Roman (238 BC–AD 456) periods provides a nearly ideal, yet still little utilized, laboratory for the study of such interactions within an insular west Mediterranean setting (Fig. 1). In this paper we present the results of a very preliminary assessment of the available literary, epigraphic and archaeological evidence for the formation of Sardinian adaptations to Phoenician, Punic, and Roman presence. The discussion of colonial–Sardinian relations was initiated by Robert Rowland (1982; 1985a) and Stephen Dyson (1985) in their pioneering studies of Punic and Roman period interactions. Our goal is to contribute, however modestly, to the existing dialogue.

It should be stated at the outset that the problem of colonial–native relations on Sardinia, at least through the Roman period, is to a great extent an archaeological one. As Rowland (1985a: 100) reminds us, we have on Sardinia a very rich material record of foreign presence spanning some 1500 years punctuated by an 'occasional bit and snippet' of literary documentation and only a slightly more robust epigraphic record. Nevertheless, we agree that an approach which integrates these material and documentary sources is essential if we are to 'actualize the potentiality inherent in the totality of the available evidence' on this complex cultural phenomenon (Rowland 1985a: 100). We have attempted that integration here, in a preliminary way: the literary and epigraphic observations provide an historical context within which the archaeological evidence is interpreted.

Phoenician-Sardinian Relations (c. 900–500 BC)

1. Literature and Epigraphy

The literary evidence for foreign colonization of Sardinia before the Carthaginians in the late 6th century is quite limited. We read from Diodorus Siculus (5.35.5) that the Phoenicians, in pursuit of their commercial enterprises in west Mediterranean silver, 'in the course of many years prospered greatly, thanks to commerce of this kind, sent forth many colonies, some to Sicily and its neighboring islands, and others to Libya, Sardinia, and Iberia'. Epigraphic evidence is little better: two inscriptions from Nora, a well-excavated Punic-Roman city on the south coast, have been dated by Cross (1984) to the 11th to 9th centuries BC. One, the Nora Stone, is thought to be a commemorative plaque celebrating the victory of a Phoenician army over native tribesmen in the battle of Tarsis, assumed to refer either to Nora or a nearby town. Pausanias (10.17) lists Nora as Sardinia's earliest city, but credits its founding to the Iberians under their legendary leader, Norax.

---

[1] Quotations of ancient authors are from the Loeb Classical Library translations.

Fig. 1 Map of Sardinia showing the principal regions and cities.

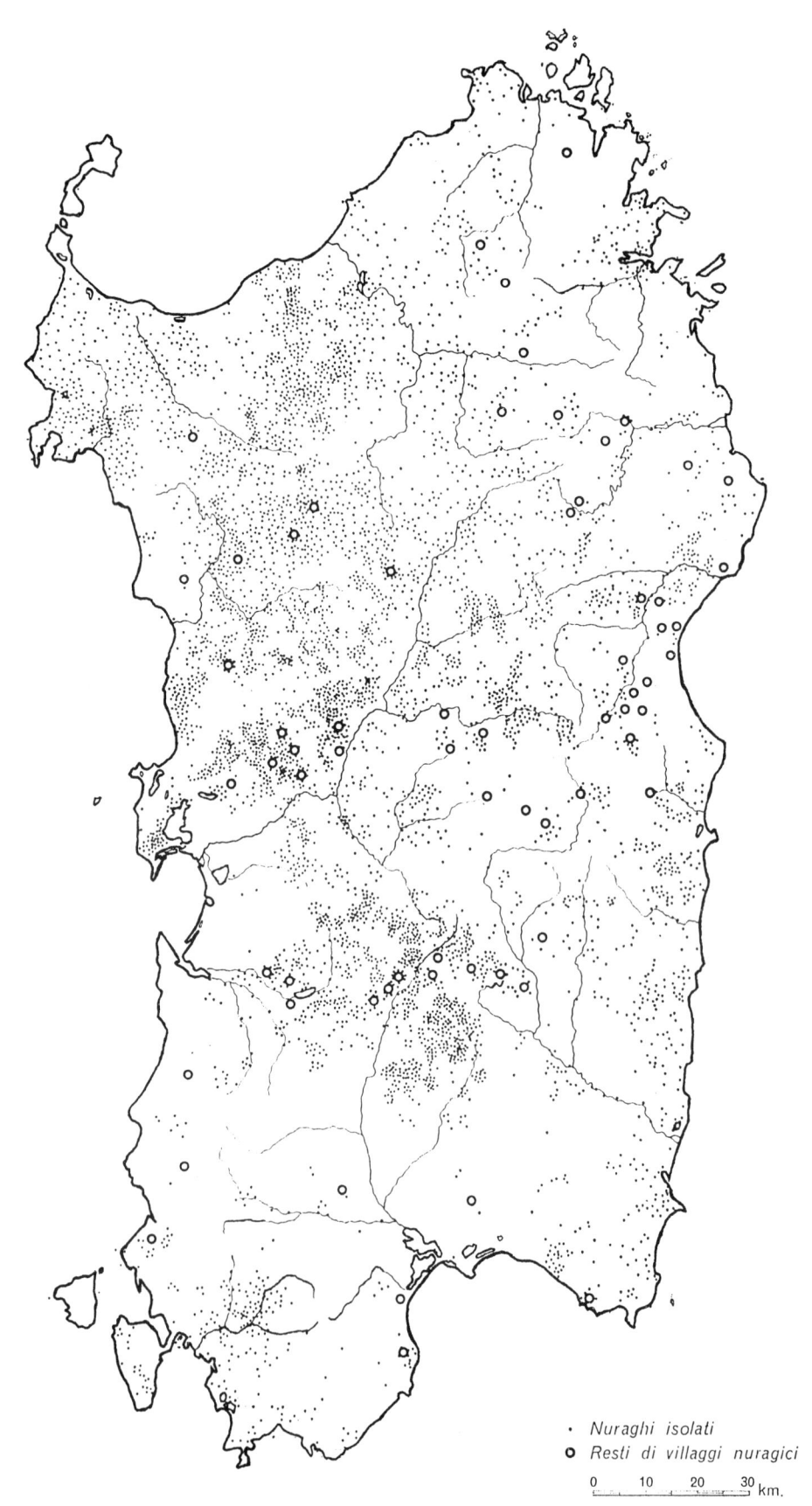

Fig. 2 Distribution of known nuraghe-settlements (after Mori 1975).

2. Archaeology

Any attempt to reconstruct in detail from archaeological data the nature of native Sardinian culture at the time of the Carthaginian incursions at the beginning of the 5th century is necessarily fraught with difficulties. Although rich in quantity, the quality of archaeological evidence is uneven and often poor. While at least 7000 Nuragic settlements have been mapped (Fig. 2), fewer than 150 have been excavated, and only a fraction of these on a large scale using modern techniques. Moreover, less than a dozen are dated chronometrically and thus chronological control more often rests upon less than secure comparisons of the still poorly classified or dated native ceramics. Data on ritual customs are no less spotty. While some 500 tombs and 150 or so well-temples are known, few of these have survived intact into the modern era to provide precise information on the non-settlement aspects of the Nuragic culture (Moravetti 1985). Detailed analyses of *individual* sites are, therefore, with few exceptions, precluded; the goal here then shall be to identify *general* cultural patterns relevant to the problem of native–colonial interactions.

The pattern of native settlement during the Iron Age (Nuragic IV, c. 900–500 BC) appears generally similar to that of the preceding Late Bronze Age (Nuragic III, c. 1250–900 BC) (Lilliu 1988: 355-470). The typical residential site during both periods was the nuraghe-village which covered some 0.25 to 5 hectares (often within a circuit wall during the Iron Age); it typically comprised a centrally located nuraghe which could vary in size and complexity (corridor, single-tower tholos, multi-tower tholos), and a surrounding village of up to several hundred stone-walled huts. Settlement populations ranged from fewer than 20 to perhaps 500, with the average being about 40 people (Webster 1991a). Excavation evidence suggests that Iron Age settlements had long histories of occupation, most having origins in simple nuraghe-homesteads of the Middle Bronze Age (c. 1500–1250 BC) (Lilliu 1982). Estimates of the size of the pre-Carthaginian period native population range from about 200,000 to 300,000 (cf. Lilliu 1982: 81) with densities of fewer than four people per sq km in the south Campidano to over 24 per sq km in the Marmilla, Marghine, Logudoro and Anglona (Lilliu 1988: 486 fig. 177).

As elsewhere in the Mediterranean, settlement distribution patterns during the Iron Age reflect a complex interplay of economic and sociopolitical factors over very long periods of time. At the insular level the distribution of nuraghi appears to reflect local concerns for both subsistence and security. Although sites can be found in virtually every setting (Fig. 2), sites are clearly clustered within the west central regions, often (54%) between 250 and 500 m amsl (Lilliu 1988: 487). The pattern is not readily explainable in terms of agricultural productivity alone, however. Indeed, an analysis of site locations in relation to soil quality shows a preference for good and moderate soils (81% of sites), while not only the poorest soils (13% of sites), understandably, but also the best soils (6% of sites) were generally avoided (Fig. 3). The Campidano, for example, includes most of the island's best agricultural soils, and has attracted intensive farming settlement since the Punic period (as well as during the Neolithic and Chalcolithic). The low numbers, and in some areas, absence of nuraghi in this zone has understandably fueled debates over whether or not nuragic sites were at one time present in these fertile lowlands and have simply been destroyed by later land clearance and building (cf. Rowland 1988: 767). But as recent survey work by Rowland (1982; n.d.) seems to indicate, it is unlikely that these and other fertile lowland regions (e.g. the lower Tirso valley) were ever heavily settled by the indigenous Sardinians.

Several reasons can be suggested for this. First, while potentially very productive, and hence attractive to commercial Carthaginian and Roman agricultural interests, the lowland soils are subject to chronic drought, receive little annual rainfall, and require irrigation to be consistently productive (Mori 1972; 1975). Also, many of the richer alluvial deposits require deep plowing and the landscape generally lacks the stone needed to build secure nuraghe-settlements. Such conditions seem incompatible with what we understand about Nuragic cultural adaptations. The available floral, faunal and technological evidence seem to indicate that the Nuragic people maintained a subsistence-level agro-pastoral economy characterized by local self-sufficiency and little surplus production. Non-intensive methods of cereal agriculture, probably involving the use of the light scratch ard for shallow plowing and the long-fallow system are suggested, in conjunction with ovicaprine-bovine-swine husbandry (including transhumance in the upland regions) and often supplemented by hunting and rarely fishing (Lo Schiavo 1981; Webster 1987: 69-91; Webster and Michels 1986: 226-29; Wetterstrom 1987: 93-104; Rowland 1987: 147-61). Such non-intensive mixed-farming is typical of Bronze and Iron Age economies elsewhere in Italy (cf. Barker 1972). Moreover, if we have correctly interpreted the functions served by nuraghi, it is clear that the necessity for a fortified residence against local and

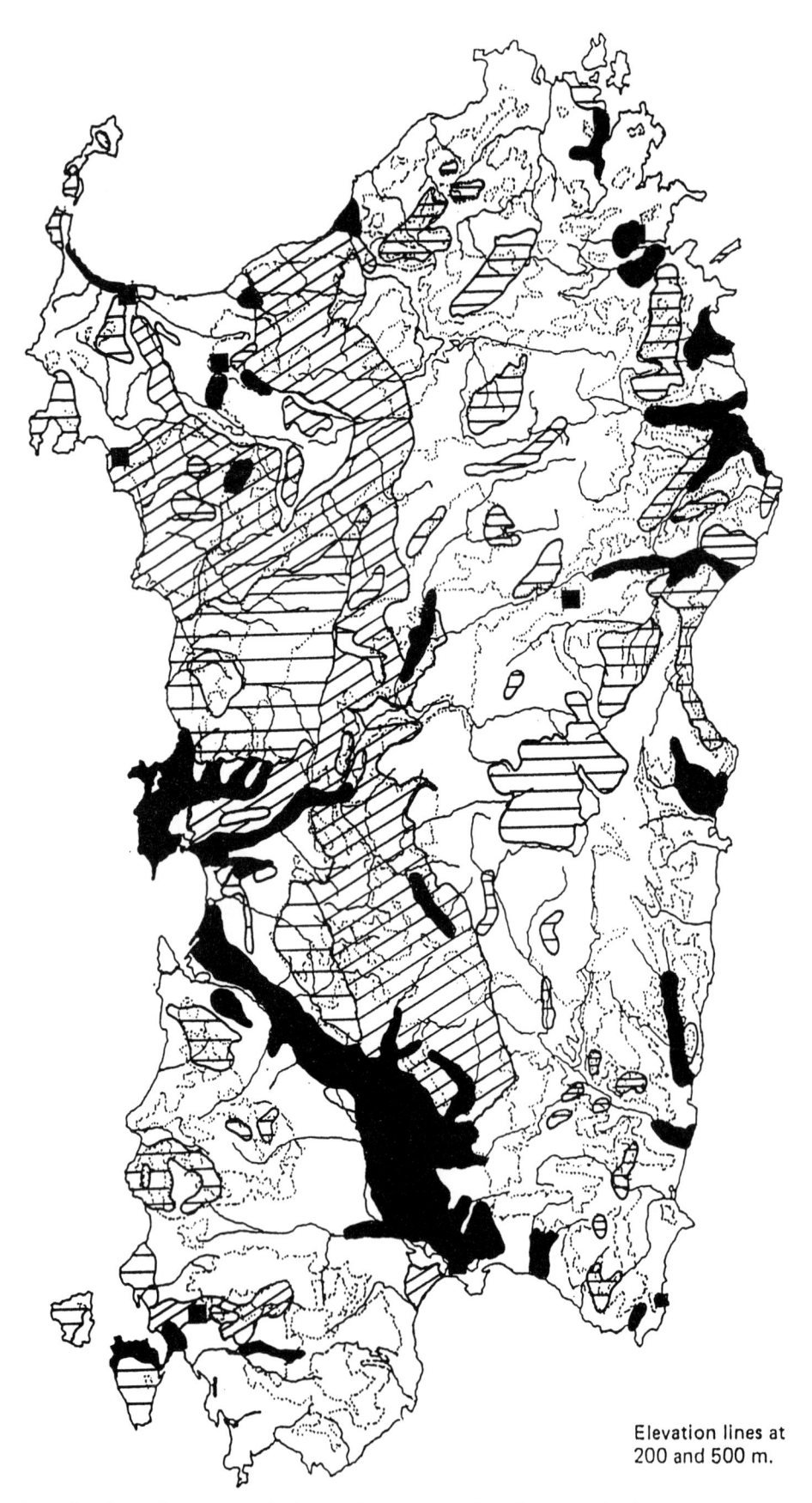

Fig. 3 Distribution of major soil groups ranked according to agricultural potential (after Mori 1972; Mancini 1966). Very good (black), good (slanted lines), moderate (white), and poor (horizontal lines).

Elevation lines at 200 and 500 m.

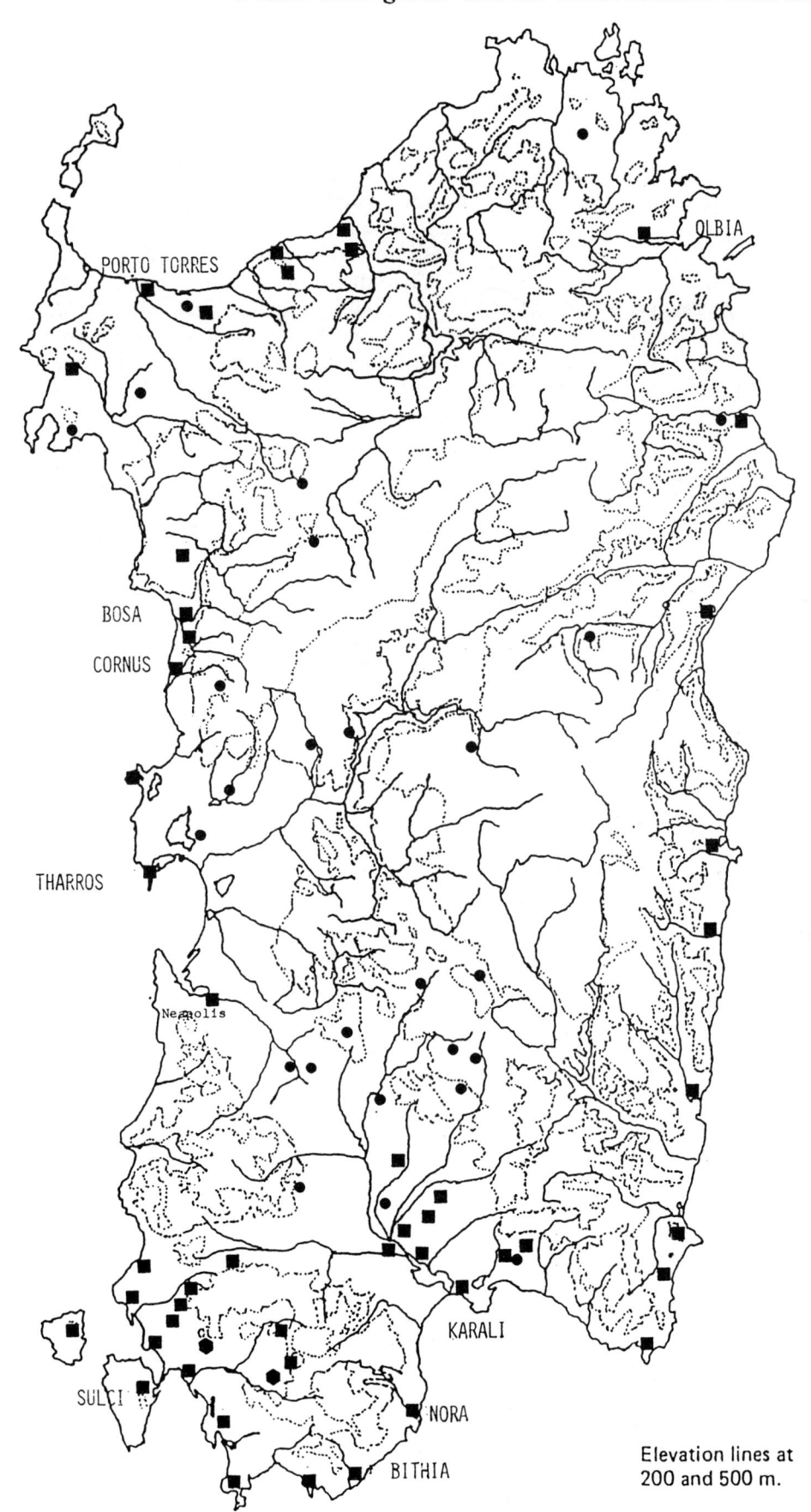

Fig. 4 Distribution of nuraghe-settlements with evidence of Phoenician (c. 1000–500 BC) trade contact (circles), Phoenician settlements (squares), and Phoenician forts (hexagons).

regional level threats to family and wealth (e.g. livestock) has great antiquity (cf. Webster 1991a). Thus, although the Iron Age pattern of settlement distribution contrasts with that of all subsequent periods including the modern (cf. Mori 1972), it makes sense in light of Nuragic economic and sociopolitical constraints: the middle altitude regions simply provided the optimal combination of minimally productive, easily-worked soils, adequate rainfall (400-600 mm), and readily available building stone (cf. Webster 1991b).

From the limited data available it also seems clear that Iron Age Sardinia was never unified politically. Instead, a large but uncertain number of more or less autonomous, hierarchically organized, subregional and perhaps regional-level polities coexisted. Organizationally, these probably spanned the entire range of pre-state level societies referred to by anthropologists as chiefdoms, an interpretation not contradicted by later classical references to the native Sardinians (Webster 1988; Webster 1991a; Webster 1991b; Lewthwaite 1985; Becker 1980; Phillips 1978). On the ground, such polities may correspond geographically to the sub-regional site-aggregates now recognized in many regions (e.g. Logudoro, Lilliu 1982: 58-59; Ozieri, Ozieri 1985; Marghine, Gallin 1989; Michels and Webster 1987; Trexenta, Lilliu 1966). In the Marghine, for example, individual aggregates (polities) covered 50 sq km or less and comprised up to 60 nuraghi in addition to a variety of civic-ritual sites (collective-tombs, well-temples) (Webster 1991a). By the Late Bronze Age, member settlements can be ranked on the basis of nuraghe size and complexity, and although still less clear from ongoing excavations here, it is likely that nuraghi were the fortified residences and/or store-houses of a local petty-elite where the greater or lesser size of the structure, as well as its supporting village, reflected the relative status, influence, and wealth (as measured in dependents, clients, livestock, trade exotica, and craft goods) of its owner (Webster 1988; 1991a). The largest settlements within any aggregate, typically multi-towered complex nuraghi with large villages of several hectares (e.g. Porcarzos-Borore, Santa Barbara-Macomer), probably housed sub-regional level chiefs and their several hundred supporters (Webster 1988; 1991b).

Evidence of Iron Age trade and exchange patterns is still quite limited, particularly regarding the movement of native products. Native bronzes (ingots, tools, figurines), rarely iron, and associated objects (moulds, crucibles, scrap hoards) are thinly distributed over the island, usually occurring within nuraghi or civic-ritual sites (Lo Schiavo 1986). Since only a single possible pre-colonial foundry, Sa Sedda'e sos Carros (Oliena-NU), has been found thus far (Lilliu 1988: 467; but cf. Gallin and Tykot in press), it is likely that metal-working was a small-scale industry controlled by local elites for the purpose of immediate use and prestige exchange (Lo Schiavo 1986: 245; Balmuth and Tylecote 1976: 196). Decorated 'geometric' native pottery has a similar widespread distribution and probably moved along similar elite-exchange networks. We might also assume on the basis of environmental variability that some exchange occurred between the more heavily agricultural lowland and more heavily pastoral upland settlement (cf. Rowland 1982; Dyson 1985).

Foreign exchange during the Iron Age is indicated by the frequent finds of non-Sardinian materials in nuraghi, tombs and well-temple contexts. Many of these derived from east Mediterranean sources presumably by way of the Phoenician sites, which first appear along the coasts as trading posts in the 10th/9th century, then as permanent settlements by the 8th (Barreca 1986a; 1986b) (Fig. 4). Excavations have confirmed the locations of at least five major coastal settlements (Karali, Sulci, Nora, Tharros, Bosa and perhaps Bithia) as well as several interior sites which seem to have been Phoenician frontier forts or outposts (e.g. Settimo San Pietro and San Sperate near Karali, and Monte Sirai and Pani Loriga near Sulci: Barreca 1986b: 155), all of which, along with architectural remains, have imported Phoenician, Greek and Etruscan pottery and bronzes of the 8th–6th century (Bernardini and Tronchetti 1985: 285-306). On less firm grounds Barreca (1986b: 155; 1986c) would expand the list to a total of 56 Phoenician sites distributed around the entire coast and in some locations (south and southeast) extending inland some 20 km, which he feels gives rise to 'the model of the "polis" surrounded by territory in which smaller settlements rose'. In any case the coastal sites, founded at easily defendable, calm water ports, were apparently intended as commercial ports-of-call for the transport of Sardinian metals (mainly from the Sulcitano-Iglesiente) to the Near East (see Barreca 1986b: 159 and above). However, finds of Sardinian bronze boats and pottery jars in Etrurian tombs (Vetulonia, Populonia, Vulci, Cerveteri) and in Sicily (Pantalica, Lipari) suggest additional markets (Lilliu 1988: 423). Lilliu (1988: 420-26) and Weiss (1986) have interpreted these bronze boats as possible evidence for more direct Sardinian–Etruscan trade, perhaps involving Sardinian animal products such as skins, wool and meat.

Apart from indications that at least some nuraghe-settlements located on or near Phoenician sites were destroyed or abandoned (e.g. Pani Loriga-Santadi, Barreca 1984: 140; Tharros-Sinis, Barreca 1987: 26), there is little evidence that the greater distribution of native settlements was significantly disrupted by Phoenician colonists. In fact, numerous native communities survived on the outskirts of the major ports until the Carthaginian period (cf. Tore and Stiglitz 1987). While it is usually supposed that the nearest Sardinians were expelled by force from new Phoenician sites (cf. Barreca 1987, and the reading of the Nora Stone, above), it seems just as likely that some were incorporated or 'adopted' into the new proto-urban communities, perhaps even inter-marrying with the colonists as is possibly evinced in finds of 8th/7th century Nuragic bronzes within otherwise wholly Phoenician tombs at Tharros (Barnett 1987: 39).

Imports of Phoenician, Etruscan, Greek and Cypriot origin are known from at least 30 Nuragic sites. The finds are usually small, portable, prestige items (e.g. Phoenician, Greek and Cypriot bronze figurines and lamps, Italian and Cypriot fibulae, and Greek and Etruscan pottery), usually found in nuraghi or civic-ritual sites, never in great numbers (Lilliu 1988: 420-25; Barreca 1979: 35; Bernardini and Tronchetti 1985: 285-306; Lo Schiavo 1978). Lilliu (1988: 423) has inferred a directional pattern of exchange from their distribution, involving movement of goods, probably among nuraghe-elite trade partners, between Phoenician Karali in the south Campidano inland toward the northwest through the Trexenta, Marmilla, Arborea and Sinis on the west coast near Tharros and the lower Tirso valley (Fig. 4).

There is some evidence to suggest that social differentiation was increasing in native communities within the regions of heaviest foreign exchange. All four known examples of elite individual burial customs which contrast with the traditional collective cist-burial rites, are located here: the 'warrior's grave' (with sword and bronze) from Senorbì-Trexenta; the 'tomb of the Sardinian prince' (with *bronzetti* of archers) in Sardara-Campidano; the grave of Is Arutas-Cabras; and most notably, the elite 'aristocratic' necropolis (with monumental 'heroic' statuary) of Monte Prama-Cabras (cf. Lilliu 1988: 430-31; Tronchetti 1986: 41-59). As elsewhere, the appearance of individualizing burial rites in Iron Age Sardinia is thought to reflect the emergence of an elite 'aristocratic' social class (Tronchetti 1986: 49; Bernardini 1982; Lilliu 1988: 433). It has been widely argued that the availability of imported prestige goods may provide an important avenue for political aspirants to increase their wealth and status through luxury acquisitions (Whitehouse and Wilkins 1989; Wells 1980; Haselgrove 1982; Kipp and Schortman 1989). In this regard communities in the Campidano–Trexenta–Marmilla–Arborea–Sinis zone enjoyed the advantages of close, direct access to the principal Phoenician ports, as well as generally superior potential for agricultural intensification and the generation of the surpluses in produce, crafts, and labor dependencies required for trade (cf. Tronchetti 1986: 49; Webster 1990). It is significant that while only 34% of all known nuraghi were located on very good or good soils, nearly two-thirds of those that were contained foreign trade goods. One could argue from this that status competition among emergent elites within the densely populated south central zone was intensified with the arrival of the Phoenician traders, giving rise to more pronounced status, wealth and occupational differences than elsewhere on the island. Whitehouse and Wilkins (1989) have argued that such intensified competition for imported prestige goods may not necessarily have promoted increased centralization, at least for native–Greek relations in southeast Italy. Indeed, the resulting tendency may be toward a fragmentation of the existing centralized hierarchy if (1) previous authorities (chiefs) are unable to exclude non-elite households from participating in trade; and (2) the goods needed for trade can be produced by the household in the domestic mode of production (Whitehouse and Wilkins 1989: 120). By all estimations, Sardinian–Phoenician trade did not involve specialized production methods or require centralized organization or great con–centrations of products or labor, but rather small-scale, local production of metal, ceramic and agro-pastoral goods. Significantly, there is some evidence of the predicted decentralization with increased social differentiation in the changing patterns of settlement in some sites. At Su Nuraxi-Barumini, to take the best example, Lilliu has interpreted the replacement of a Late Bronze Age architectural hierarchy of undifferentiated circular hut compounds around a central elite nuraghe residence with a non-centralized plan of socio-economically differentiated nuclear family houses (*rundhaus*) around a partially built-over nuraghe (now used for storage) as inferring the breakdown of a Bronze Age monarchy (chieftaincy) and the development of class society comprising an aristocratic oligarchy, artisans, peasants, and slaves. Similar changes may be detected at other sites (e.g. Genna Maria-Villanovaforru, Lilliu 1988: 446-50; and Duos Nuraghes-Borore, Webster 1988).

Lilliu (1982: 174) also postulates a new regional level of integration in the appearance of Iron Age sanctuaries (e.g. Santa Vittoria-Serri, Abini-Teti, Santa Cristina-Paulilatino, Matzanni-Vallermosa) neutrally located to function as civic-ritual and mercantile centers of a 'panhellenic' or 'national' type. Whitehouse and Wilkins (1989: 115-16) have similarly interpreted the Greek-type sanctuaries in south Italy as serving an integrative function as proto-emporia administered by a native elite but occupied by alien merchants.

Whether one agrees with the application to Iron Age Sardinia of the full implications engendered in the concept of an aristocratic society, it seems undeniable that polities within some regions of the island (e.g. the Campidano–Trexenta–Marmilla–Arborea–Sinis zone and perhaps the Sulcitano-Iglesiente) had by the end of the Iron Age become more complex organizationally than had those in other regions. We must assume therefore that when the Carthaginians initiated a military takeover of the island around 500 BC, a considerable amount of interregional variation existed among the Sardinian and Phoenician–Sardinian populations in terms of sociopolitical complexity, economic emphases and levels of trade (cf. Dyson 1985: 237), and that such cultural variability in the subject population greatly conditioned the nature of colonial–native relations during both the Punic and Roman periods.

In sum, Phoenician–Sardinian adaptations during the Iron Age varied across three socioenvironmental zones: (1) a coastal-lowland zone with high agricultural potential but with sparsely settled, acculturated native settlements, and proto-urban Phoenician/Phoenician-Sardinian coastal settlements; (2) a middle altitude uplands with good to moderate agricultural potential, and in the Iglesiente rich metal resources, supporting the most densely settled and highly organized (sociopolitically and militarily) native populations in active trade with Phoenician coastal ports; and (3) an interior mountain zone with low agricultural potential which supported comparatively sparse and poorly-organized, pastoral native tribes having only sporadic trade contact with the coast.

Punic–Sardinian Relations (c. 500–238 BC)

1. Literature and Epigraphy

Carthaginian colonization is better documented. Pausanias (10.17.9) writes 'when the Carthaginians were at the height of their sea power they overcame all of Sardinia...(and) like those who preceded them founded cities in the island, namely Caralis and Sulcis'. The Carthaginians began establishing trading centers along the Mediterranean coasts soon after Carthage's own foundation by Tyre in the 9th century BC, and, like the Phoenicians, their main interest was metal acquisition (Diodorus Siculus 5.35.4-5). By the 6th century BC, the expanded sea routes and ambitions of the Greeks and Etruscans fueled rivalries. Carthage failed to stop the Greek colonization of Massilia, c. 600 BC (Thucydides 1.13.6; Justinus 37.1), but a combined force of Carthaginians and Etruscans managed to break the westward thrust of the Greeks in the decisive battle of Alalia, c. 540 BC (Herodotus 1.165-167). Greece had become less of a threat and Etruscan power was diminishing in the shadow of early Rome.[2] Carthage responded by consolidating her hold on colonies like Sardinia. Following a number of sanguinary campaigns against the Sardinians by Hasdrubal and Hamilcar (Diodorus Siculus 4.29.6; 5.15.4-5; Justinus 18.7; 19.1; Pausanias 4.23; Polybius 3.22-23), the island was regarded as a pacified Carthaginian colony by 509 BC. In addition to her mining interests, Carthage soon came to depend heavily upon Sardinian grain (Diodorus Siculus 11.20.405; 21.16.1).

Constitutionally, Sardinia appears as the foreign region closest to Carthage herself. Mentioned closely together in treaties, we may assume that they were taxed and governed in much the same way (Polybius 3.22-23; cf. Aristoteles, *Politikon* 2.8; Bondì 1988: 126-31). The system of *sufetes* and a people's assembly are well attested (Amadasi 1967: 83-136 nos. 9, 32, 34, 36, and neo-Punic no. 8; Justinus 12.13; Orosius 3.20) and, according to Bondì, Sardinia was the only territory outside Carthage with a centralized military command. As in other colonies, Carthage employed mercenaries in her dealings with Sardinia which drew parts of the native population into direct colonial control and into interaction with foreign soldiers of varied nationalities and ethnic origins (Pausanias 10.17.9). According to Diodorus Siculus (14.95.1) 'the Carthaginians brought together troops from Libya and Sardinia as well as from the barbarians of Italy...and no less than 80,000 in number'.

All Sardinians were not comfortable with the

---

2 The sources indicate that the Greeks had earlier nurtured plans to colonize Sardinia (Herodotus 1.170; Pausanias 4.23.5-6), but these plans seem never to have been realized (Thucydides 6.90.2; Aristophanes, *The Knights* 172-173).

idea of foreign rule. According to Diodorus, many 'fled for safety to the mountainous part of the island' (5.15.4) where they could lead a free, pastoral life and occasionally raid the lowlands (Pausanias 10.17.9; Diodorus Siculus 4.29.6; 5.15.4-5; Strabo 5.2.7). The troublesomeness of the mountainous tribes is a recurring theme in sources of this period. While several native groups are mentioned, the Balari and Ilienses appear to have been the best known (Pausanias 10.17.7; Strabo 5.2.7; Diodorus Siculus 5.15.4-5; Solinus 4.1; Livy 41.6.6). These tribes were still bellicose in Roman days and an inscription dating to the early Empire from the Berchidda area may help locate the Balari in the Goceano, while the Ilienses are thought to have been located just to their south; both are rugged, mountainous, interior regions (Meloni 1971: 242).[3]

The texts mention a number of Punic cities or towns on the island, although most often Caralis and Sulcis (Pausanias 10.17.9; Strabo 5.2.7; Claudianus, *De Bello Gildonico* 1.518-22), both on the southern coast. Strabo states, 'As for the cities, there are indeed several, but only Caralis and Sulci are noteworthy.' But from inscriptions we know of Punic settlements on the northeast (Olbia) and west (Bosa) coasts, while the interior has yielded little epigraphical evidence (Amadasi 1967: 83-136).

2. Archaeology

Approximately 106 Punic settlements have been identified archaeologically (Fig. 5) (after Barreca 1986b; Rowland 1982). Eleven or twelve coastal cities were founded on expanded, and more heavily fortified, Phoenician centers. With the exception of Olbia, these were located on the west and south coasts presumably to take advantage of the developed Phoenician harbors and to provide direct access to the soil-rich Campidano and mineral-rich Sulcitano-Iglesiente (23% of the Punic settlements occurred on very good soils, 27% on good soils, 43% on moderate soils and 7% on poor soils). The possibility of a number of earlier Phoenician posts on the east coast (see Fig. 4) need not imply the existence of later Punic settlements here in view of the latter's narrower commercial interests. The remaining 95 or so Punic sites in the interior comprise a variety of small agricultural (and presumably) mining settlements, heavily fortified frontier forts, shrines and burial sites (Barreca 1986c; 1987). While most appear to have been established during the Punic or preceding Phoenician periods, others are clearly native sites: nuraghe-settlements, sanctuaries and well-temples which were transformed in varying degrees to Punic (or 'Punicized') shrines, necropoli, forts, or settlements. Some 50 native sites have evidence of Punic contact or visible influence ranging from 'Punicized' sites with typical Punic features (masonry, facilities) to sites with but a few Punic or Punic-age trade items (pottery, jewelry, coins). Some of these, at least ten, have documented contact with earlier Phoenician centers. Thus, the nature and intensity of colonial–native interactions during the Punic period was quite variable and one might assume that the ethnic composition of resident populations was as a result equally diverse (e.g. Phoenician, Punic–Phoenician, Punic, Phoenician–Sardinian, Punic–Sardinian, Sardinian).

The mapped distribution of sites (Fig. 5) suggests there were two principal zones of Punic occupation: the Campidano and its adjacent upland of Gerrei, Trexenta, Marmilla, Arborea, Abbasanta and Planargia; and the Sulcitano lowlands and its adjacent Iglesiente uplands. In the first region one finds some evidence for the continued application of a three-zone model to Punic–Sardinian interactions as Dyson (1985) has argued from the literary sources.

Sites in the Campidano (Dyson's lowlands) reflect the spread of a modest number of agricultural settlements from Karali and its hinterlands onto very good and good soils toward the northwest along the Riu Mannu and Riu Cixerri; and from the hinterlands of Tharros, Othoca and Neapolis toward the southeast, and up the Tirso to the west and north through the Sinis peninsula and west coast at least as far as Bosa. Several pieces of evidence suggest that colonial–native interactions here were generally peaceful. Apart from the urban fortifications built at least in part as defense against Greek and Roman attacks (cf. Barreca 1987: 27), Punic forts are not found in the

---

3 The Sardinian 'genealogies' provided by Diodorus Siculus, Cicero, Strabo, Pliny and Pausanias name Libyans, Greeks, Etruscans, Iberians, Trojans, Corsicans and Carthaginians as contributing to Sardinian blood. Pausanias states that the word Balari means fugitives, and that the Ilienses were descendants of a Trojan influx. With the Balari, Strabo lists the Iolaes/Diagesbeis, the Parati, the Sossinati and Aconites, of which we know only that the three latter lived 'in caverns'. The Gallilenses and the Patulcenses are easier to locate. An inscribed bronze-tablet recording border-quarrels between then was found at Esterzili (*CIL* 10.7852 = *ILS* 5947). But whatever the tribal names, these mountaineers were people discontented with the presence of colonial forces. We may simply call them native Sardinians, as the Romans did (Livy 23.40.10), although they were probably of several ethnic components. Their resistance was overruled at times, but never extinguished (Diodorus Siculus 5.15.4-5; Pausanias 10.17.9).

458 *Sardinia in the Mediterranean*

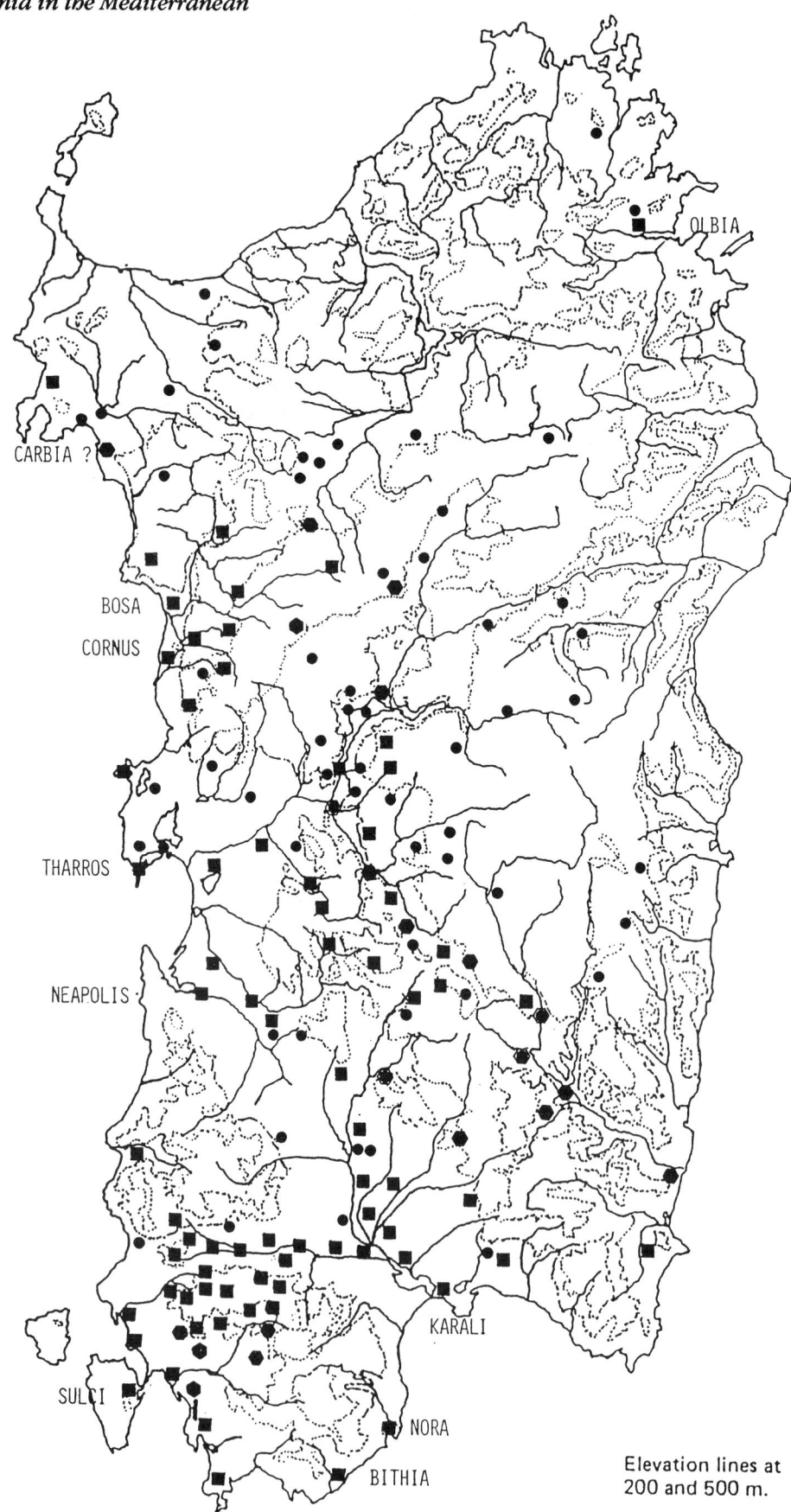

Fig. 5 Distribution of nuraghe-settlements with evidence of Punic trade contact (circles), Punic (c. 500–238 BC) settlements (squares), Punic forts (hexagons), and nuraghi probably used as Punic forts (circles within hexagons).

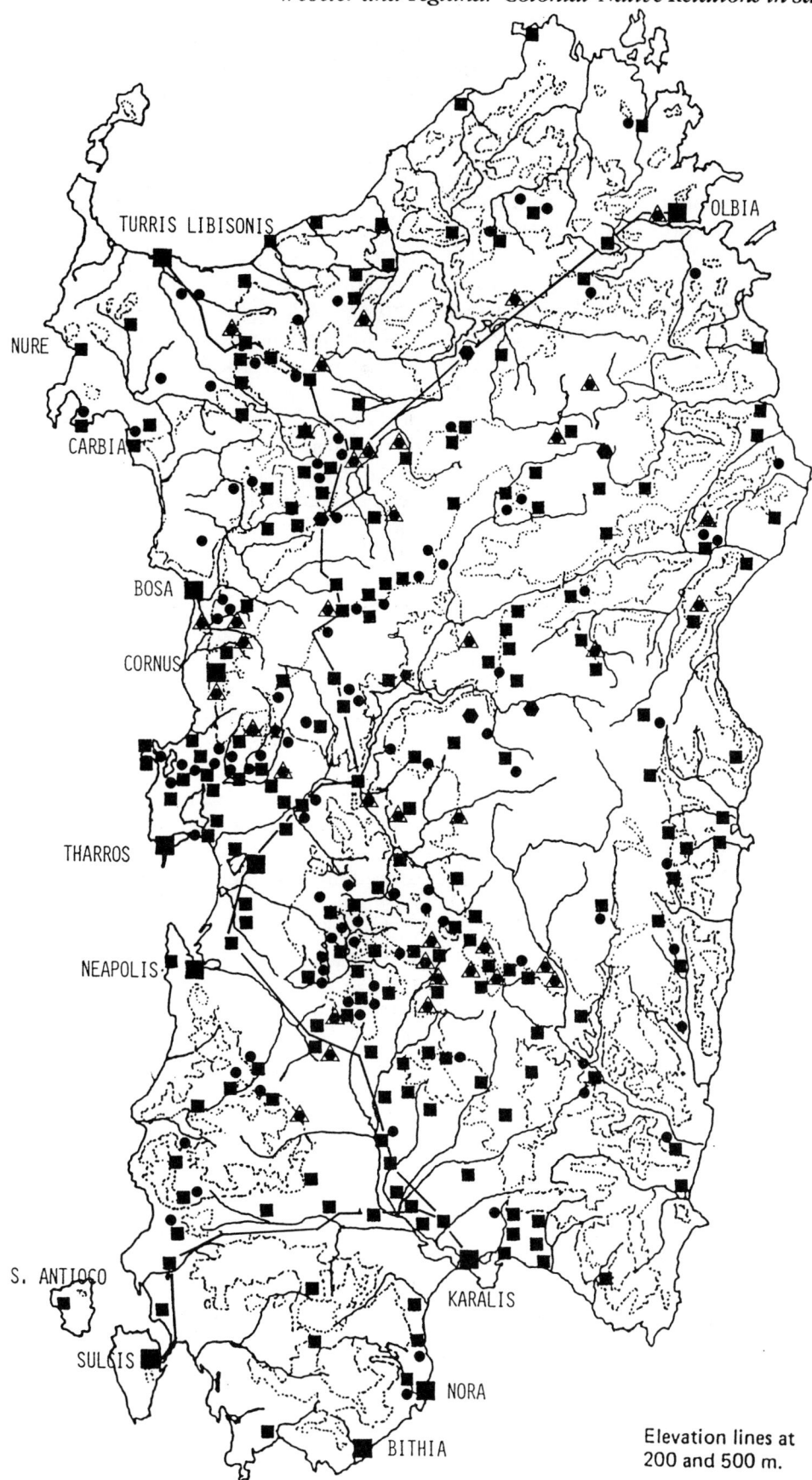

Fig. 6 Distribution of nuraghe-settlements with evidence of Roman (c. 238 BC–456 AD) trade contact (circles), Roman settlements (squares), Roman forts (hexagons), and nuraghi with associated Roman architecture (circles within triangles).

lowlands, nor are there the kinds of evidence of Punic destruction of native sites as in adjacent regions. For reasons already discussed, native settlement of the Campidano was relatively sparse and lowland natives probably offered little resistance to the colonists who themselves appear to have been concentrated in a small number of scattered settlements, presumably *latifundia* (Rowland 1982; Tore and Stiglitz 1987). In fact it is just as likely given the long experience of the lowland Sardinians with Phoenician contact that many were absorbed into the Phoenican-Punic culture, some urbanized, others acculturated within a native or Punic-Sardinian context (cf. Dyson 1985: 243). Systematic surveys in the hinterland of Karali (Rowland 1982) and Tharros (Tore and Stiglitz 1987) suggest that many native settlements occupied during the Iron Age (and also during the Roman period) were abandoned during the Punic phases (e.g. 2 out of 17 nuraghi in Sinis have Punic materials: Tore and Stiglitz 1987; 2 out of 10 nuraghi in Serramanna have Punic materials: Rowland 1982; and 1 out of 29 nuraghi in Bauladu has Punic materials: Dyson and Rowland 1988). Punicized native cult places include Cuccuru Is Arrius-San Salvatore, Monte Prama-Cabras (Tore and Stiglitz 1987: 653), Cadreas-Narbolia (Barreca 1987: 27; 1985: 325), and Sant'Anastasia-Sardara (Barreca 1985: 323). The few nuraghe-settlements in the lowlands that do have Punic period occupation (e.g., Nuraghe Lilloi and Nuraghe Prei Madua in the Sinis: Tore and Stiglitz 1987: 655; Nuraghe Is Tanas and Nuraghe Santa Maria Monserrato in Serramana: Rowland 1982; and Nuraghe Ortu Còmidu in Sardara: Balmuth 1986) probably represent well-integrated Punic-Sardinian communities.

In contrast, the evidence from the upland, middle-altitude zones (200 to 500 m amsl; Dyson's intermediate zone) bordering the Campidano to the northeast (Gerei, Trexenta, Marmilla, Arboria, Abbasanta, Planargia and Marghine) is quite different. While not of great economic value to the Carthaginians, these uplands were of primary political interest. The existence of a series of Punic fortifications, in conjunction with evidence of the destruction and/or abandonment of some nuraghi (Lilliu 1962: 103, 107; Moscati 1968: 28; Michels and Webster 1987; Webster 1988) dating to the 6th to 4th century, suggests the implementation of an aggressive strategy for protecting the Campidano and its agricultural enterprises through military pacification and administrative control (cf. Dyson 1985: 242; Rowland 1982: n. 35). Barreca (1986c: 14) and Rowland (1982: 20-22) have identified a tentative series of some 14 late Punic (c. 350–238 BC) forts spaced approximately 15 kms apart beginning at either Bosa or Carbia and proceeding inland to the southeast, finishing near the mouth of the Riu Flumendosa. At some points an earlier frontier line may be indicated by the archaic Punic (c. 500–350 BC) forts at Furtei, and perhaps by S. Nicola Gerrei and S. Andrea Frius in Gerrei and Trexenta, and possibly by Macomer in the Marghine. The areas encompassed were the most heavily populated and complexly organized of native settlement on the island during the Iron Age. A long history of intensive native competition and no doubt conflict over access to foreign prestige goods in this zone, and the disruption of previous networks via Phoenician ports with Carthaginian settlement, would have made these upland groups a serious threat to lowland Punic commercial operations and thus in need of control. It is significant in this regard that some forts were built on or near sacked and/or abandoned nuraghe-settlements, such as Santa Brai-Furtei, Goni, Casteddu and 'Ecciu-Fordongianus (Barreca 1985: 310; Barreca 1986c: 15; Rowland 1982: 20-22), and which included the major sub-regional or regional level Nuragic centers of Su Nuraxi-Barumini and Arrubiù-Orroli.

Evidence for settlement disruptions behind the frontier line is more equivocal. Apart from the Punic settlements identified by Barreca (1986b: fig. 11) there are few, perhaps only 15 or so, native sites which can be securely dated to the Punic period. Some of these are nuraghe-settlements turned into Punic shrines such as Lugherras-Paulilatino or Punicized sanctuaries such as Santa Cristina-Paulilatino, Abini-Teti, and Santa Vittoria-Serri (Barreca 1986c: 36) which bespeak acculturative efforts within the context of important native civic-ritual sites. The very large center of Nuraghe Losa in Abbasanta seems simply to have been abandoned (Lilliu 1985). The paucity of evidence for Punic period native settlement in this zone has recently been underlined by surveys in the Paulilatino-Fordangianus areas by the Maryland-Wesleyan University project, which reported diagnostic Punic materials from the surface of only 6 of the 89 nuraghi examined, while 58 produced Roman and native ceramics (Dyson and Rowland 1989; 1990b). At least two explanations are possible. The first is that many native settlements were in fact abandoned during native–Carthaginian conflicts on the frontier, as Barreca (1986c: 28-39) has suggested. Or, as Dyson and Rowland (1990a: 530) believe, 'the Carthaginians never developed that type of ceramic commercial network that made possible the spread of Roman materials into so many native communities'. Although only future research will resolve this question, some clarification may be possible by considering the preliminary results of ongoing investigations by the Pennsylvania State University of 40 nuraghe-settlements in Borore in the Marghine (Webster 1988; 1991a). Of the five neighboring sites tested thus far, four (Duos Nuraghes, Toscono, Urpes and San Sergio) appear to have been abandoned based on a series of obsidian dates and stratigraphy for periods of a century or more between 500 and 238 BC. At Duos Nuraghes, with the longest series of 136 dates, only six fall within the period of Punic presence (487 ± 114 BC, 458 ± 60, 468 ± 101, 403 ± 101, 289 ± 99, 275 ± 104) and these are on the early or late end of the range. Excavations have revealed clear evidence that the village was at least partially destroyed following the late Iron Age occupation: both nuraghi were partially razed, an east village hut was burned, and the village cistern was spiked with stones (Webster 1988; 1991a). The few Punic items recovered include several sherds of painted cream ware and an amulet depicting a frog (possibly the Punic spirit Bes). It is also clear that Duos Nuraghes, like Toscono, Urpes and San Sergio, was reoccupied during the Republican period, as indicated by obsidian dates, diagnostic pottery and coins, and continued as a native settlement well into the Medieval period (Michels and Webster 1987; Webster 1988). Significantly, the fifth site tested, the protonuraghe of Serbine, located only 2 km from Duos Nuraghes and Urpes, has revealed chronometric and cultural evidence for continuous occupation from the Iron Age through Early Roman periods. The finds include Punic cream ware (5th–4th century), nine obsidian flakes dating from 384 ± 89 to 243 ± 116 BC, several 4th-century Punic coins, and a complete Massilian Greek transport amphora found *in situ* and dated to the 4th century. Serbine's presently unique status as a Punic period native settlement among Borore nuraghi is not easily explained on the basis of its pre-Punic period importance, since it is one of the smallest structures in the group and had a walled Iron Age village estimated at less than 0.25 hectares. Nor have pre-Punic levels revealed evidence of foreign trade. The site's single evident advantage is in its close proximity to Borore's only alluvial bottoms along the Riu Murtazzolu and thus its possibly greater potential to produce under intensive cultivation the agricultural resources needed for a large immigrant population of displaced/resettled Sardinians. It may be pointed out in this context that over one-half of our still small sample of 'Punic' Nuragic sites occur on very good soil compared to only 34% of all known nuraghe-sites. Our reconnaissance work around Serbine does indicate a much larger Punic/Roman period population. It is possible that what we are documenting in Borore is a reorganization of native settlement pattern under Carthaginian control, toward the formation of a frontier administration which relied upon both a strong military presence as well as a network of well-positioned native administrators (clients), around which were resettled local groups and over which this new Punicized native elite had peace-keeping responsibilities for which they were paid in trade exotica and money.[4] Only additional excavation data can determine the merits of this hypothesis and its applicability to the intermediate (frontier) zone as a whole. It does suggest the intriguing possibility (Dyson 1985: 244) that the influx of new wealth into previously unimportant nuraghi may have had the effect of undermining rather than fortifying the old Iron Age 'aristocratic' order.

Beyond the frontier in the mountainous interior of the Barbagia, Nuorese, Goceano and Gallura there are few if any Punic settlements (Rowland 1982: 26; Barreca 1986b: fig. 11.1). Only a dozen or so nuraghi have Punic materials, mostly small numbers of coins and jewelry. The coins are found here singly or in hoards of up to 3000 (Pozzomaggiore) (Rowland 1982). Several authors (Rowland 1982; Dyson 1985; Moscati 1966: 246-47; Lilliu 1948: 341) have suggested that money was acquired by the mountain natives through raiding, as pay for mercenary activities, or through the sale of pastoral products during annual transhumant journeys to lowland winter pasture. Although possible, there is really little archaeological evidence for these activities. What does seem evident is that the more pastoral mountain tribes had little direct contact with lowland Punic or Punic-Sardinian groups. Less highly organized than native Sardinian groups in the exterior regions, they probably posed little serious threat to the lowlands, and less able to produce large exportable surpluses, were of little economic value to Carthaginian commercial interests. As a consequence the interior natives were the least affected by Punic colonization.

Punic–Sardinian relations southwest of the Campidano in the Sulcitano-Iglesiente are still poorly documented. It is clear however from the large number of Punic sites that these were per-

---

4 The use of native administrators within the occupying colonial government is well documented in early British colonial policies for the governing of hierarchically organized native African polities (e.g. Ngoni, Barnes 1951: 199-200; Sukuma, Richards 1959: 239, 243; Interlacustrine Bantu, Richards 1959: 355).

haps the most densely colonized regions outside the urban centers on the island, presumably owing to the richness of metal ores. But even though Rowland (1988: fig. 35) has tentatively identified eight Roman-period mines in this region, none can be said with certainty to be Punic. Thus we may only point to the paucity of prime agricultural soils in this region as the reason for a non-agricultural focus to the Punic colonization here. Colonization probably proceeded inland from Sulci and as in areas to the northeast of the Campidano was militaristic. Five forts are known, at least one of which—Pani Loriga—was a converted nuraghe-settlement (Barreca 1984: 140). Heavy native resistance is also indicated by destruction levels at the Punic fort of Monte Sirai (Barreca 1970: 19-20). As noted above, native populations here were probably highly organized (confederated polities) with military potential. A pattern of Punicized native cult places or sanctuaries, for example, Temple of Sid-Sardus Pater (Antas), Matzanni (Vallermosa), and a few nuraghi with Punic remains, may indicate a Carthaginian policy of native depopulation in this region. The very large settlement of Serucci (Gonnesa) was abandoned by this period if not earlier (Usai 1984), while Nuraghe Cixerri (Iglesias) was used as a funerary monument (Barreca 1966: 20, 151).

The paucity of Punic sites in the north in Logudoro, Anglona and La Nurra is not easily explained since much of this is good farm land where numerous Roman and Roman-age nuraghe-sites occur (Rowland 1988). Only two possible Punic settlements are known: Carbia near Alghero and Lago di Baratz in La Nurra (Barreca 1986c: 16; Rowland 1982: fig. 4). There are no indications of a fortified frontier system further south; no reports of Punic age destruction levels in nuraghi. Punic finds at native sites are also quite limited, and apart from stelae at Lazzaretto and Nuraghe Palmavera (Barreca 1979: 36) they are comprised of small ceramic finds, jewelry, and coins from an additional six or seven locations (Rowland 1982: fig. 4). It is probably significant that both Nuraghe Palmavera and Nuraghe Santu Antine (Madua 1988: 254), both very large complexes and probably regional or sub-regional centers of native authority, appear to have survived the Punic period and conducted some foreign trade in ceramics. Thus, Punic-Sardinian interactions in the north, albeit limited, seem to have been more symbiotic and peaceful than further to the south. The failure of Carthage to control and colonize these regions may perhaps be seen as a calculated decision based upon a weighing of this region's less than excellent agricultural and mineral resources against the cost of pacifying a very densely settled and highly organized native population. The same might be said for Olbia in the Gallura where control of a very small native hinterland can be seen in terms of the quite limited agricultural potential and close proximity to the mountains (cf. Rowland 1982: 30).

Roman–Sardinian Relations (c. 238 BC–AD 456)

1. Literature and Epigraphy

During the 3rd century BC the Mediterranean world saw the emergence of an expansionary Roman state with broad-ranging military aims justified according to Virgil (*Aeneid* 6.851-853) by a divine mission to 'war down the proud'. By the close of the first Punic War Sardinia had passed to Roman hands (Strabo 5.2.7). The Romans had negotiated with Carthage as early as 509 BC for trade access to the island but were explicitly denied rights to settle there (Polybius 3.22-23). They may have even made plans for Sardinia's colonization as early as 378 BC (Diodorus 15.27.4; Theophrastus, *Hist. Plant.* 5.8.2), and Polybius (1.24.6-7) states 'the Romans, I should explain, from the moment they concerned themselves with the sea, began to entertain designs on Sardinia'. Their chance came in 240 BC when a mercenary revolt against Carthage fomented a widespread uprising on the island, and the Sardinians pleaded with Rome to intervene (Polybius 1.79.1), which it did in 238 BC. Following this, Rome's hold on the island was not relinquished until the Vandal invasion of AD 456. In Polybius's words (1.88.8-12), 'the Carthaginians, who had barely escaped destruction in the last war, were in every respect ill-fitted at the moment to resume hostilities with Rome. Yielding therefore to circumstances, they not only gave up Sardinia, but agreed to pay a further sum of twelve hundred talents to the Romans to avoid going to war for the present.'[5]

The island was seized by the consul for 238 BC, Tiberius Sempronius Gracchus (Florus 1.22.35), although the conquest was less than total and a series of revolts from both native and Punic sectors began almost immediately. In suffocating the first revolt, Titus Manlius Torquatus, consul in 235

---

5 The Sardinian plea bears a curious resemblance to the Sicilian plea that triggered the First Punic War. This latter plea and its consequences, especially the additional payment that Rome demanded of Carthage, became indeed, according to Polybius (3.10.4) the 'principal cause of the subsequent war'.

BC, seems to have found little diffculty (Orosius 4.12.2). But in 231 BC we read that Marcus Pomponius Matho led a campaign against the rebellious Sards 'but could not find many of the inhabitants, who as he learned, had slipped into caves of the forest, difficult to locate; therefore he sent for keen-scented dogs from Italy, and with their aid discovered the trail of both men and cattle and cut off many such parties' (Zonaras 8.18). By 227 BC this first phase of military pacification was over, and Sardinia passed to normal praetorian rule (Solinus 1.5). Although theoretically the island 'became subject to the yoke' of Roman authority (Velleius Paterculus 2.38.2), actual 'Romanization' of its inhabitants took place only very gradually and was never complete. In the 'Mad Mountains', as the unpacified interior was called (Florus 1.22.35), little had changed since Punic times: the bellicose natives continued to reject foreign rule and resisted pacification efforts (Livy 23.40.3; 40.34.13; 41.6-15; Strabo 5.2.7; Varro, *De Re Rustica* 1.16.2; Diodorus Siculus 5.16.6). When, after several skirmishes, a serious uprising took place in 215 BC, Torquatus was sent back to Sardinia. The leader of the rebellion was one Hampsicora, thought to have been a Punicized native elite from Cornus. Although Hampsicora, who had gained support among the mountain tribes and the Carthaginians under Hasdrubal, joined the rebels with hopes of regaining the region (Livy 23.32.7-11), the Romans prevailed. The rebels were slain and the rebellious cities harshly taxed for punishment (Livy 23.40.1-23; 23.41.7). The unrest compelled the Roman legions to remain stationed on the island until 208/207.[6]

Roman demands on Sardinian produce, especially grain and textiles (Livy 23.32.8-9; 29.36.1-2; Valerius Maximus 7.6.1) seem often to have been excessive, putting significant strain on the island's economies and reducing in turn Roman popularity, especially among the old Punic and native elite—one probable reason for Hampsicora's revolt. The internal problems with the mountain tribes were also burdensome, and in 178 BC, 'the Ilienses, reinforced by the Balari, had attacked the province while it was at peace' (Livy 41.6.6). A Sardinian delegation to Rome begged the Senate for help. Sardinia now 'by reason of the seriousness of the war, was made a consular province' (Livy 41.8), and a descendant of the earlier veteran of Sardinian campaigns, Gracchus, was sent to subdue the uprising. 'For Sardinia two legions were ordered to be raised, each of fifty-two hundred infantry and three hundred cavalry; also twelve thousand infantry and six hundred cavalry from the allies of the Latin confederacy, and ten ships of five banks of oars' (Livy 41.9.1-3). This is an impressive force and Gracchus's campaigns not surprisingly met with success: 'He led the army into the country of the Sardinian Ilienses; he fought in pitched battle with both tribes. The enemy was repulsed and routed and stripped of his camp' (Livy 41.12.5-6); 'more than eighty thousand of the enemy were slain or captured' (Livy 41.28.8-9). Gracchus's triumph in 175 BC was followed only by two others during the Republic: that of Aurelius Orestes in 122 BC (Livy, *Periocha* 60), and Caecilius Metellus in 111 BC (Velleius Paterculus 2.8.2; Eutropius 4.25).

Strabo (5.2.7) states that 'it is not profitable continuously to maintain a camp in unhealthy places', referring to Sardinia's malaria problem, but such costs were apparently greatly outweighed by the island's resource wealth.[7] The Romans kept up the Phoenician/ Carthaginian tradition of metal extraction, as the city-name Metalla attests (Miller 1916: col. 408; cf. Solinus 4.1.3) and salt was also exploited (*CIL* 10.7856; Amadasi Guzzo 1967: 91-93 no. 9). Cereal grains were the principle wealth, however, and Sardinia became an essential supplier to Rome itself.[8] Political contenders of the late Republic were well aware of this and both Lepidus in 77 BC (Exuperantius 6) and Sextus Pompeius in 40 BC (Dio Cassius 38.31.1) tried to take advantage of Rome's dependency by blocking Sardinian exports. In the Civil War, Sardinia sided with Caesar against Pompeius (Florus 2.22; Dio Cassius 51.18), with the exception of Sulcis which had supplied a Pompeian admiral and was later rigorously punished (Caesar, *De Bello Africano* 98). Establishing reliable relations with the Sards proved difficult, and Cicero (*Pro Scauro* 44) complained 'what province is there save Sardinia that does not contain a single state that is a friend of the Roman people, and free?' The mountain tribes seem not to have assimilated with the subdued people during the transition from Republic to Empire either, but remained separate

---

6 Livy 27.22.6. We also know from Livy (32.1.6) that in 199 BC land was given to the soldiers in Sardinia 'who had served for many years'.

7 Sardinia maintained her reputation for unhealthy (malarial) climate throughout antiquity; see Pausanias (10.17.6); Livy (23.34.11); Tacitus (*Annales* 2.85.3); Claudianus (*De Bello Gildonico* 1.505-25).

8 On Sardinian grain, see Plutarch, *Pompeius* 50; Appianus, *De Bello Civile* 2.40; Cicero, *De Leg. Man.* 12.34; Claudianus, *De Bello Gildonico* 1.508-509; Strabo 5.2.7; Diodorus Siculus 4.82.4; 11.20.4; 21.16.1; Florus 2.22. The office mosaics at Ostia may allow us to assume Caralis and Sulcis as the two principle grain exporters (see *CIL* 10.7856; 14.4142 and Becatti 71-73).

entities as *civitates barbariae* (Taramelli 1928: 269-74; *CIL* 14.2954). Towards the end of the Republic, however, Roman citizenship was 'conferred upon many members of tributary states in Africa, Sicily, Sardinia' (Cicero, *Pro Balbo* 9.24; see also 18.41 and *Pro Scauro* 43). According to Schneider (1981: 480-82), several cities became *municipae*, but up to the days of Pliny the Elder (3.7.85) the only true colony was Turris Libisonis. In Imperial times there is evidence for other colonies, like Usellus (*CIL* 10.7845).

In 27 BC under Augustus, the province was governed by the senate through *proconsoles* (Dio Cassius 53.12). But just as normal praetorian rule during the Republic by necessity of unrest was punctuated by periods of consular intervention, normal Senatorial rule was relinquished at times for that of the emperors themselves. In AD 6, Augustus intervened because of serious unrest (Dio Cassius 55.28), and during the early Empire, a *praefectus provinciae* was temporarily installed (Meloni 1971: 242). In AD 19, Tiberius exiled 4000 men to Sardinia (for superstitions) to help control banditry (Dio Cassius 57.18; Tacitus, *Annales* 2.85.5; Josephus, *Ant.* 18.83-85). Border conflicts are attested in Nero's reign (*CIL* 10.7852 = *ILS* 5947, Tablet from Esterzili, see note 3), but he nevertheless returned Sardinia to the senate in exchange for Greece (Pausanias 7.17.3). Trouble continued in the intermediate regions between mountains and plains through the reign of Galba (*CIL* 10.7891), and Vespasianus switched Sardinia back to his jurisdiction in AD 73/74 (*CIL* 10.8023; 10.8024). Under both Domitianus and Nerva, we know of cohorts in the Nuoro area (*CIL* 10.7883; 10.7890). In the early 2nd century AD, Trajan raised Aquae Hypsitanae, which lay on the road between Caralis and Turris Libisonis, to the status of a market center: *Forum Traiani*, present day Fordongianus (*CIL* 10.8012; 10.8013; Miller 1916: cols. 409-410).

For the later Empire, the literary sources are scant. However, we know that road-building continued as all known milestones date to this period. The most important of these were the Caralis-to-Turris Libisonis and Caralis-to-Olbia routes. Some secondary and tertiary roads penetrated the interior, but about their intended function we know little, and few inscriptions have surfaced.[9] Roman militarism and commercialism in the island was no doubt greatly facilitated by the road network (at least by the Imperial period). However, it is also apparent from the documentary records that such Romanization need not have involved the replacement of all previous institutions. Indeed, the sufet-system introduced by the Carthaginians still existed in the 3rd century AD (Amadasi 1967: 133-36, Neo-Punic no. 8). From the *Codex Theodosianus*, we know that Sardinia was kept within the Diocesi Italica through the tetrarchical reforms and subsequent modifications. When the Roman Empire was divided, Egypt's grain exports were directed to the East, and grain supplies from both Sardinia and Sicily became even more important to the city of Rome during its final Imperial phase.

2. Archaeology

Roman Sardinia is richer perhaps than any preceding period in terms of archaeological evidence for both native and colonial settlements. However, we are still plagued with serious problems of data quality. Few sites have been systematically excavated and/or well published, and dating is often imprecise so that outside the larger urban centers, where pottery is often the sole chronological marker, sites can only infrequently be dated more precisely than generally in the Roman period, or sometime between 238 BC and the Vandal invasion of AD 456 (cf. Rowland 1988: 768). Part of the difficulty results from the persistence of Punic cultural attributes (as well as language, Tronchetti 1984: 238) well into the 3rd century AD. Archaeology records the very gradual fusion of new Roman elements into an existing Punic-Sardinian and Sardinian culture. As a result, sites are often extremely difficult to date in the absence of coins or chronometric evidence. Therefore, our approach here shall be to regard all Roman sites together as a single chronological sample for the present purpose of revealing broad changes in the pattern of colonial/native relations from the preceding Phoenician and Punic periods.

Most is known about the larger Roman coastal cities and interior towns, some from excavations (e.g. Olbia, Turris Libisonis, Tharros, Cornus, Karalis, Nora, Sulci); for others (e.g. Neapolis, Bithia and about 16 additional major settlements) the evidence is principally literary and epigraphic (Barreca 1984). These were all thoroughly provincial urban settlements—most founded upon earlier Phoenician-Punic centers—and expanded to include the full range of Roman public and private architectural features: temples, commercial and residential quarters, *thermae*, aqueducts, theaters, gridded street plan, and

---

9 The Sardinian milestones are collected in *CIL* 10.7996-8033 and in Sotgiu (1961). The itinerary of interest here is the *Itinerarium Antonini*; the maps are the *Tabula Peutingeriana* (Castorius's world map) and Ptolemaios's *Geographia*. This evidence is well compiled in Miller (1916: cols. 406-410) for as far as Sardinia is concerned.

defensive walls. By at least the Augustan period an extensive network of primary and secondary roads connected all the major settlements and extended well into the interior (Barreca 1984; Meloni 1975; Belli 1988).

Of the numerous smaller rural Roman sites we have a far less detailed picture, although it is here that a potential wealth of evidence exists for studying Roman–Sardinian relations. We are greatly indebted to the tireless and thorough efforts of Professor Robert Rowland, Jr, who has culled through the numerous, scattered field reports of more than a century of exploration to produce several invaluable inventories of rural Roman as well as Roman period native sites on the island (Rowland 1981; 1984; 1988). From these, supplemented by additional recent field studies (Rowland 1982; Rowland 1985a; Dyson and Rowland 1988; Dyson and Rowland 1990a; Dyson and Rowland 1990b; Lilliu and Zucca 1988; Michels and Webster 1987; Webster 1987; Meloni 1987; Tore and Stiglitz 1987), it is possible to map over 200 locations for rural Roman settlements numbering over 300 individual sites, including rustic villas and military posts (34 of 66 have baths and 42 have mosaics), and a variety of residential and commercial buildings occurring singly or within hamlets, villages, or estates (i.e. *latifundia*, cf. Lilliu and Zucca 1988) (Fig. 6). Also, some 18 mines have been tentatively identified. Apart from surviving architecture and a range of familiar ceramic types (imports and local copies of black glazed, *terra sigillata italica*, *terra sigillata chiara*, thin-walled, and included wares) the range of artifacts includes statues/statuettes of deities (73 locations), *timiateria* (Ceres) (21 locations), gold and silver (34 locations), bronze and other jewelry (107 locations), glass (65 locations), crude stele (27 locations), and sarcophagi (38 locations).

In addition, at least 132 locations report native sites with Roman remains. Most are nuraghe-settlements, numbering over 530, with evidence of Roman period use. And the vast majority of these contain variable quantities of prestige goods: imported and local-imitation fine-ware pottery, bronze (coins and jewelry), small figurines and, rarely, gold or silver. Significantly, some 60 have Roman-style architectural features (bricks, walls, tiles), and a few even mosaics (Rowland 1988: 766, 780). A fewer number of reused native burials have Roman materials: *domus de janas* (11 locations), giants' tombs (11 locations), burials *a tafoni* (3 locations), and burials *ad enkytrisinos* (jar) (27 locations).

The geographical patterning of Roman and Roman-native settlements appears to reveal significant changes in colonial–Sardinian interactions from the Punic period. Considering first the locations of Roman sites, two impressions become clear: first, the greater number and density of sites; and secondly, their wider distribution into virtually all regions of the island. While urban development remained a west or south coast phenomenon, the remainder of the shoreline is more or less continuously, if in some places only scarcely, settled, including the east coast where some previous Phoenician/Punic locations were used. Most of the rural Punic sites show continued use into the Roman period (Rowland 1988: 288). But with the addition of new Roman sites to the number of locations by the late Imperial period, one might safely assume at least a 300% increase in colonial populations from the earlier Punic period.

The distribution of rural Roman settlements in relation to soil quality clearly corroborates the increased emphasis on agricultural colonization predicted from literary sources: about 40% of the sites occur on very good soils, compared to 25% of Punic sites. Mostly this results from the larger number of new settlements, many presumably agricultural *latifundia* in the Campidano, especially in the Sinis peninsula and lower Tirso (Tore and Stiglitz 1987). But a great expansion of settlements into the interior is also evident, notably in the little Punicized northern regions of Logudoro, Anglona, Nurra and parts of Gallura, where soils are generally good to moderate. The east coast settlements also supported a string of interior sites in Baronu, Ogliastra and Sarrabus where soils tend to be even poorer. Most strikingly, the previous Punic frontier line has been advanced considerably inland with Roman settlements and supporting roads now extending well into the mountainous interior of Goceano, Nuorese, and Barbagia. Furthermore, the new frontier appears to have been less well defended militarily, having proportionally fewer military installations, for example, Biora, Valentia, Austis, and Sorabile in Barbagia; Caput Tyrsi in Nuorese; Luguidunec in Goceano; and numerous civilian sites in between (Tronchetti 1984: 248). Curiously, the southwest in Iglesiente and Sulcis, apart from the mines, has little evidence of extensive Roman settlement.

If nothing else, it seems clear from the settlement distribution that Roman interest in Sardinia went beyond its principal agricultural focus and included, as some literary sources suggest (see above), a range of agropastoral as well as mineral acquisitions (cf. Rowland 1984). And what of native settlement? Although only between 7% and 8% of all nuraghi are currently known to have evidence of Roman age occupation, these approximately 530 sites are still ten times the number of Punic nuraghi. And, if recent results from intensive regional surveys in Serramana (Rowland 1982), Bauladu (Dyson and Rowland 1988), Fordongianus (Dyson and Rowland 1990b), Paulilatino (Dyson and Rowland 1990b), Usellus (Dyson and Rowland 1990b), Barumini (Lilliu and Zucca 1988), and Ozieri (Amanda, in Rowland 1982) are at all representative of the island as a whole, we can predict that from 40% to 85% of the known nuraghi in any particular region were inhabited by natives who traded with Rome. This implies a native population of some 112,000 to 224,000, or 40-85% of the estimated Iron Age population of 280,000.

Clearly this is significant in light of the evidence noted above for possible massive 'demilitarization' and the resulting depopulation of some native zones during the Punic conquest. Several possible explanations for the greater number of Roman nuraghi suggest themselves. First, it is possible that native depopulation and/or resettlement during the preceding Punic period were not as extensive as might be inferred from the paucity of Punic finds at nuraghi (for reasons of sampling error noted above), and the high percentage of Roman nuraghi implies rather a very high degree of continuity of Iron Age nuragic settlement into the Roman phases, the explanation preferred by Dyson and Rowland (1989; 1990a; 1990b). But against this argument we note the results of a number of stratified, and in some cases chronometrically dated, excavations of nuraghi (e.g. Domu S'Orku-Sarrock, Lilliu 1962: 74-76; S'Uraki-S. Vero Milis, Tore and Stiglitz 1987; Losa-Abbassanta, Lilliu 1985; and five sites in Borore: Urpes and Toscono, Michels and Webster 1987; San Sergio and Duos Nuraghes, Webster 1985; Webster 1988), which indicate native reoccupation of these settlements following periods of abandonment during Punic times (see above). Additionally, nuraghi that did support Punic period use in all cases continue into the Roman period, for example Ortu Còmidu-Sardara (Balmuth 1986; Serbine-Borore, Webster 1991c). Thus, native reoccupation of a still undetermined magnitude is likely to have been a significant feature of the Roman period. And while we are far from inferring the local or regional variability in the rates and extent of such a trend, the reports in some regions of a clear predominance of Imperial over Republican age ceramics in nuraghi (cf. Dyson and Rowland 1988: 136) is probably evidence for such variability in reoccupation rates. Also significant in this context is the evidence from the five dated Borore nuraghi suggesting that Roman period native occupation was typically intermittent (see below, and Michels and Webster 1987; Webster 1988).

An alternative explanation might attribute a large-scale Roman period native reoccupation of nuraghi to historically recorded Roman provincial land tenure and fiscal policies. Both Meloni (1975: 94-99; 1987: 124) and Tronchetti (1984) have read Cicero (*Pro Balbo* 18.41; 9.24) and Livy (23.249; 23.32.9; 23.48.7; 23.41.6) as evidence for large-scale Roman programs involving confiscation of land (presumably from the Punic and Punic-Sardinian aristocracy) and its reassignment to a variety of Roman and Italian entrepreneurs as well perhaps as to natives (with usufruct rights). Also administered was a comprehensive system of taxation (*stipendium, frumentum, imperatum, vectigal*) paid in currency and in-kind as agro-pastoral products—a policy still in force at least until 54 BC (Tronchetti 1984: 246). This could explain both the great proliferation of small Roman rural settlements island-wide (cf. Rowland 1984), as well, perhaps, as the break-up of the presumably fewer large Sardinian and Punic-Sardinian nuraghi-settlements, which during the Punic period may have served as centers of colonial–native administration, especially in the intermediate zone. Finally, this may account for the resulting reestablishment of occupation at many previously abandoned nuraghi.

In addition, Rowland (1985a: 109) has argued that large numbers of natives captured during Roman pacification campaigns against interior tribes (e.g. Gracchus's capture of up to 80,000 of combined Ilienses and Balari as reported in Livy 41.28.8-9) were resettled as tenants on lowland agricultural estates. But archaeological verification of this hypothesis must await more excavations of interior-zone nuraghi.

Lastly, it is important to recognize that even if one assumes massive native depopulation under Carthaginian rule, for example 50% of the original population of 280,000, by the time of the Roman takeover in 238 BC, it is quite reasonable to expect the remaining native population to have fully recovered to previous Iron Age levels by no later than the early Imperial period, given even very low rates of population increase.[10]

The geographical patterning of Roman-period

---

[10] Elsewhere, Webster (1991b) has estimated an average annual rate of population increase for the Borore sub-region, from c. 1800 to 500 BC, of about 0.350% per year. Assuming a similar rate of increase following a Punic period reduction of the native population by say 50% or 140,000 natives island-wide, one can predict a full recovery to the pre-Punic population level of an estimated 280,000 natives within about 250 years, or by the 1st century AD.

nuraghi is also revealing. First, a relationship between high agricultural potential (hence tradeable and taxable surplus produce) and Roman/native contact is less clear than during the Punic period. Bearing in mind the unevenness of these data, only 18.5% of Roman nuraghi occur on very good soils, compared to 28% of Punic nuraghi; while 40% occur on good soils and 28.5% on poor (comparable to the 23% of all nuraghi). This may suggest that trade and tribute exchanges involved a broader range of traditional native agropastoral and perhaps hunted products. Thus, while Roman rural settlements were oriented strongly toward access to farm land, the native settlements that were thus used, and which interacted with them, were not necessarily located for the same reasons. Visual inspection of the mapped distributions of the two site types does suggest, however, that mutual distance was a factor: locations with more Roman rural settlements tend to have, not surprisingly, more Roman nuraghi; apparently Roman–native interactions tended to be local. And the results of the few surveys we do have strongly support a pattern of diminishing intensity of Roman–native contact with distance from the heavily Roman coastal areas. In the hinterlands of Tharros, 86% of Bauladu nuraghi (Dyson and Rowland 1988) and 83% of Usellus nuraghi (Dyson and Rowland 1990b) report Roman materials, and in the Cagliari hinterlands of Villasor–Samassi–Serramana, 70% are Roman (Rowland 1982). Farther inland and higher (c. 100-300 m amsl) at Fordongianus and Paulilatino in the lower Tirso valley, about 60% of the surveyed nuraghi are Roman (Dyson and Rowland 1990a; 1990b), while in the Marmilla around Barumini (c. 200-400 m amsl) only 40% of nuraghi are Roman (Lilliu and Zucca 1988). In the even more remote interior of Goceano, around Ozieri, only 34% of known nuraghi have Roman remains (Rowland 1982: 108). Significantly, within the Ozieri area, a distance factor is also suggested since 40-44% of the nuraghi below 400 m—where all 19 rural Roman settlements occur—have evidence of contact, whereas none of the 24 above this elevation are Roman (cf. Ozieri 1985: 20, 56).

Can one reconcile these new observations with the three-zone model of colonial–native interactions applied to the Punic period? Tronchetti (1984: 246) accepts the Romans' own two-zone taxonomy: *Romania*, comprising the coastal cities and Romanized agricultural hinterlands supporting Roman, Punic, and acculturated Sardinian populations; and *Barbaria*, made up of the unpacified tribes of the interior mountains. While acculturation and probable urbanization of lowland Sardinians, beginning in the Iron Age, certainly continued during the Roman (cf. examples of local Sardinian-produced *ceramica grigia* pottery in nine 'Roman' tombs at Tharros dating to the 2nd–1st century BC, Barnett and Mendleson 1987), the sheer numbers of on-going nuraghe-settlements in urban hinterlands such as the Sinis peninsula (Tore and Stiglitz 1987) makes one wonder about the real extent and nature of acculturation here and also encourages us to question the traditional assumption of widespread latifundistic developments (cf. Rowland 1985a).

Also, there is some evidence for the persistence of a culturally distinct intermediate zone of interaction at roughly 200-500 m elevation, although perhaps greatly modified from the Punic. A rough plotting of all known locations of nuraghi having Roman architecture (wall, bricks, tiles, mosaics) shows that 69% of them occur at these elevations where it will be remembered Iron Age populations were dense and well organized; and during the Punic period the zone had been demilitarized and the refugee populations possibly resettled onto fewer large Punic-Sardinian administrative centers. Only 10% occur above 500 m and 21% below. From the very few excavated it seems likely that these are not Roman settlements but Sardinian: Roman-style houses of a new emerging native elite. The use of colonial-style architecture by native elites as a means of prestige display is of course well documented for British colonial Africa (cf. Fraser 1968: fig. 53) and we should expect no less from Sardinian aspirants. Nuraghe Truvine in Ploaghe, for example, apparently had a mosaic floor as well as typical native and Roman artifacts (Rowland 1988: 780). In the commune of Barumini, seven Roman settlements and 11 (out of a total of 27 nuraghi) Roman nuraghi occur, at least one of which—the nuraghe Marfudi—has a small 'Roman' house of Republican date. The stratified midden suggests domestic use, not unlike that within a nuraghe, with both local native ceramics (including *ceramica grigia* as found in tombs at Tharros as noted), and imported and locally imitated Roman *sigillata*. Neighboring Roman sites identified as villas, *latifundia* (for agricultural and pottery production), and baths suggest a flourishing rural community of Punic-Romans and Sardinians spanning the late 4th century BC to the 3rd century AD (Lilliu and Zucca 1988).

Significantly, the concept of the 'nuraghe-villa' implies the intensification of native prestige competition (and therefore the agro-pastoral economy), especially among intermediate zone communities similar perhaps to those characterizing the Iron Age. There is some evidence for this in floral and faunal remains excavated from Borore nuraghe-settlements. Bone samples from test pits at Toscono reveal a general increase in caprine- over cattle-raising during the Roman phases, as well as a possible reduction in the stature of sheep/goats, both perhaps reflecting an intensification of sheep-raising as well as the introduction of smaller woolly fleeced breeds (Webster and Michels 1986; Webster 1987). Increases were also noted in Roman samples of grass seeds and legumes, indicating possibly intensified pastoralism (cf. Wetterstrom 1987; Webster and Michels 1986). Also, a comparison of Late Bronze Age fauna from Duos Nuraghes with Roman period fauna from neighboring Toscono suggests sheep were raised to a later age at Toscono before being slaughtered, a practice consistent with agro-pastoral intensification throughout Europe in which animals are raised less for meat than for secondary products (i.e. milk, cheese and textile material, cf. Barker 1972), the last also indicated by finds of spindle whorls and loom weights (Michels and Webster 1987). These data altogether support a hypothesis of intensification of the agro-pastoral economy in Borore after 238 BC and are consistent with the idea of renewed intensive levels of prestige goods acquisition among an emergent local native elite, in conjunction with increased tribute demands by Rome (Webster and Michels 1986). The very considerable differences noted among Borore sites in Roman trade wealth seem also to suggest that resulting status differentiation did not necessarily parallel those established during the Iron Age but instead represent a 'new' order. For instance, the single tower nuraghe-settlement of Toscono has a far greater quantity and variety of Roman items and is much larger in occupied area than either Duos Nuraghes (two central towers) or Urpes (quadrilobate tower). Only the small protonuraghe of Serbine, where a large Punic settlement existed, has perhaps as large and rich a Roman occupation.

Evidence for Roman–Sardinian hostilities is traditionally drawn from the few statements noted above of campaigns against the unpacified interior tribes (e.g. Corsi, Balari, Ilienses of the Gallura, Goceano, and Barbagia respectively) where we have at least one report of the killing or capturing of 80,000 natives (Livy 41.12.5-6). But as Dyson (1985: 257) is quick to point out, such a figure, even if grossly inflated, implies severe population pressure in *Barbaria*. Indeed, this is over one-quarter of the estimated Iron Age population for the island, clearly too high for these traditionally scarcely-inhabited regions. It seems more likely that this and other such campaigns, especially from the late Republican period onwards, refer to Roman military responses to periodic revolts or depredations of the newly developed Roman–Sardinian polities of the intermediate zone. Periodic abandonment of all five of the excavated Borore nuraghe-settlements during the Roman phases has been well documented through chronometric dating (Michels and Webster 1987; Webster 1988) and may document such engagements. At least at Serbine, our ongoing excavations have shown rather convincingly that the central proto-nuraghe structure was sacked and partially destroyed at least twice during the Republican and Imperial periods. Finally, Strabo's mention that the natives were effectively attacked while attending large celebrations is certainly more likely to refer to attacks upon the large intermediate-zone sanctuaries such as Santa Vittoria-Serri and Abini-Teti (both having Roman remains and the latter possibly sacked, Rowland 1988: 783), than anything known in the interior mountains (cf. Lilliu 1988: 460). The likely fragility of Roman–native interactions in the intermediate zone, where relations probably oscillated between symbiotic integration and mutual hostility, does not however obviate the probability, as Dyson (1985: 267) suggests, that at least the better organized among the native polities became faithful 'border client groups' aiding the few garrisoned Roman posts in the security of the frontier against the interior tribes. About these later groups we have at present little archaeological information.

Conclusions

Our purpose here has been the preliminary assessment of evidence for changing colonial–native relations in Sardinia from c. 1000 BC–AD 456. In covering this long period we were able to make rather fuller use of the relatively few literary and epigraphic references than of the much richer archaeological record, which was necessarily selectively culled for problem-specific evidence. Moreover, we are well aware of the unevenness across all these data in terms of quality. Only the results of additional regional level programs of systematic survey and excavation (e.g. Rowland 1982; Rowland 1985a; Dyson and Rowland 1988; Dyson and Rowland 1989; Dyson and Rowland 1990a; Dyson and Rowland 1990b; Michels and Webster 1987; Webster 1988) will allow us to really gauge the representativeness of our current body of observations for the colonial periods.

Still, we have begun to discern temporally specific patterns of colonial–native adaptations which are offered here as provisional models. The evidence of settlement patterns suggests the application of a three-zone model of colonial–native interactions as early as the Iron Age. The coastal lowlands, lying mainly below 200 m elevation and being sparsely inhabited by Nuragic groups, although of great commercial agricultural value, became gradually urbanized after the appearance of Phoenician centers as early as the 11th century. Phoenician–Sardinian relations here seem to have followed a peaceful process of acculturation and integration involving the abandonment of most native villages in the urban hinterlands and presumably the incorporation of these native populations into Phoenician–Punic–Sardinian coastal cities and towns by the late 4th century. The process was similar perhaps to that inferred for Greek–native southeast Italy (Whitehouse and Wilkins 1989: 118). The likelihood that these same urban hinterlands and the same nuraghe-settlements were frequently resettled by natives during the Roman period remains a largely unexplained but potentially significant phenomenon; but native population growth, the settlement of captured interior natives as tenant farmers, and the introduction of new Roman land tenure, fiscal and administrative policies will no doubt have been important factors. Colonial–native relations in the intermediate zone—the middle altitude (roughly 200-500 m) interior uplands—appear to have undergone significant and complex changes in native adaptations as a direct result of colonial contacts. During the Iron Age the densely settled, hierarchical, chiefdom-like polities which had developed during the previous Late Bronze Age were transformed into increasingly stratified, although possibly less centralized, oligarchic organizations as a result of intensified elite status competition fueled by the enhanced access to foreign trade goods through Phoenician trading centers on the coast. Again as noted, similar developments have been inferred for Greek–native interactions in southeast Italy during the same period (Whitehouse and Wilkins 1989: 120). The military conquest of the intermediate zone by Carthage after c. 500 BC may have temporarily halted the development of Nuragic trade-control-based oligarchies since native populations appear to have been greatly reduced and/or resettled, possibly within a series of colonial–native administrative centers similar perhaps to those identified in the Roman Danubian frontier (Bartel 1989: 180). But with the Roman takeover of the island in 238 BC native patterns of settlement similar to those of the Iron Age reappear here as in the coastal lowlands, and there is evidence for increasing social differentiation between and within native villages suggestive of the emergence of a new social order of native elites founded on differential access to Roman luxury goods. By contrast there are few indications that the interior mountain regions of the island underwent significant cultural modification as a result of colonial contacts or of interactions with more complexly organized native polities in adjacent regions. The interior mountains probably remained, as literature tells us, the reserve of relatively unacculturated, unpacified, 'barbarian' tribesmen into late Imperial times. Such cultural continuity or persistence on the part of the mountain tribes is explained at least in part by the constraining effects of their more acephalous organization, and hence their lower receptivity to trade goods with less functional than prestige value (see Fulford 1985: 105), and by the limitations of an agro-pastoral economy with relatively low productive potential for supporting extensive trade-exchange relations with lowland colonial and/or native groups.

Another conclusion safely drawn even now is that colonial–Sardinian adaptations during each period were conditioned by a potentially wide array of natural, techno-economic, sociopolitical, and historical factors operating over long time periods. It is apparent that colonial patterns of settlement, for example, are not to be explained by reference solely to the documented commercial or political motives and agendas of the Phoenician, Punic and Roman powers, nor even the known distribution of targeted resources on the island. Of equal importance will have been the island's cultural setting—its extant variety and distribution of sociopolitical organizations and economic adaptations—since these will have directly conditioned the subject populations receptivity or resistance to alternate colonial strategies and thus will have greatly determined the relative costs and benefits of programs of conquest, pacification, resettlement, administration, trade-exchange, acculturation and integration (cf. Fulford 1985: 105-106). Moreover, because colonial–native interactions will have involved some degree of mutualism, we must be as sensitive analytically to evidence for acculturation or change in the 'conquering' colonial populations as well as in the subject native populations, and address as seriously the question of colonial adaptations to Sardinian presence as that of Sardinian responses to colonial presence (cf. Barreca 1987).

References

Amadasi Guzzo, M.G.
1967 Le iscrizione fenicie e puniche delle colonie in occidente. *Studi Semitici* 28.

Balmuth, M.S.
1986 Sardara (Cagliari). Preliminary report of excavations 1975–1978 of the Nuraghe Ortu Comidu. *Notizie degli Scavi di Antichità* 37(1983): 353-410.

Balmuth, M.S., & R.F. Tylecote
1976 Ancient copper and bronze in Sardinia: Excavation and analysis. *Journal of Field Archaeology* 3: 195-201.

Barker, G.
1972 The condition of cultural and economic growth in the Bronze Age of central Italy. *Proceedings of the Prehistoric Society* 38: 171-208.

Barnes, J.
1951 The Jameson Ngoni. In E. Colson and M. Gluckman (eds.), *Seven Tribes of British Central Africa*. London: Oxford University Press.

Barnett, R.D.
1987 The burials: Survey and analysis. In Barnett and Mendleson 1987: 38-48.

Barnett, R.D., & C. Mendleson (eds.)
1987 *Tharros: A Catalogue of Material in the British Museum from Phoenician and Other Tombs at Tharros, Sardinia*. London: British Museum Publications.

Barreca, F.
1966 Monte Sirai III. *Studi Semitici* 20: 9-59.
1970 *Ricerche Puniche in Sardegna. Ricerche Puniche nel Mediterraneo Centrale*. Roma: C.N.R.
1979 *La Sardegna Fenicia e Punica*. Sassari: Chiarella.
1984 Santadi, Loc. Pani Loriga. In E. Anati (ed.), *I Sardi. La Sardegna dal paleolitico all'età romana*, 139-40. Cagliari: Jaca Book.
1985 Sardegna nuragica e il mondo fenicio-punico. In E. Arslan, F. Barreca and F. Lo Schiavo (eds.), *Civiltà Nuragica*, 308-28. Milano: Electa.
1986a Phoenicians in Sardinia: The bronze figurines. In M.S. Balmuth (ed.), *Studies in Sardinian Archaeology, Volume II: Sardinia in the Mediterranean*, 135-54. Ann Arbor: University of Michigan Press.
1986b The Phoenician and Punic civilization in Sardinia. In M.S. Balmuth (ed.), *Studies in Sardinian Archaeology, Volume II: Sardinia in the Mediterranean*, 155-86. Ann Arbor: University of Michigan Press.
1986c *La Civiltà Fenicio-punica in Sardegna*. Sardegna Archeologica: Studi e Monumenti 3. Sassari: Carlo Delfino.
1987 The city and site of Tharros. In Barnett and Mendleson 1987: 21-29.

Bartel, B.
1989 Acculturation and ethnicity in Roman Moesia Superior. In T.C. Champion (ed.), *Centre and Periphery: Comparative Studies in Archaeology*, 177-85. London: Unwin Hyman.

Becker, M.J.
1980 Sardinia and the Mediterranean copper trade: Political development and colonialism in the Bronze Age (1). *Anthropology* 4(2): 91-117.

Belli, E.
1988 La viabilità romana nel Logudoro-Meilogu. In A. Moravetti (a cura di), *Il Nuraghe S. Antine nel Logudoro-Meilogu*, 331-95. Sassari: Carlo Delfino.

Bernardini, P.
1982 Le aristocrazie nuragiche nei secoli VIII e VII a.C. Proposte di lettura. *La Parola del Passato* 203: 81-101.

Bernardini, P., & C. Tronchetti
1985 La Sardegna, gli Etruschi e i Greci. In E. Arslan, F. Barreca and F. Lo Schiavo (eds.), *Civiltà Nuragica*, 285-306. Milano: Electa.

Bondì, S.F.
1988 L'organizzazione politica e amministrativa. In S. Moscati (ed.), *I Fenici*, 126-31. Milano: Bompiani.

Cross, F. M.
1984 Phoenicians in Sardinia: The epigraphical evidence. In M.S. Balmuth and R.J. Rowland, Jr (eds.), *Studies in Sardinian Archaeology*, 53-65. Ann Arbor: University of Michigan Press.

Dietler, M.
1989 Greeks, Etruscans, and thirsty barbarians: Early Iron Age interaction in the Rhone Basin of France. In T.C. Champion (ed.), *Centre and Periphery: Comparative Studies in Archaeology*, 127-41. London: Unwin Hyman.

Dyson, S.L.
1985 *The Creation of the Roman Frontier*. Princeton: Princeton University Press.

Dyson, S.L., & R.J. Rowland, Jr
1988 Survey archaeology in the territory of Bauladu. Preliminary notice. *Quaderni della Soprintendenza Archeologica per le Provincie di Cagliari e Oristano* 5: 129-39.
1989 The University of Maryland-Wesleyan survey in Sardinia-1988. *Quaderni della Soprintendenza Archeologica per le Provincie di Cagliari e Oristano* 6: 157-85.
1990a Conservatism and change in Roman rural Sardinia. In A. Mastino (a cura di), *L'Africa Romana. Atti del VII Convegno di Studio, Sassari, 15-17 dicembre 1989*, 525-35. Pubblicazioni del Dipartimento di Storia dell'Università di Sassari 16.
1990b University of Maryland-Wesleyan University Archaeology Research in Sardinia. *Old World Archaeology Newsletter* 14(1): 18-19.

Fraser, D.
1968 *Village Planning in the Primitive World*. New York: George Braziller.

Fulford, M.G.
1985 Roman material in barbarian society, c. 20 BC–c. AD 400. In T.C. Champion and J. Megaw (eds.) *Settlement and Society; Aspects of West European Prehistory in the First Millennium BC*, 91-108. New York: St Martin's Press.

Gallin, L.J.
1989 *Architectural attributes and inter-site variation: A case study: The Sardinian nuraghi*. PhD dissertation, UCLA. Ann Arbor: University Microfilms International.

Gallin, L.J., & R.H. Tykot
in press Metallurgical activity at the Nuragic village of Santa Barbara (Bauladu), Sardinia, Italy. *Journal of Field Archaeology*.

Haselgrove, C.
1982 Wealth, prestige and power: The dynamics of late Iron Age political centralization. In C. Renfrew and S. Shennan (eds.), *Ranking, Resources and Exchange*, 79-88. Cambridge: Cambridge University Press.
1987 Culture process on the periphery: Belgic Gaul and Rome during the late Republic and early Empire. In M. Rowlands, M. Larsen and K. Kristiansen

(eds.), *Centre and Periphery in the Ancient World*, 104-124. Cambridge: Cambridge University Press.

Hedeager, L.
1987   Empire, frontier and barbarian hinterland: Rome and northern Europe from A.D. 1–400. In M. Rowlands, M. Larsen and K. Kristiansen (eds.), *Centre and Periphery in the Ancient World*, 125-40. Cambridge: Cambridge University Press.

Kipp, R., & E. Schortman
1989   The political impact of trade in chiefdoms. *American Anthropologist* 91: 370-85.

Lewthwaite, J.
1985   Colonialism and nuraghismus. In C. Malone and S. Stoddart (eds.), *Papers in Italian Archaeology IV: The Cambridge Conference*, 220-51. BAR International Series 243. Oxford: British Archaeological Reports.

Lilliu, G.
1948   Rapporti fra la civiltà nuragica e la civiltà fenicio-punica. *Studi Etruschi* 18: 323-72.
1962   *I Nuraghi. Torri preistoriche della Sardegna*. Verona.
1966   L'architettura nuragica. In *Atti del XIII Congresso di Storia dell'Architettura* 1: 17-92; 2: 9-77.
1982   *La Civiltà Nuragica*. Sardegna Archeologica: Studi e Monumenti 1. Sassari: Carlo Delfino.
1985   Abbasanta. Loc. Nuraghe Losa. In E. Anati (ed.), *I Sardi. La Sardegna dal paleolitico all'età romana*, 157-59. Cagliari: Jaca Book.
1988   *La Civiltà dei Sardi dal Paleolitico all'età dei Nuraghi*. 3rd edition. Torino: Nuova ERI.

Lilliu, G., & R. Zucca
1988   *Su Nuraxi di Barumini*. Sardegna Archeologica: Guide e Itinerari 9. Sassari: Carlo Delfino.

Lo Schiavo, F.
1978   Le fibule della Sardegna. *Studi Etruschi* 46(2): 25-46.
1981   Economia e società nell'età dei nuraghi. In E. Atzeni *et al.* (eds.), *Ichnussa: La Sardegna dalle origini all'età classica*, 255-347. Milano: Libri Scheiwiller.
1986   Sardinian metallurgy: The archaeological background. In M.S. Balmuth (ed.), *Studies in Sardinian Archaeology, Volume II: Sardinia in the Mediterranean*, 231-35. Ann Arbor: University of Michigan Press.

Madau, M.
1988   Materiali-fittili di età fenicio-punica. In A. Moravetti (a cura di), *Il Nuraghe S. Antine nel Loggudoro-Meilogu*, 243-71. Sassari: Carlo Delfino.

Meloni, P.
1971   Stato attuale dell'epigrafia latina in Sardegna e nuove acquisizioni. In *Acta of the Fifth Epigraphic Congress*, 241-45. Oxford.
1975   *La Sardegna Romana*. Sassari: Chiarella.
1987   Southern Sardinia during the Punic and Roman age. In N. Sciannameo (ed.), *The Province of Cagliari—Environment, History and Culture*, 122-31. Cagliari.

Michels, J.W., & G.S. Webster (eds.)
1987   *Studies in Nuragic Archaeology*. BAR International Series 373. Oxford: British Archaeological Reports.

Miller, K.
1916   *Itineraria Romana*. Stuttgart.

Moravetti, A.
1985   Le tombe e l'ideologia funeraria. In E. Arslan, F. Barreca and F. Lo Schiavo (eds.), *Civiltà Nuragica*, 132-80. Milano: Electa.

Mori, A.
1972   *Illustrativa della Carta della Utilizzazione del Suola della Sardegna*. Roma: C.N.R.
1975   *Sardegna. Le Regione di Italia*, XVIII Torino: Unione Tipografic.

Moscati, S.
1966   La penetrazione fenicia e punica in Sardegna. *Memoria dell'Accademia dei Lincei* 12: 215-20.
1968   *Fenici e Cartaginesi in Sardegna*. Milano.

Ozieri
1985   *Museo Archeologico Ozieri*. Ozieri.

Phillips, P.
1978   Aspects of research in Sardinian protohistory. In H.M. Blake, T. Potter and D. Whitehouse (eds.), *Papers in Italian Prehistory I*, 93-96. BAR International Series 41. Oxford: British Archaeological Reports.

Richards, A.
1959   *East African Chiefs*. London: Faber & Faber.

Rowland, R.J., Jr
1981   *I Ritrovamenti Romani in Sardegna*. Studia Archeologica 28. Roma: L'Erma di Bretschneider.
1982   Beyond the frontier in Punic Sardinia. *American Journal of Ancient History* 7(1): 20-39.
1984   The countryside of Roman Sardinia. In M.S. Balmuth and R.J. Rowland, Jr (eds.), *Studies in Sardinian Archaeology*, 285-300. Ann Arbor: University of Michigan Press.
1985a   The Roman invasion of Sardinia. In C. Malone and S. Stoddart (eds.), *Papers in Italian Archaeology IV. The Cambridge Conference*, 99-117. BAR International Series 246. Oxford: British Archaeological Reports.
1987   Faunal remains in prehistoric Sardinia: The current state of the evidence. In Michels and Webster 1987: 147-61.
1988   The archaeology of Roman Sardinia: A selected typological inventory. *Rise and Decline of the Roman World Part II: Principate, Vol. 11.1*, 740-875. Berlin: Walter de Gruyter.
n.d.   Where did all the nuraghi go? MS on file, University Park: Department of Anthropology, The Pennsylvania State University.

Schneider, E.
1981   La Sardegna in età Romana. In E. Atzeni *et al.* (eds.), *Ichnussa: La Sardegna dalle origini all'età classica*, 479-84. Milano: Libri Scheiwiller.

Sotgiu, G.
1961   *Iscrizioni Latine della Sardegna I*. Padova.

Taramelli, A.
1928   Un omaggio della 'civitates barbariae' di Sardegna ad Augusto. *Atti del Primo Congresso Nazionale di Studi Romani*, 269-74.

Tore, G., & A. Stiglitz
1987   Ricerche archeologiche nel Sinis e nell'alto Oristanese (continuità e trasformazione nell'evo antico). In A. Mastino (a cura di), *L'Africa Romana. Atti del IV Convegno di Studio, Sassari, 12-14 dicembre 1986*, 633-58. Pubblicazioni del Dipartimento di Storia dell'Università di Sassari 8.

Tronchetti, C.
1984   The cities of Roman Sardinia. In M.S. Balmuth and R.J. Rowland, Jr (eds.), *Studies in Sardinian Archaeology*, 237-83. Ann Arbor: University of Michigan Press.

1986   Nuragic statuary from Monti Prama. In M.S. Balmuth (ed.), *Studies in Sardinian Archaeology, Volume II: Sardinia in the Mediterranean*, 41-59. Ann Arbor: University of Michigan Press.

Usai, L.
1984   Gonessa, Loc. Serrucci o Seruci. In E. Anati (ed.), *I Sardi. La Sardegna dal paleolitico all'età romana*, 106-109. Cagliari: Jaca Book.

Webster, G.S.
1985   Field Report of Excavations at Duos Nuraghes and San Giorgio in Borore, Sardinia 1985. *Old World Archaeology Newsletter* 9(3): 14-18.
1987   Vertebrate faunal remains. In Michels and Webster 1987: 69-91.
1988   Duos Nuraghes: Preliminary results of the first three seasons of excavation. *Journal of Field Archaeology* 15: 465-72.
1990   Labor control and emergent stratification in prehistoric Europe. *Current Anthropology* 31(4): 337-66.
1991a   The functions and social significance of nuraghi: A provisional model. In B. Santillo Frizell (ed.), *Arte Militare e Architettura Nuragica. Nuragic Architecture in its Military, Territorial and Socio-economic Context. Proceedings of the First International Colloquium on Nuragic Architecture at the Swedish Institute in Rome, 7-9 December, 1989*, 169-85. Acta Instituti Romani Regni Sueciae, Series In 4°, 48. Stockholm: Svenska Institutet i Rom.
1991b   Monuments, mobilization and Nuragic organization. *Antiquity* 65: 840-56.
1991c   Test excavations at the protonuraghe Serbine. *Old World Archaeology Newsletter* 15(1): 22-25.

Webster, G.S., & J.W. Michels
1986   Paleoeconomy in west-central Sardinia. *Antiquity* 60: 221-29.

Weiss, A.
1986   Nuragic bronze boat models and Sardinian riverine commerce. *American Journal of Archaeology* 91(2): 203.

Wells, P.S.
1980   *Culture Contact and Culture Change: Early Iron Age Central Europe and the Mediterranean World.* Cambridge: Cambridge University Press.

Wetterstrom, W.
1987   A preliminary report on the plant remains from Nuraghe Toscono. In Michels and Webster 1987: 93-104.

Whitehouse, R.D., & J.B. Wilkins
1989   Greeks and natives in south-east Italy: Approaches to the archaeological evidence. In T.C. Champion (ed.), *Centre and Periphery: Comparative Studies in Archaeology*, 102-25. London: Unwin Hyman.

Winter, F., & H. Bankoff
1989   Diffusion and cultural evolution in Iron Age Serbia. In T.C. Champion (ed.), *Centre and Periphery: Comparative Studies in Archaeology*, 159-72. London: Unwin Hyman.

Riassunto

L'adattamento sardo alla presenza fenicia, punica e romana sull'isola viene esaminato mediante l'uso di dati letterari, epigrafici ed archeologici.

Durante l'Età del Ferro (c. 900-500 a.C.) i tipici insediamenti locali consistevano in un nuraghe con un villaggio circostante la cui occupazione risale spesso alla Media Età del Bronzo (c. 1500-1250 a.C.). I siti sono concentrati nelle regioni centro-orientali della Sardegna, preferibilmente su territori fertili. Gli studi sulle faune e sulle flore e le testimonianze tecnologiche sembrano indicare che la popolazione nuragica praticava un'agricoltura e pastorizia di sussistenza caratterizzate da autosufficienza locale e da un surplus minimo. I nuraghi stessi avevano la funzione di residenze fortificate per una *local petty elite*. Ceramiche decorate e oggetti di metallo venivano probabilmente scambiati tra *elites*.

Gli insediamenti fenici lungo le coste erano per la maggior parte porti commerciali per lo sfruttamento dei metalli sardi. Alcuni insediamenti sardi probabilmente coesistevano con i fenici presso queste comunità proto-urbane, e prodotti fenici, etruschi, greci e ciprioti sono stati trasportati in numerosi siti nuragici. L'apparizione di riti di sepoltura individuali indica l'aumento di una stratificazione sociale nuragica nella Sardegna centro-meridionale; un processo dovuto in parte alla disponibilità di questi beni prestigiosi. Alla fine dell'Età del Ferro, l'organizzazione sociale dei gruppi indigeni nelle regioni di Campidano, di Trexenta, di Marmilla, di Arborea, di Sinis, di Sulcitano, e di Iglesiente era probabilmente più complessa dell'organizzazione sociale delle altre regioni.

In questo articolo si sostiene che l'adattamento fenicio-sardo durante l'Età del Ferro varia a seconda di tre zone socio-ambientali:

1. una pianura costiera con un potenziale agricolo molto alto, ma con pochi insediamenti, e con insediamenti costieri fenici/fenicio-sardi proto-urbani;
2. un altipiano con un potenziale agricolo abbastanza buono, e ricco di risorse minerarie dell'Iglesiente, con numerosi insediamenti di popolazioni indigene con un'ottima organizzazione sociale, politica e militare, e impegnate in attività commerciali con i porti fenici;
3. una zona interna montagnosa con un potenziale agricolo relativamente basso, abitato da tribù pastorali scarsamente organizzate e che avevano solo contatti sporadici con la zona costiera.

Queste variazioni culturali all'interno delle popolazioni indigene hanno condizionato fortemente la natura delle relazioni tra coloni e nativi nei successivi periodi punici e romani.

I Cartaginesi, dopo numerose campagne

sanguinose contro i Sardi, hanno acquistato il controllo dell'isola nel 509 a.C. e in aggiunta agli insediamenti costieri, essi hanno stabilito numerosi siti, santuari e cimiteri nelle regioni di Campidano e Sulcitano e negli altipiani adiacenti. Non sono state ritrovate fortificazioni puniche nei bassipiani, e ciò sta ad indicare che in quella zona le relazioni tra indigeni e coloni erano probabilmente pacifiche. Le popolazioni sarde dei bassipiano sono state probabilmente assorbite nella cultura fenicio-punica, alcune urbanizzate, altre acculturate in un contesto nativo o punico-sardo.

La presenza di forti punici e la testimonianze della distruzione di alcuni nuraghi negli altipiani adiacenti, sta ad indicare che queste regioni sono state amministrativamente controllate. Durante l'Età del Ferro, queste erano regioni densamente popolate con un'organizzazione sociale assai complessa. Al di là della linea di frontiera, sembra che numerosi insediamenti siano stati abbandonati, e le tribù pastorali delle regioni montagnose avevano scarsi contatti con i gruppi punici o punico-sardi. Il fatto che la regione settentrionale della Sardegna non avesse risorse minerali o agricole, ha influenzato la decisione di Cartagine di non controllare e non colonizzare le regioni settentrionali.

L'occupazione romana della Sardegna è iniziata in seguito ad una rivolta mercenaria nel 240 a.C., ma fonti letterarie ci informano che anche dopo questa rivolta ci sono state agitazioni tra cui la ribellione capeggiata da Hampsicora nel 215 a.C. Anche se sono stati identificati centinaia di insediamenti romani rurali e costieri, residenze private, costruzioni commerciali, poderi, miniere, e 132 siti indigeni con ritrovamenti romani, testimonianza dell'incorporazione graduale di elementi romani nella cultura punico-sarda e sarda, questi siti sono difficili da datare vista l'assenza di monete o testimonianze cronologiche.

Esistono comunque differenze dal periodo punico nelle relazioni tra coloni e nativi. Il maggior numero e densità di siti romani, e la loro distribuzione su tutte le regioni dell'isola, riflette l'intensità dello sfruttamento romano delle risorse agricole, minerarie e pastorizie dell'isola. Sembra che numerosi nuraghi siano stati rioccupati dopo essere stati abbandonati durante il periodo punico, questo è forse dovuto a regole di tassazione e proprietà romane. I nuraghi situati vicino a insediamenti rurali romani, sembrano avere a disposizione più prodotti romani, e l'intensità di queste relazioni tra romani e nativi diminuisce con l'aumentare della distanza dalle zone costiere romane.

Per i Romani la Sardegna includeva *Romania*—le città costiere e le zone agricole romanizzate—e *Barbaria*—le tribù bellicose delle zone montagnose interne. Ma gli Autori suggeriscono che la vasta percentuale di nuraghi con architettura romana, a circa 200-500 m di altezza, formano una zona intermedia culturalmente distinta dove un nuovo emergere di un'*elite* nativa ha adottato forme architettoniche di stile coloniale per indicare una posizione di prestigio. Testimonianze archeologiche confermano un'ipotesi di intensificazione di un'economia agro-pastorale presso questi siti, per acquistare beni prestigiosi e per soddisfare i tributi richiesti da Roma. Queste zone ad una altitudine media, sono probabilmente servite anche come zone cuscinette contro le tribù delle zone interne, di cui abbiano poche informazioni archeologiche.

Le regioni montagnose interne non sembrano aver subito significanti modifiche culturali in seguito al contatto con i coloni, mentre le differenze negli insediamenti nativi e le relazioni con i coloni delle zone costiere ed intermedie devono essere viste in due modi. In aggiunta ai motivi politici e commerciali dei coloni, la varietà e la distribuzione della organizzazione politica ed economica delle popolazioni locali ha condizionato le strategie di occupazione e di sfruttamento praticate dai coloni. Dal momento che colonizzazione è per definizione in parte un fenomeno vicendevole, dovremmo esaminare seriamente sia l'adattamento dei coloni alla presenza sarda che l'acculturazione delle popolazioni native.

Carthaginians in the Countryside?

Robert J. Rowland, Jr

Introduction

In the 8th and 7th centuries BC, the Phoenicians began to develop permanent settlements in Sardinia while also continuing to utilize temporary emporia. These settlements were situated on islands and promontories or adjacent to lagoons. Because some of these places were continuously occupied through the Roman period (Nora, Bithia, Tharros, Bosa) and even to the present day (Cagliari, Sulcis-S. Antioco, Othoca-S. Giusta), we are not able to secure their foundation dates with precision. As far as we can tell, Olbia was not founded until the mid-4th century, and there remains a general dearth of sites in the northern portion of the island; this problem is addressed elsewhere in this volume by Tore.

One interpretation of the 9th-century Phoenician inscription from Nora has it commemorating a Phoenician victory over indigenous Sardinians (Cross 1986: 120), so that some instances of Phoenician colonization (or, in this case, 'pre-colonization': Bondì 1988a) may well have been bellicose; elsewhere (Bithia, Tharros and Sulcis: Tronchetti 1986: 104-105), the presence of indigenous material in Phoenician tombs might suggest the existence of amicable relationships between colonists and natives or at least between their ruling classes, but one notes the ample presence of weapons in those tombs (Zucca 1989) which might with equal plausibility suggest the opposite.

As early as the mid-7th century, the Phoenician coastal settlements began to expand the territory under their control. The fort at Monte Sirai-Carbonia (Moscati 1983; Barreca 1984; see Moscati 1988: 577 for additional references), soon followed by Pani Loriga-Santadi (references in Moscati 1988: 577), was established as a military colony by Sulcis to secure control over the coastal plain. In due time, if not immediately, a frontier system ringing the Iglesiente was created (Tronchetti 1988: 32-33, 46-47, 53, 64-65; Frau and Monticolo 1990), with the consequence that settlement in the protected zone became relatively dense and need not concern us much here; nor will we linger in this discussion concerning the settlements in the southeast around Villasimius, Muravera and Villaputzu (Zucca 1984; Ledda 1989: 324-39; Ledda 1985: 312-15; Marras 1982: 51-59).

It would seem that the Phoenician levels at San Sperate attest to an early colony sent out from Cagliari; Phoenician material at Cuccuru Nuraxi-Settimo S. Pietro and at M. Olladiri-Monastir might be evidence for immigrant settlement or for commercial and other contacts between native and immigrant cultures. The settlement at S. Sperate was a 'proto-urban' agglomeration of houses with rectilinear mud-brick walls with stone foundations and numerous rooms; there is also evidence of bronze working (Ugas and Zucca 1984: 12-13). At Cuccuru Nuraxi, a sacred well was constructed over the ruins of a Nuragic tower; associated material includes a large amount of Phoenician, proto-Corinthian, Corinthian and Etruscan along with locally made pottery (Ugas and Zucca 1984: 9-12). At Monastir, the assemblage revealed by a plow included bricks, imported pottery and amphoras, and carbonized material; the area could have been a sacred zone, an incineration cemetery (therefore not indigenous) or one or more structures which were burned (Ugas and Zucca 1984: 20-30). Other Archaic imports in this region and elsewhere are most likely to be objects of trade. San Sperate and Monastir are adjacent to the Mannu river, and the settlements there can be seen as representing the first stage of an expansionary process along this key route to the interior; as we know, they were followed by the establishment of forts in the 6th century at S. Brai-Furtei (Ugas 1981: 83) to the north and in the 5th century at Monte Luna-Senorbì to the northeast (Salvi and Usai 1990; additional references in Moscati 1988: 577).

Carthaginian Settlement

Shortly after the middle of the 6th century, Carthage intervened directly in Sardinia by sending an expeditionary force which was at first defeated (leading to the installation of the

Rowland: Carthaginians in the Countryside? 475

Fig. 2 Ceres figurines (circles) and other shrines (triangles).

Fig. 1 Punic 'cemeteries' in Sardinia.

Magonids in power in Carthage; cf. Bondì 1988b: 174-80). Over the course of the next century, however, Carthage vigorously pursued a policy of active imperialism which resulted, around 450 BC, in the establishment of an interior frontier system, of which Monte Luna was an integral part. At about the same time they entered Sardinia, the Carthaginians established a series of alliances with the Etruscans which soon resulted in their combined success in the so-called Battle of Alalia c. 535 BC. By the late 6th century, the Carthaginians had been so successful that, in their first treaty with Rome (Polybius 3.22.8-9), they could assert control over all trade by the Romans in Libya and in Sardinia.

After the establishment of the Carthaginian frontier, Punic influences on the native populations both within and beyond their sphere of control intensified. If the Romans and others could trade in Sardinia only in the presence of a Carthaginian official, then it seems likely that internal trade might also have been similarly restricted and that the Punic forts, in addition to the obvious military function, served as the nodes of exchange between Sardinian-Carthaginians and natives, and between diverse groups of indigenous inhabitants. There also may have been non-military sites (e.g. S. Maria di Monserrato-Serramanna) which functioned as emporia. From the 5th century on, imported goods at native sites increased dramatically; but, I here suggest, there is insufficient evidence to postulate any widespread colonization of the countryside by the Carthaginians. Although some colonization surely took place (Isserlin 1983: 157-64),[1] even including additional immigrants from North Africa (Bondì 1982: 114-16; 1990: 462-63), most of the evidence is best explained by the effects of Punicization on those Nuragic folk who lived within the widening zone of Carthaginian influence. To be sure, Carthage's 'politica del territorio' was aimed at 'garantirsi l'approvvigionamento di ingenti quantità di grano' (Bondì 1988b: 194), but securing these provisions from the natives required no more than some (armed?) units of tribute collectors, not a wholesale displacement of the indigenous population. There is an enormous difference between 'frequentazione punica' (Bondì 1988b: 184) and 'frequentazione nell'epoca punic'.[2]

---

1 Isserlin (1983: 159 n. 6) cites Barreca's observations (*Monte Sirai* 3: 168) that scattered homesteads or small villages rather than *latifundia* seem to have been the prevailing form of settlement; contrast, however, the remarks of Meloni (1984: 13-26).

2 It is not surprising that there are some relics of the Punic language in Sardinian (Paulis 1990); what is striking is that there are so few of them, in marked

Evidence for Punic Settlements

Evidence for Carthaginian settlement in the Sardinian countryside comes primarily from cemeteries, burials and habitation sites with Punic material. The presence of Punic shrines or votive figurines may also be indicative of Carthaginian settlement, as are sites named Magomadas (i.e. 'new settlement'). The following sections examine this evidence to see if it is sufficient to demonstrate Punic settlement, or is only the result of Carthaginian trade and influence on the indigenous Sardinians.

1. Cemeteries

Several cemeteries in the territory of Sanluri (Fig. 1, no. 26) (Bidd'e Cresia, Brunku sa Battalla and Mar'e Idda: Paderi *et al.* 1982) may have been exclusively Punic, for the modes of burial and all of the grave goods and other materials that have been reported are Punic of the 4th and 3rd centuries BC; Mar'e Idda is the cemetery for the village of Sa Ruina-Stuppoi so they should count as one site, not two. Elsewhere in the same territory, Punic burial customs and grave goods are found at sites with long antecedant occupations or at least with some Nuragic material, perhaps belonging to a Nuragic village without a central nuraghe (Brunk'e Mesu, Corti Beccia, Corti 'e Sa Perda-Su Pauli, Padru Jossu-Fundabi Andria Peis-Giliadiri, Sa Mitzixedda, Uraxi Mannu), suggesting either that the indigenous population had adopted new mortuary practices or that they had been replaced by colonists: we simply cannot tell for certain, but the former seems more likely. Other 'Punic' sites in the territory of Sanluri may also have been indigenous villages (Bia Collanas, Brunku Predi Poddi, Pauli Murtas, Sa Ruina-Stuppoi, S. Caterina); when Barreca (in Paderi *et al.* 1982: 45) says that the habitations 'si sovrappongono a centri di età nuragica', it is not clear if he means all the habitations, or only some of them, or even if they are new settlements at old sites rather than merely continuous occupation of those sites.

Punic cemeteries in the countryside could be interpreted either way; unfortunately, in too many cases we simply have too little information to make a well-informed judgment and we have far too few actual graves. Attic pottery or Punic amphoras, for example, are not limited to mortuary sites. And even when we have a burial,

---

contrast with the number of Latin words in Welsh (cf. Jackson 1953). For the relative paucity and limited geographical extent of Punic personal names and toponyms, see Rowland (1973), and Zucca (1990).

Rowland: Carthaginians in the Countryside? 477

Fig. 4 Other sites with Punic material.

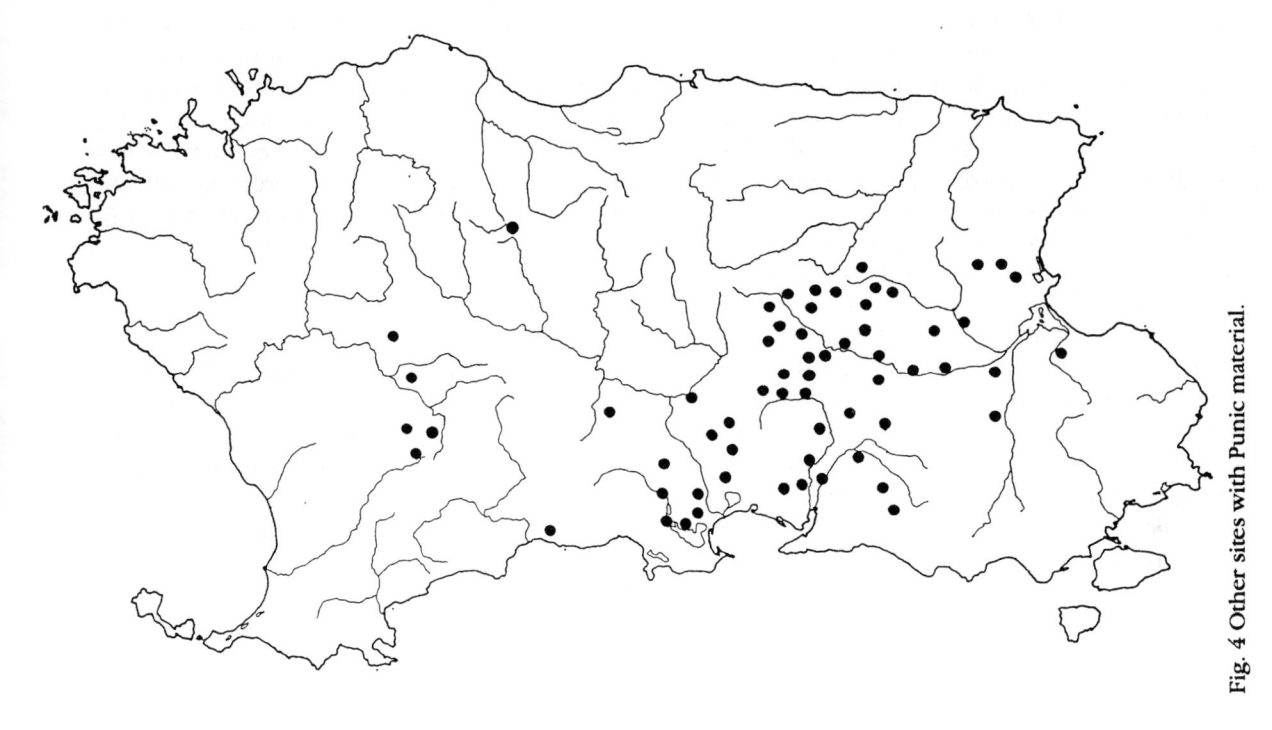

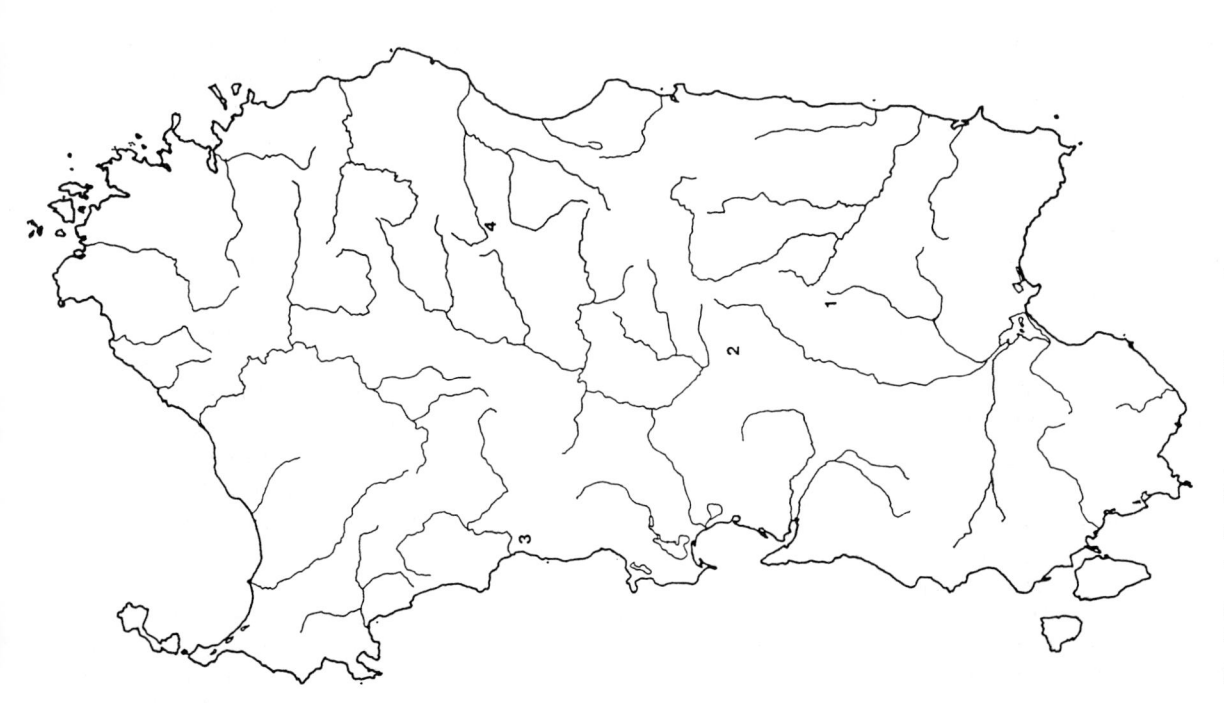

Fig. 3 Sites in Sardinia named Magomadas.

as for example the one at Bau Marcusa-Barumini (Lilliu 1938–39: 148), it is not clear in every case that a burial is Punic rather than indigenous with Punic material.

Burials with Punic material (Fig. 1)
1. There is a Punic settlement with necropolis dated to the late Punic period at S'Ungroni-Arborea, about 4 km from Othoca-S. Giusta (Barreca 1986: 280; Zucca 1987: 116); nearby, there was a Bonnannaro period cemetery (Lilliu 1988: 276).

2. A small cemetery at Assemini (Barreca 1986: 280) is to be expected in the suburbs of Cagliari.

3. A single trench grave with 3rd or 2nd century pottery at Bau Marcusa-Barumini has been converted by Barreca (1986: 281) into 'tombe'; the burial was located 'a breve tratto dal Nghe Bruncu e Topis' and should be considered the final resting place of an indigenous worthy.

4. Punic burials of several types were discovered in the last century at Decimomannu, that is, in the outskirts of Cagliari (Barreca 1986: 294).

5. At S'Occidroxiu-Furtei there is a Punic necropolis of the 4th and 3rd centuries (Barreca 1986: 298).

6. The late Punic incineration and inhumation burials at S. Lucia-Gesico may be related to the new settlement, Magomadas, not far distant (Zucca 1984: 185-95; Barreca 1986: 299).

7. There are two Punic necropoleis in the territory of Guasila, at the localities Padru Estas and Riu Sa Mela (Barreca 1986: 300).

8. A schematic representation of a human face on local basalt is said to come from 'l'ambito di una necropoli' at S. Paolo-Milis (Barreca 1986: 303).

9. The necropolis of S'Arxidda-Mogoro, probably belonging to the settlement at Cracaxia, included a stele with the symbol of Tanit (Zucca 1987: 134; Barreca 1986: 303), and the settlement at the nuraghe Nuraghes is called Punic with a necropolis (Zucca 1987: 135): the sites are about 2 km from one another.

10. A rich Punic necropolis was reported in the early part of this century at Montiju de Conzau-Mores, with mostly late Punic incineration burials, and there was also a single cremation burial at S. Maria de Sole-Mores (Barreca 1986: 303).

11. At Genna Sintas (Siutas on the IGM map)-Nuraminis, where there is a nuraghe, Punico-Roman tombs have been reported (Barreca 1986: 305).

12. Barreca (1986: 308), citing Zucca's research, records a Punic settlement and its necropolis at S. Luxiori-Pabillonis; Zucca (1987: 135) himself, however, calls it a simply a Punic settlement.

13. Chamber tombs were claimed by Spano for unspecified locales in the territory of Pimentel, but these have been identified as reutilized *domus de janas*, about 6 km south of Guasila at S'Aqua Salida-Pimentel, and are dated to the late Punic period (Barreca 1986: 309; E. Usai 1984: 113-18).

14. A single burial at Serra Santu Martinu-Riola Sardo yielded archaic material (Tore and Stiglitz 1987: 167).

15. Reutilized *domus de janas* at Coroneddas-Sagama included Punic coins among the grave goods (Barreca 1986: 312), but it is not clear if there were other objects which would more securely indicate a Punic burial rather than simply one or more burials during the Punic period.

16. There are chamber tombs at Guardia Bue and Guardia Nadali-S. Anna Aresi, a zone thickly settled during the Punic period (Barreca 1986: 314).

17. There are several cemeteries at S. Sperate (Barreca 1986: 313).

18. Punic period burials have been identified at Bingia Arena and Punta Zinnigas, both near S. Vero Milis (Tore and Stiglitz 1987: 167), and there is an archaic necropolis adjacent to the nuraghe S'Urachi (Tore and Stiglitz 1987: 167). Other archaic material found in the area of Nuraghe Melas-S. Vero Milis might have belonged to a cemetery (Tore and Stiglitz 1987: 167), while there is a cremation cemetery near the sea at Sa Marigosa (Tore and Stiglitz 1987: 168).

19. A Punic settlement with necropolis has been claimed for Roia Sa Lattia-Sardara (Zucca 1987: 142).

20. The Punic burials at S. Marina-Serramanna (Barreca 1986: 319) seem actually to have been found at S. Maria di Monserrato (V. Angius, in Casalis 1849: 933), a Nuragic site that may have served as an emporion during the Punic period.

21. At Bruncu 'e Mola-Terralba, there was a 'vast' necropolis with inhumation burials in cists (Barreca 1986: 322; Zucca 1987: 142).

22. At S. Giovanni-Uras was a Punic settlement with necropolis (Barreca 1986: 322; Zucca 1987: 145).

23. There are cist burials at Nureci-Villamar about 1 km from town across the Fl. Mannu and chamber tombs within the confines of the town of Villamar (Barreca 1986: 323).

24. A single tomb at Villaperuccio contained an inscribed gold ring and a possibly Punic bronze figurine (Barreca 1986: 324).

25. The necropolis with a cist and a 'cappuccina' burial at Su Carroppu de Sa Femina-Villaspeciosa about 1 km northwest of town will probably prove to be extensive (Barreca 1986: 324).

2. Shrines and Votive Figurines (Fig. 2)

Shrines to Demeter-Kore, later Ceres, are also likely to be indications of a Punic settlement, and in publishing a partial inventory of sites several years ago I noted that 'the distribution...confirms that her worship is essentially a continuity of Punic cult' (Rowland 1988: 793). Nonetheless, we cannot exclude the possibility that, at some places—especially those where there are no other Punic or Punic-period objects or evidence for Punic period settlement—the native Sardinians adopted a ritual which seemed efficacious for a prosperous harvest. These shrines often continued into the Roman period. Some of the sites where Ceres figurines were found are tombs rather than shrines; nonetheless, the presence of cult figures in a mortuary context eloquently attests to the existence of the cult in the locality. Similarly, a single example at a nuraghe (Madau 1988: 253, 259 no. 25) is evidence for the cult, but not for a shrine, which should require more than one figurine. In publishing the Ceres material from the Nuraghe Genna Maria-Villanovaforru, Caterina Lilliu also provides a more up-to-date list; one can certainly agree with her that 'il loro numero è in realtà certamente maggiore, dati i frequenti indizi in tal senso offerti da conoscitori delle campagne sarde' (C. Lilliu 1988: 109-27).[3] The number of sites and amount of material will both certainly increase over time, but it would seem unlikely that the basic distribution pattern will radically change. Although both Caterina Lilliu and Giovanni Lilliu include material from Barreca's inventory of sites (which is also not complete), they do not include all of the sites, perhaps because it is not always clear from his laconic notices whether or not they continued into the Roman period. Barreca's inventory includes the following sites which do not appear on the 'Roman' lists: Genn 'e Gruxi (Genneruxi in Zucca 1987: 118)-Arbus; Nuraghe Cadreas-Narbolia; Madonna del Rimedio-Oristano; Donigala Fenugheda; S. Cristina Sacred Well-Paulilatino; Is Arisca Burdas-Riola Sardo; Bidda Maiore and Nuraghe S'Uraki-S. Vero Milis.[4]

There are other votives or shrines in various places which most likely reflect Punic inspiration if not actual settlement, including seven in the territory of Cabras on the outskirts of Tharros (Barreca 1986: 287) and others in the suburbs of Cagliari (Barreca 1986: 289, 302-303). In the locality Zairi-Gonnosfanadiga was a collection of late Punic votives (Barreca 1986: 300; Zucca 1987: 123). The votives at Nurri are, as Barreca admits, somewhat problematic; they may be related in style to those from Bithia and Neapolis and might find some confirmation in the recent discovery of a 'Sardo-Punic' funerary stele (Barreca 1986: 305). The opening of the new museum at Padria now gives us a better appreciation of the Punic and Punico-Roman votives found at Is Canalis or S. Giuseppe-Padria; there was certainly an extensive Punic settlement there along with a fortification. The existence of a hand of Sabazius and a head of Mithras among the Roman period material allows one to think that the place served then as a market center, perhaps continuing one of its major Punic-period functions (Rowland 1981: 96-98; Galli *et al.* 1989; Galli *et al.* 1988; Angiolillo 1987). At Santu Iaci-S. Nicolo Gerrei was a late Punic temple of Eshmun-Aesculapius (Barreca 1986: 315). Ex-votos at Linna Pertunta-S. Andrea Frius, Mitza Salamu-Dolianova (Salvi 1990; 1989: 13-16), Sciopadroxiu-Vallermosa (Barreca 1986: 322), and Sa Mitza-Villaurbana (Barreca 1986: 325) show clear Punic inspiration, but do not prove Punic settlement.

3. Sites Called Magomadas (Fig. 3)

Sites called Magomadas in the territories of Gesico (1) and Nureci (2) and in Planargia (3) are unquestionably Punic foundations (Zucca 1984: n. 25), as is also the Macumádas in the territory of Nuoro (4), about which nothing else is known; this last may have been a small emporion (Paulis 1990: 607-608). Cultural influence from these places surely radiated into the surrounding countryside, for example to the Nuraghe Noddule-Nuoro.

4. Sites with Punic Material (Fig. 4)

At other locales, the existence of (usually) a small amount of Punic or related (e.g., Attic) material—in many instances no more than one or a few amphora fragments—at a native site suggests Punic influence on or trade with the natives

---

3 In his extensive, but likewise not exhaustive, discussion of Nuragic survivals in the Roman period, Giovanni Lilliu (1990: 431-37) provides a brief summary of some of the sites and their material, particularly Su Nuraxi-Barumini, where, however, *timiateria* are lacking, surely leading to the conclusion that it was not, in fact, a Ceres shrine ('gli oggetti del deposito sono stati supposti lo scarico della stipe votiva d'un sacello rustico, dedicato forse a Demeter e Core': p. 433).

4 This gives us then the following communes: Aidomaggiore, Alghero, Antas, Arbus, Barumini, Cabras, Cagliari, Cornus, Donigala Fenugheda, Florinas, Fordongianus, Ittiri, Macomer, Muros, Narbolia, Narcao, Nora, Nurra, Olbia, Olmedo, Oristano, Ossi, Padria, Paulilatino, Ploaghe, Porto Torres, Pula, Riola Sardo, Romana, S. Vero Milis, Sassari, Sorso, Tharros, Villanovaforru.

rather than an 'insediamento punico' (cf. Rowland 1982). Even where there is no nuraghe, it may be that the Punic material, found usually by survey archaeology, attests to the existence of a settlement of natives rather than of immigrants. Even the extensive amount of Punic material found at Nuraghe S. Antine-Torralba (Madau 1988: 243-71) has thus far failed to lead to the suggestion that there was a Punic settlement there. The many sites reported to have some Punic material are listed in Table 1.

Conclusion

This survey has shown that, although there is an enormous number of places where Punic material has been found, the number of places which can be demonstrated to have been Punic is relatively restricted. Roman coins or pottery at sites in Scandinavia or southeast Asia are insufficient by themselves to justify calling those sites Roman; in the same way, a few Punic objects in a grave or village are inadequate grounds for claiming that the burial or community in question was Punic rather than native. This is not to suggest that there were not in fact some Punic colonists and explorers who settled in and farmed portions of the Sardinian countryside; what I do suggest, however, is that we need to be more sophisticated in distinguishing between a Punic (or, for that matter, a Roman) site and a native site with material of the Punic (or Roman) period. This distinction is particularly important when the archaeological evidence is used in support of models of Carthaginian (or Roman) settlement and relations with the indigenous Sardinian population.

Acknowledgment

Figures 1-4 were drawn by Robert H. Tykot.

Table 1

Punic material at Nuragic sites (by territory)

Territory	Site(s)	Reference(s)
Abbasanta	Nuragic village Losa, giants' tomb Chirighiddu	Barreca 1986: 279
Albagiara	Nuraghi Bingias, S. Luxiori (Lussorio)	Barreca 1986: 279; Rowland and Dyson in press
Allai	Tomb with a single Punic coin and a carnelian	Barreca 1986: 280
Arbus	S. Antine, giants' tomb Bruncu Espis	Barreca 1986: 280
Baressa	Codinas	Barreca 1986: 281
Bauladu	Nuraghe S. Lorenzo	Barreca 1986: 281
	Nuraghe Santa Barbara	Rowland and Dyson in press
Bonnannaro	Nuraghe Malis	Barreca 1986: 281
Capoterra	Lu Loi	Barreca 1986: 289
Escolca		Barreca 1986: 291
Furtei	Punic 'centers' at Domu 'e Is Abis, S. Uria, S. Brai	Barreca 1986: 298
Genoni	'Settlements' at Cixius, Pran'e Preidi, Domu'e Biriu, S. Perdu	Barreca 1986: 299
Genuri	Nuraghe S. Marco	Barreca 1986: 299
Gergei	One 'settlement'	Barreca 1986: 299
Gesturi	A total of eleven 'settlements'	Barreca 1986: 299; Lilliu 1985
Gonnosno	Nuraghe Tramatza	Rowland and Dyson in press
Guasila	'Settlements' at Sa Tellera, Funtan'e Baccas, Bruncu Is Araus	Barreca 1986: 300
Guspini	Eight 'settlements' (some noted as [?])	Zucca 1987: 123-31
Isili	Villa Corlotta, Nuraghe Longu, Casteddu Pigas	Barreca 1986: 301
Ittireddu	M. Zuighe	Barreca 1986: 301
Las Plassas	Nuraghi S'Uraxi, Etzi	Barreca 1986: 302
Mandas	Bangius, Ardiddi	Barreca 1986: 302
Marrubiu	Nuragic village Ruinas	Barreca 1986: 303; Zucca 1987: 133
Modolo	Unspecified locale	Barreca 1986: 303
Mogoro	Arratzu, Bonorzuli, Is Nuraxis	Barreca 1986: 303; Zucca 1987: 133-35
Monastir	Piscina S'Aqua	Barreca 1986: 303
Nuoro	Nuraghe Noddule	Barreca 1986: 305

Table 1 (continued)

Punic material at Nuragic sites (by territory)

Territory	Site(s)	Reference(s)
Nurachi	Is Ollaius	Barreca 1986: 305
Nuragus	S. Millanu, S. Elia	Barreca 1986: 305
Nurallao	Bidda Beccia, Pranu Fas	Barreca 1986: 305
Nuraminis	M. Leonaxi	Barreca 1986: 305
Nuraxinieddu	Nuraghe Su Cungiau de Funtana	Barreca 1986: 307
Oristano	Nuraghe Baumendola	Rowland and Dyson in press
Ozieri	Two sites	Barreca 1986: 308
Pabillonis	Sa Fronta; Nuraghi Fenu, S. Luxiori	Barreca 1986: 308; Zucca 1987: 135
Palmas Arborea	Perda Bogada	Barreca 1986: 308
Riola Sardo	S'Urachedda Is Ariscas (also Prei Madau) Nuraghe Civas	Barreca 1986: 312
Samassi	Is Argiddas	Barreca 1986: 312
S. Gavino Monreale	Seven 'settlements'	Barreca 1986: 312; Zucca 1987: 136-38
Sanluri	Eleven 'settlements'	Barreca 1986: 312; cf. above
S. Nicolo d'Arcidano	'Settlement' at S. Pantaleo	Zucca 1987: 138
Sardara	Barumeli, Canale Linu, Lixius, Cuccuru Linu, Axiurridu, Arigau, S. Caterina; nuraghi Arrubiu, Perra, Ortu Còmidu	Barreca 1986: 318; Zucca 1987: 138-42
S. Vero Milis	S. Perdu, Sa Tonnara	Barreca 1986: 318
Selargius	S. Rosa	Barreca 1986: 319
Selegas	Nuraghe Nuritzi	Barreca 1986: 319
Senorbì	Turrugas, Gotti de Siliqua, Palas de Binu, Corti Auda	Barreca 1986: 319
Settimo S. Pietro	S. Marca, Bia Crabonaxa	Barreca 1986: 320
Siamanna	Nuraghe Canureu	Rowland and Dyson in press
Siliqua	Santu Iasccu, S. Margherita, Medau Casteddu, S. Pietro, Puaddas, Campanasissa	Barreca 1986: 320
Sini	Nuraghe Su Senzu	Rowland and Dyson in press
Siurgus	Donigala	Barreca 1986: 321
Soleminis	Sa Cavana	Barreca 1986: 321
Suelli	Nuraghe Piscu	Barreca 1986: 321
Thiesi	Nuraghe Fronte Mola	Barreca 1986: 321
Terralba	Coddu 'e Is Abois, Coddu Is Damas, Ena S'Anguidda, Pauli Margiani, Pauli Nicasu, S. Chiara	Barreca 1986: 322; Zucca 1987: 142-44
Tuili	Nuridda	Barreca 1986: 322
Turri	Nuraghe Sissiri	Barreca 1986: 322
Uras	Nuraghe Su Nuracci	Barreca 1986: 322; Zucca 1987: 145
Villanovafranca	Nuraghe Tuppedili	Barreca 1986: 323
Villaspeciosa	Is Crus, Is Olieddus, Lacana de Biddazzone	Barreca 1986: 324
Villaurbana	Nuraghi Melas, Canale Scolu; Sparau Crabia	Barreca 1986: 325; Rowland and Dyson in press

References

Angiolillo, S.
    1987   Il teatro-tempio di Via Malta a Cagliari: una proposta di lettura. *Annali della Facoltà di Lettere e Filosofia dell'Università degli Studi di Perugia* 24 ns 10 (1986–87) 1 (Studi Classici): 57-81.

Barreca, F.
    1984   Venti anni di scavi a Monte Sirai. *Nuovo Bullettino Archeologico Sardo* 1: 143-57.
    1986   *La Civiltà Fenicio-punica in Sardegna.* Sardegna Archeologica: Studi e Monumenti 3. Sassari: Carlo Delfino.

Bondì, S.F.
    1982   Intervento. *Archivio Storico Sardo* 33: 114-16.
    1988a   Problemi della precolonizzazione fenicia nel mediterraneo centro-occidentale. In E. Acquaro et al. (eds.), *Monumenti Precoloniali nel Mediterraneo Antico,* 242-55. Roma.
    1988b   La dominazione cartaginese. In *Storia dei Sardi e della Sardegna.* I. *Dalle origini alla fine dell'età bizantina,* 173-203. Milano.
    1990   La cultura punica nella Sardegna romana: Un fenomeno di sopravvivenza? *L'Africa Romana* 7: 457-64.

Casalis, G. (ed.)
    1849   *Dizionario Geografico-Storic-Statistico, Ecc.* Vol. 19. Torino.

Cross, F.M.
　1986　Phoenicians in the West: The early epigraphic evidence. In M.S. Balmuth (ed.), *Studies in Sardinian Archaeology, Volume II: Sardinia in the Mediterranean*, 117-30. Ann Arbor: University of Michigan Press.

Frau, M., & R. Monticolo
　1990　*Sulcis: Guida archeologica*. Firenze.

Galli, F., F. Lo Schiavo, V. Santoni & G. Tore (eds.)
　1989　*Padria—Museo Civico Archeologico*. Padria.

Galli, F., V. Santoni & G. Tore
　1988　Padria. In G. Lilliu (a cura di), *L'Antiquarium Arborense e i Civici Musei Archeologici della Sardegna*, 117-28. Sassari.

Isserlin, B.S.J.
　1983　Phoenician and Punic rural settlement: Some archaeological considerations. In *Atti del I Congresso Internazionale di Studi Fenici e Punici, Roma, 5-10 novembre 1979*, 97-106. Roma.

Jackson, K.
　1953　*Language and History in Early Britain*. Edinburgh.

Ledda, R.
　1985　*Censimento Archeologico nel Territorio del Comune di Muravera*. Quartu S. Elena: Sardalito.
　1989　*Censimento Archeologico nel Territorio del Comune di Villaputzu*. Cagliari: Edizioni Castello.

Lilliu, C.
　1988　Un culto di età punico-romana al nuraghe Genna Maria di Villanovaforru. *Quaderni della Soprintendenza Archeologica delle Provincie di Cagliari e Oristano* 5: 109-27.

Lilliu, C. (a cura di)
　1985　*Territorio di Gesturi—Censimento archaeologico*. Cagliari: Amministrazione Provinciale di Cagliari, Assessorato alla Cultura.

Lilliu, G.
　1938–39　Scopertà di una tomba in località Baumarcusa ed altre tracce archeologiche in Barumini. *Studi Sardi* 3: 147-55.
　1988　*La Civiltà dei Sardi dal Paleolitico all'Età dei Nuraghi*. 3rd edition. Torino: Nuova ERI.
　1990　Sopravvivenze nuragiche in età romana. *L'Africa Romana* 7: 415-46.

Madau, M.
　1988　Nuraghe S. Antine di Torralba. Materiali-fittili di età fenicio-punica. In A. Moravetti (ed.), *Il Nuraghe S. Antine nel Logudoro-Meilogu*, 243-71. Sassari: Carlo Delfino.

Marras, L.A. (ed.)
　1982　*Villasimius: Prime testimonianze archeologiche nel territorio*. Cagliari.

Meloni, P.
　1984　Cartaginesi e Romani in Sardegna: Latifondo e monocoltura. *Sardegna: L'uomo e la pianura*, 13-26. Reprinted 1990. Sassari.

Moscati, S.
　1983　Un secondo quadriennio di scavi a Monte Sirai. *Rivista di Studi Fenici* 11: 183-91.

Moscati, S. (ed.)
　1988　*The Phoenicians*. Milan.

Paderi, C., O. Putzolu & G. Ugas (eds.)
　1982　*Ricerche Archeologiche nel Territorio di Sanluri*. Cagliari.

Paulis, G.
　1990　Sopravivenze della lingua punica in Sardegna. *L'Africa Romana* 7: 599-639. Sassari: Gallizzi.

Rowland, R.J., Jr
　1973　Onomastic remarks on Roman Sardinia. *Names* 21: 82-102.
　1981　*I Ritrovamenti Romani in Sardegna*. Studia Archeologica 28. Roma: L'Erma di Bretschneider.
　1982　Beyond the frontier in Punic Sardinia. *American Journal of Ancient History* 7(1): 20-39.
　1988　The archaeology of Roman Sardinia: A selected typological inventory. In W. Haase and H. Temporini (eds.), *Aufstieg und Niedergang der Romischen Welt: Geschichte und Kultur Roms im Spiegel der Neueren Forschung*, 740-875. Berlin: de Gruyter.

Rowland, R.J., Jr, & S.L. Dyson
　in press　Survey archaeology around *Colonia Iulia Augusta Uselis*. *Quaderni della Soprintendenza Archeologica per le Provincie di Cagliari e Oristano*.

Salvi, D.
　1989　*Testimonianze Archeologiche*. Dolianova.
　1990　La continuità del culto. La stipe votiva di S. Andrea Frius. *L'Africa Romana* 7: 465-74.

Salvi, D., & L. Usai (eds.)
　1990　*Museo Sa Domu Nosta*. Cagliari.

Tore, G., & A. Stiglitz
　1987　Gli insediamenti fenicio-punici nel Sinis settentrionale e nelle zone contermini (ricerche archaeologiche 1979–1987). *Quaderni della Soprintendenza Archeologica per le Provincie di Cagliari e Oristano* 4: 161-74.

Tronchetti, C.
　1986　Intervento. *La Sardegna nel Mediterraneo tra il secondo e il primo millennio a.C. Atti del I Convegno di studi 'Un millennio di relazioni fra la Sardegna e i Paesi del Mediterraneo', Selargius-Cagliari 29-30 novembre 1985*, 104-105. Cagliari.
　1988　*I Sardi: Traffici, relazioni, ideologie nella Sardegna arcaica*. Milano: Longanesi.

Ugas, G.
　1981　Furtei-Santu Brai e Santa Uria. *Archeologia Sarda* 1981: 83.

Ugas, G., & R. Zucca
　1984　*Il Commercio Arcaico in Sardegna: Importazioni etrusche e greche (620-480 a.C.)*. Cagliari: Angelo Viali.

Usai, E.
　1984　Pimentel (Cagliari) Loc. S'Acqua Salida. In E. Anati (ed.), *I Sardi: La Sardegna dal paleolitico all'età romana*, 113-18. Cagliari: Jaca Book.

Zucca, R.
　1984　Macomades in Sardinia. *L'Africa Romana* 1: 185-95.
　1987　*Neapolis e il Suo Territorio*. Oristano.
　1989　La necropoli fenicia di S. Giovanni di Sinis. *Riti Funerari e di Olocausto nella Sardegna Fenicia e Punic*, 90-98. Quaderni della Soprintendenza Archeologica per le Provincie di Cagliari e Oristano 6 (Supplemento).
　1990　Le persistenze preromane nei poleonimi e negli antroponimi della Sardinia. *L'Africa Romana* 7: 665-67.

Riassunto

Gli studi dell'Autore cercano di determinare la vera estensione della colonizzazione punica in Sardegna tra l'VIII secolo a.C. e il periodo romano. Sembra infatti che sia esistita una vasta colonizzazione punica nell'isola, e la domanda è la seguente: anche se presso numerosi siti sardi sono stati ritrovati reperti punici, possiamo affermare, basandoci sul ritrovamento di questi reperti, che ognuno di questi siti è in realtà punico?

Durante l'VIII ed il VII secolo a.C. i Fenici hanno cominciato a sviluppare insediamenti permanenti in Sardegna, ma le date di fondazione di molti siti sono ancora sconosciute. A partire dalla metà del VII secolo, insediamenti costieri fenici hanno iniziato ad espandere il loro controllo territoriale. Sulcis ha stabilito forti a Monte Sirai (Carbonia) e a Pani Loriga (Santadi). La fondazione di altri siti ha poi portato al sorgere di un sistema di fontiera che attorniava l'Iglesiente proteggendo gli insediamenti situati all'interno.

Reperti fenici ritrovati presso San Sperate mostrano l'esistenza di una antica colonia proveniente da Cagliari. Ritrovamenti presso Cuccuru Nuraxi (Settimo S. Pietro) e presso M. Olladiri (Monastir) indicano l'esistenza di insediamenti di immigranti o l'esistenza di contatti commerciali tra le popolazioni locali e le culture immigranti. Presso Monastir e le aree adiacenti sono stati ritrovati reperti archeologici che includono vasellame importato e materiale carbonizzato, che potrebbe indicare l'esistenza di un cimitero con cremazioni o l'incenerimento di strutture locali. Gli insediamenti presso San Sperate e Monastir potrebbero rappresentare il primo stadio di espansione punica, attraverso una rotta chiave, verso l'interno della Sardegna. Questa sarebbe poi stata seguita nel VI secolo dalla fondazione fenicia di forti presso S. Brai (Furtei) nella zona settentrionale e nel V secolo presso Monte Luna (Senorbì) nella zona nordorientale.

Subito dopo la metà del VI secolo, Cartagine ha mandato una spedizione punitiva in Sardegna che però è stata sconfitta, il risultato di questo avvenimento è stato l'installazione della dinastia Magonida a Cartagine. Il continuo imperialismo militare ad opera di Cartagine durante il V secolo ha provocato il sorgere di un sistema di frontiera nell'hinterland sardo ca. 450 a.C., compreso Monte Luna. Il controllo territoriale è stato successivamente rafforzato da un'alleanza con gli etruschi. Dopo il primo trattato con Roma, Cartagine ha acquistato il controllo di tutto il commercio romano in Libia ed in Sardegna.

L'influenza punica sulla cultura locale sarda sembra essersi intensificata in questo periodo. È possibile che i forti punici all'interno della Sardegna siano serviti come punti di commercio tra i sardi-cartaginesi e i diversi gruppi di abitanti locali. A partire dal V secolo in poi, l'esistenza di merci importate presso siti locali è aumentata drasticamente; esistono però sufficienti testimonianze per sostenere che esisteva una vasta colonizzazione cartaginese nella campagna sarda? Anche se è avvenuta una colonizzazione che include ulteriori immigranti provenienti dal Nord Africa, l'Autore afferma che l'esistenza delle numerose testimonianze puniche è dovuta più che altro ad una punicizzazione delle popolazioni sarde che vivevano nella sfera di influenza cartaginese.

Testimonianze di insediamenti cartaginesi nella campagna sarda provengano principalmente da cimiteri, da sepolture e da siti con materiale punico. La presenza di santuari e di figurine votive puniche e di siti chiamati Magomadas sembrano indicare l'esistenza di insediamenti cartaginesi. L'Autore elenca tutti gli insediamenti sardi che presentano testimonianze appartenenti alle categorie sopra menzionate e include una descrizione delle testimonianze correntemente esistenti presso ciascun sito.

L'Autore sostiene che anche se esiste un considerevole numero di luoghi in cui è stato trovato materiale punico, il numero di testimonianze certamente punico è relativamente ristretto. Alcuni oggetti punici ritrovati nel tempio di un villaggio rappresentano una base insufficiente per affermare che un determinato sito è punico anziché sardo. L'Autore conclude affermando che è necessario che in futuro archeologi prestino maggior attenzione nel distinguere gli insediamenti punici da quelli sardi e quindi nel mostrare gli effetti dell'influenza punica in Sardegna.

Roman Sardinia and Roman Britain

Stephen L. Dyson

On first reflection, Roman Britain and Roman Sardinia would seem to be odd places for comparison. Sardinia was one of the first external provinces conquered by the Romans; Britain was one of the last. Sardinia is located centrally in the Mediterranean and had been visited by other Mediterranean groups long before the Roman conquest; Britain lies on the fringe of Europe and had operated mainly in the sphere of northern Iron Age Europe. Even in the scholarly archaeological traditions, there are differences. The archaeology of Roman Britain is one of the most developed spheres of Roman provincial studies. In Sardinia, archaeologists have tended to concentrate on the Nuragic period with much less attention paid to the archaeology of the Roman occupation.

Comparison of the Roman acculturation of a Mediterranean province and one located in temperate Europe is additionally important because of their chronological differences. Roman frontier and provincial administration has to be viewed as a cumulative experience, and it should be revealing to juxtapose territories acquired during the beginning and end of that process. There are also important lessons to be learned from the highly developed tradition of Roman archaeology in Britain for an area where provincial archaeology has lagged behind.

Roman Sardinia and Roman Britain, however, are not all contrasts. First, they are both large islands, and the study of island environments and island archaeology has attracted increasing interest among archaeologists (Kirch 1987). Secondly, both are islands with two distinct geographical, and to a certain degree cultural, zones. Each has a small lowland region, located near its coast and closely linked to a neighboring high culture area: Iron Age continental Europe in the case of Britain, and the classical Mediterranean in that of Sardinia. In both instances, this lowland area was bordered by a much more extensive highland zone with different ecology and cultural traditions. In each province, the lowland area was conquered and Romanized relatively quickly, while control of the upland areas was much slower and more difficult. Finally, in both areas, certain key questions relating to Romanization and the continuity of native cultural traditions are being rethought as new archaeological evidence is collected and synthesized, and new historical models tested. Rural Romanization, a key area of archaeological rethinking for both provinces, is the central focus of this paper.

The geographical setting that shaped pre-Roman and Roman developments in the two islands can be described briefly. In both instances, one fertile, lowland corner played an exceptionally important role in the island's historical development. For Sardinia, this is the Campidano, a rift valley which stretches northwest from Cagliari toward Oristano. Cultivating its heavy soils was probably not easy for the farmers of the Nuragic period, and the area appears to have been of limited importance during that era. The Phoenician settlements such as Nora and Tharros were established in well protected coastal areas more to the southwest and west, and depended on trade more than agriculture. The Carthaginians and the Romans, however, fully exploited the Campidano and closely linked it to the larger world of the Mediterranean. For both it was the bread basket of Sardinia. The standard image of the socioeconomic organization of the area under both conquerors is a world of *latifundia*: great estates worked by slave labor (Meloni 1975: 39, 187). At least in the Roman period, these lowland *latifundia* were supposed to have centered around great houses or villas (Rowland 1977: 462). A possible example of the remains from such a great estate house is the mosaic room found at Villaspeciosa (Tronchetti 1984: 257-58).

The Campidano is ringed by the high country that covers most of the island. The transition zone between the Campidano and the rugged interior is one of the regions with the highest concentration of nuraghi (Guido 1964). Traditionally, the inhabitants of these nuraghi had been linked in a precarious symbiosis with the lowland areas. The Nuragic warriors are often depicted as warrior-pastoralists who needed seasonal access to the lowlands for the transhumance of their herds, and were partly tied into the trading networks of the Mediterranean invaders, but who were also raiders preying on the lowland settlements (Lilliu 1963).

One of the main tasks of the Roman administration was the elimination of these unstable elements, at least in the border zones. The ancient sources mention wars of extermination (Dyson 1985: 246-59). Most historians have acknowledged that the interior mountain strongholds of Sardinia were at best brought under tenuous Roman control, even under the Empire. The history of the imperial garrisons in Sardinia is not that well known. However, it is certain that some units remained on the island well into the Imperial Period (Meloni 1975: 299-317).

While tensions certainly divided highland and lowland, there were also symbiotic relationships. Especially important was the pastoral connection. Some Sardinian scholars may have exaggerated the contrast between the fierce pastoralists of the uplands, and underestimated the degree to which the Nuragic folk of the uplands grew grain as well as raised sheep. Nevertheless, the importance of sheep-raising in the hill country was considerable. This led not only to trade, but also to a transhumant economy, which linked highland and lowland together.

These elements of lowland versus highland, of farming versus pastoralism, and concerns for limited rural security in the upland areas shaped the development of Roman Britain as well. Much of the best agricultural land is concentrated in the southeast of the island. There the later Iron Age cultures reached their highest state of development with social hierarchy and considerable concentration of political power. Contacts with continental Europe, both in the later Iron Age and in the post-Caesarean conquest periods, were intense and the economy complex. In contrast, the uplands were poorer and more isolated. They also were more dependent on pastoralism, although, as has been the case with Sardinia, this lowland–highland, pastoral–agricultural contrast may have been exaggerated (Millett 1990: 10-17).

These uplands also represented a rather insecure, inner frontier zone, not dissimilar to conditions in the interior of Sardinia. It is true that the military frontier rested for much of the period on Hadrian's Wall at the Tyne–Solway isthmus. Detailed archaeological research, however, combining aerial photography and test excavation, has shown that many more forts behind the wall remained occupied longer than scholars had previously suspected (Simpson 1964). As in the mountains of Sardinia, the unrest of Roman Britain was bound to affect the development of the countryside.

Lowland–highland contrasts, agricultural–pastoral interaction and a reasonably widespread rural insecurity all create parallels between Britain and Sardinia. The role of these factors has to be evaluated against the background of what might be called an ideal Roman rural landscape, a world that did exist in extensive areas of Italy, and which has been projected by both Romans and archaeologists on much of the landscape of western Europe (Percival 1976; Mielsch 1987). This rustic world was based on the twin elements of the small town and the villa-farmstead.

By the end of the 1st century BC, the Romans had made the small town the basis of rural life in much of Italy (Potter 1987: 63-93). The towns combined administrative, market, social and cultural functions. They had temples, fora, town halls, markets, theaters and amphitheaters.

Clustering around the towns were the villas. While the villa has sometimes been viewed in splendid isolation, the Romans clearly linked them to the towns. Roman agricultural theoreticians might aim for total autonomy, but the reality was that individual farmers, large and small, depended on the towns for a range of goods and services, and made them the center of their local social and political life (Potter 1987: 94-124).

It is a truism that the Romans imposed this Italian rural system on much of the rest of the western Empire, disrupting and largely destroying previous native rural societies, if not the native population itself. Britain, as one of the last western provinces conquered, provides a good case study of this fully developed mode of rural Romanization. At first glance, it would seem to confirm nicely to that pattern. There is considerable evidence for the destruction of those pre-Roman centers of power: the hill forts. A complex network of towns developed, ranging from major economic and administrative centers like London, Colchester and York, to small market towns and posting centers (Wacher 1975; Burnham and Wacher 1990). Roman Britain appears to have rapidly developed a flourishing curial class, which emerged, in part, from the Iron Age elite.

The villas of Roman Britain have long been studied, and investigations ranging from antiquarian research to aerial photography have documented large numbers of them, ranging in size from stately homes to the relatively small and modest corridor villas (Todd 1978; Branigan and Miles 1989). The high quality Roman provincial archaeology that is to be found in Britain has allowed the development of individual villas to be reconstructed. This was probably an autocthonous process. Modern scholars agree that external colonization into Roman Britain was very limited. Moreover, a number of Roman villas in Britain overlie native farmsteads, suggesting continuity of land ownership (Millett 1990: 94). The spread of town and villa culture has been seen as a good example of the process of turning the natives into Romans, a process which is succinctly, but vividly, described by Tacitus in chapter 21 of his *Agricola* (Millett 1990: 94-98).

However, a shift in research emphasis and the use of new models of cultural development have shown that this picture of a rural Roman Britain is more complex than first thought and that the extent of change produced in the Roman countryside by the Roman conquest was more limited than initially conceived (Cleary 1990: 30-33, 100; Millett 1990: 117-23). Since the villas are such visible features in the archaeological landscape, they have tended to be observed and recorded more readily than the more humble non-Romanized farmsteads and agricultural settlements. Increased emphasis on a total landscape archaeology has produced more evidence for the continuity of pre-Roman forms. The villa is now seen as a relatively limited part of the Romano-British landscape. This is true even in the southeast of England, where the villa culture seems to have flourished most (Millett 1990: 111-23).

In the consideration of rural development in Britain, the highland-lowland contrast again comes into play. The villas of Roman Britain were heavily concentrated in the lowland zones (Millett 1990: 118 fig. 48). This is not merely a result of the pattern of archaeological investigation; techniques of aerial photography have revealed features like military camps in abundance in the Midlands. Villa culture followed Iron Age patterns of development and anticipated to a certain degree the differences in prosperity that divide the north and south of Britain today. Towns were established in the midland area, but they do not seem to have been as numerous or to have had the complex hierarchy that characterized the towns farther south. Clearly, much of the rural population continued to live in conditions not dissimilar to those that existed before the Roman conquest. A major difference was that more groups in society had access to Roman goods than before. Similarly, the rural world of Roman Britain was still largely a native one. This restoration of the native peasantry to its proper place is not limited to Roman Britain, as the research of the late Edith Wightman and others have demonstrated (Wightman 1975).

This process of revising our perspective on the complexity of Roman rural development in Britain has interesting implications for Sardinia. The parallels between the two island provinces have already been noted. If Britain represented one of the last instances of the imposition of the rural Italian model on an external province, Sardinia can be seen as one of the first. Given the early Roman conquest of the island, Sardinia should have paralleled Italian developments in many ways.

While Romanists working in Sardinia have acknowledged the geographical and cultural peculiarities of the island and the limits of interior Romanization, they have generally described the changes in the rural landscape outside the mountains in terms that characterized Romanization elsewhere in the west. The natives were either exterminated or forced to abandon their highland Nuragic settlements, at least in those areas relatively accessible to the Campidano. What grew up in its place was the standard Roman rural culture of villas and towns. More than in Britain, this was seen as not only a replacement culture, but in many places a replacement population.

The problem with these generalizations about rural Sardinia is that they have remained in effect without major efforts to test their hypotheses with detailed archaeological investigations. For any Roman rural landscape that should mean a combination of intensive surveys and the systematic study of the towns which would have formed the focus of a villa society. Just such an aim has been behind the Maryland–Wesleyan (now Loyola–SUNY-Buffalo) research project in western Sardinia (Dyson and Rowland 1988; 1989). The general zone of investigation lay at the juncture of the lowland Campidano with access to well-established ports like Tharros and Othoca (modern Santa Giusta) and the mountainous interior. The foci of this research were the *territoria* of two Roman towns of some importance: *Forum Traiani* (modern Fordongianus) and *Uselis* (modern Usellus). *Forum Traiani* had a long history as a religious, administrative, commercial, and military center (Zucca 1986a). By the 6th century AD it had become the headquarters for the Roman military administration of Sardinia. The full Roman name of Uselis was *Colonia Iulia Augusta Uselis*. Colonial status was rare in Sardinia. This status for Uselis suggests that either it had received a settlement of Roman colonists, possibly veterans in the Julio-Claudian period, or had achieved a high level of Romanization by the Imperial period (Zucca 1986b).

Romanized towns generally required a highly Romanized *territorium*. The lowlands around both *Forum Traiani* and *Uselis* would seem well suited for the development of a Romanized villa-farmstead agricultural system. An intensive survey should produce some evidence for this rural Romanization. Models for such developments can be found in the Ager Cosanus and the Ager Veientanus in Etruria (Dyson 1978; Potter 1979).

One other feature that made these two areas attractive for research in rural Romanization was that both had a high density of Nuragic sites. These dominated the Sardinian highlands that were in close proximity to the lowland areas the Romans would have had to control; the Romans should not have tolerated this situation. The natives would either have been exterminated or at least forced to abandon the highland Nuragic sites and settle in the lowland areas. They would have been reduced to some form of serf or tenant status. In either case, the Nuragic sites would have been abandoned during the Roman period.

A full scale review of the results of the survey up to this point have been published elsewhere (Dyson and Rowland 1988; 1989) and only the general conclusions need be reviewed here. The first surprising result was that the bulk of the Nuragic sites continued to be occupied in the Roman period. In the Fordongianus survey area, 83 of the 121 sites investigated produced evidence for Roman occupation: 20 showed evidence for Republican occupation, 17 for Early Imperial occupation and 55 for Mid-Late Imperial occupation. In the Usellus area, as of the end of the summer of 1990, 103 of the sites investigated had Roman material: 23 showed Republican, 20 Early Imperial and 43 Mid-Late Imperial. For control purposes, it is interesting to compare these figures for sites occupied in the Roman period with the numbers and percentages for sites with Nuragic material or obsidian. For *Forum Traiani* and *Uselis*, the figures are respectively 96 and 99. Given the fact that a number of sites yielded no datable occupation evidence and that presumably all Nuragic sites at one time had Nuragic pottery, the comparative percentages for Roman occupation are impressive indeed. Clearly here, as in upland Britain, there is strong evidence not only for the material, but also the cultural continuity of native life.

A strong native presence does not preclude the development of an alternative Romanized landscape, as the latest evidence from Britain shows. To test this possibility, we devoted the summer of 1989 to an intensive lowland survey around *Forum Traiani*. Our methodology, based on the experience of the Ager Cosanus and information from other Roman-oriented Italian surveys, was skewed toward the maximum recovery of Roman sites. However, five weeks of intensive investigation only produced one to three probable Roman farmstead sites of the type so common in the Ager Cosanus. The investigations around *Uselis* have not yet been as systematic, but again little or no evidence for Roman villas and farmsteads has appeared. Clearly these 'highly Romanized' areas of Sardinia, located at the border of the two major geographical zones, preserved much of the rural landscape from the Nuragic past. In this respect Roman Sardinia seemed to have paralleled the Roman Britain of the Midlands more than the Britain of the southeast.

Our research has not yet included systematic investigation of the two town areas that formed the central places for the rural *territoria* that we have surveyed. However, we have done some research at the urban sites and can draw upon the collected evidence of long term antiquarian and archaeological studies in the two areas. Fordongianus still has impressive remains of Roman public baths connected with the thermal springs, apparently dating to the second century AD (Zucca 1986a: 18-29). The Roman city is supposed to have had an amphitheater, but the remains to be seen today are exiguous at best (Zucca 1986a: 17-18). The town was surrounded by a wall in the early Byzantine period (Procopius, *De Aed* 6.7.12-13; Zucca 1986a: 4-6 fig. 1), traces of which were reported in the 19th century; little or nothing of these fortifications can be seen today. The modern town of Fordongianus has developed over much of the Roman site, and although occasional reports of mosaics and other residential remains have been made, they are not numerous (Zucca 1986a: 29). The modern buildings show almost no trace of reused Roman material, and there is little evidence for portable finds. Altogether, this scattered, limited evidence hardly suggests a major Roman settlement.

Even less impressive is the evidence for urban life at *Uselis*. Documentary information on town life includes not only the designation of the town as a *colonia*, but also an important inscription dating to AD 158 found in Cagliari that mentions municipal officials from *Uselis* (Meloni 1975: 225-27). However, the supposed site of the town center (modern Santa Reparata) shows only a scatter of pottery with no building remains. The lack of architectural remains is striking for a place that was very possibly a Julio-Claudian colony and maintained an active civic life into the 2nd century AD.

This paltry evidence raises the larger question of the nature of Roman town life in the rest of Sardinia, outside of the coastal zone and the older Punic and Roman centers like Cagliari, Nora, Tharros and Porto Torres (Meloni 1975: 201-64). The best collection of basic information on these interior towns comes from the road itineraries. These mention a number of places which were, among other things, presumably *mansiones* or posting stations on the Roman road system. For the purposes of this short paper I have selected 14 of these towns and considered the Roman remains found there, using mainly the data on finds collected by Rowland (1981).

This summary picture of urban remains in interior Sardinia is hardly impressive. The lack of evidence for public amenities is especially striking. Of course, much of the information is derived from the antiquaries of the 19th century; the descriptions are often vague and the observations cannot be tested with modern-day observations. However, evidence for structures like theaters, amphitheaters and forum-related civic structures are almost non-existent. The most common remains seem to relate to baths (here see also Rowland 1981: fig. 3 with the find-spots of bath structures located on a map of Sardinia). This prevalence of bath structures may well be related to the Nuragic tradition of spring cults as much as to any Roman civic improvements.

Again, when comparisons are made with Roman Britain, the best parallels are not with the major urban centers like Verulamium, Lincoln and York, but with the *mansiones* and the small agricultural centers. These settlements do not usually produce evidence for major public buildings, but they do show a level of structural Romanization that is hard to match among the centers of interior Sardinia (Burnham and Wacher 1990). It is true that the British settlements have been the object of more systematic investigation than those in Sardinia; however, the late start of Romanization in interior Britain, as compared with Sardinia, must be kept in mind. The evidence suggests that outside of the coastal areas, town life in Roman Sardinia was much less developed than even the interior of Roman Britain.

A response to this can be that a world of great estates did not need such local town life. The Romano-Sardinian magnates could have made their villas largely self-sufficient and travelled to the larger centers like Caralis and Tharros for their urban needs.

However, the question arises concerning the extent of the evidence for villa development anywhere in Sardinia. Here again distinctions in Roman villas have to be kept in mind. There were coastal villas or *villae maritimae* which have a strong resort function, even if combined with productive activity. The Tuscan villa of Sette Finestre and the Sardinian villa at Porto Conte belong in that category (Carandini and Settis 1979; Manconi and Pianu 1981: 146). Then there were suburban villas (*villae suburbanae*) located near major towns, which allowed the owner to combine urban activity, *otium* and productive agricultural activity. A number of these probably existed around Cagliari (Rowland 1984a: 297). Finally, there were the true *villae rusticae* located away from the coast and away from major centers. Those have been the major focus for discussion in consideration of the Roman villa as a productive unit.

Again, a paper of this length does not allow for a systematic review of all the evidence related to the Roman villa in Sardinia. Rowland (1981; 1984a) provides the best collection of find reports relating to villas in Sardinia. Most striking is the fact that relatively few sites can be identified definitively as Roman villas. In many instances the described remains may have belonged to a villa, a military settlement, a *vicus*, or other types of Roman settlements. In Rowland (1984a), I counted mention of some 23 definite villa sites and 21 possible or probable villa sites. These are scattered throughout the island with several located around major cities. Only around Olbia are the remains sufficiently concentrated to suggest a Romanized landscape, in this instance mainly made up of *villa maritimae* and *villa suburbanae* (Panedda 1953; Rowland 1981: 78-88). While villas certainly did exist, the current evidence strongly suggests that by the standards of Roman Britain, this was a countryside with a low villa density. In Roman Britain, about 500 villas have been dated to the 4th century alone (Millett 1990: 186). This general picture, derived from scattered reports of villa sites, seems consistent with the detailed information collected in the Fordongianus and Usellus surveys.

This should not be seen as so surprising, if again we take Sardinia out of the world of the highly developed Mediterranean provinces and compare it to a region like Britain. Pre-Roman Sardinia was an area of very limited and very specialized urbanization (Tronchetti 1988). Phoenician *entrepots* became Punic and then Roman trading centers. Further, there was not much of a tradition of pre-Roman, proto-urbanization to build upon. Only the most complex of the Nuragic centers like Barumini could even come close to the social and economic complexity of the major British *oppida*. In Britain, the Roman towns developed in relation to this Iron Age oppidum tradition (Millett 1990: 55, 74). In areas where Iron Age central authority was lacking, such as the Midlands, neither the town structure nor the villa structure fared well. In Sardinia, outside of the Punic coastal zone, traditions of central authority were weak and the basis of urban development lacking. There was lacking not only the centers that might become cities, but also a native elite that could develop into the Roman curial class.

Nor is the lack of villas in Sardinia that surprising. While much is said about Sardinian *latifundia*, we know from the classical sources that grain, the characteristic agricultural product of Sardinia, was most effectively produced on smaller farmsteads (Rowland 1984b). The effectiveness of Nuragic agriculture has clearly been underestimated. It was based on the experienced exploitation of a particular, often harsh environment. As Millett (1990: 56-57) has noted for Roman Britain, the Romans would not have wanted to disrupt a system that clearly worked and yielded the surplus they needed.

Events in the early history of the Roman occupation of Sardinia may have led to a further reduction of that combined Punic-native landowner class which seems to have developed in the Carthaginian period and would have formed the basis of the Roman *latifundia* system. The early history of the conquest of the island was punctuated by organized resistance and revolt which seem to have centered in just that group. Most famous was the revolt of the Punicized Sardinian, Hampsicora (Dyson 1975: 1 4-46). The suppression of these revolts certainly reduced the number and power of these major landowners. Moreover, it made the Romans appreciate the virtues of an acephalous native society in Sardinia. The true Nuragic groups had their restless, rebellious side, which could be a nuisance. They required constant low-level diplomacy and occasional military actions. However, this sharply divided native society would not form the basis of major revolts. Respect for native institutions led to relative peace and moderately regular payment of taxes. Markets at the various centers drew the natives into the Roman consumer culture.

Millett (1990: 1-2), in his very fine book on Roman Britain, draws on a concept of the late art historian Otto Brendal and makes the point that Roman culture has to be seen as a dialogue between a complex Mediterranean high culture and a variety of valid native systems. The secret of its success was compromise and not total domination. The tendency of Romanists based in the Mediterranean is to think in terms of the changes that Rome wrought. The juxtaposition of Roman Britain and Roman Sardinia results in a different, more complex view. Seeing the way that the views of Roman-British archaeologists have shifted away from Romanization toward native cultural continuity, one can rethink the meaning of Roman domination in the whole Empire. Turning the Roman-British experience back to Sardinia, a province that was geographically in the Mediterranean, but in terms of many environmental and cultural qualities was very different from the Mediterranean, leads to a very different view of the complexities of the Roman Empire.

Acknowledgment

Archaeologists in North America owe a great debt to Miriam Balmuth for impressing on us both the complexity and fascination of the cultural history of Sardinia, and the many archaeological and historical challenges that work on the island. This essay is a small token of thanks for the role she has played in stimulating my own interest in things Sardinian.

Table 1

Fourteen Roman towns in Sardinia

Roman town (modern name)	Roman remains
Ferraria (S. Gregorio)	Pottery and Imperial coins with vague references to a 'città romana'.
Aquae Neapolitanae (near Sardara)	Remains of Roman baths, tombs and remains of at least one Roman building in area.
Biora (Serri)	Nuragic sanctuary of S. Vittorio, which had extensive Roman remains. Other traces of walls, tiles, tombs and pottery in the area.
Valentia (Nuragus)	Large number of tombs, new pavement laid in Roman period around sacred well.
Augustis (Austis)	Remains of antique construction, remains of a cistern with pipes leading out to a public fountain, pottery, tiles.
Sorabile (Fonni)	Remains of Roman construction, perhaps *mansiones*. Under church, tessellated Roman pavement, lead pipes, remains of a bath and other construction remains.
Ad Medias (Abbasanta)	Bust of woman, coins, figurines, traces of Roman road, burials with coins and pottery. Some reuse of Nuragic and earlier tombs. Remains of a press.
Macopsisa (Macomer)	Burials and tombstones, Roman bridge. Remains of walls and bricks with stamps. Roman pavements.
Molaria (Mulargia)	Ruins and foundations of Roman structures, burial urns, pottery, coins.
Gurulis Vetus (Padria)	Extensive Roman remains including capitals, mosaic, cisterns, painted plaster, column fragments. Remains of thermal bath. Abundant scatters of coins and pottery.
Aquae Lesitanae (Benetutti)	Roman remains near the thermal center of S. Saturnino.
Lugidio (N. Signora di Castro)	Burials, coins and mosaics. Remains of Roman fort. Bridge, burials, walls, remains of aqueduct, lead pipes.
Gemellae (Tempio)	Cistern, tombs, Roman walls.
Erucium (Bortigiadas)	Roman remains, possibly tombs.

References

Branigan, K., & D. Miles (eds.)
    1989   *The Economies of the Romano-British Villas.* Sheffield: Department of Archaeology and Prehistory.

Burnham, B.C., & J. Wacher
    1990   *The Small Towns of Roman Britain.* Berkeley: University of California Press.

Carandini, A., & S. Settis
    1979   *Schiavi e Padroni nell'Etruria Romana.* Bari: De Donato.

Dyson, S.L.
    1975   Native revolt patterns in the Roman Empire. In H. Temporini and W. Haase (eds.), *Aufstieg und Niedergang der Romischen Welt,* II, 138-75. Berlin: de Gruyter.
    1978   Settlement patterns in the Ager Cosanus: The Wesleyan University Survey, 1974-1976. *Journal of Field Archaeology* 5: 251-68.
    1985   *The Creation of the Roman Frontier.* Princeton: Princeton University Press.

Dyson, S.L., & R.J. Rowland, Jr
    1988   Survey archaeology in the territory of Bauladu. Preliminary notice. *Quaderni della Soprintendenza Archeologica per le Provincie di Cagliari e Oristano* 5: 129-39.
    1989   The University of Maryland, Wesleyan survey in Sardinia-1988. *Quaderni della Soprintendenza Archeologica per le Provincie di Cagliari e Oristano* 6: 157-85.

Esmonde Cleary, A.S.
    1990   *The Ending of Roman Britain.* Maryland: Barnes & Noble Savage.

Guido, M.
    1964   *Sardinia.* New York: Frederick A. Praeger.

Kirch, P.V. (ed.)
    1986   *Island Societies: Archaeological approaches to evolution and transformation.* New York: Cambridge University Press.

Manconi, D., & G. Pianu
    1981   *Sardegna.* Bari: Laterza.

Meloni, P.
    1975   *La Sardegna Romana.* Sassari: Chiarella.

Mielsch, H.
    1987   *Die Romische Villa.* Munich: Beck.

Percival, J.
    1976   *The Roman Villa.* Berkeley: University of California Press.

Potter, T.
    1979   *The Changing Landscape of South Etruria.* New York: St Martin's Press.
    1987   *Roman Italy.* Berkeley: University of California Press.

Rowland, R.J., Jr
    1981   *I Ritrovamenti Romani in Sardegna.* Roma: 'L'Erma' di Bretschneider.
    1984a   The countryside of Roman Sardinia. In M.S. Balmuth and R.J. Rowland, Jr. (eds.), *Studies in Sardinian Archaeology,* 285-300. Ann Arbor: University of Michigan Press.

1984b	The case of the missing Sardinian grain. *The Ancient World* 10: 45-48.
1990	The production of grain in the Roman period. *Mediterranean Historical Review* 5: 14-20.

Simpson, G.
1964 *Britons and the Roman Army*. London: The Gregg Press Limited.

Todd, M. (ed.)
1978 *Studies in the Romano-British Villa*. Leicester: University of Leicester Press.

Tronchetti, C.
1984 The cities of Roman Sardinia. In M.S. Balmuth and R.J. Rowland, Jr (eds.), *Studies in Sardinian Archaeology*, 237-83. Ann Arbor: University of Michigan Press.
1988 *I Sardi. Traffici, relazione, ideologie nella Sardegna arcaica*. Milano: Longanesi.

Wacher, J.
1975 *The Towns of Roman Britain*. London.

Wightman, E.
1975 The pattern of rural settlement in Roman Gaul. In H. Temporini and W. Haase (eds.), *Aufstieg und Niedergang der Romischen Welt*, II.4, 584-657. Berlin: de Gruyter.

Zucca, R.
1986a *Fordongianus*. Sassari: Carlo Delfino editore.
1986b Colonia Iulia Augusta Uselis. *Studi Sardi* 26: 303-45.

Riassunto

Anche se esistono delle ovvie differenze tra la Sardegna Romana e la Britannia Romana, un paragone tra le due può essere utile, sia a scopo archeologico che a scopo storico. Entrambe le isole presentano un'area pianeggiante e un'area montagnosa, ed in entrambi i casi l'area pianeggiante è stata conquistata, e romanizzata, in poco tempo. Per entrambe le isole si stanno riesaminando ipotesi riguardanti la romanizzazione dei territori e la continuazione delle tradizioni locali, basandosi su nuovi ritrovamenti archeologici e su modelli storici. Il tema principale dell'Autore è la romanizzazione rurale, che è considerata un'importante area di revisione archeologica per la Sardegna e la Britannia.

In Britannia come in Sardegna la pianura è stata importante per lo sviluppo storico dell'isola. La regione sarda del Campidano è stata una regione agricola per i Cartaginesi ed i Romani. L'immagine standard dell'organizzazione socio-economica romana di quest'area è il latifundia—una estesa tenuta lavorata da schiavi. Sembra che i Romani abbiano cercato di controllare i pastori nuragici che vivevano nella regione montagnosa intorno al Campidano, così come hanno cercato di controllare le tribù nordiche della Britannia. L'Autore afferma, comunque, che la storia delle guarnigioni imperiali in Sardegna è ancora incompleta. Tensioni hanno diviso la regione pianeggiante da quella montagnosa, ma allo stesso tempo relazioni simbiotiche sono esistite tra i due territori e sono state causate dalla transumanza dei pastori e dalla produzione di grano dei contadini. Questa produzione ha messo in contatto la Sardegna con il resto dell'area Mediterranea in quanto la Sardegna era un'esportatrice di grano nell'età romana. Gli stessi contrasti tra la regione pianeggiante e quella montagnosa, la stessa relazione agricolo-pastorale, ed i legami con il resto del mondo—Europa continentale in questo caso—sono esistiti nella Britania romana.

L'oppidum romano, base della vita rurale italiana, è stato imposto da Roma su una vasta zona dell'Europa occidentale. Gli oppida avevano funzioni amministrative, economiche e culturali. Ville sono poi state erette intorno agli oppida e erano da questo dipendenti per quanto riguarda le merci, i servizi, le opportunità sociali e politiche. Le ville romane in Britannia sono state studiate a lungo e gli studiosi hanno considerato il tipo di vita condotto nella villa come un buon esempio in cui le popolazioni locali sono state trasformate in popolazioni romane. Ma ulteriori ricerche nella Britannia romana hanno visto questo fenomeno come una continuazione della cultura locale, non come un'interruzione.

Come nella Britannia romana, anche nella Sardegna romana, le nostre conoscenze socio-economiche stanno subendo delle revisioni. Una tradizionale interpretazione della Sardegna romanizzata descrive lo sterminio della popolazione locale e l'abbandono forzato degli insediamenti nuragici dell'area montagnosa presso il Campidano. Tutto ciò sarebbe stato rimpiazzato dalla cultura romana dalle ville e dagli oppida, provocando non solo una sostituzione della cultura, ma anche una sostituzione della popolazione. Il progetto di ricerca Maryland–Wesleyan (ora Loyola–SUNY-Buffalo) condotto nella Sardegna occidentale ha cercato di riesaminare queste ipotesi, concentrando le sue ricerche sui territoria di Forum Traiani (odierna Fordongianus) e Uselis (odierna Usellus). Secondo il modello tradizionale, i siti nuragici sarebbero stati abbandonati durante il periodo romano, ma l'indagine mostra che i siti nuragici in questi territori erano occupati nonostante la presenza romana; ciò indica una continuità culturale della vita locale e una preservazione del modello di insediamento nuragico. È possibile che questo sia accaduto nel resto della Sardegna? L'Autore analizza 14 mansiones romane nell'hinterland sardo. Le rovine semplici e non complesse delle strutture civiche, indicano che in queste località non è esistita una vera vita cittadina romana. Questo fa pensare che l'hinterland sardo fosse costituito da tenute romane autosufficienti - villae rusticae. L'Autore sostiene che nella campagna sarda esistevano poche ville; certamente poche se ci basiamo sugli standards della Britannia romana. La mancanza di ville non è affatto sorprendente. Il grano, prodotto più efficacemente dalle piccole fattorie nuragiche, era un elemento economico molto importante. I romani non hanno certamente voluto interferire con un sistema che funzionava e che produceva il surplus richiesto per l'esportazione. Nella Sardegna romana quindi non assistiano ad una dominazione, ma ad un dialogo tra una complessa cultura mediterranea e una complessa cultura locale. Questa revisione ci aiuta a riesaminare il significato della dominazione romana durante l'Impero.

Sardinian Amphora Studies: Past and Future

Elizabeth Lyding Will

Miriam Balmuth's research and excavation in Sardinia have contributed materially to the renewal of interest in Sardinian antiquities throughout the scholarly world. She has also devoted great energy and attention to stimulating and fostering research on Sardinia by scholars from a wide variety of archaeological and historical disciplines. The result, as this Festschrift in her honor so clearly proves, has been a flowering of studies that have thrown light on Sardinian antiquity from many perspectives.

As far as Roman amphoras are concerned, the study undertaken at Miriam Balmuth's request of the small assemblage of amphora fragments from her excavation of the nuraghe at Ortu Còmidu led later, again at her suggestion, to a survey in 1983 of the amphoras stored in the major museums and collections on the island (Will 1986). I had never before made a systematic survey of the amphora material in an entire area; that survey could not have been accomplished without her energetic help. Time restrictions meant that permissions, transportation, and the process of locating, identifying, studying and photographing each piece had to be accomplished on a strict schedule. The results both of the study of the pieces from Ortu Còmidu and of the amphora survey added important information to our knowledge of the Roman period in Sardinia. On the basis of chronological evidence provided by the series of Roman amphoras found in the excavations of the Athenian Agora, amphora imports into Ortu Còmidu covering a period of about 500 years were identified. The survey helped to document a similar story for the island as a whole.

Miriam Balmuth's excavation at Ortu Còmidu was done with meticulous care. One need cite only the fact that small, unstamped amphora fragments, objects not treasured by most excavators, were treated with the same deference accorded other finds (Balmuth 1986: 377-78 figs. 30: 5, 35, 37-38; Will 1986: 214-15). Though few in number, those fragments provide a broad outline of the nuraghe's history during the Roman period, a type of history that is at present not available for many other Sardinian sites. Both stamped and unstamped amphora fragments have in recent years been published in Sardinian journals by scholars such as Acquaro, Boninu, Lo Schiavo, Moravetti, Righini Cantelli, Rodero Riaza, Sotgiu and others; but at the time of the 1983 survey the material available for study in the major museums and collections consisted chiefly of whole amphoras and, occasionally, very large fragments. A few smaller fragments from the Spargi wreck were on display in the Nino Lamboglia Museum of Naval Archaeology in La Maddalena and occasional fragments were seen elsewhere. But the small group of Ortu Còmidu pieces stored in the National Archaeological Museum in Cagliari provided the only complete amphora record of any of the sites and collections studied. For the most part, the amphora material examined during the survey consisted of whole or slightly damaged jars. Many of them came from the sea, where amphoras are regularly found in an undamaged state. Finds of unbroken jars on land are rarer, and those identified in the survey were probably for the most part from tombs. For every whole jar excavated on land, dozens of amphoras are found in fragments. At the time of the survey in Sardinia, such fragments were apparently stored or consigned to excavation dump heaps. While the whole jars provided very useful information, the fragments could have given a much more complete record. The material available for study in 1983 provided a valuable outline of Sardinian economic history during the Roman period, but study of fragmentary finds would have helped to flesh out that outline and to document the history in more detail. In that connection, it is encouraging to note that recent digging on the island seems to be practicing 'total retrieval' and recording all amphora finds.

Earlier Sardinian archaeologists were not alone in overlooking amphora fragments. Until total retrieval became accepted archaeological practice, amphora fragments found at sites throughout the Roman world were saved from excavation dumps or other forms of anonymity only if they bore stamped trademarks, or graffiti, or painted inscriptions. A wealth of precious information about economic history was thereby lost. We can hardly blame the excavators; money and storage space were limited. It seemed logical to keep and study only those objects of evident value or about which one knew something. Roman amphoras had never been thoroughly studied, and the fragments looked so nondescript that excavators threw them aside as coarse ware or, worse, locally made coarse ware. The implication of both phrases seemed to be that what was coarse, unless it bore some kind of inscription, would never throw light on antiquity. I remember as if it were yesterday a conversation I had 40 years ago with a young excavator at a site in the eastern Mediterranean. I was looking over his finds for the day and exclaimed in amazement that an amphora handle in the group came from a jar manufactured in southern Spain in the early Empire and was seldom found in the Aegean area. He hardly heard my words. The piece was unmarked and therefore of no interest. It was, I later learned, consigned to a dump. But the practice of total retrieval brought about a change in attitude. During the 1950s and especially the 1960s, it slowly became accepted procedure. At the town of Cosa and Port of Cosa (Tuscany) excavations, for example, every amphora fragment, no matter how unpromising its appearance, was kept. When I later studied and classified the pieces, a most valuable picture of the economic history of the town and its port emerged (the publication of the amphoras from the town of Cosa is forthcoming; on the port amphoras, see Will 1987a). The amphoras shipped from the port and the town have thrown new light on the Republican wine trade with the West and with the Celts in particular. The imports into the town of Cosa during the Empire can also be closely documented. What was saved from the excavation dump proved to be precious historical evidence.

Three other excavations in which the study of amphora fragments has led to important chronological and historical insights might be mentioned. At none of these sites has a complete amphora been found; the tale is told by fragments alone. Manching, a Celtic city on the Danube north of Ingolstadt in central Germany, can be dated by the close study of Roman wine amphora fragments from between c. 200 BC and the 80s or 70s BC (Will 1987b; 1990). These dates are in accord with those indicated for the founding and destruction of the site by other categories of objects discovered there. They do not agree, however, with the dates of c. 150–50 BC suggested for the amphora fragments in their original publication (Stöckli 1979). In my 1987 study of the Manching finds, I discussed the complexities of amphora dating and the numerous variations, as far as shape is concerned, that are possible within each category of jar. In that respect, a specialist has a distinct advantage over a nonspecialist. Stöckli did not distinguish among the various early types of amphoras represented at Manching, and he confused some of those types with a later category. Manching is an example, then, of the rich historical record that amphoras represent; but it also suggests the complications of fragment typology. I will return to that topic below in some remarks about the need for care in the analysis of fragments.

Another excavation in which fragmentary Roman amphoras have helped to clarify chronology is the palace of Diocletian at Split. Here, many pieces, chiefly of olive oil amphoras, were found from 1968 to 1974 in the American-Yugoslav Joint Excavations (Will 1989). Little was known about the history of the site before the building of the palace and after the death of Diocletian. The amphoras indicate that there was a certain amount of trading activity at the site before the building of the palace and as early as the 1st century BC. Most of the fragments, however, date to the 4th and 5th centuries AD, an indication that the site remained a center of importation after Diocletian's death in 313. Importation continued into the 6th and possibly the 7th centuries AD.

A third site where fragmentary amphoras, both Greek and Roman, are proving to be of considerable use chronologically is Arikamedu, on the southeast coast of India (Will 1991). Excavations are still in progress, but study of the fragments originally published by Sir Mortimer Wheeler and his Indian colleagues (Wheeler *et al.* 1946: 41-45) indicates that the earliest amphoras, Greek Koan jars, date from as early as the 2nd century BC. Only a few of the latest fragments now appear to be later than the end of the 1st century AD. Wheeler felt that the site dated to the first two centuries of the Empire, but he was writing at a time when very little work had been done on amphora chronology. He also failed to publish all the fragments he found at Arikamedu. Only pieces of wine jars were published, whereas study of his finds now stored in the museums of Pondicherry, Madras, and Delhi reveals several fragments of jars for Spanish and Istrian olive oil and Spanish garum. Once again, amphoras are helping us to see a more complicated picture of ancient economic history.

Amphoras have a useful story to tell. For the story to be accurate, the amphoras must be studied with great care. Measurement of heights, widths and diameters is essential for accurate typology. When only a fragment of a jar is preserved, it can easily be confused with fragments from jars similar in appearance or fabric. The several types of amphoras manufactured in the 2nd and 1st centuries BC in the Cosa area, for example, all made of the same clay, can only be distinguished by measuring diameters, in the case of rims, and width and thickness, in the case of handles. Also diagnostic for accurate typology are the estimated greatest diameters of belly fragments, demonstrating that all fragments must be carefully measured. The Romans were adept at producing by hand objects that were surprisingly uniform in size (even down to small parts of the jars). We know now the standard dimensions of the chief types of amphoras (see discussions in Will 1987a; 1987b, and elsewhere). There are, as I have mentioned, variations that must always be taken into account in the case of each category; but on the whole it is easy to assign fragments to type if the critical measurements are taken.

Total retrieval and close measurement of fragments bore fruit in the case of Ortu Còmidu. Only five Roman amphora fragments were found, but they showed that wine came to the area from central Italy in the latter part of the 3rd century BC. In the early 1st century BC, olive oil was imported from the Adriatic region. Spanish garum was used at the site in the Augustan period, and the importation of Spanish olive oil in the 1st century AD signalled the end of exportation of oil from Italy itself and the replacement of Italian products by provincial producers. A fragment of an African olive oil amphora of the 3rd century AD dates from the time when Africa was replacing Spain as the chief exporter of olive oil.

In general terms, the material studied in the 1983 amphora survey of the major collections on Sardinia paralleled the evidence at Ortu Còmidu. Wine and a little olive oil reached the island from Italy during the late Republic. With the advent of the Empire and the decline of Italian agricultural production, almost all importation of wine into Sardinia ceased. We must assume that domestic production of wine took its place. At the same time, there was a dramatic rise in the importation of olive oil into Sardinia, initially from Spain, which took over from the Italian exporters in the Adriatic area, and later from Africa, which in its turn took over from Spain. During the Empire garum also became a major import into Sardinia from Spain.

The amphora evidence from Sardinia helps confirm and complete the picture of Roman trade in the western Mediterranean in general. The island imported from Italy for as long as possible and then turned, at least for oil and garum, to the same export centers which served the Italian peninsula during the Empire. From this evidence we see that Sardinia was an integral part of the western Mediterranean economic community during the entire Roman period.

Amphoras can provide precious historical evidence about the Roman period in Sardinia. Miriam Balmuth recognized that fact and saw to it that a beginning was made toward filling a gap in our knowledge of the history of Roman trade in the western Mediterranean. Future excavation on the island can add much to that picture. In addition, a comprehensive study of the amphoras already excavated would also be of great value. The amphoras identified in the 1983 survey should be studied in detail and either published or, in some cases, republished. Collections of fragments should be identified, analyzed and published. In this way the role of Sardinia in the economic history of the western Mediterranean will be understood in far greater detail than is possible on the basis of our present evidence.

References

Balmuth, M.S.
1986   Sardara (Cagliari). Preliminary report of excavations 1975–1978 of the Nuraghe Ortu Còmidu. *Notizie degli Scavi di Antichità* 37(1983): 353-410.

Stöckli, W.E.
1979   *Die Grob- und Importkeramik von Manching.* In W. Kramer (ed.), *Die Ausgrabungen in Manching* 8. Wiesbaden: Franz Steiner Verlag.

Wheeler, R.E.M., A. Ghosh & K. Deva
1946   Arikamedu: An Indo-Roman trading-station on the East Coast of India. *Ancient India* 2: 17-124.

Will, E.L.
1986   Amphoras and trade in Roman Sardinia. In M.S. Balmuth (ed.), *Studies in Sardinian Archaeology, Volume II: Sardinia in the Mediterranean*, 210-28. Ann Arbor: University of Michigan Press.

1987a   The Roman amphoras. In A.M. McCann, J. Bourgeois, E.K. Gazda, J.P. Oleson and E.L. Will, *The Roman Port and Fishery of Cosa*, 170-220. Princeton: Princeton University Press.

1987b   The Roman amphoras from Manching: A reappraisal. *Bayerische Vorgeschichtsblätter* 52: 21-36.

1989   Roman amphoras. In S. McNally and I.V. Schrunk (eds.), *Diocletian's Palace*, VI, 58-113. Dubuque, IA: Kendall Hunt.

1990   Celtic importation of Roman wine in the second and first centuries BC. In R.R. Holloway (ed.), *Rome's Alpine Frontier*, 25-30. Providence: Brown University Art and Archaeology Publications.

1991   The Mediterranean shipping amphoras from Arikamedu. In V. Begley and R. De Puma (eds.), *Rome and India: The Ancient Sea Trade*. Madison: University of Wisconsin Press.

Riassunto

Secondo la professoressa Will, una nota esperta di anfore romane, è importante preservare e studiare i frammenti d'anfora recuperati durante gli scavi archeologici. Il ritrovamento fatto da Miriam Balmuth ad Ortu Còmidu è l'esempio di uno studio attento e paziente di frammenti d'anfora. Il ritrovamento sopra menzionato ha condotto nel 1983 ad un'indagine sulle anfore conservate nei musei sardi che ha aumentato la nostra conoscenza del periodo romano in Sardegna.

La collezione dei frammenti d'anfora di Ortu Còmidu, oggi conservata nel museo archeologico nazionale di Cagliari, è una delle poche collezioni complete di frammenti d'anfora sino ad ora ritrovate. Troppo spesso accade che i frammenti d'anfora ritrovati, vengono 'immagazzinati' e dimenticati o addirittura scartati. Dal momento che è raro ritrovare anfore intatte, scartare o ignorare frammenti d'anfora significa non considere evidenze inestimabili delle storia economica del Mediterraneo romano. Per questa ragione è assolutamente necessario che tutti i ritrovamenti fatti durante gli scavi archeologici vengano conservati.

Oltre ad Ortu Còmidu, ci sono stati altri tre studi effettuati presso tre siti, che hanno rivelato importanti scoperte sulla cronologia e la storia del mondo romano. Lo studio di frammenti ritrovati a Manching, una città celtica sul Danubio nella Germania centrale, ha rivelato una possibile revisione delle date di fondazione e distruzione di questo sito. Numerosi frammenti di anfore, nella maggior parte dei casi contenitori di olio d'oliva, sono stati ritrovati presso il palazzo di Diocleziano presso Spalato. Alcuni cocci risalgono addirittura al I secolo a.C., ma molti risalgono al IV e al V secolo d.C. Ciò sta ad indicare che in questo luogo esisteva un commercio prima che il palazzo fosse costruito, e che il sito è rimasto un centro d'importazione dopo la morte di Diocleziano nel 313 d.C.

Presso Arikamedu, nella costa sud-est dell'India, sono stati ritrovati e si stanno ritrovando frammenti d'anfora che completano i ritrovamenti precedenti fatti da Mortimer Wheeler, pubblicati nel 1946. Questi studi successivi stanno estendendo la cronologia del sito. C'è da aggiungere che una revisione di frammenti non pubblicati, conservati nei musei di Pondicherry, Madra e Delhi, ha rivelato l'esistenza di un'importazione di olio d'oliva dalla Spagna e dall'Istria, e un'importazione di vino da Roma e dalla Grecia.

La pubblicazione di ritrovamenti riguardanti anfore sarde, fatta da numerosi studiosi, ha aiutato a confermare e completare le ipotesi riguardanti il commercio esistente nel Mediterraneo occidentale. I frammenti ritrovati ad Ortu Còmidu mostrano che questa regione importava vino dall'Italia centrale durante il tardo III secolo d.C., olio d'oliva dalla zona adriatica durante il primo secolo a.C. e *garum* dalla Spagna durante il periodo Augusteo.

Il fatto che l'olio d'oliva venisse importato dalla Spagna durante il I secolo d.C. sta ad indicare la fine delle esportazioni italiane di questo prodotto e la sostituzione dell'olio italiano con quello proveniente dalle provincie. Il materiale studiato nell'indagine della collezione di anfore sarde del 1983 conferma questa ipotesi per tutta l'isola. L'Autrice conclude l'articolo sostenendo che è importante continuare gli studi su questo tipo di materiale (frammenti d'anfora), che è importante ripubblicare e rivedere materiale precedente e identificare le nuove collezioni di anfore.

List of Contributors

Enrico Acquaro
Consiglio Nazionale delle Ricerche
Istituto per la Civiltà Fenicia e Punica
Via Salaria Km 29,500, Montelibretti, C.P. 10
00016 Monterotondo Stazione, Roma, Italia

Maria Giulia Amadasi Guzzo
Università degli Studi di Roma "La Sapienza"
Dipartimento di Scienze Storiche Archeologiche
  e Antropologiche dell'Antichità
Via Palestro, 63
00185 Roma, Italia

Tamsey K. Andrews
Widener Library
Collection Development, Room 84
Harvard University
Cambridge, MA 02138

C. Atzeni
Università degli Studi di Cagliari
Dipartimento di Ingegneria Chimica e dei Materiali
Piazza d'Armi
09123 Cagliari, Italia

Piero Bartoloni
Via S. Satta, 36-38
09047 Selargius, Cagliari, Italia

Marshall Joseph Becker
West Chester University
Department of Anthropology and Sociology
West Chester, PA 19383

Paolo Belli
Consiglio Nazionale delle Ricerche
Istituto per gli Studi Micenei ed Egeo-Anatolici
Via Giano della Bella, 18
00162 Roma, Italia

Paolo Bernardini
Soprintendenza Archeologica per le
  Provincie di Cagliari ed Oristano
Via Angioy, 15
09124 Cagliari, Italia

Renée Bonzani
University of Pittsburgh
Department of Anthropology
Pittsburgh, PA 15260

Joseph Cesari
Direction Régionale des Affaires Culturelles
Circonscription des Antiquités Préhistoriques de
  Corse
19, Cours Napoléon—B.P. 301
20176 Ajaccio Cedex, Corse, France

John F. Cherry
Faculty of Classics
The University of Cambridge
Sidgwick Avenue
Cambridge CB3 9DA, UK

Jean M. Davison
Department of Classics
481 Main Street
University of Vermont
Burlington, VT 05405-0218

Lucia Manca Demurtas
Sebastiano Demurtas
Via Carlo Meloni, 21
09170 Oristano, Sardegna, Italia

Stephen Dyson
Department of Classics
State University of New York-Buffalo
Buffalo, NY 14260

Maria Ausilia Fadda
Soprintendenza Archeologica per le
  Provincie di Sassari e Nuoro
Ufficio Operative di Nuoro
Via Ballero 30
08100 Nuoro, Sardegna, Italia

Maria Luisa Ferrarese Ceruti
Università degli Studi di Cagliari
Scuola di Specializzazione in Studi Sardi
Piazza Arsenale, 8—Cittadella dei Musei
09124 Cagliari, Italia

Ornella Fonzo
2 Via E. Lai
09128 Cagliari, Sardegna, Italia

Barbro Santillo Frizell
Klassiska Institutionen
Sölvegatan 2
22362 Lund, Sweden

Noël H. Gale
Zofia Stos-Gale
University of Oxford
Department of Nuclear Physics
Isotrace Laboratory, Keble Road
Oxford OX1 3RH, UK

Lenore J. Gallin
Institute of Archaeology
University of California, Los Angeles
Los Angeles, CA 90024

Franco Germanà
Viale Mameli, 32
07100 Sassari, Italia

Claudio Giardino
Via F. Dall'Ongaro, 95
00152 Roma, Italia

Jean Guilaine
Centre National de la Recherche Scientifique
Centre d'Anthropologie des Sociétés Rurales
56, rue du Taur
31000 Toulouse, France

Gerard Klein Hofmeijer
Instituut voor Aardwetenschappen
Rijksuniversiteit Utrecht
P.O. Box 80 021
3508 TA Utrecht, The Netherlands

Linda Hurcombe
University of Exeter
Department of History and Archaeology
Queen's Building, The Queen's Drive
Exeter EX4 4QH, UK

François de Lanfranchi
Centre d'Etudes et de Recherches Archéologiques
Musée Départemental de Levie
20170 Levie, Corse, France

Giovanni Lilliu
Via Copernico, 4
09131 Cagliari, Italia

Fulvia Lo Schiavo
Soprintendenza Archeologica per le
  Provincie di Sassari e Nuoro
Viale Umberto, 89
Sassari 07100, Italia

Fabio Martini
Università degli Studi di Siena
Dipartimento di Archeologia e Storia delle Arti
Sezione di Preistoria
Via delle Cerchia, 5
53100 Siena, Italia

L. Massidda
Dipartimento di Ingegneria Chimica e dei Materiali
Piazza d'Armi
Università degli Studi di Cagliari
09123 Cagliari, Italia

David Gordon Mitten
Department of the Classics
Harvard University
Cambridge, MA 02138

Alberto Moravetti
Istituto di Antichità ed Arte
Facoltà di Magistero—Università di Sassari
Piazza Conte di Moriana
07100 Sassari, Italia

Giuseppe Murru
Soprintendenza Archeologica per le
  Provincie di Sassari e Nuoro
Ufficio Operative di Nuoro
Via Ballero 30
08100 Nuoro, Sardegna, Italia

J. Brian Peckham
Biblical Department
Regis College
15 St Mary's Street
Toronto M4Y 2R5, Ontario, Canada

Patricia Phillips
Department of Archaeology and Prehistory
University of Sheffield
Sheffield S10 2TN, UK

David Ridgway
Francesca R. Serra Ridgway
Department of Archaeology
University of Edinburgh
16-20 George Square
Edinburgh EH8 9JZ, UK

Robert J. Rowland, Jr
Loyola University
Office of the Dean
6363 St Charles Avenue
New Orleans, LA 70118-6143

U. Sanna
Dipartimento di Ingegneria Chimica
 e dei Materiali
Piazza d'Armi
Università degli Studi di Cagliari
09123 Cagliari, Italia

Vincenzo Santoni
Soprintendenza Archeologica per le
 Provincie di Cagliari ed Oristano
Via Angioy, 15
09124 Cagliari, Italia

Paul Y. Sondaar
Instituut voor Aardwetenschappen
Rijksuniversiteit Utrecht
P.O. Box 80 021
3508 TA Utrecht, The Netherlands

Maud Teglund
Institut für Antikens Kultur och Samhallsliv
Gustavianum, Uppsala University
S-753 10 Uppsala, Sweden

Giovanni Tore
Università di Cagliari
Dipartimento di Scienze Archeologiche
 e Storico-artistiche
Piazza Arsenale, 8
Cittadella dei Musei
09124 Cagliari, Italia

Carlo Tronchetti
Soprintendenza Archeologica per le
 Provincie di Cagliari ed Oristano
Via Angioy, 15
09124 Cagliari, Italia

David H. Trump
University of Cambridge
Board of Extra-Mural Studies
87 de Freville Avenue
Cambridge CB4 1HP, UK

Caterinella Tuveri
Soprintendenza Archeologica per le
 Provincie di Sassari e Nuoro
Ufficio Operative di Nuoro
Via Ballero 30
08100 Nuoro, Sardegna, Italia

Robert H. Tykot
Department of Anthropology
Harvard University
Cambridge, MA 02138

Giovanni Ugas
Soprintendenza Archeologica per le
 Provincie di Cagliari ed Oristano
Via Angioy, 15
09124 Cagliari, Italia

Pierfortunato Virdis
Dipartimento di Ingegneria Chimica e dei Materiali
Piazza d'Armi
Università degli Studi di Cagliari
09123 Cagliari, Italia

Gary S. Webster
Department of Anthropology
The Pennsylvania State University
Mont Alto Campus
Mont Alto, PA 17237-9799

Aviva Weiss Grele
Department of Anthropology
The Pennsylvania State University
University Park, PA 16802

Elizabeth Lyding Will
Department of Classics
Amherst College
Amherst, MA 01002

Tabula Gratulatoria

Erica Hoadley Adams	Charlotte Bobrecker	Patricia Crawford
Monni Adams	Elizabeth Coppedge Bohn	Frank Moore Cross
Frank G. Alvau	Ladislaus Bolchazy	Lorraine Curry
Mary-Jo Cipriano Amatruda	Larissa Bonfante	Peter M. Day
Z. Philip Ambrose	Elie and Batya Borowski	Joseph F. Desmond
Ralph Appelbaum	Amy Brauer	Jeanne C. Dillon
Mario Aste	Estelle Brettman	Marcia N. D-S. Dobson
Enrico Atzeni	Peter J. Brown	Wanda V. Dole
William S. Ayres	John Brownson	Owen P. Doonan IV
Eric C. Baade	Victoria Bunker	Sterling Dow
Ernst Badian	Edmund M. Burke	Julia Dubnoff
L.H. Barfield	Jose Bustamante	Elaine Kasparian Elliot
Graeme Barker	Mr and Mrs Pat Capone	Ernestine S. Elster
Jane A. Barlow	Trish Capone	Edith P. Erickson
George F. Bass	William G. Cavanagh	Mr and Mrs De Coursey Fales
Arthur Beale	Madeline H. Caviness	Mary Ella Feinleib
Marilyn M. Beaven	K. Kenneth Chakemian	Thomas R. Fenn
Robin F. Beningson	Effie Filopoulos Chigas	Mary E. Finnegan
Janet Bennett	Count Cinelli	David N. Fixler
Carl Sandler Berkowitz	Marie Cleary	Carolyn H. Frazer
Luigi Bernabò Brea	Clemency Chase Coggins	Elizabeth Gardner
Mark R. Besonen	Howard Comfort	Eleanor M. Garvey
Philip P. Betancourt	John Demetrius Costas	Sol Gittleman
David A. Bloom	Carlene Weber Craib	Lia Glovsky

Cyrus H. Gordon
Esther Stoddard Graves
Christopher Gray
Andrew R. Greenbaum
Nina Duncan Groeneweg
Lin Haire-Sargeant
Birgitta Pälsson Hallager
Judith P. Hallett
Anthony Hands
Anthony F. Harding
Richard J. Harrison
Alice Ryerson Hayes
Robert C. Hilton
Steven W. Hirsch
Amy K. Hirschfeld
R. Ross Holloway
Sarah Hood
Gertrude Howland
Debra Hudak
Jane W. Hudson
Mr and Mrs James D. Hume
Patricia A. Johnston
Richard E. Jones
Martha Sharp Joukowsky
Alexander Kaczmarczyk
A.J. Kalis
Norma Kershaw
Ann O. Koloski-Ostrow and Steven E. Ostrow

Christine Kondoleon
Neal A. Konstantin
Guenter Kopcke
Fran Lanouette
Roland A. Laroche
Gilbert Lawall
Robert R. Laxton
Paula Kay Lazrus
Heather Lechtman
W. John Lees
Albert Leonard, Jr
James G. Lewthwaite
Katina T. Lillios
Elisha Linder
Alex M. LoPriore
Mary Louise Lord
Susan S. Lukesh
David Marchand
Jeanne M. Marty
Miranda Marvin
Jean Mayer
Anna Marguerite McCann
Brian E. McConnell
Laura Maniscalco McConnell
Gioconda Cinelli McMillan
Alan McPherron
Edward H. Merrin
Regina F. Merzlak

Leo Mildenberg
Warren G. Moon
Andrew M.T. Moore
Barbara P. Moore
Susan Tufts Moore
Lynne D'Arcy Morgan
Martha A. Morrison
Navyn Naran
Joan Neumann
H.G. Niemeyer
Christine Richards O'Shea
Janna Owen
Susan Lewis Papa
Luigi Peano
Joanne H. Phillips
Ann Pizer
Lourdes Prados
Geraldine Ramer
George Rapp, Jr
Harold Raynolds, Jr
Peter L.D. Reid
Roberta J. Richard
Brunilde S. Ridgway
Eleanor Robbins
John Rosser
Anne Rossi
The Royall House Association, Medford
William and Elizabeth Ruf

Justin Runestad

Christina A. Salowey

Mario Sanges

Sondra and Milton Schlesinger

Shirley J. Schwarz

Jane Ayer Scott

Mr and Mrs Edward Shapiro

Philippa D. Shaplin

Charles Shumaker

Albert J. Sibson

David Smart

Cyril Stanley Smith

Paula Bacon Smith

S. Amber Somes

Steven J. Spieczny

Lawrence E. Stager

Kay E. Stein

Karen Stockert

Ruth S. Thomas

Dennis Trout

Lucia Vagnetti

Emily Vermeule

Paolo Visonà

Gisela Walberg

Jane C. Waldbaum

Nora Wecker

Howard Weintraub

Al B. Wesolowsky

Sandra Hurst White

Shelby White and Leon Levy

Malcolm H. Wiener

Irene J. Winter

James R. Wiseman

Marianne Witherby

Susan Wood

Luke W. Yeransian

The Authors

The Editors

Indexes

Index of Place Names

Abbaia 178, 183
Abbasania 490
Abealzu 126, 138, 172, 174
Abini-Teti 221, 233, 250, 257, 259, 260, 308, 316, 333, 352, 406, 456, 460
Abu Simbel 412
Acco 412
Achladia 249
Achzib 412
Addeiu 230
Aetokremnos 32, 34
Ager Cosanus 487
Ager Veientanus 487
Aghios Ilias 249
Agios Petros 33
Aidomaggiore 176
Aidu Arbu 183
Aiodda 222, 225
Akhili 33
Aladorza 187
Alambra 325
Albitretu 114
Albucciu 188, 198, 319, 351
Alcacer do Sal 421, 423
Alghero 58, 333, 431, 438
Alikes 249
Al Mina 356, 357, 386, 388, 413
Ampurias 435
Amrit 411
Andria Peis 476
Anghelu Ruju 135, 137, 141, 144-48, 151, 153, 156, 163, 164, 168, 170-72
Antas 144, 414
Antigori 306, 307, 315, 322, 336, 351, 355, 359
Arad 412
Araguina 29, 30, 39, 45, 48, 118, 120, 139, 155
Arbu 183
Arca de Calahons à Cattla 132, 136
Archanes 239, 248, 249
Ardiddi 480

Arenas 329, 338
Arene Candide 170
Argiddas di Samassi 222
Ariete di Perfugas 170
Arigau 481
Arikamedu 494, 496
Arkalochori 322
Arkines 249
Armenoi 322
Arratzu 480
Arreganyats 128
Arrubiù-Orroli 460, 481
Arslan Tash 412
Arzachena 126, 132, 169, 319
Assemini 478
Asine 310
Assur 351
Athens 239, 248, 357, 363
Athlit 412
Aurras 183
Austinaccia 112
Austis 465, 490
Axiurridu 481
Ayia Irini 225, 239, 248
Azor 412

Baccu Simeone 319, 331, 333, 340, 346
Baciolo 339
Balaiana-Luogosanto 144
Ballarino 339
Bangius 183, 480
Barcellona 74
Bar Hadad 412
Barumeli 481
Barumini 268, 301, 303, 308, 406, 409, 488
Basi 74, 79, 82
Bassit-Posidaion 388
Bauladu 176, 460
Bau Marcusa 478
Baumendola 481
Bau Nuraxi 319

Beaume-les Créancey 300, 301, 303
Belloussia 249
Benetutti 490
Bia Collanas 476
Bia Crabonaxa 481
Bidda Beccia 481
Bidda Maiore 479
Bidd'e Cresia 476
Bidistili-Fonni 308
Bidui-Birori 195
Bilippone-Dualchi 182
Bingia Arena 478
Bingias 480
Biora 465
Biriola Dualchi 178, 182, 183, 192
Birori 176
Biriai 170, 223
Bithia 308, 379, 374, 375, 386, 403, 414, 418, 454, 464, 474
Bizzicu Rosu 122
Bucche del Rodano 431
Bolotana 176
Bonarcado 176
Bonifacio 118, 124
Bonnanaro 126, 127, 137, 138, 144-48, 151-53, 156, 333, 341, 346
Bonorva 176, 431
Bonorzuli 480
Bonu Ighinu 84, 118, 120, 126-28, 137, 138, 147-49, 153
Boqueirão de Pedra Furada 35
Bordasse à Conilhac-de-la Montagne 132
Bortigali 176
Bortigiadas 490
Bosa 357, 413, 454, 457, 460, 474
Bosa Vetus 429, 431, 438
Boun Marcou 130
Brodu 169, 172
Broglio de Trebisacce 336
Brunk'e Mesu 476
Bruncu 'e Mula 478
Bruncu Espis 480
Bruncu Is Arcus 480
Bruncu Perda Crobina 64
Brunku Madili 188
Brunku Madugui 178, 182, 184, 188, 222, 233
Brunku Predi Poddi 476
Brunku sa Battalla 476
Budas 183
Buddusò 431
Burinna Spring 239, 248
Byblos 410
Byrsa 426

Cadreas-Narbolia 460, 479
Cagliari 367-76, 414, 418, 426, 427, 474, 487
Calabona-Alghero 321, 336
Calanchi 109, 112, 115, 117, 126
Calzola-Castellucciu 108, 109, 117
Capanne Vecchie 339
Campaniforme 150
Campanisissa-Siligna 481
Campiano 339
Campo dei Forestieri 64
Campo Pisano 327
Campu 'e Cresia-Simaxis 171
Campu Lontanu-Florinas 225, 227
Canale Barisoni-Torpe 321, 328, 338
Canale Linu 481
Canale Perdera 64
Canale Scolu 481
Canale Serci 328
Ca'n Canet 33
Canchedda 178, 180, 183
Cannatello 307
Canureu 481
Capaci 166
Capo di Gelidonya 310, 318-20, 322, 323, 335, 336, 337, 345, 413
Capo Marargiu 330
Capo Perora-Arbus 143, 156
Capo S. Elia 140
Caput Tyrsi 465
Caralis 488
Carbia-Alghero 460, 462
Carbonia 164
Carcu 120
Carrarzu Iddia-Borringali 183, 192
Carthage 386, 419, 423, 426, 427
Cassaros 183
Casteddu 460
Casteddu Pigas 480
Castellaro Vecchio 74, 79
Castelli di Bonvei 330
Castidetta-Pozzone 114, 117
Cave della Ceca 60
Cerveteri 384, 454
Charkadiu 33
Chercos di Usini 225
Chirighiddu 480
Chiusazza-Malpasso 166
Chiusazza presso Siracusa 167
Chorreras 421, 423
Ciutulaghja 107, 122, 126-28
Civas-Riola Sardo 481
Cixeiri-Iglesias 462
Cixius 480

Coattos 180, 183
Coddu'e Is Abois 481
Coddu Is Damas 481
Coddu Vecchiu di Arzachena 223
Cudinas 480
Codrovulos-Pantallinu 41
Codrovulos 29
Conca Cannas 59, 60, 62, 64, 70, 85
Conca Illonis-Cabras 164, 170
Concoli Corongiu Acca 109, 142, 143, 156
Conca s'Ollastu 59, 64
Coni o Santu Millanu Nuragus 250, 251, 259, 260
Connau Piscamu 183
Contrapiana 183
Corbeddu 30, 34, 36, 39, 40, 44, 45, 47-56, 63, 75, 79, 138, 139, 155
Cordes Mountain 134, 136
Corinth 239, 248
Cornus 464
Corona 225
Coroneddas-Sagama 478
Corongiu 'e Maria 183
Corongiu Marxi e Su Iriu-Gerzei 180
Corongiu-Pimentel 163
Corrre'boi 327
Corte Anda 170
Corte Nou 130, 131
Corti Auda 481
Corti Beccia 476
Corti 'e Sa Perda 476
Cos 494
Cossoìne 381, 383
Costa Tana-Bonareado 221, 233
Cova d'En Daina 130
Cuzzo del Pantano-Matrensa 227
Crastu di Ghilarza 225
Crastu-Soddì 182
Cruci 122, 127
Cuccureddì-Esterzili 230
Cuccureddus 414
Cuccuru Arrius 304, 315
Cuccuru Is Arrius-San Salvatore 460
Cuccuru Linu 481
Cuccuru Nuraxi 230, 400, 474, 483
Cuccuru Porcufurau 62
Cuccuru S'Arriu 137, 139, 144, 155, 157-74
Cuccuru Tiria 305, 315
Cucru Is Abis 60, 62, 64, 70
Cumpulaghja 122, 124, 126, 127
Cunculu-Scano Montiferro 182
Cuntorba 114, 117
Curacchiaghiu 29, 30, 39, 45, 48, 120, 122

Daphne 412
Decimomannu 478
Decimoputzu 319
Dela Laïga à Cournanel-Aude 132
Demengaki 71, 81
Dolianova 132
Domu 'e Biriu 480
Domu 'e Is Abis 480
Domu S'Orku 466
Donigala 481
Donigala Fenugheda 479
Donori 176
Dor 412
Dualchi 176
Duos Nuraghes 215, 271-86, 289, 455, 461, 466, 468

'Ecciu-Fordongíanus 460
Elath 412
Elephantine 412
El Sec 386
Ena e Leperes 183
Ena S'Anguidda 481
Englianos 249
Enkomi 318, 326
Enna Sa Vacca 130
Eretria 356, 413
Eri Manzanu-Bono 431, 438
Esterzili 457, 464
Etzi-Las Plassas 480
Euboea 32

Faenza 65, 76
Faurras di Villamar 222
Fenan 334
Fenosu-Palmas Arborea 165, 170, 183
Fenu-Pabillonis 481
Figa la Sarra 114
Filigosa-Macomer 135, 136, 163, 165-67, 170, 172
Filitosa 114, 117
Finucchiaglia-San Francesco d'Aglientu 176, 183
Fiurita 114
Flumenelongu-Alghero 308, 310, 333, 341, 346, 431, 438
Fonni 176, 490
Font de la Vena 132
Font del Roure 128, 136
Fonte Mola 182, 188
Foronia 434
Forraxi Nioi 307, 308, 331, 333, 340, 341, 345
Fraigada 183
Franchthi 32, 39, 71-73, 82
Friarosu 182, 188, 222

Frontilizzos 178, 183
Fronte Mola 481
Fruscos 180, 183, 188, 222
Funtana 319
Funtan 'e Cresia-Ortueri 333
Funtana 'e Deu-Lula 250, 256, 257, 259-61
Funtana e Landiri 183
Funtana Figu 60, 62
Funtana Janna 308, 333
Funtana Mela 195
Funtana Raminosa 307, 321, 327-29, 338, 346
Funtana Suei 178, 180, 183
Funtan'e Baccas-Guasila 480
Funtanedda-Sagama 191
Furtei 460
Fustiolau 59

Gadoni 307
Gagai 183
Gaione 62, 74
Gàiro-Ogliastra 381, 383
Galla 178, 180, 183
Gallura 107
Galtillì 310
Garlo 230, 234, 242, 248
Gaudo 135
Gazza e S. Caterina 180
Gennamari 328
Genna Maria 200, 201, 229, 234, 307, 351, 455, 479
Genna Olidoni 338
Genna Sintas-Nuraminis 478
Genna Udda 183
Genn 'e Gruxi 479
Genoni 176
Ghilarza 176
Giuanne Malteddu 29, 41
Giribaldi 75, 77
Glipha 33
Gonnesa 176
Gori 460
Gotti de Siligna 481
Goulet 118, 126
Gournia 322
Gozo 445
Gozzura 328, 338
Gramont à Soumont-Hérault 132
Gremanu-Fonni 250, 251, 254-57, 259, 260
Grotta del Guano 122
Grotta dell'Inferno 29
Grotta dell'Uzzo 73, 82
Grotta di S. Bartolomeo 58

Grotta di Filiestru Mara 29, 74, 76, 77, 79, 84-89, 97, 165
Grotta Rifugio 137, 139, 155
Grotta Sa Korona 29
Grotta Verde 29, 118, 126
Guardia Bue 478
Guardia Nadali 478
Guate-Mala 212

Hof ha-Carmel 310
Hagia Triadha 318, 322, 336
Hala Sultan Tekke 325, 326
Hastru Longu-Fonni 176, 183

Ibiza 386, 426
Ibn Hani 227
Iglesiente 307
Intenscias 29, 41
Ingurtosu 328
Is Argiddas 481
Is Arisca Burdas-Riola Sardo 479
Is Arridelis di Uta 162-66, 170-72, 174
Is Arultas 139, 140, 155, 455
Isca Maiori 170
Is Canalis 479
Is Crus 481
Is Gannaus di Giba 163
Is Nuraxis 480
Is Olieddus 481
Is Ollaius 481
Is Palmarola 73, 75, 79, 82
Is Pantelleria 73, 75, 79, 82
Is Pianosa 65
Is S. Antioco 58, 60
Is S. Pietro 58, 60
Is Tanas 460
Ittireddu 176, 319
Ittiari 225

Jappeloup 130
Joppa 412

Kalavasos-Ayios Dhimitrios 321, 322, 325, 326
Karales 431, 434
Karali 454, 460, 464
Katarraktis (Achaia) 249
Karatepe 411, 417
Katakalou 249
Karphì 239, 248
Keri 227
Khalde 411
Khaniale Tekke 358, 363
Khust 77

Knossos 32, 73, 239, 248, 249, 322, 357, 363
Kolophon 249
Kommos 269, 320, 322
Kourion 321
Kuau 182
Kuntiller Ajrud 412
Kyme 319
Kythnos 325, 345

Lacana de Biddazzone 481
Laccu Sa Vitella 59
La Crucca 141, 155
Ladrofurti 225, 227
Laerru 29, 41
Lago di Barratz-La Nurra 462
La Londe-les-Mouses 130
Lanzi 339
La Pesta 339
Lapithos 325
Laterza 135
Lavrion 325
Lazzaretto 462
Lefkandi 356, 357, 363
Leptis Magna 445
Le Trebine 60
Levie 118
Lighedu-Suni 182
Lilloi 460
Li Lolghi 223
Li Muracci 132
Li Muri 106, 122, 132, 136, 144
Liori 178, 180, 183
Linna Pesttunta-S. Andn'a Frius 479
Lipari 58, 59, 69, 74, 75, 77, 79, 307, 315, 358, 454
Liltoslongos 168, 171, 172
Lixius 481
Llanera 130
Logudoro 454
Longone 118, 126
Longu 480
Losa 200, 201, 268, 460, 466, 480
Lu Brandali-S. Teresa di Gallura 144
Lugherras 460
Luguidunac 465
Lu Loi 480
Lu Maccioni 139, 140, 155

Maa-Palaeokastro 325
Macomer 176, 460, 490
Macumádas-Nuoro 479
Madonna del Friddo 44
Madonna del Rimevio-Ositrano 479
Magomadas-Gesico 479

Magomadas-Nuseci 479
Magomadas-Planargia 479
Malafà 227
Malakunanja 35
Malchiltu 144
Malia 322
Malis 480
Mamoiada 176
Manching 494, 496
Mandra Antine 171, 172
Mannu-Suni 195
Mantzanni 462
Mar'e Idda 476
Marfudi 467
Maroni-Vournes 322
Maroula 33
Marze 114
Masone Perdu 128, 136
Masua 307, 327
Mathiati 318, 326
Mwatzanni-Vallermosa 456
Mavrata 249
Mazarakata 249
Medau Casteddu-Siligna 481
Medeon 249
Megiddo 239
Melas 478
Melas 481
Melos 58
Mene 178, 180, 183
Mersa Madakh 421, 423
Mesu 'e Montes 163
Migalona 114
Mikro Kokkinokastro 33
Milis 176
Minza-Castellucciu 112
Mitos-Pyrgos 239
Mitza Sa Tassa 60
Mitza Salamu-Dolianova 479
Miuddu 192
Molinello-Anguera 227
Molimentos-Benetutu 171, 172
Monte Arci 57-60, 62, 64, 65, 69, 74, 75, 85, 94
Monte Arribiu 308, 316
Monteatini Val di Cécina 335
Monte Baranta 190
Monte Barbatu 112, 114
Montecatini 328, 339
Monte Canu-Sorso 397
Monte Claro 126, 137, 138, 145, 148, 150, 164, 170
Monte d'Accoddi 102, 142, 156, 165, 166, 168-72, 180, 190, 198, 223, 305, 315

Monte de S'Ape-Olbia 273
Monte Grosso 120
Monte Lazzu 120
M. Leonaxi-Nuraminis 481
Monteleone Rocca d'Oria 368
Monte Luna 426, 474, 476, 483
Monte Maiore 29
Monte Mannu 328, 336
Monte Manzanu 180
Monte Olladiri-Monastir 165-69, 171, 172, 229, 397, 400, 474, 483
Monteponi 327
Monti Prama 357, 360, 406, 407, 455, 460
Monte Putzolu 191
Monte Rotondu-Sotta 122, 126, 127
Monte Sa Idda 308, 316, 358, 363
Monte Serai 454

Monte Sirai-Carbonia 373-75, 414, 462, 474, 483
Monte Sissini 324
Monte Sparau 60, 64
Montessu 103
Monte Tamara 327
Monte Traessu-Giave 59
Monte Trebina 58
Monte Urpinu 58
Monti Urtigu 58
Monte Valerio 336
Montevecchio 328
Monte Verde 35
Monte Zara 229, 230, 234
Monte Zuighe 431, 438, 480
Monti Cau-Sorso 431, 438
Montiju de Conzau-Mores 478
Moreddu di Cheremule 172
Moru Nieddu 183
Motorra 128, 136
Motya 386
Mozia 421, 426, 427
Mulargia 490
Mulineddu 183
Muntagnola 114, 117
Musuleu 122, 127
Mura 'e Coga-Sindia 195
Mura Fratta 178, 180, 183
Muravera 474
Muros 58
Murtedu 109, 117
Muru Mannu di Tharros 222
Mycenae 239, 248, 318, 319

Najac à Siran-Hérault 132, 136
Narva 183

Nastasi 319
Neapolis 365, 373-75, 439, 447, 464
Nea Skala 33, 34, 39
Nebbio 118
Nichoria 249
Nicolai e Nebida 143, 156
Nieddue 307
Noddule 250, 251, 259, 260, 479, 480
Nodu de Sale 192
Nora 357, 367-75, 377, 386-88, 392, 413, 414, 418, 426, 448, 454, 455, 464, 474, 484, 487
Norbello 176
N. Signora di Castro 490
Nuciaresa 126
Nuraddeo-Suni 195
Nuraghe Antigori 65
Nuraghe Losa 60
Nuraghe Sfundadu 190
Nuragus 490
Nurattolu 187
Nuraxi Figus-Gonnesa 143, 156
Nuraxi Longu 183
Nuraxinieddu 171
Nurdole 250, 251, 254, 257, 259, 260, 296-303, 400
Nureci-Villamar 478
Nuridda-Tuili 481
Nuritzi-Selegas 481
Nurri 176

Olbia 368, 431, 434, 438, 439, 441, 442, 447, 457, 462, 464, 474
Olièna 333, 341, 346
Olmedo 431, 438
Ono 180, 183
Orasu Nou 77
Oredda 168
Orgono 182
Oridda 143, 156
Orolo 195
Orotelli 176
Orreddo-Silanus 187
Ortucchio 170
Ortu Còmidu 84, 90-94, 97, 231, 289, 365, 460, 466, 481, 493, 495, 496
Ortueri 333, 341, 346
Osilo 58
Ossi 308, 333, 341, 346
Osteria dell'Osa 205, 206, 209
Orroli 319
Orrubiu-Orroli 201
Othoca 474, 486
Ovodda 381, 383

Oxylithos 249
Ozieri 126, 137-39, 148, 153, 454

Paderi 222
Padria 431, 490
Padro 132
Padru Jossu 137, 141, 144, 145, 147, 148, 153, 155, 156, 476
Palaeperphos 412
Palaggiu 105, 112, 132
Palaghju 126
Palaikastro 322
Palaiochori 227
Pala Sa Murta 59, 64
Palas de Binu 481
Palmaera 142, 156
Palmarola 58, 59, 69
Palmavera 198, 200, 229, 462
Panchéraccia 115
Pani Loriga-Santadi 454, 455, 462, 474, 483
Pantalica 308, 454
Pantallini 29
Pantalleria 58, 59, 69
Pascialzos di Cargeghe 225
Paulilatino 176
Pauli Margiani 481
Pauli Murtas 476
Pauli Nicasu 481
Pedralba 142, 156
Pedra Oddetta 183
Peiro Signado 76
Peppe Gallu 180, 188, 272
Perda Arrubia 62
Perda Bogada-Palmas Arborea 481
Perda Lunga di Austi's 130, 136
Perda s'Oliu 327-29, 338, 346
Perdas Urias 58-60, 64, 85
Perdosu 183
Perdu Corra 336
Perfugas 40, 76, 431
Perla e Pazza 180, 183
Perra 481
Pescale 65, 74, 76
Phaestos 310
Piano Conte-Serraferlicchio 166, 172, 174
Piana di Curinga Stentinello 74, 77, 82
Piano Quartara 166, 172
Pienza 74
Pira Inferta 59
Pirosu-Su Benatzu 308
Piscapu 183
Piscina S'Aqua 480
Piscu-Suelli 400, 481

Pithecusae 386
Pithekoussai 355
Planu Dentis 307
Pobulus 183
Podere Casanuova 163
Poggiarella 106, 107, 122, 126, 127
Polada 124, 126, 127
Polibio 434
Ponte Etzu 178, 180, 183
Ponte Secco 102, 168
Populonia 454
Porcarzos-Borore 214, 454
Poros 333
Porto di Cosa 494
Porto Conte 431, 488
Porto Torres 431, 435, 487
Porto Vecchio 122, 127
Pozzomaggiore 461
Pozzo-Olmedo 431
Pranu Fas 481
Pran'e Preidi 480
Pranu e Sanguini 327-29, 338, 346
Pranu Multeddu-Goni 106, 108, 117, 128, 168, 169, 172, 174, 304, 315
Prei Madua-Riola Sardo 460, 481
Presa-Tusiu 120, 122, 126, 127
Preideru 29, 41
Prida 192
Pruna 178, 180, 183
Pteleon 249
Puaddas-Siligna 481
Puig Ses Lloses 130
Puisteris 164
Pulighitta 183
Punta Feuraxi 59
Punta Muroni 64
Punta Pizzighinu 64, 70
Punta Su Zippiri 62
Punta Zinnigas 478
Putzola 183
Pyla-Kokkinokremos 325, 326

Qasile 412
Quattro Fontanili-Veii 356

Ras el Bassir 356
Ras Ibn Hani 321
Ras Shamra 230
Rinaiu 105
Ronaldone 135
Ripoli-Grotta di Piccioni 170
Rio Tinto 421, 423
Riu Acqua Bella 59

Riu Altana 29, 40, 41, 44, 48
Riu Cannas 62
Riu Murus 59, 62
Riu Sa Mela 478
Riu Solacera 64
Roia Cannas 58, 59
Roia Sa Lattia 478
Rosas 321, 327-29, 338, 346
Routsi 249
Ruinas-Marrubiu 480
Ruju-Buddusò 397, 407, 409
Rusumini 115

Sant'Anastasia di Sardara 229, 264, 268, 397, 400, 460
S. Andrea Frius 460
Sant'Andrea Priu 135
S. Antine-Arbus 480
Santu Antine-Torralba (SS) 198, 200, 201, 277, 278, 286, 431, 438, 462, 480
S. Antioco-Bisarcio 305, 315
Santa Barbara-Bauladu (OR) 287-93, 347, 351, 354, 480
S. Barbara-Macomer (NU) 195, 200, 201, 454
S. Benedetto 139, 140, 155
Santu Brai Furtei 400, 460, 474, 480, 483
Sa Caddina 183
S. Calogero 235, 238, 239, 246-48
S. Caterina 476, 481
Sa Cavana 481
S. Chiara 481
Sa Coa de Sa Multa 40, 41, 47, 48
Sas Concas 169
Sa Corona 169-71, 178, 184, 223
Sa Corte Noa 305, 315
Sa Coveccada 132
San Cosimo 223, 225
Santa Cristina 262, 264, 269, 270, 310, 456, 460, 479
Sa Domu 'e S'Ortu 180, 183
Sa Duchessa 321, 327, 328, 330, 338, 346
S. Elia-Nuragus 481
Sas Enattos 328, 338
Saint-Eugène 130
Sa Figu 225, 233
Sa Figu di Ittiri 225, 227
S. Francesco d'Aglientu 176
Sa Fronta-Pabillonis 481
S. Gemiliano-Sestu 58, 163, 164, 165, 170, 171, 229
San Giorgio 225
S. Giovanni 478
S. Giuseppe 163, 165, 172, 479

Santa Giusta 400
S. Gregorio 490
Santu Iaci-S. Nicolo Gerrei 479
Santu Iasccu 481
Sant'Imbenia 356, 360, 363, 400, 431, 438
Sant'Iroxi 223, 233
Sa Jacca-Busachi 188, 222
Sa Korona Monte Majore (SS) 304, 315
Sa Korona-Villagrica 188
St Léonard 134
S. Lò-Bosa 192
S. Lorenzo 480
S. Lucia-Gesico 478
S. Luxiori-Albagiara 480
S. Luxiori 478, 481
Sa Mandra 'e Sa Guia 333
S. Marca 481
Sa Marchesa 321, 327-29
S. Marco-Genura 481
S. Margherita 481
S. Maria de Sole-Mores 478
S. Maria in Paulis 307, 329, 331, 333, 345, 358, 363, 431
Santa Maria Monserrato 460, 476, 478
S. Maria-Nabiu 439
Santa Maria Zuarbara 62, 70
Sa Marigosa 478
S. Marina 478
San Michele 149, 164, 168, 169, 171, 172
S. Millanu 481
Sa Mitzixedda 476
Sa Mitza 479
Santa Naria 112, 114, 117
S. Nicola Gerrei 460
S. Nicolò Gerrei 445
Sos Nurattolos di Alà dei Sardi 230
Sta Nychia 71, 81
San Pantaleo 132, 481
S. Paolo-Milis 478
Sa Pedrosa 29, 41, 44, 48
Santu Pedru de Alghero 163, 164, 168, 170, 172, 174
S. Perdu-Genoni 480
S. Perdu-S. Vero Milis 481
S. Pietro-Siliqua 481
S. Pinta 60, 64, 70
Santa Reparata 487
S. Rosa 481
Sa Ruina-Stuppoi 476
San Salvatore 268
Sa Sedda 'e Sos Carros 307, 454
San Sergio 215, 461, 466
San Simeone-Bonorra 431

San Sperate 454, 474, 478
Sa Tassa 64
Sa Tellera-Guasila 480
Sa Tonnara 481
Sa Turricola-Murros 221, 233
Sa Turriga 168
Sa Ucca de Su Tintirriolu 122, 139, 140, 155, 163-65, 169-71
S. Uria 480
S. Vincente 144
S. Vito dei Normanni 225, 233
Santa Vittoria-Serri 229, 230, 264, 268, 400, 456, 460
Sagama 176
Sahul 35
Salamis 412
Salvaticu 114
Samaria 32
Samos 413
S'Aqua Salida-Pimentil 478
Sardara-Campidlano 308, 319, 455, 490
Sarde Melas 183
Sarepta 411
Sarule 308
S'Arxidda 478
S'Aurrecci 225
Scaffa Piana 120
Scala di Giocca 98
Scalza Murta 114
Scarlozza 178, 180, 183
Sciopadroxiu 479
Scoglio del Tonno 336
Sec [tombe de] 132
Sedilo 176
Selinunte 413
S'Ena S. Juanni 178, 180, 183
Seneghe 176, 180, 183
Senorbì 367-75, 455
Serbine 187, 215, 461, 466, 468
Serra Cannigas 170, 171
Serra Crabiles 141, 147, 148, 153, 155
Serra Coastula 182
Serra 'e sa Furca di Mogoro 164
Serra Ilixi 318, 319
Serra is Auras 171
Serramanna 460
Serra Santu Martinu 478
Serra Orrios 230
Serri 490
Serruci-Gonessa 462
Sette Finestri 488
Settimo S. Pietro 58, 308, 454
Settiva 109, 120, 122, 124, 126, 127, 134

Seulo 143, 156
Sidon 411
Sinis 460
Siniscola 223, 308
Sinnai 176
Sisaia- 143, 156
S'Iscia e sas Paras 143, 156
S'Isera de Abbasanta 187
Sisini 230
Sissiri-Turri 481
S'Isterridolzu 142, 156
Skorba 62
Skouriotissa 318, 326
S'Occidroxiu 478
Sollacaro 117
So'n Matge 30, 33, 39
So'n Muleta 30, 33, 39
Sonnixeddu 58
Sorabile 465
S'Orreri 143, 156
Sparau Crabia 481
Spargi 493
Spartines 33
Sphakia 249
Split 494, 496
Stazzona 105, 112
Steni Vala 33
Strette 29, 30, 39
Stylos 249
Su Benatzu 229, 358, 403
Su Carroppu de Sa Femina 478
Su Carroppu 29, 74, 76, 118, 126, 139, 155
Su Coddu 165-72, 305, 315
Su Crucifissu Mannu 102, 141, 142, 148, 156, 162, 163, 16, 169, 172, 174
Su Cungiareddu de Serafini *see* Tanì
Su Cungiau de Funtana 481
Su Cungiau de Is Fundamentas 163, 164, 174
Su Igante 397, 409, 431, 438
Sukas 413
Sulcis 355, 367-75, 377, 384, 386, 388, 414, 418, 419-23, 431, 434, 454, 464, 474, 483
Su Lidone 250, 251, 259, 260
Su Littu 98-105
S.'Ulivera 180, 182, 183
Su Montigiu 'e Sa Femmina 98
Su Mulinu di Villanovafranca 222, 225, 227, 233
Sumboe 182
S'Ungroni 478
Suni 176
Su Nou de Pedramaggiore 191
Su Nuraxi 198, 200-202, 229, 234, 301, 337, 455, 460, 479

512 *Sardinia in the Mediterranean*

Su Nuracci 481
Su Paris de Monte Bingias 59, 64
Su Pirastu-Ussana 163, 171
Su Senzu 481
S'Urachedda Is Ariscas 481
S'Urachi 478
S'Uraki 199, 201, 400, 466, 479
S'Uraxi 480
S'Urbale 229
Su Tempiesu 250-53, 256, 257, 259, 260
Su Varongu 70

Tacco Ticci 57
Tanca Sar Bogadas 128
Tanì 141, 150, 155, 156
Taormina 307
Tappa 114
Taravo 112
Tarsus 356, 357
Taulera 142, 143, 156
Tivulaghju 126
Tell Abu Harwam 412
Tell Keisan 412
Tell Sukas 356, 386, 388
Tell Tainar 356
Temperino 339
Tempio 176, 490
Temple of Sid 462
Termitito 336
Terramaini 163-67, 169, 170-72, 174
Terrazzi Zannini 44
Terreseu-Santadi 169
Terrina 108, 115, 117, 305
Teti 333
Teti Abini 340, 341, 346
Tharri 431, 434
Tharros 365, 367, 368, 373, 374, 375, 386-88, 392, 412, 414, 418, 424-28, 439, 442, 444-47, 454, 455, 460, 464, 467, 474, 484, 486, 487, 488
Thapsos 307, 336
Thasos 33, 345
Thebes 310
Thiesi 176
Thorikos 227, 233
Tilariga 198
Timna 334
Tires Llargues 130, 136
Tiryns 239, 248
Tivolaggiu 106, 107
Tolinu 192
Tomba Branca 172
Tomba del Duce di Vetulonia 397
Tomba dell'Emiciclo di Sas Concas 172, 174

Tomb of Huy 321
Tomb of Rechmire 321
Torralba 176, 308
Torpe 328
Torre 114
Torre Mordillo 336
Torriciola 112
Toscanos 419, 423
Toscono 207, 215, 276-78, 289, 461, 466, 468
Tramatza 480
Trattasi di Villanovafranca 222
Treasury of Atreus 227, 230, 233
Trubas di Lunamatrona 222
Tronza 183
Truba Niedda 327, 329, 338
Truvine 467
Tumulo della Speraoza 355
Tuppedili 481
Turri 187
Turris Libisonis 464
Turragas 481
Tusari 183
Tylissos 239, 248, 318, 322
Tyre 356, 411, 412
Tzipanéas 58

Ulinu 178, 183
Ulu Burun 310, 318-20, 322, 323, 335, 336, 345, 413
Urasa 183
Uraxi Mannu 476
Uri 407, 431
Urpes 207, 2125, 276, 277, 278, 289, 461, 466, 468
Usellus 486, 482, 491
Uzzo 79

Valentia 465
Valle Chiara 114
Vascolaggiu 106, 107, 126
Veii 206, 360
Velulonia 450
Viale Colombo 163, 164, 169
Villa Corlotta-Isili 480
Villagrande Strisaili 319
Villanovaforru 308, 319, 330
Villaperuccio 478
Villapurzu 474
Villasimius 474
Villasmundo 356
Villaspeciosa 484
Villenueve-Tolosane 134
Vounous 321
Vulci 384, 454

Yabneh Yam 412

Zakros 239, 248, 322

Zembra Island 65
Zinjirli 411
Zoppo 122, 127

Index of Authors

Acanfora, O. 172
Acquaro, E. 421, 434, 493
Acquaviva, L. 114
Adams, R.M. 212
Adler, M. 212
Adovasio, J. 36
Agosti, F. 139
Allen, J. 35
Almagro, M. 222, 297, 300
Almagro Bash, M. 308
Almagro Gorbece, M. 301, 308, 396
Alroth, B. 442
Amadasi Guzzo, M.G. 413, 429, 434, 435, 439, 441, 442, 443-45, 456, 457, 463, 464
Amiran, R. 421
Ammerman, A. 62, 74, 75, 77
Anderson, P.C. 84
Anderson, W.P. 419, 424
Andrefsky, W. Jr 74, 75
Andrews, D. 200
Angiolillo, S. 479
Antona Ruju, A. 144
Araña, V. 60
Aranguren, B. 163
Arca, M. 29, 41
Arnal, J. 134
Arnaud, G. 112
Arnaud, S. 112
Arribas, A. 222, 386, 387
Aru, A. 185
Assorgia, A. 59, 63
Atzeni, E. 29, 76, 106, 107, 128-31, 139, 140, 163-65, 169, 171, 178, 221, 222, 229, 230, 305, 307, 317, 347, 349, 351
Atzori, M. 94, 163, 171
Aubet, M. 434

Bacigalupo Pareo, E. 443
Badas, U. 229, 308
Bafico, S. 274, 277, 356, 400, 429, 431
Bagolini, B. 74
Balmuth, M.S. 90, 198, 205, 207, 213-15, 233, 271, 289, 305, 317, 318, 347, 355, 360, 384, 439, 454, 460, 466, 493

Bankoff, H. 448
Banti, L. 336
Baraq, D. 410
Barfield, L.H. 74, 76
Barker, G. 451, 468
Barnard, A. 211, 215
Barnes, J. 461
Barré, M. 390
Barreca, F. 216, 264, 268, 269, 310, 317, 347, 413, 419, 429, 431, 434, 435, 454, 455, 457, 460, 461, 464, 465, 474, 478, 479
Barnett, R. 386, 387
Barnett, R.D. 411, 455, 467
Bartel, B. 469
Bartoloni, P. 206, 268, 305, 308, 355, 356, 360, 366, 384, 386-88, 400, 407, 414, 419, 421
Buss, G.F. 310, 317, 321, 322, 323
Bats, M. 367
Baumgarten, A. 411
Bear, L.M. 320
Beazley, E. 263, 264
Beccaluva, L. 59
Becker, M.J. 206, 307, 454
Belli, P. 233
Belluomini, G. 59
Bérard, J. 223
Berger, P. 442, 444
Bernabò Brea, L. 58, 166, 221, 239, 307, 308
Bernardini, P. 233, 355, 360, 384, 386, 396, 397, 400, 403, 406, 407, 419, 434, 454, 455, 469
Biagi, P. 74
Bigazzi, G. 59, 64
Bietti Sestiere, A.M. 206, 355, 435
Bikai, P.M. 412, 419
Binder, D. 74, 75, 77, 78
Binford, L.R. 36
Birmingham, J. 299
Bíró, K.T. 77
Birocchi, E. 307
Bisi, A.M. 267, 310, 347, 403, 406, 413, 419
Blinkenberg, J. 299
Bloedow, E.F. 73, 78
Boardman, J. 356, 357, 359, 386
Bogucki, P.J. 77, 78

Index of Authors

Bonadonna, F. 59
Bonanno, A. 214
Bondi, S. 304, 386, 387, 396, 406, 413, 414, 429, 435, 456, 474, 476
Bonfante, L. 360
Bonifay, E. 115
Bonnet, C. 388
Bonzani, R.M. 65
Bordreuil, P. 410, 411
Botto, M. 413, 434
Bowmer, M. 206
Branigan, K. 485
Breglia Pulci Doria, L. 355, 388-90, 434
Briard, J. 115
Briend, J. 419
Brize, P. 388
Broglio, A. 165
Broneer, O. 239
Brumfiel, E.M. 71
Bruni, E. 142
Buchholz, H.-G. 298-301, 317, 321
Buchner, G. 58, 355
Buhl, M.L. 419
Bunnens, G. 410, 411
Burnham, B.C. 485, 488
Businco, L. 143
Cacciatori, A. 157, 165, 169
Cadogan, G. 239
Calegari, G. 40
Calvi Rezia, G. 74
Campbell, J. 90
Camps, G. 74, 108, 109, 115
Canalis, V. 163
Cann, J.R. 58, 59
Carancini, G.L. 435
Carandini, A. 488
Carlisle, R. 35
Carneiro, R. 213
Carpenter, T. 364
Carratelli, G.P. 318
Carter, J.B. 268
Casalis, G. 478
Cashdan, E. 210
Caskey, J. 239
Casson, L. 310
Castaldi, E. 120, 143, 170, 171, 223
Castiglioni, C.O. 40, 58
Catling, H.W. 321, 323
Cavalier, M. 58, 166, 221, 233, 239, 307
Cavalli-Sforza, L. 138
Cavanagh, W.G. 199, 233, 355
Cavet, S. 410
Cazalis de Fondouce, P. 134

Cello, G. 304
Cecchini, S. 429, 445
Cesari, J. 105, 109
Chabot, J.B. 439, 441-43
Chamorro, J. 308
Chapman, R. 76, 77, 206
Charles, R. 142, 143, 148
Chenorkian, R. 115
Cherif, Z. 424
Cherry, J.F. 28-30, 32, 33, 55, 71-73, 318, 334
Chiera, G. 388
Cintas, P. 421
Clark, J.G.D. 90
Cleary, A.S. 486
Close-Brooks, J. 206
Cocchi Genick, D. 65
Cocco, D. 106, 128, 129, 168, 169
Coffyn, A. 308
Coldstream, J.N. 355, 356, 360, 412, 413
Coles, J.M. 323
Collins, M. 35
Conchon, O. 32
Conqui, L. 58
Constantini, L. 73
Constantinou, G. 307, 321
Contu, E. 144, 163-65, 168-72, 180, 188, 198, 199, 221-23, 227, 229, 230, 233, 250, 307, 317, 333, 358
Cosseddu, G. 143
Coulon, C. 59
Courbin, P. 356, 387-89
Courtin, J. 74-77
Craddock, P.T. 307, 347
Cremonesi, G. 165, 170
Cross, F.M. 357, 410, 413, 448, 474
Crummett, J.G. 61
Culican, W. 411, 412
Cunisset Carnot, P. 297, 299, 301
Cutroni Tusa, A. 444

D'Agostino, B. 206, 434, 435
Davies, N. 310
Davis, J. 239
Davison, J.M. 355, 384, 387-89
Davoli, G. 250
Day, P.H. 306, 322
Dayton, J.E. 413
DeBoer, W. 210-12, 215
De la Marmora, A. 57, 58
Delibes de Castro, G. 301
Delibrias, G. 35
Della Vida, L. 441, 442, 444, 445
Delpino, F. 308, 360

Demakopoulou, K. 334
Demartis, G. 163
Demas, M.V. 325, 335
Demurtas, S. 176, 178, 180, 182, 187, 188, 198, 214, 222, 225, 227
Deneauve, J. 421
Depalmas, A. 74, 75, 169, 170
Deriu, A. 355
Deriu, M. 59
Dermitzakis, M.D. 31
Desborough, V. 356
Descoeudres, J.P. 360
Desio, A. 258
Dessau, G. 335
Dessi, C. 178
De Vino, B. 304
De Vos, J. 31
Diamond, J. 34, 74
Dietler, M. 448
Dillehay, T.D. 35
Dincauze, D.F. 28, 30, 35, 36
Di Paola, G. 59
Di Salvo, R. 206
Dixon, J.E. 59, 71, 325
D'Oriano, R. 301, 368, 429, 434
Dothan, M. 268, 412
Drennan, R. 211
Duday, H. 139
Dunbabin, T. 223
Dyson-Hudson, R. 210
Dyson, S. 448, 454, 456, 457, 460, 461, 465-68, 485, 486, 489

Earle, T.K. 71
Efstratiou, N. 32
Elayi, J. 410, 411
Eph'al, I. 413
Esteva Cruanas, L. 131
Evans, A.J. 239
Ewer, R.F. 210
Exel, R. 62

Faccini, F. 142
Fadda, M.A. 188, 227, 229, 250, 274, 278, 296, 403
Fagan, B. 35, 36
Fantar, M. 441, 444, 445
Fasani, L. 165
Faulkner, R. 310
Fenu, A. 140, 141
Ferrarese Ceruti, M.L. 109, 128, 142, 162, 163, 168, 169, 171, 221, 223, 246, 305, 306-308, 317, 319, 322, 335, 355, 413
Ferron, J. 414

Finley, M. 400
Finzi, C. 424
Fiorelli, S. 333
Fisher, R.A. 325
Floris, G. 137, 143, 144
Fonzo, O. 289
Fornaciari, E. 141
Fosch Nieddu, A. 163, 165-67, 170
Foschi, A. 29
Francaviglia, V. 58, 60, 62, 64, 73
Fraser, D. 467
Frassetto, F. 142
Frau, M. 474
French, E.B. 335
Frenzel, G. 324
Fried, M. 211
Fulford, M.G. 448, 469

Gailey, C. 212, 213
Gale, N.H. 60, 71, 305, 307, 317, 318, 320, 321, 323-25, 328-31, 333-36, 351, 358, 359
Galili, E. 310
Gall, H. von 239
Galli, F. 163, 165, 319, 479
Gallin, E. 199, 205, 207, 214-16, 187, 307, 347, 454
Galinsky, K. 389
Garbarino, C. 324
Garbini, G. 424, 434, 441, 442
Garibaldi, P. 78
Garnsey, P. 216
Germanà, F. 50, 137, 139-44, 148
Giardino, C. 306-308, 349
Gibson, J.C.L. 411
Ginge, B. 206
Godart, L. 310
Gouder, T. 426
Gouin, L. 351
Gras, M. 233, 308, 355, 431, 434
Green, S. 211, 212
Gregl, Z. 205
Grosjean, R. 105, 107-109, 112, 114, 115
Groube, L.J. 35
Guglielmi, M. 310
Gubel, E. 410
Guido, M. 213, 484
Guidon, N. 35
Guilaine, J. 74, 130
Guzzo, P.G. 299, 301

Halbherr, F. 318
Hallam, B. 29, 59, 60, 74
Harverson, M. 263, 264
Haselgrove, C. 448, 455

Hastorf, C. 212, 213
Hatzidakis, J. 239
Hauptmann, A. 335
Hedeager, L. 448
Held, S.O. 32
Hencken, H. 308
Herrmann, G. 411
Hiscock, P. 35
Hodge Hill, B. 239, 244
Holloway, R.R. 384, 389
Holt, P. 390
Houwink Ten Cate, P.H.J. 411
Hug, E. 137
Hult, G. 230
Hurcombe, L. 83-85, 87, 93, 94
Huss, W. 439, 443-45
Hutchinson, R. 239
Hyslop, J. 212

Iakovidis, S. 239, 244
Isserlin, B.S.J. 413, 476

Jackson, K. 476
Jehasse, J. 109
Jenkins, G. 424
Johnson, G. 212
Jones, R. 35
Jones, R.E. 306, 319, 322, 336
Joussaume, R. 105
Jssel, A. 143
Junghans, S. 335

Kagan, D. 390
Karageorghis, V. 307, 335, 412, 431
Karo, G. 239
Kearlsey, R. 356
Keegan, W. 34
Keeley, L.H. 83, 84
Kelly, R. 210, 412
Kestemont, G. 410, 411
Kilian, K. 221, 239, 244
King, R. 214
Kipp, R. 455
Kitch, P.V. 484

Klein Hofmeijer, G. 29, 30, 40, 44, 49, 50, 73
Knapp, A.B. 318, 326, 334
Koehl, R.B. 411
Kowalewski, S. 212, 216
Krahmalkov, C.R. 413, 445
Kromer, B. 78
Krysko, W.W. 351
Kus, S. 212, 213

Kuznesof, E. 212, 213

Laqarce, J. 321
Lai, G. 163-71
Lancel, S. 419, 426
Lanfranchi, F. de 29, 30, 62, 107, 122
Lauro, C. 59
Laviosa, C. 310
Laxton, R.R. 199, 233, 355
Lech, J. 77
Leclant, J. 426
Ledda, R. 222, 474
Lewis, R. 424
Lewthwaite, J. 29, 30, 33, 76, 198, 205, 214, 289, 454
Libertini, G. 307
Lidzbarski, M. 439
Liègeois, J. 108, 109
Lilliu, C. 479
Lilliu, G. 108, 109, 125, 130, 137-43, 148, 171, 178, 180, 188, 198, 200, 204, 205, 214, 221-23, 225, 227, 229, 230, 250, 264, 277, 301, 305, 308, 317, 319, 347, 351, 352, 357, 360, 396, 397, 406, 429, 431, 435, 451, 454-56, 460, 461, 466, 467, 468, 478, 479, 485
Linder, E. 268, 412
Lipiński, E. 412, 439, 441-44
Liverani, M. 434
Lo Porto, F. 221, 225
Lo Schiavo, F. 115, 171, 188, 201, 204, 223, 233, 299, 301, 304-308, 310, 317-19, 322, 323, 333, 335, 336, 351, 356, 357-60, 397, 400, 403, 406, 412-14, 419, 429, 431, 434, 435, 451, 454, 455, 493
Laddo, R. 58
Longworth, G. 60
Lopez Roa, C. 308
Loria, R. 140, 163, 165, 169-71
Lovisato, D. 58
Lucia, G. 144, 322, 403
Lugliè, C. 165, 170
Lynch, T.F. 35

Mackey, M. 60, 62, 71
Macnamara, E. 307, 322, 329, 358, 360
Madau, M. 250, 254, 367, 368, 384, 386, 387, 400, 429, 431, 462, 479, 480
Maddin, R. 333
Maddoli, G. 359
Maetzke, G. 188
Maggi, R. 78
Mahjoubi, A. 444, 445

Maiori, A. 239
Malone, C. 74, 76
Manca Demurtas, L. 176, 178, 180, 182, 187, 188, 198, 214, 222, 225, 227
Manconi, D. 488
Manfredi, L. 424, 444
Manly, B. 324
Mann, M. 212
Manning, S. 319, 335
Manouvrier, L. 137, 140, 142, 144, 148
Mansur-Franchomme, M.E. 84
Mantovani, P. 58
Manunza, M. 163, 164, 170
Marcello, A. 304, 324
Markoe, G.E. 410
Maroni Bovio, J. 167
Marras, L. 387, 414, 474
Martelli, M. 396
Martin, R. 137
Martini, F. 29, 30, 40, 45, 50
Mass-Lindermann, G. 421
Massoli-Novelli, R. 317
Masson, O. 439
Mastino, A. 223, 429, 435
Maxia, C. 137, 140, 141, 143, 144
Mazza, F. 387
McDougall, J. 60, 62
Meeks, N.D. 307
Meister, K. 389
Mellegni, F. 139

Meloni, P. 223, 384, 386, 389, 429, 434, 435, 442, 445, 457, 464, 465, 476, 485, 487
Meltzer, D.J. 35
Mendelson, C. 386, 387, 467
Menzel, D. 212
Merkel, J. 317, 325, 333
Meulengracht, A. 73
Michels, J. 60, 62, 74, 205, 207, 212, 215, 216, 289, 451, 454, 460, 461, 465, 466, 468
Miege, J. 289
Mielsch, H. 485
Miles, D. 485
Miller, K. 463, 464
Millett 485, 486, 488, 489
Milliken, S. 73
Mitova-Džonova, D. 230, 242, 245
Mohen, J.P. 115, 299
Molleson, T. 206
Monticolo, R. 474, 484
Moravetti, A. 168, 171, 187, 188, 198, 199, 214, 255, 229, 274, 278, 451
Morel, J.P. 365, 384, 388

Mori, A. 451, 454
Morris, C. 212
Moscati, S. 310, 366, 384, 386, 388, 396, 414, 419, 421, 424, 426, 431, 435, 439, 441, 460, 461, 474
Mosso, A. 307
Muhly, J.D. 305, 307, 317, 318, 322, 330, 331, 335, 336, 359, 413
Müller, H.P. 411
Muller, J. 76, 77
Murra, J. 212, 213
Muraru, A. 77
Murray, O. 262, 318
Murru, G. 250, 258
Mussche, H. 227
Musti, D. 400
Myers, T. 210, 211, 215, 299
Mylonas, G. 239

Nandris, J. 77
Naveh, J. 413
Nebbia, P. 109
Neppi Modona, A. 239
Neve, P. 239
Nicolardot, J.P. 299
Nicosia, F. 304, 384, 387, 396, 397, 400, 431
Nieddu, G. 400
Niemeyer, H.G. 358, 359, 387, 388, 421
Nissardi, F. 50, 307, 308

Oded, B. 411
Oyuela-Caycedo, A. 212, 213

Paderi, M.C. 222, 225, 476
Page, D. 388
Pais, E. 223, 308, 429, 435
Panedda, D. 434, 488
Pardee, D. 411
Pareti, L. 388
Paribeni, R. 318, 336
Parpola, S. 411
Patterson, T. 212, 213
Paulis, G. 429, 433, 435, 376, 479
Paynter, R. 211, 212
Pearson, L.I.C. 384, 388, 389
Peckham, B. 410-13
Peebles, C. 212, 213
Pendlebury, J. 239
Pélon, O. 227, 239
Perazzi, P. 163
Percival, J. 485
Perea Caveda, A. 426
Perenti, R. 139
Peretti, G. 109, 112

Peretto, C. 29
Perlès, C. 32, 71-75, 77, 78
Perlman, S. 211, 212
Peroni, R. 221
Pesce, G. 419
Peterson, N. 210
Phillips, P. 75-77, 84, 90, 454
Pianu, G. 488
Piperno, M. 29, 73
Pigorini, L. 58, 318
Pisano, G. 424, 426
Pitzalis, G. 29, 30, 40
Plantalamor Massanet, L. 227
Planton, N. 239
Popham, M.R. 357
Potter, T. 485
Prausnitz, M.W. 412
Pritchard, J. 239, 368
Puddu, M.G. 230
Puech, E. 411
Puglisi, S.M. 120, 221
Pulak, C. 310, 318, 322
Puxeddu, C. 58, 74, 164

Quillard, B. 426
Quojani, F. 166

Radcliffe-Brown, A. 211
Radi, G. 59, 170
Randall-MacIver, D. 355
Reid, P. 77
Rellini, U. 307
Renfrew, A.C. 58, 59, 73, 212, 214, 215
Reverte, J.M. 206
Ridge, J.D. 328
Ridgway, D. 206, 308, 355-57, 359, 387, 431
Ridgway, S. 360
Riederer, J. 347, 349
Riquet, R. 139
Rita Larrucea, M. 227
Rizzo, M.A. 355
Roberts, R.G. 35
Rocco, B. 426
Root, D. 210, 211, 213
Rossi, G. 274, 278
Rouse, W.H.D. 442
Rovini, D. 403
Rowland, R., Jr 215, 290, 355, 448, 451, 454, 457, 460-62, 464, 466-68, 476, 479, 480, 484, 487-89
Rowlands, M. 211, 213
Runia, L.T. 206

Sahlins, M. 210

Saïdah, R. 411
Saliby, N. 227
Saller, K. 137
Salvadei, L. 206
Salvi, D. 474, 479
Sammartino, F. 65
Sangas, M. 419
Sangmeister, E. 222
Sanna, R. 162, 164-66, 170
Santillo Frizell, B. 199, 235, 262, 264, 267
Santillo, R. 235, 267
Santoni, V. 139, 157, 164, 165, 169, 172, 178, 188, 221, 222, 230, 233, 264, 397, 400
Sauzade, G. 134
Sebis, S. 180, 287, 347
Semenow, S.A. 83, 84
Sergi, G. 141
Service, E. 212
Settis, S. 488
Schaeffer, C. 321
Schneider, E. 464
Schortman, E. 455
Schubert, H. 222, 227, 421
Segert, S. 443
Serra, P. 424
Shackleton, J.C. 29, 32, 33
Shaw, J.W. 269, 320
Shefton, B. 388, 390
Shelford, P. 71
Sherratt, A. 77, 78
Simmons, A.H. 32
Simpson, G. 485
Skeates, R. 73
Smith, C. 210-12
Snodgrass, A.M. 359
Soja, E. 215
Solanilla, V. 424
Sondaar, P.Y. 29-32, 36, 40, 44, 49, 50, 52, 53
Spano, G. 58, 318
Sparkes, B. 368
Spoor, C.F. 30, 31, 50, 139
Stanner, W. 211
Stech, T. 305, 317-20, 331, 336, 359
Stern, E. 412
Stiglitz, A. 455, 460, 465-67, 478
Stöckli, W.E. 494
Stos-Gale, Z.A. 305, 307, 317, 318, 320, 323-26, 328-31, 333-36, 351, 358, 359
Svoronos, J.N. 318
Sznycer, M. 412, 439, 441-43, 445

Tanda, G. 29, 76, 142
Tangheroni, M. 351

Tarling, D. 60
Taramelli, A. 58, 141, 170, 171, 229, 230, 235, 250, 251, 307, 439, 464
Tarrus, J. 129
Tatton-Brown, V. 321
Taylor, H. 347
Teixidor, J. 443
Thaler, L. 31
Thimme, J. 317
Thompson, D. 212
Thompson, H. 367
Thomsen, P. 239
Tiñe, V. 74-77, 165-69, 198
Todd, M. 485
Tomasello, F. 225, 227
Toms, J. 206
Tore, G. 264, 360, 400, 403, 429, 430, 431, 433-35, 455, 460, 465-67, 478
Torrence, R. 71-73
Traverso, A. 165, 166, 168, 169
Tronchetti, C. 216, 355, 357, 364-68, 384, 386-88, 396, 397, 400, 406, 407, 419, 431, 454, 455, 464, 465, 467, 474, 484, 488
Trump, D. 29, 65, 74, 84, 140, 163, 165, 169-71, 198-201, 214, 215
Tsirkin, J.B. 387
Tusa, S. 221, 227
Tuveri, C. 250
Tykot, R. 57, 59, 62, 71, 287, 307, 347
Tylecote, R.F. 207, 305, 307, 317, 318, 323, 325, 333, 347, 349, 351, 454

Uberti, J.L. 421, 426, 441
Ulzega, A. 45
Ugas, G. 65, 144, 165-71, 180, 221-23, 225, 227, 229, 230, 233, 355, 396, 397, 400, 403, 406, 474
Usai, E. 478
Usai, L. 163-72, 397, 400, 403, 462, 474

Vagnetti, L. 246, 306, 319, 322, 323, 336, 358, 359, 412
Vaughan, P. 71-73, 78, 83

Vercoutter, J. 321
Verdelis, N. 239
Vigne, J.D. 28-31, 55, 289
Volkommer, R. 389
Vuillemot, G. 419

Wace, A. 239
Wacher, J. 485, 488
Wachsmann, S. 321
Warren, S.E. 59-62, 71, 74, 76
Washington, H. 58
Watanabe, K. 411
Webster, G. 199, 204, 205, 207, 211, 213-15, 271-74, 276, 289, 451, 454, 455, 460, 461, 466, 468
Weisgerber, G. 307
Weiss, M.C. 30, 62, 108, 207, 454
Wells, P.S. 455
Wetterstrom, W. 451, 468
Wheeler, R. 318, 320, 494
Whitehouse, R.D. 448, 455, 456, 468
Wiener, M. 335
Wiessner, P. 213
Wightman, E. 486
Wilkins, J.B. 448, 455, 456, 469
Will, E.L. 493-95
Williams Thorpe, O. 60, 74-77
Wilshusen, R. 212
Wilson, E. 210, 412
Winter, I.J. 410, 411, 448
Wittenberger, J. 210
Wright, R. 239

Xella, P. 441

Yadin, Y. 268
Yoffee, N. 212

Zanardelli, T. 58
Zucca, R. 355, 365, 396, 400, 407, 429, 431, 434, 439, 444, 465-67, 474, 476, 487
Zuffardi, U. 320, 324, 327, 328, 336
Zwicker, U. 307, 323